# BOOKS BY DAVID HALBERSTAM

*The Noblest Roman*

*The Making of a Quagmire*

*One Very Hot Day*

*The Unfinished Odyssey of Robert Kennedy*

*Ho*

*The Best and the Brightest*

*The Powers That Be*

# The Powers That Be

# The Powers That Be

DAVID HALBERSTAM

ALFRED A. KNOPF    New York    1979

Copyright © 1979 by David Halberstam

Grateful acknowledgment is made to Oxford University Press for permission to reprint an excerpt from *A History of Broadcasting in the United States,* Vol. 2, *The Golden Web,* by Erik Barnouw. Used by permission of Oxford University Press.

Library of Congress Cataloging in Publication Data

Halberstam, David [date]   The powers that be.

Bibliography: p.    Includes index.
I.   Press and politics—United States.   I.   Title.
PR4888.P6H3        070.4′0973      78–20605
ISBN 0–394–50381–3

Manufactured in the United States of America

FIRST EDITION

*For Jean Sandness Butler*

# Contents

# Prelude

On September 10, 1960, Samuel Taliaferro Rayburn arrived somewhat early in El Paso, Texas, for a Democratic Party rally. The particular rally featured Rayburn's personal protégé, Lyndon Johnson, the Democratic candidate for Vice-President, and the young man about whom Rayburn had considerable personal misgiving, John F. Kennedy, the presidential nominee. Rayburn at the time was seventy-eight years old and in his sixteenth year as Speaker of the House of Representatives. His health was already slipping, he was in fact dying of cancer, though he did not yet know it. He had not been feeling well in recent months but he steadfastly refused to see a doctor. He had a rural suspicion of doctors in general and, in addition, he feared that any report that he had even seen a doctor might quickly spread through the House and spur rumors of his declining health and thus weaken his mandate and inspire challenges to his rule. At the time he thought he was suffering from no more than a severe back problem. In addition, his eyesight was fast failing, he could no longer read, and this too was a closely guarded secret; only his most trusted associates were allowed to read to him in the privacy of his own chambers. Those around Rayburn who cared deeply for him realized that as his body failed his political control was probably ebbing as well; more, that he had probably stayed on as Speaker too long, that he was living off his past reputation and strength, and that it was only a matter of time before Sam Rayburn had to give up what he prized above all else, the Speakership of the House. (Once, a few years earlier, traveling back from a Sunday picnic with his good friends Lyndon and Lady Bird Johnson, he had pointed to the Capitol dome as they first saw the Washington skyline and he had said, "Lady Bird, how do you like *my* building?" saying it modestly, more as a matter of love than of ego; this was what he had done with a half century of his life, this and nothing more.)

On that day in El Paso while waiting for Kennedy and Johnson to arrive, however, he was restless, he had a half day on his hands and precious little to do, and so he turned to the people with him and said that he wanted to go over and see Mexico, would that be all right? Are you sure? one of them asked, feeling the trip might be a strain, but he said yes, he had a notion to go over there to see Mexico. Which was unusual, for though Sam Rayburn had helped marshal the Congress of the United States to play its role as this nation sprang to world-power status, he had never been interested in foreign travel or the world outside. He had hated junkets and mocked those members who regularly went on junkets. To his mind, the rest of the world was outside his realm of competence, he did not need to travel to see it. He accepted what the President said the world was like, since the President knew more about these things and the President of the United States would have no need to lie. The world outside, he believed as an act of faith, did not relate to domestic politics. He had, for the record, as a young congressman, once visited the Panama Canal, and it was also believed, though this was in question, that he had once attended dedication ceremonies of some sort in Mexico many years earlier. So, depending on the count, this was—after forty-eight years of national service, many of them at the most crucial and sensitive level—this was to be either his second or third trip outside the United States. With him that day as guides were the El Paso congressman J. T. (Slick) Rutherford; his assistant, Larry L. King, later to be a nationally known writer; and one of Rayburn's nephews, then stationed at Fort Bliss. So they drove over to Juárez, and there the old man sat and stared, his eyes fixed on the wonders of Juárez, until finally it was time to go back. At which point they turned the huge car around and headed back across the Rio Grande, and as they crossed the river and reached the checkpoint, the American immigration officer waved them to a halt and asked them to declare their nationality. Rayburn, who was also becoming hard of hearing, could not hear the guard, and so the guard yelled, a little more angrily this time. After all, he was simply dealing with another very old, very bald man. *Declare your nationality,* he shouted, and there was again a pause, and this time the guard shouted again, not unlike a drill instructor, and this time the Speaker answered back, not his nationality, but his identity, *Sam Rayburn! Sam Rayburn!* and he yelled it with the same ferocity that he had used in gaveling down countless demonstrations at countless Democratic conventions, and it was like a gavel flashing in the El Paso air, and the officer looked and there was a flash of recognition and a flash of fear, and he quickly waved the car through. So they drove back over the Rio Grande and into El Paso and drove through that city, and finally Rayburn, who had been very silent, turned to Rutherford and King and said, "Well, it looks pretty much like I thought it would," and suddenly King realized that the old man still thought he was in Juárez.

He seemed in a somewhat grumpy and sour mood in the car, but that was not surprising, he had been that way on and off for several weeks. He was still bothered by the forthcoming election campaign. Everyone knew he hated Nixon, he had never made any secret of that, Rayburn was a man of the party and of old-fashioned loyalties and he believed that Nixon had slandered the Democratic Party and some of his friends. But Rayburn was still wary of Kennedy, he had not completely accepted him as a man of presidential stature. Kennedy represented much of what he was coming to distrust in politics. Jack Kennedy had served under Rayburn in the House, but he had not been a particularly diligent member; he had stayed around only long enough to run for the Senate, and when he had been elected to the Senate, he had used that body primarily as a base from which he could run for the presidency. Rayburn disliked this, it was a sign of the younger man's fierce ambition. Worse, Kennedy was someone who was closer to many journalists than he was to most of his colleagues in the Senate.

Sam Rayburn, that year, had of course been for Lyndon, but Lyndon was a reluctant and petulant presidential candidate; his grand design called for everyone else to take a risk and stop Kennedy in the primaries while he stood on the sidelines. Rayburn and others had pushed for Lyndon to run a more active campaign, they had in fact put together a campaign complete with an opening announcement, and then, at the last minute, Johnson had reneged. Rayburn, furious, had turned to Horace Busby, Johnson's speech writer, and had asked, plaintive and exhausted, "Why is Lyndon always like this?" Johnson's campaign had, of course, failed, since it was never a campaign, and Rayburn had hated the way that Kennedy forces had controlled the convention in Los Angeles. They seemed to be cold and merciless young men. He was still uneasy about the idea of a Catholic running for the presidency, the South that he knew had too much racial and religious hatred and he was afraid that Kennedy's candidacy would simply stir things up. When Kennedy had first offered the vice-presidency to Johnson, Rayburn had been one of those most opposed to the idea. But then overnight he had changed his mind and he had told Lyndon to take it, not out of love for Jack Kennedy but out of hatred for Richard Nixon. He had told Lyndon the ticket could win only if he was on it, and it was imperative that Nixon not be President.

That day in El Paso they finally got the old man back to his hotel room, and Rayburn asked Larry King to turn on the television set because Richard Nixon was about to make a speech. Nixon was Rayburn's personal bête noire in politics. Now, as King was fiddling with the dials, he began his diatribe against the Republican candidate. "Look at that face, that hateful face. Boys," he confided, "a few years ago I made the mistake of saying that Richard Nixon had the most hateful face of the five thousand people I served with in the House and someone violated that confidence and it got into the papers and it embarrassed me and I had to apologize. But it's *true,* he has a hateful face, the worst face of anyone I ever served with." The Speaker normally liked all politicians, finding even in their weaknesses and idiosyncrasies a sign of their humanity, but Nixon was different, Nixon had not only attacked friends of his, Presidents and Secretaries of State, but accused them of a lack of loyalty.

Now, as he watched Nixon speaking on the tube, he turned to King and asked him to see if he couldn't fiddle with that machine so they could hear the voice but not see the face. Could he please remove the picture? So King poked around with the dials until he made Richard Nixon a nonperson and finally only a voice emerged from a vast screen of snow. "That's better," said the Speaker. But as Nixon continued talking King noticed an almost chemical change in Rayburn. He seemed to be changing color. Nixon was attacking the

Democrats while promising not to attack them, and this seemed to affect the Speaker profoundly. Rayburn began now to denounce not just Nixon but the entire proceedings. It was, thought King, as if the old man were dismayed not just by the candidate himself but by the whole process he represented. "Look at what they're doing, putting someone like him on that machine. It's all going to be like that Checkers speech, trying to trick people into electing him. They're going to try and trick people into making him President." It was clear, King thought, that Rayburn was appalled by the entire new process of politics, the new and different tempo, television, modern advertising, polls, all that. The new modern manipulation was so different from the manipulation that Rayburn knew and trusted and practiced, where Rayburn and a few others dealt the cards, knew each other and looked into the faces of the men they were dealing with the next day. A new age was coming where things were moving faster, and where fewer and fewer people turned the face off the television set. As he went on he sounded more and more querulous. He liked everything about the old age of politics and nothing about the new.

Eleven years later a crew of CBS television reporters was in Johnson City, Texas, interviewing Lyndon Johnson for his televised memoirs. There was a curious ambiguity to the project: Johnson, the first of two Presidents to feel himself driven from office by the press, was still angry at the media for his demise, CBS not excepted, and yet Johnson, the politician-memoirist-business-man, was not only telling his side of the story but making hundreds of thousands of dollars for the combined book-documentary project. His mood and his temper thus sharply fluctuated. On one particular day the former President was in an unusually relaxed mood, and a senior CBS producer named John Sharnik asked him what had changed in politics between his early days in Congress some thirty years before and the final days of his presidency. Sharnik asked his question quite casually and was stunned by the vehemence of Johnson's answer. "You guys," he had said, without even reflecting. "All you guys in the media. All of politics has changed because of you. You've broken all the machines and the ties between us in Congress and the city machines. You've given us a new kind of people." A certain disdain passed over his face. "Teddy. Tunney. They're your creations, your puppets. No machine could ever create a Teddy Kennedy. Only you guys. They're all yours. Your product."

It was like a news explosion. The pace had been so slow before Roosevelt, so relaxed and genteel. Washington, after all, was not that big a dateline. There had been only a handful of reporters there who really mattered and who covered national events, five or six of them perhaps. They were all gentlemen emulating the style of Richard Oulahan of *The New York Times* and J. Fred Essery of the Baltimore *Sun,* the beau ideals of the time, very properly dressed, men who wore fedoras and carried walking sticks. The walking sticks were symbolic, they were a sign of the more leisurely professions; after Franklin Roosevelt came there would be no more walking sticks. To their colleagues they were *Mister* Oulahan and *Mister* Essery. Mister Essery even wore a starched shirtfront. Croswell Bowen of International News Service had arrived in the late twenties and he, new in town and much influenced by *The Front Page,* had deliberately affected a style that was in part rumpled and in part seedy; but he had quickly gotten the message and soon was appearing with both a fedora and a walking stick. They were all men in their forties and fifties, it was not yet a young man's beat. They were the cream of a new crop of journalists, they covered the activities of dignitaries, and their clothes, as much as anything else, put some distance between them and other reporters, those who covered murders and other police stories. They were very deliberately making the profession more serious; why, Hoover himself was said to be personally fond of Oulahan, and later, while still President, attended Oulahan's funeral, a mark of great distinction for Oulahan. They all carried calling cards, they never rushed from one office to another; they knew all the people they spoke to by name and they as rarely as possible used the telephone, the telephone was a sign of being rushed, it seemed a mark of discourtesy. Besides, there was always time to visit news sources in person, the government was so small, there were so few sources of information. The State, Navy, and War Building housed the entire American military and national security complex, such as it was. They would drive to the Ellipse in the morning, parking their cars there, a good hundred yards away from the White House itself, complaining bitterly to each other how inconvenient it was all becoming with this new heavy traffic; then they began their rounds. The first stop was often the Interior Building, because it was usually good for a story on Indians. In the twenties in Washington the Indian story was a big one, Indians were one of the few major concerns of the federal government. Then, often traveling as a small group, they would go on to the War Department Building. Secretary of State Kellogg saw them very regularly, though there were those who did not think Kellogg a particularly good source of information. Sometimes they saw General Pershing as well. Then they went to the White House and tried to see the President. There was no need for White House credentials as such, everyone knew everyone else, if there was a new reporter his colleagues vouched for him. One reporter covered the entire executive branch in those days—the White House, State, War, Interior, Commerce—so if a colleague covered the Congress two men might make up the entire bureau. (Thirty years later ten or twelve reporters might be necessary to cover a comparable number of departments, and most of their work would be done by phone; there simply wasn't time for very much human contact.)

When journalists visited President Hoover they submitted their questions for him in writing. On occasion he deigned to answer them. In writing, of course. Increasingly, as the weight of the Depression bore down on him, Hoover declined to respond at all. Indeed, his press secretary suggested on occasion that the reporters would do well not even to use the terms "financial crisis" and "unemployment" in their stories without checking with the White House press office. Some of them thought that bordered on censorship. Complaints were made and the White House backed down. Most of them were disappointed with Mr. Hoover. Before becoming President he had been a much-admired figure, a talented administrator with an international reputation for having brought food to a starving world after World War I. Washington journalists were in fact the very ones who had built his reputation, for, in truth, Herbert Hoover, outwardly stiff and formal, particularly as President, had been, before taking office, a very good source of news, very accessible, very manipulative, a very good all-around leak. But Hoover had changed even before the Depression, when he ran for the presidency in 1928. It was as if he were a different and now more important man and such close contact with working reporters was below not just his dignity but that of his intended office. He was very good, it turned out, at outlining the flaws and weaknesses of government as long as someone else was in charge of the government.

As the Depression grew worse, Hoover had turned inward; he had been unable to deal with the terrifying turn of events. Immobilized politically by his fate, he grew hostile and petulant. He blamed reporters for his problems and his diminished popularity, as if his hard times during the Depression were their fault and the economic chaos was primarily a public relations problem. He became obsessed with what was written about him, and punitive toward reporters. "Knowing that the newspapers made him, he assumes with equal ease they can destroy him," wrote Paul Anderson, one of Washington's better reporters. There were more and more squabbles between the President and the press; on several minor occasions, such as when reporters wrote about a Marine guard being bitten by one of the dogs at Hoover's fishing camp, there were investigations launched to find out who their sources were. It was a bad time for the nation and a bad time for the President. The country was in economic collapse, and the entire nation waited to hear what Hoover was going to do. The President was largely silent. In his first year, he had held twenty-three press conferences and handed out eight press statements; in his last year as President, when the country most desperately wanted contact with him, wanted leadership and wanted a voice, he held only twelve press conferences and handed out twenty-six statements.

Franklin Roosevelt changed all that. He was the greatest newsmaker that Washington had ever seen. He came at a time when the society was ready for vast political and economic change, all of it enhancing the power of the President and the federal government, and he accelerated that change. The old order had collapsed, old institutions and old myths had failed; he would create the new order. In the new order, government would enter the everyday existence of almost all its citizens, regulating and adjusting their lives. Under him Washington became the focal point, it determined how people worked, how much they made, what they ate, where they lived. Before his arrival, the federal government was small and timid; by the time he died it reached everywhere, and as the government was everywhere, so Washington became the great dateline; as it was the source of power, so it was the source of news.

Roosevelt promised reporters two press conferences a week and, with astonishing regularity, he held to that: 337 in his first term, 374 in the second, 279 in the third. United Press carried *four* times as much Washington news in 1934 under him as it did in 1930 under Hoover; *one fourth* of all the world news on the Associated Press wire in those days came from Washington. Suddenly everything was faster, the pace was quicker, there were so many more events, so many more government agencies, so many more sources, so many more stories. "You've got a mouthful now," Roosevelt had said as an early press conference was ending. "Better run." Run they did, there was no more time for walking sticks, no more time to put questions in writing, no more time for calling cards. The world had changed from one administration to another. Power in the wake of the Depression was waiting to be taken, and Franklin Roosevelt was going to take it, and those in the media were going to be his prime instrument.

God, did he make news! Every day there were two or three stories coming out of the White House. He intended to make the whole federal government his, make it respond to his whim and vision, he did so, and in that struggle he became this century's prime manipulator of the new and increasingly powerful modern media. Thirty and forty years later, politicians like John Kennedy and Lyndon Johnson would study how Franklin Roosevelt had handled the press, it was a textbook course in manipulation. The entire nation waited on him; if newsmen misread the rules and transgressed even slightly, he could come down hard and quickly, indeed quite brutally, on them. But the personality was secondary. Far more important was the fact that he was the best source in town. He understood exactly what journalists needed and when they needed it, and he understood from his Albany days that the very high public official who gives the greatest amount of information can dominate the story, often define the issue in question and thus dominate the government. Let no other government official dare try and take the play away from him and thwart his will. He was skilled at taking reporters behind the scenes, into the very heart of the mechanics of government, what was being done and why, explaining, in terms highly suitable and favorable to him, the working of the processes. He was thus divulging a staggering amount of information, all of it difficult to get by any other means, all of it sympathetic to him. And everything was happening so quickly that the reporters never had time to go to other sources; if they tried, they might make today's story better, but they would surely be beaten on tomorrow's. Roosevelt was as much teacher as spokesman, and he was always aware of every nuance, of the constituency and mandate he was trying to create. He tried to shape every story. "If I were writing that story," he would often say, "I would write it along the lines. . ." Then he would dictate their leads. In terms of public policy it was a tour de force, nothing like it had ever been seen before. "The best newspaperman who has ever been President of the United States," Heywood Broun called him. "The White House school of journalism," Raymond Clapper, one of the most distinguished of Washington reporters, labeled the entire operation.

It was, by contrast with previous operations, strikingly informal. There simply wasn't enough time for formality, and besides, Roosevelt's touch, that splendid patrician touch, required informality, without it he would have appeared a snob. In another time he might have seemed overbearing, but in the midst of the Depression, when the nation had lost its faith, it took comfort in the fact that he was so sure of his destiny and his role. His destiny would become theirs. His confidence seemed inspiring. He knew the reporters by their first names and he laughed with them and exchanged small talk and, totally at ease with himself, he was totally at ease with them. He constantly assaulted the nation's newspaper publishers for their conservatism, which, given the greater class consciousness of the era, did not hurt him with working reporters. He went before the Daughters of the American Revolution and began his speech, "Fellow immigrants . . ." and the reporters covering him loved it. He even made up nicknames for them. Felix Belair of *The New York Times* became Butch because Roosevelt thought there ought to be someone named Butch at a paper as serious as the *Times*. His touch always seemed so sure. He was so confident of himself, so sure that he was the ablest man in the country to govern, so aware in his own patrician way of his right to be doing what he was doing, that he seemed totally natural as President; it was a great art and he made it seem artless. It was astonishing in that era that someone so wellborn could have so intuitive a common touch; some friends thought it had come from the polio, that this had sensitized him and made him aware of the pain that others, less fortunate, suffered. It made him no less confident, and it made him far more aware.

He was a cripple. Those who covered him never wrote about it because Steve Early asked them not to, and the White House photographers never took his photo in a wheelchair or on crutches because Early asked them not to; those were different days and reporters respected certain rights of the President. (Felix Belair, working for *Time* a few years later, was with Roosevelt at Hyde Park when he had voted in the 1940 election. He had gone inside the voting booth and a lever had jammed. "This goddamned thing doesn't work," came that rich familiar voice from the voting booth, and Belair had filed it and *Time* had printed the quote; Roosevelt was enraged—no one believed in those days purer of soul that the President of the United States could lapse into profanity. Reporters had always shielded the public from presidential profanity and Roosevelt denied that he had been blasphemous.)

Nor did the journalists covering him think of Roosevelt as a cripple, he seemed to radiate such immense power and force, a kind of magnetic vitality.

The first time that Felix Belair, then newly assigned by the *Times* to the White House, met Roosevelt was after a press conference in 1936. Steve Early, as was his wont with new reporters, had waited until the conference was over and then he had brought the new man up to meet the President. The first thing that Belair noticed was the head, how massive and forceful it was, a head waiting for a great artist to sculpt it. Then the hand. The hand was enormous, like a Virginia ham, Belair thought, as it swallowed up his own hand. "Mister President," Early was saying, "do you know Felix Belair of *The New York Times?*" Then that voice, rich and powerful, so sure of itself, sweeping over Belair: "No. I don't believe I've had the pleasure, but I've read his stuff." Could it be more perfect? He even had the phrasing right, why, that was the way other newspapermen spoke to each other about their work, *I've read his stuff.* Just one of the boys. Whenever it suited him.

He was very good with the boys, the five or six or seven regulars who traveled with him on all trips, able to be one of them when he chose, even on occasion playing poker with them. Once he had blown up at one of the regulars at a press conference, and he immediately realized that he had gone too far and come down too imperiously. Later the reporter apologized for being a little sleepy because they had all been up until 4 A.M. playing poker. Poker, the President said, that sounded like a good idea, he hadn't played poker with them in a long time. He turned to Marvin McIntyre, his other press secretary, and told him to get together a buffet dinner, they would all play poker that night. So they played that night and Willard Edwards of the Chicago *Tribune* played and he was also a few drinks ahead of the others, and, as if carrying out the *Trib*'s editorial opposition to Roosevelt, he raised every time the President raised. He did not do this very well, and Roosevelt kept winning the hands, but it did not deter Edwards. "Colonel McCormick's money is better than any goddamned New Deal money," he kept saying. McIntyre, watching, was shocked and made a signal to the other reporters to get Edwards out of there, but Roosevelt waved him off. He was taking the Colonel's money and he was in no hurry to get rid of the Colonel's man.

Roosevelt's hold on his press corps was very powerful. In part he was brilliant at the mechanics of their craft and they, like everyone else, were members of the society, he held their hopes in his hand just as he did those of their readers. The years of the Depression had been so bleak; reporters, like everyone else, had wanted a savior, wanted him to succeed, wanted the New Deal to work. It had rained heavily on inauguration day and there was mud everywhere but it had not dimmed their anticipation of the new era. At one point along the parade route Turner Catledge of the *Times* had looked down and seen a new dime. He had picked it up and said, "Now I know everything's going to be all right." Any symbol would do. So Roosevelt began with the benefit of the doubt and, indeed, more. He was also very skilled, once in office, at using peer pressure to keep reporters in line, isolating any journalist who asked too difficult a question, making him look ridiculous. There was a small group of regulars who sat in the front-row seats at all White House press conferences and who were totally Roosevelt's men. They laughed at every joke and pun; the others called them The Giggle Club. There was no doubt that the President used them effectively; not only would a potential dissident feel the quick lash of the President's tongue, but he might also hear what seemed to be the laughter of his colleagues. When Bob Post of the *Times* asked, in 1937, whether the President was considering a third term, Roosevelt had answered, "Go sit in the corner and put on a dunce cap," and everyone had laughed. Another time, angered by the isolationist writings of John O'Donnell of the New York *Daily News,* the President had awarded O'Donnell an Iron Cross. Once, when he was feuding with Arthur Krock of the *Times* and Felix Belair asked a question he did not like, Roosevelt had answered, "I bet little Arthur sat up all night framing that one." Much laughter. Another time, when Belair seemed to doze off at a press conference while Roosevelt was going through a tirade against fat-cat publishers, a favorite theme, the President had exploded, "Belair! I don't care what paper you represent! You're here on my sufferance and when you're here you will take notes!" It was a shattering moment for Belair, the President of the United States shouting at him. There were not many moments like that but there were enough to remind the regulars who was in charge, informal or not, family atmosphere or not. Once, after the 1942 election, Richard Harkness, then with United Press, had written in his overnight story that Roosevelt had voted the straight Democratic ticket. The next day Harkness was sitting with other reporters when an enraged Roosevelt sought him out. "You have destroyed the secrecy of the ballot! How dare you announce that I voted in any way? How dare you say I voted straight Democratic or anything else?"

But those moments were the exception. It was a reporter's dream, there was so much energy, so much action, so much access. Roosevelt had an intuitive grasp of the way the press worked, could be worked. His sense of timing was impeccable; he once told Orson Welles that there were two great actors in America at that moment. Welles, he said, was the other one. Besides, the rhythm of the times, the great inventions and the changing shape of society, were working to centralize power. The coming of radio and airplanes was breaking down regionalism and making the nation, in a clearer sense, one. Radio was a network, one man's voice was heard across the entire country. Issues became national rather than parochial and regional. In the old era Washington was filled with journalists who covered regional issues for their regional papers; when the Roosevelt era was over Washington was filled with reporters who were often highly trained specialists who wrote of national implications for the entire country. The speed of decision was becoming faster and faster and, as it did, local governments simply could not keep up with the growing power and affluence of the federal government. The federal government's taxing power increased as its mandate increased, and as its taxing power increased, so did its real power. Technology was bringing the central state a longer and more powerful reach. The central state could reach areas previously isolated. More, it could perform functions, deliver services, and make judgments inconceivable in another era.

Nor was this an isolated phenomenon. It was happening throughout the world. In Germany and in the Soviet Union, powerful highly centralized governments had taken power, and their very rise strengthened the coming of the centralized government in America. Highly centralized totalitarian states were deeply threatening; if power was more clearly centralized elsewhere, might not a democracy prove vulnerable, might not, in an age of increasingly swift and destructive bombers and other weapons, democracy be too slow, too awkward? So the coming of totalitarian states strengthened the American presidency, giving the President leverage which he used not just against the adversary states but against the American public, Congress, and press, arguing the needs of national security. Similarly, as the peacetime Roosevelt years ended and World War II began, the focus was to change from domestic issues, about which the Congress was informed and felt itself equal, to foreign policy and national security, where Congress felt itself ignorant and clumsy and thus inevitably subservient.

All this began in the thirties, the arrival of new forces that were to make the American presidency for some forty years almost unchallenged in its power, and it all began under Franklin Roosevelt. A lesser man, a more modest man, might have shrunk from all these possibilities and implications as he took office, but Roosevelt welcomed them; he welcomed the chance to change things, to expand the powers of the government, and he knew immediately how to create his own new mandate.

He was, of course, subtly but quite consciously elevating the importance of the press. If he wanted direct access to their readers, then they had to have direct access to him. He was more often than not going directly to the media rather than to the Congress with information; and he put more energy into his press relations than into his congressional ones. There was a changing institutional balance. If on occasion print reporters were angered by his increased use of and chumminess with radio reporters, then people in the Congress and some Democratic Party politicians were irritated by the fact that he seemed to court media people in general more than he did them. He simply needed the Congress and the party structure less.

As he used the media more often and more directly, they became more influential; they became more and more architects of the national agenda, making more decisions on what the great issues were rather than just responding to the decisions of others. The press corps was becoming a different, more serious, and better informed body. Reporters became, with their greater role in the Roosevelt years, more influential and more prestigious around town, more sought after; similarly, as the stories became more serious and more complicated, the people writing them became better qualified, better educated, and more serious.

In those early Roosevelt years reporters like Catledge and Belair, who had covered the Congress in the old era, could almost feel the tide changing, the Congress becoming weaker; no one on the Hill even seemed to know it was happening. One moment in 1937 seemed to crystallize it for Belair: the President was at Warm Springs and he had been driving around in his manually operated car and he had stopped where the reporters were gathered, for an impromptu outdoor curbstone press conference. The setting seemed to emphasize the informality of it, the President driving up in front of waiting reporters, teasing them—*Are you all right? You probably want something from me to write about?* Then he had quickly gotten down to business. There was a major congressional struggle on at the time on the question of devaluing the dollar; the President wanted the devaluation and big business in general opposed it. The news had come in that day that the Senate had voted for devaluation, which did not surprise Belair. What did surprise him was Roosevelt's tone. He was boundlessly full of himself that day, more so than usual, and he seemed exalted by the triumph. "This proves," he said, "that the Senate of the United States cannot be bought." Belair was scribbling down the words, but even as he did, he was thinking, *Who ever said that it could be bought?* It was the colossal arrogance of it, it symbolized to Belair how completely Roosevelt had taken over the town, how personal an instrument of his will he had made the office, it was his possession and so was everything else in Washington. It was as if it were now *his* Senate. If the Senate responded as he wanted, it was a good Senate, otherwise it was a bad one. It often seemed in those years, Belair thought, as if a new kind of politics had come into existence, so forceful and all-encompassing was the power of the President. He could reach past anything that stood in his way, the opposition party, the Congress, his own party, the Supreme Court.

Part of it was the special quality of the moment; the Depression gave Roosevelt vast political freedom and also permitted him, as a media figure, to play exactly the kind of role in exactly the type of theater he wanted— Roosevelt the friend of the common man, his opponents the friends of the old, discredited, exploitative order. There was also one large new ingredient in the political composition of the country and that was radio. Roosevelt had made radio his own personal instrument and had changed permanently the institutional balance of politics. Radio had been a powerful force in the country for almost a decade; by the time of his inauguration it was already the most important means of entertainment in the country and it represented a means of merchandising that was beginning to rival and even threaten magazine advertising. But it had been scarcely used as a political instrument. Herbert Hoover, in desperate political trouble, needing all the assets he could muster, had not deigned to use radio. Men of his generation looked at it with contempt. It was beneath their dignity. Hoover's rare broadcasts had been awkward, stilted, pedantic, words written and spoken in governmentese. Rather than humanizing the President, they had merely confirmed the impression of an uncaring man in a distant office. Yet the instrument was there and sooner or later some shrewd politician was going to make a powerful national connection.

The first broadcast had been made in 1920 and the public response had been quick and enthusiastic; by 1922 there were some 220 radio stations in the country. The sets themselves, simple models, sold for about ten dollars. Stores were not able to keep them in stock, manufacturers had to rush forward their orders. By 1923 there were already 2.5 million sets in the country. Millions of Americans had made radio the focal point of their households, scheduling their day around their favorite programs. When "Amos 'n' Andy" was on the air, the nation simply stopped all its other business and listened. When Pepsodent sponsored "Amos 'n' Andy" its sales tripled in just a few weeks. The way was clear. Those companies which were highly dependent on popular taste, like toothpaste and cigarettes, saw the light; by 1931 the American Tobacco Company spent $19 million to advertise Lucky Strike on radio. Was it surprising then, with audiences and sales like that, that Franklin Roosevelt, free of charge, was soon selling himself and the New Deal on radio? He was the first great American radio voice. For most Americans of this generation, their first memory of politics would be of sitting by a radio and hearing *that* voice, strong, confident, totally at ease. If he was going to speak, the idea of doing something else was unthinkable. If they did not yet have a radio, they walked the requisite several hundred yards to the home of a more fortunate neighbor who did. It was in the most direct sense the government reaching out and touching the citizen, bringing Americans into the political process and focusing their attention on the presidency as the source of good. Roosevelt was the first professional of the art. He had practiced for it as governor of New York. The first time he had used radio as President he had turned to Carleton Smith of NBC, the one radio man allowed in the room, and had said, "You'll never have any trouble with me, I'm an old hand at this." Which he was. Smith (whom NBC had chosen to replace Herluf Provenson because the Roosevelt people thought Provenson was too close to Hoover) had a stopwatch that Roosevelt always used to time himself. He called it "that famous watch." Smith was impressed by Roosevelt's ability to stay almost exactly within the prescribed time limits. When it was over he would always turn to Smith and ask: How did it go? Was I repetitious? Were there any lapses? There rarely were; it was a consummately professional performance.

Most Americans in the previous 160 years had never even seen a President; now almost all of them were hearing him, *in their own homes.* It was literally and figuratively electrifying. Because he was President he had access to the airwaves any time he wanted, when he wanted. Indeed, because he was such a good performer, because his messages so bound the nation, the networks wanted him on more often regularly, perhaps once a week (an offer he shrewdly turned down, aware of the danger of overexposure, telling a network official that people cannot stand the repetition of the highest note on the scale for very long). "You guys want him to do everything," Steve Early, Roosevelt's press secretary, once told Carleton Smith. "I don't want the Boss to do very much. We want to conserve him."

He spoke in an informal manner, his speeches were scripted not to be read in newspapers but to be heard aloud. He worked carefully on them in advance, often spending several days on a speech, reading the words aloud, working on the rhythm and the cadence, getting the feel of them down right. When aides questioned the immense amount of time he devoted to just one speech, Roosevelt said that it was probably the most important thing he would do all week. He had an intuitive sense of radio cadence. Unlike most people, who speeded up their normal speech pattern on radio, Roosevelt deliberately slowed his down. He was never in a rush. He had often memorized a speech before he began, and so he seemed infinitely confident, never seemed to stumble. The patterns of the speech were conversational. His very first words reflected his ease: "My friends," he began. *My friends.* That was it, they were his friends. Nor were they a passive audience. At that desperate moment in American history the American people were not cool, not aloof, they needed him and they wanted him to succeed; what could be more stirring than to be told by that man with that rich assured voice that the only thing they had to fear was fear itself.

It was all so personal. This was not some distant government official talking in governmentese, this was a voice connected to a warm human being; he knew them, he had visited them. He spoke of his wife and his children, even his dog. Some thirty-five years later an astonishing number of Americans who did not remember the names of the dogs of Harry Truman, Dwight Eisenhower, and John Kennedy, remembered the name of Franklin Roosevelt's dog because he had spoken with them about Fala, *my little dog Fala,* about Fala's Irish being up over Republican criticism. It was an awesome display of mastery. It was as if sitting in the studio he could visualize his audience sitting around their radios in their homes, and he spoke not to the microphone but to those homes. If it was very hot in Washington he might turn to an aide and ask, over the open mike, for a glass of water, and apologize to his audience, and that too humanized him, the President needed a glass of water. His touch was perfect. Often, when the speech was over, because newsreels were becoming a bigger and bigger factor in American life, Roosevelt would then repeat vital parts of the speech for a newsreel camera. But the camera was not allowed in to film the broadcast itself; it was simply too noisy in those days.

Nearly 50 million Americans listened to most of his speeches. They were in a real sense his own captive audience. Not by chance was he the first three-term and then four-term President in the nation's history, rising above tradition, above opposition party, above his own party's will. (No longer did politicians need the party to raise a crowd. Now the radio did it. Yet few professional politicians of the day understood radio or how to use it. Carleton Smith of NBC tried to do a program with members of Roosevelt's Cabinet and had a terrible problem. Jim Farley, the Postmaster General and ablest professional politician of his generation, simply could not pronounce the word "with." It always came out "wit," making Farley seem like a hack.) Thus did Franklin Roosevelt outdistance even his own party. He had changed the institutional balance and he changed the nature of the presidency; from now on it was a personalized office, less distant from the average American. Until March 1933, through a world war and a Great Depression, the White House had employed only one person to handle the incoming mail. Herbert Hoover had received, for example, some 40 letters a day. After Franklin Roosevelt arrived and began to make his radio speeches, the average was closer to 4,000 letters a day.


The White House reporters, of course, resented the coming of radio, and even more, the coming of the first radio correspondents. Never mind that radio inevitably whetted interest in government and thus increased readership, never mind that radio would act as a kind of monitor and force journalism to improve, ending the Hearst style of reporting, what was at stake was turf. Suddenly there was a new kind of reporter around, reporters who, to the eye of the print traditionalists, weren't reporters at all. They were pretty boys with slick voices and worse, they seemed to have stunningly quick access to vast audiences. Carleton Smith of NBC was the first radio correspondent at the White House. His job was to place a microphone in front of the President and tap Roosevelt on the shoulder when the network hookup was ready. NBC in those early days was the dominant company. Poor Bob Trout, the first CBS man, had to stand outside the door. The first time that Roosevelt saw a CBS microphone he asked, "CBS? What's that?" But CBS gradually got into the act. John Charles Daly succeeded Trout. Daly was not so much a correspondent in the early days as he was a special-events man; he was supposed to cover the launching of ships and to help broadcast concerts by the Army Band on Mondays and the Marine Band on Wednesdays. Daly—smooth, strikingly handsome, with a rich voice—inspired even more resentment among the print reporters, particularly from Belair of the *Times* and Walter Trohan, the feisty correspondent of the Chicago *Tribune.* Trohan in particular did not like radio and he especially did not like John Charles Daly. "That man's no reporter," he used to complain to his colleagues. "He's never worked in a city room. He's never covered a story. *I think he's an actor. "* What makes you think he's not a reporter? Belair asked. "Because reporters play poker when they're not working and that man is off in the woods practicing lines from Shakespeare, listening to his own voice," Trohan answered.

Daly, of course, was not shy. He had his job and part of it was to push for access. That part was made easier by the growing size of the audiences; no one had to tell Franklin Roosevelt where people gathered. Gradually the status of Carleton Smith and Daly changed; correspondents they wanted to be, correspondents they were. Soon they rode in the third car in presidential caravans. In those days position was based on circulation; the wire services were in the first car; the specials, men like Belair and Trohan, in the second; and the networks in the third. That was not good enough for Daly and he kept arguing that the networks in status were in fact equal to the wire services. That was a staggering presumption for the times and at first not only did the print reporters resist it, but more important Steve Early refused to accept it. But Daly persisted; on occasion, he argued, the networks had a greater circulation than the wires, although in sum the wires had a basic circulation that was higher. But certainly more people heard CBS than read the *Times*. Finally Early, after consultation with his boss, agreed, and at the start of a presidential trip, Early changed the rating system, putting the networks in the second car. As they all rushed to their cars Daly and Smith found Walter Trohan in the second car. "You son of a bitch," Trohan told Daly, "this is our car." Not any more, it wasn't. Daly summoned Early, who forced the Chicago *Tribune* and *The New York Times* to car three. When Felix Belair complained mildly to Early later, the press secretary apologized. "It's not that we like them better," he said. Radio had arrived.

I

# 1/CBS

He was young and the industry was younger. He had started in the family cigar business, which was very successful, but he was nonetheless restless for something a little different, he did not simply want to repeat his own father's successes. He did not know very much about radio, which was then very new. A friend had one of the early crystal sets, and Bill Paley tried to buy a radio for himself, but in those days radios were not for sale in stores, and so he had to have one made. He became a devoted radio listener, the little machine seemed to open up a much larger world, and he often found himself staying up very late at night listening. He also found that many of his friends were doing much the same thing. One summer in 1925 when his father, Sam, and his uncle Jake were away and he was in charge of the company, he experimented a little with the advertising budget and for the grand sum of fifty dollars a week sponsored the "Miss La Palina Hour" on WCAU, the local Philadelphia radio station. Miss La Palina was, of course, named after the cigar, which was in turn named after the family, Paley, and for the fifty dollars he got not only the singer but a ten-piece orchestra as well. When Jake Paley returned from the trip and very quickly spotted the fifty-dollar expenditure, he was furious; Jake Paley was not a frivolous man and he did not do frivolous things like listen to the radio. He demanded to know what the money had gone for and his nephew tried to explain. "That's nonsense," said Jake Paley, "that machine is never going to work," and so Miss La Palina quickly departed Philadelphia's airwaves. But in the next few weeks Sam Paley, who was a very smart man and a very good listener, was struck by how many people stopped him on the street to ask what happened to the "Miss La Palina Hour." He wondered aloud to his son Bill how he could spend half a million on print advertising and get so little response, and then spend only fifty dollars for radio and everyone missed his singer. Soon Jake Paley checked the books and found that sales had gone up because of the radio advertisements. Shortly after that Miss La Palina went back on the air, and very soon after that Bill Paley went into radio.

Sam Paley had made his money in cigars, the Congress Cigar Company, and indeed the woman on the wrapper of the La Palina was said to resemble

Goldie, wife of Sam, mother of Bill. Sam Paley's father, Isaac Paley, had been a prosperous businessman in Russia; he had been in the lumber business in a small town outside Kiev, and he had been a good deal wealthier than most Jews in Russia in the latter part of the nineteenth century. But he was discontented with the restrictions which the Russian society placed on Jews and the anti-Semitism that hung so heavily in the atmosphere at all times, and so he had often thought of emigrating to America. Unlike most Eastern European Jews who dreamed of America as a distant miracle and who, if they came to this country, came blind and by steerage, Isaac Paley, deciding that America was worthy of his interest, had bought a first-class ticket and taken an investigatory trip to the United States. He had liked it here, and had returned to Russia to bring over his entire family, including the youthful Sam, around 1890. Isaac Paley had settled in Chicago, investing his money in a number of stocks. He envisioned a life of genteel semi-retirement, sitting around the samovar with his friends, discussing serious intellectual subjects, sipping tea the Russian way through the sugar, enjoying the intellectual ferment of the old world while buffered by the greater freedom of the new one.

He did not intend for his son Sam to work; he wanted him instead to be a full-time intellectual. Unfortunately Isaac Paley's investments were not worthy of his dreams, the stocks went bad and he lost all his money. So as a boy Sam Paley went to work to support his father, something that Isaac Paley never entirely realized. Sam Paley was very bright and ambitious and entrepreneurial and soon he was rolling cigars and selling them, and soon after that there were others working for him, and soon after that there was a factory, and after that, other factories. He was a man of great driving energy and a genuine skill in the blending of tobacco. He had a feel for the texture of tobacco, how to take two or three different strains and anticipate the blend that they would create. He proved to be a masterful cigar maker, the most successful one in the country at the time, and his success was genuine. He eventually sold the business for $30 million just before the Depression.

Since he had had a dilettante for a father, Sam Paley was more determined than most men that his own son would be a serious young man and would know the meaning of hard work. Not only would Bill go to the best American schools, to the Wharton School of Finance and Commerce at the University of Pennsylvania, but he would be required to work at every level of the cigar company from the bottom up. So Bill Paley did just that and he found that the cigar business was a hard taskmaster, there was very little room for either generosity of spirit or of bookkeeper error in the making of cheap mass-produced cigars. The edge of profit was simply very thin. Sam Paley was pleased by how well his son did in the business, Bill was a good tobacco buyer and he was a very good salesman, particularly gifted at making other people believe that what he wanted was what they wanted as well. But Sam Paley was not a dogmatic man; it was not necessary for his son to take over the family business for Sam Paley to validate his own life. So in 1928, when through family friends and in-laws the chance came along to buy into a fledgling radio network called CBS, Sam Paley, already impressed by radio's possibilities, quickly encouraged his son to get in on it, and put up some $400,000 of the family money. The Congress Cigar Company had just been sold to Dillon Read and while he and Jake had five-year employment contracts as part of the deal, Bill did not. He was free to go to CBS. Sam was enthusiastic about his son's idea: he had decided that one of two things would happen with CBS. Either it would very quickly turn out to be a bust, and thus smaller than the cigar business, in which case he would get his son back with very little heartbreak, or it was going to be very big, in which case it would turn out to be liberating for a talented young man like his son, William Samuel Paley. Radio turned out to be bigger than cigars.

At the time the Paleys bought into CBS, Bill Paley was all of twenty-seven years old. Because the network was being very poorly run, he had intended to spend some time in New York reorganizing the business structure before returning to Philadelphia and the family business. He never went back to cigars. In those days, NBC, all of two years old itself, was the dominant network, so dominating that it had in fact been split into two networks, the Red and the Blue. (The Blue network, at government order, was sold and became ABC in 1941.) Whether CBS would even survive when Bill Paley took over was highly questionable. Radio had no past, the present was very shaky, and most solid responsible people did not seem to think there was very much future. To the degree that network radio existed, NBC was it: NBC controlled the wires, it had signed up the best concert stars for its programming. CBS in 1928 owned no stations of its own, had only sixteen affiliates, lost money, and was housed in one small floor in the Paramount Tower.

Bill Paley changed all that. He was for fifty years the supreme figure of modern broadcasting, first in radio, then in television. Very simply, he merchandised more products for more different companies, and sent out more different entertainers on more different programs, than anyone in the history of mankind. His was one of the staggering success stories of the American twentieth century, a century whose early genius seemed to flower in production and whose later genius emerged, fittingly enough, in sales and promotion. Bill Paley was right at the center of the era's most powerful forces, he had combined the prime energies of American huckstering with the explosive new potential of American technology. He and his imitators achieved vast power and influence over American taste and culture. He made the American home the focal point of the American marketplace. Whereas at the turn of the century only an occasional door-to-door salesman visited the American home, by the middle of the century a ceaseless stream of the most subtle electronic impulses created by the nation's most richly rewarded hucksters was beamed into this new marketplace, relentlessly selling not just the American dream but an endless series of material products through whose purchase that dream might be more quickly achieved.

He was in any real sense the father of modern broadcasting, a towering figure in this newest of professions, his maturity spanning almost the entire history of the institution. He was, in the savage, predatory world of broadcasting, not just the first, but the best. For almost fifty years he had swum in waters with some of capitalism's greatest sharks and there were no tooth marks on him. He was tough and shrewd, and he survived and endured, creating with his desires and ambitions the modern structure of broadcasting, with its brutal ratings system and its unparalleled profits. He more than the other early figures of broadcasting was fascinated by entertainment and programming; it was devotion to every detail in programming which made him so important in American life, for he helped determine what the nation first heard and then saw in its home every night. His chosen instruments, particularly with the coming of television, were by the end of the sixties more dominant in most American lives than newspapers, churches, and often the family itself. It was his decisions which created broadcasting as it exists today, with the power and tastemaking centralized in the network. He brought to his new career an extraordinary assortment and blend of skills; he was a shrewd and imaginative businessman able to see the future and carve it up, even as it was just arriving; he was a wonderful salesman, subtle, low-key, well briefed on each client, with the marvelous ability to make his ideas seem as if they had originated with the client; and in addition he had a natural feel for entertainment. He both loved it and could judge it.

That last was a crucial advantage. There were other men who were good businessmen and others who were deft salesmen, but the feel for talent, that was something else, and it was essential in so public and volatile a profession as broadcasting. He had an absolutely brilliant ear and later, as television arrived, a brilliant eye as well. He had almost perfect pitch in terms of entertainment. For almost half a century, he had a better idea than anyone else in the country of what would play and what would not play to the largest possible audience. He was totally without sentiment: he knew what was good and would sell, what was bad and would sell, and what was good and would not sell, and he never confused one with another. If his own personal taste happened, as it did, to be exquisite, he never confused his taste or that of his very silky friends with that of the larger audience. He was very simply a genius at mass entertainment.

The critical years were the early ones. What he had from the start was a sense of vision, a sense of what might be. It was as if he could sit in New York in his tiny office with his almost bankrupt company and see not just his own desk, or the row of potential advertisers outside along Madison Avenue, but millions of the American people out in the hinterlands, so many of them out there, almost alone, many of them in homes as yet unconnected to electricity, people alone with almost no form of entertainment other than radio. It was his sense, his confidence that he could reach them, that he had something for them, that made him different. He could envision the audience at a time when there was in fact no audience. He not only had the vision, he knew how to harness it, he could see that the larger the audience, the greater the benefit to the network, because it would mean that many more advertisers would want to participate. If the larger audience meant better advertisers, then it also meant more money, which meant better programs, which meant larger audiences, and which meant that more stations would want to affiliate with CBS.

Whereas in those days NBC was trying to make a large part of its money from its affiliate stations by *charging* them for carrying many of its shows, Paley envisioned a different route, designed to reach the maximum audience as directly as possible. It would make things easier and cheaper for the affiliate and thus inevitably minimize the affiliate's role. All he wanted was a guarantee of the maximum audience. The larger the audience, the more time he could sell. To achieve that goal, he had something to offer—indeed to give away— by making his programs available to affiliate stations. As Erik Barnouw writes in his excellent history of American broadcasting, *The Golden Web:*

> He began by making the entire sustaining [unsponsored] schedule *free* to affiliates. At any time during network hours—ten to twelve hours daily—the affiliates could plug into CBS without cost, using its offering of the moment. The affiliate was under no obligation to use any of the sustaining programs but could use all. To many stations the arrangement was a windfall, particularly as the Depression deepened. It was also convenient, eliminating much haggling and bookkeeping. In exchange for the bonanza Paley wanted something: an option on any part of the affiliate's schedule for sponsored network series. He found little resistance to this. The option meant that Paley could sell time to a network sponsor without any uncertainty as to clearance. He could sign a contract with a sponsor for time coast to coast, then instruct the affiliates to clear the time. At first, this required only two weeks' notice.

The small station owners loved the idea; they were desperate for entertainment and lacked the resources to develop their own programming. Now they were getting something for nothing. And there was a geometric progression to it, since the richer CBS became, the stronger its programming, which made CBS that much more desirable. And if CBS preempted, the more the stations were paid. The very announcement of Paley's new idea almost doubled the number of affiliates. In the first year of his stewardship CBS went from a gross earning of $1.4 million to $4.7 million, and to $28.7 million by 1937; the number of stations reached 114 in the first decade he was there. Success had come and it had come very quickly.

He was perfectly suited to this new profession. All his personal qualities seemed to aid him, he was a sensualist and hedonist who was, at the same time, a rigorously disciplined and organized businessman. This meant that he could be at ease with and understand the entertainment part of his coming empire, while still dealing with the business part. There he was as alert, farseeing, and coldhearted a taskmaster as the cigar business had ever produced. More than anyone else in broadcasting, he always knew the entire profession: he knew more about the entertainment side than the other businessmen, and more about the business side than the other entertainment people. He was always ahead of everyone else.

No one read a business report better than Bill Paley; he had an unerring instinct for the bottom line, just as he always seemed to ask the right question at every business meeting, the one question which uncovered the fatal weakness in any proposal. It was, thought a colleague, as if he could sense, from the tone of someone else's voice, the level of confidence, where the flaw lay. When the voice was confident, Paley dozed, and when the voice faltered, suddenly, like a crocodile awakened, he bore in. But it was more than just a pure business sense that made him so successful. The world, after all, was filled with coldhearted, shrewd accountants. Paley had something else, flair, an extra sense about talent, a touch and feel for it. It was all intuition, all taste, there was no way it could be studied or memorized. He could, in 1931, three years after taking over the network, go on a shipboard cruise and by chance hear the early records of a then unknown singer and know instantly that the singer was big, very big, and send back a cable telling his subordinates to sign Bing Crosby immediately. Some thirty years after he first heard Bing Crosby he took Blair Clark, one of his news executives, to the opening night of *Camelot,* and Clark was absolutely astonished by Paley's sense of the show. It was as if Paley were always a beat ahead of everyone else in the theater, laughing at the lines and keeping time with the music. At first Clark, who knew that Paley had put up some of the money, was sure that the Chairman had seen the show before, but he soon realized he was wrong. It was simply that Bill Paley's sense of entertainment was so true, he was just that much quicker than anyone else in the audience. In the same instant, he could hear it, *understand* it, consider it, and know it was going to work. So that was an advantage, a gift of the gods, an ear totally pure.

He had a sense of taste that was almost equally pure. If he chose to limit the amount of true excellence that he broadcast on his network, it was not from failing to recognize it, it was rather a shrewd calculation of the levels and the limits of what the traffic would bear at a given time. It was skill at rationing the number of tasteful things that could be done, enough to sustain the network's carefully orchestrated reputation for excellence while not so much as to affect the bottom line. He was thus able, at moments when the network needed prestige rather than money, to put on a quality program and prove once again that CBS was different, better, nobler than the other networks. For despite what he programmed to his fellow Americans during most of his career, Paley's own sense of aesthetics was eerily fine and instinctive. He was the kind of man who could walk into a room and, with precious little formal training, always pick out the finest painting or the most valuable antique in that room. More, he understood not just aesthetics and taste but the value of them, and the limits of that value, that everything in its way had a price tag. In the forties he had once spent a week in Paris looking for antiques with his correspondent David Schoenbrun as his guide, and when the trip was finished he took Schoenbrun aside to thank him for a wonderful visit, he had after all met only the best people and eaten at only the best restaurants. "David," he had said, "this has been a perfect trip and you have been a perfect host and because of that I'm going to give you a very valuable tip." Schoenbrun's ears pricked up, for he knew that Paley traveled only in the company of the shrewdest and richest businessmen in America. "Don't buy Matisses and Picassos, David," said the Chairman of CBS to the Paris correspondent of CBS, "they've gone too high on the market now. Buy Rembrandt because Rembrandts are the best. They're the best buy now and they're always going to be great. You remember that and remember that Bill Paley told you so." Schoenbrun, in no position to make use of such information, was even more annoyed a few years later when he realized that Paley had been right as usual, Rembrandts *had* gone up more than Picassos and Matisses.

He was also, particularly in the early days, a marvelous salesman. He knew what he wanted, and he knew what he was selling, and he could always put himself in the position of other people. He was so sure that radio could help, it made him almost irresistible. He could see their products selling out in that new wonderful market that he had just invented—aspirins and laxative being swallowed, tires being put on cars, cigarettes being lit up. In those days NBC was large and somewhat overconfident and CBS was small and open and tried harder, and its best salesman was Bill Paley, young and charming and energized, and very available. He was filled with enthusiasm and the fun of what he was doing, the promise of it all. David Sarnoff at NBC was an engineer turned businessman, ill at ease with the hucksterism that he had wrought, and he did not condescend to sell, but Bill Paley loved to sell. CBS was Paley, and he sold it as he sold himself. He loved being a salesman, he was selling his own dreams, he was relentless about it. When the network was young he had fearlessly taken on George Washington Hill, the head of the American Tobacco Company, the most important of all possible radio customers, a man totally committed to NBC.

In the revolution that was taking place in American merchandising, the coming of bigger, national markets and high-powered instruments to reach them, George Washington Hill was at the time as important a figure as Bill Paley. Though it was the height of the Depression, American Tobacco's sales were booming and the main reason they were booming was that Hill was a revolutionary in terms of advertising technique. He was the pioneer of the high-powered, big-budget era of oversell, where the sales campaign often became as important as or more important than the product itself. In an age when advertising budgets were quite small, he was spending six million dollars a year on advertising, and he believed instinctively that, all other things being equal, it was not so much what the product was that counted as what you *said* the product was; he believed that if you said loud enough and often enough that Luckies were different and better, people would believe that they were different and better, even if the tobacco was essentially the same. He loved short snappy ideas; it was for instance his idea to push the blindfold test. If the average person tried smoking with a blindfold, Hill claimed, he would find out the difference between Luckies and other brands. Pushed hard enough, the gimmick finally became believable to an astonishing number of people. He pushed other slogans: "Luckies Are Kind to Your Throat"; "Lucky Strike Means Fine Tobacco"; "Lucky Strike Green Has Gone to War"; and he was a pioneer in promoting the sale of Luckies to women, ending age-old taboos. "Reach for a Lucky Instead of a Sweet," he advised, and women did. He was a small, fierce competitor, ruthless in competition and wildly successful, and he paid himself about a million dollars a year in an era of marginal income tax; he received all other businessmen in his office, where he always wore an enormous cowboy hat, a reminder that they were on his ground rather than their own. His business, so dependent upon public taste, was a natural for radio, and there was no more important client for Bill Paley than George Washington Hill.

But in 1928 and 1929 Hill was still advertising over nine NBC stations and no CBS outlets. The failure to sell American Tobacco, which was in those days much larger than CBS, in some way deprived CBS not just of money but of legitimacy. Paley felt it was essential to break that monopoly, and in mid-1930, through the pioneer public relations man Ed Bernays, he finally arranged an audience with George Washington Hill. Paley emphasized to Hill that CBS had a young, energetic creative team, which was an advantage since radio was so new. After he had spoken George Washington Hill handed him a blank piece of paper. "Ideas, young man," Hill said. "I buy ideas. I want ideas. So put your ideas on this piece of paper and give them to me. I want creativity." Paley went back to his staff and they came up with a number of ideas that surprised even them; with their freshness and obvious salability and confident of his success now, he brought them back to Hill, who pronounced them absolutely first-rate. "It's true," he said, "you are creative, and these are good ideas." Then Hill went down the list, and as he did, he discussed each idea admiringly, and then managed to find some fault with it. But this encouraged Bill Paley. Hill was listening, they were getting close. So he and his staff went back to the drawing board and again they came up with fresh ideas and again George Washington Hill at once admired them and then managed to suffocate them. The third time this happened, always at first so encouraging and then finally so disheartening, Paley finally decided that the only ideas that George Washington Hill really fell in love with were his own. So Paley baited a trap. He waited a good long while before he went back to see Hill and then he mentioned that he and his CBS staff had pretty well exhausted their supply of ideas. That was too bad, said Hill. They did have one little idea, said Paley, but it was almost surely wrong for American Tobacco. What was that? asked Hill, his interest piqued. Well, said Paley, the sell very soft, almost reluctant, a little martial music, a live band, five times a week, fifteen minutes a day. Martial music, said Hill, now very much interested, martial music was always popular, everyone loved martial music. Suddenly he was very interested, and he called in his staff and he marched around the room playing imaginary John Philip Sousa marches, his own one-man band. It was now his idea. A program of band music, he said to his staff. Vince Riggio, his sales manager, listened and said he didn't like it. So Hill strutted around the office a little more, playing all the parts in the band, *oom Pah—oom Pah,* and Riggio said he still didn't like it, and at that moment Bill Paley was ready to strangle Vince Riggio, but Hill marched around his own desk once more, kicking his knees high: *"Every-one loves martial music!"* he shouted, trying to sell his own idea to Riggio. "Now I'm beginning to get it," said Riggio. So it was that Bill Paley had very cleverly taken one of his own ideas and deliberately orphaned it so that Hill would think it was his own, and so it was that the American Tobacco Company sponsored martial music five times a week for fifteen minutes on CBS, an important breakthrough for the young network.

He was just so much smarter than everyone else in the business, so much more subtle, he could sell not just entertainment and products but an aura as well, the idea that CBS was different, somewhat classier, more statesmanlike, and more devoted to the commonweal. If in the early days CBS was attacked by some critics for broadcasting too many laxative commercials, then typically, in 1935, Bill Paley announced somewhat grandly that his network would stop using commercials for laxatives and other products of questionable taste. He was much applauded for his statesmanship, and nobody paid very much attention to the small print in his announcement which had said that the new policy would not apply to existing CBS contracts. Since in those days the laxative people stopped advertising during the slow summer months and signed new contracts in the fall, this simply meant that CBS could tighten the screws on the laxative people and keep them from taking a summer vacation. That year it broadcast more laxative commercials than ever before.

For Bill Paley was tough, that above all. He did not just build an empire, he protected it as well. There was nothing sentimental about him, he knew what he wanted for himself and for his network and he would take on all challengers, be they other networks, the government, demagogues, or rivals within the company. He could be on occasion charming and gracious and witty, and he survived and endured and no one got a piece of him. Other men came and served his purpose and during their passage, whether long or brief, were generously rewarded; they too could bask in the reflected power and glory of the network, but then their time had come and their purpose was done, or they had become too ambitious, or they did not measure up, and they were gone. He could say of Frank Stanton, the other great corporate figure at CBS, the man who had done so much to protect him from the roles he chose not to play and who had done so much to tidy up the reputation of his network, after Stanton had performed a particularly unpleasant chore, "I've always had a guy like Stanton for jobs like that." He would always have it his way, he was one of those men for whom the rules are written and then rewritten, but it made no difference, for he would have broken them anyway. He alone could break the rule on mandatory retirement at CBS, and he could be almost innocent about it, he had not so much broken the rule, he would explain later, as the board had implored him to stay on and he had been pleased and flattered that they liked him so much and so he had stayed. Others came and served and then left, usually involuntarily and often somewhat bitter, but he remained, exuding year after year, decade after decade, a special vitality, an almost animal energy. Indeed, when he was in his seventies a young woman spent some time with him at a dinner party and was struck by how well he looked, zestful, full of life, and she had mentioned this to Truman Capote, then a friend of the Paleys. "He looks just marvelous, doesn't he?" she said, and Capote agreed. "Yes," he said, "he looks like a man who has just swallowed an entire human being."

So he could hold power all those years, always without illusion. There was about him a distance, he was apart, one did not approach him lightly, he was spoiled as few men were spoiled, being not just rich but powerful and influential as well. And unlike Presidents, who were often rich and powerful, his power remained, they came and went, Roosevelt had come and gone, and more than *thirty years* after he had gone Bill Paley still held power. He had things his way, life existed on his terms. He saw the people he chose to see, and he did not see the people he did not choose to see. There were those that thought they were his friends, but had misjudged him or simply misread the rules. Nothing reflected that more than the unfortunate experience of Ralph Colin, who, for some forty years, served as Paley's and the company's lawyer. No one served Paley more loyally during all those years, no one had witnessed more of Paley's deeds, the good ones as well as the less good ones, than Ralph Colin. Both men had been very prominent in the world of New York culture, a part of the Museum of Modern Art crowd. In 1969 Bill Paley, then president of the board of the Museum and acting there as he did at CBS, bent the rules of the Museum and summarily fired a director named Bates Lowry without consulting the other board members. Ralph Colin, then a board member, had, for reasons which must later have puzzled both men, challenged Paley's decision saying that Paley had broken the rules, though it made no difference; Lowry remained very much fired. It was a fatal mistake. The MOMA meeting at which Colin challenged Paley ended at 5:30 P.M. on a Thursday. The very next morning at 10 A.M. Paley summoned Colin to his office. The Chairman did not stand when Colin entered the room, nor did he motion his long-time associate to a chair; he simply said he had given long and careful thought to the matter and had decided to terminate their relationship, but that Colin would still represent the company. A few months later, when Paley was on vacation, Frank Stanton was dispatched to tell Colin that his firm had lost the CBS account as well. The sting was very real for Colin, an urbane and civilized man, and the incident bothered him for some time. Eventually he called Paley and asked to come by and see him. Colin quickly made clear to the Chairman why he was there. He was bothered by this particular scar, he said, the abrupt loss of a great friendship. It was still awkward, he explained, particularly because they still saw each other at so many social and cultural functions, concerts, museum openings. Could they at least retain the semblance of their friendship? he asked. Ralph Colin long remembered Bill Paley's reply. "Ralph, we were never friends. You were my lawyer."

A revolution was taking place in communications and advertising in the thirties and young Bill Paley was at the very center of it, enjoying every moment, the excitement, the challenge, the victories. He seemed perfectly cast for the part. He was young and handsome and rich and smart, and the enthusiasm, indeed the avidity for life, for every phase of it, seemed to jump out from him. He bought a handsome triplex in Manhattan and got Lee Simonson, the best theater designer of that period, to design the rooms for it. At an estimated ten thousand dollars a room, Simonson created an effect that was, not surprisingly, wonderfully theatrical—a barroom with chromatic lights that could be controlled in any number of ways by a person lying in bed, a piano concealed in a wall with only the keyboard projecting out, and radios built into every room. Nor were the possibilities of Paley's costuming neglected: the closets were built to house as many as three hundred Paley suits, and there were special racks for a hundred ties and a hundred shirts. For Bill Paley, make no mistake, was not just an executive, he was something of a ladies' man and a man-about-town, there always seemed to be a beautiful woman on his arm.

Success was coming to the descendants of Isaac Paley in America and it was coming quickly and it was very sweet. All things or almost all things would be possible for Bill Paley despite his Russian-Jewish roots. This was and is a point of some sensitivity with Paley. When a recent book about CBS by a reporter named Robert Metz described Paley as a Russian Jew, Kidder Meade, Paley's PR man, whose great value as a public relations man stemmed in part from the fact that he was *not* Jewish, sent out a letter purporting to correct factual inaccuracies, noting among other things that Paley was an American Jew, not a Russian Jew. Well, yes, he was, and perhaps, as the Yiddish expression goes, God's ear is at Kidder Meade's lips, but in the world of American Jewry, Bill Paley was a Russian Jew, which in those early days was not as good as being a German Jew. German Jews were a good deal more socially acceptable, and they were viewed both by the Wasp establishment and by themselves as being more upstanding and respectable than Russian Jews, who were generally regarded as long of hair, disheveled of dress, and radical of thought. Those who knew Bill Paley when he first came to New York thought that he would have liked to be taken up by Our Crowd, the bastion of German-Jewish respectability, but Our Crowd was having none of it. The smell of cigars was still on his money and radio was new and flashy and perhaps vulgar. A Sulzberger would do; a Paley (who knew, after all, what the name had been before Paley?) would not. Paley's friend Ben Sonnenberg thought there was something a little poignant about him in those days. He was consummately charming but he did not seem to know it, he was the head of a new company with enormous potential but he did not yet fully comprehend its reach, and he was far more interesting and vital than so many of the stuffy people whose acceptance he seemed to want and need. Paley never ceased to be a little ambivalent about his origins, both about being Jewish and about being a Russian Jew. He was proud of his background, but as he grew older and more successful he did not necessarily want to be reminded of it. As he tried to put it aside, hang around not just with Wasps but with super-Wasps, it somehow always lurked in the background. It worked on him so powerfully that it could even warp his normally keen sense of popular entertainment. His aides secured an early option on *Fiddler on the Roof,* which they were sure would be a smash hit. They were surprised when Paley, after reading the script and listening to the music, turned it down. To Mike Burke, one of those who suggested he buy it, Paley said, "It's good, but don't you think it's too Jewish?" Burke, startled by the comment, answered that no, as a non-Jew, he did not.

The Jewishness was always there, he was always aware of it and sensitive to it. More sensitive, in fact, than many of his friends who, liking Paley, finding him bright and charming, wanted him to join their clubs or move to their exclusive islands. When they encouraged this, Bill Paley was always a little nervous. He was pleased by their intentions, but wary of the outcome. In the late fifties Philip Graham, by then publisher of the Washington *Post,* had suggested that Paley join the F Street Club. The perfect club for him in Washington, Graham said, just the right combination of men, men who were powerful, attractive, effective. Bill Paley would be at home there. Paley, know-ing the Byzantine ways of clubs and restricted apartments and exclusive is-lands that wanted no Jews, was nervous. He did not really like the idea of clubs, he told Graham; his experience was that he was better off without them. But Graham, a man of infectious enthusiasms, said not to worry about *that,* these were modern, serious, humane men, and he, Phil Graham, the prince of the city, would personally lobby it through. He was as good as his word. Or almost as good as his word. He lobbied for Paley with great vigor and intelligence. But a few weeks later when his friend Shirley Clurman ran into him on the Washington–New York shuttle, he seemed almost desperate, his normal en-thusiasm for life totally absent. Mrs. Clurman asked what was wrong. "Oh God," said Graham, "this is one of the worst days of my life—this is the day I've got to go to New York and tell Bill Paley that he was blackballed at the F Street Club."

If as a young man he was blocked from the staid and somewhat stuffy world of Our Crowd, then he quickly moved into what was then called Café Society, the forerunner of the Beautiful People, where success and achievement were more respected than blood and tradition. These were people who were famous, glamorous, and visible: writers, stars, athletes. The celebrated, and the almost celebrated, and of course the celebrators. He was very much a man-about-town in that world and he was seen with only the best-looking women. In 1932 he was married for the first time, to Dorothy Hart Hearst, who was just divorced from John Randolph Hearst. She had been one of the most beautiful girls in Los Angeles, bright, vivacious, quick, a favorite of old WR himself. The home she created for Bill was an exciting place, a salon filled with energy and excitement, people like David Selznick, the famed journalist Herbert Bayard Swope, and some of the new Roosevelt brain trusters. The people had to be successful and they had to be involved. She was a fan of Roosevelt and so, in a somewhat milder way, was he. When people sat around criticizing the New Deal and Roosevelt, he often defended the new administration. Those who knew Bill and Dorothy Paley in those days liked the idea of their being together, not just because they looked so attractive but because friends sensed that Dorothy Paley was a good influence on Bill, somewhat more political, somewhat more liberal, and something of a conscience for him, and because she brought to him people who were a counterbalancing influence to the people and the values with which he was surrounded at work. She was, friends thought, a woman with a strong ethical sense, and they often heard the word "principle" coming from her. But there was in her also, they thought, a certain dangerous tendency to show that she was smarter than Bill and on occasion a tendency to correct him. Bill Paley, friends noted, was not a man who wanted to be corrected by his wife in his own home.

Broadcasting is a curious profession. It is the most powerful instrument in the world for merchandising soap, and it is potentially the most powerful instrument in the world for public service, and it has always been caught between the duality of its roles: public service because it is licensed by the government, and thus, like it or not, it owes something to the society, and merchandising, because its material norms are relentlessly driven upward by the marketplace and the stock market. So there is an inevitable conflict of great proportions built in here, one that the public-service side rarely wins. No matter that news and public service have brought television most of its finest hours and most of its true respectability. No matter that most of the speeches by network officials justifying most of what they do at *all* hours are based on the First Amendment. No matter that it is a photo of Ed Murrow, not one of the cast of "The Beverly Hillbillies," that hangs on Bill Paley's office wall. Over the years the instinct for merchandising has always been more powerful, particularly since most broadcast executives in their hearts regard news and public service as a form of charity. Indeed, many of the great moments in broadcasting, first in radio and then in television, have come almost involuntarily; when a particular network was behind in programming and had a weak schedule, it had little to lose and therefore might, for a time, emphasize public service. Boosting news and public affairs became the cheapest way to forge ahead and build a reputation.

Robert Kintner did the nation (and ABC) a public service in 1954 by televising the Army-McCarthy hearings, his the only network that did, a move of some heroism made much easier by the fact that in those days ABC was so pathetically weak that in fact it had nothing else scheduled and had precious little to lose. Later, when Kintner brought exciting news-oriented years to NBC, it was a move again dictated by need; CBS was beating NBC in almost everything else, so why not make an effort in news, make the station more exciting, break in relentlessly on regularly scheduled programs, which were not rated very high anyway and thus easily sacrificed. Only later, within all networks, as the schedules strengthened and had their own momentum and the ratings went up, did the unwillingness to interrupt programming mount.

When in the early years at CBS Bill Paley made his first big move into public affairs, this was largely dictated by the fact that NBC was so strong in entertainment that the easiest way for a newcomer to make a reputation was in news. It was quick and it was cheap, and it had the added advantage of prestige and respectability; even if it did not immediately bring the network a direct cash profit, it sold the network indirectly by giving it an aura of class. By 1930 it was obvious to Bill Paley, first, that the public-affairs section of CBS was going to be increasingly important, and second, that this was going to be a very sensitive and difficult area. Clearly a network could do remarkable things in public affairs, and just as clearly it was going to be an area filled with controversy, dispute, pressure, anger, and possibly even lawsuits. Paley himself felt totally inadequate to deal with this, he had neither the training nor the taste for it. He did not like dispute and contentiousness. So that year, only two years after he had taken over CBS, he made a move that would have immense impact on the structure and texture of the network as it finally developed. He hired a man named Ed Klauber. Klauber was to play two roles at CBS. The first was to organize and define the news and public-affairs section of the network, setting the standards for broadcast journalism. His second and somewhat less specific role, closely related to the first, was to become the heavy for Bill Paley, the first in a long line.

Klauber's most important job, however, was to set the standards for broadcast journalism; forty years later he was regarded by most senior broadcast journalists as the father not just of CBS and its glory days in both radio and television but of all network news as we know it today. That he was brought into the network and given so remarkably free a hand was a mark of Paley's interest and commitment; Klauber educated Paley on the importance of news, but only because Paley wanted to be educated. Klauber could not have been Klauber without Paley and without Paley's belief that this was the right thing to do. He was a dour, morbidly shy, difficult man, autocratic and tyrannical. He came from a background in print journalism at *The New York Times* and he brought to the undisciplined, unprofessional, and often seedy world of radio public affairs a hard-edged knowledge not only of what news was but of the responsibility implicit in serious journalism.

Before 1930, when he came to CBS, radio news was almost totally corrupt; to the degree that it existed at all, it was often an offshoot of advertising. Now Klauber transferred his own knowledge of journalism, learned at an elite newspaper with an elite audience, to a new medium with a mass audience. In effect he created the vehicle which made the coming of Ed Murrow and his reporters possible a decade later. He saw the dimensions and possibilities of radio news, he did not underestimate his audience, and he believed that the American people were ready for good serious news programs. Unlike most senior print journalists of his era, he did not automatically fight the coming of radio (Ed Murrow, for example, was not considered worthy of being a member of the London Press Club when he first arrived in England), and he was above all worried about the quality of the news, that it not be too opinionated, too personal. Klauber was not bothered by the potential damage that advertising could do by selling commercials over radio, he felt people could make up their minds about buying cars or mayonnaise, that this was within the range of their experience, that radio could not over a period of time induce the public to buy an inferior car. News, he felt, was quite different. Ordinary Americans did not have the basis to judge journalism, the subject matter was often people, places, and events far outside their experience. His presence at this moment was of key importance: without Klauber radio might easily have gone the way of hyped-up Walter Winchell news broadcasts, or perhaps it might have degenerated into such vacuity that finally the government would have stepped in and given Americans a government-controlled broadcast system like that of France. Instead Klauber very quickly set standards for objectivity so rigorous that CBS news within a decade had a higher level of integrity and intelligence than 90 percent of the American printed press. Forty years later, Fred Friendly, one of his lineal descendants, gave aspiring young journalists a printed card displaying Klauber's standards of fairness: "What news analysts are entitled to do and should do is elucidate and illuminate the news out of common knowledge or special knowledge possessed by them or made available to them by this organization through its sources. They should point out the facts on both sides, show contradictions with the known record and so forth. They should bear in mind that in a democracy it is important that people not only should know but should understand, and it is the analysts' function to help the listener to understand, to weigh and to judge, but not to do the judging for him." A nice intelligent definition of journalistic responsibility; forty years later it could still make people very angry.

Klauber had a sense of standards and a sense of excellence and intelligence. He wanted quality people doing quality reporting. It was Ed Klauber who lobbied over a very long period to bring his great friend Elmer Davis (he had been the best man at Davis's wedding in 1917) to CBS. Most other people at CBS were dubious of the idea. Davis might be a very eloquent journalist but he seemed to have an arid voice and style. Davis himself was doubtful; he resisted Klauber's offers for a long time, but he finally succumbed in 1939 and became a model commentator. He was a wonderful short-essayist, he used words with economy, and he always made his point, and his arrival at CBS in 1939 marked a triumph of intelligence over vocal felicity. By contrast, H. V. Kaltenborn, another early news analyst, was a great problem, and there were constant wrangles between Klauber and Kaltenborn over Kaltenborn's extraordinary affection for the first-person singular. At CBS it was believed that Kaltenborn would never be a first-rate analyst until he filed down the capital *I* on his typewriter. It was not, Klauber argued, that CBS wanted to take away his freedom of speech; he could say just as much as before, but could he please say it in a more subtle way? Instead of saying "I think, I believe, I know for a fact," he would be better off if he attributed his opinion to others. The ultimate Klauber triumph over Kaltenborn, as later recounted by the newscaster, came in 1940 when Wendell Willkie, running for the presidential nomination, made a major speech. Kaltenborn drafted his comment on it: "I listened to Wendell Willkie's speech last night. It was wholly admirable." Then, aware of Klauber's dictates, he crossed it out and rewrote his broadcast: "Millions of Americans of both parties listened to Wendell Willkie's speech last night. Most of them agreed it was wholly admirable."

Paley was a willing and eager sponsor of Klauber's move into news and public affairs, he knew that this area was important and that it was good for the network. He was, as the Kaltenborn episodes showed, also aware that it was a difficult and sensitive role, that the amount of anger and controversy it generated was enormous, and that he needed some very tough front man to handle the more odious part of being a brilliant young broadcasting proprietor. That job became Klauber's; years later it was Frank Stanton who perfected the role, turning it into an art form, who ran the unpleasant errands for Paley and made all the appearances before congressional committees, but the first person to play it was Klauber, both inside and outside the institution. He was heavy, awkward, clumsy, rude, no one particularly liked him, he had little charm, whereas everyone liked Bill Paley, he exuded charm, and so Klauber was the perfect foil for Paley. Klauber did not need to be liked, instead he was obsessed by improving the institution, defending it against enemies. In that sense he was quite selfless, almost innocent. It was Edward Bernays, the pioneer public-relations man, who had first recommended Klauber to Paley, sensing that Klauber, whom he also did not particularly like, might be excellent in a large and growing organization. Very quickly it was Klauber who handled all the tough jobs for Paley, but he never had anything to do with advertisers since he was too graceless and too abrasive.

In 1931, when Father Charles Coughlin, with radio as his amplifier, began to emerge as a new and very serious political problem, it was Klauber who dealt with him. Coughlin in those days was using radio in an unprecedented and terrifying way and his shows were becoming more and more political and more and more anti-Semitic. Klauber went out to see Coughlin and suggested that the Father send in advance scripts for screening; the good Father immediately devoted his next sermon to a nonpolitical theme—that is, to CBS's attempt to censor him—and suggested that his faithful write to CBS in protest, which more than one million listeners did. The response was shattering, it showed how emotional the times were; it was, after all, the height of the Depression, and this episode gave the first real insight into both the political power of radio and the vulnerability of the medium without some kind of established standards. Klauber and Paley soon worked out a shrewd formula which limited Coughlin's right to air time while at the same time seemed to oppose censorship, indeed appeared to open radio to even greater religious freedom. There would now be a regular CBS church hour, it would be free, all religious leaders, of course, liked that, and most wonderful of all, it would rotate from denomination to denomination each Sunday. Thus the silencing of Coughlin while being generous to religion.

Klauber's role in those years was very important. Not only was he setting and defining the internal standard of news; he was determining how broadcasting would treat politics and politicians. Mainly because of Klauber, CBS was soon to be the leader in public affairs, and as it defined its own policies, eventually those rules and standards became in varying forms the policies for the other networks. Roosevelt's use of radio in his first term showed how powerful and effective the new instrument could be. By 1936, as the presidential campaign neared, the pressure on the part of all politicians to exploit radio was mounting. Klauber found himself rejecting, for example, the attempt of the Republican Party to use slick paid political commercials by Madison Avenue copywriters. Politics, he decreed, was too important for this kind of commercialization and fake dramatization, and political spots had to be more serious.

That year he also set an even more important precedent bearing on access to modern broadcasting, one which determined that broadcasting would be, to an uncommon degree, a presidential vehicle. It seemed so natural at first: the President wanted to go on radio, the nation wanted to hear him, the networks themselves were delighted to be the conduit, it made their role more prestigious. Though everyone agreed that the American people really wanted to hear the President and thus he was speaking as a national leader and not simply as a politician, the ugly disturbing question always remained. At what point was the President speaking in a national emergency (in this case the Depression), and at what point was he just a very shrewd professional politician using both this new device and the nation's trauma to strengthen his own domestic political position? Was he a President or a politician? Where did you draw the line, and who could draw it, and who if anyone was permitted to answer him?

In 1936 this issue came to a head when Roosevelt gave his State of the Union speech. It was, not surprisingly for an election year, intensely political. In fact it was his campaign platform, nothing more, nothing less. It was carried by CBS as by other networks. The Republicans were appalled by it; Roosevelt had been beating them to death with radio anyway, and now here to inaugurate an election year was this nakedly political speech. John Hamilton, the chairman of the Republican National Committee, went to the networks to ask for equal time. NBC said it would give access on one of its two networks; Mutual, which was a conservative network, readily granted Hamilton what he asked. Next Hamilton went to see Paley, then in his New Deal incarnation. Paley directed Hamilton to Klauber. Klauber listened to Hamilton complain that Roosevelt's speech had been patently political, that it was possible to make a judgment on a speech like this, there was a line between national interest and political propagandizing. Then Klauber said no, he would not give Hamilton time. It was a crucial moment. Klauber, himself sympathetic to Roosevelt and the New Deal, said that this was an official message of the President, it had not been labeled as political and thus no political party, which after all had no real constitutional function, could do over radio what Roosevelt had just done. Klauber thus helped define presidential prerogative; the right of presidential access was already strong, now he was setting a precedent that made it infinitely harder for potential presidential opponents and critics to reach the airwaves.

Forty years later Klauber's precedent still held and the real questions had never been examined. The entire process had strengthened the presidency immeasurably and comparably weakened the party system. Since the President realized that he could not be effectively answered by his political opponents, the instinct to use radio and later television was greater. In the same way, as the opposition party showed that it had less and less access to the most powerful new means of communication, its attractiveness to potential candidates and its role in American life were significantly diminished. Part of the party's job had always been to raise crowds for politicians. Now it had lost that job and been cut out of a vital part of the national dialogue.


In 1937 there was a position opening up as head of CBS's European division. It was in effect a business job, scheduling European officials for CBS broadcasts; above all, it was not journalistic. For a time it appeared likely to go to a young man named Fred Willis, who was charming, sociable, and if not actually British *seemed* to be British, which was just as good. A friend of his named Victor Ratner asked if it was true, since the job was considered something of a plum. No, said Willis, he had thought it over, but he wanted a real future in the company, and the one thing he was sure of was that you should never get that far from headquarters. So the job went instead to a young man named Edward R. Murrow.

Murrow. The right man in the right place in the right era. An elegant man in an up to then inelegant profession; one of those rare legendary figures who was as good as his myth. Whose presence is so strong that it still lives; because he was what he was, in many ways CBS News is today what it is. Shy and anguished and often awkward in personal conversation, but totally controlled and brilliant as a communicator, a man who spanned the oceans and who more than anyone else made broadcasting respectable for a generation of other talented broadcasters, and, having done this, almost two decades later when radio was respectable and television was not, by going to television made it journalistically legitimate and honorable. A man who was in a way more an educator than a journalist and whose career and the technology which he was part of were one of the conduits of America's transformation from a sleepy post-Depression isolationist nation to a major international superpower. In effect he educated the nation as it slowly, awkwardly, entered the larger world and found itself becoming a superpower. If later he started covering the effects of that new international role on the domestic political process, and if much to the dismay of his superiors this new subject matter made him a target as well as a reporter, well then, that was another story. What was important in the beginning was the special quality of excellence he and the men he hired set for broadcasting; men who were in his image, and who thereupon brought men to CBS and the other networks in *their* image. Though he was depressed and exhausted and professionally emasculated when he left CBS in 1961, much of what he had helped to create still lived. His legacy was a tradition of reporting from which the corporate officials, whatever their private feelings, simply could not back down.

His was a unique coming. No other broadcast journalist would ever again accumulate the prestige both inside and outside the company that Murrow had. There were many reasons for this: part of it was that it was all so new, radio broadcasting so experimental, that when he proved to be so good and the story proved to be so big there were not a lot of complicated internal systems to keep him down and limit him. Indeed it was quite the reverse, as his comet ascended, so too did that of CBS; he took CBS with him, the network was the direct beneficiary of his excellence; he was, at the start, bigger than the network. So there was little desire to restrain him, to keep him within the narrow limits of objectivity, in part because of the very nature of the war he was covering. It was not the Vietnam War. It was not something complicated and divisive; rather it was seen as the story of the survival of Western civilization, the most heroic of all possible wars and stories. He was indeed reporting on the survival of the English-speaking peoples. A commentator who went as far as Murrow and who wholeheartedly supported the cause of the democracies (and who did not balance Hitler against Churchill) did not offend his audience or any large part of his audience; rather he came to symbolize and embody the passions of that audience. When it was all over, he was in his own way as much a hero and a personage of that epic era as Eisenhower himself. There was during those great years no need to see the German perspective, to report what the isolationists felt; journalists simply trusted their own intelligence and instincts (Murrow, appalled in later years by growing pressure to balance out viewpoints for the sake of an artificial fairness, compared this with balancing the views of Jesus Christ with those of Judas Iscariot).

It was a heroic time, and he was one of the certified heroes of it. In a less heroic or a more dubious war—Korea and Vietnam come to mind—where American survival was not at stake, no American commentator would make a comparable reputation either with the public or his own company. In Vietnam those correspondents who made their reputations also became controversial, respected by the elite and by their peers but anathema to the government, and often an embarrassment to their companies. What Murrow did was distinctive to that war and that era, and to Murrow. He not only earned an awesome reputation with his working colleagues (Elmer Davis would note that he was shocked that such magnificent reporting could be done by someone who had never worked in a city room); he was also an ornament to management. He opened the great doors of the English country estates for his boss, Colonel William S. Paley.

In normal times there would have been no way for Murrow to have been Murrow; excellent reporting might have pleased the intelligentsia and his colleagues but angered vast portions of the public and the government and placed him in constant confrontation with management. But World War II was special and he was special, the first great professional radio voice in the sense that Roosevelt had been the first great radio voice of a politician, a voice steeped in intelligence and civility and compassion and sensitivity. It also, and this is crucial, allowed him to accumulate enormous capital within the company. This meant that when he came back to America he was a superstar with prestige and freedom and respect within his profession and within his company. It was his subsequent, and hardly hasty, decision to spend that capital and to be an outspoken correspondent on the domestic scene that was to make him a corporate liability; it was a decision by the best of the broadcast correspondents on the best of the networks and it was to underline quickly the limits of freedom that actually existed within broadcasting. He was the same Murrow with the same high standards, but there was a great deal of difference between covering a heroic war and revealing domestic warts (as indeed the same heroic General Eisenhower of World War II was the somewhat less than heroic Candidate Eisenhower who did not defend his friend George Marshall from the slanders of Joseph McCarthy). There are many different variations of courage. Murrow was to find that out.

He was ungodly handsome, Walter Pidgeon playing Ed Murrow, television looks before television existed; Bill Shirer, meeting him for the first time, was shaken by how handsome Murrow was, just the kind of smoothness that you would expect in a corrupt profession like broadcasting, thought Shirer. Murrow was not a trained journalist and that was an asset because there was a vast difference between the words and rhythms of print journalism and the words and rhythms of spoken English; he had nothing to unlearn. The spoken word is colloquial, print journalism when read aloud is by necessity stilted and forced. Murrow was descended from Southerners who had moved to the Far West and he and the rest of his family retained a sense of old-fashioned high English, an almost poetic language which is fast disappearing from the land. As a young man he had worked as a logger, and this had not only expedited the changing of his name from Egbert to Edward it also gave him an appreciation of the shrewdness and intelligence of ordinary people and an uncommon ability to talk with them. He learned to master simplicity and understatement. Later, in college, he studied drama and voice with excellent teachers at Washington State and this had honed his sense of timing and rhythm in language. (In particular, one speech teacher, Ida Lou Anderson, had sensed his potential; later when Murrow was in England she suggested the pause in "This . . . is London.") His spoken English was thus unusually effective; he knew, unlike most reporters, how to use pauses and the absence of words as effectively as the words themselves. He had just the right touch; enough drama in his voice to make what he was doing work but not so much as to be phony and a ham. It was a matter of taste; Murrow had perfect taste.

He was not an intellectual, and many of the men he hired—Bill Shirer, Eric Sevareid, Alex Kendrick, Howard Smith, David Schoenbrun—were far more cerebral than he, but he was a brilliant communicator; he could take something happening in one part of the world and make it comprehensible and recognizable thousands of miles away. This was a very special talent, and it does not necessarily come with brilliance, for brilliant men are often able only to reach other brilliant men, they end up talking largely to themselves. But rooted in the middle class as he was, Murrow could make use of his own difficulties in understanding the complicated pressures of a shrinking world. Again and again he taught younger reporters at CBS to try to think of friends they had left behind in some small town, and to try to envision themselves standing at the bar after one or two drinks and explaining what they had seen that day—and use the exact same language.

If he was a communicator he was also in the best sense an educator. His passion was not for the scoop but for intelligence, for the audience to understand what was going on in the world. He had come from the world of education and his first job at CBS had been running its educational service. It was hardly a powerful job, but he had helped in bringing European intellectuals to America and he had a paramount sense of the importance of learning. Education was central to reporting. In 1945, after the war was over, he became impressed with the knowledge of French and France of a bright young interpreter at Eisenhower's headquarters. The name of the aide was David Schoenbrun, and Murrow asked Schoenbrun what he planned to do when he returned home and Schoenbrun said that he hoped to go back to teaching high school French. Murrow paused for a moment and asked him, "How would you like the biggest classroom in the world?"

Murrow was in Europe as the CBS European director when Hitler pressured the Austrians into Anschluss. He was not expected to broadcast himself but he was caught up in something which had a force of its own; the cream of American journalism was now in Europe—John Gunther, H. R. Knickerbocker, Bill Shirer, Jimmy Sheean, Dorothy Thompson—and Murrow was inevitably drawn to their world. When the Germans moved into Austria, Murrow overnight became a journalist. He was a natural for his role and he was a part of a vast change: it was the dawning of a new and sometimes terrible modern age; life had been vastly speeded up; the speed with which Hitler had come to power had been speeded up by science and technology and radio; the speed with which Hitler could move was intensified by modern weaponry, "blitzkrieg" it would be called, the name summoned visions of lightning and thunderbolts, and now the speed with which Murrow could report back to America had the same lightning force. Murrow's voice symbolized the shrinking of the world; what affected Europe now affected the United States, and intuitively the masses of Americans knew this, knew they were bound to events in Europe. Where newspapers had often been edited for a special elite, Murrow was a voice of the elite to the mass.

In 1938 the whole country watched and waited on events in Europe and they watched and waited with Ed Murrow. In the first major piece ever written about Murrow, an extraordinarily perceptive article in *Scribner's Magazine* in December 1938, a young writer named Robert Landry sensed the coming of the new journalistic order:

> [Murrow] has more influence upon America's reaction to foreign news than a shipful of newspapermen. This influence has not been generally recognized partly for the reason that the newspaper correspondents have tradition on their side, and partly because the networks have played up their commentators rather than their correspondents (like Murrow). But the influence is there, great and growing—and obvious to anyone who knows both radio and the press. Murrow has three advantages over correspondents for the greatest American newspapers: 1. He beats the newspapers by hours; 2. He reaches millions who otherwise have to depend on provincial newspapers for their foreign news; 3. He writes his own headlines. That is to say he emphasizes what he wishes—whereas the newspaper correspondent writes in cablese—then has his copy edited, maybe rewritten and then published under a bank of headlines in which he has no say.

Thus did Landry precisely identify a change in the journalistic order, the mass impact of the broadcast journalist and the ability to put a personal touch to the news.

In addition to doing his own reporting Murrow set out to hire one of the great teams of foreign correspondents. The first of these was William L. Shirer, who had been covering Germany since the rise of Hitler and was exactly the kind of informed, intelligent journalist that Murrow was looking for. Shirer wrote of their first meeting in his diary for August 20, 1937: "I have a job. I am to go to work for the Columbia Broadcasting System. That is *if* . . . I have a job *if* my voice is all right. . . . Who ever heard of an adult with no pretenses to being a singer or any other kind of artist being dependent for a good, interesting job on his voice. And mine is terrible." Shirer was absolutely right about his voice; he was by no means a natural broadcaster and CBS headquarters was not amused or delighted with his early reports. Finally Murrow had to cable Klauber asking whether CBS wanted a slick voice or a great journalist. Murrow carried the day and Shirer became the first of a series of reporters hired for reasons of substance rather than style. The decision in the long run was to be of great benefit to CBS; it meant that the voices were often diverse, rarely mellifluous, but always filled with intelligence and knowledge. The Murrow boys became what one CBS colleague not entirely admiringly called a kind of philosopher-king-intellectual-journalist. Their broadcasting techniques were often secondary to their knowledge of an area. Howard Smith was soon hired and then a young print journalist named Eric Sevareid, a man who always seemed just slightly inhibited by a microphone.

But Shirer was the first; he and Murrow covered the Anschluss together in 1938. Anschluss, the submission of Austria to the Germans, had been expected. In March 1938 Murrow was in Warsaw arranging an educational program. Shirer was in Vienna. He called Murrow. They had their own prearranged code. "The opposing team has just crossed the goal line," said Shirer. "Are you sure?" asked Murrow. "I'm paid to be sure," answered Shirer. That meant that the German troops were crossing the border. Murrow chartered a plane, himself the only passenger, to get to Vienna, so he could report it. He stayed in Vienna for five days and then flew to London for a fuller report: "It was called a bloodless conquest and in some ways it was, but I'd like to be able to forget the haunted look on the faces of those long lines of people outside the banks and travel offices. People trying to get away. I'd like to forget the tired futile look of the Austrian army officers, and the thud of hobnail boots and the crash of the light tanks in the early morning on the Ringstrasse, and the pitiful uncertainty and bewilderment of those forced to lift the right hand and shout 'Heil Hitler' for the first time. I'd like to forget the sound of the smashing glass as the Jewish shop streets were raided; the hoots and jeers aimed at those forced to scrub the sidewalk. . . ." Gradually they picked up other correspondents and stringers and thus was born almost of necessity the CBS "World News Roundup." Night after night as the tension mounted and Hitler threatened the peace of the entire world, the story came to America by radio. In New York, H. V. Kaltenborn, who was anchoring the show, would come on and say, "Calling Ed Murrow, calling Ed Murrow . . ."

This was the beginning of an era. Hitler moved against Poland and swept across France, and Murrow based in London became *Murrow,* his voice linking England to America. For the two years before America entered the war and even when it finally entered and England's survival seemed to hang in the balance, his was the common voice. If most politicians and most elitists of a generation (with the exception of Hitler and Roosevelt) scorned radio and still thought print more important, the British at every level were acutely aware of Murrow's power and influence; their necks were on the chopping block, their very survival was at stake, and they realized more quickly than most societies that power was changing and that Murrow was more important than American ambassadors or print journalists. As desperate as their situation was, it was clear that Murrow more than anyone had the power to help them. He was their ambassador not just to the American government but, more important, to the American people.

He was perfectly cast. It was a dark and somber time, and he had a dark vision of mankind and of himself. He had warned his wife, Janet, before their marriage to beware of his depressions, his despair and his moodiness, his black periods. "Ed," Janet Murrow said of him, "is a sufferer." There was always a kind of sadness to him; he could say to his colleague Dick Hottelet about his youth, "I never learned to play." A puritan who could never entirely accept his success and who was ill at ease with happiness and pleasure. He was always gracious but always very private; despite impeccable manners he kept everyone at a distance. He might reveal to his closest friends his thoughts, but never, if possible, himself. He came from the kind of semi-Calvinist home, said his friend Sevareid, "where there were too many rules and not enough love." The anguish and the ambivalence always remained, even at the moments of his greatest success, as if symptomatic of the contrast between his hard and difficult upbringing and the silky world which he had now been privileged to enter by dint of his awesome success. He was always on the very edge of being formal, in tone and in dress; the clothes were expensive, the cuff links very fancy, he was in fact just short of a fop; anyone else in journalism dressing like Murrow would have looked like a fop. He had, Charles Collingwood later learned, almost not hired the young Collingwood for CBS because the first time they met, Collingwood, who was a young man-about-town, was sporting a pair of very loud argyle socks, then much in fashion with the flashier younger set, and Murrow was not entirely sure a man in socks that loud was entirely proper for CBS, Rhodes scholar or no. He never, even in the most casual conversation with friends, spoke a sentence which did not sound as if it was ready for the air. He was a fine wing shot and quite willing to hunt with the British at the great estates, but, like many poor country boys, he could not swim and no one could get him in a bathing suit near the water. His dignity was paramount. Once Sevareid and Murrow were about to board a plane at La Guardia together and Sevareid was quite casually and even more sloppily eating a bag of popcorn. To Murrow, so easily recognizable to the public, it somehow seemed beneath their respective dignities, and, offended by Sevareid, he very deliberately walked several feet ahead of him as if to disassociate himself from popcornism.

The British loved him. They knew exactly what he was broadcasting (many of his broadcasts were replayed for British armed forces and it was a source of sustenance to them to know that this was what America was hearing). And so he was taken up by the very elite of British society; in a country where doors opened reluctantly if at all, suddenly all doors were open. His job would have opened many doors in any event, but coupled with his charm, his looks, the fact that he was distinctively American and did not go British made him even more popular; he was a reminder of what America was. He quite consciously avoided British mannerisms, British accent, British words. In America he was a hero and a voice, albeit often a faceless one. In December 1941 he came to America for a series of personal appearances and a major dinner was held in his honor—a star-studded celebrity night, virtually in effect a state occasion. On one side of him sat Archibald MacLeish, the poet of the Roosevelt administration, and on the other side, Bill Paley. And MacLeish heralded him as poets rarely herald journalists, in this instance for having destroyed "the most obstinate of all superstitions—the superstition against which poetry and all the arts have fought for centuries, the superstition of time and distance." It was an incredible moment for a young man of thirty-five. Five days later he was invited to the White House for dinner with Franklin Roosevelt. It was to be an informal occasion, Roosevelt wanted to hear Murrow's informed judgments on Britain's status and potential. The dinner was delayed by events; the date was December 7.

# 2 / Time Incorporated

Harry Luce had been ready for war. More than almost any other major publisher, Luce was an interventionist. He had been furious with Roosevelt for not moving to a wartime footing quickly enough. Sometimes in years to come he would mutter darkly to friends about his fear that Roosevelt would, in his phrase, "escape history." That meant that he would be seen as a great wartime leader instead of a man who in Luce's opinion had been terribly negligent in preparation for its coming. The Japanese had taken things out of his hands. But Luce was ready. Nor was he unhappy about the domestic political consequences. The New Deal, he told friends, was dead. It had been seriously wounded the moment that the first planes had been built for Lend-Lease. Now, with the United States at war, it was over. Harry Luce did not mind.

Henry Robinson Luce. Harry. Everyone called him Harry, it was a sign of terrible ignorance to call him Henry, though he was not a good old boy, he was not easily approachable, and he did not grant intimacy easily. But Harry it had to be. Once when he was trying desperately to get Dwight Eisenhower to return from SHAEF and run for the presidency, he reported enthusiastically to his managing editors that he was making progress, that Ike was coming along, his prayers were being answered, and he began by reading the latest letter from the great man: "Dear Henry," it began. "Well," he said a bit sheepishly, "we'll allow him one more chance. . . ." He was the outsider, the poor boy at both Hotchkiss and Yale who later towered over his contemporaries but never really became an insider himself. He would have loved to be one of the inner club where the greatest decisions are made with the softest voices ("Why don't the Rockefellers like me?" he once asked a friend plaintively.

"I'm sure they like you," the friend answered. "Then why don't they ever ask me over for dinner or an evening of cards?"). But he was a curiously artless man, graceless and brusque and lonely, rude inevitably even to those whose favors and good will he coveted; he could only be what he was, he could never be facile or slick, though on frequent occasions his magazines were.

He was a big man, little ideas and little concepts and little men did not interest him; he was always in search of giants. He was ever restless, ever dissatisfied, he was not a man of inner peace. He was fascinated by men; men, not the great rhythms of history or economics, were the key to the past and he was a big man himself. He was a major figure of American journalism, the leading innovator of more than two decades, and perhaps only Walter Lippmann in a different way was as important a figure of the same era. He was also a major figure in American politics, and he frequently crossed back and forth between the two, as did his magazines, so that Luce's printed version of what he felt events should have been often obscured what they in fact had been. He and his magazines would be the true voice of American life at the midcentury, what he had hoped would be the American Century, the real voice of Christian Capitalism, closer to what the country's real drive and impulse were than the countless critics who decried him and what they deemed to be his conservatism.

He was the son of a missionary and he took his Presbyterianism seriously. Very seriously. It hovered above his life, forcing him to work ever harder to exert his will in greater areas and to take as little joy from his material successes as was humanly possible. Religion was a living force, it required genuine obligations, hard work, and sacrifice, permissiveness was never to be rewarded. He was the Calvinist as journalist, as a poorly briefed Richard Nixon once found out. Nixon had come to dinner at the Luce headquarters before the election in 1960, hoping to get the Luceian nod. Someone had clearly briefed Nixon about Luce and his religion, telling Nixon that a discussion of predestination was the key to Luce's heart. And so in the middle of the dinner when they were all talking about religion, Nixon said that if he were not a Quaker he would rather be a Presbyterian than anything else, because it was so easy. There was a long moment of stunned silence at the table, all the editors looking at Luce, waiting for him to explode. For about thirty seconds the air hung silent and then Luce decided to let it go, but it did not lead Richard Nixon down the corridor to Harry Luce's heart. Son of a missionary, Luce was part missionary himself, and like any true missionary, he had both mission and vision; he knew what his calling was. He started *Fortune* magazine because as an emancipated young capitalist in the late twenties he thought most American businessmen were narrow sleepy Babbitts unworthy of their roles and their duties and he wanted to seek out the handful of worthy businessmen and hold them up as examples. Similarly he was fascinated by religion and philosophy and was a serious lay theological scholar who did more than anyone else to interest his fellow Americans in these subjects and to popularize men like Niebuhr and Tillich. But he did as little as he could to popularize Sartre. He did not like Sartre, thought him too vague, too fuzzy, and even more than he disliked Sartre, he disliked Sartre's existentialism, which he suspected would inspire a kind of permissiveness that could threaten true Western culture. So he worked long and hard to keep Jean-Paul Sartre off the cover of *Time*. His magazines would play no part in the propagation of ideas and values unworthy of true Western culture. He would strengthen not weaken the West.


He was large on the landscape. Always the editor, always in charge. Roy Alexander, a managing editor who had come from the St. Louis *Post-Dispatch,* where Pulitzer was always known as "the proprietor," for a time referred to Luce that way, but Luce did not like it, "proprietor" implied just business ownership, and he was the *editor,* let there be no doubt about it, and just to make his point he had a tendency to patronize his top business associates. It was a means of letting them know that *Time* was first and foremost an editorial product and then and only then a business success; thus he, Luce, was first and foremost a journalist, and only afterward an eminently successful business-man. His professional accomplishments were dazzling. He was the man who invented the concept of a weekly news magazine. Once when talking with students at Brandeis, he was informed that he had no right to call *Time* a news magazine since it was full of opinions largely his own. His response was very simple and typical: "Well, I invented the idea, so I guess I can call it anything I like." With *Life* magazine, a publication global and dazzling, he brought photojournalism to a height never reached before. With both these magazines he quickly outdistanced and thus powerfully influenced the tepid, bland, and often ignorant journalism of the day; *Time* in the thirties, run by a bunch of green young Yale graduates, was in effect teaching older newspapermen how to report, showing that there were greater dimensions to stories than had previously been permitted. Politically he was a belligerent democrat, a muscu-lar Christian, as hopeless an Americanophile as only someone born twelve thousand miles away could be; very early in this century he sensed the coming of America's new power and range, America would be the superpower in the super-century.

Even on the eve of World War II, when the nation's future seemed darkest, he foresaw the American Century, and he almost seemed to welcome the challenge of the war, it would test America's worthiness. Though he was much mocked, in time it did become the American Century. Yet this caused new problems, for the American Century brought an arrogance of power and values that bothered his critics, who worried about both America's imperial course after the war and *Time*'s enthusiasm for that course. For him and for many of the elite of his generation, born as they were near the turn of the century, too young for World War I, the idea of America's attaining the full zenith of its power was an idealistic one, a true goal. For it was, he thought, an age when America and Americans had to be educated to their power and their responsibilities. To him the idea that the American Century might bring *too much power* was totally alien, to him the danger was of too *little* American power. His American Century was a noble concept, convinced as he was of the rectitude of our culture and our values and our energy; the world would want these same things, on our terms and by our definitions, and it was our clear duty to spread them. He would stand watch to ensure that our politicians matched and fulfilled their responsibilities. No wonder, then, that men like Walter Lippmann and Bill Fulbright, men increasingly full of doubts, were never favorites of *Time* magazine; they were clearly unworthy of the challenge ahead. In truth, he despised them. But all this made Luce and *Time* the most important and influential conservative-centrist force in the country for more than two decades. He was one of the first true *national* propagandists; he spoke to the whole nation on *national* issues, one man with one magazine speaking with one voice, and reaching the entire country. He was not interested in regional or parochial concerns and he tended either to belittle them or to ignore them. Rather, his vision was of the whole nation.

It was, however, the irony of his life that the more passionately he believed in something, the more ruthlessly he wanted to sell it, the more his own prejudices showed and offended readers. ("Mister Henry Luce is like a shoe salesman," said Earl Long, a governor of Louisiana who was not an admirer, "but all the other shoe-store owners stock all different sizes of shoes, but Mr. Luce, he only sells shoes that fit hisself.") In areas where he was less passionate, less committed, he was often far more influential. He cared more deeply about politics than anything else, but curiously it was the back of the book—art, education, books—that probably touched his fellow citizens more immediately than the front, where Luce's opinions on political issues and the future of the West were more clearly outlined. His greatest influence may have been in broadening American culture, in involving millions of middlebrow Americans in the arts, in theater, in religion and education.

Similarly, for editors of countless newspapers, he broadened the definition of news. Until he arrived, news was politics and crime, but Luce's curiosity recognized every tiny part of the social fabric—medicine, the law, even the press itself—as something newsworthy. He was as much educator as he was journalist and propagandist. Yet he had a strong sense of the nature of his reader and he would on occasion, when he thought the magazine was becoming too eastern, tell his sophisticated staff, "I want more corn in the magazine. Yes, I know you don't like it, you're too Ivy League and sophisticated, but we need more corn in it." If he was going to lead them to a promised land, he was not, on the way, going to lose touch with his following. He had a powerful sense of what people should read, what was good for them to read, and an essential belief worthy of the best journalist, that any subject of importance could be made interesting. Thus the cover story, the personalizing of issues so that a lay reader could become more interested and more involved in serious reading matter. The cover story alone had a major impact on the journalism of our age.

He had, long before polls and demographic studies became fashionable, an intuitive sense of demographics; he had a sense of a changing nation, that there were more and more better-educated people who needed better and more concise and sharply honed information. Local newspapers, even in big cities, he believed, were not answering their questions. Thus the story of *Time* magazine is also the story of the explosion in American education in this century. In 1900, according to U.S. government statistics, less than 1 percent of the country was enrolled in high school; in 1939, the early years of *Life,* that figure, rapidly escalating, had grown to 5 percent. The original prospectus for *Time* estimated that there were one million college graduates in the country and said that *Time* intended to get as its readership every one of them. It was clear from the start that Luce was trying to take advantage of the rising level of education. He believed fiercely in it, he envisioned an America where the mass, not merely the elite, was educated, and he caught the rising wave of that phenomenon. Those editors who were blind to it—Hearst comes to mind—saw their once powerful empires slowly dissipate. *Time* magazine at the start was aimed at the new young college-educated American, the modern men and women of the age. It was at the beginning flip, fresh, and smart-aleck, reflecting not just the style of Luce but that of his Yale classmate Briton Hadden; there was in the early issues of *Time* more than a touch of young college kids in raccoon coats on their way to football games. Then after Hadden's untimely death Luce assumed more and more editorial control. The magazine changed, it was more serious, less flip, there was, after all, so much of the world to be serious about. What was it the gay, ebullient Hadden had said to his more stolid, more responsible friend Luce, watching him walk across the Yale campus, deadly serious with both thought and obligation? "Watch out, Harry, you'll drop the college." Some thirty years later, when Clare Boothe Luce was ambassador to Italy, Luce confided to his colleague Emmet Hughes that he was very worried about Clare. Why? Hughes asked. "Well, she has to be persuaded to stop carrying the entire world on her shoulders," Luce said. Hughes began to laugh. "Harry," he said, "you're just the man to do it."

But if he made *Time* more serious, he also made it more political, intensely political and partisan. This came to produce an inner conflict in both the man and his magazine. For Luce loved journalism and journalists and he had a driving relentless curiosity; that was part of him. But the other part was the missionary, the believer, a man whose beliefs and visions and knowledge of Truth contradicted and thus outweighed the facts of his reporters. His curiosity versus his certitude. If he willed something to be true hard enough, then it must become true, whatever the evidence. If the evidence was contradictory, he would find other evidence, and if he could not find other evidence, then he would find someone as sure as he was in the vision so that the evidence was not needed. This was the flaw in *Time,* for all its brilliance, and it was part of the larger contradiction in Luce himself, particularly in that era. In the conflict between curiosity and ideology, ideology tended finally to win out, at no small price to himself and to many who worked for him, and many more who read him.

He was a true ideologue of the West. He was a man of that incredible era when this nation rose to the height of its power and, steeped in American lore as a young boy growing up in China, loving the legend of Teddy Roosevelt, the most muscular Christian of them all, he had an acute sense of America's destiny. He was too young for World War I, and deprived involuntarily of that experience, sure that American power and influence should and must expand, he was an early and relentless interventionist at the time of World War II. His mission was to prepare Americans for their responsibilities. Even before World War II ended he was a post-war ideologist. Communism was to him intolerable, it was in conflict with his basic religious and philosophical tenets. He would not shy from the great ideological struggle, not from a struggle with Soviet Communism in the American Century. Russia was still an ally while he readied himself for the Cold War, much to the consternation of some of his correspondents who took a more moderate line. He welcomed the Cold War as a worthy challenge to America, he knew which side was right and which was wrong. On the eve of ideological battle, his mind was not clouded by doubt. He was a man of will, incredibly willful, men could change history, could turn the currents, and his magazines and his own sense of the West's destiny reflected that. What he did he always did with a certain ferocity. Once watching him drive a golf ball, which he did ineptly (he was a poor athlete), his friend and confidant the Reverend John Courtney Murray laughed and told a friend, "You have just witnessed something special, the only man in the world who can drive a golf ball two hundred yards by sheer force of will." Luce as a young boy was burdened by a terrible stammer but, by that same force of will and special tutoring, he reduced it until the stammer virtually disappeared. (It remained noticeable at moments of stress. It was said of Time Inc., an environment natural enough to the Organization Man, that at certain high levels most executives tended to have just the slightest corporate stammer.)

Harry Luce did not often take time for social niceties, sports like tennis or golf, all the potentially hedonistic callings, there were too many serious global challenges. His clothes were always wrong, always rumpled and ill-fitting. It was not in him to dress well. Food was fuel, nothing more. He set a terrible table at home and there were legendary stories of Luce offending (probably deliberately, though no one was ever sure) maître d's at fabled French restaurants throughout the world, Luce puncturing soufflés as he talked. Luce: "Got anything good to eat here?" Maître d', slightly stunned: "Well, we are particularly proud of the *canard à l'orange.*" Luce: "I know what that is. It's a duck with orange sauce. I'll have it but hold the orange sauce and give me applesauce." Once, during World War II, he grabbed one of his star reporters, John Hersey, and took him to a fancy New York restaurant for lunch because Walter Graebner, the magazine's London correspondent, was back and was going to talk about the war. Graebner never managed to speak as Luce, filled with passion and energy, totally dominated the table during a prolonged, rich, and bountiful lunch. Graebner and Hersey sat silent during the meal, and after dessert was finished listened absolutely astonished as Luce absentmindedly called over the headwaiter and berated him because their order had not been taken. How long, Luce demanded of the man, did he intend to keep them waiting?

Always functional. No time for frills. Life was work and sacrifice, not splendor and materialism. When Time-Life was about to construct its new building, Luce, who through *Architectural Forum* had done so much to expand the knowledge of American architecture, was adamant about not creating anything fancy. It would, above all, not be a monument. Nothing like Lever House, the Seagram building, or the CBS building, concrete and glass as an extension of a man's myth. "No," he replied when colleagues pressured him, "I want a building for work." Finally near the end of the planning an architect named Max Abramovitz wanted Luce to expand just a bit. A great mural by Fritz Glarner, he said, was what the building needed most to give it an extra quality. Luce seemed resistant, so Abramovitz pushed harder: "Harry, look at what Michelangelo did for the Pope on the ceiling of the Sistine Chapel." Luce would eventually agree to the Glarner mural but for the moment the idea was very alien. A mural? He looked at Abramovitz quizzically. "But that was good for the Pope's business. What good is a mural going to do for mine?"

To him America was not just a country, it was an idea and an ideal. His magazines would celebrate this. Holding forth on this theme, he came inevitably to believe what he had just heard, even if by chance he had just heard it from himself. That which he had said became print, and that which he had printed became true. He sought to make America what it should be, and thus, of course, in the pages of *Time* America *became* what it should be. The dream realized. There was a curious innocence about all this. Whatever he did not choose to see about the darker side of life in this country, he did not see. In 1954, when the Supreme Court ruled against segregation in the public schools, Luce, son of a missionary, was vastly relieved. "Well, that's good," he said to his editors, "that takes care of that problem." As far as he was concerned the problem of race and segregation in America no longer existed.

He was the exile come home, the boy always in search of his native land, and to him America was always a more wonderful place; he was seduced by the mythology of the land as no native-born American could ever have been. As a boy he had heard from his father stirring stories of the Founding Fathers and of Teddy Roosevelt, the greatest of the Reverend Henry Winters Luce's heroes. Those years in China, many of them spent as the only American in a British school, where he had to fight against constant British assaults upon his origins, made him more intensely American, more accepting of American values than most men of his intellectual achievement.

This attitude colored his magazines as well. It was as if Luce's publications were more midwestern in origin and tone than the New York base indicated. He was possessed, for all his shrewdness and intelligence, by a kind of American innocence. He was by his own admission a square, which he thought a highly laudable quality, and it was one of the things which kept him in touch with his readers. Once, coming out of a Goldwater rally in 1964, a friend mentioned how boring the rally had been, how square all the people were. "What's wrong with that! What's wrong with that! I'm a square too," he said. It was easy for him to be in touch, his own taste frequently ran to corn. One of his few conflicts with Louis Kronenberger, his talented drama critic, was over Kronenberger's dislike of *South Pacific,* a musical Luce loved. He was capable of asking Edward Albee, the playwright, why he wrote such negative things—in fact, why were all major playwrights so negative? Why couldn't Albee, Luce suggested, write a musical comedy based on the life of Paul Hoffman (the Studebaker industrialist and foreign-aid expert and a great Luce favorite)? All wonderfully Protestant and wonderfully American.

He was a remarkably uncynical man; he was a believer. Yet he was fascinated by cynicism and hedonism in others; if he did not exactly like or admire his old friend Joe Kennedy, he was nonetheless intrigued by him, fascinated that he could dance so close to evil without being stricken. On the night of John Kennedy's acceptance speech at the Democratic convention the two men sat together in Luce's apartment, talking about both their sons, and Joe Kennedy had suggested what Harry should do about young Hank: "Why don't you just buy him a safe congressional seat?" Luce was appalled. "What do you mean by that? You can't do *that!*" "Come on, Harry," said Kennedy, "you and I both know how to do it. Of course it can be done." Similarly he hated corruption as only a Protestant reformer can. He had no Latin or Mediterranean tolerance of it, or belief that corruption was generic to the human species. To Luce it was evil and he campaigned against it at home and abroad and each year *Time* bureau chiefs around the world would receive the annual cable suggesting that HRL wanted material for the all-out big story on the problem of worldwide corruption. Stamp it out. A better world. A world that would never be.


Power, not money, fascinated him and moved him. Indeed, in keeping with his sense of what America was and where it was going, he originally intended to call *Fortune* magazine *Power.* He liked making money, it commanded respect, it was better to make it than not to make it, and it allowed him great journalistic freedom; the more successful he was, the freer he was of the demands of his own business people. He spent exorbitantly on his publishing empire, but he had little interest in money personally and he hated to use it on himself, he was too good and strict a Calvinist. So he spent reluctantly, both for himself and for his beautiful second wife, Clare, and they fought over money, over which one of them would be able to use the one Luce car in the earlier days of his marriage when he was already a millionaire, and over the fact that his dress shirts turned yellow with age, which annoyed her, and over whether it was time to redecorate the house. Why redecorate, he would ask, when it's already been decorated? "Harry," she once asked, "are we rich or are we poor?" He avoided the answer. She repeated the question. Finally he admitted they were rich. "Good," she said, "then I can redo the apartment."

azine, was responsible
ually made *SI* so success-
become big business in
e stayed with the magazine
. At another time he wanted
me interested in murder and
loved being one step ahead of
nger from Phoenix to inquire
d just had its one thousandth
e fact that was.) Once, meeting
sion column for the *Herald Trib-*
ver watched television because he
ested that Crosby could make a lot
would tell which of the upcoming
agazine he outlined was similar to the
most successful ventures of our times.

radio and television. As far as he was
, and it was not really journalism. He was
1898, and in his era journalism meant print.
both radio and television; there was a time
C network for very little, finally he went into
halfheartedly and bought five stations which
out. The stations were profitable but he took no
Most of what they showed struck him as silly,
rather than expanding it. When friends talked to
ed to tune out. In the end, as television grew more
riously challenged the kind of magazine he had
*Look*—there were those close to him who thought
part of something so vast and so powerful. Yet his
d not want to stray; that was his field and his signature

atur was important to him. He thought a publisher like
ger of *The New York Times* lacking in responsibility
id not sufficiently dominate his reporters' copy. As the
essence was it printed. As far as he was concerned,
g his duty, giving up far too much power, taking no real
he printed. (He was sometimes puzzled by the fact that
njoy higher credibility in the public mind than *Time*
iked the actions of the giants of television, taking a vital
it over to the worst kind of huckstering, where the
learly profit. Though he had an ostensible friendship
—all emperors must accept the company of their peers
ainful of him, and in 1964 when Paley and Frank

Another time Clare wanted to buy some pearls and Luce delayed and delayed in giving her an answer, but he finally said yes. At which point she went out and bought a pearl necklace for about $300,000. He was staggered when he saw the bill, and he immediately demanded that one of his women staffers come up and explain about pearls to him. "Why do women like pearls? What's the difference in pearls? Those pearls you're wearing, how much do they cost?" A couple of hundred dollars, she answered. "Then why should others cost so much more when no one can tell the difference? Why do women like the more expensive ones?" He became inevitably, absolutely absorbed by the subject of pearls and saw to it that *Life* did a good-sized story on pearls.

The pleasures that money could buy were not pleasures to him. It was power he loved. When he divorced his first wife, Lila Hotz, to marry Clare, he was exceptionally generous, but as far as is known he never gave her any *Time* stock. That was crucial, money was one thing, but stock in the magazine was another, it was power. He did not want his money anywhere but in *Time* magazine, and that was the bane of his financial advisers, who thought he should diversify just a little. "Harry," Clare once asked, "don't you think it's a mistake to have all your eggs in one basket?" "It's all right," he answered, "as long as it's my basket." That was the place for his money, in Time-Life, which was the one thing he really loved. Once during the late thirties he was offered a wonderful chance to get in on an early oil-drilling group, one of those chances that was only for the very rich, the big boys. It was also an opportunity to go in with people he was then very much in awe of and wanted to be associated with, the Dillons and Rockefellers. It was a marvelous deal, a sure winner, and an entrée to the right club as well. All it took was an initial investment of two hundred thousand dollars for which Luce went to the bank. But good deal or no, Luce, who was already a multimillionaire, did not like going to the bank, he hated the idea of *owing* money, it smacked of being poor. The deal was a winner from the start and it very quickly hit some wells, but this sort of thing required additional insertions of money to keep drilling. About a year later the partners came back for more money and Luce was annoyed. Did you tell me they would come back for more money? he asked his adviser Allen Grover. Yes, Grover answered. How much are my wells worth? Luce asked. Grover explained that it was a complicated procedure because there was a group of investors, and it was hard to know exactly. But Luce insisted that he wanted to know how much his wells were worth. Grover found out and reported back that they were worth approximately a million dollars. At which point Luce immediately insisted on selling, which irritated the other members of the syndicate because they had to find someone to take his place. He finally got his million dollars, but it was a dumb thing to do socially, it alienated people whose association and friendship he had long coveted and it was an even dumber thing to do in business terms. The company eventually became something called Astral Oil and his original investment and a little more would eventually have become ten million dollars. The bank loan he had taken at the time was, in terms of his personal worth, minuscule, but he was uneasy about it, he hated owing the bank money and he wanted all his money in *Time* stock. That was what mattered and that was what was useful.

Which was the way he felt about money and financiers. He did not like men whose preoccupation was simply the acquisition of money, people with no goal, no mission in life other than sheer materialism. He looked down on them. He liked the Rockefellers because, in addition to being rich, they were doers, they had causes and were involved. He was an old friend of Joe Kennedy but there was a part of him that did not entirely respect Joe, the fact that Joe was too much of a financier, too interested in money for money's sake. He was contemptuous of Bill Paley of CBS, whom he knew well, because Paley owned such an awesome instrument for education and social change, as Luce saw it, and yet contented himself with using it to make money, not to expand people's minds (though the idea of Luce trying to dominate an entire television network with his views and attitudes did not make his closest associates feel easy).

In part this contributed to his almost scornful attitude toward the business types at *Time;* he was visibly impatient with them and took pleasure in being patronizing and condescending with them in front of his editorial people. He did this because he sensed that the business people were afraid of him and that many of the journalists were not, and he liked to push on the raw nerve. At *Time* there was a group called the President's Committee. It met every Thursday and it consisted of Roy Larsen and the publisher, and the top business people of the magazine, but Luce did not like to go to the meeting; much to the annoyance of the business side, he deputized Allen Grover to represent him, as if he could not find the time to lend his presence and his concern to these petty subjects.

He was the editor, let there be no doubt about that. He would take all responsibility for whatever *Time* and *Life* printed. He was in charge. No one else need apply. Once, when one of Luce's top journalists, Bob Manning, was a little restless and thinking of leaving the fold, Luce flew to Europe to meet with Manning and try to dissuade him. But the meeting proved fruitless, and when Luce came out, looking somewhat discouraged, he encountered the *Life* photographer Carl Mydans. "Is he going to stay, Harry?" asked Mydans. No, Luce answered, he is not. "Why not, Harry?" Mydans asked. "He wants to be me," Luce said.

If Luce was partly the Calvinist missionary who knew his mission and knew his duty, he was also very much the journalist. He was insatiable in his curiosity, he wanted to know everything about everybody, he was always hammering away with questions, almost neurotically. Indeed, close friends thought that Luce was on almost all occasions so dogged an interrogator because he wanted a shield for his shyness. If he was asking questions, then he did not have to talk, and it also prevented people from asking *him* questions. Thus for all *Time* correspondents there was the nightmare of Luce on the move, arriving in their city, immediately demanding to know what every building was, what every incident meant. Luce in Paris during the fifties, visiting the bureau, asking suddenly, "Are the French happy?" "Harry,"

Stanton cracked down on Jim Aubrey, CBS's merciless programmer, Luce took a certain pleasure in it. In his opinion (and that of many others) Paley and Stanton had tolerated Aubrey's personal excesses as long as the ratings were high, but then when the ratings showed a sign of slipping they had become for the first time concerned over Aubrey's personal behavior. *Life* was doing an article on the subject; Luce, hearing about the piece, wanted to see it before it was published. "What's this about my friend Bill Paley?" Luce asked Ed Thompson, the managing editor of *Life*. Thompson explained the article carefully. Luce, rather than being upset, was absolutely delighted. "Damnit, it serves those sanctimonious sons of bitches Paley and Stanton right. Can't we make it tougher?" Thompson had to point out that in terms of libel they had already gone as far as they could go.

A curious blend of a man. Part sophisticate and part hick. At once shy and incredibly arrogant. At once surrounded by all the men of his empire ready to do him service, and painfully, desperately lonely. He felt so awkward, he had in some curious way so little real sense of his position and accomplishment. Once, after a dazzling evening with intellectuals and celebrities at the home of his friends Richard and Shirley Clurman, he turned to Shirley and asked her how she managed to assemble so glittering a group of people. "It's very simple, Harry," she said, "we just tell them you're coming." He could not accept what he had become: he could not enjoy his wealth, it was as if beautiful and lovely things were sinful to him, life had to have a purpose and things which were simply pleasant or beautiful of themselves had no purpose. His boyhood had been rigid, Henry Winters Luce was a stern figure, Harry's stammer had not come from nowhere, there were always rules to obey and standards to be met and, after they were taken care of, more rules to be met.

The Luces had been influential in China, but the Harry Luce who arrived in America to be educated at Hotchkiss and Yale was desperately poor, virtually—as were most missionary kids—a charity case. Mish-kids, they were called. At prep school he was an outsider, Chink Luce, wearing funny clothes copied by poor Chinese tailors from models in hopelessly outdated American magazines. He looked and felt terribly different from those spoiled eastern prep school kids. Their families had known each other forever, these young men had played with each other from the day they were born, they wore the right clothes, and said the right things, and laughed at the right jokes. Sitting there at the school table, hearing his contemporaries complain about the school food, which, by the standards he had known in China, was very elegant, he felt badly out of place. He was different, peculiar. Desperately serious and ambitious. Years later, near the end of her life, Pearl Buck, the other great and successful child of Chinese missionary parents, had reminisced with Luce about growing up as missionary kids. How wonderful it had been, how special and regal she had felt, Miss Buck said. She was absolutely stunned to hear Luce say, *No, it had not been wonderful, he had hated it, he had felt so different at*

*Hotchkiss and Yale, he had hated being that poor, and was painfully embarrassed by it.* Miss Buck was startled by the violence of his response, but it was a cry so deep, a revelation so painful by a man who so rarely revealed himself, that it was like meeting an entirely different Harry Luce. Once a friend of his pointed out how odd it was that he was so reverential to many of the big-business tycoons, few of whom could really touch him in genuine accomplishment. "You're right, I suppose," he answered, "but you have to understand that there's nothing worse than being a missionary child. The pain and poverty is just terrible. A missionary deals with all of the important people in the community, but he's never really one of them. He doesn't have their position or money or real status. So when I'm with all these big men in industry there's still a part of me that's the son of the missionary with the local VIPs." No wonder, then, that he had so fierce a desire to succeed, and that he so hated the idea of failure, and his most special intolerance was for those whom he considered losers.

In the same way, he admired men who had the ease about them which he so clearly did not. Part of his vast admiration for Dwight Eisenhower, friends thought, was that Ike was so totally different, Ike had so natural an ease and grace, he could walk into a group of men, even without his title, and very quickly gain respect and affection. Luce yearned to be accepted by the social and business elite but he never really was, he could not bring himself to be more graceful. His edges were always too sharp. His very strength was his lack of grace, it made him a better journalist, he was an unfinished man in the best sense, and in conflicts between his social peers and his reporters he usually sided with his reporters. He was simply too strong and too irascible to gain the favor of the people he coveted. So much of his life finally was lonely, he understood almost everything about his magazines' professional life and so little about his personal life. It was hard for him to reach out to people in a personal way. Once as a young man riding a subway back from a business meeting in Wall Street, he turned to his aide Allen Grover and said abruptly: "Allen, do you understand women?" Grover answered that sometimes he thought he did, though surely not always. "Well, I don't," Luce said curtly, closing the subject. Even at the height of his power there were poignant scenes of the Luces giving a cocktail party in Phoenix at 5:30 P.M., and at 5:30 on the nose Harry Luce, the most powerful publisher in America, standing at the door like some nervous debutante at her first ball, wondering whether anyone was going to come, after all.

He was, in those grand years of the forties and fifties and early sixties, the most powerful conservative publisher in America, and in the fifties at least as influential as the Secretary of State, yet there was a part of him that felt he had been shunned. He wanted a title, he wanted recognition. Perhaps a job in the Cabinet. An honorary degree. He had achieved so much and yet he seemed to crave recognition that was far beneath him. Near the end of his life he was tired and often worn out and yet he seemed to desire this kind of acceptance more and more; all too often he sat on the dais of the Waldorf-Astoria for some

Another time Clare wanted to buy some pearls and Luce delayed and delayed in giving her an answer, but he finally said yes. At which point she went out and bought a pearl necklace for about $300,000. He was staggered when he saw the bill, and he immediately demanded that one of his women staffers come up and explain about pearls to him. "Why do women like pearls? What's the difference in pearls? Those pearls you're wearing, how much do they cost?" A couple of hundred dollars, she answered. "Then why should others cost so much more when no one can tell the difference? Why do women like the more expensive ones?" He became inevitably, absolutely absorbed by the subject of pearls and saw to it that *Life* did a good-sized story on pearls.

The pleasures that money could buy were not pleasures to him. It was power he loved. When he divorced his first wife, Lila Hotz, to marry Clare, he was exceptionally generous, but as far as is known he never gave her any *Time* stock. That was crucial, money was one thing, but stock in the magazine was another, it was power. He did not want his money anywhere but in *Time* magazine, and that was the bane of his financial advisers, who thought he should diversify just a little. "Harry," Clare once asked, "don't you think it's a mistake to have all your eggs in one basket?" "It's all right," he answered, "as long as it's my basket." That was the place for his money, in Time-Life, which was the one thing he really loved. Once during the late thirties he was offered a wonderful chance to get in on an early oil-drilling group, one of those chances that was only for the very rich, the big boys. It was also an opportunity to go in with people he was then very much in awe of and wanted to be associated with, the Dillons and Rockefellers. It was a marvelous deal, a sure winner, and an entrée to the right club as well. All it took was an initial investment of two hundred thousand dollars for which Luce went to the bank. But good deal or no, Luce, who was already a multimillionaire, did not like going to the bank, he hated the idea of *owing* money, it smacked of being poor. The deal was a winner from the start and it very quickly hit some wells, but this sort of thing required additional insertions of money to keep drilling. About a year later the partners came back for more money and Luce was annoyed. Did you tell me they would come back for more money? he asked his adviser Allen Grover. Yes, Grover answered. How much are my wells worth? Luce asked. Grover explained that it was a complicated procedure because there was a group of investors, and it was hard to know exactly. But Luce insisted that he wanted to know how much his wells were worth. Grover found out and reported back that they were worth approximately a million dollars. At which point Luce immediately insisted on selling, which irritated the other members of the syndicate because they had to find someone to take his place. He finally got his million dollars, but it was a dumb thing to do socially, it alienated people whose association and friendship he had long coveted and it was an even dumber thing to do in business terms. The company eventually became something called Astral Oil and his original investment and a little more would eventually have become ten million dollars. The bank loan he had taken at the time was, in terms of his personal worth, minuscule, but he was uneasy about it, he hated owing the bank money and he wanted all his money in *Time* stock. That was what mattered and that was what was useful.

Which was the way he felt about money and financiers. He did not like men whose preoccupation was simply the acquisition of money, people with no goal, no mission in life other than sheer materialism. He looked down on them. He liked the Rockefellers because, in addition to being rich, they were doers, they had causes and were involved. He was an old friend of Joe Kennedy but there was a part of him that did not entirely respect Joe, the fact that Joe was too much of a financier, too interested in money for money's sake. He was contemptuous of Bill Paley of CBS, whom he knew well, because Paley owned such an awesome instrument for education and social change, as Luce saw it, and yet contented himself with using it to make money, not to expand people's minds (though the idea of Luce trying to dominate an entire television network with his views and attitudes did not make his closest associates feel easy).

In part this contributed to his almost scornful attitude toward the business types at *Time;* he was visibly impatient with them and took pleasure in being patronizing and condescending with them in front of his editorial people. He did this because he sensed that the business people were afraid of him and that many of the journalists were not, and he liked to push on the raw nerve. At *Time* there was a group called the President's Committee. It met every Thursday and it consisted of Roy Larsen and the publisher, and the top business people of the magazine, but Luce did not like to go to the meeting; much to the annoyance of the business side, he deputized Allen Grover to represent him, as if he could not find the time to lend his presence and his concern to these petty subjects.

He was the editor, let there be no doubt about that. He would take all responsibility for whatever *Time* and *Life* printed. He was in charge. No one else need apply. Once, when one of Luce's top journalists, Bob Manning, was a little restless and thinking of leaving the fold, Luce flew to Europe to meet with Manning and try to dissuade him. But the meeting proved fruitless, and when Luce came out, looking somewhat discouraged, he encountered the *Life* photographer Carl Mydans. "Is he going to stay, Harry?" asked Mydans. No, Luce answered, he is not. "Why not, Harry?" Mydans asked. "He wants to be me," Luce said.

If Luce was partly the Calvinist missionary who knew his mission and knew his duty, he was also very much the journalist. He was insatiable in his curiosity, he wanted to know everything about everybody, he was always hammering away with questions, almost neurotically. Indeed, close friends thought that Luce was on almost all occasions so dogged an interrogator because he wanted a shield for his shyness. If he was asking questions, then he did not have to talk, and it also prevented people from asking *him* questions. Thus for all *Time* correspondents there was the nightmare of Luce on the move, arriving in their city, immediately demanding to know what every building was, what every incident meant. Luce in Paris during the fifties, visiting the bureau, asking suddenly, "Are the French happy?" "Harry," answered a bureau member, "how can you tell whether an entire nation is happy or not? How can you even tell whether one person is happy?" "Well," Luce answered, "that's what we pay you for, to find out things like that." Luce in Milan at a championship soccer game between the two best soccer teams in Europe. Eighty thousand Italians at the game coming out of their seats at a particularly frenzied moment, Luce turning to a *Time* reporter to ask: "How many of them are Communists?" Legendary stories of reporters for *Time* preparing for a Luce visit by studying the route that Luce was expected to take, airport to center of town, memorizing it so that the next day as Luce barked out his questions they would be ready. Frank White, a senior correspondent in Europe in the immediate postwar years, once took Luce through West Berlin, getting everything right, until finally Luce pointed to a bomb crater. "What's that? What's that?" he demanded. "Harry," said White, "that's a hole in the ground." The one *Time* correspondent who deliberately refused to play the game was a sometimes acerbic man named Israel Shenker. Shenker, knowing that everyone else on the staff was geared up for landmarks, professed total ignorance of sights in Rome, a city Luce knew well from his tour as the ambassador's husband. Once Luce and Shenker were traveling together when Luce spotted a huge edifice. "What's that? What's that?" he asked. "I'm sure I know what that is. . . ." Shenker answered that he did not have the vaguest idea. "I'm sure I know it," said Luce. Finally the Italian driver, half bored, leaned back and said, "It's the Colosseum." He was interested in people only to the degree that they could tell him something, slip him a fast fact; losing interest if they did not have a reservoir of facts for him, he would quickly turn to someone else. That was his quick fix, information. The people who worked for him joked about it, yet they were aware that it was enormously stimulating to them, that endless maniacal curiosity. Who are the most important men of the half century? he might ask. What has happened to all the dethroned European royalty? But it was exhausting as well as exhilarating for staff people working with him or traveling with him. *Time* magazine was his life, he had no personal life, it consumed twenty-four hours of his day. There were no respites, no time-outs. If he was at the airport in Brussels and his plane was delayed two hours, then he immediately became restless—whom could he visit? The Prime Minister? The editor of a leading paper? Above all, that time must not be wasted, questions must be posed, answers must be received.

But it was that endless curiosity, almost a hick curiosity—our best editors have always been at least partly hick, everything is new and fresh and possible for them, they take nothing for granted—that made him such a great editor and so energized his publications. Even when he was well into his sixties he would come down and edit *Life* or *Time* for a week or so each year, and his people felt the energy that transformed the magazines, made them vital. He had a profound sense of other people's interests. He started *Sports Illustrated* even though he had remarkably little interest in sports. He stayed with it when it was a very expensive loser and most of his associates wanted to junk it, because his instincts told him the audience was there and growing (ironically, television, which had helped kill his beloved *Life* magazine, was responsible for the explosion in sports and leisure life that eventually made *SI* so successful). He knew somehow that sports was about to become big business in America, that others were interested in it, and so he stayed with the magazine even when it was twenty-five million dollars in debt. At another time he wanted to start a magazine called *Murder;* he had become interested in murder and thought other people were interested too. (He loved being one step ahead of his editors and he once phoned Otto Fuerbringer from Phoenix to inquire whether Fuerbringer knew that Chicago had just had its one thousandth gangland murder. What a wonderful obscure fact that was.) Once, meeting John Crosby, who was then writing a television column for the *Herald Tribune,* Luce complained bitterly that he never watched television because he never knew what was good on it. He suggested that Crosby could make a lot of money by starting a magazine which would tell which of the upcoming programs were worth watching. The magazine he outlined was similar to the then nonexistent *TV Guide,* one of the most successful ventures of our times.

Luce himself was not interested in radio and television. As far as he was concerned, it was not his business, and it was not really journalism. He was very much a man of his era, born in 1898, and in his era journalism meant print. He resisted chances to go big into both radio and television; there was a time when he could have had the ABC network for very little, finally he went into television rather late and rather halfheartedly and bought five stations which he never really cared much about. The stations were profitable but he took no real pleasure in their profits. Most of what they showed struck him as silly, narrowing the field of vision rather than expanding it. When friends talked to him about television he seemed to tune out. In the end, as television grew more and more powerful and seriously challenged the kind of magazine he had helped invent—*Life* and *Look*—there were those close to him who thought he regretted not being a part of something so vast and so powerful. Yet his love was print and he did not want to stray; that was his field and his signature was on everything.

His own imprimatur was important to him. He thought a publisher like Arthur Hays Sulzberger of *The New York Times* lacking in responsibility because Sulzberger did not sufficiently dominate his reporters' copy. As the copy came in, so in essence was it printed. As far as he was concerned, Sulzberger was shirking his duty, giving up far too much power, taking no real responsibility for what he printed. (He was sometimes puzzled by the fact that the *Times* seemed to enjoy higher credibility in the public mind than *Time* did.) Even more he disliked the actions of the giants of television, taking a vital instrument and turning it over to the worst kind of huckstering, where the prime concern was so clearly profit. Though he had an ostensible friendship with Bill Paley of CBS—all emperors must accept the company of their peers —he was privately disdainful of him, and in 1964 when Paley and Frank

Stanton cracked down on Jim Aubrey, CBS's merciless programmer, Luce took a certain pleasure in it. In his opinion (and that of many others) Paley and Stanton had tolerated Aubrey's personal excesses as long as the ratings were high, but then when the ratings showed a sign of slipping they had become for the first time concerned over Aubrey's personal behavior. *Life* was doing an article on the subject; Luce, hearing about the piece, wanted to see it before it was published. "What's this about my friend Bill Paley?" Luce asked Ed Thompson, the managing editor of *Life*. Thompson explained the article carefully. Luce, rather than being upset, was absolutely delighted. "Damnit, it serves those sanctimonious sons of bitches Paley and Stanton right. Can't we make it tougher?" Thompson had to point out that in terms of libel they had already gone as far as they could go.


A curious blend of a man. Part sophisticate and part hick. At once shy and incredibly arrogant. At once surrounded by all the men of his empire ready to do him service, and painfully, desperately lonely. He felt so awkward, he had in some curious way so little real sense of his position and accomplishment. Once, after a dazzling evening with intellectuals and celebrities at the home of his friends Richard and Shirley Clurman, he turned to Shirley and asked her how she managed to assemble so glittering a group of people. "It's very simple, Harry," she said, "we just tell them you're coming." He could not accept what he had become: he could not enjoy his wealth, it was as if beautiful and lovely things were sinful to him, life had to have a purpose and things which were simply pleasant or beautiful of themselves had no purpose. His boyhood had been rigid, Henry Winters Luce was a stern figure, Harry's stammer had not come from nowhere, there were always rules to obey and standards to be met and, after they were taken care of, more rules to be met.

The Luces had been influential in China, but the Harry Luce who arrived in America to be educated at Hotchkiss and Yale was desperately poor, virtually—as were most missionary kids—a charity case. Mish-kids, they were called. At prep school he was an outsider, Chink Luce, wearing funny clothes copied by poor Chinese tailors from models in hopelessly outdated American magazines. He looked and felt terribly different from those spoiled eastern prep school kids. Their families had known each other forever, these young men had played with each other from the day they were born, they wore the right clothes, and said the right things, and laughed at the right jokes. Sitting there at the school table, hearing his contemporaries complain about the school food, which, by the standards he had known in China, was very elegant, he felt badly out of place. He was different, peculiar. Desperately serious and ambitious. Years later, near the end of her life, Pearl Buck, the other great and successful child of Chinese missionary parents, had reminisced with Luce about growing up as missionary kids. How wonderful it had been, how special and regal she had felt, Miss Buck said. She was absolutely stunned to hear Luce say, *No, it had not been wonderful, he had hated it, he had felt so different at*

*Hotchkiss and Yale, he had hated being that poor, and was painfully embarrassed by it.* Miss Buck was startled by the violence of his response, but it was a cry so deep, a revelation so painful by a man who so rarely revealed himself, that it was like meeting an entirely different Harry Luce. Once a friend of his pointed out how odd it was that he was so reverential to many of the big-business tycoons, few of whom could really touch him in genuine accomplishment. "You're right, I suppose," he answered, "but you have to understand that there's nothing worse than being a missionary child. The pain and poverty is just terrible. A missionary deals with all of the important people in the community, but he's never really one of them. He doesn't have their position or money or real status. So when I'm with all these big men in industry there's still a part of me that's the son of the missionary with the local VIPs." No wonder, then, that he had so fierce a desire to succeed, and that he so hated the idea of failure, and his most special intolerance was for those whom he considered losers.

In the same way, he admired men who had the ease about them which he so clearly did not. Part of his vast admiration for Dwight Eisenhower, friends thought, was that Ike was so totally different, Ike had so natural an ease and grace, he could walk into a group of men, even without his title, and very quickly gain respect and affection. Luce yearned to be accepted by the social and business elite but he never really was, he could not bring himself to be more graceful. His edges were always too sharp. His very strength was his lack of grace, it made him a better journalist, he was an unfinished man in the best sense, and in conflicts between his social peers and his reporters he usually sided with his reporters. He was simply too strong and too irascible to gain the favor of the people he coveted. So much of his life finally was lonely, he understood almost everything about his magazines' professional life and so little about his personal life. It was hard for him to reach out to people in a personal way. Once as a young man riding a subway back from a business meeting in Wall Street, he turned to his aide Allen Grover and said abruptly: "Allen, do you understand women?" Grover answered that sometimes he thought he did, though surely not always. "Well, I don't," Luce said curtly, closing the subject. Even at the height of his power there were poignant scenes of the Luces giving a cocktail party in Phoenix at 5:30 P.M., and at 5:30 on the nose Harry Luce, the most powerful publisher in America, standing at the door like some nervous debutante at her first ball, wondering whether anyone was going to come, after all.

He was, in those grand years of the forties and fifties and early sixties, the most powerful conservative publisher in America, and in the fifties at least as influential as the Secretary of State, yet there was a part of him that felt he had been shunned. He wanted a title, he wanted recognition. Perhaps a job in the Cabinet. An honorary degree. He had achieved so much and yet he seemed to crave recognition that was far beneath him. Near the end of his life he was tired and often worn out and yet he seemed to desire this kind of acceptance more and more; all too often he sat on the dais of the Waldorf-Astoria for some

boring self-congratulatory dinner program and friends, seeing his face gray, would ask why he was doing it, and Luce would answer, "Because it is expected of me." He wanted in the Eisenhower years to be Secretary of State, but Foster Dulles was there and Foster Dulles was *Time* magazine sprung to life. Once during the Eisenhower years he was offered an ambassadorship and he said no, telling friends that "the only ambassadorship I would take is to a restored democracy in China," an assignment not entirely within the control even of Ike and Dulles. China, of course, had spawned him and China haunted him. He had made his stand there, and when China had gone Communist he had refused to accept the verdict of history, he had continued his war long after Chiang had given up on his. So it was that in the American mind his name was inextricably linked with China. One thought of Harry Luce and then thought of China. He was, wrote A. J. Liebling, the maître d' who at a smorgasbord is always trying to unload a bit of unwanted Chiang Kai-shek on unsuspecting guests.

He was an unabashed patriot in a profession which plays down overt patriotism. The American flag was never far from the pages of *Time* and *Life*. The Reverend Luce, aware that his children knew only China, had constantly emphasized to them that America was not like China, America was different, the corruption they saw here was Chinese, not American. He passed on an idealized version of America that was to remain with Harry Luce for most of his life. Harry Luce was a booster, but a special one; boosters are usually small-time with narrow scope, with more than a touch of Babbitt in them, but Luce had scope, he was fascinated by great issues, and he was no small-time Babbitt. But the booster part of him made the intellectual community, which he often longed to be part of, that much more suspicious. He was, after all, a devout Republican. That was strike one. Then he was a committed practicing Christian. That was strike two. Could a man of these faiths be really acceptable? He became eventually a man without an intellectual-cultural base: too square for the critics, too critical for the squares.

   For his beliefs were central to his life, his Americanism, his Presbyterianism, his Republicanism, his belief in the capitalist society. It was also his obligation to make sure that his readers knew right from wrong. If in 1952 it was better for the nation to elect a Republican President, then it was *Time*'s job to expedite this, which the magazine zealously did. After its coverage of the first Eisenhower-Stevenson campaign, in which *Time* had brutalized Stevenson, an associate challenged Luce, telling him these had not been questions of truth with a capital *T*, they were, after all, simply political questions. Luce dissented strongly. "Eisenhower was right for the country for a large number of reasons, therefore it was *Time*'s duty to explain why the country needed Ike. Any other form of objectivity would have been unfair and uninvolved," he said. If this bothered some intellectuals, it nonetheless helped connect him to his readership, and it helped to set his publications apart. They were middle-

brow even if the people working for him were not, and this was one reason
he was so successful.

There was a major difference between his two most important and influential magazines. *Time* was more clearly and openly the political instrument of
the Luce empire, the Papal Nuncio or the *Pravda* of the organization setting
down the line. Within the organization, the men who were more ambitious in
the corporate sense, the men who wanted to rise in the company, went to work
there. *Time* was more filled with internal intrigues than *Life*. *Life* was different, less political, more open; it was more dependent upon pictures and thus
more tied to events themselves rather than to interpretation of events. The
people who went to work there were more interested in the fun and excitement
of their profession than their careers per se. *Life*, by its dependence upon
photography, made itself closer to the human heartbeat. Luce, by the late
thirties, had come to hate Franklin Roosevelt, but Roosevelt could still dominate the pages of *Life*, that powerful face, that cocky, zestful tilt of the head,
produced wonderful, forceful pictures, and pictures were *Life*'s business. Indeed, one of the reasons for Luce's early enthusiasm for Wendell Willkie (not
surprisingly, the other early major Republican sponsors of Willkie were the
Cowles brothers, who published *Look*) was that Willkie too had a wonderful
face for the era of modern photojournalism. He was a Republican who did not
look like a Republican, the rarest of things in those days, a Republican with
sex appeal.

All of this made *Life* fairer. In *Time*, Luce was outlining to Americans
their responsibilities and duties, and often explaining Truth. He believed that
if something appeared in *Time*, people would believe it, because after all if it
appeared in *Time*, he, Harry Luce, believed it. In *Life*, he was reflecting
America to Americans, in a sense reflecting the heartbeat of a nation. It was
a difference Luce was acutely aware of. Once, when someone was threatening
to sue *Life* over a series of articles, Luce in annoyance turned to one of its
editors, Ralph Graves, and said, "I always thought it was the business of *Time*
to make enemies and the business of *Life* to make friends."


There was in liberal intellectual circles such deep antagonism toward Luce for
his coverage of China, and for the partisan quality of his domestic political
coverage, that intellectuals often overlooked or disdained the great achievement of Luce as a publisher, his extraordinary inventiveness and his continued
incredible success, publication after publication. There were several reasons for
his immense success: his own curiosity, his sense of the audience, the ability
never to underestimate their intelligence but never to overestimate their
sources of information. Then, too, his own odd sense of excellence. He hired
high-quality, talented people and managed to keep at least a fair share of them
from resigning in protest. But there was a constant struggle between Luce and
many of his most able and talented people, torn and anguished as they were
by the sometimes strict ideological limits that Luce imposed. In the early days

of the magazine the struggle was often between Luce and some of his editors, but later it all sifted down, the editors gradually became more clearly extensions of Luce himself and the struggle was increasingly between Luce and some of his best reporters. In both instances many of his best people wondered why they stayed. It was not just the money, though the money was good, better than most newspapers at the time, and the expense accounts were lavish. Rather it was also because the jobs were fun, the institution was filled with energy, and there was of course always the possibility of influencing so important an institution. That and the fact that they were often touched by Luce's own personal magnetism. If the magazine was often dogmatic, he very rarely was. He loved to argue, convinced of course as always that he would win, a conviction validated usually by what the magazine printed the following week. It was no accident that many of his best people, including men and women who left his employ, often ended up fonder of him than they were of the magazine.

All of this made Luce's life a little more difficult, but it also gave his publications a gloss and strength that a lesser publisher might not have tolerated. Why, he often wondered aloud, were all the talented writers liberals? Why was his staff always fighting him? Once, in a moment of pique, he turned to a young woman on *Life* named Dora Hamblin. "I hope," he told her, "that when you grow up you will get to be the editor of a great big magazine. And that everyone who works for you is a Republican." Yet his own vision always dominated, though not so completely as to drive out his ablest people. He was willing to incorporate some of their reporting, but never so much that their reporting would outstrip or challenge his vision. He was in charge. Let there be no doubt about it. That was the way it should be.

Gradually over the years, as *Time* magazine became richer and more influential, there developed a more or less continuous battle over politically sensitive stories between reporters in the field and the editors in New York. This was just as Luce wanted it, for he had given his real power to his editors. He may have actually liked the reporters better, may have taken more pleasure in the vitality of their company and delight in the fact that they always seemed ready to argue with him, but there was never any doubt that *Time* was an editor's magazine. The reporters filed from the field, often brilliant dispatches, and then the editors overseeing the writers set the tone for the story and decided what might go in, and what would not go in. That there might be an ethical contradiction in this never occurred to Luce. Once when he was in Los Angeles he told his friend Paul Ziffren, the liberal lawyer, how he had known that Nasser would win out in Egypt over Naguib in their power struggle. How could you be so sure, Harry? Ziffren had asked. "Because I was there and met all those people and spent some time with the correspondent right before it all happened," Luce said proudly. "Lucky for the correspondent that you were there," Ziffren answered, "because otherwise it all would have been cut out in New York. You know, it always amazes me, Harry, how you can keep such first-rate people when you treat their copy the way you do." "Listen," Luce answered in a special moment of total candor, "I don't pretend that this is an objective magazine. It's an editorial magazine from the first page to the last and whatever comes out has to reflect my view and that's the way it is." But it was the very same contradiction between the editors in New York and the staff in the field that often made the internal struggles at *Time* so interesting. Thus the *Time* reportorial staff, which was by the sixties as good as any in the country, was often up in arms against its own product, a posture that bothered Luce not at all. He wanted quality, but he wanted quality on his terms.

He was from the start, whatever his politics, a publisher ahead of his time. *Time* arrived at almost the same moment as commercial radio and in several ways it was the direct and immediate beneficiary of it. For the coming of radio had by the late twenties changed the way most Americans got their news. Newspapers were no longer the prime or only means of communication in the country, though few publishers realized it yet. Radio was faster, it was delivering more and more impulses to millions of homes. Names and places were flashing into homes in endless quick spot newscasts, not always connected, not always sorted out. Radio was expanding the information business in a huge leap, and newspapers were behaving as if things were still the same. Most of the nation's newspaper publishers did not react to this, but Luce did. He knew that his messenger was not the first to reach his audience, that radio was there possibly whetting the appetite of the audience for better information. Therefore *Time* had to sum up better and answer different questions. It had, above all, to pull things together. So it did; it set events in context. It named foreign countries, explained that they were the size of Oregon or Montana, gave a brief outline of their politics, helped readers to pronounce difficult names, and used graphics as newspapers had never used them. It personalized complicated foreign issues. In the process it broke the rather suffocating norms of American journalism, and eased the profession into a more natural style of storytelling.

What was remarkable about *Time* in the early days was how small a staff actually put out the magazine. In the beginning it had no reporters of its own. Instead it piggybacked. A small staff sat in New York with subscriptions to a few papers around the country, clipping and pasting, and using a few dictionaries and the telephone with skill. Yet the form was successful because the time was right; *Time* was taking issues that people were increasingly aware of from daily newspapers and radio broadcasts and explaining what it all meant. All of this was Luce. He was absolutely sure that the readers he wanted to reach were both busy and curious; they had less time to read and they wanted more information. There were, he told his colleagues, two kinds of news, slow news and fast news. Slow news meant, he said, more depth, more questions answered, more time to reflect. Slow news involved the reader more; fast news did not. Fast news arrived and was gone. The field was completely open in slow news, that was *Time*'s business. Besides, he said, there was more money to be made in slow news than in fast news.

.   .   .

The early issues of *Time* had not seemed particularly political. In the thirties it began changing, becoming a magazine in which the politics were as important as the information. Given Luce, the politics were not surprising, Republican and pro-business. Suspicious of Democrats and organized labor. Internationalist, unexpectedly so for that period; more, its internationalism was not just the easy internationalism of the Atlantic. *Time,* because of Luce, cared about Asia as well, particularly China.

In domestic politics Luce's Republicanism was asserting itself more and more in terms of growing hostility toward Roosevelt and the New Deal. The intensity of that feeling was a little surprising. *Time* prided itself above all on being young and modern, and the people who worked for it saw themselves as modern, and the audience it wanted to reach was modern. Most modern young Americans in those days were very much under Franklin Roosevelt's spell; the memory of the worst of the Depression was too strong and the personal magnetism of Roosevelt's appeal too powerful. For some readers Luce's antagonism was puzzling. Clearly part of it was political. Roosevelt was a Democrat and that was, considering his background, something of an affront in itself. For Luce's Republicanism was something almost organic to him, as much a part of him as his Presbyterianism. Indeed, the two were of a piece; it was as if, believing in the things he did from his religion and his God, it was impossible to be anything but a Republican, it was for him shared values, shared vision, shared ethic. To Luce's eye, Roosevelt was not a traitor to his class; his view was more subtle than that. That Roosevelt could do what he had done, become a Democrat (semi-kin as he was to the sainted Teddy Roosevelt), meant that he was a man to be watched. He was not, in Luce's view, straight. It was not a matter of whether Roosevelt had violated the nation's political norms, he had violated *Luce's* norms. What many of his fellow Americans considered Roosevelt's magic touch with the Common Man, Luce saw as an instinct to patronize. Yet that Luce should end the decade so bitter toward Roosevelt was, despite his Republicanism, somewhat surprising. Much of Roosevelt's criticism of capitalism was not very different from Luce's own; and if Roosevelt was slower than Luce in moving against Hitler, he was nonetheless well ahead of most of his party and his country.

Part of the antagonism, friends of Luce thought, was personal. Some friends traced it back to a handful of dinners that the Luces and the Roosevelts had shared at Hyde Park, dinners which had not worked out well, there had been at the end a coldness and an anger. It was not the easiest foursome of the decade: Roosevelt, patrician and patronizing; Clare, young, outspoken, willful, beautiful, and conservative; Luce, forceful, often insensitive, often awkward; Eleanor, strong-willed, as political as Clare and disliking almost everything about her. Somehow in all this Roosevelt had treated Clare cavalierly as just a young pretty (silly) thing, which above all else she was not, and it had been a mistake. Luce in those earlier days was not yet *Luce,* he was the editor of a lively up-and-coming magazine, but he was not yet the great press lord he was to become, and there had been serious offense given, Harry had been angered over the treatment of Clare, and she was not a woman who would easily forgive or forget or permit him to forgive or forget. These feelings had not helped Franklin Roosevelt in the pages of *Time,* and Luce's bitterness toward Roosevelt remained long after he had warmed toward other of his old antagonists.

Yet it was not altogether remarkable that Roosevelt had not taken Luce quite seriously as a publisher until it was too late. The *Time* magazine of the twenties was clever rather than powerful, and slick rather than political, and Luce was hardly a formidable figure. He had been thirty-four years old when Roosevelt was first elected in 1932, the publisher of a snappy, lively magazine. When Luce published his first issue of *Life, Time*'s circulation was about half a million. Not bad, but not awesome either. The real power was to come while Roosevelt was in office and it was the birth of *Life* magazine which crystallized it. For *Life* was a stunning success, the reaction of the American people far outstripped not just the printer's capacity to produce copies but Luce's own limited calculations on its possibilities. The success was immense and was to transform the entire company, making it not only richer and more powerful but an empire. *Life* not only was rich in itself; it made *Time* rich and thus infinitely more powerful.

The birth of *Life* reflected Luce at his best. He had envisioned the magazine as it was to be, and he had pushed his printers hard for the production techniques that would make *Life* possible. Equally important, he had not faltered when the very success of *Life* threatened to bring down his entire company. His editorial instincts always took precedence over any cautionary sense of the bottom line.

There were at the time of *Life*'s birth several successful magazines— *The Saturday Evening Post* and *Collier's* among them—but they were not really photo magazines. They were not keyed to news; they were produced at a more leisurely pace, containing short fiction and longer serials and nonfiction articles scheduled months in advance. Yet the possibilities of a new photographer's magazine had always been there. Cameras were modern and could readily produce brilliant and realistic photographs of the world unposed. It was a seductive idea, seeing the world as it was instead of as it had often been seen before, as frozen for and by a Speed Graphic. The old world had been of people saying "cheese." A number of editors and publishers had explored the possibility of a magazine which would come out every week and which would emphasize the work of talented, highly mobile photographers, the right photographer capturing the right scene at exactly the right moment. But they had always been frustrated by technological limitations. It was, they soon discovered, simply impossible to bring out a magazine like that under that high-speed deadline pressure at a cost that was not prohibitive.

Normal printing was both too slow and too expensive. The normal ink that was used in high-quality printing, thinned with linseed oil, was simply too slow to dry. It dried by oxidation, which meant that if it were run on a high-speed press on cheap paper it would be badly smeared and the impressions ruined. A good news-photo weekly demanded a fast press run and expensive high-quality paper. So the prospect seemed unlikely, and reluctantly a series of editors and entrepreneurs had been forced to shelve their idea. This included Harry Luce himself, who, as early as 1932, had begun his own investigation into a weekly photographic magazine. He did not know very much about photography but he sensed immediately the drama inherent in it, and was sure that readers wanted it. His first dummy was called *Newsreel.* But the technology was not yet feasible.

As *Time* magazine became more and more successful, Luce became more restless. Success had never made him complacent, if anything it had the opposite effect, the more successful he was, the greater his obligation and responsibility to do more; success was not a reward per se but an acknowledgment that he owed even more. Once in the early forties, his first Washington bureau chief, Felix Belair, who had moved over from *The New York Times,* was appalled at how hard Luce was working when his magazines were so successful and asked him why. Luce answered as if he had smelled something distasteful in the air. "Felix, sometimes I actually think you're a hedonist." So it was not surprising that, with the increasing success of both *Time* and *Fortune,* in 1935 he began to think again of his photo magazine. He knew exactly what he wanted. He wanted large photos but photos that did not sit by themselves. His photos would tell a story. It would be a magazine for everyone. *Dime,* he intended to call it, to show that it was inexpensive. But the idea of magazines called *Time* and *Dime* was too much, too good an opportunity for every comic and would-be comic in the nation, and reluctantly he switched to a working title of *Show Book of the World.* He envisioned a staff of brilliant photographers going all over the world, telling human stories every week. At first he talked only to close aides, not even to his printers, because he was wary of gossip, wary that some other company might pirate his idea.

By coincidence at exactly the same time, independent of Luce, his printers in Chicago (the Donnelley Company, which printed *Time*) had started to experiment with several new techniques which might expedite the printing process and make a new glossy magazine possible. One technique was called heat-set printing, in which a heating system would be built into the press. In this system the ink would be dried not simply in the air but with the aid of a burner. Another was the arrival of a fast-drying ink, made not from linseed oil but with a petroleum base, and it was perfect for the heat-set printing. Flash-dry ink, it was called. There was still a problem with the paper. They needed to find a paper high enough in quality to do justice to photos and yet not so expensive as to be prohibitive for a mass-circulation magazine. The Donnelley people had heard of a new procedure developed to produce something called machine-coated stock. The procedure took rather ordinary paper and coated it while it was on the press, giving it a slick coating that was perfect for quality photographic reproduction. Though this process had been tested, it had not yet been put in production, but the Donnelley people were confident they could use it.

So within a year there was the coming together of the technological pieces which would make a new slick photographic magazine possible. Just then, Luce was beginning to draw up dummies for his projected new magazine. In December 1935, Tom Donnelley was in New York with one of his salesmen, H. P. Zimmermann. They had a few hours after lunch before catching the Century back to Chicago and they decided to drop in on Luce. "I've got something for you to take back to Chicago and worry about," Luce said, and outlined his vision of the new magazine. It would cost five or ten cents, it would be large, and it would have to be of good quality. A year earlier they would have had to turn him down. Now they simply asked for a few months and told Luce to go ahead with his part of the planning. They seemed confident they could do it. Two months later C. G. Littell, one of the company's executives, came into Zimmermann's office with a few samples of what they could do with the new heat-set press process. "You can go ahead and sell this process now," he said. He had hand-rigged some machines for his trials. By chance the next day Zimmermann got a call from Luce in New York. "Is the Ford of the printing industry ready to talk about producing a new weekly news magazine?" he asked. It was so important a moment to the printers that Zimmermann coerced Littell, who despised selling, to come to New York. There they explained the new system to Luce and told him it could print *Life* as fast as it was now printing *Time.* Luce was delighted with the trial sheets they brought him, they were exactly what he wanted. For the next several months the printers continued their experiments, rigging old presses with gas-burning heaters, becoming more confident all the time. Finally they were absolutely sure of the process. There were, however, a few problems left. First, it would take time to buy and equip the new presses that were needed for this technique, and second, the new machine-coated paper was not yet available.

But Harry Luce was impatient, he had not come this far by waiting on other men—he was a man to lead, others could catch up. He wanted to go ahead and he did not want to wait. If he waited, perhaps some other publisher might beat him to his idea. If Tom Donnelley had been able to do it in the dry runs by makeshift rigging of his presses, then he would just have to rig a few more. A few Donnelley officials blanched at the suggestion, but it was a potentially huge contract and finally they agreed. As for paper, they would go ahead using expensive ready-coated stock, losing money at the start if need be. They would transfer to the cheaper paper when it was available. They ran more trial magazines, one called *Dummy,* one called *Parade,* and one called *Rehearsal.* On November 19, 1936, some eight months after the first experimental use of heat-set printing, *Life* magazine appeared.

Anticipation for this new magazine was already high. Sight unseen there were already 230,000 charter subscribers. Luce was quietly confident. He told friends he would risk $1 million from his fledgling company to see *Life* survive, or go, as he said, "to an honorable grave." He and his colleagues had envisioned a somewhat limited success for the magazine, a circulation of perhaps

400,000 gradually rising to 1,000,000 over a period of years, and they had planned their advertising rate accordingly. The rate was designed to tempt and encourage new advertisers rather than to extract maximum immediate profit. To their astonishment, *Life* was a success beyond anyone's wildest calculations. It had an entire market to itself. It appeared in the days before television; it was an inexpensive lively magazine opening a window on the entire world; it was filled with photos of the people that readers had heard about over the radio. These were not stiff posed photos but modern candid photos of people and events.

In small town after small town, people lined up on the appointed hour to buy their copies of *Life*. Usually there were not enough copies to go around. In Worcester, Massachusetts, where the business people were testing circulation patterns, the allotted 474 copies were sold out in a few hours. Gradually each week the number of copies for Worcester was increased, and still they were gone. First 3,000, then 4,000, then 9,000. Finally the newsdealer in Worcester cabled asking for 12,000 copies. It was not only beyond all expectations, it was beyond all production capacities as well. The Donnelley presses in Chicago simply could not deal with the demand. Instead of printing the expected 400,000 copies a week, they were printing 1,000,000, keeping all their presses running until the very last moment when it was time to retool for the next week's issue.

But that was only a part of the problem. *Life* was threatening to swallow up the entire company. All the prepublication advertising notes had been based on a very low circulation; they expected to take a while to find readers and were willing to lose a little money at the beginning. That would be normal, a means of pumping life into the new magazine. But now their losses were enormous. This kind of success was costing Luce something like $50,000 a week, and many of the advertising contracts were fairly long-term. Suddenly the entire company seemed to hang in the balance. The decision that faced Luce and his colleague Roy Larsen in those early weeks was whether to keep the circulation down, which would also keep their losses down but might in the long run stifle the magazine, or to meet the demands of the readership, no matter how huge, and lose money. The magazine was in effect giving its advertisers what amounted to free ads. The dilemma was a terrible one. The losses that *Life* might incur could reach $5 or $6 million before it all turned around, if it turned around. In those days *Time* was making a profit of only $2 million a year. They would need to borrow millions and millions of dollars from the banks to keep their small company afloat. There was a certain Frankenstein potential in *Life*'s success. Luce had only one response, and Larsen agreed; the most dangerous thing for a publication to do was to fail to meet its readers' demand. So they decided to print 1,000,000 copies of *Life* and go to 1,500,000 as quickly as the Donnelley machinery would permit. It was a crucial moment in the Luce publishing history, for out of that came the success of *Life*, and *Life* enriched the entire Luce world; in making *Life* rich and powerful it made *Time* rich and powerful and it made Harry Luce rich and powerful. It was, in the pre-television era, the kind of journalistic and advertising vehicle that television was eventually to become.

In June 1941, when Harry Luce went to China, he was at the height of newly discovered power. He was accumulating more and more money and more and more journalistic muscle. The coming of *Life* magazine had changed the entire Luce operation. Before the appearance of *Life,* Luce was the publisher of a moderately successful and influential news magazine with a circulation of 630,000 copies a week. But *Life*'s astonishing success had transformed everything, it had turned Time-Life into an empire, and Luce into an emperor.

The world was becoming smaller, a great war had already started. America might not be in it yet, but it was very real to Harry Luce, who was an all-out interventionist, and he intended to make it real for his fellow Americans. It was a great story, which demanded to be covered on a scale that only *Life* and its brilliant photographers could match. It was as if *Life* magazine and World War II required each other. Events, all of them dramatic, demanded to be seen and covered. All of this demanded the creation of an ever larger staff in the field. Not just for *Life,* but for *Time* as well. *Time* was no longer just a clip-and-rewrite shop. It was now sending its own people into the field, but with a special attitude that distinguished that company from all others for more than two decades, a damn-the-expense-charter-the-plane-or-yacht attitude. These were Luce's men and women, his ambassadors to the world, an extension of him and his will. They would go first-class. Nothing would stand in their way.

Everything seemed to feed itself. Events made *Life* and *Time* more important, and sales went up, and as sales went up, advertising went up and both *Life* and *Time* became richer. Luce of course poured the money back into the product, always trying to improve it, and followed his personal instincts in deciding how the power would be used. The first real flexing of Luce's muscle had been very much an outcome of the success of *Life*. *Life* had to an uncommon degree, along with *Look,* its junior partner, helped invent Wendell Willkie and make him an instant national political figure. "Invent" is precisely the right word. Willkie, like Roosevelt, was one of the first modern media figures, using the then modern media to circumvent the will of what normally would have been a resistant party system. Whereas Roosevelt was doubly blessed, the voice a wondrous instrument, the face a treasure for the new and modern photography of the age, Willkie was somewhat lacking in voice, but rich in face. Willkie seemed to Luce perfect for the American Century, internationalist, modern, yet from the heartland. The barefoot lawyer from Wall Street had his roots in Indiana. The face was rugged and clean, strong but not pretty. The hank of hair reassuringly fresh and unspoiled. That hank of hair told it all, Wendell Willkie was healthy but not slick and greasy. A straight shooter. *Life* magazine could sell Wendell Willkie and it did, at least to the Republican Party. That Willkie was able to gain the nomination and challenge Roosevelt was very much a sign of the newfound power of Luce and his magazine (it is dubious whether *Time* could in that era have pushed Willkie to the nomination, *Life* was the crucial driving force). *Life* and *Look* in those days were the equivalent of CBS and NBC, and that Willkie was so attractive in their format made him an instant political success. Had he run against anybody but Franklin Roosevelt he might have won. Roosevelt's third victory might have weighed heavily on Willkie, but it did not weigh that heavily on Luce, the 1940 election had taught him a great deal about his power and his reach; he had challenged a President and he had made his will known both within his party and in the society at large. With the Democrats dominating Washington, his was now probably the single most important and influential Republican voice in the country. Luce was now a national press lord, ready and eager to spread his gospel.

Luce was also, as American entry into World War II approached, the most powerful man in America who was interested in Asia. That is, of the small elite of Americans that were intensely pro-interventionist, almost all were men and women of the Atlantic. But Luce was unique, his roots were across the Pacific, he was a man whose interest spanned both oceans. As he saw it, if America's past was linked to Europe, then its future was linked to Asia. He had an abiding connection with China, a fact that the embattled Nationalist government of China was acutely aware of. He was convinced of both the importance and the inevitability of postwar Chinese-American friendship. Preferably between Chiang and some Republican President. In a sense he was by 1940 already the Nationalist ambassador to America. It was not just his magazines, but his *March of Time* newsreels, showing the brave Chinese standing up to the barbarism of the Japanese, which became perhaps the most successful and influential propaganda of its time in making Americans care and think about China and identify with Chiang Kai-shek. He cared desperately about China. Whereas few other journalistic organs even bothered to staff China in those days, Luce had several people there. Among them was correspondent Theodore H. White. In June 1941, Luce flew to China to see the country and to meet his staff. Perhaps no professional relationship was to prove as rich and frustrating and embittering for Luce as the one with Teddy White.


Teddy White was then all of twenty-six, the doyen of the Chungking press corps, where he was regarded with a mixture of awe, respect, affection, and amusement. When word of Luce's imminent arrival reached Chungking, there was a good deal of betting about how Teddy would greet his boss. Luce was an imposing figure, and Teddy's editor, and yet Teddy was an inveterate first-namer. Finally the other reporters decided that Teddy would probably walk up to the plane and say, "Hello, Mr. Luce. I'm Teddy White. Now, Harry, what we're going to do today is . . ." which is precisely the way he *did* greet Luce. They were, from the start, the odd couple, Harry and Teddy. Luce, with his enormous head that made him seem much larger than he was, huge eyebrows, consumed by his obsession with China—an obsession as much spiritual as national, for his China lived as much in his soul as anywhere else. Teddy White, who in terms of looks and origins could not have been more different, small, gnomelike, a wonderful rich sweet-ugly grin and terribly weak eyes. He was Jewish-left instead of Presbyterian-right. He was having, at the time he met Luce, his own very different love affair with China. His view of China was harder-edged, less spiritual, more cerebral. Rarely would Luce's split personality between the total journalist and the total missionary be so severely tested as on China, and probably never would he have such ambivalent thoughts about any individual as he did about Teddy White, whom he often considered the best journalist he had ever employed, and whom he also considered the reporter who had done the most to lose China, the other country he most dearly loved.

Teddy White was young and full of energy. He had come to China straight from Harvard, where he had graduated in 1938 with a summa cum laude in modern Chinese studies. He had not waited for his graduation but had immediately caught a bus for Ann Arbor, Michigan, there to spend the summer at the University of Michigan learning colloquial Chinese. From Ann Arbor he started the first leg of a Sheldon Travelling Fellowship. That fellowship, highly prized among his peers, was supposed to take him all the way around the world, but when he reached China he was immediately seized by the excitement of a huge nation in the middle of its own revolution. He resigned the fellowship and stayed on, going to work in the Nationalist government's Information Ministry for a man named Hollington Tong. John Hersey spotted him there in the spring of 1939; Hersey, gifted, handsome, wonderfully graceful, Luce's favorite and for the moment surrogate son, was in those days *the* star of *Time* magazine; Hersey, then all of twenty-five, had been making a trip through China when he stumbled on this rather small, enormously energetic figure of twenty-four who was neither a sartorial nor a cosmetic wonder and who seemed to know everyone and everything. Hersey was astounded; he was used to hiring stringers (part-time reporters) for *Time* but this young man was special, he seethed with excitement and life, he was always in a rush, journalists twice his age deferred to Teddy White in checking their stories. He was, Hersey thought, full of information, but White's information was more than just facts, it was information that had been synthesized, facts connected into patterns. Teddy could see patterns where others could see only isolated facts. What was even more astonishing about him, besides all that almost electric energy and intelligence, was that he did not even work for a paper, he was simply doing this on his own, it was so natural for him. Hersey hired White on the spot as a stringer for *Time,* which meant that he was writing articles on speculation at twenty-five dollars a shot. From the start he was better than any other stringer *Time* had. He was, it turned out, a born journalist. There was always something concrete in his reporting, he knew how to transfer an image from the air and put it on paper, how to make others see what he wanted them to see. Early in his career with *Time* he had gone behind the Japanese lines with

Chinese horse cavalry and he had come back with a great story, for which he was awarded the first by-line that the magazine had ever given. Even as a stringer, he was a star. Other journalists might be stars in manner or in style; Teddy White's stardom was in his extraordinary intelligence.

He was, when Luce met him, something of a curiosity for someone in Luce's employ. He was so different. First off, he was Jewish, and *Time* in those days simply did not hire Jews. Jews were very much a *they*, they were not yet in the mainstream of American letters, let alone Luceian letters; indeed, for another fifteen years it would be difficult for Jews to join the foreign staff of *Time*. They could be hired and they could work as stringers, but whether they could go on the masthead if their names were too Semitic was another thing. For the Luce publications, like Luce in those early days, were very Waspy and old-school; until the very end of his life Luce was still capable of turning to a Jewish editor and asking, "And what do our Jewish friends think of that?" Teddy White was not bred as *Time* reporters had been, and if he had gone to the old school he was by no means *old-school.* And he did not look like *Time* reporters, who tended to be tall and handsome. But he was so good that Luce later told friends he could not believe it, that someone with such different origins could know and love China as he did.

White, for his part, delighted in Luce, in his ravenous curiosity, his zest for life; he was awed by the notion that someone who represented such might and majesty and power could be so interested in him. The two men seemed to have an almost magnetic attraction for each other. Luce was intrigued to discover that White could synthesize things better, analyze better, he seemed to be one step ahead of Luce even on Luce's beloved China. White in turn was drawn by Luce's energy; this was a man fascinated by great issues, strong-willed but not, he thought, dogmatic. There were, of course, differences but they did not seem important at the moment. Luce believed that big men made and dominated history. Thus he was obsessed by the importance of Chiang. White, growing up poor in Boston during the Depression, had been deeply affected by the radicalism of the thirties. He thought that larger forces like economics were crucial, he did not think that one great man's will alone changed history. Thus he did not consider Chiang to be as important as Luce did. But they did not argue about this, there were too many other things to do and share and talk about.

They shared, of course, a common passion for China and right from the start they had a wonderful time together. Luce, receiving the Super-VIP treatment from the Nationalist government, was being tightly sequestered in Dr. Kung's mansion. He wanted to get out and feel the city, so on the second day White sneaked him out in a rickshaw and they went through downtown Chungking, which was caught in the worst of wartime poverty and deprivation. Luce became totally alive, trying to remember the language of his childhood, becoming more and more excited. "Correct me! Correct me!" he yelled at White when he spoke in Chinese, and White corrected him a little, but gradually Luce's Chinese began to come back and he became full of himself, as if young again. He seemed to want to talk to everybody, and White was astonished, here was one of the two or three most powerful publishers in America jabbering away with the poorest peasants in a nation touched by the worst of a terrible war. Exulting in this. All his boyhood images were coming back, he talked excitedly about what it had been like being a boy in China. For a moment the past and the present all blended. It was a romantic and heroic moment in China, the government of Chiang was withstanding a brutal assault by the Japanese. There were daily bombings and only the most primitive kind of human air-raid signals to give any warning. Even as Luce and White rode around Chungking, the Japanese were bombing, and Harry and Teddy from time to time dove into shelters. But the Japanese bombing only seemed to make Luce more passionate. White had an impression that Luce wanted to grab a rifle and shoot down a Japanese plane, this was real life, he had missed World War I, and now he was getting a chance again. Everything seemed larger than life, everything more real and more passionate, friendships total and final. The common bond was a love of China, and more, an awareness of its importance. Luce was entranced by White. After a few days in Chungking he told White to pack his bags, he was coming home with him. "You're going to be the Far Eastern editor of *Time.*" It was a fascinating trip back, Clare Boothe Luce was along and White was detailed to explain Asia to her; at Wake Island when Luce was busy he gave White a very detailed schedule of what he wanted his wife to see and know. Then as they neared America a brief warning from Luce: "Teddy, it's different back at the office. Everyone's door is open to me, but my door is open to none. We're friends, Teddy, but my office door is closed."

White did not stay long in New York. America was about to enter the war, and he wanted to get back as quickly as he could to his beloved China. On the day after Pearl Harbor, which ironically was the day that Luce's father, the Reverend Henry Winters Luce, died, White had gone by to pay his respects to the editor, to say how sorry he was. But Luce waved aside the condolences, he seemed almost relieved by events, "Teddy, he lived long enough to know that China and America were allies again," Luce said.

Those days saw the beginning of a special relationship between the two men. They had their passionate friendship, then a terrible break, then gradually, ten years after that, a reconciliation and the renewal of friendship. Luce seemed, Teddy White thought, to hover over his life. A fierce and willful man, with a first-rate mind and a consuming urgency. Life was an urgent business. He believed devoutly in Christianity, but he believed that Christianity had to be strong and forceful, there was nothing tame about Luce's God. He wanted strong men worthy of strong deeds. Yet if Luce seemed to hover over White's career, then White, one of hundreds and hundreds of journalists he had hired, was to haunt *him* even more.

Teddy White was a new American statistic sprung to life. Near the turn of century, a new kind of immigrant, no longer the good, reassuring Anglo-

Saxons and Scandinavians, but Russian and Eastern European Jews and Italians, began to pour into the country. Among them in 1891 had been David White, sixteen, late of Pinsk, son of a rabbi, who had run away from home. He arrived in Boston with nothing but his dreams. In his early years he was a peddler, but he taught himself English and drove himself to go first to night law school at the YMCA, because it was free, and finally to Northeastern. He became a lawyer and, much to the disappointment of Teddy White's mother, a determined socialist, David White specialized in clients who were penniless. He was intensely political, convinced that capitalism was an exploitative system, and he passed on his beliefs to his four children. In 1927, when Teddy was twelve, the boy and his brothers stayed up all night on the night that Sacco and Vanzetti were executed, lest he ever forget what capitalism did to the workingman.

They lived in a Jewish ghetto in Dorchester. Mary Winkeller White was far more ambitious than her husband, and harbored—like so many of their neighbors—a passion for education for her male children. It was the key to the new world. Her son was bright and energetic, the schools were free, his teachers were much taken with him. He did well and eventually entered the famed Boston Latin School, one of the great public schools of America. There generations of poor ambitious youths first began to escape the poverty of their backgrounds. But not immediately: on October 29, 1929, the day of the Great Crash, White wrote in his diary: "No money all week, Pa brought home $2 today. Mama is crying again." Two years later his father was dead, the family of five was drawing eleven dollars a week in welfare, and White, much humiliated by the welfare money, finished his last year at Boston Latin.

Though Harvard had accepted him, he could not afford to go. He was sixteen. He taught Hebrew, he sold newspapers, sometimes shouting the headlines in Latin when he spied an old Latin School classmate. He even joined with a friend to collect used papers from the cars at the end of a trolley run, refold them, and turn them back to the distributor for a tiny additional profit. But then after two years Harvard offered him a scholarship. There was also a scholarship for newspaper boys and he won that. Together they came to four hundred dollars, which was what Harvard cost. His college days contained none of the pleasures normally associated with young Harvard gentlemen of the prewar era; he was a commuter and commuters were grinds, there was no place for them in the social life. They arrived, they studied, and they were whisked away by the MTA. It was as if they could be tolerated academically so long as they were not seen socially. Harvard to them was a classroom and a way station, little more, often more wounding than nourishing. Harvard rarely touched a commuter, even a gifted one like Teddy White. But he was the exception, he was lucky. He caught the attention and the admiration of a brilliant young scholar named John King Fairbank. Fairbank was to become the single most influential American academic authority on China of two generations, but in those days he was a novice professor a few years older than his prize student in the then desperately underdeveloped specialty of Sinology.

More than anyone else at Harvard, Fairbank reached out to the young Teddy White. White himself had chosen Chinese studies, although he was never exactly sure why. Fairbank took in this penniless student and made him feel at home, and cared for him and gave him entrée to a larger world. "He would explore my mind and rearrange it and teach me above all to think, not just in Chinese studies but to think," White remembered. Fairbank and his wife, Wilma, became something close to proxy parents for Teddy White. Years later during the war when Wilma Fairbank came through China and they were passing a gully where the bodies of Chinese soldiers were washed up and there was a terrible stench, Wilma Fairbank turned and asked, "Is that the way dead bodies smell, Theodore?" and Teddy White felt for the first time in his life truly grown-up, he knew something that these people who opened the world to him did not.

Fairbank did not think Teddy White would have a fair chance in the elitist diplomatic service of that day. It was still very much a gentleman's calling, and though Teddy White was in the best sense a gentleman, he was not what gentlemen thought a gentleman was. He would make a fine scholar, but Fairbank thought there were other possibilities, all that energy and curiosity, a skill with words, though perhaps a bit purple. Teddy should be a journalist. For a graduation present he gave him a secondhand typewriter and six letters of introduction for China. It was the making of a journalist. Teddy White never, the rest of his life, wrote anything without imagining John King Fairbank reading it.

In China, he was very good right from the start. Older correspondents were amused by the sight of him—short, wearing a pith helmet, pockets bulging with notes, socks, candy bars—but charmed that someone could be so cocky and unsuave and so openly excited about life. When Carl and Shelley Mydans, a talented husband-and-wife photographer-and-reporter team, arrived in Chungking for *Life,* they remembered how scared they were of him. Teddy, after all, was a big-time war correspondent. He, of course, was terrified of *them,* since they had come out from the home office and had been staff members far longer than he. One day they were sitting nervously in a bomb shelter when White turned to Shelley Mydans and asked her how many words a day she filed. "About ten thousand?" he asked. "Oh," she answered, "about that. What about you?" "Oh, I do about that myself." The truth, she later thought, was that on a good day she might manage a thousand words and that was probably what he filed. But they were all so young and so green and so scared.


Teddy White had the great reporter's gifts: limitless energy, a fine mind, total recall, and an ability to synthesize material. He was, despite his passion, his love of the story, surprisingly hardheaded. As time passed he watched as Chiang turned inward. The heroic moments for the Nationalists had been the early ones, when the Japanese had attacked: that assault had at first made the

Chiang government more legitimate, more truly nationalist. It had evoked for a brief time the very best of both ruler and populace. But the challenge was beyond bearing, the dual pressure of China coming into a modern age plus the attack by the Japanese; the government was simply too fragile. Now after Pearl Harbor, with American aid mounting, Chiang's preoccupation was less and less with the Japanese, and more and more with the Chinese Communists, a civil breach that had always been at the center of his mind. But now it was too much, it was as if his faults, which had always been there, were being magnified by events. Teddy White watched first with sadness and later with increasing contempt. He began to report that China was not Chiang, that Chiang was increasingly a weak and unrealistic instrument, a China that never would be.

His editor, who loved him and was intrigued by him and thought he was the best journalist he had ever hired, did not believe him. To be critical of the Chiang government, to see it for what it was, cut too deeply into him, it was like disavowing not just his own principles but those of his parents, of betraying old friends and family. It was all so personal, interwoven with his family, his boyhood, his religion, and his obligations. He was profoundly a man of obligations. That all this should be challenged by *Communists* was too much. It could not be accepted. Years later, when he was an old man and China was Communist, he once asked Dick Clurman how old he was. Clurman answered that he was twenty-nine. "I'd like to be your age again," Luce said wistfully, and Clurman asked why. "Well, I grew up in a little town called Tengchow and it's been taken over by the Communists. I'd like to go back one day and see it as a free town." It was, thought Clurman, a seminal Luce story. To criticize Chiang's China was like criticizing his family. As years passed, long after the collapse of Chiang and as more and more evidence of his weakness and corruption became available, Luce did not regret that he had come down so hard on Teddy White; quite the contrary, he regretted that he himself at one crucial point might have wavered and that he might have held back potential support to a floundering Chiang. It came at the end of the Marshall mission in 1946 and Charles J. V. Murphy, one of his more conservative writers, had produced an all-out pro-Chiang piece. George Marshall's people had asked that Luce hold back on the piece because it might disturb the fragile coalition they were trying to arrange between Nationalist and Communist forces. Luce held the piece back and never quite forgave himself.

He was also in those years a different man from the Luce of the early period. He was more sure of himself now, more dogmatic in dealing with his own people in New York. He had been rewarded by increased circulation and profit and success for the rightness of his ways, and that did not lessen his obligation, it increased it. As World War II began, America and its reach expanded and so in a parallel way did that of Time-Life. Luce had a profound sense of America's duties and mission in the American Century. He was, even at the beginning of the war, already looking to the future. His vision of the Soviet Union was a dark one, he anticipated most of his journalistic contemporaries in identifying the foreboding rigid quality of that society. But he went further. To him it was a moral question. The Soviet Union was not just a bad society but an evil one. This would not be just one great power threatening another, but an evil system locked in a titanic battle for the future with a righteous one. The Communists represented what he hated most. They were godless, they did not value human freedom as he defined it. It was not a dislike, it was a genuine hatred and it profoundly affected his magazines; his feeling took him beyond journalism to the edge of crusade. The missionary in him answered the challenge. He did not, as the war progressed, think his reporters were sufficiently anti-Communist. Oh, they were bright and keen, and they saw what was on the surface, but they lacked the full scope to see the entire struggle in the epic moral terms it deserved. They did not understand, and so he wanted to balance their viewpoint out, to make sure that the magazine was not tilted by their good intentions.

John Hersey, who knew him better than anyone else on the staff in those days, felt that he was hardening and that the magazine was hardening. (Hersey, also the child of missionaries in China, was Luce's favorite. People thought of him as Luce's successor, and Luce did as well, Luce was always talking about the fact that this was a young man's company. Why, he said, he would turn over the reins when he was forty. A few years later, when he had passed forty, he was still talking about its being a young man's company. Why, he said to Hersey, I intend to turn it over to people like you when I'm fifty. In 1964 he retired at the age of sixty-six.) When Luce was younger, Hersey had found him very open on crucial issues; in the earlier days it was possible to negotiate a story with him, to discuss the possible ways of writing it. But as *Time*'s power grew and his personal power grew, there was less flexibility. His was a world of fewer grays, where Truth was an ultimate thing. There was less and less discussion of a story, more and more dictation from Luce. His increased dogmatism was a problem for his new staff of working reporters. *Time*'s Washington bureau chief, Felix Belair, quickly found himself alienated from the magazine and its version of events. "Harry," Belair told Luce in 1944, shortly before quitting *Time* and rejoining *The New York Times,* "I don't think you'll ever be happy with us and our report. Frankly, I think you're wasting the hundred and fifty thousand dollars a year you pay for our salaries because we're sending you what is, and you're putting in the book what you think things *ought* to be." Belair expected Luce to be annoyed by his comment and was surprised when Luce enthusiastically agreed. "That's exactly it, Felix! But that's the function of enlightened journalism, to lead, to put in what ought to be."

That Communism might be a form of government to unleash powerful historical forces in China and expedite its entrance into the modern age was something Luce refused to accept. Refusing to accept this, he refused to accept the reporting of his ablest reporter. He had, after all, other sources, sources in

Washington, particularly in the Nationalist government and among conservative missionaries, and they were lobbying very hard with him. The Nationalist
government was acutely aware how vulnerable its position was in China and
how even more vulnerable it was in the United States. To the Chinese Nationalists Luce was simply the most important man in America. They not only
lobbied him hard, they lobbied him skillfully, they let him know how much
they depended on him, how much they *needed* him, how much they owed him.
They played on his sense of obligation. So the columns of *Time* and *Life*
belonged lock, stock, and barrel to the Nationalist government. Flying to
Chungking during the war was itself a sign of status and priority. The plane
was an old junker and normally the inflation was so desperate that it was
simply filled with paper currency. When reporters like Carl and Shelley Mydans were able to fly in, replacing a day's currency, they knew at once how
important they were, or rather how important the magazines they worked for
were.


The tension between *Time*'s home office and the field had started in 1943. But
in America at large there was little sense of that. Press censorship was heavy-
handed, and the American government was loath to publicize the failings of
an ostensible ally. At the same time the all-out campaign to picture China as
the beleaguered but gutsy underdog ally of the United States, the selling of the
Gimo, in which Luce and his publications were playing the major role, was
at its height. The Mydanses, stationed in Chungking for *Life,* found that they
had total access to the Gimo and the Missimo, they could photograph them
eating together, or with their wonderfully photogenic dog. The Missimo,
Shelley Mydans thought, had a highly developed sense of Western propaganda, she was light-years ahead of most Asians in understanding American
publications and making herself accessible, knowing what reporters and photographers wanted. Madame Chiang's tour of the United States in 1943, largely
organized by Luce, was a striking success. It was the high point of Chinese-
American friendship, so carefully propagandized and orchestrated not just
through the magazines but through the *March of Time.* Brave, Western-loving
China, gallantly resisting barbarous Japanese. The China that *Time* and *Life*
portrayed was very attractive, a handsome chief couple, soldiers who in their
drills looked impressive; the China that existed was failing and failing fast.
Slowly but surely America was starting to learn the difference.


In March 1943, Teddy White heard of a terrible famine in Honan Province and
with great skill and cunning he made his way there. Years later he felt that
of all the reporting in a forty-year career he was most proud of this story; the
reaction in America was so sharp, the kickback so immediate, that finally even
the Nationalist government had been forced to respond, and perhaps millions
of lives had been saved. It was a terrifying experience for White. He rode in

on horseback; he had to keep whipping his horse to make it move, otherwise
the desperate starving mobs would kill the horse for food, and if they killed
the horse, then White would be left behind and he would die too. He slipped
his story out past the censor. Millions, he reported, were dying and there were
already three million refugees. The root of it, he wrote, was that the army was
insisting on collecting a grain tax from these poor peasants, despite several
crop failures. Nor had the Chiang government been willing to send in any
grain. The story had enormous impact in the United States, where many
Americans liked China because it was the kind of country that made you feel
better about yourself—you could send aid so that a benign government could
feed its hungry peasants. Typically, Chiang did not even believe the story.
Fortunately for White, someone had photographs of these peasants and
Chiang was finally convinced. Madame Chiang tried to have White fired. But
the reaction was so great that grain was indeed sent in. To White, who was
increasingly convinced of the rigidity and incompetence of the regime, it was
one more symbol of the failure of Chiang, and of his isolation from reality.
"The country," he wrote Luce, "is dying almost before my eyes."

    The contrast between Teddy White's China and Madame Chiang's China
worried people like Pearl Buck, who felt that when Americans discovered the
reality of China they would quickly become disillusioned. Miss Buck wrote
Luce asking him to publish an article in *Life;* hers was a far more realistic
portrait of the isolated Chiang, and of the growing oppressiveness and clumsiness of the regime. Her article worried Luce, not the truth of it, but the effect
of it. Was it too critical of Chiang? he wondered. Would it allow Americans
who were already uninterested in Asia to justify their isolationism, and give
an already reluctant American government an excuse to cut back aid? It was,
he wrote in a memo at the time, the most important propaganda question since
1939. "But we believe in truth. Yes, however deeply our nation has suffered
propagandistically both from Moscow and Berlin, we believe in the strategy
of truth. . . ." Explaining to White why he was printing the Buck piece, he
wrote in a remarkably revealing letter shortly after the Honan story, May 1943:

> In Chungking you are, of course, daily confronted with all the
> things that are not being done as well as they should be. But just think,
> Teddy—the great fact is that Chungking is still there! That's the fact
> that you have to be concerned about explaining. . . . You have always
> had immense faith in China and in the Generalissimo. . . . Perhaps
> you felt that you had communicated too much faith—or too easy a
> faith. I simply write you to say you need have no such fears. It is still
> the faith—and not the defects of the faith—which it is most of all
> important to communicate.

It was a touching and poignant letter no other editor could possibly have
written: the essence was not facts or analysis or scoop, but faith. Faith above
all.

But White was quickly losing faith. He loved working for *Time,* he loved Luce, but he was having a harder and harder time trying to reconcile what he saw with what the magazine printed. Early in 1944 he came home for a rest. He wanted to write free of Chinese censorship and he wanted to see if he could get an article through Luce. He was apprehensive about the growing difference between the two of them. He was for continued aid to China, but for more controls and for a more realistic attitude toward Chiang. He and Luce in effect collaborated on the article. It bore White's by-line, but it paid homage to Luce's views as well, and it was essentially a compromise. Their last compromise. It was critical of the regime, told of how Chiang withheld some of his best troops from fighting against the Japanese in order to seal off the Communists, and concluded that the amount of aid that was arriving was pitifully small. Finally it asked for more aid to China. White was pleased that the article had worked out as well as it did. "When I came back to New York I was told you would never let anyone publish anything like the things I wanted to say. I was scared as hell, Harry, at what would be an inevitable clash between my convictions and your policy," he wrote Luce.


That inevitable clash was not far off. Even in the brief time White had been away, events in China had deteriorated considerably, and now on his return he found that his colleagues thought the article too soft. Despite Japanese advances, Chiang's chief concern seemed to be the Communist armies. There was now mounting American pressure on Chiang to make some kind of deal with the Communists to create a common front against the Japanese. Chiang was paying lip service to this, but to him the real struggle was the domestic one. Lieutenant General Joseph Stilwell, Chiang's chief adviser, was becoming increasingly frustrated with Chiang; Stilwell was something of a god to most of the Chungking correspondents, they were in awe of his combination of intelligence and bravery, and honesty and concern for the people. Stilwell was sick of Chiang, whom he called Peanut, and he was sick of a government built on lies. He hated above all a Generalissimo who would treat his own soldiers as barbarously as Chiang treated his. Stilwell wanted more authority for himself, he wanted to move Chiang's troops against the Japanese and make more effort to find some sort of accommodation with the Communists. Almost all the major correspondents in Chungking were sympathetic to Stilwell and accepted his view of the situation and his frustrations, not the least of them White, who deeply admired the general. (He edited Stilwell's papers after the war.) White's reporting was bleaker, his sense of hopelessness about the government greater, his own frustration greater. So too was his sense of being cut off and alienated from his own publication; it was bad enough dealing with both the Chinese censor and the American government, but it was as if there were censors back in New York on *Time.* His office in Chungking carried a sign saying: "Any resemblance to what is written here and what is printed in *Time* magazine is purely coincidental." For he was also becoming, in the middle of 1944, aware of a resistance from his own magazine that bordered on antagonism. The new foreign editor of *Time,* appointed in the summer of 1944, was a man named Whittaker Chambers.

Chambers. His name is stamped indelibly on that era. Much of an intellectual generation that came to maturity in the thirties and forties defines itself on how it feels about Whittaker Chambers and Alger Hiss. Chambers was a brilliant, brooding man, a child of the century, caught in the worst and most savage of its ideological storms. Not by chance was his autobiography called *Witness.* Survivor of a miserable childhood, an early member of the American Communist Party, he turned with the same passion and intensity of commitment that he brought to belonging to the Party to fighting it. He was as much on a wartime footing when he left the Party as when he was in it. Chambers saw the world through a unique and darkened prism, the inevitability of total conflict between the West and Communism, everything was seen and measured on that scale. "The only American in *The Brothers Karamazov,*" in the words of Alfred Kazin. He had had a special vision when he was in the Party and just as special a vision when he was out. It was not just ideological, it was conspiratorial as well. He was convinced that some of *Time*'s more liberal foreign correspondents and editors were either wittingly or unwittingly agents of the Comintern, and they were also in a conspiracy to have him fired from his job. In time this became true, he became so great an obstacle to them and their reporting that they did in fact conspire to have him removed. His relationship with the men in the field was very different from the normal antagonism which marked editor and correspondent. Many editors dislike correspondents, believing that they have all the fun and glory. This was different; to Chambers, correspondents were the enemy and did the work of the enemy.

His rise to that job and the timing of it was not happenstance. Luce was very much aware of Chambers's attitudes. He was, in fact, precisely what he wanted; someone who, like himself, and unlike his reporters, saw the entire field of battle. If most of his correspondents were more liberal than he wanted, then very deliberately he intended now, with the postwar era in sight, to tilt the magazine more to his fancy, and to employ more conservative editors. Luce knew that his field reporters hated Chambers but that did not bother him a bit. Chambers was a lightning rod for him. Hersey, the favored son, sensing that Chambers was an extension of Luce, turned down a potential job as managing editor because he knew he would be in constant conflict with Luce; White, less shrewd in those days, thought the job was to get past Chambers and to get to Luce directly. The correspondents in the field had to filter their copy through Chambers. Luce liked the idea of it, and liked the idea of playing the semi-innocent to their problems, knowing they were thus ever more dependent upon him. He could look more benign, more centrist with Chambers around. White, totally frustrated in China, felt the key to his chances was his personal relationship with Luce. Chambers was a wonderful vehicle for Luce, talented, brilliant, disliked by most of his colleagues. Yes, Luce would say, Whit is a difficult man and he does have his faults, but the magazine needs someone like him—he *understands* the Soviet Union. The magazine, he said, was becoming too liberal and Chambers was the man to resist that thrust. Among those he had in mind was Teddy White. He was more and more unhappy with his China hand. "Teddy's become a partisan," he was telling friends in mid-1944, "he's given up on Chiang. He's become too involved in the story." Before long he was adding that Teddy was too left, too close to the Communists.

In Chungking, in 1944, there was a sense that the magazine was changing, building up for something different. Annalee Jacoby, the widow of Mel Jacoby, a *Time* correspondent killed earlier in the war, was working now with White. In the early fall of 1944 she interviewed Chiang. It was a mild interview, of mild questions. She sent it off and both she and White were stunned later when it came out completely rewritten; worse, questions that had not been asked and answers that had never been given were printed. It was more anti-Communist and more upbeat about victory. She and White made inquiries and found that the story was the work of Chambers. White still thought the problem was Chambers and not Luce, but Mrs. Jacoby was less trusting. That year had been a terrible one for both White and Jacoby. The censorship in China was heavy-handed, there was a growing sense of estrangement from the home office, yet they were charged with covering a major convulsive story of awesome historic implications.

White increasingly saw Chiang as the real enemy of China. He had become more and more impressed, as had Stilwell, with the Communists. They were on the rise now, they touched something powerful in the people, their treatment of the peasants seemed in direct contrast to that of Chiang's forces. White, educated in the Depression and post-Depression days, saw Marxism as a powerful and vital force, and now it seemed to be on the move in China. He was not an ideologue of the left, but he was sympathetic to it in those days and he was not surprised by the success of Mao's people. The Communists had won the support of the Chinese peasants. In Mao's words, the people were the ocean in which they, the fish, could now freely swim. It not only made them politically and militarily more effective than the Nationalists, it made them seem more sympathetic as human beings. They were a new breed, they had suffered through the Long March and survived, and it was as if they had kept their rendezvous with history. White's reporting reflected this now. He kept insisting that the Chinese Communists were real and important, and must be brought into both the government and the war. Luce was enraged. He would not accept the fact that his China and his Chiang no longer existed.

All of this was tearing White apart. He had a tremendous story, and he knew it better than any other American reporter in China and he could not be heard. His editors had turned on him. Worse, his name was running in the magazine masthead, but what was being printed represented the reverse of his views. At that point, right before the final break with Luce, he received a terribly important letter from his old Harvard professor John Fairbank, then with the Office of War Information in India and perfectly aware of what was happening in China. The letter was shattering. Up to then White and Fairbank had corresponded in an amiable, father-and-son way. This letter was different, it was a letter of great brutality. I am ashamed of you and your friends are ashamed of you, Fairbank wrote. This is an epic moment and this is the time for you to state your case. Your country is being lied to on a crucial issue. White had by then become increasingly dubious that he could survive a confrontation with Luce over China and he was already planning to write about his experiences. He had already done some work on the book which became *Thunder Out of China;* Fairbank's letter stiffened him. From then on the book became a certainty, not just an idea.


In the summer of 1944 all of Stilwell's and White's predictions came true. Chiang's troops came completely apart during what was called the East Asia Retreat. White and Stilwell were there when it happened. It was not a retreat, White wrote, but a collapse. Chiang, White later wrote in *Thunder Out of China,* had made the fatal mistake of trying to fight the Japanese while clinging to the old feudal fabric, and he had ended up unable either to defeat the Japanese or to preserve the old order. In Washington authorities were shocked by the Chinese collapse and Roosevelt in early July cabled what was virtually an order to Chiang telling him to place Stilwell in "unrestricted command of all your forces." American reality was for the first time about to meet Chiang's reality; America wanted to win the war against Japan, that was primary; Chiang wanted to stay in power, that was primary, the war was secondary. Roosevelt's command was terrifying to Chiang, it might mean that Stilwell would aid the Communists. He balked. He challenged Roosevelt and he won; Roosevelt recalled Stilwell. For the embattled and impassioned Chungking press corps, admiring as it was of Stilwell, this was the ultimate event, the accommodation to everything that was wrong, and the lowering of the American flag. It was a very big story, the kind for which a correspondent is willing to risk expulsion from a cherished assignment. Brooks Atkinson of *The New York Times* simply smuggled himself aboard Stilwell's departing plane in order to report. White let out all stops. He smuggled out a version which he knew would end his assignment if printed. "Chiang has outlived his historical usefulness," he began. The Gimo, he wrote, was "a man of almost appalling ignorance. He is not only ignorant, he is unaware of his ignorance." Luce was furious. Nothing of White's file went into the magazine. The cover story on Stilwell in the November 13 issue was a Chiang puff piece, Chiang was better because his ideology was more acceptable to us. White was bitter when he saw the cover piece, it was the exact opposite of everything he believed and had filed. He wrote Luce a thirty-page letter that was virtually an ultimatum: If you persist in this policy, he wrote, you are not only wrong, but you are harming China and you are harming the United States. Luce was enraged by the effrontery of White, as well as by his politics. "He's on the other side," he told friends. White was told to restrict himself to combat rather than political reporting. This was fine with him, he told friends, since *Time* clearly did not need a correspondent in China anyway.

They had one last fight at the time of the Japanese surrender in 1945. *Time* was planning a cover story on Chiang. White was convinced that there would be a civil war and Chiang would lose it. Along with his file for what was to be the forthcoming cover story, White sent an advisory cable, once again angering Luce as much with his personal behavior as with his political reporting.

> If Time Inc. adopts the policy of unquestioningly, unconditionally supporting [Chiang's] hand, we will be doing a monstrous disservice to millions of American readers and to the Chinese whose personal concern this is. . . . We hope that you will select facts in an impartial, judicious manner warranted by the enormous dimensions of this tragedy. For Jacoby and myself this piece is a testing stone. . . . We feel our policy should be nonpartisan, directed to a middle-road democratic peaceful solution. If this is determined otherwise, we shall consider this a repudiation of ourselves as reporters and will want to be relieved of the current assignment and return home at least to put the case directly before the editor in chief for final settlement of our status and China policy.

For Luce this was one ultimatum too many and a challenge, and from a man who was now clearly siding with the enemy. How could he, Luce asked friends, have been fooled by White in the past? Had White changed, or had he always been on the other side? But to have sponsored a man like this! That was a serious flaw. "We desired nothing except nonpartisan reporting," Luce replied. "We realized this might be an unreasonable request in view of your avowed partisanship. . . ." White received the cable at the same time he was granted permission to cover the surrender on the battleship *Missouri.* He was deeply offended because almost nothing of what he and Jacoby had filed had gone into the magazine. There was no meeting of the minds, nor could there be, any more. White would cover the surrender and then return to New York to meet with Luce and perhaps await reassignment.

White came home after the surrender and he and Mrs. Jacoby began working full-time on the book that became *Thunder.* He had told Mrs. Jacoby that he was still sure he could turn Luce around on China but it was beyond all that now. The lines were drawn, the easy access was gone. They had one very long and frosty conversation. It was no more Harry and Teddy. While he was working on *Thunder,* White awaited his next assignment. Charles Wertenbaker, the head of the news service, had promised Moscow, which was the assignment White badly wanted. But then there was a silence. Perhaps Moscow had not been promised after all. Part of the reason for the problem

over Moscow was Luce's growing resentment over what he considered the
dubious loyalty of his stars like Hersey and White, a feeling they were making
their reputations on his time and then exploiting him; but even more of it was
a suspicion of White's politics. Was the man firm enough to send to Moscow?
More and more, as what was to be the Cold War approached, Luce categorized
people as hard or soft. Hard men were worthy; soft men might easily be dupes.
Finally, with Moscow still in the offing, Luce applied a *Time* magazine kind
of loyalty test. Would White take *any* assignment *Time* offered, any job from
office boy to managing editor? White said no. Would, Luce continued, White
take any post in the *Time* foreign service?—adding that perhaps Cuba was a
possibility. Once again White said no. It was, of course, a good-soldier test;
*Time* magazine, with many attractive jobs and many equally unattractive ones,
placed great emphasis on being a good soldier, more loyal to the company than
to your own individual preference. But there was no good soldier White: "A
very rugged character is Teddy," Luce wrote in a memo at the time. So there
was no place for him at *Time* and he resigned. He had been sharing a small
office with Carl Mydans, and the day that he quit they went out for lunch,
talking about what Teddy was going to do next for a living. That afternoon
Arthur Schlesinger, Jr., who was a Harvard classmate, dropped by and while
Schlesinger was in the office the phone rang: the Book-of-the-Month Club had
just bought *Thunder*. White was always pleased that he had quit *before* getting
the Book-of-the-Month news. It would have been less dramatic if the order had
been reversed.


*Thunder,* which he wrote with Mrs. Jacoby, combined all of White's skills. It
was a brilliant and prophetic book, the result of the ten years he had invested
in China, four at college and six on the mainland. It was a rare book in that
it combined remarkable historical insight with special passion and urgency. It
was also surprisingly tough-minded, it dealt not with the China he wanted but
the China that was; there was relatively little illusion about the Chinese Communists. The book was an immense success, it sold 43,000 copies in the regular
trade edition and over 400,000 in the Book-of-the-Month edition, the third-
largest sale ever for the BOMC at that time. White and Jacoby had hoped that
it would change the view of Washington toward the Communists, and they
were essentially disappointed. But the book was nevertheless potent. It
sounded the death knell of respectability for Chiang's support in the United
States. His popularity had already crested during the war, but the increasing
reports of his regime's harshness and incompetence had damaged him, the
Stilwell firing had hurt him further, and now he was no longer viewed by
Americans in general as a real leader. Rather, he was seen more and more in
terms of American domestic political perceptions, the liberal left turning on
him, the far right standing firm with him. It was a dangerous loss in terms of
his American legitimacy, and *Thunder* diminished it even more, leaving what
was to be a terminal taint on his regime.

Luce himself was bitter about the book. Years later when he spoke of George Marshall's mission, a hopeless attempt to patch up a Chinese truce, he would speak angrily about White's influence on Marshall. Why, the first day that Marshall had set foot in China, according to Luce, he was "carrying that book by that ugly little Jewish son of a bitch." For Luce it was like losing a test of wills to someone he had hired; worse, he had lost what was in effect his homeland to someone he had hired, *someone he had made.* What was perhaps worst of all, some who knew him well thought, Luce in his heart was aware, despite the ferocity of his arguments, that White was more right than he. Could it really be that the Communists deserved China? That was a terrifying thought. In subsequent years *Time* columns referred on occasion to pinko Teddy White, which hurt White. But White was even more wounded by an interview that Luce gave to the St. Louis *Post-Dispatch* in which he said that he had had to fire Teddy White because he was a Communist. In those post-China years, as the shadow of what came to be known as McCarthyism descended, White was not having a very easy time professionally. Despite his immense talents, no one seemed eager to hire him. He was considered left-wing by editors, and places like *The New York Times* would not take him on despite his gifts. His books were banned from American overseas libraries, he had serious passport troubles at various times. So he was doubly wounded when he heard what Harry Luce had said about him. After all, they had once been close friends, and White was a deeply sentimental man. A man of God, a veritable Bishop Odo of Bayer, he thought (referring to a Christian bishop who in the name of God and good works used to go around beating his opponents over the head with a huge spiked club, all in the name of Christianity). One did not cross God's man lightly, Teddy White thought, and clearly Harry Luce was God's man, and just as clearly Teddy White had crossed him.

White himself did not return to China. He sometimes talked disdainfully of his successors who wrote what Luce wanted, enthusiastically reporting Nationalist victory after Nationalist victory until the Communists walked into Nanking. Luce, however, did return several times to China. In 1945 he came back in imperial manner, the returning raj, the most honored guest of the regime, two floors of the largest hotel given over to him and his staff, carpenters and painters rushing around for two weeks before his arrival to fix it up, a red carpet literally rolled out for him. Endless state dinners and guided tours made their impression. After several days Luce summoned his staff for a dinner and explained how well the government was doing, how the countryside was calm, the talk of growing Communist power vastly overrated, the Kuomintang beloved. He had seen it and been there. Shelley Mydans of *Life* had spent the war in China, the latter part in a Japanese prison camp, and because of serious eye troubles she had been allowed to move around the Chinese countryside in order to get medical treatment. Listening to Luce that night, she had been appalled, and she had dissented, telling him that she was certain of real resentment against the government in the countryside, that the political flow seemed to be toward the Communists, that the Communists were in fact the

constant subject of favorable talk in the countryside. He just brushed her off;
it was not something he wanted to hear, particularly from a woman, she
thought.

So he refused to see the Communists coming, and refused to accept their
take-over, and when they did win, he did the most dangerous thing a journalist
can do, he adopted a policy of nonrecognition toward events. China was not
to his liking, therefore it did not exist. China remained Chiang, even in exile
on a small island. And here the role of the Luce publications in the dark era
that followed the fall of China was crucial, as they pushed their own obsession
onto the American people. The influence of a publication is always greater in
direct proportion to the distance of events; it was hard for Luce to sell Dewey
over Roosevelt to the American people in 1944 because they were in a position
to judge for themselves what Roosevelt was or was not. But China was distant,
few Americans had any direct contact or involvement with it. Therefore the
power of the publication increases, the ability to define information rises,
particularly when the publication becomes as obsessed as *Time* was on China.
The Luce publications at that moment, the late forties and early fifties, were
simply the most powerful and influential national organ in the country, particularly within Republican and centrist groups. *Time* and *Life* were truly dominant, and their failure after the events to tell the truth was critical. *Time* helped
foster a belief that China had gone Communist not because of deep historical
forces culminating in revolution (forces which would prove as difficult for the
Soviets to deal with as they would for Americans), but because of conspiracy.

In the years after he left *Time,* Teddy White was dismayed by what
his old magazine was doing to the American people on the subject of
China. White was by then a grown man, shrewd and independent, and he
was very much aware of the limits of the power of the press, but on this
issue he thought the role of the press and of Luce was decisive. If Harry
Luce, he thought, had accepted the collapse of Chiang's regime, if he had
been willing to accept and explain why it had failed, the subsequent
American political story might have been very different. Had we been open
and understanding about these events instead of frozen and wrong, we
might have saved ourselves two terrible wars. The Luce publications were
among the worst deceivers, and they were not above punishing those who
had been right. For it was the fall of China and the trauma that fall produced here (lovable, friendly, subservient Christian China turning overnight into 600,000,000 angry, hostile Communist Chinese) that led
squarely to the excesses of the McCarthy period.

Luce himself was not a McCarthyite, but he thought a certain amount of
McCarthyism, within bounds that *he* could set, was good for the country. It
could put the liberals a little on the defensive, make them a little nervous,
lessen liberal criticism of capitalism. But he was wary of McCarthy, and his
publications turned eventually against the Wisconsin senator; his record on
McCarthy himself, admirers could point out, was better than some others in
that dark period. The real story was nevertheless more complicated than that.
Luce put the Democrats on the defensive, he made Acheson seem a soft-liner,

and above all, he helped freeze the debate. Luce allowed McCarthyism to take place, he created a vacuum in which the misinterpretation of events led to conspiracy theories. He had no sympathy for those men who had been right and were about to be sacrificed to the witch-hunters, he remained bitter about Marshall and Acheson and the State Department. His publications formed a major obstacle to anyone trying to restore any reality to American Asian policy. He never really recognized Communist China and never accepted the verdict of history. At a personal level this might have been admirable—Harry Luce had not betrayed old friends, he had honored his father's memory—but at a journalistic level it was intensely dangerous. He was unbending. In the pages of *Time* Chiang had never slipped from power and never slipped from grace. Once, during a 1960 trip around Asia, Luce stopped off in Taiwan with Roy Alexander, then editor of *Time*. Alexander met a young Chinese priest who talked with some excitement about Mao's achievements on the mainland and Alexander, a conservative man himself, passed this on to Luce with some surprise and a measure of respect. But Luce was having none of it. "What do you want us to do, Roy," he asked, "give up?" Harry Luce would not give up; he knew which China he loved, and which was the real one.

That 1960 trip was fascinating. Despite the fact that Chiang was old and doddering and senile, Luce was still a hero worshipper. "I was in the home of my friends," he wrote of Chiang in a memo to his staff. He was in Taipei for several days and he saw the Generalissimo and Madame Chiang morning, noon, and night. Day after day. It was, thought Stanley Karnow, the correspondent who was with them, the most exhausting thing he had ever been part of; Karnow, who was some thirty years younger than Luce, was absolutely worn out by the schedule, by the drone of Madame Chiang advising Luce on foreign policy. There she was, Karnow thought, some fifteen years after the events, and she was repeating her litany endlessly to Luce, telling him how the important thing was to drive the Commies out of the State Department. This, he thought, more than six years after the decline of McCarthy. That appalled Karnow, but what impressed him even more was how sophisticated Madame Chiang and Chiang were in playing to Luce. They flattered him ceaselessly, they told him how important he was to them, how dependent they were on him, how great a man he was. That, thought Karnow, was the key. On the last day there the Luce group was scheduled to go directly to the airport, and even Luce, thought Karnow, seemed relieved by that, there was only so much you could say to the Gimo after all. But on the way to the airport the word came that Chiang wanted to see him again. Even Luce flinched. "What will I say to him that hasn't already been said?" he asked Karnow. As they were about to enter Chiang's great office, Luce turned rather brusquely to Roy Alexander, as sometimes was his wont, and told him to wait outside. Then he and Karnow entered. It was a memorable scene.

Luce asked Chiang: Well, Mister President, how do you see the world perspective in the period ahead?

Chiang answered: I see great dangers lying ahead.

Luce leaned forward. What dangers? he asked.

Chiang answered: I see great dangers.

What kind of dangers? Luce leaned forward just a little bit more. Can you explain, Mister President? Can you be more specific?

Chiang answered again in his semi-mystical way: There are big dangers ahead.

Thus ended the interview, but as they walked out Alexander rushed up to Luce. "What did he say, Harry?"

Luce answered, "Watch out in the period ahead."


The break with Teddy White was a bitter one for Luce, the loss of a favorite correspondent and the loss of a favorite country. For ten years the two men did not talk, and in those years Luce was often bitterly cruel in what he said about White, in the tone of a spurned ex-lover. White himself went on to other glories; he moved to Europe, retooled himself in another culture, wrote a memorable book about the rebirth of Western Europe, called *Fire in the Ashes,* and with his rare combination of great talent and great independence carved out a career as a self-employed journalist. He also became one of the leading political writers for *Collier's.* Then in 1956, while White was still living in Paris, mutual friends brought him together with Luce. Both were a little nervous about meeting, but it worked, they talked long into the night about everything but China, and their mutual energy was kinetic again. A year or so later, when *Collier's* folded, White, who was still considered in some circles a little left-wing, was wondering what he would do for work. He received only two phone calls offering him jobs. One was from Ed Murrow, the other was from Harry Luce, who called to say that he was sorry about the news. Then he added, "I don't know who was right or wrong on China, but it's time to come home, Teddy." But White had decided that he would never again sign on with a large corporation, that it was all too uncertain. However, he did start writing again for *Life* and he was treated with special sensitivity by Luce himself, who was wary of ever again having a confrontation with his star. In the remaining years that the two men worked together, Luce asked White to rewrite only one thing. White had produced a piece about Averell Harriman, and he had mentioned that Harriman had been Skull and Bones at Yale and since Luce was Bones, and the name Bones was never supposed to be in print, this would be a problem coming out in his own magazine. Would Teddy please change it? White would. They ended up good friends though still with some reservations about each other. White still marveled at Luce's vitality and drive, and his capacity to dominate. In 1964, they were in San Francisco during a political convention and Luce invited White to have dinner with a group of *Time* correspondents. It was a pleasant dinner but Luce very early in the evening went into one of his prolonged monologues. No one else could talk. Finally White, no small talker himself, interrupted and spoke for a few minutes. At which point

Luce resumed the monologue. Thereupon one of the younger men in the bureau also interrupted and began to speak. "Don't interrupt me! Don't interrupt me!" Luce ordered. "Teddy can." At which point he looked over at White. "But don't interrupt me too much, Teddy! Don't interrupt me too much!"

Luce's politics hardened in the postwar years and *Time* had become increasingly Republican in its tone. He had been stunned by Truman's defeat of Dewey in 1948. Then in the fall of 1949 China had fallen, the Democratic administration had failed to save Chiang, and that was too much; Truman, and even more Acheson, would have to pay the price. *Time* was now committed and politicized, an almost totally partisan instrument. The smell of blood was in the air. There was a hunger now in Luce to put a Republican back in power. It was as if Luce, between elections, stood as the leader of the opposition, a kingmaker who had failed to produce a king. The fall of China and the rise of a postwar anti-Communist mood had produced the essential issue to use against the Democrats: softness on Communism. If the Democrats for almost two decades had exploited the Great Depression as their essential issue—all Republicans wore top hats and forced all laboring men into breadlines—now Republicans, with Luce at their forefront, were fixing on foreign affairs as the Democrats' Achilles' heel. It was a brutal time; serious foreign policy issues with emotional overtones were made more emotional by Luce; his magazine encouraged a kind of political primitivism. *Time* tried to convince its readers that the disaster in Asia had been caused by bad and unworthy Democrats at the State Department. It also encouraged them to think that a Republican administration would deal more forthrightly and more morally with the Communists, roll them back a little. *Time*'s heroes during the late forties and early fifties were men like Foster Dulles and Douglas MacArthur, who talked of bringing moral standards to foreign affairs. Of MacArthur, *Time* was particularly worshipful, writing in that period when he was the Consul General of Japan: "Inside the Dai Ichi building, once the heart of a Japanese insurance empire, bleary-eyed staff officers looked up from stacks of papers, whispered proudly, 'God, the man is great.' General Almond, his chief of staff, said straight out, 'he's the greatest man alive.' And reverent Air Force General George E. Stratemeyer put it as strongly as it could be put . . . 'he's the greatest man in history.' " Acheson was the villain, savaged by Luce in those years. Clearly Acheson was not a patch on MacArthur: "What people thought of Dean Gooderham Acheson ranged from the proposition that he was a fellow traveller, or a wool-brained sower of 'seeds of jackassery,' or an abysmally uncomprehending man, or a warmonger who was taking the U.S. into a world war, to the warm if not so audible defense that he was a great Secretary of State." Clearly the lines were being drawn. Luce had once told Felix Belair that Belair did not understand what being a Republican really meant, that it was like being part of a family.

Never was that pull so strong as with the approach of the 1952 election. Luce felt it was of prime urgency that the Republicans win, in order to save the party, and thus in effect save the Union. If the party, already out of power twenty years, were out of power twenty-four years, it might mean the end of the two-party system. To this end he had been attacking the Democrats for four years, and in 1952 he was prepared to go all out. Though later most intellectuals and liberals were to remember *Time*'s harsh handling of Adlai Stevenson as the mark of Luce's desperation, at the upper level of the company that was always considered the minor decision. The real decision, the real hard and difficult choice, had been the decision to destroy an old friend like Bob Taft. That decision, one which was as much moral as it was journalistic, was terrible for Luce. Years and years later, when he had been drinking, he would confide to friends that it was the worst thing he had ever done—that he never believed that he could have been so hard to an old friend like Bob Taft. Luce did not care about Stevenson, and the protestations of liberal intellectuals fell off him lightly, but Taft was an old friend, a Yale man, a Bones man. Luce and Taft had old ties from the early days when *Time* was printed in Ohio. Dave Ingalls, Taft's campaign manager, had been a college classmate, and, better still, a member of Bones. His wife, Louise, a member of the Harkness family, had been a crucial financial contributor in *Time*'s early days. More than anything else, Taft epitomized the kind of rectitude—there was no other word —that Luce demanded and so rarely found in politicians. Taft was intelligent, serious, honorable, conservative, moral, principled. Precisely the kind of man that *Time* normally would have sponsored. Taft had been denied the nomination in 1948, now by all rights it was his. He could be defeated only if Eisenhower were invented as a candidate. To desert Taft now, to betray him at this late date at the very pinnacle of his career, was a terrible deed for Luce to commit, and yet this was precisely what he did. Luce in 1951 and 1952 went all out to find and sponsor a more liberal Republican who could beat Bob Taft. Perhaps more than anyone else he worked to persuade Ike to run and, with a few other key people, he organized and arranged Ike's early campaign before the General could return from SHAEF. In the truest sense he was Ike's sponsor. In his later years Luce took personal credit for gaining Eisenhower the nomination.

If that is perhaps slightly exaggerated, there is considerable evidence to support at the very least a major, powerful role. He had decided by late 1951 that a Taft nomination would be a disaster, that Taft simply looked too much like the stereotype of a Republican, the cold small-town bank manager who refuses a loan, and that his nomination might again reelect a Democrat. He wrote in a memo at the time: "I thought the American people should have the experience of living under a Republican Administration and discovering that they were not thereby reduced to selling apples on street corners."

He worked very hard personally to convince Ike to run, flying over several times to see him. He was absolutely dazzled by Ike, like a little boy in love for the first time. Ike was everything Luce was not, he was from the heartland, he had been in war, he was always at ease, and he had the ability to gain instant respect from whatever group he was in. He was Luce's vision of America sprung to life, the embodiment of what Luce thought an American soldier should be. He came from Abilene. With that grin and that toughness, he certified the reality of American democracy. Luce proudly sent key members of his staff to Paris to meet Ike and let some of the magic rub off, and he warned Ike through the pages of *Life* that if he held off too long on his decision it might be too late. When Ike finally allowed his name to be entered in some of the primaries but refused to give interviews, Luce nevertheless sent Robert Elson, one of his more talented writers, over to interview the General, assuming rightly that an exception would be made. But Elson found Eisenhower uncommonly vague about the one thing that mattered, politics. The interview was something of a flop, and Elson cabled back: "Ike says, 'No matter what anyone says or does I am determined to be absolutely honest with myself. . . . A lot of people talk to me of issues. Certainly there are issues . . . but the word has become a cliché. . . .' All of which is not to say that Ike does not feel deeply on a number of subjects. He feels for instance that there is altogether too much of a tendency to think that the emergency has passed . . . he is friendly to Chiang and would put no obstacle in way of Chinese undertaking to liberate themselves from Mao's tyranny. . . ." So Ike became Luce's man, even though Luce from time to time complained that he felt ideologically closer to Taft and did not know where Ike stood on issues. That, of course, was precisely why the Republican Party had chosen Eisenhower. He had no political past. There was nothing to haunt him. He was associated with no camp. He did not even seem to know himself which party he belonged to. Thus did Luce bring Eisenhower into the race, and thus did *Time* and *Life* go all out for him.

This was not just journalism, this was a cause. The Taft people were stunned and bitter, they had always regarded Luce as a personal friend and his magazines as essentially sympathetic; if *Time* had held the center for Taft, the nomination was his. But instead Luce had gone and brought this man, Eisenhower, who was hardly a Republican in the first place, into the campaign, and was doing everything he could to destroy Taft, to take away that which by all rights was his. More, *Time* was one of the leaders of the group which tried to describe the normal factional struggle at the convention, the struggle over contested delegations, in terms of good and evil. Portraying Bob Taft as a crook. That, in many areas of the Midwest, would never be forgotten or forgiven. Perhaps the single most important and dramatic thing *Time* did was run an article which simply laid out the arithmetic of the nomination. It was a devastating piece which showed that the states the Republicans most desperately needed to swing the election were the ones where Ike ran well. By contrast, Taft was strong in states where the Republicans would win anyway, or where the Democrats surely would win. The article had been ordered up by Max Ways, a highly respected *Time* editor. Ways had been switched over to national affairs from foreign affairs right before the election, exchanging places with Tom Griffith, who was regarded as the house liberal, and the switch with Ways was generally interpreted within the magazine as Luce battening down the hatch and tightening security. Ways had written the piece without telling Luce about it, and thousands of copies were quickly delivered to the Republican convention in Chicago—some critics said in fact there was a special press run ordered to get them out there a little earlier. The Ways article had a finality to it: it said in effect, in this deeply Republican journal, to a party that had been out of power for twenty years, that if you want to win, you have to go with Eisenhower. The price of political purity is defeat. There was no doubt that it played a decisive role with swing delegates. Luce was bothered a little by the article's potential morality—pragmatism over true belief—but he was delighted by how effective he knew it was going to be, how clearly it stated the case. He told Ways they would lose a lot of old friends, but he accepted that as part of the job. He asked Ways only one question: "How do we explain that our backing Eisenhower is not a case of expediency versus principle?" The answer they worked out, which satisfied Luce, was that if Ike were unworthy, then this would represent expediency at its worst, the dumping of a worthy man who could not win for an unworthy man who could win. But since both men were highly qualified and only one of them could win, they were obligated to go with the man who could win. Years later, when Luce was visiting California, he asked his liberal friend Paul Ziffren about the Clarion Tower in Washington. Why did they dedicate it to Taft? he asked. There were so many other senators equally important, or perhaps even more important, to whom there were no buildings dedicated. "Why this for Bob Taft?"

"God, Harry," Ziffren said, "you're the last person who should ask that."

"What do you mean?" Luce asked.

"Harry, don't you know that's the Clarion Tower of Expiation? It's a way of getting rid of the guilt from 1952," Ziffren said. Then he added that Taft deserved better than being accused of trying to steal an election.

"You're right," Luce said, "we never should have done that."

But if Luce regretted what he had done to Taft, much of his staff was appalled by what the magazine subsequently did to Adlai Stevenson. Rarely had Time's partisanship shown so openly as in the 1952 presidential campaign. For Luce the choice was so clear, so mandatory, that it was no problem at all. Truth demanded that he and Time prove to the nation why it should elect Dwight Eisenhower. It was all that simple. Yet Stevenson was an attractive figure to many of Time's writers and editors. Tom Matthews, the managing editor, and Stevenson had been Princeton classmates and were old friends. When Stevenson had first appeared as a potential Democratic national figure, Time had approved. He was then simply a reformer of the right kind and background challenging more traditional Democratic politicians. But once he received the nomination, that was a different thing, he was challenging Dwight Eisenhower. Time became much tougher with him. Much of the staff was very unhappy, but Luce had little patience with his staff's unhappiness. It was a bitter autumn for the house liberals, there was a terrible fight between Matthews and the conservative editor Otto Fuerbringer over a particularly tough cover story Fuerbringer had written on Stevenson. Matthews, like much of the staff, felt that Luce could not be reached at all, fairness meant nothing to him, ideology guided him. There was talk of rebellion and protest, though in the end nothing happened.

Later, after the election, knowing that much of the staff was dissatisfied with *Time*'s coverage, Luce gave a dinner at the Union Club for the entire staff. Some of the liberals on the staff thought this might be a peace offering, a gesture of conciliation on Luce's part for the heavy-handed election coverage. But it was quite the reverse. Luce was in a triumphant, arrogant mood, ready, it seemed, not so much to find common ground as to accept surrender. There was a touch of brutality to the evening. He said in effect that he was the boss, and that it was not for them to agonize and wring their hands over his product. If there was to be any agony, let it be his. "I told you I was your boss. I guess that means that I can fire any of you. I don't know anybody around here who's got a contract, have they, Roy [Alexander]? So I could fire any of you. I could fire all of you until Roy got hold of me and said, 'This guy is crazy,' and put me in Matteawan or something. But I don't know anyone who can fire me. Sometimes I wish there were. Well, as long as I don't get fired, I propose to serve as *Time*'s editor-in-chief." It was a blunt putdown of his staff, and after hearing it, Matthews, already frustrated and embittered by the experience of the Stevenson cover story, went out for a drink with friends and told them there was nothing to do but resign. Most of the top editors were very fond of Matthews, he was an attractive, urbane man, reasonably apolitical, responsible for much of the increased excellence in *Time*'s cultural sections. That night he seemed totally depressed as he talked with his colleagues about the future. The others hated what had happened, but finally agreed that it was Luce's magazine. For most of them it was impossible to leave. But Matthews did resign the managing editorship, and accepted another assignment from Luce in England. *Time* and *Life* gave Eisenhower sweetheart coverage while he was in office. *Time*'s Washington bureau became an extension of the Administration. Eisenhower did not change American foreign policy very much, but the rhetoric of the Administration escalated and became more harsh, and as it did the rhetoric of *Time* softened and became more benign.

# 3 / The Los Angeles Times

The Chandlers thought *Time* magazine just a little liberal. Not, mind you, as liberal as most major eastern publications, but eastern and a bit fancy nonetheless. Particularly for a Republican journal. The Chandlers were more conservative in those days, in the early fifties, and if they had a sister publication anywhere in the country it was the Chicago *Tribune.* Taft was more to their liking than any other politician. Ike was acceptable, but they had their doubts. Their doubts, moreover, were respected, for they were special, they were the *Chandlers,* they were California, conservative, rugged, unaffected by the social changes of the last twenty years.

It is a dynasty, one of the few remaining in American society, surviving the dual contemporary onslaught of modern inheritance taxes and normally thinning genes. Its power and reach and role in Southern California are beyond the comprehension of Easterners, no Easterner can understand what it has meant in California *to be a Chandler,* for no single family dominates any major region of this country as the Chandlers have dominated California, it would take in the East a combination of the Rockefellers *and* the Sulzbergers to match their power and influence. In California the Chandlers are *the* dominant family, their touch has been all-inclusive; the men are born to their roles and bred to their responsibility; their women are not lightly selected, because in this family a marriage implies not just the present but the future; one has a sense of the oldest male Chandler of a generation choosing the woman of his life while thinking of genes and bloodlines and generations to come. They are *Chandlers;* their bustling prosperous region exists to an uncommon degree because they envisioned it that way.

They did not so much foster the growth of Southern California as, more simply, invent it. There is water because they went and stole water. The city is horizontal instead of vertical because they were rich in land, and horizontal span was good for them, good for real estate. There is a port because they dreamed of a port. They had settled in a garden of nature, and where nature failed they and their friends provided. If God had not been sufficiently generous in giving this paradise adequate water, then Harry Chandler and a few of his cohorts would simply go and rape the Eden of the Owens Valley some 230 miles away of its water, and the water would turn arid valleys into a prosperous urban garden. Who is to say that the history of the West and the history of California would be better if Harry Chandler had been someone who thought the law applied to him, and the Owens Valley, rather than Los Angeles, had prospered? Los Angeles is the major city in America most resistant to the power of labor unions, not because it evolved naturally that way but because first General Harrison Gray Otis and then Harry Chandler fought the unions in a constant ongoing struggle that was nothing short of war, mobilizing all other businessmen under their wing, tearing the entire city apart with a bitterness that lasted some sixty years.

General Otis was a zealot, an angry choleric man, who had gone out to California after the Civil War. He wedded his paper to his prejudices and he founded the dynasty. But it was Harry Chandler, his son-in-law, who brought it scope and imagination and strength (the strength of the family is in its Chandler origins, not the Otis ones, and to this day members are a good deal prouder about being Chandlers than they are of being Otises). The General was an impetuous swashbuckler, poised for the slightest provocation, ready to punch out with either his fists or his newspaper at all who dared offend him. The newspaper was a strident extension of his prejudices and passions and ignorance; he was one of a breed of frontier newspapermen as anxious to fight as he was to write, more often than not loud and boisterous today and gone tomorrow. Harry Chandler was different, he was an entrepreneur, a businessman first and foremost. A pirate visionary. He had come to the General first as a young circulation distributor, quietly taking over the General's circulation lists without the latter knowing it, until he had one day made the General an offer he could not refuse, at which point he became the business manager of the paper. Thus a dynasty, conceived in no small way, in a kind of commercial blackmail. Shortly afterward, in the way that these things are sometimes done, Harry Chandler also became the General's son-in-law.

He was very different from the General. He had no time for anger, for petty feuds and squabbles, he was, in the most hardheaded and calculating way imaginable, a dreamer, and he was always dreaming of the future of Los Angeles, of growth and profit: the commercial future of Los Angeles, tied as it was to the commercial future of Harry Chandler. That was of the essence. The paper was the instrument of his and his friends' commercial interests; it would speak for his passions—water, a port, annexation of Mexican land (he owned a lot of land in Mexico too), crushing unions. It would help slay the politicians he wanted slain (by and large Democrats) and elect those he wanted elected (Republicans), all of which was done with such great success that Jerry Brown, elected in 1974, became only the third Democratic governor of California in this century, one of the two others being his father. Harry Chandler was the classic entrepreneurial wheeler-dealer. He was, in the phrase not used in those days, upwardly mobile. He did not shout like the General, and his vision was far bolder and broader; if he was going to steal the water from the Owens Valley, it was not just for the benefit of Los Angeles, it would help irrigate otherwise arid and valueless land in the San Fernando Valley, vast sections of which just happened to be owned by Harry Chandler. What other reason to have, so to speak, a green thumb? He did not need to shout or flaunt his power.

It was simply there. He and his five or six business associates could, as if they were architects, design the future of a city, its growth and its limitless possibilities, and above all their share of it.

The paper reflected all of that; it was ancillary to the essential cause of the Chandlers, which was commercial profit and commercial expansion. Journalism, as an expression of restraint and judgment on a community, journalists as the spiritual monitors of a community, those were things Harry Chandler never heard of. His was advocacy journalism of a primitive kind, brutal economic advocacy. If in the nineteen twenties and thirties and forties much of the eastern seacoast was a developed, increasingly refined society with a journalism to match, there was nothing of that sort in California; there the mud was still on the boots of the first families, it was a frontier land, and Harry Chandler was the son-in-law of a frontier editor.

He was the patriarch of the family. He had eight children of his own and he wanted nothing less from his own children, eight each they must sire, he said, and he disapproved of those who fell short. When he came to visit his son Norman, the favorite (it could not be otherwise, Norman was the first son), he made it clear that he did not like the fact that Norman and Buff Chandler slept in separate beds. Harry Chandler, visiting Norman, looking at the bedroom, shaking his head, muttering, "I don't approve of that, I just don't approve of that." He raised his own family very strictly. The food was simple, alcohol extremely rare, the house was not grand, there was a very low Yankee ceiling to pleasure, as befitted the son of Moses Chandler, who also lived a simple spartan life, and who at the end of his life, though his son was wealthy, had contrived to run a piece of string from his house to the outhouse so that, as his eyesight failed, he would be able to find the facilities at night. There was no high life in the home of Harry Chandler, no Chandler was spoiled in that generation, there was to be no divorce. Young Chandlers were brought up to work hard; a sense of obligation hung in the air. Chandlers as young men did physical work, they were not to be overprivileged. Harry Chandler as a young man had done hard physical work and he had been justly rewarded; if Norman Chandler did hard physical work as a young man, perhaps he too, and his heirs to follow, would be justly rewarded as well.

Harry Chandler passed on his sense of dynasty to the next generation. Norman, first male born of Harry and Marian Otis Chandler, was gentler than his father, more introverted and private, less the buccaneer. A man worthy of holding on to wealth, if not necessarily the sort of man to go out and accumulate it on his own. A shy man, full of a sense of responsibility and obligation to his family and to his community. Norman Chandler, unlike his father, did not like the tumult, violence, roughness, and combat of the political and economic pit; he was an excellent businessman yet nonetheless quick to delegate as much responsibility as he could in order to spare himself the pain of dealing in the fierce and often harsh world that his father had passed on to him. His coming might have signaled the beginning of the end of the Chandler line, for at a certain point in the history of most great families the blood thins, initiative and incentive diminish, privilege, arrogance, and weakness breed, rather than drive and hunger. Could the line survive beyond Norman Chandler, mild, gentle, a man who dreamed wistfully of spending his life on the Tejon Ranch which he really loved? He was a man who under normal circumstances might have lapsed readily into the status quo, too gentle for the stern duties of a dynasty.

But he married, surely in full realization of the needs of his role, the perfect wife: Dorothy Buffum of Long Beach, a restless, highly energized woman of soaring ambition, ambition for her husband, for herself, above all for her son. She became the Chandler incarnate, more Chandler than the real Chandlers. Buff, who was a favorite of Harry Chandler's, always talking to him about politics, a subject that bored most of his children, including to a degree, his first son. Buff as a young woman, lying down on the floor, ear cupped for voices from downstairs, listening as Harry Chandler (who often did business at home, and who was by then hard of hearing) held court with his various business associates. Buff, traveling to Washington with Harry and Norman, listening through the keyhole as Harry did business with Herbert Hoover and other Republican luminaries in his room at the Willard Hotel. She had a rage, nothing less, to be someone and do something; a rage and a drive as strong as anything that had ever burned in Harry Chandler. A Buffum of Long Beach was not, in the pecking order of those days, no matter how rough and primitive the pecking order, quite as good as a Chandler. The Buffums ran dry-goods stores, and there were some of Norman's older sisters who did not think she was quite good enough for their beloved, much-adored younger brother and they made the mistake of letting her know that, a mistake they would rue long afterward. But if anything these snubs drove her even more to succeed, to impose her will, indeed if one part of Los Angeles society would not accept her, then she would, with the might and majesty of the Los Angeles *Times* and its women's pages, redefine Los Angeles society.

She was an intense, volatile, passionate woman, at once vulnerable and brutal, capable of hurting and being hurt, astonishingly resilient. Above all, she was not a woman for the status quo. Her arrival ensured that the dynasty survived and expanded during Norman's tenure, but, more important, the intensity of her will and the fierceness of her spirit profoundly affected her son Otis and thus perpetuated the dynasty for one more generation. If she saw her husband relaxing at night, slumping slightly in his seat in full view of guests, she might say to him—loud enough so that others could hear—*"Posture, Chan! Posture!"* He would then sit a little straighter. Or if he were having, as sometimes was his wont, one drink too many, she would stop it. "No more drinking, Norman!" And that would be that. Only for his benefit, for he would look right, he would look the part of a scion of a great family. Nor would he ever be able to relax, to recline on his laurels; if she found him sitting in the same chair every night after dinner, she would make him move, explaining to friends that she never wanted him to be too comfortable, to become a creature of habit. He would be pushed to his ultimate responsibility, there would be no softness permitted. Comfort would be dismissed. Duty, obligation summoned.

Norman Chandler, his son Otis Chandler could say many years later, had no more freedom of choice than he himself did. For that sense of obligation was shared by the son as well. There were times when he was young that Otis Chandler thought he wanted to be a doctor—Otis in a green surgeon's smock, hands steady, ready to operate. His own man, doing his own thing. But it was never in the cards; he thought about it a lot, but never really *seriously*. No one ever told him he could not be a doctor, but it was known that he was supposed to be publisher of the *Times*. It would have been an act of unparalleled rebellion for him to be anything else, and so he dutifully and quietly, for he was a quiet, somewhat reticent young man, fulfilled the required role for a Chandler, he worked hard as a boy—much harder than most young people, no Chandler was to be spoiled—he worked so hard shoveling manure in his father's orchard that he never, as a grown man, would touch his wife's garden, lovely though it was. He fulfilled his parents' dreams, he was a star athlete, indeed a world-class athlete at Stanford, just missing an Olympic medal, he went off to the Air Force as an officer and when he finally arrived home from his military duty, showing up on a Friday with his wife and child and rented truck, he was greeted enthusiastically by his parents. There was a pleasant family dinner that Friday night, his parents were pleased that the Korean War had not taken too large a toll from him, and on Saturday, when he got up, Norman and Buff handed him the detailed outline for a seven-year work program which put him through every stage of the paper—press room, mailer, delivery room, advertising, city room. He was to start work the following Monday. He did. He did very well at it. In fact, the mailers voted him Apprentice Most Likely to Succeed during his tour there. Such is role and obligation.

Norman Chandler was, in terms of California history, the transitional man, the man who bridged the era of the pirates and the era of his son, Otis, the head of a modern, civilized, highly sophisticated, computerized empire in which the voice of the *Times* and the voice of good-government reformers sounded on occasion perilously similar. He was a simple man, Norman Chandler, fearsomely good-looking, the Marlboro man, with a touch more elegance, perhaps a touch of Cary Grant in him. Strangers were inclined to like him even before they knew him, just because of the way he looked. ("Don't ever," Buff Chandler, perhaps in reaction to being told so often how handsome Norman was, once told a friend, "tell a young man he is very good-looking. It doesn't do him or anyone around him any good.") A man whose personal qualities were gentle, almost sweet, very human, in virtual contrast to the editorial policies of his paper, which were narrow and harsh and ignorant. A close friend saw him as a figure from Edna Ferber's *Giant,* a good man within his framework, the more personal the requirement, the better he was, but a man of limited vision, his sense of a larger world and the social requirements it demanded very narrow. It was not that he was cold or unjust, it was more that he was simply unworldly. When he heard voices he responded well, but he heard a very narrow range of voices. He did not like contentiousness or disputatiousness.

He liked being publisher very much—since destiny did not permit him to be a rancher—and he was very good at it, or at least he was very good at the business side of it. He had no feeling for the editorial side, his parents had neglected to put him through a training period there. It was a world he did not understand; he could not write and he would not know a news story unless he read one. He had once been at his club in Northern California and witnessed an air crash and several days later was telling friends at the paper about it and one asked why he had not phoned it in, since it was a very good story. He was surprised by this (though in terms of ignoring stories this still put him behind Arthur Ochs Sulzberger of *The New York Times,* who, as a young man, happened to witness the extraordinary collision at Le Mans in 1955 which killed eighty-three people, did not realize that this was something that might possibly interest his readers, and failed to phone it in). Since he did not really understand the editorial side, he ran essentially the paper which he had inherited from his father, along with its existing prejudices, which happened, of course, to be those of his father.

At heart Norman Chandler was a very conservative man, not a kook right-winger of the sort that California in the middle of the twentieth century was producing—people furious with change, and searching for a world that would never be again and probably never was in the first place—but a serious, dogged Taft Republican, a man with a devoted belief in property rights and the perquisites of the ruling class. He had, after all, grown up in a much more ordered, much less volatile world where far more privilege existed and where privilege was much less on the defensive. Indeed, in his youth it was poverty, not privilege, which was on the defensive. (Norman's grandfather in 1886 had defined in the pages of the *Times* what kind of companions he wanted in Los Angeles: "Los Angeles wants no dudes, loafers and paupers; people who have no means and trust to luck, cheap politicians, failures, bummers, scrubs, impecunious clerks, bookkeepers, lawyers, doctors. The market is overstocked already. We need workers! Hustlers! Men of brains, brawn and guts! Men who have a little capital and a good deal of energy—first-class men!") Norman believed in privilege and its rights; one of the most serious and revealing disagreements he had with his son, Otis, was over a state referendum which would allow millions of citizens access to the California coastline; Norman believed the coastline belonged to those few property owners who held land, he had no sympathy or feeling for the 20 million who did not. He used his paper as forcefully as he could on the side of the rich and the powerful, be it oilmen or land developers, and he and his close friends, the heart of the Los Angeles conservative establishment, constantly sponsored politicians at every level who were committed to the status quo. He disliked most of the changes of the twentieth century, the constant assault upon property, the diminution of privilege. Yet he was not a man to fight blindly against progress, he was too tolerant and civilized for that. He accepted what was and what would be and, as the paper under his own son seemed to sponsor change, he accepted that with his usual good grace and charm, doing all he could to protect his son from the rest of his even more conservative family, and speaking with undisguised pride of how well Otis was doing, how it was time for an older generation to accept the vision of a younger one. (Indeed once, flying back from a newspaper convention in Washington, he found himself seated near Paul Conrad, the remarkably talented, provocative, and very liberal cartoonist of the *Times,* the bête noire, in fact, of all of Norman Chandler's own friends. How did Conrad like working for the *Times?* Norman Chandler, gracious as ever, asked. "Just fine now," answered Conrad, "although I would never have worked here in the old days." "You're goddamn right, you wouldn't have!" said Norman Chandler, but he said it with a smile.)

Because he did not need or particularly want public acclaim or approval and was in fact quite shy about public appearances, and his wife was exactly the opposite, at once wanting and desperately needing acclaim, it became part of the legend of Norman Chandler that he was a weak man married to a strong woman. This was by no means true. Buff Chandler was very strong, very much the more public of the two, the more outspoken, the seemingly more forceful. Norman Chandler was content to be out of the limelight, yet he was in his own way very forceful, and he had things very much his own way, and there was little that happened in the paper or in California or Los Angeles politics for a very long time that he did not want to have happen. There was beneath all that sweetness and gentleness a very hard line beyond which he simply could not be pushed, and while this rarely showed in public, it was always there. That was it, he had made his decision, the curtain had come down. His wife, more passionate, more volatile, would often miss the signal and keep arguing and then he would say, in a voice that meant the argument was over, *That's enough, Buff,* or *You don't know what you're talking about, honey.* The argument would end, an argument which had never really been an argument anyway since he had not really consented to join it.

Part of what others interpreted as weakness was actually his security, a total sense of himself and the fact that he did not need to scratch or scramble, he had the luxury of elegant manners under which he could conceal his own very strong will. In his later years a bust of Norman Chandler was commissioned from the noted sculptor Jacques Lipchitz. It was Norman's due as part of a dynasty; the bust would stand in the entrance of the *Times* building, just as busts of his father and grandfather already stood there and as a bust of his son would someday stand there, grim proud reminders of both human mortality and bronzed immortality. The bust of Norman Chandler that Lipchitz produced is not a piece that many of his friends like. They find it too harsh, too cold, and they miss the gentleness of their old friend. The truth is that Lipchitz had a very hard time with Norman Chandler as a subject. He liked Norman Chandler very much but he could not in the artistic sense find him, and days and then weeks in Rome passed, Lipchitz searching the face for his subject, becoming more and more restless and frustrated, complaining, "I cannot find Norman, I cannot find Norman." The tension in the room grew all the time, Norman restless with the sittings, Lipchitz working on a tiny model. Then one day Lipchitz shouting, *I've found him, I've found him!* Norman Chandler had been thinking, and without knowing it his face had set, and Lipchitz had seen in that instant the real baron of the Chandler family, he had connected the face to the empire, and he had toughened up his maquette and made it much stronger. The lesson being that the sweetness was there but so were the other qualities necessary to run that empire.

The paper that Norman Chandler published in the forties and much of the fifties was parochial and reactionary, a voice for the property holdings of the Chandlers and their close friends. If journalism in the East was gradually improving, often out of necessity because of a rising educational level in the society, Los Angeles (and what was to constitute the Sun Belt) was different. It was a world still close to the frontier, still isolated, still being defined. It was a more isolated island in America in those pre-television, pre-jet days, it was less a part of the American mainstream; whatever main standard of American journalism was being set in New York, Los Angeles was alien to it; in Los Angeles no one cared what they did in New York, New York was distant, too liberal, too polluted by foreigners and labor unions. It was the joke of Herman Mankiewicz that the classic Los Angeles *Times* headline was: "LA Dog Chases LA Cat over LA Fence." S. J. Perelman could write of traveling across the United States by train and stopping at Albuquerque: "I asked the porter to get me a newspaper and unfortunately the poor man, hard of hearing, brought me the Los Angeles *Times.*" The paper was so bad that in 1946, before he opened bureaus in other American cities, Ed James, the managing editor of *The New York Times,* sent Gladwin Hill, one of his best reporters, to Los Angeles because he so distrusted the Los Angeles *Times* and the Chandlers. James was afraid to have *The New York Times* working off the carbons of the Los Angeles paper.

Unlike what was happening in the East, in the West the land was still being divided, the fortunes still being made, the frontier mentality was still very vivid. It was the right, indeed the duty, of a good newspaper to fight for its owners' economic privileges, not to sit on the sidelines while the future of those interests and the future of the community were swept away by reformers. The nation was midway through the twentieth century, and here an almost nineteenth-century view of order held forth: a small group of men who controlled the community and who knew what was good for the community because in their own eyes they *were* the community.

That belligerent activist conservatism was as much a part of the dynasty as the blood itself. They considered that they had invented Southern California, they were the keepers of the flame, their editorials said so, and in their hearts they believed what they wrote. The struggles they had fought with their enemies, particularly the labor unions, were not those of the normal publisher against an opposing faction, but were in the truest sense wars, they were total, there was blood on both sides, the resulting memories and bitterness shaped the spirit not just of a powerful family but of the entire region. Members of the dynasty looked upon themselves as the founding imperialists of Southern California.

It had started with Harrison Gray Otis. *General* Otis. General in title, but even more in spirit. A fierce man. One had a sense of fire coming out of his nostrils, Otis always at the ready for an insult or a slight. There was a smell of cordite to his words. He was not a man to be crossed, he demanded total loyalty on all issues by all friends. Either that or they were no longer friends, in which case they were enemies. He was a man who came equipped with a full spleen, he was righteous about his past, ferocious about his future, a man not given to argument, for argument implied that there were two sides to an issue. He was born in Marietta, Ohio, in 1837. His own parents had been Vermont farmers who moved to Ohio in 1800, "staunch, stalwart, intelligent, God-fearing people of the Methodist faith," he later called them. As a boy he worked as a printer's apprentice and as a printer. When the Civil War broke out, Otis, then twenty-four, enlisted almost immediately, rose to captain, and saw a great deal of action, and was wounded twice; he was breveted after the war with the rank of lieutenant colonel. He returned to Marietta and started publishing a small newspaper, but was bored and restless, and in 1876 moved West to Santa Barbara to edit the Santa Barbara *Press,* and finally, in 1881, at the age of forty-four, a driven man who had been in some way drifting for almost fifteen years, sure of his destiny but never finding it, he arrived in Los Angeles. His happiest days had been in the Army; he was quick to volunteer in 1898 during the Spanish-American War and, commissioned a brigadier general, he led troops in the Philippines in 1898 and 1899.

His love of the military remained with him. He called his home in Los Angeles the Bivouac. Another house was known as the Outpost. The *Times* was known as the Fortress. The staff of the paper was the Phalanx. The *Times* building itself was more fortress than newspaper plant, there were turrets, battlements, sentry boxes. Inside he stored fifty rifles. He loved, even in civilian life, going around in his uniform. He was a man for whom combat, military or personal, was far more exciting and more rewarding than peace and calm. His motto and that of the *Times*—it seemed appropriate—was *Stand Fast.*

*Stand Firm. Stand Sure. Stand True.* His voice seemed to thunder at all times, whether he was shouting at an enemy or asking someone to pass the salt. He brooked no slights, however innocent, upon his person. An unsuspecting fellow resident of Los Angeles once greeted him in the morning, slightly mispronouncing his name. "Good morning, General *Ah*tis," the poor man said. "It's *Oat*tis, you goddamn fool," he answered back.

When Otis arrived in California he found what he was looking for, a land that was not just a home but a future and a cause. In 1882 Los Angeles was a dirty, sleepy country town of 5,000 about to start the most astonishing record of growth for any city in the country's history; his arrival was fortuitous, but his role in the city's growth was pivotal; he was quite possibly what historian Morrow Mayo called him, "the chief figure in the whole history of Southern California." His pen was as fierce as his demeanor. Of the Democratic Party he wrote: "A shameless old harlot." Labor leaders: "Corpse defacers." Hearst: "Yellow Yawp." H. H. Boyce, a onetime colleague and then rival editor: "A coarse vulgar criminal." Hiram Johnson, the reform governor of California: "A born mob leader—a whooper—a howler—a roarer." His most bitter fights were with the labor unions. The conflict was totally personalized and he came to see organized labor as the single greatest poison for the American future and, more specifically, the future of Los Angeles. He hated San Francisco, which was a union city, and the pages of his paper were filled with purple choleric assaults upon it. He was as sure of his own rectitude as he was of the sins of his enemies.

Not surprisingly, he inspired loathing of a comparable intensity, and came to seem the embodiment of the blustering, bullying, unfeeling capitalist. He fought all reform attempts in California with every means at his disposal, becoming a central figure in California politics. In 1910, running for governor of California, Hiram Johnson, the leader of the progressive movement, was speaking in Los Angeles when someone in the audience shouted out: "What about Otis?" Johnson, every bit as good at invective as the editor, answered: "In the city of San Francisco we have drunk to the very dregs of infamy; we have had vile officials, we have had rotten newspapers. But we have nothing so vile, nothing so low, nothing so debased, nothing so infamous in San Francisco as Harrison Gray Otis. He sits there in senile dementia with gangrene heart and rotting brain, grimacing at every reform, chattering impotently at all things that are decent, frothing, fuming, violently gibbering, going down to his grave in snarling infamy. He is the one thing that all Californians look at when, in looking at Southern California, they see anything that is disgraceful, depraved, corrupt, crooked and putrescent—that is Harrison Gray Otis." That was in public; heaven only knows what they said of him in private.

When Otis settled in Los Angeles in 1882 he went to work at fifteen dollars a week for a newspaper called the *Times,* and later bought a share of it. Los

Angeles in those days did not seem to have a particularly bright future, it was a town without a port, it was not yet connected to the rest of America by any major spoke of transportation, its water supplies were limited. But there was land. A drought in 1864 had forced the Spanish ranchers to break up their vast estates in order to pay taxes and that had been the beginning of the Los Angeles real estate business. It had a wonderful climate. Then, in 1883, the Southern Pacific completed its southern route, and the boom began. Suddenly a new Mecca was attainable by those of less than pioneer blood. Los Angeles offered hot sun and cheap land and cheap labor. In the first year of the railroad 5,000 new residents came to Los Angeles, doubling the population. In 1884 Southern California oranges took first place over Florida oranges in an international exposition in New Orleans. It was a significant moment. Everything, it seemed, grew better in this new Eden. In 1885, the Atchison, Topeka & Santa Fe connected *its* link to Los Angeles and the railroad competition was on.

Rival lines started advertising furiously back East for passengers, emphasizing the wonders of this new world, land, sun, happiness, a land for builders and dreamers. It was the signal for a boom, cheap land and low-cost transportation. First the Santa Fe cut its one-way fare from the Midwest to Los Angeles from $100 to $95; then the Southern Pacific cut its fare. Then the Santa Fe. Then the Southern Pacific. Down went the fare from $80 to $70 to $60 to $50. Suddenly, from any place in the Midwest, Southern California was only $15, then $5, and finally, at the peak of competition, $1. Kansas City to Los Angeles for *One Dollar,* it was the American dream in full glaring life.

On they came—boomers, high rollers, some to live, some to exploit, some to have, some to be had. Five trains a day entered Los Angeles filled with prospectors or prospects. People bought land they had never seen, land which might not even exist. In 1884 the population was 12,000; by 1886 it was 100,000. The annual freight carried by Wells Fargo alone went from 300,000 pounds to 7,000,000 in the same period. The recorded real estate deals (and only half were recorded) went from virtually nothing to $8 million a month to a peak of $13 million a month in July 1887. A town was becoming a city overnight. Among the chief and most immediate beneficiaries was Harrison Gray Otis, who did not fail now as he had in Santa Barbara; he had predicted the future and the future had come to him and one of the best things about the future was that land sales required land advertisements and the best place to advertise for land was in the local paper, particularly the *Times.* One of the best things about the future was that it was making Harrison Gray Otis a rich man even in the present.

He had bought into the *Times* in 1882, just before the boom, and his luck was very good. He shared ownership with H. H. Boyce and after a short time, not surprisingly, the two men could not get along. General Otis was not a man to share power or agree to committee decisions, and it quickly became a simple question of who would buy out whom. Finally they agreed on a price of $18,000. If Otis could in one month raise the money, which seemed a very great deal at the time, Boyce would sell to him; otherwise, Otis would have to sell to Boyce. Otis raised the money and took complete control of the paper in 1886. Boyce used his $18,000 to start a new paper, the *Morning Tribune,* which meant that there now were three daily morning papers in the city—the *Times,* the *Tribune,* and the *Herald.* Whether the *Times* could survive in competition so fierce was doubtful.

Enter Harry Chandler. He was a younger man, born in Landaff, New Hampshire, in 1864, twenty-seven years after the General. As Otis was typical of the men who came to California because they were restless with civilian life after the Civil War, Harry Chandler was typical of another kind of California migrant, someone who came to California for his health. He had suffered pneumonia as a student at Dartmouth College, having made the mistake of swimming in an almost frozen river, and had been sent West by his family to recover his health and repair his damaged lungs. He arrived there at the age of seventeen, was thrown out of several boardinghouses because he was a lunger, and was eventually taken in by a doctor who was also suffering from a serious lung disease. The doctor had some fruit orchards in an area near what is now Hollywood. The work there was good for young Chandler's health. The doctor had a wagon and he told young Chandler he was free to do with the fruit what he could. It was unsalable locally since it was so bountiful. So, being an enterprising young Yankee, Chandler took to carting the fruit farther north into areas where only grain was grown and where the Mexican farm hands were desperately thirsty. On that first day Chandler made a profit of $19. Since his overhead was negligible and his market was captive, and because he was also very thrifty, in two years he had saved almost $3,000.

Harry Chandler was always thinking ahead; if General Otis was always searching for his next enemy and his next feud, Harry Chandler was always searching for his next big chance. He soon decided it lay in newspaper circulation. He liked working out of doors, his health seemed to depend on it, and so very carefully and quietly he began buying up the circulation routes of the local papers. In those days circulation men were independent of newspaper owners, it was in effect a sublet, they controlled areas and handled particular pieces of territory, almost as jobbers. In a short time Harry Chandler came to control the entire 1,400-person list of the *Times;* at the same time, using dummy connections, he was also taking over the lists of the *Herald,* the *Tribune,* and other local papers. It was a profitable business and the more he made, the more he plowed back, expanding his lists all the time, keeping very quiet about it. Harry Chandler did not need to be out front. He worked best when as little as possible was known of his intentions. He very quickly was making more money than the three or four newspaper owners combined.

In 1885, with total control over the *Times* circulation list, he became a major figure in the *Times*'s ascendancy. He did this by helping to kill off a major rival. The competition between the *Times* and the *Tribune,* both morning papers, was particularly fierce, a competition born out of blood and hatred.

Boyce had already sued Otis twice for libel, and it was clear that only one of the two papers would eventually survive. Chandler now proposed to Otis (indeed, he later boasted quite openly about the deal he had pulled) that they starve out Boyce's *Tribune*. Otis said it could not be done. Chandler said it could be done and done easily, and as Otis listened he soon agreed. Through his dummy operation Chandler controlled the circulation list of the *Herald,* and had considerable control over the *Tribune* routes. It would be easy, he said, to play the *Times* and the *Herald* together against the *Tribune.* If a *Times* reader was about to change, Chandler would make sure that he went to the neutral *Herald* instead of the *Tribune*. If a *Herald* subscriber was going to change, Chandler would make sure he went to the *Times.* He would also work on *Tribune* subscribers to drop their paper. He helped here by making sure from time to time that the *Tribune* delivery boys went on a prolonged picnic in the country and did not get back in time to get the paper out. Only General Otis and Harry Chandler would really know what was happening. It was a delightful scheme and it worked. Within two years Boyce was forced out of business and his equipment sold, at five cents on the dollar, to another dummy figure, acting, incidentally, as it turned out, for Harry Chandler, who was gaining more leverage all the time.

Thus in the years following 1886, when the boom took place, General Otis, aided by his very smart young assistant, Harry Chandler, was already running a thriving paper and was in a perfect position to benefit the most. His competition was in decline. Circulation and advertising doubled, tripled, quadrupled. The little paper of 1,400 circulation that Harry Chandler first knew was on its way. It made General Otis a rich and successful man, and very soon after, it made Harry Chandler, as befits a young, ambitious, enterprising fellow, Otis's circulation manager, then his business manager, and finally his son-in-law. It was the beginning of a great dynasty, the bond being H. H. Boyce's circulation list. Horatio Alger could not have imagined it better.

Otis and Chandler had arrived at their partnership at almost the exact moment the railroad link was completed. They were immediate beneficiaries of the boom, but the boom did not last long, it was simply too inflated, too explosive, too much madness in the air. What went up was going up too quickly, and so just as quickly it began to come down. The banks became very nervous, too much money was being lent on far too little real property. They began to pull back. By 1888 the boom had collapsed. Suddenly people were leaving Los Angeles as quickly as they had arrived, two and three thousand a month. The banks stopped lending on all but the most valuable real estate located right in the center of town, and then only on pre-boom values. The assessment figures for the county, which during the boom had gone from $32 million to $65 million, now dropped to $20 million, far below the pre-boom level. Everything seemed to come apart, bankers disappeared, town leaders committed suicide. General Otis, still rich, was still the boomer. During the worst of the collapse he still looked forward: "Let our wide pasture be changed into highly improved farms. Let the arid wastes be provided with an abundance of water. Plant new orchards and vineyards. Build new railroads."

But writing was not enough; in 1888, on General Otis's motion, the Los Angeles Chamber of Commerce was born. It was to become one of the most energetic and chauvinistic booster organizations in the world. His idea was simple enough: if people did not come to Los Angeles on their own, or if the right kind of people did not come, Los Angeles would seek people, more, it would seek the right kind of people, good God-fearing, hard-working midwestern farmers, strong of back, strong of values, people who would neither cheat nor be cheated. Certainly midwestern farmers, tired of those long bleak winters, would be delighted to move to this new Eden. With Otis and to a lesser degree Harry Chandler as the driving force, with the cooperation of both railroads, California was sold to the Iowa and Minnesota and Nebraska farmers. If the Midwesterners would not come to California, then California would come to them, and so it did, California on wheels, in a fully organized, brilliantly conceived all-out propaganda effort that would make even the most modern huckster proud. California produce was shipped to the Midwest, to be sampled at the lowest possible cost; papers, pamphlets, books, all boasting of the wonders of California, usually written by the *Times*'s editorial writers, were distributed. No place in the Midwest was safe from the invasion of huckstering Californians, and in particular, the coming of California produce. The children of Grant Wood were being given a chance to become the children of sunshine. Why resist? In they poured, good, simple, God-fearing, and, best of all, innately conservative.

It was a crucial step for both General Otis and Harry Chandler, they were no longer merely journalists in a frontier town, if indeed they had ever been. Now they were the chief architects and the chief builders of the new society, men who did not merely aid in the growth but in effect invented the city, not just a growing community of which they were a vital and important part, but rather an extension of their will; they had willed it to grow and be great when others had lost faith, they did not just speak for the city, they *were* the city. The act connected the *Times* to the upper level of Los Angeles society, and it marked the real beginning of the *Times* as the paper of the Los Angeles business establishment, the paper of the powerful and the rich, the voice of Los Angeles money. Even in harder times to come, even when Hearst entered the scene and did better in terms of circulation with his instinct for sexy headlines and his dreadful red-baiting, the *Times* remained in a special niche because of its service to the business elite, so that even when it was not doing well in circulation it always did well in advertising.

That was part of the legacy of the bust. The other, far more important historically, was that the bust produced the first clash between the *Times* and the labor unions. The event was to produce, overnight, a permanent scar on Los Angeles, making it in the two decades to come one of the bloodiest battlegrounds between labor and capital in the nation, and making the *Times* one of America's most reactionary papers. For the next sixty years, the *Times* was not just a voice of anti-unionism, but an outspoken, relentless instrument for all conservative policies and candidates, wedded to the Republican Party but wary of the party lest it become too soft. *Time* magazine, quite conservative itself in the thirties, could say of General Otis that he "lived to make the *Times* the most rabid Labor-baiting, Red-hating paper in the United States."

Yet the beginning was innocent enough. When the strike of typographers on the four papers began in 1890, the union leaders believed that Otis was their friend, that he would personally work to settle the dispute peacefully. He was, after all, a former union printer himself, he carried a union card, he had paid his dues in the past, he seemed to be their colleague. They completely misread their man. He felt they were bullying him, he was above all else not a man to be bullied, and he became their foremost enemy. The conflict began in the wake of the boom, when times were bad. Everything was shrinking, in particular advertising in the four daily papers. All four papers asked their printers to take a 20 percent pay cut, in hopes that they would settle for a 10 percent cut. The local union replied with an ultimatum, refusing to discuss terms and threatening to strike unless they were given an additional year extension on their contract. The owners were given twenty-four hours to agree, and when they failed to do so the typographers walked out. It was a very brief walkout, a job was too important, the money was tight. A day later they went back to work at the *Tribune* and four months later at the *Herald.*

The controversy was worked out smoothly and relatively easily with three of the papers. But Otis would have none of it, he would not stand for this kind of labor bullying, they had tried to push him around, to strong-arm him. There had been the threat of violence in their demands and he would not back down. If they wanted a fight he was always ready. They had walked out on Harrison Gray Otis, so be it, they would never walk back in. He raged at his fellow publishers for giving in so easily. He, Otis, was a man of courage, no one would push him around. Labor unions, he decided, operated by the threat of their numbers against the wealthy, who were usually too rich to want a fight. Well, he was different. So he imported scab labor to take the place of the printers, eulogizing his new workers: "These men came to Los Angeles much as the first settlers of New England came from the old country to escape religious intolerance and to gain personal freedom to worship as they saw fit. Like their hardy, selected forebears, these liberty-loving Los Angeles immigrants were pioneers who laid the foundation for the future growth of their adopted land."

It was the beginning of twenty years of brutal industrial strife. Other unions declared for the typographers; Otis, taking command of Los Angeles business, pushing, threatening, blustering, forced the business and industrial side to mobilize as forcefully and as cohesively as labor; in the past, in confrontations like this, capital had often lacked leadership; this time it had a commanding officer. Soon it was no longer just a labor struggle. Rather, given the bellicosity of both the unions and General Otis, given the tension of the times, post–Civil War America at the height of its industrialization, it was all-out war. A struggle that divided an entire city, and became a focal point for the entire nation, and into which both sides, labor and capital, poured talent and resources. General Otis declared war on the union, then on all unions; his paper grew obsessed with unionism. The police became the instrument of the ruling establishment. There were constant fights between union men and scabs. Los Angeles became known as scab city or, in the pejorative term of union men, "Otistown." Other unions, rallying behind the typographers, boycotted not just the *Times* but any store that advertised there. Union wives would go to a store, order a large number of items, and then as they were being wrapped up, would ask innocently if the store advertised in the *Times*. If the salesgirl said yes, a wife would cancel the order and walk out. Otis was just as fierce, no one would ever accuse him of a lack of passion or courage; he assaulted anyone who gave in to the unions. In 1894 there was a railroad strike which tied up all produce and brought commerce in the city to a halt; it seemed from reading the paper that the strike was not against the railroads but against the *Times*, and against the General personally. The railroad battle became particularly bitter, six companies of U.S. Infantry were brought in to restore law and order.

Now Otis moved again. After the railroad strike ended in 1896, he united all the town's business and industrial leadership in one group, the Merchants and Manufacturers Association, or M&M as it was known, whose basic pledge was to employ no union man, to break all unions, and to make Los Angeles the greatest open-shop city in the world. Any employer who dealt in any way with labor, who employed union men, or who seemed even partially sympathetic to labor's cause, came under total pressure. Owners were first urged and then threatened; the banks, who were of course central to M&M, cut off credit. All of this was the work of Harrison Gray Otis. He loved it; this was battle; this was life. From 1907 to 1910 a state of war existed in the city. At the height of the struggle Otis took to riding around Los Angeles in a huge touring car with a cannon mounted on it. The city became a testing ground for outside interests; what happened in Los Angeles would, it seemed, determine what happened elsewhere in the country. The stakes were very large. The Los Angeles business leaders, spurred by the knowledge that the West was opening up, believed that if they could keep the unions out, they would make Los Angeles infinitely more attractive, both to capital and to settlers, than San Francisco.

Which troubled the business establishment of San Francisco. Labor costs in San Francisco, one of the most heavily unionized cities in the country, were around 30 percent higher than in Los Angeles. Los Angeles was reaping the benefit; by 1910 its population was 350,000. San Francisco employers were telling their labor leaders either to lower their demands or to make sure that Los Angeles was unionized as well. So the San Francisco union heavies began to move their toughest people into Los Angeles. The Structural Iron Workers were the shock troops. They were tough, fearless men, the union men most dreaded by business leaders. In 1910 they arrived in Los Angeles and the city was torn apart. There were strikes everywhere. Management was desperately pouring in tough strikebreakers from the Midwest; the unions had their own gorillas. Anti-picketing laws were enforced by the local police, but the union men paid no attention. There were trials of union men, but something interesting was happening. The climate of opinion, which had been favorable to business in the early part of the struggle—all those good midwestern farmers wanted no part of unions, they were for good, simple, basic Americanism—was beginning to change. In trial after trial the union men were acquitted. Public opinion was shifting to the side of the unions.

On the night of October 1, 1910, there was a series of explosions at the Los Angeles *Times*'s printing plant, giant explosions that literally shook the city. The first was heard at a distance of ten miles, and it was followed by five more. Printers' metal inside the plant became shrapnel. The entire building, given the high amount of gas and the volatility of the ink, was soon in flames. Twenty *Times* employees lost their lives. It was to be a watershed moment in the long, bitter Los Angeles labor struggle. The General was away checking his land-holdings in Mexico when it happened. But when he returned he quickly wrote a blistering editorial in a paper printed at the auxiliary plant his son-in-law had wisely lined up: "O you anarchic scum, you cowardly murderers, you leeches upon honest labor, you midnight assassins, you whose hands are dripping with the innocent blood of your victims, you against whom the wails of poor widows and the cries of fatherless children are ascending to the Great White Throne, go, mingle with the crowd on the street corners, look upon the crumbled and blackened walls, look at the ruins wherein are buried the calcined remains of those whom you murdered. . . ." Later, when Clarence Darrow was about to take on the defense of the two men accused of dynamiting the plant, he was shown the editorial. "But how could anyone make those charges," he asked Job Harriman, one of his local defense assistants, "when the firemen were still poking around in the ruins and no one could have known what caused the explosion?" "Ah," said Harriman, "you don't know Harrison Gray Otis."

Each side blamed the other for the explosion; there had been dynamite incidents involving labor in recent months and the *Times* said it was a bomb. The union people said that gas had ignited the building because Otis took such meager and inadequate safety precautions and ran such a sweatshop. There were reports of printers being carried out of the building earlier in the evening overcome by gas. National attention focused on the case. General Otis went on a national lecture tour, a hero to all American businessmen, someone willing to stand up for what was right. Perhaps, answered Eugene V. Debs, if it was indeed a bomb that had gone off at the *Times*, it had been put there by *Times* executives themselves to turn the tide of public opinion against the unions.

Seven months after the explosion, agents of William J. Burns, the private detective agency hired by management, arrested two men, Ortie McManigal and J. B. McNamara, in Detroit. The arrest was made illegally, as was the extradition of the two men. They were literally kidnapped in the Midwest and taken forcibly to Los Angeles. McManigal broke after a few days and said that his companion, McNamara, had dynamited the *Times,* and that the dynamite and other equipment had come from McNamara's brother, J. J. McNamara, secretary of the feared Structural Iron Workers Union. The trial of the two McNamaras became one of world and national focus, as if this alone could settle all the strife and answer all the questions which had torn Los Angeles apart for so long. Intense fund raising took place on both sides. Clarence Darrow, the greatest attorney of his age, the spokesman for the poor and the dispossessed, agreed somewhat reluctantly to defend the McNamara brothers. All labor and its allies rallied to them; labor men, made suspicious by the nature of the arrests and the way the accused had been spirited to Los Angeles, were convinced that they were being railroaded. There had, after all, been similar cases in the past. Samuel Gompers, the head of the American Federation of Labor, came out to Los Angeles in September 1911 to declare the McNamaras innocent, to affirm labor's commitment to them, and to give a plug for defense attorney Job Harriman, who was running for mayor of Los Angeles as a Socialist candidate. It appeared that Harriman was running well against the *Times* candidate and might become the next mayor of Los Angeles. *A Socialist mayor.*

Unfortunately for Darrow and labor, the McNamaras were guilty. Darrow had a spy in the prosecution camp and became intimately knowledgeable about the case that was building against his clients. He sent his own hired investigators to check out the prosecution's evidence and each time he did he was appalled by how well the prosecution case stood up; there was evidence and it was very strong. The Burns detectives had been trailing McManigal and McNamara long before the *Times* explosion. One day Darrow, dejected and dispirited, walked into the McNamaras' cell and said, "My God, you left a trail behind you a mile wide."

But even as the evidence was mounting that the McNamaras were guilty, so was the average workingman's conviction that they were innocent and a genuine cause. Harriman looked more and more the winner as mayor. Darrow's position in all this was very delicate. He hated violence. He also hated the idea of the death penalty, which now seemed sure for two of his clients. It was possible that the prosecution might use the trial to get at even higher officials in the labor movement. Some labor officials were sympathetic to him on this point, others were willing to risk the trial, indeed anxious for it, even if the McNamaras were guilty. If they were hanged, then labor simply had two more martyrs. It would not be a defeat.

But the *Times* had its problems as well. A victory in the trial could mean a defeat in the long run, the political tide seemed to be flowing the other way, Harriman looked a sure winner; Otis might win the battle and lose the war. Besides, Darrow was a dangerous adversary in court; in a Darrow trial with all the world watching, it might be Harrison Gray Otis who seemed to be on trial. So a deal was worked out. The intermediary in all this was Lincoln Steffens, the muckraker, a curiously innocent man with a rather naïve view of Los Angeles businessmen (both Otis and Chandler told Steffens they were for letting both McNamaras go scot-free, it was only the prosecutor who insisted on trying the case, and Steffens apparently believed them). Steffens, working primarily with Chandler, arranged for the men to plead guilty before the election, whereupon J. B. McNamara would get a life sentence and J. J. McNamara, fifteen years. Otis, a substantially different man from Chandler, was outraged when he first heard the suggestion of a deal. He was, after all, the true believer; he not only wrote those fierce words; the secret of his success was that he believed them as well. Over his dead body would there be a deal. He would see those sons of bitches hanged for what they did. He raged at Chandler, but his son-in-law, a shrewder, more materialistic man, thinking more of the economic future than of the vengeance at hand, calmed him down. He did not want, Chandler kept assuring him, a victory in the case if it meant a Socialist mayor. It took some time, but finally the General listened to Chandler. In the long run, Harry Chandler argued, it would be better for the General's own cause if they took the deal, for the guilty plea would kill the labor movement in Los Angeles, move most fair-minded citizens away from organized labor and undermine labor leaders with their workers.

He was right, and the deal was struck. On December 1, 1911, four days before the election, Darrow, never telling his deputy Harriman of what was happening, pleaded the McNamaras guilty in court. Overnight Harriman's campaign ended; the next day the streets of Los Angeles were littered with Harriman buttons and badges; he was beaten by 30,000 votes. Darrow was shouted down and humiliated in public, called a traitor by those who had long adored him. The Socialist movement in Los Angeles, which had been on a crest in Los Angeles and elsewhere just a day before, was dead. Los Angeles became a reactionary city harboring both political extremes, each bitter, unforgiving, and conspiratorial toward the other.

The role of the Los Angeles *Times* in this twenty-year struggle was crucial, it had led the fight, it had won the war, it had seen and prophesied a conservative victory, and it had been right. The winning general was Harrison Gray Otis; he was proud of his role, more assured than ever by his victory. He knew now who the real enemies of American society were. Such was the special heritage of the Los Angeles *Times,* such was the special passion of the Otis-Chandler dynasty, a passion against labor, against social reform of any kind, against any politicians even lightly tainted by labor. War it had been, war it remained. For some thirty years members of the Otis and the Chandler families joined relatives of some of the victims on the night of October 1 for an annual memorial service for the dead employees, a last rite for a distant past that was not so distant.

That Harry Chandler held sway over General Otis in the decision not to try the McNamaras was of great and lasting importance, for it signified a crucial change in the paper, the end of one era and the coming of another. The age of General Otis, harsh, angry, combative, was passing, and the age of Harry Chandler, one of economic empire, was arriving. They were very different men and they ran very different papers. Otis was a ranter, a shouter, a man rich in bile and polemic; he was not a man to confine his prejudices to his own dining table, he loved the paper because it enlarged his audience and amplified his voice. He was polemical by instinct, journalism was not so much an extension of business interests as it was an extension of personality. Harry Chandler was totally unlike him. He had no real interest in newspapers as a means of informing a larger public or of expressing his own beliefs. He could not write and, unlike a lot of editors and publishers who cannot write, he did not pretend to be able to. He did not seek combat or enemies, he sought empire, he wanted above all to extend his reach and his economic power. Southern California was new and virgin and it was waiting to be taken. He intended to take it and take it he did, mainly through the careful use of his newspaper. The *Times* under him was in no way the diary of a growing city. Rather it was the instrument and weapon of a vast and expanding economic order. Its job was to tame, intimidate, and silence potential enemies of that order, and at the same time to encourage friends and allies, to allow finally the order to grow as quickly as possible with as little interference and debate as possible. Its job was not so much printing information as withholding it; it would sanitize the large, significant political and economic developments within the city, boost the ones the Chandlers wanted boosted, while printing minor stories about crime.

The paper, particularly after the McNamara trial, had huge influence in Southern California, rich, powerful, forceful, potentially ruthless. Behind it always in the early decades of the twentieth century, there was the cold, shrewd eye of Harry Chandler. An awareness of that made economic association with Chandler highly desirable, and his enmity equally undesirable. Harry Chandler was not just a publisher, he personified the existing economic order, an existing order which had, with its victory over the labor unions, destroyed the main obstacle to its will. No wonder that in the future the men of this order would rail against the possible regulation of their activities by the federal government. It was the role of the paper to create and sustain a political system that protected the economic system, to select and anoint conservative politicians, almost always Republicans, and to destroy potential opponents, almost always Democrats. The paper did this with stunning success; it had its own political reporters, Kyle Palmer at the state level and Carlton Williams at the local level, who were not so much reporters as they were fixers and bosses; they moved against opponents with precious little mercy, and they created politicians who were in the image of the *Times*'s editorial page. The politicians whom the *Times* invented and sponsored were of a kind. They were for something called Americanism, and they were against foreign influences, for true industrial freedom, which was a favorite *Times* slogan, against socialism and labor unions and Communism and public housing.

Harry Chandler was a brilliant operator; he thought big, he thought in terms of a larger community, ever expanding. His just share of that expanding city did not mean so much the newspaper that new residents bought as the houses they lived in. He had little time for the feuds and the fights which marked the reign of General Otis. He never sought the spotlight. He never swaggered, his voice was always lowered, but he was quietly and shrewdly ruthless. More, he was never greedy, because a greedy man might create too much opposition. As he planned and divided the future of Los Angeles, he made sure that other key power brokers had a share too, lest they oppose him. Where General Otis might have fought men who were too much like himself, Harry Chandler coopted them and brought them along. There was a slice for everybody, everybody who mattered, that is. The trademark of a Harry Chandler deal was a clique of a few powerful rich men, most of them land barons and dealers, one or two big moneymen with connections to the big banks, a lawyer and a politician or two to grease the local skids and take care of legal problems, perhaps a judge to keep things safe, and perhaps the paying off of a few lower-ranking people somewhere down the ladder. All done of course with maximum secrecy.

His reach was enormous. He was in land, in oil, in shipping, in cattle, in construction, in rubber tires. He helped create new sections of the city like Hollywood, because it was to his advantage and that of his friends, and he helped bring the movie colony to California. The aviation industry came to California in the early twenties because Harry Chandler had taken a liking to Donald Douglas and had written a check for $1,500 and had given Douglas a list of nine other businessmen from whom he could expect similar contributions, a list which, with Chandler's introduction, was like a solid-gold loan. The $15,000 it brought enabled Douglas to move his aircraft company to Southern California. He guided the destiny of Los Angeles, a city built not so much by city planners to their specifications as by economic royalists to *their* specifications. The real estate holdings of Chandler and his friends dictated that the city would spread more and more widely. Similarly, he and his friends helped kill any semblance of major public transportation for the modern Los Angeles, not only because they had a vested interest in extending the city as broadly as they could, but because they believed in the automobile and had a vested interest in the sale of gas, in the use of tires, in the sale of cars, in the construction of freeways, and, of course, in the sale of outlying real estate.

Real estate was at the center of his empire. He was a man of land, and he had a gift for it, a touch for how to put together the big deal, to create a new instant suburb, to entice public officials to bend the laws to make services available. He and his friends had a knack for taking a useless piece of outlying soil and, by means of political leverage, making it profitable, buying at desert prices and selling at new subdivided oasis prices. In the twenties, the years between the wars when a kind of middle-class dream was becoming reality in

California, the dream of a small one-family home, there were some 3,200 new subdivisions started in Los Angeles which produced more than 250,000 new building lots. No one was more important in creating the atmosphere for that growth and no one benefited from it more directly than Harry Chandler. (Indeed, he often neglected his other properties; when Norman Chandler finally took over the Los Angeles *Times* in 1941—he had been over the previous ten years gradually assuming more and more responsibility as Harry Chandler had entered his seventies—he found the paper in serious economic trouble. As an economic entity, it had never been important to Norman's father—Harry liked to deal at a bigger, faster table.) Of the Los Angeles *Times* in the thirties and forties it was said that there was one simple key needed to understand the editorial page on all issues: "Think of what is good for real estate."

It was a power clique that existed almost without opposition. The classic Harry Chandler coup—his trademark was all over it and he was its principal beneficiary—was the decision of the Los Angeles business elite to steal the water from the Owens Valley. The rape of the Owens Valley, for what happened was nothing less than that, is the story of a very shrewd, very rich power elite in a major city determined, in its desperate need for more water, to let nothing stand in its way, particularly the water rights of a separate, distant, smaller community. For that was the key to Los Angeles's growth—water. The climate was wonderful, land was plentiful, the only limit imposed by nature was water; it was thus a powerful political issue. "If you don't get the water," William Mulholland, the city's water superintendent, used to say of additional sources of supply, "you won't need it."

There was, however, one potential source of water, so far away as to be almost laughable, and that was the Owens Valley, some two hundred miles northeast of Los Angeles. Little of the acreage in that valley was irrigated, most of it was wasteland, but the land that did have water was like the Nile Valley, rich and lush. At the turn of the century there was a move made to develop the entire valley and make fertile the barren land. In 1902 the U.S. government under Teddy Roosevelt, increasingly interested in land development, created the Bureau of Land Reclamation with the specific idea of reclaiming otherwise useless land, particularly in the Southwest. By good fortune for Harry Chandler and his colleagues, a man named J. B. Lippincott was named the Bureau's supervising engineer for California. Lippincott, who was to become one of the great double agents of all time, had done considerable work as a water consultant for the Los Angeles city government, and he was well acquainted with the city's power brokers. In June 1903 he and an engineer named J. C. Clausen began surveying the Owens Valley with the ostensible idea of capturing the spill from the Owens River and using that water to irrigate the surrounding land, creating a new rich and fertile development region for small farmers and homesteaders. Lippincott and Clausen began approaching local farmers about relinquishing their water rights; they were seen as friends and benefactors; most of the local farmers and ranchers, hearing that a huge government project was in the air, cooperated. Clausen was clearly committed to the redevelopment of the Owens Valley, he thought the project a natural, but Lippincott had other ideas. Quietly he had begun talking with his powerful friends in Los Angeles about the idea of bringing the Owens water to the city by means of a two-hundred-mile-long aqueduct.

Meanwhile, even as the Owens farmers slept on, a syndicate—which included General Otis and Harry Chandler and a few of their friends—began to make some crucial land purchases. First, in October 1903 they took an option on a 16,000-acre ranch in the San Fernando Valley. The option was relatively inexpensive and a few months later, cutting the original owner of the ranch in on the deal, they bought the spread, paying only $500,000 for it. The land went cheap because it lacked water. There would soon be other comparable deals, one for a ranch of 46,000 acres. It was all very hush-hush. Harry Chandler told a few friends that something was up, he couldn't tell them all about it yet, but they ought to get in on it. Which they, of course, knowing him, knowing how good his word was, did.

It was all of a piece, wonderfully synchronized. On July 28, 1905, Lippincott, against the angry opposition of his engineer, Clausen, recommended dropping the Owens redevelopment plan and suggested that the federal government instead yield the water in the area to the city of Los Angeles. The California reclamation chief ruled for Lippincott and Los Angeles. The next day the Los Angeles *Times* broke the secrecy embargo on the entire story and bannered the possibility of new water for the city. The next step was a bond issue to pay for the land and water rights. Supported by all important factions in the city, it passed by a margin of 14 to 1.

The two pieces of land in the San Fernando Valley, purchased by the Chandler syndicate for about $3 million, were estimated to be worth up to $120 million when it was over. The largest shareholder was Harry Chandler. He held on to the choicest pieces of real estate, and this landholding became the basis for the vast Chandler fortune. He gradually became the largest land baron in Southern California, a partner and shaper in every deal large and profitable, and enemy of all those who might oppose or try to regulate his enterprises. At the time of his death, his estate was worth an estimated half a billion.

If the Los Angeles *Times* was a joke to Perelman and Mankiewicz, it was a joke to few other people who lived in Los Angeles in the thirties and had to deal with the paper socially or politically each day, a situation made worse by the fact that the main alternative to the Chandler paper was Hearst. For all of Norman Chandler's personal attractiveness he published a paper devoid of fairness and justice. He did not know better and he did not intend to know better. His paper slew his enemies—Democrats, labor unions. Norman Chandler was publishing in the tradition of his father and grandfather, and publishing for his peers, the big boys in the California Club, the conservative anti-labor barons of Southern California. The friends of the Chandlers were written about as they wished; their enemies were deprived of space, or attacked. What was not printed was as important as what was printed. The *Times* sanitized and laundered the operations of a rich anti-labor establishment and its politicians; it repeatedly used red scares to crush any kind of social-welfare legislation. It gave its enemies no space and no voice. If a newspaper at its best reflects and hears all factions of the community, letting them play their will out as openly as possible, examining the legitimacy of each case on its merits, trying to limit the emotions and passions, then the *Times* was a manifestly unfair newspaper; it appealed to ignorance and prejudice and it fanned passions.

It was intensely, virulently partisan. The *Times* was not an organ of the Republican Party of Southern California, it *was* the Republican Party. It chose the candidates for the party; if anything the Republican Party was an organ of the *Times*. Fairness had nothing to do with it. In 1934, Turner Catledge, then a young political reporter for *The New York Times,* went out to the West Coast to do a story on Upton Sinclair and his radical political movement. Sinclair was then running for governor in a passionate and heated campaign against Frank Merriam, the Republican candidate. Catledge picked up the Los Angeles *Times* after he arrived, looking for news of Sinclair. There was none. He thereupon looked for a schedule for Sinclair so he could at least find out where the candidate was speaking and perhaps drive out to hear him. He found none. All he could find about Sinclair was a story saying that Sinclair was attacking the Bible and was un-Christian. That night Catledge went out for dinner with the *Times*'s chief political correspondent, Kyle Palmer, and, still wanting to cover some Sinclair rallies, asked Palmer where Sinclair was speaking. Kyle, who was very charming, replied, "Turner, forget it. We don't go in for that kind of crap that you have back in New York of being obliged to print both sides. We're going to beat this son of a bitch Sinclair any way we can. We're going to kill him." Which they did.

Indeed, though Catledge did not know it at the time, Palmer's real role was not political correspondent. He was on loan to the Motion Picture Industry Association, in particular to Louis B. Mayer, and his job was to use the formidable talents of Hollywood against Sinclair. He was very good at this. Though the industry was relatively new, its potential as a propaganda vehicle was immense, and the industry ginned out a series of fake newsreels aimed at defeating Sinclair which played relentlessly at all movie theaters in the state. They were not run as political advertisements but as real news footage, and they were very effective. One showed a crowd of bums allegedly waiting at the California border to pour across in case of a Sinclair victory. Another showed a little old housewife about to vote for Merriam. Why? asked the interviewer. "Because I want to save my little home. It's all I have left in this world." Another, the most effective of all, showed a wild-looking man with a long beard, clearly a foreigner and a foreigner of the worst sort, with a very heavy accent, the kind a Russian would have. He told an interviewer he was voting for Sinclair. Why? asked the interviewer. "Vell, his system vorked vell in Roosia, vy can't it vork here?" But that was the way Kyle Palmer operated, masterminding the Republican cause, cheerleading for it, striking down or ignoring wayward Democrats. In the thirties, in the forties, in the fifties. In

1958, a year in which California politics was particularly turbulent, Don Irwin of the New York *Herald Tribune* went out to do a major piece. He dropped by to see Kyle Palmer, and found him very pleasant, very gracious, and quite informative about the Republicans. What about the Democrats? Irwin asked. "Oh, we don't bother with them," Kyle answered.

That was his job, that was his mandate. He knew whom he worked for and what they wanted. He exercised awesome power over four decades, he was the voice of the Los Angeles *Times;* Harry Chandler had begun it, he had created Kyle Palmer, and in time Kyle Palmer and the Los Angeles *Times* created Richard Nixon. Palmer was that powerful, a Dick Daley of Southern California. He was wonderfully ingratiating, and cynical. He made careers and he broke them, sometimes the same career. He chose the candidates for the Republicans, dictated policies, floor-managed legislation in the California legislature, told governors which bills to sign. He was a journalist and a political writer, but in a real sense he was a kingmaker. As a result of Hiram Johnson's fight against the railroads, all state offices were made civil service in an attempt to remove them from the temptations of corruption, and because they were civil service there was no patronage. Thus, at the most basic level of politics, the usual reward a party could offer, jobs, did not exist. Consequently the party structure of California in the early part of this century was already as weak as it was to become by the 1960's in the rest of the nation. The Democrats were critically dependent on patronage. In the vacuum created by the weakness of the party apparatus, the newspapers became powerful. Thus California was forty years ahead of the rest of the society; it was dominated early in this century by media politics.

Palmer became the political boss of California; whom he chose and whom the *Times* listed on its ballot became the automatic choice of hundreds of thousands of voters on election day, many of them brand-new migrants to the state and therefore particularly dependent on the *Times.* When Frank McCulloch, later to be an editor of the *Times,* as a young journalist first went out to Los Angeles for *Time* magazine, he inquired about state politics and was told repeatedly by sources that he ought to check out a particular question with Mister Republican. *Mister Republican.* The very title seemed to reek of majesty and power, and McCulloch was somewhat surprised to find that Mr. Republican was, in fact, a working newspaperman. The Little Governor, others called him, not always in endearment. His job was to prepare and anoint candidates, to push legislation, to keep the statehouse free of radicalism. Other reporters in Sacramento might wait for several hours outside the governor's office, hoping for a quick audience with the governor, a fast briefing, only to find Kyle emerging from an hour-long session during which he had briefed the governor on what the Chandlers wanted. Kyle Palmer liked to boast of how he had dictated policy for Governor Frank Merriam; how when Merriam had hesitated on signing a bill that would help Kyle and Harry Chandler's friend

Asa Call get his insurance company through a difficult post-bankruptcy time, he, Kyle, had called the tune. Merriam had turned him down as the clock neared midnight on the last day of signing, and finally Kyle—he liked to tell this story himself—had said, "The *Times* wants you to sign that bill, Governor," and finally the governor had capitulated. He always did, Kyle liked to say. There were other quick glimpses of Kyle too, Kyle making all politicians —Goody Knight, Pat Brown, Earl Warren—come by his office to pay homage when they were down in Los Angeles. A requisite part of the L.A. Visit. Homage to Kyle. "Just going by to kiss his ring," Pat Brown would say. Kyle being visited at the same time by Goody Knight, the governor, and by Teddy White, the writer, and seeing White first, deliberately keeping Governor Knight waiting in the outer office. Politicians, after all, even governors, must learn who is boss.

Kyle Palmer at the center of the action. Loving the excitement and the laughter and the wheeling and dealing of it. The phone always ringing. All visiting Republican politicians coming by to see him. Other reporters trying to interview Herbert Hoover in the early forties when Hoover was on a brief visit to California, Hoover brushing by them because he was in a rush, he was due at Kyle's house to talk, to listen, and then to grant an exclusive interview. Everyone needed Kyle, there were always people coming by the office at the *Times,* or going by Perrino's, where he always lunched and held court, the best table, knowing he would be there, in order to get a chance to talk with him. Kyle watching them, telling a dinner guest that a particular person was lunching there only so he could drop by Kyle's table on the way out, and then twenty minutes later watching the person approach the table. A young state assemblyman named Smith, coming by and mentioning a possible race for Congress, and Kyle saying very clearly: No, this was not the year, and if the young man did not take the hint, then a subsequent column saying that Smith was thinking of running for Congress but there was a stumbling block, and the stumbling block (unsaid, it didn't need saying) was, of course, Kyle Palmer. Kyle at the center, rushing back and forth from hotel room to hotel room in 1948 locking up the ticket for his friend Earl Warren with Tom Dewey. Kyle, after all, could broker the California delegation, and Warren was a friend, a bit too liberal perhaps but not as liberal as some liberals thought. The same Kyle who, some enemies suspected, for there was never any evidence, had a good deal to do with splitting the California delegation away from its favorite son, Warren, for Ike in 1952 and helping Nixon get the vice-presidency (Buff Chandler sitting in a booth near the Warrens in Chicago during Nixon's nomination, receiving looks of cold anger from Virginia Warren, was sure herself that Kyle had a hand in it). Kyle always at the center, bringing back nuggets of gossip, wonderfully titillating scraps for Buff and Norman, keeping them on the inside, all the wonderful tidbits that his readers never saw, so that years after he had finally left the paper Buff could turn to Nick Williams, the editor of the *Times,* and say that she and Norman did not seem to be as well informed as they used to be.

He had started under Harry Chandler, apprenticing for the job under Robert Armstrong, the influence peddler of the time, who served as the Washington bureau chief for the paper, and more importantly Harry Chandler's and thus Los Angeles's chief lobbyist in Washington. Armstrong was a former Warren Harding press officer, and he was not only Harry Chandler's man, he was a key aide to Herbert Hoover in the twenties, and he solidified Chandler's connections to Hoover. While Armstrong worked at the national level, Palmer, who had covered his first statewide campaign for the Chandlers in 1918, handled California, building over the years an enormous interlocking series of connections which served as his power base. When Armstrong retired in 1932, Palmer took over both state and national responsibilities. He was very much Harry Chandler's man. Chandler was an activist and he liked the hurly-burly of politics himself, and he was not a man to pass on too much independence to those who worked for him; in effect, Kyle was deputized as Harry's ambassador to politics and to Sacramento. The real decisions at first were Harry Chandler's. Kyle might be on the lookout for young and talented politicians, but the choice was made by the publisher. Harry Chandler knew exactly what he wanted: he created the Axis, a three-newspaper combine with the Oakland *Tribune* and the San Francisco *Chronicle,* so that those three conservative papers, acting as one, could totally dominate California politics.

It was very different with Norman Chandler. He had no real taste for politics, it was tawdry, harsh, clamorous, and dirty. Better to keep politics at a distance. He did this by giving Kyle Palmer a free hand. Kyle Palmer, not Norman Chandler, wielded the great political power at the *Times* because it was known that Kyle spoke for Norman, had his proxy, and since the population was shifting in the state, Southern California rapidly becoming more populous and powerful than Northern California, Kyle became the dominant member of the Axis. He was short and dapper and clever and pleasantly cynical about himself. He was a dedicated conservative, the voice and manipulator for the monied class, and his conservatism was important, but his love of politics was more important. He preferred Republicans but was always looking for someone on the other side of the aisle who would deal as he would deal. He loved the high life and it kept him in constant trouble and constant debts. "I'll never be a millionaire," he liked to say, "because I enjoy living like one too much." There were many wives, and always alimony and money problems, and he was said to be on more payrolls than the *Times*'s, and there was a small scandal when he in fact turned up on the payroll of the local race track, which happened to be a powerful force in California politics. It was even said that Democrats of good heart and conservative inclination built him his last house. The wives tended to look a little like each other and they did change rather regularly. Harry Chandler, who liked Kyle very much, was nonetheless annoyed by Kyle's high living and at one point, when Kyle failed to make good on a note that he owed him, simply moved Kyle from the house he was living in at Malibu and installed the young Norman and Buff in it. This started a legend that Norman and Buff always got Kyle's used houses.

He was a simplistic man. He had been around power and had exercised it and there was an arrogance to him, he knew who counted and who did not. He knew the right side and the wrong side. About labor pickets, he could say, to other journalists, that they simply should be taken away and shot. He knew what a newspaper's function was, and he was not bothered by larger horizons. When in 1959 a young man out of Harvard named Alan FitzGibbon had gone by to talk to him about a job, Palmer had asked what kind of reporting he wanted to do. Foreign reporting, answered FitzGibbon. "Listen, we've got one man as it is in Switzerland and he costs us forty thousand dollars a year," Palmer said, "and he doesn't bring in a single ad." So much for the larger world. He was cocky and brash and self-mocking, and he knew that politics was settled in back rooms among the boys; he hated reformers, not just for what they stood for, but for the way they went about it, so serious, so intense, they did not have any fun with it, there were no handsome dinners, there was no laughter. He wrote in a dreadful florid style, eighteenth-century avuncular. In the late thirties and forties he seized on anti-Communism as an issue, socialism had, after all, been a part of the Sinclair campaign, the threat of radicalism was everywhere. He did not really believe that Communists were anywhere and everywhere, but it kept the Democrats on the defensive, and prevented them from using economic issues against his own people. He was not interested in complicated economic debate; he was for something called the free-enterprise system.

He was a good tactician; he held the imprimatur of the Chandlers for a very long time and he did not want to surrender it. It had come from Harry Chandler, and Norman did not seek it, but Kyle Palmer was always a little wary of Buff, Buff was an activist in her own right, with her own dreams of power, perhaps an ambassadorship, and he knew she resented the fact that he gave the big political dinners, that when Nixon or Warren came back from the East the dinner was always at Kyle's house. Thus Buff, more than Norman, was a potential rival political center. So when Goody Knight, upon being elected governor, tried to make an end run around Kyle by appointing Buff to the Board of Regents, Kyle knew exactly what it meant. It meant that Goody Knight wanted a direct line to the Chandlers, bypassing Kyle Palmer, thus perhaps lessening Kyle's leverage on Goody (whom he liked but who was not, by far, his favorite). So Kyle went immediately to see Buff and asked her, "Well, I guess you want me to go soft on Goody now, don't you?" "No," she said, "what do you mean?" "Well, he's put you on the Board of Regents and now I'll have to go soft on him." "No," she said, giving him precisely the answer he wanted, "you write it just the way you want."

The conservative part of him was very real. He did not like liberals or labor unions; they were to him essentially alien, and perhaps even dangerous if unchecked. He had been born in Tennessee in 1892 and his mind was set in the mores of that period, agrarian, no labor unions, a simpler life. His relationship with Warren revealed his roots. He liked Warren, he was so smart and able and professional, and Palmer respected the fact that of all the major Republican politicians he had dealt with over thirty years he had the least leverage with Warren. For Kyle to push a man for a judgeship with Warren, he would explain, would almost surely backfire. Warren could not be dealt with like that. He was so damn stubborn. "Our Swedish friend," he called him. Our Swedish friend. Swedes were stubborn. Yet he was impressed by Warren, he was smart and shrewd and he was a winner, he knew how to balance the forces, he could move between the labor unions and the world of the Chandlers and somehow satisfy both. Palmer became virtually the go-between for Warren and the big-money boys of Southern California, not just the Chandlers' ambassador to Warren, but more Warren's ambassador to the Chandlers, selling Warren to his more conservative friends in Los Angeles, warning them if they did not take Warren they might eventually get something worse. But he was always bothered by Warren's liberalism, and in 1954, when Warren had gone to the Supreme Court and had handed down the *Brown* v. *Board of Education* decision desegregating America's public schools, Kyle Palmer was furious. His Tennessee roots were very strong. He believed as devoutly in segregation as any Tennessean. Shortly afterward Warren was back in Los Angeles and he went for the ritual lunch at Perrino's. They invited a mutual friend to join them over coffee, and the friend was surprised, upon arriving, to find the political writer of the Los Angeles *Times* berating the Chief Justice of the Supreme Court of the United States. The subject was race and the desegregation decision, and Kyle, normally so cool and cynical, was in a rage, the people of this country would not stand for this decision, it would never work, it would destroy the country, God had not intended the races to mix. It was against everything that made America great. It was not a short spiel, but a genuine filibuster, and it went on and on, reactionary and embarrassing, and finally at the end Warren, always cool, got up, put his arm gently around Kyle Palmer, and said, "Kyle, you and I will always be friends," and walked away.

Most politicians were his friends. They liked him even when he cut them up; at the end he had pushed Goody Knight out of the governor's chair and almost broken his heart, but Goody still liked him. Pat Brown liked him too. Pat was one of the few Democrats who could deal with him, and Pat did it well, coming down to Los Angeles to give his civic-club speeches against crime and drugs—Pat was the hot young district attorney of San Francisco then, it was a good vehicle for a liberal to use to come to power in California— dropping by to see Kyle. Kyle using Pat against Goody Knight as a foil when it looked as though Goody was getting a little too close to labor (there would be sudden references in Kyle's column to the possibility of the popular, well-liked Pat Brown making a try at the governorship). They were all good friends, he liked them all, but of them all there was one favorite, one politician whom he cared for almost as a son, nurtured, protected, and tutored and sponsored, and that was Richard Nixon.

# 4/CBS

The instinct for the high life was there before the war, but the war years heightened it. The best of British society was open to Ed Murrow, he was perhaps the most celebrated American in London in those most passionate years, and so it was open to his handsome young friend Colonel Bill Paley, as it might never have been in self-sufficient peacetime society. Murrow, in fact, was like the ultimate credit card for Paley in England, nothing was denied him, and everything was possible. Some of Paley's friends thought that it was in England during the war that he realized for the first time the real social possibilities that his new power base might generate. After the war, plainly, his social life was more important to him and it was slightly different than before. Then there had been people around who might have challenged him and argued with him, men and women of high intellectual and political accomplishment who were not awed by Paley's position and who were his real peers. After the war he was still the driving relentless businessman, but he was closing himself off more, seeing people a little richer, a little more social, a little less likely to challenge him. His first marriage was finished and Dorothy Paley was no longer there to goad him to see a wide variety of people.

The war had made CBS bigger and richer and far more respectable. It had once been young and vulnerable, and Paley had had to work diligently to sell it. On the eve of the war one third of the network's schedule was commercially sponsored; by the end of the war, two thirds was sponsored. Now the company sold itself, its power and influence was accepted, the war had shown how dependent the society was upon it, how dependent the *powerful* were on it. It was a guaranteed success, and likely to be even more powerful in the years to come, with television presumably just around the corner. Now the company was secure and it needed to be protected, and he wanted to protect himself. Now others needed him more than he needed them, and there were more people added to the staff whose job was not so much to sell the company as to protect it.

In 1947 he was remarried, this time to Barbara Cushing Mortimer. It was the ultimate social marriage for him; Babe Cushing was one of the most beautiful and social women in America. Her father was a legendary Boston surgeon and her mother was determined that she and her two sisters would be raised to marry well and be perfect hostesses; she instilled in them manners and poise and charm, and as a reward for her labors one daughter married Vincent

Astor, another Jock Whitney. Babe was lovely, and slim, and gracious; more, unlike so many of the leading ladies of the world of high fashion and high society, there was nothing mean or hard about her. She seemed to be without envy or guile. One of her special gifts seemed to be kindness. Her taste was impeccable, she was not so much an arbiter of fashion as she was fashion itself, what she did was of itself stylish and where she went became of itself fashionable. She led a certain kind of life effortlessly and perfectly, she could set the best table in the best way and serve the best dinner and wear the best clothes and it was all done as if without effort. Other women took their signals from her, she seemed to take her signals from something inside her. So it was not surprising that Bill Paley, who liked and wanted and got the best in everything, courted her and married her; she was, after all, exquisite and a man seeking perfection would want to marry her. (Years later, bemused by Babe Paley's beauty and elegance and the comparable elegance of one of her peers, Marella Agnelli, the wife of the owner of Fiat, Katharine Graham asked Truman Capote which of these two extraordinary ladies was more beautiful. Capote, aware of the difficulty of the decision—there are, after all, some choices that should not be made—had evaded the question, but Mrs. Graham had persisted and finally he had given in. "Well, my dear," he had said, "I do believe that if they were both in Tiffany's window Marella would be a little more expensive.") It was a very good marriage for Bill Paley and there were those who thought he was marrying not just a woman but a whole society as well. He got Jock Whitney as a brother-in-law, and he entered a new and very elegant world, very rich, very exclusive, and very conservative.

There was one footnote to the marriage. The wedding was very small and private and very few friends were invited. No one from the company. Well, yes, Ed Murrow was invited, but Murrow, after all, in those days was not just an employee, he was perhaps the most admired nonpolitical figure in America, and so it was an honor to be his friend, and of course to have him and Janet at the wedding. But Paley did not want his business associates there. He had, in fact, gone to his colleague Frank Stanton, who had recently become President of CBS, and he had borrowed some film to be shot for the wedding (Bill Paley was never one to throw around his own money; years later Babe Paley complained frequently to friends how hard it was to run a house on as tight a budget as he laid out; why, they could not even take magazines at the house, she said, because he took them at the office) and he had explained that no friends would be invited, it would be very small. Which Stanton accepted, and did not mind until a few days after the wedding, when Paley dropped off the film to be developed at CBS, and Stanton had the rolls developed and looked at them, and yes, there were Bill and Babe, and there were Jock and Betty, and there was . . . *Edward R. Murrow.* Since Stanton was already intensely jealous of Murrow and his immense public reputation and his then almost unique personal friendship with Paley, he was deeply wounded, it was an indication to him that no matter how great his title, how large his earnings (and they became very large), how great his public reputation, he was ultimately no more than an employee. The incident did not readily leave Stanton's mind. In the decade to come, the breach between him and Murrow grew, manipulated in their separate roles and their powerful ambitions as they both were by Bill Paley. They came to despise each other, though each was ostensibly working for the same thing in broadcasting, and when Fred Friendly once asked Stanton why he could not heal this terrible breach with Murrow, Stanton —the memory of the wedding and the film still fresh with him—mentioned the incident as part of the problem.

Paley had the good life now. He had bought the old Pulitzer place in Manhasset, where most of his neighbors turned out to be Whitneys or better. He filled the house with perfect antiques and the world's greatest art and he and Babe constantly looked for new things, and they traveled in great style, once flying into Paris from London in a chartered plane, but having to wait at the airport briefly because their *luggage* was coming in a second chartered plane. He saw fewer of his old friends. Slowly and subtly he was becoming more conservative in his politics. He had once liked Franklin Roosevelt but now he was almost always with Republicans and he sounded more and more like a Republican himself. Not a right-winger, of course, not a Taft man, he was too modern for that, the person he really liked, as did his new closest friends, Walter Thayer and Jock Whitney, was his old wartime boss, Dwight Eisenhower. Why, Ike was just the kind of modern man that good modern Republicans could agree on and get behind.

He was a different man heading a different company. The success of broadcasting in the immediate postwar years was staggering, the beginning of an era of almost mindless profit. World War II had brought America kicking and screaming into the modern world. It had revved up America's industrial capacity, had brought new, highly centralized managerial systems to many American corporations, and had turned the entire society into a dominating world economic giant. America was rich while the rest of the world was poor, and it was the first modern society to experience a genuinely national explosion of middle-class appetites. Those possessions which were limited to the rich in most societies, be it education or housing or automobiles, were by the late forties becoming available to the middle class here. Modern advertising benefited from the explosion and expedited it; it was an age in which advertising came into its own, as the audience became larger and more national, the possibilities for a company became larger, and the percentage of their budgets that large companies devoted to advertising grew as their reach grew larger. Delivery systems that once might have limited companies to regional sales were now wonderfully quick, and that meant that a larger constituency required this new national medium. For twenty-five years, and with only a few minor pauses, starting in 1946 the American economy surged ahead, an entire society seemed to reach for the middle class, for cars and more cars, and houses and dishwashers and washing and drying machines. All things, all luxuries were suddenly possible. There were profits for all, and particularly for the new instrument of mass circulation, radio, and then television. In material terms and in terms of merchandising it was a golden era; rarely in so short a period would so many expensive goods be purchased by so many people.

Yet the economic surge was not matched by comparable political health, the country's two main indexes were not in any synchronization. As the economy surged ahead, America's political spirit seemed to shrink; it was a dark time politically, an era of national suspicion that ended in witch-hunting. This contradiction between economic well-being and political sickness produced at CBS a tension that was almost unique. Here was the network making more money than it had ever made before, profits were so great that the heads of the network ignored the political darkness around them and anything else that might interrupt or slow down that material success. Yet at the same time the network's news organization was supposed to cover the growing national hysteria. It was vital for a great news organization to have, at its core, some form of conscience, but a conscience in that decade ahead seemed likely to prove unusually expensive for the ever richer parent company.

For Bill Paley in the late forties was moving to make his network the unchallenged leader in broadcasting. He had always hated being number two, he wanted above all to be the best and have the best of everything, the best network, the best art, the best friends. (Once when Mike Dann, the programming executive, after long months of delicate negotiations had arranged for a CBS special on Picasso, an achievement of some size, particularly because Picasso spoke some English, he went to Paley knowing that the Chairman, a lover of great art, would be very pleased and fascinated. Paley was delighted to a degree, though he dampened Dann's pleasure by saying yes, Picasso was good, "but I'd rather go after Matisse. You know, Mike, on today's market a Matisse is worth much more.") That NBC with its enormous head start was number one for so many of the early years rankled him, even if the rival network did have vastly superior technical facilities, but there was a certain condescension in his voice when he talked about General Sarnoff, who he felt had no serious interest in broadcasting and did not really care about his profession. CBS during the Paley-Murrow years might be first in prestige and quality, but it was nonetheless number two to NBC in programming, advertising revenues, and profit, and always had been. Bill Paley had never really accepted that status. He had systematically worked to make CBS better in all departments and he had done this by trying at the start to hire the best people; he had, after all, a far greater instinct for talent than Sarnoff and he always wanted the best. Sarnoff was not like that, he thought *he* was the best, and he wanted no one around to threaten him. He once told Ralph Colin, Paley's lawyer, "Bill likes to surround himself with geniuses. I don't want anyone around as smart as I am."

In 1948 Paley was ready to move. He believed that television was coming on very quickly and he had a strong private belief that with the advent of television only the very best in radio would survive, and he also sensed that a lead in radio might carry over into television. Quietly, through intermediaries, he started feeling out some of NBC's star radio comedians, who, it seemed, were not so much restless with NBC as they were with the U.S. government, which was in their eyes taxing them at an outrageous rate. With the help of Lew Wasserman of MCA, Paley devised a scheme whereby the entertainers would be taxed as companies, not as individuals. Jack Benny, for instance. It was a crucial moment, radio was at its zenith and Jack Benny was its biggest figure, the superstar of Sunday at 7 P.M., the man with the highest rating. Benny's contract was up, and he had an opportunity to set a pattern that his colleagues might follow. Here the difference between Paley and Sarnoff was essential. Paley loved entertainment; when a star was coming to CBS for lunch, Paley was at his best, flowers, charm, style. He was in entertainment and stars were everything, he loved being with them, and his touch was sure. Twice a year he would go to Hollywood and meet with his entertainers, and he was wonderful, he was thoroughly briefed and prepared on each star. Are you happy? he would ask. Is the show working? And then he would turn on that charm, *Bill Paley cared,* the charm never seemed to fail.

Sarnoff was different; he was an engineer, a man of radio and equipment. He had never even met Jack Benny, his greatest star. He was convinced that the key to NBC's success was its engineering advantages, its big clear channel stations. *We're the pipes,* Sarnoff told associates, the pipes were the main thing. That was what mattered. He believed that he owned the best theater in the nation and he had the greatest sound system in the world, so he felt he could put on whatever he wanted; the sound system was so good and the seats were so comfortable. He was not a man of entertainment, he was instead a poet of technology, he understood and loved the instruments themselves, genuinely loved touching them, loved the smell and the language of the lab. He had been a protégé of Marconi, his office boy at fifteen, he had risen to early fame in 1912 at the age twenty-one by being the wireless operator who had kept in touch with the sinking *Titanic.* Then he was a visionary in a new and revolutionary field, he would rather be with his engineers than with his stars, he understood their dreams as he did not understand those of entertainers. He had dreamed in the early twenties of installing something called a Radio Music Box in every American home, and by the thirties, when radios were in fact finally arriving in people's homes, he was already pushing for some strange new thing called television. Competitors, appalled by his relentless sense of the future, bought ads portraying Sarnoff as a gorilla wrecking the radio industry and labeling him (they meant it pejoratively in those days) a televisionary.

Bill Paley could not understand David Sarnoff, could not understand the thrust of his life. Paley himself had no feel for the technology. Technology, in fact, intimidated him, he seemed more than a little allergic to Peter Goldmark, the brilliant CBS scientist who had invented the long-playing record and who had pioneered in color television, and Peter Goldmark believed of his boss that no matter how well an invention tested beforehand, when Bill Paley touched it, it came apart. In contrast to Colonel Bill Paley, who loved café society, General David Sarnoff was in his life style at least a modest man, a Russian immigrant who never made any great personal fortune from his position at NBC; indeed, the difference between his wealth and Paley's was something that always bothered him. Sarnoff was a correct and proper man, sensitive about his own simple background and his position in America and the need to be worthy of his place. He was ill at ease with the ostentatious way the Jewish tycoons of Hollywood lived and threw their money around; to his mind it was vulgar and precisely the kind of thing that caused anti-Semitism. He wanted no part of it and he wanted no part of a system that built up stars with huge vulgar salaries (once finding out the enormous amount of money that NBC was paying to Jackie Gleason, he complained angrily, noting that this was more money than he received. "But, General," said Pat Weaver, another NBC official, referring to a Gleason trademarked pratfall, "you can't do the fall").

Predictably, Sarnoff was not anxious to compete with Bill Paley in wildcat money offers for comedians, people of that ilk. He was encouraged in this by some aides who said that comedians like Benny weren't important anyway, their time was past, it was soon all going to be television anyway and people like Benny would not be able to stand up to the camera. So Sarnoff did not meet Paley's offer and Benny switched. The moment Benny left, Sarnoff said: All right, we'll put Horace Heidt in his slot at seven o'clock. *Horace Heidt.* Sarnoff, having failed to adjust for Benny, was now locked into a bad policy and watched the others leave: Edgar Bergen and Charlie McCarthy, Amos 'n' Andy, Red Skelton, Burns and Allen (at the last minute Sarnoff, desperate, switched his policy and paid a small ransom to hold Bob Hope). But Paley had stolen NBC's Sunday night. Horace Heidt was an instant failure and Benny was bigger than ever. Even more important, this was not just the last gasp of radio talent on a dying medium. It gave CBS a vast head start over NBC at the moment in 1949 when television was beginning to come into the mainstream and when ownership most desperately needed programming and stars.

A few days after the raid a very angry David Sarnoff called Bill Paley to ask how he could do it—how he could violate the long-standing unwritten agreement they had not to raid each other. How could he do it?

There was a long pause and then Paley's voice (the one time, said Ike Levy, an early friend of Paley and a large CBS stockholder, he could ever remember Bill Paley being sheepish):

"Because I needed them."

Indeed he had. Within a year CBS was first in programming and revenues and profits. And not very long after that there was a sense among some of the CBS news correspondents that if Bill Paley had needed Jack Benny and Amos 'n' Andy badly a year earlier, he now needed his reporters just a little less. They became a little less important, as David Schoenbrun shortly found out. He was the distinguished CBS correspondent in Paris at the time, a man who seemed almost to own Paris, indeed it seemed almost part of the American perception of France, *David Schoenbrun in Paris.* In Paris he received a phone call from Bill Paley and Bill wanted a small favor. Jack Benny and Mary Livingstone would soon be traveling through France on their vacation and Paley would like David to keep an eye on them. Paley knew how influential David was in Paris, and this was important to the company—crucial contract negotiations were going on with Benny and it was important to show Jack Benny what a great organization CBS was, how much influence it had, *even in France,* and Bill Paley did not have to underscore how important Jack was to the company. To the company. Besides, David would just love Jack and Mary.

Which was not true. Very quickly David Schoenbrun came to dislike both Jack and Mary, and if Jack Benny had been portrayed all those years as a stingy old man, he was not anxious now that he was in France to dispel his own reputation. Nor did Schoenbrun come to like Mary Livingstone, who seemed to be nagging at him all week. But the week passed and finally Schoenbrun thought the visit was over. Then, on the night of July 13, Mary called Schoenbrun and said that she wanted some perfume, the kind that Babe Paley used, which was, of course, the best. They were, she added, leaving Paris early on Monday the sixteenth.

"I need two quarts," she said.

"What kind is it?" asked Schoenbrun.

"I don't know, but it's the best."

So Schoenbrun listed all the great perfumes and finally got to Vent Vert. "That's the one," she said.

When do you need it? he asked. By Sunday night, she said, because they were leaving very early on Monday. "You've got troubles," he said, "because tomorrow is the fourteenth, which is like the Fourth of July, and this town locks up."

"Well," she said, "Bill Paley said you owned this town and you could do anything you wanted and that when Jack saw what you could do we'd be glad to stay at CBS and not go to another network. So do it." And she hung up. "Resign," said Dorothy Schoenbrun to her husband.

But Schoenbrun's journalist instinct was challenged and off he went, racing to Balmain's store; Balmain was a friend and perhaps things could be arranged. But all he found was a security guard. Eventually the security guard admitted that Balmain was at his stud farm in Normandy and after more wrangling Schoenbrun got the private number in Normandy and eventually reached Balmain, who assured him he was crazy, that the store was closed, locked. "But it's for *Jack Benny,*" pleaded Schoenbrun.

"Who is Jack Benny?" asked Balmain.

Finally, after several calls—the honor of France, Schoenbrun assured him, hung in the balance—Balmain surrendered, called the security guard, told him the perfume was in the vault with the mink coats, the vault was opened, and Schoenbrun stuffed a briefcase full of Vent Vert, immensely pleased with himself. He called Mary Livingstone to tell her of the size of his accomplishment.

"Bill Paley said you could do it," she said, by way of thanks.

So Schoenbrun, justifiably pleased with himself over his triumph over French holidays and working habits, wrote Bill Paley describing what he had done. For the company. He never received an answer, which made him think more and more that there was a new scale of values at CBS, and that Sunday-night comedians were far more important than correspondents, even correspondents who owned France and who knew General de Gaulle on a personal basis. Things, he thought, had changed. His wife agreed: when they treat reporters as lackeys for comedians, you should quit, she said.


The take-over of the comedians sealed the balance at CBS. It was now big in radio, which was more profitable than ever, and it was soon to be big in television; by 1954, there were 32 million television sets throughout the country, CBS television's gross billings doubled in that single year, and CBS became the single biggest advertising medium in the world. The real money, money and revenues beyond anyone's wildest dreams, was in television and above all in entertainment. The possibilities of nationwide advertising were beyond comprehension; afternoon newspapers quickly began to atrophy; mass-circulation magazines, which up until the early fifties had been the conduit of national mass advertising—razor blades, beer, tires, cars, household goods—were suddenly in serious trouble, within little more than a decade they would be dead or dying—*Collier's*, *The Saturday Evening Post*, *Look*, *Life*. Television was about to alter the nature and balance of American merchandising and journalism.

At the same time the balance at CBS in subtle ways was also changing. The value of news was being undermined and its position in the company was simply being swept away by the new material force of the entertainment side. Television time was too valuable to be wasted now, it could sell for so much more. Once there had been some sort of uneasy balance, a place for both of them, they had both been of value. Now that was changing. News was becoming less and less important; entertainment was bigger and bigger and costlier and costlier. Besides, the company was beginning to grow in all directions. It was successful and because it was successful it had to be *more* successful. For success created a cash-flow problem; the more successful it became, the more it had to protect itself by diversifying; the more it diversified itself, the smaller something called CBS News became in the overall package. Programming was the key, mass entertainment was the key. (As Norman Corwin, the great writer of CBS radio plays, had already found out. In 1947 he had ridden back from the West Coast with his employer Bill Paley and Paley had suggested that perhaps Corwin's constituency was too small, too specialized. Oh yes, Bill Paley said, he liked it and appreciated it, no doubt about that, but couldn't

Corwin write for a larger audience? It was, after all, a commercial business. Facts were facts, and they had to be faced. Paley himself did not necessarily like the trend but this was reality. A few months later Corwin received a new contract which called for CBS to receive 50 percent of his earnings from subsidiary uses. It was for a writer an intolerable condition and he refused to sign, which was probably what CBS wanted him to do.)

Now, having raided Sarnoff of his talent, Paley moved to make sure that something like this would never happen again, in particular that it not happen to *him* and that the stars or the people representing the stars would not have too much leverage against a network. In the past and in radio days, the networks had not produced their own shows and thus had remarkably little control over what they were showing. In effect, the advertising agencies were dominant. Now Paley moved to take over programming; at first there was some resistance, agencies saying that they would not stand for it, but gradually it began to change. In the early days of television, as in radio, one company had sponsored a show completely; but now it was all too expensive, no single company could afford a show with the new soaring production costs. At first, companies alternated sponsorship on different weeks; then gradually they began to share programs (a tense moment—would the American people accept a program brought to them by both an auto company and a floor wax? Would this create too much chaos in the consumer's psyche?). Then more and more commercials on the same program and finally the cruelest blow of all, back-to-back commercials. All of this because the costs were always going up, no single company could sponsor Walter Cronkite's news program as, for example, Pall Mall had once sponsored Douglas Edwards all by itself (it costs now about $18 million a year to sponsor the CBS "Evening News"). So gradually CBS began to produce and schedule its own shows. It was no longer a pipeline for the work of others. Now it was all bigger stakes, bigger costs, and finally bigger risks. It involved more and more of Bill Paley's time.

He loved it, and he was good at it. He had a sixth sense about a program, whether or not it would work. At programming meetings he was always the most alert, genuinely listening, never underestimating (or overestimating) any idea. There was never any wild adventurous policy here; Bill Paley was not a great innovator; by and large he was content to let others be first and experiment and make the first mistake while he figured out how to improve it. And slowly, as CBS became richer and richer, it all became a vicious cycle, the ratings became the ultimate measure of success. Not taste, not the balance between commercial success and public accountability, but the ratings. No one was responsible. The advertisers wanted the highest ratings because they wanted the biggest numbers and so the networks had to give the advertisers what they wanted, which was, of course, simply giving the people what they wanted. A kind of golden prison.

Radio had been the perfect vehicle for serious journalism by serious correspondents. Journalism at its best is a highly personal art, and radio encouraged individualism. The technology of radio was not complicated or expensive; a correspondent, sure of a story, simply went on the air. Ed Murrow in London, Bill Shirer in Berlin. Almost nothing was required in the way of producers or technical people. One man and one engineer. Nothing to filter the correspondent. It was so inexpensive and so easy to do that it seemed to produce its own freedoms for the reporter in the field; it spun off remarkably little bureaucracy and little control from the home office. Murrow did not want his radio reporters to mimic the wire services; he wanted more original, more reflective reporting. He told his men that eight out of ten stories should be original and not patched by the wires—he would give them two out of ten himself every month or so. He wanted thoughts and ideas, a sense of the issues at play and a sense of the texture of the country they were covering. He also warned them against hamming it up on the air. "I don't want personalities," he said. "If you're a good reporter you'll become a personality. It will take care of itself. Just be intelligent and informed." Which they were; it was a point of pride with the CBS foreign staff that at the CIA the nation's chief intelligence experts began their day with *The New York Times* and the transcript of the CBS "Morning News Roundup." In the world of reportorial excellence, where analysis and intelligence are valued above all else, that was high praise.

Murrow had returned to America after the war with a certain amount of misgiving; he had told Janet that they were going home "to fight the same kind of things we've been fighting here," an odd and dark remark. His friendship with Paley was at its height, and Paley set out to make him a corporate executive. It was an ill-conceived idea and it lasted little more than one unhappy year. Rather than giving Murrow the leverage to make the news section better, it seemed very quickly that the company was using Murrow's name to make decisions that were not necessarily his seem more palatable. The most delicate problem turned out to be his old friend Bill Shirer. They had been good friends, Janet Murrow had been the godmother of the firstborn Shirer child, and in a subtle way they had been rivals as well. Murrow, deft, civilized, the ultimate gifted broadcaster in projecting mood and feeling; Shirer, a far better writer, more cerebral, a more penetrating journalist in dissecting ideas and issues. It had been a friendship not without its edge, but they were men bound to each other by a transcending common experience which had evoked the best of each of them. More, they were identified with each other completely in the public mind, for in those dark days at the start of World War II it had been their two voices, Murrow and Shirer, that the nation had listened to; listeners could not think of one without thinking of the other. After the war, when Murrow had taken his corporate job, he had suggested that Bill Shirer join him as a deputy. But Shirer was wary of the front office, he preferred to remain a journalist. He was, like Murrow, a star, and like Murrow, he had easy access to Paley; they too were bound by the great days of World War II. If Murrow was the most prestigious of CBS journalists, then Shirer was a close second; his was a very big name, particularly among intellectuals. His *Berlin*

*Diary* had been one of the most moving and affecting books of an era, journalism rich and personal.

When Shirer first came home from the war his relationship with Paley had become cooler. In 1946 he was at the peak of his reputation and he was scheduled to lecture in Chicago. Paley, knowing of the trip, suggested that he lunch with Bill Wrigley, the chewing-gum millionaire. Wrigley, according to Paley, was a great personal friend and a serious admirer of Shirer's. So Shirer had lunched with Wrigley and Wrigley had suggested that Shirer do some broadcasting for him at about $2,500 a week. The only catch was that Shirer would have to live in Chicago and broadcast from there. It was not a prospect that enthralled Shirer, who had grown up in Chicago and who did not like that city, and besides, he had been out of America for some twenty years and he loved New York and after years of travel and hotel living he was anxious to live there. So he had turned the offer down. Wrigley had called Paley about it, and Paley had summoned Shirer. *Bill had to take it,* Paley said, and his tone was unmistakable, Wrigley was one of their biggest advertisers. Shirer tried to explain how much he liked living in New York after all those years as a foreign correspondent, but Paley was growing steadily colder and steadily more insistent. Almost too late Shirer realized that this was not a professional thing but rather a loyalty thing. It was good for the company for him to sacrifice his own life style and go to Chicago. "Are you sure you want to turn this down?" Paley asked pointedly, and it suddenly became clear to Shirer that he had crossed Paley in some terrible way, that it was no longer like the old days during the war, and that he was in some way turning down far more than a job in Chicago.

This had started his troubles. There was a certain coolness from then on with Paley, but Shirer was soon to face more serious problems. In those days he had a weekly fifteen-minute radio program going at a perfect hour, 5:45 on Sunday afternoon. He liked the time slot, and the ratings were considered very good. He had a Hooper rating of 6.9, one of the highest on the air, which meant that he had about five million listeners. He had just won a coveted George Peabody Award for outstanding reporting and interpretation of news. He was, however, also on his way to becoming the most controversial major broadcaster on CBS. He was a commentator, and commentators were supposed to have opinions. That had never been very much of a problem in the past, the opinions of the major commentators were largely consensus ones. But now, as the Cold War was becoming more serious, Shirer was proving to be less of a consensus figure. Strong opinions on the Cold War were permissible at such a prime hour, so long as they were the conventional ones. Shirer was critical of the Truman loyalty program for government employees. He was critical of the Truman Doctrine for Greece and Turkey. He made unfavorable comments about the nature of the Chiang government. Very subtly the norm for most major American journalists was becoming an acceptance of the Cold War, and somehow Shirer was refusing to come aboard.

Shirer's sponsor was the J. B. Williams Company and he had experienced no sponsor problems until 1947, when it all blew up. Shirer was subsequently convinced that the problem was not so much with the Williams Company as with J. Walter Thompson, the advertising firm which was handling the account and which did not like his politics. In March 1947 the Williams Company dropped Shirer and hired another broadcaster for the same spot. Murrow, acting on orders, reassigned Shirer to another slot, but without a sponsor, which meant a considerable loss in pay. It was a dreadful precedent because it meant that a sponsor was controlling the time and the broadcaster. Murrow was not very happy with the developments but he was also a little unhappy with Shirer's most recent work; he felt that his old colleague wasn't doing enough legwork any more and at one point he publicly accused him of becoming lazy. The struggle over Shirer quickly escalated into a major controversy, with charges and countercharges in various publications. Shirer claimed that CBS was being gagged and that the network was acquiescing to it. A delegation of pro-Shirer people went to see Paley to protest, which angered the Chairman, and there was a major rally at Town Hall on Shirer's behalf, protesting CBS's pullback from its earlier liberalism. Shirer and Murrow lunched and made one last stab at trying to settle the problem and finally worked out an agreement wherein Shirer would get his time slot back and both sides would say that it had all been a misunderstanding. But Paley was furious. He blamed all the fuss, the pickets and the delegation that had come to see him, on Shirer, and he wanted Shirer out of the company. "I don't want it," he said of the settlement. Then he turned to Shirer and said, "Your usefulness to CBS is over." That was that. Shirer was enraged when during his last broadcast both Murrow and Stanton stayed in the engineer's booth ready to cut him off if he attacked CBS. They were no longer friends. Shirer left to write an unflattering novel based on a Murrow-like character. The last time they were together Shirer warned Murrow: "It's okay for me. I've been through this before with newspapers. But you're going to get it too. Don't kid yourself."

The whole thing had been a major embarrassment for Murrow. He had lost a friend, he had slightly soiled his own reputation, and the issue had raised questions that he could not readily answer. Murrow had decided that a sponsor could select a broadcaster, though it could not control content. It was, he knew, an unsatisfactory answer because the choice of a newscaster defined the tone and style of a show; there was no such thing as pure content. In addition, the Shirer decision meant that sponsors rather than CBS News had the right to advance or limit a given broadcaster's career, and that very quickly the least offensive journalist, rather than the most talented, might rise and be rewarded. It was an unpleasant incident for Murrow; he found that he was speaking with the company's voice, not his own, and it was not a role he relished. Less than a year later he was no longer a corporate figure but back in broadcasting again.

From the start Murrow regarded television with suspicion. It was there, it was clearly going to be important, and he was a communicator, and whatever else it was, it was clearly a powerful forum for communication. But, like his colleagues in print, he felt that television, after all, was somehow another world, closer to the world of show biz than to the purity of ink. In addition, he was not sure it was a good conduit for the transmission of ideas, and he was ill at ease with the sheer force of it, with what he suspected was a tendency to overdramatize, and a likely incapacity for dealing in subtleties. So in the late forties, as television journalism began to surface, the Murrow group regarded its coming with some doubt. Besides, for many of Murrow's boys there was simply far more money in radio. Indeed, only when Murrow himself started appearing regularly on television did it become respectable among them. In particular he was wary of trying any kind of hard-news formula for television; he had never really been a hard-news man, he was always more interested in ideas, in interpretation and in nuance, an essayist at heart, and there was, among those who knew him well, a sense that Murrow was also keenly aware of being Murrow, of being a little different from the pack and speaking for special things in a special way. He was by no means anxious to dilute the impact of being Murrow by the mechanics which made you little more than a ringmaster. So his moves toward television were slow at first. When he returned to broadcasting in 1947 it was to radio and his evening news show; he did, however, do some reporting and commentary for television at the 1948 convention. But he was still wary of television, and the contrivance that might have to go into it. It was a team art with producers and cameramen, sound men, many levels of technicians between the individual journalist and his audience.

The strength of Murrow and his people was that their reporting had been uniquely personal. Now that was going to change. If Murrow were to go to television he needed a producer; he found him while still doing radio. His name was Fred Friendly, and they were brought together by a talent agent named Jap Gude. Their partnership began with a series of albums of radio documentaries—"I Can Hear It Now," Murrow's narration, Friendly's technical ability—which were successful beyond anyone's expectations (students of Friendlyology noticed as the years passed that very slowly and subtly Friendly's by-line on the cover grew larger and larger, until it equaled Murrow's). Then they tried some radio documentaries, "Hear It Now." In 1951 they turned sound into sight: "Hear It Now" became "See It Now."

The combination was an unusual one. It married Murrow's great broadcasting skills, very considerable shyness, and totally enviable reputation with Friendly's great ambition and superb technical skills; indeed, there were those who thought that Friendly was more in control of his skills than he was of his ambition. Friendly was a driving, creative, restless man, at once a creator of his own legend and a destroyer of it. A man who, in the words of one friend, always came equipped with his own precipice from which to jump. He had the capacity to begin a sentence by saying he was just a simple country boy, and end it by implying that he had indeed invented Edward R. Murrow. Talented, insecure, unsure of his own respectability (the name Friendly is an Americanization of the name Freundlich, which was the original name on his mother's

side; his real name was Ferdinand Friendly Wachenheimer, a name which
would not necessarily help his career, and at the suggestion of a Providence,
Rhode Island, radio manager, at the age of twenty he became Fred Friendly).
He took great refuge in Murrow's respectability and legitimacy. He was not
in any sense a journalist but rather an immensely talented dramatist ("Watch
out for Friendly," Murrow would tell journalistic initiates who might not
know of Friendly's instinct for drama, "he doesn't know a fact").

Friendly wanted—and this fitted perfectly with Murrow's conception of
television—to do a *Life* Magazine of the Air. The excellence he brought to
CBS was not happenstance; it was as if he were driven by an inner fury to be
the best. Knowing he was going into television and knowing nothing about
film, he set out to master it. He went to the Museum of Modern Art and
studied film there, looked at everything they had, and from there to Pathé
News and studied what they had, and he demanded to know who was good
in documentary film, and demanded that they explain what worked and what
did not work. And then he set out to find the best technicians around so he
could build the best team. Using, of course, Murrow's name as the come-on.
He was aware that the name could open doors which otherwise remained
closed, and he became absolutely expert at using it: Ed wants, Ed says, Ed feels,
and whether indeed Ed said or Ed wanted or Ed felt is another thing, but it
brought marvelous results of which Murrow was equally the beneficiary.

He was almost overpowering, physically huge, a massive voice and formidable presence; he was not a man to be harnessed to a lesser figure. But part
of Friendly's strength was his excessiveness, his passion, he became excited
about what he was doing; if Fred Friendly were interested in water, the
problems of water, then the whole world had to be interested in water. There
was another thing that set him apart from a lot of others in the world of
broadcasting, and this was the fact that the bigger the show, the more difficult
the idea, the better he responded—he was excited, not frightened, by big
challenges. It was one of his most attractive qualities. If, later in his career,
when he was at higher levels in the corporation, the sweet smell of corporate
success upon occasion got him in trouble, he was to a degree saved by the
restlessness which drove him and everyone around him to excellence, and
which let nothing stand in his way. In 1954 he, at least as much as Murrow,
was the driving force in doing the McCarthy show, pushing and coaxing and
driving everyone around him. And there was one moment when they were
preparing the film that the others would long remember. The team was sitting
around watching a BBC broadcast. It was a very simple show, an announcer
reading *The Canterbury Tales* in Middle English. All very simple. And suddenly Friendly was exploding—"That's it, that's it, that's what this fight is all
about!" And someone else asked, What the hell do you mean, Fred, what does
Middle English and Chaucer have to do with it? "Damnit, for the right to do
what you want, poetry, art, and freedom of speech. The freedom to put on
whatever you want without fear."

But there was another part of Friendly that was not so entirely worthy, that was show biz, that preferred effect to reality, and when later he was running CBS News and he was told he should hire a particular reporter who had done very well in a difficult assignment, he had answered, "Yes, yes, he's good, I know he's good, *but is he a star? I only want stars.* " His talents suited Murrow perfectly, Murrow could control his excesses and Friendly could dramatize what the staider, shyer Murrow wanted to say and do it with great professionalism. Television, for better or worse, did require a show-business component, and Friendly provided that, marvelously tailored to Murrow. All of which made "See It Now" a great show, too good, finally, for its own good.

By the late forties there was already growing political pressure on broadcasting. What was to become known as McCarthyism had already surfaced in the networks in terms of blacklisting—political pressure against the network and sponsors not to use certain actors and writers who had been tainted by earlier left-wing activities. CBS, which had at one period been considered the most liberal of the networks, quickly became the most sensitive to these organized pressures from the right, and acquiesced more readily than its competitors. It was a time of great cowardice, and many talented people were kept off the air. (Years later, when it was all over and McCarthy was a demon of the past, Paley met Zero Mostel at a party, and since Mostel, who had been the victim of some of the worst of the blacklisting, was now enjoying the fruits of a second career, Paley complimented him on the brilliance of his talent, and Mostel, ever bitter and irreverent, looked at him coldly and said, *"If I'm so talented why didn't you put me on your network?"*)

There was a cleansing of the airwaves, and it extended, some thought, to the News Department. Some liberal magazine critics wrote that CBS was silencing some of its more liberal commentators, and the Shirer incident had left a bad taste in many mouths. Murrow found himself expending more and more energy in trying to protect members of his staff who were being attacked and red-baited by the right. As early as 1948 Murrow was depressed by the pressures of political reaction at home and the rising tension between the United States and the Soviet Union and the gradual stifling of free debate that the Cold War tension was producing. He was hardly a figure of the left; if anything, he was a freedom-of-speech and First Amendment man, a classic political centrist with a certain sympathy for the underdog, and a personal social inclination to move in the highest circles. But he was becoming uneasy with the increasing timidity of his own profession and his own company. Loyalty was not a major political issue, and he did not think broadcasting was doing anywhere near the job it could do in defining freedoms on behalf of those accused of disloyalty. In 1948 he encouraged his old friend David Lilienthal, the head of the Atomic Energy Commission, a man under attack for his own views, to make a speech criticizing the broadcasting industry for failing to use its influence to create an understanding of the new and complicated atomic world which America had entered. Lilienthal showed Murrow his projected speech and was surprised when Murrow asked him to make it even tougher. What was significant, of course, was that Murrow, the towering figure in broadcasting, felt so limited by the failures within broadcasting and his own lack of leverage that he had to go to an outsider to get his own views aired. Later that same year, when Lilienthal was under mounting congressional pressure to resign from the AEC, he met with Murrow again and found his friend in an unusually dark mood, talking about growing pressures against him. He told Lilienthal he did not think he could continue to broadcast much longer unless he used more and more anti-Communism in his commentaries. His contract at CBS was binding, but he was already talking about what he was going to do next.


So it was that the moment of the greatest profit in the history of merchandising was coinciding with two other events: first, the arrival of the McCarthy era and the height of the Cold War, and second, the coming of national television. It was not just the right wing that broadcasters were worried about, it was the government as well. The government was increasingly sensitive to the power of broadcasting, and this sensitivity was matched by a parallel awareness within the networks of just how many legal ways the government had to lean on the networks. All of this produced a desire among network executives not to do anything that might offend either the government or Madison Avenue. (Nothing reflected the timidity of the CBS corporate side so much as the way the network handled the status of its first Moscow correspondent, Dan Schorr. Though Schorr went to Moscow in 1955, two years after the death of Stalin and one year after the censure of McCarthy, he stayed there on per diem, as if he were a part-time employee. He was, in fact, a bureau chief. Schorr, somewhat unhappy with this lowly status, was told by Sig Mickelson, the president of CBS News, that management preferred it that way "because it's too soon after the McCarthy red scare and network blacklisting to have a Moscow bureau officially entered in the CBS directory.")

This nervousness was magnified by the added dimension of television. Television at once made the networks infinitely more powerful, and in the eyes of the networks (if not the government) infinitely more vulnerable. A story in *The New York Times* or a major magazine about the public relations machinery of the Pentagon might appear, and might also pass in the night, perhaps activating a few senators to look more closely at the issue. Similarly, the same show done on radio might have little effect. But the same material, with film, programmed to an audience of 15 million was a different thing; it became a political cause célèbre. For television represented very simply a quantum jump in journalistic and political power. The audience was so much bigger and the emotions the medium generated were so much greater that in many ways the traditional laws of journalism were no longer applicable. And very subtly and unconsciously there was a compensating narrowing in scope, in adventurousness on the part of the network, in terms of what could, would be said.

There is an unwritten law of American journalism that states that the greater and more powerful the platform, the more carefully it must be used and the more closely it must adhere to the norms of American society, particularly the norms of the American government; the law says it is better to be a little wrong and a little late than to be too right too quickly. (Television, Robert MacNeil wrote in *The People Machine,* acts as a cheering section for the side that has already won.) Part of this is born out of a need for respectability and a desire for legitimacy and a fear of disturbing the status quo, and part of it is born out of a very healthy sense that if the platform is that powerful, personal opinions are almost dangerous, that no one journalist should be that powerful. So television's major figures became in effect prisoners of their power. ("If Walter Cronkite would say on television what he says on the radio," said Lyndon Johnson, who was an inveterate radio listener, "he would be the most powerful man in America." But for precisely that reason, by the time that Cronkite was Cronkite he could not say those things.) Television was simply too powerful. It moved and reached a whole new mass of citizens who had never been readers, and even among those who had been readers it often brought a wholly new and often quite emotional dimension of response.

Thus almost from the start of television there was an unconscious decision at the networks to limit the autonomy of the network news show. The corporation which was risking so much would need to have greater controls, more restrictions. Murrow to a degree escaped that problem for a time because of his unique position within the company, his personal connection with Paley, but eventually even he, with so much capital stored up, expended it and found himself a liability to management. How that happened, how the single greatest broadcaster of an age used up his welcome (while still doing high-level, quality, accurate work), is a tale worth examining.

For a time he was special. If he was not exactly untouchable he was certainly less touchable than other mortals. But even Murrow was aware that he had to ration the number of controversial shows he could do. In addition, he made a deliberate decision to make himself palatable to his public. If from the beginning in 1951 "See It Now" exemplified in a near-breathtaking way the best of television, restless and adventurous probing into complicated areas of social and political problems, then there was also, very soon, another face of Murrow, and it was called "Person to Person." The program existed from the start much more in the world of show business than of journalism. Higher Murrow and Lower Murrow, the New York critic John Lardner called the two shows. A pure celebrity jaunt into the homes of the famous (and often fatuous). Murrow, who was not an especially good interviewer, was coupled with people who often had remarkably little to say; celebrityhood, the status of being well known for being well known, did not necessarily imply intelligence. The "See It Now" people soon referred contemptuously to the "Person to Person" staff as "the buttonhole makers." Joe Wershba, one of the most talented men on the "See It Now" team, remembered how incongruous it all seemed, the same Murrow who did those distinguished documentaries and who was broadcasting's most civilized voice doing silly patter with instant, often empty-headed stars. The first time Wershba heard of the new show seemed symbolic: Murrow was doing a show on Berlin and he was standing there at the Reichstag with Howard K. Smith and Smith was interviewing Ernst Reuter, the mayor of Berlin, and Murrow mentioned casually to Wershba that he was starting a new show with celebrities and that one of the first guests would be Lucille Ball. Lucille Ball? Wershba, who loved and worshipped Murrow, looked at him and thought: the Reichstag, Ernst Reuter, Ed Murrow . . . Lucille Ball!

Murrow from the start was clearly embarrassed about his other persona. He would periodically mutter excuses that he had originally intended to bring a wide variety of noncelebrated Americans—blacks, Indians, laborers—to the show, but it had not quite worked out that way; and from time to time he said that he did it as a way of "picking up a little change for Johnny and Jesse" (Johnny Aaron and Jesse Zousmer, his two writers), though, of course, the assumption was that he picked up a little change of his own. Paley bought the show from him for an estimated one million dollars, a gesture that was at once generous but not entirely altruistic, since it gave Paley an extra hold on Murrow ("I gave Ed the only money he ever made," Paley liked to say of it later, and it was clear that in a way the money was for far more than the show).

But it was also obvious that Murrow's reason for doing "Person to Person" was more political than financial, that it was a deliberate and conscious decision to broaden his base. Up to then he was totally political, often dark, increasingly controversial, more and more hitting raw American nerve. If he continued with "See It Now" alone, then he faced mounting political opposition with a base that lay increasingly in the elite alone, with the elite itself increasingly on the defensive. He would be a newscaster who could see only the darkness. But "Person to Person" gave Murrow a good-guy incarnation, noncontroversial, built him up as a star and a celebrity himself, and a celebrity who had a lot of friends, none of whom was controversial. He was aware of what he was doing. Why do you do it? a friend once asked him in a kind of "Say it ain't so, Ed" tone, and he hesitated for a minute and then he answered that he did the show he hated in order to do the show he loved. Later he told friends that he had been able to withstand the storm after the McCarthy broadcast partly because of the broader base of popularity he had picked up from "Person to Person." It had made him a figure *trusted*, tolerated, and indeed liked in many more homes. Naturally the two staffs, bitter in their rivalries, were acutely aware of the duality of Murrow's broadcasting incarnations: the "See It Now" people hated the idea of their great man, their prized resource, indulging himself in something as frivolous as "Person," and the "Person" staff hated the idea of the risks involved with their star in something as controversial as "See It Now." After the McCarthy show, when the senator began to pressure Murrow, Johnny Aaron charged into Wershba's office one morning and yelled, "See—you get in with shit and you get shit on your hands!"

What is significant about the Murrow-McCarthy show is that it was so significant: first, that it took so long in coming; second, that it loomed so large over what was clearly so flat a landscape; and third, that it caused such a storm. For it would have been truly unforgivable for television and for a team with the reputation of Murrow and Friendly to fail to do a major documentary on McCarthy (or indeed to wait much longer than they did to do one). It would have turned CBS in general and Murrow in particular into a joke. For there was never very much doubt or mystery about who Joe McCarthy was or what he was doing; when he was finally gone there was not very much left but the smell of evil; even in the sixties and seventies his excesses appeared gross and many who had been his supporters earlier were not very anxious to invoke his name. The only thing real and serious about him was the fear he generated; he came at a time when the society faced new and terrible inner fears and those fears were no longer dormant. He was reckless and cavalier from the start; his was an essential challenge to freedom of speech, and an astonishing number of people were cowed, or at least semi-cowed. This was true in print journalism and it was even more true in electronic journalism; if the center did not fold, it did not exactly hold either. Murrow was classically of the center, he was the best of broadcasting. Yet he did not act. McCarthy had given his first speech in March 1950, and that year passed, and then 1951, and then 1952, and then 1953. Starting in 1952, friends began to ask Murrow and Friendly when they were going to take on McCarthy. When? It was a very good question. (Indeed, when Murrow finally did take on McCarthy in 1954, Murray Kempton, the columnist, happened to be with Roy Cohn, McCarthy's closest assistant, and Kempton watched the program and told Cohn that he and McCarthy were finished. Why? asked Cohn. Is Murrow that strong? No, said Kempton, but if Murrow was moving, then it was a sure sign that the center was turning on McCarthy.)

McCarthy was a fascinating example of the weaknesses of traditional journalistic objectivity. He was a senator and thus a great public figure, and reporters could write down what he said, and as long as they spelled his name correctly and quoted him correctly, they were objective. But what McCarthy said word by word was meaningless; it was the invisible part, the inflection, the distortions of scene, the lack of follow-through, the lack of seriousness, the cumulative record or lack of record which was missing in all accounts. He made his charges and went on to his next charges, and objective journalists were considerate enough not to bother him with his record, with what he had said the week, or month, or year before. What was most desperately needed was to report on McCarthy in context, to bring some perspective to a long course of events and charges. But if the norm of the society is corrupted, then objective journalism is corrupted too, for it must not challenge the norm, it must accept the norm.

Murrow had done some radio commentary on McCarthy and he was already restless with his own limits in this period. He thought the clouds were darkening. A number of close friends had lost their jobs and he had put several people on his own rather than the company payroll as a means of protecting them. When his old friend Raymond Gram Swing had been forced out of his job at the Voice of America after a clash with McCarthy, Murrow took him in at CBS in a nonbroadcasting capacity, Ray Swing wrote for the show but he did not appear on it. But Murrow's own problems were mounting. CBS News had censored a dispatch of Murrow's from the Korean War which was critical of General MacArthur and this had led to a considerable wrangle between Murrow and Paley (Paley in years to come believed that his troubles with Murrow stemmed largely from this moment). It was a bad sign. So much of Murrow's special freedom and special status derived from the fact that he was the last CBS newsman to have easy access to the boss and that he had the personal connection born of the World War II association.

So even as he started to prepare his material on McCarthy, Murrow was in a particularly dour mood. He was seriously disturbed by the company's and his own failure to move earlier on McCarthy. Indeed, congratulated on the show, he would point out that it was not so much, that Scotty Reston of the *Times* had been saying the same things for eight or nine months. In addition, Murrow knew better than most that in journalism it is not so much what you cover which is important as what you do not. The decision to omit is often as important as or more important than the decision to commit.


A year before the McCarthy broadcast, the "See It Now" team had been told to start collecting film, though there was no talk of the exact or even rough date for the show. Murrow's own failure to act had become an issue among journalistic colleagues. Yes, he had done a number of shows protective of civil liberties, on people being pressured by the broader forms of McCarthyism, and yes, in 1953 he did a show about Milo Radulovich, the young Air Force Reserve meteorologist asked to resign his commission because of the alleged radical beliefs of his father and his sister. But he had not gone after McCarthy himself, and there was an undercurrent of criticism among colleagues and among people in the civil-liberties field. When they brought the matter up to him he answered yes, the show should be done, but he was searching for the right vehicle. That a take-out on McCarthy required some kind of special vehicle surprised some of his friends. When they persisted and demanded that he use his extraordinary forum to make an attack upon McCarthy, a speech explaining what McCarthy was, Murrow would pull back. No, he couldn't do that, it wouldn't do any good, he answered. He was aware of the problem, but it wouldn't do any good for him to simply go on television and make a speech against McCarthy. His friends were not satisfied with his answer, and for that matter, neither was he. Those who knew him well, and knew how abhorrent McCarthyism was to him, thought he had become a kind of prisoner to broadcasting's growing political cautiousness. But in late February 1954 his staff started moving ahead on the show. Murrow may have known that the Army was also going to attack McCarthy, and any further delay on his part was thus intolerable. There were also reports that McCarthy himself might go after Murrow; the senator was already telling people he had documents proving that Murrow was a Communist. When Murrow finally decided to go ahead he warned everyone on the staff what was possibly in store. He did a dry run with everyone there, asking if they had anything to hide, anything that might come out later that could embarrass them. At the same time lawyers were getting ready to go through every aspect of Murrow's own past, in preparation for McCarthy's expected counterchallenge.

There was also a part of Murrow that was uneasy about using his forum in what would inevitably be so personal a fashion; if McCarthy had broken the rules of civilized political behavior, then this meant that any responsible journalist portraying him accurately would similarly have to break his or her own rules and built-in restrictions. Television was too powerful to be used as an adversary instrument. He was worried about the balance of his McCarthy show. (Later, after it was over, when Gilbert Seldes, the fine critic, scolded him for its imbalance, Murrow was not offended, indeed was sympathetic to Seldes's point.) When he finally decided on the means of covering McCarthy it was a simple one, to let McCarthy destroy McCarthy; "the terror," Murrow said after screening some of the footage of McCarthy, "is in this room."


Murrow and Friendly kept the idea of their show a secret inside CBS as long as possible on the assumption that the less the twentieth floor knew, the better, which was, of course, fine with the twentieth floor; Paley was not about to order Murrow *not* to do a McCarthy show, any more than he was likely to order him to do one. But he certainly was not very eager to be associated with it, and there was as much institutional distance put between the program and CBS as possible. No, CBS would not buy an ad to announce the program, and no, they could not use the CBS logo in their ad. So Murrow and Friendly bought their own ad and paid for it out of their own pockets and signed it with their own names. (Twenty years later, Paley, irritated by the use of this fact as evidence of his distance from the McCarthy show, insisted that they had never come to *him* directly for permission to do the ad. Of course, the entire CBS structure was carefully arranged so that they would not be able to approach the Chairman.) Paley, asked at the last minute, did not want to screen it (both Murrow and Paley knew what his reaction would be: Ed, do we really have to do this? this is killing me). Paley did suggest that Murrow offer McCarthy equal time, a suggestion Murrow found useful, he had been thinking of the same idea, and this had the added advantage, when McCarthy demanded equal time, of not looking as if they were backing down. (Paley once mentioned to Eisenhower that he had given McCarthy the thirty minutes of free time. Ike was appalled: "Good God," he asked, "what did you do that for?") They also asked Sig Mickelson, the nominal head of CBS News—though in fact Murrow and Friendly ran a virtually separate shop—if he wanted to look at it, but Mickelson declined, he had screened nothing else of theirs. The most potent and sensitive television show of a decade was thus broadcast without any prior screening from CBS superiors; such a thing would be inconceivable a decade later.

Right before they went on there was a phone call to Murrow from Paley: "Ed, I'm with you today and I'll be with you tomorrow." A nice call. The show, of course, was very good. Long overdue and very good. Murrow afterward was haunted by the fact that the program was so late. Maybe, thought one colleague who knew him and understood the complexity of his position at the company, it was a little overdue because those who have the power to do things like the Murrow show attain that power precisely because they are not, in delicate situations like this, precipitate. Murrow let McCarthy speak for himself and then he added his own devastating epitaph: "We will not walk in fear one of another, we will not be driven by fear into an age of unreason. If we dig deep in our history and our doctrine, and remember that we are not descended from fearful men, not from men who feared to write, to speak, to associate and to defend causes which were for the moment unpopular . . ." It was a good show. On its most important test it passed without a blemish— it caught McCarthy for what he was, not for what he said he was. The finest achievement of the show was that twenty years later, in another era when civil liberties were far stronger and there was far greater willingness to defend them, the McCarthy show could be aired without any apology or explanation.

After the show there was a nice, gracious call from Babe Paley. She was Bill's proxy. The deniability had to be kept open in case the storm was too great and Murrow or the program eventually had to be sacrificed. The reaction was intense, but McCarthy had already overstepped himself, not just against Murrow, but against the Army, and finally against the Republicans. The tide was turning and the Murrow show was part of the turning. Not everyone at CBS thought so. Some members of the CBS board were furious and started putting pressure on Paley to bring Murrow under control: was he, they demanded to know, an independent entity, some sovereign state who could do whatever he wanted? The next day Fred Friendly ran into Jack Van Valkenburg, the president of the television network, and rode up in the elevator with him. He was the first member of management Friendly had seen since the show, and as they rode up they talked about the weather and their families, and the fact that Friendly was supposed to move to the Riverdale section of New York, but they did not talk about Joseph R. McCarthy. The reason, of course, was that reactions to the show were not yet in, and no television executive was about to commit himself before he found out which way the wind was blowing. A few days later Stanton called Friendly into his office; it was one of the rare times Friendly had ever been in Stanton's office. There was no talk of the quality of the show, whether it had been bad or good, or needed to be done. Just the problems and the pressures it created.

"A lot of people think you may have cost us the network," Stanton began. He meant lawyers and people in Washington with political connections.

Friendly countered by mentioning the avalanche of supportive telegrams, 100,000, an exceptionally large number.

Then Stanton, he who had invented the analyzer of taste, a machine to find out what the public wanted, took a sheaf of papers and showed them to Friendly. A special Roper poll that he had commissioned on the subject of Murrow and McCarthy. Not surprisingly, it showed that more people believed in McCarthy than Murrow (an elitist figure taking on a major political demagogue does not overnight get 51 percent of the vote), and that 33 percent of the population felt Murrow was a Communist or a Communist sympathizer. The pejorative parts of the poll, of which there were many, were all circled in orange crayon. Stanton asked Friendly what he thought of these statistics.

All the more reason to do the show, Friendly said. Which ended the conversation, except that it was an extraordinary insight into the way broadcasting management regarded journalism—not whether it was the right show done in the right way, but according to the pressures that it had to bear. Not whether it was a good show, but what the vote was. Friendly went away, as he and so many others often did, wondering whose voice he had just listened to. Was it Stanton speaking for Stanton? Or was it Stanton speaking for Paley? Somehow passing the word as it is often passed in broadcasting, to let Friendly know that there were limits to all this, you could do this show but you better be careful not to do any more like it.

In all this, both before and after the McCarthy show, Bill Paley stayed as far away from Murrow as possible. There was, of course, no reason why he should be directly involved. But those working on the programs were aware of his distance, of what might be called the deniability of it all. Which is fine, except in later years Bill Paley liked to recall those days, and as they were re-created in his mind, there was this one big trench, there were, yes, standing alone, Bill Paley and Ed Murrow, shoulder to shoulder. As he reminisced like this he often wondered why people did not give him more credit for his part in what he had done for the show.


"I'm with you today and I'll be with you tomorrow." A nice phrase. A lovely ring of loyalty to it. Except it wasn't true. The McCarthy show, and several other incidents, but principally the McCarthy show, proved to Paley that "See It Now" and Murrow as currently produced were a potential liability (if not already a liability) to the network. There was simply too much autonomy for so reckless a figure as a journalist. (In times to come Paley would talk about Murrow and journalists. Oh yes, Murrow was a great fellow, a great journalist. No, it was not true that it had ended badly between them, there were letters to prove what good friends they were, though of course Murrow had a brooding sense of life. Very difficult, dark fellow. Always taking too many risks in the war. Not a happy fellow. Too bad, really. Then, confronted with evidence of growing separation between the two of them, always came a small lecture on journalists. They were all alike. They claimed to be objective, but none of them really were. Had to watch them all. They all wanted to make personal comments. Had to fight with them all. Even the best of them, like Murrow.

Keep them from taking things away from you. Breaking the laws that they themselves had to set. You had to watch them very carefully.) There was always a fine balance between the prestige and respectability which Murrow and people like him brought the network, the laudatory columns that Jack Gould wrote in *The New York Times,* and the tension that these same shows increasingly created in Washington, on Madison Avenue, and on the CBS board itself. As television became more powerful, the reaction became more powerful. Now Paley more and more heard a certain playback from his business associates: Murrow had too much autonomy, Murrow was too independent. Besides, Paley was an out-and-out Republican now, an avowed Ike lover, and when his reporters made the Administration angry they were making his closest friends angry. It was not that Murrow's autonomy was growing; indeed, if anything it was the same as or less than it had always been; but the vehicle he was using was becoming more powerful. In January 1952, for the first time, according to Nielsen, there were more television than radio sets turned on between 9 P.M. and midnight. In 1954, the year that Murrow took on McCarthy, television's gross billings jumped 50 percent over the previous year. The candy store was becoming bigger and bigger, and it did not want, nor would it any longer tolerate, any obstreperous employees, no matter how elegant their manner.

The new affluence was not by any means matched by public accountability. As for the McCarthy show itself, which CBS would later cite as one of its finest hours, no less an authority than Murrow himself felt it was a symbol not of the network's strength but rather of its unwillingness to accept responsibility. The show had been done by Murrow, not by CBS, he told his friend David Lilienthal somewhat bitterly. He thought CBS had backed away from it and he felt strongly that on an issue of this gravity the network should have accepted responsibility for the program. What he had feared, he told Lilienthal, was now taking place, a huge growth of power and influence without a comparable willingness to accept responsibility for it. Murrow's show on McCarthy had probably salvaged television's respectability, without it the medium would have been disgraced. Always sensitive to the charges that the networks failed in the area of public affairs, senior officials would later point to the McCarthy show. The implication was clear, that they did programs like this all the time, that there was a steady stream of network courage from Murrow to "The Selling of the Pentagon" (which, significantly, was screened endlessly by layer upon layer of CBS people before it was finally broadcast— no more could a journalist, no matter how good, go straight to the public with that precious time).

The reality was quite the opposite: in exercising his freedom Murrow guaranteed that neither he nor anyone else would ever again have that much freedom or autonomy, that never again would there be a figure of broadcasting bigger than the network, and with a following and respectability and leverage so great that he could, by walking out, damage the network. The network instead would control the journalists, the shows, the hours, and, to a considerable degree, the subjects. No correspondent would ever again set the parameters of freedom on so mighty an industry. If journalists wanted that much freedom, let them found their own newsletter like I. F. Stone.

So now, quite systematically, CBS moved to emasculate Ed Murrow. First to limit the number of "See It Now" shows. Then to control the hour they were shown. Then to change the name. Then to take the show away completely. Then to separate him from his producer, Fred Friendly. It was all done very deftly, and perhaps not even that consciously; corporations are often good at this, the increments of limitation were small, just enough to cut him steadily down but never really enough to drive him away in anger. Within four years "See It Now" was dead, and in six years Murrow himself was gone. It was never Paley who did it; more often than not the hard decisions were administered by Stanton, so that Murrow seemed angrier at Stanton than at Paley and talked about the need to get back to the old days of the good Bill Paley, when it was just Bill and Ed.

Gradually, as Murrow was cut down, his place as a spokesman for broadcasting was taken by Stanton. The CBS prestige figure. A much safer one too. The Statesman of Broadcasting, as he became known. Stanton would give the good speeches and make the public statements and lobby for the good things and get in time the requisite awards. It was as if by *saying* that the company was doing something good and noble then it was in fact *doing* something good and noble. It was the ideal device, for when Murrow had made similar speeches it looked as if he were complaining about the lack of excellence, but when Stanton did it, it was always taken as a promise of future excellence, a promise not necessarily fulfilled.

The signs of the decline were small at first. The unwillingness of the company to pay for ads for the Radulovich and McCarthy shows. And then at almost the same time as the McCarthy show a quick tangle with Senator John Bricker, who was sponsoring an amendment to limit presidential treaty-making powers. His real aim was to diminish the United Nations and the covenants the United States had entered there, and he wanted U.N. covenants approved not just by the Senate and the House but by state legislatures as well. On "See It Now" Bricker debated with Senator Estes Kefauver; Murrow had insisted that each side bring a legal expert and that annoyed the Bricker people. Then it turned out that instead of an equal split of the half hour the Kefauver side by chance got 11 minutes and 23 seconds to 8 minutes and 53 seconds for the Bricker people. The Bricker people were angry and their anger was passed on to Stanton, who wanted to give Bricker another shot. Murrow was furious; he felt as a journalist that if you were fair the public knew it and supported you, and that if you started caving in to politicians it would simply feed their hunger. His attitude was regarded in the company as naïve, he did not understand the complicated realities of television and government and John Bricker was given another shot. For Murrow it was a dark omen.

He soon had sponsor problems as well, which made him more vulnerable to the network. In the past he had been sponsored by Alcoa, which was somewhat removed from the average marketplace pressure. Alcoa had remained loyal despite a considerable amount of grumbling from some of its board members. It had given Murrow complete editorial freedom, which meant that he was not dependent upon the network for that freedom. But the McCarthy show and a sympathetic program about J. Robert Oppenheimer had caused the rumbling against Alcoa to mount and to become more direct. At the end of the 1955 spring schedule Alcoa decided not to renew. At almost the same time the quiz shows had been born, a marvelous new national tranquilizer, and this was not "The $64 Question" of the old radio days, not in super-rich America in its super-century, this was "The *$64,000* Question." A super-contest, a human horse race with money dangled in front of the humans. Watching the first run of "The $64,000 Question," Murrow was appalled: the huckster part of the network had always frightened him; he had a somber sense about the commercialism of America, made even more somber by the knowledge that the industry from which he sprang was one of the prime offenders. Now his worst fears were being realized. At the end of the first run he turned to Friendly and asked: "Any bets on how much longer we'll keep this time period?"

Not very long. Soon after the final "See It Now" show of 1954–55 Murrow and Friendly were summoned to Paley's office. There, the Chairman, solicitous of their work, generous in praise of it, wondered if it wasn't too confining, coming up every week (at a regular hour of prime time, something he neglected to mention). Wouldn't it be better to do eight one-hour shows? Wouldn't this be more thorough and more satisfying? Murrow, wise to these games, asked at what hour they would be shown. Paley said at night. Murrow asked if he could continue the half-hour show if he preferred. Paley, who had a particular genius for saying no without saying the actual word, made clear there would be no more regular half hours. The schedule was tightening at the expense of public affairs; there were more important and more profitable things to be shown. The loss of the time slot was not the only setback for Murrow. Rather, the decision to go to a full hour changed the whole balance of the show and it cost Murrow and Friendly heavily in terms of spontaneity, and in some subtle ways it cost them in autonomy. For now, with that much time and perhaps without a regular sponsor, shows had to be scheduled long in advance, and agreed upon in consultation with others in the company. No longer could they just go out and do whatever they wanted and put it on at *their* hour.

The problems and the pressures mounted. General Motors said it would sponsor six of the eight, then reneged when it turned out that one of the shows was to be on the vice-presidency. GM decided in advance that this would end up as an attack on the then Vice-President, Richard Nixon, and canceled out. One of the documentaries was on the farm problem and starred the Secretary of Agriculture, Ezra Taft Benson. The Republicans decided that damage had been done to him, and asked for equal time (hardly expecting to be granted it). Murrow protested, but CBS gave the Republicans the time anyway. Murrow came very close to resigning. By the next year, the 1956–57 schedule, there were still as many "See It Now" shows, but they had been moved to what was considered a particularly weak hour, Sunday at 5 P.M., no longer in good if fluctuating evening hours. It was a sign of the network's lack of commitment and pride in the show, as if saying yes, we have to do it and this is the only slot we can bother to spare. Murrow, once the pride of the network, was a little more of a stepchild each year. Besides, shows that he considered excellent, programs on Tito and Chou En-lai, which were major journalistic beats, were followed by panel discussions that were clearly an attempt to dilute the effect of what had just been presented. The humiliations as far as Murrow was concerned were mounting, his influence was waning. Murrow himself was increasingly despondent, and depressed by the entire business. It was one thing for Murrow to have to contend with fighting powerful enemies in the field to accomplish what he wanted; it was much worse when he had to contend with powerful enemies in his own house.

The ultimate for Murrow was a program that he considered one of the least important of the year 1958, a minor, noncontroversial show. In March, he did a program on statehood for Alaska and Hawaii. It was what was known in the business as a soft show; what distinguished it was how ordinary it really was. It balanced spokesmen, some for, some against, statehood. One of the pro-statehood people, Harry Bridges, the labor leader, was asked about a statement by a congressman from Lackawanna, New York, named John R. Pillion, that Bridges would control the Hawaiian delegation. Bridges answered quite properly that Pillion was crazy. Pillion, not that crazy, demanded equal time (claiming, among other things, that the show was not balanced because the anti-statehood people were older "and by the trick of association the implication was willfully created that only 'old fuddy-duddies' oppose statehood . . ."). It was a silly letter and a silly request but CBS again caved in. Sig Mickelson, bringing the news to Murrow, felt there was a terrible finality to the decision, that to a journalist of Murrow's stature the decision to put on a dissent as silly as this on a show as mild as the Hawaii-Alaska one for reasons of such self-evident cowardice was shattering and in some way terminal. It was not unlike handing Murrow a live grenade, and he knew that Murrow would accept it as such.

The decision was straight Paley; Mickelson had argued against it and had mentioned the implications, that it might drive Murrow from the network. Paley was unmoved by any arguments; the only possible explanation for Paley's adamancy was that he *wanted* to put a live grenade in Murrow's hand. Murrow, predictably, was horrified and shocked. The decision had been made without any consultation and it was clearly a surrender to the most pointless kind of political pressure which would only bring on more political pressure. But the significant thing was not just the decision; it was the manner of the decision and the manner of the treatment. It was the end of an era, Murrow was now being treated no longer as Murrow but as a mortal, like any other television journalist. He had expended his precious capital from World War II, he had subtly been brought down to another more mortal level. The special relationship was gone. Murrow wrote a very strong letter to Paley saying that the decision to put Pillion on without even consulting him undermined his relationship with the company and made the future of "See It Now" dubious. It was precisely the letter Paley wanted and expected. A few days later Paley met with Murrow and Friendly. Murrow said that this had all become untenable and that he or Friendly had to share in the decisions on who was to get equal time when it involved "See It Now."

"But," said Paley, "I thought you and Fred didn't want to do 'See It Now' any more."

Murrow argued that he wanted to talk about the equal-time regulations —of course he wanted the program to continue. But it was already past that.

"I thought we had already decided about 'See It Now,' " said Paley, and with that both Friendly and Murrow knew that "See It Now" was dead.

For Murrow it was his most painful moment at CBS; the end of the program about which he cared most deeply.

"Are you really going to destroy all this?" he asked of Paley. It was, he pointed out, the most remarkable piece of machinery in electronic journalism.

Paley said yes, he was, he could not stand the constant stomachache it was giving him, the pain was killing him.

"It goes with the job," Murrow answered. And that was it.

On the way back to their office Murrow turned to Friendly and said, "It's all over."


It was a time of considerable personal pain for Murrow; he loved CBS and he had in a way made CBS News what it was and now he felt himself slowly being shunted aside. He was too proud to complain outright, but gradually he began to change, to become more depressed. There were hints and allusions about his troubles to friends. Small gripes which would have been unspoken in the old days. A different quality, friends thought, a little more bitter.

One day around then Charles Collingwood—who was closer to him than anyone else at CBS, Murrow's real personal heir apparent—told Murrow that he was caught in a dilemma, a choice between doing a show or going on a much-needed vacation.

"I'd go on the vacation," Murrow said.

Collingwood mentioned that he rather wanted to do this particular program.

"It doesn't make any difference," Murrow answered. "You're only important around here as long as you're useful to them, and you will be for a time. And when they're finished they'll throw you out without another thought." It was a side of him Collingwood had never seen before, but it was to be repeated more and more. They were squeezing him and pushing him aside and he knew it, but they were doing it in a subtle way, the increments were small, and he was torn by his personal anguish and his loyalty to his own people. He did not want to complain, he did not want to go public and damage the very news organization which he had helped create. But it was bad and getting worse.

In October of 1958 Murrow went before a meeting of radio and television news directors in Chicago and said: "And if there are any historians . . . a hundred years from now and there should be preserved the kinescopes for one week of all three networks, they will find recorded, in black and white or color, evidence of decadence, escapism and insulation from the realities of the world in which we live. . . . If we go on as we are then history will take its revenge and retribution will [catch] up with us." Paley was furious; Murrow had betrayed him, had fouled his own nest. Ed Murrow had betrayed Bill Paley, who had, in Bill Paley's view at least, made him rich and famous. The most dangerous thing about what Murrow said, of course, was that it was true; it was bad enough for people like Jack Gould of the *Times* to write along these lines, but at the upper levels of broadcasting Gould could be discounted, he didn't know the realities of the industry; he was not, and this is the key word, *realistic.* But to have this said by the single most respected man in the industry was very damaging. Criticism coming from *within* was too much. (Some sixteen years later when Roger Mudd, the apparent successor to Walter Cronkite, gave a rather mild speech at Washington and Lee University indicting network public-affairs policies, the response at the higher level of CBS went far beyond anything Mudd had said, and the reason was simple: he had recalled all too clearly the vision of Murrow, and a man who thought he was a little better than broadcasting, and those critical assessments, so admired when they were turned to other subjects, were not at all admired when they were turned to the home industry.)

The professional relationship was ruptured; Murrow thought Paley had betrayed the best show on the network, and now Paley thought Murrow had bitten the hand that had fed him very well.

There were still footnotes to come. That same year the fabled quiz shows turned out, as many had suspected, to be fixed, and cast a very long shadow over broadcasting. In 1959, Stanton, speaking to the same convention Murrow had addressed a year earlier, outlined stricter new codes and said there would be no rigging. The speech drew no headlines. Gould saw nothing new in it. Kidder Meade, a public relations official for CBS, called Gould to push the story. What story? Gould asked. Stanton said *all* programs. Gould, beginning to catch on, asked if that meant Murrow as well. Call him, Meade said, he's in New Orleans. So Gould called Stanton and he said yes, he meant "Person to Person" as well, it would all be spontaneous and "Person to Person" guests would be denied advance questions. Either that or there would have to be a disclaimer saying that the show had been rehearsed in advance. It was an appalling performance by Stanton—certainly the company's revenge against Murrow. The mild pre-show preparation for "Person to Person" in no way paralleled the rigging of the quiz show. Murrow, of course, was furious; he issued a statement to the *Times* saying that Stanton had finally revealed his ignorance of all news matters. It was a great day for CBS and its images; the two foremost figures of the company arguing their disputes out in the front page of the *Times.*

It was not by chance that Stanton was Paley's instrument in this attempt to humble Murrow. Murrow was in decline; at his best he had represented the talented individual, unchecked and unrestrained on the new open, enterprising network, the triumph of one man and his skills, his freedom reflecting the company's confidence in his common sense and good judgment. But now the network was becoming too big, too powerful, too rich to tolerate the skills of an individual any more, a man who thought he was better than the company. The company must come first. A correspondent would be allowed to rise only with the company's permission and only when it brought greater glory to the company. Now it was Stanton who was on the rise. Stanton did not just speak for the company, he *was* the company, he would never criticize it, each word from his mouth was as if written by Bill Paley. He was the total extension of Bill Paley's will. Which made him safer as a spokesman of broadcasting than Murrow. He could speak to the same audiences of the same soaring dreams for broadcasting and he seemed as committed as Murrow to the First Amendment, but he was, and this was of the essence, never really critical of broadcasting. Frank Stanton was a very ambitious driven man, but his ambitions were not really his own, they were always tailored to the wishes of the company. He was accustomed all those years to think, not of what was good for him, but of what was good for Paley and the company. Years later, when he had left the company involuntarily with no small amount of bitterness, some friends asked him what *he* thought about a major magazine article, somewhat unflattering both to himself and to the company. "Bill won't like it" was his first response.

Stanton had no feel for entertainment and he rarely meddled in that side. He was a man of systems and he brought structure and discipline and a sense of respectability to the sprawling company. That sense of order was something deep and visceral to him, it was not something he had learned while at CBS, he had simply always been that way; indeed, as a little boy delivering newspapers in Dayton, Ohio, he worked diligently to make sure that his route, unlike those of other newsboys, did not sprawl, that it was concentrated in one area. He therefore traded off customers who were outside his base camp to other paper boys, creating a highly dense and profitable enterprise. He had little intuition or feel, he seemed the ultimately constrained man, tightly wound, totally controlled, always holding back his own emotions, a Puritan among so many Babylonians. (In 1968, Peter Goldmark, the brilliant CBS inventor, demonstrated the new video-cassette system by showing two films. One was a British educational film called *The Sex Life of a Grasshopper,* a very serious and much-praised if slightly dull examination of a grasshopper's procreative instincts. Goldmark, who thought the film excellent if somewhat turgid, was stunned when Stanton was furious with his choice. Stanton considered it lewd and immoral, and improper for CBS use.)

It is not surprising that one of the things that had helped advance Stanton's career in the early days was his attempts to quantify the success of various programs, studies that later led to the rating system. There was a kind of surgical cleanliness about him and his work, even his handwriting seemed too precise, almost too perfect. His taste in art was very good, but it was cold, almost sterile. He loved order, his own desk clean every night, the new CBS building, his creation, cold, austere, almost frightening. Black Rock, as it was known within the profession, reflected him more than Paley; he had picked the granite for it himself, and sometimes behaved as its guardian, fighting off those CBS employees who wanted to break the clean lines and desecrate his vision by performing such human and uncorporate acts as putting photos and posters on the wall, or putting more plants in their offices than his rulings decreed. (Once an executive from the Museum of Modern Art, making a tour of the building with Stanton, awed by the ferocious interior cleanliness of this massive building, so many rules so carefully obeyed, had finally seen Paley's office, very different from all the other offices, with its warmth of color and richness of furnishing, including a cigar-store Indian, a small offering to Jewish roots. He turned to Stanton and observed: "Well, here's one that got away from you, Frank.")

Stanton's father had been the manual-arts teacher and supervisor in Dayton and he had subscribed to all the manual-arts magazines, and Stanton had grown up with a love of design. It was Frank Stanton who had come up with one of the great CBS inventions, the tiny dot on the CBS stationery that ensured that all CBS letters typed by all CBS secretaries would begin at the same point and have the right balance. He was acutely conscious of image, he cared about it and thought about it. He had a doctorate in psychology from Ohio State and he was one of the few Ph.D.'s in America who insisted on being called doctor. In the cheap huckstering world of broadcasting, a world he never felt at ease with, the title seemed to add respectability and prestige. It was also a Stanton law that a news program could never be called a "show," it had to be a "program."

He was the embodiment of the modern corporate man. Indeed there was something chilling about him. He had almost no personal life. His world was his work. He was totally driven, he worked seven days a week, often eighteen hours a day, and he liked to let people know it, it added to his legend, and thus his power at the company, that Stanton never slept. If a CBS reporter did a particularly good broadcast on a Sunday, then there might be an immediate phone call from Frank Stanton, which not only flattered the journalist but advertised the fact that Frank Stanton was on the job. Even his idiosyncrasies added to his legend: an electric system that lit up his desk and let him know when his secretary was away from her desk, and another system that, when he went home at night, held an elevator and also readied his car. We must not, after all, waste our good minutes.

So he was the company man. Paley ran the entertainment side, and Stanton ran the corporate, and he was the official spokesman of the company, and the two men balanced their talents, which were so very different, to the benefit of each other and the company. It was Stanton's job to be out front, to speak for the company and to protect Paley. Paley did not like venturing into the public sector, there were too many vultures out there. Paley did not like to go to Washington and above all he did not like to testify before Congress, because he knew he might lose his temper. Paley did not tolerate fools lightly, and he felt there were a lot of fools in Congress. Stanton loved to testify, he loved the moment, the spotlight, sitting there at the Capitol with the senators all prepared and the reporters waiting with their pencils poised. There was no better congressional witness than Frank Stanton, he went down to Washington several days early and he stayed in his hotel room and he went through practice runs, and he was always prepared and gracious. He loved being the first witness at a hearing and CBS lobbyists were told to make sure Stanton was first, because the first witness was usually the star, drew all the attention, made most of the headlines. Besides, senatorial questions tended to become sharper as a hearing progressed, which meant that the first witness often had an easier time.

It was an art form and he had mastered it, the art of being at once flexible, deflecting hostile senators, and speaking for broadcasting and for the First Amendment, cloaking in a subtle way the enormous profit they were all making. He always looked so good and so proper that when he was testifying the idea of the vulgarity of most of what television did, and the obscene amount of profit it made, seemed very distant. Yes, he always seemed to be saying, there had been faults and excesses in the past but CBS was pledged to a better day. His voice, thought some colleagues, was always more true and sure in arguing for public service when he was *outside* the institution than when he was *inside* it. Yet it seemed indecent to connect him to the Wasteland. It was not surprising that he soon gained the reputation of the Statesman of Broadcasting. He stood for doing all the best things in all the best ways in broadcasting, and when it was over he had made more than $20 million out of CBS.

He and Murrow had disliked each other from the start and they had been rivals from the start, a rivalry that Bill Paley had played on and encouraged. Both were young ambitious Protestants in a company where the proprietor was sensitive about being Jewish (indeed, for a time during the McCarthy years Stanton had been known on Madison Avenue as the *goy between,* the Protestant who would do Paley's dirty errands). Stanton had been envious of Murrow's wartime reputation, and Murrow in turn had a few years later been envious of Stanton's growing position in the company, his influence and his access to Paley. That access seemed to be increasing precisely as Murrow's was diminishing. Murrow was privately contemptuous of Stanton and often called him "the bookkeeper." Sometimes he called him the "image maker." Once, Murrow told a friend in the news division that it had been their job to make CBS better than it was, but it was Stanton's job to make CBS *look* better than it was. Murrow had never realized that it was Paley who had changed, that Stanton existed purely as an extension of Paley's new will as Murrow had been an extension of his older one, and that everyone was playing his proper role in this. Murrow to the end tried to believe in Paley as he had once been and refused to admit what he had become, and he believed the great hope of CBS was getting back to the good Bill Paley of World War II.

In 1956 the quiz scandals had provoked one of those periodic bursts of network good intentions to do more in the public sector. Promises were made about moving into one of the most neglected areas of broadcasting, a good high-level network children's show (perhaps to be produced by all three networks in conjunction; a promise made to the FCC and forgotten as soon as the pressure from the quiz shows died down). Now in March 1959 Stanton promised that CBS would sponsor regular one-hour documentaries in prime time. Once a month. Then perhaps biweekly. Then perhaps once a week. Then the kicker: "if the networks are permitted to retain their present structure . . ." It sounded like a documentary series that was suspiciously like "See It Now." But without Murrow. Then the corporate genius showed: on the Murrow-Friendly team it was Murrow's name that was special, Murrow whom they feared. At the same time they knew that Friendly was intensely ambitious, delighted to be associated with Murrow. But they also knew there was a part of him that wanted a reputation of his own, "Fred Friendly Presents." Or Fred Friendly inventing the new Edward R. Murrow. Besides, Paley and Stanton dealt all the cards, they knew that with everyone in CBS News desperate for air time it would be impossible for either Murrow or Friendly to say no to any major offer of time. So in effect Paley and Stanton were offering the same time as "See It Now" enjoyed, but they were splitting Murrow from Friendly.

They made Friendly an offer he could not refuse. He was called into Sig Mickelson's office alone and offered the new monthly documentary. Friendly was surprised by the offer, he wondered whether it had been cleared with the twentieth floor; but Mickelson assured him that not only had it been cleared, but this was what *the twentieth floor wanted.* Was the offer made to the Murrow-Friendly team? Friendly wondered aloud. No, answered Mickelson, but Murrow was going on sabbatical anyway. Murrow certainly would be the reporter on some shows but other correspondents would be used.

So the predictable happened. Murrow encouraged Friendly to take the job, the offer was simply too good, the time too precious. Friendly was the best documentary producer at CBS; if someone else took the assignment and failed, it might be bad for television journalism. It was a moment of corporate genius, only men with great corporate skills could work out arrangements like this. Murrow was split from Friendly. "See It Now" became "CBS Reports" (once Paley and Stanton, searching for a name for the new show, asked Murrow for a suggestion. "How about 'See It Now with Ed Murrow'?" he answered sardonically). They gave air time to Friendly, who was in no way a corporate threat, and cut Murrow off from any regular and direct access to television air time. He was now even more of a supplicant. Friendly, in retrospect plagued by guilt, always wondered whether he should have resigned then and there, whether he had let down the man who had made him. He did not resign. And Murrow was now a great name, but a name without air time.

Which was exactly what the corporation wanted, as Friendly found out a year later when Murrow was coming back from his sabbatical. Friendly wanted to fill alternate weeks of "CBS Reports" with a show called "Face the Nation Debates." Two major figures would debate each week. His superiors quickly picked up on the idea, for them it was an ideal show, it filled the time slot easily and inexpensively and had its own built-in answer to any charge of imbalance. If, for example, the spokesman for the liberal side was beaten, that was his and liberalism's fault, not the fault of CBS. Friendly from the start had wanted Murrow as the regular moderator. Paley bought everything but Murrow. "What's wrong with Howard Smith?" he asked. "What have you got against Eric?" One did not cross William S. Paley lightly.

So Murrow returned with his future at CBS very much in doubt. If he was an ornament to his profession, his superiors deemed him almost too risky a one. Sig Mickelson, negotiating a renewal of Murrow's contract, found that he had come up with a figure acceptable to both himself and Murrow but that after months and months of querying he could never get a response from management. Murrow himself had little taste for the fight any more, particularly a fight against his own people. He was tired now and eroded physically and spiritually. His dark and somber view of life was coming all too true, and in particular he was depressed about his own profession. He saw it more and more a vehicle for manipulation rather than for broadening understanding. All those years of smoking, all that nervous energy and tension had taken their toll. Those cigarettes and drinks were finally depressants, not stimulants, and now he was worn out. His future at CBS was very unclear. Fortunately for him in 1960, with his contract still unsettled, Jack Kennedy was elected President and Murrow came under consideration for the top job at USIA. The other leading candidate, ironically enough, was Frank Stanton. Kennedy was advised by friends that Stanton was a far better bureaucrat but that Murrow offered his administration badly needed prestige, particularly among liberals who were still suspicious about the senator's own timid conduct during the McCarthy period. He considered the choice for some time, there was no love lost on Stanton, but the appointment was also a way of getting Stanton out of CBS. Finally he decided that Murrow's name would help both his administration and the USIA. The Kennedy offer, said Janet Murrow years later, was a "brilliant and timely gift."

When the offer came he was ready to go. It was hard to believe that this was the same man who just twelve years earlier had reigned supreme in his profession and who had received an under-the-table offer from NBC asking him to write out whatever figure he wanted, *just name the price.* Now he was almost unemployable in broadcasting. The day the news came from Washington he was in the middle of anchoring a radio show called "Background," a Friday-for-Sunday taping. He was sick of it all by then and he wanted out, totally out, so he turned to his colleague Blair Clark and asked if Clark would fill in and anchor the program. Clark said he would and asked Murrow what he should tell the listeners to explain Murrow's absence. Murrow answered, not snappish, but with cold suppressed fury, "Tell them I've gone to serve my country."

On April 27, 1965, Ed Murrow died of lung cancer. It had been a long and painful and exhausting illness. That night CBS, under its head of news, Fred Friendly, broadcast a memorial program "to the most distinguished commentator in its history." It was made up of tapes from his television broadcasts and voice-overs from his radio days against still photos. It was powerful and moving, not least because the friends of his who happened to narrate it— Sevareid, Collingwood—were the best voices of broadcasting. The afternoon before it went on, Friendly received a phone call from Kidder Meade, Paley's chief PR man.

Is anyone going to speak for the company? Meade asked.

Friendly answered that he didn't know what that meant. This was a show, he said, about Ed Murrow, who had worked for CBS.

Are you going to be on? the PR man continued.

No, said Friendly, it was going to be very simple. Murrow and some of his boys.

What do you think, said Meade, of the idea of the Chairman going on for two minutes?

Oh, said Friendly, slightly taken aback, do you think he really wants to?

Yes, said Kidder Meade, I'm very sure he'd like to.

And so on the occasion of the death of Edward R. Murrow, William S. Paley, who had done so much to make him and almost as much to break him, and who wanted to be sure that the company got credit for Murrow, went on the air to say that he personally would miss Ed Murrow, as would everyone else at CBS.

In 1973, as Watergate moved its way, Janet Murrow watched television news regularly and often felt frustrated by the lack of commentary. She thought that of the various commentators Bill Moyers most resembled Ed, and he was on public television. Her son, Casey Murrow, lived in Vermont and taught school and did not own a television set.

# 5/ The Washington Post

He was the incandescent man. Phil Graham walked into a room and took it over, charming and seducing whomever he wished, men and women alike. No one in Washington could match him at it, not even, in the days before he became President, John F. Kennedy. He was handsome and slim and when he smiled, at first shy and then bold, everything stopped. He was the Sun King. He was brilliant and witty, alternately serious and imaginative, tracking his own intellectual course, away from the accepted judgments of the day, thoughtful, reflective, then suddenly almost in the same sentence irreverent, almost blasphemous. He seemed to stand there at the great parties in the greatest homes of Washington, a city which deified, above all, power, and mock great events and great men; though, of course, he was a man who had sought power, and who had, by the strength of his marriage, his newspaper, his own personal brilliance and energy, a direct line to almost any figure of power in the city. He could laugh at it all, the foibles and the folly of man, and then retreat at night and make a quick call to Felix Frankfurter, or Dean Acheson, or Lyndon Johnson, or even Dick Nixon. In one sense he was different from most men in Washington: he cared as much about the power of the mind as he did about the naked tangible power of votes and influence. Yet that difference simply made his a more electric presence. No one, no politician could work a room the way he did. Everyone wanted to talk to him, to sit next to him at dinner, to bask in the excitement and originality of his mind, to feel the quick warmth of his smile and his wit. When his daughter Lally was graduating from Madeira, the top finishing school of Washington, he had been asked to give the graduation speech, and the headmistress had introduced him as the publisher of *The New York Times*. He had grinned and without missing a beat had begun, "I can't tell you how pleasant it is to be here at Foxcroft today. . . ." He seemed to fly higher and faster than anyone else, there was a quality about him that was almost feverish; it was as if he were racing against time. He had no time for or interest in conventional ideas, he was always thinking of deeds at once adventurous and risky; he was in the best political sense an adventurer. He had only contempt for those who played it safe; life for him was something that you played almost as much as you lived. He loved the excitement of it all, moving the pieces; above all, he hated boredom and people who bored him.

Everyone adored Phil Graham. In a city of heavy conversations, phrases portentous with conventional wisdom, he was funny and outrageous, his laughter was contagious, as he laughed others laughed too, and for a moment felt freer. People in Washington were so serious, and even the bright men were politicians and in the end they were selling something, usually themselves; he was different, if he was selling himself it was by mocking the very act of being important; he was irreverent before it was fashionable. He also had that rare ability to make almost everyone he dealt with feel for a brief few moments that he or she was the most important person in that room. In a city where most important people were hell-bent on proving that *they* were the most important people in the room, that was a priceless gift.

He seemed in the somber atmosphere of Washington a man who thought that life was fun, who loved the wild gesture, and who also loved to deflate the pomposity of the moment. During the Eisenhower administration he had once been seated at dinner with George Humphrey, Ike's Secretary of Commerce designate, and his wife. The Congress had just ordered Humphrey to sell some stock and Mrs. Humphrey had gone on at great length protesting the injustice of it all. She was very whiny about it and, worse, she bored Phil Graham. "Mrs. Humphrey," he said, "in this town complaining about being the wife of the Secretary of Commerce is like burping at the dinner table in Cleveland."

Nor did he spare himself from his irony. He loved to tell of how the one man he wanted to meet was J. Robert Oppenheimer, and how he had schemed to arrange a meeting, and finally after much conspiring of various friends it had been arranged, and Phil Graham had cautiously and shyly approached the great man at a dinner party. As he neared Oppenheimer's circle he heard the great man discuss a book he had just finished, and wonder of wonders, *Phil Graham had just read it too.* He had bided his time and then at just the right moment, Phil Graham had given his interpretation of the book, being careful to be erudite without being too self-conscious, and feeling pleased that he had spoken deftly, and the great man would be impressed. "Is that your real opinion of the book, Mister Graham?" he heard Oppenheimer say, and he nodded his assent. "Then it is clear, sir," said Oppenheimer, a man of true intellectual arrogance, "that you have not read it in the original Sanskrit." Or the grand gesture: Phil at a fancy publisher's dinner noticing that his friend Clare Boothe Luce was wearing absolutely grotesque shoes, and asking her why. Clare answered that she had constant trouble with her feet. At that point Graham asked to see the shoes, took them, threw them away, and picked her up and carried her out of the hall. He loved the outrageous gesture, the fun of it.

Yet he was a serious man, perhaps in some ways too serious for his own good, with a penchant for taking the flaws in the world a little too personally. He had arrived in that town as a very bright young man at a glorious moment for very bright young men, the height of the New Deal, he was a Frankfurter law clerk, the brightest of the bright young men—not just a Harvard Law School graduate, not just a former editor of the *Harvard Law Review* (the distinguished Harvard law professor Henry Hart had said that not only was

Phil Graham ready to be editor of the *Harvard Review,* indeed he was ready
to be dean of the Law School, even as a student), but a Frankfurter protégé.
In a city wired for bright young lawyers, and especially wired for Felix Frankfurter's boys, he was Frankfurter's favorite young man. The proxy son who
argued with Frankfurter all day long. He was the envy of his contemporaries
in Washington. Everyone talked of his future. Many thought he might become
a Supreme Court Justice. Or perhaps even President of the United States. It
was the common opinion that the lowest job he would hold would be Attorney
General of the United States.

Then as a young man he had fallen desperately in love with Katharine
Meyer, the tall, shy, somewhat awkward daughter of Eugene Meyer, a formidable figure of the Washington political-financial establishment. The courtship
had lasted at least fifteen minutes, she had been dazzled by him, above all he
made her laugh, this serious, young woman who so clearly felt ill at ease in
her family's ostentatious splendor, and who had had the confidence systematically driven out of her by a willful egocentric mother. Kay Meyer had not
laughed easily. She was a shy, uncertain yet curiously strong young woman;
he in turn had been moved by her, the shyness, the subtle inner grace and
almost hidden reservoir of strength. They were, in the days right before World
War II, the *jeunesse dorée* of Washington, the fabled youth. All Washington
had gone to the engagement party. Much later, as the sense of being a son-in-
law festered and seemed to tear at his very spirit, some wondered whether he
had married Kay Meyer for her money and for her father's newspaper.

The truth was very different. He was, despite his genuine log-cabin origins, very rich himself; his father had been a dairy farmer outside Miami and
as the city had expanded, so Ernest Graham had moved into real estate as well,
gradually building a considerable fortune out of both real estate and his dairy
products. More, the Washington *Post* in 1939 was hardly the awesome, intimidating, and dominating instrument it was to become some thirty years
later; rather, it was at best the number-three paper in town and journalism was
not the celebrated, increasingly respectable profession it was to become. He
had married her because he had fallen in love with her; indeed there were those
of his friends who wondered whether Kay was good enough for *him,* and
indeed a career in journalism, which was not an entirely serious profession,
appeared to them likely to deter him from the more important work that
awaited him.

But he was the activist, the wheeler-dealer, and he used his paper accordingly; in most things, particularly race, his activism was liberal and essentially
benign, but it was always carried out, even if with the best of intentions, at the
price of the paper's essential integrity. He was a good man, there was no doubt
of that, and he sought a better life for people, and he would use his paper
accordingly. In 1950 there were serious riots in Washington over the integration of a publicly owned swimming pool. It was a hot summer and racial
tension had been mounting in that Jim Crow city for some years. That summer
the *Post* assigned a young hotshot reporter named Ben Bradlee to the story
and Bradlee was out in the field for a very tense and dangerous thirty-six hours,

covering what had become major riots. It was very bad on the first two days and there was considerable indication that it was going to really blow and become much worse. So on the first night Bradlee returned to his office about 10 P.M. to see how the paper had played what was in his mind a very big story. He was exhausted and more than a little scared, but at least he had something to show for his risk. He picked up the first edition, quite sure he would have the lead story, and he looked and looked, but it was not on page one, nor, as he looked, in the first section, nor on the first page of the second section, and so he kept turning and finally he found it very deep inside the local section, a tiny story describing the events in a tearoom manner and calling them an incident. *An incident,* Jesus Christ! Bradlee was furious and he started shouting, *the great goddamn liberal Washington* Post *was running from its own shadow, the great liberal* Post. Bradlee was furious, he had nearly been beaten up, and he had been scared, and it was a great story, and his paper called it an incident. Just then he felt a finger on his back and it was Philip Graham dressed in a tuxedo, and Graham said, "That's enough, buster." Graham beckoned him to go upstairs, where he met Oscar Chapman and Julius Krug of the Interior Department, both in black tie, and Clark Clifford of the White House, also in black tie. At that point Graham asked Bradlee to describe what had happened, a narration that Graham had spared his readers, and when Bradlee was finished, Graham very quickly hammered out the details of a deal he wanted: the Washington *Post* would run the stories and tell everything the way it was, unless the Administration immediately closed all pools for the summer and reopened them the following year on an integrated basis. Bradlee listened, half appalled, half admiring, as Graham set his terms and the others gradually consented. It was, he decided, the quintessential Phil Graham story, using his paper as he saw fit for his definition of social good, benign, liberal, but also very much the instrument of his power, not choosing to let the people of Washington know and decide things in their own awkward, clumsy way.

He was gifted and graceful with the English language, though he had not come up through the editorial ranks at the *Post;* he had a special feeling for the language going back to a childhood when his mother impressed upon him a love of words. He could phrase ideas and feelings well, and he loved doing that, language mattered. Once, right after he had taken over *Newsweek,* he was scheduled to meet with the magazine's top executives for the first time. Osborn Elliott, his editor, impressed on him the importance of the meeting, that everyone there wondered who he was and where he intended to take the magazine. So Graham sat down and made a few notes and then went before them and said, very simply, that what he wanted in journalism was the best of ideas and sense of time and place and events; he knew it was a flawed profession, but he wanted *Newsweek* to be, in his own words "the first rough draft of history." The first rough draft of history. There is no better description of the profession at its best.

He was brilliant and restless and his brilliance and audacity bordered sometimes on the reckless. Just after he had taken over the *Times-Herald* in Washington, making him overnight the most important publisher in the nation's capital, he was considered for the cover of *Time* magazine, a form of national recognition he badly wanted. It was an important moment for him, but it was also delicate, the *Time* people, particularly Luce, were suspicious of Graham and his liberalism. But a few of the younger *Time* editors liked Graham and they set up a lunch, and they wanted him to make a good impression, if for no other reason than the better the impression, the more likely the cover story. They had coached Graham on the questions he was going to be asked and what kind of answers to give so as not to offend the more senior men of *Time*, and they had pleaded with him not to be blasphemous, which was something of a Graham specialty. He appeared and put on a truly dazzling performance, at once sympathetic and for him quite restrained until near the end of the lunch when one *Time* editor had asked him how he, a liberal, justified running in the *Post* so conservative a columnist as George Sokolsky. "Well," he answered, "I figured that every newspaper needs at least one shit columnist."

He was, thought one close friend, a man torn between two equally powerful and conflicting orbits, between freedom and responsibility. It was as if there was one Phil Graham who sought absolute freedom, the ability to be beholden to no one, the happy irreverence that went with a life of no restraints; and at the same time he wanted to influence events, to be a mover, to be at the side of the most powerful men in the country. He was a man caught between wanting to mock events and wanting to be at the center of them. He had, after all, not followed his own career, where brilliance and excellence might have provided him some form of freedom as his own base, but had, no matter how reluctantly, accepted his father-in-law's request—indeed desperate plea—to run the *Post*. No matter how shrewd his stewardship, no matter that he was, in business terms at least, a much more successful publisher than Eugene Meyer, he continued to see his success as somehow derivative. At first the cloud this cast over his accomplishments was small, but in his mind it always grew, haunting him, eating at him, sapping at first his self-respect and finally his very humanity. But it had always been there, it was not by chance that on the day he joined the *Post* a group of his closest friends, sensitive to his doubts, wrote a letter to the editor, duly printed of course, extolling the virtues of Philip Leslie Graham, saying *how lucky the* Post *was to get him,* which of course it was, being one of the most poorly managed papers in all the continental United States. But he was caught in a terrible dilemma of his own making: the greater his success at the *Post,* the greater the influence of the paper, the greater the property, then the greater his link to the Meyer family, in his own mind and that of some of the general public. The greater his success, the less it was his own. The doubt hung there just at the apex of his success, at the very moment when his contemporaries, men like Jack Kennedy and George Smathers and Lyndon Johnson, were assuming power themselves. He complained bitterly to friends, as he became more ill, as his madness grew, about how much he had done for the *Post* and how little recognition he got; he turned, in his last years, on Meyer; he made himself a prisoner of his early choice, his lack of freedom. Once, in 1961, hearing that one of his top *Newsweek* people, Kermit Lansner, was planning to buy a brownstone on the West Side of New York, Graham, always generous, immediately offered to lend him the money to buy a house on the more chic, more expensive *East* Side. Lansner turned him down. "Why not?" asked Graham. "Why are you rejecting what I'm offering you?" "Because I don't need the money and I don't want to be beholden," Lansner said. "Listen," said Graham, "don't kid yourself, we're all beholden. Have you ever looked at my life?"

His consciousness of being a son-in-law grew stronger as he grew older, the belief that whatever recognition he was gaining was somehow not his, as if there were an asterisk alongside his curriculum vitae. At the end, when he was very sick, he became bitter about old man Meyer, Meyer who had deliberately given him the paper at a startlingly young age, and indeed had given Phil —rather than his own daughter Kay—the majority of the voting stock so that he would in fact not feel indebted and not feel like a son-in-law. When Phil Graham had been younger he had boasted to friends like Shirley Povich, the *Post* sportswriter, that Meyer was different, that most rich men deliberately put their fortunes and their influence outside the reach of their sons-in-law, that the younger men rarely had access to the power or the money. He was lucky. What he wanted, Meyer gave him. If he wanted to acquire the *Times-Herald,* then Meyer, whatever his reservations, went out and tried to buy the *Times-Herald.* He had been, he said, the rarest of things, a spoiled son-in-law. But later, when he was sick, it was different, and he raged against old man Meyer, against his children, and against his religion. The Meyer family, he said, had never appreciated him, had never given him credit for what he had done for them. The truth was that Meyer had loved him like a son, cared for him and loved him as much as he cared for and loved his daughter (Meyer loved Kay, but he loved and *admired* Phil). He was a beloved son to his in-laws, among other things the peacemaker in the ongoing wars between Eugene and Agnes Meyer. He was not unappreciated; he was simply a very troubled, very haunted man. The person who doubted Phil Graham the most was Phil Graham.

Near the end many of the people around Phil Graham began to realize he was a very sick man. There had been signs in the past, but they had either been ignored, misinterpreted, or covered up. But they had always been there, almost from the very beginning. The twelve-year-old boy who had gotten in such a fierce argument with his Sunday-school teacher, Mrs. Dale Miller, that he had been ordered to leave the class. The college boy whose drinking sprees were so violent that his father pulled him out of school for a term. The young man in the Army who wrote letters home confessing days with visions of such plunging despair alternating with such ecstatic happiness that he did not entirely understand himself. The talented young Frankfurter law clerk, who, having dazzled the best minds of the city, on occasion in the privacy of his home came completely apart, scenes of tears and deep depression, telling his young wife that he was not worthy of what others expected of him. Perhaps in the early days only Katharine had a sense of the darker spirits inside Philip Graham, and she loved him so much, was so in awe of him, that it seemed to her nothing more than the tension of a brilliant young man who pushed himself too hard under too much pressure.

In the late fifties there had been more obvious signs of his mental frailty. He was out for several months in 1957, worked sporadically in 1958 and 1959. At the *Post* the code word for his illness among top executives was "Problem A." Though he was the publisher of the most important paper in the nation's capital and though newspapermen often argued among themselves about the need to be more candid in reporting about the health of high officials, his illness was shielded from the public and from most of his friends and employees. His illness was now on a downward spiral; the respites between the bouts of the sickness became shorter and shorter, the symptoms more pronounced and more virulent. He was like a piece of once fine machinery that has aged and begins to break down, the breakdowns coming more frequently and more seriously until by the end he was a desperately sick man who raved at his closest friends and his family. In his last two years he turned on his wife, started a highly public affair with a young woman, and threatened to divorce Kay Graham *and* take the company away from her.

It was a fascinating conflict. Washington's most important publisher, the publisher of *Newsweek* as well, a close friend of the President, an even closer friend of the Vice-President, mad, threatening legal action against his wife. Phil Graham clearly out of control, crashing the White House, demanding to see the President and haranguing him on a variety of issues until John Kennedy finally told Kay that she had to do something about it, he simply could not take it any more. There was some talk of a new treatment involving lithium. Fritz Beebe, Graham's counselor, suggested it, but Graham had a morbid fear of drugs, what they might do to him, a loss of control, and he rejected the idea. The extraordinary drama rolled forward, watched and discussed by Washington at large, and most of all by those personally involved in the *Newsweek*–Washington *Post* publishing empire. Top executives of *Newsweek* in New York sat discussing among themselves what they would say if summoned to court; would they testify that their boss, the man who had hired them, and whom they loved, was indeed mad? And was he mad? Who finally was likely to control the *Post* and *Newsweek*, which way would it go? It was the stuff of theater, so much power and influence resting on so brilliant and troubled a human being. Nothing, of course, was written about it.

·   ·   ·

Philip Leslie Graham was born in the Black Hills of South Dakota in 1915. His father was a miner and when the price of gold dropped after World War I, Ernest Graham had moved to another frontier, South Florida, where he first managed a sugarcane plantation in the Everglades. A group led by a man named George Earl had optioned hundreds of thousands of acres of land. Graham, who had studied agriculture as well as mining at the Michigan School of Mines (later Michigan State), was to run it for them, which he did until they were virtually wiped out by the severe 1926 hurricane, at which point they dropped the cane and went instead to a truck-farming operation. By 1932, with the Depression in full sway, the Earl group simply walked out, and Ernest Graham took over the land for himself and began working it as a dairy farm. He started with some 3,000 acres, and pretty soon he had a couple of hundred head of cows. Times were very tough for a long while, and in fact when Phil Graham was young they lived on a houseboat in the Everglades.

The home was in some ways almost primitive, in other ways sophisticated. Florence Morris Graham, Philip Graham's mother, had been a schoolteacher. She might follow her husband from failure in the Dakota gold mines to the very edge of a great swamp, but she was an educated woman, civilization there would be, books and magazines there would be. George Smathers, Graham's boyhood friend, remembered that this was the first home in which he had ever seen *The Saturday Evening Post* and *Time* magazine. Phil Graham himself boasted of the fact that even in their worst and poorest years, his mother had subscribed to *The New Yorker,* and that she had always talked to him about books and theater, telling him that these were part of an important and attainable world. The contrast between the mother and the father was a sharp one; Florence Graham was gentle and spiritual; Ernest Graham was a stern and unbending man; managing a cane plantation in the twenties was not for the gentle of spirit, and he often settled disputes with his fists. He became eventually a state senator who fought against the poll tax in Florida, and once made an unsuccessful try for the governorship of the state.

The dairymen of Miami, of whom Ernest Graham was one, were destined to become very rich. The city was growing faster and faster, always expanding, swallowing up its outskirts; that meant there was a continuous land boom. The Grahams became one of the wealthiest families in Florida. By the time Phil Graham married Kay Meyer (which shocked Ernest Graham, he being suspicious of great eastern wealth) he was already assured of a fortune, the log cabin and the houseboat had receded far into the past. But this did not affect his feelings about his background, particularly his almost romanticized sense of his mother, that she was a rose in the desert, a smart, gentle, sophisticated woman who pushed him toward a better education and a better life, letting him know that there were people in other cities living better lives and dreaming better dreams and doing things that were exciting and important. His mother died when he was in his teens, but in her last days she had gone to a friend named W. I. Evans, a leading lawyer in the region, asking him where Phil should go to law school. Evans had answered Harvard. Thereupon Florence

Graham, as her son would tell the story, had exacted a deathbed promise from her husband that young Phil would be sent to Harvard Law. So even from the start he was a young man caught in a conflict between a tough, harsh father and a gentler, somewhat wistful mother; as he told stories of his boyhood, she loomed larger and larger, and Ernest Graham loomed tougher and tougher.

When Phil Graham went off to the University of Florida he charmed everyone. He was tall and skinny, six foot two and a hundred and ten pounds, and he was brighter and quicker than anyone around. His friend George Smathers thought Phil Graham came as close to having total recall as anyone he had ever met; Smathers was also a good friend of Jack Kennedy and he thought Kennedy pretended to have total recall while Phil Graham really had it. At Florida he seemed inattentive in class, appeared to do no homework, and then boom, at the end of the year, there it was, straight A's. It was a style his own, intellectual-cool, look no hands, and others imitated him, trying to match that inattentive, irreverent style, and some of them flunked out of the University of Florida in the process. Only Phil Graham could do it with such ease and grace, and yet get such good marks. He was different, smarter, funnier; other students broke the rules, and the professors raged and flunked them out; Phil Graham broke the rules and the professors beamed and gave him A's. He was, some of his friends thought, quite high-strung. "Nervous" was the word in those days; no one saw it as a dark side, all his contemporaries were charmed that someone that bright could get such good grades and still be a good old boy, drink so much, play so hard. The only problem was that he did not handle his liquor very well; sometimes when he was drinking he seemed out of control, and there was a moment when Ernest Graham, hearing what was going on at Gainesville, drove up to the university, grabbed his son, and literally marched him out of school. There was something fierce and unrelenting about the old man. Not just Phil was afraid of him, most of his friends were too. He pulled Phil out for a semester and when he returned he was a much chastened young man, more serious.

He wanted to go on to law school and Harvard Law it would be. On arrival in Cambridge he looked like something of a hayseed, tall, thin, country. Will Rogers come to Harvard Square. There was an old joke among first-year law students at Harvard that each member of the class is told to look to the person on his right and then the one on his left, because one of the three of them would not be there by the end of the year. Phil Norton, who became a friend, had looked over and had seen Phil Graham and had decided that since he was so self-evidently a hick, Graham would not be there at the end of the year. He was wrong. Philip Graham was a star at Harvard Law. In those days it was *the* law school in America, it was the best ticket around, it took the bright young men from America and it put them on the conveyor belt for the powerful institutions of America which needed fresh raw young brains. It did not teach morality or ethics or social conscience; rather it taught function and utility and success. In the thirties it was a uniquely exciting place because it was linked directly to the great events and activities of Washington through the body and mind of Felix Frankfurter, who dominated both Cambridge and Washington. It was Frankfurter with his Washington connections who picked out the brightest young men and guided them to the capital, where, under his auspices, they took command of the center, youthful legends forming a network of their own, influential beyond age and title, inspiring both respect and fear.

At Harvard, Graham had become very close friends with Ed Prichard, who had come from Kentucky by way of Princeton and was a backcountry boy genius himself, funny, full of charm, country-slick and country-shrewd, sure to be a senator from Kentucky and perhaps more. It was clear to the other young men who knew him that Pritch was touched with greatness, that he was going to excel, not just in school but in life, that he was brilliant and funny and good with people. Pritch had arrived at Harvard in 1935, having met Frankfurter the year before when the great professor was lecturing at Princeton; Frankfurter, much taken with Prichard, had invited the young man to look him up when he arrived at Harvard. Prichard had not done that and in his second year he met Frankfurter on the street. "Where have you been, Mister Prichard?" Frankfurter asked. "Why haven't you come by to see me?" Prichard allowed as how he had been waiting for an invitation. "Oh, so you're one of those young men who have to have an engraved invitation from Tiffany's? All right. How about Sunday for lunch?" The story added greatly to the legend of Ed Prichard.

After Graham and Prichard became friends he brought his young friend to Frankfurter's Sunday lunches. Frankfurter had an unhappy marriage and no children of his own, and Pritch and Phil Graham became his surrogate sons. They were bright, but they were outrageous, and that was what Frankfurter wanted, he was the immigrant Jew looking for the American experience and he wanted Peck's Bad Boys, both deep out of the American grain, as his sons. He not only tolerated their contentiousness, he seemed to encourage them to argue with him and to shout him down. It was his proxy American boyhood. He did not want them to be dull and dry, he wanted what was perilously close to rudeness. A friend remembered one time a few years later, when they were all in Washington and when Frankfurter was holding forth and arguing with Prichard, then his law clerk. Suddenly Frankfurter looked over and saw his law clerk holding his head in his hands. "Pritch!" he snapped. "What are you doing?" "Counting the diversions in your argument, Judge," Prichard answered. Others watching the three of them in action, arguing and fighting and squabbling with each other, feeling that the two younger men were almost deliberately rude to Frankfurter, were appalled. Once Herbert Bayard Swope, a guest at Eugene Meyer's house, watched their act and finally took Meyer aside. How could he stand it? They were so rude, so boorish. Why, Frankfurter, Swope said, was as bad as the two boys.

At Harvard, being Felix Frankfurter's protégé gave Phil Graham an added cachet. He was already doing well academically, he was to finish tenth in a class of four hundred, and he had that special style, almost homespun in the elite atmosphere of Harvard. He could do what all the other very bright young men could do and yet he somehow put a distance between himself and his work, he seemed not to care that much. In his last year he was elected editor of the *Harvard Law Review,* the chosen of the chosen. The larger world of Washington and New York was created so that the editors of the *Harvard Law Review* would have some theater worthy of both their talents and their ambition. He was very good at the *Law Review.* Most brilliant young men paid the price of being too bright too young, they were awkward and self-defeating in personal contact. But Phil Graham seemed to have been born with grace and charm and subtlety in dealing with others; he was by instinct a good politician. As editor of the *Law Review,* he dealt with some of the great prima donnas of the academic legal world, students and, worse, law professors. He was deft at editing their copy, understanding in improving their work, and he had a special gift, which was to serve him well the rest of his life, for dealing with talented, egocentric people. He could take what they wanted to do but had not yet fully accomplished, improve upon it and make them see what he wanted, and yet make them feel that it was they, rather than he, who wanted to improve it.

So he was, at Harvard Law, marked for greatness. Nonetheless, a terrible question hung over his last year. Frankfurter had gone to the Supreme Court in 1939. Who would become Frankfurter's law clerk, Prichard or Graham? Pritch was a year ahead of Graham but he had stayed on to do a year of graduate work at the law school. The clerkship was the ultimate cherished prize, even more valued than the editorship of the *Law Review.* It announced to the outside world, particularly in New Deal Washington, who was the brightest star of the year. Both men were favorites of Frankfurter. It was a difficult question, and Frankfurter finally solved it by naming Prichard as his law clerk in 1939–40 and working out a deal whereby Graham would clerk that year for Stanley Reed; then, the following year, when Pritch was finished, Graham would move over and clerk for Frankfurter. In football it is known as red-shirting, in the arms race as stockpiling. So it was that both men clerked for Felix Frankfurter.

He graduated from Harvard Law School in 1939, two Supreme Court Justices eagerly awaiting his services. He had Frankfurter's voucher and that was the only one needed in those days, indeed it was nearly the only one that existed. Those were great and exciting days to be in Washington. Franklin Roosevelt was President, his New Deal seemed to be in midstream, World War II was approaching, the government slowly but inevitably was readying itself, constantly centralizing. Power was passing, and passing quickly, from the legislative branch to the executive branch, and the executive branch needed bright young men. A man's youth was not a hindrance in the executive branch, rather it was an asset, young men worked long hard hours and they gave undivided loyalty, they wanted to get ahead, the New Deal and the nation needed them. No one stood on past performance and past reputation, it was an age where there seemed to be shortcuts to power for the bright young men; speed and energy were of the essence and the bright young men were speedy and energetic. As the New Deal plunged forward with all its new alphabet agencies, it needed young men and women to run them, and someone had to recommend the young men. The chief talent scout was Felix Frankfurter. Sympathetic in those days to the growing power of the federal government, equally well connected in both government and academe, he was the ultimate connector. Washington was a smaller town, and Harvard Law dominated other law schools as it would never do again. The government was changing and it wanted a new prototype, not some hack produced out of a connection to a local city boss, but a bright clean young lawyer–wheeler-dealer produced by Harvard Law School; Frankfurter was thus in a position to deliver jobs and patronage as no mayor of a big city could still do. In those days Frankfurter's position was unique; he had intellectual authority and he had moral authority and he had political connection. He kept abreast of everything, he read more than anyone in town, if a bright young man arrived in town who was by mishap not already one of his protégés, Frankfurter was quick to annex him. He was a brilliant and skillful wheeler-dealer, he kept in touch with all sorts of people; when Frankfurter died, I. F. Stone, the radical journalist, said of him, "There goes my only subscription on the Supreme Court."

Frankfurter's influence on a generation of bright young men was enormous. They constituted a sort of freemasonry, an American intellectual underground, an American equivalent of the British Fabians. Anyone playing the game that Washingtonians loved (and needed) to play, trying to decide who would be running the city in fifteen or twenty years (so they could get early bets down), looked to the Supreme Court law clerks, particularly the Frankfurter clerks. Contemporaries looking around somewhat enviously at who would be in charge in Washington did not doubt that it would be Phil and Pritch, they were so smart, so well connected, so talented. They had everything; no one else seemed to be able to keep up with them; why, they finished each other's sentences. No two men seemed to have so brilliant a future. How tragic, then, that Ed Prichard would, as a still young man, his entire future in front of him, go to jail for ballot stuffing in Kentucky; and Phil Graham would, on the threshold of his best years, take his own life.

It was a glistening time. Never were the issues clearer, never was talent so badly needed. So much was happening, so much was possible, so much was ominous. It was the summer of 1939 when they had gone to Washington, the summer when much of the rest of the world went to war. Later they would look back on those months with great nostalgia, the fun, the excitement, the involvement in great issues. A group of them, all bachelors, all bright, all headed for great things, had taken a house together in Virginia. Pritch, of course, who was the funniest of them. And Phil. And Butch Fisher, who later headed the Disarmament Agency, and Graham Claytor, head of the Southern Railroad, who later became Secretary of the Navy. Johnny Oakes, then a young reporter for the Washington *Post*, kin to *The New York Times* family, later editor of the editorial page of the *Times*. John Ferguson, later Ambassador to Morocco. Bill Cary, who later headed the SEC. All the best young men, all—with the exception of Oakes—lawyers, all ready to run the world, all doing the work that a few years earlier would have been done by men twice their age.

They lived at a place called Hockley House over in Arlington, Virginia, and there were a hundred and fifteen acres; perhaps the house was a little seedy, but all in all it was fun. Dean Acheson's butler had recently been caught in an amorous embrace with Dean Acheson's cook and Acheson had been forced to fire the butler, and so they had hired him, and he gave Hockley some class. There was dinner every night, and if you had guests, you signed them in, and the bill for room and board came to about a hundred dollars a month. The house pulsated with excitement, a sense that history was moving every day and they were in direct touch with it.

It was that summer that the dinner-table discussion began to change. Gradually it was no longer just domestic events that they discussed, it was more and more Europe, the approach of war. Phil Graham was very left of center in those days, he not only read the local newspapers, he read the *Daily Worker* and he was very anti-Hitler, part of that, of course, was from Felix, part of it was from his own instinct. He and Pritch gradually became part of a group that worked hard for America's military preparation and its early intervention. As he did, his ideology began to diminish, he became more interested in the war effort than he was in ideological definition or purity. The group met regularly at Bob Nathan's house, preparing strategies to get the United States into war. Others there were Wayne Coy, for whom Phil Graham later went to work, Isidore Lubin, Lauchlin Currie, and Isaiah Berlin. Berlin was the most brilliant of them all, flashing, original, almost too quick for his own good. He was with the British Mission and he was connected to Frankfurter, and to all Frankfurter's bright young men; he was so quick and passionate that the words and ideas seemed to tumble out. Shayeh, he was called, the Hebrew diminutive for Isaiah, and you had to have a practiced ear to understand him. Once they all went out to Justice Brandeis's house and Brandeis said to Berlin, "Mr. Berlin, I count myself quite fortunate—I've been with you thirty minutes and I've been able to understand almost 25 percent of what you've said." Berlin, of course, was close to everyone important in Washington and so was another friend of theirs, Jean Monnet, who was very close to Berlin, and because the French government was technically Vichy, he was posted to the British Purchasing Office. It was an exciting time. There was an immediacy to events, a passion to life, and they had an almost electric connection to it.


It was Johnny Oakes who first took her to Hockley House. Johnny Oakes was always very serious, the good proper son of the German-Jewish aristocracy, and nephew of Adolph Ochs, and he had always done well in everything, first at Princeton and then as a Rhodes scholar at Oxford. He was handsome and obviously very able, but no one had ever accused Johnny Oakes of having too light a touch. He had known about Kay Meyer, and when she returned to Washington after working as a reporter in San Francisco, he had started taking her out and had brought her to Hockley. He was very interested in her, and though he worked for the paper that her father owned, his own family was so well connected at the *Times,* which was a great paper compared to the *Post,* that no one could really accuse him of careerism. He was too stolid, too somber to marry for reasons of career. He thought that Kay and he were serious, and friends of theirs thought they might get engaged. They would have been a wonderfully serious young couple.

She was tall for women of her generation and just a little awkward. She did not think of herself as pretty, and God knows, her mother had told her often enough that she lacked style. But most of the young men she knew liked her looks, particularly when she smiled. She had a pretty, almost tentative smile, and it was made even more attractive by the shyness, the sense that she was vulnerable and the reticence that marked her manner. She had been to Vassar, which she had not liked, and then the University of Chicago, some-what against her father's wishes, and then she had gone on to San Francisco, where she had done some labor reporting and had become a friend of left-wing labor leaders like Harry Bridges. She was a little left herself, it was quite permissible in those days, and friends thought she was made extremely self-conscious by the contrast between her political beliefs and the grandiose style of the Meyer home in Washington—Crescent Place, it was called—with end-less servants and rooms. She had not really wanted to return to Washington, for which she had no great fondness, it was a city that had bored her in the past; it was filled with stuffy young men who seemed to be part of a preordained social order, and who were not interested in what was going on around them, except for dinners and parties. She was not very good at that kind of socializ-ing. Those men were very heavy and she did not want to go out with them, nor did she like men who were too serious. And then at Hockley House she met Phil Graham. He was alive and exuberant and outrageous, filled with stories, at once brilliant and serious and then mocking the solemnity of the very mood he had created. He did what no one else had ever done for Katharine Meyer before. He made her laugh and he made her feel young and pretty and he got her outside herself. He was like no one she had ever met before, he was so alive and life seemed to mean so much to him, there was so much energy. Because she was very bright she sensed immediately that he was a man who was always going to break the rules, a man who would always need to be forgiven. And she would always forgive him.

The first thing he said to her, as she later remembered it, was that he was going to marry her. The next thing was that he did not want her father's money. Not a penny. Instead, they were going to move to Florida and they were going to be poor and she was going to have only two dresses, and he was going to enter Florida politics. The words delighted her, they liberated her from the weight of being Eugene Meyer's daughter, sought for her dowry. It was a very brief courtship. Perhaps a month. He was the handsomest and most winning young man she had ever known, there was no one he could not charm. Even her mother, whom she had never been able to win over, who disapproved of everything she did, adored him. Everyone smiled upon them. Her father was a great figure in Washington, so he was her sponsor; and Phil was a Frankfurter protégé, so he was Phil's sponsor. Frankfurter and Meyer had been great friends during World War I, and although Meyer had suspected that Frankfurter had become a little too radical in the ensuing years, they had remained friends, it was a powerful alliance, two titans in the city, both aligned on the major issue of that day, intervention in World War II. Phil Graham was finishing up his year with Stanley Reed. He and his friend Pritch had been immediately welcomed into the Meyer home, sponsored as they were by both Felix Frankfurter and Kay Meyer. It was a world unlike any they had ever seen. Agnes Meyer was a grande dame and she ran a grand salon, and it featured not the boring banker friends of Eugene Meyer, but Thomas Mann and Paul Claudel and Toscanini and the great photographer Edward Steichen. Pritch was startled once in 1940, when Wendell Willkie was running for President and someone had thrown an egg in his face, to hear an intense discussion of the ideology of the act. What did the egg on the face truly represent? Steichen had looked at Willkie's egg-splattered face and announced that it was the photo of a gangster reaching for his gun. Agnes had dissented. It was, she said, the face of a poor average American wiping away the insults of left-wing thugs. Pritch sat in wonder as an entire evening was devoted to the philosophy of the thrown egg.

Phil Graham had not known Kay very long before he did indeed ask her to marry him, and she accepted, and then in ten minutes he got wildly drunk; it was the first time she had seen the wild side of him. The next day when he came by to pick her up he was clearly embarrassed, and he brought Pritch along, so that they would not have to talk about what had happened the previous night. But there were not too many scenes like that; they were the perfect young couple for the new meritocratic Washington. They represented, if not the city's society past, then the future of Washington society. They had a brief engagement and on June 4, 1940, less than a year after Phil Graham had arrived in town, he was married to Katharine Meyer on the grounds of the Meyer mansion in Westchester County, not far from New York City. At that very moment the British, seemingly badly defeated, were pulling back in disgrace from the continent of Europe. It was a dark moment for the West. The family and only a few close friends were invited. The feistiness that seemed to mark their world was very much in evidence at the wedding luncheon. Frankfurter was there and at the luncheon he and Steichen started talking about whether Communists should have freedom of speech. Suddenly it was no longer a discussion but a fierce argument, and Frankfurter was saying no, they should not, they were a fifth column, and Steichen, Pritch, and Graham were on the other side, that freedom of speech belonged to everybody, or it belonged to no one. No, shouted Frankfurter, enough was enough, these were not loyal citizens. It got out of hand, it was too violent, there was real shouting, and Felix had to take Kay Graham away for a walk, it was all too tense; she noticed as they walked away that there was even a tear on Pritch's face, it had been so intense.

In order to marry Katharine Meyer, Phil Graham had had to ask permission not just of her parents but of Felix Frankfurter as well; there was a tradition among law clerks, going back to Holmes's time, that they were supposed to work full-time and have no personal life. Felix granted his permission. He approved of her and approved of the marriage, he was not averse to annexing the Washington *Post* for his sphere; thus sanctioned, they really could marry. From then on Frankfurter reprimanded her young husband if he did not keep her fully informed of what was happening at the Court. "Phil, did you tell Kay what Hughes said in court yesterday? Did he, Kay? . . . He didn't? Phil, don't you know that Holmes told his wife everything?" No, Jedge, Phil Graham said, it was part of his special privilege, his role as the feisty son, that he was allowed to call the great man Jedge, and allowed to argue with him constantly. It pleased the young Kay Graham that so Olympian a figure of Washington doted on her husband and it seemed to confirm how wonderful the young man she had married was. She was impressed by the way her husband stood up to and argued with Frankfurter. They argued incessantly. There was a particularly bitter fight over the decision to deport Harry Bridges, and Phil had not wanted to write the opinion. They had argued all day long and into the evening. Finally it was time for Phil to go home. He was no sooner in the house than the phone rang and it was Felix, and they argued some more, and finally Phil said—Kay would long remember the words, the audacity of them, they seemed to symbolize the whole relationship—"I just don't care what you do, Jedge. I just don't want to see you make yourself look silly." He had refused to write the decision; she was very proud of him.

He went immediately from being Frankfurter's law clerk to a job where his principal responsibility was gearing up America's industrial capacity for the oncoming World War II, trying to get industry ready for what surely awaited this country. He was by then fiercely anti-Hitler, that was his obsession. Hitler cast a specter that was terrifying. Officially his first job was as a lawyer for the Lend-Lease Administration and then he worked in the Office for Emergency Management. In fact, he was part of a small group that Roosevelt had created to break the bottleneck of production problems. He was brilliant at his job, cutting through red tape, getting things done, slipping past the bureaucracy, which was in no way as passionate as he was about preparing America for war. He was smart and clever and fearless and dazzlingly well connected. He was very skilled at pinpointing where a problem existed and even more fearless in attacking it. He was also Frankfurter's protégé and Eugene Meyer's son-in-law and important people tended to take his phone calls as they did not take the phone calls of most twenty-five-year-olds.

The job was huge, America was still very much asleep, it took comfort from the shelter of two great oceans; industry was just coming off the Depression years and beginning to prosper and was in no rush to convert to wartime needs; business was not filled with visionaries. In the late summer of 1941, for example, Graham and Joseph Rauh, then a colleague and later to be known as one of the most influential liberal lawyers in Washington, were working on a study of airplane production. It was at the time when Roosevelt was talking about clouds of American planes. Graham and Rauh checked the production figures, which were still secret, and they found that Roosevelt's prediction was somewhat excessive. America had in fact produced only one four-engine plane in the month of August. Some cloud. They passed this information along to Wayne Coy, their superior, with a note that something ought to be done about it, and Coy soon after received an angry note from Harry Hopkins saying that this was sloppy legwork, there were many more planes on the way. To which Coy added his own note, chastising his young troubleshooters and demanding more accurate research. So they decided to go by and see Robert Nathan, who produced the statistics, telling him that he had cost them dearly with their boss. Nathan looked at his charts for a long time and finally said, "Yes, there's been a serious mistake." Graham turned to Rauh and said, "We've done it this time, there's our ass." "Yes," said Nathan, "there was no bomber produced in August." So they went back, reinforced now, stronger than ever, and pushed Coy to push Hopkins and keep the pressure on.

Which was difficult. The government was slow to move, industry was even more hesitant. That was the real problem, Phil kept saying, if you could only move industry ahead, if you could only convince them to make some minor sacrifice and convert to wartime production, then you had broken the logjam. Walter Reuther, who had been an ally of theirs, was thinking along the same lines, and they came up with the idea of government loans to industry to encourage wartime conversion. It was as much Phil Graham's idea as anyone else's. He drew up the bill himself, wheeled and dealed it to get it through Congress, and then grabbed a cab to take it around town to make sure that every cabinet member signed it. It was a classic example of Phil Graham's joy in making connections and moving pieces, he loved the game and he was very good at it, audacious and shrewd. His contemporaries thought he was the most effective member of that small cabal. The rest of them could think and dream, but Graham was a doer as well. They often wondered about him, so slim, almost frail, and yet so much energy, they wondered if it could all hold together. There was no doubt in the minds of most of his contemporaries that he was the most able young man of his generation in Washington, he seemed touched by a larger spirit, his course guided by something beyond him, so talented, so able, so good-natured that he did not even inspire envy in a city rich with envy.

Among those who noted and admired his talents was Eugene Meyer. Meyer was sixty-five when Graham married his daughter. He loved the newspaper, it was not just a source of power, he was accustomed to power and influence, it was more than that, it was a source of pleasure. He saw his ownership purely in terms of public service (indeed, when he had mentioned the first time to one of his star reporters, Eddie Folliard, that he considered it an act of public service, Folliard, who was in the tradition of the old police reporters and who had never heard a publisher talk like that before, rather liked the idea; began to think of *himself* as a public servant). He did not need to prove that he could be a success in any field, he had already done that, and he was unusually tolerant in sponsoring editorial views that were more liberal than his own; indeed, he deliberately sought more liberal voices in order to make the paper more vital and less stuffy. He had learned the hard way that he could publish a good paper only if he could get good people and that he could get good people only if he gave them considerable editorial freedom, freedom often at the expense of his own views.

He wanted to keep the paper in the family, but for a long time he had seen no successor. His own family was wracked with tensions and divisions; he and Agnes Meyer were both forceful, unyielding people on totally different wavelengths and their marriage was an angry, often chaotic one; it had left its scars on their children. He had one son, who had no inclination at all for journalism. Of his four daughters, Kay, he liked to boast, was most like him, there was an inner intellectual toughness to her and he could not push her around at the table, she was more likely to argue back, particularly when he offered his Herbert Hoover nostrums. That was all very well, it was good to have a spunky daughter, but he was a German-Jewish patrician of the old generation, a smart daughter was a wonderful blessing, for a smart daughter could then marry a *smart son-in-law.* But one did not turn something important like a newspaper over to a woman. It simply was not done. Besides, there was a part of Kay, for all her intelligence and will, that was unsure and uncertain, she was more sure of her politics than she was of herself.

But if Kay Graham was not eligible to be publisher of the Washington *Post,* Phil Graham was something else. Meyer loved Graham, thought he was the most brilliant and gifted young man he knew; he was successful with his peers, successful with older men, he used language well, he managed to be original and yet somehow diplomatic when need be. He was the only member of the household who could get on with everybody else and he had become, in a relatively short time, the mediator of family disputes. When old man Meyer began, as he frequently did, to reminisce about his high-level jobs during World War I or how he had put together Allied Chemical, stories that bored his wife and interested none of his children, he now had an avid listener in Philip Graham. Indeed, it was part of the legend of the Meyer household that whatever Agnes Meyer's faults she was a good deal more interesting than the old man, that she talked less about Fun and Games with Calvin Coolidge, or Riding the Range with Herbert Hoover. But Phil Graham was genuinely interested in Meyer's world, and Meyer came to care for him as he would a favored son.

In 1942, when Phil Graham joined the Army Air Corps, Eugene Meyer took him aside and asked him to make a commitment: when he came back from the war, he would take over the *Post*. Meyer desperately wanted the paper to stay in the family. Otherwise, the old man said, he would have to start looking elsewhere for an alternative choice. But Phil was the man he wanted, he was proud that this gifted young man was a part of his family. It was not an easy choice for Phil Graham. More than most young men he had other possibilities and other dreams: he not only loved the world of politics, he knew he was good at it. He was, in his own mind, still decided upon a return to Florida, practicing the law, which he loved, and eventually running for the Senate. Politicians in those days were considered far more important than journalists. Besides, taking on the *Post* committed him to a course he had always been wary of, it made him potentially, in other people's minds, a kept son-in-law, and it locked him professionally into the Meyer family. But he also loved the idea of newspaper work, he had a particular love of language, he wrote well himself, and there was a part of him that was excited by the possibility of making the *Post* a truly great paper. Newspapers might have as much to do in shaping the course of public events as politicians, he thought.

He did not jump at the offer, in the beginning his doubts outweighed his desires, but Meyer was very persuasive. The paper, he insisted, needed Graham, it was being badly run and Meyer was too old and too late to the newspaper business to correct things and run it properly. But it could do great things in Washington, Meyer insisted, an honest enlightened paper was what the city badly needed. Graham thought about it for a while and discussed it with Kay. She told him the decision was his, she hesitated to take him on a course different from that of his dreams. (Florida politics was still all right with her.) He talked it over with his friends. Joe Rauh was puzzled, Phil seemed to be playing Hamlet over a decision that Rauh would have made with ease. The *Post* to him was a golden opportunity, though later Rauh would come to understand Graham's hesitation. But Washington exerted a powerful pull, he was already there, he was well connected there, and he had already invested something of himself in the city and in his friendships. Perhaps the crucial decision had been the first one, made without even the knowledge that it was a choice, the decision to clerk in Washington for the Supreme Court Justices rather than to return to Florida immediately. Once he was part of the Washington scene it was that much harder to go back to a small Florida town and work his way back to the capital; there would be no other bright young men, no great events, no comparable excitement in Florida. After long and troublesome reflection he told Meyer that he would join the paper when he returned from the war.

He spent the war doing intelligence work in the Pacific, working on breaking Japanese codes; later he was in the South Pacific as a staff officer picking bombing sites. He did not have a particularly bad war, the South Pacific was a bitter and dirty theater for some, but he was a staff officer, a talented and valuable one, and he emerged as a major in the fall of 1945.

On December 8, 1945, the Washington *Post* announced that Philip Graham would become associate publisher on January 1. The paper that he took over was no great plum. It was erratic in content (I. F. Stone had once called it an exciting paper to read because you never knew on what page you would find a page-one story), weak in both advertising and circulation. It was not the class paper of Washington, the afternoon *Star* was; it was not the dominant paper in the morning, the *Times-Herald* was. It had only about 25 percent of the city's total daily newspaper circulation. It survived mostly through the largesse of Meyer. He poured his money in, enough to keep it afloat and respectable, never enough to make it great, although certainly enough to make it personally very costly. The annual loss, over the first twenty years that Meyer owned the *Post,* was somewhere between a million and a million and a half dollars. Even during the war years, when it was hard not to make money publishing a paper, Meyer had not been particularly successful. He had made a total profit from 1942 to 1945 of a quarter of a million dollars, this at a time when every other paper in the country seemed to be making vast profits. Worse, Meyer had made a bad mistake on the use of his limited newsprint. Given a small amount of newsprint and a correspondingly small paper, he had unwisely chosen to give much of the space to advertisers rather than to the editorial side, believing that if he was good to advertisers in their hour of need, they would remember it and show their loyalty to him after the war, when space was again plentiful. They, of course, did nothing of the kind. When the war was over and newsprint was again available, they did what they had always done, they advertised in the Washington *Star.*

The *Star* was good and rich and smug in those days. It was the paper of the well-educated and well-bred of Washington, the last vestige, it would turn out, of a Washington that was coming to an end, Washington as a pleasant, genteel southern city. It was the paper of old Washington society, traditional, settled, often landed. In tone and style and outlook it could almost as easily have been published in Richmond, Virginia. It was a paper for people who knew each other well, as their families had known each other well, where titles mattered and foreign diplomats mattered, and arrivistes, unless they happened to be President of the United States, were slow to make the social order. Blacks lived partially hidden lives, they existed to appear only at the appropriate moment in the appropriate dress to serve someone a drink or a dinner. They did not hold jobs in the government, they did not protest about their conditions, and they were deemed to be both happy and largely invisible. The *Times-Herald,* by contrast, had no illusion about being a class operation; it played handily to the passions of the moment, which, in the late forties and early fifties, were abundant.

The *Post* was different, it was a paper which found its identity, liberal, enlightened, internationalist, before it found its real numerical constituency.

Meyer had taken it off the scrap heap and the humiliation of a bankruptcy auction and had given it immediate legitimacy when he bought it in 1933. The city room had been painted and the old office game of lighting matches under cockroaches, a favorite of *Post* reporters for years, had ended. Shirley Povich, traveling with the Washington Senators baseball team, had heard about the sale when he reached St. Louis, where the Senators were playing, and he received a cable saying that a new, as yet unnamed owner had bought the paper and his 15 percent pay cut was being restored. Meyer was big-league, he could invest what was, by existing *Post* standards, big money into the operation. But he did not, he frequently pointed out, intend to endow it permanently, the paper was sooner or later going to have to pay its own way. But it was in a weak position, it split the morning sale with the *Times-Herald,* and that readership which was to form the heart of its constituency—young, well-educated people brought to Washington by the New Deal and a generally expanding central government—had not yet arrived in any numbers.

Several years after he had bought the Washington *Post,* Eugene Meyer was seated in front of his building surveying the passing scene, watching his city from the steps of his paper. It was lunchtime and Povich passed Meyer and asked if he needed a lift into the center of town. No, said Meyer, as a matter of fact, he was going to be picked up in a few minutes for his weekly bridge game with Newbold Noyes, associate editor of the Washington *Star,* at the Metropolitan Club. Povich noticed that Meyer seemed unusually pleased with himself. "And do you know who my partner is today, Shirley?" asked Meyer. No, answered Povich. "Ely Culbertson," said Meyer with a large grin. Eugene Meyer, thought Shirley Povich, was not a man who liked to lose.

He had not lost very often. He was the son of immigrant Jewish parents; his father was Alsatian French, his mother was half German, half English. He was born in Los Angeles, California, in 1875 and he had gone to Yale, where he did three years' worth of work in two years. He was serious and somber and he intended to be a very great success. He had thought everything through. As a young man he devised a larger plan for his life. He would devote the first twenty years to his education. In the next twenty years he would become very rich, then marry and start a family. The third twenty years he would devote entirely to public service. Then at the age of sixty he would grow old gracefully. To an astonishing degree he kept to that schedule. He became a shrewd, subtle financier, a man who was far ahead of his time in the use of political and economic intelligence and analysis. He understood research and he understood the impact of political forces upon the market long before it was fashionable. He paid well for good political and economic analysis and he was always better briefed than most of his peers. Unlike most young men playing the market, he did not run with the pack, he was far more scientific, and he was, on occasion when the market fell out on others, able to avoid losses. "Watch out for this fellow Meyer," J. P. Morgan once said of him, "because if you don't he'll soon end up having all the money on Wall Street." Could there be higher praise? Meyer seemed to deal in everything—copper, oil, chemicals—and he was a genuinely creative man: he put together what became the giant Allied Chemical Company. Though he passed up a chance to become one of the two largest shareholders in General Motors, he made millions out of the Fisher Body Company. When he was forty years old, two thirds of the way through his grand plan, his net worth was valued at nearly sixty million dollars.

In 1917, two years behind schedule, he went to work for the Wilson administration as a dollar-a-year man advising on material for Army uniforms. He was to serve in government jobs under Wilson, Harding, Coolidge, and Hoover, and later Harry Truman. All of his jobs were important. Many of them had to do with the financing of World War I and the reconstruction of Europe after that war. It was a distinguished career and it had confirmed Meyer as a true internationalist, a man of America and Europe, something that would be crucial to the tone of the paper he would renovate. When he was fifty-six, with the Hoover administration leaving office, Meyer left government. The final Hoover years, because of the Depression, had not been pleasant. He had been a target of anti-Semitism and he had been bothered by the inaction of Hoover. His old friend had seemed to draw in, and had been unwilling to face the reality of the national crisis. Their friendship had ended badly. Meyer left Washington, depressed and saddened.

He did not really know what he wanted to do with the rest of his life. He had turned out to be far more active than his original grand plan had assumed. He thought from time to time of getting into the newspaper business. In 1920 his friend Adolph Ochs had invited him to come to work for *The New York Times* in a major capacity. Meyer would even be allowed to buy some of the *Times*'s preferred stock. But it quickly developed that Ochs had wanted Meyer to run the *business* side of the paper. The idea did not appeal to him; if he was to remain a businessman, then he would remain a big one, not a man committed to upping circulation and cutting costs of a daily newspaper for the greater good of Adolph Ochs. But the idea had stayed with him. In 1925, with the Hearst organization publishing both the *Times* and the *Herald* in Washington, Meyer had lunched with William Randolph Hearst and he had asked to buy one of the two papers. He knew that Hearst was losing more than one million dollars a year in Washington. "I always buy newspapers," Hearst had answered, "never sell them." Hearst had asked Meyer why he wanted to buy the paper. Meyer had quickly explained that the Hearst formula, then so successful elsewhere, what he called a newspaper for the working proletariat, did not pay off in Washington, which was not a workingman's town. Thus Hearst had ended up competing with himself for the same audience. "I can understand why you want one outlet in Washington to influence legislation," Meyer said, "but you don't need two papers for that purpose, especially two that are fighting one another and costing you a lot of money."

But Hearst was more interested in losing money than in selling, and after that Meyer's attention had shifted to the Washington *Post.* It had once been one of the most prestigious of the city's newspapers but in recent years it had come on hard times. Ned McLean was the publisher of the *Post* for seventeen years, during which time he had systematically destroyed the existing paper and its reputation. He was a boy disguised as a man, a pathetic spoiled figure, the third generation of a wealthy family where the strength of the income and the strength of the genes did not stay in tandem. His only real interests were horse racing, hunting, and chasing women. His wife, Evalyn Walsh McLean, whom he had honored by buying the Hope diamond for $154,000, once described him as a classic example of "unearned wealth in undisciplined hands." He had come to the *Post* uniquely ill-prepared for his responsibilities and he had run a reactionary, almost childish newspaper much despised by the working newsmen of his day. He was a serious alcoholic, and he had used his own money cavalierly; as his personal fortune dwindled, he had drawn on the resources of the *Post* to sustain his lesser habits. His only political interest seemed to be a connection with the Harding administration, which he much admired; and McLean became so close to it that he was tainted by the Teapot Dome scandal and had to spend several hours on the witness stand during the Senate investigation.

By the late twenties it was clear that the *Post* was going to be sold and it was only a matter of who would buy it. In 1929 Meyer moved after the *Post*. Meyer had checked with Adolph Ochs and Ochs had told him that a paper ought to be worth about $5 million if its gross amounted to half of that sum. But Meyer had no way of knowing what the paper's gross was and he was wary of showing interest for fear of driving the price up. In May 1929, through intermediaries, he offered $5 million for the *Post*. He thought it was an offer that could not be refused but in the end the McLeans turned it down. Still, he now knew what he wanted, which was a newspaper, and he knew where he wanted it, which was Washington, and he knew what kind of paper it should be, serious and respectable, filled with news about international affairs. It must be in Washington because that was the right audience; he was fond of quoting Lord Northcliffe to the effect that of all American papers he would prefer most to publish the Washington *Post* because every morning it reached the breakfast tables of all members of Congress.

He had become restless with his retirement in Mount Kisco, on his estate in the countryside north of New York City. The house was enormous and filled with servants. (Once before, when they were in Washington, Agnes had left for the summer house with much of the staff, and Gene had complained about how many people she had taken. "But I left you with a butler, a cook, and a housemaid," Agnes had protested. "But you know that I can't stand camping out," he had answered.) One day in the Mount Kisco house he had put his hand on the banister and come up with dust. "This house is not properly run," he had announced. "You'd better go and buy the Washington *Post,*" Agnes answered. Which he soon proceeded to do. Ned McLean had run it further into the ground, the Depression had undercut its value even more, and on June 1, 1933, it was sold at a public auction. Meyer, fearing that the price would skyrocket if it were known that he was a bidder, used a dummy buyer named George Hamilton. Hamilton's instructions were to bid in increments of $25,-000, and not to go higher than $2 million. For $825,000 Meyer won the auction. The *Post* was his. The paper was in dreadful condition. It was down to twelve-page editions, it could not pay its newsprint bill, and it was $500,000 in debt. Most of its best reporters had left because of McLean-ordered salary cuts, the plant was in terrible physical shape, and its circulation had dropped to only 63,000 (compared to *The New York Times*'s 466,000). But it had a certain amount of honor in its past, it had an Associated Press franchise, which was much rarer in those days, and it was what Meyer had always wanted.


He was a genuine tycoon, and his coming put the staff members in awe. Eugene Meyer was big-time, he was the kind of man who could, and in fact did, make up for the *Post*'s losses from the income on his other investments. He had already lived a full and rich life. He was often pompous and pedantic but he was interested in large issues and he transmitted that interest to his staff. He was not second-rate and he had a splendid sense of his own value and his own ability. He feared no one. He could say of Bernard Baruch, a legend to most younger men, that he was a bit of a con man and not really that talented. He told Alan Barth, one of his editorial writers, who was about to go on a trip with Herbert Hoover, "Hoover's not a bad fellow, but he's not really very bright, so you'll probably have to take care of him." He was feisty on occasion and when Jesse Jones, the head of the Federal Reserve Board, took exception to a *Post* editorial and tried to fight with Meyer, the publisher later said that it was a good thing for Jones, who was a foot taller and fifty pounds heavier, that others had stopped the scuffle. "Otherwise I feared for him," he told friends. "You know, of course, that I took boxing lessons from Gentleman Jim Corbett." Meyer did not exactly have the common touch; once, during the Depression, explaining why he could not give his staff raises, he said that everyone must make sacrifices. "You should realize," he told the assembled reporters, "that I have made no addition to my collection of French Impressionists since I bought the *Post.*"

It would be a long haul to turn the *Post* into a viable paper. It was caught in a crowded daily field, and it shared the morning slot with serious competitors. On occasion, despite the fun he was having with the paper, Meyer wondered if he had made a mistake in buying it. It was such a terrible drain. He quickly arranged his property so that the losses of the *Post* could be played off against the taxable income from his other properties and investments. Even so, it was very expensive. The *Post* lost money for some twenty-two years. Very late in Eugene Meyer's life, long after the paper had become immensely profitable, columnist Marquis Childs was talking with him. Childs observed that though Meyer had done many public-spirited things in his lifetime, by far the most valuable was the decision to rescue the *Post* and turn it into an important quality newspaper. "Yes," said Meyer, "you're absolutely right." He thereupon proceeded to tick off just how much money he had lost in every single year of the paper's existence. "Why, one year," he said, still somewhat in shock from the experience, "it even cost me more money than my entire income!"

As publisher he had everything to learn. He had moved into an entirely new and different world. He was a brilliant man but he was in no way street smart. Almost immediately Cissy Patterson, publisher of the rival *Herald,* tried to take away his four best comic strips, *Dick Tracy, Winnie Winkle, Andy Gump,* and *Gasoline Alley.* "Are comics important?" Meyer asked an aide. He was told that they were and so he decided to fight her for the publication rights. The case went all the way to the Supreme Court, and while it was being heard both papers ran the disputed comics. Finally the Court ruled for Meyer. That displeased Cissy Patterson, who had once been a good friend. She sent Meyer a small beautifully wrapped gift box. He opened it up. Inside was a raw chunk of beef. A pound of flesh. At first Meyer did not understand the present, but Agnes Meyer did. "Of course, a dirty Jewish Shylock," she said. Meyer was shocked by the act. Publishing was more contentious a profession than he had imagined.

He boasted later that he had made every mistake in the book. He hired the wrong people and he was clumsy in his personnel relations, and he really did not care about local news or about sports. But from the first he knew two things, what type of paper he wanted to publish and whom he wanted to reach. That gave him a sense of clarity about the future, and slowly, inevitably, he put together the kind of staff that could give him the type of paper he wanted, a paper with a serious, distinguished editorial page which was interested in the larger world, a modern internationalist paper.


Meyer had brought the paper back from the near dead and, as long as he was publisher, it would not die. But whether it would truly live, whether it would grow and expand, was another question. The *Post* seemed doomed to split the morning market with the *Times-Herald* and, given the educational level of that time, the kind of paper that Meyer wanted to publish seemed destined to a perpetual small share of it. Nor was the *Post* a good paper by classic journalistic standards. There was precious little real reporting in it; Meyer did not really invest in reporters, it was not the vision he had of a newspaper; he had grown up in another age, where you owned a newspaper in order to have an editorial-page voice, not where your power came from the sum of the efforts of a group of distinguished reporters. He cared about having a voice, particularly in Washington, Eugene Meyer speaking every day to the Congress, to the Supreme Court, to the President. He did not see journalism as a profession of reporting; only *The New York Times* in that era had a large and expensive staff of reporters assigned to cover the world. In those days few sensed that the real power of journalism was the power to define, the power to cover or not to cover. News was not yet viewed as subjective; all events were perceived as of predetermined importance, the presence of a reporter added no particular dimension. Therefore the power of the Washington *Post* at the time was to be judged by the strength of its editorial page. Editorial writers were sophisticates, men who had been to college, smoked pipes, and were often specialists; reporters, by contrast, had not been to college, wore fedora hats, waited for events to take place, and wrote brittle snappy leads about them. So the *Post* scrimped on reporting; the other major news outlets staffed Franklin Roosevelt, not just at the White House but out of town, but the *Post* did not; Eddie Folliard, the *Post* White House reporter, did not even make the trips to Hyde Park. Whereas the *Times* by the late thirties had five or six national reporters covering Washington, the *Post* had one; whereas the *Times* had fifteen foreign correspondents, the *Post* had one man doubling at State and the White House. The *Post* covered the world mostly by writing down what the State Department said was happening in the world. "The *Post*," Ferdinand Kuhn, the paper's first full-time diplomatic correspondent, once remarked, "will cover any international conference there is, as long as it is in the first taxi zone."

Meyer above all wanted excellence on his editorial page. He found out quite early that he could not dictate editorials himself and still have a quality editorial page. It was a discovery that few publishers ever take the time to make. So he decided to hire the best writers he could, giving them maximum freedom (except on the subject of tariffs, an important issue, he trusted no one but himself there), and it was this decision that gave the *Post* of the thirties and forties its special reputation. It was cheaper to hire a handful of very good editorial writers who did not run up huge expense accounts in foreign lands than it was to hire a lot of reporters. Indeed, when in 1957, a decade after Phil Graham took over, the *Post* decided to send its first man overseas, to London in fact, the reaction of John Sweeterman, the very tough and very able business manager, was: "Walter Lippmann works in Washington, why does he have to work in London?" Thus the editorial page gave the *Post* its special, albeit somewhat inflated, reputation as one of America's best newspapers, intelligent, humane, enlightened, the conscience of Washington, integrationist when the city was segregationist, internationalist when the nation was isolationist, civil libertarian when the nation was locked into witch-hunts. It was a liberal paper in the best (though journalistically limited) sense and it seemed to care in the most farseeing way about the future and traditions of a free society.

In that sense the paper's voice seemed removed from the fears and narrowness of the nation at its worst times. Much of this was the product of Meyer's ownership. He had been a success for so long in so many arenas, he had served five different Republican Presidents, he was so secure about his position in public life that he was above petty parochial pressure, beyond conventional needs of social acceptance. He did not feel threatened by public or peer disapproval or the threat of social ostracism. He was curiously modest about dealing with editorial talent, he made suggestions almost timidly, and he knew the limitations of his own beliefs. Wanting in 1945 to hire a then unknown young editorial cartoonist named Herbert Block, he sent Block a trial subscription so that Block could see if he approved of Meyer. Above all, he made it clear that he feared no one, and he passed this on to his editorial writers in subtle ways. During the war Henry Morgenthau, Jr., then Secretary of the Treasury, came by for lunch, and Meyer, who always seemed to have a cigar in his mouth, passed out cigars after the meal. A dark shadow came over the Secretary's face. Was it not known that Mr. Morgenthau did not tolerate smoking, not just in his office, but in the entire wing of the Treasury Building? The cloud darkened as Meyer lit up. "Excuse me," said Harry Dexter White, one of Morgenthau's bright young men, to Meyer, "we never smoke in the Secretary's office." "We're not in his office," Meyer said, and kept right on smoking. It was a wonderful signal to editorial writers, it meant that they were as free as Meyer not to be intimidated; Meyer clearly regarded Morgenthau, not as most people in Washington did, as a very powerful man bearing a great name, but simply as Henry Morgenthau, Sr.'s, not terribly bright son. It was the kind of signal that good journalists love. For gestures like that and for the general freedom he gave them, they came to admire Eugene Meyer; they thought him quite capable of being very stuffy and pompous, but they also counted themselves lucky for having a publisher so rich and successful that he did not care what people thought or said about him as long as he thought he was right.

The first editor of Meyer's editorial page was Felix Morley. Meyer had given him great freedom, but they had split apart in the late thirties over the transcending issue of the day, American preparedness and intervention in the war in Europe. Morley was a Quaker and a pacifist and he was horrified by a course that was going to take America into a major war. Meyer and Morley argued increasingly on the direction of the paper on this most crucial of issues, and in August 1940 Morley resigned. For a time it appeared that Elmer Davis, the distinguished radio commentator and perhaps the nation's best political essayist, might take the job, but Davis at the last minute withdrew and suggested that Meyer instead hire an editorial writer from the *Christian Science Monitor* named Herbert Elliston.

It was Elliston, working under the umbrella of Meyer, who brought the *Post* editorial page to genuine greatness. Elliston was a tough Yorkshireman who had traveled all over the world and spent many years in China. He was self-educated and fiercely literate, he was afraid of no one, he did not covet small-bore social acceptance, he believed that an editorial should make one point and make it clearly, and he expected to back up whoever wrote the editorial. He did not want his editorial writers, as was the fashion then, to write what amounted to birthday greetings: *We hear that Mr. Smith is the new Ambassador to France and we wish him well and know that the entire Washington community joins us.* He was an internationalist before it was fashionable, and while he was humane on social issues, he was not a man to bleed too much; he had a very strong sense of how harsh life could be. Those who worked for him were in awe of Elliston and they took sustenance from his self-evident personal strength; whereas some editors in a variety of subtle ways, words never spoken but feelings transmitted, communicate doubt and timidity, Elliston communicated confidence and fearlessness. He did not worry about diversity; unlike the editorial page of *The New York Times,* where the editor dominated and went to each writer separately, discussing which editorial he should produce, the *Post* was more democratic. There was a meeting each day and various editorial writers argued back and forth with each other, some of the talk very strong, none of it personalized. Nor did Elliston always insist on consistency; in later years Merlo Pusey, a classic conservative Republican, and Alan Barth, a true Hugo Black libertarian, debated over the Court and sometimes one prevailed, sometimes the other. Elliston thought consistency less important than vitality and intelligence and passion. In consequence, during the forties and fifties the Washington *Post,* a paper which was for most of that time losing money and which had serious overall flaws as a newspaper, had the most distinguished editorial page in the country.

There were two men who were crucial to that success. One was Herbert Block, the cartoonist, probably the most important cartoonist of his day, sharp, powerful, almost brutal, who created, among other things, an image from which Richard Nixon never entirely escaped. The other, less well known to the general public but perhaps even more influential in setting the paper's tone, with its passion for liberty, was Alan Barth. He was for a generation of younger journalists in the late forties and fifties one of the great role models, and many young students at eastern colleges in the fifties thought of journalism as a potential career because Alan Barth was writing editorials for the Washington *Post.* He and Herblock made the *Post* in some ways a great paper even when it was, by most standards of the profession, almost a bad paper. Barth was a gentle, modest man, passionate about liberties and freedom; he was by instinct a liberal, but his strength went far beyond traditional liberalism. It was a total unbending belief in civil liberties, an ability to stand back from the heat of contemporary passion and to express his ideas with great force and lucidity. He was considered by many of his colleagues simply the ablest and most talented editorial writer they had ever met, a man both intelligent and passionate, more passionate than most intelligent men, and more intelligent and reasoned than most passionate men. He had the ability to be intensely and vitally involved in the day's events and yet the capacity to see beyond them and put them in historical perspective. He was gentle enough to care about the minor human concerns that often matter less and less to very successful men, and tough enough of mind and spirit to pay the price for the most difficult of avocations in this country, the full-time pursuit, not of happiness, but of liberty.

Barth had grown up in Beaumont, Texas, worked on a paper there and reported from Washington during the war, and had met Frankfurter, who was fascinated by him and his intelligence. It was Frankfurter who in 1943 recommended Barth to Eugene Meyer. During the war Barth was working for the Office of War Information when he received a call from Meyer asking him to

come by and talk about a job as an editorial writer. Barth was quite prepared
to say no, he thought the *Post* essentially conservative and he was a committed
New Dealer. But he was impressed by Meyer—for all his accomplishments and
his self-evident rich man's vanity there was a touching honesty and modesty
to the way Meyer propositioned him. He treated Barth not as most publishers
treat job applicants; he simply reversed the procedure, it was as if Barth were
inquiring into Meyer's qualifications and so he proceeded to outline his qualifications. He was, he assured Barth, not a very good publisher. He thought that
with the right people he could make the paper better. He explained how he
had spent the first third of his working career becoming rich and the second
third in government service. Now he was publishing the *Post* and he wanted
nothing but to use the *Post* as a vehicle for public service and public good. He
knew he could not impose his views on talented men, therefore he was willing
to listen to talented professionals. "I want you, Mr. Barth," he said, "because
I think the paper is too conservative." "Are you really sure," Barth asked him,
"that you want a total libertarian on your page?" "Absolutely sure," he
answered.

So Barth became an editorial writer; the connection for him had been
Frankfurter and so he was somewhat surprised when, just before he started,
Frankfurter took him aside and said, "You realize, of course, that from now
on you have no friends in government." No friends in government, the end of
a friendship with Frankfurter? That stunned Barth; why, part of his value to
the *Post* he had thought was his contacts with people like Frankfurter. Would
this mean a terrible new almost monastic existence? What Frankfurter meant,
he soon discovered, was not for Barth to cut himself off from Frankfurter but
to cut himself off from *Morgenthau,* who was also a Barth friend and for whom
he had once worked. Frankfurter prescribing a Caesar's-wife test naturally
exempted himself; he liked nothing better than to have a direct line to the
Meyer-Graham family and to influence the paper's policy, as Barth discovered
as he began to break with Frankfurter in subsequent years over issues of civil
liberties.

The *Post* hired a brilliant, passionate libertarian at almost precisely the
moment that liberties were to come under a kind of siege. Perhaps that always
happens after a period of both domestic innovation and a war; perhaps there
is always a period of disillusionment and contraction, a nation turning in, of
men and women out to revenge earlier wrongs, and other men and women
slightly ashamed of their recent past. The stage was set for an epic test. The
*Post* was not a rich paper; it was not a national paper, yet it was a local paper
in a national city, which was in this case almost as important. If it did not reach
out to cover the world or the national theater, that did not matter, for in this
case the national theater came to the paper. What was called McCarthyism
was to an uncommon degree a Washington phenomenon, and thus a Washington story; though the name became symptomatic of a larger virus, and there
were episodes of McCarthyism throughout the country, the focal point was
Washington. The aggressors were, by and large, senators and congressmen,

they had their own investigating committees, their main targets were in the federal government. This assault created tension and fear which engulfed the entire city, leaving scars that lasted for decades; it was a great story and a great moment which the *Post* did not seek, but which sought it.

Alan Barth thought he had the best job in the world. He would get up every morning and walk from his house in Cleveland Park to the *Post* building and his mind would be filled with the arguments for the day ahead. He was going to face Merlo Pusey in editorial conference and he had to muster his thoughts. Pusey, whom Barth very much admired, was an intelligent Taft conservative; Pusey had been sponsored at the paper earlier by Charles Evans Hughes, as Barth had been sponsored by Frankfurter. He and Barth opposed each other on almost every issue dealing with the Court, they liked and respected each other, each had a total belief in the integrity of the other, and they came to realize gradually that each made the other a better editorial writer, each pushed the other beyond cliché. Barth would argue for his point of view and Pusey would ask, what is the law, what is the constitutionality of that? It was, thought one man watching the two of them every morning, like a miniature debate parallel to the great debate taking place between Hugo Black and Frankfurter on the Court, with Barth increasingly the proxy for Black, and as Frankfurter turned more conservative on the issue of liberties, Pusey the proxy for Frankfurter. The two Justices had been in an epic struggle of their own—Frankfurter had once dominated the Court completely, but Black was slowly pulling the Court away from Frankfurter and making it more libertarian. It was a powerful and compelling ongoing argument on personal rights and the limit of the Court, and over the meaning of the Fourteenth Amendment. Barth, who knew both Justices well and counted them both as friends, was fascinated by the struggle. Barth would finish a Frankfurter opinion and he would be in awe: Felix, he would think, is *absolutely* right, and then he would finish the Black dissent, and he would decide, no, *Hugo is absolutely right.* Gradually he found himself siding more with Black than with Frankfurter and gradually carrying the editorial page with him until one morning he received a phone call from Hugo Black himself, who said, "I never thought I would live to see the day that you or Phil Graham would ever say anything in opposition to Felix." It was a wonderful life, he thought, when those debates were taking place, the best of all possible jobs in the best of all possible places. That part of it he loved, though as the fifties turned and the worst of the McCarthy period was upon us, there were long periods when nothing was pleasant, when everything seemed stained by the fear in the land, when basic liberties seemed terribly on the defensive, terribly without friends. The few institutions that stood firm, like the Washington *Post,* found themselves on the defensive too.

All of which placed a special burden on the young publisher of the *Post,* Philip Graham. He was different from Meyer. If he was more liberal in the classic sense of that word, he was also much younger, and, at the moment that he inherited the paper, much more ambitious. Meyer had made his mark in countless ways before becoming publisher, his place in history was assured, indeed he had ordered up a house biography just to make sure that his story lived. If during his stewardship, the *Post* continued to lose a million dollars a year, no one thought that meant that Meyer could not handle money. But Phil Graham was different. He had been only thirty-one when he came to the *Post,* having forsaken a bright future in other fields, and so while he was at the *Post* he was driven, not just by what he might or might not achieve at the paper, but by the career he might be missing elsewhere. His reputation was still to be made and it could not be made by being Eugene Meyer's son-in-law, a stewardship at the *Post* marked by the loss of a million dollars annually. He became obsessed, as Meyer was not, by financial success, by a black-ink bottom line, in part because a strong paper needed a secure financial base and in part because he had to prove his own ability. That drove him finally toward respectability, toward caring about what advertisers said in a manner that normally he would have disdained. More, Phil Graham's real love was politics, not journalism, he wanted to be not just an observer of the action, but a mover, at the very center. He had convictions, strong ones and almost always benign ones. But he was a wheeler-dealer. He was quite prepared to trade off *Post* editorial support on minor issues in order to get some congressman or senator to back a major issue that he truly cared about. He was wheeling and dealing as early as 1948, trying to get Fred Vinson to take himself out of the field for the Democratic nomination. He helped invent Estes Kefauver's national career by suggesting that he investigate crime in America, and when Kefauver seemed reluctant, he had turned to him and asked, "Don't you want to be Vice-President?" Graham had become, by the late forties, perhaps the single most important mover within the city of Washington. He was the friend of the powerful, adviser to them, doer, activist; his instructions to the city editor, Ben Gilbert, left no doubt that the paper was to be an instrument for social progress. Stories that reflected badly on integration or home rule simply would not make the paper. So Phil Graham was bringing a new era to the *Post;* he was more involved than Meyer, he knew more about talent than his father-in-law, he cared more about words. He was also more worried about the economic vulnerability of the paper than Meyer and he inevitably and almost unconsciously sought respectability more than Meyer did. He was a classic insider; he hated for the *Post* or its writers to look as though they were not on the inside and connected. Very gradually he became more and more concerned about political respectability. If he was to deal with powerful politicians, he had to be realistic, he could not be too radical, his paper must not look as if it were a base camp for eggheads. That produced a growing schism between Graham and his best editorial writers.

Above all, he was concerned about the paper's economic future. As the paper was viewed in Washington, so was he. He was bright, he understood the future and the economic difficulties newspapers were to encounter. It was not enough that it was a civilized voice at an uncivilized time, that was fine, but it was too dangerous. He became concerned that the *Post* not be considered too left-wing, too out of step with the times (no matter how dreadful the times, one ought to keep partially in step with them). In addition, he was obsessed with getting rid of the morning opposition paper, the now-merged *Times-Herald.* He was convinced, rightly, that only one of the two papers would survive, and he was determined that it would be the *Post.* If both survived, which he thought unlikely, both would be weak. If the *Post* could buy out the *Times-Herald,* then its future was infinitely brighter; if it could not, it was doomed to a small share of the city's morning readership, never being rich enough to hire a real staff, and thus forever deeding over power in the city to the afternoon *Star.* Besides, television was on the horizon, and television was going to affect newspaper circulation in some way, though he was not exactly sure how.

So the *Times-Herald* became an obsession with him. When Cissy Patterson, the publisher of the *Times-Herald,* died in 1948, Graham was eager to move. He talked to Meyer, and they were ready to make an offer for the paper. Meyer believed totally in his son-in-law: what Phil wanted, Phil got. But Mrs. Patterson had turned the paper over to seven faithful employees known in Washington journalistic circles as the Seven Dwarfs. A year later, when they were in serious financial trouble, Graham was ready. He made an offer of $4.5 million for the paper, all of it Meyer's money, and he and Meyer were prepared to offer an additional $1 million for Mrs. Patterson's shares in the trust that controlled both the Chicago *Tribune* and the New York *Daily News.* For a brief time it looked as if the sale might go through, and Graham was alternately euphoric and depressed, depending on the latest rumor. That summer Kay had rented a small house in Narragansett, and Phil was commuting on weekends. Each weekend he seemed to grow more and more confident. "I'm 90 percent certain," he announced one weekend. They went together for a long walk on the beach, both terribly excited. All their dreams and their future seemed tied up in this. They sat on the beach, and Phil said, "Let's close our eyes and imagine the future and what it will be like when we get the *Times-Herald.*" They did, and Kay later asked him what he had been thinking of. *"The look on Sam Kauffmann's face when he hears the news."* That was it, of course—Sam Kauffmann, publisher of the *Star,* owned the town and condescended to the Meyers and Grahams, and with the other papers splitting up the morning advertising, Kauffmann could afford to keep his rates down, thus starving his competitors. He knew he had to acquire the *Times-Herald* in order to make a run at the *Star.* But the lawyer for the seven owners was apparently playing games with Meyer and Graham. They increased their offer but they never had the inside track, which belonged to Colonel Robert R. McCormick, the conservative isolationist Chicago publisher.

In the end McCormick took over the *Times-Herald.* The Meyers made one last attempt. Agnes Meyer, fierce competitor that she was, offered to throw in the house on Crescent Place, a grand ostentatious Taj Mahal of a residence, worth in those days one and a half million dollars. But it did not work. The Colonel had won. It was a crushing blow for Graham, he thought it was the end; Colonel McCormick with his vast assets and resources coming to Washington. "I'm going to die for six weeks," he told Kay, "and then I hope I'll be all right." With that he went into a serious depression, pulled away from his friends, would not go to bed, stayed up all night reading, mostly biographies of newspaper titans. After a few weeks he announced to Kay that it was all right, that he had studied the lives of newspaper giants, and they had all put it together in their late twenties or early thirties. "I'm still in my early thirties," he said, "we're going to make it." With that he seemed to bounce back, if anything more single-minded about the idea of merger than before. But there was no doubt it was a serious setback. During the days when it all seemed possible, that the *Post* would buy out the *Times-Herald,* he had seen the future clearly: one morning paper in Washington. He knew both the political and the financial consequences of that, and it had been snatched away, perhaps for good, the paper in the hands of a man who was an archenemy.


So the *Post* entered a period of difficult change in a highly vulnerable position. This was not the financially secure semi-monopoly paper which some twenty years later was to take on the President of the United States. It was instead an articulate, fragile paper which regularly lost money and which seemed to have a gift for making powerful enemies, and whose young publisher was searching for financial security and political respectability. Phil Graham was committed to liberties, yes, there was still part of him that was the young man who had argued with Frankfurter over the rights of Communists to freedom of speech. But he was also anxious for legitimacy, to be near the center of action, to come to some accommodation with the contemporary mood, trying to do that, if at all possible, without giving up too many of his principles. The *Post* was being constantly attacked in the Congress. The *Uptown Worker* it was called. It was also being red-baited by the *Times-Herald.* All of this placed Phil Graham under terrible conflicting pressures; he was by the standards of his peers a very dedicated and serious libertarian, but he also wanted respectability and to be seen as someone who was responsible. If his editorial writers went too far, it might cost the paper its legitimacy with advertisers, with the public at large, and, most dangerous of all, it might permanently jeopardize his chances of ever buying the *Times-Herald.* This put him in a conflict, sometimes open, with certain of his editorial writers. They were dreamers, too pure, he thought. He was a man of the real world. "Fifth-floor liberals," he called them, and it was not a term of either respect or endearment. In his own mind, he was a man of the real world, making real decisions, hard choices. He believed in civil liberties, but he often thought the editorial page too pure, the paper seemed on a course somewhat beyond what he wanted or what he could finally control. Barth was simply so strong, his voice so clear, in meeting after meeting he could carry the board, and his editorials never drifted, liberty was to him, after all, not a divisible commodity; the darker the climate, the clearer his voice, the more confident of the American past and future he seemed. It made the *Post* seem to stand alone, and it made Phil Graham very nervous. If Graham was somewhat uneasy with his editorial writers, they, in turn, were aware that they were making him nervous, that there was a difference between him and Meyer, that he was somehow a little more vulnerable to outside pressures. There had been subtle warnings from Graham as the fifties began, warnings that were really more than pleas: Couldn't the editorial writers be a little more balanced? Couldn't they be a little more aware of the pressures on the paper?

This came to a head in April 1950, when Earl Browder, the head of the American Communist Party, a man against whom there were no espionage charges, testified before McCarthy and refused to give the names of other people. Barth believed that if you care about freedom you defend unpopular people and unpopular causes, and that some of the most important court cases in history had been fought over some of the least attractive people. So he wrote a powerful editorial which seemed years later exactly what a good paper would want to print, but which in the heat of the moment seemed to make the paper vulnerable to charges of Communist sympathy.

> In refusing to identify and stigmatize certain persons whose names were presented to him . . . Mr. Browder was patently in contempt of the committee's authority. But the contempt was pretty well earned by the drift and character of [the] questions . . . Mr. Browder was as responsive as anyone could have wished to those questions relating directly to the McCarthy charges. . . . [Other senators] saved the sub-committee from engaging in a kind of persecution that might have resulted in its punishing Mr. Browder for adherence to fundamental American decencies. Not everyone in America tests a man's loyalty to his country by his willingness to betray his former friends. The apotheosis of the informer is not altogether accomplished in the United States. . . .

Graham had been on his way to New York by train when he read the editorial and he was furious. He absolutely exploded. This was simply too much. It was one thing to defend liberty when liberty had to be defended, but this was gratuitous, it was looking for trouble. If it was a clear case, a high government official unjustly accused, that was one thing—one could defend Dean Acheson, for he was a good American—but Earl Browder, the head of the American Communist Party! It put the *Post* in bed with the CP, much to the pleasure of the paper's enemies. It was as if Graham was saying that it was all right to be libertarian, but do you have to go looking for it, and Barth was answering, *You don't have to look for it, it is here.*

The enraged Graham decided he was going to fire Barth, since Barth could not be restrained. Graham told Frankfurter about it and Frankfurter, friend to both, lover of liberty and pragmatist, told him it would be a dreadful mistake, yes, the editorial was bad and unnecessary, and yes, Communists abused rights, but it was not that bad, Barth was a valuable man, a good man, and besides, the danger to a paper with a reputation like that of the *Post,* if it fired its principal editorial writer, was incalculable. Only partly mollified, Graham printed a couple of critical letters with this editor's note: "The purpose of the editorial, which we regret did not seem to come through, was to show what a sorry mess we have come to when a Communist can [take] the public position of upholding political freedom and opposing the doctrine of guilt by association. . . . The real question is the value of the testimony of Communists, former Communists, and temporarily exiled Communists, where that testimony, of dubious credibility, may do permanent injury to persons of good character." In a private memo, Graham told a friend that the editorial was just plain wrong, and that it had somehow slipped by Elliston. Barth, hearing of this and appalled by the publisher's note in the paper, was furious himself; he and Graham were never really friends again. He was aware of the pressures on his publisher, he was aware that they had very different responsibilities, that Graham was responsible for the survival of the paper as he was not, but he was angered nonetheless. He knew Graham was creating the base for a more successful paper, but he preferred the stodginess of Meyer.

Graham was clearly trying to hold on to the center; shortly after the Barth piece he personally wrote a three-column editorial that sought to condemn in equal terms the Communists and the witch-hunters (witch-hunting could "drive out of the government the very brains which alone can give us victory in the Cold War"). It also called for a Commission on National Security which, unaffected by the passion of the moment, would give serious answers to the question of Communist infiltration. Nothing, of course, came of the commission. When in February 1951 the Chicago *Tribune* wrote a long story calling the *Post* the Washington edition of *Pravda* and attacking Graham, Meyer, Elliston, and particularly Barth, Graham was very upset. Unlike most of the people around him, he took the attack seriously. Graham suggested to Meyer that he might think of suing and Meyer wisely shrugged him off. But he was clearly being more and more affected by these assaults, he was getting too much playback from advertisers and from political friends of his, and he was afraid of being isolated. So he wrote a long internal memo answering all the charges, meant primarily for the use of his advertising salesmen in answering advertisers. Implicit in all this was the idea that Barth had become some sort of liability to the paper. In 1953 Barth wrote an editorial attacking the FBI's technique of gathering irrelevant information in its investigations and making the information a part of a person's dossier. Graham killed the Barth editorial, and when Barth rewrote it as an article for *Harper's,* and Graham asked him to withdraw it, Barth refused. That ended all personal relations between them.

.   .   .

It was a difficult time for Graham. In 1950 he was thirty-five years old, his own ambitions were considerable; he was no longer a boy wonder, he did not want to lose his place on the power escalator; yet he was putting all his effort into the paper and nothing seemed to change there. He was no doubt better on the issue of McCarthyism than almost any other figure in Washington. But he was surrounded by major politicians who played it cooler than he. McCarthyism was a dreadful thing, of course, but they were not about to get involved. They were made as uneasy by the hunted as by the hunter. There was something unseemly and messy about being a target of McCarthy, as if a *serious* person simply would not have let it happen. Graham wanted to be connected to the center, but the center, on this issue, had turned to mush. The sooner McCarthy was gone, the easier it would be for him. Therefore in the early fifties much of his own political activity went into trying to stop McCarthy. He contributed generously to the campaigns of Republican centrists. He sought and sustained a mild uneasy flirtation with Nixon, telling friends that there was more to Nixon than they thought, that he believed Nixon had the capacity for growth, that they had to see Nixon in private to get a real sense of the man. He worked very hard to get Eisenhower to run in 1952, which was in part an attempt to connect the *Post* to the Republican center, to a warm smiling general from the heart of the Midwest, and in part a belief that Ike could stop McCarthy as the Democrats could not.

After Eisenhower and Stevenson were both nominated he discussed with his editorial writers the possibility of the *Post* breaking its recent tradition of not endorsing candidates. The editorial writers assumed that the *Post* would back Stevenson and said it was a good idea. The paper came out for Dwight Eisenhower. Eisenhower was difficult enough for the *Post* writers to swallow, but Nixon too! That was hard. When the Nixon slush fund story broke, the *Post* at first, like many papers, called for his removal from the ticket. But after Nixon had given the Checkers speech Graham personally wrote the *Post* editorial, saying that Nixon had "eloquently and movingly" answered the charges against him, that he had not used the fund for his personal ends and it was thus not a case of moral turpitude but simply an error in judgment. Graham's friends and editorial writers were furious. It was one thing to sponsor Ike, it was another to champion Nixon; Nixon had been a hatchet man for the Republicans on the very issues that Graham cared about. When a friend of Graham's protested, he said that he knew Nixon privately and Nixon was good in private. The friend was appalled, he said he was not interested in private assurances, rather he cared about the public record. Don't be so pure, Graham had answered, it was time to be realistic. As for Ike, Graham's commitment was total, he not only committed the *Post* editorially, he was a serious fund raiser for Eisenhower, and he was the master of ceremonies for the key Eisenhower-Nixon fund raiser in Washington right before the election. He also, in the service of Eisenhower and Nixon, censored Herblock's cartoons in the two weeks before the election. It was the first time Herblock had ever been censored. Yes, Graham told friends, he knew Ike was not running the kind of campaign he had hoped for, and yes, he had doubts about Nixon, he wasn't stupid, was he, but this was the only way to stop McCarthy. On election night, as the results poured in showing an Eisenhower landslide, he walked over to a reporter named Murrey Marder, who up to then was one of the two reporters in Washington doing diligent dogged coverage of McCarthy.

"Poor Murrey," he said.

"What do you mean, Phil?" Marder asked.

"It looks like we'll have to find you another beat."

"You're wrong, Phil," Marder answered, "you're going to have to find me another man to help. It's going to be twice as rough."

Marder, of course, was right. He knew McCarthy, he knew the committee, and he knew the timidity of the rest of the Republican Party. After all, McCarthy had been an asset, he had put the Democrats on the defensive, and if he did violate liberties, if he did go a little far, so what. It always takes a few broken eggs to make an omelette. Besides, Marder sensed, if the Republicans had tolerated McCarthy before when he was weaker, they would be less willing to challenge him as month by month he grew more powerful. Marder and one other reporter in Washington, Phil Potter, a relentless, driving man from the Baltimore *Sun,* had been almost alone for several years in covering what was called the Red Beat. They had shared their work and they had lived their beat as few reporters do, the madness, the tension, the political hysteria, the fear of libel. It was totally exhausting; when it was all over Potter had a feeling that he had not eaten or slept in four years, that he had been living in some terrible endless tragedy. Whereas Marder was a restrained reporter, Potter was a man who seemed to be moved by great physical force, outspoken, opinionated. During the various McCarthy hearings he would astonish admiring colleagues by coming back to the *Sun* bureau and writing a first draft of a story in which all his anger, all his rage at what McCarthy was doing would come forth: "Joseph R. McCarthy the no good lying son of a bitch from Wisconsin . . ." Then, having vented his spleen and released his anger, he would tear up the story and sit down and go to work. Often when Potter had finished for the day he would go to the National Press Club, where he would find some of his colleagues and tell them that they had to start covering McCarthy, trying to explain what McCarthy was like, what he was doing. It was, he thought, missionary work. Most of his colleagues thought he was simply too involved. A story was a story. If Joe said something you reported it; that was all it took.

Only Marder seemed to agree with him that this was a time in which the press was being badly exploited. Marder was on the Red Beat because Al Friendly, who had preceded him, had become so exhausted by the assignment that he had finally asked to be pulled off. Friendly (no relation of Fred Friendly of CBS) had been the first *Post* reporter on the story and he and the *Post* executives had decided very early on that they had to get away from the routine way of covering the senator, that the essence of what the press was doing was a kind of blind amplification of unproved charges. It was a great journalistic shell game of its kind, hit and run: McCarthy charges, press picks up, passes on, never checks, charges are forgotten, McCarthy goes to next town, reveals a new set of charges, press again uncritically passes them on. McCarthy had shrewdly and ruthlessly seized on the weakest part of the mechanics of journalism, the desire of reporters to have a hot story, and the ability of a senator—who was after all a high public official, and thus a serious man—to make a charge. Because he was a serious man the charge became, if not reality, at least news. The boys in the Senate press gallery occasionally had minor qualms about what McCarthy was doing and what their role in it was, but there were always excuses: *he was a senator,* their editors wanted it, the play was good, Joe might be right, you could never tell. Sure, they had doubts, but only a columnist could express doubts. Thus it was news. So it was not just McCarthy who was violating the essential bond of trust and civility in a free society, it was the press that was a willing accessory.

McCarthy, of course, knew it. He learned quickly and he had a crafty instinct for the mechanics of it. He knew all the deadlines, knew at what time in the afternoon to break a story in order to make the morning newspapers. He knew that Sunday was a slow news day, so that any charges he made on a Sunday got particularly good play in the Monday newspaper. He was just being a good guy. One of the boys. Wasn't that what they wanted? The press boys would gather outside his office. He would walk in after a day on the floor and he would invite them in and he would rummage through his files for some worn-out, discarded charge and he would hand it to them. Here's one for you, boys. Joe was just being helpful. He was good at it. He knew that the key was the wire services, they were uncritical, never judgmental, always in a rush, that they in particular loved those bulletins. McCarthy Charges. McCarthy Claims. He was always making news, providing something for the local radio stations, which desperately needed something new. He always had fresh meat for them. He knew how to play the wire services off against each other, a little something for AP, and then the next day a little something for UP, and then something for INS. If AP had something, then UP wanted it a little more, and then suddenly it was on both wires at night, coming into the city rooms of a thousand newspapers, that much more legitimate, forcing other newspapers which had their own correspondents to match the stories. So it was a cycle, a cycle directed by Joseph R. McCarthy. Besides, it was a story, it had been a story the week before, it had been a story yesterday, it would be a story tomorrow. It was not just McCarthy who was making the charges, why, there were other men, serious men, senators muttering gravely that where there was smoke there must be fire. It was so easy, all you had to do was go by and talk with Joe, and he would give you, I mean *give* you, a new charge, reach right there in the drawer and hand you a charge. That most of these charges were empty, that he was self-evidently not serious about anything but headlines, did not matter. In the journalism of that era, that they made news was enough. Marder and Potter, with Homer Bigart of the *Trib* joining them from time to time, were the two who were trying to hold him to some kind of record, to bring some form of accountability to the road show. Joe, of course, was still a good old boy with them. Trying to be helpful. Why, he knew the two of them were just trying to do their job, they had to do it to please their editors. A quick stop-time photo of the era: McCarthy walking into a room of reporters, saying, voice slightly lowered, "Now, boys, this is off the record." A favorite ploy. Potter is there and he says, "Joe, I'm not listening to anything from you off the record." "Come on, Phil, I'm just trying to be a good guy, just trying to help out." So finally Potter goes into another room and McCarthy asks if any of the wire boys want to leave the room and of course they do not, and so a few hours later the story comes clicking across on the agency wires just as McCarthy had intended.

At the *Post* they had worried from the beginning about how to cover him. Was the very act of coverage itself a way of helping him? It was fine to give brilliant critiques of McCarthy on the editorial page, but if the front page were turned over to him day after day, didn't that mean the *Post,* no matter how unwillingly, was playing his game? In the beginning they had assigned Al Friendly to the Red Beat; Friendly, who had come out of Army Intelligence, was one of the bright young men whom Phil Graham had brought to the paper when he took over. Friendly had felt strongly that he could not just wait for McCarthy's charges, that this was a reckless demagogue who broke all the rules of trust for a public figure, that the traditional rules for covering a public figure were based on standards of restraint which McCarthy had systematically violated. So what McCarthy was doing, what it all really meant, had to be carefully spelled out. It was either that or ignore him, and ignoring him was more dangerous. As a cardinal rule, newspapers must not ignore what they do not like or find distasteful. So the *Post,* with Friendly covering, had gone to longer and longer stories. But the Red Beat depressed Friendly; for the first time in his life he felt his work eating away at him, he was taking it home every day, he was, he knew, letting his prejudices and his passions overwhelm him. At home the tension would not go away and he would have to take out his carpenter's tools and work into the night making cabinets and restoring furniture.

Finally he and Russ Wiggins, the editor of the *Post,* both decided that it was too much for him, that it was time to take him off the beat before he came apart. They replaced him with Murrey Marder, who was in retrospect the perfect choice for the assignment, quiet, intelligent, dogged, meticulous. There was nothing flashy about a Marder story, no one ever accused him of deft or imaginative prose, but he was above all else careful and fair. He had covered the Hiss case in 1949 and then, as a reward, had gone to Harvard on a Nieman Fellowship for a year. The year at Harvard, a school then very much under assault, had strengthened both his belief that this was a historically dark moment and his resolve to do something about it. He was moved one day in a class on Asian studies when historian John Fairbank had put aside his usual lecture about the Sung Dynasty and come back to the present day to read aloud from a newspaper. Mr. X, he read, had just been named as a Communist sympathizer and a traitor. "Who knows who Mister X is?" Fairbank had asked his class. "Maybe it could be you. Maybe it could be me." As it turned out, it *was* Fairbank, he had become a target, and Marder remembered the incident when he returned from the Nieman and was assigned to the Red Beat. Doggedly, he worked out a means of covering McCarthy. Hold him to the record. Not just what he said yesterday, but the day before and the week before. Explain not just this charge, but what happened to the previous charges. Give the people on the other side, the accused or the semi-accused, a chance to answer. Always explain the meaning of the charges. Try above all not to be a megaphone for McCarthy. Expose him to maximum scrutiny.

The best thing about the Washington *Post* in those days, for all its myriad weaknesses, was that it was very much a reporter's paper, it was not bound by too many rules and too much bureaucracy, it would allow a good reporter working a good story a good deal of freedom. There was simply an agreement that Marder would do all he could to put McCarthy in perspective, to get into the paper some subjective sense of what was really happening. It meant immense physical problems for the *Post.* Marder was methodical and very slow, and his stories were always long and they were always finished at the last minute. He was trying to get the extra dimension long after other reporters had put their McCarthyized versions on the wires and gone home. Nor could his stories be bitten off at the end, in the time-honored tradition of the profession, for the last paragraph in his story might be as important as the first. For Marder it meant staying late and going to the composing room to protect what he had written from being chopped off. It was an exhausting business, the stories were complicated and they were not easy to put together or edit. But if the rest of the nation was getting mostly McCarthy's charges, the *Post* readers were getting something fuller. The stories were also, unkind as it was to say so, a colleague noted, tedious, and McCarthy, after all, had never been tedious. Isn't there some way we can make this shorter or punchier? Al Friendly, by then the assistant managing editor of the *Post,* asked. No, said Marder, you can't be punchier. What about trying to synthesize it more? Friendly asked. No, said Marder, it's either this or going back to letting him use us. There really isn't any shortcut. Which Friendly understood, but both he and Wiggins agonized over it nonetheless, didn't giving McCarthy all the space somehow help him, direct more attention to him? "Aren't we making him bigger?" Friendly asked. It was a constant worry, and Marder would answer that McCarthy was there, he was not an apparition, he was indeed making these charges, he was destroying the lives of real people, and he would not vanish simply because the Washington *Post* wanted him to vanish. Besides, he said, either you believed that a full and fair and honorable explanation of the man and what he was doing was all your readers needed and would in the end bring him down, or there was no sense in being a journalist. The principle was at the heart of a democratic society. Yes, Wiggins and Friendly would answer, but still . . . wasn't it too much? Yes, he answered, it was too much because McCarthy was too much. Even when Ferdinand Kuhn, one of the most respected reporters on the paper, came up to him and said, "Murrey, how can you stand it? I mean, every day, the poison. Doesn't it destroy you?" Marder had answered that you had to believe that if you print the truth and enough facts, in the end it will be all right. You just have to believe that.

The paper, he thought, was very good about this. He had a sense of both their confidence and their trust in him, and yet at the same time he was conscious of their constant nervousness about the course they were on. There were times, he could tell, when the *Post* clearly would have liked a respite, when his editors felt exhausted by what he was doing and where it was taking them, and by the fact that until very late in the game the *Times* was not there with them. If only the *Times* had committed a full-time reporter to cover McCarthy the way he and Potter had been assigned. The *Times* had once assigned a reporter named Clayton Knowles, but Knowles had a left-wing background himself, had briefly been a member of the Communist Party, and that had proved embarrassing to the *Times* and not only had they pulled Knowles off, but for a long time they had seemed defensive and failed to put a reporter on McCarthy. Marder and Potter sometimes wondered what the problem was with the *Times.* Was it a sensitivity to the fact that some of their own people were vulnerable to subpoena? Or was it merely a technical lapse, a failure to create a Red Beat? Or was it arrogance, a belief that the *Times* was above that kind of saturation journalism? Marder realized that he was often on very thin ice, but he was also aware of having the trust of his superiors, and it made him more careful than ever. His editors worked hard to protect him from direct pressure, but it was always there; years later Kay Graham took his wife aside and said, "Your husband gave us many sleepless nights, but I prayed that he was right and thank God he was." The prayers were not very different from some of the ones he was offering himself. He and Potter felt very much alone and vulnerable. He had a terrible sense of how dangerous it all was. Was not every story close to libel? And close to a violation of liberties? Once he had written a story trying to disprove a McCarthy charge and had said that five people were *not* Communists. In the composing room the word "not" was somehow dropped out and the story came out saying these people *were* Communists and he had felt desperately ill. From that time on he tried to write his stories even more carefully, with a composing-room-proof construction, so that a dropped word could never again reverse his meaning. It was exhausting and exhilarating and terrifying. Once he had been in an elevator with Walter Winchell, who was then a great fellow traveler of McCarthy, and Winchell had pointed a finger at him and had said, "We're going to get you and we're going to destroy you."

But if liberties were being destroyed, he thought, and no one else was willing to be the watchdog, who but journalists would do it? He was watching people's careers being destroyed, their lives going down the drain. He remembered a particularly poignant moment, going out to talk to Edmund O. Clubb, one of the China hands already coming under attack. Marder tried to get Clubb to give his side of the story and Mrs. Clubb had tried to help him, pleading with her husband, "Edmund, please tell Mister Marder what happened, please tell him your side." Clubb answered, "I can't, I'm a member of the Foreign Service. The institution will protect me and we in the Foreign Service do not speak out against the congressional branch." In the end, no one protected Clubb.

McCarthy, of course, was playing up to Marder and Potter.

"That was a good story you did today, Murrey, I thought I'd call Phil Graham and tell him what a good job you're doing. He ought to give you a raise."

Then, noticing the dark look on Marder's face, McCarthy said, "Come on, Murrey, haven't I always been a good boy with you? Haven't I always been available?"

"Joe," Marder answered, "you haven't answered a call of mine in two years."

"Why, that's impossible. I can't believe it."

"Joe," said Marder, "cut the crap. You know and I know that your secretary has instructions not to put through any phone calls of mine."

"That's not true."

So Marder was barely back in his office when the phone rang. Joe being good old Joe, giving him a story, pledging Marder to secrecy, and two hours later, of course, the same story was over all the wires.

Marder's big story, the one that was the beginning of the end for McCarthy, came in the fall of 1953, when McCarthy seemed at his peak and Eisenhower, rather than taking him on, was giving way to him. Even the entire United States Army seemed in retreat before his advancing squad. McCarthy had held hearings earlier at Fort Monmouth, New Jersey, and there had been very good headlines out of that: *Communist Agents in the Sensitive Signal Corps Area.* Hot stuff. There were supposed to be thirty-three espionage agents there, and it had been a good road show, even by McCarthy standards. The hearings had struck Marder as particularly sloppy and careless, and he began to check around. He had very good sources in the Army, people who hated the fact that the Army was accommodating McCarthy and who were keeping their own records on McCarthy. They told Marder that these were bogus cases; in fact they were not McCarthy's cases at all, that Joseph R. McCarthy, R.-Wisconsin, had done no investigating of his own, but had simply piggybacked on some security cases that the Army had looked into and then thrown out. There was no question of espionage in any of these cases; rather they were dossiers filled with tiny bits of information, people who had gone to Front meetings or who had read the *Daily Worker.* There was not a single solid accusation of spying, the Army counsel told Marder. The charges were, even by McCarthy's standards, shockingly flimsy. So Marder decided to go up to Fort Monmouth and talk with the accused.

Not everyone on the paper thought it was a good idea. Phil Graham was opposed to it, simply on practical grounds. He thought it was a no-win situation, that you could never prove innocence, not in a match with a man who had only to imply guilt. And even if Marder were to prove that these particular people were innocent, who knew about a huge Army post like this, 25,000 men and women, there might well be a few Communists, Graham said; it was all a very risky business. But Graham did not tell Marder not to go, so he went and spent several days talking with the accused and some of their lawyers, coming away absolutely convinced that there was nothing to the McCarthy charges, that for all the smoke and blathering, McCarthy had not found a single Communist. He also knew there was considerable danger in stating this forthrightly in the *Post*, because it was already under terrible political pressure. "I might," he told Russ Wiggins, the editor, "cost you the paper. There's just no guarantee that there won't be other Communists and that we won't get hung." Wiggins told him, "You write what you have to. We'll worry about the paper."

The stories were very good and very strong, and most important, they changed the balance of the struggle. They were a clear challenge not just to McCarthy but, in a far more important way, to the United States Army as well. For months it had been in political retreat before the forces of Joe McCarthy. The Army knew McCarthy's charges were baseless, but it was afraid of a fight. Shortly after the Marder articles appeared, Robert Stevens, the Secretary of the Army, held a press conference. Stevens had been trying as hard as he could to appease McCarthy, but now he was in a vulnerable position because he was being questioned by a reporter who knew exactly what his dossiers contained. Yet he was in no way anxious for a confrontation with McCarthy. He might hate what McCarthy was doing, and he might, in his heart, be contemptuous of McCarthy, but there was a game to be played, and the game at the time, not just at the Army but elsewhere, was the surrender of a certain number of hostages to slow the wolves. But at the press conference Marder was, for such a mild man, quite relentless, asking question after question, giving Stevens no daylight, no respite. His colleagues, who usually interrupted any other reporter, deferred; either they had no interest in the case or they knew something important was happening and for once they were willing to stand on the sidelines. Slowly, inevitably, Marder was cornering Stevens, and Stevens knew it, knew he was being set up, that Marder was offering him a chopping block upon which Stevens could place his very own head. Stevens ducked and faked and equivocated and finally, cornered, he admitted, yes, that there had been no accusation of spying in the Fort Monmouth cases. Up until then the Army had been giving ground, looking the other way, fuzzing its statements, but Marder had drawn a line that Stevens would have preferred to leave undrawn. Later Stevens pointed out that he had not volunteered the information, that he had been forced into it, but it was too late. The Army had been forced to hold turf. Thus the stage was set for the Army-McCarthy hearings.

At which point Phil Potter played an important role. Potter genuinely hated McCarthy. But he had watched Stevens that day and he knew what had happened and that this might be the turning point. He had remembered something he had filed away a long time ago. It was about television. McCarthy had been on television regularly, but mostly in brief news clips of the television shows of the day, brief flashes. Nothing very lengthy. There had been one or two fully televised hearings, including one concerning Reed Harris, an official at the USIA. McCarthy and a few people around him had liked the way those hearings had gone; everyone told McCarthy how good he was. It was in the nature of people, seeing their hero in the white hat go after the baddies in the black hats, to applaud. But to those who had paid attention, there were some minor warning signals. A few of the lower-ranking staff members, people who had little access to McCarthy himself, checked the mail and got a surprise. The mail was, in fact, very troubling. Most supporters of McCarthy at that time saw him as a lonely knight. There was a Communist menace and it was very large and it was peopled by Communist thugs, and in its way was only Joe McCarthy, standing a lonely vigil. That was the impression conveyed by the headlines, and of course by McCarthy himself; his tendency toward excess and bullying had been obscured. But on television the scene was different. The accused did not look like thugs, they looked like simple, pathetic, often rather frail people, accidental victims, clearly misplaced. And McCarthy did not look like Gary Cooper in *High Noon;* he looked like a bully browbeating his opponents, interrupting them, leaning on them, pushing them around. The mail on the Reed Harris case was very bad. One of the low-ranking staff members had mentioned this fact to Phil Potter and Potter had filed it away. Then, as the Army-McCarthy hearings were about to begin, Potter remembered what he had heard and told Senator John McClellan about it. Give up on other procedural matters, he recommended to McClellan, but above all hold on to the right to televise the proceedings. McCarthy had been a little dubious about televising the hearings and this time McClellan had insisted, he held firm, and, being conservative, he was invulnerable to attack by McCarthy. So televised hearings there would be. It was a fateful decision. For if NBC and CBS were too busy and too rich and too nervous to televise these hearings, then ABC, with an almost empty schedule, was not. Kintner decided to put them on, and there, day after day, Joseph R. McCarthy did in Joseph R. McCarthy.

II

# 6 / The New York Times

They were good friends, the Restons and the Grahams. Scotty Reston loved Phil Graham, and they often played golf together. Scotty was a superb golfer who had for a time considered a professional career, and if Phil was not exactly a skilled golfer he was nonetheless an audacious and enthusiastic one, bringing to the propulsion of a ball so small a great zest; he would, even as he teed off, tell of what a great shot he was going to hit, what a shame it was that NBC and CBS were not there to record this most singular event. Scotty, of course, delighted in that as he delighted in all of Phil Graham's multiple enthusiasms and energies, the way that Phil always seemed to take over a room when he entered, breathing more life and energy into everyone, and breaking the social amenities in a way that Scotty himself would never have dared, making everyone laugh and at the same time keeping them off balance by homing in on their weak spots. Reston, good strict Calvinist that he was, admired that charm, and that high-powered, seemingly loose energy, the ability to risk so much and get away with so much. He himself was too old-fashioned a man to be like that, he was not without his humor and his light touch, but these qualities were far more subtle and reserved in him. Our Scottish Pope, Phil called him, and it was a charming nickname, applied not without affection and accuracy, and also not without a certain amount of edge, for it would remind Reston and others that perhaps Scotty was a bit stiff and traditional, a bit too much the Calvinist in his daily life and in his columns. But it was Phil Graham of the *Post* who was very much in constant pursuit of Scotty Reston of the *Times.* Graham wanted desperately to hire Reston and bring him across the street from the *Times,* where he had become the symbolic journalistic figure of the city and that generation. At the *Post,* Phil Graham hoped, Reston would begin the process of turning his somewhat local paper into a truly national journal, perhaps even a miniature of the *Times* itself. The attempt at seduction was almost constant, the offers generous—two, three times what Reston was already making.

It was not by chance that he had picked out Reston. Reston was the dominant Washington journalist of the fifties. For slightly more than a decade James Reston owned that town as no print reporter would ever own it again. He had the most powerful platform in Washington at a time when there was no real competition, and he used that platform with a shrewd combination of force and subtlety. He was very aggressive without seeming to be aggressive. He used the telephone brilliantly but his voice was never demanding. There were long pauses between the words. His voice showed that he was never in very much of a hurry. That meant he was trustworthy. He had become, by the early fifties, the journalist that all the young reporters in America admired and wanted to work for, a symbol not of journalism past, but of journalism to be, fair, civilized, intelligent, and internationalist. There was nothing small or parochial about him; he was interested only in large issues, which meant big stories. At the center of his work was America's involvement with the world. As the press was slowly, almost unconsciously, institutionalizing itself, beginning to set national standards for itself, he, by the quality of his work, and his personal status and conduct, seemed to represent what journalism might become, a serious and respected profession.

He was Walter Lippmann's close friend, and more, he was the great political columnist's protégé, even more than Lippmann was far more the role model for working reporters, since he was a working reporter himself. The more Reston in his columns ventured into the world of theory and great ideas, the more awkward he seemed; the closer his columns stayed to the reporting he had done that week, the stronger they were. In that sense he was no Lippmann, though on occasion, with mixed results, he tried to emulate him. His best work, like that of other reporters, was shaped by the brutality of deadlines, and he thus brought Lippmann's philosophy to a working pragmatic level. He was, as Lippmann was not, a practitioner of daily reporting (a difference of which he was acutely aware, that he could talk to people as Lippmann could not; he was proud of the fact that he could get in his car and drive into the backcountry and stop and interview a farmer. "Can you imagine Walter doing that?" he had asked friends, a touch of pride to his voice).

His power in the Washington of the fifties was unique. At the start of the decade Arthur Krock was still the *New York Times* Washington bureau chief, but Krock was not working the town as Reston was, Reston was connected to all the men in their own forties and fifties who were now about to be powerful, the best kind of sources. But he had the power of *The New York Times* and it was in those days an awesome platform, any government official who had an idea or a viewpoint or a document wanted it in the *Times,* so Reston became the proxy for all the paper's national and international reporters. It was a remarkable moment for a paper; the *Trib* was in sharp decline, television had not yet arrived, and radio in peacetime was not the powerful force it had been during the war. Of the news magazines, *Time* was too partisan and *Newsweek* was too weak and bloodless. The *Times* owned the town, *The New York Times* was, in fact, what journalism in America aspired to.

.  .  .

"How do you like the new century?" Adolph Ochs had written his mother in 1900. "It certainly opens auspiciously for us." Indeed it had: in 1896, when to his family's dismay Ochs (already deeply in debt) had bought the floundering *Times* for $75,000 in borrowed money, its circulation was about 9,000, it was $300,000 in debt, and it was losing more than $2,500 a week. But Ochs was a formidable man. By 1900, despite the Spanish-American War, which was a bonanza for his yellow competitors, his *New York Times* had reached a circulation of 82,000, it was comfortably in the black, and the future was his. He was a journalist by way of the printshop and the business side; he had no college education and he did not pretend to be a writer or a pundit. He had a passion to succeed and be respectable, not a passion to inform. But he knew a lot about printing, and he was a very shrewd businessman and he had a particular genius for turning necessity into virtue. If all the best comic strips of the day had been signed up by competing newspapers, then Adolph Ochs would make it a point of honor that the *Times* would never run comics. If the two most successful papers of the day, both in New York, Pulitzer's *World* and Hearst's *Telegram,* had with their lively, often overheated journalism taken over mass circulations of more than 300,000 each, then Ochs would not compete with them for *their* readers. Instead, as well suited his personal manner, serious, formal, a young man of rectitude, he would bring out a paper for the *good* people of New York, serious, formal, well educated. It would not, his slogan said, soil their breakfast linen, that being an age when people still had breakfast linen.

So he had arrived, it was a new era, and a new century. *The New York Times* when he took it over had a grand total of two telephones and two typewriters. Most of the reporters wrote their stories in longhand and were much offended by the din created by the younger men who actually typed. This became something of an office conflict. Finally one of the *Times*'s handymen built a large table with a felt top to muffle the sound and the typists were placed in a far corner of the room. The *Times* in addition would print news that was muffled. Ochs wanted nothing that would shock or offend or cause controversy. Since he could not win a segment of the market by being lively, he would win by being serious. He would emphasize news, serious, worthy news, the kind of news that respected men of finance and state would want to read. New York was the financial capital of the country at the time and so Ochs decided to fill his paper with as much news as he could to interest these men; all the news of finance, all market reports, all real estate deals, all government announcements, particularly the long and dull ones which other newspapers ignored, were welcomed to the *Times.* Ochs listed all fires in the city, and in addition he listed the names of all store buyers who arrived in New York to shop. That alone was one of his crucial decisions, it helped make the *Times* *the* paper of the retail fashion business, and it increased its advertising leverage overnight. The *Times* was becoming a paper of record. A dull record perhaps, but that did not bother Ochs, he liked a dull paper, and he did not mind if people thought him a bit dull as long as they treated him with respect. He did not want controversy, he wanted to be sound, respectable, and safe. Important people spoke well of a publisher who put out a sound but boring paper; they did not speak so well of a publisher who put out a lively paper that on occasion chronicled their divorce cases.

All of this was very much in keeping with the man himself, the patriarch of the family, founder of the Ochs-Sulzberger newspaper dynasty. Adolph Ochs, born in 1858, was the son of German-Jewish immigrants, proper though by no means successful or rich people. In fact, his father, Julius Ochs, who had settled in America in 1845, was something of a failed dreamer, if not an outright dilettante. Young Adolph had quit school at the age of thirteen and become a printer's apprentice in order to support his family, and had become publisher of the Chattanooga *Times* in 1878, needing his father's signature on the papers since he was not yet twenty-one. He was a serious and determined young man, old long before his years. One did not think of Adolph Ochs smiling; he was a man whose tie was always tied.

He was very sensitive about being Jewish, which was a dominating characteristic about him and the dynasty he founded. They were good and respectable German Jews at a time when the nation was being flooded with Jewish immigrants from Russia and Poland; the German Jews, who had seemed more German than the Germans in the old country, now if anything seemed more Protestant than the Protestants in the new. But the Eastern European Jews, given to beards, long hair, and radical political theories, did not fit in. The smell of the old world and old grievances was about them. Their presence stirred anti-Semitism (Adolph's brother George believed that those immigrants with their old world ways caused anti-Semitism not just against themselves but against older, better-behaved, more established Jews; if they would just tidy themselves up, cut their hair, and behave themselves things would be all right). Ochs, good citizen that he was and intended to be, coveted the respect of the good people of the Gentile world. He was what was then called a White Jew. He was determined to show, principally through his newspaper, that Jews were hard-working, trustworthy, and made good citizens. He wanted to succeed, to make the paper profitable, but in truth he wanted and coveted respectability far more than he coveted material profit. That was crucial to the tone of the paper. He wanted the best people to read his paper, and as they did, to think well of him and his kind.

Whereas other publishers had traditionally used their newspapers to amplify their political opinions and were intensely partisan, Ochs wanted none of that, he had no particular political opinions, other than that America was a good society. He wanted as little partisanship as possible. Partisanship, to him, was always dangerous; it could backfire. Whereas other publishers with powerful egos loved being at the center of public attention, Ochs hated the idea, it was his style to avoid public attention as much as possible, since public attention was always a little dangerous; if you were a Jew and you were successful, particularly in that era, people were bound to resent it. That translated directly into the tone of the paper's columns; he did not want to make people unhappy, he did not want controversy, he wanted to make as few judgments as possible, and he wanted as weak an editorial page as possible. He wanted to be respectable rather than powerful; he did not want the controversy that went with power. He seemed a stodgy, somewhat pompous figure. Much of what he said at editorial meetings often seemed silly or even childish. Yet his instinct about the possibilities of a given paper was uncanny, and all his major decisions turned out to be the right ones. The brilliant Herbert Bayard Swope, the most scintillating editor of his time, frustrated by the odd combination of Ochs's pedestrian manner and his relentless success, once called him "a subcalibre genius."

Ochs was immensely hard-working, certainly the best businessman of all the publishers in New York at that time. Besides, events were coming his way. It was the right era for the type of paper he was publishing. He was presiding at the *Times* at a time when America was coming of age and entering the world, and when the level of education was constantly rising. All the forces unleashed in the world were going to make for a smaller world where people were more concerned with international and national events, and all the educational forces were conspiring to create a better readership.

So he had made the *Times* a success almost from the start. In the beginning he had improved the typeface and used better ink and it had all worked; in the first year the circulation had gone from 9,000 to 21,000 and by 1898 the circulation was up to 25,000. Then in 1898 his success was for the first time seriously threatened and he responded brilliantly. The Spanish-American War, rich as it was in the jingoism of the era, was exactly what Hearst and Pulitzer loved, and they moved in what seemed like battalion strength, they filled gunboats with reporters, photographers, illustrators (when Frederic Remington, the great artist, had complained that there was too little action, Hearst had wired back that *he* would furnish the war, and Remington would furnish the pictures). They loved a story like this, rich as it was with blood and flag. Their coverage was full, lavish, and properly gory. Ochs tried working in concert with other newspaper editors, but there was no way he could match the giants. His success was stalled, his circulation began to drop, and his ownership of the paper, fragile as it was with heavy debts incurred back in Chattanooga, seemed in jeopardy. Then in October he made his decision. The *World* and the *Journal* each cost two cents an issue. He could not match either in war coverage, so he would compete with them in price. Ochs announced that he was dropping the price of the *Times,* so serious and respectable and priced accordingly, from three cents a copy to *one cent.* It was a stroke of genius. Some said that the paper was seeking a new audience and would start to sensationalize the news. Some of the *Times* reporters, restless with the prohibitions against being stylish, were overjoyed. But they were wrong, and Ochs was right, the paper remained what it had been, and the circulation soared. Ochs defended his decision by pointing out that once the paper was put together and ready to print, it cost him less per copy to print 100,000 copies than, say, 40,000, that the real expense came before the first issue was printed, the cost was in the printers and stereotypers.

It was a stunning victory. The Spanish-American War, ironically enough, was the making of the *Times*. A year later Ochs's circulation was 76,000, triple what it had been before he cut the price. Advertising multiplied along with circulation. Ochs had created and now strengthened his base. The *Times* had a solid part of a market that was bound to increase and become more affluent every year, just as his competitors were slicing up shares that were bound, in the near future, to diminish. It was, above all, a respectable newspaper. (When Ochs purchased the paper he sponsored a contest for a slogan. The winning slogan, absolutely dreadful, "All the World News, But Not a School for Scandal," was, mercifully, never used.) It wanted the attention of the governing class, the right and proper people, and it did not like offending that class. Whereas other newspapers of the age were to a large degree a reflection of their readers' appetites and tastes, the *Times* was different, it was an almost unconscious reflection of Ochs's desire for status, and as such it was a reflection of governing-class norms, more conservative and status quo–oriented than it suspected. It told the right people in government and finance what they needed to know, and inevitably it came to reflect the concerns and ambitions of those people. It was not by any stretch of the imagination a popular paper. If it were to become popular, which it did by midcentury, then people would have to grow up to the level of the paper.

Ochs was also a good patriot. Like most newcomers to America, he was unusually sensitive about his semi-immigrant status. In 1908 William Bayard Hale, one of his best reporters, received a rare two-hour audience with Kaiser Wilhelm. The Kaiser took advantage of the interview to rant and rave against foreign powers, most noticeably the British, for the entire time. It was an extremely bellicose interview, part of being a good Christian, the Kaiser said, was the ability to go to war. War, after all, was not a bad idea, a little "jolly good fighting" was good for a nation. "We are Christians by forcible conversion," he added. All in all it was a very explosive, powerful interview and Hale did not even dare cable it back to his paper. When he returned home, Ochs, his managing editor, Carr Van Anda, and several other editors studied the material. In the end they decided to send Hale to Washington to show the interview to President Theodore Roosevelt. Roosevelt was astonished by the bellicosity of the Kaiser's words. "I don't believe the Emperor wanted this stuff published," the President said. "If he did, he's a goose." Roosevelt said that he did not have the power to kill the interview, but in his opinion it never should be published. The *Times,* he added, could save mankind by killing it. So the interview, which turned out to be a very real and prophetic reflection of not only what the Kaiser said but indeed what he meant to do, was killed.

A decade later, near the end of the war, there was a disturbing incident in which Ochs's patriotism was severely questioned. Austria, one of the enemy powers, was putting out peace feelers. The *Times* editorially welcomed peace with Austria, but the war was going well for America, passions were too high, everyone wanted complete and total victory, and there was a violent reaction against the *Times* editorial. The paper became the target of a major jingoistic hate campaign. Denunciations came pouring in against Ochs, many of them citing his German-Jewish ancestry. Woodrow Wilson himself was reported furious over the editorial. Ochs and his top people met with Colonel Edward House, Wilson's prime aide, not so much to defend the editorial as to proclaim their patriotism. But it was a terrible moment for Ochs. Old friends turned away from him. He was absolutely shattered. He was sure that everything he had worked for was going to be lost, that he was going to lose the *Times.* He went into a deep and prolonged depression. He thought for a long time of retiring, placing the paper in the hands of trustees, all of whom would be publicly chosen. It reminded him again how fragile his position was, how easily it could be undermined. The crisis passed but his depression lasted.

It was not his first or his last depression, for he was almost surely a manic-depressive. There are no exact records concerning his illnesses, and much less was known about mental illness in those days (nor were family members as anxious to face the realities of illness), and his family, which still controls the *Times,* carefully smudged the descriptions of his sickness in the authorized history of the paper. But there was talk about his melancholia, and his occasional prolonged periods of depression. In truth he was a man of enormous energies, and when he was up and on a high and believed in what he was doing, nothing could stop him. He was confident, forceful, and autocratic. (Being told that he looked a great deal like Napoleon, he answered, "But I am very much taller than Napoleon.") When he was up, he believed he could achieve anything, and he would work endless hours, his touch was stunningly sure. But even as a young man his ferocity of ambition made others around him uneasy; he had bought the Chattanooga *Times* when he was scarcely out of his boyhood, and he had made a success out of that. But then he had lost a great deal of money on land speculation and no matter how successful the Chattanooga paper was, it could not get him out of debt. The purchase of *The New York Times* was a way of getting out of debt. When he first bought it, other members of his family were absolutely appalled, this was one more manifestation of what had been considered his quirkiness, and they thought seriously of committing him. Later, during the years of his greatest triumphs, the illness seemed to hang more heavily upon him, there were long, long periods of deep depression when he seemed almost immobilized, when he could not work and when he simply stared out into space for hours on end. During these depressions he became totally convinced that he was going to lose the *Times,* lose all his money, and that his death was close at hand. (During one of his depressions he became obsessed with the subject of death, and though still a reasonably young man bought a plot of land for his grave, writing to his family that he was very pleased with the purchase because it was "on nice high ground. Very desirable. No malaria.")

He was not in any sense a man of news. He knew that he wanted a serious paper but he did not know exactly how to put it out, how to translate his general sense of what the paper should be into reality, how to make it more than lists. He knew he needed an editor of comparable vision and great technical skill. In 1904 he hired Carr V. Van Anda. It was the combination of the two men, Ochs and Van Anda, which was to make the *Times* the truly dominant national institution it became, for Van Anda knew how to take Ochs's vision and turn it into a daily reality. Carr Van Anda was the legendary editor of his era. He was a brilliant and original man, perhaps even, thought some of the men who worked for him, an authentic genius. He was also cold and domineering. Everything in his manner advised his staff to keep its distance. His reporters stood in terror of him. There was no small talk in his discourse. Among themselves *Times* reporters referred to his look as "the Van Anda death ray." Everyone was called Mister (indeed, even Van Anda and Ochs called each other Mister Van Anda and Mister Ochs). He was not easily approachable. Once, rather late in his career, after a sportswriter was given what was then the most precious of *Times* commodities, a by-line, a delegation of reporters went to see Van Anda and ask if they too could have by-lines. "The *Times* is not running a reporter's directory," he said, declining their suggestion. That was that. He was not much interested in literary style and he did not care about good writing. He wanted news, news and facts. The grayer it was, the better. In that sense he was a man after Ochs's own heart.

He was not particularly caught up in politics; his real passion was reserved for science, which was fortunate, since this was an era of vast and rapid changes in the natural sciences. Van Anda was trained as a mathematician. He was absolutely fascinated by science and math and they took him to the study of astronomy and physics and into modern exploration. He had scored one of his great beats during the sinking of the *Titanic*. The news that the *Titanic* had struck an iceberg broke very late, at 1:20 A.M. Then there was complete silence from the ship. Since the information was so fragmentary and the *Titanic* so unsinkable, other New York editors published the bulletins but reiterated the fact that the ship was unsinkable. Not Van Anda. He studied the information, pondering the silence from the ship, he did his own mathematical calculations, and he decided the *Titanic* was in fact sinking. The *Times* alone led with that. It was a great beat on an immense story. His legend was made. A few years later it was made even greater when Einstein was visiting Princeton. Einstein at the time was just beginning to publish his mathematical formulae in America. A *Times* reporter covered a lecture and brought back an immensely complicated mathematical formula from the lecture. Van Anda studied it, and decided there was a mistake in it. The reporter called the Princeton math department, where a mathematics professor checked the equation on the blackboard where Einstein had written it down and reported that the *Times* man had copied it accurately. But because Van Anda was taken so seriously, the professor said he would bring it up with Einstein personally. Einstein scanned the notes and called back. "Yes," he said, "Mr. Van Anda is right. I made a mistake in transcribing the equation on the blackboard." Thus are legends secured.

Van Anda had been the managing editor of the *Times* for ten years when World War I began. It was the perfect story for the *Times*, serious, complicated, distant, multifaceted, multifronted. The *Times* now had the resources and the growing sense of tradition to be able to cover it properly; few other American papers had either the inclination or the will to do so. It was also the kind of journalism that Van Anda knew and understood and loved, and he went all out. He wanted more coverage than any other paper; he was determined, above all else, to be comprehensive. The *Times*'s reporters at that time were perhaps not the era's most brilliant, indeed the paper was still using a lot of stringers, reporters who were not on the staff but took regular free-lance assignments. Still, in terms of totality of coverage, there was nothing like the *Times*. That was the *Times*'s trademark, to be the most comprehensive. As many as twenty reporters were covering the war at once. Van Anda was fascinated by it all, his mathematical mind was captivated. He would study all the maps of Europe, trace the movements of the various armies, decide himself where major battles would probably take place, and then with a surprisingly prophetic instinct, dispatch his correspondents accordingly. The *Times* was also printing a Sunday rotogravure section filled with powerful photos of the fighting. Television and radio and newsreels had not yet arrived, and photographic camera techniques had improved markedly in the fifty years since the Civil War, and there was a power, a starkness, and an immediacy to these photos that had never been rivaled in the daily press. It was perhaps the most dramatic reflection yet of war. In 1913, on the eve of the outbreak of fighting, the *Times* had a daily circulation of 242,000 and a Sunday circulation of 158,000; in 1918, the last year of the war, the daily was 352,000, and the Sunday circulation was over *486,000*. The *Times* was ever more dominant as the paper of an influential and expanding class.

It held an enviable position, the vital center. It was judged in the partisanship of the era to be above partisanship, and that was a style in which the more modern young educated Americans preferred to think of themselves. The war had brought America far more directly into world affairs. A governing class needed a paper like the *Times*. In the early days under Ochs the *Times* had been called, with some accuracy, a paper owned by Jews, edited by Catholics, and read by Protestants. That began to change in the thirties; there was a new generation of Jews who became *Times* readers and that made the paper even stronger. Many of these new readers were not yet college-educated, but in terms of their seriousness about the world, their own literacy, and above all their ambitions for their children, they might just as well have been; college educations were on the immediate horizon for them. They or their parents had come from the old country, and in some ways they were still bound to it, if only by fear and hatred. But they permitted the *Times*'s editors the luxury of putting out an international paper while still having a surprisingly broadbased local circulation. Probably no other city in the country could claim a constituency like that. For the editors of a serious newspaper they represented an enormous boon. They meant that the *Times* could make a virtue of its seriousness, its internationalism.

The thirties were the years in which the *Times* solidified its position. The *World*, which had been a great paper under Pulitzer, had died, victim of an appallingly weak business side. At one point in 1930 Pulitzer had offered the *Morning World* to Ochs for virtually nothing, telling him that the acquisition would give the *Times* an instant morning circulation of one million. But it was the Depression, money was tight, and Ochs, who was uncommonly wise about papers' constituencies, refused. In fact, he did not want the *World* circulation even as a gift. He did not think that very many readers would switch; after all, they had had innumerable chances in the past to become *Times* readers and had rejected the opportunity. If they went anywhere, he suspected it would be to Hearst's *American*. He thought the acquisition might well prove a burden, certainly pushing up his production costs and then his advertising costs, and thus disturbing the subtle harmony of his entire operation. So he decided to stay put. (Later, when the *World* went out of business, he predicted at an editorial meeting that the *Times* would get 75,000 more daily and 100,000 more Sunday readers from Pulitzer's paper. His earlier prediction was far more accurate. The death of the *World* touched the *Times*'s circulation not at all.) But papers were dying all around him. In 1927, just before the Depression, there were twelve papers in New York and three in Brooklyn; that number was now fast declining. The *Times* with its sophisticated readership had a firm hold on the class retail advertising, and when the *World* folded the *Times* scored one serious victory: it took over the *World*'s leadership in classified advertising. That was important; classified-advertising leadership was a prize for any paper, so much money coming in for so little work. When the *World* first died, there were other papers which simply republished the *Times*'s classifieds, unchanged, in order to support their claim to be number one in total linage.

So, year by year, the *Times* was in a stronger position in the morning, while other papers were becoming weaker. Broadcasting was beginning to change reading habits, radio was hurting afternoon newspapers and especially hurting papers like the Hearst press. By the mid-thirties, it was clear that the *Times* was locked in a struggle with the *other* serious morning establishment paper, the *Herald Tribune*, which was very much like the *Times* in tone. Like the *Times*, it emphasized good reporting, but its staff was a little smaller and a good deal livelier. There was by the beginning of the forties a suspicion that only one of the two would survive, the good gray *Times* or the good, not quite so gray, *Trib*.

Ochs had taken his dynasty well into the new century, but it was in the reign of Arthur Hays Sulzberger, his son-in-law, that the *Trib* was in fact beaten. Sulzberger had married Ochs's only child, Iphigene, to no great enthusiasm on the part of the patriarch. If marry she must, he would have preferred she marry someone with a background in journalism. Sulzberger was a very handsome man, scion of a very old and aristocratic New York Jewish family. He was intelligent and gentle, reasonably sure of his place in society, modest by comparison to Ochs. As a young man learning the business, it did not seem to bother him that others might regard him as the son-in-law. Ochs had been in no particular hurry to advance Sulzberger's career, nor did he seem to like the idea of getting older. When he was in his sixties he issued an edict forbidding the *Times* to refer to people in their late sixties and early seventies as "old." He had brought Sulzberger along quite slowly and he had once told him quite late in his life not to push him. "I'm not dead yet," he had said. Yet Iphigene Ochs Sulzberger was his princess. She, like the paper itself, was a genuine extension of Ochs and his dreams. In 1902, when President Theodore Roosevelt had autographed a photo for her, Ochs had been impressed and proud. His dreams would be realized. "Perhaps this incident may impress you with the importance of the training Iphigene should have," Ochs told his wife. "She will be much courted. Her good will shall be placed at a high value. There is nothing beyond her reach if I live ten years longer and meet with no mishap." Ochs lived some thirty-three years longer, and there was little beyond Iphigene's reach and she was indeed much courted. She was smart and well educated and socially conscious. Ochs had taught her to muffle her views slightly, so that she should not seem too demanding or too sure of herself. She learned that lesson well. Much of what she said was understated, particularly to the various editors of the paper, and it was easy to mistake the fact that she was very strong-willed.

It was *her* family's paper, not her husband's, and she could raise a decisive voice. On the question of who would succeed him as publisher, Ochs gave one vote to Sulzberger, one vote to his nephew, Julius Ochs Adler, and one vote to Iphigene Sulzberger; in May 1935, one month after Ochs's death, not surprisingly Sulzberger became publisher of the *Times*. He was modest, he knew the limits of his own knowledge about newspapers, and he was not a man to presume to have knowledge he did not possess. Nevertheless, he wanted to upgrade and modernize the paper while holding to its tradition of excellence. His wife was very much a part of his decision making. It was not an age in which a German-Jewish father, no matter how adoring, would turn over a paper like the *Times* to his daughter, but she put her stamp on the paper in endless subtle and not so subtle ways. She was the enduring symbol of the family in this century; she was the one who at the age of eleven had helped lay the cornerstone for the new Times Tower with these words: "I dedicate this building to the uses of *The New York Times*. May those who labor herein see the right and serve it with courage and intelligence for the welfare of mankind, the best interests of the United States and its people, and for decent and dignified journalism, and may the blessing of God ever rest upon them." Strong words and sentiments and she believed them. Of the four publishers of the modern *New York Times* she was the daughter of one, the wife of the second, mother-in-law of the third, and mother of the fourth; thus she more than anyone else was part of the living organic continuity of the family and the paper.

She had a very strong idea of what the paper should be and, even more important, who should represent it, particularly overseas. She did not care so much about the style and manner of the *Times*'s local reporters, and they were a diverse group. But the foreign correspondents and the Washington correspondents were of a type, they had to be Gentlemen. In addition to possessing the right skills, they had to be fine young men, intelligent and proper, they had to be the right kind of people, attractive—if not physically (although that did not hurt), then at least as human beings. They must not have rough edges or New York accents and they must not embarrass the *Times* among the important people of the world. They were chosen much as the State Department chose its ambassadors, and they became the elite. They were more often than not quite well-educated, attractive Protestants, and they tended to be soft-voiced and never too aggressive. Though the paper was Jewish-owned, it was not eager in the thirties and forties and fifties to send Jewish reporters overseas or to place them in executive posts.

In 1948 A. M. Rosenthal, who was Abraham to his birth certificate, Abe to his friends, but, in the euphemistic tradition of the *Times,* A.M. to readers of his by-lines, then one of the most talented young men on the staff, went to Paris on a temporary assignment. What Rosenthal coveted most in the world in those days was a place on the prestigious foreign staff, and though he had reported with distinction from the United Nations, he had not yet been promoted to foreign correspondent. While in Paris, someone stole a twenty-dollar traveler's check from his hotel and Rosenthal raised a considerable fuss, threatening to deduct the amount from his bill. The French concierge, much annoyed, immediately called the *Times* bureau and protested to C. L. Sulzberger. Sulzberger, then both correspondent and foreign editor, as well as nephew of the publisher, thereupon decided that Rosenthal was the *wrong sort* of young man. He had made a fuss and might possibly stain the reputation of the *Times.* Sulzberger, without mentioning the incident to Rosenthal, blackballed him for some seven years from the foreign staff.

The family was determined that the paper not seem to be too Jewish. In 1937, when editorial-page editor Rollo Ogden died, Arthur Krock thought he had been promised the job, then one of the most prestigious on the paper. But Sulzberger gave it instead to John Finley, much to Krock's dismay. "It's a family enterprise," Sulzberger said, "and it's a Jewish paper and we have a number of Jewish reporters working for us. But in all the years I've been here we have never put a Jew in the showcase." Then Krock replied that his mother, whom he much admired, was not Jewish, only his father, who was something of a ne'er-do-well, was Jewish. By the laws of the prophet, he added triumphantly, you're not Jewish unless your mother is Jewish. Sulzberger looked at him and said, "Arthur, how do you know all that if you aren't Jewish?" Krock, for his part, as Washington bureau chief, hid his own Jewishness and most assuredly did not want Jewish reporters in his bureau. When he had beaten back the umpteenth attempt of New York reporter Warren Moscow to join the bureau, Felix Belair, one of Krock's favorites in the bureau, accosted him. "There are some people here," said Belair, "who think you're anti-Semitic." "Well," said Krock, "maybe I am." So it was that the *Times* had, in effect, a double standard of who could work for it and where they were assigned.

Slowly and steadily Arthur and Iphigene Sulzberger upgraded the paper and the quality of the reporters. Soon the foreign reporting, if not as brilliant as that of the Chicago *Daily News,* was the most comprehensive in the country. The paper had become, almost without anyone realizing it, a family trust; the paper enhanced the family and the family enhanced the paper. Sulzberger, perhaps even more than his father-in-law, believed in putting back what he had taken out. The instinct of the family was not to make money, it was to put out the best paper possible, and to make enough money to make that possible. Their real goal was not wealth, although they became very wealthy, or power in the classic sense of being able to dictate policy to politicians they had installed. Rather, it was the greatness of the paper and the respect and prestige that this could bring to them. That was what they coveted, the foremost of those German-Jewish families, respectability and professional (if not social) acceptance. It was much more important than money, anyone could have money and money if anything only intensified resentment and anti-Semitism. The *Times* would be a symbol of the Jew as a good citizen. Whatever convictions Arthur Hays Sulzberger held about most things in his life, his sensitivity to anti-Semitism never abated. Above all, he did not want the paper to be too Jewish in tone, and he did not want too many Jewish executives. He, like many senior Jewish leaders of his generation, did not want Jews in places where they might attract attention and create controversy. In 1939 he was among a group of Jewish leaders who urged Franklin Roosevelt not to appoint Felix Frankfurter to the Supreme Court, for fear that it might increase anti-Semitism. During World War II, with the rise of anti-Semitism internationally, he suffered terrible nightmares about his own and his family's vulnerability. It was a very real fear to him. These fears touched the paper itself, and there is no doubt that when in 1970 Spiro Agnew began his orchestrated attacks upon media owners, this touched the rawest of nerves in the *Times* executive office and in other great media centers, where Agnew's attacks were viewed as thinly coded anti-Semitism, and the nervousness was underscored when the Agnew attacks were followed up by a vast increase in anti-Semitic mail.

All of this desire for respectability and a place in the society became part of the family tradition and became a trust, something larger than the family evoking the best of its spirit and values, part of the governing characteristic of the family and of the newspaper, the paper and the tradition. That it was a family business meant that the tradition and sense of obligation could to some degree be passed on; the young members of the family were exposed to it early and often. They determined their own levels of profit, which were often, right through the sixties, dangerously low, and they showed their books to no one except each other and the IRS. By contemporary financial standards they were old-fashioned and arrogant, but they made the paper better. Beyond that they had fashioned something with a life and dynamic of its own. The editors and reporters who came to work for the *Times* because of its tradition intensified the tradition; they became as much a part of the paper as the family.

While Van Anda's distrust of stylish writing survived, and much of the paper read as if written by the same people who wrote government documents, the *Times* was gradually becoming somewhat more professional and less formal. The beat was picking up. The reporting was becoming more sharply defined. The laissez-faire editorial policy of the twenties, when New York simply tended to print what came in, was changing. Whereas in the twenties the various Washington correspondents of the *Times* decided themselves what they wanted to cover—which meant that three reporters might cover the same assignment, with all three versions printed in the paper—by the middle of the thirties there was an assignment desk to prevent this kind of repetition. The paper was becoming streamlined. As World War II started, Arthur Hays Sulzberger made a crucial decision that enabled the *Times* to become the dominant paper of New York and thus of the country in the fifties and the sixties. Throughout the thirties the *Times* had been locked in solid, intense competition with the New York *Herald Tribune*. The business underpinning of the *Times* was considerably more secure, it had a lock on the New York retail-store advertising, and it made the *Times* Sunday edition in particular a valuable part of the property. On the eve of World War II both papers were doing well: the *Times* had a circulation of 481,000 to the *Trib*'s 347,000. If anything, in the past few years the *Trib* seemed to be gaining on the *Times* just a little. The *Times* did better in the city of New York; the *Trib*, more Republican, did better in the suburbs, which in that era were also more Republican. In 1942 the government decided to ration newsprint, and the two papers made absolutely different decisions on how to apportion their limited amount of space. Sulzberger, believing that this, above all, was not a time to profiteer, and was instead a time for maximum coverage, put a sharp limit on advertising and used his space for news. His advertisers complained and threatened but he would not yield. The decision was different at the *Trib*, where for years they had envied the *Times* its superior hold on New York's department stores. Helen Reid at the *Trib* saw this as a chance to pass the *Times* for good in advertising linage. Suddenly, *Times* profits were indeed down, and *Trib* profits were way, way up. In 1942 the two papers were almost even, and then in 1943 for the first time the *Trib* pulled ahead in department-store advertising. But it was a victory of the most pyrrhic sort; the *Times*, with its massive coverage of World War II, had consolidated its position with readers more than ever, its claim to true seriousness now was virtually unchallengeable. As soon as the war was over, the newsprint restrictions were relaxed and the *Times* surged ahead, leaving the *Trib* far behind. Only one serious morning paper would make it and the *Times* had won. The *Times* would become ever richer and more prosperous, and the *Trib* would no longer be able to sustain itself as a healthy number two, as it had before the war. It would be caught in all the terrible pressures of a changing era, new competition from broadcasting, and strong competition from new suburban papers. By 1950 the results were beginning to come in, the *Trib* had remained static at a time when there was no longer such a thing in the newspaper field as remaining static. The *Times* had gained all the new readers, its lead was now 544,000 to 340,000, and by 1960, 686,000 to 352,000. The race was over before the *Trib* really knew it was a race. In 1955, in what was to be a symbolic move, Homer Bigart, the greatest of the *Trib*'s reporters, Pulitzer Prize winner in World War II, Pulitzer Prize winner in Korea, the archetypical *Trib* man, fearless, tough-minded, and irreverent, had become disgusted with the frustrations of his shop and walked across the street to ask for a job at the *Times*. "Homer," said Turner Catledge, the *Times*'s managing editor, "what took you so long?" (Two Pulitzers or not, Bigart had to go through the *Times*'s normal highly bureaucratic personnel procedure; "What do you think of Eisenhower?" asked the editor in charge of personnel. "He was trying to find out," Bigart told friends later, "whether I was a Commie or not.")

The difference between the papers was even more marked in the Sunday editions. The *Times* since Ochs's day had been the paper for the top department stores not only in New York but throughout America. Indeed, designers and manufacturers announced their new lines not through professional journals, but by using *The New York Times Magazine*. There was no way the *Trib* could compete. The *Times*'s heavy Sunday edition made the entire paper richer and stronger; the *Trib* on Sunday drained the resources of the paper for the other six days. The Sunday *Times* had an unbeatable combination. Lester Markel was the editor and his formula guaranteed that every Sunday the views of Arnold Toynbee and Barbara Ward were sandwiched between the latest in garment-industry ads, equally appealing to those concerned about the future of the Western world and those concerned about the trends in Western underwear. The numbers told the story: in 1940 the *Times* outcirculated the *Trib* on Sunday 836,000 to 544,000; by 1950 it was 1,173,000 to 675,000 and by 1960, when the battle was almost over, 1,371,000 to 521,000.

So the *Times* had in the first half century risen to be the most influential paper not just in the country but in the world. More, it had significantly changed the nature and tone of journalism, moving away from the intense partisanship and parochialism of a previous era, when papers existed only as an extension of a publisher's political or commercial will. What Ochs and Van Anda and their successors had done was to create a paper where the power was invested, not in the publisher, not in the editorial page, but finally in the reporter. The publisher deliberately diminished his own role. It was journalism which left it to the reader to make judgments. The *Times*'s role was only in selecting where the reporters should go and what they should cover; in contrast to the editorializing of a previous generation, that role seemed small enough, though in the decades to come, given the lack of alternative sources of information, it too would become a center of constant controversy.

James Reston was acutely aware of the advantages conferred by his platform; he never had any illusion about how much of his success was due to working for the *Times.* Years later, when one of his bright young men, Max Frankel, deeply dissatisfied with the assaults upon his writing by the New York copy desk, decided to resign and go to *The Reporter* magazine, Reston had a long talk with him. He had agreed with everything Frankel said about the editing. "But, Max," he had finally added, "think of the platform. Can you really give up the platform?" Reston had a lock on Washington, as he well knew; Bob Donovan ran a good bureau for the *Trib,* but it simply lacked muscle; the Washington *Post* was influential and respected within the city, but its power came more from its editorial page than from its reporting, and had it been published anywhere else in the country it would have been just another well-intentioned paper. *Time* and *Life,* the Luce publications, were rich, but they were feared more than respected. That gave the *Times* a unique position, and Reston was a man to make the most of it. As Washington bureau chief, moreover, he was powerful within the institution of the *Times,* which in turn added to his power in Washington. He was an absolute favorite of Iphigene Sulzberger, he was the pride of Arthur Sulzberger, and he was closest of all to Orvil Dryfoos, who had married the Sulzbergers' oldest daughter, Marian, and who was the anointed publisher-to-be. This gave him an enviably direct pipeline to the top of the paper; he could get choice space for his stories any time he wanted. (He had, after the Republicans took office, convinced John Foster Dulles to give him the secret Yalta papers, and he had been able to do this by promising Carl McCardle, Dulles's press officer, that they would be printed in their entirety.) No one in New York had leverage comparable to Reston's. In 1962, dissatisfied with the way Turner Catledge was running the paper, he had gone to him and said bluntly, "Turner, you are neither managing nor editing this paper, and I am telling you because I am going to tell Orvil." His position within the paper was that strong.

This duality of power gave him a special status. He could hire almost at will, without clearing his people through New York. Upon being appointed bureau chief in 1953 he deliberately went out and tried to hire the best young journalists in America to stock his bureau, thus enhancing his bureau's reputation and prestige, as well as his own. It was, he said, a wonderful opportunity; all the best young reporters in America wanted to come to Washington and the *best of them* wanted to work for the *Times.* That made his ivory hunting much easier. He could speak with contempt of another famed *Times* bureau chief, noted for filling *his* bureau with average reporters. "He only hires second-raters in order to make himself look better," Reston would say. "Me, I only hire the best because that makes me look better." So he filled his bureau with a stunning array of the best reporters in America—Russell Baker, Allen

Drury, Tony Lewis, Tom Wicker, Ed Dale, John Finney, Neil Sheehan, Hedrick Smith. "Scotty doesn't want a bureau," Mimi Baker, the wife of Russell Baker, once said of him. "He wants a harem." They were of a breed, serious, well educated, male (Reston was not at ease with women who worked, they seemed alien to him, and when he once offered Mary McGrory of the *Star* a job he also noted that she would have to work part-time on the switchboard). A Pulitzer Prize or a Nieman Fellowship did not hurt. His men often had graduate degrees and they were usually specialists in some field—science, economics, urban development. They were reporters trained to cover an increasingly complex government which demanded a higher and higher degree of specialization, and they had to be men worthy of the *Times*. (In 1957, in his constant search for new talent, he asked Russ Baker if there were any new bright young men in town. "Well, yes," said Baker, "there's this bright guy Ben Bradlee who's just back from Paris." "Bradlee," said Reston, "yes, I've seen him around. He looks like a bit of a cad.") He had the toughness, arrogance almost, to make sure his men received the proper amount of respect. No one would push Reston's men around. Once during the early Kennedy years when the Administration was at the height of its arrogance, particularly in its image making, Reston decided that Ted Sorensen had been bullying his new and not yet entirely established man at the White House, Tom Wicker. So he picked up the phone and he called Sorensen and rather gently suggested that it would probably not be a good idea to push Wicker around. "We were here before you got here, Ted," he reminded Sorensen, "and we will be here when you are gone."

He was a man of the center, probably more liberal than conservative though not overtly so, certainly dedicatedly internationalist in a time when that was the accepted norm of the city. He was at heart an optimist in his thinking, which pleased the Sulzberger family. He was, as Murray Kempton once wrote of him, classically a man of the *Times*, that was his real life's blood. The *Times* had made him what he was, the *Times* was what he knew. Once during a newspaper strike he had written irately about the injustice of striking the *Times*, that it was like striking an old lady. "Besides," he wrote plaintively, "how do I know what I think if I can't read what I write?" He believed in the American experience; as it had worked for him, he believed it would work for others. He had been born near Glasgow, had come to America at the age of eleven, and had grown up in Ohio, where he was a superb athlete and an indifferent student. It was not until he met and pursued the local judge's daughter, Sally Fulton, and raised himself to her standards that he began to do well academically. That was a turning point for him. He saw his marriage as the key to his life, it had given him stability and a center and a worthy ambition, and he believed that this was central to the success of most men, the right kind of wife. He annually wrote a column along these lines for the *Times*, about the good women of Washington who stand quietly behind their successful men, and it was less and less warmly received by a generation of modern young women. He had worked for a time for the old Cincinnati Reds baseball team as a public relations man, and had gone from there to the AP in London, where he had quickly impressed people. Ferdinand Kuhn had spotted him for the *Times,* he had been hired in 1939, and his advancement had been meteoric. During the war he had worked for a time in Arthur Hays Sulzberger's office as Sulzberger's personal assistant, and he was exactly the kind of young man that the Sulzbergers liked to represent the *Times.* London had been a moving experience for him; the sense of England as a democracy coming together under the terrible weight of German bombs had added to his personal belief in the democratic process. He had gone from there to the Washington bureau and he had in 1945 won a Pulitzer, the first of two, for stories on the Dumbarton Oaks Security Conference, which laid the groundwork for the United Nations. Reston had been given a set of the secret Allied papers for the conference and had drawn on them brilliantly during the conference. His stories, informed as they were, had created a great stir among the high officials there. Every nation thought its particular rival had leaked Reston the papers. Actually they had come from the ultimate outsiders at the conference, the Chinese delegation. "Always look for the unhappy ones," Reston counseled young reporters.

He was a very good, very tough reporter. He knew how to work a town, how to take a tiny chunk of information and make it grow and add small bits to it until finally they were of a piece. He had a fine anticipatory instinct for news, for where it was about to happen, and he was deft and skilled over the phone. No one was better at taking a tiny fragment of information and calling a source and pretending he had far more, so that the source would be gulled and would begin to talk. It was a specialty of his, anticipating the beat. In 1956, after Eisenhower had suffered a heart attack, the big political story was whether he would run again. Dr. Paul Dudley White, Ike's cardiologist, was scheduled to testify before a Senate committee that summer, and throngs of reporters had gathered, hoping to interview Dr. White about Eisenhower's health. At the appointed hour White's cab pulled up at the Senate, the crowd of reporters surged forward, and out of the cab popped Paul Dudley White and James Barrett Reston. Having collected a bureau of all-stars, he liked nothing better than to go out periodically and break the biggest story of the week, just to show the hot young tigers around him who was still the best. But he did this with the best of taste, and there was no resentment. His journalistic assessments were usually terse and pithy; in his columns he seemed more sentimental and particularly during the sixties he seemed to work very hard to balance forces which no longer balanced.

No one in the fifties wrote better about American domestic politics. ("Who the hell does Scotty Reston think he is telling me how to run the country?" Dwight Eisenhower once said angrily after reading a Reston column.) His pieces on the changing of the guard from the Eisenhower to the Kennedy administration, reflecting on the different Americas they had sprung from and represented, were absolute models of lucid and imaginative journalism. He held the center and he had authority and access, and he used his platform brilliantly so as to bring even more access. He became, like Walter Lippmann, a symbolic figure in Washington. He was not an intellectual and his larger global views were shaped mostly by Lippmann; but he profoundly affected the thinking of other working reporters, he was the working reporter writing about things they had to deal with, and he had a powerful effect upon his peers. In truth, it was the ripple effect: Lippmann affected Reston and Reston in turn affected the top print people, who affected the broadcast people in defining issues and terms in Washington. Everyone spoke well of him, even the people in the top echelon of the State Department who normally looked down on such journalists as plebeian roughnecks. He wanted journalism to be better, to have better-educated and more serious reporters, to have, above all, a higher purpose. He was bothered by much of journalism, he wanted it to be more serious, less frivolous. He wanted weight to stories and he wanted reporters to come to terms with larger issues. He was discouraged, he often told his young reporters, by the fact that, by the very definition of news, newspapers know how to cover explosive noisy events, but not the subtle, less tangible, and often more important changes within a society. "We cover revolution better than we cover evolution," he would say. In addition he set high ethical standards for the bureau. Whereas Arthur Krock had enjoyed the social possibilities of Washington and had often promoted his social friends through the *Times*'s columns, Reston was far more strict. He did not push his friends, he told young reporters that they need not run soirées to get news in Washington, and it was a point of pride with him that when he went to the White House he carried a pencil and a notebook with him.

Everyone wanted to hire him. It was as if by hiring Reston you could overnight turn an ordinary paper into a major national newspaper, for you would get not just Reston but the Reston touch and the Reston beacon, the bright young reporters he had already hired and the ones he would hire next. His pull was at that moment even greater, it seemed, than that of the *Times*, the *Times* was serious but gray, but Reston was serious and wrote well; young men who had doubts about working for the *Times* had few doubts about working for Reston. He more than anyone else over a generation had opened up the possibilities of *writing* on the *Times*. "Don't write," he counseled one reporter about to go overseas, "as though you're writing for *The New York Times*'s foreign desk. Write as though you're writing letters home to friends."

Phil Graham had failed in his first attempt to lure Reston away from the *Times* to the Washington *Post*, but he nonetheless persisted. Graham was not entirely at ease with Russ Wiggins, whose background was in some ways so similar to that of Reston and who had also worked in Arthur Hays Sulzberger's office. Graham found in Reston a lighter and more congenial touch. The essential offer was for Reston to come over as editor of the editorial page but there was also a promise that he would soon become editor of the Washington *Post.* Graham was clearly dissatisfied with his own paper, and he felt strongly that Washington deserved something better. Yet there was also a curious ambivalence in his attitude. "I want a miniature *New York Times,*" he would say, and then they would talk about what they might do and how to do it and then the ambivalence would show, the doubts would surface. The *Post,* he would say, was not yet ready to be the *Times.* It needed strong local coverage. The *Post* had to cover Washington, there was Alexandria and Arlington and Maryland to cover. Why, he said, the *Star* had always triumphed in the past on the strength of its local news. "The first thing we have to do," he said, "is win in Washington. You don't want to go national too soon." He wanted Reston, the ultimate symbol of national prestige, and at the same time he was wary of the course Reston might set, that he might try and emulate the *Times* too quickly.

That the mandate was so unclear bothered Reston. That and the fact that Graham, whom he loved, whose political instincts he respected, was nonetheless a prototypical wheeler-dealer. He loved to move the pieces on the board. It was not enough for him to sit on the sidelines, as Adolph Ochs and Arthur Sulzberger and even Eugene Meyer had done, and wait for events. He was too impatient. Reston, good Calvinist that he was, was, like most *Times* men, grateful for the degree to which the paper liberated him from doing his publisher's dirty work and flattering his publisher's favorite politicians. Could he really, he wondered, be the kind of editor he would want to be if his publisher were a not so secret player on the stage? Much bothered by the problem, Reston sought out his friend Lippmann for advice. There were two Walter Lippmanns, as friends of the sage had come to know. There was the one of his columns, serious, abstract, often theoretical, if anything too theoretical, a man who seemed far above the daily pettiness of life. Then there was the other Lippmann, immensely shrewd, tart and pragmatic, a man who could measure the bureaucratic odds very coldly in almost any given situation. Lippmann strongly advised Reston against going to the *Post.* Not only was he nervous about Graham the publisher—he had seen too many dangerous acrobatics on the old New York *World*—but he did not think the *Post* had the resources that Reston would expect. Only the *Times,* he said, had the resources, the money, the prestige, the foreign correspondents, the connection to academe that a man like Reston needed. More, the *Times* needed Reston. Lippmann was, in sum, very negative about the *Post* offer, he knew Graham and he knew the city and he warned Reston that Phil Graham was not yet ready to put out the kind of paper that Reston wanted. Besides, he felt the conflict within Graham was too much; charming though he was, he was as much the politician as he was the publisher. So finally Reston turned down Phil Graham's offer again. He was too much a man of the *Times,* he was very happy there, and the *Times* had given him everything he had ever wanted and had given it to him at an early age. He was not able to leave the paper that had made him and then compete with it, in no matter how gentlemanly a manner and for no matter how lofty a cause. Perhaps, he thought later, it was just as well, perhaps he would have tried to make the *Post* an international paper too quickly, and even have hurt it. Instead the *Post* would have to wait for a younger man to become its editor. Someone who even looked like a bit of a cad.

# 7/CBS

Nineteen forty-eight was the last year of the radio convention; by 1952 everything had started to change. The cameras had begun to arrive, and more important, they were connected to a genuine, if embryonic, national network of stations. But 1952 was the watershed; it was a year in which the Democratic and Republican parties could still make decisions of their own about what the convention etiquette and rules would be; by 1956 that was past, no logistical decision at a national convention could be made without consulting the networks, the two were locked into a terrible symbiotic relationship that allegedly benefited both. In 1952 the rules were still being set. When a young California senator named Richard Nixon was nominated for the vice-presidency by the Republicans, and hordes of reporters gathered around trying to get the first great exclusive, Don Hewitt, a CBS producer in the broadcast booth, suddenly and imaginatively told his floor reporter to take his headset off and give it to Nixon so that Cronkite and Murrow in the broadcast booth could interview him. Naturally Nixon wanted to talk to them and to the nation, and so while print reporters furiously waited—and could not hear the questions, only the answers—CBS stole an exclusive. It was this same Hewitt, one of the most imaginative men in television (a man born to be a television producer or managing editor of the New York *Daily News,* according to his friends), who on his way to the meeting hall at that same convention happened to have breakfast one morning at a local greasy spoon. At the moment he was puzzling how to identify people on the floor. The camera, after all, was constantly moving, flashing on important delegates, and the producers wanted to identify the VIPs without breaking the running commentary of Cronkite. He and a colleague named Perry Wolff were talking about this dilemma, how to blend the camera with the spoken word, when Hewitt noticed a sign with movable letters advertising the day's specials—hamburger 35 cents, soup 20 cents.

"What would you like?" the waitress asked.

"That board," Hewitt said, and bought it for twenty dollars. Thus was one of the great staples of television born—supers, the type superimposed upon the screen.

It was that kind of convention. The old was making way for the new. It was held at the Chicago Amphitheatre instead of the Chicago Stadium because the former was better for television. The average citizen might not yet have a television set, but there were gatherings in homes and bars to watch. Delegates coming to their seats in the convention hall found small notices pleading with them not to read newspapers in their seats because the camera might fasten on them while a great Democrat was giving a great speech and thus make all Democrats look foolish.

There was not yet at the beginning any sense of the sheer power of television, although both conventions would change that, and as politicians perceived television's force they immediately put more and more pressure on the networks to bend them to their will. No one was more aware of this than Sig Mickelson, who in 1952 was in charge of the CBS television team. He reveled in it. It was all very free, he thought, one of the great assignments. You could operate by instinct without consulting your superiors. When he went back four years later, in 1956, it was very different. It was not that he was no longer in charge. It was simply that there were three corporate superiors there: Stanton, the president of the company, the vice-president for Washington, and the legal vice-president. Which meant that things were different for Mickelson —there were people looking over his shoulder, asking him later why he did certain things, questions which inevitably took away a journalist's boldness— and made an editor second-guess his instincts a little too much. What Mickelson was experiencing in 1956 was one of the great changes in broadcasting. The drive in television news was no longer for pure excellence, a drive to be better and faster than the other two networks, though, of course, excellence still mattered. Now it was that old drive, but tempered with an awareness of the *implications* of the news, of what the reaction to a controversial story might be in high places. An awareness of the amount of kickback per story. The power of the medium was simply too great to let nature take its course.


In 1952, for the first time television profoundly affected the choice of the candidates at both conventions, and thus indirectly the capacity of the party regulars to control their own organizations. Democrat Estes Kefauver had been catapulted into national prominence with his televised hearings on crime. He was, though it was not widely perceived at the time by the intelligentsia, a deceptively fine television figure, not naturally handsome, but nonetheless looking worthy of trust, neither too quick nor too slick, honorable rather than too smart or flashy. His manner was of a country boy trying to retain his honor among the big-city boys in Washington. The reality, of course, was quite different. Kefauver was the ultimate sophisticate, a Yale Law School graduate with an extraordinary capacity to control his own ego, and the conscious ability to project himself as a man of integrity into millions of homes. "I've met millions of self-made highbrows in my life," said his friend Max Ascoli, the editor and publisher of *The Reporter*, "but Estes is the first self-made lowbrow." He had already angered the party officials by his investigations of gambling and rackets, which repeatedly embarrassed big-city Democratic administrations, and the Democratic Party leadership was out to challenge him on that basis alone. More, his sampling of the political water in New Hampshire had quickly underscored Truman's vulnerability, and had turned Truman into a powerful enemy.

But in a much larger sense Kefauver had also, by running for the presidency, challenged the existing political structure, and he had gone intuitively to a new power base, the primary route, using the media as a connecting link of access to the population instead of the party machinery. He set a pattern for the diminution of the party structure. In the past the party officials had dominated the choosing of the candidate (unless, as in the case of Roosevelt, there was a sitting President determined to force them down); they had, of course, allowed for regional balance and ethnic composition, but it had been their choice, made their way, in their hotel rooms. All that was quickly changed; Kefauver was going over their heads. Television was giving him the access and exposure that the party machinery would have loved to deny him. So if he entered the convention as a man of the people with his own delegates, the one thing the party machinery could not do was to reject him and nominate someone who clearly looked like a party hack. It would have split the Democratic Party.

Above all, at Chicago, Truman wanted to beat Kefauver. The President knew that his own time was up, he wanted to defeat the man who had wounded him, and—as he viewed it—wounded the party. His vehicle for this reflected extraordinary political shrewdness. For Adlai Stevenson did not look or sound like a man of the party. In a changing era, when party loyalty was diminishing nationally, when there was a mounting suspicion of smoke-filled rooms, and when greater affluence had liberated Americans from their economic and social commitment to the party, Stevenson was the ideal choice. Because he was in fact very much a man of the party. Stevenson himself, with his soaring rhetoric, tended to forget this from time to time, but the party pros never did. He came to the nation through the courtesy of the Daley machine. The Daley machine of Chicago had propelled him into the governor's mansion in Springfield, Illinois, and Daley himself had protected him and kept him clean (and perhaps slightly innocent) in the savage jungle of Illinois politics. Stevenson never challenged the machine (some twenty years later, his son at first tentatively and then more openly made the break with Daley) and Daley himself was smart enough to know that Stevenson toned up the image of the machine. Thus in 1952 Stevenson was a perfect foil for party professionals wanting to knock off a difficult, irreverent, and potentially troublesome insurgent. Stevenson had a record of regularity without sounding or looking regular. Whether Truman and the others would have gone to Stevenson had Kefauver not challenged the party machinery is a moot question. But if Stevenson was at least partially a beneficiary of television, he seemed not at all aware of it. Indeed, his dislike of the camera and the medium became a major political handicap, particularly against a natural politician like Dwight Eisenhower, who adapted readily and easily to a new weapon.

. . .

For Stevenson was a man born in 1900, a man of an earlier generation and above all a man of print. Stevenson loved old-fashioned speech and its rhythms and cadences and pauses, a speech that had a classic balance to it, as if somehow it had just been translated from the Latin or Greek. He was more than fifty years old before television came into the average household; he did not watch television, and his friends did not watch television, and all of them, not watching television, were somewhat contemptuous of people who did. The night of Richard Nixon's Checkers speech—which was perhaps the single most important moment in the 1952 campaign, and above all a moment when the Democratic candidate for the presidency should have been in front of a television screen—the candidate was sitting at his home in Libertyville, Illinois, where there was no TV set. A young member of his staff named Newton Minow, who was only twenty-six and thus much younger than the other Stevenson people, and who, unlike them, *owned a television set,* called his wife in Chicago to *hear* what she had *seen.* It was not the first time something like this had happened to Minow and he argued regularly and strenuously (or as strenuously as one could argue with as civilized a man as the Governor) that it was not really important whether he or his friends watched television, but millions of Americans did, and if what appeared on the screen was not reality it made little difference as long as they felt it was. Stevenson, of course, disregarded warnings like this, television was not within his framework. He considered it essentially demagogic. In any case he loved his own words and the audiences that responded right there in front of him to his own words. Which meant that even when the Democrats, hard-pressed for cash, bought television time, it rarely went well—the Governor could never quite tailor his speech to the time and the hour often expired with him still speaking; more, he was often not so much speaking as reading, which made the effect even more awkward.

When some of the Stevenson people discovered through their sources on Madison Avenue that Dwight Eisenhower was planning a series of special one-minute spots designed for saturation use in crucial areas, they became excited. Louis Cowan, a television producer who later became President of CBS, picked up the news along the advertising grapevine and quickly confirmed it. This was something absolutely new: the use of almost straight advertising techniques in national politics. There was, Cowan thought, a very real possibility of matching that effort and thus neutralizing the effect. Stevenson was no war hero, but he was articulate and there was no reason why spots could not be cut from some of the better moments and lines of his speeches. The Governor did not agree. He was absolutely appalled by the idea, first that Eisenhower would do this, and second that events might force him to do the same. Cowan, who was an old friend, had never seen him so angry and so indignant: "This is the worst thing I've ever heard of. Selling the presidency like cereal. Merchandising the presidency. How can you talk seriously about issues with one-minute spots!" Cowan, who had expected Stevenson's immediate response to be negative, was nonetheless stunned by the vehemence of it. The candidate would not use television in any modern way himself, and he would not watch Eisenhower using it. Even the network correspondents assigned to cover him and wanting to get him on their news shows not so much for ideological reasons as for professional reasons—if Stevenson got on the air *they* got on the air—kept coming up with suggestions. Perhaps they could put a soundless camera in his working room? Or in his car? And they could dictate a voice-over on how he spent a typical day? "Certainly not," the Governor said.

So for an entire campaign he did it his own way. Perhaps in retrospect that is why the 1952 Stevenson campaign is remembered with such nostalgia by his supporters among the intelligentsia, the fact that there was still old-fashioned eloquence despite the coming of a new medium, and because in the face of the McCarthy darkness his voice seemed so calm. His failure to adapt to new techniques, to pander (his own word), probably made his supporters love him all the more, and probably also narrowed his political base. On election eve the Democrats had arranged for a mass rally in Chicago. The lineup of speakers was to be Truman first. Then Alben Barkley. And then Stevenson. Lou Cowan, who was in charge of the program, was very anxious to combat the negative impact of Stevenson's divorce. Ike was not just a war hero; Ike was also a family man who could put a Mamie in the White House. So Cowan wanted to feature as subtly as possible Stevenson's sons. A small gesture. The camera would flash to the three sons and then, just as Stevenson was about to go up to the podium, young Adlai would touch his father lightly on the back and say, "Good luck, Dad." Good luck, Dad, something warm, to show that yes, Stevenson was all right, a family man, albeit an imperfect family. Not Checkers perhaps but something a little warm. Young Adlai had, of course, said he would do it. It was the biggest gambit that Cowan could make toward showmanship, but gradually his conscience began to bother him, that and the fact that if the candidate resented it, the incident might disturb his concentration and ruin the speech. So at the last minute Cowan mentioned to Stevenson what the plan was. "Lou, old boy," said the first Democratic candidate for President in the television age, "we don't do things like that in our family."

The Eisenhowers of Abilene turned out to be a little more flexible than the Stevensons of Bloomington. Just a little bit more flexible, for the truth was that no matter how much he owed his nomination to television, Dwight Eisenhower, the returning war hero, disliked and distrusted television, thought it a tool of demagogues, just as in a somewhat milder form he had earlier disliked and distrusted radio.

Eisenhower's first tutor in the art of using both instruments was David Schoenbrun. As a young staff aide, Schoenbrun had talked to General Eisenhower on a number of occasions about radio and he had sensed immediately

Eisenhower's vast distaste for the entire business. The more he talked about what De Gaulle had done, had used radio to make himself the voice and spirit of France, even in exile, the more Schoenbrun realized he was making the wrong argument, that Eisenhower was uneasy with De Gaulle's grandiosity and his ego, and he was convincing the General not so much of the potential of the instrument as of its dangers. "Do you realize how frightening this really is?" Ike would ask. Schoenbrun would argue that radio was there, it was powerful, it had to be used, and that the General had to come to terms with it, for he knew that part of the General's hesitancy was his own feeling (quite accurate, it turned out) that he did not use radio well. Ike, he said, had to learn to use it. "I guess so," Ike would say, and then continue his resistance to radio. "Listen, it's there and you have to use it," Schoenbrun once said. "Suppose I can't?" Eisenhower answered.

Eisenhower bridled if Schoenbrun even referred to radio as being part of the press. To him radio people were clearly in another, less reputable category. He kept talking about the possibility of dangerous people taking it over and exploiting it. "What's to stop a demagogue from taking over? Who's to set the limits on it? What are the controls?" After Schoenbrun went to work for CBS they continued their arguments and Schoenbrun would mention that at CBS Paley, Stanton, and Murrow were good and serious men, men of honor and restraint. When he talked like that Eisenhower would reject the argument. "I don't like it," he said. "I don't like the idea of something where you have to depend upon the integrity of the man and not the integrity of the institution."

With CBS News in Paris after the war, Schoenbrun had remained close to Eisenhower. Sometimes it seemed that part of his job was to relay to the General an endless series of requests for appearances from CBS in New York. Eisenhower, of course, turned them all down. Immensely vital in personal contact, he became wooden and stilted in front of the camera. In early 1952 Murrow arrived in Paris to film a "See It Now" segment with Ike, and the General had been terrible, clumsy and awkward. He had refused to look at the camera, and he had mumbled and coughed. The show had been a disaster and afterward Eisenhower talked with Schoenbrun and he suggested that perhaps Schoenbrun might coach him a little. The ethics did not seem particularly questionable, and since this would give the correspondent even greater access to Eisenhower, Schoenbrun accepted. The first thing he told Ike was that there was a problem with his head because of the baldness. "I know I'm bald," said the leader of the Western forces that had crushed Nazi Germany, somewhat testily. "What else can you tell me?" "Well," said Schoenbrun, "you tend to lower your head and that elongates it, and makes it seem longer and balder, like an egghead. Maybe you can tilt your head the other way, back a little." So slowly the head was tilted back, but not with any great enthusiasm. At one point when Schoenbrun made a suggestion about the possible use of makeup, Eisenhower snarled angrily at him, "Why don't you just get an actor? That's what you really want." It was always difficult for him, he read poorly and the words seemed alien to him as they came out. But he stayed with it. It was all difficult and strange but he knew he had to do it, because he knew he was going to run for the presidency. Once, in 1951, after Eisenhower and Schoenbrun had done a television program, Schoenbrun suggested that Ike work a little harder on his television preparation and learn to memorize lines because he had so much trouble reading them. Why should he bother? Eisenhower asked. "Because you're going to run for the presidency," the correspondent answered. "What makes you think so?" Eisenhower said. "Well, you do have a man sitting in a room off your headquarters writing a book called *Man from Abilene,*" Schoenbrun said. A few months later Eisenhower left Paris and came home.

When he came home he found that he needed television and needed it badly, like it or not. Robert Taft had control of the party apparatus, and that left Ike dependent on media. So, somewhat aloof and distant (Ike liked to flash that famous grin when it suited him, not when some aide told him to), he reluctantly adapted to modern politics. He made the transition better than his two opponents, Adlai Stevenson and Robert Taft, both of them more traditional politicians, both of whom had more to unlearn. Perhaps his career as a military man helped him; his was a profession in which a good leader constantly had to adapt to new weapons, whether he liked them or not, and television was clearly a new weapon. So though he disliked doing television shows in practice and disliked the implications of television even more in theory, Dwight Eisenhower set a series of political television firsts: the first candidate to have his announcement for the presidency televised live; the first candidate to use spot commercials; and later, as President, the first to have his press conferences televised.

From the very start, when he made his announcement in Abilene, it was a television event, not the least because his old friend and officer Colonel William S. Paley, now just Citizen Paley, was almost as much an admirer of Ike as he was of television. Just before Eisenhower's initial announcement Paley had asked Sig Mickelson in the News Division why CBS didn't just go out there and cover Ike live in Abilene. Mickelson had checked it out and found that live coverage would be very, very expensive, they would have to lay cable all the way to Abilene and that would mean thousands and thousands of dollars. Usually news like that cooled Paley off quickly. But not this time. "I'll call AT&T and tell them to get going and you start planning on the coverage," Paley had said, which made people in the News Division believe that there was more to the coverage than journalistic interest.

So on June 4, 1952, the stage was set for live television coverage from Abilene. CBS had brought Schoenbrun back from Paris to cover Ike, hoping to exploit his Paris connections, and Schoenbrun was assigned to cover the great moment, which was scheduled for the old parade ground in Abilene, a symbolic event—the old soldier come home, the good midwestern boy in the true midwestern setting. But it turned into a disaster. Just before Ike was to speak, torrents of rain began to fall. Ike was soaked, his few hairs plastered to his forehead, his glasses fogged up and dripping. Aides tried to move the speech to a nearby barn and on the way Ike stumbled on a cable and he began to rage openly: To hell with all this, I'm not going to do it.

The next day there was supposed to be a press conference at the Abilene movie house. The print people tried to bar television and television cameras, claiming that television would corrupt the proceedings and turn it into a zoo. The wire-service reporters up to then had always been the fastest, and they threatened to have platoons of Abilene Boy Scouts at the ready to shuttle out with bulletins to the waiting wire connection. At first it was expected that Schoenbrun would be the one pool reporter allowed in with one camera, but as the print protests mounted, it seemed likely that all television cameras would be barred. Murrow was with Schoenbrun and he called Paley; Paley liked challenges like this, the fight for access was great fun (television was traditionally better at fighting for access than at using it once granted), and Paley ordered another camera team to be ready to film the Eisenhower people barring the Schoenbrun team. Jim Hagerty, Ike's press officer, was there and he told Schoenbrun that he was acting under pressure from the print people, though Schoenbrun suspected it was Ike himself, that the previous day's humiliation had confirmed all his darkest doubts about television and how it would make a fool of him. But Hagerty realized the stakes were big, that the last thing he and the General wanted was the occasion of Eisenhower's home-coming to be marred by scuffling over television cameras by police and journal-ists. If Eisenhower were to challenge Taft successfully, he was going to need all the help he could get from television. So the Eisenhower people said okay and at the last minute Schoenbrun was let in. But the technical arrangements were more primitive than usual and in the confusion Schoenbrun found himself with no return circuit from New York. That meant in effect that he was broadcasting the live press conference of Dwight Eisenhower, but that he was deaf; he had no sense of whether he was being heard in New York. It was his big moment and it was a horror—as first Hagerty and then Eisenhower spoke and answered questions, Schoenbrun repeated the questions and repeated the answers, and his superiors in New York, enraged by his performance, screamed pointlessly at him to shut up.

Not that Ike had anything to fear from the cameras. Quite the contrary. In the fight for the nomination against Robert Taft, the embodiment of the center of the party and a party which was still regarded by many Americans as the party of business, the more exposure of both Eisenhower and Taft, the better for Eisenhower. Since Ike's Republican roots were virtually nonexistent, his leverage *within* the party absolutely minimal, the more closed the race for the nomination, the better for Taft. The more open and ventilated, the more the Republican leadership had to respond to a broader sampling of opinion, the better for Eisenhower. In an era when class consciousness still lived and so did the Depression-days image of Republicans, Taft had serious problems. He was Mr. Republican and he *looked* like Mr. Republican. Television was cruel to him, he looked cold and unsmiling, what warmth he had as a man was remarkably well concealed; he looked like a representative of the rich, unused to dealing with people from the other side of the tracks. Television could, if used properly, reflect Ike's very considerable charm, that unique warmth and strength that had regularly made other and often more talented men trust him and use him to conciliate. The more primaries, the more open the convention, the better for Ike. Television brought home in a terrible way the great problem Taft had, the argument *Time* magazine was to make so persuasively, that he could not win, that those who were for him were for him passionately, but that he could not expand his base.

The Taft people clearly understood all this and even before the convention they had talked about barring radio and particularly television from the convention. Schoenbrun was traveling with Eisenhower on a whistle stop in the Midwest when he heard the news about barring broadcast journalists from some of the proceedings and he had immediately gone to see the General to tell him that this was a big chance to get the American people on his side (and to help all television reporters, of course, because if television was barred from the convention, so was David Schoenbrun). Schoenbrun suggested that Eisenhower attack the Taft camp for trying to shut the American people out of the convention. Ike would say that he had been fighting all these years to defend freedom and democracy and to tear down the Iron Curtain in Europe, and now here at home the Taft people were trying to erect an Iron Curtain at the Republican convention. Jim Hagerty was present at the meeting and he told Ike that he'd better listen, that this was a serious moment, that his only hope was for an open convention and he badly needed the cameras there. But Eisenhower still seemed reluctant, the television cameras might help him and might hurt Bob Taft, but that did not mean he liked them. Finally, quite unhappily, he agreed to make a statement at the next stop, along the lines that Schoenbrun had suggested. Schoenbrun, lacking radio facilities, decided to send it out first as a news bulletin over CBS, but he wanted to let one other reporter in on it, because he was sure that if his story came in and no wire or major newspaper corroborated it, his superiors would put it aside. But if there was a major story supporting it on the wires, they would go with him. So he tipped off Don Whitehead of AP about the speech and at the next stop they rushed out to file it, feeling they would get a one-stop beat on their colleagues. They sent it out, and slipped back on the train, expecting to find their colleagues excited by the new statement and somewhat irate that they had been scooped. But they found nothing at all, Ike had failed to mention it, although by now the news of Ike's statement was ringing out around the country. He had simply forgotten about it. So they rushed to see Hagerty and he was appalled and pledged that the candidate would correct the omission, and they made an unscheduled stop at which Ike rather awkwardly made a haphazard reference to an Iron Curtain coming down on Chicago, but this time he failed to mention television. Schoenbrun was sure that the General, either consciously or unconsciously, was blocking the thing out. So they had to stop the train a third time and finally Ike made his ringing denunciation against what Bob Taft was trying to do to television coverage of the convention.

. . .

At the convention television was a powerful if still not fully understood force. Taft had a considerable lead entering the convention, but he was about 100 votes short of the nomination. The Eisenhower strategy was to challenge Taft in a number of southern states, hoping to slow him down, and to give as much exposure as possible to the idea that the Taft people were a narrowly based wing of the party. Reporters, particularly television correspondents, found the Eisenhower people unusually cordial and helpful at the convention, anxious to give as much access as possible and to make any confrontation as public as possible. The Eisenhower strategy was relatively simple: the longer the convention went on, the more the national population saw Ike's grin and Taft's cold face, the more pressure there would be on delegations to go for Ike. Television was their main weapon. The aim was to take a national convention, which had once been a private closed affair belonging to the party, and turn it into a national forum, meaning that it inevitably became in tone and in response more national and less partisan. If the audience, and thus the constituency, was national, then inevitably the convention had to respond to the audience or offend the audience by looking too partisan. This accelerated the trend toward candidates who were, in style, background, and looks, independent, as opposed to candidates who too clearly bore the stamp of their party and their regions and who looked like politicians. Ike was the first beneficiary of this trend.

In effect the Eisenhower people, with Henry Cabot Lodge doing much of the planning, decided to try role casting at the convention. Lodge cast the convention as one would cast a play. Taft would be the old-fashioned cold Republican candidate surrounded by arrogant party professionals who were afraid of the people's will and who thus had to stop the unpolitical good guy, the man of the ordinary people, Dwight Eisenhower, from getting the delegates he rightfully deserved. The Taft people stepped readily into the roles designed for them. So did the press. When the credentials committee met to consider contested delegations, Lodge arrived on his own a little early and let in both radio and television correspondents. It put him in a no-lose situation. A few hours later when the Taft-oriented committee showed up it was appalled to find that its most sacred chambers had been opened to broadcasting. The Taft people on the committee voted 60 to 40 to remove the television and radio equipment, but in so doing they played right into Lodge's hands. They appeared as they had been cast, a small cabal trying to close the convention so they could steal votes, keeping out reporters who were representative of the American people. The Taft people were causing to unite, as one, the Eisenhower people, television reporters, and the general public. Inevitably, just as Lodge had anticipated, this brought increasing pressure on Taft to compromise on the delegates. So Taft moved quickly to work out a settlement on the delegates, but Lodge refused—he wanted the confrontation much more than he wanted the eight additional delegates whom Taft was willing to cough up. It was a shrewd strategy. Slowly the convention slipped away from Taft, more and more people at home began to call their delegations to complain about what Taft was doing to Eisenhower, time worked relentlessly against Taft, and hour by hour as the convention went on it became clearly apparent that Dwight Eisenhower was a more attractive figure than Robert A. Taft. And maybe a better politician.

The subsequent Eisenhower campaign saw for the first time in a national campaign major use of the combination of a new American art form, the linking of advertising, political, and television skills. The Republicans went to Batten Barton Durstine & Osborn for help. BBD&O designed a format for a thirty-minute appearance by Ike. It would not be what old-style politicians expected, a twenty-nine-minute speech with a few quick flashes of the crowd and a cut to an adoring Mamie. For they were not selling, so to speak, the great thoughts and eternal wisdom of Dwight Eisenhower. They were selling Ike the hero. And a key to selling a hero is, of course, a hero's welcome. Ike would enter the hall from the back. Shot of crowd going wild, people cheering, craning to see him. Cameras on faces of crowd. Camera on Ike, looking duly modest, beaming, fatherly, understanding why they loved him but properly modest about it. Ike on the podium. Then a flash to Mamie. Shouldn't every hero be called Ike, and shouldn't he have a Mamie? A brief speech by Eisenhower, and then the only thing to match a hero's arrival—the departure of a hero. The crowd still excited. Flash to American flags. All very well done.

In addition the Eisenhower people laid in with a powerful last-minute pre-election blitz of commercial spots. Rosser Reeves, an advertising man who was a volunteer and not a member of BBD&O, thought that most television programs by politicians were too formal, too long, and too expensive, and that there was a great danger that they might give the average television viewer more of a politician and less of his favorite program than he wanted. Reeves thought it might be far better to do snappy one-minute commercials. His idea was proposed to the inner Eisenhower group, which liked it and decided to go very hard on spot commercials. A special fund was set up; eventually one and a half million dollars was budgeted for them, which was very big money in those days. The basic question for Reeves was which Eisenhower to sell: an Eisenhower cleaning up the mess in Washington? Ike cleaning out Communists? Ike bringing fiscal responsibility? Or Ike as a man of peace who might end the Korean War. Reeves went to the *Reader's Digest* and got its mailing lists, which were then considered the best in the country and certainly not elitist. Three sample mailings of 10,000 each were sent out to *Digest* readers asking them to decide which campaign technique they thought would be most effective. Not surprisingly the results were overwhelming for Ike the war hero who was a man of peace. The committee immediately came up with a slogan: "Eisenhower, the man who will bring us peace." It was brought to the General for routine approval, and he, much to the surprise of his associates, demurred; he could not guarantee peace. There were no guarantees in the modern age, he said. Slightly thrown off by this eruption of old-fashioned ethics, the committee went back to the drawing board and came up with an even better slogan:

"Eisenhower, man of peace" (thus, of course, the subliminal counterslogan—Stevenson, man of war). Reeves then collaborated with the General, sixty-second commercials written by Reeves, approved with some mild modification by Eisenhower; citizens hired for the occasion posing questions to the General. Eisenhower went ahead with it, though telling friends that he was somewhat amazed that his career had come to this, it was not what he thought an old soldier should do. The commercials were used in the last few weeks in saturation quantities. Ike won overwhelmingly. He probably would have anyway, but a precedent had been set in which politics, advertising, television, and big money were all enmeshed. The coming of modern manipulative arts to modern politics.

That fall Marya Mannes, writing in *The Reporter* on the campaign, caught the flavor in a ditty called "Sales Campaign":

> *Hail to B.B.D. & O.,*
> *It told the nation how to go;*
> *It managed by advertisement*
> *To sell us a new President.*
>
> *Eisenhower hits the spot,*
> *One full General, that's a lot.*
>
> *Feeling sluggish, feeling sick?*
> *Take a dose of Ike and Dick.*
>
> *Philip Morris, Lucky Strike,*
> *Alka-Seltzer, I like Ike.*

There was one major footnote to the 1952 Stevenson campaign and that was the 1956 campaign. For if 1952 had been a disaster, then by 1956 there was at least an attempt being made within the Stevenson camp to recognize that television had been invented. By then the men around Stevenson, principally Bill Blair and Newt Minow, had convinced the candidate that some television professionalism was necessary and so Stevenson made a stab at it. In early 1956 Stevenson called a young television producer at WBBM in Chicago named Bill Wilson and suggested they meet. Wilson, who became very fond of Stevenson, did not readily forget their first meeting, in part because it was with such a famous figure and in part because it was an odd mixture of Stevenson's uneasiness and snobbishness and because Stevenson was so profoundly uncomfortable even talking about the idea of television. "They tell me," he began, "that you're in television and they tell me that I need someone like you." Which, of course, made Wilson feel every bit as uncomfortable as the Governor. So they did a brief investigation of Wilson's background, quickly discovering that he was the right sort of person, properly bred, who had gone to the University of Chicago and not USC or UCLA, some place near *Hollywood.* Wilson quickly learned how sensitive Stevenson was to any attempt to change him or sell him, and he kept cosmetic application to a minimum, getting the cameras to shoot high on Stevenson so he would not look dumpy. To the degree that someone from the demagogic world of television could get on well with Adlai Stevenson, Bill Wilson did, though that was in large part because the candidate was afraid of television and kept his own distance. Wilson attempted from the start to humanize the Governor, and he thought Stevenson potentially very good on television. Stevenson did not like being thought of as stiff and, placed in a group of serious but friendly citizens asking questions, he forgot about the camera and concentrated on them and he often became charming and warm. So during a prolonged primary fight for the nomination Wilson scheduled informal local television appearances, paying often no more than $100 for the air time and placing the candidate with interested but sympathetic local Democrats. He told the panelists to ask difficult questions because Stevenson improved in discourse in inverse proportion to the banality of the questions, and the shows were deemed a considerable success by almost everyone but the Governor himself.

Stevenson, of course, preferred his beloved formal speeches and he never understood what was going on. Wilson recalled in particular one night show in Florida. Stevenson asked if they really had to do this program and Wilson said yes, it had been scheduled long in advance. "But do you know where I could be tonight? I could be speaking at a downtown civic club." Wilson asked how many people would attend. "One hundred and fifty," said the candidate. "Governor," explained Wilson, "we may reach thousands and thousands of people tonight." Stevenson listened reluctantly. "I don't understand it at all," he finally said, "I simply don't understand it at all." Nonetheless, Wilson had the upper hand during the primaries, though it all changed once Stevenson gained the nomination. For suddenly the telecasts were no longer local, they were national and big money was at stake and with two hundred thousand dollars riding on thirty minutes no one was about to have the candidate share the air time with average citizens no matter how good their questions and how much they humanized him. So the appearances became very formal, very stiff, Stevenson reading from his speeches, rigid, cold performances. He loved it; he was more comfortable with his words this way.

There was, Wilson thought, one moment that seemed to symbolize the whole thing, the vast chasm between the candidate for President and the new medium which had already become the major conduit for reaching people. They were at the Democratic convention and it was about 1 A.M., when Wilson was awakened by a phone call from the Governor, asking him to come to Stevenson's hotel room immediately. "I'm having terrible trouble with my television set—the reception is very bad, and I wonder if you could drop down and fix it." That summed it all up, thought Wilson, you could figure out his mental processes completely: He has trouble with his television set. He needs someone to fix it. Who's in television? Wilson. Wilson's in television. I'll call him to fix the set.

.  .  .

The 1952 Democratic convention was important in part because it brought a
new face to the American people, a face that would be known in television
history. The CBS team going to Chicago knew that it was going to be on the
air live for endless hours and it needed someone to hold the broadcast together.
The word for that in the trade, but not yet in the popular vernacular, was
anchorman. Murrow himself, still at the peak of his influence, was not much
interested. Nor were many of his colleagues. Walter Cronkite, however, was.
Walter Cronkite was not one of the Murrow Boys. Cronkite in 1952 was
perhaps the one rising star within the company who was outside the Murrow
clique. There was a time in London during the war when he might have made
the connection with Murrow. He was a United Press correspondent in London
and a very good one. He was, in the eyes of Harrison Salisbury, the man then
running the UP bureau and an exceptionally good judge of talent, the best on
his beat.

It was the fall of 1942 and the American military presence was minimal
and the first B-17's were just arriving in England. Cronkite had the Eighth Air
Force story, then the prime journalistic assignment in the war. Every day
Cronkite and the other reporters went out to the various air bases and interviewed the young fliers as they came back. It was a terrible time; the attrition
rate was very high—twenty planes would go out, fourteen might come back.
The essence of the story was the hometown angle, the reporters never wanting
to get too close to these young men because they might be gone the next day.
Cronkite was involved in a fierce competition with other very able reporters,
Gladwin Hill (then of AP, later of the *Times*) and the legendary Homer Bigart
of the New York *Herald Tribune*. Cronkite was very good, very fast, always
driving, always looking for an edge; indeed, at one point he translated the
accepted unit for bombs, which was a long ton, 2,200 pounds, into regular tons,
so that, to Hill's dismay, UP's tonnage was always a little heavier than that
of AP. All of the reporters had pushed the Army Air Force brass to allow them
to go aboard a mission and finally, in late February 1943, permission was
granted. Four correspondents would be allowed to go. The big story, of course,
was the B-17's, which were new and very effective and faster than the B-24's,
but it was decided that for reasons of morale among B-24 pilots, one of the
four reporters had to go with them. Hill and Cronkite immediately argued that
a wire man dared not go with the B-24's, not so much for fear of the Germans,
but in case the other wire service might fly in a better, faster plane and thus
get a quicker, better story. So finally Bigart and Dick Post of the *Times* had
to draw for the B-24. Post lost and he never came back. Cronkite flew the B-17
and when he came back that day he wrote his lead: "American Flying For-
tresses have just come back from an assignment to hell—a hell 26,000 feet
above the earth. . . ." "You're not really going to file that, are you, Walter?"
asked a slightly appalled Bigart. Yes, I am, Cronkite answered, and the story
was eventually anthologized in the *Treasury of Great War Reporting*, though
perhaps as much for Cronkite's later success as for the story's style.

But he was a very good, very aggressive young reporter and he had caught

Murrow's eye, and Murrow decided to offer Cronkite a job. Murrow arranged for them to lunch at the Savile Club, which Cronkite in the great tradition of middle America thought was the Saddle Club (which may help explain why he has been so successful as an anchorman). They lunched amicably. Murrow offered the job and Cronkite, who was making $67 a week, accepted it on a handshake; it was for $125 a week plus fees, which Cronkite, like most print reporters, thought were surely nonexistent—they were, in fact, likely to triple his salary. Cronkite returned to bid farewell to his colleagues at UP, and Salisbury, a very shrewd operator, immediately said that this was too bad because that very moment a huge raise had come in from New York for Cronkite of $12.50 a week. Indeed, at Salisbury's urging, New York had doubled that, which meant a grand total of $25 in raises, or $92 a week. Cronkite was impressed by this vast commitment of UP's resources and this double sign of its belief in him, and because he loved United Press with the simple fanaticism of the devoted wire-service reporter—the greatest thrill in the world is to beat AP by ten minutes, that is a kind of nirvana, or at least a ten-minute nirvana—he turned down Murrow. That produced a certain tension between them over the years. Murrow simply could not understand the value system of a man who would prefer United Press over the more elite world of CBS. Cronkite stayed with United Press during the war and did a lot of classic wire-service reporting, soldier-action-hometown, it-was-rough-but-we-had-to-do-it journalism. He was very good and brave, almost foolhardy, and he gained a reputation as one of the best combat correspondents of the war. When the Germans launched their major winter offensive in the Ardennes, cutting off Bastogne, Cronkite was quick to rush to the front with Patton's relief force. That relief mission reached the outskirts of Bastogne, and Cronkite, eager for an eyewitness story, perhaps the first one from the embattled town, got out of his jeep and slowly and methodically crawled toward a barn. He eventually spotted a GI. He moved toward the soldier and finally started interviewing him in the Ernie Pyle tradition: Soldier-what's-your-name-and-hometown?

"Well, gee, you ought to know that, Mister Cronkite," the soldier answered.

"Why's that?" Cronkite asked.

"Well, sir," said the kid, "I'm your driver."

He finished the war with UP and there was no doubt of his excellence; the brass there thought highly of him and he was awarded, as a sign of his success, the Moscow bureau. Those were days of minimal creature comforts in Moscow, and he and his wife, Betsy, were warned that they had to bring everything to Moscow, which they did, and on the day they departed someone mentioned to Betsy Cronkite that she would do well to buy a lot of golf balls since there were none available in Moscow, which she immediately rushed out and did, buying hundreds and hundreds of them; an exceptional supply, considering that (a) Walter Cronkite did not play golf and (b) there were no golf courses at all in the Soviet Union. Moscow in 1946 was not very great fun, nor for that matter was United Press; the Russians were fast discontinuing their policy of limited friendship to brotherly Western correspondents, revoking the marginal privileges that had once existed; in addition, the financial generosity of United Press, which was always somewhat limited, seemed to diminish. The UP car was of antique proportions and did not run, and when, during one of the worst winters of recent Russian history, Cronkite asked for permission to buy a new car since even the Russians were complaining about the condition of his vehicle, his superiors suggested that he get a bicycle.

Things like that often undermine a correspondent's confidence and Cronkite quickly asked to be brought out of Moscow. He came home to America for a year with a promise that he would soon return to Europe as the number-one man on the entire Continent. His salary was then a hundred and twenty-five dollars a week, and, with family obligations growing, he asked for more. The UP executives assured him, probably accurately, that he was already the highest-paid man on the staff. Which was fine except he still wanted more; yes, he said, he loved United Press, which he truly did, he loved scooping people and getting the story straight and clean and fast with no frills—even years later, reminiscing, there is a kind of love in his voice talking about the old UP days, how much he loved UP, how he liked the feel of dirt in his hands, he was not at home with a lot of commentary—but love or no, there had to be some money. So Earl Johnson, his superior, said that he thought it was time that he and Walter had a little talk, since Cronkite apparently did not understand the economic basis of United Press, an economic attitude which was legendary among most journalists and secret only to Cronkite. "No, I guess I don't understand it," Cronkite said, and so Johnson explained: "We take the best and the most eager young men we can find and we train them and we pay them very little and we give them a lot of room and then when they get very good they go elsewhere."

"Are you asking me to go somewhere else?" Cronkite asked.

"No, no," said Johnson, though adding that a hundred and twenty-five dollars a week is a lot of money for us, though probably not for you.

So Cronkite returned to Kansas City, whence he came, on a kind of extended leave, and while he was there he saw an old friend named Karl Koerper, who was a big local civic booster and the head of KMBC, which was a CBS affiliate. And Cronkite, who was disturbed by what he had found in Kansas City, told Koerper at lunch that Kansas City seemed to have died, there was no spirit and excitement any more. What had happened? Then he answered his own question, it was the death of the Kansas City *Journal.* You get monopoly journalism, he said, and something goes out of a city, a sense of excitement and competition. When newspaper competition dies, something dies with it. Kansas City is a duller town now, Cronkite said.

"What do you mean?" Koerper asked.

"It's your fault," Cronkite continued. "You radio guys cut the advertising dollars so much that you drove the newspapers out but you haven't replaced them. You have no news staff."

"We certainly do—we have eight men," said Koerper proudly.

"Do you know how many reporters the Kansas City *Star* has?" Cronkite asked.

"But that's their principal business," Koerper answered.

"There!" said Cronkite, seizing on it. "That's the answer!" So the upshot of the conversation was that Walter Cronkite was hired in 1948 by Karl Koerper to work as Washington correspondent for his station and a series of other Kansas and Missouri stations, which was the beginning of Walter Cronkite's career as a broadcaster. He was thirty-one years old, he was from the world of print, and more, he was from the highly specialized, fiercely competitive world of wire-service print. But he went to Washington; his salary was $250 a week and he was working for a string of midwestern radio stations. Somehow in the snobbery and pecking order of American journalism there was something slightly demeaning about seeing Walter Cronkite, who had been a big man during the war, hustling around Washington as a radio man for a bunch of small midwestern stations, although Cronkite did not find it demeaning since he liked the excitement of Washington and since he intended to return soon to Kansas City as general manager of the station.

He worked in Washington for about a year and a half, not entirely satisfied, but not all that restless, and then the Korean War broke out and he got a phone call from Ed Murrow asking whether he might be willing to go to Korea and cover the war for CBS. Would he? Well, Murrow better believe that he would, it was the kind of assignment he loved and wanted, it was exactly where he wanted to be. There was, Murrow said, no great problem with KMBC since it was a CBS affiliate and that type of thing would be easily straightened out. In the meantime, Cronkite should get himself ready to go overseas again. But there was some delay because one of his children was about to be born. Then in the middle of all this, the freeze on ownership of stations ended and CBS bought WTOP, which had been a locally owned Washington station, wanting it as a major outlet in the Washington area, a kind of political flagship. The station television news director asked Cronkite to do the Korean story every night, and inquired what he needed in the way of graphics, which turned out to be chalk and a blackboard. Everyone else was trying to make things more complicated and Cronkite, typically, was trying to make them more simple. He worked so hard in preparation for it, backgrounding himself, going to the Pentagon to develop independent sources, that his mastery and control of the subject were absolutely unique. He simply worked harder than everyone else, and in a profession as embryonic as television news, peopled as it frequently was in those days by pretty boys, he was an immediate success. He had that special quality that television demands, that audiences sense, and that is somehow intangible—he had *weight,* he projected a kind of authority. The people in the station knew that he was stronger and more professional than

anyone else around and very soon he was asked to do the Korean War story
twice a day, and then, very soon after that, the entire news show, and then two
news shows a day. He was an immediate hit, a very good professional reporter
on a new medium, and he soon began to do network feeds from Washington
back to the network news show in New York. Korea began to slip away as
an assignment.

Among those most aware of Cronkite's talents was Sig Mickelson, who
was then in charge of television news at CBS. He was in effect the head of the
stepchild section of CBS News, trying to build up television, but doing it very
much against the grain, since in comparison with Murrow he had no bureaucratic muscle, and since all the stars of the News Department were in the
Murrow group. Mickelson was quietly strengthening the rest of the News
Department. He had known Cronkite in earlier incarnations and from the start
he had seen Cronkite as the man around whom he could build the future
television staff. As the 1952 convention approached, radio was still bigger than
television, although the convention itself would help tip the balance in favor
of television. The Mickelson group wanted a full-time correspondent who
would sit there all day long and all night long and hold the coverage together,
not get tired, and have great control over his material. Mickelson asked for
Murrow, Sevareid, or Collingwood, the big radio stars. But the radio people
told Mickelson to get lost. Instead, negotiating through Hubbell Robinson,
they offered a list of reporters who were ostensibly second-stringers. On the
list was precisely the name that Mickelson wanted, that of Walter Cronkite.

The Murrow group had never really considered Cronkite one of them and
there was a certain snobbery about it all; Cronkite was somehow different from
the others; it was not just that they had been stars longer than he, they were
of a different cast and a different type and it would be crucial in the difference
between television news reporting and radio news reporting. Cronkite was
then, and he remained some twenty-five years later, almost consciously a
nonsophisticate, and he is even now, much as he was then, right out of the
Midwest, and there was a touch of *The Front Page* to him, he was almost
joyously what he had always been, a lot of gee whiz, it was all new and fresh
even when surely he had seen much of it before, and it was as if he took delight
in not having been changed externally by all that he had seen. He was above
all *of* the wire services—get it fast and get it straight and make it understandable and do not agonize over the larger questions that it raises. The Murrow
men—Sevareid, Howard Smith, Collingwood, Shirer, Schoenbrun—were
notoriously cerebral and had been picked for that reason; they had been
encouraged to think and analyze, not just to run as sprinters. They had dined
with the great and mighty of Europe and they had entered the great salons and
taken on the mannerisms of those salons; they were, whether they wanted to
be or not (and most of them wanted to be), sophisticates. If they had once
worked for organizations like UP, they were glad to have that behind them
and they did not romanticize those years. Sevareid, for example, came from
Velva, North Dakota, which was smaller than St. Joseph, Missouri, where

Cronkite came from, but Sevareid had left Velva behind long ago and there was a part of Cronkite which had never left St. Joe, and which he quite consciously projected.

Cronkite had come to the 1952 convention knowing that it was his big chance. He had come thoroughly prepared, he knew the weight of each delegation and he was able to bind the coverage together at all times. He was, in a field very short on professionalism, incredibly professional, and in a job that required great durability, he was the ultimate durable man. By the end of the first day, in the early morning, the other people in the control booth just looked at each other, they knew they had a winner, and a new dimension of importance for television; they knew it even more the next day when some of the Murrow people began to drift around to let the television staff know they were, well, available for assignment. Cronkite himself had little immediate sense of it, he was so obsessed by the action in front of him that he had no awareness of the growing reaction to his performance. It was true that people kept coming up and congratulating him on his work and it was true that there seemed to be a new attitude on the part of his colleagues, but he still did not realize what had happened. On the last morning of the convention, when it was all over, he went for an early-morning walk with Sig Mickelson along Michigan Avenue. Mickelson said that his life was going to change, he was going to want to renegotiate his contract and he would need a lot more money.

"Do you have an agent?" Mickelson asked.

"No," said Cronkite.

"Well, you better get one," Mickelson said. "You're going to need one."

"No, I won't," Cronkite said.

"Yes, you will," Mickelson said.

As President, Eisenhower adapted quickly to television, but he did not seize upon it as his successors would; it was there and if he did not use it someone else would, so he used it. He treated the press much as he treated the nation. Reporters were pleasant, well-behaved enlisted men; no matter how much physical proximity he gave them, and it was in fact considerably limited, it was understood that they were there not to ask too many questions or to be impertinent. It was a role that they readily accepted, in part because they sensed his larger mandate, his special position, and because they themselves shared some of the fears which had given him that special mandate, the fears of McCarthy at home and the fears of a monolithic, ruthless totalitarian enemy, and they did not want to be accused in even subtle ways of helping the Other Side. Eisenhower did not know the names of the reporters who covered him, with the exception of Merriman Smith, the UP correspondent and dean of the White House press corps, who had the privilege of opening and closing press conferences. Eisenhower knew Smith's name, or at least came fairly close to knowing it, calling him *Merriam,* Ike coming in again and again to press conferences and saying, "Hello, Merriam." He did not manipulate the press

very much, largely because he did not need to. It was almost as if there were
a natural law, that the greater the American perception of Communists as an
external threat, the greater the willingness of the people, Congress, press,
public opinion, to grant the President control of a broad and unquestioned
national interest and not to try to dissect it; as the sense of the Communists
as a threat receded, beginning at the very end of the fifties and the start of the
sixties, so for the first time came a growth in our willingness to perceive
different dimensions and gradations in our national interest.

Eisenhower had in Jim Hagerty a superb technician and a man perfectly
constituted for the General's Olympian relationship with the press. He was
technically a master, superb at all details, brilliant at not losing baggage, and
making sure that hot meals were still hot and that phones were always available. As he was masterful at the minutiae so he was also deliberately weak on
substance; he had successfully sealed up the White House and there were
perilously few leaks—in part because the kind of people who worked for Ike
were not the kind of people who talked to reporters anyway, sharing the
essential Eisenhower view that all reporters were corporals; and in part because the nation did not seem to want leaks from the White House, there
seemed little appetite for inside details of Eisenhower's policies, particularly
anything that might reflect incompetence. A locked-up situation like this
meant that reporters were almost totally dependent upon Hagerty, and he in
turn exercised very sophisticated control over the press. He took marvelous
care of the reporters' physical needs and he unleashed a great glut of informa-
tional trivia. No nation ever learned more about what its President ate for
breakfast than the people of the United States of America under Dwight
Eisenhower. If the President were meeting with the British Prime Minister in
Bermuda, reporters would get an almost Andrew Wyeth–like portrait of what
the room looked like, where each chair was, who sat next to whom, what each
dignitary wore. Indeed, one of the great early Art Buchwald columns mi-
micked an imaginary Hagerty briefing during a summit conference: *Q.* What
did the President say to the Secretary of State, Jim? *A.* He said, "Good night,
Foster." *Q.* And what did the Secretary of State say to the President? *A.* He
said, "Good night, Mister President."

Hagerty was a print man, he was not only a former *New York Times*
political reporter, he was the son of a famed *Times* political journalist; he had
worked for Tom Dewey as a press secretary and he had been instrumental in
getting Dewey to use television naturally and effectively during his 1950 gubernatorial campaign. He was equally effective in moving Eisenhower toward
acceptance of modern communications. Within a year of Ike's election Hagerty had supervised a televised cabinet round table, with the cabinet officers
carefully rehearsed (with the help of BBD&O) in the delicate art of spontaneity. The next year cameras were let into an actual cabinet meeting with
the cabinet members working off rehearsed lines. But far more important, from
the moment Eisenhower came into office Hagerty intended to televise his press
conferences; it was only a matter of adequate technology so that it could be

done as naturally as possible (he was very sensitive to technology; after he finally allowed television into Eisenhower's press conferences, Hagerty always personally checked each camera before every conference to make sure that it made no distracting noise). In particular Hagerty did not want to subject the General to the fierce lights necessary for a live performance, and in those days film was not fast enough to permit more subtle lighting. The networks, of course, were pushing for televised press conferences; it would not only be a breakthrough for the President, it would be a breakthrough for them, as they made the President bigger so he would make them bigger, make them more legitimate, they would, after all, not just be passing on to their audience a bunch of comedians and tap dancers, but the President of the United States, and that was serious business.

In 1954 the networks told Hagerty that they had come up with a film sufficiently fast to limit the intensity of the lights. Hagerty asked for a dry run and, playing the part of the President himself, and with network correspondents playing the part of other White House reporters, they ran a trial conference. It worked, Eisenhower liked what he saw and decided to let the cameras in. Hagerty was well aware of the inevitable explosion from print reporters and he asked the networks to keep it a secret. A day before the scheduled conference Hagerty announced to the writing press that cameras were coming. There was, of course, a violent reaction, with the most intense protest coming from representatives of the three wire services. For this was a real loss of power; above all, the wires had offered one thing in American communications—speed, not wisdom or depth or intellect. Simply speed. Now here was television challenging the wire services on the biggest of national stories. The three wire-servicemen, all senior correspondents, complained bitterly to Hagerty; Hagerty in turn called the networks—his loyalty, after all, was only to Dwight Eisenhower—and suggested that since they and thousands of their stations were wire-service subscribers, they might just call the wire-service executives and remind them of this. The network executives did, and shortly thereafter the word came down to the White House wire reporters to call it off. The first time the cameras entered the press conference Hagerty demanded the right to edit the film in order to prevent any mistakes (there was one egregious mistake: Ike had referred to the French problems in Indochina as taking place in *Indonesia*—but if he was not good at naming Asian countries he was better than his successors at staying out of them). The film was edited and soon released and after a few more conferences Hagerty decided not to bother editing. The conferences were not yet live, and Eisenhower accepted rather than exploited the new medium. The real exploitation would come with the man who followed him in office, John Kennedy.

Dwight Eisenhower had decided to make television an instrument of presidential power. Sam Rayburn, in his beloved House of Representatives, had made the exact opposite decision. It might be turning into a wired world, but he was

not going to wire the House. Rayburn didn't *like* the print press; he despised
and feared television. It simply multiplied all the dangers of the press without,
as far as he was concerned, bringing any benefits. He hated House members
who longed only to run for the Senate, and senators who longed only to run
for the presidency. He was appalled by what he felt television had done to the
Senate by the mid-fifties. It had become a major launching platform for presidential campaigns. He thought television had ruined the Senate as a serious
body. "All they do there is preen and comb their hair and run for President.
It's like a presidential primary over there," he said. He would complain to his
friends that these senators were no longer rooted in their districts, no longer
connected to their people and to the daily lives of their constituents. Instead,
he said, they were linked to cameras and machines that made them look good.
"I hate what it does," he said, and meant it. He made a deliberate decision to
keep television out of the House, not just out of the main chamber but (unlike
the Senate) out of the committee rooms and the corridors as well. It was one
of his most important legacies: the rest of Washington might be modernizing,
that was all right with him, but he was having none of it. Print was bad enough.
But at least you could make a deal with certain print reporters and they
honored it. But who could make a deal with the camera? When people pushed
him to go on television himself he refused. "I won't sell their cereal for them,"
he once told Marquis Childs.

Also, and this was equally important, television threatened the House
leadership in a generational sense. In the Rayburn years seniority had become
the only test for leadership. Thus the leadership was very old, the dominant
figures were all in their seventies and eighties; they were men who certainly
had not risen to power because of their attractive appearance. Often it was
quite the reverse. Television encouraged youth, it helped the young Jack
Kennedy in his 1960 presidential quest, it liked vigor. And it made old men
look even older. Age was the ally of the House leadership. The more isolated
their district, the easier it was for them to hold power. Television broke the
isolation; besides, with a single appearance a very junior, very articulate, very
handsome congressman might cast a larger spell than a committee chairman.
That was very threatening. The camera was thus more than an impertinence
or an annoyance; it could become a genuine danger to the very power structure
of the House.

Rayburn was so totally a man from another age, representative of politics
past. Television, jet airplanes, computers—all that was alien to him. He hated
airplanes and refused to fly if at all possible. Once, in the immediate postwar
years, he was forced to fly with General Eisenhower for a major homecoming
ceremony in Denton, Texas. "How many engines has this machine got?" he
asked an aide after boarding. "Four," the aide answered. "Is that all?" he said.
In an age when most powerful public officials used the auto pen for signing
things, he still did all his serious business in pencil on the back of a used
envelope. (In 1960 he had gone off to see the newly elected President of the
United States to ask for a job for the son of an old Texas friend. "Ramsey

Clark," Rayburn had written on the back of a crumpled envelope.) He told his aides that when he got a letter written by hand in pencil he took it more seriously than fancy typed letters because he assumed that when someone who was barely literate wrote a letter it was really important to the writer.

Sam Rayburn was the last towering figure of the House of Representatives, a man whose name was and is still linked with the giants of the past—Longworth, Clay, Cannon. He served for sixteen years, half again as long as Henry Clay, the previous Speaker with the longest term. Those men had been rivals of the President himself. In the Washington of another era they could and did challenge the President's will. Rayburn had come to power as the world was changing and that other era was ending. As terrifying modern weapons appeared on the scene America and other nations, reluctantly or no, began investing more power and authority in their central governments. Yet Rayburn had presided over the House during years in which much of its power was fading. This was not his fault, it was simply a fact of the times; during those years the world had become smaller, the velocity of life had picked up, the society had become urbanized. The executive branch was becoming involved in every aspect of daily life, and the ability of the Congress to deal with the growing complexity of modern life was diminishing. There were simply too many issues. The centralization of power during this period, the thirties through the sixties, was based in part on the rise of inventions like radio and television and computers which permitted—indeed demanded—a common culture and politics. The issues had shifted from domestic to foreign affairs. But Rayburn fought change. He did not want radio or television in his chamber, he did not want congressmen to expand their staffs to keep pace with a rapidly expanding federal bureaucracy. He did not want the Congress participating in foreign affairs, even when he privately doubted the President's course.

All of this made the House vulnerable to the forces of modernity, which rival institutions were quickly exploiting. For Rayburn had chosen to hold and wield power in a very personal sense, not in an institutional manner, as some of his more formidable predecessors had done. That was fine, and during his tenure the institution did not suffer particularly because he was so strong of mind and character and body, but when he was gone the institution was doubly vulnerable. The forces of modernity were more powerful than ever and he was replaced by small, vastly lesser men—McCormack, Albert, midgets really, men uniquely ill equipped to lead an archaic institution under serious assault. It was Rayburnism without Rayburn. They held to his norms and his prejudices without his strengths and his intelligence; as he had worked against modernizing the House rules, so did they; as he had placed too much power in the hands of the committee chairmen, so did they; as he had blocked modern broadcasting from covering the House, so did they.

At the time Rayburn died, television was preparing to go from a fifteen-minute news show to a half-hour one, and thus became the dominant form of communications on the national level. Yet for year after year following his death his successors barred cameras from their building. That Sam Rayburn did not choose to let television cameras near the House meant only that the House suffered; the President was televised every day. For the failure to use television was a serious institutional handicap. If the House was not seen performing its most important functions on television, then, as far as most people were concerned, it was not doing anything; if it was not doing anything, it might just as well not exist. That did not bother Rayburn. He seemed, if anything, aware of the limits of parliamentary democracy in the latter part of the twentieth century, and he worked to limit the dangers of it, to make sure that the House did not thwart presidential will. Indeed, his own career in the House symbolized the end of one era and the beginning of another. He had run for Congress and won in 1912 and entered the House in 1913; he had arrived in Washington just in time to witness the inauguration of Woodrow Wilson, a man who saw himself, and his office, in almost Olympian terms.

He was comfortable within the House, uncomfortable in trying to use his power outside of it. Inside the House all his good qualities seemed to apply. He was farm boy, strong, broad-shouldered, so that he seemed much taller than in fact he was. His friend and protégé Dick Bolling thought Rayburn was the first image politician Bolling had ever encountered: a calculated and deliberate exterior prepared for his colleagues, formidable, gruff, slightly querulous. Everything seemed to advertise the fact that Rayburn was not a man to be crossed, that the penalties would be severe. The set of the body was powerful and he was very much aware of it. But if he was an image politician, he required physical proximity to exploit it; his power did not carry over modern communications. Indeed, one reason he did not like television cameras was that they did not reflect the physical strength of his body. He felt that television made him look short and bald. He was equally suspicious of newspaper photographers; and he was convinced that they conspired to make him look balder and smaller than he was, thus diminishing his power.

He often boasted that he had served *with,* not under, Presidents of the United States, but the truth was very different. He had indeed served under them and he had, on most crucial issues of the era, turned the House into an extension of the executive branch, making it an offering to the President. This was not a happenstance thing, it was very deliberate on his part. He talked often in great privacy about the limits of his own knowledge, the limits of the knowledge—indeed, the ignorance—of his colleagues. Their backgrounds were terribly narrow and he was appalled by the idea of their getting involved in areas of national security. He often talked in private about what the Industrial Revolution had done to America, how it had changed this country and made it more complicated, and how this had worked against a debating society like the House. He simply did not think the House could hack it in a modern industrial society, that if it dominated or even partially checked the President, this could easily weaken the nation against potential totalitarian adversaries. Therefore his mission was in effect to protect the somewhat fragile presidency from a potentially obstreperous and parochial Congress.

He came, as the power of the press increased, as more and more reporters appeared in Washington, to dislike the press more. The press was clearly making his own job more difficult. He was trying to hold together a complex decentralized institution where compromise was of the essence, and these reporters—buzzards and vultures, he called them in private—were only interested in sensationalism; every time they appeared they made the art of compromise harder. To him the ideal House member was someone who got ahead by going along, by keeping his or her mouth shut. The type of congressman the press liked and seized on was someone who was always talking, always giving press conferences, always threatening the thin balance of compromise. Exposure threatened compromise; exposure incited ego and vanity, and too much individualism. Rayburn was convinced that any dealings he had with the press were at the expense of his real business, which was compromise.

He simply did not really like most reporters or take their craft seriously. Martin Agronsky, one of the few reporters the Speaker liked and trusted, and even more important one of the few to capture him on tape and film, used to argue with Rayburn about this, pointing out that give and take with the press was part of the public process. Agronsky found a deep-seated resistance, an abiding distrust. It was not that reporters had treated Rayburn badly or betrayed a confidence. To the contrary, most of his dealings had been favorable. It was simply that in his eyes reporters were not serious. They were upstarts. They were playing with the public process without ever having paid a price. They were not his equal by terms of service or by terms of the Constitution, but then they wrote about him and suddenly they were his equal. He hated it.

In all the years he held power Sam Rayburn never had a press secretary. Late in his career, during the fifties, he had talked with one of Lyndon Johnson's staff members, Booth Mooney, about coming to work for him. It was all decided, but in the end Rayburn did not have the nerve to tell Lyndon that he was taking Mooney. Rayburn suggested that Mooney tell Johnson, and Mooney in turn said he would prefer it if the Speaker brought the matter up. "Well," said Rayburn, "I guess we'll just have to forget it." (Johnson later told Mooney he wouldn't have liked working for Rayburn in the House anyway. "Too slow," he said.) Rayburn avoided the press; he and Johnson would often go to the White House when Eisenhower was President, and as they left, Johnson would stop to talk with the assembled reporters. Rayburn would speed ahead. "I don't know why Lyndon lets those buzzards catch him every time they want to. I don't want to talk to them." When he did talk, it was always on the most confined, and confining, terms. Thus the few favored reporters who gained access to him and to his inner circle did so only at a very high price—a prohibition against using most of what they were getting at the time or being allowed to use it only on his terms, playing on his terms— reporters, in effect, as good old boys. Which was fine for Rayburn, he did not

seek greater exposure, he was content to run the House; after his brief flirtation
with the national ticket in 1944, he had been content to be Speaker; he did not
really want a lot of exposure, he sensed that his own reticence would make it
easier to restrain others.

Sam Rayburn's rules were the bane of broadcast journalists covering the
House (though not necessarily of network executives, who were thus spared
the necessity of putting on potentially long and expensive House sessions). The
correspondents' working conditions were primitive, everything was done to
make their day as difficult as possible. They regularly protested but to no avail.
Once, in the late fifties, they banded together and decided that the time had
come to send the Speaker a formal petition, and so they gathered and wrote
out a very formal if somewhat ponderous letter of protest: We wish to interpose
our strenuous objections to the barring of radio and television coverage.
. . . They had Bob Menaugh, who worked in the press gallery, deliver it to the
Speaker. Which Menaugh did, though not without some trepidation, knowing
of Rayburn's sensitivity to petitions. Menaugh arrived just as the Speaker was
about to leave his office.

"I've been instructed to bring you this letter," Menaugh said.

So Rayburn, who was already standing, picked it up and began to read
it aloud, mocking it as he read: "We wish to interpose . . . our . . . strenuous
. . . objections . . ."

He looked at Menaugh, tore it up, and said, the word sounded like it had
four syllables: "Sheeeeyit."


Thus were the cameras kept out of the House. The decision was to have a
profound impact, making the House less able to compete with the executive
branch, and diminishing its importance in the eyes of the public. Rayburn did
not like television and it threatened his view of order, so he cut it off. The lesser
men who followed him continued to observe his edict though clearly they were
by then living in a television age. Characteristically, the only time the Congress
of the United States appeared on television during this era was when the
President of the United States came to the House to deliver his State of the
Union speech. Then the congressmen could be seen dutifully applauding, their
roles in effect written in by the President's speech writers. As the presidency
grew and grew beyond all accountability it was perhaps not by chance that
when the House of Representatives at last admitted television to a committee
hearing room, it was for the beginning of impeachment proceedings against a
President of the United States.


The extraordinary commercial success of television had not been without its
price; the great quiz shows turned out, not surprisingly, to be rigged. This
shook the nation; if the people of America could not trust a television game
show to have straight answers to straight questions, what could they trust?

That one of the people involved, Charles Van Doren, was the scion of the American literary aristocracy, bearing one of its great names, seemed to indicate that we were all, if not guilty, at least vulnerable, temptable. In the Congress the reaction to the rigging was very strong and the networks were clearly on the defensive. At CBS the pain and the reaction were very real. For some time Bill Golden, the brilliant CBS designer, had been suggesting to Murrow and Friendly that they investigate the quiz shows, that the word around town was that they were rigged and that it would be better for the entire television industry if it were a television team that broke the story. But nothing came of it, the story broke in print, and the industry was seriously, justifiably—and only briefly—damaged.

Among the prime victims at CBS was Lou Cowan, then president of the television network. Cowan was considered a humane liberal figure in broadcasting—he had served as Stevenson's chief media adviser in 1952 and earlier during World War II he had helped produce serial shows which focused on the problems of Negro soldiers, thus helping to give some identity to blacks. As president of CBS, he had been committed to both Murrow and Friendly and had worked hard, against growing commercial pressures, to get extra time for news specials (often in desperation calling Bob Kintner at NBC, finding out what he was doing, and then using Kintner and NBC's growing appetite for public affairs as a wedge to force CBS to be more responsible). More than once he had been encouraged by Stanton when the two of them privately discussed putting pressure on Paley for more public affairs, only to find that, once in Paley's presence, Stanton did not back him up as Paley systematically assaulted their arguments. This had come to a head in 1956 at the time of the crisis in Lebanon, when the world seemed poised on the brink of war and Eisenhower had sent in American Marines. Cowan, at the urging of the News Division, had put the United Nations debates on live, Stanton had given permission and indeed had seemed enthusiastic. But Paley had subsequently returned from a vacation in a rage about the misuse of time and the loss of revenue, the fact that war had not broken out showed how false the alert had been. Stanton, much to Cowan's bitterness, had not backed Cowan up. Cowan had exploded; he told them he had only come to CBS in the first place because of the Klauber-Murrow tradition, because of its reputation for service.

But his position was a fragile one. It was further eroded by the quiz scandals, since in addition to being a supporter of public affairs, he was a huckster as well. He had invented "The $64,000 Question," and while he claimed innocence of the rigging—his position throughout was that the program had such immense natural drama that it did not have to be rigged—he was nonetheless an inevitable target. Either his subordinates had rigged it under his very nose, in which case he was guilty of gross incompetence, or he was somehow involved. Either way he lost. At a time like this the networks needed a fall guy, and Cowan became the main fall guy at CBS. Stanton issued a series of public statements expressing confidence in Cowan's innocence, while at the same time pushing Cowan very hard to resign: the good of the *company*

demanded that a head roll and that the head be a high one. Stanton told Cowan
not to communicate with anyone else at CBS and suggested that he resign for
reasons of ill health (Cowan had been ill at the very moment of the scandal).
Cowan instead went public and insisted that his health was excellent, but
because of pressure from Stanton he was indeed resigning. So the quiz scandals
came home to CBS. A gross commercialism had caused the scandal and the
troubles seemed to reflect network greed, the triumph of dollars over ethics.
The question of who would succeed Cowan at CBS would tell a great deal
about William S. Paley and about the future of CBS and of American broadcasting.

The choice was James T. Aubrey, Jr. Even now, some twenty years later,
the name has an almost distinctive resonance. Jim Aubrey. The huckster's
huckster. A man so nakedly open about what he was and what he wanted—
that is, the greediest side of the network so openly revealed and displayed—
that even the other hucksters were embarrassed. What differentiated him from
the others was not so much that he was worse than they were as that he did
it with such abandon and with so little apology. CBS had always stood for
class, for quality, and for civility. Aubrey once said to one of his aides, a man
already despondent about what he felt television had done to him, making him
harsh and ruthless: "The trouble with you, Bill, is that you're not a killer.
You'll never make it here." Aubrey said unabashedly what others in the
network world refused to admit even though they knew to be true of themselves and their work.

He was a man so fierce and rapacious, who climbed to heights so dizzying
and by such ruthless means that his career seemed like a bad novel—and
indeed spawned several (bad) novels. A man who, when announcing excessive
CBS annual profits, could note in passing that they would have been even
higher if CBS had not wasted so much money on public affairs programs. Who
could, on the day after John Kennedy's assassination, tell Blair Clark, who was
the head of CBS News and a very close friend of Kennedy, and at that terrible
moment obsessed with trying to convey on television both the drama of tragedy and mourning, and the struggle of the American government to hold
together: "Just play the assassination footage over and over again—that's all
they want to see." Who could say of the idea of producing *The Glass Menagerie*
on CBS, "You think I'm crazy? Who wants to look at that? It's too downbeat.
The girl's got a limp." Whose greatest legacy to television was a program called
"The Beverly Hillbillies," a series so demented and tasteless that it boggles the
mind, depicting as it did, in the words of Murray Kempton, "a confrontation
of the characters of John Steinbeck with the environment of Spyros Skouras."
When he took over as network president in 1959, Jim Aubrey was almost
unique among his fellow Americans; he thought network television programming too highbrow. He set out to lower it and lower it he did, to a rising graph
of CBS corporate profits. From the start Bill Paley knew what Jim Aubrey was,
and from the start Bill Paley let him have his way; nobody remembers Jim
Aubrey with much pride, but he is a more exact replica of what network

programming became and the reasons for it than Ed Murrow ever was, though they were both extensions of Bill Paley.

If television had been indecently prosperous before Aubrey, he made it ever more so. When Aubrey took over in December 1959, CBS's net annual profits were $25.2 million; two years later they had more than doubled. Between 1961 and 1964, Aubrey's last year, they reached a high of $49.6 million, an extraordinary jump over the past and over the other networks. He was so brutally and primitively successful at what he did—no matter what questions his professional conduct raised, how terrible the shows, the profits always rose, the stock always went up—that there was some belief in Wall Street just before his downfall that he could in fact take the network away from Paley. Not because he was a better man, but because his system worked and Wall Street admired that, even if it meant not watching television themselves. When he was finally fired, five years after taking over, because his private behavior had flashed too often into public behavior, CBS stock dropped nine points on the market. "That puts my net value to the network at twenty million," Aubrey said.

A few weeks after the fall of Aubrey, a young writer named Michael Mooney approached Elmo Roper, then closely connected to CBS, to ask why Aubrey had been fired at this particular moment. After all, there was nothing exceptional in his behavior, nothing that he had not already done either professionally or in his rather dramatic personal life.

Roper had answered, "Young man, Mr. Aubrey has made us so rich that we can now afford to worry about our image."

The Aubrey-Paley relationship was unique. Stanton may have been the one corporate figure who survived over decades with Paley and managed, at a terrible price, to survive, the ultimate corporate man who suffered the ultimate loss of individuality. Aubrey, who was finally destroyed and thrown out, was different. During his brief imperial reign he treated Paley with what bordered on contempt. Aubrey was a peculiar man; like most Americans, he disliked everyone he worked for, but unlike most other Americans, he took few pains to conceal it. Rather, it was as if he felt compelled to show what he felt about his boss. It was a relationship edged in money and hate; it was as if there was a mechanism in Aubrey that had to insult Paley, to condescend to him: a programming meeting in California where Paley began to talk and Aubrey, almost offhandedly, just the right amount of condescension, handcrafted: *Bill, let me take care of that.* Or in his voice when Paley would call him on the phone: *Yes, Bill,* his voice a little bored, *I think we've taken care of that.* Or with a close friend sitting in his office when his secretary would announce that Paley was on the phone and he would wink and say, "Tell the Chairman I'll call him back." Yet it worked, and Paley accepted it, even though what Aubrey did was almost brutally to throw away the façade of artistic pretense that CBS had so prided itself on. But it worked because the profits were so great. That above all, even as Aubrey flaunted his contempt for Paley's sense of image, sense of class. It was all so brash and so crude. Paley loved the stars, the talent, and Aubrey was deliberately rude and autocratic to them; tired of Jack Benny, who was beginning to slip, the sainted Benny who had helped to make CBS television what it was, Aubrey once said as bluntly as he could to Benny, "You're through." There was pain in all this for Paley, but the ratings were remarkable, just remarkable, and so he tolerated it. He tolerated it because it worked.

Aubrey's success was very simple: he had a killer instinct for the lowest common denominator, and unlike others who had that instinct, he had no shame, no interest in respectability, or at least the traditional forms of respectability. He knew that if he followed his instincts he could make money and generate ratings and that money and ratings generated a respectability all their own. His particular vehicle was his belief that television as a mass instrument was not being sufficiently exploitative of the mass, it was not reaching the large rural mass out there. He was convinced that the people who ran television were too urban in their orientation, too educated, and too interested in pleasing people who did not watch television. They were, he was sure, neglecting a vast and less educated rural audience (or at least the children of rural people, for whom television was likely to be the prime if not the only form of entertainment). He took control of the programming department as no one other than Paley had ever done before and he ran it by his own strict standards. He wanted rural comedies and detective stories. Later he went to sexy ladies, and there was in fact a famous Aubrey memo that turned up in the hands of congressional watchdogs, calling for more "broads, boobs and busts." He wanted no old people. Youth was better. No physical infirmities. No social issues. No maids—people did not identify with servants. Lots of action and as little thinking as possible. "I don't want any more seamy sociological scripts," he told one aide. "Goddamnit, I want happy endings. I can't communicate with the creative people. They just won't listen. The trouble with the creative people is that they don't know the public. The people out there don't want to think. I come from out there." A special kind of honesty—he did not think he was better than the audience, better than what he was showing.

He did not, unlike so many timid colleagues, apologize for what he was doing. His whole history at CBS was studded with irony. He had become president because of the quiz scandals, and he had replaced bogus shows with banal ones. At a time when American intellectuals and congressmen and editorial writers congratulated themselves on the freedom of American arts as opposed to the limits of Communist arts, the truth was that in the most powerful new vehicle for the arts Americans lived under a tyranny of ratings and the dollar. Aubrey brought to television not just "The Beverly Hillbillies," but "Mr. Ed," a show about a talking horse, "Petticoat Junction," and "The Munsters." Paley was embarrassed by much of this. He disliked "The Beverly Hillbillies," and he told friends that "The Munsters" was a bad cartoon. But happy or unhappy, he who had made the ratings such a fixture—the only God was Nielsen—could not argue with what he had wrought. Paley had argued against "The Munsters," telling friends that it would disgrace the network; but Aubrey wanted the show, he felt the public was ready for monsters. He was right. In fact he was right a lot of the time. Given the standards for success that existed at the networks, it was hard for him to be wrong. By 1963, CBS had 12 out of the top 12 daytime shows and outdrew NBC and ABC together by 6 to 4 in the evening hours. Advertisers were spending a cool million every evening at CBS. Who would fight Aubrey? Who would want to? Who would risk a machine that coined money?

Aubrey at the same time fought constantly with the News Division. The News Division caused problems and it made Washington angry. While for many that was the major problem, for Aubrey it was secondary. His concern was that the News Division took up too much air time, air time which could be used to sell detectives and hillbillies and monsters. Sensing that Sig Mickelson wanted to take Charles Kuralt, one of television's most literate and civilized young commentators, and turn him into another Ed Murrow, Aubrey waged an all-out fight against Kuralt, demeaning him at every opportunity, mocking his work and his looks, in effect dampening the possibility that Kuralt might be a threat to his profits. He issued a directive in 1962 to cut back on the News Division's tradition of preempting prime time on special occasions. This was a crucial move because the News Department had systematically over recent years been locked out of regular prime time and any additional barrier between it and regular access to the air confirmed more clearly its second-class status. Aubrey was appalled at the importance that CBS attached to the political conventions, not realizing that in addition to pleasing Wall Street and Madison Avenue, it was important to please Pennsylvania Avenue as well. He stomped out of the 1964 Republican convention after two days, telling David Susskind, one of his friends in those days, "This damn thing is going to cost us ten million dollars. Who wants to listen to news? . . . If I had my way we'd have some guy come on at eleven P.M. and say, 'The following six men made horse's asses of themselves at the Republican convention,' and then he'd give the six names and that would be it." It was not by coincidence that his rise and the spectacular profits of CBS in those years saw a comparable decline in CBS News and a rise at NBC. CBS News was just less important, less emphasis went into it. Meanwhile Kintner was pushing his Huntley-Brinkley show. NBC was promoting the news, putting money into its news department, ripping out its regularly scheduled shows for news. The Cronkite team was getting less and less support. In 1964, just before the conventions, Aubrey told a close friend, "The only thing Paley and I agree on is that we're not going to blow all that fucking money on the conventions this year." The lack of emphasis was painful for CBS News people but the price was still to be paid; at the 1964 convention CBS was decisively beaten in the ratings by NBC.

# 8/ The Los Angeles _Times_

Kyle Palmer, political correspondent and kingmaker, had picked Nixon out very early and nurtured him. Nixon, he told his friends, was the best young politician he had ever seen, the best tactician. It was born into him, Palmer said, his very reflex was for tactics, he had an intuitive sense of the chessboard. He was the quickest to learn. Palmer had decided from the start that Nixon had the quality and the scope to go national. Kyle Palmer had not been a member of an informal group in Los Angeles–Whittier that had advertised for young enterprising congressional candidates, but his friends were part of it (indeed, Jack Garland, Norman Chandler's favorite brother-in-law, was a member), and Palmer had been looking for someone like Nixon. The presence of Jerry Voorhis, steadfast New Dealer, in the House seat was a constant irritant, particularly to a political czar who controlled almost everything else. Worse, many of the Chandlers and their friends lived in Pasadena, which was included in the Voorhis district. There are two versions of what had happened. The first was that the original committee was something of a front for Palmer and that he had picked Nixon from the start. The other was that the committee picked Nixon and that Palmer very quickly fastened on him, sensing that Nixon was doing well, and shortly thereafter took him to Norman Chandler for the official laying on of hands. The latter story is more likely the right one. It is unlikely that Palmer would pick up Nixon and invest seriously in him until he thought he had a reasonable chance of winning; Palmer did not like losers. But he quickly took Nixon under his wing in that campaign, urged him to hit hard on the anti-Communist line. The New Deal era was passing, he said, so Nixon should tag Voorhis to it, to the CIO-PAC, attack the bumblers in Washington, put him on the defensive. At the same time, in the pages of the Los Angeles _Times,_ often in Palmer's own column, _The Watchman,_ there began the evolution of the White Knight Nixon. Young. Clean-cut. War veteran. Quaker background but not afraid to fight. Family man. Straight shooter. Not afraid to duck the issue of Americanism. ("Nixon has ability and courage. He will stand up and fight for what he believes to be right and he swings from the floor.")

The trouble for Jerry Voorhis had, of course, begun even before the arrival of Richard Nixon. It was 1946, a year after the end of the war, fourteen years since the first election of Franklin Roosevelt, and all the pent-up tensions and frustrations over wartime sacrifice, plus the smoldering resentments against the New Deal, were in the air. It was a very bad time for a liberal congressman. The mood of the country, particularly in the West and the South, was shifting dramatically. In addition, the conservative assault on Voorhis had begun earlier in the California State Assembly with a clever redistricting of his base. The move had a certain logic, the district had been awkward, but nonetheless Voorhis was the loser. An assembly district that went 5–1 Democratic was subtracted from his congressional district. Overnight he was vulnerable. At the same time he noticed that the Los Angeles *Times* was keeping up a steady drumbeat against him, trying to isolate him, not just as a Democrat but as a left-winger, slightly wild and woolly, a red hot. The *Times* had two people in its Washington bureau, Warren and Lorraine Francis, who wrote primarily about the *Times*'s favorite water projects. Voorhis had more or less considered them friends. They had, to be sure, never written anything favorable about him, but they had seemed personable and pleasant and they had never done him grievous damage either, had never tormented him in the past. They started now. Suddenly there was a rash of stories that portrayed him—falsely—as the leader of a radical faction within the California Democratic delegation. There was no truth to it, and Voorhis encountered no problem with his Democratic colleagues, but it was embarrassing and, worse, he had been placed on the defensive. It clearly helped to isolate Voorhis in the public mind as being a little different, a little radical, not even a good Democrat. A troublemaker.

The campaign was carefully orchestrated, and there was no doubt, among those in Washington who knew how the Los Angeles *Times*'s political coverage worked, about who was the sponsor of it. Nor, as Voorhis quickly learned, was there any way to protest. He tried, but there was no easy denial. What could he do, call up Norman Chandler and complain? What would he get for that? Probably another attack. Attacks upon him could be printed but no answers given. The *Times* simply dominated his district. The attacks usually came from Kyle Palmer: "Voorhis was once a registered Socialist and that streak will not rub out. Public ownership, cooperatives and 'escape from monopolistic control' are favorites with him. Voorhis is not above all the smart little stunts Congressmen indulge in to make the folks back home feel good —even to keeping track of and sending birthday greetings or cards to the newly born. He has trimmed of late on his leftist friends, even wishing the CIO-PAC would not endorse him. . . ." Voorhis could get no real coverage of his campaign; nothing that he said explaining his record could make this or almost any other paper in his district. He could not even get his daily schedule printed. If he wanted the *Times* to print the announcement of a rally he had to buy an advertisement and even then they sometimes edited it. Midway through the most difficult campaign of his career, fighting for his political life, he could feel himself becoming a nonperson.

Richard Nixon had no complaints about the press coverage of that campaign. There was a traveling claque which went around with him and which often seemed not just to applaud Nixon but to drown out Voorhis. It bordered on bully-boy tactics. This was the beginning of Nixon. He was the local boy ready to make good, upwardly mobile, ambitious for all the good things that his sponsors seemed to have, unquestioning of them, their values; status and power were their own rewards and bore their own legitimacy. He was bright, eager, a winner. He had run against Voorhis and beaten him, they were in his debt as much as he was in theirs; Voorhis had been a special thorn and Nixon had removed that thorn; now Kyle Palmer adopted Nixon. He guided him on issues, emphasizing that Communism was a no-lose issue, it put Democrats on the defensive, no one wanted to defend Communism, thus it always worked. He made sure that Nixon saw Norman and Buff Chandler, and their friends, and he tutored him on the various members of the inner circle—Norman, Asa Call, Frank Dougherty, what they were like, their interests, their vulnerabilities. He told Nixon that when he came back from Washington and went to dinner with his sponsors, he should always give them a nugget, a bit of gossip, a feeling of being on the inside, something they would not get elsewhere. He made sure that when Norman and Buff were in Washington, Nixon would find ample time to see them, to escort them around, to give a dinner in their honor. Washington and Nixon became linked together. At the same time that Palmer was explaining to Nixon how to deal with his new sponsors, he was selling his new protégé to the elite, particularly to Buff and Norman. This young man was not just a congressman. He was going to be a senator. Not just that, but there was nothing stopping him from being a *President.* He was the best young politician Kyle had ever seen, Norman and Buff should take him very seriously, be proud they had a special relationship with him.

Thus began the connection. It was a very special relationship. The *Times* sanitized Nixon, printed whatever would make him look good, and ignored anything that might be damaging. Kyle Palmer was the sole journalist who had access to Nixon at all times, who could walk in and see him without an appointment, without even checking with Rose Mary Woods. It was an almost fatherly relationship; in fact, in 1950, preparing a Senate seat for Nixon, Palmer had written: "Nixon is young enough to be old, and wise enough to be prudent and his perceptive qualities are exceptional. In fact the flattering references which our fathers formerly made to an exceptionally promising junior—that he had an 'old head on young shoulders'—applies with all its homely implications to this young man who grew up here, became a lawyer, went to war, and returned to win a spectacular victory in his first bid for public office." The connection of the *Times* was through Kyle; Norman and Buff stood back just a bit. They were not that directly involved, they were not that personally close to Nixon, but he was useful to them, and potentially even more so; his future, if Kyle was right, seemed limitless.

Yet he was of a different class, he was not *of* them, and they did not want to be any closer to him than necessary. Buff had always found something lacking in him, and years later, when it all had gone sour and he had disgraced himself, she would remember that she always thought he was a little tacky. Indeed, the first time she had met him, on election night in 1946, when all the good winners dutifully came by the *Times* building (as they now go by the television studios) for the anointing by Palmer, she had not liked him. Nixon with his parents and brothers had gone upstairs to the Chandlers' private suite in the building, where there was a buffet. Someone asked the Nixons what they wanted to drink and the Nixon women said milk, so the Nixon men also said milk, and then as Buff was going out the door for milk, Nixon had taken her aside and asked for a bourbon—"Can you get me a straight bourbon? I don't want my mother to see me drinking it." It was a quick flash, but she did not like it, a grown man concealing a drink from his mother. But she did not let it stand in the way of the *Times*'s sponsorship of Richard Nixon. The Nixons, after all, were politicians, people to be used, not liked. They would use him, he would use them. They did not need to be friends.

So Richard Nixon had gone off to Washington with the backing of the most powerful media figure in his entire region. He would have no further problems with the Republican Party in California for Kyle Palmer *was* the Republican Party, and he was bound to have enthusiastic coverage in the *Times*. Kyle Palmer had anointed him, looking not just to the present but to the future; sixteen years later, sick, dying, Palmer could tell his friend Asa Call that Nixon was the politician who justified his career. And Palmer would be a better friend to Nixon than Norman Chandler, because Norman was in the end too much the gentleman. Kyle had fewer scruples about using the *Times*'s influence.

Almost as soon as Nixon arrived in Washington, moreover, he made another journalistic connection that was to prove immensely useful to his career. Years later, when Nixon argued that the press and the liberals—he linked them together—hated him because of his position on the Hiss case, because he had been right and they had been wrong, it would be difficult to remember that the situation had really been quite completely different in those days, that in fact most of the working press had been far from hostile during the Hiss case, and Nixon was regarded by the main working reporters as the prime and most reliable source on the committee. In addition, one very powerful reporter had befriended, advised, and guided him through the proceedings. Bert Andrews of the New York *Herald Tribune* had sometimes seemed to be more of a Nixon staff man than a working journalist. Richard Nixon would be offended, much later in his career, by the relationship between Bob Woodward and Carl Bernstein and their governmental sources, but it was in fact only a delayed replay of his own special relationship with Bert Andrews.

In 1947, Bert Andrews was the *Trib* bureau chief, which made him Washington's number-two newsman. He was classically the rewrite man turned reporter, very facile, very quick, a story banged out in ten minutes. He was of the old breed of reporters, he liked action stories, stories with accusations and drama, and he did not like policy stories, or stories that were heavy with issues. He liked stories out of the House Un-American Activities Committee because they were exciting and filled with charges and countercharges.

In the fifties, as more complicated stories about foreign policy became more important, his star descended somewhat. But in 1947 he was a formidable figure, at the height of his fame. He had just won a Pulitzer Prize, for stories about abuses of security procedures. That had for a time created the image of Bert Andrews as a reporter who was vitally interested in the civil-liberties aspects of public policy; in truth, his sympathies ran the other way.

Andrews had picked up on Nixon as a comer very early. Nixon was a member of HUAC, and HUAC produced big stories in the late forties. Perhaps there was more heat than light in many of them, but they were played as very good stories nonetheless. The two men quickly became friends and soon Nixon was a frequent visitor to the *Trib* bureau, an Andrews protégé. Robert Donovan, then a much younger reporter, remembered being in the office and watching Nixon with Andrews, Nixon somehow very awkward and unfinished and Andrews turning and saying, after Nixon had left, "Bob, I can make that fellow President of the United States."

They had become very close, each was a valued connection for the other, Nixon a bright young man on the rise, with his HUAC connections a good source, Andrews with a powerful eastern newspaper at his disposal, a rare connection for an ambitious young western congressman. When Nixon had first been tipped off by some excellent sources about the Hiss-Chambers case, he had come immediately to Andrews and had shown him the secret testimony of the confrontation between the two men. Andrews, as Nixon had expected, had immediately smelled a rat, and he had told Nixon that Hiss was lying. That was what Nixon thought Andrews would say, and it was what he thought too, but the comment had steadied Nixon's hand. There is considerable reason to believe that he knew well in advance how good a case he had, and that by going to Andrews he was getting not only confirmation of his instincts but an unofficial commitment that as he plunged ahead, he would, if he entered a major confrontation, not be alone, he would have the influential *Herald Tribune* with him. Two days later he took Andrews with him to meet Chambers for a mock grilling of the witness. At that meeting it was Andrews who had asked for a tangible relic of the Hiss-Chambers friendship, and Chambers had taken out a book of bird paintings by Audubon that Hiss was supposed to have given him. That helped nail it down for both of them. By this time Andrews was not just a reporter covering a story, he was friend, adviser, press officer, and reporter for Nixon. He was to get some very good stories for the *Tribune* in return, but his role was special. He had steadied Nixon and advised him, and kept him aware of other developments on the case through his sources at the White House. A few months later, when the so-called Pumpkin Papers first surfaced, while Nixon was on vacation, it was Andrews who sent Nixon a series of urgent telegrams telling him to return as quickly as possible because big things were happening.

Andrews proved to be an invaluable connection and friend. He not only helped brief the younger, rawer Nixon on strategy, he helped legitimize him with other reporters. Nixon would often come to Andrews's room at night and discuss strategy with the journalists. His press relations as the proceedings wore on were, contrary to later myth, quite good. He was a good source, he was considered the soundest and most cautious member of the committee. If there had been an instinct on the part of some liberal editorial writers to side with Hiss at the beginning (Hiss, after all, was clearly elegant and distinguished, and Chambers was sloppy and inelegant), then, as the evidence mounted, first reporters and then editorial writers changed. It was Hiss who finally suffered from bad press relations. Nor was Hiss very much of a symbol to working reporters. Most of them thought he was guilty of perjury.


Nixon's relationship with the Los Angeles *Times* continued to be very profitable and the Hiss case had not hurt him with his sponsors back home. He got wonderful coverage, his every attack on the Reds printed, applauded, his deeds written large and heroically. The easiest of political deeds in the late forties, a HUAC speech, was transformed into a gutsy, courageous stand. Not only were his assaults upon his enemies amplified, but their rebuttals silenced. Typically, the slush-fund incident of 1952, the biggest story in the nation at the time, did not make the Los Angeles *Times* for three days, and when it finally did it was written, on Kyle Palmer's instructions, as a *rebuttal,* NIXON AN- SWERS CRITICS. The paper gave Nixon enormous leverage and clout at home, but it was not by any means the healthiest of relationships; it spared Nixon from the normal give-and-take of politics and journalism, it bred in this most fragile of egos a sense that he could attack others without being attacked in return; it allowed him to rise to higher and higher levels of politics without ever testing his ability to take the normal strain and criticism of politics. It made him think that no one would dare attack him—for few in California did —and it made him believe that his lesser moments, if known to journalists, would not be printed, and that finally, if journalists did write normal, balanced, tough-minded analytical stories, they were virtually personal attacks. Few other major politicians came out of a metropolitan area so pampered.

It all created in Nixon a sense that he could get away with things, that the press was crooked and could be bought off. That there were, in fact, special rules. It meant that other politicians in his own area and in his own party lived in fear of him. (In California, Earl Warren, Goodwin Knight, and Bill Knowland, all three Republicans, despised Nixon and deeply distrusted him and believed he was less honest than other politicians, but they were very cautious about it, he was the Chandlers' boy, if they crossed him in any incident a Nixonized version might appear in the *Times* to their detriment.) In 1954, when Goody Knight was governor, Nixon made a deal with Knight that gave Knight the right to name the chairman and the vice-chairman of the California delegation, and Nixon the right to name the treasurer. Knight thereupon went sailing on a honeymoon and Nixon immediately broke the agreement and moved to name the top men. It was a real power struggle; control of the California delegation in 1960 was potentially at stake. Knight, alerted by a ship-to-shore radio of Nixon's move, returned, rallied his troops, and held his turf. It was, by most newspaper standards, a wonderful story, the two top figures in California politics, both potential presidential candidates, struggling over the state's delegation, one of them clearly having broken his word, but no word of it ever appeared in the state's most powerful paper. It was not, by the standards of the Los Angeles *Times,* a wonderful story—it showed Nixon breaking his word to a fellow Republican.

But that was the way the Los Angeles *Times* did it. In late 1949 Kyle Palmer called Richard Nixon in Washington and asked, "Dick, have you thought of running for the Senate?" Nixon answered that he had not thought of it at all, which was not exactly true. In truth, he had for several years thought of little else. "Well," said Kyle, "I wish you'd give some thought to it because we'll all support you if you do." Later Palmer phoned his friend and money raiser Asa Call. "My friend," he said, "the telephone is an astonishing instrument. It is absolutely amazing what you can do with just one call." Thus was it done. A Senate seat from one of the two most powerful states in the Union arranged for a two-term congressman. The oligarchy was all lined up, a few more phone calls were made, the money was arranged. (It was all very simple. After the election there was a deficit of $5,000. Call hated this, he hated untidiness, so he went home and mentioned it to his wife, and Mrs. Call said she would like to make up the difference for Mr. Nixon and so she wrote a check for $5,000, it would be her pleasure.) There would be plenty of money, the oil companies were not displeased, tidelands after all was the central issue of the time. There would be access to the media, Norman and Kyle would fix that. So the seat was cleared. There was a misguided Republican named Raymond Darby who wanted to run for the Senate himself, but Kyle made it plain that this was not his year; Darby, somewhat innocent, was more insistent than most, so Kyle struck up a deal: What about running for lieutenant governor? *Raymond Darby would make a terrific lieutenant governor.* Lieutenant governors often became governors. We can promise you, Kyle said, the support of the Los Angeles *Times. The support of the* Times. Ray Darby knew what that meant and he stepped aside and technically, yes, the *Times* did support him, but Kyle was interested in Goody Knight for lieutenant governor that year, Goody was still quite conservative in those days, and Kyle wanted a check on Earl Warren (later he would use Pat Brown as a check on Goody as Knight became too close to labor). So he pulled the rug out from under Darby, and while the *Times*'s official support went to Darby, its real support—full coverage—and the money of its friends went to Knight; Darby predictably perished in the primary.

So it was set up for Nixon to run against Helen Gahagan Douglas. Here again the *Times* was instrumental. The issues of the campaign were totally redefined. Instead of tidelands and the rights to offshore oil, the central issue of the campaign and the principal one upon which Mrs. Douglas was running, it became Communism. It was all red-baiting. Pink lady. If anything, the editorial voice of the *Times* was even harsher than that of Nixon. Mrs. Douglas's voice was never heard. She was never covered; she was only attacked, that was all that was permitted. Any conservative Democrat who backed Nixon made page one. If a Marine fighting in Korea sent back a five-dollar campaign contribution to Nixon—to keep America the way it had been when he left—it was fully reported. Any women's volunteer group was given great news space ("This is the group that did such a fine job in the primary and they want to repeat it and keep Helen Gahagan Douglas out of the Senate next November 7"). There was no way, other than buying ads, that Mrs. Douglas could even get her schedules into print. It was a wonderful free ride for Nixon; he could speak to civic clubs and by raising his eyebrows even imply that there was something sexual going on between Mrs. Douglas and Harry Truman (there was not, of course), and it was never reported. There was no attempt by any newspaper to assign a reporter to a candidate and have the reporter record the charges of that candidate; thus the candidates were unusually free to say what they wanted without any real accountability.

That Helen Gahagan Douglas was in trouble even in a clean campaign was beyond doubt. The Cold War was at its height, Stalinism seemed a dark and immediately threatening specter. The country, disillusioned, was turning inward from the liberalism of the thirties and forties. Mrs. Douglas seemed the embodiment of a period that people were now turning away from, liberalism on domestic issues, trust of the Soviet Union. When the Korean War began in June, her position was made even more vulnerable; when, in October, the Chinese Communists entered the war, her candidacy became hopeless. Up to then she had been doing quite respectably in the polls. With the entrance of the Chinese, her position collapsed, the nation became even more nervous and conservative.


If the opening up of a Senate seat, the removal of serious opposition, and the savaging of an opponent were a help to Nixon in 1950, it was little compared to what the *Times* and Kyle Palmer did for him in 1958. That was the year that California's political muscle on the national scene seemed at an apex. Earl Warren was no longer governor, he was now Chief Justice of the Supreme Court, but Goody Knight was governor and highly popular, a very good vote getter, attractive to Democrats, a genuine possibility for the national ticket. Bill Knowland was Senate Minority Leader, and Richard Nixon was Vice-President, the leading possibility for the presidency. But Nixon's future was not a sure thing, particularly given Eisenhower's only partially concealed personal doubts about him. One possible problem for Nixon was control of his own delegation; Kyle Palmer would probably try to help him, but Goody Knight and an assortment of other California politicians were potentially antagonistic. At best Nixon might take a divided home-state delegation to the 1960 convention.

All of that changed in late 1957 when Bill Knowland suddenly announced that he was coming back to California to run for governor. There were various reasons for Knowland's decision: his wife, unhappy with his style of life in Washington, wanted him home, and Knowland, who had been appointed to his Senate seat, was under the misapprehension that he was an enormously popular figure. Sacramento was just a steppingstone: Bill Knowland, stolid, dull, slow, had, God Save the Mark, presidential ambitions. When the news of Knowland's announcement reached Los Angeles it shocked everyone, in particular Kyle Palmer, who was accustomed to making these decisions himself and then instructing the Bill Knowlands of the world where their duty lay. Gladwin Hill of *The New York Times,* who had his office in the *Times* building, wandered into Palmer's office to find him absolutely white, stunned, muttering, *How could he do it, how could he do it to me?* It was, thought Hill, probably the first time that Kyle Palmer had ever been caught by surprise by a Republican politician. Though he had written of Knowland glowingly, indeed unctuously, in the past, his granitelike integrity, his great political acumen, Kyle Palmer in fact thought Bill Knowland stupid and pigheaded and a considerable political liability. Now suddenly Bill Knowland was coming home, hoping perhaps for the Republican presidential nomination. The fact that the sitting governor, Goody Knight, was a Republican and a *Times* protégé made things more difficult, even though Knight had been flirting with organized labor and was pledged to fight a particular *Times* favorite, a right-to-work bill. Knowland, by contrast, had decided to make right-to-work the keystone of his campaign. Looming just as large was the control of the California delegation for 1960; here were two potential titans about to struggle over the delegation, something that properly belonged to the ultimate *Times* protégé, Richard Nixon.

If the *Times* moved quickly against Knowland it could either force him out of the race or strengthen Knight immeasurably (although there was a danger there, it might in the act strengthen Knight against Nixon by making him look like a giant killer). So, quietly, a Nixon-Palmer strategy was worked out: they decided to force Goody Knight out of the race and make him run for the Senate, and allow Knowland to make the governor's race. The advantages for Nixon were self-evident: even if both won, Knight was a far more attractive, far more broadly based politician than Knowland, thus a far more serious threat to split the delegation in 1960. On the other hand, Knight, if he won, would be a very junior senator and no longer a force in California politics, while Knowland as governor would be so awkward and hamhanded he would no doubt alienate diverse elements in the state and become a very vulnerable figure. Further, they might just lose and cancel each other out, leaving California bereft of Republican leadership and leaving Richard Nixon a clear shot at the Republican nomination in 1960.

So the pressure began immediately on Goody Knight to switch. Phone calls from Kyle Palmer. Then regular references in Kyle's column to Knowland's integrity, and inferences that Knight was in cahoots with labor, and thus tarnished. An October 1957 Kyle Palmer story saying that Knowland was beating Knight handily in the polls. The polls were unnamed and never seen. Clint Mosher, a California journalist, who was a friend of both Nixon and Knight, called up Knight to warn him that there was a deal between Nixon and Knowland. "They've got you, Goody," he told the governor. "Nixon just told me he would go into every county in the state for Knowland against you." The big Southern California money to which Knight had had easy access in the past was cut off. Oh, perhaps a few hundred thousand dollars could be raised. But not the million and a half they needed for a run at the governorship. There was, Howard Ahmandson, a millionaire insurance man and Knight's chief fund raiser, said, all the money they wanted if Goody chose to run for the Senate.

The irony was not lost on Goody Knight. Even so, he did not quit. He was an ebullient, energetic man, much smarter than most people thought— he had decided early on that it did not hurt politically to hold back on some of his intelligence and to look a bit of the bumbler. He loved being governor, he was an extremely popular governor, and he did not want to run for the Senate. He did not want to lose a Senate seat, and for that matter he did not particularly want to win one either. So Knight hung on as the pressure for him to switch mounted, and finally he went down to Arizona for a few days to make up his mind. He took with him his wife, Virginia, and Clem Whittaker and Leone Baxter, who were the top Republican public relations team in California and who were encouraging him to make the race for governor. And for five days it was like a scene from a slightly overdramatic play. Goody getting up in the morning, enthused, knowing he could win—he *could* win, that was at the heart of it, if he could only get by the *Times*-dominated Republican primary. He would do it, he would run, and, encouraged by Baxter and Whittaker, he began to do a little jig, *I will run, I will run, the hell with them, I'll raise the money myself, I'll go for the governorship and I'll raise the money from ordinary people.* It was Goody upbeat, Goody ready to take on the powers. And then every day, late in the afternoon, Kyle Palmer would call and he would threaten, there would be no money, no support, and besides, there was this scandal in the Knight administration. A bad appointment Knight had made because of his wife, Kyle hated to print it, but he had all the facts. Goody knew which scandal he was talking about, Kyle didn't want to print it, but he was a newspaperman and newspapermen printed stories. The paper was pushing for it, he did not think he could hold out much longer. Only old-time friendship had allowed him to hold out this long. Goody listened, he did not talk very much, all the talking was being done at the other end. When the call was over the governor of California was beaten; he would lie down on the couch in the fetal position, a man broken. Then slowly the others would bring him back, they would try to breathe oxygen back into him, telling him he was a popular governor, he could do it, and slowly, by dinner, he would be coming back, confident again, and by the next morning he would be ready to run, hat in the ring, surging with confidence, and then would come Kyle's call again and Kyle would warn him, I can't keep it out of the paper any more, it's too hot, it's going to kill you, there won't be any Senate seat left, there won't be anything left. Goody would fold again. There were other calls, all orchestrated. A call from Howard Ahmandson on how hard the money was to raise. Then one from Buff herself, that was unusual, the Chandlers usually kept a certain distance, but the stakes were big, and Buff was telling him how wonderful it was, Washington was an exciting city, Goody and Virginia would love it, reminding Goody how much the *Times* had done for him in the past (a veiled threat of what it would be like if the *Times* were on the other side). It was, she said, all arranged, it was wonderful, just wonderful, Goody's announcement would come on the White House steps with Ike's blessing and both Ike and Dick would be there.

So finally Goody Knight bowed to the pressure and announced his withdrawal from the gubernatorial race. Thus encouraged to run against Knowland instead of the more popular Knight, Pat Brown announced for the governorship and he in turn convinced Congressman Clair Engle to run for the Senate. It was a disaster for the Republican Party, the worst in this century. Knowland doggedly held on to right-to-work as his main issue, despite Kyle Palmer's warnings: Palmer thought it was all right to be reactionary but you ought to have the sense to mask it when you ran for office; you were never to give an opponent that good an issue, your job was to put him on the defensive, talk about things like Communism, hide your own vulnerabilities. The party went down to flaming defeat. Both Knowland and Knight were beaten; Pat Brown became the second Democratic governor of California in this century. In the embers Richard Nixon stood alone, the surviving Californian of national stature. There would be no challenge to him for control of the delegation. In a post-election interview, asked about the wreckage of the Republican Party, Norman Chandler said that it really wasn't so bad, that the great hope for the party for the future was Richard Nixon.


The *Times,* thanks to Norman Chandler's decision to use its limited newsprint during World War II for news instead of advertising, had become in the postwar years the leading paper of the area. Hearst had gone for maximum advertising, but it had been, like most things the Hearst organization had done in the middle of this century, short-lived profit, while Norman Chandler had expanded the news in his paper at precisely the time that there was a great new migration to California, defense workers come to work and servicemen passing through. He had made the *Times* the paper of the new immigrants. The financial success of the *Times* in the postwar years had even encouraged Norman and Buff to start their own afternoon tabloid, the *Mirror,* in 1948; it was their personal venture into journalism, *theirs,* not Harry Chandler's or General Otis's, and they cared desperately about its survival. They were at once proud of the *Mirror* and ashamed of it. (The problem was that the *Mirror* was a tabloid, and Norman and Buff had no taste for a tabloid, it offended their sensibility. The better the story, by tabloid standards, the more likely it was to offend them. Norman was an almost delicate man in terms of taste, and when Ed Murray, the editor, published racy stories, he would always ask, "Do we have to run this? Do we have to put this in?" Buff was always more blunt. If she didn't like a particular story, she would simply call Murray and say, "You're down in the gutter again.") Since the *Mirror* was new and uncertain, an arriviste paper in a circulation war at a time when afternoon papers were by and large doomed, they were willing to try all kinds of different measures to make it work, such as, on occasion, printing real news. The *Mirror* was for that reason less controlled and more open, a better newspaper with a better staff, and it was more able to see the city as it really was. The *Mirror* could not afford the luxury of turning away from the excitement of daily life the way the *Times,* fat, secure, could.

But Norman Chandler wanted to be a good publisher. He was less and less happy with what he was hearing about his own operation. It was clear to him that what he had inherited was no longer keeping up with the times. Besides, Buff was pushing him toward a different kind of journalism. She was, starting early in the fifties, becoming increasingly aware that the *Times* was regarded with absolute contempt within the profession. She and Norman could go to the newspaper conventions and they would always be treated kindly by their peers, the Sulzbergers and others, but there was no doubt that the paper was despised; on the occasion that working newsmen voted on which papers they respected and which they did not, the Los Angeles *Times* ranked at the very bottom, exceeded only by the Chicago *Tribune.* She was too proud a woman for that. It clearly bothered her more than it did Norman. The other thing she was much more aware of than Norman was the change in the community. Not only were there millions of new people in greater Los Angeles, but they were different, they were younger and better educated, they had come there not to retire, but to live, to educate their children, and this was changing the city, it was no longer so isolated and so parochial and it was going to demand a different kind of newspaper. So she pushed Norman to change the paper, to get rid of the editor, L. D. Hotchkiss, whom she thought was small-time and second-rate, to change the structure of the *Times*'s governing board, to change the entire operation. All the time grooming her son, her heir, to take over.


Buff Chandler. A woman before her time. A feminist in pioneer country. Always, above all else, a presence. Fierce, intense, driving. Easily wounded, easily moved to tears, yet resilient, always ready to work the next day. A mover, always driving and pushing. A relentless woman. "I pushed Norman Chandler every day of his life," she once said to a friend, and no one doubted her, least of all the friends of Norman Chandler. She was the woman who kept the Chandler dynasty alive, pushed Norman to reach beyond his parochial orbit and touch a larger world, drove by the most subtle pressures her son, Otis, to deeds of excellence (not by chance was he a world-class shot-putter).

She was the most important Chandler of modern times, her mark was every-where in downtown Los Angeles, the cultural world of the city would not exist without her. She had, almost single-handedly, threatening, and scratching and intimidating and intriguing, raised the money for the downtown music center and the two theaters next to it, raising $18 million with her battalion of women when the normal means of financing had failed. Pushing everyone to the breaking point, knowing everyone's weakness, Buff on the phone, virtual con-tempt in her voice: "Twenty-five thousand? . . . We're not talking about *that* small a gift." Buff driving her women, who in turn drove their husbands for money lest they be omitted from the Los Angeles social hierarchy (as dictated by the Los Angeles *Times*). The greatest fund raiser, said the composer Johnny Green, since Al Capone. The Dorothy Chandler Pavilion was an idea accom-plished, culture brought instantly to the western wasteland, a huge building standing outside the downtown *Times* office (in an area where Chandler real estate holdings were considerable, and whose value was not diminished by the coming of the center), so that Norman Chandler, modest, self-contained, rarely needing tangible assurances of who he was, could look outside his office at the *Times* and see this Taj Mahal that his wife had willed, and he had said rather poignantly, "I wonder if anyone will ever name a closet after me." So they did, they named the elegant offices on the top floor of the *Times* building the Norman Chandler Pavilion, which was both kind and proper, everyone should have a pavilion of his or her own. A few months after that ceremony Jack Benny was at a function and saw Norman and Buff walking toward him and turned to a friend and said, "Here they come, Mr. and Mrs. Pavilion."

But she was *somebody,* her imprint was on that city as that of very few men or women were on few cities. Let no one doubt it, let no one seat her improperly at a dinner party, at a place anywhere beneath what the first lady of Los Angeles should receive, or they would hear of it; let no society writer for the Los Angeles *Times* at a dinner honoring Ronald Reagan make the mistake of saying that Mrs. *Otis* Chandler had been seated next to the governor —Missy, whom Buff did not like—or Buff would become furious, the writer had gotten it wrong, it was Mrs. Norman Chandler who had been seated next to the governor (whom she despised, by the way). Queen Victoria, her friends called her, with great affection. Madame Queen, Norman Chandler's sisters called her, with very little affection. Not everyone loved her, people in that community were fiercely divided over her, nothing she had ever done had been without a price, and those who had been lacking in sufficient commitment, or who had sponsored rival projects, or who had opposed her, had felt the lash. She was a trailblazer, a woman to break the rules and set new guidelines, but let no one blaze a trail slightly more modern or unconventional than hers, or set lines somewhat more radical. If she were tearing up the guidelines of the old social life, she would nonetheless remain the arbiter of the new one, she could become very angry with a women's-page editor who moved too quickly on the issue of abortion or anything that she was not yet ready for. Perhaps no one had as much to do with the changing of Los Angeles from a provincial hidebound community to a modern, somewhat more sophisticated and infinitely more tolerant modern *city* (it had always in the past been a very large, sprawling small town), from changing the Los Angeles *Times* from a reactionary provincial paper to a modern national one, than Dorothy Chandler. Not bad for a Buffum of Long Beach.

The Buffums of Long Beach, though not as good as the Chandlers of Los Angeles, were, of course, good people, hard-working, religious, very successful; Buffums is now a very large and very successful department-store chain. Charles Buffum, father of Dorothy, had even been mayor of Long Beach. He was a good man, Christian and God-fearing, who had come out to California from Illinois in 1902. The women in the family were more sophisticated. His wife, Fern Smith, had graduated from Knox College, an excellent school in Galesburg, Illinois, and an aunt named May Smith had taken a degree in medicine at Ann Arbor, which was very unusual for a woman in that age. So the Buffums were a little more refined than some people thought and it was not surprising that all three Buffum children went to Stanford, which was where the best people in California sent their children. Dorothy, the youngest of the three, was not a serious student; she seemed to be in a rebellion against going where her older brother and sister had gone, and she spent most of her time dancing her way through Stanford. One spring night she was at a dance and there were a bunch of Dekes sitting in a large window seat, not dancing, half inside the room, half outside it. They were, she remembered, wearing old clothes, it was their special snobbishness, if you were a Deke you did not have to dress up. She looked up at them, and like many people who looked for the first time at Norman Chandler, she thought he was the handsomest man she had ever seen. He was wearing very casual clothes, and he was not dancing, and he was just sitting there taking it all in, as if it was his due, which it was. He gave no sign that he had noticed her. He was clearly a prince, but it was doubtful she was a princess. In those days she had to pass the Deke house on her way to the sorority house every day, and it was part of the rites of spring and the rites of the Dekes that these young gods would sit on the lawn and watch the girls pass in review. After a while she realized—it was something she sensed, she walked very proudly and she never actually caught him staring at her—that he was watching her closely. After all, she did have very good legs. Like many young Stanford women of that era, she walked a little better and a little slower when she walked past the Deke house, and in due course Norman Chandler did what she wanted him to do, he asked her out. Norman Chandler liked movies, and they went to a lot of movies that year, and in the middle of his senior year, Norman Chandler, restless for the real world, left college to go to work for the Los Angeles *Times*. Shortly afterward he married Dorothy Buffum.

In those days the world of the right people in Los Angeles was Pasadena, which was very conservative and very traditional, with a very set kind of status. The men ventured downtown every day and did whatever they did, which was usually what their fathers had done before them, and the women stayed home and did what they had always done, women's things, they reared children and had lunch with each other and went to teas and played each other in bridge, and they waited their rightful turn in the social pecking order. The social order was already set, and there was very little change because old families remained old and new families did not lightly crash in, as new money did not lightly crash in downtown. It was all very stratified, and pleasant, particularly if you were essentially listless. Not many fresh winds blew through Pasadena. It was for Buff—high-spirited, energized, her place in the order already preselected and unchangeable—a dreadful existence. She was not interested in women's small talk, she was interested in politics and deals; she liked talking to Harry Chandler about making and breaking governors and senators. She was not a woman to sit around and eat delicate sandwiches with the other women while the real dealing was going on in another room. Besides, there were immediate problems with Norman's sisters, who were older than he was and who had dominated him in the past, particularly Ruth, who was beautiful and very smart and the oldest and who had had great influence over Norman.

The unspoken message from the sisters was that Buff wasn't quite good enough for Norman, that she was a notch under them in status, they were the *real* Chandlers, she was an appendage who would have to adjust to their will and wait her turn. If this was not really a testing time (her in-laws later tended to think she exaggerated it), it nonetheless seemed so to Dorothy Buffum Chandler; years later, talking to friends about those days, recalling hurts suffered, the snubs rendered, she still broke into tears. She felt very much snubbed and put down by the sisters; she felt they treated Norman condescendingly, like a little boy, and treated her even worse. In part because of the wounds and snubs suffered early, Buff Chandler deliberately tried to separate her husband—physically, spiritually, and ideologically—from the more conservative world of his family, and to move him into a new, more modern, more meritocratic world. (Once, near the end of his career, Norman was asked by Jim Bassett, who was writing a house history, to name the peaks and valleys of his career; before he could even say a word Buff burst in: "Norman never had any peaks and valleys. He was totally a status quo person.") Throughout her life people argued whether she was a liberal or a conservative; the truth was that she was neither. She was instead, for a variety of reasons, a person restless with the status quo, a ventilator, a person unafraid of new ideas and new perceptions and new people. She liked change, but not too much change, change on her terms and for her benefit. In that sense, if not in the classic philosophical sense, she was a liberal. She opened windows and let in air, she did not live in the past. Thus she hated Pasadena and the teas and the timidity of women's talk and she prevailed upon Norman to move from there. In time, after Harry Chandler's death, she refused to go to the family Thanksgiving dinner, and the Chandler family became more clearly divided and the resentments against her grew.

But in the beginning she was simply a very vital, very underemployed, very unhappy young woman looking for her place. Women in those days did not work, certainly not upper-class women. Even in the marriage there were problems; it was vitally important in this family to produce heirs, but instead there were miscarriages. Finally she was able to have children, first a daughter, Camilla, in 1926 and then, more important for the dynasty, Otis in 1928. In 1932 she fell into a terrible depression. She seemed to withdraw totally from the world around her. At first she and Norman both thought this was a natural problem, that time would cure it. But the depression instead grew deeper, and became a kind of desperation. First she did not want to see anyone, then she refused to eat. Then she refused to go out. There was a diminishing amount of confidence, a diminishing pleasure in life. She believed she had failed in life and in particular had failed Norman. But Norman Chandler had a friend who had seen a psychiatrist, and one day the friend came by the house and talked with Buff, and told her that her symptoms were more serious than they realized, that this might not just be some passing unhappiness, and that psychiatry might help. He gave Buff the name of a pioneer woman psychiatrist in the area, Josephine Jackson. With Norman's approval Buff visited her. Psychiatry was rare and unusual then, and people who went to psychiatrists often were made to feel tainted, as if there were something wrong in going. It took more than a little courage, particularly coming from that class, to go ahead with treatment.

Dr. Jackson did not visit patients, nor did they visit her. They left their own homes and lived with her and about eight other patients in an old rambling house. The doctor only accepted people who interested her, those she thought might be worth saving. It was like an early commune in a sense; the patients and Dr. Jackson all ate together, and they would go and have walks with each other and then have private psychiatric sessions. The treatment lasted for several months and at the end of it Buff Chandler was greatly changed. Dr. Jackson had convinced her that she was bright, vital, and interesting, that there was nothing wrong with her except her idleness, that she had a genuine role to play and that she must become involved. There was a life different from that decreed in Pasadena, Dr. Jackson said, and she had not been wrong to be unhappy, indeed she *should* have been unhappy, it would have been terrible if she had been happy. Life, Dr. Jackson insisted, demanded involvement.

Involvement there would be. Norman Chandler was a shy and private man. He had a very small circle of close friends and even these he kept at a distance. "Everyone loved him," his wife once said of him, "and no one knew him." He was a man who did not like to reveal himself, and there was, even with the closest of friends, even with his family, a barrier there, lines that were never crossed. Years after Norman Chandler died, Buff could say to a friend who thought they had had a very good marriage, that she felt in all those years she had never really reached Norman Chandler. For a man that shy, the life of a publisher of a major metropolitan paper in a modern era was often difficult. He recoiled from public responsibilities and public duties, speeches, awards, civic functions, all the blathering. She by contrast ventured forth with great zest, she had no fear of the spotlight, only of the places it did not reach. He had, she thought, married her in part because he knew he needed someone like her to complement him, someone who could deal with the public and who knew what kind of a speech to make, who would often write the speech herself. She often thought he had married her knowing he needed someone to push him; if so, he had found the right person.

She was always driving him, pushing him to get outside the world from which he had come, to move to Hancock Park, to get together with the new businessmen who were coming to power in Los Angeles, men like Tex Thornton, who was running Litton Industries; she steered him, above all, away from the old order. Much of this went against his grain; he preferred to do things as they had always been done, he was very orderly, clothes carefully hung out every night before he went to bed, collar stays already in the collars. He was, she once told a friend, the most methodical of men, he wanted everything the same today as it was yesterday. As she pushed him he would often say: "That's enough, that's change, I don't want to change." But there was also a part of him that knew he *had* to change and that the paper had to change, that the world was changing and even more immediately the community was changing. (Though if she changed the order, it was not exactly making a revolution; if a society reporter for the tabloid *Mirror* published, after a gala ball, a huge photograph of bored chauffeurs leaning on their limousines, that society editor was quickly looking for another job.) So she constantly pushed him into areas where he normally might not have ventured. He was most at ease in the world of business; he ran the business side of the paper and he ran it well. In fact, no one in those years ran a newspaper better in the strict financial sense than Norman Chandler ran the Los Angeles *Times.* Starting with the strong non-union base that General Otis and Harry Chandler had created, he was far freer than most publishers to experiment in modern technology. Buff never interfered in the business side, but in the public side she was always in there pushing and demanding, fighting for early air-pollution studies and legislation, fighting for better conditions and pay for women, molding the women's sections of the two papers to her own causes and visions.

The importance of what she did through the women's pages should not be underestimated in the history of contemporary Los Angeles. Wounded and rejected by one social order, Buff Chandler set out to redefine the social order of the entire city. The instrument of this change was the society section of the Los Angeles *Times.* There she rewarded the people she admired, and punished and eliminated those who did not, so to speak, measure up. This was a very considerable lever of power used by a woman of great skill, drive, intelligence, and, on occasion, ruthlessness. Some of what she accomplished was bound to happen anyway; everywhere in America it was becoming harder for old families to hold their positions, but in Los Angeles Buff Chandler certainly expedited the process. In the past, the society pages reflected the traditional order, discreet mentions in the *Times* columns of Junior League and DAR functions, just enough use of names to remind both the outside world and the inside world who was on the inside. Nothing vulgar.

Now, starting in the fifties, it began to change; never too rapidly, mind you, one did not let in the barbarians too quickly, one still kept standards. Now she featured a new kind of woman, a doer, an activist who was a community leader, women who were friends of hers and who were involved in her favorite activities. Sponsored by the *Times,* Woman-of-the-Year awards went to selected Los Angeles women. These were women who had done something, community and social activists. (Not political; political activists in civil rights were not among the early winners. If women came from the world of politics in those days they better be Pat Nixon, or Rose Mary Woods, or Betty Robbins Haldeman, mother of Bob Haldeman. Mrs. Cesar Chavez need not apply.) While other members of the staff participated and suggested names, it was clearly a Buff Chandler production. Those she wanted to reward were rewarded, and those she did not like went unnamed, their star never to shine. The message was clear: this was the new Los Angeles society, these were the right people, the role models.

She made up a similar rewards system at the *Mirror.* She came in one morning and summoned all the women's-page editors to a meeting and announced that she had come up with a new idea. Again a system of honors. This one would be called Best Dressed for Your Life. The society reporters would scurry around Los Angeles and find people who had interesting jobs and lives and were dressed for these lives in a comfortable way. They would be the winners. Muriel Beadle, one of the editors, said that she thought it was a bad idea and a dreadful title, and that there was no way it would work. She had an impression, as the meeting went on, that Buff Chandler had not heard a word, Buff never raised her voice, but Best Dressed for Your Life it would be. Again, like the Woman-of-the-Year Award, it reflected the new order that Buff wanted to create.

Then finally she created her own particular favorite: the Amazing Blue Ribbon 400, this being the elite of elite organizations in Los Angeles, the shock troops of the fund-raising drive for the music center; only the select could join, the best people of the new meritocracy, the lucky few gaining the right to give $1,000 a year to the music center, thus an immediate $400,000 a year for funds for the center. Though the title sounded, as one member said, like an unwieldy trapeze act, and though there were those skeptics who thought the membership might be larger than 400, might even be 550, it was nonetheless an important group, well featured in the pages of the *Times,* and lesser souls clamored to get in. When in 1976 Betty Ford, then the wife of the President, visited Los Angeles, she lunched with the Amazing Blue Ribbon 400, and one member suggested to Buff that it might have been nice to have Ethel Bradley, the black wife of the black mayor Tom Bradley, to the lunch. Buff said it was simply out of the question. Mrs. Bradley was not, after all, a member.

But the group was a success, and it did raise money for the music center, and in the process of all this Buff Chandler was quietly forging her new social order. In the past there had been two main centers of power. One was East, or downtown, Los Angeles, the old money, the old businesses, the old establishment, largely Protestant and not just Republican but very conservative, which read and approved of the *Times* and which had always determined policy for the city and the state in the past. The other was the newer, flashier establishment of West Los Angeles, principally Beverly Hills, younger, more modern, more extravagant, more ostentatious, more liberal, more Democratic, more Jewish, and which, if it read the *Times* at all, read it primarily to disapprove of it. The twain had never met; the good ladies of Pasadena did not, by and large, shop in Beverly Hills; the Los Angeles Country Club did not admit Jews, indeed it prided itself for a very long time on the fact that it did not even admit actors. In the past West Los Angeles was a small power center, it represented Hollywood and little more, and Hollywood was self-evidently gauche and as such easily dismissed. But the wartime and postwar years had changed that. There had been a great influx of new industry to Southern California (mostly in the scientific and defense fields) and this had brought a wave of migrants different from those of the past, younger and better educated and more determined to play a part in the community's affairs. The center of this new power wave was in West Los Angeles; it was not by chance that Tex Thornton had located his Litton Industries in the very heart of Beverly Hills.

In certain ways Buff Chandler more than anyone else bridged the gap between the two worlds and connected the communities. She found out, first, in saving the Hollywood Bowl from closing in 1951, one of her first major civic accomplishments, that the good families of the old Los Angeles were either not interested in music or not easily separated from their money or, most likely, both. The new Los Angeles, perhaps because it cared more for culture, and perhaps because it was less secure and more eager for status and acceptance, or perhaps for both reasons, was the perfect source of energy and money. The Hollywood Bowl lesson was not one that she easily forgot, and in 1954 when she began her four-year-long battle to raise eighteen million dollars for the music center, it was the new money, much of it Jewish and much of it arriviste, that was crucial to her success. The new people, moreover, were her battalion commanders in the awesome job of fund raising. Inevitably that pulled her more and more to West Los Angeles, she lunched not just at Perrino's but at Le Bistro, and as her world became broader-gauged, so did Norman Chandler's. These were the people who had worked hardest and supported her most loyally during the most important struggle of her life. Besides, she was impressed with the ability and intelligence of men like Lew Wasserman, the head of MCA, and Paul Ziffren, the top lawyer of West Los Angeles. They were different from most of the people she had known, in the acuteness of their minds and their zest for life. She once asked Norman Chandler why they didn't put Lew Wasserman on the board of CalTech, a symbolic appointment in the parochial world of Los Angeles, where boards like CalTech represented that which had been and that which was about to be. Lew Wasserman was, she said, smart, intelligent, his advice was always good. She pushed for it repeatedly and so one day Norman Chandler called up Lew Wasserman and asked to have lunch, and they lunched together and in the middle of it Norman mentioned that Lew would be just right for the board of CalTech. Lew Wasserman said that was very flattering, but Norman ought to know a few things, first that Lew Wasserman did not want any nonessential trouble or tension in his life, second that, as Norman knew, he was Jewish, third that he was a liberal Democrat, and that he thought this was all too difficult a package. Norman Chandler said not to worry, there would be no fight, in fact the board had voted unanimously on his nomination that morning. That was the way things were done, and that was how the bridges of a very odd community were built. It was a parochial community becoming a modern one; the music center was in some strange way the visible tip of the iceberg.

Buff Chandler sensed the change in Los Angeles quicker than her husband because she knew what was happening in the world of the arts, and there the changes were taking place much faster than they did in the world of the California Club. She had been conservative enough in her earliest political incarnation. As befit a prize student of Harry Chandler, her politics were good straight Republican, a little more moderate as the fifties approached than those of Norman. Probably, thought her friends, she felt more at ease with the other leading moderate Republicans in California than she did with the archconservatives, among whom were numbered, of course, most of Norman's family. At the 1952 convention she had been for Eisenhower and Norman had been for Taft; Bob Taft was a genuine political extension of Norman, a man of the old values and a man with a true belief in the rights of property. Besides Taft was not, like so many California conservatives, a hater. Buff had finally told Norman during the convention, and she had meant it, that he was not to come to her bed until he changed, and she kept her promise. No Ike, no sex. Finally during the convention they had gone to a reception for Taft, as her version of events went, and Norman Chandler and Robert Taft had been isolated together and talking privately when a photographer approached them. Taft berated the photographer. Norman, who took himself seriously as a publisher, told Taft never to talk to anyone from a newspaper like that again, and quickly left the reception. On the way out he told Buff that he was switching to Ike, and thus was permitted to return to her bed.

But politics interested her less and less as the fifties passed; she was gradually moving away from politics to the arts. There was a greater role for a woman in the arts, men were less resentful of a woman as a powerful driving figure. As she became more interested in the arts she also became more and more aware of the new Los Angeles and its diversity, its power and resources and vitality. As far back as 1957, grooming her son, Otis, to become the publisher of the tabloid *Mirror,* she had talked with Frank McCulloch, then of *Time* magazine, about the future of the city. McCulloch was acknowledged as being by far the best newspaperman in Los Angeles at the time, and she was asking him very blunt questions about Otis and the *Mirror* and his future. Was he really an able newspaperman? she asked. It was typical of the Chandlers, McCulloch thought with some admiration; they were always planning very far in the future, and they were always, when it came down to important things, very tough-minded and blunt. How good was Otis? she asked. Was he ready to take over the *Mirror?* It wouldn't be a mistake, would it? When would he be ready? Perhaps, she mused, almost to herself, in about three years. She hoped, she said, that Otis would represent the new version of Southern California, a younger, fresher, more enlightened audience, less tied to the past. Perhaps he could reach these new young people in a way that the older, more staid *Times* could not. The entire region was changing very quickly and perhaps Otis could be the symbol of something new, speak to the new people and for them. It was, thought McCulloch, who had dealt at some length with the Chandlers in the past, a typical Chandler performance. Nothing was left to chance, they thought everything out. Here was Otis three years away from taking over the paper and yet they were planning everything out in detail, trying to find out if he was really good enough: a dynasty required careful planning. McCulloch was even more impressed some three and a half years later when they finally promoted Otis to publisher, not of the *Mirror,* but of the *Times.* The *Mirror* by 1958 and 1959 was sinking deeper and deeper into debt, and while it might under some conditions have been a good place for young Otis to take a trial managerial run, the sickness was clearly terminal. It was all right on a dying property like that to keep putting a certain amount of money in, the tax write-off canceled out much of the loss, but you did not taint your prime resource, your only son. It must never be said of Otis Chandler that he was the chief executive of the *Mirror* when it was dying. Above all, Otis must not be stamped as a loser. No Chandler was a loser.

Among the forces that had made the Los Angeles *Times* a very conservative paper in the forties and most of the fifties were the conservatism of Harry Chandler and the vast shadow that he cast; the innate traditional conservatism of Norman Chandler; the conservatism of the community and of Norman's peers at the California Club; and the conservatism of the Family, which was very much an extension of Harry Chandler. The Family was even more conservative than Norman because the force of modern business had propelled him, involuntarily or not, into a changing world, while they had simply sat on the sidelines. That conservatism was something that hovered constantly in the background as first Norman and Buff, and then later Otis, began to change the paper in the fifties and early sixties. But though the Family had the power to react angrily to decisions and thus intimidate Norman and Buff and their editors to some degree, they had no direct power over the newspaper. Norman and Buff were, in the real sense and in the eyes of the public, *the* Chandlers. They made the decisions, they stepped out into the spotlight as Chandlers never had before. Their names were always in the paper, Mr. and Mrs. Norman Chandler did this, went there, were seen at, which was, by the standards of the past, very un-Chandlerlike, the Chandlers had tried to keep their names out of the paper. (Told to make sure that a story about a Stanford alumnae association was in the paper and mentioned Buff by name, L. D. Hotchkiss, the tough abrasive old editor of the *Times*, whose main job in the old days was looking out for the Chandlers' interests by making sure that their names and their interests did *not* get in the paper, would simply shake his head and say, "It isn't like the old days, it just isn't like the old days.") Which was very hard on the rest of the Family. Yes, they were Chandlers too, it was their family and their paper too, but all the power was invested in two people, one born a Chandler, more passive, the other, born a Buffum, more active. The rest of the Family felt themselves each day more powerless, more passed by, less a part of decisions, less connected to this paper which, the members were sure, was less and less what their father would have wanted. Nor was any of this made easier by the fact that Buff was imperious in triumph. She deliberately, to the degree that she could, cut them off. Perhaps the men, the brothers and the brothers-in-law, could, on occasion, hunt with Norman (the Garlands worked very hard and not very successfully to serve as a bridge between the factions, in part because Norman liked hunting with his sister's husband Jack Garland), but the women were cut off. There was no role for them. They, of course, still adored Norman and whenever he showed up at family occasions the affection and warmth for him was very real; that made Buff, if anything, a very convenient foil for him. The Good Norman and the Bad Buff.

Thus as the modern era approached, as the fifties passed, as Norman grew older, Buff Chandler saw her job as limiting the influence of the Family in corporate and editorial matters, all the time preparing the way for the accession of Otis Chandler, which, of course, was precisely what the rest of the Family did not want. Norman was one thing, he may have been under her influence but he was their brother, and he was conservative, but Otis was worse —he was, they thought, young, he was liberal, and he was in many insidious ways even more under her influence. The more outsiders who replaced family members, the better for her; the more the paper and the company expanded and acquired other properties, the more it would have to issue and sell stock, and the more that happened, the more the new stockholders would be entitled to representation on the board. The more outside representation on the board, the weaker the family influence, and thus in her mind the better for Norman, and, far more important, because Norman was all right, his position was secure, the better for *Otis*. She understood the need for new managerial techniques and expansion; but for Buff Chandler good management techniques were not just good business practice, they were good politics. Norman too by the late fifties was leaning that way, he wanted to make the company more modern; he had seen how narrowly it had survived the Depression, he was aware of the fragility of its cash flow. He would often talk to friends about what might happen if a rich powerful labor union decided to come in and run an opposition morning newspaper without worrying about profit, simply to bleed the Chandler product. He was interested in changing the structure of the paper, he was hearing more and more from friends like Tex Thornton how important it was to expand, that if he did not expand, his property would die, so he too was interested in moving forward.

Thus the stage was set for an ongoing family struggle that was at once business and editorial, at once political and personal. Upon it hinged control of the paper, and whether it would expand and if so how, and most of all, who in the years to come would edit and publish it. The classic family-owned enterprise that Harry Chandler had conceived was potentially an endangered species, the property either to be devoured by taxes, given modern tax and inheritance laws, or bitten so heavily as to be perennially weak and vulnerable. The financial position of the *Times* in the early fifties was by no means secure or sound; there were more newspapers in Los Angeles in those days, more people carving up a smaller pie, the city was not as rich as now—indeed, the country was not as rich—and the *Times* was not even the number-one paper in circulation. Hearst's *Examiner* was still far ahead, though it was not so successful in advertising as the *Times,* which was the paper of the business establishment. Harry Chandler's holdings had been vast, but they had not been orderly, and in the end the newspaper had been surprisingly poorly run. Norman, while not nearly the visionary predatory force his father had been, was a far better and more orderly businessman in the traditional sense, and he had slowly brought order to the family holdings. If not the man to create an empire, Norman was the man to hold on to it.

During the forties Norman had worked very carefully to build the company up and to solidify its financial position. When a financial expert named Ted Weisman, who was also a friend, told him in the early fifties that his stock, which was on occasion sold over the counter, was desperately underpriced, Norman Chandler quite casually agreed. Almost appalled by what he took to be the nonchalance of Norman's attitude, Weisman protested that he had studied the books and knew the paper's assets, and the stock was ridiculously low. *Ridiculously low.* "You should be much higher in your value," Weisman told Chandler. "Yes, I know," Norman Chandler said. "What good is book value? What good will it do? I know what our potential is, but we have to build up earnings. We'll do it, but it will take time, and most people going into the market don't have the patience. They want the quick return. What good is potential if you don't earn money on it? We're going to improve and we're going to earn money and it's going to take time."

To another friend he could talk in great privacy about the paper, he knew it was not a good paper, he knew he did not have good people, he knew it was rooted too much in the past. He wanted, he said, to bring in new people, people whose loyalty was to excellence, not just to the family name. The paper was becoming reactionary, it lived too much in the past and it was not keeping up with the times, and if it was not careful it would die. He needed good people, but how did you find good people? How did you change a paper? he mused. Then he began to answer his own question: it was very difficult to change this particular paper because of the complexity of the Family, there was only one person who could change it, who if he did not actually change the Family could at least bring the Family with him, and that was Norman Chandler. The Family would accept him, in fact had to accept him, so the Family would accept the changes he made, however reluctantly.

It was typical of the Chandlers that they expanded and strengthened their operation first on the business side; the editorial expansion that came later was in reality an inevitable by-product of the business success, the rationale being: we have all this power and money and leverage, why not use it for something? The first of the outsiders Norman hired was Al Casey, who came from Railway Express and later went on to American Airlines. He was bright and brash and funny and very tough. (Once, in a struggle with the *Times* board over whether or not the paper should pay a dividend, Tex Thornton had spoken up against Casey, who wanted to pay a dividend; Casey wanted the dividends because many of the Chandlers had little else in the way of income and he had counted the votes before the meeting and he was sure he had it locked up. But Thornton had argued so persuasively that the dividends were turned down, which infuriated Al Casey. He thereupon went out and acquired a company for the *Times* that was in competition with Thornton's Litton, thereby under the rules of the company forcing Thornton to resign from the board. It was a trick that Thornton did not find amusing, and he did not speak to Casey for several years.) When Casey arrived in 1963 it was the era of acquisitions and mergers. There was no way a company could stand still in corporate America any longer; either it expanded and broadened its base or it was swallowed up. Swallow or be swallowed. (Norman Chandler, in fact, liked the acquisition game. Once he wandered into an editorial meeting, looked at his son, and asked, "Thought about buying any newspapers lately?" Otis said no. "Well," said Norman, "I see where there's one for sale in Florida." He paused. "Costs only about twelve million. You ought to check out your tax situation. . . .")

No longer would the *Times* be a small company which published two newspapers. It would become a conglomerate, and it was the real leader in the American newspaper profession at this, and some fifteen years later, papers like *The New York Times* and the Washington *Post* were just catching on to what Norman Chandler and his bright young men had done. No company was better at the acquisition game than the Times Mirror. Norman was committed to corporate expansion because he wanted to strengthen his company; Buff was committed for that reason and also because she wanted to diminish the role of the Family. Thus she was delighted with the coming of outsiders to the board, and she also helped push for the use of an outside team of management consultants. In the late fifties McKinsey and Company began studying which way the *Times* should go in the future; much to Buff's delight, the firm always recommended modern procedures and corporate expansion.

The struggles over expansion were central to the future of the company, and within the Chandler family they were in almost equal parts fights of blood and ideology. On one side was the Norman Chandler branch, the new outside directors, men like Harry Volk, Frank King, Tex Thornton, and Al Casey; and on the other side was the rest of the Family, led by Norman's oldest sister, Ruth, Lady Crocker. Casey and Thornton in particular carried the burden for expansion, for the need to issue more stock in order to acquire new properties. The arguments in favor of issuing the stock, that this was the new sound managerial technique, that *only* by issuing the stock and expanding could the Family retain control, all these arguments simply fell on deaf ears. Thornton and Casey argued that the company could not stand still, that it would be taxed to death, that they were moving from a generation of seven heirs of Harry Chandler to a generation of fifty heirs, that the future of their own children was threatened, that the next generation might thus lose control—and the benefits. All these were alien arguments. The answer from the others was always the same: *Our father did not want us to sell, he wanted us to keep control. This is our company.* Behind it all, of course, was the tension between Buff and the rest of the Family, particularly Lady Crocker, who hated Buff and who was in many ways just like her, strong, smart, willful, and unbending, both of them struggling for power within the Family. Buff had far more access to Norman and access to power, so Buff over the years gained power and Ruth lost it. Al Casey would detail a proposal and give the reasons for going ahead with it, and Ruth would listen and say, "You're a nice young man, Mister Casey, but you're just an agent for Mrs. Chandler." "You know, sometimes," he would answer, "what she wants is consistent with the best interests of the paper." "Don't tell me, Mister Casey," Lady Crocker would say, "don't tell me."

She was, he thought, very smart and very tough; he liked her. He would make a presentation, a very good one, and when he was through she would look up and say, "You know what's wrong with your proposition, Mister Casey?" "No," he would say. "You're scared, Mister Casey, you're scared." "No, I am not," he would answer.

"Yes, you are. I can tell."

It was rough. Business deals loaded with all the tensions of blood. Norman Chandler was not very much help in these sessions, in part because he did not like arguments and fights, but even more because, on questions like this, he did not have very much leverage with the Family, he was seen as an agent of Buff. What he said, they believed, was what she said. The outside board members were better, they were regarded as being partially tainted but essentially purer of motive. At the meetings, various members of the Family would often ask questions, but Lady Crocker rarely did, she made up her mind, she did not like any of it, she was quite convinced that these men too were agents of Buff. Once at the end of a long and bitter session she turned to one of the directors and said, "You know, I'm not as bad as you've been told." It was an illuminating moment, there was no question in her mind about who, in this struggle, the adversaries were.

There was an underlying quality of brinksmanship to the struggle. For there was a codicil to the Harry Chandler will that said that if any member of the Family committed an imprudent negative act, he or she lost *all* inheritance under the trust. All inheritance. That was no small lever for the Norman Chandler branch, particularly in a family where the trust was central to most of the incomes. Norman Chandler and his professional aides, armed as they were with management studies, could conceivably go to court and claim that a particular member of the Family had blocked the expansion despite expert recommendations, and that this was imprudent, and cut off that member from all financial privileges. It was a very good weapon, and it hung there in the background, Norman and all his professional advisers and *expertise* versus the rest of the Family and their emotions. The Family did not want a court case, but no agreement could be reached and at one point of impasse it was suggested, just suggested, mind you, that in exchange for the Family's going along with the stock issue, Buff would leave the board and leave her office at the *Times*. It was, of course, just an idea, though one that was highly salable to the rest of the Family. One of Norman's management consultants mentioned the possibility of the deal to Norman, who, of course, mentioned it to Buff, and she remembered all the wounds, all the hurts; it was clear in her own mind who had caused her breakdown, and she would not move aside. No modernization was worth that much. So they continued to negotiate, and to pressure and to threaten the lawsuit, and finally Lady Crocker came around. "I don't want to be a dog in the manger," she said, and the Family was persuaded to issue stock and go public. It was the first family-owned paper to go public. In 1964, at the time of a second major stock issue, the Times Mirror Company was listed on the big board of the New York Stock Exchange.

Thus the Los Angeles *Times*, with its new professional leadership, moved more quickly and readily into the boom that awaited certain select newspapers than any other major paper in the country. Norman Chandler was smart and he created a sound economic base for his property, and unlike other family owners, he went outside the family for management. Most newspapers of that period were dominated by a family mentality, overloaded at the top level with family members—competent or not—and beneath them layers of tired family retainers waiting for the gold watch. The retainers were usually dreadfully underpaid and not very professional because the family executives, taking both dividends and salaries, believed they were actually living on their salaries and had little idea of what they were paying their executives. Not at the *Times*. One of the things that the outside management consultants had demanded and that Norman had accepted was the idea of paying top executives very well, with strong pension plans; otherwise the *Times* would not be able to compete with other booming companies.

Suddenly in the late fifties everything was coming the way of morning newspapers, and particularly those in certain areas; no newspaper was in more of a boom area than the Los Angeles *Times*. More and more people were arriving in Southern California to hold more and more jobs, there were more and more businesses, which meant more and more homes, more and more ancillary businesses, more and more subscribers, more and more advertisers. Every new industry meant new jobs, which meant new subdivisions, which meant new supermarkets, which meant more pages in advertising. It was a period of phenomenal growth and one of the main beneficiaries was the *Times;* television was cutting into the news function of afternoon papers, but television did not satisfy all reader curiosity nor was it a particularly good instrument for certain kinds of advertising. The Hearst paper, the *Examiner,* was still there, but its high circulation was based on headlines, which made it particularly vulnerable to television news. Besides, no newspaper corporation in the country was as poorly run in the postwar era as the Hearst empire, the narrowness and shallowness of the political view exceeded only by the incompetence of the corporate side. (Marion Davies, the great and good friend of old W. R. Hearst, had sensed the weakness of the progeny and had thought his son George Hearst, who was to run the *Examiner,* particularly reckless. She had once, when Norman and Buff were young, invited them to dinner so that George could be exposed to an attractive hard-working couple not much older than himself, and Buff and Norman did indeed arrive for dinner, but their industriousness proved not to be contagious and George Hearst proceeded to run the *Examiner* into the ground.) The *Times* began to dominate the morning market and the morning market was all that mattered any more. Those who were rich in the morning market became richer. Not only were afternoon papers competing with television, they were also competing with changing systems of living. A city like Los Angeles sprawled in every direction and the delivery system for an afternoon paper was impossible. A circulation manager might face thirty miles or more of congested highway every afternoon between his press and many of his customers. It was a boom time for morning papers, and none was in better shape than the Los Angeles *Times.* This was crucial, for the major changes in editorial complexion and dimension that were soon to take place were in a large part the direct result of such extraordinary financial success.

The inflow of money in that period of the late fifties and early sixties was very liberating, first to Norman Chandler, and even more so to Otis Chandler; it allowed them to change the editorial product quite dramatically, with a good deal of the Family's normal ideological nervousness assuaged by mounting financial rewards. Norman Chandler had wanted to begin changing the paper by the middle of the fifties, but he did not really know how to go about doing it. His editor during the forties and fifties was L. D. Hotchkiss, a bellicose angry man, tyrannical with his staff, limited in his vision, and, above all, careful not to tamper with the Chandler interests. If Hotch did not know exactly what should go into a Chandler newspaper, he had a very good idea of what should *not* go into a Chandler paper. He and Kyle Palmer worked closely together; Kyle wrote the stories that promoted the Chandler political interests and savaged its enemies, and Hotch made sure that nothing appeared that damaged those interests. He was a hard man in the tradition much associated with the old Chicago city rooms, orders barked and never questioned; he tolerated no dissent, no discussion, no questioning or diluting of his authority. He was a very short man and was said to dislike members of his staff who were taller than he was. Most of his staff was, of course, taller than he. L. D. Hotchkiss was the editor, there was no managing editor, and let everyone on the staff know that. Once in the fifties a man named Jim Toland was editing the home-news Sunday magazine for the *Times* and *Time* magazine was doing a survey of magazines like this for its press section. The *Time* people interviewed Toland, and he was rather pleased about this, he was making it in the big time, and he mentioned it to his superior, Nick Williams.

"Did you," Nick Williams immediately asked, "refer to yourself as editor of the magazine?"

"Yes," said the innocent Toland.

"When is the piece supposed to run?" Williams asked. Toland told him.

"There's still time," Williams said, and he raced to the phone, called a friend at *Time,* and asked *Time* to drop Toland's title.

"Look," he later explained to Toland, "there's only one editor here and his name is L. D. Hotchkiss, and you had better know that."

Toland only semi-believed Williams and a few months later he asked Hotchkiss if he could run in his magazine a small index listing himself as editor.

"Of course not," Hotchkiss said.


Of all the staff members at the Los Angeles *Times* no one had a better sense of the whimsical explosiveness and anger of L. D. Hotchkiss than Nick Williams, who was the senior deskman for many years and who was in charge of putting the paper together every day and who was in effect the managing editor of the paper, lacking only the pay and the title. He had felt with great regularity the edge of Hotch's tongue and anger, and he had for many years survived in his job, at a price. He had developed a set of ulcers that were said to be coveted by medical science for their sheer grandeur. It was said of Nick Williams that he never dared put too much distance between himself and the *Times*'s men's room because of the tension in his stomach. It was not an easy life for Williams, when he went home at night he quickly took his first two drinks; they were not, as with most men, small comforts that eased the entrance into a gentler world, they were, in fact, virtually a fix, a form of need. It was a job with precious few benefits, he was not paid well, and for many of those years he secretly wrote pulp fiction under another name in order to educate his family. Those few who knew him well, and knew that he was a man of a very special sensibility, a remarkably cultured and erudite man, wondered why Nick Williams put up with it. It was a question that often ran through his own mind. But he hung on, thinking he would like to become editor and he would like, if it were possible, to change the *Times.* He waited some twenty years. Then one day in 1958 L. D. Hotchkiss came up to him in the city room, frowning a little more than usual. "Norman wants to make you managing editor," he said.

"What do I do?" asked Williams, for managing editor or no, he was wary of crossing L. D. Hotchkiss.

"You go upstairs and thank him," said L. D. Hotchkiss.

Which Nick Williams did.

He went upstairs and he received his instructions from Norman Chandler, and they were quite surprising. Nick, Norman said, was to take hold of the paper. "I want you to push," he said, meaning that he was to take the paper away from Hotch, which would not be easy. "Then I want some investigative reporting, I want to find out what's going on. I want reporters to go out there and dig." That was unusual too, and there was for a moment a quick question in his mind as to whether Norman Chandler really understood the consequences of that order. "And," continued Norman Chandler, "above all I want the paper to be fair." That last was particularly significant to Nick Williams because it confirmed, as he had suspected, that Norman Chandler thought the paper had not been fair in the past, that it was the wrong kind of newspaper. It was a very stark admission, shattering by Chandler standards. Nick Williams was getting, in effect, a charge to change the paper, and Norman Chandler was choosing his man very carefully and, it turned out, wisely.

He had also chosen a man he could work with easily, and he had seen things in Nick Williams that few others at the time had spotted. For Nick Williams was a very deceptive man. He did not look or seem like a man destined to be the great editor of a powerful expanding national newspaper. He looked like someone who ought to be sitting on the neighborhood bar stool, or indeed might just have fallen off it, rumpled, unprepossessing. The voice high and squeaky and almost country. Yet he was at once the most shrewd and intelligent of editors, a man deeply erudite and broad-gauged in his interests. No one knew more about the paper, about every little department, than Nick Williams, and no one knew more of the sociology, of the vast polyglot of little communities that constituted greater Los Angeles. He was always, in that most impossible of all constituencies, out studying his readers, he could often be found traveling around on Sundays in different communities, scouting, getting a feel, having breakfast in some roadside shop, trying to understand his readers and why they read his paper. Tough, strong, wise, immensely appreciative of talent, he was perhaps the ablest major American newspaper editor of his generation. Certainly no other editor took a paper from one century to another so quickly, so cleanly, and with such excellence, and yet no one knew his name. Part of it was the location of his paper (the judgments on American culture are made in the East and published in the East), but most of it was the nature of the man. He was not an image editor, he did not seek recognition. He would go, year after year, to the various conventions of publishers and editors, little known, virtually unrecognized, and hide in the background, while men who could not carry his typewriter but were brilliant at the politics of editors' associations, good at conventions, good at playing the game, gave their bold speeches on freedom of the press, speeches that had little to do with the timid papers they usually produced back home. Nick Williams was, in fact, terrible at those meetings, he would feel very ill at ease and indeed one year he had drunk perhaps a little too much and there was a very stern lecture from Norman Chandler: "Character! Character! Nick, I would rather have character than talent!" (The next day Norman called and apologized. "I was a little rough, wasn't I? Let's go get a drink.") He had studied Greek at the University of the South at Sewanee, and he knew and loved the classics, and he knew the paper so well that he brought to every confrontation or potential confrontation not just the authority of his title but the advantage of absolutely superior and very detailed knowledge. He simply knew much more about everything on the *Times* than anyone else. He was not threatened by the fact that people underneath him might be more talented than he, and in that sense he was virtually unique as an editor. He did not think he wrote well, but in truth he was a very good writer, though most of his writing was done either in internal office memos or in letters to readers. He was old-fashioned enough to answer personally all letters that came to the *Times,* and many of his letters were gems. He could, on the cancellation of a once beloved but now boring comic strip, personally write three hundred letters explaining his decision. He could also be biting in letters, such as the one he wrote to Walter Annenberg when that former publisher turned diplomat wrote from London complaining about a story by the *Times*'s London man, Bob Toth. "Dear Walter," wrote Williams. "It seems to me that you are looking at Toth as if he were working for the Philadelphia *Inquirer,* and he was looking at you as if you were a servant of the United States of America."

He was, and the job required this above all else, a man of great political skill. He was at once respectful of the past and of tradition and yet equally respectful of the talent and creativity of those restless with the past. He knew the Family and the community and the levels of tension, he knew just how much tension and pull Norman Chandler could absorb at any given time. He knew exactly the limits of change, how much elastic was in the rubber band. He would move forward, but he would never do so precipitously, and if he were doing something audacious, he would in no way *seem* audacious or belligerent; there was something mild and unassuming about him that softened the blows to the Family as the paper changed. Yet he was very good at holding the line for his people, protecting them from assault from without, be it from politicians or members of the Family or, even worse, Buff Chandler, who was often displeased by Martin Bernheimer, the music critic, who was not sufficiently admiring of *her* protégé, Zubin Mehta. (Nor had Bernheimer helped himself with Mrs. Chandler when she, a lover of astrology as well as music, had rushed up to him and said, "Isn't it wonderful, Martin, Zubin is a Taurus." "Yes," he had answered, "he conducts like one.")

So it was that Nick Williams became managing editor first, and then soon after, in 1958, editor, some twenty-seven years after he had first joined the paper. He began to change the paper slowly; the charge from Norman was somewhat less pronounced in practice than in theory. It was clear that Norman Chandler was quite bothered by the way that Carlton Williams, the *Times*'s kingmaker at city hall, was emulating Kyle Palmer and throwing what was ostensibly Norman's weight around. His first job, Nick Williams thought, was to separate the paper from the Republican Party, to gain some degree of independence in coverage of politics (old-time *Times* readers were stunned during the 1960 national campaign when the *Times* covered not just Richard Nixon but Kennedy as well; the idea of printing what a Democrat was saying about a Republican was unheard of). But the resources for a great paper were not yet in place; Norman Chandler wanted to change the paper but he had not approved any real change in the editorial budget. It was as tight as ever. The paper was better in that it was no longer bad, but it was not better in that it was good. One of Williams's first moves, encouraged by Norman Chandler, was to hire Frank McCulloch away from *Time* magazine; McCulloch was then the *Time* bureau chief in the West, assertive, driving, a man who exuded a kind of civilized macho and impressed foot reporters and high executives alike. He had impressed the Chandlers while doing a cover story on them in 1957, they had gradually become friends with him and they periodically checked with him for journalistic estimates. In 1960 he was hired as managing editor and, very soon after, the *Times* began to change. McCulloch was a creative, hard-headed newsman, and he began to push the paper almost immediately. He had none of the subtlety of Nick Williams, he believed in investigative reporting and he was a fearless hunter of sacred cows. He moved aggressively on the paper from the first day he was there, perhaps too aggressively for Nick Williams.

It was, of course, not only Frank McCulloch who had arrived. For one other person had come to the *Times* in executive capacity in April 1960 and that was Otis Chandler, bearing both of the family names, the scion of the dynasty. The dynasty had worked. It had delivered on schedule, indeed ahead of schedule, a new publisher, tall, handsome, muscular (he had his own gym in his office and would on occasion lift weights there). He was serious, methodical, somewhat humorless, and remarkably hard-working. He was the son clearly of both Norman and Buff, but he was in some way even more Buff's son. The parents had set an exhausting schedule for him, no Chandler would be spoiled. Norman had insisted that his son work hard (during the war when Otis was young the Chandlers had taken in a young boy from Hawaii, a then-endangered place; Otis had come to hate the other boy, because he had been spared the rough physical work schedule that a Chandler was given daily). Otis as a boy had to bike eight miles to school every day from the ranch in the Sierra Madre.

But the sense of Buff, of her intense will, was deeply ingrained in Otis Chandler. Her role in the dynasty had been basic, to push Norman, and to provide a male heir. The latter had not been easy. It was as if she had willed herself to have a male child, and willed him, when born, to be special. There was one moment when he was eight that was particularly revealing. Otis had been taking riding lessons, and as Buff watched one day young Otis was thrown from a horse. His body had lain there terribly still after the fall, and she had known instantly that he was very seriously injured, and she had gathered him up and rushed him to a hospital, one hand on the wheel, one on her son's hand, feeling the pulse give out, the hand grow cold. At the hospital Otis was pronounced dead. "My son is not dead!" she had cried, and gathered him up and rushed, wildly now, to another hospital, Huntington Hospital in Pasadena, shouting in the car all the way that Otis is alive, Otis is alive! and there as she was arriving she saw Dr. Leon Campbell, a friend, and he had reacted instantaneously, giving Otis a shot of adrenaline in the heart, and the boy had begun immediately to have life signs, nor had his pulsebeat stopped long enough to damage the other organs. In her own mind, if not in the eyes of medical science, she had very simply willed him to live. Nothing less. It was that kind of relationship. She and Norman had never dictated any set rules to Otis Chandler on what he was to accomplish, but all that energy, all that high tension and will had created its own commitment, the obligation for the son always there, it was never put into words what he owed, it never had to be, he owed everything.

As he advanced in his career, as he went up the Chandler ladder to the Chandler title, she had always backed him vigorously. Anyone who knew her heard constantly of Otis: had they seen what Otis was doing lately? had they read Otis's editorial? Otis, she said, had a feel for the paper, he could write, just like his great-grandfather. Buff Chandler, her friends decided, good Protestant credentials notwithstanding, was a Jewish mother of the worst sort, a member of that category of women whose own lives were only partially fulfilled and would be fulfilled not so much through their husbands as through their sons. She was always grooming Otis for more, for the top job at the *Times;* at the heart of her drive and her intense investment in her son, friends thought, was an essential belief, deeply felt but never expressed, that *she,* by training and ability and qualifications, rather than Norman, should have been publisher of the paper; thus Otis, more an extension of her than Norman, was more qualified to run the paper than his father. By 1959 she was saying the unthinkable, telling Norman that it was time for him to think about stepping aside for Otis at the *Times.* Lightly at first, you could only push Norman so far at a given time. Norman, she decided and said, was no longer that interested in the paper, his interest had shifted more to the corporate side, the acquisitions, he was more at home there, he liked the business side, he could read a balance sheet better and faster than anyone else around. No one could make a better assessment of a potential acquisition than Norman Chandler. He was carrying the two jobs, publisher and head of the Times Mirror Company, and she thought it too much (she also, friends thought, wanted to install Otis while Norman was at the peak of his health and power; if Norman became sick Otis became that much more vulnerable). Why not make Otis publisher? she asked.

Norman Chandler did not really answer her at first, it was not a suggestion he really wanted to hear. That was only a part of her thinking; in truth she felt that the *Times* badly needed to change and change quickly, that Norman was incapable of understanding why and how it needed to change, he was too static, too locked into place and past. The paper, she thought, needed new energy and a new vision and Norman was not a visionary person. He was too cautious. His generation, she told a friend, was passing; she did not think *her* generation was passing, she did not see herself as part of Norman's generation. So she continued to push, wanting the full leverage of Norman's position if there were to be a family struggle over Otis. Some six months after she had begun to talk seriously with Norman about the switch, the management consultants came out with a confidential report which said that if the company were to continue to grow, the corporate side would be even more important and the two jobs, one of publisher, one the head of the entire company, should be separated. It was precisely the ammunition Buff wanted and, indeed, expected, and this time there was more give. It was the hardest thing Norman Chandler ever had to do; he loved being publisher of the *Times,* it was not just his job, it was his birthright, his station, indeed his heritage. This time he listened to her, thought about it a long time, decided she was right (she was always, he once told a friend, about twenty steps ahead of him in political moves). He would become chairman of the Times Mirror Company and his son, Otis Chandler, would become publisher of the paper. Buff was, as ever, willing to accept credit: "I thought it was time to pull my Norman pawn out and put my Otis pawn on the board," she told T George Harris of *Look*. (Harris filed the quote to his editors, but it was never printed; the word was that the Chandlers had asked that it not be used.)

It was conducted almost as a coup d'état. Otis himself did not know of it until it was over and done. The problem, of course, was the Family. The outside directors were for it, Norman and Buff were for it, but the Family was rebellious. If Norman was to go, the Family wanted his brother, Philip Chandler, who was general manager and in charge of production, and the Family might, just might, be able to block Otis if all the members held together. There had, however, been an earlier recommendation from the management consultants that the chief executive officer of the company be able to serve for at least fifteen years, in order to give the organization stability. Philip Chandler, already fifty-one at the time of the recommendation, would be too old. It was a perfect weapon against him. It all came down to Norman. He was torn between blood on one side and blood on the other; he cared about Philip, but he also thought that Philip was a bit of a nuisance, always complaining about the paper and what it was publishing, never really carrying his weight. But to the rest of the Family, Otis bore a special stigma, that of Buff. No one else in the Family wanted him, he was thirty-two, too young, too liberal, and too much a Buffum. The problem for the rest of the Family was that they had, in truth, no candidate. Norman Chandler had worked his way up through every level of the company, and Otis Chandler had done even more, he had spent seven years in training, from the toughest manual jobs to the craft of reporter; few publishers in America had ever assumed their title as well grounded in their own newspapers. He had worked and he had studied, and filled notebooks with his ideas of how the operation could be improved. No other Chandler had ever invested so much of himself or herself in the paper as Otis had done. No cousin of Otis's generation had paid as high a price, if indeed any price at all.

Once again it was a face-off with the Family, which only gradually, reluctantly, came around. Otis Chandler became the publisher of the Los Angeles *Times*. It was not done without scars. Norman Chandler, who could be sweet and gentle and, on occasion, very tough, expedited the retirement of his younger brother, and there were those in the Family who believed that Philip had in fact been fired. It was a bitter blow for the other Chandlers, and it added pain to the anger they already felt about Otis taking over. Since everyone adored Norman, the blame again was placed on Buff. Thus the coming of Otis, forcing as it did the exit of Phil, exacerbated tensions. The split within the Chandlers became wider than ever, made worse by the fact that to the other Chandlers Buff, her coup accomplished, now seemed more domineering, more outrageous than ever; when Otis made decisions, decisions that profoundly changed the course of the paper, they could not believe that they actually originated with Otis; they did not take him seriously, it had to be Buff using Otis. To Buff, these were people from the past, their day was done and she did not deign to hide her feelings. Nor did she have to, she had won. Otis was publisher.

Who knows Otis Chandler? The elusive man. Who reaches him? What are his passions? There is to him, despite the drive for excellence, despite the drive for quality, an odd sense of distance, as if there were a space around him, a moat that no one quite crosses. Otis: polite, intelligent, decent, industrious, hard-working, controlled, terribly controlled. His passions are curious ones, they are not passions of the gregarious, they are passions of the loner—building his body, shooting rare beasts at high altitude by himself (indeed, Otis Chandler was appalled when Lyndon Johnson had invited him to the ranch for the first time and had taken him deer hunting, which meant in Texas driving around the ranch in an air-conditioned Lincoln, wearing a silk shirt, and shooting at terrified deer from the car, while Secret Service agents ran back to collect the dead carcasses. It was not Otis Chandler's idea of a hunt and it was hard for him even in the presence of a President to conceal his distaste), fixing and tinkering with rare antique cars, riding a dirt bike on the back trails of California, surfing, racing expensive supercharged cars at high speeds. He has very few close friends. (He had one, Jack Burke, and for his trouble Jack Burke got him deep into financial scandal that is only now, a decade later, lifting from his head; he has another, Evelle Younger, the attorney general of California, a man largely disliked by almost all of Otis's journalistic associates, indeed a friendship that is considered by top editors to be something of an embarrassment to the paper.) He is by any scale the ablest publisher in America in business terms, and he has had a record of caring deeply about excellence. He also cares deeply about image, about giving speeches and gaining recognition for himself and the paper, partly because its West Coast location robs the *Times* of much of its legitimate recognition. He is good at the public functions demanded of a publisher, better than his father ever was, and yet there is no ease about it, it is an almost mechanical performance, neither stilted nor natural, it is something that has to be done, and as such he will do it and do it well, because he is a Chandler. (A few years ago, all *Times* executives were subjected to a psychological test. Otis eventually took it; it showed that he was very much the loner, and so he consciously worked to be more at ease with people.) He is, by normal standards of American cosmetology, very handsome, tall, powerfully built, and yet there is again something missing, the look is not easily confident, he has what one friend called troubled eyes. No publisher in America improved a paper so quickly on so grand a scale, took a paper that was marginal in its qualities and brought to it excellence, as Otis Chandler did, no publisher as rashly escalated the salaries of working journalists, well above what *The New York Times* and the Washington *Post* were paying, as Otis Chandler, and yet it is almost impossible to think of him as a man whom reporters by instinct would be comfortable with.

There is always a sense of a man out of place. He is not a news animal, he does not have that inner passion or special zest for it, the restlessness to be the first to know and the first to tell that makes reporters such great professional gossips. Indeed, if he were in another profession, if for some reason the Chandler dynasty had rested on other companies, it is somehow hard to imagine Otis Chandler as a serious newspaper reader. Perhaps the business section of the *Wall Street Journal.* Yet he is a good publisher, he listens carefully, by and large he chooses good people, he defuses the various pressures on himself and his staff well. He has always been more liberal politically than other members of his family and other people he grew up with; he had become in the mid-sixties a close friend of Robert Kennedy; they had liked backpacking together, doing outdoor male things, and Otis had been on his way to the Ambassador Hotel the night that Kennedy was shot. Once, a year after that assassination, he had turned to a friend and said, "I guess there's no one who represents us any more." The friend asked who "us" was and Otis had answered, "The black and the young and the poor." Part of which is true, by Chandler standards he has a right to say this, but by the standards of most Californians he is above all else a Chandler, and that ties him, no matter what else, to the existing financial and political establishment, to certain obligations and connections and corporate responsibilities that do not burden the rest of the black and the young and the   poor. There is about him an almost innocent aura, as if Otis were from another generation, a rich kid from a generation when rich kids really were different from everyone else, and learned all he learned, which is quite considerable, not from the streets but from special private lessons. A kennel-bred dog, one friend said, a damn tough kennel-bred dog.

It was not, after all, a profession he chose. It was chosen for him. But if he had to do it, he would do it and do it well. There was always that drive for excellence, always the goals. Otis, the 130-pound gangly prep school track star who became interested in weights and systematically built himself up to 220 pounds of pure muscle to become a world-class shot-putter at Stanford, second in meet after meet only to the great Jim Fuchs, missing the 1952 Olympics because he sprained a wrist on his throwing arm at the last minute. The football coach at Stanford pleaded with Otis, in those days when 220 pounds meant a mountainous lineman, to go out for football. No, he said, I want to win the NCAA title this year. That was his goal, Otis, even as a boy, was very goal-oriented. But he refused for another reason—in his heart, football, particularly playing the line, was too anonymous; who knew the names of the interior linemen in those days, who knew what they did? He did not want the Chandler name to carry him, he wanted to carry the name, to do it on his own, he wanted not just his excellence, he wanted no one to doubt his excellence. If he was a championship shot-putter, it was clearly his own victory, he had not earned it because he was the scion of a great family. Always from the time he was young he had that special drive. Even as a young man he was both willful and methodical; in a thousand subtle and not so subtle ways Buff Chandler had driven herself and set goals, and in some way this had been passed on to her son. Otis with goals, Otis wanting upon graduation to join the Air Force's officer training program, and needing to lose 17 pounds because they took no one heavier than 217. Otis starving himself for days, finally on the last day just making the weight, and gaining all 17 pounds back in celebration that night. Even now as a grown man the goals remain: which rare sheep to hunt for from which high altitude to order to once again enter the hunter's record book; which rare car to bring to mint condition. (As late as 1978, when he was fifty and thus much much older than the other entrants, he competed in a major auto race, the Six Hours of Endurance, at Watkins Glen in New York. He and his teammate, John Thomas, finished sixth. He had hoped to finish tenth at best; at one point he was clocked at 152.6 mph.) He is very willful. Missy, his wife, told friends years ago that she had known Otis as a boy and knew if she married him that he would have to get his way, that it could be no other way. It was a life remarkably devoid of freedom of choice, prescribed by an overwhelming sense of duty and obligation and an obsessive desire to gain recognition on his own within his unchosen profession.

He was a very hardheaded businessman, and a very tough one, and he was that way even before taking over the *Times*. It was Otis Chandler, not Norman, who had pushed for the closing of the *Mirror*, who had said that it was a loser and they had to get rid of it. Norman had hated to close the *Mirror*, it was like disowning a child, he had cried during his farewell speech there, but he had been driven by Otis to cut his losses. The afternoon market, Otis had argued, was not then and never would be what they hoped, there would be no public transportation, the city was sprawling farther and farther, not higher and higher. Delivery systems were impossible. Thus the Chandlers had made the deal, at Otis's insistence, with the Hearst people, and miraculously, the Hearsts (no one had ever accused the Hearsts of that generation of being smart) had dropped their morning paper, the *Examiner,* which was a winner in a morning market, in trade for the Chandlers dropping their afternoon paper, which was a loser. An instant bonanza for the Chandlers.

It was a truly remarkable deal, stunning, among others, people at the Justice Department, but the top officials there soon found that they were locked in. A man named Jack McKinney, who worked for the Hearsts, had earlier gone to see Lee Loevinger, the head of the antitrust division of Justice in the Kennedy years, and he had explained the dilemma—the organizations losing money on two papers—and Loevinger had made a terrible mistake, he had said something which no one in the antitrust division should ever say, he had said to McKinney, "Well, why don't they each drop one paper?" Later when they did each drop one paper, Bobby Kennedy went around the table with his highest aides and he got the same answer from each member: it's highly illegal, but you'll never convict them because the head of your antitrust division suggested the deal. It was an absolutely staggering deal. Hearst confined itself to the afternoon market, which was shrinking nationally, and particularly so in Los Angeles, and in the process it gave the Chandlers clear title to the morning market, in effect a morning monopoly. It was done at precisely the time when local television news shows were on the rise, thus spelling even further grief for afternoon papers, whereas having a morning monopoly was like having a license to print money. It was the most important deal of the era in California journalism; the Hearsts had simply deeded title to the future to the Chandlers. Norman Chandler in the end was overjoyed; though he had lost something like twenty-five million dollars on the *Mirror* in its thirteen years, he now began to call it the best investment he had ever made, and in an interview upon his retirement, asked about his best decisions, he referred to starting the *Mirror* because in the end he had left his son a monopoly in the morning field.

For years Otis Chandler had been filling up notebooks about procedures at the *Times* that were wrong and outdated, methods that could be improved and modernized. He knew the paper was weak editorially, and he knew the essential structure on the business side was sound, but could be modernized. He also knew whatever reputation he was to make would have to come from the editorial side, because the paper was already a considerable business success. So he set out working with Nick Williams almost immediately to improve and upgrade the staff, to pay better; within three or four years the *Times* was paying the best salaries in American newspaper journalism. He was filled with ambition and drive, and the search for excellence and recognition; the Washington bureau had loved it in the mid-sixties when he had met with the staff and had announced, "We're going to spend as much money as it takes to be the best newspaper in the country and I mean, specifically, *The New York Times.*" The future seemed limitless. He believed strongly that journalism had to change, that it had to adapt to television rather than fight it, that newspapers had to give readers an extra dimension now that they were no longer the fastest carrier of news. Thus they had to provide other services. It was not a revolutionary idea among reporters, but it was a novel view for a publisher, since to the degree that publishers were aware of television in those days it was simply as something to dislike. He also believed, and this was crucial, that a quality operation paid, that the more you put in, the more you took out. He believed it and he made it come true. He was also in part lucky. The country in the sixties was in a vast economic upsurge, and nowhere was that more evident than in California. His timing was absolutely right, and if he had not been so successful financially, he might have been very vulnerable to the Family. Nonetheless, he demanded a quality operation and he made it pay. The editorial budget for the first year he took over, 1960, was $3.6 million; by 1976 it was $19 million. Even allowing for inflation, it had far more than doubled. But the daily circulation in that period went from 536,000 to 1,010,000. Sunday circulation went from 924,000 to 1,275,000, and advertising linage, from 80 million lines to 116 million.

Otis not only intended to improve his own paper; suddenly he was forced to, because for the first time he faced some serious local competition. The poverty of California journalism had long tempted eastern publishers to try some sort of publication out West; Harry Luce had thought of it, so had the Cowles people and they had even started a small suburban daily in the Valley, and the editors of *The New York Times* had often considered it, as a means of making their paper truly national. In 1961 *The New York Times*'s executives began serious preparations for a West Coast edition, a miniature edition of the eastern daily, slightly tailored for the California market. By then Otis Chandler had taken over, he already had a blueprint for his own expansion, and he was in no way pleased with the idea of an eastern invasion of his terrain (he later thought long and hard of ringing *The New York Times* with a series of small suburban dailies, to exploit the changing demography of New York and the exodus of middle-class whites from the central city). The relationship between the *Times*'s western edition and his own expansion was a sensitive point. He intended to upgrade the Los Angeles *Times*'s reportorial staff and open new bureaus anyway, but there was no doubt the challenge from New York expedited the process; it led him, among other things, to open a joint, and on occasion unwieldy, news service with Phil Graham of the Washington *Post* and that in itself required new foreign bureaus. In the fall of 1962 *The New York Times* began publishing its western edition. It was never intended as a threat to the local paper in terms of advertising but as a clear challenge in terms of prestige. The paper never took hold; its circulation varied between 75,000 and 100,000 and it constantly lost money. In 1964 Arthur Ochs Sulzberger, the new publisher of *The New York Times,* closed the paper, but it had served a purpose, it had helped spur Otis Chandler in his drive to improve his own paper, and it had reminded the elite of Los Angeles of how weak a newspaper they had been getting.

But much of the change in the Los Angeles *Times* would have taken place anyway, Otis Chandler was ambitious and committed to excellence. It was financially the most successful newspaper in the country, the best run, and the richest. It had an extra advantage, of course: the battle that General Otis had won some fifty years ago against the unions had permitted the *Times* to pioneer in the use of modern technology while unions were blocking modernization at comparable papers. Its profits over the last several years have averaged over $30 million a year, far far greater than those of the Washington *Post*, which often had a profit one third that figure, and *The New York Times*, which made a profit only one seventh as large.

The way was clear. The first increment of change was almost invisible to the naked eye. A small change really. Kyle Palmer was in semi-retirement by 1960, but the local version of Kyle, Carlton Williams, was still very active. Democrat Sam Yorty was running against Norris Poulson, the Republican mayor whom the *Times* had sponsored and helped invent. Poulson was, in fact, the *Times*'s boy. So as the campaign opened Carlton Williams prepared to do his usual job, which was to destroy the Democrat. He came up with one story about Yorty that was particularly vicious, just short of libel, if indeed short. Williams turned the story in, and Frank McCulloch, who had recently taken over as day managing editor, looked at it, thought that this was exactly the kind of story that the *Times* had always published which had made it look so bad in the past. He thought about it a very long time, and he decided that they could not publish this, he had not, after all, left *Time* magazine for the Los Angeles *Times* in order to destroy Sam Yorty for the Chandler family. He took the story to Nick Williams, and Williams pondered it and then agreed, this was the past, they did not publish stories like this any more. When they told Carlton Williams he screamed bloody murder. Why had they sent him over half the country checking out Yorty? He had always written stories like this, it was the way they did things. He had always done this kind of reporting. Exactly, McCulloch said, that's the problem. It took a lot of courage on Nick Williams's part, McCulloch thought, he was in effect ending an era, and he was doing it without talking to Norman or Otis.

If that was the first step, a more important one was to come shortly afterward. In 1960 throughout certain sections of the country, a new conservative group was quietly organizing. It was all being done informally, friends calling friends, vouching for this new organization. All very good people, very respectable, pillars of their community. Upper middle class, or very rich. Mostly in the South and what was to be known as the Sun Belt. People who didn't like the way things were going. Alarmed by the rate of change, the lack of control. All the trouble in the South. The Negro thing, all that protest, so much of it on television all the time, those television cameras encouraging *them* to protest even more. The country getting out of control. The United Nations. Communists. Socialists. Earl Warren. It was time for someone to stand up for Americanism. Stop being ashamed of being Americans. Didn't anyone want to speak up for free enterprise? Time to use the Communists' own techniques against them. Bombard newspapers with letters. Take over town meetings. Infiltrate the PTA. Suddenly, without any overt publicity, it was burning like a brush fire. No one had written about it, no one had identified it as a movement, but a movement it was, it wanted to impeach Earl Warren, that, after all, was a perfectly respectable part of the American Dream. Warren had done dark and sinister deeds, but then, so too had Dwight Eisenhower.

It was the coming of what was to be known as the John Birch Society, a semi-clandestine operation of very respectable leaders, bound together in uncompromising resentment against the direction the society was moving. It was not surprising that Southern California was one of the hotbeds, the particular rootlessness of the society had always lent itself to powerful extremes of both the left and the right, there was, in the volatility and evanescence of the culture an atmosphere ripe for extremism, each side with its own utopian dreams, each side driving the other to a more polarized position. Then too, Earl Warren came from California and he was a particular bête noire for the radical right, living proof to them that the Republican Party was just as corrupt and radical as the Democratic Party. So it began in Southern California, with great bundles of hate mail pouring in to newspapers about Warren: Warren was a Communist and should be impeached. Both Nick Williams and Frank McCulloch became aware of the mail; it is unclear who noticed it first, Nick Williams thinks *he* spotted it, and Frank McCulloch thinks he mentioned it to Nick. But they both began to pay attention and think of doing some reporting on this phenomenon, the mail was so virulent and so similar in wording, so clearly organized. Finally Williams went to see Norman Chandler; Otis was already publisher but Norman was very much around, particularly on matters like this.

"I'm getting a lot of mail saying Earl Warren is a Communist," Williams said.

"That's strange," Norman Chandler said.

"Do you think he's a Communist?" Nick asked.

"Of course not," said Norman (in fact, the principal problem with Warren, he often said, was not his politics but his charm. Warren, Norman Chandler said, could always charm him out of anything he wanted, and he insisted that Kyle Palmer deal with Warren at all levels, otherwise Warren would talk him out of anything he wanted done).

"Maybe we ought to look into it," Williams said, and they did. McCulloch looked around the city room, he had only been there a few months, he was very new, and he wanted a staff reporter who was very careful and cautious and who knew something about the law. Smokey Hale, the city editor, recommended Gene Blake, a mild-mannered, quiet, hard-working veteran reporter. Blake, like most Americans at the time, had never heard of the John Birch Society. He began by getting hold of their Blue Book, with all their plans, and he was shocked, it was like a journey into the shadows. The words of Robert Welch, Blake thought, were devastating. A secret world. He spent a month on the legwork and on March 5, 1961, the *Times* ran the first of a five-part series on the Birch Society. It was mild, remarkably understated, nonjudgmental reporting, almost too bland, if anything; if the Birchers were being hanged, they were being hanged with their own words. If any other paper in the country (except possibly the Chicago *Tribune*) had published the articles, it would have meant nothing. But coming in the Los Angeles *Times* it was startling. The Birchers were Pasadena, the *Times* was Pasadena, the Chandlers, both literally and figuratively, were Pasadena. This was not some fringe group the *Times* was dealing with, this was the very heart of its traditional constituency. The *Times* was venturing not into the heart of the lions' den but into the den of the Christians.

When Blake was finished he got a very nice note from Otis congratulating him and saying that Otis was about to write the accompanying editorial. "Prepare yourself," the note said, "here comes the onslaught." Otis had been appalled by the articles, he was, by the standards of Pasadena, unusually liberal, he had gone to prep school at Andover, where he had been easternized, his years as a star athlete had moved him into a world at least partially black, in the Air Force one of his closest friends had been Mal Whitfield, the great black runner. He may have been, from the viewpoint of some of his reporters, the most conventional of men, but by the standards of Pasadena, whence he had come, he was a very unconventional one. When he saw the five articles, he went to Nick Williams and demanded that they write a very strong editorial. Williams had a very shrewd sense of how much heat the organism could take at any given time; if the *Times* was changing from one constituency to another, which it clearly was about to do, it must, he thought, do so slowly. In reaching for a new audience and a new California, it must be as careful as possible not to offend the old one, the people who had made the paper, financially at least, so successful an institution. Nick Williams was a subtle man (he used to say privately that the responsibility of a truly great newspaper was to educate the elite and pacify the masses) and he wanted to change with invisible increments of progress with no marked break from the past. Therefore he wanted a low-key editorial, carefully reasoned, something that did not explode and insult, with as little emotion as possible. So he gave it to Kerby Ramsdell, who was a very conservative editorial writer, and Ramsdell wrote a tightly reasoned editorial saying that the kind of thing the Birch people were doing, however well-intentioned, *was not the American way,* it was not constitutional, it was destroying rather than saving liberty.

Nick Williams was quite pleased with it and took it to Otis Chandler. Otis found the Ramsdell editorial too soft, he wanted something much tougher. He could tell immediately that Nick was resisting. Williams's glasses went up on his forehead, a sure sign, which Otis Chandler had come to recognize, of Nick's resistance. Perhaps Williams's voice just a little scratchier: "Do you really think so? Those people out there have been our people," he said. "Nick," said Chandler, "we're a Republican paper and this is our constituency, and if anyone has a responsibility, we do." Nick's glasses were still on the forehead, and Williams was rubbing his forehead, yet another sign of resistance, asking a few more questions, trying to be sure that his young publisher knew what was coming. Then Williams decided that it was Otis's newspaper and he could do what he liked with it and he sat down and wrote a much tougher editorial, taking, of course, the requisite swipe at Communism ("the godless materialism and blood-soaked tyranny of the Communist conspiracy") but also tearing into the Birchers for their attacks on Roosevelt, Truman, Eisenhower, both Dulles brothers. "The *Times* does not believe that the arguments for conservatism can be won—and we do believe it can be won—by smearing as enemies and traitors those with whom we sometimes disagree." Otis was delighted with the editorial, he signed his name to it and placed it on the front page. Nick Williams, even more than Otis Chandler, knew what was to come, that the reaction was going to be very militant and very organized, and it was. Circulation departments of most newspapers become nervous when there are as many as 30 cancellations because of an article, and in this case there were 15,000. *Fifteen thousand.* Later there was some evidence that the cancellation was done on home delivery—stop delivering your Communist rag to my home—and those very people simply bought the paper at newsstands. It was a staggering reaction. For the *Times* this was like a declaration of independence from the past, from the days of General Otis and Harry Chandler, when the *Times*'s slogan had been *Stand Fast. Stand Firm. Stand Sure. Stand True,* and from the dusty philosophy that had lived after they had died, and a sign of the coming of a new and different newspaper.

It was also the making of Otis Chandler, he was very much the publisher, he was showing his freedom, this was real journalism. *His newspaper was standing up against wrong.* He reveled in that. But it also made him more cautious, more directly aware of the pressures to which he had become heir and from which his father in the past had often shielded him. The Family was furious. Philip Chandler and his wife, Alberta, were big Birchers, she had used her home for a reception for Robert Welch, and there was talk of a rebellion against Otis. It was a very bad time, and Otis Chandler did not particularly like it. He went with several other publishers to a meeting of the local advertising club and the others were cheered while he was booed, and shot-putters do not like being booed. If the Birch stories and editorial gave him his independence, they also taught him how fragile it was, how much independence had to be rationed, that there were limits of freedom. Very shortly afterward the *Times* did a series on the blessings of Americanism, and covered with enthusiasm Fred Schwarz's Christian Anti-Communist Crusade, while Blake did a series on the evils of Communism.

For all of that Norman Chandler was not displeased by either the Birch stories or the reaction to them. A few months after the incident Gene Blake happened to run into Norman Chandler at a reception and he approached the former publisher cautiously, not knowing what his attitude might be. He found to his surprise that Norman Chandler, whom he barely knew, reached over and grabbed him warmly and asked, "When are we going to hit those Birchers again?"

So the paper was changing and changing quickly, in its attitude toward politics, and Richard Nixon, who had been invented and nurtured by the old regime, would soon learn that. In 1960 the Chandlers gave their all for Nixon, there was even some talk about Buff becoming an ambassador. President Nixon, after all, would remember his friends. The coverage of the campaign had been fairer than in the past, a reporter had even been assigned to Kennedy, but there was no doubt about the tilt, the favorite son was Richard Nixon, this was to be the culmination of fourteen years of Kyle Palmer's planning. Yet the campaign in California was fascinating, an instant reflection of how quickly the state was changing, how powerful the new demographics were. For Jack Kennedy was clearly touching something new and emotional and powerful in California, something young and physical and vigorous, as Kennedy seemed young and physical and shorn of the past. It was new media politics, the politics of being a star. The crowds were incredible, large, intense, self-evidently sexual, filled with the first political teenyboppers, all this the result of the intrusion of television into political life. It was like nothing that veteran reporters had ever seen. One afternoon late in the campaign, returning from a series of wildly enthusiastic rallies, Donald Shannon of the Los Angeles *Times,* who was the pool reporter with Kennedy, said to the candidate that it looked very good in California, but Kennedy was dubious. "No," he said, "I don't think so, the Los Angeles *Times* is against me and that's very tough, I think it's going to cost me California."

It was very close in California right up to election eve and the paper was still divided, part the old *Times* and part the new *Times,* and the night before the election Norman Chandler decided to go all out, the warlord in him still lived, and he wrote a hellfire and brimstone editorial damning Kennedy as a media prettyboy, and praising Nixon as the last best hope of mankind. This was not the sweet graceful Norman, this was the Norman Chandler whom Harry Chandler had sired and Lipchitz had found in his sculpture. He had phoned it in to Nick Williams and he knew from the response that Williams had not liked it, but he had bulled it through over Williams's cautious doubts, it was like a last gasp of old-fashioned Chandler prejudice, right of property. Perhaps Kennedy was correct, perhaps given the closeness of the race in California, the *Times* did swing just enough weight to give the state—if not the election—to Nixon.

Election night, however, was not pleasant; the Chandlers had, after all, nurtured Richard Nixon all those years, so the least he could do was be a winner. Those who spent election night with Buff and Norman had a powerful sense of the disappointment and frustration of the Chandlers. The anger was very real and, curiously enough, it was not aimed at John Kennedy, it was aimed at Richard Nixon. How could he have blown this lead? How could he have let this happen? How could he be a sitting Vice-President in a time of peace and prosperity and be beaten by a callow youth like Kennedy? *How could he have done this to them?* After all, look what the Chandlers had done for him over the years. He had let them down. But then, and this was not said directly, though it was in their tone, they had never liked him that much anyway.

# 9/ The Washington Post

They were two old men and they were both approaching death and each had
something that was valuable only to the other. Their views on most issues
could not have been more different. Colonel Robert R. McCormick, who was
seventy-three in 1954, the crusty publisher of the Chicago *Tribune,* a man who
had breathed the chill of his own isolationism into a vast American region, was
the owner of the Washington *Times-Herald.* And Eugene Meyer, who was
seventy-eight, and who symbolized, perhaps more than any other businessman
of his era, international cooperation and links with the democracies of Europe,
was the owner of the Washington *Post.* They saw the world just about as
differently as was possible. One, for example, considered Joe McCarthy a
savior, the other thought him a plague. But one of the things that they had
in common was that they both owned newspapers that were at least partially
crippled as long as the other's newspaper continued to exist. Nor were their
respective papers of very great value to a potential outside buyer. What good
was it for an outsider to buy the *Times-Herald* as long as the *Post* was still
there sharing the morning market? What good to buy the *Post* and struggle
for oxygen with the *Times-Herald?* Each paper was of value primarily to the
other; if one could swallow the other, success seemed guaranteed; if they both
continued, failure too was probably guaranteed. It was a situation that obsessed Phil Graham, the need to buy the *Times-Herald.* He had come close
in 1949, when the paper had seemed to be for sale after Cissy Patterson's death.
But Colonel McCormick had bought it, spent millions renovating the plant,
and made Graham's dream seem more distant. The very columns of the
Colonel's paper seemed to indict the *Post* every day.

But McCormick was old now and he was sick and Washington had not
turned out to be very much fun for him. He had tried to transfer his highly
successful formula from the Midwest to Washington—he called it bringing the
United States to Washington (in effect, it was an ongoing attack upon the
government of the United States)—but it had not worked at all. His voice and
his prejudices had suited the Midwest at the time, but when he had brought
his anti-eastern, anti-intellectual, anti-English tone to a city that was somewhat Anglophile, quite eastern, and increasingly well-educated, he had been
in trouble. Though he had invested several million dollars in new machinery,
McCormick had continued to lose anywhere from a half million to a million
a year on the *Times-Herald.* Most important, Washington had never been
pleasant, he had never felt at ease there, he believed all those things he had

written about it, and it had colored whatever appreciation he might have had of life in the capital. Now old, his health failing, as Meyer's was not, he was trying to sum up his life. He did not like loose ends, and he considered the paper in Washington a loose end, badly run in a city that he did not understand and did not care to understand. Besides, he liked Meyer, Meyer was smart and successful and rich and he admired those qualities, and Meyer had stood by him in a moment of mutual self-interest when membership in the Associated Press was limited to one paper in each city, and each had been trying to keep the AP service from a rival upstart paper. This had taken place much earlier and most other publishers, fearing Roosevelt and knowing his hatred for McCormick, had stayed away from the fight; but Meyer, having a comparable problem in Washington, had been McCormick's surprising ally.

That had softened McCormick's feelings toward Meyer and in 1954, through the intermediary of Kent Cooper of the Associated Press, he made his overture to Meyer. Cooper helped expedite the deal because he feared that the constant warring between two morning papers in Washington would simply weaken journalism in the nation's capital. In January 1954, Meyer received an enigmatic note from Cooper asking whether he might be in Florida in the near future, since there was the possibility of a business matter to be discussed. Meyer immediately thought of the *Times-Herald*. He called Cooper and asked if this opportunity might be in journalism? Yes, Cooper answered. In Washington? Meyer asked. Yes, Cooper answered again. Meyer said that as a matter of fact he did intend to be in Florida very soon. Phil Graham was already there, and they quickly met with Cooper. The deal was very simple. McCormick wanted to sell. Did Meyer want to buy? Yes, he did. How much? Well, said Cooper, the Colonel wanted to get back the $4.5 million he had paid for the paper plus an additional $4 million he had spent for presses and equipment. That was fine, said Meyer. There was no haggling. Nonetheless, there were a number of tiny details to wrap up and that took two months. Graham, who had seen the prize slip away once before, became nervous and tense.

There was one last-minute hitch. Bazy Tankersley, the Colonel's niece, who was running the paper, who did not want to lose control, and who hated Meyer, protested the sale and asked for a chance to raise the money on her own. McCormick gave her permission to try to raise an equal amount of money provided that she did not tell why she was doing it. Fearing the coming of Meyer-Graham liberalism, she desperately tried every conservative millionaire she could think of: Robert Wood of Sears, Roebuck; Joe Kennedy; Sid Richardson; H. L. Hunt; and Clint Murchison. If only they had known then what some of them and their ideological descendants were to know later! But all she could raise was $4 million and McCormick was impressed with neither the money nor her stewardship. The paper was to go to Meyer; Meyer he knew and Meyer in some way he trusted. Meyer might be a little liberal, but he was sound, he knew money, he was not going to do something rash. McCormick did not think of himself as selling to Graham, Graham was someone much younger and thus much less important; in McCormick's mind it was Meyer's money, thus it would be Meyer's property. To him the *Post* was Meyer, as it had been for some twenty years. In reality, it was by then Graham's paper. (It was not unlike the moment in 1970 after Captain Harry Guggenheim, the owner of *Newsday,* the Long Island daily, hired Bill Moyers to be his editor with many promises that Moyers would eventually inherit the paper. When Moyers turned out to be quite liberal, the Captain was appalled, and knowing his life was near the end, he tried to think of a very good sound conservative publisher whom he could sell to. He immediately thought of his old friend Norman Chandler, a wonderful Taft Republican, and he called Norman, who was delighted by the idea, and the deal was made in a few minutes. What Norman did not mention was that his son, *Otis* Chandler, now ran the family's properties, and Otis was ideologically very close to Moyers.)

Whether McCormick would have dealt as readily with Graham is another question. But it was in fact Graham's deal, he had thought of nothing else for a decade. He had talked incessantly about it, to Meyer, to Kay, to his business people, he had worked to keep his editorial page from placing the *Post* in an untenable position, he had worked to reassure Alicia Patterson, who was part of the Patterson-McCormick family, that Meyer in his attempt to buy the *Times-Herald* in 1949 had not been trying to make a run on the Colonel's stock or take over the Colonel's company. For Graham, taking over the *Times-Herald* had always been the key to the future. Now the future was his. The day before the deal was consummated he was so excited that he had to talk with someone to let off steam and yet he did not want to break that closely held secret in so gossipy a town. So finally he called Shirley Povich, the sports editor, then covering baseball spring training in Florida, a man who was privy to all, and who could keep a secret. "Shirley," he said, "hold your breath for twenty-four hours. I think we finally have it."

In March 1954, the *Post* bought the *Times-Herald.* As the final negotiations were proceeding, each time there was a potential roadblock Meyer simply opened his wallet and swept away the obstacle. Settlement for older employees? Pay it. The Colonel's fleet of trucks? Buy them. The Colonel's house in Washington? Buy it. Nothing was going to stand in his way on this deal that his son-in-law wanted so desperately. Graham became tighter and tighter. He loved extreme secrecy in all his deals and now he was more careful than ever. He made sure that John Hayes, one of his executives, had the initial check of $1.5 million made out to Hayes and not to the Tribune Company, for fear of a leak. He made sure that Hayes went to Chicago by train instead of plane because it was safer. He installed direct phone lines for quicker and more private communication with Chicago. Then it was done, the merger had taken place. The *Post,* with shaky resources and aging physical property and a circulation of 204,000, had taken over the *Times-Herald,* with a circulation of more than 250,000 and a handsome new physical plant. The lesser animal had inhaled the larger one. Congratulations, wired Walter Lippmann, to the canary that swallowed the cat. Graham, as a courtesy, that morning called Bob Addie, one of the best *Times-Herald* sportswriters, asking him to go to work for him. Addie, who had not yet heard of the merger, said no. "But I just bought your paper," said Graham. "Good morning, boss," said Addie.

The *Times-Herald,* it turned out, was solid gold in its books, worth far more than the *Post* paid. The *Post* executives had thought the *Times-Herald* circulation figures inflated, but they turned out to be very real, the paper had been losing money only because of the Colonel's enormous investment in new machinery, and on the eve of the merger it was about to turn the corner and start showing a profit; now it would make money not for Robert R. McCormick but for Philip L. and Katharine M. Graham. Graham was determined to do everything he could to hold the *Times-Herald* readers. The paper's banner, much to the annoyance of the top editorial people, proclaimed the Washington *Post* and *Times-Herald* in equal type (a situation that was not to last). In the beginning Graham was determined to preserve all vestiges of the old order, all comic strips, all features, all columnists. He hired a top lawyer from Covington and Burling to study and secure the *Times-Herald* contracts for strips and columnists, and to make sure that no one got away, and to check at the same time the *Star*'s contracts so that he might spirit away some of its best people. Most newspaper professionals, looking at the vast difference between the two papers and imagining the comparable differences between their readers, had warned Graham that he would be lucky to keep only a fraction of his new circulation. But Graham believed otherwise, he thought if he gave readers what they had come to expect, the comic strips, the sports coverage —he thought the sports coverage was crucial in a situation like this—he could hold a surprisingly large part of the *Times-Herald* circulation. The *Post* already had two full pages of comic strips, now it was adding sixteen strips more. It took an enormous effort by everyone involved to get out the first edition, which had 64 pages. For the first Sunday edition, Graham—wanting to hold on to every single subscriber—pushed his entire staff to the limit; he put out 500,000 copies of a 228-page edition. Each copy weighed 2 1/2 pounds. It was an exhausting chaotic period, but it worked. It was the most brilliant merger in daily newspaper history and it was Phil Graham's tour de force. Graham's belief was simple. If he held circulation he would hold advertising, and he turned out to be right.


At the Washington *Star,* the leading newspaper of the city, the senior executives were not very worried by the merger. They did not take the *Times-Herald* seriously, it was a scummy paper, and they did not take the *Post* seriously, they had dominated it for more than twenty years and the prevailing view was that it was a bad paper because Meyer and his family did not know how to publish a good paper. This was not really Meyer's city, he was an outsider. The *Star* had always been the dominant paper in the past, thus it stood to reason that it would always be the dominant paper in the future. The executives did not see events changing, the coming of television, the rise of a formidable opponent in Phil Graham. Nor did they sense the shifting nature of Washington's readership, the coming of more and more rootless young people to work for an expanding Federal bureaucracy in Washington, most of them liberal. For them the merger was the union of two bad papers, and an untenable marriage given the ideological problems of the two. As a result, the *Star* did not move, it had never tried to buy the *Times-Herald,* it did not expand at the time of the merger, it did not make any gesture of competition, it did not, as some wanted, come out with a morning edition. At the executive level of the *Star* the high guess on how much of the *Times-Herald* circulation the *Post* would keep was 80,000. Most estimates were closer to 50,000. They were wrong. Very wrong. Almost, it turned out, terminally wrong. Of the *Times-Herald's* daily circulation of 250,000, the new paper kept *180,000;* of its Sunday circulation of 250,000, the new paper kept *200,000.* It was a signal victory for Graham. In four months the combined paper had a morning circulation of 381,417 daily and 393,580 on Sundays. Almost overnight the *Post* had become ninth in circulation in the nation. In 1943 the *Post* had had 24 percent of the circulation among the four papers in Washington in existence then; in 1953, just before the merger, the figure was 24.3; ten years later, in 1963, with only three papers in Washington, it had 46.7 percent of the circulation. This was not an ordinary business deal, this became the foundation of the new, modern, rich, powerful Washington *Post.* It made the paper wealthy and virtually unchallenged, an institution, in effect, unto itself.

This was the beginning of a new era for a new kind of newspaper. The *Post* would no longer be weak and thinly staffed, dependent on the U.S. government for its sources of information, unsure of its place in the matrix of politics. Soon the *Post* would be a strong, wealthy paper, supreme and unchallenged in its own market, no longer competing with other papers (they had largely been destroyed by television), rich enough in resources to have whatever staff it needed and wanted, indeed, a paper so powerful that it would rival not only other great newspapers but the very institutions in government that it once so timidly covered. The first step, the crucial hurdle, was the acquisition of the *Times-Herald.* That determined the future with a finality that no one at the time realized. Particularly the people at the *Star.*

The *Star* had always been *the* paper of the old Washington, a small southern city. It had been run mainly by two families, the Kauffmanns and the Noyeses, and they had proliferated and produced endless offspring, all of whom found their way into the swelling executive ranks of the paper. They knew personally all the top merchants of the city, and they got, through personal connection and because for many years they ran the city's best newspaper, the lion's share of the advertising. The *Star* dominated the city's politics, its economic structure; all the release dates for city officials' news stories were timed to give the *Star* the advantage. Buildings like Union Station were built because the *Star* wanted them built, segregation was retained because the *Star* wanted it retained. The *Star* had not particularly liked the New

Deal or Franklin Roosevelt, but it regarded them as passing fancies. Instead, its own city was passing. The government, which dominated Washington, was no longer a genteel government of genteel men all of whom knew and vouched for each other; it was, rather, a massive government in which power and position counted. The head of the paper from 1949 to 1963, the crucial years during which the city and its journalism were changing so dramatically, was Sam Kauffmann. He was a strong, forceful, stubborn, arrogant man, filled with prejudices; he did not like blacks, but then he liked Jews even less. He did not take Eugene Meyer seriously, he looked down on Meyer as a newcomer to the city, a neophyte in publishing, and a Jew. He did not foresee what television might do to afternoon papers, he did not realize that it was in the process of changing newspaper reading habits profoundly. Nor did he foresee the coming of Phil Graham. Kauffmann told Newbold Noyes that the *Post* would keep only about 5,000 of the *Times-Herald* circulation. He was, of course, ludicrously wrong; he had no idea how much money the new *Post* would make, or how much Graham would put back into the paper. Graham would spend money to make money. He went after the best executives he could get, hiring, for example, John Sweeterman, who was to become his forceful business manager, from Dayton for $36,000. Graham was off and running from the start. By the time the *Star* did move, it was too late, the *Post* had taken over the area. In 1954 the *Star* owned the city; a decade later it was weak and frail and barely holding on.

The *Post* in its weakest pre-merger years had been carried primarily by its expanding broadcasting properties. First WTO radio, then WTOP television, then the Jacksonville radio station. Graham from the start had been fascinated by television. He was not entirely sure whether it was going to destroy print journalism or not, but far more than most print executives, who merely feared it or were contemptuous of it, he knew something was happening, and he wanted a part of it. Meyer could not have disagreed more; he was of an older generation, he did not like broadcasting, which he found cheap, noisy, and hucksterish, and he did not want to invest in it. In 1947, some ten years before television became any kind of force in journalism, Graham hired John Hayes, who had operated the American Forces Network of radio stations during World War II, to be his broadcast man. In 1950 the *Post* bought its first television station, which became WTOP; Meyer reluctantly accepted the idea though he did not like it. At least it was in the Washington area. In 1952 Hayes recommended buying a radio station and television station in Jacksonville, Florida. Meyer adamantly opposed the idea for a long time. Finally Meyer asked Hayes who else wanted the station. "Phil wants it badly," Hayes answered. "Well, let's buy it then," Meyer said. What Phil wanted, Phil got. The Jacksonville station was bought in 1953, and others in Miami and Cincinnati were to come. Graham was not just ahead of Meyer, he was ahead of the Sulzbergers and the Chandlers as well. Most print men of that generation were, like the Sulzbergers, made uneasy by broadcasting. Even when broadcasting was profitable, the money seemed tainted to them. Not to Graham. He was acutely aware that his other properties were carrying the *Post* through the thin years. If a reporter received a raise from Graham he sometimes received along with it a small lecture pointing out that his paycheck had come from WTOP.

Now, with the merger completed, the *Post*'s economic base was enviable. John Sweeterman, the business manager, helped hold on to the new circulation and became a formidable force within the paper's structure itself, systematically defeating the editorial executives who tried to draw up new, larger budgets. It was Sweeterman, as much as Graham in those early months, who made sure that the paper got out on time, and who insisted on retaining what some *Post* editors thought were the overly conservative features of the *Times-Herald*. Sweeterman extracted from Graham a commitment not to remove the *Times-Herald* logo for ten years; it was, however, reduced in size for the first time seventeen days after the merger. It was also Sweeterman who worked to turn the Sunday section into a broader-gauged package, geared more to entertainment and filled with special sections, and to make the daily paper a more attractive package for middle-class readers. It had in the past been the paper of Washington's new elite, now Sweeterman was pushing for a wider audience. This was crucial for the business success of the *Post* and was essential to its eventual editorial success. Big-time teams of reporters were expensive, having the reportorial teams and the legal staffs needed to challenge the government was the luxury of rich semi-monopolistic papers. It was a curious irony of capitalism that among the only outlets rich enough and powerful enough to stand up to an overblown, occasionally reckless, otherwise unchallenged central government were journalistic institutions that had very, very secure financial bases.

Where the readers went, the advertisers soon followed and followed quickly. It happened first in classified because classified was always closer to the pulse of the paper and closer to the pulse of the community; it was not by chance that Eugene Meyer, the millionaire publisher, constantly solicited classifieds from every Washington cab driver who dared have him in his cab. It had always been Meyer's dream to pass the *Star* in classified advertising; that to him would be proof that his paper had truly reached the city, reached the real working people. In 1955, a year after the merger, a bright young man named James Daly was hired to become the *Post*'s classified-advertising manager and on his first day in the office he met Eugene Meyer. "Mister Daly, how long will it take us to pass the *Star* in circulation?" Meyer asked. "That's an unfair question," said Don Bernard, Daly's boss. "I haven't even shown Mister Daly his desk yet!" But Daly predicted five years. "Five years," echoed Meyer, "that's all right. I think I can live that long and I want it before I die." They passed the *Star* in four years, in 1959. Financial success came so quickly that it was far beyond Graham's or Meyer's anticipation. In 1954 the *Post* cut its losses to $250,000. Then, beginning in 1955, it made a profit of $2 million a year. The *Star* before the merger had beaten the *Post* in advertising two to one; in fifteen years that ratio was reversed.

. . .

The *Post* had become the most influential newspaper in one of the two most influential cities in America. Financial, social, and cultural ideas and images might be formed in New York, but political ideas were formed in Washington. The *Post* reached every member of Congress and the Supreme Court and the executive branch, every working Washington journalist from every other newspaper now read it. It made Philip Graham the prime political mover in Washington, and thus a national figure of considerable magnitude. He was no longer just a flashing, scintillating young man of high promise running a financially sluggish newspaper. He was now a brilliant, forceful, driving, often reckless, often aggrandizing man backed by a powerful rich newspaper. "A montage of the American dream," *Time* magazine called him in a flattering cover story that seemed to excuse him from what Harry Luce would have considered his youthful indiscretions. He was the foremost figure of the new Washington. He knew everyone worth knowing, he was fighting to break the old guard, to bring home rule, to end segregation. He was an activist and the *Post* would be an instrument of his dreams. He loved every minute of it, of being involved.

His marriage was not that good but it was not that bad, he was not dependent on Kay—Meyer had seen to that, Phil had the majority of voting shares—she was a middle-class wife who stayed in the background and watched him with a combination of admiration, fear, and, on occasion, resentment. He was dazzling and she was dutiful. Serious social occasions terrified her, she knew that she would not measure up, that she was ungainly, and did not know how to dress. If they were going to a fancy occasion Phil would call up Nancy White at *Harper's Bazaar* and arrange to have Nancy get something for Kay so that it would not be too great a disaster. Try and protect her, he had said. It was all quietly humiliating. She felt clumsy and somehow he made her feel clumsier; she seemed locked into her insecurity. She did not know how to set a good table. They had had Adlai Stevenson for dinner once and at the last minute Phil had gone downstairs to get some wine and it had been sour, and that had been a fiasco. Yet she was in awe of him too, and she loved him and she was proud that everyone made such a fuss over him, even if it did seem to take them to a social level which was beyond her ease. She felt best when they were with old friends from the days when he had been a law clerk, people who loved them both, and who were not always so fancy and so important, with such people she could be quite relaxed. Old friends began to notice that there were, in fact, two Kay Grahams. One was the woman who accompanied Phil to parties, and who seemed awkward and unsure of herself, determined never to say anything when he was talking, or to cost him even a tiny share of the spotlight. The other was the Kay who, when Phil was busy or out of town, came alone and who though shy and reserved seemed to be a woman of considerable intelligence, depth, and curiosity. Once, when they had just been married, they had been having a dinner party and he had said, "Do you know the first thing that Kay does every morning?" There was a pause and then he said, "She looks in the mirror and says how lucky she is to be married to me." Everyone laughed at the time, it seemed to be said with kindness and with so little malice that it was fun, and besides everything that Phil said made people laugh. But he would not have been able to say something like that now, it had become a little too true, he had seemed to grow more dashing and she had grown dowdier, and there would have been nothing to laugh about.

She worried sometimes about how hard he pushed himself. She alone in those years had an embryonic sense of the two faces of Phil Graham, not that she was prepared to say anything about it. But she knew the difference between the man who was totally engaging and witty at a party and the man who, when they were alone afterward, could so swiftly slip into a mood of despondency and self-denigration. It did not seem very serious, but it was unsettling nonetheless, and she worried. He became too exhausted when he tried to do too much. She wished he would slow down; now that he had everything they wanted, the paper, the seeming guarantee of success and a secure future, he became not calmer and more relaxed but, if anything, more driven. Because he had more, there seemed more to do. Because he was more influential, there was more to influence. Because he was more important, he felt compelled to reach for more. He was dabbling more and more in politics in the fifties. Working actively at almost every level in Washington affairs. In national politics he had very quickly become disillusioned with Eisenhower; Ike was a status quo man, and Graham was not. Gradually he was more and more drawn to Lyndon Johnson, then the Senate Majority Leader. The original connection had been through his boyhood friend George Smathers, but the friendship soon flowered on its own. Graham saw Johnson as a political extension of himself, liberal, pragmatic, partially populist, from a semi-deprived southern background. A man who knew the real world and who, unlike most wheeler-dealers who were purposeless in a moral sense, had an overall sense of moral purpose. Graham had become convinced, after the 1954 Supreme Court decision integrating the public school system, that it was important to have a President who could heal the divisions within the country.

He became one of Johnson's top unpaid advisers, speech writers, and promoters. He was, very simply, Lyndon's man, and to the degree that he could tilt the paper toward him he did. But he also worked outside the *Post.* He tried hustling Lyndon to his liberal friends—*you're going to like him, he's better than you think*—with varying degrees of success (it was not so much the accent that put the liberals off, it was the smell of oil and gas that tainted Johnson's public image). He tried to get his friends to become full-time speech writers for Lyndon. (He told Emmet John Hughes that all Lyndon needed was someone who could teach him how to talk north of the Mason-Dixon line. He set up a meeting for Hughes to work with Johnson, but Hughes, a man with a rich old-fashioned cadence to his writing, soon realized the almost total cultural and intellectual gulf between them, and canceled out.) He was always working on Lyndon to go national, trying to overcome Johnson's own immense paranoia about eastern liberals who might never accept him; Johnson legitimately feared the risk of trying for a position as a national liberal only to find himself rejected by the liberals and cut off from his southern base. Phil kept telling Johnson that the only way he could reach for the presidency was to act on civil rights, to move away from the image of segregationist, and that he could do this by shepherding a civil-rights bill through Congress.

In 1957 he had pushed Johnson to try; the southern segregationist power in Congress was at its height, and most of Lyndon's top advisers were Southerners and very wary of the uncharted waters ahead. The showdown on the bill came that summer. At the time, Phil Graham, overworked, tense, nervous, was resting out at his country place and Lyndon called him back to Washington to help hold the liberals in place while Johnson worked the conservatives. Kay was with Phil when Johnson's call came. She was immediately apprehensive about the prospect, she knew that Phil was exhausted, that something might be seriously wrong with him, and that this might be a lull before one of the storms. She argued against his going back to Washington, but Lyndon held the day and so Graham went back and worked as an assistant whip for Johnson. They were virtually living together, working over strategy every night, manning phones during the day, cajoling people, articulating the case for the bill. That was only part of it. Graham also strengthened Lyndon's nerve when periodically he became discouraged and petulant and wanted to cut out entirely. At one point it became clear that the southern power was very strong, that its procedural muscle outstripped the northern voting power and the bill would have to be seriously compromised. In fact, by liberal terms, the guts cut out of it. Now Phil Graham's role was crucial. He was constantly on the phone with his liberal friends—he had a considerable amount of both credibility and leverage with liberals; as the publisher of the most important liberal paper in the city, he could to a large degree stake out the liberal position in print—and he now argued that a weakened bill was better than no bill. The first part of the loaf was the hardest to get, he said, and they could set a precedent by passing this civil-rights bill, which would make the passage of future, tougher bills easier. It was crucial in dealing with something as emotional as civil rights to have a precedent. There had been a moment when it all hung in the balance, when Graham was lobbying ferociously, when the civil-rights group seemed in rebellion against Johnson's compromise, and when finally two people turned the tide for the bill, Roy Wilkins of the NAACP and Graham's old friend Joe Rauh, the ADA lawyer. They helped carry the day and the next morning there was a six-o'clock phone call from Phil Graham to Joe Rauh. The call woke up the exhausted, groggy Rauh. The first thing he heard was the exuberant voice of Phil Graham. At first Rauh wondered whether he had overslept, whether it was *his* clock that was wrong, Graham's voice, after all, did not sound like a morning voice.

"Do you know what Lyndon said about you today?" Graham asked excitedly.

"God, Phil, how the hell can I know what Lyndon said?" answered the still startled Rauh. Today, after all, was not yet today.

"Lyndon said you saved his bill," replied the exultant Graham. Exultant, Rauh thought, at 6 A.M.

The *Post* printed little about how the bill had been gutted, about the backstage manipulation that had gone on. It handsomely praised Johnson's handling of the bill, claimed he had not watered it down, and said that he had become the common denominator between North and South. Thus it was his personal triumph. That was precisely the role that Graham wanted for Johnson and had been trying to entice him into. The shoe had, not surprisingly, fit.

But Kay Graham was right. The civil-rights struggle had drained him, it had taken from him precious energy that he simply did not have. He returned to his farm exhausted; yet almost as soon as he came home the crisis at Little Rock blew up and he suffered his first major breakdown. It would become clear later—it was not clear at the time, for so many doubts about him were obliterated by the force and charm and magnetic quality of his presence—that he was not a well man. His successes at the *Post* had not relieved the pressure on him; they had only increased his responsibilities and put him closer to a kind of frenzy. Powerful as he was, fewer and fewer obstacles stood in his way, more and more other powerful men sought his counsel and his help; fewer people were now eager to argue with him or ignore him or tell him no. They sought his advice and his companionship, both for the quality of them and for the muscle that accompanied them. He was like a skater going faster and faster as the ice became thinner and thinner, while at the same time the wind resistance was getting milder and milder.

Little Rock triggered his first major breakdown. There had been smaller ones before, but only Kay had really known about them and they had been treated as minor episodes of exhaustion. Meyer simply thought Phil was too thin and too nervous. Kay had a feeling that these symptoms were part of something more serious, but she had no real understanding of mental illness, no one to turn to; it is hard for ordinary worshippers to diagnose illnesses among the gods. Those who saw him the most, after all, loved him the most. She had a foreboding sense of what was ahead. She had learned gradually over the years to protect him, how, on occasion, to allow him to disappear for a few days without anyone knowing that he had in fact disappeared or that there was a serious reason for it. She had witnessed the scenes of despair almost from the time they were married, the sudden change in personality from exuberance to darkness, and she had learned, in part she thought, how to deal with it, how to talk him out of it.

Why Little Rock hit him so hard is still something of a question. Certainly part of it was the exhaustion that had come from counseling Lyndon Johnson during the civil-rights debate, a chore that had come to him when he was already tired. Certainly part of it came from the fact that Little Rock symbolized the first tearing of the national fabric in modern times over the question of race, and that he, with his southern roots, took it personally. Certainly part of it came from the expanded role and increased power that had followed the merger. He expected more of himself, and he saw himself in a larger role, and now he could do anything that he wanted to do.

Not very much was known about the illness. Some doctors suggested that it might be in part biochemical, that the system for some reason, perhaps stress, produced imbalances that affected the brain, causing certain cycles. First the manic cycle, moments of frenzied energy, the ascent when all things were possible, when nothing could go wrong, when nothing could be denied him, and when history was his. During these cycles, he was in fact absolutely brilliant, his mind and his spirit racing ahead of everyone else, creative, original, seemingly able to see into the future, absolutely sure of his touch. Then the depressive cycle, a period of great hopelessness, of tearful, brooding scenes, with an awareness of nothing but failure and flaw, deeply self-denigrating, when he despaired about what he was and what he had done and literally could not get out of bed. Any suggestion from a friend about his true value and worth was turned away by his own scorn and a confession of some dreadful recent sin.

It was Little Rock that touched off the first of these major cycles in Phil Graham. Later many other American cities were marked by racial chaos, their names part of a painful ledger, but in 1957 Little Rock seemed to stand alone. The Supreme Court had in 1954 ordered desegregation of southern schools with all deliberate speed, and that speed had been deliberate indeed, but finally, three years later, Little Rock Central had been ordered to accept nine black students. Orval Faubus, the governor of Arkansas, suddenly interposed himself and the state government and said that he would prevent integration there. He encouraged local resistance, and for several days the black children were driven away from the school by mobs. Eisenhower was still President, his was a passive presidency, and he was slow to act; he had not particularly liked the Supreme Court decision and he seemed in no rush to force Southerners to comply with a law he disliked. So when he failed to move immediately, this created a vacuum; the world watched while a country governor in Arkansas challenged the President of the United States.

At this point Phil Graham moved into the vacuum. His activities seemed frenzied. He became a self-appointed manager of the Little Rock crisis. He was on the phone day and night to everyone: the White House; presidential advisers Sherman Adams and Maxwell Rabb; Nixon; Bill Rogers; Harry Ashmore, the Little Rock editor; Brooks Hays, the Little Rock congressman; black leaders Thurgood Marshall and Roy Wilkins. Trying to think of anyone Ike might listen to. Calling his reporter at the White House, Eddie Folliard, to pass on notes to Ike. Calling Ike's friends to get him to move. Trying to move Faubus a little, wondering what might affect Faubus, thinking of Truman, Truman was a good Baptist and a traditionalist, maybe Truman could call Faubus. But who would call Truman? Brooks Hays, the Little Rock congressman, that's who. Hays was a national lay Baptist leader and so Graham called Hays to call Truman to call Faubus. Anything. There was a touch of desperation to it all. Always trying to move the pieces. A brainstorm: maybe Ike with his immense prestige could enter the school with a black child on one hand and a white child on the other. When the White House rejected that, he had another idea. Maybe Ike could take one child by the hand and he, Phil Graham, could take the other and they could walk in together. There was hysteria to it, six phones going at once, pushing himself harder and harder, taking more and more responsibility upon himself, as if it were his fault if it did not work, his fault and his failure. More and more obsessed. Calling his friend Joe Rauh at 3 A.M.: "Joe, I've got to have Thurgood's phone number right now! I've got to talk to him now! We can do this tonight." Using his office as a battalion headquarters, keeping in touch with Ashmore down in Little Rock all the time, passing on Ashmore's battle reports to Sherman Adams and Bill Rogers. Telling Ashmore that Rogers was important because he affected Nixon, and Nixon was good on this one, Nixon was arguing with Ike to take charge. Nixon, he told a somewhat surprised Ashmore, was better than what people thought of him (after it was all over, Graham asked one favor of Ashmore, he asked him to write a note to Nixon thanking him for his help during the crisis, which Ashmore dutifully did). Day after day he manned his phones in the war room; he did not sleep at night. He seemed constantly on a high. It was, thought one friend, as if for a time Phil Graham thought he was President of the United States, and all this was his responsibility. Or at least a proxy President. At one point he decided that Lyndon Johnson should go to Little Rock and intercede. He called Johnson, who was in Texas at the time. Given the delicacy of the issue and the intensity of his own ambitions, there was nothing that Lyndon Johnson wanted less to do than to intervene personally at Little Rock, and he told this to Graham. Graham began to scream at Lyndon, who screamed back at him, and for a time relations between them cooled. Another friend, Max Rabb, Eisenhower's aide on minority questions, thought this was a different Phil Graham from any he had ever seen before; the old Phil Graham had been cool and irreverent and self-mocking, but this was a new man, desperate, obsessed, frenzied. Almost a kind of madness. Every other word seemed to be *must*, as if time were ticking away on him, a man bedeviled who did not even have time to listen, because evil was on the march. Ike finally did move, he went from doing nothing to sending in the 101st Airborne, and so finally the Little Rock crisis ended. When it did, Phil Graham collapsed.

He took time off from work and went to his country estate at Glen Welby in Virginia. Only a very few *Post* executives were told how serious his illness was, that it was a nervous breakdown. At Glen Welby he seemed paralyzed. He closed the drapes and would not get out of bed. Katharine Graham tried to deal with him, but she, shy and unsure of herself, feeling herself limited in her use of language in comparison with him, how could she talk him into anything? He was the one who could use words; nonetheless she tried to make him see how much people loved him and respected him and needed him. He, by contrast, poured out a desperate account of his own shame. His mood was black. When she mentioned his charm, he ridiculed her—wit and charm, he said, that was only a means of keeping people at a distance. That way he would

get to know a lot about them and they would learn nothing of him. He told
her of a man who had come to see him for something and he had charmed
the man, made him laugh, seduced him, told the man he needed a haircut, led
him to a barbershop, and left him there, still dazzled. He told the story and
as he told it he hated the Phil Graham he was describing.

Eventually the down cycle ended and in 1958 he gradually regained some
composure and came back to work. But it was the beginning of an increasingly
erratic time. There were some good periods but they were briefer and briefer,
and his hold seemed more and more tenuous. He was in and out of the office
for most of 1958 and 1959, his behavior was more and more fragile, but few
people knew it, most people saw him only during the good periods when he
was as bright and winning as ever. His closest friends knew that he was
seriously ill and worked hard to protect him during the bad times. "I've been
told to be on my best behavior," he told Arthur Schlesinger in one of these
periods, mocking his exaggerated good manners. In those moments he seemed
almost immobilized by his own sense of the darkness. He might call a friend
like lawyer Edward Bennett Williams and they would go off to a restaurant
on the wharf where he would not be recognized and they would talk for hours,
Graham despondent, sorrowful, sure of his doom. He was convinced that he
was a terrible person, sin hung heavily in the air, and there was now an almost
incurable instinct for self-destruction. There was, friends thought (though
often in retrospect), starting around 1958, the beginning of a discernible pattern, the attempt in his self-rage and his self-destructiveness to destroy, not just
himself, but those closest to him, both in his family and in his work. Strangers
in some ways were more immune, but he could lash out at friends and family
as if he were lashing out at himself. In addition there was one other strain
which began to show under this stress, and that was a deep and increasingly
bitter resentment about being a son-in-law, a growing hostility toward the
aging and somewhat defenseless figure of Eugene Meyer, and, perhaps more
appalling to his friends than anything else, the beginning in this rare and
intensely humane man of feelings of anti-Semitism toward Meyer and other
members of his family. It was the sign of a man who was much sicker than
they had all realized.

The illness increased Graham's power mania. It was not enough to be
around politics and politicians, now more than ever he had to be a participant,
and a peer of the very powerful. It brought him closer and closer to the center,
like a moth to a flame. He became more intimate than ever with Lyndon
Johnson. He became, after the civil-rights struggle of 1957, Lyndon Johnson's
northern interpreter and advertising man, selling him to people, counseling
him, sending him books that he should read. He was always trying to improve
Lyndon's image and widen his base. He decided in Johnson's last months as
a senator that Lyndon and Lady Bird needed a far larger and grander house
than they owned, something befitting the Senate Majority Leader and possible
future President. An official residence, large enough to be Lyndonesque. Since
he had Lyndon's power of attorney, he simply went out and bought the house

himself, a huge grotesque place. He knew that it was quite terrible and he immediately told Kay that he did not want to hear her and her friends Polly Wisner and Evangeline Bruce, powerful figures of Georgetown all, talking on the phone about what a dreadful house Lyndon had bought. The three women talked all the time on the phone, the Nine O'clock Network, he called it, and he always said he wanted to buy time on it. He knew the power of smart intelligent wives in Georgetown, their ability to set the tone and decide who was in and who was out, and he knew how sensitive Lyndon already was to Georgetown snobbery. "I don't want the word going out on your network that Lyndon's just bought an atrocious house. It's just fine for him," he told her. He had earlier told Johnson that he needed a program if he was going to reach the presidency and he had sat down and written out a program which Johnson later considered the forerunner of the Great Society. Now, as the 1960 election neared, he became a member of the Johnson inner circle and was one of the men who helped evolve Johnson's basic strategy. It was, they all thought, a realistic strategy. It called for Johnson to fight Kennedy in a few safe primaries but not to expect to have as many votes as Kennedy at convention time. Perhaps Kennedy would be ahead 500 delegates to 300, a nice lead, but far short of the desired number. In that case, the strategy assumed, most liberals who had never particularly liked Kennedy would go to Stevenson, and Kennedy would sink. Thereupon, the professional politicians, fearing and disliking Stevenson, would go to Johnson as the alternative safe candidate. Built into the strategy was one essential assumption: that somewhere along the way Kennedy would slip. That was central to the strategy and it never happened.

That summer, Phil Graham made a subtle transition from Lyndon Johnson to Jack Kennedy. It was easy enough to do. They knew each other. In 1958 they had been together at a dinner party and Phil had told Kennedy, "Jack, you're very good. You're going to be President someday, but I think you're too young to run now, and I hope you won't." Kennedy had taken up the challenge immediately. "Well, Phil, I'm sorry but I'm going to run. I'll tell you why. One, I'm better than anyone but Lyndon and he can't win. Two, if I stand around and let someone else have it for eight years he may be able to dictate his successor. And three, if I wait around in the Senate for eight more years I'll become a lousy senator." That was a man Phil Graham could understand, and they became, guardedly enough, friends. He and Kennedy were indeed in many ways startlingly alike, the same style, the same humor, the same quickness, the same low tolerance for boredom. Besides, Kennedy looked more and more like a winner. It was clear to Graham on the eve of the Los Angeles convention that Lyndon Johnson's presidential campaign was a lost cause. Graham was never a man for lost causes. Yet he had other ideas of what he wanted to happen at the convention. He was no journalist at a convention, trying merely to find out what was happening. This was a power broker using the leverage of his paper to wheel and deal, a broker for the liberals. The benign broker.

As the convention opened he brooded over an idea that had intrigued him for some time, the idea of a Kennedy-Johnson ticket. To most people that was inconceivable, the two men had simply said too many harsh things about each other. But Graham thought it was a genuine possibility and, more important, he also thought it the strongest possible ticket. On the first day of the convention, July 11, he and Joe Alsop went by to see Kennedy to ask him to take Johnson for the vice-presidency. Graham made the pitch, which was very basic, Johnson was the best man available, and he would bring strength to the ticket in precisely the areas where Kennedy was most vulnerable. Kennedy listened and immediately agreed, so immediately in fact that Graham thought Kennedy was merely going through the motions and paying lip service, and he repeated his advice again, cautioning against a lip-service offer to Johnson. Kennedy must assume, Graham warned, that Johnson would decline and he must argue all of his doubts away. Again Kennedy agreed and then he mused aloud whether, since the balloting was about to begin and since he still needed a few votes, he could get any votes out of the Johnson thing. Graham then passed on a bit of this information to his newspaper. Not all of it, for fear that too much might embarrass Kennedy and jinx his plan. So it was that the Tuesday *Post*'s lead story said somewhat discreetly that the word from Los Angeles was that Kennedy would offer the vice-presidency to Johnson.

Graham also passed the word to Johnson that Kennedy was considering him. On Tuesday, Graham was scheduled to have lunch with Johnson anyway and now he wanted to go into step two of his operation, getting Johnson to release Stevenson from his neutrality pledge so that Stevenson could nominate Kennedy. He also wanted to talk Johnson into taking the vice-presidency. There was no other way, he could no longer reach the presidency himself, the numbers were too tough. But to his dismay he found Johnson in an ugly, contentious mood, unwilling to back down. Johnson had just been given a chance to talk to a joint session of the Texas and Massachusetts delegations and he was ready for battle. This time he was going to pull out all the stops, he was going to eat Kennedy raw. Kennedy was just a kid, Joe Kennedy's rich little kid, and he was using that medicine, whatever it was, some kind of drugs for his back, and it was about time someone said something about it, and about old Joe Kennedy and Hitler. "I'm going to put it on the line," Johnson said. Graham was appalled. "The hell you are, you're tired as hell and you're going to take a nap while I write you a speech." Which he did—a high-road speech about wisdom and conciliation and experience, part of which Johnson gave and part of which he discarded in order to attack Kennedy's health and his father.

All of which made Graham's job far more difficult. He was becoming increasingly frenzied, as the events of the convention moved faster, and as liberal opposition to Johnson mounted, and as the clock seemed to be working against him. He was the kingmaker, or the would-be kingmaker. He quickly had another idea. A message from Kennedy to be read by Stevenson asking the convention to draft Johnson for Vice-President. But that did not work. It was clear to him that the problem now was Johnson and the people around him. So he found himself running back and forth feverishly between hotel rooms, arguing with Johnson, trying to keep the Kennedy people in line, trying to offset Bobby Kennedy's distaste for Johnson. (Years later, when Johnson as President began to turn against Kay, Bobby Kennedy was angered. "How dare he," he said. "Without Phil he never would have been on the ticket.") He was exhausted and almost wild; Kay began to worry about him, but she barely saw him. It was so difficult, communications were terrible, everyone seemed out of synch; when the Kennedys were ready, Johnson was petulant; when Johnson was ready to take it, Bobby Kennedy was promising people that it would not be Johnson. Then back to Johnson, who had been ready to take it a few hours earlier, but whose feelings were hurt now, and who would accept the vice-presidency only if Kennedy drafted him for it. Graham played the key role, darting back and forth, keeping the thing together, keeping it from coming apart at both ends, finally triumphing. The great surprise ticket, Kennedy and Johnson. His ticket.

So he was the kingmaker, he had helped broker the convention. He loved it, he was exhilarated, he had helped put together the right people at the right time. His friends. Jack and Lyndon. Jack and Lyndon and Phil. He returned that night to his room absolutely exhausted and drained. "We've got to get away from here," he told Kay. "I've got to rest." She knew what that meant.

No word of what he had done appeared in his paper or any other major publication. It came out for the first time a year later when Theodore White published the first of his *Making of the President* books. If anything, the disclosure that Graham had done this did not hurt his reputation, given the values of journalism and politics in those days, rather it enhanced his reputation as an insider, a man of power close to power.


He was also clearly sicker than ever now, the highs were more creative and more brilliant, the lows more despairing than ever; he was, ironically enough, becoming more and more powerful as he was becoming sicker and sicker.

# 10/CBS

Jack Kennedy was the first television President. In no way could he have been elected President without television. It was that simple. He meshed politics and television with such charm and style and dispatch that the intellectual elite of the country, which might normally have regarded the cross-blend with trepidation, rich as it was in potential for demagoguery, enthusiastically applauded him (the applause being generated in large part because the alternative to Kennedy was Richard M. Nixon). Television loved him, he and the camera were born for each other, he was its first great political superstar; as he made television bigger, it made him bigger. Everyone using everyone. The media using the President, the President using the media. His presidency made owning and watching a television set politically mandatory, and television not only made him President but helped swing the institutional political balance toward the presidency and away from other centers of power, meanwhile growing as a major center of power itself. It was an inevitable coming, but Kennedy with his sure instinctive sense for new political possibilities, his inordinate self-confidence, and his striking good looks simply expedited the process. He understood immediately when taking office the dynamics of it, that television executives respect power; he understood that television producers love film and thus that the President and the executive branch could virtually go into the business of producing film, producing their own shows, that the opportunity for television spectaculars was all his. The President traveling to other countries was an event, a special that reporters and cameras would follow, not just dutifully, but enthusiastically, as they would never follow a Senate Majority Leader or a Supreme Court Justice or a lowly governor. He learned by instinct that he could in fact make his travels (often events with a primary partisan political orientation) the subject of huge national interest, and that he could thus induce network journalists to drop, almost unconsciously, their normal critical facility and take their places instead as part of the pageantry, heralds of it, as it were, and not much more. He came to understand too that the farther he was from Washington, the less he was seen as a partisan political figure and the more he was viewed as being President of all the people (the China trip of Nixon was to be the apex of this phenomenon). And to see how, the less knowledgeable and secure the correspondent was thus far from home, the weaker his own sources of information, the more he needed to depend upon the President's own organization for information. An interesting transformation for the network journalist: the ability to get on the air, which was crucial to any reporter's career, grew precisely as the ability to analyze diminished. In such ways John Kennedy wrote the book on television and the presidency, a book which both Lyndon Johnson and Richard Nixon studied carefully, both of them feeling very much in his shadow; each shrewdly sensing the weaknesses and vulnerabilities of the networks and playing upon them. Partly as a result, there was an enormous jump in presidential power in the decade that followed. It was in fact an expansion so great and so unchecked, with so little attempt at rebalance, that Fred Friendly, a good liberal television executive who was in 1960 anxious to help counsel a good liberal President-elect on television and went down to Washington to help advise the new President on how to be more effective and more spontaneous, could a little more than a decade later call the office "an electronic presidency" and could complain to his old associate Walter Cronkite in the summer of 1974 about the fact that Cronkite, by going on Nixon's clearly dubious trip to the Middle East, was escalating by his presence the importance of the trip.

John Kennedy may not have been weaned on television like the generation of the sixties, but he nonetheless understood it from the first, knew that it was becoming more powerful all the time and knew that it was more likely to help him than his adversaries. More than most Washington politicians, he had a sense of the power of the press on a national scale, a knowledge that had been passed on to him like a legacy by his father. Old Joe Kennedy knew the strengths and weaknesses of the press unusually well; he had cultivated men like Harry Luce and Arthur Krock when he was in Washington in the Roosevelt days (and had made it a point to be having dinner with the potentially dangerous Luce the night his son accepted the Democratic nomination for the presidency). Joe Kennedy knew that if reporters were not entirely likable they could be extremely useful and a surprisingly high percentage of them were, under special conditions, worthy of trust. Joe Kennedy had long used them as a source of power and information. Now his son Jack Kennedy was doing the same, aided by the fact that by style, education, intellect, humor, breeding, he genuinely felt more at home with a certain level of Washington journalist than he did with most politicians, and the journalists—new breed, well educated, as nicely tailored at Brooks Brothers as any Wall Street banker or lawyer —reciprocated that friendship. Thus from the start, when other potential presidential candidates had been building their sources of national power through the Senate (Johnson, Humphrey) or through the party (Nixon, Humphrey), Kennedy had cultivated direct access to the nation through journalists. With party officials, with other senators, he was a junior legislator who had to wait his turn; with journalists he was an attractive bright politician who whetted the nation's curiosity and thus made news.

His timing could not have been better; at that very moment the media were becoming a far greater power base in the country; television was the key, making the press not just a part of the prism but indeed a major political factor. And as television was important, and television journalists important, so print reporters in Washington were important too, for while they did not command the huge audiences of the great network reporters, they nonetheless affected the way the public chose to react. They defined issues and helped set the attitudes and myths of Washington, spelled out who was good, who bad, what the key issues and areas were, and thus profoundly affected the attitudes of those men who commanded the national mass audiences. Television, rather than making them weaker, had amplified their power. When Jack Kennedy lunched and charmed Walter Lippmann he was charming not only Lippmann but James Reston as well, because Lippmann affected Reston profoundly, and not just Reston but in turn the *Times* and other print Washington bureaus, and not just the print Washington bureaus, but the reporters who worked for CBS and NBC. The lunch could reach out like small ripples. If in 1960 during the primaries a major *Times* columnist like James Reston thought a particular candidate could not win, it was now as important as a major party boss thinking he couldn't win.

Kennedy also had a very good sense of the true long-range source of journalistic power, that it was better to cultivate reporters themselves (and cultivate them indirectly—that is, cultivate them not so much by simply inviting them to dinner as cultivate them by sharing an interest, be it in their profession or the book they were reading, the issue they were fascinated by) than to try to connect to the top of the hierarchy (Johnson and Humphrey were forever trying to court publishers and top network officials). Kennedy was above all a cool professional politician and he made the transfer to television without losing a step, learning not so much from instructions and from paid television professionals as by his own instincts, and of course from shrewd advice from those around him. Not the least of them Joseph P. Kennedy. In 1959 Sander Vanocur, then a young NBC correspondent, was stationed by the network in Chicago and soon found himself being cultivated by Jack Kennedy's brother-in-law Sargent Shriver, who was a good friend of Vanocur's friend Newt Minow. Unlike Minow's other friend, Adlai Stevenson, Sarge Shriver owned a television set and knew how to turn it on and knew who was on it. So one evening there was a party at the Shrivers' home and a ruddy-faced sandy-haired older man walked over to Vanocur and said, "You're Sander Vanocur, aren't you?" Vanocur allowed as how he was. "I'm Joe Kennedy," said the man. "I saw you at Little Rock. You did a good job down there. I kept telling Jack to spend more time and pay more attention to guys like you and less on the print people. I think he's coming around." Which was very nice, to have your father encourage you to be good to the cameras.

It was television that in 1956 had helped catapult Jack Kennedy, then just one of many bright young faces in the Democratic Party, to instant stardom, made him a national figure, television capturing his grace and attractiveness in defeat. He had entered Chicago one of many hopefuls and left a national figure. During the subsequent 1956 campaign Bobby Kennedy had been detached from the Kennedy team to ride with the Stevenson group and study the mistakes they were making, which was an unusually rich assignment, and at one point during the tour Bobby had leaned over to Newt Minow and said that Stevenson was vastly underestimating the impact of television, something with which Minow quickly and painfully agreed. Then Bobby Kennedy said that when he had been a boy there were three major influences on children— the home, the church, and the school—and now there was a fourth—television. The decade moved quickly, and within a few years television would rank among those influences at least second.

They were flying to West Virginia, the presidential candidate and his own private pollster, and their mood was not exactly lighthearted. They had over the past year and a half become unusually close. Never before in American history had a major presidential candidate so depended upon the advice and skills of a pollster, using polling much as an airplane pilot uses radar to chart and comprehend what he can no longer see for himself. But now it all seemed on the verge of blowing up in the candidate's face. A year earlier the pollster Lou Harris had taken a poll of West Virginia and it had showed the candidate Jack Kennedy leading Hubert Humphrey, his only potential opposition in West Virginia, by a margin of some 70 to 30. Indeed, the results were so good that for a time the only concern in the Kennedy camp was whether or not Humphrey could be lured into entering the primary there. When a few months later Humphrey in fact entered the West Virginia primary, the Kennedy people had breathed a collective sigh of relief. In their view they had set a major ambush for Humphrey and he had just walked into it. Perhaps, they thought at the time, they could end the entire primary struggle right then and there in West Virginia. But in Wisconsin, a few weeks before the West Virginia primary, everything went wrong. For the first time in the 1960 election, the issue of John Kennedy's religion had come to the surface. Wisconsin had seemed like Humphrey territory, so similar in politics and economics to his native Minnesota that he had often been called the third senator from Wisconsin. But the religious issue had hurt Humphrey, many good Republican Catholics had seized on the primary as a chance to cross over and vote for Kennedy, and perhaps aided by that crossover, he had carried the state. But the victory in Wisconsin, the winning of it, now haunted him in West Virginia, where a year earlier, at the time of Lou Harris's first poll, no one had known or cared that Kennedy was Catholic. Finding that this handsome young man might in fact do the Pope's work, the good backcountry Protestants of West Virginia had almost completely reversed themselves. With some three weeks to go in the primary Humphrey was leading 60–40, and Kennedy's entire campaign seemed in jeopardy. If the bandwagon stopped in West Virginia, so great was the potential opposition to him that it might never start again.

Kennedy's very use of Louis Harris as his own private full-time pollster marked a key change that took place in the political balance in 1960. Kennedy's decision to go all out in using Harris's polls to guide in the selection of primaries and issues during the general election was something dramatically new. In 1952 the advertising agency BBD&O had done a little polling for

Eisenhower on a marginal scale and the intellectual critics of America had not
been pleased. It smacked of political manipulation. Now Kennedy was going
all out, Harris was a certified and valued member of the Kennedy inside team,
and was in fact probably far more influential with the candidate than any party
professional. The political party system was in the process diminished, losing
one more of its roles to modern media, of which the new breed of pollsters was
unquestionably a part. The coming of Franklin Roosevelt's welfare programs
had deprived the Democratic Party of one of its central functions, the ability
to deliver services and jobs to the urban needy; the coming of national television had deprived both parties first of their ability to offer access to aspiring
candidates and second of their ability to control their own conventions, which
increasingly were to become celebrations, not of the parties, but of the national
networks. Now with polling the parties were losing yet another traditional
function, the reporting by the party people at the bottom to their leaders about
what grass-roots Americans were thinking and what was bothering them. That
represented a considerable part of the party's historic reason for being, and an
important aspect of the party's ability to keep a political leader accountable.

Now it was different. Party professionals were quickly being phased out
by professional pollsters who had no need to answer to the average citizen. Nor
were the pollsters like the old-fashioned professional pols who had worked
from the bottom up and knew their wards; the new pollsters came from the
top of the society and they paid attention on behalf of, not the least powerful
people of the society, but the most powerful ones. It smacked of a far more
manipulative society; the pollsters dropped in to listen but they did not stay
the next day to provide any services, as the old pols might have done. The
pollsters were busy modern men, they lived, not in the small towns of America,
but in New York and Washington, and they were close to the most powerful
politicians, public figures, and media executives of those two cities. Indeed, as
more and more powerful newspapers and networks moved into doing their
own polling, the best of the pollsters worked *for* the media and were very much
a part of them. Lou Harris, for example, went from his work with Kennedy
to the employ first of the Washington *Post,* then *Newsweek,* CBS, *Life* magazine, NBC, and finally ABC.

The birth of this was in West Virginia. Jack Kennedy had publicly
released the Lou Harris poll and put Harris directly on the spot. Now *both*
of their careers were in jeopardy. They had been working together for almost
two years. Kennedy looked on most professionals with barely concealed disrespect. Not only were they rarely on his side (they were against him because
of his religion, which more often than not was *their* religion as well), a serious
sin in Kennedy's eyes, but they bored him, which was also a serious sin, and
finally, to his mind they all too often did not keep up with their own profession,
they knew less about their districts (and how those districts could help John
Kennedy) than Lou Harris did. Harris was quite capable of coming in and
using his team of people so effectively that he could tell Jack Kennedy exactly
what he needed to know about the districts, *what they could do for him.* They

had virtually the same turn of mind, Kennedy and Harris, they looked for the same things in numbers, the implications of numbers. Whereas other politicians tended to regard numbers from a poll as static indices, Kennedy was acutely aware of nuance, of subtlety of trend. Whereas up until that time pollsters like Gallup had produced numbers but had deliberately given as little interpretation of them as possible, Harris was fascinated as much by the implications of the numbers as he was by the numbers themselves, he was more sociologist and political analyst than he was mathematician. But he had never before seen a politician read a sheet of numbers like Jack Kennedy; in most cases, Harris had had to spend hours with politicians trying to show them what the numbers meant, and that was never necessary with Jack Kennedy. More, unlike other politicians, Kennedy knew the limitations of polls; unlike Lyndon Johnson and Richard Nixon, he was not mesmerized by them and he did not find in them any final truth. They were, to his mind, merely straws in the wind, not, as Lester Markel of *The New York Times* had once warned, the wind itself.

In 1957 Harris had done a poll of Kennedy-Nixon for Dick Lee, the mayor of New Haven and a friend of Kennedy's, and Kennedy was impressed with him from the start. In 1958, as Kennedy tuned up for a national campaign, he faced a Senate reelection fight. One of the side issues was the question whether he would run a stronger race than Foster Furcolo, the Democratic gubernatorial candidate. They had won their primary elections by very similar margins, and in the general election, with both facing relatively weak opposition, it became a macho thing, how they would run against each other. Most experts thought the two would run in an almost dead heat with virtually the same margins. But Lou Harris had studied the demographics of Massachusetts and had discovered that Kennedy had a chance to eclipse Furcolo dramatically. Kennedy, he suggested, was far more acceptable to new, more independent voters. Those voters lived in the suburbs of Middlesex County and in western Massachusetts. Kennedy, he proposed, should make an extra effort there, even though they were areas that Democrats normally wrote off. Kennedy did, though few were aware of it. Right before the election most newspapers had Kennedy and Furcolo running absolutely even races; Harris had Kennedy winning by some 73 percent with Furcolo in the mid-50's. It turned out to be probably the most accurate poll he had ever taken, and it cemented their relationship.

So as the 1960 campaign started Harris had become an insider, a member of the inner policy group, determining which states they would run in and which to avoid, and which issues they would emphasize. It was an expensive service. Some of the Harris polling was done with extraordinary density, 23,000 people were polled in Wisconsin alone, a remarkable number, but then Joe Kennedy did not intend that his son should lose a presidential race for lack of spending money. The total bill was some $300,000, a huge figure for those days. The Wisconsin polling had been particularly helpful; there were those who thought that without it Hubert Humphrey might have won in Wisconsin. But then the religious issue had risen and was boomeranging in West Virginia. Time was running out and Kennedy was behind and he was very angry about it all. Suddenly it seemed that all his opponents were gathering together to use West Virginia against him as a club, a proof that a Catholic could not win. Not yet at least. There was no tangible sign of Lyndon Johnson there, but the smell of him was everywhere, Robert Byrd of West Virginia was Lyndon's man and he was working there night and day for Hubert Humphrey, with whom he had little ideological or personal connection.

It was as if everything else Kennedy achieved would be thrown out because of West Virginia. Between Wisconsin and West Virginia he had won in Indiana, a state with a comparable ethnic balance and index of prejudice, home of the Ku Klux Klan, but he had won unopposed. Stuart Symington had at the last minute resisted the temptation to challenge him. With Indiana, Kennedy hoped for some concession, even a partial one, from his critics that a Catholic could draw votes in the backcountry. But the night of the Indiana primary he had flown into Washington, and even as he was leaving his plane, an aide had handed him the next morning's Washington *Post*. Kennedy stood there in the headlights of his own plane on the tarmac, reading the editorial that said that Indiana was not the test, *West Virginia* was the test, and as he read, he pounded his right fist into his left hand in helpless rage, cursing the *Post*, the good goddamn liberal Washington *Post*.

So West Virginia it would have to be. They had very little time. They massed all their people, their in-laws and cousins and college roommates, and they invaded West Virginia, and there was no hamlet in that state small enough to withstand the twin invasions: the first, this curious assemblage of well-tailored lean young men with strange Massachusetts accents, and the second, the other delegation, that of Lou Harris's people, nice well-behaved young people who were trying to find out how the good burghers felt about politics and religion. Kennedy was using Harris to find out where he needed to make his effort, and whether he should openly confront the religious issue. Harris had prepared a series of polls designed specifically to test the depth of religious tension. ("Is there a tunnel being dug from Rome so that the Pope can have a secret entrance to the White House if Kennedy wins?" Kennedy was appalled by questions like that. "Lou," he once asked, "how many did you poll with this one?" "About seven or eight hundred people," answered Harris. "You don't think that's a little dangerous, that you might be planting the idea with some of these people?" Kennedy asked. "Well, that's the risk," Harris answered.) Slowly, gradually, Kennedy began to close the gap. But a few days before the election Humphrey was still ahead. Harris at that point was pushing very hard for Kennedy to meet the religious issue head on. Everywhere he went, he told Kennedy he found that he had one problem, and one problem alone, his religion. Without it, he would have no problem dealing with Humphrey. Most of Kennedy's Washington office, including Bobby Kennedy, were strongly opposed to raising the issue, claiming that it would only fan the flames. What Harris was reporting was that the flames were already there. You could not ignore the issue, because it was already *there*. That was Kennedy's own strong impression, but the polls confirmed it. His father was bitterly opposed to his raising it; Joe Kennedy, who had been victim of so much prejudice in his own lifetime, hated the idea that his son might even seem to be apologizing for his religion.

But Kennedy went ahead anyway. In the last few days he began to discuss his religion openly, telling his audiences that he could not believe that he had forfeited his chance to become President of the United States the day he was baptized. Then two days before the election he made a dramatic statewide television appearance with Franklin Roosevelt, Jr. He talked about how serious an issue this was, of how deeply he believed in separation of church and state. He then repeated the oath of office, swearing on an imaginary Bible, held in Roosevelt's hands. Then he told his audience that if he ever violated that oath of office he could and should be impeached. Then Kennedy repeated the part of the oath which ended "so help me God." He paused and said, his voice very soft, that anyone who violated the oath of office, in addition to his civil offense, was committing a sin against God, for he had sworn the oath on the Bible. He paused again and quietly repeated that phrase: "A sin against God, for he had sworn on the Bible." That did it. The next day, checking voters in the tiny precinct of Chesapeake, Harris could feel the change. He knew Kennedy had it. Late that night, feeling jubilant, Harris returned to Charleston and as he was walking down the main street he spotted Hubert Humphrey and one aide, both exhausted, both carrying their own luggage. "Lou Harris! Lou Harris!" Humphrey shouted, ebullient as ever. "I wish to God that I were rich enough to afford you, because if I did I could win this election." "Hubert," Harris answered, "if you swear to God, you're raising the religious issue."

Jack Kennedy had run in 1960 with two fundamental problems facing him: he had to destroy an age-old prejudice against a Catholic becoming President; he had to overcome a suspicion of what was considered his youth and immaturity. The Catholic issue was critical, particularly within the Democratic Party, where the principal kingmakers were all Catholic and thus exceptionally nervous about rippling the Protestant waters. What he had to present to the party apparatus was a fait accompli, a clear popular mandate to show that he was a winner, so that either they would be smart enough to want him or at least, failing that, they could not turn him down without shattering the party. In challenging the party apparatus, the primary route was crucial, and television was crucial to that. It was also crucial in helping Kennedy over the other hurdle—by its emphasis on the cosmetics of a candidate, it helped significantly lower the age that Americans deemed mandatory for a major politician.

Johnson chose not to challenge Kennedy in the field, believing him to be just a brash young man and that the seriousness of Johnson, who dominated the Senate, would be clear to the party; so the only major figure running against

Kennedy in the primaries was Hubert Humphrey. Humphrey was the embodiment of the politicians of the thirties; he had learned nothing from the days of Roosevelt, nothing new from 1948 on. He still gave the old radio speech, and not a particularly good one at that, a little too hot and a little flowery and a little too long, and he still talked about himself in the third person, it was just a matter of taste and banality, the idea of Jack Kennedy or Adlai Stevenson regularly referring to himself in the third person was inconceivable. So he gave the radio speech though the radio speech was dead; it had died at the 1956 convention when Frank Clement of Tennessee had keynoted the convention with a thundering overheated, overlong, overkill speech from the past and overnight ended his career as a national politician. Humphrey, in contrast with Kennedy, did not know how to hold the respect of most reporters covering him, he did not entirely trust them or confide in them, and they found little quality of depth to him, that which he said on the platform was what he said to them in private. The qualities of introspection and reflectiveness that they particularly treasured were missing. To them he was of good heart, high-spirited, but somewhat weak, probably a little glib; he did not grow in their respect the more they were exposed to him. But he was perceived by reporters covering him to be intellectually promiscuous, a little too eager to please all groups. (He did not readily change; those perceptions of him and his inability to adapt to the technology cost him bitterly in his career. In early 1969, after his defeat for the presidency, he finally agreed to appear on "Face the Nation," and representatives of the show and his press aide conferred at great length beforehand to see if they could limit his soaring Humphreyisms, that is, keep him short. And for once it worked, he was excellent that day, his answers were short and interesting, he seemed to be listening more to their questions instead of to his answers. It was a new Humphrey and afterward his press people and Sylvia Westerman, the producer of the show, congratulated themselves that this was indeed a new Humphrey, but within a week he was on other shows and it was the same old Hubert Humphrey babbling away, talking as if in order not to listen, his own sad way of concealing the considerable intelligence he had.)

Kennedy, by contrast, in 1960 had been working on his television approach for several years, traveling around the country, meeting local pols, but also working out connections with the media, in effect trying out his television style as a kind of road show, knowing immediately that the talking heads and the long thirty-minute formal speeches were out, that people did not want a long semi-formal lecture, that a certain spontaneity was needed—a show, a drama, a cliff-hanger, an element of combat and conflict of will. He discovered that even in a hostile press conference with hostile questions there was drama, and he could benefit from the drama and the hostility. He mastered the greatest art of television, of appearing to be spontaneous without in fact being spontaneous.

In overcoming the suspicions of his religion Kennedy's greatest asset was his looks. He was not only handsome; he did not look like a Catholic, or what non-Catholics feared a Catholic would be; Dick Daley of the Chicago machine looked like a Catholic and a boss, Pat Brown, intensely human, harboring the same ambitions as Kennedy, looked like a Catholic, Al Smith looked like a Catholic, but Jack Kennedy looked like a star. He was stylish and fresh and clean, his tailoring and his coiffing reeked of elegance and tradition, the first Irish Brahmin, the Irishman as Wasp. He more than any of the other candidates knew the importance of appearance, he wore expensive suits, he massaged his scalp and groomed his hair, he buffed his nails. Those bitterly prejudiced against Catholics, those who in Kennedy's phrase thought the Pope already had his suitcase packed and was only waiting for the inauguration, they were hopeless. But there was a far wider segment of the American population that might be considered mildly anti-Catholic. To this group the sight of the young, slim, modern, attractive Kennedy, free as he seemed to be of restraints and prejudices of the past, erased their suspicions. Television helped, it meant that instead of one quick glimpse of Kennedy in the town square, they were able to regard him again and again in their own living rooms, where he did not seem out of place or unwelcome. Indeed, they now might want to vote for him to prove that they had no prejudice.

In addition, slowly, gradually, starting in 1959 television was creating a new role for him as a politician. He was becoming a star. He had, for television and particularly for that era before people became suspicious of glamour, star quality. The excitement he created on television helped him enormously with print. He was dashing, he had an air of mystery; reporters and editors, like their readers, wanted more, not less, of him. He seemed always on the move as if there were miles to go before he slept; he never wore an overcoat or a hat if possible. He was his own casting director and he did the job well. The Kennedys were perceived as exciting and different from ordinary people. They were star-crossed. They were handsome and had handsome wives. Actors and actresses and great athletes and astronauts wanted to be around them. Theirs was like a great dramatic novel being played for the entire nation, being played out, as it were, on television. All of this began with Jack Kennedy; he was so good, so smart, so fresh, so intuitive, as he manipulated from the very first with a powerful new weapon without seeming to manipulate. That was his real skill. Manipulation *au naturel.*


He also knew the great inner truth about the Catholic prejudice and that was not to hide it. Thus after getting the nomination in 1960 he was always looking for the right forum in which to confront the issue. His meeting in that year with the Houston ministers was an example of his mastery of a great new skill in televised politics: deliberately allowing someone else to rig something against you that is, in fact, rigged for you. Their ambush of you becomes instead your ambush of them. One's opponents in a conflict like this are bound to be emotional and overwrought, they will always appear aggressive and fanatical. In contrast, Kennedy appeared calm and cool, with a fine sense of himself, and he had dealt with these questions a thousand times; by contrast, the ministers posing the questions not only were highly emotional but laboring under the impression that Kennedy had never dealt with these issues before. So instead of being thrown to the lions, John Kennedy was being thrown to the Christians, their turf, their anger; the angrier the questions, the ruder the hosts, the better for Kennedy, he would have the sympathy of the real audience, the one watching on television. The Houston audience was, much to its own surprise, a prop audience. Kennedy appeared to be parachuting behind the lines, and some of his aides warned against it; but his instinct was true. This self-confidence was supreme, it worked exactly as he intended; Sam Rayburn, up to then dubious of Kennedy, and probably sharing a few of those prejudices himself, was ecstatic. "He ate them raw," Rayburn said. Kennedy had arranged for the debate to be televised and the moment it was over a Houston advertising official called Kennedy headquarters to let them know it was pure gold. It became a staple of the campaign, hundreds and hundreds of copies of the film were made and it was shown whole, used for spots, played and played again, and, most significantly, used as a means of advancing him —with Kennedy coming into a given area they could build interest in him this way. The film had what television loved, real drama, real confrontation, and there he was, a real live war hero, walking into the pit and winning. With film like this (which you did not have to show if it had turned out poorly), and with money, you could pick your audience, and you could show yourself as you wanted to be shown.

There were two other key moments at which television helped change the balance for Jack Kennedy. The first came on the eve of the convention. Kennedy was far ahead on the delegate count, but he was still shy of the nomination. Just as the convention was to start, Harry Truman attacked Kennedy's youth and inexperience and listed a number of candidates he preferred—Johnson, Symington, Robert Meyner, Chester Bowles. The Kennedy people were furious and, if not scared, certainly concerned. They had worked very hard to have all the pieces come together and they did not at this late date want it all to start coming apart on them. They also knew they had to answer Truman and that this might be a chance for the candidate to exploit an issue which until then had haunted him. Robert Kennedy called Bob Kintner at NBC. (The choice was in part because Kintner as a young reporter in Washington had been a good friend of Joe Kennedy, and in part because the Kennedys, quite justifiably, were very upset with CBS, very unhappy with Stanton's extremely close friendship with Johnson, and felt that they never got a fair break from CBS. They were absolutely convinced that Stanton was Johnson's media errand boy.) So Bobby Kennedy told Kintner that his father had suggested that he make the call, Joe Kennedy had said that Kintner was all right and could be trusted and that *NBC owed the Kennedys free time.* "We don't owe you a thing," Kintner said; when Kennedy started to protest, Kintner recommended that he read the FCC regulations. At which point Kennedy asked if Kintner had any ideas. Well, said Kintner, who had hyped NBC's public affairs coverage and loved instant specials, that was another matter. For example, he said, if Jack Kennedy, the leading candidate for the nomination, held a news conference to answer a former Democratic President, that would be worth covering and certainly NBC would want to cover it. Bobby Kennedy asked Kintner if he would call the other networks. Kintner said no, he could not, it would not be proper. But Kennedy persisted, expressing his doubts about CBS and Stanton, and finally Kintner agreed to call Stanton but insisted that Kennedy himself would have to call Leonard Goldenson at ABC. Kintner also said that he would have to offer a comparable platform to Johnson and Symington, the other announced candidates. Johnson, with his own misconception of modern media and his enduring incapacity to understand Kennedy as a politician and what he had been doing for the last three years, declined the offer of a press conference and on hearing that Kennedy would hold one told Kintner, "Terrific—he'll destroy himself." Kintner called Stanton to say that NBC would cover the Kennedy press conference. Stanton, still committed in his heart to Johnson, was doubtful about it and asked why, and Kintner said because NBC thought it was a good news story. Stanton expressed his reservations about the story, which heightened the growing bitterness in the Kennedy camp over CBS and in particular over Stanton. So on July 4, when Kennedy held a press conference, only NBC was covering it live at first, though midway through CBS started arriving with cameras.

It was a perfect forum for Kennedy: he had been challenged and attacked, and now he was again able to ventilate what had been a dangerous submerged issue. Kennedy was at his best, deft, self-deprecating, funny. Above all, and this was crucial given the particular nature of the charge, he was very much unrattled, very much in control of himself. It was all very cleverly done. Truman had said that it was a closed convention. Well, Kennedy rejoined, Truman apparently considered an open convention to be one where the convention met, studied all the candidates, reviewed their records, and then nominated the candidate of Truman's choice. As for his youth, he pointed out that his fourteen years in the House and Senate gave him more time in national elective office than Woodrow Wilson, Franklin Roosevelt, and Harry Truman at the moment of their ascension to the presidency. He was also, he said, older than George Washington when he led the Continental Army, older than Jefferson when he wrote the Declaration of Independence, and older than Columbus when he discovered America. It was an absolutely marvelous rejoinder, not a speech but a *performance,* as much theatrical as it was political. It allowed Kennedy to enter the convention exactly as he wanted, gracefully, self-assured, and very much in control; en route he manhandled Johnson at a joint session of the Texas and Massachusetts delegations. That things went well at the convention did not, however, mean that Kennedy lost his residual distrust of CBS; it was simply to him one more occasion on which Stanton had tilted toward Johnson and made things as difficult as possible. But the incident at the convention was minor compared with the biggest day that Kennedy had on television that year, his first debate with Richard Nixon.

. . .

It was the day that changed politics. Before it, politicians had looked like
politicians and bosses were still bosses; after it, nothing was the same; the
bosses were on their way downhill and the candidates looked different, the
tailoring was better, cut tighter at the waist, the hair was a little longer
because television made normal-length hair look thin. Even the smells were
different, the old smell of cigars replaced by the smell of cosmetics,
though, in deference to the *machismo* of the candidates, some networks,
like CBS, had an iron rule that no photographers were allowed in the
room where a candidate was putting on makeup. Afterward candidates
and their managers planned schedules not so much by cities or states as by
television *markets;* that was the television word, and it fit—they were
there to sell themselves. Television shifted the entire balance and nature of
political exposure; during an old pre-television campaign, perhaps fifty
thousand people might view a presidential candidate in a given city on a
very good day, and perhaps three to four hundred thousand might see him
in an entire campaign. Now millions and millions could see the candidate
in one night. Replacing the bosses was a new breed of taste arbiter, men
like David Garth and Jerry Rafshoon and Charles Guggenheim, television
advisers to political candidates. Garth, for example, could claim respect
and power so great that his very willingness to take on a candidate made
that candidate a serious contender and meant that money would come in.

The first debate, in 1960, had changed it all. John Kennedy had gone in,
if not exactly an unknown, certainly the underdog, and he had come out
looking a winner, while Richard Nixon had in one brief appearance squand-
ered the advantage of eight years of the vice-presidency, and had come out
looking a loser. The effect was so great that it was sixteen years before two
presidential nominees again debated, though the entire nation wanted more
debates. There was simply too much to lose. The big winner that night in 1960,
of course, had been television, more specifically the networks. Television was
legitimized as the main instrument of political discourse. It was a great night
for the networks, the debates were something they had wanted for years.
Indeed, in 1952 Frank Stanton, the President of CBS, had broached the idea
to Dwight Eisenhower, asking him to debate Adlai Stevenson on television.
Ike, who always deferred to staff expertise, asked if Stanton had checked with
Ben Duffy of BBD&O, his principal media adviser. Stanton said he had. "And
what did he say?" asked Eisenhower. "No," said Stanton. "Well, that's my
answer," said Ike.

The mystery, of course, was why Richard Nixon had agreed to the debates. He had surprised his own staff by doing so. Previously he had emphasized to his campaign aides that there would be no debates, and that no one
on the staff was to mention debates. It was *verboten.* "In 1946, a damn fool
incumbent named Jerry Voorhis debated a young unknown lawyer and it cost
him the election," Nixon told one staff meeting, as if to emphasize how

strongly he felt. The political aides in the room, like Leonard Hall, who had been the head of the Republican Party, felt reassured hearing Nixon talk like that, for there was nothing to win and a lot to lose. Hall was a good deal less assured a few weeks later when Nixon, acting entirely on his own, consulting with no one, announced that he *would* debate Kennedy. Hall was shocked when he heard the news from a friendly reporter. Though Len Hall was principally responsible for keeping Nixon on the ticket in 1956, though no one had worked harder to facilitate Nixon's road to the nomination in 1960 than Len Hall, though he was an acknowledged good, shrewd, professional politician, Nixon had not consulted him at all. It was a symbol of the changing times; the candidate simply needed the political machinery less and less, there was new technological machinery now available that took the candidate directly to the people over the heads of the professional politicians. A foolish decision, Hall thought, giving away something you didn't need to give away. Some of the Nixon people heard that David Sarnoff, the head of RCA, had been the last person to see Nixon before the announcement, and the rumor went round that somehow Sarnoff was the villain, that he had twisted Nixon's arm. Years later Hall accused Sarnoff of costing them the 1960 election, but Sarnoff had said, "I'm not the son of a bitch. If he had asked me whether to debate, I'd have said debate, but it didn't come up."

Ted Rogers, who had been Nixon's television adviser for a decade and who knew Nixon's thinking on television more intimately than most, thought three things had influenced Nixon's decision. First, a kind of arrogance of elation in the wake of the good reception to his acceptance speech at Los Angeles, an occasion when everything had worked perfectly. Second, a fear that if he failed to debate Kennedy the issue would haunt him throughout the campaign, that everywhere he went a hostile press would ask him why he was afraid to debate Kennedy. And third, Rogers thought, Nixon's feeling that something like this was inevitable, that it was a good thing for the country, and that the technology should be speeded along. Nixon had often talked to Rogers about how politics was changing, about days to come when people would vote right in their own living rooms; this, in a way, was a chance to be part of history. Though Rogers was surprised by Nixon's decision to debate and somewhat annoyed that he had not been consulted either, he was not displeased. He was of television, and it was good for television, therefore it was good for him. Besides, he thought the Vice-President was invincible in a situation like this.

Rogers had advised Nixon for ten years at that point, with a diminishing amount of pleasure in his role. He had been one of those bright young men who left World War II and went right into the then brand-new world of television. He had done some commercial shows such as "Amos 'n' Andy" from the West Coast, and he liked very much what he was doing. In 1950, a friend of his named Jim Lamb, who was a member of a group trying to find a Republican candidate for the Senate, called and said that the group was having trouble over the question of political television. Lamb said that the group was divided: half of the people thought TV was totally worthless, and half thought it was of some value but far too expensive. So could Rogers come by and explain this strange new world to them? Rogers went to a breakfast meeting presided over by Murray Chotiner. Rogers himself knew nothing about politics and was not particularly interested in that world, so the stories he told the group were not of political impact but of commercial impact—what happened the day after a new product was advertised, how it was sometimes entirely sold out within hours. The increased power of the visual sense over the audio sense was incredible, almost beyond measurement. He also warned that if they did decide to push a candidate by means of television, it was important to have a consistent campaign plan and follow it through. They could not start and then peter out.

A few days later Chotiner called to say they were planning to run Nixon for the Senate. Would Rogers help? Rogers lunched with Nixon shortly after that and liked him. Nixon seemed young and fresh; he was, like Rogers, a Navy veteran, the kind of young political figure who had been produced by World War II. What Rogers especially liked, because he was thinking in television terms, was that Nixon did not seem like a politician; he was not, in those days, stylized, a poseur, overblown. Rogers felt that Nixon would be reasonably easy material to work with; he had nothing to unlearn. Nixon seemed open, accepted a certain amount of criticism, and was a good listener. Rogers quickly emphasized the importance of brevity in television, telling Nixon that the medium was so forceful that no one needed thirty minutes. Rogers warned him even then that people did not like it when their favorite programs were preempted.

Rogers did not go to Washington after Nixon was elected senator. In fact he was somewhat surprised, in 1952, right after the Republican convention, to get a call from Nixon summoning him to Denver to meet with the Eisenhower team. Rogers stayed with Nixon throughout the campaign, practicing what he called preventive television, that is, trying to make each broadcast as simple as possible, trying to limit artifacts and intrusion. On the famous Checkers speech, he drew a chalk line around the desk and told Nixon that as long as he stayed within the line, the camera could reach him. Rogers had his doubts about putting Pat Nixon on that night, thinking it might be improper. But Nixon insisted. It was, Rogers thought, as if it were the Nixons against the world. In her husband's mind, her honor and reputation had been attacked just as his own had been. Rogers had no idea what Nixon was going to say that night, and when the speech was over, with Nixon bursting into tears at the end, deeply moved by his own words, Rogers, like many others, thought it masterful. It had clearly saved Nixon's place on the ticket, and it had turned the flow of the campaign around.

But there were doubts about it later. It was as if somehow in saving himself Nixon had paid too high a price. He had made himself even more the issue—not his politics but *himself.* There was a growing feeling among the political and journalistic taste makers of the country that Nixon was not quite acceptable for very high office. He had gone just a little too far. (The taste makers sensed that perhaps Dwight Eisenhower shared their opinion, although Ike welcomed Nixon back on the ticket.) In the daily and weekly *Variety,* the headlines over the two articles on the Checkers speech reflected the reaction. Echoing the titles of popular soap operas, they proclaimed: JUST PLAIN DICK and DICK'S OTHER INCOME.

There was something else that Rogers noticed about the Checkers speech —the powerful impact it had, not just on the nation and not just on Eisenhower, but on Nixon himself. From then on, as far as Rogers was concerned, Nixon became an electronic candidate. He had an immediate consciousness of the power of television. From then on, he did not care much about the writing press (though he liked reporters of all sorts less and less). *He had done it his way,* with no impertinent questions and answers at the end. Suddenly television was magic. Rogers, who liked much of the writing press, noticed immediately Nixon's changed attitude toward reporters. Up until then he had been very cautious and solicitous in the care and feeding of reporters, and reasonably accessible. But from then on it changed. If the bus was ready to roll and they weren't there, he'd simply say, "Fuck 'em, we don't need them." The Checkers episode had taught Nixon first that the national press was potentially antagonistic and harmful to him, personally, and second that he could go over their heads.

When the campaign was over, Rogers was glad to get back to California; he wanted no part of Washington. He was not entirely sure now that he liked Richard Nixon, who was not an easy man to reach, growing more and more distant, more and more turned into himself, more and more suspicious. From the start, Rogers had been disturbed by certain of Nixon's idiosyncrasies; now they were getting worse. Even as a young candidate he had been sure that the technicians in a television studio were going to try something on him—pull a plug, kill a mike—and Rogers had constantly argued with him that they were professionals. No, Nixon argued, they were labor, they were Democrats. He had always been painfully shy—about himself, about his habits and looks. It was almost unbearable for him to talk about anything personal. It was as if talking about such things, or about his own body, was sissyish, as if these were fears and restraints picked up as a boy and not outgrown as a man. Rogers could not remember another man who seemed to have such a strong aversion. Rogers wanted Nixon to let his hair grow longer for television, but Nixon did not want even to think about it or hear about it. Then there was the problem of perspiration. Nixon did not seem to sweat heavily under normal conditions, but conditions of tension and stress made him sweat profusely, a psychological sweat. (When Jack Kennedy entered the TV studio for the second debate, he was annoyed to find that the temperature was about sixty degrees and that some Nixon people had been in there during the afternoon, tampering with thermostats, trying sweat control.) But discussion of sweating was forbidden; it was simply too painful for Nixon to deal with. These problems had always existed, but now, as the decade of the fifties wore on, Rogers noted in the man far more anger and hostility.

Rogers kept in some touch with Nixon during the early vice-presidential years. He sensed that the office had not brought Richard Nixon very much happiness, that it had only made him a more difficult man, more aware of the antagonism toward him. For all the cheerleading Nixon did for the President, he was excluded from decision making, excluded from social pleasures at the White House, summoned forth by Ike only for some unpleasant task.

Rogers returned to work in the 1956 campaign. The job made him uneasy. The candidate seemed more and more difficult, less and less accessible; there were more periods of black despair, and they lasted longer. Jim Bassett, the Los Angeles *Times* editor who had been seconded to run the campaign and who was Rogers's closest friend in the Nixon camp, seemed shaken one day and confided to Rogers that Nixon had thrown a prolonged tirade against the press in his room at the old Brown Palace Hotel in Denver. Some anti-Nixon story in the paper had touched it off and the scene had been genuinely scary, not the simple flashing anger most politicians displayed, but the uncapping of a well of deep overwhelming resentment. He was like a caged animal, Bassett reported, a man profane and insecure who had totally lost whatever control he once had. There had been minor scenes of the sort in the past but nothing like this. Later in the campaign Rogers saw exactly what Bassett was talking about. Rogers had arranged for a televised appearance of Nixon and a group of college editors at Cornell, Rogers's old school. It was to be all open questions and answers.

"How are you going to control it?" Nixon asked before the show started; Rogers said he wasn't.

"What if there are left-wing plants?" Nixon asked, and Rogers said that he should answer the questions as best he could, that if they were posed in too hostile and loaded a way it would only make Nixon look better.

The conference was a heated but successful appearance. Television critics wrote that it was Nixon's best appearance during the campaign. Despite his unhappiness, Nixon had in fact handled himself well, but when it was over he had gone after Rogers in their small private plane, screaming at him, "You son of a bitch, you put me on with those shitty-ass liberal sons of bitches, you tried to destroy me in front of thirty million people." He had to be physically pulled off Rogers by Phil Potter of the Baltimore *Sun,* and it was a terrifying moment for everyone.

Ted Rogers had not intended to work for Nixon in 1960. Normally the higher the office, the more challenge and the more fun, but Rogers, like others, had found that as Nixon rose in politics it became less fun; he turned inward, the bitterness grew, he confided less, he seemed less accessible, and he seemed more and more to need scapegoats. So this time Rogers turned down the offer to handle television. But in the spring Len Hall flew to California, went to Rogers's boss (who was a good Republican), and arranged for a transfer without Rogers's permission.

By the time Rogers reached Washington, he was excited again. The chance to handle a presidential campaign had challenges of its own; his television suggestions were to be used at the highest level—that was a challenge. So, in early June, the campaign leadership, all old and loyal Nixon people, assembled for an informal meeting with the candidate to try to outline the kind of campaign they would run: Hall, Bassett, Jim Shepley, Bob Finch, Rogers. It was the kind of meeting they had held many times before, Nixon talking informally, the others responding. Rogers in particular was thinking about the convention, about how to modernize it, to make it shorter and more interesting and cut out some of the boredom. It was a convention, he pointed out, that was more likely to be a ratification than anything else. It was like old times, the give-and-take, with Bassett wisecracking in the background. Rogers found himself excited to be back. The following Monday there was a phone call from Len Hall and Hall sounded a little embarrassed. This time, Ted, Hall said, the boss isn't all that interested in your ideas. What? Rogers asked. Well, said Hall, more embarrassed, this time it's different, this time he's going to make all the decisions himself—he's only interested in your ability to execute them. Besides, Hall added, even more embarrassed, he didn't think you were respectful enough to him. At that point Rogers said he might as well go home, he had no intention of being a highly paid go-fer. But Hall argued that it would loosen up as the campaign went along. He said Nixon had just emerged from eight years with Ike where he had been the most visible go-fer in the country, and now he was reacting to those years of servitude. He was not allowing anyone the title of campaign manager. He wanted all the credit himself. Nixon was bitter about the past, bitter about Ike, openly contemptuous of Ike's political ability. Both Bassett and Rogers were staggered by the transformation; Nixon had changed in a decade from a reasonably approachable young man to a political megalomaniac. No one could tell him anything. He had decided that he was the ultimate politician. (Bassett was even more shocked a few weeks later when he was in a room with Nixon and the candidate looked around, noted that all of the handful of people in the room were Catholics, and then proceeded on a twenty-minute deadly serious monologue on what a great Pope he would have been, how well he would have run the Vatican.) Both Bassett and Rogers wanted to go home, but Bob Finch was sent around to say how damaging it would be if two high officials resigned. So both men stayed, reluctantly.

As the campaign progressed, there was one immensely important change in the relationship of Richard Nixon to the men closest to him. This was the decline of Leonard Hall and the rise of a young assistant named Bob Haldeman. The shift symbolized the decline of the role of the party and the rise of the importance of new national media. Len Hall was then the leading Republican Party official in the country, known by everyone and liked by almost everyone. In the late fifties the party structure still mattered, it could still deliver, and Leonard Wood Hall *was* the party. He had literally grown up in it, his father had been Theodore Roosevelt's gardener at Oyster Bay, and the party was his true heritage. He was an immense man who was too smart to be as jolly as he seemed; he had once been a New York congressman, but his true interest was the party. Eisenhower, as President the titular head of the Republican Party in the fifties, had completely deferred to Len Hall on all political matters. That had increased Hall's influence immensely. He was a moderately conservative man himself, and close to Richard Nixon. He thought him the best solution to the seriously divided Republican Party, acceptable to both main factions. During the Eisenhower years probably no one in the country did as much to advance Richard Nixon's career as Len Hall. In 1956 Eisenhower had wanted to leave Nixon off the ticket; he did not particularly like him, and besides some of his eastern associates like Sherman Adams were pushing him to get rid of Nixon. Eisenhower summoned Hall and told him he wanted Nixon off the ticket. Moreover, he wanted Hall to break the news to Nixon himself. It was one of the least welcome tasks imaginable for Hall, but, accompanied by Bob Humphrey, another party official, he called on Nixon to tell him the news. Nixon was shattered. His face turned very dark. "He's never liked me," he said to Hall, "he's always been against me." At that point, acting on his own and in what he considered the interest of the party, Hall set out to save Nixon's skin, and started his own private campaign to keep Nixon on the ticket. He kept Eisenhower's request a secret and he decided to prove to Eisenhower that he needed Nixon on the ticket and that anyone else would tear the party apart. Hall privately commissioned a series of polls designed to measure the appeal of various vice-presidential candidates, including Frank Lausche, a Democrat. His polls showed Nixon running far ahead of anyone else, with Lausche second. Hall showed the polls to Eisenhower and Ike grasped his meaning instantly. Nixon stayed. Hall had saved Nixon's job and thus virtually assured him of the 1960 nomination.

He went to work early for Nixon and by 1959 he was calling in every due bill he had among the party faithful. When Nelson Rockefeller made his abortive try for the nomination in late 1959, it was Len Hall who drove him out, Hall who steadied his troops in the field when Rocky made his raids, and who day after day showed Rockefeller the evidence of Nixon's strength among the county chairmen. There was, it turned out, precious little gratitude on the part of Nixon for all that help. Len Hall would not be his campaign *manager,* Nixon himself would be filling that position.

Richard Nixon seemed in 1960 to be the luckiest of young men. He was only forty-seven years old, he had been Vice-President for eight years, with the presidential nomination virtually tied up. For eight years he had been able to build up his national image and national connections. In his own mind, however, he was a victim. He felt he had been badly treated both professionally and personally by Eisenhower and the men around him, consulted only when they needed him, otherwise kept in the servants' quarters. All this had sharpened his resentment. He had entered politics to rise above what he had been, and he had succeeded, but he also had not succeeded. He was Vice-President but he had never been invited to the social quarters in the White House. He had remained the outsider, and Ike's aloofness always reminded him of his lack of real status, of how fragile his purchase on the society was. Not just Ike but Mamie as well, it had been there in everything they did. When the Nixons were preparing for the South American trip, Pat had called Mollie Parnis, the dress designer, who catered to the wives of many of Washington's most powerful figures, asking for some help in clothes. Miss Parnis had mentioned this to Mamie Eisenhower, for whom she regularly designed, and Mamie was appalled by the idea. "No, no, dear," she had said to Miss Parnis, "don't do that. Let the poor thing go to Garfinckel's and buy something off the rack." Now finally he was out of Eisenhower's shadow, he was his own man, there was no access even for someone as loyal as Len Hall.

Hall watched the erosion of his position with great sadness and some sense of annoyance; now that Nixon had the nomination he did not need the party or its advice. He did not need journalists. All he needed was television and enough money to buy the time. He became closer to Haldeman. Like many in the early Nixon group, Hall considered the union of Nixon and Haldeman particularly tragic, one man so private and desperately shy, the other so rigid, narrow, and unbending. ("Nixon," James Shepley later said of that campaign, "was by nature an excluder. Haldeman liked to exclude people. When Nixon's needs met Haldeman's abilities, you had an almost perfect formula for disaster.") It was to Hall like darkness reaching for darkness, Nixon so vulnerable to isolation, Haldeman so given to it. Hall told friends that he thought Haldeman was the goddamnedest man he had ever seen in politics. He had an instinct, not for politics, not for the fun of the game, the give-and-take and byplay, the dealing with diverse groups and keeping them in line, but for power, for being as close to the source of power as he could and cutting out anyone else. It had always been a problem getting Nixon to deal with groups that he did not like or felt were different; now here was a man Nixon liked and admired who told him he didn't have to do it. Hall had always been bothered by one problem, which was that Nixon did not sleep well. Because he did not sleep well he kept a Dictograph near his bed, and he often woke up and dictated memos. These memos had in the past been among the angriest and most paranoiac documents around and Nixon's friends agreed to ignore them as much as possible. Haldeman seemed to relish acting on them, letting the midnight Nixon live. Whereas the nature of the political act was to bring people in, Haldeman seemed to want to keep them out. He never bothered to argue or explain or persuade. He seemed to like orders, either giving them or taking them. If he represented Nixon at a meeting and a subject came up, you could never tell whether he was speaking for himself or Nixon. In the final days there were signs that the campaign was picking up, particularly in Texas, California, and Illinois, three very important, powerful states. Hall and a few others pleaded desperately with Nixon to discard his promise of visiting all fifty states by going to Alaska in the final days of the campaign. Instead they asked him to concentrate his last precious hours in those big swing states. But he could not reach Nixon and he could only reach Haldeman and Haldeman did

not even bother to argue. Nixon was going to Alaska, he said, and that was
that.

It was a terrible campaign, Hall thought. The only time he could reach
Nixon was after a major mistake had been made. Then for a brief period Nixon
would be receptive. Nixon wanted to do everything himself, he wanted no
other voice, no other partner. In those same final weeks, as Hall had smelled
the chance for a victory, he had pushed hard to get Eisenhower to campaign
more, believing that in a close election Ike might make the difference between
winning and losing. Hall had found that Ike was amenable to the idea. Ike,
it turned out, had been wounded by Kennedy's attacks upon *his* record and
he had become partisan. Hall had finally arranged a meeting of the two men
and he was confident that this would do it, that Nixon, as they had agreed,
would ask Ike to step in and campaign more. So they had gathered, and Nixon
began by saying, right off, "Mister President, I think you've done enough
already." Ike flushed a violent red, but he said nothing and the meeting quickly
broke up. Hall had barely returned to his office when the phone rang. It was
Eisenhower demanding that he come back to the White House immediately.
When he arrived the President was still in a rage. "Did you see him? Did you
see him?" Ike did an imitation of Nixon, hunched over, shoulders bent, head
down. "Did you see that? When I had a front-line officer like that in World
War II, I relieved him." Then he paused and he smiled a little. "He doesn't
look like a winner to me."


Rogers's opposite number in the debates was Bill Wilson, who had in 1952 and
1956 been television adviser to the ultimate reluctant dragon of American
politics, Adlai Stevenson. Wilson and Ted Rogers had not met before the 1960
debates, and charged as they were with the responsibility of arranging them
and setting the ground rules, they approached each other with great caution.
By the end they were friends, brought together by mutuality of problems—
frustrations with their candidates and distrust of the networks. Both men
sensed that the networks were more interested in promoting themselves than
either Richard Nixon or Jack Kennedy, an impression that was later confirmed
when, during the moments of greatest tension just before several of the debates,
the candidates would arrive to find some high network executive in the studio,
ready to introduce one of his chief advertising clients to a potential President.
The two television advisers were also, and this was important, different from
those around them. They were incredibly young. Wilson was twenty-nine in
1960 and Rogers was thirty-one. They were not political, and in their very
presence hung a kind of heavy threat to the older professionals. They looked
different and they dressed different and they *were* different. They discovered
very early in the game that the networks were trying to split them apart, to
use one of them against the other, and they soon learned to be wary.

In particular they were both anxious to have the camera take what were
called reaction shots, that is, let the camera focus on Kennedy while Nixon

was talking, and vice versa. The network executives didn't like the sound of this. It seemed potentially editorial and they were nervous about becoming too editorial, too involved; they wanted the prestige but with as little responsibility as possible. But both Rogers and Wilson insisted that it was the natural thing for the camera to do, since it was the instinctive thing for the audience to do, to check the reaction of one candidate while the other was making points against him. Reaction shots they wanted, reaction shots they would have.

Wilson sensed early in the negotiations that the Nixon people were less confident about the debates, perhaps because they had more to lose, and he was under dual orders from Kennedy: not to lose the debates, and to press every advantage by keeping the Nixon people off balance. Wilson was confident in large part because his candidate was confident (later he decided that the lack of confidence on the part of the Nixon people might have been an extension of Nixon's own insecurity). Jack Kennedy had not yet admitted Bill Wilson to his inner circle; Wilson had not been with the Kennedys long enough for that, and he was still a little tainted by his Stevenson association—weren't the Stevenson people losers?—but enough other Kennedy people trusted him and so Kennedy did too. And Jack Kennedy, Bill Wilson quickly recognized, was absolutely sure he could take Richard Nixon on television.

One thing had impressed Wilson during those endless meetings with the network and Nixon people and that was how much access Rogers seemed to have to Nixon; he was always saying yes, but he would have to check that with the boss. The truth was quite different. As the first debate approached, Ted Rogers, who was largely responsible for the debates, was in truth totally impotent. He not only had no authority of his own, he had no connection with the candidate. He had no access at all. He could not meet with him. He could not reach him by phone. The situation was, Rogers thought, suicidal, particularly since television had made this politician; he owed his career to it, he believed in it. When Rogers called the plane to leave messages, he was never sure if they got through. Nixon had been ill at the beginning of the campaign, and the word filtering back to headquarters was that he was not recovering well, that his strength was still limited. Still, he continued to press on relentlessly in an exhausting campaign. It was as if his schedules had been made up by people who had never heard of television and how it could lighten a candidate's burden. Rogers saw Nixon occasionally on the evening news shows and did not like what he saw. He thereupon would call his liaison aboard the campaign plane, Bill Rogers (no kin, later Secretary of State), and Bill Rogers, who was increasingly regarded in the Washington headquarters as a man who pretended to have access and control when indeed he lacked it, always assured him that Nixon was fine. Has he lost weight? No, he's fine. Have you got him on a milk-shake diet? No problem. Ted Rogers himself flew out to Kansas City to talk with Nixon about the first debate and never saw the candidate. I know your problem, Rose Mary Woods said, but there's nothing I can do. There was no discussion. It was to be the most important event of the campaign and the television adviser could not reach the candidate. Rogers asked that Nixon come to Chicago early to rest and relax and go over the details. He was never sure the message even got through. So it was that Edward A. Rogers, who was in charge of television for Richard Nixon on the most important night in Nixon's life, finally got to see his candidate at four-thirty on the afternoon of the debate. He was allowed thirty minutes with him. The main thing the Republican nominee for President wanted to know was how long it took to drive from the Blackstone to the studio. Rogers was shocked; the candidate looked better suited for going to a funeral, perhaps his own, than to a debate. His face was sickly gray and seemed to sag. He was nearly exhausted. He had lost some twenty or thirty pounds and his frame had hardly been robust to begin with. His shirts, and this was crucial, were two or three sizes too large, thus emphasizing the appearance of illness. His campaign people had not even bothered to buy him new shirts. Rogers was stunned; this was a sick man and nobody had said anything.

That night, on the way to the studio, Nixon struck his knee on the edge of the car door and a look of terrible pain crossed his face. He turned even more gray. Rogers asked if it was the same knee he had injured earlier and Nixon said yes. Inside the studio the candidates were asked if they wanted makeup. Each said no; each was afraid to use it for fear the other might then turn it down and the headlines would read: KENNEDY TAKES MAKEUP, NIXON REFUSES IT. The difference was that Kennedy had just come from campaigning in an open car in California, and his skin was always marvelously receptive to the sun. Rogers was not surprised. He had been hearing from friends out in L.A. that Kennedy was experimenting with something new called Man Tan. Anticipating just such a thing, Rogers had made sure an aide named Ev Hart was on hand. Nixon trusted Hart, and Hart quickly made Nixon up with Shavestick. Rogers was worried, but there was little choice; there was the danger of perspiration, but without any makeup the camera would make Nixon look like a Herblock cartoon.

The problems that Bill Wilson was having were immensely simpler. He was dealing with a more confident candidate. He might be something of an outsider in the inside Kennedy world, but he had all the professional access he needed, and his candidate understood precisely what was wanted. Wilson sensed that Kennedy was bothered by him because he came from the Stevenson camp, and even more because he came from the world of television rather than from politics; thus there was no real way to calibrate his professionalism or his toughness of mind. Kennedy was worried that someone from the world of television, who dealt with comedians and show people, that sort, might try and get him to do something out of character. He took small gestures seriously; he would not hold his hands too high, as Ike did—that seemed unnatural and imitative. He was always bothered about what kind of greeting to give to laborers. He didn't want to just wave—these were working people and that might seem too weak a gesture—so he finally decided on a semi-clenched fist. People from the world of television might not understand such restraints. (One night during the campaign, when Kennedy was going to make a television appearance in Harrisburg, Pennsylvania, Wilson got a phone call from Bobby Kennedy, who asked if Wilson had done similar shows for Stevenson, which was not, in Bobby's opinion, any particular recommendation, and then Bobby said, "Well, okay, but you better not fuck up." Just to be safe, Bobby called David Lawrence, who was still the political boss of Pennsylvania, to make sure that Lawrence leaned on Wilson a little. And Lawrence did, with a mildly threatening phone call. Wilson did not know whether to laugh or cry; as if Dave Lawrence knew anything about television. In later years, as he advised other candidates, Wilson noticed that he was being treated with less suspicion. Instead, there was an attitude almost of *dependence,* as if the candidates believed that the television advisers could remake them using some special magic.)

But that night in Chicago, Bill Wilson was quite pleased; his candidate had come to Chicago early, rested and tanned. He had, in a relaxed way, drilled himself with potential questions from his staff (Jim Shepley in the Nixon campaign had prepared comparable material, but Nixon never used it). The station, WBBM, just happened to be Wilson's old station, and he knew all the technicians and the cameramen, so he was confident, which relaxed Kennedy even more. While they were in Kennedy's dressing room at the station, the question of makeup arose and someone said that Nixon would not come out of his dressing room until Kennedy had *his* makeup on, and Kennedy knew what that might mean. Kennedy asked Wilson if the press was out there, and Wilson said yes, and Kennedy said, "Fuck 'em, I won't do it." He was not about to be ambushed by Nixon. But Wilson insisted that he needed some kind of makeup, mostly to close the pores and keep the shine down, and Kennedy asked if Wilson could do it, and Wilson, who knew the neighborhood, ran two blocks to a pharmacy, bought Max Factor Creme Puff, and made Kennedy up very lightly.

"Do you know what you're doing?" Kennedy asked.

"Yes," Wilson said.

"Okay," Kennedy said. Wilson was impressed by how relaxed he was. On such decisions—Max Factor Creme Puff instead of Shavestick—rode the future leadership of the United States and the free world.


A few minutes later, both candidates emerged from their dressing rooms, and Don Hewitt, who was in charge of producing the show, took one look at Nixon and was scared. He looks terrible, Hewitt thought, and if Nixon looked terrible the show might look terrible. He went over to Ted Rogers and asked if Rogers was satisfied with the way Nixon looked, and Rogers, for whom it was all too late, said yes. Hewitt was still worried and he feared a charge that CBS had rigged the show against Nixon, and that the victim, of all innocent people, might be Don Hewitt. So he went to his own two superiors, Sig Mickelson and Frank Stanton, and told them he thought they had real problems with Nixon and that they better take a look. Stanton took a look, then asked Rogers if he was *sure* Nixon looked all right. Rogers said yes.

It was a disaster for Nixon, and in a way a triumph not just for Kennedy but for the new medium; within hours no one could recall anything that was said, only what they looked like, what they felt like. That night the entire nation watched, and presidential politics came into living rooms in an intensely personal way. All feel, all senses. To paraphrase Emerson: "I cannot hear what you are saying because what you are thunders so loudly." Never was it more true. All the insecurities and doubts and inner tensions of Nixon were there for his fellow countrymen to see. He looked terrible. He sweated terribly. The sweat began to roll down his face. Rivers of sweat over a gray face. In the control room, both Rogers and Wilson were monitoring the debate and keeping close track of the number of reaction shots. Rogers had a feeling that at that moment Don Hewitt was the most powerful man in the country politically; he controlled the camera, and the camera was all-powerful. And now, suddenly, something curious happened in the control booth: Wilson and Rogers switched sides. Whereas in the earlier moments Wilson had been demanding reaction shots of Kennedy (cool, patrician, slightly disdainful as Nixon talked), now he was demanding more reaction shots of *Nixon,* and Rogers was demanding more of *Kennedy,* anything to get that brutal, relentless, unsparing camera off the face of Nixon. It was a madhouse in the control room, Wilson pointing at his sheet, shouting at Hewitt, "You owe us two more of Nixon, you've had sixteen of Kennedy and only fourteen of Nixon," and Rogers shouting, "No, no," and Hewitt yelling at both of them to keep quiet so that he could work.

Obviously neither Kennedy nor Nixon entirely realized what had happened that night. Nixon left the studio thinking he had won, though talks with aides quickly disabused him. Kennedy had some inkling of what had happened because as he left the studio Mayor Richard Daley, who had so far shunned him in Chicago, was suddenly there, entering with his phalanx of supporters, which was a strong indication that, at the very least, Kennedy had not lost. The Kennedy group left Chicago and flew to Lorain, Ohio, at 2 A.M. In Lorain, they started the day at 7 A.M., and suddenly they knew what had happened. The crowds were enormous, larger than anything Kennedy had drawn so far, and they were more enthusiastic and more *personal.* Kennedy had been in their homes the night before. They kept pushing toward the car and every twenty or thirty feet someone would yell, "Hey, you really did a job on him last night," or "You really got him last night." It was, thought Pierre Salinger, who was riding with Kennedy, as if people had been watching a prizefight and now were proclaiming the winner.

At almost the same time, the Nixon people were learning what a disaster it had been for their tiger, and clearly there had to be a scapegoat. A convenient one, as he had somehow sensed he would be, was Don Hewitt. For a long time afterward in the Nixon inner circle his was a villainous name; he was blamed for forcing Nixon into a situation where he would use faulty makeup and for focusing the camera on Nixon too often. Though in the end there were only four debates, at one time there was the possibility of a fifth and Hewitt was scheduled to produce it. The Nixon protest against Hewitt was so strong that CBS discussed having someone else handle it. Hewitt protested in turn, saying that to take him off the debate was to admit that CBS had erred, a very dangerous precedent. The CBS people finally agreed and decided to keep Hewitt on the debates. But there was no fifth debate.

One scapegoat was not enough, however, and Ted Rogers seemed likely to become another. There was some talk, particularly from Haldeman, that perhaps they ought to change television advisers, and Nixon himself picked it up. Perhaps Ted ought to go back to California. He did not, however. He stayed on and was given more access to the candidate, but by then it was all too late. The advantage Nixon should have been able to exploit as Vice-President had been blown, and there was no way to undo the damage.

Though Ted Rogers stayed on with the campaign, he did not like any part of it. He was dismayed by the candidate, by the growing meanness of spirit in the operation, and he found himself wondering whether he could, in fact, vote for the man he worked for. He did not vote against Nixon, but when friends asked him whom they should vote for, they found his answers surprisingly tepid and noncommittal. He wanted no more of politics and after the campaign he tried for a nonpolitical job at Metromedia. He was turned down at first, though all his credits were good. No one wanted the man who had managed the worst disaster in television history. So at Rogers's request, Len Hall wrote a letter to the Metromedia people saying this was cruel, that Nixon had been his own television man and simply would not listen to anyone.

A few weeks after the election, Len Hall was down in Florida with Nixon. There were just a few old friends around and they all went out on a boat. Finally, Hall asked the question he had always wanted to ask: Why did you decide to debate? For a long time Nixon simply looked up at the sky, his eyes closed, his face drawn and tense. And Hall waited, but there was never an answer.


Several years later, when Nixon was thinking of running again, he was appearing on a CBS show produced by Don Hewitt. Nixon asked Hewitt several questions about makeup. Hewitt replied that the best makeup in the world was a good natural tan. Nixon seemed to listen carefully, and in years to come Hewitt often wondered whether he was responsible for the houses in San Clemente and Key Biscayne.

# 11 / The Los Angeles Times

The presidential election of 1960 had been disappointing for the Chandlers and for Richard Nixon, and for Nixon things were soon going to be even more disappointing. Nothing reflected this more than the changing role of Jim Bassett, the man who had been groomed to be the next Kyle Palmer, the *Times*'s own controller of California politics. Bassett was a pleasant genial man, much better liked by colleagues than Palmer; he was a Republican, but he was a far more independent man. He had written the best seller *Harm's Way,* and that had given him a degree of independence that few people working for the Chandlers enjoyed. He had first met Nixon in 1948 while serving as political editor of the *Mirror* and he had liked him. To Bassett's eye, Nixon was by California standards rather centrist. Bassett had written a long piece that Nixon approved of. Then, in 1952, Nixon had called Norman Chandler, at the suggestion of Kyle Palmer, and asked for the loan of Bassett, and it was granted, Bassett was immediately transferred to Nixon's staff as a press secretary. The job of press officer in 1952 was relatively easy, the press seemed rather sympathetic, certainly not in any major way antagonistic, most of the reporters thought the accusations of the slush fund minor; they even, in response to Ike's statement that Nixon must be clean as a hound's tooth, formed a Hound's Tooth Club, which served as a kind of bond between the candidate and his traveling reporters. It was a rare moment, when Nixon was one of the boys. Then, in 1954, Eisenhower, bothered by the lack of energy in the Republican Party, asked Norman Chandler for the loan of Bassett to improve the press relations of the Republican National Committee. Chandler had complied, and Bassett was again dispatched; leaves for the greater good of the Republican Party, which was also the greater good of the Republic, were easy to come by. Bassett had spent long hours with Nixon that spring, it was the height of the McCarthy period and Nixon was running all of Ike's dirty errands on it, resentful, forced to make speeches he did not want to make, answering McCarthy, feeling used, which he was, and unappreciated, which he also was. Bassett and Nixon had become closer during this period, and in 1956 Nixon had asked him to return as press secretary but really as an ex officio campaign manager. Nineteen fifty-six had produced a darker Nixon, there were grim scenes, temper tantrums, rages against the press, tirades against Ike. He had been harder to reach, more isolated, more convinced of the brilliance of his own political judgment, more contemptuous of Ike and the people around him. It had been a disquieting experience. Bassett, like Ted Rogers, the television expert, had seen a side of Nixon that was deeply disturbing.

In 1960, when Nixon had called Norman Chandler again and asked for Bassett, the publisher had immediately agreed. But for the first time Bassett had reservations. He had less enthusiasm for the enterprise. Bob Haldeman was clearly on the rise within the Nixon camp. So this time Bassett set some conditions with Norman Chandler before he left. He told Norman that he would go only on the condition that he did not have to stay in Washington if Nixon was elected. He wanted to come back, not to the *Mirror,* but to the *Times,* as political editor, which was Kyle Palmer's title. Norman Chandler agreed and the deal was made and Bassett went off to Washington, this time with an even better title, planning director, ostensibly the number-three man in the campaign hierarchy. Like everyone else who had ever given Nixon good advice, he was isolated during the 1960 campaign and he could not reach the candidate. When Nixon first mentioned his bizarre idea of campaigning in all fifty states, Bassett had argued vehemently against it. Nixon had asked why, and Bassett had said that while Nixon was in Alaska, Kennedy would be in five major eastern states drawing crowds and making news. Nixon had suddenly turned angry and accused him of being a pimp for the eastern press. "That's all you think about, the eastern press," he had said, and he had said it angrily. Nixon had of course gone to Alaska and during that time Kennedy had not gone to five major states, he had gone to eight, and it was symbolic of the way Nixon had turned victory into defeat.

Bassett had returned to California to work for the *Times.* He found it now to be a very different paper. Norman Chandler had switched jobs, Kyle Palmer had retired, and Otis Chandler had taken over. Nick Williams, anxious to break with the past, had retired, along with Kyle Palmer, the title of political editor, which he thought a particularly odious relic of another era. There would instead be a political analyst. That was fine with Bassett, who had no desire to be a kingmaker. He had hardly been back in California a few months when it became clear that he might be joined on the local political scene by Richard Nixon. Nixon, beaten for the presidency, was looking for something to do and he was under growing pressure from people like Len Hall and other major eastern supporters to run for the governorship of California. Hall was convinced that if he was to remain in national politics Nixon needed a platform within the existing political structure. It was a serious misreading of the new structure of politics; Hall, an old-timer, a man of the apparatus, did not understand how diminished the structure was in importance, that in the new age the media were probably more important than structure, that Nixon by simply being Nixon had a platform, a former Vice-President, a presidential candidate, a man with ready access to all media, national and local, a man in effect with a portable platform. He did not need to be governor of California to be a national figure; indeed, if anything, the job might limit him, it might tie him to local issues instead of liberating him to comment on national and international ones.

Besides, Len Hall and Lee Folger, who were the men principally pushing for the race, did not understand California politics, they had an essential eastern disrespect for it, they thought things were as they used to be, that the *Times* could dictate its choice, and that the incumbent, Pat Brown, was an obvious clown. In the Nixon inner circle when the final choice was being debated, Bassett, wearing his two hats, attended, and he found himself virtually alone in opposing the race. Why shouldn't he run? Nixon asked. "Well, for one thing," Bassett said, "you might lose." There was a moment of stunned silence. *Richard Nixon lose to Pat Brown?* Pat Brown was a bumbler, everyone knew that (even Pat Brown knew it and used it to his advantage, he was very shrewd and he knew it humanized him, he had brought self-deprecating humor to a fine art as a political weapon). "The second reason," Bassett continued, "is that you'll have to deal with things you like least in politics—local issues, roads and water. Things you don't like even at the national level. No foreign policy. Even if you win you're going to lose because you'll be tied to issues that you hate." As he talked Bassett had a sense that Nixon shared his reservations, that it was not a race he particularly wanted to make, but the pressure was very heavy, and besides, there was nothing else he knew or wanted to do. All his life he had been running for things, he had no other passion or interest, he was alive only when he was running.

There was one other person who advised him not to make the race. That was Norman Chandler. Nixon went by to see Norman, for what he assumed would be the conventional blessing and laying on of hands; Nixon would coyly pose the idea of the race, Norman would beam happily at the prospect of the prodigal son returning to California. So Nixon posed the idea and Norman said no, he did not think it was a particularly good idea (the Chandlers, after all, were quite happy with Pat Brown, who paid them regular homage). Perhaps, he suggested, it was not a race that was exactly right for Nixon. Did he really want to be governor of California? There was something else that he did not mention to Nixon, that the *Times* was a very different paper, the rules had changed, it was Otis's paper now and he could no longer hand-deliver the *Times* to Nixon as he had in the past.


Indeed the rules had changed. Nixon had already gotten a light taste of that. He had bought a house on a special deal in a prosperous new Los Angeles subdivision called Trousdale (a subdivision made possible in part by the Teamster welfare fund). It was, like a number of his financial dealings, questionable. It was a knockback deal and Nixon got a $300,000 house for about $90,000, the owners of the subdivision wanted his name to give their new area respectability. Nothing really out-and-out illegal, just slightly tainted, and this time there were stories about it, and some appeared in the *Times,* raising some questions. When the first story appeared, Nixon called Frank McCulloch in genuine bewilderment. "What's wrong with what I did?" he asked. McCulloch answered that it was not really very attractive. "Why not?" he asked, "I'm a private citizen." McCulloch answered, "Well, you're not entirely a private citizen, Dick. You have been Vice-President of the United States and you may well have a political future." "I don't see what's wrong," Nixon said. "Well, I wouldn't do what you did," McCulloch said. (Later during the campaign when Nixon became embittered over the political coverage of the *Times,* he called up McCulloch to ask if this new coverage were in some way tied to his purchase of the house, and McCulloch, half surprised, half appalled by the question, had to explain no, it was not.)

But the times had changed. Richard Nixon had never been placed under any real scrutiny before, scrutiny by reporters on issues that they knew and understood, in some cases issues that they knew and understood better than the candidate. In the past when he had run in California, there had been no scrutiny, no analysis, no holding him to the record; on the contrary, he had been the instrument of the leading papers, they had cleared the way for him and had devastated his opposition. When he had campaigned no reporter had stayed with him day by day to hold him to a given record, or to ask him questions about inconsistencies. Even when he had run for the vice-presidency, it had been a different press corps, satisfied by and large with the charges, the headlines they would bring: NIXON CLAIMS, NIXON CHARGES, NIXON ATTACKS. Always the Reds to stand up to. Just meet the deadline and get the lead. In 1958 there had been the beginning of an attempt to hold him to the record; the word had filtered back to Washington that the 1956 campaign had been particularly ugly, that Nixon in some of the far western states had been particularly brutal in red-baiting a number of Democratic senators, of slicing the truth in his charges.

But there was no real record, and so in 1958 *The New York Times* had assigned staff men to follow him everywhere and to bring a tape recorder with them—actually it was an old-fashioned wire recorder—and whenever Nixon spoke the *Times* man would hold the mike high enough to catch him. This greatly angered him. One of the reporters assigned was Russell Baker, later to be the *Times* humorist, a man who felt a certain degree of sympathy for Nixon, and he knew that the candidate hated the wire recorder (indeed, some of the Nixon people in retaliation began to hold a wire recorder on the press in the back of the plane), and once during a Wyoming airport press conference when all the local reporters were asking slow-pitch softball questions, Baker had asked a tough question and Nixon had blown, a quick flash of anger. "That was just the kind of question," he said, "that you had to expect from *The New York Times.*" He had gone into a five-minute tirade about the *Times.* Later he sought Baker out on the plane and apologized, it was a sore throat that was bothering him, he explained, he wasn't feeling well. He had meant no harm. He really liked the *Times.*

Nineteen sixty-two promised to be wide open. The issues in the past had always been beyond the capacity of reporters to question, issues of foreign affairs, Nixon had met with heads of state and reporters had not. Nixon was an expert in foreign affairs and few of them had ever left the United States. Reporters did not know about foreign affairs, they accepted what he said and wrote it down. But California was different, California, as large and complicated in its mechanism as some countries in Europe, a big state with immensely complicated social issues, education, highways, water problems. Most of the reporters had covered these issues personally, they were intimately involved in their complexity, as Nixon was not.

Besides, and this was crucial, the nature of the press corps in America was changing very quickly in that decade. It was going from the old Chicago Page One School—write it and write it fast, and don't worry about the implications —to a new, far better educated, more sophisticated generation. A generation of journalists was flowering who had graduated from some of the nation's best schools and who saw their career, increasingly, as a profession. Journalism as a profession. Which meant that there were obligations and rights and responsibilities that went with it. They were better paid, more responsible, and more serious. They were not so easily bent, not so easily used. Editors were becoming fairer and they could not dominate their reporters as they might have done a generation earlier; reporters were specialists. Journalism as a career had a much greater component of public service. Nowhere was this more evident than on the Los Angeles *Times*. Norman Chandler was no longer publisher, Buff Chandler's interests were shifting from politics to the arts. The new publisher, Otis Chandler, was not interested in kingmaking, he was interested in good, responsible journalism. One of the first steps, aimed at de-Republicanizing the paper, was to staff both candidates running for governor in 1962. If the *Times*, as the leading paper in California, covered both men, then other papers would too. Both Williams and Frank McCulloch agreed in 1962 to measure the length of Nixon and Brown stories to make sure they were equal in length as well as, they hoped, texture. All of which meant that Pat Brown was the first Democrat to get equal time in the Los Angeles *Times*. Kyle Palmer was gone, dying of leukemia; he would die during the campaign. (He had left the paper a few years earlier to go to Hawaii, and Hotchkiss, needing him badly, had begged him to come back, but his original departure had cost Palmer his pension rights and now at the end he was sick and broke. Norman Chandler, a hard man when it came to the rules, had refused to bend, and finally Nick Williams had put Palmer on his own personal payroll as a political adviser.) Jim Bassett was the top political writer, but though he was close to Nixon he was also more independent, and his stories reflected it. All during the year, Kyle Palmer kept calling Bassett, trying to get more pro-Nixon stories into the *Times*, and when that failed he would call Nick Williams to warn him that Bassett was not as good a friend of Nixon as he pretended to be, a circumstance that Nick Williams prayed was true. There was, however, something else new on the *Times* and that was Dick Bergholz. Bergholz was a very tough reporter who had come over from the *Mirror* when it folded. Norman Chandler had been a little uneasy about Bergholz in the beginning —did he really want Bergholz on his staff?—and he had checked with his friends the Copleys, who ran the San Diego *Union*, where Bergholz had previously worked, and they, good conservatives, had vouched for him. But Bergholz was something new in terms of the *Times*'s political staff, tough-minded, aggressive, almost combative. It was not so much what he wrote, which was fair and balanced, but his manner, which bordered on the abrasive. It was not his way with Nixon alone, it was his way with all politicians—saying, in effect, don't worry about me, I can be rough on anyone.

Nixon had started out above all trying to be on his best behavior, trying to wipe out memories of the Nixon past, the Nixon who had cut reporters off during the 1960 campaign. This time it would be the high road, and he would be very accessible. He was available to reporters who wanted to see him, even reporters from the smallest dailies. Autographed copies of the recently published *Six Crises* were mailed to all reporters. A party was held for the press at the new Trousdale house. (Even then the past haunted him. Reporters, looking around the house, began asking where Checkers was, and Pat Nixon answered that Checkers was old and the rug was new and white and Checkers could not be trusted.) But the campaign quickly became a terrible one for Nixon. He was, thought his friends, chagrined about running for governor, his heart was never in it, he never involved himself in the issues beyond a superficial reading of the briefing papers. The whole operation made him more vulnerable than he had been in the past, more vulnerable to a tougher press corps. Early in the campaign Nixon called a group of reporters together and said he wanted to give them a briefing on Brown's campaign, but not for attribution, and Bergholz had quickly said no, none of that, don't pull your Washington game on us, Dick, either we can use it or don't say it. Nixon was stunned—a reporter talking to him like that, particularly a reporter from the Los Angeles *Times*. It was like that for much of the campaign. He would make a speech saying he was going to clean up the mess in Sacramento, and he would get back on the plane and reporters would ask him: What mess in Sacramento? Specifically, which agencies was he talking about? He wouldn't be specific. He had no real interest in the issues of California, that became very clear very early, his knowledge was very thin. Soon reporters began to write that. Sid Kossen wrote a piece for the San Francisco *Examiner* saying that Nixon knew little about the state, had no real interest in the issues, and was talking in the most vague generalities. The next day two of the biggest money people in California appeared at *Examiner* publisher Charley Mayer's office demanding his firing. The publisher said he would not fire Kossen. Then they asked if Kossen could at least be taken off politics and Mayer simply laughed. Kossen was convinced that it had been done directly at Nixon's request.

If he had tried to be sunny at the beginning of the campaign, that did not last long, the polls were not good, he had no real issues, Pat Brown was not such a bumbler after all. Pat Brown, it turned out, had taken speech lessons and lost thirty pounds. He was a marvelously earthy politician, the exact opposite of Nixon, who cherished his privacy and whose attempts at being one of the boys always seemed so stilted. Pat Brown was wonderful with the boys, if anything he was too much one of the boys (the style of his son Jerry was almost the exact opposite). Pat Brown was gregarious and available and politics was always fun. As the campaign began to go badly, Nixon seemed to

darken, the line went harder. Jack Langguth, then a young reporter for the
*Valley Times Today,* and later a successful novelist, saw Nixon in the beginning as a man caught between two conflicting spirits, a good one and a bad
one, but as the polls sank and the darker spirit dominated, Langguth decided
he was wrong, it was simply a conflict of two strategies. Now, as Nixon was
falling, he was seizing on the Communist issue. He began to charge that Pat
Brown was soft on Communism, and then he held one of those alfresco
informal airplane press conferences, not just Nixon the candidate, but Nixon
the campaign manager: Well, fellows, this is the issue that's taking hold and
we're going to hit it very hard, this is the good one. The questioning from
Bergholz and others became very tough on the issue of Brown's Communism.
Bergholz asking: Is he a Communist? No. Is he a Communist sympathizer?
No. What I mean, fellows, is I don't think Governor Brown understands
Communism. I've dealt with the Communist leaders. I know what they're like.
Which was certainly essential to being governor of California. It was very
tough questioning, unlike anything he had ever had before in California, and
other reporters watching Bergholz question Nixon could almost see him flinch.
It was not just what Bergholz wrote, but even more his manner. To most
politicians that was simply Bergholz being Bergholz, Bergholz was rough with
all politicians, part of the game, but to Nixon, with that terrible sensitivity,
everything always so personalized, it was not Bergholz being Bergholz, it was
Bergholz being against Nixon. It was *personal,* a vendetta, and there were
complaints from high Nixon people to Norman Chandler about Bergholz, but
nothing was done, the die was cast, the paper had changed. Nixon was convinced that Bergholz was trying to help Brown, picking up things on the Nixon
campaign and phoning them in to the Brown people, which was not true. The
Nixon campaigns in the past had always been based upon the destruction of
the opposition. The opponent, rather than Nixon, became the issue. That was
a Kyle Palmer specialty, lesson one. Thus the Communist issue was the great
ace in the hole, the opponent was always on the defensive.

But in this campaign the electorate was more sophisticated and so was the
press, and Pat Brown was not that easy a target. He had been governor of
California for four years, which meant that he had not been in office too long,
and he had been a good governor, a serious humane public figure. There were
no scandals in his administration and no one was very angry at him. The image
he projected was of a man able, affable, and good-hearted instead of brilliant.
When Nixon went to the Communist issue Brown defused it well with the
reporters. He told of being scared when Nixon announced that he was going
to drop a major bomb on the Brown camp: he had woken up in some motel
on the road and felt a warm arm next to him. "Damn that Nixon," he thought,
"he's slipped a hooker in on me, that's his big bombshell." He had discovered
in the midst of his panic that it was his wife who had joined him late at night.
Then he added, his voice filled with disbelief and scorn: "Can you imagine
anything dumber than him going around charging me with being soft on
Communism. Me, a practicing Catholic." He was eminently better with the

press than Nixon was; Nixon would try for at least ten minutes a day to be a good fellow with reporters, always a little stiff, always stilted, as embarrassing to the press as it was to Nixon. Pat Brown, at the end of the day when they were exhausted and yet bound to each other by the schedule, joining the boys at the bar, telling stories in which he was often the clown, explaining which mistakes he had made that day. He seemed the least manipulative man in American politics, and yet in his own special way, the confession of error, one of the shrewdest manipulators.

As the campaign progressed, there were increasing complaints from the Nixon people to the *Times* executives. Haldeman was particularly incensed. When Nick Williams received complaints from old and loyal subscribers, his stock answer was that the paper was no longer a Republican paper. Those who knew Norman Chandler thought he was somewhat rueful and not entirely at ease with the new course. All of which brought little solace to Nixon. In the final weeks of the campaign the Cuban missile crisis occurred and took away whatever issues he had. It was the Democrats who looked strong and firm in dealing with the Communists; Richard Nixon, who had so long portrayed himself as the man who stood up to the Communists, had been reduced to a yes man for Kennedy. The Cuban missile crisis was the final blow, events were outside his control. It was all over. He was being beaten in a race for an office he had not even wanted (during the last days he had told a television reporter he was running for governor of the United States and the Los Angeles *Times* had printed the mistake and that had hurt), and in his mind it was the press that had done it. It was not in him not to blame himself, or bad luck, or bad timing. So in his mind it was the newspapers of California that had done him in, in particular the one which had first sponsored him. The *Times* was no longer his friend; clearly it had become his enemy. No matter that right before the election, the *Times* had finally endorsed him, the endorsement by traditional Chandler standards was halfhearted. But it was the reporting he hated, and which he believed was one-sided; the truth was that the reporting on his and Pat Brown's race was fair and balanced, what every politician hopes to get from the major metropolitan paper, a fair break and a decent hearing. It was simply that he had never encountered equal treatment before in California and he found it devastating.

It gnawed on him and festered. Particularly the Los Angeles *Times* coverage and particularly Bergholz. Above all, Bergholz got under his skin, the tough questioning. To his mind they had deliberately assigned a reporter who had disliked him (in truth, the *Times* switched Bergholz and Carl Greenberg, the other campaign reporter, back and forth to balance the coverage). Coming from Nixon such complaints were ironic. He had often boasted from the podium that he was of the two-fisted bare-knuckles school of politics, that there was nothing he liked better than a rock 'em, sock 'em campaign. Give it hard, take it hard. The truth was that he was much too shy, much too private, much too vulnerable for that kind of politics; his skin was far too thin for what he had let himself into. He liked to think of himself as heir to Harry Truman, but Truman was tougher, a far more confident man, and he had gone up the ranks much more slowly. Truman was fifty-one years old when he first went to the Senate, and his rise had come in the forties and fifties before the press was so powerful, the glare of the camera so all-encompassing. When Truman said that if you didn't like the heat you got out of the kitchen, he meant it. Nixon was, by contrast, desperately sensitive, full of self-doubt, his very self always on the line, the nerve always too raw, the ego too fragile. Every hurt was always remembered, every enemy noted, each attack became in some way more personal. Usually politicians like this, with egos that vulnerable, are winnowed out of politics fairly soon, they come apart under the stress, or they realize they simply do not have the taste for the brutality of the public arena, a knowledge that to give, you have to take, but Nixon had been different, he had been a wunderkind, his career had leapfrogged him far ahead of a normal politician's pace, senator at thirty-eight, Vice-President at forty, he had been given a bye over the normal early barriers, he had never really had to run the gauntlet before. It was a situation made for disaster; the pressures were mounting, each job was at a higher level and brought greater scrutiny, and yet he had developed no inner resources with which to deal with the increased tensions.

"*I have no complaints about the press coverage,*" he began. It was the night of his defeat, and the boil had burst. All the pent-up frustrations and resentments from that campaign and campaigns past spewed forth. There was no doubt in the minds of the editors of the Los Angeles *Times* that it was aimed at them in general, and Bergholz in particular. Nixon had been drinking, which was always dangerous for him, he did not drink well, liquor did not become him, his mood often turned angry, the self-pity mounted. This time he was out of control, he was exhausted, and it had been decided that he would not meet with the press. Herb Klein was at the hotel podium, explaining this to reporters, when suddenly he looked up and saw Nixon approaching, and Klein felt an immediate flash of foreboding. It was a terrifying performance, Nixon naked, without restraints, filled with the sense of the injustice of the world against him, rich in self-pity. It was Nixon describing how he really felt, Nixon the victim, singled out by an unfair, unjust society for ideological reasons (as if there had been any real ideology involved in his campaign for governor against Brown). For politicians, losing is always pain, but if you like politics, you like the game, you are enriched by the give-and-take, but Nixon had by his own admission never liked the give-and-take, the physical contact of it, and therefore when he lost, everything was lost, it was an emptier process for him than for others, the process was only a means, never an end, winning, getting ahead were the only things, thus when he lost, everything was lost. So that early morning he singled out the press and the metropolitan press in particular. He singled out the Los Angeles *Times* for printing the governor of the United States flub, and he singled out Bergholz's colleague Carl Greenberg, whose reportage had been innocuous, as the one good reporter in the press corps. It was an unsettling moment even for those who had always disliked him, watching a man who had lost his restraints and was shorn of his dignity. He could not stop himself, this man who above all else prided himself on control and cared above all for his privacy. It was a performance unmatched in recent American politics. To reporters it was not surprising, they had always suspected that he had felt that way. But the special bitterness he reserved for the *Times* was surprising. Greenberg was so embarrassed at being singled out as the one good reporter that he immediately offered to resign, but Frank McCulloch told him to forget it, things like that can happen to anybody. That morning when Bergholz and McCulloch went to work they found television crews staked out by the *Times* building asking for comments. What could they say?

Later that fall Norman and Buff Chandler went on vacation in Europe and they ended up in Venice, in a small restaurant. They were seated at the front of the restaurant near another couple from Southern California, and they were exchanging amenities when Norman turned to Buff and said, "You won't believe who just walked in." She looked up just in time to see Dick and Pat Nixon heading for the back of the restaurant. The Chandlers were nearly finished, but Norman made the meal drag on. "I want to see what happens," he told his wife. Sure enough, the Nixons eventually got up to leave and as they passed by they barely acknowledged the Chandlers, but stopped for a long time talking warmly to the other Californians before departing. "That's very odd," the other man said, "we barely know him." (Norman, who loved the incident and the story, embellished it; in his version Nixon came by and talked to the other couple and then turned to the Chandlers and said, "I'm sorry, I've forgotten your names." Buff, who did not love the story, told it as well, but she did not embellish it, and years later she was still angry over it.)

# 12 / Time Incorporated

On the night of the inauguration in January 1961, Harry and Clare Luce sat in the imperial box with Joe and Rose Kennedy. Luce, of course, was bothered by it all, his final endorsement of Nixon in *Life* had been quite tepid, he had a sense of guilt after the election that he had gotten too soft, and he repeatedly asked friends whether he had failed Nixon, whether he had let Kennedy charm him too much. Even the inaugural was not without its problems. Luce was bothered by Kennedy's tendency to call him Mr. Luce, instead of Harry, and Kennedy wanted to be called Jack, which Luce, with his reverence for the

American presidency, thought improper. So all kinds of elaborate signals went on that night between *Time* executives to make sure that the nomenclature was right. Finally Hugh Sidey, *Time*'s White House correspondent, called over to Dick Clurman, the chief of correspondents, "All's well in heaven tonight. Luce is calling him Mister President, and Kennedy is calling him Harry."

That kind of tolerance in Luce of a liberal Democrat was not without its price. One did not sit readily in the box of a potential adversary or fraternize lightly with the enemy. Luce had made it very clear in the days before the inauguration who he considered to be an acceptable candidate for Secretary of State (Chester Bowles and Fulbright were unacceptable); later he took credit for the selection of Dean Rusk. He made it equally clear that he would tolerate no softening of the line on Communism, particularly in Asia, where Democrats were known to be soft. Any Democratic President moving ahead of Luce's pace on this issue would have *Time* and *Life* to reckon with. Kennedy himself was already cautious about moving in that direction, but *Time* and *Life* were further obstacles and potential adversaries in the event of any change in American Asia policy. *Time* had its policy and its reservations about too soft a President; Kennedy had his policies, and the pressures from his own liberal constituency. The relationship was one of constant tension.

It was against that particular background that John Kennedy viewed *Time* and *Life* as key to the independent center, and potentially a highly antagonistic one. He was, above all else, a marvelous contemporary politician with a shrewd sense of the sources of power, and unlike most politicians, he understood that those sources were not static. He had arrived at a moment of flux in the pattern of American political power. Some sources were growing weaker, and some stronger, and by nature Kennedy had a grasp of the new balance. He knew television and print were becoming more important all the time and that this was a source of strength for him; he could always sell himself to the media. Magazine editors liked the Kennedys because Kennedy covers always sold well. He knew exactly how much good and how much harm each reporter could do him, and he knew their personal idiosyncrasies, how to evoke the best response out of each one.

The news magazines and the columnists offered the best target, they were more judgmental, therefore they could, potentially, do him more damage; but at the same time he could, potentially, influence them more. The news magazines were prisoners of their style and their deadlines. Coming out only once a week, not being first with the news, they needed a special kind of access, the little anecdotes and tidbits which showed inner knowledge. What the candidate had for breakfast, who his tailor was, how he worked on a speech. Colorful little details which seemingly told a lot. That, of course, gave the President a special advantage. There was, in effect, more room for him to maneuver with the news magazines.

In 1959 as he geared up for his race, he did not have a particular problem with *Newsweek*. *Newsweek* was running a bad second to *Time* and needed good exciting Kennedy coverage. Besides, the correspondent covering him, Ben

Bradlee, was a neighbor and a very close personal friend, and indeed it was to a degree Bradlee's friendship with Kennedy that had catapulted Bradlee ahead in his own career. But *Time* was a potential adversary, far more likely to be conservative and antagonistic. This explained why, in a senator's office —and later a presidential administration—obsessed by a good press, all reporters were equal, major reporters for major outlets were more equal, but most equal of all was Hugh Sidey of *Time*. Kennedy was acutely sensitive to Time-Life, he believed that, in the pre-television era, it was the most influential instrument in the country. Nothing, he claimed, helped him gain early national recognition so much as a favorable *Time* cover story. He used to tell friends that there were Republicans and Democrats, and then there was a vast middle group, politically uncommitted. This middle group, he said, decided the election, and *Time* magazine influenced that group more than any other part of the press. *The New York Times* and Scotty Reston were enormously influential with other Washington journalists, but *Time* to him was at the center of the spectrum; it was national and it reached people throughout the country. It was not just the sheer numbers of the people it reached, perhaps two million, it was who they were: influential people respected by their peers, people whose words were often listened to.

In the late fifties Jack Kennedy therefore paid more and more attention to Hugh Sidey of *Time*. Sidey was reasonably fresh from working in the Midwest, and like many other young men coming to Washington, he was impressed by the fact that the status of a reporter there was different from that back in the hinterlands, where they were often regarded as carriers of some kind of plague. In Washington reporters were not only stroked during the day but invited to the best homes for dinner at night, a change in status so total as to be bewildering. Sidey was assigned to cover the various Democratic senators then eyeing the presidency, and he quickly found that two of them, Stuart Symington and Hubert Humphrey, seemed neither to know how to deal with the press nor to care, and that two of them, John F. Kennedy and Lyndon B. Johnson, cared a very great deal about the press in general and *Time* magazine in particular. (The first time that Sidey appeared in Johnson's office he found that the Senate Majority Leader was better briefed on Hugh Sidey than Sidey was on him, and Johnson gave Sidey the full treatment, composed of equal parts of how important Lyndon Johnson was and how important Time-Life was.) Johnson knew Sidey's deadlines perfectly, knew that Friday was the big writing day in New York, and thus Thursday the big filing day in Washington, and so he set aside six o'clock every Thursday for *Time* magazine, and he would call Sidey and say, "All right, it's *Time* magazine time," and Sidey would troop over punctually and they would drink scotch, which Johnson claimed publicly was bourbon. Johnson would outline what he had done that week or, more accurately, what he wanted *Time* to think he had done. He would, he repeatedly emphasized, rather have one story in either *Time* or *The New York Times* than three or four elsewhere, it was his way of becoming a national figure. Curiously, of the major figures preparing for the

1960 race, the only one who seemed to Sidey distant almost to the point of being antagonistic was Richard M. Nixon. Perhaps Nixon, being a Republican, assumed he would have *Time*'s support without working for it, and perhaps he was the same way with the rest of the press, but even the top people at *Time* had a certain amount of difficulty seeing him. Even Luce couldn't see Nixon readily. The bureau people would call Nixon's office and say that Luce was going to be in town and would like to see the Vice-President. The answer would come back that Nixon had a very busy day, there was a full desk, many complicated responsibilities. Since on the same trip Luce would often be seeing Eisenhower and since access to the President of the United States was very easy, there was always a bit of annoyance with Nixon.

There was, of course, no problem of access with Jack Kennedy. Everyone in his office was available, most particularly the senator himself. He was very much aware of the potential hostility of *Time* and he was aware in 1960, when Otto Fuerbringer became managing editor, that Fuerbringer and his deputy, Jim Keogh, were likely to be very antagonistic toward him. His essential strategy then was to try to neutralize the New York office, and he set out to study the magazine as another politician might study the interconnections of Democratic ward heelers in New York or Pennsylvania. He mastered the structure of the magazine, the pay scale, the power of the managing editor over the senior editors. When a lowly researcher ended up doing a large number of stories involving him, he made sure that the researcher had direct access to him. In particular he was obsessed by Fuerbringer and his role. What was Otto's relationship with Luce? Did Luce dominate Otto? Was Otto his own man? Fuerbringer, he knew, was the key man, he handled the day-to-day controls. Kennedy knew that the reporters in the field by and large did not like Fuerbringer. He found out very early in the game that Otto was likely to be hostile to him, that it was not personal, just political. He became uncommonly sensitive to every nuance in the magazine. Once, after becoming President, he surprised Luce, who had paid him a White House visit, by asking, "What's the matter, Otto out on vacation last week?" Luce seemed surprised by the question and asked why. "Because the magazine was different last week, the tone was different." And Luce was shocked, because Fuerbringer had in fact been out sick all week.

Kennedy also worked consistently with *Time* reporters, repeating relentlessly to them his belief that there was no way he would get a fair shake from *Time,* knowing, of course, that this would make them bend over backward to be fair, giving him a slightly better edge. In 1959, when he was gathering steam for a run for the presidency, a group of Methodist bishops came to visit him in Washington. It was an important story for Kennedy because the religious issue was hanging heavily on him and it was important to him that the story be fair, that it at least not make his religious problem more serious. The early copies of *Time* arrived at the Washington bureau on Sunday night and Kennedy's office called to ask for a couple of early copies. So Sidey trundled along to the Senate, dropped them off, and went up to the gallery. From there he watched the senator, who was then on the floor debating labor law, slip the magazine into his desk and surreptitiously read it during the debate. Finally Kennedy looked up at Sidey in the gallery and smiled, not a big smile but a smile nonetheless. A few hours later Sidey saw him and asked what he thought and Kennedy answered, "Okay, okay. Not bad, considering it's *Time* and Harry Luce. Not bad."

There were a number of reasons besides Kennedy's astute courting why the Luce publications were giving him a fairer shake than liberal Democrats normally got. One was a crucial difference in Luce's attitude. He had had, in Eisenhower, his own President for eight years; the fierce partisan hunger of 1952 had been assuaged. And then he, like many of his readers and correspondents, was fascinated and charmed by Kennedy himself and the Kennedys in general—all those driving, ambitious, single-minded people, all that money, all that glamour. Despite ideological reservations about the young senator (and he had considerable), at a personal level he came to prefer Kennedy to Nixon. "I don't know, I don't know," he told a group of his editors right before the election. "I just don't like Nixon. I guess we have to support him, but I don't like him." Then he waited. "You know, I never liked Nixon. But I *like* Kennedy. I don't agree with Kennedy on most things, but I *like* him." A few years later a friend asked Luce how he felt about Kennedy and he answered, almost angrily, "He seduces me." "That's not so bad, Harry," the friend said. "Yes, it is," he answered. "When I'm with him I feel like a whore." Kennedy himself reciprocated in kind, he not only took Luce and his magazines almost as seriously as Luce did himself, which was the ultimate compliment, but he liked Luce as well. He was used to dealing with curmudgeons, he had one in his own family. He once asked Sidey, "How's old Lucey?" Lucy? Sidey thought he heard. Lucy Who? "What Lucy?" "You know," said Kennedy, "old man Luce. I kind of like him. He's just like my old man. What he's got, he made himself and I respect that."

So part of it was a kind of curious personal attraction and style. Kennedy had come to New York for a *Time* editors' lunch during the 1960 campaign and a huge crowd of gaping office workers had filled the cavernous lobby of the Time and Life Building. Luce had been impressed by that, it was an instant demonstration of Kennedy's raw political sex appeal. But the other part of it, so far as Kennedy's fortunes were concerned, was pure luck. Otto Fuerbringer, who was considered by most senior *Time* people to be more papal than the Pope, more Luceian than Luce, came down in the summer of 1960 with a serious and disabling aneurysm. He became subject to a fierce numbing headache, and right after the Republican convention in 1960 he had to withdraw from operating duties. Normally if a managing editor of a major publication became ill it would have little effect upon a political campaign; managing editors can change at *The New York Times* without the astute reader ever knowing, the paper is so much a product of its parts, the managing editor's hand is so rarely visible. Not *Time* magazine. At *Time* magazine the managing editor is all-powerful, it is an editor's magazine, and if the editors to an uncommon degree determined the tone of the reporting, the managing editor above all others determined how the editors felt. The managing editor was an extension of Luce's will, the man whose job it was to keep the rest of the potentially too liberal staff in line.

To this day the campaign of 1960 has a special connotation within *Time* magazine, it is known not so much as the year of Kennedy's election but the year of Otto's aneurysm. Tom Griffith, the assistant managing editor, was made acting managing editor. At first Luce, somewhat wary of Griffith's reputation for a kind of mild liberalism, turned to Roy Alexander, who had recently vacated the managing editor's job. But Alexander said Griffith could do the job. Griffith was a disciple of Tom Matthews, a talented writer in his own right who was known as the house liberal in the upper echelons of *Time*. Griffith had been somewhat uneasy with *Time*'s partisanship during earlier election years, and in 1956 he had written Luce a poignant note warning his editor that too much bias was showing too often. He said that in the past *Time* had cheated a little at election time, but cheating was now in danger of becoming a "four-year proposition." He told Luce that *Time* lacked the power to win general elections, and its attempts to sway voters so openly only diminished the magazine's influence. Griffith had hoped to be managing editor of *Time* himself, but it was simply not in the cards politically. He was the consensus choice of most of the senior working journalists of the organization, a superior craftsman, an open-minded man, and a good listener, but he was not considered trustworthy enough in the ideological sense to hold so pivotal a position. Luce was aware that he had been the popular choice with most of the senior working staff. Just before Roy Alexander retired, Luce was in Paris with his then Paris bureau chief, Frank White, and he asked White who should succeed Alexander. Even as the words were out of Luce's mouth, he pulled back the question. "Never mind, I know who you're going to name, and he's a very good man, but he isn't going to get the job." Griffith was a figure much respected by younger *Time* writers and editors. He was also fond of Luce and he displayed that affection in two books dealing with the press in general and *Time* in particular, books in which he never mentioned the name Fuerbringer. So when Griffith took over at *Time* for the campaign of 1960, he was determined to put out a fair magazine, not for the benefit of Kennedy or the liberals, but for the benefit of *Time*. He felt *its* credibility was at stake, that its reputation for abandoning journalistic fairness every four years was a serious problem; he was reminded of a letter that Franklin Roosevelt had allegedly written William Allen White saying that for three and a half out of every four years White was an admirably fair journalist. At that time Louis Banks was editing national affairs and Griffith conferred with him, and though Banks was probably a little more conservative than Griffith they had a feeling they could work together. Very early on Griffith decided that the coverage of both candidates should be equal in length and equally critical, equal on what the candidates had said and on their speaking style. Then he feared that that might end up too saccharine and so he added another touchstone, which was to find the worst thing that could be said about either candidate that week. But because that sounded too *Time*-ish, too snippety, he added another touchstone: the best thing that could be said about either candidate that week.

Griffith was aware that he was in a special situation. He was sure that he would not have been able to hold the same job in any good conscience under the conditions that existed in 1952. Very early in the campaign a story came in that Griffith sensed was probably a little more pro-Republican than the facts called for; Griffith called Banks in, they edited it together, and finally Griffith said to him: We may disagree on politics but let's not misjudge each other's motivations, let's always know where we stand. So it worked well, the reporters in the field were surprised by how balanced the coverage was, morale in the office went up, it seemed a different magazine. Luce himself never complained about the coverage, there were never any kickbacks on stories, and at the end when *Time* had predicted the electoral count correctly Luce seemed pleased. He told Griffith he had done a fine job, to go out and buy himself a case of champagne, which indeed Griffith would have liked to do. Or at least he would have liked to drink one bottle if Luce had sent it up. But the idea of going out to a store and ordering a case of champagne and sending the bill to Harry Luce seemed a little improper.

If Luce, and much of the staff of *Time,* and the President-elect of the United States were pleased with the fairness of *Time*'s coverage, there was one man who was not pleased, and that was Otto Fuerbringer. He never said a single word to Griffith about the coverage, not even mild words of congratulation, and shortly after his return Fuerbringer visited the writers in national affairs. Far from congratulating them on the fairness of their work, he launched a harsh attack on them. They were not, he said, tough enough. It was not a pleasant occasion. At the same time, since Fuerbringer was returning and Griffith was moving aside, Lou Banks decided to have a dinner party honoring Griffith. Among those invited were Fuerbringer and Jim Keogh, Fuerbringer's very conservative deputy. But shortly after accepting the invitations, both canceled out. Banks saw the handwriting on the wall and quickly made a transfer out of *Time* to *Fortune.* Griffith shortly afterward was moved to a job at *Life.*

At almost the same time that Fuerbringer was returning, John Kennedy, by then the President-elect, sensed that something had changed in the magazine. It was the interregnum period between the election and the inauguration and one night the Kennedy plane landed at Palm Beach and the President-elect disembarked. He stood for a moment on the runway, reading an early copy of *Time* in the lights of the plane, his finger pointing at the type as he read, his face growing colder and colder. "This is wrong . . . this is wrong . . . this is wrong . . ." he started saying. He immediately summoned Sidey from the waiting press group.

"Sidey, I hear Fuerbringer is back."

"Yes, he is, Senator."

"Sidey, you assured me he was virtually at death's door. . . . You've failed me." And he stomped off, absolutely furious.


The early sixties were great years for journalism. The Kennedys themselves, who were always good copy, helped guarantee that, and organizations like *Newsweek* and *The New York Times* and the networks were all expanding their coverage, the bureaus were all getting bigger. *Time* was no exception. The *Time* news service was flowering under Dick Clurman, who slowly was building what became in the sixties one of the great journalistic stables in the world. Yet the very growth of the news service created internal tensions within *Time* magazine, for as far as Fuerbringer was concerned, *Time* was an *editor's* magazine. The more that Clurman upgraded the news service, the more, in effect, he was inevitably challenging Fuerbringer's domination of the magazine, since the more and better the reportage from the field, the harder it was to ignore. Fuerbringer was very much in control of a tightly structured pyramided magazine where he held total editorial power. But Fuerbringer had no control at all over the hiring and the assignment of reporters. He made several attempts to take over the news service and to gain control of the hiring but Luce always fended him off. Clurman completely controlled the hiring; he could offer his reporters good jobs, good—very good in those days—pay, unusually generous expense accounts, no boring or trivial stories. Yet he had no control over whether or not their work got into the magazine. This made for a constant conflict between the two men, between New York and the field, and that was precisely what Luce wanted. No one was totally fulfilled except perhaps Harry Luce. Sidey was Clurman's man, and Clurman's star, but neither could control what happened to Sidey's files. That was Fuerbringer's job. Fuerbringer in turn did not particularly like the idea of Sidey covering the Kennedy White House, and right after the election, at a meeting of Luce's managing editors, he brought up the subject, suggesting that Sidey was too close to Kennedy and his people—which was true in a way; he *was* too close, which was what *Time* wanted, the access; nor had being too close to the Eisenhower people ever bothered *Time*'s editors in the past eight years. Access and friendship were of the essence then, all publishers wanted their White House reporters to be too close. Fuerbringer went on briefly about the need to transfer Sidey, and Luce listened and finally interrupted him. "Well, we've had enough of that. We'll go on from here."

Which put Sidey in a constant conflict between his magazine and the Administration. Nineteen sixty-one for Kennedy was a difficult year with a high degree of failure, and *Time,* to him, seemed particularly critical, almost joyful at his difficulties. It was a year in which Kennedy deliberately made as much of his administration open and available to Sidey as possible. His treatment of the press in a situation like that was in direct contrast to what that of Nixon would be. Nixon under pressure turned only to reporters from publications already favorable to him; Kennedy, in trouble, turned to those most critical and dubious of him, and if anything tended to take those already for him a bit for granted. If he was to speak on a Monday, which was after *Time* closed, he made sure that Sidey saw a copy of his speech in advance. If *Time* were doing a cover story on any aspect of the Administration, everyone in the White House was made available. Luce was invited for lunch quite regularly, and if the lunch went well there might be two or three weeks of semi-favorable coverage before the magazine slipped back to the norm.

But the tension and the resentment were always there. It was, thought Sidey in retrospect, always the little things that set Kennedy off; it was as if the President could bear the criticism on major issues from *Time,* but his control slipped when it came to minor things, some idiosyncrasy in the family, a reference to old Joe Kennedy, to Jackie's tennis lessons. He took the little things so seriously, he was intent upon his image, about not making a fool of himself. The Kennedy people themselves were convinced that *Time* was after them. To them Sidey was the good guy of the operation, but they were wary of the bottom line. Even after a cover story at the end of 1961 named him Man of the Year, Kennedy was furious. Kennedy called Sidey: "I hear you sons of bitches have done it again." What was the problem? Sidey, somewhat bewildered, asked. "Kenny O'Donnell's seen the cover and you've ruined me." The cover had been done by Pietro Annigoni, an Italian artist whom Jackie liked. The sitting had not gone well. Annigoni sat in the Oval Office for five days and complained that Kennedy had never posed for him. Annigoni was told to paint Kennedy as he saw him, and he did, but it was a darker, more shrouded figure than most people, including the President, wanted. The *Time* editors immediately knew there was going to be trouble. Jim Keogh asked, "Pietro, how did you do it?" "Well," he said, "this is what I saw." Kennedy looked tired, one eye seemed to be slipping off into space. "He's made me look cross-eyed!" Kennedy complained. "Well," said Annigoni, "he *is* cross-eyed."

On another occasion Luce happened to be visiting Kennedy shortly after *Time* had run a story cutting the size of a Kennedy crowd from 80,000 to 40,000. Kennedy was, of course, outraged. Normally he took his anger out on Sidey, but this time he took it out on Luce, raking him over in a private meeting, telling him that his magazine simply was not fair, that it did not try to be fair, that Fuerbringer did not care about the truth, that the truth was not in *Time* or Fuerbringer. All this time Sidey had been waiting outside for Luce. Suddenly the two men emerged from the Oval Office together, the tension showing on both their faces. Kennedy grabbed Sidey. "Here he is, here's Hugh Sidey! He's a fair man, one of Washington's fairest reporters! Sidey, if you went out on Pennsylvania Avenue and found a reasonably fair workingman and asked him if *Time* was fair to me, what would he say?" Sidey looked from Luce's face to Kennedy's face, both of them taut with strain, and for a moment he wished he were back in Iowa. Finally Sidey heard himself mumble that what Kennedy said might be true but that the Washington workingman was not representative of all workingmen since Washington was a company town. They left the White House with Luce visibly shaken and a little gray. He was caught between his Republicanism and his patriotism. "I don't like it," he kept saying, "I don't like to have the President of the United States feel that way about me and about the magazine. I don't like it at all." He waited a day before he called Fuerbringer to pass on the news, that the President had been complaining about him. "Well, what do you want me to do?" asked Fuerbringer. "Nothing," said Luce.

The day that John Glenn was to finish his first space orbit had started as a day of singular pleasure for Hugh Sidey; it was, after all, a glorious moment for the President of the United States and for the nation, and thus for a man whose main job was to cover the President. Here was something momentous, successful, and easy to get into his magazine on his own terms. Sidey was sitting with a few colleagues in the White House press room watching the imminent splashdown—all systems A Okay, in the vernacular of that time and place—and Sidey, like the others in the room, felt the measure of pride and relief that all Americans in the sixties felt who could assume that their system and their technology now matched that of the Soviets. Suddenly Kenny O'Donnell, who was on most occasions a good source and a friend, barged into the press room, grabbed Sidey, and said, "You've done it again! You've done it again!" O'Donnell summoned Sidey to the Oval Office and on the way Sidey asked what was the matter, and O'Donnell said it was serious, very serious: a mention in the People section of *Time* that the President of the United States had posed for the cover of *Gentlemen's Quarterly*. Sidey immediately relaxed, thinking it a small matter. When he got inside the Oval Office the President of the United States, who, like most of the nation, was watching the heroics of the astronaut on television, pointed to a copy of *Time* magazine and said, "This goddamn magazine is just too much, too goddamn much. Where did you get this ridiculous item about me?" Sidey was at that point still too much caught up in the euphoria of this day of national triumph, and he failed to see the face of John Kennedy and he began to laugh. Suddenly Kennedy cut in on him, his voice very cold and very angry, telling Sidey that this was serious, that it was not something to laugh about. Even as Kennedy was talking, Sidey began to feel Pierre Salinger and Kenny O'Donnell edging away from him. Even as Tazewell Shepherd, the President's naval aide, was trying to prepare the phone call to Glenn, who had just splashed down, Kennedy was still berating Hugh Sidey of *Time* magazine. It was pure unrestrained presidential Irish anger. "What do you mean I posed for them! What do you mean! Why did you do this! I never posed for them. I'll be the|laughingstock|of|the country. They'll remember me as the man who posed for *Gentlemen's Quarterly*. People always remember the wrong things, they remember Arthur Godfrey for buzzing a tower and Calvin Coolidge for wearing those hats and they'll remember me for this." While he was talking, Admiral Shepherd interrupted to say that Colonel Glenn was on the line. Without breaking stride, Kennedy nodded, moved toward the phone, continued his harangue of Sidey: "Sidey, you son of a bitch, see if you can get this right," he said. And then without a pause, he was on the phone, butter melting in his mouth: Colonel Glenn, how marvelous, how proud the whole nation was of him, what a great moment it was for all Americans, how proud John Kennedy personally was of him. He continued that way for several minutes, finally put the phone down, and went right back to Sidey, as if there had been no interruption: "You sons of bitches, you always do this to me. That damn magazine of yours!" It was, Sidey thought later, a chewing out such as a journalist rarely gets from the leader of the free world, but it was also access, wonderful access for him and for *Time*.

So it was, with each side trying to use the other, to manipulate the other, and with Sidey caught in the middle, squeezed at both ends. The job required not just journalistic ability but diplomatic skill as well. Sidey had to negotiate between two formidable forces, knowing just how hard to push, and to defend, both with the Kennedys for *Time* and with *Time* for the Kennedys. He subdivided himself with considerable ability. He was a very good dual ambassador and it worked finally to his advantage, giving him exceptional access. But then gradually, in the last year of Kennedy's life, Sidey noticed a change, not so much in Kennedy's feeling about the magazine's fairness as in his estimation of its importance. The equation had changed with the coming of television. In Washington the power of print was slipping and slipping quickly. Television gave greater access, so television got better access. It was felt among journalists throughout the city, the anger as Kennedy permitted television into his press conferences, and even greater irritation when he held conversations once reserved for the giants of print like Arthur Krock with the three network representatives. What could be more humbling for the leading print journalists than to sit and watch their television sets just like their fellow citizens back home? Those conversations were crucial, they not only bypassed the traditional press conference procedures, they were—and this was most painful of all—a better, more substantive, more intelligent forum. They tended to show the President in a very attractive light, where he could explain his side of things. The old order was changing and television was now dominating. Once in early 1963 Kennedy asked Sidey how *Life* magazine was doing. "Well, it's not like the old days," Sidey answered. Kennedy asked what the problem was. "Well, I don't really know; the ads are off, it must be television," Sidey said. For Kennedy that must have been one more bit of evidence of a changing balance. For *Life* it was particularly painful; *Life*'s power in Washington for some twenty-five years had been awesome, a dominant national vehicle. Everyone wanted good coverage, a good play in *Life;* the Eisenhower people had for several days held back photos of the first satellite from everyone else to give *Life* the first break. It had always been like that. But now that power was ebbing, there was a new and more dramatic medium on the scene.

In 1963 even as favored a reporter as Sidey felt his access diminishing, he knew there was a new and powerful rival in television. But he was intrigued that his editors in New York did not yet seem to sense it. They were very much involved in their own world, the power to bestow a cover remained, as far as they were concerned, the power to make or break a career. Sidey himself could still see people, but it was a little harder, there was a little more effort involved in seeing a top White House aide, and there was perhaps just a little bit more of a sense that the balance had changed slightly, that if a White House source saw you he was doing you a favor and you owed him something. At the beginning of the Administration, Sidey had been seeing Kennedy once a week and the Kennedy minions any time he wanted, but by 1963 it was drying up: perhaps he saw Kennedy every three weeks. At the time of John Kennedy's death, Sidey had not seen him in a month. Television was simply more important to a President and easier to deal with, and the President could almost always dictate the terms. An election year was coming up and television was sure to be the dominant medium, the ultimate presidential tool. In fact, Sidey had an impression near the end that Kennedy was seeing him largely for old times' sake, because they had been friends, and because Kennedy, who was a terrific gossip, liked to keep in touch with print reporters as much to hear as to talk, and because Kennedy himself had a special interest in the printed word. With another President, Sidey sensed, the changeover might have come sooner and more abruptly.

In 1960, at the time of the Democratic convention, Lyndon Johnson had made a last-minute visit to New York, where he had appealed for Luce's support in his try for the nomination. *Time,* in an issue that came out *after* the nomination, had put Lyndon on the cover, which had surprised some of the magazine's political reporters. It was generally considered an anti-Kennedy gesture by Fuerbringer. In this instance *Time* got lucky, because Kennedy surprised the convention by naming Johnson the nominee for Vice-President. But it had rankled some of the Kennedy people. Three years later, when John Kennedy was assassinated, Otto Fuerbringer decided to put Lyndon Johnson on the cover instead of the deceased slain leader. This was the traditional *Time* policy, to go with the new leader; *Time* did not like to put dead people on its cover. But there were many people at *Time* who thought this a serious mistake, particularly because the nation was still mourning Kennedy (*Time* in its Publisher's Letter rather grotesquely boasted that Kennedy was its number-one subscriber). Some editors thought that Johnson went on the cover because Fuerbringer liked him more than he did Kennedy. *Newsweek* ran Kennedy.

A few days after the assassination there was a luncheon of the top *Time* magazine executives. Sidey was invited up from Washington to talk about Lyndon Johnson. He began by saying that Johnson was an incredibly able man, perhaps in terms of governance the most able man to sit in the White House in years, but that he was also a flawed man. *Time,* he said, would do well to watch him carefully, for, more than most politicians, Lyndon Johnson lied and deceived, although often on small matters and often with no awareness that he was lying or deceiving. As he talked it became clear that Fuerbringer did not like what Sidey was saying. Finally he interrupted to say that these things didn't matter, so what if Johnson was crude and a liar—he'll be a good President. But, curiously enough, Hedley Donovan, Luce's editorial heir and now editor-in-chief of Time Inc., who was usually the most cautious man at these meetings, interrupted and commented that perhaps they should all pay a little more attention to what Sidey was saying. Donovan said that he did not think you could divide your character: if a man lied on small things he might well lie on big things as well. Later, after Sidey had left, there was another attempt by Fuerbringer to get Sidey off the White House, but Dick Clurman held the fort and Sidey's job was saved again.

# 13 / The Washington <u>Post</u>

It was later said in newspaper circles that Phil Graham purchased *Newsweek* because he and Kay were in New York one weekend and Kay had a cold and could not go out and so she asked Phil to go downstairs and buy her a magazine, and he did, buying *Newsweek*. The truth is somewhat different. *Newsweek* in the fifties was a more peaceful, stuffier version of *Time*. It had none of the brilliance or zest of *Time,* and none of the excesses of Luce. Its staff was considered better than the magazine, and many of the people there were dropouts from the Luce empire. Its circulation was 1.3 million, far behind *Time.* It was a weak alternative for those who found *Time* simply too prejudiced; *Newsweek* was prejudiced too, but in a blander way. It was owned by a number of people, principally Captain Vincent Astor, and the principal editors were the Malcolm Muirs, father and son. In 1959 Vincent Astor died and it became known around New York that the Astor Foundation was thinking of selling the magazine. Jim Cannon, one of the senior editors, and Osborn Elliott, who was then the managing editor, and generally considered the ablest man on the magazine, decided to try to buy it themselves. They had very good credentials, they had a very good idea of what they wanted from the magazine, they knew all the other bright young men in the business, and they considered themselves the ideal pilots for *Newsweek*'s future. All they lacked was money. For a time Elliott and Cannon tried to raise money on their own, but newspapermen, no matter how well bred and connected, do not by and large inspire confidence in bankers, and the sum they needed was $11 million. They had brought in a third conspirator, a brash young man in their Washington bureau named Ben Bradlee, and the three of them talked together almost every night about how to take over the property and get it away from the Muirs. The competition was getting intense, there were other buyers

around, the Muirs themselves were trying to put together a group, and pro-
spective owners kept taking Elliott to fancy but secret lunches behind huge
potted plants to see if they could get an inside track. Finally one night Bradlee
called up Elliott and said, "Oz, old buddy, I've been thinking a lot where the
smart money in this town is and I've decided it's in Phil Graham's pocket. Why
don't we go see him?"

None of them knew Graham very well; Bradlee had worked for him
briefly at the *Post* in the late forties. He had liked Graham's irreverence and
he had not minded in 1951 when he had asked Graham for a leave of absence
to try for a coveted Nieman Fellowship at Harvard and Graham had given him
the kind of answer Bradlee loved, "Fuck you, Bradlee, you've already been to
Harvard." The three men discussed the idea of Graham and they decided that
he was a good bet, younger and more modern than most publishers, and richer
than most people they knew. Bradlee called Graham and by invitation went
to Graham's house that night at 9 P.M. He stayed until 4 A.M., feeling at the
end that he had been very brazen, that he knew nothing of finance or the
commerce of magazines, and very aware that he was asking a man for some
$11 million. But he also thought that you ought to try to influence your fate,
and that this was a magazine that had a chance to be good, if not great, and
that he did not want to go to work for *Time*. Graham was, of course, immediately interested. All his senses started clicking. He asked Bradlee to put everything he had said down on paper and Bradlee did, staying up all the next night
preparing a fifty-page memo. Graham became even more interested. He was,
Bradlee found out later, in the midst of one of his manic periods and, being
quite aware of this, had asked Bradlee to fill in Fritz Beebe, the Graham lawyer
and financier. "Fritz," he told Bradlee, "is very good, he cools me off when
I'm too hot." At the moment he feared he was too hot. But this time Beebe
didn't cool anything. He pushed Graham forward, he smelled a very good deal.
Beebe did not know that much about journalism or communication, but he
knew it was an uncommon business opportunity; there was $3 million in the
till at *Newsweek*, as well as some other desirable properties.

Graham's handling of the *Newsweek* deal was brilliant. It reflected the full
dimension of the man. He was by then in the midst of a terrifying illness and
yet he still could be absolutely bold and lucid, creative and charming. Though
the official selling price for *Newsweek* was $15 million, in the end no more than
$75,000 really changed hands. It was one of the great steals of contemporary
journalism. Graham personally took command of the deal, he was aware that
there might be competition, that S. I. Newhouse might come in, and he knew
how Newhouse operated, which was to figure out the bid and come in one
dollar higher, and so he set out to make the most of his personal connections.
Graham sent Bradlee to see Brooke Astor, the widow of Vincent Astor,
because Bradlee's parents had, of course, been good friends of the Astors (old
Be Bradlee, Ben's father, had always complained bitterly, after the Bradlees'

annual visit to the Astors in Maine, that no man in the world was as stingy in putting wood on a fire as Vincent Astor); then Graham himself courted and thoroughly charmed Brooke Astor, promising that he would continue the magazine in the journalistic tradition of Captain Astor—which was particularly touching because Captain Astor had set no journalistic tradition at all. He mobilized Elliott to talk to her as well. Mrs. Astor liked all these bright, attractive young men and she told friends that Philip Graham was the most audacious and charming young man she had met in years. Meanwhile, Al Friendly, who had once worked for Averell Harriman, was dispatched to Rome, where Harriman, who owned about 30 percent of the stock, then resided. Graham also worked on a banker named Alan Betts, a man not readily susceptible to charm, who represented the Astor Foundation, and even here his touch worked.

It turned out that the main competition was Doubleday, the book-publishing house. The day before the bids were officially opened, Betts had gone to see Elliott and Gibson McCabe, the business manager of *Newsweek,* and he had told them that the two bids were almost identical, and that the Astor board would respect their feelings as to which buyer they favored. He could, in fact, guarantee that the board would act according to their wishes. Both Elliott and McCabe, who were in on the Washington *Post* deal as deeply as they could be, coughed and said that they preferred the *Post,* the idea of joining up with the energy of a powerful news-gathering organization fascinated them, and they liked the electric personal quality of Phil Graham. To their surprise, Betts, usually so reserved, said, "I couldn't agree more. I've never been so impressed by a man in my life. Why, do you realize that he has set up a special telephone line from his suite at the Carlyle to my office? And just a few days ago he was in here and he made out a check for two million dollars as a down payment." Graham had, of course, operated with his usual combination of style, secrecy, and paranoia. There were secret phones, code names (earlier on D day there had been a call to the suite at the Carlyle and a voice had said simply, "Uncle Harvey has the money," which meant that Fritz Beebe, who did, indeed, have an Uncle Harvey somewhere in his background, had the money from Prudential Life). After the final meeting with Betts, Elliott went to a phone booth and called the secret number at the Carlyle and Bradlee answered, and Elliott said to tell Phil to go out and get drunk. "Drunk happy or drunk sad?" Bradlee asked. "Drunk happy," Elliott said.

In March 1961 Graham bought *Newsweek.* The overall price was $15 million, which included a half share in a San Diego television station, which they immediately sold for $2.5 million, and there was $3 million in the till. It was an absolute steal.

That night they all celebrated, the Grahams and the Elliotts and the Bradlees, and Phil was like a little kid. He was wearing a homburg and he kept bouncing up and down in the back seat of the limousine, crushing the top of the hat. Kay was not that enthusiastic about the purchase of *Newsweek,* she was wary of what Phil did in his manic moods, but she was pleased for his happiness. She did not want to spoil his fun and so, although she had heard the news that morning for the first time, she waited until the next day to tell him that the doctors had found a serious spot on one of her lungs.


The *Newsweek* deal changed two things overnight. It made *Newsweek* almost instantly big-time; all the potential for a quality publication had been there, the literacy rate in the country had been rising, and *Time* had not entirely filled the gap, particularly with younger readers. All it took was getting rid of the top editorial management, bringing in a few talented reporters, and adding a high-powered business side. The essential structure of the magazine was sounder than most people suspected. Here Graham moved quickly. If he had been a little slow to pour money and resources into the editorial side of the Washington *Post,* even after it had started making money, he did not hesitate with *Newsweek.* He began to pour in money, and the staff and the bureaus expanded; it was very quickly a real competitor to *Time.*

Now, suddenly, instead of just being the publisher of a national newspaper, Phil Graham was a genuine press lord. He had a powerful monopoly national paper in Washington and a powerful new national magazine in New York; his position seemed on the rise at the very moment that Luce's was in decline, in part because of the beginning of the withering of *Life* magazine. The Luce empire by 1961 was weaker than it had been a decade earlier; the Graham empire was expanding.

This was a period of great restless creativity for him. Kay was uneasy with it, he seemed almost beyond restraint. He not only acquired *Newsweek,* he bought *Art News.* Later that year he had another idea. He had always wanted to amplify the *Post*'s coverage, to create some kind of news service. *The New York Times* had a news service, syndicating its stories to more than a hundred papers, and it was not only very profitable for the *Times,* it vastly increased its national influence. He had wanted something like that for the *Post* but he had always lacked the resources. Now in 1961 he watched from a distance the changes young Otis Chandler was making on the Los Angeles *Times.* He started checking out Chandler and every report was good. John Sweeterman, his business-side man, knew the Chandlers and assured Graham that young Otis was a very serious modern young man, determined to improve and upgrade the *Times.* "You know, I've always wanted a news service, and if they're going to be that good, maybe we can hook up. They've always been financially successful and editorially weak, and we've always been editorially successful and financially weak. So we're at about the same place." Graham put Sweeterman in charge of working out some arrangements with Otis Chandler. Quickly the details were settled; each paper would put a certain number of foreign correspondents in the pot, being sure to match each other, and they would at first try not to overlap and duplicate each other in foreign capitals. It was a terribly important moment, it committed each paper to having a foreign staff, it moved each that much further away from parochialism, and it vastly amplified the power and influence of both papers as the news service grew and grew; by 1978 more than three hundred and fifty subscribed. When it came time to name the news service, the *Post* editor felt it should be called the Washington Post–Los Angeles Times Syndicate, since the *Post* was by far the more prestigious of the two papers. Sweeterman suggested this at the final meeting. "No, John," said Graham, acutely aware of Chandler sensitivity to eastern snobbery, "we'll call it the Los Angeles Times–Washington Post News Service." He had in a very brief period taken an idea that no one else had, and that others scoffed at, and not only made it come alive but made it work. It was Phil Graham at his best.

It was time now to make real another dream. Phil Graham had always wanted Walter Lippmann for the *Post. The* Washington columnist would have long ago made the *Post the* Washington paper. Graham had pursued it with some intensity over many years. But then after he bought *Newsweek* he had a brainstorm. He had wanted desperately to make *Newsweek* big-time, and big-time as quickly as he could. What better way than to have Walter Lippmann as a columnist for *Newsweek* once a month? Overnight that would give *Newsweek* the intellectual respectability it had always lacked. Graham had broached the new idea to Lippmann and the eminence, who was immune to neither flattery nor money, had gradually let himself be seduced. But not seduced cheaply. He came to the *Post* and *Newsweek,* it was said, for $100,000 a year, an immense sum in journalistic circles at that time, the money to continue until he died, and with his wife, if she outlived him, to receive a handsome annual figure.

So the stage was set. Graham was euphoric. All that was required was for Lippmann to sign the contract. At this point he became wonderfully secretive. He called Jim Cannon, still a *Newsweek* editor and now Graham's own man in New York. He had worked out a plan worthy of the CIA. Charley Paradise, Graham's personal secretary, would be flying from Washington to New York under an assumed name, carrying the Lippmann contract. Cannon was to say nothing to anyone else, and to meet him at the airport. He was to receive the contract, which was in an envelope without the *Post* letterhead. He was to take the envelope to a famous law firm. There he would find Lippmann already accompanied by his lawyers. Lippmann would identify himself as being Walter Lippmann. Cannon was to hand the letter to Lippmann and no one else. He was to sit there and be witness while Lippmann discussed it with his lawyers. He was to wait for Lippmann to sign it. He was to receive it from Lippmann and verify with the lawyers that it had been signed. Then he was to leave and immediately call Graham on a secret phone. Graham would be waiting. Cannon was not to mention this to anyone else, particularly Cannon's great buddy Oz Elliott, the editor of *Newsweek.* Graham would do that himself.

. . .

Nothing better symbolized the changing role of the press, necessitated by the changing role of America and its entrance into the world, than the emergence of Walter Lippmann as the national philosopher-journalist. For some thirty years he served as the nation's foremost columnist and his impact upon two generations of America's most important and influential journalists was almost beyond measure. "He has given my generation a wider vision of our duty," James Reston, one of his chief disciples, once wrote of him. As America moved into a new international orbit where it was in constant conflict with other great powers, it was Lippmann who filled the desperate need for intellectual depth and who was able to put these conflicts into some kind of context. Whereas the previous towering journalistic figures of Washington had been renowned because they knew the city, or the President, or the Speaker of the House, Lippmann stood out because he knew the world. Certainly few journalists of Lippmann's own era had any preparation for the new role; they might, at best, come alive at a Republican or Democratic convention. In an age when journalism was making a forced transition from the *Front Page* mentality and a preoccupation with local news into dealing with a world whose presence was both immediate and threatening, Lippmann was fittingly enough rooted not in journalism but in academe. His role models were not journalists but the great figures of the Harvard Philosophy Department. When he was an undergraduate James and Santayana had pleaded with him to remain on as a faculty member, the better to follow in their own footsteps in a profession so carefully separated from the world at large. He was a journalist who had never covered a story, had never worked in a city room, and had never rushed to a fire. Perhaps, in another, calmer age, he, like his patrons, might have remained at a safe distance from the heat and fire of great events; after all, Santayana had once casually remarked to the young Lippmann, "I see by my small Spanish paper that Taft has been elected President."

But events were too pressing, the world was closing in, distance was shrinking. Lippmann was twenty-five when World War I began, and he eventually served as an intelligence officer. The war belonged to his generation, he could not ignore the implications: the end of American isolation, be it the political isolation of Washington or the intellectual isolation of academe. So it was that this talented young man, who at the age of twenty-five found out about the approach of World War I only because a much-desired walking tour of the Alps was canceled, left the field of abstract philosophy and entered the more immediate world, as first an editorial writer and then eventually a columnist. There was an element of shrewdness to it. Not only was he moved by these events, which were now irresistible and could not be ignored, but he was drawn by the audience that his comments on these events offered him. At Harvard he would have been part of an elite within an elite, his books highly praised and read by a small but brilliant fraction of the intellectual world; as a columnist he would reach a far greater audience. The forum amplified his voice; people listened to him because he wrote at the very moment when they most needed help and guidance. He became, not the distant disconnected philosopher, but instead the chronicler of the most important events of a terrifying age, his audience made constantly larger by the immediacy of his subject. Over the desk where he wrote was the original of a Thurber *New Yorker* cartoon that had a woman saying to her husband: "Lippmann scares me this morning."

As the daily columnist he gradually stood alone. No one else had the territory that Lippmann had, the knowledge, the range, the intelligence, and above all the confidence in himself and his judgments. Those of his protégés who were a generation younger looked to Lippmann with undisguised awe and admiration; they had come to journalism through the traditional routes, they had written the requisite police stories and chased fire engines and they had done all that a bit better than their peers, moving ahead in their profession, and they had finally come to Washington. If after their arrival in Washington they wrote stories about foreign policy, then they did not dare inject their own viewpoints, of which they had none, or their own expertise, of which they also had none. Rather they relied almost exclusively upon what some American or possibly British official told them at a briefing or at lunch. The closer journalists came to great issues, the more vulnerable they felt. Lippmann was different; this was, after all, the young man who while still in his twenties had helped draft Wilson's Fourteen Points. He did not need a quote from someone in the State Department to steady his hand.

His very career seemed to mirror America's entrance into the world. As a freshman at Harvard he had written an article in a student monthly, and the great William James, the emeritus philosophy professor, had walked across Harvard Yard to the freshman dorm just to meet this prodigy. His classmate John Reed, who later chronicled the Russian Revolution, introduced Lippmann to friends as the future President of the United States. James Truslow Adams predicted that Lippmann would be Secretary of State, or at the very least, if things did not pan out, governor of New York. Theodore Roosevelt called him the most brilliant young man of his generation. When the war was over he had returned to become an early editor of *The New Republic,* then editorial-page editor of the New York *World.* The *World* under Pulitzer was a dazzling paper, it was built upon the star system, and nowhere so much as on the editorial page, where there was a genuine galaxy of talent: Lippmann, Arthur Krock, Allan Nevins, and James M. Cain, the novelist. But the business side was never very strong, and the *World* was seriously mismanaged. When it died in 1931, Lippmann became a columnist. It was to be his decisive incarnation. He was forty-two at the time. The offer came from Mrs. Ogden Reid, who ran the *Herald Tribune,* a paper with a devoutly Republican editorial page. The *Trib* was not a reactionary paper, it was in fact the embodiment of the eastern Republican establishment; it did not actually want to turn back the clock, but it was in no rush to move it ahead either. Lippmann, who had flirted briefly with socialism in his youth, accepted the offer.

Many of his more ardent liberal admirers were appalled, a typical state of affairs that symbolized the ongoing tension between Lippmann and the liberals, who always wanted Lippmann to be more liberal than, in fact, he was. As they were internationalist at the time, so was he; as they were humane and people of good will, so was he; as they were liberal and tended to prefer social change, so he, quite often, did not. For he was not an ideologue. He was a man with a passion for rationality and civility and order, all of those achieved with the coolest intelligence possible. He wanted America to become an adult society in an orderly, civilized world. Anger, passion, gunshot dismayed him and threatened him. He was, after all, the only son born to very prosperous German-Jewish aristocrats, and he had been a somewhat spoiled, somewhat precious young man, very intent upon controlling his feelings, deeply sensitive about his background. (When Lippmann turned seventy, a group of his younger colleagues and admirers published a book of essays in honor of him. His childhood friend Carl Binger, by then a nationally known psychiatrist, was asked to write about Lippmann's boyhood. Binger said he would be glad to. But, he emphasized, there was one thing he knew he could not mention and still retain Lippmann's friendship. He could not say that Walter was Jewish. Otherwise Walter would never forgive him, and would never speak to him again. Binger got around it by noting that Lippmann had attended Dr. Sachs's School for Boys, which was where the Our Crowd people in those days sent their sons.)

His column was immensely successful from the start; it was vital to the *Trib* and to an uncommon degree it made the *Trib* competitive with the *Times*. If the *Times* gave readers far more news, then Lippmann at the *Trib* made the world seem far more understandable. In 1939, after eight years of writing the column in New York, he moved to Washington. That too was symbolic. His years there marked the coming of the United States to superpower status. In his mind Washington was not just the capital of the nation, it was on its way to becoming the capital of the West. Lippmann would stay there, a man of Washington, genteel and civilized, for the next twenty-eight years.

He had never worked in a city room, but journalist he was. *Today and Tomorrow,* he called his column. He believed that he owed his readers one thing above all else, the kind of intelligence and perspective necessary to prevent them from being surprised by the transcending events of the day. He did not write of the minutiae of government, of the daily swirling Washington rumors or the small factional fights within the bureaucracy which at the moment often loomed so large to his peers. His sights were always on the larger horizon. Nothing petty interested him. He was quite capable of burying very big scoops in his columns. He seemed somehow, perhaps because of his travels, perhaps because of his background, much more a man of the world, much more the true internationalist than other journalists. His passport seemed to show less in his writing, and he seemed above much of the pettier unconscious nationalism that infected most of his colleagues. He was history's child. It was not by chance that he was impressed by the possibilities of the Chinese-Soviet split some ten years before the State Department, nor was it surprising that, unlike the State Department, he saw the war in Vietnam very early on, not in terms of monolithic Communism, but in terms of traditional Vietnamese nationalism.

The younger journalists of the day who honored him and learned from him—Reston, Marquis Childs, Richard Rovere, John Chancellor, Eric Sevareid, Murrow—imprisoned as they were by deadlines, were moved by the fact that he brought, above all else, so much intelligence and so large a sense of history to his daily work. He seemed in outlook to be timeless, untarnished, a man of the nineteenth century drafted to cover the furies of the twentieth. The others felt themselves overwhelmed by events; and only Lippmann seemed always to have time to think. Where they were most vulnerable, he was at his strongest. In the post–World War II years, when America reluctantly accepted vast new global responsibilities, Lippmann was already in his mid-fifties, an emeritus age by most journalistic standards; he had in effect spent an entire life preparing for this moment, while they were bright young men whose skills had in some cases—at least in their own minds—propelled them far beyond their normal range. While they still apprenticed, Lippmann was already *there,* ahead of not only them but the Secretary of State as well, it often seemed.

He had enviable control of his life. Other journalists were prisoners of events, tearing up long-planned vacations at the last minute as the United States or the Soviet Union unveiled some new charge. But Lippmann never did. At the beginning of the year he knew his entire schedule, when he would be in Washington, when he would go to New York for his annual two weeks of theater, when he and Helen would give the first of their two annual parties, when he would go to Maine for the summer, and when he would take his annual trip to Europe. Later in his life, during presidential-election years, Lippmann would slightly alter his summer vacation schedule and return briefly from Maine. He did this, heaven knows, not to cover the conventions themselves, he did not intend to be *that* direct a witness to history, it was simply that his house in Washington had far better television reception than his summer house in Maine. But the rest of his life was like a metronome. He would rise at a certain hour in the morning, read the required paper by 9 A.M., then write the column in longhand. At 12:30 a yellow cab dispatched by the Washington *Post* would come by to pick up the copy. Then and only then would he depart for a working lunch at the Metropolitan Club. Reston, his protégé, once wrote facetiously of the single physical hardship in Lippmann's life, the continuing struggle between the sage and the resident mockingbirds who disturbed his work. Wanting neither to harm them nor to listen to them, Lippmann had solved this delicate dilemma by padding his chimney to muffle their voices.

His younger colleagues were aware that he was in his own way a very good journalist. He used *The New York Times,* the only paper in America with a large staff of foreign correspondents, as his private news service. He kept in close touch with Reston for a regular fill-in on domestic politics. Whenever there was a bright young *Times* reporter back from a distant part of the world, Lippmann, through Reston, arranged a lunch. There was hardly a significant young correspondent in Washington that Lippmann had not flattered with a luncheon invitation—whereupon the pundit proceeded with what in a less civilized man would have seemed the most predatory kind of brain picking. "They say," he once told a young reporter back from Africa, "that I have to know something about Africa. But I'm already having a difficult enough time with Asia. Can you please help me and tell me something about Africa?" Who would not jump at the honor of turning over everything in his brain? The only quid pro quo to this—Lippmann got all the information he wanted and gave none, let no younger reporter dare ask *him* a question—the younger reporter was able to say that he had lunched with *Lippmann,* tangible evidence of a career on the rise. Lippmann was thus very good at staying young, at not aging and becoming a prisoner of his past experiences. (Indeed, this freedom from the past could be troubling. Near the end of his life it was decided that someone should write the definitive biography of Lippmann, and Richard Rovere of *The New Yorker* was chosen to do the job. Rovere was very pleased about the assignment and began interviewing Lippmann about his career. On occasion he would ask him why he had taken certain positions, or what his role had been in certain important political events, or how he recalled things that had happened, say, twenty or thirty years before. Lippmann was satisfactorily forthcoming, indeed generous with circumstantial detail. But as Rovere began checking the old man's recollections against other sources, including Lippmann's own diaries, he discovered many discrepancies. So many, in fact, as to imperil the entire project. Finally, in frustration, Rovere withdrew from the assignment.)

But he shaped a generation. By his presence he made the profession infinitely more respectable, infinitely more honorable, and that much more, in fact, a true profession. In particular his influence upon men like Reston and even younger men like Ben Bradlee, the rising stars of newer generations, was immense. Journalism was not just facts and bulletins, journalism must explain things, journalism must embrace ideas.

In hiring Lippmann, Graham paid him what most of his associates thought was an exorbitant sum. Kay thought so too. Years later, after Lippmann died, there was some talk about endowing a Lippmann Chair at the Nieman Foundation at Harvard, but when Harvard officials talked with Kay Graham about it, they found her very cool, even though Walter had been one of her great friends; her family, she felt, had already endowed Walter Lippmann when he was alive. But in some ways Phil had been right, Lippmann was worth it, there was only one Lippmann and having Lippmann as part of the empire was worth the money. Later, pleased with how well Lippmann was working out for *Newsweek* and the *Post,* Graham decided to give him a huge car as a present and, being delighted with his own generosity, was deeply wounded when Lippmann did not like the car and wanted to exchange it.

There were quick flashes of Phil Graham's illness exposed now even to people on the outside. A young reporter for *Newsweek,* thinking of leaving for another job, met with Graham. Graham, who wanted to keep him, was absolutely charming at first, nothing but warmth and praise; when it became clear a few minutes later that the reporter was serious, that he really intended to leave, Graham changed to instant rage: "All you little pricks are all alike, you're in it for nothing but what you can take from us." The top people at the Washington *Post* had been aware of his sickness for some time, but the highs and lows were coming faster and faster and they seemed more and more dangerous. In the beginning no one at *Newsweek* suspected the illness, they did not know him as well, he was in Washington, they were in New York. All they saw was a quick, energetic, brilliant man, almost too quick for his own good, who always seemed three steps ahead of them. He was very good to them, he kept his promises to expand the budget and bring in new people, and he was wonderfully informal. (When he had held his first meeting with his top editors at the Carlyle he had asked Elliott what kind of men they were. "How informal do I have to be? Do I have to wear shoes and socks for them?" Elliott had said no, of course not, they're informal, and so they all showed up at his room and he had come to the door naked except for a towel. Elliott had said yes, informal, Phil, but isn't this a bit too informal? But the lunch had gone well, until suddenly someone had looked down on the floor and there was a white pill, clearly a Miltown. There was an argument over whom it belonged to: Phil Graham thought it was his, but one of the editors thought it was *his.*) In the first few weeks after he bought the magazine he was very much present, but then he had stayed away and his editors thought he was simply showing confidence in them. The truth was that he was in a very deep depression and out of touch with everyone. Then, about a month after he bought the magazine, came the Bay of Pigs, engineered as it was by his best friends at the White House. Oz Elliott had called to give him news of it, thinking that on events of this gravity the publisher at the very least should be informed. "You'd better," Elliott said, "cast your mind back over the last eight years of Ike and think if there was anything as bad as this."

There was a long pause at the other end of the phone and Elliott thought for a moment that something might have gone wrong with the wire. But then he heard Graham's voice saying, "I'm still here, but for the first time in my life I'm trying to think before I speak. . . ." Then there was another pause, and finally he said, "No, I guess not, but in the long reach of history it will seem very small." And so it was that *Newsweek* did not come down very hard on the Bay of Pigs.

Nor did the Washington *Post* say very much about the Bay of Pigs. There was a nice genteel chumminess between the top people at the paper and the top people in National Security, even during the Eisenhower years; a centrist consensus of direction, a unity against the enemies, both abroad and at home, and that was even more true now that Kennedy was in office. Kennedy and Graham were of the same generation, the same background, the same attitudes, and the same purpose. They saw each other too often socially and trusted each other too much. Reporters who, covering a labor dispute or a political dispute, might have kept themselves distant from even the most subtle manipulation, were remarkably vulnerable to the seductive call of National Security. The call of the Good Citizen. The need of the Nation to stand as one. This was particularly true in Washington, where the government was the one business and the most sacrosanct part of that business was dealing with foreign countries, particularly covert dealings; the government's norms were more sacred in Washington, its ability to isolate violators socially more real. There, all the good and responsible people in journalism had grown up with all the good and responsible in government; they had gone to the same schools together. The CIA in particular seemed to specialize in well-born, genteel figures who moved smoothly in and out of the same drawing rooms as the most influential Washington journalists, their very civility an unspoken promise that they would not be a part of unseemly deeds. It was an illustration in microcosm of the social vulnerability of the press. In addition, as Washington was a company town, Phil Graham, by dint of his power base and his personal energy and his creativity, was the company manager.

When the Bay of Pigs was being planned, Chalmers Roberts, the *Post*'s national security reporter, knew from good sources that something was coming; he had been briefed a few days before the landing by Jack Kennedy himself. After checking with his superiors because it was a story of such magnitude, Roberts had written only that anti-Castro Cubans were about to fight Castro Cubans for control of the island and that the anti-Castro Cubans had the blessing of the Kennedy administration. (In a revealing moment in his own history of the Washington *Post,* Roberts told of the *Post*'s failure and of his own role. "The fact was," he wrote some sixteen years later, "that Graham, Wiggins, Friendly and Roberts found no fault with such a CIA operation and hoped it would succeed in what they perceived as the national interest.") Karl Meyer, an editorial writer with strong Latin-American connections who knew something of the events beforehand, found himself quashed in his attempt to get anything in the paper. It was a crucial moment; it was the ability to stand apart from the government on an issue like this that separated a great and independent paper from an ordinary rich but docile paper which, free country or no, took its signal from the government. Graham's voice sounded from the editorial page, in tones he might have used in talking to Jack Kennedy himself: the events in Cuba, the *Post* wrote, were "only one chapter in the long history of freedom which has encompassed many great disasters and many darker days before men have combined their wit and determination to write a brighter sequel." Graham also killed an editorial critical of the Bay of Pigs written by Bob Estabrook, his editorial-page editor, pulling it without even consulting Estabrook.

The personal connections helped. Another administration might have fared as well; certainly powerful American newspapers, particularly in 1961, did not lightly challenge the course of American foreign policy. But the fact that it was Kennedy made a difference. Kennedy, after all, was so likable, so charming about his connections with publishers and reporters, he made it easier for journalists to believe in his essential good will. Because of that charm and intelligence they gave him the benefit of the doubt. It was impossible for important journalists of that era to believe that such a man would carry America on a course into darkness, that on certain issues he might be far from candid, or that the machinery of the government was too powerful even for a man of such ability. Thus the *Post* at the time of the Bay of Pigs did not criticize the most important issue of that disaster, the fact that the machinery was in part out of control; for one thing, the editors of the *Post* were simply too close to the machinery.

In New York there was some uneasiness about the Bay of Pigs. After all, New York was two hundred miles away from Washington and people there were less in awe of Washington's great names and great titles. Not everyone in New York was enthralled by Graham's closeness to Kennedy. Indeed, it was for some of the middle-ranking *Newsweek* editors not just the Kennedy-Graham friendship that was so bothersome, it was that Bradlee was also very close to the President. For Bradlee's reward for the purchase of *Newsweek* had not been just a finder's fee, or a chance for stock options. It had been something even better: he had been given the Washington bureau of *Newsweek*, something he probably would have gotten on merit anyway, although career advancement always seemed to be a little faster and a little easier for Bradlee than for most people. He had, in the immortal words of his friend Art Buchwald, battled his way up through the school of hard knocks of St. Mark's and Harvard. He had returned to Washington from Paris in 1957 and moved to P Street in Georgetown, and his neighbor on that block, only five houses down, had been Jack Kennedy, just preparing for his presidential race, and the friendship had flourished. Kennedy loved to be surrounded by super-Wasps anyway, and Jackie, lonely and unhappy in Washington, had liked Antoinette (Tony) Bradlee. ("Will you be my best friend?" she had once asked Tony plaintively.) Jack Kennedy had also liked Tony Pinchot Bradlee very much. ("Oh, Jack," Bradlee quoted Jackie saying in his book *Conversations with Kennedy*, "you know you always say that Tony is your ideal." The President replied, "Yes, that's true," and then a second or two later added, "You're my ideal, Jacqueline.") It was all just a little tricky, for Kennedy was also, apparently unbeknownst to Bradlee, having a prolonged affair with Tony Bradlee's divorced sister, Mary Pinchot Meyer. Otherwise it was all very pleasant and charming. Bradlee and Kennedy were in many ways uncommonly similar men, their values, their drives, their charm were strikingly of a kind, if Bradlee had been a politician he would have been Kennedy and if Kennedy had been a journalist he would have been Bradlee. (*That Special Grace* was the title of Bradlee's first book, a brief memoir of the Kennedy style.) There was a nice snobbery to it all, so that when the Kennedys were in the White House there were often evenings when politicians were invited over to watch movies (which was considered a plus, you had entertained them without having to talk to them, "only fifteen minutes of our time," in Jackie's words), and then after they departed, the Kennedys and the Bradlees would share a small private buffet dinner.

That had been a terrific connection for *Newsweek,* still fighting the larger, richer apparatus of *Time,* a sense of a unique connection. Which was not entirely true; Kennedy, controlled as ever, might see Bradlee more socially, and might give him very real access, but he made sure that Hugh Sidey of the potentially hostile *Time* had as much access as anyone else, if not more. There were, in fact, few clear journalistic triumphs for Bradlee over Sidey; Kennedy might complain regularly to Bradlee about Luce and his publications, what sons of bitches they were, but he rarely gave Bradlee much of a lead. Most of it was almost a matter of visibility, almost of gamesmanship, Bradlee being with Kennedy in Washington the night in 1960 he won the West Virginia primary, and flying at the President's invitation back to Charleston that night in the *Caroline,* so that Sidey could watch Bradlee get off the plane right behind the President.

The nation had an insatiable appetite for the Kennedys and so the top *Newsweek* people loved the Bradlee connection; there would be a story deadline on Friday, everyone sitting around, and at the last minute Bradlee would call in and would talk about what an unidentified high source had said, and everyone knew who it was, it was the President himself. Bradlee did not even have to say it, it was all too cool for that. There was a wonderful sense of being on the inside and knowing the inside things. *Newsweek* had Bradlee and *Newsweek* was connected: *Newsweek* knew what Kennedy had for breakfast. It was Kennedy using Bradlee for his purpose, which was to have a direct conduit into *Newsweek;* and Bradlee using Kennedy for his purpose: it had not hurt his career to have a direct connection to a politician so clearly on the rise. And *Newsweek* was using the connection for *its* purpose, which was to close the gap on *Time.* Later, in another era, as journalists put themselves and their ethics under more scrutiny, there would be some uneasiness about the relationship between Kennedy and both Graham and Bradlee. (Indeed, when Bradlee wrote his book about those years, a book that did not help his reputation, coming as it did right after his paper had played a major role in the unseating of Richard Nixon, there were friends of his who explained his action by saying that he had written it to warn young journalists against the same course.) But at the time the executives of *Newsweek* loved the relationship. There was a feeling that there was a new leadership in the nation and a new style at work in the country, and that *Newsweek* rather than *Time* was taking advantage of it.

Phil Graham was, by the end of 1961, a desperately ill man. The depressions were deeper now and far more terrifying; his highs were more frenzied, there were fewer and fewer restraints. He knew he was very sick; in the last years of his life he was institutionalized three times, twice voluntarily. More and more often he told friends in his darker moments that he faced a choice of living as a very sick man who everyone thought was crazy or perhaps committing suicide. His public behavior was becoming more and more erratic. A brilliant performance on the board of COMSAT, the communications satellite corporation, which Kennedy had asked him to run, was punctuated by a fistfight with a lawyer. There were endless haranguing calls to both Johnson and Kennedy. At first, Johnson, who had no idea that Graham was ill, was puzzled. "What's wrong with Phil?" he would ask. "He just seems so different." Then, as the illness became more serious, Graham began to taunt Johnson. "You'll never be President, Lyndon," he would say. "This is the end of the line. Just Vice-President." Johnson, insecure in his own new incarnation, and deeply wounded by the cruelty, cut himself off from Graham. Kennedy tried to retain the friendship; he once told Bradlee, holding his thumb and forefinger close together, "The line is drawn narrow between rationality and irrationality in Phil." Graham would sometimes stomp past the White House guards on his way to Kennedy's office. Once when he began berating Kennedy over the phone, the President tried to calm him. "Do you know who you're talking to?" Graham shouted. "I know it isn't the Phil Graham that I love and respect," Kennedy answered. He saw a photo in the *Post* of a columnist escorting Kay to a benefit and he tried to have the columnist, who was totally innocent of any involvement, fired; at the same time his own affairs were mounting, and he was becoming less discreet. He raced around Europe hiring correspondents for *Newsweek* and promising others raises and transfers until finally Oz Elliott called him and said that this was totally disrupting the magazine and unless Graham stopped he would have to find himself a new editor. "Osborn, old buddy," Graham answered, "I love you," thus totally disarming Elliott.

He seemed in the last year or so always on the edge of firing Russ Wiggins, the *Post* editor, and Al Friendly, the managing editor, and at one point he beseeched Kennedy to fire Wiggins for him. During the New York newspaper strike in the winter of 1962–63, he involved himself and became a self-appointed negotiator, much to the annoyance of the other publishers. He quickly became enamored of Bert Powers, who headed the printers' union, which annoyed the publishers even more. He forced Friendly to come up and write a piece on Powers, promising that if Powers wasn't as wonderful as Graham claimed, then he would buy Friendly a car. He was not entirely satisfied with what Friendly wrote, so he drafted his own editorial on the strike, which Wiggins considered so one-sided that he refused to run it, and he told Graham that he would quit the paper if it ran. Graham pulled back, but from then on he made Wiggins the main target of his anger and schemed relentlessly to get rid of him. He tried to replace Wiggins with Friendly (the two were close friends), largely, Friendly thought, because he was not quite so strong a figure and might prove more malleable than Wiggins. It was a terrible time for both men, trying to deal with and protect a man they loved, trying to put out a paper, and trying to hold on to their jobs.

It was also clear in the last few years of his life what the main preoccupation of his sickness was—his obsession with being a son-in-law. He talked about it all the time, and he argued bitterly with those who said that his success was his own. He turned against the figure of Eugene Meyer, who had died in 1959, and he began to lecture friends on what a sinister figure Meyer was, either calling Meyer a kike—the anti-Semitism was becoming more virulent—or wildly advising friends that they must not be like Meyer because he was anti-Semitic himself and had never hired Jews at Allied Chemical. Meyer, he said, Meyer was nothing, the *Post* was a terrible newspaper until he, Graham, had taken it over, he was the one who had made it a success, but they had no gratitude toward him for that, it was not in them. Old friends who knew how much Meyer had loved Phil were shocked. He turned not just against Meyer but against Kay as well; he spoke with anger about her and about his own children, they were kikes too. He was a man caught in the deepest throes of self-hatred and self-destruction, and when the manic period was over he would talk plaintively of how badly he had treated Kay, how good she had been to him, how unworthy he was. He would go from a high of total arrogance and increasing meanness of spirit to a low of total despair. He knew in moments of lucidity that he was very sick, and he was terrified of the future. He did not want to be mad, a burden to those he loved and cared about, and he did not want to be some tranquilized half vegetable. He told a few close friends like Al Friendly that rather than live half a life, he would kill himself. Those who knew him well, who knew how strong his will was, took him seriously.

His last affair told it all. It was the sum of all of his frustration at being a son-in-law, and he carried it out as publicly as he could, as if in vengeance against himself and his in-laws. It was with a young staff member of the *Newsweek* Paris bureau named Robin Webb. She was Australian, and she was, mutual friends thought, as startled by some of Graham's behavior as everyone else. They had met in Paris in 1963. Very soon he was being seen everywhere with her, as publicly as possible; more, he was announcing his intention of marrying her and yet keeping both the *Post* and *Newsweek*. It was clearly a declaration of independence from the Meyer family. He announced this to all his friends, that he and Robin would soon wed. (Once in this period he called Robert McNamara, then Secretary of Defense, who was then feuding with some of the top military personnel, to announce, first, that he was going to marry Robin, and second, that McNamara's feuds with the military were hurting the nation, and he, Graham, intended to bring them all together and settle it. At which point McNamara, who was not normally noted for his sense of humor, told Graham, "Phil, I've got a wonderful wedding present for you. I won't edit the Washington *Post* for you any more if you'll give me back the Department of Defense.") So there he was, traveling around the world with Robin, grand summit meetings of all the *Newsweek* foreign correspondents, presided over by Phil, with Robin at his side, great dinners at the Connaught in London, presided over by the two of them, Phil never looking more dashing or elegant or princely, a surrealistic scene to working reporters who were at once fascinated by what they were seeing, the audacity of it, intrigued by Phil's personal promises of both journalistic greatness and salary increases, and yet wondering all the time where Kay was, and what she thought of it all. They were, after all, Meyer properties.

And at this very moment, he was undergoing a new and almost uncontrollable urge to find religion. He began to seek out friends who had strong religious beliefs. Emmet Hughes, who had worked for *Time* and was about to go to work for *Newsweek,* was a serious Catholic, and Graham had always been fascinated by Hughes's Catholicism. Now it was as if he wanted to share it. They talked more and more about religion and on occasion Hughes would come to Graham's room in the Carlyle to find him disheveled, unshaven, but walking around reading a Bible aloud. They talked often about Graham's struggles against suicide, how hard he was finding it to hold on to life and how difficult it was to convey his despair in the world of rationalism in which he lived. "I can't talk to people in Washington any more. People like Bundy and Schlesinger. They're all very bright, but they don't know what I'm talking about, what I'm going through. The spiritual part. The desperation." He had picked up a Bible and walked around the room reading it and he seemed for a moment to be taunting Hughes. "You know," he said, "it's too bad you were born a Catholic, you really don't know what it means. It's taken me all this time to learn it. You have to come to it the hard way." He also sought out his friend Scotty Reston of the *Times,* a serious practicing Protestant. His talks with Reston were not only theological. He clearly envied the core of Reston's family life and he wanted to know what kept him so straight. Was it Reston's parents? His upbringing? Reston believed it was his wife, Sally, who held things together. Why, Graham seemed to plead, was he himself so filled with doubts and demons? It was as if he were looking for some kind of spiritual strength from men like Reston and Hughes, hoping to find, in their faith, something to sustain him in his desperation.

It was clear in the last year that he seriously intended to take control of the paper and the magazine and marry Robin; more, given what the stock situation was or at least what Meyer had given him, he might just be able to do it. Or if he failed, it would be because he had been declared insane. Only that could keep him from control. Which sent Washington, a small gossipy town at its journalistic-political heart, into a kind of hysteria. A struggle between Kay and Phil was not just a divorce but a struggle for power, comparable to a sitting President on the eve of an election jettisoning one Vice-President to choose another for his second term. The city was alive with rumors and talk. Everyone in town was fascinated. Was it true, asked President John Kennedy, summoning Ben Bradlee, that the Meyer family was trying to unload *Newsweek,* that they were unhappy with the entire business? It was, of course, important to be loyal, but it was also very much a matter of being on the right side. It would not do to be disloyal, but it would be even worse to be disloyal to the winner. That might put someone on the wrong side of a very powerful publisher, whoever he or *she* might be. In *Newsweek,* in the New York offices, the top editors sat and discussed whether or not the man they worked for was sane, and what they would do if called to testify in court. In Washington, where the Grahams were an essential part of the social scene, where everyone loved and admired Phil yet cared about Kay, there were sharp divisions. Phil People and Kay People. It was, one friend of both of them thought, an interesting division, some men tending to side with Phil, their wives with Kay, particularly if they were a little middle-aged and not that attractive. No one was sure what the stock deal was. There were reports that Phil had the majority share. He just might pull it off. He might not be mad, he might just be a little eccentric. The sides were very sharply divided. (Indeed, years later when Kay Graham decided to publish the Pentagon Papers, Jim Rowe, an old Washington traditionalist and a committed hawk, told Ben Bagdikian, with some anger, about her decision, "Look at her over there, surrounded by nothing but Phil People and turning her back on the people like us who were Kay People.") Some people tried to straddle. One high *Newsweek* executive failed to pass all of Phil's loyalty tests and so, one day, Phil Graham waited until the executive had gone home and then moved every bit of furniture and belongings out of his office, put an entirely new name on the door and new furniture in, so that the next day when the aide came to work, he found his office gone. He had been turned into a nonperson.

It was a terrible time for Kay. The humiliations seemed endless, some small, some large. It was as if every phone call might bring some new slight. Where there were no real slights, she could imagine them. Once, near the end of it, she had come to New York to go to the ballet with some friends, Kay People all. The *Newsweek* office had arranged tickets, but the secretary had made a mistake and got them for the wrong evening, and so when Kay and her friends showed up at the ballet they had been turned away. She was sure it was a deliberate attempt by Phil to humiliate her in front of her closest friends. Only the most apologetic letter from the secretary finally softened the blow. She was in pain, of course, not just for herself but for him as well. She loved him and she knew he was out of control. She was at once terribly wounded by him and at the same time trying desperately to save him. When he announced he was leaving her and that he was going to take control of the paper, his doctors told her not to fight him overtly, that his behavior was already so erratic that any challenge on her part might push him over the edge. So on the surface at least she acquiesced; she would, it appeared, turn over the paper to him.

Her mother, Agnes Meyer, was not so acquiescent; she was in that year far more ready to challenge Phil than Kay was. Agnes was a born battalion commander, a woman who had always seemed to prefer her son-in-law to her own daughter. Phil's charm had always worked with her, he called her "Grandma" and he could cajole her into almost anything, even writing a check for a million dollars to keep a baseball team in Washington. "Come on, Grandma, let's just write that check," and Agnes had in fact written the check. But now she threw her troops to her daughter; she was not about to let this man take the newspaper away from her grandchildren and walk away with the Meyer property. ("Isn't it curious," she said in the middle of the struggle, "that none of this has even gotten into the newspapers?") She threw a huge party for Kay at which most of Washington turned out in a show of loyalty. And she let Phil Graham know he could not fire Russ Wiggins and Al Friendly.

Nevertheless, he seemed to mean what he said about taking the paper. He went to his lawyer friend Ed Williams and said that he wanted Williams to get him a divorce so he could marry Robin. That seemed very final. At this point Williams played a central role. He and Phil Graham were very close (a friendship in part cemented by the fact that Williams in *his* first marriage had married the daughter of the head of the very prestigious law firm for which he worked), and during the last years of the illness they had become even closer. Ed Williams did not know Kay Graham very well, nor did he have any particular feeling for her, but he knew that Phil Graham was a very sick man and that this divorce and remarriage, with all its implications, should not now take place. Perhaps another time, when his friend was better. So he saw his job as slowing down Phil's demands and the divorce process while still remaining his friend and confidant. It was not altogether easy. Starting in early 1963, as Graham was coming off his New York newspaper strike high, and continuing for some six months, Williams ostensibly worked for Phil, trying to get the divorce for him, conscientiously playing the role of the one person in Washington who was not going around saying that Phil Graham was crazy. Why, they were buddies and Ed was going to get Phil's divorce for him, Phil was all right, he knew what he was doing. All the time, however, he was working to slow things down. Kay Graham had no knowledge of this. As far as she was concerned, Williams was a Mephistophelian figure, a member of the Red team, trying to steal the paper from her and her children. But during those six months, back and forth it went, Graham pushing, and Williams stalling, waiting for Phil to come off the high and working to get Robin out of the picture.

Which finally happened. In 1963, Phil and Robin had gone to Phoenix for a publishers' convention. The two of them had been there a week and it had been a very hard week. He was announcing that he was going to marry her and perhaps marry her right down there. He had been drinking a great deal and he was a little rough with her; his behavior was clearly more erratic now than ever. The night of the main banquet he had been drinking very heavily and was very abrasive. One of the speakers was Ben McKelway of the Washington *Star*. Speeches at publishers-and-editors meetings are usually by definition reasonably self-indulgent, a lot of talk about the greatness of the press and the freedom thereof, and McKelway's was by most measures an ordinary speech, but it was too much for Phil Graham. He took the podium and made an extraordinary wild and obscene speech, attacking everyone there: they were all fat bastards, they were afraid of the truth, he would not wipe his ass with their papers. It was mostly obscenities, not without some measure of truth, of course, and there seemed no way to end it until McKelway's wife walked up to the podium and very gently took his hand and told him he was very good, but he had said enough.

In Washington they knew it was worse than ever and they dispatched two psychiatrists to Phoenix. They also decided to send Emmet Hughes, who was the best man to deal with him when he was in this shape. Hughes got together with the psychiatrists and it was the first time in his life that he had had to use physical force on someone: the three of them wrestled Graham down and injected some drugs into him. Jack Kennedy had sent a presidential plane for him, and they finally got him aboard, but not before he had punched out a house detective at the airport. They flew him back to Washington in the presidential plane and they brought him through the private Butler Aviation wing of National Airport. There is a small lobby there, and it was filled with a number of Washington *Post* executives, all in their gray suits, all very nervous, and one old lady who was clearly with a different group. Finally Phil Graham, clad only in a bathrobe, walked into the waiting room, surrounded by psychiatrists and retainers, and the woman looking at this bizarre troop was absolutely terrified. Her terror clearly showed on her face. Sick as he was, Phil Graham had not lost his touch and he looked over and saw the panic on her face and said reassuringly, "It's all right, miss, I'm only dying of cancer."

Shortly after that he returned to Kay. Then, in late June of 1963, he had himself committed voluntarily to Chestnut Lodge, a private psychiatric center in Rockville, Maryland. There he seemed to be getting better. In fact, there were reports that he was virtually taking over the hospital. It was the early summer and the weather was good and Kay had come down to see him every day, bringing him lunches, and they had played tennis each time she had come. The reports of his progress were so good that gradually a trickle of nonfamily friends were allowed down there. In late July, Oz Elliott was permitted to come and he found Phil Graham in a surprisingly good and mellow mood. Elliott had brought with him the first computer printout on one of the most enterprising pieces of reporting that *Newsweek* had ever done, a study of black America. The printout itself, which had been done in conjunction with pollster Lou Harris, was absolutely fascinating reading, each statistic seemed to whet the appetite for more. Elliott and Graham were, on this beautiful day, sitting on a lawn reading them and at the other end of the field a patient was shouting endless obscenities. They tried to ignore him for a while but finally Graham said, "How do you like my friend?" Elliott asked, "Does it go on often like this?" "It goes on all the time," Graham said. There was a long pause and then Graham said, "When I first got here I was afraid I would sink to that level. Now it's getting better. I can't see the shore on the other side yet, but I know it's there." Elliott was pleased with the day, with Graham's fascination with the study, with the sense of ease he seemed to have about himself. He seemed to be getting better; everyone thought he was getting better. Because of that he was permitted to leave the center on weekends. And on August 3, 1963, at the age of forty-eight, Phil Graham, one of the brightest men of his generation, a man who had done so much but in his own mind accomplished so little, took a shotgun and killed himself. Kay was in a different room of the house at the time.

Later there were two somewhat contrary views of what had happened. The two doctors thought that what had happened was a characteristic of manic-depressives, that it was as if he had been walking on a piece of level ground and then had suddenly fallen through a trapdoor; they felt they had made a serious mistake in letting him go, since he was not yet ready for so much freedom. In that sense he had always been a problem, a patient almost too smart and too manipulative for his doctors. But a few friends like Scotty Reston and Dick Clurman felt differently, they felt he had known exactly what he was doing, that he had come home and measured his life and known how sick he was, that he was not in any real way getting better, nor was he likely to, that he could never again be the man he was, not without all kinds of drugs slowing him down. *He might never again be taken seriously.* He was, in effect, making a clinical diagnosis of himself as mentally crippled and the only thing left was to commit suicide.

# 14 / CBS

Charles de Gaulle, living in a society that had one state-controlled television network, spoke for all chief executives: he used to say that all print reporters were against him, but that television, television belonged to him. It was the classic statement of a politician about journalism. Print can be too querulous, can do too much analyzing of motive, too much spreading of doubt, but broadcasting, particularly as used by the chief executive of the country, had none of those drawbacks; it was powerful and direct. Print responded primarily to the questions of readers; broadcast was always conscious primarily of the power and station of the public official. Which is certainly the way Jack Kennedy looked at it. If Republican politicians believed that all reporters were Democrats and thus hostile, Jack Kennedy, like most Democratic politicians —including Franklin Roosevelt—believed all publishers were conservative and thus Republican, and thus stacked against him. Kennedy cited as evidence how few papers were Democratic, how few had supported him. Television, he decided, was the balancing weapon and he told the men he appointed to the

Federal Communications Commission (an area in which he had little basic interest) that the only advice he could give them was to keep the networks and the stations fair. Nor did he find very much opposition among the networks; whereas a few months ago they had withheld their favors and their courtesies, now they were eager to please. Was there a feeling at CBS that they had somewhat isolated themselves by tilting a little to Johnson? Well, they would quickly change that. Blair Clark, who had only a few years earlier been an assistant to David Schoenbrun in the CBS Paris bureau and who was a very close college friend of Jack Kennedy's, was almost overnight made general manager of CBS News. No, Clark was assured by his superiors, this had nothing to do with his very close association with Kennedy, the job was in the works anyway. Be that as it may, right after the assassination he was moved out of it.

In truth, however, the Kennedy candidacy and presidency created a whole new balance of power. Not only was the influence of the opposition party diminished but in a far more basic way the whole balance of government was changed, with the presidency growing in power at the expense of other branches of government. It was no longer Democratic President against Republican opposition, but Presidents against all else, with partisan differences muted. Truman, Eisenhower, Kennedy, Johnson, Nixon found themselves more tied to the office than to their parties, and above all bound together by the commonality of their institutional opposition. Television, given all that potential institutional opposition, became a crucial weapon. An unwritten electronic amendment to the Constitution, one former public official called it. All this really began in the Kennedy years. It was a combination of many things: Kennedy's own style and looks and confidence; the coming of television sets to so many homes; the vastly improving technology that allowed cameramen and reporters to cover candidly things that might have been barred to them in the past; the arrival in the middle of his administration of the half-hour news show, which immediately doubled the possibilities of political news and made the national television theater show twice as long—in effect doubling the audience; and finally the inability of other branches of the government, official and unofficial, to gain access to television in any comparable way.

Television not only changed the balance of power, it became a part of the new balance of power; if no one clearly understood that at the time, Kennedy nonetheless knew that it worked for him, and where other politicians felt more threatened by a new order he adapted with ease. Other Presidents had used the press and the press conference as a means of reaching and informing the country and listening to it at the same time; Kennedy quickly moved to live press conferences as a means of building up not just his ideas but himself. Some members of his staff, Rusk and Sorensen, were against it, fearing a faux pas would bring the world to the brink of war. Kennedy from the start was sure it would work, and so it did: he made it an extension of political theater, he used reporters as pawns to help him look better, smarter, shrewder, more capable and in control; indeed, mastery of the press conference in a way became a substitute for mastery of the political climate; he had more seeming control than real control.

The Bay of Pigs, for example, was a total disaster and completely Kennedy's fault, *but it was not a televised disaster,* there were no cameras on the scene; and though the response to the Bay of Pigs was televised, Kennedy had the power, and the authority, and the cool, to handle it, putting off all serious questions about why it had happened in the first place on the basis of national security, and thus in a marvelous tour de force accepting responsibility, appearing completely in control, and yet explaining nothing. No wonder his popularity soared. Similarly, a year later during the Cuban missile crisis he used television and an external threat to bind the nation to him. Space shots were to be covered—space shots were national, and space heroes were to be presidentially welcomed and hailed, their success merged with his; he was thus identified with the program, which was successful and modern, and with the astronauts themselves, who were young, handsome, virile, brave, and much admired. Astronauts showed that America was on the move; astronauts and Kennedy and Jackie showed that America *and* Jack Kennedy were on the move, and it was not by chance that the Kennedys as a clan quickly adopted and sponsored the first space hero, John Glenn. In those days domestic concerns were minor, or at least judged to be minor; the nation and the government were still totally focused on foreign policy and foreign crises, and the *President* was the spokesman for the national interest or at least what was judged to be the national interest in foreign policy. Now he not only defined the national interest, he had increasingly a *national* vehicle and a national voice; it was a very powerful combination.

If Kennedy had sensed what television could do for him as a candidate, he knew even more clearly what it could do for him as President. He knew not only that he could get television time for himself whenever he wanted, but that he could put on his people, be they McNamara or Schlesinger or O'Brien, any time he wanted, and that they, often nothing more than White House assistants, could get more exposure than senior senators. Indeed, what was remarkable about Kennedy was his inbuilt sense of the danger of overexposure; that alone made him unique since in that era most politicians who understood the importance of television clamored for more and more time. Yet at the very start of his administration Kennedy had asked Pierre Salinger to check out how many fireside chats Roosevelt had given, telling Salinger he had decided to use them as a guide. Why? Salinger asked. Because the public remembered them, Kennedy explained. The reason they were memorable, Salinger soon found, was that there had been so few, one or two a year. "You see," Kennedy told Salinger, "the public thought he had been on all the time and yet he had carefully rationed them." Besides, he added, television was far more powerful and dramatic than radio and thus there was even more need to be restrained in its use. So when Salinger or other Kennedy aides would request that he make a particular appearance, the President would hold back, he had been on, he would say, a week ago or two weeks ago. He was not eager, he told Arthur

Schlesinger, Sr., who asked him to do more television, to become the national bore.

He could, he realized, pick the time and the place and the setting for his statements, even the style. When he wanted to pass the Trade Bill of 1962, which was historic and difficult legislation, he knew that it would take as long as eight months to sell and he had decided to give Bill Lawrence of ABC a half-hour interview as a means of starting the campaign. They had dutifully filmed it and the film turned out to be bad. Let's redo it, he said, and they did it over. He moved to grant the leading correspondents of television a status rarely granted to working broadcast correspondents in Washington in the past. Lawrence, who transferred from the *The New York Times* to ABC, was one. Sander Vanocur of NBC was another favorite. He became an instant star, he seemed to be in the Kennedy style, his connections with the Kennedys pleased his bosses, who were gratified at having their ambassador to the White House so favorably thought of (had Nixon been elected in 1960, Vanocur might easily have gone into a journalistic eclipse). Kennedy, of course, believing that owners and publishers were conservative and that his best chance lay with working reporters, was acutely aware of who covered him, who were, so to speak, his boys. So at the time of the inauguration when CBS decided to assign George Herman to the White House, Kennedy, not entirely pleased by the decision, brought the subject up with his old friend Blair Clark. Kennedy asked why CBS had assigned Herman, "he's not one of our guys, you know, the guys who covered us and rode with us during the campaigns—he doesn't know us." Clark reported this conversation to Herman. "He says that you won't be able to call him Jack and he won't be able to call you George." Herman told Clark that in about a week it wouldn't be Jack and George anyway, it would be Mister President, and that it was quite likely in the first few months he would be scooped on announcement stories, but the guys who got the scoops would have to be protective of their sources and would have to hold back on stuff that Herman could use. "So it all evens out," he said. Which is what happened. Very soon there was no Jack and Bill and Sandy, and for a time Herman was beaten on minor stories, but then a few weeks later a high White House official came by and asked if he was still doing the "World News Roundup." Yes, he was. Well, said the aide, I would speculate that the President will go to Paris next month. It was Herman's admission to the club, and it was a significant leak; in the old days it surely would have gone to one of the major print outlets.

Kennedy used television to gain a lead on other institutions, including his own political party; the party was now diminishing as a source of power and he needed it and its machinery less and less. He could go over the head of the party to the people more directly through television. Even his dealings with someone as powerful as Dick Daley became in a way more a courtesy than a reality. With the Congress there was a similar imbalance. When he first became President the Congress seemed able to stalemate him, particularly on domestic issues. So, like Presidents before him, finding himself unchecked in foreign affairs and hogtied domestically, almost unconsciously he shifted the action to foreign affairs. It was where his real interest lay anyway, and it was where the President was strongest and where the Congress was itself weakest. The real power of the Congress was not so much to challenge the President on a given issue as to deny to the President the things he wanted, particularly in terms of the budget, but since the bulk of the vast budget was going into defense, and since Congress was uneasy about challenging him on issues of national interest, its power had diminished subtly over the years. Kennedy set the agenda for the Congress to respond to, and in the early sixties those issues were more and more in foreign policy. To this he now added the presidential weapon of television. The opposition Republican Party tried—almost pathetically—to answer. The two Republican congressional leaders, Everett Dirksen and Charles Halleck, started holding a weekly press conference, designed primarily for television. The only problem was that Dirksen and Halleck were not primarily designed for television. Dirksen was marvelously overblown, like a huge and rich vegetable that has become slightly overripe; watching him, one had a sense that he was always winking at the audience, winking at the role that he had chosen to play, the stereotype of a slightly corrupt old-fashioned senator. Their performance became known as the Ev and Charlie Show. It was like watching two burned-out old Shakespearean actors playing the role of the tired if not loyal opposition. Kennedy himself could not have cast them better; they were old and conservative and Republican and for Bad Things, and he was young and active and for Good Things. Clearly the country needed young, strong, active leadership; and you could see merely by looking at your television screen that the Congress was old and tired.

He also knew about the inner mechanics of television and the desires of television producers, he knew they wanted the best show, and generally the best show was the one that had him at his best. He easily talked CBS into doing a show with Jackie at the White House; suggesting the show, he mentioned casually the ratings of a comparable show that Sophia Loren had done in Rome. When the show was filmed at the White House and he was allowed a last-minute appearance, he knew immediately, even before it was over and before anyone had looked at the film, that his tone was wrong, that somehow he had been too flip. He asked to redo it. When the producers looked at the film they found he had been right, the first take was somehow wrong in tone. When he consented to do a television news special, an informal conversation with all three networks—which, among other things, totally cut out print correspondents—there was an agreement to film ninety minutes and cut to an hour. Some people who watched the taping noticed that George Herman seemed to ask the toughest questions and that when he did the President's answers seemed to get hazy and blurry. Naturally, when the taping was edited at the network studio, the weak answers were the first to go, not for political reasons but simply because they were not sharp and focused, *they did not make a good show*. The instinct of the producer, who did not work for the White House, was to have a show in which everyone spoke his lines, in which there was no presidential fuzziness, no vagueness, no failure, no uncertainty. Kennedy became his own best television adviser.

The door to Kennedy's office was always open, a surprisingly large number of people could drop in and chat with the President of the United States. But when the Huntley-Brinkley or the Cronkite show was on, everything stopped. No one was to disturb him. He could be disturbed if Walter Heller or Ambassador Dobrynin or Senator John Stennis were in the room, but not when the nightly news was on. It was sacred. He put, aides noticed, more concentration into watching the news than into almost anything else, you could watch with him but you could not talk. He felt that what went on these shows was terribly important. Perhaps it was not reality and perhaps it was not even good journalism, *but it was what the country perceived as reality* and thus in a way was closer to reality than reality itself. He felt he could not respond to the country if he did not know what voices it was hearing. His interest in the rest of television was much more tepid; he was a reader, not a viewer, he rarely watched the box for entertainment. Once while in office he turned on the late movie because in fact it was about himself, the screen version of PT-109. He was, like many of his fellow citizens, absolutely infuriated by the number of commercial breaks—deodorants, foot powders, and digestive aids that his wartime heroism was now selling—but unlike his fellow citizens, he could call up the head of the Federal Communications Commission the next day to complain. "Why do you let them put so many commercials on?" he asked. "It's cheap! Cheap! Cheap!" He was very angry. "I want a rule that limits the number of commercials," he told Newt Minow. Minow agreed that it was a very good idea and all he needed was more consumer-minded commissioners, and Kennedy promised to appoint them. But foreign policy was always much more fun than domestic affairs and less hassle, and so the consumer-minded commissioners never arrived. They were traded off somewhere along the way.

He knew that he could be seen as he wanted to be seen when he wanted to be seen. (When Ben Bradlee of *Newsweek* once called him to tell him how effective he had been during a television appearance, Kennedy had answered, "Well, I always said that when we don't have to go through you bastards, we can really get the story to the American people.") He also knew, and this was important, that it was as much theater as it was politics, and therefore the choice of setting and supporting cast was equally important. There was no doubt that 1964 would have been a year of travel, right before (or perhaps right after) the Republican convention. Perhaps the Soviet Union could be visited. Better he went there than Khrushchev came here, it was a better role, the handsome young President in Russia. It was a no-lose trip—if things went well, then he had brought peace; if they went badly, he could stand up to Khrushchev. Besides, the side trip for Jackie to Leningrad would be filled with what came to be known as photo opportunities. The presidency as political *cinéma vérité.* He made television bigger and more important and more respectable. If he was on occasion angry with television he usually got over it; once after the network news show seemed more critical of his handling of the steel crisis than he deemed necessary, he called Newt Minow to demand that Minow raise hell with network executives and threaten them with suspension of their licenses. Minow was appalled by the nakedness of the threat and did not do it; Kennedy called him the next day and thanked him for preventing a President from making a fool of himself. His attitude toward television was nicely summed up in a conversation he had with André Malraux. Malraux, as a representative of that great democracy where the state controlled the one network, had visited him in Washington and was shocked by the degree of independence of American news shows. He asked Kennedy why he put up with something like this—Huntleys, Brinkleys, Cronkites. Kennedy said that he didn't mind as long as he got equal time. Then he laughed. He laughed because he knew he always got far more than equal time.

John Kennedy changed the presidency more than any of his recent predecessors except for Franklin Roosevelt, who had slipped so naturally into the radio presidency. Kennedy's coming represented the confluence of the man and the technology, a new political force and a politician with the skills and instincts to exploit it. In his time style became in some ways as important as substance, and on occasion *more* important (the Kennedy staff in the first year was fascinated to see that the preponderance of mail received at the White House was about Kennedy's style rather than his policies). As radio had begun the personalizing of the man, now television was accelerating that process. If Kennedy had attractive personal qualities and occasionally questionable political ones, so he was quite ready to emphasize the personal side of the presidency; he knew exactly the benefit of an attractive wife and family, he knew how much his style helped him and eased doubts about his policies. The audience—it was an audience now—was pleased to judge him on this new scale. The process was a boon for a President like Kennedy, and inevitably a handicap for his successor, Lyndon Johnson, who was so clearly an old-fashioned nonmedia politician, a man who judged his peers and himself not on their style but on whether or not they could produce. The President was not just a political leader now, but a star, he had glamour, as did his friends, his wife, his children. Caroline and John John became the first of a new generation of princes and princesses to live in the White House. The White House marriages of the Johnson and Nixon daughters would be state events, three-hour television spectaculars. Politics became a kind of show, with the President the matinee idol.

The President was rising higher on the political landscape, the Congress and the party system were being diminished, and in addition it was a new kind of presidency, with far more potential for manipulation and far less accountability, far more able to dominate the landscape, with a capacity to transmit its will far faster and more directly. The new conditions also meant that the inner texture of the President himself and the state of his psyche became ever more important, because the possibilities of abuse were greater than ever (within five years of Kennedy's assassination, Richard Nixon would reach the White House with a staff drawn primarily not from the world of politics but from the world of the advertising agencies, the manipulative arts). And as television speeded up the cycle of life, it also intensified the pressures on the President and thus the pressures on his psyche.

As, year by year, the presidency became more and more important, so too did the White House staff, the men around the President became sub-Presidents, power centers unto themselves, more powerful than senior senators, more powerful than cabinet members, more powerful than the head of the party, acting finally as extensions of the psychological strengths and weaknesses of the President. These men were not, as a powerful cabinet member might have been, extensions of different regions and different interest groups within the country, perhaps former governors with constituencies and loyalties of their own, representing New York or Oregon or blue-collar workers as well as the President. Now more and more they were an extension of one man, loyal only to him, and reflecting his psyche as much as his politics. For better and for worse. In the case of John Kennedy the nation was reasonably fortunate; he was, by the standards of major politicians, with their enormous drives and ambitions and egos, a secure man. That meant that as President he could surround himself with men of some excellence and, more than most politicians, not confuse loyalty with ability. He did not necessarily think that dissent was disloyalty. He had the inner confidence and security to judge professional relationships on grounds other than loyalty. But in the next decade the country would not always be that lucky.

# 15 / The Los Angeles Times

What Otis Chandler, the proprietor, and Nick Williams, the editor, had signaled in the first two years of their reign over the Los Angeles Times was more intention to change than change itself. Nick Williams was slowly bringing the paper from right to center, but it was only a beginning. The staff was essentially weak. The Times had few talented reporters, and those who were being asked to come aboard were nervous about joining the main Chandler enterprise. Nick Williams might eventually establish a reputation as a strong farsighted editor, but in 1962 he was seen primarily as a second-rate Chandler apparatchik. Ed

Murray, the respected editor of the *Mirror,* offered a job by Williams when the *Mirror* closed down in 1962, refused, thinking that though Williams was offering the prospect of change, it was not within his or Otis Chandler's capabilities to put out a genuinely good paper.

But Otis was eager for change and for quick change. He was intensely ambitious (before going off to any publishers' or editors' convention he would sit by himself for long hours memorizing the photos and biographies of other key figures; he would know them, know more about them than they did about him). He was eager for national status and a national reputation and he was aware that the place to start was Washington. Washington, even more than New York, particularly in the early sixties, was where journalistic reputations were defined. Those who were powerful and well regarded in Washington were powerful and well regarded within the profession. Journalism fed off government and government centered upon Washington. So the key was a Washington bureau, foreign bureaus could come later. For the Los Angeles *Times,* a paper scorned by journalists and politicians alike, Washington was doubly important. ("What paper do you work for?" Harry Truman in 1958 asked a young reporter named Donald Shannon. "The Los Angeles *Times,*" Shannon answered. "Oh," said Truman, "that's the *second* worst paper in the country.") The *Times* was regarded with abiding contempt on Capitol Hill, and Shannon, one of the two men in the bureau, found that his phone calls were rarely returned by Democrats; in general, only Republicans would deal with him. Even at the White House with a Republican administration he felt the weakness of his position, he did not have a full-time press-room phone of his own, he had to share one with another reporter.

So much for the status of the Los Angeles *Times* in Washington in 1959. Otis Chandler was not about to stand for that; if you were a California paper going against the grain, trying to gain the most elusive of prizes, eastern and thus national recognition, then a strong Washington bureau was necessary. In addition, it would have to be done on eastern terms, that is, find people with existing reputations; you could not bring people from California and demand that they be respected. The *Times* needed instant prestige, to have on its staff someone of such stature that his presence would be an immediate signal to the entire world of journalism that Otis Chandler was serious. The obvious choice was James Reston, who dominated Washington journalism as no single reporter ever would again, but Reston was an untouchable figure; even the Washington *Post* had failed to hire him away from *The New York Times.* The other glistening journalistic figure in Washington at that time was Bob Donovan of the New York *Herald Tribune.* Donovan operated the second-best bureau in town, though he did it for a paper in decline. His own stature and that of the people around him exceeded that of his paper. He was a man of unusual grace, both professional and personal, he wrote uncommonly well under the pressure of deadlines, and there was a lovely, almost poetic quality to his work that stamped him as being different. In a profession of hard-driving arrivistes, Bob Donovan was, and this was rare in the profession, liked as well as respected. In Washington, wielding the lesser instrument of the *Tribune,* Donovan was a very good second to Reston and his name loomed almost as large.

So it was that Nick Williams, with Otis Chandler's approval—*I want the best,* he always said—went after Donovan. At first Donovan was resistant to the idea. He did not know Nick Williams and everything he knew about the Los Angeles *Times* was bad. He had made political trips to California in the forties and fifties and he despised what he had seen there, the prejudice and parochialism of the paper. But gradually he came to like Nick Williams very much and to trust him; if Nick Williams said they were going to make it a great newspaper, then he probably meant it. Nick was very candid about the problems they faced, about the complexity of the Family. But these, he said, were problems he could deal with and they would not be problems for the staff. He and Otis would protect the staff. That much he pledged. Donovan asked if they were expanding because *The New York Times* was moving out West, and Williams assured him that the plans for the improvement of the paper had been on the drawing board long before the Sulzbergers had begun their parachute jump.

So Bob Donovan thought about it, and the more he thought, the more he liked the idea. Nick Williams had offered him a lot of money, but money was not the prime factor; Donovan was very well paid on the *Trib* and he had just made a lot of money from a biography of Eisenhower and a small book on Kennedy's wartime service that had done very well commercially. What intrigued him the most was the challenge of bringing what he considered New York standards of journalism to California. The *Trib* was sliding, though he did not expect Jock Whitney to fold the paper, as he subsequently did a few years later; it was the challenge that excited him the most. He thought it was important, not just for the Los Angeles *Times,* but for the country as a whole, that the higher eastern journalistic standards be made national. So with some misgiving, for he cared about the *Tribune* and he liked Jock Whitney and he knew that his leaving might drive another nail in the *Trib*'s coffin, Donovan accepted the offer. Nick Williams had promised to deliver whatever he needed to build a first-class bureau, and so he went out and hired quality people. When it turned out that his estimates had been wrong, that the budget was inadequate, Nick simply doubled his budget. Donovan hired the best reporters in town, paying very good salaries. Because the name Reston was a very good one in Washington, Donovan even hired Scotty Reston's son Dick, to cover the State Department. The Los Angeles *Times* had purchased instant respectability. It was a symbolic moment, Bob Donovan leaving the *Trib* for the Los Angeles *Times.* Here was the most respected journalist of a once great eastern newspaper leaving to go to work for what had been only yesterday a frontier newspaper but was now on its way to becoming the richest paper in the country.

There was one other addition to the staff that year that was basic to the change in the paper. In 1963 Bruce Russell, the paper's cartoonist, died. He was an old-fashioned cartoonist who used lots of eagles for Americans and bears for Russians, and drew lots of little notes alongside them so that everyone would know which the good side was. When it was time to replace him Otis Chandler asked Nick Williams who the best cartoonist in America was, and Williams answered that it was Paul Conrad of the Denver *Post*.

"Conrad's the best available one—you can't get Herblock away from the *Post*," Williams said. "But Conrad will cause you a lot of grief."

"Then get him," Otis said.

"He'll cause you a lot of grief," Williams repeated.

"If he's the best, get him anyway."

So Nick Williams, who just a few years earlier had turned down syndication rights to Conrad, wrote to Conrad suggesting he come out to Los Angeles, and Conrad, a greatly talented free spirit, who drew far more than eagles and bears, and who had long vowed that the one paper in America he would not work for was the Los Angeles *Times,* reluctantly agreed to make a visit, on the condition that Williams meet him at the airport; he asked to be met because he wanted to explain from the first the degree of freedom he insisted upon. At the airport he told Williams that a cartoonist could not be edited in terms of content, that he would accept editing only if a cartoon did not work. If the cartoon works, it is valid; if it doesn't, then and only then is it not a good cartoon. He knew the problems; he had often been heard shouting at his editors in Denver, "You want an illustrator, not a cartoonist. Go get yourself an illustrator!"

So in the new search for excellence and despite what it would do to his stomach, Nick Williams hired Paul Conrad, and he was right: Conrad was the best. And he was also right when he said that Conrad was going to cause them a lot of grief. Conrad became almost immediately *the* symbolic figure of the new Los Angeles *Times,* every day jarring old conservative nerves. There might be a large number of talented new reporters on the paper, but they were mostly in Washington, and it was possible to overlook them. But who could overlook Conrad, overpowering the editorial page, dominating the paper, his drawings bold and powerful and often angry? There was no way to turn away from a Conrad cartoon without having gotten its point. Conrad was the enemy within, mocking them, tormenting them. So the lions of Los Angeles sat around at the California Club at lunchtime, talking about Conrad as some twenty-five years earlier they had talked about FDR. Every day Conrad seemed to make fun of them and the things they held most dear. He caused Otis Chandler more grief than any other staff member, with the possible exception of Martin Bernheimer, the music critic, and on more than one occasion Otis Chandler went to Nick Williams and said that Nick had to do something, *anything* about Conrad, and Nick would try to control him for a few days. But the potential for trouble was always there and it didn't help that the year Conrad came to the Los Angeles *Times,* 1964, was by chance the year that Barry Goldwater was running for the Republican presidential nomination.

If there was any place in the country where Barry Goldwater's appeal was real, indeed visceral, it was Southern California, and particularly among certain members of the Chandler family. However, Otis Chandler liked Nelson Rockefeller, as did his mother, and Norman Chandler was more comfortable with Rockefeller than Goldwater (it was not so much that he disliked Goldwater as that he was uneasy with the people who supported him, there was so much unchecked anger to them). So at Otis's suggestion and with Norman's concurrence, the *Times* decided to support Rockefeller. It was an important decision, the presidential nomination seemed to hinge on which way California went, and the party was badly divided between the liberal-center and its right wing. It was a delicate problem for the *Times,* which was trying to edge away from its old constituency, now intensely pro-Goldwater. Otis Chandler wrote the editorial supporting Rockefeller in the primary, and now for the first time there was a serious split between father and son. Norman Chandler read the draft of the editorial and insisted that Otis put in the traditional Republican pledge of allegiance, that the *Times* would support whoever won the Republican primary. Norman Chandler was very upset by the editorial, his son had never seen him like this before, it was clearly not easy being caught between the paper and the Family.

"We have to put it in," he said. "We're Republican and we always have been."

"No, we aren't," said Otis Chandler.

"Yes, we are, and we always have been," said Norman.

"Well then, let's change," said Otis. "We can't support Goldwater, we can't go that way."

"If you don't put that in, what can I tell my friends at the California Club? Everyone knows we're a Republican paper, that's our history. What can I tell them?" Norman Chandler said.

It was as close as Norman Chandler ever came to ordering his son to do something, and finally Otis, sensing that his father could not be pushed any further, that this was mandatory, something deep in the blood and the history of the paper, reluctantly inserted a small pledge: yes, the *Times* would support the choice of the party. It was an important lesson for Otis. He was not yet on the board of Chandis, the family trust corporation that controlled the stock, and he did not spend much time at the California Club, and he did not realize how much heat and pressure his father was taking for him, how hard Norman was working to forestall family and corporate rebellion. Those pressures had not yet really reached Otis Chandler, and they failed to reach him in part because his father was shielding him every day, using his own body and his vast good will and influence within the community and the Family to protect his son, even when he personally disagreed with him. When Norman's friends complained to him, which was often, he would simply answer that Otis was right and the critics were wrong, the *Times* was still the same, it was still a Republican paper. In his own mind this allowed him to balance what his son was doing with his own obligations to *his* father, to balance the present with the past. If people pushed further, and they often did, then he would show a bit more edge, a very little bit: "Otis is a contemporary person. He lives in a different world than you and I do, and he has to change with the times. What we should be doing is not arguing about Otis but going out and playing golf."

Later Otis Chandler was to learn just how much his father had protected him, but in 1964 he had less sense of that, he was more full of his own rectitude and his own passion, and so reluctantly he gave in and the *Times* announced that it would support the Republican nominee. Which did not particularly please his mother, who disliked Goldwater and the world of Goldwater. She was convinced that if the *Times* had given more support to Rockefeller, pushed a little harder, he might have won the primary and might have gained the nomination. She was not pleased when Goldwater won the primary, and in part she blamed the paper, and she was even less pleased when the Republican convention nominated him in a paroxysm of hysteria and anger, much of which seemed aimed at the press, and much of which she found ominous.


Buff Chandler had hated the convention, not just because she was for Rockefeller, but because she saw it as a triumph of the barbarians, the very people she had disliked and fought all her life, the California know-nothing right. Isolationists. All of them screaming not just at Nelson Rockefeller but at Buff Chandler and her son, Otis. So when Jim Bassett, then the editor of the editorial page, had come to Norman Chandler's hotel room the day the convention ended with an editorial that gave a mild pro forma approval to the convention's choice, and Norman and Otis Chandler had accepted it, she was furious. In part she was still irritated at the *Times* for its editorial during the primary. Now she told Bassett that this editorial was too weak. "Jim, this won't do at all. You have to point out how disgraceful this performance was, how dangerous these people are. We cannot have this sort of thing. We cannot." She kept arguing, and gradually Norman and Otis came around, and so Bassett, who sensed what was going to happen and was pleased, went downstairs and wrote a much tougher editorial, attacking the choice of Goldwater. Norman and Otis were rather passive about it; they might have doubts about Goldwater, but they had committed the paper to the choice of the convention and they were stuck with him. Buff was delighted with the next editorial, and Norman and Otis approved it. So Bassett cabled Los Angeles, telling them to kill the previous editorial. Nick Williams, back in Los Angeles, understood the implications immediately and called Bassett and said, "You know what's going to happen. They're going to hate this one." Bassett laughed and said sure, he knew what he was doing, but he was—Williams could sense his smile over the phone—acting under orders. Shortly after that, Robert Nelson, the business manager of the *Times* and a very forceful figure at the paper in many subtle and some not so subtle ways, read the editorial. Nelson was a very conservative force, appalled by the smell of liberalism in the newsroom. He exploded at Williams, "You can't run this, goddamnit, you can't run this. This goes against all of our friends. You damn well won't do this." Nick Williams, whose victories over Bob Nelson were not easily gained and thus were to be treasured, was not displeased with the situation. He told Nelson rather innocently that yes, it was a strong and rather unusual editorial, but it had been cleared from the top. Would Nelson like to call Norman Chandler in San Francisco? Then Williams called Bassett back, he was laughing now, and said, "You son of a bitch, do you know what you've done to me? I mean, the business types are going crazy!"

So the editorial ran, and it seemed to some almost like an attack on the Family, and with it one of Conrad's great ones, powerful and with a true instinct for the exposed nerve in the Chandler family—a cartoon of the Republican convention showing the inmates taking over the insane asylum. It was too much. The business associates of Norman Chandler were in rebellion, the Family was in rebellion. There was a serious mutiny, the first since Otis had taken over. Talk of a challenge to him, talk of rounding up votes. Word slipping out that it was Buff who was behind it all, proof that Otis was simply a pawn in Buff's hands. Otis Chandler was scheduled to go to Dallas to make a speech that day, but he had to cancel it to hold things together, and Nick Williams went in his place. He also told Williams that he had to do something about Conrad. Put some brakes on him. Talk to him. Anything. So Williams did the most gentle kind of talking to Conrad, because you did not order or threaten Con; just some explanation of how much tension could be absorbed at a given time, a hint that if Otis were gone, then Nick was gone, and possibly even Conrad would be gone. A delicate business. It was a very tense year, all in all. The family challenge to Otis failed, but there was no doubt that the incident had shaken him; gradually he was learning, despite his father's attempts to shield him, the limits of freedom. Nothing was without its price—the better things were, the higher the price.


The changing of the paper from one century to another was a difficult undertaking. Not just with the Family and the readers, but within the paper itself. It was one thing to hire a group of famed eastern reporters, and Bob Donovan all-stars, big names, big eastern by-lines, big salaries, and indeed hire a few top editors; but it was quite another thing to change the interior of a newspaper's bureaucracy, the copy editors, the assignment editors, the people who do the daily editing of the paper. There was almost no attempt to do this; the interior of the paper existed as it always had. Which meant that in addition to the normal conflict and tensions between the field and the home office—all reporters in the field believing that their most poetic lines, the ones they cared most passionately about, were being cut out by anonymous butchers, and the deskmen thinking that the reporters were living too high on expense accounts, too full of themselves and their by-lines—there was an additional problem, a conflict between new eastern journalism and the old-fashioned *Times* journalism, more cautious, shaped by different attitudes, and very much part of the paper's past. Nor was the conflict entirely accidental. Nick Williams wanted change, but he did not want too much change too quickly. If Frank McCulloch was coming aboard in 1960 as managing editor, then he wanted Frank Haven to remain as night managing editor (no one had told McCulloch, when he was offered the job as managing editor, that it was a split-level job), and Williams was not unhappy with the tension between the two of them. McCulloch was there to push the reporters, and Haven was there to control the desks, and to slow down the reporters.

The two men could not have been more different. McCulloch, a journalist's dream, driving, relentless, always upbeat, a doer, a man who had glistened at *Time,* a special favorite of Harry Luce. His energy level was extraordinary, it was impossible to think of him as a deskman, and when he came to the *Times* he was always out on the newsroom floor pushing reporters, getting them out of the office, making them look for news, changing the rhythm of a paper where, in the past, everyone had stayed inside the office waiting for the next five-alarm fire. Changing them all from passive to active.

Frank Haven had never really been anything but a deskman. During all the years that Nick Williams was slowly rising up the ladder of the *Times,* his closest deputy was Frank Haven. The two had a language of their own, they knew each other's taste and foibles so well that they could talk without speaking. Haven seemed to others strong, forceful, blunt; almost, if he could get away with it, bullying; a man with knowledge but with no vision. His world was simply smaller and more circumscribed than that of many of the bright young people who were coming to work for the paper; to them he was a stodgy, unbending man, and their private nickname for him was "the Lurch" (after a television character in "The Munsters"). He was, however, the best technician on the paper, he moved copy unusually well, and he was a much better read, much smarter man than most of his critics gave him credit for being. But he was also a man whose social-cultural mores and attitudes, human as well as journalistic, were set in another time. He and McCulloch were in conflict from the start.

Yet there was a sense, never quite stated, but always there in the atmosphere, that Nick Williams was never entirely at ease with McCulloch either, that he thought that McCulloch did not entirely understand the restraints necessary in the situation, the interior subtleties of the Family, that he pushed too hard, that he was too impetuous, too brash. So a pattern soon developed. The newer, more original stories that McCulloch assigned were often played well in the early edition, which McCulloch controlled, and then were put back inside and chopped up in the later editions, which Haven controlled. The stories that were being cut up were the ones that McCulloch liked the most, the ones that were not a product of the natural news flow but were the result of reportorial initiative. It was a very hard time for him. A friend from *Time* remembers meeting him on a plane during this period and asking what was going on and McCulloch saying, "I have to get out, I can't take the office politics any more."

More and more frustrated and restless, he became less enamored of the *Times*. *Time* magazine had always hovered in the background for him, it was his first love; the Los Angeles *Times* was not in his blood, and that in part was why he failed to make a fight of it. Had he really committed himself to the *Times*, he might have gone to Otis and fought Haven and the desks and he surely would have won. So he told Otis and Norman Chandler that he was leaving and they were genuinely shocked, they had very little sense of the tension in the newsroom, and they made several counteroffers, including more money, and an absolute guarantee of succession to Nick Williams, but it was too late, McCulloch had already given his word to Harry Luce to return to *Time* as head of the Saigon bureau.

A year later he was in Vietnam and he ran into his old friend Gordon Manning, then with CBS. What was it like, Manning asked, being the managing editor of the Los Angeles *Times*? "Oh," said McCulloch, "it was like being aboard a great aircraft carrier manned by the entire Chandler family and trying to steer by leaning from the back of the ship and trailing your hand in the water."


Thus in the sixties the Los Angeles *Times* struggled to emancipate itself from its past. It succeeded more quickly in Washington and overseas than at home, and there was a feeling that the closer the reporting got to home, the softer it became. In Washington, the members of the bureau were all new and many of them were former *Herald Tribune* reporters. But two very important editors were added to the top in California. In 1964 Ed Guthman joined the paper as national editor, and two years later Jim Bellows became managing editor for soft news. The coming of Guthman was extremely important to a paper that had basked so long in California conservatism; he brought instant prestige to the upper level of management. Guthman had during the fifties won a Pulitzer Prize for the Seattle *Times* for stories about the victims of McCarthyism, he had subsequently done major investigative stories on the Teamsters, and these stories had connected him to a young rackets investigator named Robert Kennedy. When John Kennedy was President and Robert Kennedy became Attorney General, Guthman had gone to Washington as the public affairs officer in the Justice Department. He had gotten to know Otis Chandler a little during the early sixties when Otis and Bobby Kennedy had become close friends, and he had been impressed by Chandler's awareness of what television was doing to journalism. Guthman himself felt that after the Kennedy-Nixon debates journalism had changed, that the age of television had begun, and he was appalled how few publishers recognized this and were adjusting to it. Otis Chandler had been different. He had also suggested that if Guthman were ever looking for a job, he should give him a call. In 1964, when Robert Kennedy was leaving the Justice Department, Guthman took Otis Chandler up on his offer. It gave the national staff of the *Times* a kind of instant legitimacy. Guthman was highly respected in the profession, and even though he had flacked for Robert Kennedy he had never been perceived as a flack, but rather as a man of strong social conscience whose roots were in investigative reporting. He believed it was a reporter's responsibility to be involved in issues, not to stand on the sidelines; to push forward and uncover scandal; and he would look for reporters in that image. The Iron Duke, he was called by some colleagues; even his friends did not think he was an easy man to win an argument from. In all this he was a man as different from the traditions of the *Times* as it was possible to imagine. It was one thing to hire Bob Donovan, graceful, literate, instant elegance, Donovan was not a sharp-edged digging reporter, not a man to cut against the grain—in his years in Washington he had angered few high officials; it was quite another thing to hire Guthman. Instead of instant elegance it might mean instant trouble. He became a symbol both within and without the paper of how much it had changed. A Kennedy aide at the top of the mechanism. First Conrad and now Guthman. He was immediately considered by some of the younger *Times* reporters to be a potential successor to Williams, though among genuine bookmakers he was not a real candidate. By Chandler standards he was too eastern (he was a Westerner but his Kennedy connection made him seem eastern), too liberal, and too Jewish.

Two years after Guthman came to the *Times*, Nick Williams hired another potential successor. Jim Bellows had been the Sunday editor of the New York *Herald Tribune* during its final literary flowering. In those days, as the paper had become sicker and sicker, greater and greater freedom had been given to reporters and writers. Bellows was, also by Chandler standards, a little different, perhaps too liberal, perhaps in some way *too* different. (Buff Chandler never really liked him, he did not seem quite serious enough to her. Years later he would say of that period that he had never quite fitted in, because he thought journalism should be fun and the Chandlers did not.) Bellows had been an early sponsor of people like Tom Wolfe and Jimmy Breslin; he was a writer's editor, he loved talent and style, he was at ease with talented people as not many editors were. The more talented and more creative the reporter, the happier Bellows became. If he seemed on first glance to be a potential editor of the paper, however, then appearances deceived, for he and the Chandlers were on very different courses in this most volatile decade. Bellows was a man of inherent irreverence, not only aware of the changes the society was undergoing in the sixties, but sympathetic to them. In the view of the paper's establishment, he became too far-out, he changed in dress, his hair grew longer. Other editors referred to him as "the Hippie." It did not affect his professional ability, but it made him seem an insufficiently serious figure to others.

Thus the *Times* was almost hydra-headed, two papers merged into one, or perhaps more accurately, a new modern eastern newspaper of one set of standards grafted by the miracle of modern technology onto an old-fashioned conservative California paper which wanted to change but which was rooted in another time and place. It was, in effect, a journalistic transplant, under the most difficult conditions. The superstructure of the Los Angeles *Times* had changed, but the pressures under which the paper operated had changed less. Haven was as powerful as ever, the editors underneath him reflected him and his taste, not that of Guthman or Bellows, neither of whom ever really took hold. The two halves of the paper did not mesh; indeed, Nick Williams told a friend at the time that the paper in Los Angeles did not really have the talent to handle and edit the copy coming out of Washington. Washington reporters felt that Los Angeles was holding them back, that it was too parochial; Los Angeles, by contrast, resented the cockiness, the arrogance of the new star system, and deskmen on occasion mumbled about their annoyance with eastern reporters or Jewish reporters, in phrases not very different from those soon to be used by a Vice-President of the United States.

The paper held together in the middle and late sixties largely because of the individual brilliance and authority of Nick Williams. He had a genuine appreciation of the new staff, it was exactly what he had sought and put together, but he had a respect for the old one as well: he thought Haven a good professional newsman, he felt strongly that the paper had to have this interior balance wheel. He kept the various component parts in a barely submutinous form of operation, and respect for him on the staff was almost total. But there was a constant underlying tension, most acute, as the decade progressed, between Haven and Guthman.

The decade of the sixties was an explosive time, the old order was being challenged and changed in every sense, racially, morally, culturally, spiritually, and it was a rich time for journalists. For a while there was a genuine struggle over who would define news, the people in positions of power or the people in the streets. It was as if all the social currents that had been bottled up for two or three decades, because of the Depression, World War II, and the Cold War, were exploding, and every element of the existing structure of authority was on the defensive. The first real blooming of a post-war era. Guthman and his reporters rose to the occasion, indeed seemed to relish it. They were uncommon talents: Don Bruckner, later to become a vice-president of the University of Chicago, an extraordinarily talented and cerebral reporter, covered civil rights with great sensitivity and feeling for detail; Jack Nelson, forceful, relentless, fearless, began to bore in on the FBI and some of its excesses; Stuart Loory, supremely able, supremely independent, covered the White House. Haven liked neither Loory's work nor his manner. In fact, Haven disliked most of what was going on. There was constant grumbling from him. Bruckner would do a major take-out on the blacks in Chicago. "Why do we have to print this? Can't that son of a bitch write about anything else?" Or of a Nelson take-out on the FBI: "There goes that biased son of a bitch again. Going after the establishment again." Or on a Loory story on the intricacies of the White House: "What the hell has this got to do with what Nixon said?" Can't Bruckner write about anything but civil rights? Haven would ask. Can't Nelson do anything but the FBI? Isn't there any good news out there? It was not just Haven, whose bark was often worse than his bite, who liked to squeeze people if he could but who rarely fought hard over any issue; it was also the subeditors, the sub-Havens, who, hearing their boss complain, took what he said literally, and who, hearing that he did not seem to like a certain reporter, felt freer to take liberties against that reporter, freer to muscle the work of a Loory or a Bruckner; rather than offer those reporters his shield, Haven was either consciously or unconsciously signaling to the people who worked for him that they were vulnerable.

In all this Guthman was caught in the middle. If Haven was interested in a particular story, Guthman would send the request on to Washington, but he did not put Haven's name on it, because he did not want to pressure his reporters too much. He did not want them to write a story simply because their top editors demanded it. That meant the request might go unheeded, which angered Haven, who was already sensitive about his lack of control of the Washington bureau; he had a feeling that he was being snubbed and ignored, and in fact he *was* being snubbed and ignored. Similarly, Guthman, who played it very straight, would argue with Haven over a story in the morning, fending off Haven's complaints, and then, losing the argument, would pass Haven's arguments on to the bureau as if they were his own, thus often angering the Washington bureau. He was extraordinarily loyal at both ends, so that the reporters did not know he was being pounded by Haven, and Haven did not know when he was being pushed by the reporters. Haven took his frustration out on Guthman, and it was not an entirely pleasant process. So it was that over the years Haven was bleeding Guthman just a little, cutting him up at news meetings, making him seem a little too liberal, accentuating the difference between Guthman and everyone else. Slowly, without Guthman realizing it, for he was not a good office politician, he was becoming damaged goods, increasingly vulnerable, particularly after Robert Kennedy was killed in June 1968. Haven had nothing to lose; he had reached the highest level he could aspire to. He was not going to become editor, whereas Guthman in the minds of those around him was a potential managing editor or even editor.

The Los Angeles *Times* had gradually put some distance between itself and Nixon in the years after the 1962 debacle. Nixon had moved to New York, which made things easier in the sheer physical sense, and the paper was slowly being depoliticized. Otis Chandler was not a kingmaker, he did not like the role and he did not want to be that close to the fray. But the paper was still Republican, and there was still a Nixon connection, mostly to Norman. Buff liked Nixon less and less; her interest in politics was diminishing anyway, she had been on the Board of Regents of the University of California and had acquired a considerable distaste for Bob Haldeman, who was then working for Reagan. Besides, she thought Nixon essentially tacky. There had been two unpleasant incidents in 1967. Earlier in the year he had come for lunch with the executives of the *Times,* all men with the exception of Buff, and just as they were sitting down to eat, in that clumsy and almost grotesque attempt to be one of the boys, he had told an absolutely dreadful story. "I guess I shouldn't tell this one," he had said, "but I'll do it anyway." Then the joke: "Why did the farmer keep a bucket of shit in the living room?" Stunned silence at the luncheon, no one, so to speak, able to come up with the answer. Nixon supplied the answer: "To keep the flies out of the kitchen!" A moment's grim pause, then Buff Chandler, somewhat shocked: "You're absolutely right, you should not have told that story." Then later in 1967 he and Pat had gone to dinner and an evening at the Hollywood Bowl with Norman and Buff and afterward they had returned to the Chandlers' home for a nightcap. As the evening was about to end Nixon said that he was thinking of trying for the presidency one more time and, playing directly to Buff, told her that she above all must understand what it was like to be at the center of the greatest stage in the world, that you were never satisfied until you tried it again and he never would be, he had to have one more try. At which point he asked both Buff and Norman their opinion about a presidential race, and they answered noncommittally. The evening seemed about to end when Pat Nixon surprised everyone by turning to her husband and, noting that he had asked everyone's opinion but hers, said that she most emphatically did not want him to run again, she had been through it too often in the past and it had torn them apart, there was too much pain. Besides, now, for the first time in his life, he was making a good living, the girls were at the age when they needed a father at home. So she did not want him to run, in case, she said, he was interested in *her* opinion. Buff Chandler had not liked that scene; that was no way to treat a former Los Angeles *Times* Woman of the Year. It had confirmed to her the artificiality of the man, the triumph of ambition over humanity.

But he came with the territory, and as the other Republican Party candidates collapsed in 1968, he, the drudge, the familiar long-distance runner of American politics, had stood alone and received the Republican nomination. With the nomination went the backing of the Los Angeles *Times;* it was a Republican paper, ipso facto it backed a Republican candidate, albeit in a restrained manner. Otis Chandler had some qualms about it; he did not fear Nixon as he had feared Goldwater, but he had no particular liking for him either and he genuinely liked Hubert Humphrey. There was a part of him that thought that Hubert represented the best of American politics and perhaps in a different environment, with a different family, Otis Chandler might have endorsed Humphrey. Nixon won in 1968 and he received the news of his victory in California. As he boarded the plane back East the next day, Ron Ziegler told the pool reporters that his one act that day in California had been to call Norman Chandler and thank him for all the help through the years. So it was that the Los Angeles *Times* had finally put their boy in the White House, though it was not the same Los Angeles *Times* and he was no longer really their boy.

III

# 16/CBS

Television speeded everything up. It was simple and it simplified. It was deeply dramatic, and it reached a huge new national audience; magazines like *Time* and *Newsweek* had once been considered major national outlets because they reached two or three million Americans; now the news shows were reaching a combined total of sixty million every night at roughly the same hour with roughly the same package ("a nightly national séance," in Daniel Schorr's phrase). Television could do certain things powerfully, effectively, and dramatically, and with the total truth. And it could just as easily obscure the truth, and neglect serious difficult gray areas of public policy. It could cast light on certain kinds of immorality (like legal segregation in the South) because they were so visible, tangible, and simple, but it had a much more difficult time dealing with the far more complicated problems of race in the North. Since northern racial problems did not lend themselves to either easy dramatization or quick solution, television soon lost interest in the subject.

But in this quickening of the cultural tempo, every event, every personality, every fad came and grew and often departed at an accelerated rate. As television made things grow larger much more quickly, it also had a tendency to let them die more quickly too, the roots were not as deep, more of the country was living on electronic sand rather than on real soil. The saturation point and the point of boredom came sooner. People were bored with an issue before it was solved, finished, or decided. Television heightened the interest in the war in Vietnam, heightened for the first time the enthusiasm for it, probably quickened its demise, and left people saturated, long before the war was in fact over; it was over in people's minds while it was still unfinished upon the battlefield. Television had no memory, it was not interested in the past, it erased the past, there was never time to show film clips of past events, and so, inevitably, it speeded up the advent of the future. Speed and action, that above all. Once, during the mid-sixties, Perry Wolff, a producer on sabbatical, called his friend Marya McLaughlin. "What are you doing today?" he asked. "Trying to decide whether or not to cover a demonstration which wouldn't be taking place if we didn't cover it," she answered.

For the professionals who worked in it, for the journalists, television was a departure too. It was no longer one reporter with a typewriter, or one reporter with a microphone and one engineer in New York, it was film and sound and technicians as well and, above all, producers, men who were not necessarily trained journalists and who might or might not know the significance of a given story. Producers were a new breed trained to find and exploit the drama in films. In the sixties the power moved gradually from the correspondent to the producer until by the end of the decade correspondents were calling it, bitterly, "producerism," a system in which the producers of a news show controlled the news, in which the public relations man for a government office or a senator's office could call the producer, not the correspondent, outline the story, explain the film possibility, and have the producer pencil in the story on the assignment sheet, often with the notation: "talent to be assigned." *Talent to be assigned.* Which was a complete reversal of the traditional journalistic procedure of the correspondent wending his way through the field, using his eyes and ears and sensing what is important, what is a story, and then telling the home office. This was very different, and it meant a different balance. Reporters at their best respond to events, but producers respond to more complicated stimuli—to film and to management, to the needs of the show, to ratings. Producers, even the best of them and the ones of the highest integrity, in some way belong to management, and they have a stronger sense than the correspondent of just how much exterior pressure the news show can take at a given time. Producers know that ratings are important on a mass-based news show, and ratings take into account dramatics, how good the visual is, what the audience is, how much international or complicated reportage it can absorb, what the other networks are likely to use in the way of film. Film. Film above all. Thus a different kind of news judgment: what is dramatic, what looks good, what do people want to see, and how much bad or unpleasant news will they accept. The principles of putting together a mass visual news show going to twenty million people are wholly different from the principles governing the editing of an elite newspaper like *The New York Times* with an elite audience of about one million.

The real change in power and possibility began with the coming of the half-hour news show in 1962. The difference in the way politicians regarded television in 1960 and the way they regarded it in 1964 was the difference between night and day. In 1960 television had profoundly affected the campaign and the means of exposure; by 1964 it *was* the campaign. The fifteen-minute show had been somewhat derivative of radio and it was smaller and less potent. Perhaps eleven or twelve minutes of air time. More primitive technology and film and techniques. Lots of what were known as talking heads. Then suddenly the change: twenty-two minutes, new kinds of film which were faster and faster. Smaller cameras. Soon satellite stations. Suddenly the news shows needed vast new field staffs, bureaus to be opened, time to be filled, film to be shot. In the early sixties, at the key meetings of network executives to decide whether or not to go with the half hour, the great question was whether or not there would be enough film and news. Suddenly correspondents in the field became important. Instead of forty-five seconds there might be two minutes. Overnight, correspondents had the most powerful political platform in the country. Politicians have always gone where the crowds have gathered, and by 1963 the crowds were gathering every night in their own living rooms. In some ways the change was not so obvious, either to the pols or to the public, because the 1964 election obscured it; it was a campaign without subtlety, without closeness. Johnson was so clearly going to swallow Goldwater. But what was clear to print reporters working in 1964 was that the whole schedule had changed, the campaigns were different now, no longer run to catch the main editions of the big East Coast newspapers, but run to catch the evening news shows with, above all, film. To be telegenic. Whereas in 1960 a candidate's most skillful press aides had been obsessed by how to get a positive column by James Reston or a page-one story in the Washington *Post* or *The New York Times,* now it was television first, how to make the evening newscast with good film. It was, in the words of Theodore White, who watched the process as a particularly interested observer, like going from the one-page hand-fed press to the rotary printing press.

Sig Mickelson and some of the other news executives had been looking to replace Doug Edwards as the anchorman of the evening news as early as the mid-fifties. Edwards was the original CBS anchorman, he had been given the job during the embryonic days of television. He had been fine standing off the "Camel News Caravan" of NBC's John Cameron Swayze ("Let's hop-scotch the world"), but the rise of Huntley-Brinkley was a serious challenge. Edwards did not project the kind of weight that Mickelson and the others wanted, he simply did not seem strong and solid enough a personality to anchor a new modern news show. Douglas Edwards might close the evening news by saying, *And that's the way it is,* but people might not necessarily believe that that was the way it was. Mickelson had first tried to replace Edwards (who was well aware of the pressures against him) with Charles Collingwood. For two reasons. First, because Collingwood—talented, attractive, a graceful writer, the heir apparent to Murrow, Murrow's own choice for his successor—was the member of the Murrow group who had made the transition from radio to television with the greatest facility; and second, because Collingwood, who had been in London with Paley during the war, was well thought of in the executive reaches and remained a personal friend of the Chairman. But in those days sponsors were extremely powerful; one sponsor handled the entire show and the Pall Mall people were not at all interested in switching from Doug Edwards to Charles Collingwood. Pall Mall liked Doug Edwards.

The pressure to have a new anchorman grew as the importance of the news show grew and as NBC's ratings mounted. The choice was important both internally and nationally, for it would dictate to a considerable degree what kind of news show CBS would carry. Among the towering and ambitious figures of broadcasting, the great stars, the competition for the job was intense; no major figure of broadcasting had ever been accused of a lack of ego, and the desire to be the signature figure was very considerable. Of the potential new anchormen, both Howard Smith and Eric Sevareid had already by the late fifties run into similar problems of translating their talents and their styles. Both of them were superstars and they were not just reporters, they were commentators, and their commentary was fine for a time, particularly when it came from foreign countries, but as they came home the negative pressures had increased. Sevareid angered the brass by his regular criticism of Dulles, but for a long time he was overseas, so there was not a great problem. But Smith had been in constant trouble, there was a lot of blue-penciling of his copy when he had come back to Washington, and the problems he caused were far greater than those caused by Sevareid. Part of it, friends thought, was the difference in style. Sevareid was a more subtle writer, perhaps more deft, and he learned to make a fierce point without seeming to be fierce, whereas Smith was a more forceful writer, using more sharp, straight, declarative sentences, and very direct, and there was never any mistake about what he was saying or how he was saying it.

Both Sevareid and Smith, increasingly frustrated by the growing pressures against them, had wanted to meet with Paley, but Paley was not anxious to discuss the subject. To discuss the tightening controls was to admit they existed. To discuss the difference between today and yesterday was to admit that there was a difference. Sevareid was particularly bothered by the growing militarism of American foreign policy and the lack of subtlety toward Asia, this and the inability of an organization as powerful as CBS News to point out the distinction and to show the possibility of real foreign-policy debate. Finally a meeting between Sevareid and Paley was arranged, but it was not a great success. Paley (whose friends were in the White House now, and who was getting flak from his political and social buddies on every bit of adventurous journalism undertaken by CBS) seemed very distant. Sevareid raised his questions, talked about how much more difficult it was to report and say anything now, how much more editing there was, but Paley was adamant, it was the fairness doctrine, CBS had to be fair, CBS would not get ahead of the parade, CBS newsmen could not enjoy the luxury of having a point of view. Sevareid argued that CBS News had always been the best, that during the war it had shown leadership, and that CBS must show some leadership now, must help clarify a needed public debate, that there was too much obscuring of important public issues. If newsmen had specialized knowledge, and it was agreed at CBS that they did, then they should somehow manage to convey that knowledge to the listener; there was more to all this than the government was saying. But Paley would not give an inch. He was not interested in leadership, political leadership at least (he might be interested in commercial leadership). There was no give. All he came back with was stock answers about fairness, about trust, about licenses granted by the government. It was the age-old debate about the limits of professionalism and intelligence and whether the reporter, in the name of someone else's definition of objectivity, should appear more ignorant than he really was. Sig

Mickelson, sitting in on the meeting, had a feeling that Paley had decided not to hear a word that Sevareid was saying, that all the decisions had been made long ago.

Howard Smith was a victim of the same problem. In the late fifties he had come home to report on America after more than two decades abroad. He was an intelligent, somber journalist, a complicated man who had never, during the worst of the Cold War, signed on to the idea of the Communist monolith; he had instead seen gradations of nationalism in Eastern Europe, a viewpoint not yet fashionable, and because of it he had frequently been attacked as being too left-wing. While in London he had been accustomed to a fairly flexible amount of editorializing in his weekly news commentaries. Now in America he was finding it very different. When he angered a major politician, that politician tended to pick up a phone and call a superior; he was discovering something symptomatic of all journalism, and a distinguished *New York Times* correspondent, Tony Lukas, had a name for it: the Afghanistan Principle. Lukas, who had spent six years as a *New York Times* correspondent in under-developed parts of the world, soon learned that if you were a *Times* man overseas you could be as blunt and as tart and as perceptive as you wanted to be about the local government and there was surprisingly little home-office fallout. The closer you moved to the center of power in Washington or New York, the less you could say, and if you tried to apply the same freedom of expression in describing, for example, a water commissioner in New York as you did in describing, say, the Prime Minister of India, the comment would probably not run. The basis of the Afghanistan Principle was clearly that truth survives more comfortably at a distance.

Upon his return from Europe, Howard Smith found himself under constant pressure to make his commentary milder, and there was a particular resentment of him at the executive level; he seemed to be the correspondent who most offended both the Administration and Paley's conservative friends. When in early 1961 Murrow left CBS to work for Kennedy, he was in the midst of preparing a "CBS Reports" documentary on racial policies in Birmingham. Smith was assigned to take it over. One clip of film showed Birmingham cops standing by while thugs beat up civil-rights workers. Smith, a Southerner himself, was appalled by what he saw; he had watched the rise of Nazism and Fascism in Europe and now he had come home to see some of the same signs. In his narration he quoted Edmund Burke, saying, "The only thing necessary for the triumph of evil is for good men to do nothing." CBS executives, already sensitive to mounting resentment from southern affiliates, wanted it out. (Friendly, arguing with Smith, made one vital point: the thing about television, he said, was that you didn't *need* expository commentary like this, the film was so damaging that *it* said it all.) Smith was adamant and insisted that it stay in. Blair Clark, who was general manager of CBS News, pleaded with Smith not to cause a confrontation, and warned him that Paley was eager for one. Clark met with Paley once a week and was quite aware that the name most in disrepute in Paley's mind was Howard Smith, that the Chairman had

accumulated a vast backlog of grievances against Smith and now considered
him a liability. Clark begged Smith not to force the issue. But Smith did so,
and shortly afterward left CBS for ABC.

Which left unanswered the question of who was going to be the signature
of the evening news show—Sevareid, Collingwood, or the outsider, Walter
Cronkite—a question more important because as 1961 ended it was increasingly
clear that CBS was going to go to a half-hour news show. The job was the most
prestigious that CBS had, but it was also not a commentator's job, television
was simply too powerful for that kind of commentary and that kind of personal
freedom. For the correspondents in their regular nightly appearances were an
interesting combination, part wire-service men (in terms of the narrow spectrum of personal expression and the brevity of their reports) and part superstar, known to the entire country, as recognizable on a presidential campaign
and often as sought out by the public as many candidates themselves. But the
power was so great and the time on camera so limited that the reporters
themselves often seemed underemployed. They were often serious and intelligent and sophisticated, and they seemed more knowledgeable than their
nightly reports. The difference between the insights of the CBS reporting team
on a brief spot on the news program and its performance at a national convention or during a Watergate special seemed enormous. Even a half-hour show
was like trying to put *The New York Times* on a postage stamp, and there was
a standing insider's joke at CBS that if Moses came down from the mountain
the evening news lead would be: "Moses today came down from the mountain
with the Ten Commandments, the two most important of which are . . ."

Sevareid and Collingwood might be the disciples of Murrow, and Cronkite might be the outsider who had never crashed the insider's club, but his
style was now more compatible with what the show needed. His roots were
in the wire service, he was the embodiment of the wire-service man sprung to
life, speed, simplicity, scoop, a ten-minute beat; Hildy Johnson with his shirt
sleeves rolled up. He came through to his friends and to his listeners alike as
straight, clear, and simple, more interested in hard news than analysis; the
viewers could more readily picture Walter Cronkite jumping into a car to cover
a ten-alarm fire than they could visualize him doing cerebral commentary on
a great summit meeting in Geneva. From his earliest days he was one of the
hungriest reporters around, wildly competitive, no one was going to beat
Walter Cronkite on a story, and as he grew older and more successful, the
marvel of it was that he never changed, the wild fires still burned. If in 1952
he became the CBS political anchorman, no one was going to go to the
convention better versed, better prepared, and better backgrounded, and if he
was going to cover a space shot, no one was going to sit up more nights in
advance mastering space, the history of it, filling his private notebooks on it,
and while he would now use an assistant to check out facts, no fact or perception that the assistant turned up would ever go into Walter's book (which
meant using it on the air) until the assistant could prove under the harshest
kind of questioning that he could vouch for that fact.

Yet the marvelous thing was that he did not look competitive; he looked comfortable, reassuring, and very much unhurried and in control. It was an admirable and quite lucky combination of qualities. His professionalism also made him very easy to work with; what was on the outside with him was on the inside, he liked, indeed loved, being Walter Cronkite, he had an enthusiasm for life and for his work which still smacked of an innocent country boy let loose in the big city, it was all wonder and enthusiasm. In a profession filled with immense egos, with very mortal, often insecure men blown overnight to superstar status, heady stuff indeed, Cronkite exercised a very considerable amount of control over his own considerable ego, and it rarely flashed through as openly as those of some of his colleagues. And while he was good at the show-biz part, just enough of a rich voice to make him interesting and to reassure his audience—that's the way it is—he knew where to draw the line. And he was enough of an old wire-service man to be uneasy with the new success and fame, or at least to allow that he was uneasy with the new success and fame, which was just as good, and which somehow kept things in balance. He was just sophisticated enough never to show his sophistication. There was a gee-whiz-is-that-really-true? quality about him that was a wonderful protective device, it meant that the other person was always talking, always explaining, and that Cronkite was never committing himself.

In addition, he had enormous physical strength and durability. Iron pants, as they say in the trade. He could sit there all night under great stress and constant pressure and never wear down, never blow it. And he never seemed bored by it all, even when it was in fact boring. When both Blair Clark and Sig Mickelson recommended him for the job, the sheer durability, what they called the farm boy in him, was a key factor. He was the workhorse. After all, the qualities of an anchorman were not necessarily those of brilliance, he had to synthesize others. There were those who felt that Sevareid had simply priced himself out of the market intellectually, Eric was too interested in analysis and opinion and thus not an entirely believable transmission belt for straight information. He was an intellectual, he wrote serious articles in serious magazines, and yet he wanted to be an anchorman as well, and there were those who thought this a contradiction in terms. When he found out that Cronkite was getting the job he was furious. "After all I've done for the company," he protested to Blair Clark.

The casting of Cronkite was perfect. He looked like Middle America, there was nothing slick about his looks (he was the son of a dentist in St. Joe, Missouri, and his accent was midwestern). He was from the heartland, and people from the Midwest are considered trustworthy, they are of the soil rather than of the sidewalks, and in American mythology the soil teaches real values and the sidewalks teach shortcuts. Though he had been a foreign correspondent and a very good one, in his television incarnation he had been definitively American, in those less combative, less divisive days of the late fifties and early sixties; Good Guy American. He had covered conventions, which were very American, and space shots, which were big stories where no one became very angry. When there was an Eisenhower special to do, Walter did it; he was seen with Eisenhower, and that too was reassuring. Ike and Walter got along, shared values, it spoke well for both of them. (Among those not comforted was John F. Kennedy, who, shortly after his election to the presidency in 1960, took CBS producer Don Hewitt aside. "Walter Cronkite's a Republican, isn't he?" Kennedy asked. No, said Hewitt, he didn't think so. "He's a Republican," said Kennedy, "I know he's a Republican." Again Hewitt said he didn't think so, and indeed he suspected that Cronkite had voted for Eisenhower over Stevenson and Kennedy over Nixon. "He's always with Eisenhower," insisted Kennedy. "Always having his picture taken with Eisenhower and going somewhere with him.")

Cronkite was careful not to be controversial, disciplining himself severely against giving vent to his own personal opinions and prejudices, and this would be an asset for CBS in the decade to come. He represented in a real way the American center, and he was acutely aware when he went against it. To him editorializing was going against the government. He had little awareness, nor did his employers want him to, of the editorializing which he did automatically by unconsciously going along with the government's position. He was never precipitous. His wire-service background gave him a very strong innate sense of the limits to which a correspondent should go, a sense that blended perfectly with what management now deemed to be the role of the anchorman and the news show itself. He represented a certain breed and he was by far the best of the breed. He was wise and decent enough to be uneasy with his power, and the restraints the job required were built into him. And so he was chosen to anchor the half-hour news show—a mass figure who held centrist attitudes for a mass audience.

He became an institution. His influence, if not his power, rivaled that of Presidents. Interviewing Edward Kennedy at the 1976 Democratic convention about his decision not to run for the presidency, he suggested that if Kennedy were not running for the presidency he might make less of a difference within the society. "You don't have to be a President of the United States to make a difference in this country. You don't even have to be a congressman," Kennedy responded. Then he looked at Cronkite closely. "You make a difference, Mr. Cronkite." Walter Cronkite set the standards by which others on the tube were judged. He was a grown man before his first appearance on television, and yet by the late sixties he had probably been on the screen more than anyone else in the world. In Sweden, anchormen were known as Cronkiters. He was not a great writer himself but he was a good editor and when others wrote for him his ear could always tell what would work and what would not work. He was not a great interviewer, his natural decency and cautiousness and his reluctance to seem too combative appeared to inhibit him; his questions were often not hard enough (most memorably in 1968 when he was playing straight man to Mayor Daley of Chicago). But he was an excellent synthesizer and clarifier, he worked hard in the brief time allotted to his program to make the news understandable to a great new mass of people. He managed in a decade of dark and shattering news to convey to an enormous audience that he was a good man, worthy of their trust.

As with Dwight Eisenhower, the people set him apart from his office; when things went badly the audience might be angry with television news and television reporters, but not with Walter Cronkite personally. He had a very strong self-imposed sense of what the limits of his role were, and the trust that had been given to him and the dangers of violating it, and it worked; he became over the years very simply the most trusted man in America. When political pollsters wanted to check on the credibility of potential presidential candidates, they always named Walter Cronkite too as a control against which the trust and acceptability of the potential candidates could be measured, and of course the potential candidates never quite measured up to Walter.

There was one memorable moment in 1970—when the political pressure against his institution and his office, skillfully exploited by a President who now viewed CBS and Cronkite as a major opposing power center, had mounted to a dangerous degree, and the networks were on the defensive. It was then that the value of Cronkite being Cronkite was demonstrated. The scene was a meeting between CBS executives and affiliate owners, and the prejudices and angers of the affiliates against the elitism and pessimism of the CBS News team had been deliberately orchestrated by Nixon. Resentment was at its peak. Kent State had just taken place and Agnew had just started his attacks on the press. The meeting had been bitter and there was a smell of blood in the air. That night CBS gave a banquet and the management trotted out all the stars, Jimmy Stewart and Doris Day and many others. They all walked in and received polite applause, and then suddenly Cronkite came in and the house went wild, a magnificent standing ovation from the very people who had been savaging CBS News that morning. You *can* have it both ways.


Radio had always been profitable. CBS had almost immediately, by the standards of most American companies, become extremely rich and successful. But the television profits were staggering. They represented, in terms of investment, roughly three times what a comparable hard-goods manufacturer reaped. More, the profits seemed to escalate every year, gradually corrupting and changing the nature of broadcasting. Greater profits did not mean, as some company altruists had hoped, greater experimentation, more money invested in higher-quality programming. On the contrary, profits brought merely the expectation of more profits, and policies designed to create them. The impulse to take risks in quality programming, to serve the national interest in public affairs, became weaker all the time. And the enormity of the new profits did not make the company stronger or more confident of itself. Ironically, as it became greedier, it became more nervous, more insecure. The race was getting faster and faster and the ice was getting thinner and thinner, so much was being gambled on standards which were so arbitrary. Now broadcasting was obsessed with the ratings, and the ratings had a morality of their own, they dictated their own reality and their own truth. Those who argued against the system, who argued for doing better programs, were no longer realistic, they did not understand the big picture.

For the first twenty-five years of its history the net income at CBS had averaged $4 or $5 million a year. Those were essentially radio years. Then television arrived. In 1953, television reached 21 million American homes and CBS income after taxes reached $8.9 million; by 1954, the year that CBS, by virtue of television, became *the largest advertising medium in the world,* the net income was $11.4 million; by 1957, 42 million homes had television sets and the profits after taxes had reached $22.2 million. It was a constantly ascending curve and it brought its own ruthless truth, and pushed aside other forces, other interests in the company. (Once in 1965, as the entire company seemed to be more and more obsessed by the profit drive, Fred Friendly, then the head of CBS News, had asked Bill Paley how much profit the company had made that year. "Fifty million," the Chairman had answered. "That's enough," said the bumptious Friendly. But he was wrong, it was not enough, a decade later the profits had doubled again.) There was a certain merciless quality to that drive; if CBS did not get the highest ratings at a given hour, then someone else would get them, NBC or ABC, and if NBC got them, the CBS share of that hour would become proportionately less. So it was not enough to succeed, to put on a good program that was sponsored and made a profit, now there had to be a dominance of the ratings, a super-profit. In the first decade of national television, CBS dominated, it seemed to have all of the top ten shows, its ratings were always higher and thus its profits were much higher, and its stock was stronger. Told by Mike Dann, his programming chief, that CBS had taken nine of the top ten daytime shows, Paley had shaken his head and said, "That damn NBC always hangs in there for one."

It was a juggernaut. If CBS had a program with very high ratings, that did not mean it could therefore run a high-quality show of great public service with low ratings; a quality show with weak ratings pulled down the average and canceled out the benefits of the show with high ratings. Nielsen was the new god of television; his truths were not truths, they were commandments; what was rated high was good, and what was rated low was bad. There was room for nothing else, no other value systems, no sense of what was right and what was wrong. The stakes were too great, and became greater every year. Once in 1955 CBS did a special on Mary Martin. It was a considerable occasion and so a number of celebrities were invited for a special private showing at the CBS building, including Truman Capote, who found himself seated between Frank Stanton and Bill Paley. Capote had watched the show with growing admiration and enthusiasm and when it was over he had turned excitedly to Stanton. "Isn't it wonderful!" he had said. "Well, we really won't know until tomorrow when we get the ratings, will we?" Stanton answered.

The rating system seemed to destroy all that was in its way. The lowest common denominator of taste prevailed. It was the end of what little restraint there was in the programming departments. Any sense of balance or of mix was finished. It was no longer a matter of the right audience, it was a matter of the total audience. In the mid-fifties the series arrived—in effect, drama without drama. And if the faces were like the material, often curiously bland, almost plaster, still the economics were extremely good. It often seemed that the greater the distance the network could put between its programs and reality, the greater the profit, and it was done without shame. In 1965, to its undying disgrace, CBS, the network which with Ed Murrow and Bill Shirer had so brilliantly chronicled the rise of Hitler's Germany, put on a weekly show called "Hogan's Heroes." This was a program with an almost obscenely comic view of the Third Reich; yet for many young Americans, given the power of television, given the absence of any countervailing vision of that period in history, their most formative and perhaps most memorable portrait of Nazi Germany would be the series of buffoons and clowns who paraded around on this uniquely mindless show. The immorality of the decision to place this program on the nation's airwaves was staggering, yet the competition seemed to demand it. "Hogan's Heroes" was a winner; if CBS did not put on "Hogan's Heroes," then perhaps NBC would use it and NBC would come up with a larger share of the dollar.

That was at the heart of it. The competition was so fierce and the weapons so inane. The costs for all the shows, winners and losers, were essentially the same; only when a show *failed* and the schedule had to be revised did the cost go up. Since all three networks sold by circulation, and the advertisers paid by circulation, the ratings were crucial. One network might, with the right formula, as CBS did for so many years in the late fifties and most of the sixties, make as much as $20 or $30 million a year more than its rivals on the same production costs.

There was an additional dynamic here, and that was the pressure that Wall Street began to generate on broadcasting in the late fifties. CBS had been public and listed on the New York Stock Exchange as far back as 1937, but it was only in the late fifties, with the soaring new revenues from television profits, that Wall Street really discovered the industry—and its *potential.* A lush new field to conquer. Soon the stock market was pushing its norms upon the industry. In the past the company's business people had thought in relatively simple terms of profit, making a good deal more money than they spent, a practice that permitted some balance in programming. Now they reflected more and more what was best for the *market.* In the late fifties there was an almost feverish quality to the way CBS and Wall Street responded to each other's seduction; inevitably the people within the company who best understood and followed the market gained power and influence over those whose concerns were limited to producing good television. Wall Street's pleasures were relatively simple: much higher profits, lower production costs, the acquisition of more and more subsidiary companies. This was, after all, the era of the conglomerate, a time of quick corporate shuffling designed to add and subtract companies and avoid taxes. Companies like CBS became increasingly dominated by a new generation of bright young men who knew systems, how to take an existing structure and make it far more profitable, cutting quality here, adding a minute or two of advertising there, little changes which, when carried through for an entire year, might mean millions and millions of dollars. Their loyalty was to the bottom line. Whether or not they ever watched the programs themselves, no one knew; whether they thought there was any ethical consequence to the programs they showed was a question that did not arise. "The people from Harvard Business School," Fred Friendly said years later, "taught the networks how to institutionalize their greed."

For years and years, when CBS was a small company and he was having constant problems getting the telephone company to string lines for him, Bill Paley had dreamed one dream, of having a million dollars in the bank. Now his company was churning out profits of $20 and $30 million a year, but it wasn't in the bank, that would be old-fashioned. Rather, the money was going into the acquisition of other companies, the expansion of the empire. What had always limited the sheer commercialism of broadcasting in the past was not the law, which was weak and fuzzy, nor even the marketplace, it was the inner restraint of men like Paley (who once as a young man had testified against potential congressional restrictions on broadcasting by pointing out how little of his schedule was commercially sponsored) and Sarnoff (who had not even wanted to have commercial programming). These restraints were now vanishing. The pressure from the market was simply too strong.

Then in the early sixties a new force was added to the equation that made the pressure even greater and made the network's commercialism even less inhibited. That was the coming of color television. Now advertisers were able to see their products in color, in images more attractive than anyone ever thought possible. Sales possibilities became even more seductive. It was the ultimate American dream: cowboys selling cigarettes could literally ride off into the sunset. As early as 1960 the system for broadcasting color was quite adequate, but the problem was the lack of color sets in the country and the cost of producing a color show. But slowly the number of sets began to increase. By 1962, there were about one million color receivers in the country and advertisers began to come aboard for the first time. By 1965, there were five million color sets in use, and all three networks had gone to full-time color schedules. As the coming of black-and-white television had meant a quantum jump over radio in terms of commercial opportunity, so the coming of color meant another quantum jump over black-and-white. As the possibilities of profit grew so rapidly, as the rewards of victory in the ratings grew so large, the interior restraints of the men who ran broadcasting diminished appreciably.

There had been a time when Bill Paley had orchestrated the rating system, he had been very good at it, the best in fact, and loved it, but by the mid-sixties he was more and more like the man who rode the tiger and then ended up inside—as much prisoner of the system as its architect. There were still times in the late fifties and the early sixties when, having spent the weekend with a few friends and heard their complaints about the level of television, he would come in on Monday and gather the programming people around him and there would be a burst of good intentions, of scheduling high-level quality shows. "Pleasing Bill's friends," it became known as around the network. A few weeks later most of those good intentions would ebb as the cost of putting on the quality shows became clear. Good intentions were too expensive. It would be simpler to have different people as weekend houseguests.

For the company was caught in a dilemma. It was on its way to becoming a conglomerate, it was acquiring other companies, and expanding into new fields, and the stock *had* to be driven up. It was an endless race, every victory was its own trap. Wall Street wanted growth and expansion and profit. By the early sixties Bill Paley would hold his high-level meetings to plan out the new year and he would explain that the new standard was a 15 percent annual increase. But 15 percent was a brutal figure, particularly for an industry whose profits were already inflated. (In 1974, in the midst of Watergate, CBS earned a record $34 million net profit for the second quarter, and Gordon Manning, a news executive, congratulated Robert Wood, then the president of the network, on his success. Wood, however, seemed to wince at the idea. What's wrong? Manning asked. "Do you realize that what we just accomplished now becomes the norm?—that we must go against it in the future, and if we slip below it, it means we've failed," Wood said.) Do you really have to push that hard? a colleague once asked Paley, and the Chairman said yes, he did, the CBS board forced him to (which was not exactly true, the CBS board was his own creation and he ignored it, defied it, or listened to it as his whim dictated). But what about showing some better programs? Paley's friend continued. I would love to, Paley answered; in fact there was nothing he would like more. But he could no longer do it, the company was public, and he had obligations to the universities who had bought his stock and the widows trying to raise their children who had invested their life's savings. It was no longer entirely in his hands, he said. Why, it was the worst mistake he had ever made, going public, listing the company on the big board.

The truth was, of course, that he loved it, loved the pressure that Wall Street generated, because he was good at it, he was the best, Number One. He loved pushing his stock up on Wall Street. He loved not just the sheer tangible financial reality of it, but the idea of it too. It was as if the CBS number on Wall Street, ever rising in those heady days of the late fifties and early sixties, was a daily announcement of the excellence of his stewardship, something that friends of his like Walter Thayer and Jock Whitney and the Rockefellers could understand and respect, an index not just of his leadership but of his manhood. There were those who worked for Paley who could tell from the tone of his voice in the late afternoon just how well the stock had done, whether it had risen or fallen. One or two of his associates, hearing his voice, knowing how important the market figure was to him, would even write down their own predictions so they could check the next day with the *New York Times* listing. It was, of course, big business, a point in the ratings could mean millions of dollars and likewise could mean a point or two on the market, which would mean even *more* millions of dollars. It was all so well planned and executed. They were aware of every show that added, and they were aware of every show that detracted: a documentary, for instance, might hurt the ratings, which would hurt the stock. In 1966 Bill Paley went before a stockholders' meeting and appalled his News Division by mentioning in passing that, had it not been for unscheduled news events such as space shots and the coverage of Winston Churchill's funeral, the shareholders would have gotten six cents more a share. Clearly it was going to be harder and harder for public-service programs.

In all of this Bill Paley himself was changing. He was changing as a broadcaster, and as he changed as a broadcaster he changed as a man too. He became even more isolated. He saw no one who might challenge him, no one from the world of television, and most particularly from the world of CBS, came to his home socially. It was as if the more commercial the world of television became, the more he cut it off from his social life. His social life was terribly important to him and it was very closed, very private. No one at his table discussed television. Once a young family member had mentioned rather casually how awful he thought most of the programs on television were and Babe Paley had become enraged, she had stomped out of the room, and later she accosted the young man, demanding to know how he dared to talk to Bill Paley like that, *in his own home.* For a man whose professional life brought him seemingly to the very center of public affairs and public life, his personal life was almost completely detached; it was as if there were a moat around the house in Manhasset and not very many people crossed it. The people who did were not by any means his intellectual or professional peers; instead, they were of a kind, very rich, very social, and very conservative. They could all tie a black tie and play golf, and in general they regarded most of the changes in the society with varying degrees of alarm. Bill Paley was at ease with that world, there was no one in it who challenged him, and he was accepted by these people; that seemed to matter a great deal, it was a mark of how far he had risen. He talked with enthusiasm of who his friends were, and who came to his table and whose table he went to, the doors that were now open to him. The names of royalty were mentioned.

His new social connection, of course, was expedited by his marriage to Babe Cushing. She had connected him to the inner circle of that world and, ironically enough, she had less interest in it than he. She had married him in at least partial hope of getting out of it, she was interested in expanding her vision, in meeting new and different people. Writers, artists, there was much more that she wanted to learn. The friendship with Truman Capote that ended so badly, after the publication of some thinly veiled fiction about him in *Esquire* magazine, had begun because Capote was like a university to her, he knew so much and passed on so much (while at the same time learning so much himself). The marriage between Bill and Babe Paley, featured as it so often was in the society columns and the most fashionable magazines, was not by any means an easy one. As he was spoiled in his professional life, he was spoiled at home, and she had wondered on occasion to very close friends whether he hadn't married her as much for her social entrée, for her brothers-in-law, as for herself. He was a demanding man, a perfectionist, he was accustomed to things being done exactly the way he wanted. There were any number of highly paid people on the CBS payroll who existed for that purpose alone, and he expected the same degree of perfection at home—the perfect guest list, the perfect meal, the flowers in exactly the right place; he had an incredible eye for detail and he knew when anything was out of place. Nevertheless, despite his immense financial success and the style in which he intended to live, he was not necessarily the most generous man about his home, there were many struggles over money. It was as if he had separated his worlds, one world in which he worked, and another world in which he lived and played. How different these worlds were he found in the mid-sixties when he finally realized one of his life's ambitions, to open a restaurant. It was to be at the base of the CBS building. The Ground Floor. Paley, a food nut, was absolutely fascinated by the entire business; he was always dropping in, checking the decor, sampling the soup, tasting the sauces. His pleasure was enormous when the restaurant opened and his disappointment equal when it failed to be a wild success. At one point, puzzled by the lack of its success, Paley turned to the restaurateur who was running it for him, Jerry Brody, and suggested that they might turn it into a supper club for those who eat around II P.M.—something that Paley liked to do after evenings at the theater or a concert.

"Bill," said Brody, "there ain't no supper business in this town."

"No?" said Paley, puzzled, "why not?"

"Because everyone's home watching the tube."

But he lived in the style that he wanted, in the exclusive community that he wanted, and he was in some ways content. That did not mean he was free from anti-Semitism. He had, ironically, chosen to live in a very exclusive, snobbish part of the society where the index of anti-Semitism, subtle or otherwise, was far higher than in the meritocratic world which he had long since forsaken. Perhaps he was a friend of Jock's and that was a very good connection, everyone liked Jock, but that didn't mean that a lot of people out there didn't resent him and his success and his religion.

All of this—the new possibilities of profits in programming, the ferocity of the ratings war, the growth of the entire company, the conservative world he moved in socially—took him further and further away from his News Department, which seemed not only less profitable than anything else, but somehow more threatening to the company. Now he organized the company to put more and more filters between him and the News Department, to deny access to his editors and journalists as much as possible. In his view, he had given Murrow friendship and access in the early days and Murrow had misused it, and it had been painful both professionally and personally. He was going to make sure that it never happened again. The successors of Murrow did not know him personally; men like Sevareid and Cronkite and Smith did not have easy lunches or dinners with him, that was a thing of the past. He became a far more distant figure. In 1961, at Ed Murrow's going-away party, Harry Reasoner, who had been with CBS five years and was already a rising star, anchoring the weekend news, was accosted by a tall, pleasant, attractive man who complimented Reasoner on his work and said he had been watching it with pleasure. When Reasoner's face failed to register any reaction, particularly gratitude, the tall man smiled and stuck out his hand. "Bill Paley," he said, introducing himself.

Robert Kintner had brought NBC News alive, and in doing so strengthened the entire network. He was a driving, difficult man with a great instinct for excellence and a great feel for what television was, for the excitement it could project, *and* he knew that the quickest and the cheapest way to create excitement was through an expanded news organization. The news organization could be the sinews of the network, could hold it together, and a great news organization would make a reputation for NBC and thus for Bob Kintner as well. He loved the sheer electricity of news, and he delighted in instant specials (in 1964 when Lyndon Johnson had a heavy cold there were constant bulletins throughout the day about Lyndon's health, interrupting the NBC programming schedule and blowing up the cold to massive proportions). In addition, he had come up with the Huntley-Brinkley team, which was an almost perfect anchor: Huntley, from Montana, Cronkite-like in his rock steadiness; David Brinkley, from North Carolina, the tart, slightly rebellious younger brother who could by deft tonal inflection imply a disbelief and an irreverence that the medium with its inherent overseriousness badly needed. Backing them was a team of fine floor reporters. In 1956 NBC had challenged CBS's supremacy for the first time; 1956 was the Huntley-Brinkley Democratic convention and as it went on, hour after hour, much too long, journalistic overkill, ultimately picking the same two candidates who had run in 1952, it had become a fine showcase for Brinkley's dry humor.

The sudden surge in the NBC ratings had subsequently scared CBS, indeed terrified the news executives, and Don Hewitt, the CBS producer, had panicked and had gone to Mickelson and suggested teaming Cronkite, who was then doing the anchor, with Murrow. The two big guns of CBS against the upstarts of NBC. A sure winner on paper. Ruth and Gehrig on the same team. It was a disaster. They were both the same man, playing the same role —two avunculars for the price of one. They did not play to each other or against each other as Huntley and Brinkley did. The chemistry was bad: Cronkite liked to work alone, and Murrow was not a good ad-libber.

By 1960 Huntley-Brinkley was number one in the ratings. For the first time, Paley, who loved to be number one, took notice and began to complain to his news executives—not about content but about ratings. Kintner loved it; he ordered the NBC people to close the nightly news with a statement saying that this news program had the largest audience in the world. Bill Paley was

Number Two! It grated on him terribly, but not so terribly that he would change the schedules of the five CBS-owned and -operated—O and O—stations (the five stations the FCC allowed each network to own outright, and indeed the richest source of network income) and put the Cronkite news on at 7 P.M. instead of 6:30, when it was then showing. NBC, of course, was showing Huntley-Brinkley at 7 on its O and O stations. Seven was the better hour, more people were at home then. The pleas of the CBS News Division that they be allowed to broadcast at seven too, fell on deaf ears. It was a galling problem for the news people, it taught them how little muscle and prestige they really had in the company. Paley was adamant. Somewhere deep in the bowels of CBS, the news people were sure, there was a very smart accountant who was beating them on this issue.

It was in general a bad time for CBS News. The reason was simple: the rest of CBS was so successful, so dominant under Aubrey, that any interference with entertainment by public affairs lost money, real money; NBC, by contrast, not only was fielding an excellent news team at the peak of its ability, it was weaker in programming and had less to lose by emphasizing news, by interrupting programs, by promoting its apparent love of public affairs. Every NBC program seemed to bear some reminder that the way to watch the 1964 conventions was with Huntley-Brinkley.

So at the very outset the omens were bad for CBS News and things were very quickly to get worse. Paley was in San Francisco for the Republican convention and he was in a foul mood. Because of his Eisenhower connections, he had been committed to Bill Scranton, the good, establishment, respectable candidate that season, and this had made the Goldwater people particularly suspicious of CBS. That suspicion had not dimmed when Dan Schorr, then in Europe, had done a story connecting Goldwater with certain right-wing German military men, a story that brought to the fore all the incipient mistrust of the conservative politician. The fact that the Scranton people were exploiting this particular story at the convention made Paley doubly nervous. CBS was for a time barred from Goldwater's headquarters. Paley himself panicked as the pressure mounted, and demanded that Friendly fire Schorr. Friendly, who had just taken over as head of CBS News and who was in a frenzy, kept turning to his staff and asking what he should do. The staff considered this unseemly. The obvious answer was to pay no attention to Goldwater or Paley, particularly since Schorr's story seemed valid. Friendly settled it by calling Schorr and repeatedly asking, "How could you do this to me? How could you do this to me?" as if Schorr had filed the story primarily as a way of putting Fred W. Friendly in the pressure cooker. "You've given me a clubfoot," Friendly told Schorr. The air was foul even as the convention was just starting, and Paley became convinced, as Schorr remained unfired, that he had too little control over his own News Department. Finally the Goldwater-German crisis was all resolved, there was a humiliating apology dictated to CBS by the Goldwater people and read over the air by Cronkite, and Schorr's job was saved, although his ego was bruised. But the entire incident angered the preoccupied Paley and did not put him in good spirits for the ratings disaster which was still to come.

For NBC was at its best. Its motto under Kintner had been "CBS plus thirty"—that is, whatever CBS was putting on plus thirty minutes more—and now it was paying off as immense amounts of logistical support and technology were poured in. It was not as if the two networks were out there covering a story, but rather as if it were some kind of heavyweight championship; they were there not to define the political story of that year, but to define themselves. It was less journalism than show-biz preening, tied to ego and ratings and image. Good ratings here could help the entertainment side, poor ratings might weaken the entertainment side. The network logic could be plotted easily: television, by covering the convention all day long, made the convention that much bigger; as the convention became more important, so too did the presidency become more important; and the choice of a candidate became in the public mind a more vital decision. (No wonder that in 1968 the out groups of America, finding they were not getting as much coverage as they wanted, brought their own counterconvention to Chicago, and gathered where the presidential cameras were already set up.)

In 1964 NBC's success was awesome. A debacle for CBS. At one point in San Francisco NBC seemed to have submerged the entire opposition. Kintner, of course, loved it. He had a booth of his own with a special telephone to call his subordinates—it rang on their desks when he picked it up. Julian Goodman was in charge of listening on the phone, but at one point Goodman was out of the room and the job of handling Kintner and his phone fell to a producer named Shad Northshield. The phone rang.

"Northshield," said Northshield.

"The new ratings we've got are eighty-six," said Kintner's gravelly voice.

"That's great," said Northshield.

Kintner hung up immediately. A second later the phone rang again.

"Did you get that straight—eighty-six percent?" Kintner said, and hung up.

Seconds later the phone rang again.

"It seems to me that you could give me more of a reaction," Kintner said.

"Well, what do you want, a hundred percent?" asked Northshield.

"Yes," said Kintner. Bang went the phone.


The difference between the NBC and the CBS coverage of the convention was not great; NBC was in command with a good team, and CBS with a younger floor team and a highly frenetic new level of executive leadership was less experienced. But there were not that many stories missed, because there were not that many stories to miss. The real difference was in the ratings, and it was an immense difference. Someone would have to pay. Long, long afterward, Walter Cronkite was still bothered, not just by the fact that he had been scapegoated, but because his superiors, in their discussion of what had gone wrong, never mentioned the coverage itself. He for one did not think that the coverage was very good, he thought that he hadn't done a particularly good job. But no one, when the crunch came, ever mentioned his weaknesses. And no one, certainly, thought of blaming the people who had failed to support the news program, Aubrey and Paley.

Paley had seemed irritable and restless at the Republican convention, and when Friendly and Bill Leonard, his deputy, returned to New York, that small media capital where everyone was talking only about NBC's triumph, they found his irritability had hardened. Paley now wanted drastic and immediate changes in the convention team, he was not about to remain number two. Friendly and Leonard tried to explain the performance in San Francisco, they pointed out that this was a young team, that time was now on their side, and that besides it was simply too late to change the team for the Democratic convention. They had compromised themselves slightly in their talks with Paley by mentioning innocently that Cronkite had talked a little too much during the convention. They realized their mistake immediately. Paley had seized on the comment: Yes, Cronkite was talking too much. Suddenly it was clear to them that Cronkite was going to be the fall guy, as far as Paley was concerned. Why was Cronkite on the air so much? Why did he dominate the others? Why did he talk too much? He had to go. There would be a new anchor. Paley and Stanton—usually it was Stanton who brought down the word from the corporate level but this time Paley was there as well—asked what changes the News Department was recommending. This was an ominous word, *recommending*. Friendly and Leonard said they planned to do nothing. Do you recommend, said Paley, that we get rid of Cronkite? Absolutely not, said Friendly. Then Paley told them to come back with specific recommendations in a few days. The corporation, it seemed, was about to confront the News Department. Friendly and Leonard met with Ernie Leiser, who was Cronkite's producer, and after much soul searching they recommended that it was impractical to do anything about the convention team. NBC was going to dominate at Atlantic City as it had in San Francisco and there was nothing that could be done about it. The best thing was simply to take your lumps and plan for the future.

It was not what Paley wanted to hear. This time the suggestion was a little less of a suggestion, more of a command. Come back and bring with you the names of the correspondents with whom you intend to replace Cronkite. Now they were meeting almost every day. At the next session Friendly and Leonard were still trying to hold the line, but Paley now had his own suggestion. Mudd. This terrific young correspondent Roger Mudd. Mudd, he said, was a born anchorman. (Which was perhaps true, particularly for a team that had been beaten by David Brinkley, for there was a touch of Brinkley in Roger Mudd, he was intelligent and wry and slightly irreverent, he seemed not to be overwhelmed by the gravity of occasions which, as a matter of fact, were rarely grave.) And now Paley became enthusiastic, there was nothing like this young fellow Mudd, he was terrific. And, with Mudd, said Paley, how about Bob

Trout? If Mudd was young and from the world of television, Trout was senior and a word man, Trout could really describe things. Trout, of course, was a famous radio man who could go on for hours with lingering descriptions of events. A Mudd-Trout anchor, that was Paley's idea. The great thing about being Bill Paley, thought one of his aides, was that he could put the hook to Cronkite for Mudd-Trout, and then a few months later, when Mudd-Trout had failed, he could wonder aloud why he had allowed Friendly and Leonard to force such a weak team upon him.

In all this there was no talk of substance, no talk of missed coverage or of bad reporting, it was all of image and ratings. Friendly found himself caught between his ambition and his News Department, and what bothered friends of his in those days, as he talked his dilemma out, was that he seemed or at least half seemed to accept management's right to make non-news judgments on news questions. A sacred line was being crossed without protest. Telling Dick Salant, his predecessor on the job, of the pressure and of the case Paley was building against Cronkite, Friendly said he did not know what to do. He just did not know which way to go. Salant answered: Fred, is it just ratings or is there a professional case against Cronkite? And Friendly answered, inadequately, that it was their candy store, that it all belonged to Paley. Knowing that he was being ordered to fire Cronkite, Friendly warned Paley that Cronkite would not stand for it and would quit if he lost his anchor, and Friendly was shocked by Paley's response: "Good, I hope he does." Finally Friendly gave in. It was a shocking failure, a classic example of what serious journalists had always feared about television, that the show-biz part would ultimately dominate the serious part. Among CBS working reporters Friendly's decision was not accepted; two years later, when Friendly resigned over the CBS failure to televise the Fulbright hearings, most members of his own staff thought he had chosen the wrong issue at the wrong time, that the real issue had been the yanking of Cronkite.

Friendly and Leonard flew out to California to break the news to Cronkite, who was vacationing. There was some talk of the possibility of a Mudd-Cronkite anchor, but Cronkite, a wildly proud man, wanted no part of it, he did not want to share his role with Mudd, and he knew CBS did not want him in the booth. Cronkite in his hour of crisis behaved very well. He did not dump on the company. He was properly loyal. Privately, talking with friends, he protected the company and the institution of television, saying that as a newspaper had a right to change editors if it wanted to, so too did a network have a right to change anchors. Then he held a public news conference and said yes, he thought the company had a right to change anchormen. No, he was not going to worry about it. He did not complain, nor did he agree to the suggestion of the CBS PR man who asked him to pose by a television set for an ad that was to say: *Even Walter Cronkite Listens to Mudd-Trout;* his loyalty to CBS did not extend to fatuousness. At Atlantic City he happened, by chance, to enter an elevator that contained Bob Kintner of NBC. Reporters spotted them coming out and thereupon wrote that Cronkite was going to

NBC, a rumor that helped him in his next CBS contract negotiation. All in all it could have been worse for him; he was buttressed by an inner and quite valid suspicion that a Mudd-Trout was likely to be an endangered species.

When Friendly returned from his trip to California, he called Stanton to let him know that the preeminent figure of television had been separated from his most important job, and Stanton had said (it made Friendly feel like a sinister character in a Shakespeare play—yes, the deed has been done, sire), "Good, the Chairman will be delighted." Mudd-Trout duly appeared. They were a total failure. NBC routed CBS even more dramatically at Atlantic City (some Cronkite fans going over to NBC in anger), and there was one moment during the convention (which, of course, was not a convention so much as it was a coronation) that remained engraved on the minds of the two news teams. It was the night that Johnson was to accept the nomination. Sander Vanocur of NBC had known Johnson and knew his style, and what he was likely to be feeling like, so he positioned himself near the entrance and waited and waited, guessing that Johnson at this moment might just be in an expansive mood, and then Johnson appeared and Vanocur popped up and had him. Yes, Johnson was in a marvelous, rich, anecdotal mood and—perhaps because Vanocur was regarded as a Kennedy man, what better way to vanquish the ghosts—he had gone on and on. With no one from CBS there at all. It was a marvelous exclusive and Kintner ran it and ran it all night, and when the CBS people saw it come over they were appalled. There was no one near at hand and so Bill Leonard, who was the head of the election unit and not a reporter at all, put on an electronic backpack and went rushing over, panting, and Vanocur, his exclusive done and by now running on the air for the third time, a great scoop in a scoopless convention, turned with a small smile of comfortable charity (which might later have cost him a job at CBS) and said to the President of the United States, "Mister President, you know Bill Leonard of CBS—he's a good man." Victory at Atlantic City. The end of the Mudd-Trout.

Friendly had worked hard to keep Cronkite from quitting outright, to persuade him to stay with the evening news. Cronkite did stay, and that fall CBS put together a magnificent election unit that ran far ahead of NBC up through election eve and that gave CBS the major share of the ratings. Cronkite was, of course, immediately rehabilitated; at the same time, the Huntley-Brinkley format was slipping, it had played for eight years and that was, given the insatiable greed of television, a very long time. The Cronkite show, aided by what was to be exceptional coverage of the Vietnam War by a team of talented young reporters, regained its prestige. But there are two footnotes to the tensions of the 1964 convention.

The first deals with the question of being number one. Paley had wanted to be number one without paying the price, while Friendly and the others had argued for the change in evening time slots that would allow Cronkite to come in at the better hour. But Paley had never listened. Then the dismal ratings of San Francisco stirred him, and one night during the convention, when all the indicators were absolutely terrible, Frank Stanton flew from New York to

San Francisco and gathered Leiser, Friendly, and Leonard for dinner. He had, he said, some very good news. And so with that marvelous delicacy which marks the way things are done in corporations (no admission that perhaps the News Department was right and that Paley had changed his mind—chairmen do not change their minds), Stanton said that if Friendly called the people at the local stations in New York and Philadelphia he might be able to argue them into letting Cronkite come on at seven o'clock. So Friendly made the calls, and lo and behold, his marvelous persuasive powers worked and Cronkite got just enough of a boost from the time change to regain his rating.

The second footnote deals with the man himself. For the Walter Cronkite who came back to work was a somewhat different man from the one he had been before being humiliated in public. As the next few years passed and he became even more the dominant figure of the industry, his pride intensified. In 1968 during the Democratic convention the delegates were voting on the peace plank. And suddenly, as sometimes happens at conventions, Cronkite and everyone else started using—overusing—a single word to refer to a situation. The word this time was *erosion,* which had obviously replaced *slippage,* the last convention's word. The vote came to Alabama and Cronkite mentioned that there was an erosion of two votes. He was broadcasting live and suddenly someone passed him a scribbled note: "Tell Walter not to use the word 'erosion'!" Cronkite, without missing a beat in the commentary, answered with his own note: "Who says?" Back came another note: "Stanton." Suddenly it was as if there were fire coming out of Cronkite's nostrils, and even as he continued the delegate count he wrote one more note: "I quit." So someone handed a note to pass to the brass saying: "Walter quits." And this was passed back and even as it was being passed back Cronkite was standing up and taking off his headset and reaching for his jacket. It was an electric moment. And suddenly someone was yelling, "For God's sake tell him to get back down there, don't let him leave. They're not trying to censor him. They just don't like the word 'erosion.' " So he sat down, and continued his broadcast. They might mess with him once, but no one messed with Walter Cronkite a second time.

Lyndon Johnson was a man of the thirties. He never really adapted to the new technology of his own era; typically, he was one of the few people in Washington in the late sixties who was a devoted listener to *radio.* He never really made it with television, though of course there was a time when he first came into office when it was all a honeymoon and it all worked and he reveled in it, President of all the people, Minister of Truth, anchorman for all the networks, television belonged to him, he could do whatever he wanted, no one could ever catch up with him; these were great moments, his own impetuosity enhanced by being President and a televised President at that, his surprises becoming televised surprises for the whole country. Lyndon settling the railroad strike, looking at his watch, seeing that it was near seven o'clock, deciding that he wanted to announce the news at seven o'clock on the button. Deciding to go to the CBS station—the White House was not yet set up for instant presidential specials, that would come in a few weeks, hot cameras ready for a hot Lyndon whenever Lyndon was ready for the cameras—and so suddenly the whole White House team was rushing into cars, sirens screaming, tires screeching, tearing through Washington evening traffic, and yes, at the very instant that Walter Cronkite came on the air, in strode Lyndon; Cronkite was put in the position of not so much giving the news as introducing the President of the United States, the only President we had, and Lyndon was there announcing that he had settled the railroad strike. He loved it, it was the best fun of his life, and later when he returned to the White House and an absolutely appalled Lady Bird asked why had he done it, why had he risked his life tearing through traffic like that, he had laughed and said: "Because I wanted to see the look on Walter Cronkite's face when I walked in the studio!"

He knew that he could set the agenda and, as President, simply Being There was enough, he was the message, and the other parts of the government could never really catch up (indeed, years later when it all began to slip away, when the war was darkening everything and Bobby Kennedy began to make speeches on Vietnam, Johnson showed a tendency to move the government to the Pacific en masse to compete for television time). But the fun of it was limited. As he was a beneficiary of it, so he became a victim of it; the combination of his own excessiveness and the heightened force of television was deadly. There were many pluses and many minuses to Lyndon Johnson, but in no way was he a man to ration himself, he wanted, as a politician and as a man, both to give too much and to take too much. Whereas Jack Kennedy was always aware of the danger of overexposure, Johnson was the exact reverse, he was almost maniacal about being *on,* he wanted to be on all the time. He was carnivorous and he was dealing with a carnivorous machine. When his aides, particularly the holdover aides from the Kennedy days, warned him that he was dealing with fire, that he had been on just last week, he replied, yes, but he wanted to be on this week as well, on all three networks.

If Jack Kennedy had been the first television President, or the first President made by television, then Lyndon Johnson was probably the first to be brought down by television, or at least in part by television, which finally fed not only his presidency but the forces against him, and he knew it. His real farewell to politics was not the one that most people remember, the surprise announcement on March 31, 1968, when he declared that he would not seek reelection, but a much more interesting and significant farewell given the next day in Chicago, where he had gone to face the National Association of Broadcasters and had in effect blamed them for his defeat and for defeat in Vietnam. They had turned the country against him, he believed. "Historians must only guess at the effect that television would have had during earlier conflicts on the future of this nation, during the Korean War, for example, at the time our forces were pushed back to Pusan, or World War II, the Battle of the Bulge . . ." They had beaten him, those cameras and all those punk kid reporters in Vietnam. They, the broadcasters, had beaten him, not Gene McCarthy and Bobby Kennedy and the kids in the streets. And he was more than a little right.

He was never really at ease with television. He had been wary of it in 1960 when, he knew, it had helped Jack Kennedy beat him for the Democratic nomination; in that same year there were originally supposed to be debates between the vice-presidential candidates, arranged by his friend Frank Stanton, but Johnson was quick to cancel them, he wanted no part of that. The populist part of him was ill at ease with the modernity of television. There was something else, too, Johnson as the poor Texas boy afloat in the world of eastern sophisticates, who felt he was going to be judged for the wrong reasons by the wrong people and that his roots and origins would be held against him. He felt that he could never dare to be what he really was in front of the camera. So to him television was a gimmick, and it brought out the worst in him: acting, preening, false piety. An attempt always to play someone else—Kennedy, Roosevelt, Churchill, almost anyone but Lyndon Johnson. Or when he got into trouble, the instinct to play different Lyndon Johnsons. Your friendly schoolteacher (the code was that the President had been a schoolteacher); then your friendly southwestern rancher (the President was a man of the plains and the big skies); finally, your friendly successful but honest businessman (the President had been a success in business as well as politics and was thus fiscally responsible). None of it worked. He always seemed to freeze, and it was so stilted, and there was so much of that high school elocution style from the past. Always role playing. He made the worst mistake a politician or a major television correspondent can make, he watched himself endlessly on the replay. He waited up for the late night shows, studying himself, not liking what he saw, always looking for ways to change it. This was considered a terribly dangerous thing within the television trade; you either are what you are and it works, or you aren't, but you don't tinker. Whatever was natural and human and alive in him froze. Someone, in a moment of primitive expertise, had told him to look right at the camera, and that was all he needed. From then on he fixed the camera like a man who suspected it was about to pick his wallet, and just drilled it; his eyes never wavered, never faltered. The impression was fierce, somewhat frightening. He was always playing with television, looking for a different style or a better lighting man, a better makeup man, a better pair of glasses, a larger TelePrompTer, a slicker television adviser. Always the gimmicks. Always unhappy with the way he looked: the big nose. Makeup men would come and makeup men would go, but the Rushmore features remained, casting their shadows over the rest of his face. When Johnson first took over as President, CBS had a young man named Mike Honeycutt working in its Washington bureau and one night he made Johnson up just before he went on the air. Afterward Johnson summoned Honeycutt. He was ushered into the Oval Office for a memorable meeting with the leader of the free world.

"Boy, you trying to fuck me?" asked the President of the United States.

"Sir?" said Honeycutt.

"Boy, you trying to fuck me?" Johnson repeated.

Honeycutt looked puzzled.

"Get him out of here!" Johnson roared, and a Secret Service man rushed Honeycutt out of the office, whereupon it was explained to him that the President had not liked the way he looked on the screen.

Similarly the glasses. Always a problem with glasses. Johnson squinting, Johnson with contact lenses, Johnson looking for the best eye doctor in the world, sending his staff to find the best eye doctor and Jack Valenti finally calling back with pleasure because he had found the best eye doctor in the world.

"Where's he from?" Johnson asked.

"Buffalo," Valenti said.

"Buffalo? Buffalo where?"

"Buffalo, New York."

"And you tell me he's the best? He can't be the best in the world and be from Buffalo!"

Nonetheless, the world's greatest eye doctor was rushed to Washington along with the man Frank Stanton and CBS then considered the world's best producer, Fred Friendly himself, head of CBS News. CBS was playing a very delicate game, serving CBS's audience while keeping a very close contact with the President of the United States. Small services rendered by Stanton and Friendly and CBS did not seem a great threat in those days; the idea of the danger of a super-President had not yet emerged in the liberal intellectual consciousness, and since Friendly and Stanton were mildly liberal and acutely aware of who had power, and since Johnson was reasonably liberal and very powerful, the trip did not seem improper to them. The Friendly trip—Friendly was already conferring with Johnson occasionally on other matters—was made at Stanton's request. Friendly happened to arrive at the White House the same day as the greatest eye doctor in the world, to find Johnson almost overwhelmed by the number of different glasses on his desk (a desk that had been personally redesigned by that great American carpenter-designer, Dr. Frank Stanton of CBS), and Johnson was suddenly looming over Friendly and the glasses, yelling that he didn't understand television, the only thing he understood was that everyone kept telling him how poorly he looked, how poorly he performed, that he was always squinting. And then suddenly, as the doctor was fitting Johnson with a huge device used to measure for contact lenses, Johnson—looking something like a Martian behind the optical device—started working over Friendly:

"Why don't you do something for your country?"

"What?" asked Friendly.

"Why don't you come down here and work for me?" Johnson said.

"You don't know anything about me."

"I know all about you from Walter Lippmann and Eisenhower. You come down and sit by my side and be the domestic version of Mac Bundy [an offer made to virtually anyone who went near the White House in those days, chimney sweeps, etc., the chance to be the domestic version of McGeorge

Bundy]. We'll clear it with Hoover today and announce it on Monday. You'll come to the ranch with us this weekend." At which point Friendly, who knew exactly what the job was—in its essence to reduce the Johnson nose, to make Lyndon Johnson look good on television—hesitated. He knew the job was not an easy one, since there was only one person who could do it and that was Johnson himself. Domestic version of Mac Bundy, he thought. Was he going crazy?

"I don't have any intellectuals," said Johnson as if reading Friendly's mind.

"I'm not an intellectual. All I can do is produce television shows. You might not like me. [Truer words were rarely spoken.] I might not like you," Friendly said. Even Friendly's driving ambition had some limits, and he sensed the danger ahead. He called Murrow that day, and Murrow, knowing both Johnson and Friendly, said it was the worst idea he had ever heard of. "They'll cut your balls off in four weeks," he added. Then came the phone calls, one marvelous one from Johnson, that enormous voice pouring out of the phone into Friendly's office in New York: Make up your mind, make up your mind, what do you want, do you want to sit around the 21 Club all day long drinking old-fashioneds and make a hundred thousand dollars a year, or do you want to help your country?

Friendly decided not to go to Washington to become Lyndon Johnson's television guru. Lyndon Johnson, he knew, had a special problem with television: he was haunted by a ghost. Kennedy had been so good, had been the first and had done it with such ease and skill and to such applause that Johnson, who felt himself in Kennedy's shadow in general, was particularly haunted by the Kennedy television ghost. He was, he knew, bound to be compared to Kennedy and the comparisons were bound to be unfavorable. Which made it doubly worse, because his insecurities flared in the areas where Kennedy had been strongest (or allegedly strongest), with the media and in foreign policy. There was no problem in the areas *he* felt strongest in: dealing with the Congress, domestic politics, finding a consensus among divergent forces. If, thought Pierre Salinger, who briefly served as a holdover press secretary, Johnson had come along at a different time, it might have been easier, the comparison with Kennedy might not have been so direct. Johnson would call in favored reporters and talk about television and in particular about how overrated Kennedy was on television. He, Lyndon Johnson, had watched him and didn't think Kennedy was all that hot. Quite overrated. Of course, he would continue, he thought television was an overrated political tool in any case. He probably wouldn't be on that much. He didn't really want it or need it.

The more he talked about it, the more obsessed he was by it; he tried to charm and cajole the television reporters who were covering him; he told them that if they played ball with him he would make them big men; why, he always claimed, he had made Frank Reynolds a big star at ABC, which was not exactly true. And he could not quite understand why they did not respond.

His recourse then was to go over their heads, to squeeze their bosses a little, it had always been a favorite move of his, to try to pressure and flatter publishers and heads of networks, and he never realized how much working reporters hated it. But he was more successful with this in broadcasting than in print, because the networks thought themselves, or liked to think themselves, vulnerable. His connections with men like Stanton and Kintner were very close; Stanton was his man, but so too was Kintner, Kintner had been an old friend in Washington during the New Deal days and Kintner later even went to work for him (unsuccessfully and unhappily). He loved to call when Kintner was head of NBC, catching Kintner in his limousine on the car phone, and they would discuss what was happening and what was going to happen.

Not everyone at NBC was happy about the closeness of that relationship, any more than the CBS people were happy about the Stanton-Johnson axis, and there was one moment during the 1964 convention when something happened that many of the top news people had long feared and dreaded. The convention was Johnson's anointing, everything was to go on schedule, there was to be no dissent. (He was in those days still scared of Bobby Kennedy and surprisingly nervous about his hold on the Democratic Party.) Dissent did, however, occur, just once; it came from the picketing of the Mississippi Freedom Democratic Party, young blacks and whites protesting not Lyndon Johnson's presidency but the lily-white nature of the Mississippi delegation. That angered him nonetheless, and so in a rage he had picked up the phone—he was, after all, a direct man, he was not much given to intermediaries and to deniability—and he called Kintner and he bellowed into the phone: "Get those goddamn cameras off those niggers! Get them off right now!" Kintner passed down the word to his associates and there was a quick scurrying in the executive levels of NBC News to find out what was happening and to see what else there was to cover, and by the time the order was ready to be given to cover something else, the cameras mercifully were already off on another incident.

He knew from the start that television was an enormous weapon, that he could get on whenever he wanted. Indeed, his years saw the rise of the unofficial network policy of giving the President time. In the past the networks had always asked the reason—was the national interest involved? Now he merely asked and they gave. He knew that the Congress could not compete, that he could give whatever figures and facts he wanted and there would be no rebuttal, and that only the television correspondents themselves, and even they to a marginal degree, blocked his way. He went to great pains to have his appearances filtered as little as possible by the White House correspondents. Whereas Kennedy thought of the exchange between President and journalist as part of the game, and knew that the process of give-and-take, or more accurately the semblance of give-and-take (he was taking more than he was giving), worked to his benefit, Johnson was far more careful in approaching the journalistic minefield. In addition, Kennedy, and this was crucial, knew that the presidency did not endow him with any immortal qualities that he did not already possess, that he was still a working politician who happened to have at his disposal great new technological advantages. But Johnson, like Nixon to follow him, being less confident, less secure, wanted the presidency to invest him with qualities that were not already there and did not necessarily belong to mortals. He was the President. He was special. He was above other human beings, he was above his fellow citizens, who were no longer citizens but subjects. A democratic monarch, which meant that he did not like that last vestige of democracy, working reporters who kept nibbling away at him.

He tried to change the rules of presidential television, to expose himself less and less to questioning and to use the medium more and more as a forum for his (regal) pronouncements. Soon there were fewer and fewer press conferences and those that took place seemed to be mostly occasions for announcements. Lyndon as anchorman. When a reporter complained that they had not had a press conference in a long time, Johnson answered that he didn't have anything to announce. When the reporter answered that this was not necessarily the function of the conference, Johnson became quite annoyed. He was ill at ease with any kind of open dialogue with television reporters, although, ironically, it would have been the perfect forum for him; the questioning of a few intelligent journalists would have evoked the sheer force and above all the incredible knowledge of government that Lyndon Johnson possessed. For in truth, there was no one in this century who knew more, both in detail and in large perspective, about the intricacies of the politics of the United States. If only, Dan Rather thought, he would have said, "All right, you think I'm a wheeler-dealer and you're right, but just watch my smoke, and I'm doing this for you," people might have responded to that. But Johnson would not permit it. "I can't compete with Walter Cronkite," he once told his aides, "he knows television and he's a star. So when I'm with him I'm on his level and yet he knows what he's doing and so he does it better and so I lose."

He did not like press conferences anyway; he had begun to believe his own myth of the presidency, and he felt that the authority of the President was diminished by all those mortals asking questions. They had not earned the presidency, and yet there they were pretending to be his equal (a theme repeated frequently by his successor). When the evening news showed one of the White House correspondents casting the slightest doubt on one of his announcements, he summoned from the past his old friend Sam Rayburn. "Sam," he would say, "tell them where to go and what to do." When asked what that meant, he answered: to run for sheriff, to pay their bills, to know his side of the issue. Who had elected them? He began to see, particularly as things went sour, only the negative part of the instrument, not the possibility of using the instrument as a presidential weapon. He had forgotten that television once raised him above everyone else; now all he remembered was the injustice of it, the part that he couldn't control. And what injustice. That boy Rather, playing these games against him, and Rather was from Texas and worked for CBS. "I thought you were my friend," he would say to Stanton. "I thought you and Walter were my friends and look at what you and that boy Rather do to me." Rather perplexed him. "I could help that boy, I don't understand him, I have friends at CBS. I could make him a star." Which he believed, and when Rather, who in his flinty way would never give Johnson a handle, stayed outside the Johnsonian reach, the President was hurt. "Why did that boy do that to me? . . . Why, I remember him when he was on the roof during that storm in Houston, and I could help him." The tension with Rather had existed from the start.

For Dan Rather was, whatever else he might be, not one of Lyndon's boys. He was one of the worst offenders, in Lyndon's eyes a Texan gone eastern, a boy who should have known how to help his country (by helping Lyndon Johnson, of course). The Texas thing had helped in his original assignment to the Johnson White House; Rather had come from the CBS affiliate in Houston, had distinguished himself first by physical courage and then by sheer energy and hard work, and had later covered the South for CBS during the early sixties when the coming of the half-hour news show meant the expansion of the domestic bureaus. With Johnson in the White House, CBS executives had wanted someone with a Texas accent to cover him. They decided that Rather had extensive Texas contacts (which he did not), he would know Johnson's staff people (he protested that he knew no one on the staff but was assured by one executive that there was a Mary *Rather* on the staff . . . perhaps she was a distant cousin . . . they could become close friends, Dan and Mary). Rather had protested immediately his lack of knowledge of and kinship to Mary Rather and his superiors had finally accepted this, though suggesting that he could at least help in translating some of that Texas language into English. Rather did know enough about Lyndon Johnson to realize that it was almost impossible for a journalist to have any kind of close relationship with him and still keep a modicum of self-respect, and he was wary about the idea of covering the President while expecting the Texas thing to work.

Rather in those days was the most junior of the network correspondents, and his CBS colleagues remember that the edges were still rough, the blue suit a little shiny, the country still showed. Curiously, being the outsider, the graduate of a backcountry school instead of Harvard, some of the advantages of eastern sophistication that haunted Lyndon Johnson (and twisted Richard Nixon) bothered Rather too, because he lacked them—a sense that Easterners had more and knew more than he did. But in his case, instead of poisoning him, it seemed to give him an added edge, drove him to work harder. He was not afraid to learn in mid-career; he was an unfinished man, and at an age when many of his colleagues had stopped growing he was still learning. But Johnson from the first misread him, thought he could have a slice of him, and greeted Rather accordingly: Lyndon Johnson was glad to see Dan Rather, Lyndon Johnson knew he could count on Dan, he was not like these eastern boys who didn't understand a Texan, "you understand me and you're going to help me." Rather had winced at that. Oh God, I'm really in for it, he thought.

It never worked well, not from the start. Johnson liked to brand everyone and everything around him and he found Rather to be a man not easily branded. There were reporters from papers and networks more sophisticated,

more professional, and more experienced than Dan Rather, but few who had
so strong a sense of their own value and their own independence. His father,
a construction worker who laid oil pipelines in Houston, had seen to that. Irvin
Rather was a strong and capable man, the only person his son had ever known
who had finished all the courses advertised on a matchbook cover, and thus
gained an engineering degree. He was a proud man and his stamp was on his
son. His position was difficult. Great newspapers do not like their White House
reporters to be in an adversarial position with the White House; networks,
being more timid and more accountable to the government, like it even less.
So his problems were potentially dual: difficulties with the President could
easily become difficulties with his superiors. He was thus more vulnerable than
the average White House correspondent. The first attempt at branding him
took place very early, at the first White House press conference Rather covered. Lyndon Johnson simply refused to see him or acknowledge his question.
For a print reporter this might mean very little, but for a network journalist
it is absolutely shattering. All his bosses were watching, a lot of institutional
manhood was riding on it, it was imperative for Rather to show that he had
the clout to do his job. To go unrecognized at two presidential press conferences might cost him that job. So while his CBS bosses gathered around the
tube in New York, Dan Rather again and again kept jumping out of his seat
as if there were a spike in it, trying to get the attention of the President, but
to no avail. What was worse, Johnson recognized his main competition, Nancy
Dickerson, and even worse, by name. *Yes, Nancy.* Rather was devastated, and
he decided he could not let this happen again, his very career was at stake.

So he carefully rehearsed what he intended to say and he sought out Jack
Valenti, who was the nice guy in the White House, and considered friendly to
all reporters. With Valenti, Rather laid it out—he thought this was deliberate
on Johnson's part, and if it was, then he, Dan Rather, was going to kick back,
no one was going to ignore him. But Valenti was very soothing: Rather was
wrong, Johnson was not against Rather, *Lyndon Johnson liked Rather,* he
thought a lot of him, Rather reminded him of young friends he had known
in Texas. The White House was *for Dan Rather,* Jack Valenti was authorized
to say that. The problem was the President's eyesight, he had a terrible problem with his eyes and could not see ten feet without his glasses. He was looking
for Rather, but had been unable to see him. Now, these other reporters, he
knew them because of their outlines, their shapes were familiar. So Rather
knew that Lyndon Johnson was putting a mark on him, teaching him a lesson
before the assembled multitude of CBS executives. And Rather found that at
the next conference he was quickly recognized, even though he was seated
much farther back. The President's eyesight, he noticed, had greatly improved.

But recognition did not solve the problem. It was not so much that Rather
was so tough a reporter as that a President, particularly this President, resented any departure from his own definition of events, any independence of
judgment, finally any independence on the part of a journalist. So Rather
bothered him. He was puzzled—why, I could help that boy, why is that boy

so hard on me? And the pressure on Rather mounted—the phone calls from Johnson to his bosses, the complaints, the gentle lectures on how to be a good boy. Then in mid-1964 (a time when ostensibly everything was going almost perfectly for the President, all according to schedule) suddenly came a harsh lecture administered by the President himself: "You did a good job down there in Texas and then you got up here to the big time and the first thing you've done is fallen in with all these eastern people, *The New York Times* and the *Time* magazine. So you've come to the big city and fallen for their eastern ways. Well, you've made the biggest mistake of your life. The best thing you've got going for you, the best thing about you, is that you're all Texan, and I'm all Texan, and what you're doing, playing Easterner, is a phony and I know it's a phony and you better get it right."

Which changed nothing. It was fascinating for Rather to know that the President of the United States cared so much about his career. But he continued to do what he was doing and the White House continued to get angrier. In late October, a number of international events came together—Khrushchev fell from power, the Chinese exploded the bomb—and, allegedly under the pressure of events, Johnson demanded air time to go before the nation. It was an interesting moment, the height of a presidential campaign. The networks gave him the time for what was predictably a political speech and the Republicans screamed bloody murder. Rather, doing the instant analysis, was told by his bureau chief, Bill Small, to hold it to a minute, which Rather did, a very brief piece which said in effect that the Goldwater people say this is a political speech at a political time and they have asked for equal time and it will be interesting to see what the networks do. Anyone watching might have added that it would also be interesting to see what they would do about Rather. Johnson was furious and he passed on his complaints to Stanton, who passed them on to Friendly, who passed them on to Rather. In fact, Friendly tore Rather apart, telling him how irresponsible his journalism was. How could Rather do something like this?

Johnson's mood remained negative right through to election eve, when he invested a great deal of energy in not recognizing Rather (who in desperation had positioned himself next to the fair Nancy Dickerson of NBC). It ended like something in a Marx Brothers movie, Rather chasing around trying to be one step ahead of Johnson so that he could get that desperately needed interview, Johnson skillfully avoiding seeing him, finally late in the evening going for Rather's third-string backup man and giving *him* the exclusive. It was not long afterward that Rather was transferred out of the White House and assigned to London. There were various reasons: Rather had asked for an overseas assignment and CBS wanted a bigger name at the White House and Harry Reasoner was available. London was considered a plum, and Rather had asked to go overseas, but there was a part of him that sensed that the complaints had had an effect and that one reason he was in London was that brief comment on Johnson's speech. He didn't stay long in London, the Vietnam War was blowing up, and like most correspondents of his generation, living in the shadow of the Ernest Hemingway of Spain, he wanted to be part of it, and he went there in 1965.

Among the documentaries that CBS did not make in the sixties, and one that clearly would have been of more than just passing interest to its vast audience, was the study of how Lyndon Johnson, in addition to being a powerful figure in the Congress, became a very rich man. Such a documentary would, of course, have been embarrassing to Lyndon Johnson; worse, it would have been embarrassing to CBS. For among those who had lent their skills and their institutions to the augmentation of the Johnson fortune was Dr. Frank Stanton, President of CBS, and he had done it with the full knowledge and cooperation of Bill Paley. The relationship between Johnson and Stanton was, by Johnsonian standards, special. It went beyond the normal bounds; and he treated Stanton with a respect and deference he showed to very few men—perhaps Clark Clifford, perhaps Abe Fortas (in large part because Stanton, like Clifford and Fortas, understood Johnson well and had great reservations about accepting any job under him). Johnson displayed kindness toward Stanton, a respect for his professional abilities and for his commitment to Lyndon Johnson that he displayed to very few others. "You always come through, Frank, and I am grateful for it," he wrote in a note to Stanton in 1964, and those were very rare words for Lyndon Johnson, he liked to keep most people off balance, and in his heart he felt that no one really came through for him. As early as the mid-fifties Johnson would tell reporters covering him that Frank and Ruth Stanton had just been down on the ranch the past weekend dove hunting with him, and Frank Stanton was probably the finest man in the United States, the Johnsonian eye fixing the CBS correspondent, and any man lucky enough to work for Frank Stanton could count his blessings. The years, the endless favors, the trips to the White House for Stanton, did not weaken that tie and some sixteen years later, when a television documentary team (from CBS naturally) came down to film Johnson's memoirs, the former President took them across his ranch and then pointed to a small hill and said: Yes, right there, that spot there was where Frank and Ruth Stanton were going to build their house, Lyndon Johnson was going to give them that little spot of land, and they were all going to settle down there and be neighbors.

And so it was that Frank Stanton, president of a company that among other things should have been analyzing power and wealth in America, was indeed over the years very close to a President who was steadily becoming wealthier and more powerful, as Stanton was becoming wealthier and more powerful and the company was becoming wealthier and more powerful. The relationship was filled with all sorts of minor improprieties, and Stanton is just sensitive enough these days when he talks about Johnson to put a little more daylight between them; no, they were never really that close, although yes, Johnson did offer him that land down there on the ranch, and yes, he did redesign the presidential desk ("Besides being a high calibre communications executive," Johnson had written Stanton at the time, "you are also a wood-work craftsman. My desk is far more handsome than it used to be, and there is a tidy look that it didn't have before"), and yes, he often did take care of Johnson when he came to New York as a senator and a congressman. The relationship made people in the CBS News Division very uneasy when Johnson was President. They knew that Stanton was in constant touch with Johnson, and they were sure that in his own mind Stanton had his priorities straight, that he was helping a friend who happened to be President, helping CBS in Washington, and alleviating the sting of some of its correspondents. But they did not like it. There were so many things that were going on, and they were not really informed of them. Stanton was always busy advising Johnson. He lent Johnson Joe Stern, a top CBS engineer, for consultation on technical matters, on White House television reception; he helped find experts for Johnson; he used CBS personnel to install three TV sets in Johnson's bedroom in August 1964, and then a few months later three more in Johnson's White House. He sent in constant reports on the business community's attitude. He told Johnson when his cosmetic look was good. (He wrote of one photograph of Johnson in *The New York Times Magazine:* "One of your best photographs and I like your collar very much." Of a televised Johnson appearance he wrote criticizing the use of McNamara and Clark Clifford as unnecessary props since "there is no official more awesome than the President of the United States.") It was hard at times to tell where Stanton's loyalty really lay. Though he had been the initiator of presidential debates and had always pushed for them, when in 1964 Johnson broke the short-lived tradition by refusing to debate Goldwater, most people in television were appalled, but not Frank Stanton. When Tom Wicker wrote a *Times* column criticizing Johnson, it was Stanton who wrote a letter to the *Times*, defending the presidential circumspection.

Johnson had first gone to CBS in 1938 when he was a young congressman and very unsure of himself, particularly in New York, which was well known to be a den of slick eastern sophisticates, all of whom specialized in skinning poor old Texas country boys. He had been trying to get some sort of network affiliation for Lady Bird's fledgling radio station, an affiliation that might allow the station to survive. His welcome in New York had hardly been overwhelming, and it had emphasized in his own mind, he would tell friends later, his own gawkiness and clumsiness. He had finally gone to CBS to see Paley, who in those days was still very open, and Paley's secretary had announced that there was a very tall Texan waiting out there in a big hat and boots who said he was a congressman. Paley went out to meet him and the Texan, according to Paley, had said, "Mister Paley, I have this here ticket for a two-hundred-and-fifty-watt station in Austin and I'd like to join as a CBS affiliate." That was a very small station indeed and Paley explained that they had an affiliate in San Antonio and one in Dallas, but had sent him nonetheless to a young man on his staff in charge of this kind of research. The young man was Frank

Stanton and he knew what a congressman was and he looked at his map and found that there was a strong station in Dallas and a strong one in San Antonio and right there in the middle, in the crease between their coverage, was little Austin, not threatening Dallas and not threatening San Antonio. Who will ever know what would have happened if it had been some other noncongressional station owner coming up from Austin with a station that CBS clearly did not need? What we do know is that Stanton said that this was just the place for a good small station, a fine place to put a CBS affiliate, for which Lyndon and Lady Bird were eternally grateful and eventually a good deal richer. The key to the Johnson wealth was that station and the Johnsons never forgot it.

It of course made for Frank Stanton, who became the chief lobbyist for CBS, a powerful friend who was to become still more powerful. Stanton had treated him with great courtesy in that first meeting, making an extra link between the two men. Stanton served in one way as a kind of eyes and ears for Johnson with the establishment; there would be phone calls from Johnson or from Lady Bird asking for help, because Lyndon didn't know those people in New York, could Frank give some advice on this? And of course the Johnsons coming to New York and Stanton laying on the limousine, and taking care of theater tickets, and arranging all those New York favors. Little ones, and sometimes big ones. Even when Johnson was President there was a special place for Frank Stanton. Lyndon Johnson dealt with Stanton and no one else in the White House did. The Johnson White House was reasonably open, particularly on domestic affairs, and staffers cut across lines at all levels, but Stanton was set apart, Johnson handled that himself, and he would say to an aide, "Call Frank Stanton and tell him . . ." and then more often than not check himself in midsentence and say, "No, I'll call Stanton myself." A special niche. Stanton not just as connection to the most powerful broadcasting corporation in the world, but as a connection to the very center of the American business establishment, Stanton serving as a kind of Johnsonian intelligence agency in New York, keeping Johnson informed, as in December 1967, when a group of establishment figures met in Bermuda to discuss the seeming deadlock of the war. It was Stanton then who called the White House to report on the meeting, claiming (erroneously) that they had demanded Rusk's resignation.

The connection served them both well. The gentlest scratching of the biggest backs around. The Austin radio station prospered and when television arrived there was no competing television station in Austin for years and years. Some were unkind enough to regard it as something unique in American broadcasting, monopoly ownership. And it was a very rich station, even if it was small, and it managed to be richer than other small stations. Large companies were known to do a disproportionate amount of advertising on it, and sometimes this was very subtly done, on the *radio* station, where it was less noticeable than on the television station. Lyndon Johnson was fond of that little station and even while he was President he carried around with him a piece of paper that showed the spot sales for the week, and there were calls right through the vice-presidential years to the big advertising agencies from key members of Johnson's staff, and sometimes from Lady Bird herself, expressing disappointment at failures to advertise. Stanton himself was always there to give advice, if there were a challenge from a UHF station, and Johnson would call to tell what the latest problem was and Stanton would always look into it. Lou Cowan had once walked into the office of the president of the network to hear Stanton calling various affiliate stations in Texas saying that Senator Johnson was going to be on "Face the Nation" that Sunday and he, Frank Stanton, hoped that these stations would be carrying it.

Stanton served on the United States Information Agency board, a clear conflict of interest, and during the years of the Vietnam War was a committed hawk, working constantly to let the heads of his News Department know his displeasure with dovish reports or programs. Once, after Bill Fulbright was finally allowed on "Face the Nation," Stanton called Friendly the moment the show was over to say what a rotten thing that was to do to the President of the United States. In 1965, Friendly arranged a lunch for Paley and Walter Lippmann which Paley had sought, and which was difficult to arrange because both Paley and Lippmann were hard to pin down on schedules. Friendly had assumed Stanton would co-host it, and on the day of the lunch was surprised to see Stanton eating separately in the CBS dining room, thus snubbing Lippmann, who was then Johnson's foremost opponent on the war. Stanton later became furious when Murray Fromson of CBS reported that American bases in Thailand were being used as staging areas for the bombing of North Vietnam. He complained bitterly to Friendly that this was a violation of embargoed information, a position neither true nor defensible by any serious news executive, since the North Vietnamese knew precisely what was being done at the Thai bases; it was only the American people who had been kept ignorant. Friendly pointed this out to Stanton, who said yes, that's true, but it might prove embarrassing to the government anyway.

Week after week at the news executives' lunches with Paley and Stanton, Stanton passed on the complaints he had caught from Johnson that week, the litany of presidential anger, how much heat he had caught, how angry Lyndon was. News executives, watching this performance, wondering what was behind it, what it all was supposed to mean, felt that Stanton had placed himself in a totally impossible position, trying to have it both ways, the statesman of broadcasting and the chief CBS lobbyist. He was clearly trying to let CBS News know how much tension it was already causing (and thus in a not so subtle way letting the News Department know it should not go any further, that any additional coverage might be too much) while at the same time trying to let them know that he, Frank Stanton, was shielding them from the heat. The newsmen present had to admire the complexity of the performance, and yet they were utterly appalled by it.

A few years later, after Johnson had left the White House and was working on his book, the then Vice-President of the United States, Spiro Agnew, began attacking the media and particularly the networks. Aaron

Asher, who was Johnson's editor on the book, asked him what he thought of the Agnew attacks. "It's all wrong," he said. "All wrong. They'll all end up screaming the First Amendment, and it's not going to do him any good. They'll get back at him. Whenever I had real trouble with those network commentators I'd call up someone like Frank and I'd say, 'What the hell are you trying to do to me? What are you people screaming at me for?' And it would quiet down for a while, and then they'd come back at you again and you'd have to phone up again."

The crucial moment for Lyndon Johnson in setting the nation's path on Vietnam was the Tonkin Gulf incident. There he handed the nation, its Congress, and its press corps a fait accompli. He chose the timing of the incident at his pleasure, when it suited him, and he chose the place, where it suited him. By choosing this particular incident, what *seemed* to be an American response to North Vietnamese provocation, the whole situation was wrapped in the flag; by choosing a locale where there was no possible competing source of information, where there was no *New York Times* or Washington *Post* or CBS correspondent stationed, he totally controlled the flow of information. Only he and a few other men knew what had happened and why, only he and a few other men knew what the American response was. If the normal flow of information at a moment of crisis such as this already favored the President, then he had very carefully and deliberately chosen an incident where the control of information favored him far more than usual. In this case, working reporters had only one real source of information, his White House. Everything worked like a charm, every institution played its role just as he wanted, no other institution could challenge the presidency, no other institution could catch up with it. The bombers were on their way before the American people even knew it, and the bombers became their own rationale, each bomb dropped became a rationale for the next one, no real American in those days dared doubt the use of his own nation's bombers.

Americans had been trained during the war and the post-war years to trust their Presidents, and the President, after all, had all the information. Now he could dole it out as he chose, define the issue as he wanted; events were moving too quickly for anyone to doubt, indeed events had already moved, and journalists were desperate to have a share of them, and so the government, shrewd and knowing about the forms of journalism, used those forms against a free press; it handed out information as it chose, secure in the knowledge that if its information did not exactly reflect the entire truth, it nonetheless fit the forms that journalism wanted and demanded. What other source of information was there? It was a classic example of what the presidency had become, how it could move more quickly and effectively than countervailing institutions. The President's reach, with jet planes and television, was extended, he could move quicker over longer distances now, he could reach a national audience at will to justify his actions. He brought to his decisions, moreover, the added rationale of national security, a rationale which for the past twenty years had been strengthening the presidency and weakening the Congress. By definition, issues of national security could not be debated openly in Congress; they were secret. This aided Lyndon Johnson immeasurably in the Tonkin Gulf incident; because the crucial fact about that incident, the one fact that might have stimulated profound public debate, was kept secret. This was the role of the CIA. Rather than the simplistic story that formed the center of the White House position—that the North Vietnamese, unprovoked by us, had assaulted our ships—the truth was the reverse. Through secret CIA operations —34-A raids, they were called—we had systematically been provoking the North Vietnamese, running PT-boat raids against their naval bases, deliberately jamming their radar. We had provoked them, but our citizens did not know of this; all they knew about was North Vietnam's response. All this meant that the Congress had been manipulated and it meant that most of what the best of the nation's reporters wrote in the days after Tonkin was, in fact, lies and distortions. It was the most dangerous example of what a free society can do to itself when it emulates a closed society.

But he had gotten what he wanted, an incident he could use to produce an all-purpose resolution from the Congress. And the Congress quickly played its appointed role. In a matter of a couple of hours—thanks to reaction time of the modern age, to the swiftness of the new weapons—the President had placed both country *and* Congress in a position where they had to back him up and back him up immediately, where he could control and regulate the precipitating events and control the information flow, and where he could make issues more, not less, emotional, so that the Congress must deal with them, not at the level of common sense, but at the level of patriotism and emotion. He would give them, when he was ready, the flag, and they would salute it. Tonkin Gulf was the incident he had been looking for—he had, in fact, ordered a draft resolution prepared several months earlier for just such an eventuality.

One man knew what Johnson was doing. Wayne Morse understood that the combination of speed and information was crucial, that the faster things went, the better for the President; and that control of information was equally crucial, because the case that Johnson was presenting was, he sensed, extremely dubious. Johnson was pushing hard for an instant resolution, and William Fulbright, head of the Senate Foreign Relations Committee, was acquiescent. He was in those days playing his friend-of-the-family counselor to the President rather than a constitutional role, and in that capacity was floor-managing the Tonkin resolution. He and Johnson had been close in the past, he had been Johnson's personal Secretary of State when they were both in the Senate, and Fulbright had not yet accepted the fact that Johnson had gone on to greater things with greater men of greater reputation; Fulbright believed that when it came to the crunch of war in Vietnam, the President would consult with him. And so, as events swept along, Fulbright was willing to play his role. Morse argued fiercely with him (years later a reporter interviewing Morse about those days was surprised to find him more bitter at Fulbright than at Johnson). Morse wanted time and Fulbright said no, there was no time, they had to rush the resolution through. What's the rush? asked Morse. What's the hurry? Morse knew the only way to get cross-checks on the information was through a senatorial hearing with witnesses. Not just the President's witnesses, but competing ones—Matthew Ridgway, George Kennan, Lightning Joe Collins, and others—and he knew that if he could ventilate the issue, then the Administration was in trouble. The more questions raised, the more difficult it might be for the Administration. So Morse asked for time to call witnesses. But Fulbright resisted, there wasn't time, the President needed the resolution *now*. Otherwise the Communists would know we were divided. Fulbright had his way—the President's way.

Tonkin Gulf was probably the high-water mark of the era, for by crossing this particular Rubicon, by going too far, by exceeding both his mandate and common sense, Lyndon Johnson was unleashing forces that ultimately would work to limit the President and the presidency. Few, however, noticed at the time. Most were caught up in the rush of events, planes hurtling toward Asia, pointers moving briskly over charts of depots. A few were made uneasy by the rush to decisions, the haunting lack of information. Among them was Ed Murrow. He was sick and dying, out of CBS, out of the government by then, full of misgivings about both the war and Lyndon Johnson, and that night as the news unfolded on the screen, Murrow did something he had never done before, he called up his onetime protégé Fred Friendly, by then the head of CBS News, and tore into him. In the past when Murrow had been angry with Friendly he had handled him quietly and sometimes his silence was the most eloquent form of his anger. But this time he was in a rage: "By what God-given right did you treat it this way? What do we really know about what happened out there? Why did it happen? How could you not have Rather and the boys do some sort of special analysis?" Friendly was shocked by his anger, and felt a certain guilt because he had that day been on the phone with Dan Rather, and Rather had said that it all smelled a bit tricky, and Friendly had told Rather for God's sake not to say anything along that line on the air. Friendly simply did not know how to cover something as elusive as this, how to raise the questions. He was still, like the country, more hawk than dove, and the whole thing scared him. And he was also in quite close contact with the Johnson administration. There was some talk about coming back on the air later that night—perhaps a midnight special—but that too was dropped.

# 17 / Time Incorporated

Johnson was handling television well in the early days of the Vietnam War. It was taking its line from him, and from his White House, letting Washington define the situation in Saigon. Television was on Johnson's side, part of the Johnson team. Print journalists were proving more difficult. Particularly *The New York Times*. The *Times*'s reporters in Saigon, and a few others. Johnson found this annoying because the *Times* supported most of his domestic legislation. Vietnam was another matter, and it infuriated him. He was the second President to feel that way; his predecessor had felt it just as strongly.

On October 22, 1963, the publisher of *The New York Times,* Arthur Ochs Sulzberger, was scheduled to meet with President John F. Kennedy. It was their introductory meeting and Sulzberger, then thirty-seven years old, was apprehensive about it. Though he bore both names of the *Times*'s family dynasty, he had been publisher for only five months and he had been in no way prepared for the job. His parents had decided much earlier that Orvil Dryfoos, their son-in-law and Sulzberger's brother-in-law, was much more suitable as publisher of the *Times*. Then Dryfoos had died suddenly of a heart attack and Punch Sulzberger (his very nickname seemed somehow a reflection of the family view that he was a little lightweight) had been thrust into the job. This had occurred only a few months earlier. He had never met with a President before and he was very nervous. He knew that he did not carry with him the real respect of the institution he headed; it was said among working reporters on the *Times* that his main responsibility had been taking care of the office air-conditioning units. That day, as he walked over to the White House, he had turned somewhat apprehensively to Scotty Reston and asked, "What do I say to him? What does he say to me?" Reston, aware of Punch's uneasiness, had assured him that it would only be a matter of small talk. "He'll ask you about your children and you ask him about his."

The talk never quite got around to families. Kennedy was furious about the American reporting from Saigon. Worse, the handful of reporters in Saigon, at one time effectively cut off from contacts within the embassy, had, as the policy collapsed, become so well connected that they found out about almost any development or factional fight within the embassy more quickly than did Kennedy's own top people. He was particularly irate over my own reporting for the *Times* from Saigon. Because I had the *Times*'s platform and because I was the only full-time resident reporter for an American newspaper in Saigon, I had excellent connections. At the time, I had been in Vietnam for some fifteen months. I was twenty-nine years old and reasonably brash and aggressive. My reporting, like that of my colleague Neil Sheehan and others, had already been regularly disputed, attacked, and condemned by the White House.

"What do you think of your young man in Saigon?" Kennedy began.

"We like him fine," Sulzberger said, somewhat taken aback.

"You don't think he's too close to the story?" the President asked.

No, said Sulzberger, he did not. (In fact, the *Times* was very nervous about the entire situation. It hated the idea of one of its reporters being controversial and it hated the idea that it might be blamed for being soft on Communism. In addition, some editors disliked what they felt was my lack of balance and wished my reporting were more conventional, with more articles directly quoting high-level offices about how well things were going.)

"You weren't," suggested the President, "thinking of transferring him to Paris or Rome?"

No, said the publisher of the *Times,* he had no such plans. He left the office somewhat shaken. It had been a very cold day. He immediately canceled arrangements for my scheduled vacation so it would not look as though the *Times* were caving in. The lines between President and press over Vietnam were being drawn.

Vietnam was a war in which journalists made their reputations and generals lost theirs. It was the first of two traumatic national crises—Watergate was the second—in which the essential combatants were not the President and the opposition party nor the President and the Congress, but the President and the press. Both the presidency and the national press corps had become infinitely more powerful over the preceding thirty years. Each had been the beneficiary of most of the major changes in the society, the new technology that produced an explosion of communications and also centralized power, the rising educational level, and the new place of America in the world. The President now had new methods of reaching people through broadcasting. He had the budget and the issues to dominate Congress. The transcending issues in the twenty years after World War II were not such things as the farm program, where the Congress felt itself on familiar ground, they were issues of foreign policy, which belonged to the President. All these changes had enhanced *presidential* power. Such manifestations of America the Superpower as the CIA were, in effect, presidential agencies, a part of the executive branch. They passed their information on to him, and it became his information. The only alternative source of information was the free press, but the combination of the Cold War and the McCarthy period had made the press hesitant to challenge the Administration, willing to accept its norms and definitions.

The great heads of the media were anxious to be good and loyal citizens, and the working reporters themselves had almost without question accepted the word of the White House on foreign policy. The height of this credulousness had come during the Kennedy years. Kennedy had shrewdly made the most verbal and articulate members of his administration available to the press, their information made more pure and less political by the fact that many of them came from academe or seemed to come from academe. They were historians and economists, experts and not politicians. The result had been an amplification of the Kennedy myth. The press corps might be congenitally skeptical in assessing the intentions and ambitions of domestic politicians, but it brought no such toughness of mind to the politics of foreign policy. No one recognized the fact that for more than a decade American policy in Vietnam was, in the minds of its architects, directly related to American domestic politics, that a series of American Presidents tried to hold Saigon so that they would not lose Washington.

Washington was a presidential town and a journalists' town. Eager ambitious hostesses in the sixties much preferred a White House assistant to most senior senators, and most senior journalists to all but a few White House stars. The only real debate had been earlier in the decade over containment and that had been quickly taken care of; by the early sixties there had been no serious foreign-policy debate in fifteen years. The unspoken assumption was that debate would help the enemy. But by the time the Kennedy administration was inaugurated, it was no longer just a matter of stopping Soviet tanks from crossing into Western Europe, of Western Christian democratic societies that wanted an American umbrella. It was now more and more a question of threatening unrest in underdeveloped parts of the world, where the Western umbrella was also potentially a neocolonial one, where it was no longer just a question of Communism versus capitalism, but of colonialism versus neocolonialism. Beyond that, the Communist world was clearly no longer a monolith, the split between the Chinese and the Soviets was growing more serious every day. The world was changing, but in American foreign policy the issues were not changing.

Nevertheless, the cracks were beginning to appear in the concrete. In early 1961 Tad Szulc of *The New York Times,* who had very good Latin-American sources, picked up the story that the CIA was recruiting and training Cuban exiles at a camp in Guatemala. The training camp was something of an open secret. *The Nation* had written an editorial about it in 1960, but there had been an almost deliberate attempt by the rest of the American press not to know too much about it. The Gentlemen's Agreement still held. When word leaked out in Washington that the *Times* planned to run the Szulc story, President Kennedy called Scotty Reston, the *Times*'s Washington bureau chief, and tried to get him to kill it. Kennedy argued strongly and passionately about what the Szulc story would do to his policy and he spoke darkly of what the *Times*'s responsibilities should be. Reston, somewhat shaken, called Orvil Dryfoos, the publisher, and passed on Kennedy's arguments. They were quite chilling—the blood of dead men in the expeditionary force might be on the hands of the *Times*'s editors. Indeed, the *Times* might be responsible for canceling the entire plan. Reston suggested toning down the story and removing the references to the forthcoming invasion. Dryfoos agreed and ordered the story sanitized. It was a rare instance of a *Times* publisher interfering with the paper's reporting. Some editors in New York were absolutely enraged, and they demanded that Dryfoos meet with them. It was a very heated meeting. Dryfoos was clearly surprised by the degree of anger among his own people. Theodore Bernstein, one of the assistant managing editors, argued that there was a difference between national security and the national interest and it was not the job of *The New York Times* to aid the national interest as defined in secret by John Kennedy. But he lost the argument. A much sanitized Szulc story appeared under a much smaller headline. Secrecy was a curious point. If Tad Szulc knew, then it was not a very great secret, certainly not in the leaky world of Cuban exiles and counterexiles. Certainly Fidel Castro knew as well. The only ones who did not know were the Americans. Well, they would learn soon enough. That era was beginning to end: the President of the United States had, with one phone call, made the publisher of *The New York Times* a partner to a clandestine operation. He had asked for the secrecy of wartime in a time of peace and he had shifted the burden of illegality to a publisher and a bureau chief. It was a decision that was to be very troubling to a generation of senior journalists in the years to come, no matter how much they loved their country.

The Bay of Pigs was a fiasco; Kennedy later told Turner Catledge that he wished the *Times had* run the story, it might have saved him a disaster. But the old rules still held. A few days later Kennedy held a press conference. He was absolutely charming and magnanimous. He took full responsibility for the Bay of Pigs (he had no choice, there was, after all, no other President). When reporters asked questions about what had happened and why, he would not answer them on grounds of national security. The reporters let him do it. Kennedy remained angry about the Bay of Pigs; though they had not published much about it before the event, most editors seemed to enjoy criticizing him after it. In the weeks after the fiasco he talked more and more about the need for self-censorship. He suggested the creation of a committee of senior editors to work as a kind of unofficial board of censors in a case like this. It was an idea he never followed through on. But a few weeks later he addressed a meeting of American publishers in New York and gave a surprisingly hostile speech calling for increased self-censorship: "The newspapers which printed these stories [mild stories about the recruitment of Cuban exiles printed before the operation] were loyal, patriotic, responsible and well meaning. Had we been engaged in open warfare they undoubtedly would not have published such items. But in the absence of open warfare they recognized only the tests of journalism and not the test of national security. And my question tonight is whether additional tests should now be adopted. . . . Every newspaper now asks itself with respect to every story: 'Is it news?' All I suggest is that you add the question, 'Is it in the interest of national security?' . . ." Nothing came out of this speech, either, for the tide was beginning to go the other way. The next crisis would be Vietnam. There would never be any debate over the Kennedy decision to expand the minimal Eisenhower commitment there. It was a presidential time, it was the height of the Cold War, there were Communists out there, and so he just did it. What was to become a major foreign-policy struggle, over not just Vietnam but the limits of power, began as a press struggle, the White House version against the reporting of a small handful of newsmen.

On one hand there was the official version put out by the highest American officials in Washington and Saigon, all very carefully orchestrated, and apparently built upon the idea that if Americans said often enough that things were going well, things *would* go well. In the meantime, even if things did not go well in Saigon, if people in America believed they were going well, then the Kennedy administration had bought some time. Slowly, inevitably, the Administration put more and more pressure upon its people in Saigon to report optimistically. The top people in the embassy in Saigon did so, and so did some of the most ambitious officers in the field. But among lower- and middle-ranking American and Vietnamese officials, there was the working-level view. It was a view shared by the American reporters. They could see what was really going on, and they refused, in their reporting, to fake it. Once this battle was joined there was a massive effort, on the part of the White House and its ancillary agencies, first, to discredit the reporters professionally and personally, and second, to force officials of the U.S. government at the working level to echo the voice of Washington. The American government was fighting less a war than a public relations campaign.

It was billed in Washington and in New York and in publications sympathetic either to the White House or to the Pentagon as a press struggle, implying that it was a struggle of reporter against reporter. It was never that. Among the six or seven resident reporters in Saigon between 1961 and 1964, there was remarkably little disagreement over the essential direction and facts of the story, over how badly the war effort was going, how incompetent and hostile an instrument of American policy the Ngo family was. If there was any disagreement over the progress of the war, it was not among resident correspondents, it was on the part of *visiting* journalists like Joe Alsop and Marguerite Higgins, who were there not so much to report on the war as to strengthen policy. Alsop, the most imperial and imperious of American journalists, once lectured a group of resident reporters about the progress of the war. One of the Saigon reporters replied in some detail about how poorly things were going. Oh, that, Alsop said, who cares about that? That had nothing to do with it. You're naïve to report so pessimistically. It was unpatriotic on the part of the local men, and it would, of course, cost them their careers. "You'll be like those fools who lost their jobs in China. I tried to help them. I tried to warn them," he said, "but they never listened. But I testified for them at their hearings, and never fear, I shall testify for you as well." Generous as ever, he proceeded to write columns saying that their negative reporting was undermining the war effort.

The Kennedy White House, unused to reporters it could not con and who were outside its reach, began a publicity campaign to sell Saigon through Washington-based reporters to the American people. (Though Jack Kennedy, shrewd cool pol that he was, was not about to fall for his own propaganda. That might be the fate of Lyndon Johnson, but not Kennedy, who told his historian-aide Arthur Schlesinger on several occasions that he could find out more about Vietnam from the dispatches in the *Times* than he could from all his own cables.) Men like Pierre Salinger and Kenny O'Donnell, who were on very good terms with working White House reporters, referred regularly to the problem with the reporters in Saigon. They were too young. They did not know what war was about. They rarely went into battle. They sat around and drank and reinforced their own pessimism. Some White House and Pentagon spokesmen talked about dangerous political radicalism among the reporters. The Pentagon got rougher, it attacked not just the reporters' accuracy, but their manhood and their patriotism. A Pentagon briefer told reporters that a *Times* reporter had been shown a photo of Vietcong bodies and had burst into tears. The reporters in Vietnam were sissies. It was bad enough in the Kennedy years, when there were only 15,000 Americans there. But in the Johnson years, when there were 100,000 and then 200,000 Americans in Vietnam, the campaign stepped up. Whenever a Washington-based reporter headed for Saigon (the White House and Pentagon encouraged trips like that, visiting reporters had few sources of their own and thus were dependent upon the high-level briefing officers assigned to them), Johnson liked to see the reporters and do the briefing himself. "Don't be like those boys Halberstam and Sheehan," he would warn. "They're traitors to their country." It was rough stuff.

The struggle was basically over information. How well was the war going? How large a war was it? Gradually, the White House was committing not just men and resources to Vietnam, but its credibility as well. It was putting its word against that of a handful of reporters in Saigon. In the beginning it looked like an absurd mismatch. For more than twenty years before, the Americans had trusted the word of their President. *The President knew, he had all the information.* Day after day the White House could win in this kind of confrontation, it had all the great names on its side, it could put on any member of that dazzling administration at prime time to explain how well the war was going. His spokesmen were famous, and they were experts and they were men of good will. It was a bit like Watergate: in the beginning everyone believed the President. The polls reflected that. There were Rusk and McNamara and Bundy on television explaining how well the war was going. Who could make the case against them? The reporters were young and unheard of. Their sources worked deep in the bowels of the American operation in Vietnam and gave information, usually very good information, only in exchange for anonymity.

They could not go on television and they could not be quoted by name. In Vietnam, there was a rule of thumb among working reporters: the better the information, the more anonymous the source. In Saigon, the officers who were willing to be quoted by name were always optimistic. Ambitious colonels who wanted to become generals were quite willing to be quoted by name. They either knew nothing of what was going on in the field or cared nothing. By contrast, the resident reporters found that a great deal of time and effort went into protecting sources. There were periodic Army and CIA investigations of reporters' sources. Not of whether the stories were accurate, but of who the sources were. From time to time resident correspondents received plaintive cables from their desks in New York asking why their colonels would not let their names be used. "If my colonel uses his name in dispatches," one reporter cabled back, "he no longer colonel."

Yet the Saigon reporters themselves were remarkably free of peer pressure. Washington hierarchies meant nothing there. Nor did acceptance by the top level of the American Embassy mean anything. It might have been different in other capitals where ambassadors and generals still had a certain cachet, but in Saigon the journalists very quickly came to the conclusion that the top people in the embassy were either fools or liars or both. To the degree that the reporters responded to any social pressure and wanted any acceptance, it was from the American officers who were actually involved in the fighting. That was the only group whose respect they coveted. Lieutenant Colonel John Vann distinguished himself not just in combat but also in the eyes of newsmen for his willingness to report honestly, despite the pressures from his superiors. When he left in mid-1963, a group of reporters went to the Tan Son Nhut airport to see him off. They gave him a small engraved ashtray signed with their names which simply said: "John Vann, Good Soldier, Good Friend."

The reporters *were* young. Their training was not in war reporting but in political reporting, which was an advantage. They were not connected to the military from other, happier wars, and they were too young to have seen friends' careers crushed by the McCarthy era. In that sense they came to the story remarkably clean, carrying no excess psychological or political baggage. What obsessed them was *the story*. They had no other motivation, no other distraction. Almost all of them were single. They worked seven days a week and eighteen hours a day and they knew above all else that they were riding a great story. They also very quickly after arrival amassed a network of sources in Saigon. Given a government of monumental incompetence and an American mission that dutifully parroted every mindless statement of the government, many of the military's best-informed people, the most passionate and most knowledgeable, turned to the reporters as outlets. These were officers, both American and Vietnamese, who were immensely frustrated by the deafness of their superiors. They talked to reporters reluctantly, often near the end of their tours. The reporters' only problem was separating professional gripers and whiners from informed tough-minded critics of the war. Though most of the reporters had been trained in political rather than military reporting, it was an irony of Vietnam that their military reporting was generally a good deal better than their political reporting. They had the best possible military sources in the country, but their political reporting was limited by the absence of serious skilled Asia experts in the American Embassy. The McCarthy era had taken care of that. Thus the historical perspective was often lacking, as well as an understanding of how deeply rooted the political sickness was. Reporters are rarely very much better than their sources and their political sources in Saigon were regrettably limited in their larger vision.

For a time the White House attempted a number of gimmicks in dealing with the press problem. A better public information officer. Better briefings from higher-level officers. Perhaps if people in the embassy were nicer to the reporters things might work out better. None of these, for extremely basic reasons, worked at all. Frustrated, the White House tried a new tack. VIP's would be flown over periodically. The VIP would be interviewed as he arrived in Saigon and he would proclaim light at the end of the tunnel and inevitable victory. These predictions of imminent victory would go out over the wire services from Saigon. The dateline seemed to validate the statements. Then the VIP would fly back to Washington, where he would hold another press conference, claiming that after an extended look at the battle region he was more confident than ever that victory was at hand. Then there would be a second set of stories.

But that was just the beginning. Soon there was even better proof that if the Administration couldn't deal with the Vietnamese Communists, it was learning how to handle the American press corps. By 1965 the embassy was offering a briefing every afternoon at 5 P.M. It became known as the Five O'Clock Follies. An American military spokesman, usually a major, put forth what were said to be the day's military developments. The briefing officer had never been to these battles, he could not vouch for the information he was giving out, he had no sense of what really happened, but he gave it out anyway. Most of the information was based on what American officers said had happened and what South Vietnamese officers said had happened. It was a known fact of Saigon life that as the information went up from company to battalion to division and to Saigon the statistics changed, Vietcong casualties tended to rise dramatically. All of these battles were victories. At the daily briefing the American Army won the war a thousand times against the Vietcong and North Vietnamese. The air war was a favorite, since it was so much harder for a reporter to check the facts about an American bombing raid. The briefing officer told how many planes had winged over North Vietnam that day, how much tonnage they had dropped, how many factories, bridges, bicycles, and kilos of rice were destroyed. As the officer spoke, reporters scribbled notes. All of this could be printed and credited to an American military spokesman. Thus it was news.

It was a cynical performance. That none of it could be vouched for bothered few of the spokesmen. They were simply doing their jobs. The better reporters, those who were more experienced and had sources in the field, soon stopped going to the briefings. The briefings were far from the horror of Vietnam, the ambushes, the minefields that blew off the legs of young kids. Yet the best reporters of the war thus had their stories neutralized by the wire services, whose dispatches, based on the briefings, were printed with surprising regularity on the front pages of the nation's great newspapers. Some reporters complained bitterly to their editors, telling them to bury the briefing story inside. To little avail. In terms of news management, it was a great success. In terms of dealing with the Vietnamese Communists, it had no effect at all.

Otto Fuerbringer. Otto to everyone. He was the most controversial man within *Time* magazine, immensely influential, perhaps the most influential conservative of his generation in journalism, but outside the magazine almost no one knew his name. He was the symbol of both Luce's and the magazine's division —divisions between ideology and journalism, and between editor in New York and reporter in the field. Though some of the most bitter struggles of which he was a part took place in the sixties, these conflicts and divisions went back to the late forties. For *Time* had been a house badly divided for that long. It had started over China in the forties, reflecting Luce's intense personal anguish over the Nationalists' defeat, and it had extended into the fifties, a decade of intense partisanship at the magazine, in part because of the loss of China. The earlier favorites of Luce—men like Tom Matthews, Charley Wertenbaker, the chief of correspondents, and John Hersey—all generally considered liberal, had seen it coming with the arrival of men like Roy Alexander and his protégé Fuerbringer in the late forties. "The hard-eyed boys," Hersey and the others called them, meaning that they took a harder line politically. Soon Hersey, who told Luce that *Pravda* contained roughly the same amount of truth as *Time,* and Wert and Matthews would be gone. The new men, Hersey thought, reflected not just Luce's own ideological hardening, but his determination to make sure that the all-important editorial control of the magazine rested in safe hands, hands that were if anything a little more conservative than his own.

Alexander was the first of these men to arrive and eventually to come to power. A hearty, extroverted man, he was immensely popular with the staff. He was a former assistant city editor of the St. Louis *Post-Dispatch,* and—more important—he was an admirer and friend of the American military. He had joined *Time* as a writer in 1939, and had written much of the magazine's military coverage during the war, and afterward had retained extensive friendships with America's top military officers. Alexander was a conservative man, deeply anti-Communist, a devout Catholic who went to Mass every day before work. Yet he was also considered by those who worked for him to be fair. He was a man, thought his subordinates, whom you could talk to on a story, and even those who disagreed with him were personally fond of him. In the world of Time Inc., corporate as it was, great value was placed upon being what was known as a Good Soldier—knowing the exact limits of individualism the company tolerated and when to sacrifice yourself for the good of the institution. Within Time Inc., Alex was known as one of the best soldiers of them all, a man who knew by instinct exactly how hard to press and not to press on each story. He was a good man to go drinking with after work, and it was later said of Roy Alexander that he was not a hard man nor did he need to be a hard man, for he had Otto Fuerbringer with him to play the heavy.

Fuerbringer too had come from the *Post-Dispatch,* joining *Time* in 1942 as a national affairs writer and becoming an assistant managing editor in 1951, very much Alexander's right-hand man. Fuerbringer was a formidable and often disturbing figure to many of the top people at *Time.* No one doubted his professionalism, which was of the highest order. His technical skills were legendary. Yet many of the top people at *Time,* who were charmed by Luce's openness, his zest for life, his abiding restlessness and curiosity, and were bothered by the magazine's lack of the very same qualities, its arrogance and coldness, increasingly saw Fuerbringer as their villain. That Fuerbringer was in fact Luce, or the vital part of Luce, was not something they wanted to accept. It made it seem that there was just a little more chance to win an argument if only Harry could be reached! For Fuerbringer was a striking figure, a man of presence, and he held power decisively and did not encourage dissent. He seemed to have learned less from Luce about curiosity and more about the Mission. He seemed to lack doubt, and his own certitude was reflected in the magazine's certitude. He believed in a strong America. He *knew* which voices were committed to making this country strong and powerful, and he could guess which ones were aimed at weakening the national purpose. Fuerbringer, unlike most of his colleagues, did not really fit in with other journalists, and his mind did not seem like that of a journalist; he was a man, said one colleague, "who arrived too early at a place where you could not argue any more." It was Fuerbringer who had written the famous cover story on Adlai Stevenson that had helped trigger the departure of T. S. Matthews. Matthews had later described the piece as "a clumsy but malign and murderously meant attack." Fuerbringer himself had been angered by Matthews's refusal to discuss the piece with him. It had been a bitter moment in *Time*'s history and the scars had not easily healed.

In the late fifties, as Alexander's term neared its end, the decision of who would replace him became a central one within *Time* magazine. The managing editor was an enormously powerful figure: he defined the coverage and the tone and the line and he dominated the senior editors, who dominated the writers, who dominated the reporters. Fuerbringer clearly was the odds-on favorite; he was viewed as probably being Luce's choice, and certainly being Alexander's. Yet many of the most talented senior people were alarmed at the prospect of Fuerbringer taking over the magazine, and for them Tom Griffith was the consensus choice. But Griffith, who was long on journalistic skills, was nonetheless short on Truth or what passed for it at the corporate level, and it was never really in the cards for him to get the job. Luce was not close socially to Fuerbringer, as he was with some of his top people, theirs was an almost purely professional relationship; and the editor-in-chief was also very much aware that a great many of his best people had serious reservations about Fuerbringer. In a way, that touched on the very ambivalence within Luce, and the resistance both bothered him and impressed him.

In the year before Fuerbringer's ascension, Luce had a series of dinner conversations with one of his favorite writers, Emmet John Hughes (who also was a close friend of Phil Graham). Hughes was the prototype of a Luce favorite, a deeply intelligent Catholic intellectual, a man who, like Luce, shared an almost theological sense of the future of Western civilization, though he was considerably more liberal than Luce. Hughes was handsome and cultivated and considered by many to be Time-Life's best writer, and Luce enjoyed his company. They could talk at many levels—theology or politics, this world or the next one. They shared many interests, and Luce, so graceless himself, admired Hughes's social skills. He had lent Hughes to Eisenhower in 1952, as a speech writer, and it was Emmet Hughes who had written the most important sentence for Dwight Eisenhower that year: "I shall go to Korea." Though later Luce became embittered by a book Hughes wrote that was highly critical of the Eisenhower administration, in 1958 and 1959 no one was closer to Luce than Hughes, and Luce often told others that he wished Emmet had a little more career drive. Hughes might discuss Calvinism ably, but he did not live it, he was—by *Time* corporate standards—just a little lazy.

For a variety of reasons Hughes had almost total contempt for Fuerbringer. Much of it was ideological: Hughes was connected to the liberal-center of the party with the Rockefellers, Fuerbringer was to the right of its center. Much of it was personal: Hughes was acutely conscious of his own social connection with Luce and he was almost haughty in his treatment of Fuerbringer. In the prolonged series of dinners he and Luce had in the late fifties, the main subject was Fuerbringer's ascension to the throne. Later Hughes decided that they should be called the Why Otto Should Not Be Managing Editor Dinners. At these dinners Luce was in effect questioning his closest personal friend on the magazine about his forthcoming choice. Back and forth it went. Luce would begin by listing all the reasons why Otto should be an editor—he was a superb technician, a very complicated railroad ran on time, Fuerbringer ran pictures well, he had a brilliant sense of when to run a cover and when not to. Then Luce would add: "I don't know anyone at *Time* who knows more about more different things than Otto, isn't that true?" To which Hughes would always reply, no, it was not true. "But Otto knows opera and art and music," Luce would insist. Hughes, who looked down on Fuerbringer and considered him something of a trivia expert on these subjects, not a real expert, would answer, "I don't know anything about opera or art, but I do know politics and politics is essential to your magazine, and I know Otto doesn't know a goddamn thing about the world of politics." On and on these dinners went. It was as if Luce were testing not Hughes but himself, forcing Hughes to come up with the full litany of anti-Fuerbringer judgments. All of

Luce's own doubts came out. Why, he asked, does everyone tell me Otto shouldn't be managing editor? Why is everyone so suspicious of him? Again and again Hughes ran through it, the feeling that Fuerbringer on many crucial subjects had a closed mind, that he simply wasn't sufficiently open-minded intellectually. He warned Luce, above all else, that if Otto was chosen as managing editor, he would get *Time* into a lot of trouble, and that his mistakes would not be small, technical ones, missed deadlines, misspelled names, but the larger, more dangerous ones, the misshaping of truth. Hughes also had a sense that sometimes, as he argued, he was helping Fuerbringer's case. This was confirmed by a conversation he had with Allen Grover, who was a special assistant to Luce and his close personal friend, and who finally told Hughes, "Harry hears you about Otto. He may even suspect you're right, but he also wants a managing editor who's going to say yes." Finally, at the last of these dinners, Hughes told Luce, "I'll go through it one more time, Harry. I think you've made up your mind. In fact, I know you have. I'll withdraw all my objections to him if you'll tell me about one single incident in all the years you've known Otto when he took a position different from you on any significant issue." There was a very long silence and finally Luce began to laugh. No, he said, he couldn't think of any. Shortly after, in March 1960, he made Otto Fuerbringer the managing editor of *Time* magazine.

Otto was *Time* magazine sprung to life, a living extension of the very magazine he edited, which was not surprising, since he took most of his opinions from, of course, *Time* magazine. He was a strong man in a strong job. Even his nickname reflected it. The Iron Chancellor. Later, after he had retired, few *Time* people who believed that they had opposed him could remember very many arguments with Otto Fuerbringer. They were right; the truth was, there *were* very few arguments, the nature of the job and the structure of *Time* magazine did not leave much room for argument unless the managing editor liked argument, and Otto Fuerbringer did not like to argue. As he did not choose to argue, no one argued back; as no one argued back, he was convinced that no one disagreed with him. He ran the show. He had the key to the printing press and he had a strong hand and he was sure of his vision and that of Harry Luce and he was certain that these visions were one and the same. Mostly colleagues would recall that when they tried to dissuade Otto from something, there would be a cool almost quizzical smile on his face, that of a cat who has just eaten a very tasty bird. The smile was always there. Once a senior researcher from *Time* was crossing Madison Avenue when she saw a vaguely familiar face. For a long time she tried to place him. Finally she had it! Otto without his smile. It was, she thought, like seeing the neighborhood butcher dressed in suit and tie.

He was a man to dominate a system created to be dominated. When he first came to power there was a complicated system of conveyor belts that brought Roy Alexander the copy. Fuerbringer immediately changed the system and moved the desks. Someone asked him why. "I did not become managing editor of *Time* to sit in the hall in front of that trolley," he answered. Others noted that he installed a warning system that rang on senior editors' desks with a sound not unlike a London air-raid siren. There would be no doubt who was in command. He was a superb technician, decisive in his judgments, able to hold the many disparate parts of *Time* magazine together at all times, to know the stage and condition of each major story. He was, in that very complicated and difficult job, like a masterful air-traffic controller, he knew where the big stories were but he never lost sight of the minutiae; he plotted the course of thirty stories in his mind all at once and fitted them all together under terrible deadline pressures. He was probably the best single technician in *Time*'s history. And even his critics felt his sense of timing on cover stories was exquisite. Indeed, it was one of the ironies of his tour that though he was probably most remembered within the shop and within the profession for his dogmatic views on Vietnam, it was his idea to put the Beatles on the cover as 1965's Men of the Year. The idea was not received warmly. Luce did not seem to know who they were; Luce's heir apparent, Hedley Donovan, was dubious, Beatles did not lightly track on his most solemn curve; Henry Grunwald, whom Fuerbringer thought might have been an ally, seemed apathetic, perhaps the Beatles were too lowbrow for this son of Vienna; and Jim Keogh, Fuerbringer's very conservative deputy, was violently opposed. "Suppose," he argued, "there's a big battle in Vietnam that week with a lot of Americans killed and we come out with a cover on the Beatles?" So Fuerbringer went instead with General William C. Westmoreland, cast in bronze, a Man of Purpose, though by the time Westy was chosen and being cast, Luce had become excited by the Beatles and seemed disappointed that the choice was Westy. But it was like a symbol of his tour, Otto went with Westmoreland instead of the Beatles.

He was a conservative man, the son of a German Lutheran theologian, and his roots were in the conservative tradition of the Missouri synod of the Lutheran Church. He had gone to Harvard and been managing editor of *The Crimson* before going back to St. Louis to work for the *Post-Dispatch*. He joined *Time* during World War II. He was never really a man of New York and in fact was deeply suspicious of the New York intellectual and journalistic worlds that influenced his colleagues so strongly. In addition, he deeply distrusted *The New York Times*. He hated the fact that in so many circles the *Times* was considered good and *Time* was considered bad. He also believed, and this was a very important part of him, that journalists *did* by and large have a liberal bias, and that it usually stemmed from their backgrounds, and thus it was very much a part of his job to serve as a counterweight to their reporting.

Fuerbringer's formative professional experience had been writing military stories for *Time* during the war. Some of his friends thought that had been an important experience for him. Had he served with the military during the war, he might have been a little less susceptible to the patriotic call of the generals;

during those years, in another, far more legitimate war, he had come to believe what the highest military people said. He was old-fashioned in his patriotism, and suspicious of those who challenged it. (His suspicion was strong enough to extend beyond *Time;* in the mid-sixties he attended the Harvard *Crimson* annual dinner and listened to a speech by *Newsweek* national affairs editor Jay Iselin, another old *Crimson* man. The speech was mild enough but during the course of it Iselin opined that covering Lyndon Johnson was not especially easy because Johnson could not always be trusted to tell the truth, scarcely a radical statement. When Iselin was finished he was startled to see an enormous, imposing, and decidedly angry man descending on him. It was Otto Fuerbringer. "I have never heard such an unpatriotic speech in all my life," he declared. Fuerbringer's hands, Iselin noted, were now about to grip Iselin's lapels. "I am not prepared to stay in the same room with a man who makes a speech like that." He stomped out.)

Otto Fuerbringer was in sum a conservative man, and he was also classically a man of *Time* magazine. Yet there was always some question about Otto in the minds of some of his colleagues: Was he a conservative in the ideological sense or in the bureaucratic sense? Was he *Time*'s Bill Buckley or was he *Time*'s Bob Haldeman?

Nothing in the decade of the sixties was as divisive as Vietnam, and nothing cut to the heart of the divisions already existing both ideologically and structurally at *Time* like Vietnam. Vietnam came to dominate the decade that Otto Fuerbringer ran *Time* magazine. Like many others, he did not see the full threat at first. In fact, in 1960, shortly after he had taken over, he was talking with Stanley Karnow, the Hong Kong bureau chief, one of a series of Hong Kong bureau chiefs who were to cause him grief, and Karnow, already worried about developments in that area, mentioned Vietnam. Fuerbringer told him not to worry, there would not be a war. Why not? asked Karnow. "Because we've got the Seventh Fleet right offshore and if they try anything we'll blow the hell out of them." Karnow tried to explain the limitations of the Seventh Fleet in a guerrilla war, but it was, after all, a classical conventional American answer to that problem and a lot of American conventional wisdom was going to be shattered in the sixties.

But this came later. At first *Time* loved the war, was more eager for it than the Kennedy administration; if anything, the rigidity of the Luce magazine on the subject of China and Asia was an enormously restricting force upon Kennedy. He knew that if he changed his policy on China, or if he seemed soft on Vietnam, *Time,* as Harry Luce had pledged to Joe Kennedy, would tear him apart. *Time* was connected to the Pentagon as Kennedy was not. Mert Perry, a *Time* reporter in Saigon, amused by the vast number of *Time* dignitaries who came to Vietnam on VIP trips, called it "*Time* Magazine's Disneyland." Luce himself clearly realized Vietnam was in part his baby. In 1963, during the height of the Buddhist crisis in Vietnam, he ran into his former London bureau chief, Bob Manning. Manning was by then Assistant Secretary of State for Public Affairs. "I hear *we're* in trouble in Vietnam," said Luce.

. . .

In the spring of 1962, Charles Mohr, who was then a rising young star for *Time* magazine, had asked for assignment to Nairobi. *Time* at that moment did not have a Nairobi bureau, but because he was something of a favorite of Luce's, *Time* duly opened a bureau there for him. Mohr was a young man on the way up in the organization; he had come to *Time* from the United Press and joined its Washington bureau and had been an immediate success, moving quickly to the White House. He was an ideal reporter, energetic, irreverent, bright, loving his work, a wonderful mimic, able to ingratiate himself with a broad spectrum of people. He had covered part of the Eisenhower years for *Time* and had achieved a small footnote in history by asking Dwight Eisenhower the question that provoked one of his most famous answers, what Richard Nixon had specifically done as Vice-President. Answer: "Well, if you give me two weeks . . ." He had asked for assignment to India, a country that had always fascinated him, much to the dismay of Luce, who disliked India intensely, it being discordant, noisy, smelly, and filled with Indians. Luce liked having Mohr at the White House. "But who's going to carry my messages to Ike? You have all that access!" he had told Mohr. "Well, Harry, I'm just a messenger, I just give them to Jim Hagerty. The President really likes your notes, he *likes* to hear from you." "No, no, I get through because you're there. The President really likes *you*," Luce had answered.

The friendship between Luce and Mohr had been cemented during a meeting of the World Council of Churches in India in 1961, at which Luce was a special delegate. For two weeks in an alien country that Luce abhorred, they spent twenty-four hours a day together, often in brutal heat. Once in Madras there were ugly street urchins selling coconuts; Mohr, desperately thirsty, bought two. Luce refused to drink because the kids were so dirty. "But, Harry," Mohr argued, "you can't get sick from it; it's all in the shell." Mohr had smuggled in some whiskey and later offered some to Luce. Luce was upset by this, he hated the idea of breaking the law. "What's going to happen to us if we get caught?" he asked. "What's going to happen to us if we don't have the whiskey?" Mohr answered. So they solved the problem by letting Luce drink the whiskey, but acknowledging that he knew nothing at all about how Mohr had come to have it. That had brought them even closer together, and since Mohr was one of the most talented people on the staff of *Time,* in print as well as in person—the two are often different—Luce became uncommonly proud of him. While Mohr was preparing to go to Nairobi, Hong Kong suddenly needed a man. Stanley Karnow wanted to work on a book, and Mohr was asked if he would take Hong Kong for six months of temporary duty. Mohr said yes, and those being the days of super-affluence in the Luce empire, he and his wife and two children were flown to Hong Kong. Southeast Asia, given the expanding war in Vietnam, soon became a full-time assignment. Though he was later to be stationed in Nairobi, as he had always dreamed, it would not be for *Time* magazine.

Mohr, of course, knew that Asia was a problem spot on the *Time* globe, that the shadow of Communist China hung heavily over the entire area. Karnow confirmed this, he did not want to cover Asia any more, he thought events were going to get worse in Indochina. Karnow made it very clear to Mohr that the job was his permanently for the asking, that he, Karnow, did not intend to return. Almost as soon as Mohr arrived in Hong Kong in May 1962, he was ordered to Saigon for a crash cover on the American general Paul Harkins. Mohr flew in immediately and for the first time met his stringer Mert Perry, a very wise and able reporter who filled him in on the growing American commitment. With Mohr was a young man named Jerry Rose, who was trying out as a *Time* correspondent and who had been in Vietnam earlier (he was later killed there), and both he and Perry kept emphasizing to Mohr that the American euphoria was wrong, that this was a very hard struggle, that the American presence was potentially far more futile than anyone realized. Mohr himself argued back vociferously. Like most American newcomers to Vietnam, journalist or not, he believed in the raggedy-ass theory of the Vietcong, that a light touch of American power and determination would bring them to heel very quickly. Every time Mohr made a point based on what he had learned in his high-level Saigon briefings, the growing optimism over the statistics, Perry would simply say, well, yes, MACV said that and they were all generals and surely smarter than he was, but every time he, Perry, went out in the field it was very different and it didn't work. Mohr's own education began very quickly. He soon found that, in fact, Perry was right; that what was being said in the field was very different from what was being said in Saigon. In July, he got a very early lesson in the war, going out on a mission with a Vietnamese unit during which there was very little contact with the Vietcong. Some local villagers were finally rounded up and were tortured very brutally by the Vietnamese. An American adviser with the unit attempted to get the ARVN —Army of the Republic of Vietnam—soldiers to handle the prisoners better, trying to explain what he had done in Korea. Later, they were eating lunch in one of the village huts, with some women cowering in the background, and a Vietnamese officer brought over a testicle and asked if they wanted to eat it. The American adviser was furious. It was, Mohr later realized, a typical day in Vietnam, one in which nothing happened and yet everything happened. He filed the story and told Perry that night that he doubted that any of it would get into *Time* magazine. He was not disappointed.

What was interesting about Charley Mohr, in the light of the controversy that later arose over his reporting from Vietnam, was what a distinctly nonideological man he was. If anything, some of his friends suspected that he covered war so well, so bravely, and so intuitively, first in Vietnam and then —perhaps even more brilliantly—in the Middle East, that he might just like war a little too much. He was a very good combat correspondent and he had his sources, and they were all in the field, and they told him that no one in Saigon was listening to their reporting, that their own generals were either fools or liars. Starting in early 1963 he began to warn that this war was not even being fought, let alone being won, and he was also suggesting that the

Ngo family, rather than being a fine instrument of American anti-Communism, was a rotting, archaic, deeply self-destructive vehicle. This put him in almost immediate conflict with his editors, particularly Fuerbringer, who liked the war and took what was essentially a Pentagon position on it (a little more muscle and they'll all fold). It was clear to Mohr not only that his editors were more enthusiastic and confident about the war than he was, but that they were also closely wired in to the Pentagon and the more hawkish elements of the White House, and that almost everything he filed was being knocked down by some very high government official. Very early he realized there was a major split between himself and his editors, a split that went far beyond the normal foreign bureau–home office tension.

This sense of things was heightened in the fall when he went back for home leave and met with various senior editors. They were, he discovered, more sure of their knowledge than he was. They *knew.* He lunched with Fuerbringer and they talked at length about the war, and Mohr said that he thought the military statistics were all dangerously inflated, that things were much worse than anyone thought, and that the real danger was the Ngo family. The family was, he said, a terrible instrument, a bad ally, deeply anti-American in its heart. It was not just anti-Communist, it was anti its own people. What surprised him most was Fuerbringer's contempt for what he was saying. Fuerbringer answered that Mohr was naïve; we didn't want these people to like us, he said, we were going to use them. Mohr answered back that this was not the point; the government was incompetent. It was a discussion that went nowhere, though Mohr felt that Fuerbringer was willing to forgive him for being so naïve because they had been friends in the past.


So Mohr returned to Hong Kong knowing that he was probably on some sort of collision course with his editors. They were euphoric in their optimism, it was an extension of the mindless optimism of the American Embassy in Saigon, and yet every time he came back to Saigon the war seemed more hopeless, the government less flexible, the power and thrust of the Vietcong more formidable. Little of this was reflected in what was printed. *Time* was very upbeat about the war, though there were little tidbits of Mohr's files occasionally getting in, just enough to keep him marginally satisfied. But the tensions were growing at both ends. Anyone with a sense of Asian history could see in the collapse of the feudal Ngo regime an exact replay of the collapse of the Chiang regime; anyone familiar with *Time* magazine might see in the frustrations of Charley Mohr an exact replay of the frustrations of Teddy White. In the summer of 1963, with the Buddhist crisis in Saigon, this all came to a head; all the weaknesses in the Diem government that he had warned his magazine about became increasingly visible to the naked eye. There were days during the Buddhist crisis when Mohr could slip a couple of good paragraphs in, and then there were weeks when the hand in New York seemed to be made of iron.

In August he was asked to prepare a file on Madame Ngo Dinh Nhu, an assignment he jumped at, since she was the real symbol of the family, the true voice of its arrogance and isolation. Mohr took on the assignment with full energy, sending in a file of a hundred pages that not only characterized her and the rest of the family, but tied their weaknesses to the shortcomings of the government in Saigon and in the field. It was Mohr at his best, it amounted almost to a small publishable book, and when it came in the response in New York was wildly enthusiastic. Everyone in New York seemed to be sending Mohr cables telling him that this was the greatest file ever, that he was unique among *Time* reporters in the field. He was very flattered. But what the file said was devastating. It left an impression of almost total futility about the venture in Vietnam. And that posed a considerable problem: Luce's vision of mission and truth called for one kind of story, the file from Mohr called for another. So John Gregory Dunne, the writer in New York, tried to thread the needle, attempting to get in as much about the arrogance and insensitivity of the family as possible while, of course, not entirely surrendering Fort Saigon. Dunne was pleased with what he did and he was sure that Mohr would be pleased as well. But Mohr was hard to reach, he was off in the Philippines on a long-overdue vacation, and when he finally saw the story he was furious; he felt they had contradicted all his reporting in the last three paragraphs. The end of the piece said that Diem was the best we could get, that things were not so bad.

For Mohr, it was the final straw in what had been a year of cumulative frustration. He wrote his superiors a violent letter. (Fuerbringer later claimed that Mohr had at first praised the story and had only turned on it when he returned to Saigon and found that his colleagues did not like it, but Mohr denied this.) The letter denounced the Ngo family and said that *Time* was making a dreadful mistake in tying itself and American policy to Diem. Mohr closed his letter by seeming to taunt Fuerbringer: Why, he asked, do the pro-Diem editors of *Time* keep referring to the Saigon press corps as anti-Diem? His letter created a storm in New York. Here was the lowly reporter challenging the almighty, all-powerful managing editor. It was no longer just a journalistic ideological trespass; now, far more serious, it was a hierarchical one. If Fuerbringer could have fired Mohr at that moment, he surely would have done so, but Mohr, like Hugh Sidey in Washington, was the property of chief of correspondents Dick Clurman. Fuerbringer told Clurman that he did not trust himself to answer Mohr's letter because it was so insulting, so Clurman answered it, telling Mohr that he could not write a letter like that to the managing editor, he could not challenge his motivation and his honesty, he was way out of line. Clurman wrote that Mohr reflected a "peculiar embattled myopia. . . . You work in a small, crucial corner of the world. You are relatively isolated from other world news, and for reasons that I don't quite understand, you develop something near to paranoia about the respect accorded your work. Most pointedly, you develop considerably less respect for the seriousness and integrity of your New York colleagues than they do for you. . . ." To which Mohr wrote back to Clurman, with a copy for Fuerbringer, that he did not take back his letter and was not sorry for it. He reiterated the urgency of what he had said about the future of Vietnam, but he was willing to let the matter drop. Charley Mohr did not know it, but as far as Otto Fuerbringer was concerned—that is, as far as getting anything into the magazine—he was dead.

Fuerbringer was angry. The incident only strengthened his conviction that the root of the problem in Saigon was the American press. He was hearing this from many of his sources, some of whom were high in the Pentagon. The war was going well, these sources said, but the problem was a young, immature American press corps. So Fuerbringer ordered up a press story. Those who worked for other outlets in Saigon later believed the *Time* press piece was aimed at them; those who worked for *Time* magazine in New York and who knew Otto Fuerbringer thought the piece was aimed at Charley Mohr. Fuerbringer had tried this before, but Mohr's files on the Saigon press corps had been, not surprisingly, too sympathetic to the reporters for Fuerbringer's taste. This time he ordered the story without cabling Saigon. Later, some people thought that part of the ensuing damage might not have occurred if Henry Grunwald had been at *Time* that week. Grunwald was the foreign editor, and in the past, bloodshed over Vietnam had been avoided largely through Grunwald's skills. He was not only one of *Time*'s most skilled writers and editors but one of its more subtle politicians as well, and there was no one better at working his way through the minefield of Vietnam than Grunwald, keeping everyone just a little unhappy, keeping Fuerbringer unhappy and Mohr unhappy, though of course keeping Fuerbringer less unhappy than Mohr. But Grunwald was on vacation, and a writer named Ed Hughes, who was considered more of Otto's man, was sitting in.

In the World section, Greg Dunne was asked to write the week's Vietnam story. He was also aware that a press piece was being readied and that people in the Press section were running for cover. All week, colleagues kept coming by to laugh and congratulate Dunne on his good fortune in getting the Vietnam assignment. He was very nervous about it, even more so on Friday, when a strong file came in from Mohr that began: "Vietnam is a graveyard of lost hopes." Dunne admired Mohr greatly, but he also wondered if there wasn't some more subtle way of telling the story. It was a passionate, emotional time in Saigon, and Mohr had filed a fierce, relentless, powerful piece. Dunne agonized over it, went out for a drink with his fiancée, a young lady named Joan Didion, and proceeded to get very drunk. He decided he would not return to the office but would call in sick. Miss Didion stiffened his spine; if he were a man he would go back and write the truth, which he finally did, half drunk, staying up most of the night, turning out the worst piece of writing he had ever done for the magazine but keeping it faithful to Mohr's file. Under the *Time* system, Hughes, the senior editor, was then to edit and rewrite it. Dunne did not see Ed Hughes's rewrite until six the next night, and the story was of course completely turned around. At the bottom of the story, where the managing editor traditionally placed his initials, Fuerbringer had written: "Nice." Dunne thereupon asked to be relieved of Vietnam assignments and was given in the next few months only the most insignificant foreign stories. A promised raise did not materialize. He decided to leave the magazine and a few weeks later wrote Otto Fuerbringer a pleasant note that said that although they had had their disagreements, he regarded his years at *Time* as well spent. Fuerbringer wrote back a warm note, asking, "What disagreements?"

That struggle was secondary to the one taking place in the Press section. Luce had always understood that information was power and, unlike other publishers, was not bashful about savaging other publications and journalists. The magazine strengthened its own vision by denouncing other visions. Not by chance had its Press section battered Walter Lippmann in the past. Throughout the Vietnam War, *Time* did much of its heavy-duty advocacy through the Press section, attacking anyone critical of the war, praising anyone who liked it. It was a powerful weapon, and it was frequently and often brutally employed. In this case, there was no doubt what Fuerbringer wanted, and the man who normally would have written the piece, Ron Kriss, came up with an airtight excuse not to write it. At which point Fuerbringer chose John Koffend. Koffend was a charming, handsome, somewhat cynical writer at *Time* who had in fact not wanted to be a writer there. He had been happy reporting science for the magazine from Los Angeles, when his talents caught someone's eye and he ended up writing *Time* copy in New York. That week, following orders, Koffend wrote a first version of the press piece. Fuerbringer demanded that he rewrite the story, which Koffend did. Again Fuerbringer demanded that it be rewritten. Finally, it was virtually dictated by Fuerbringer. It took the straight Pentagon line, with a touch of the White House, and was a violent, all-out attack upon the reporters in Vietnam: they knew nothing, they simply sat around and drank and reinforced their own cynicism.

The story was finished on a Friday, and on Saturday morning Dick Clurman went to Fuerbringer and told him two things: "First, you are entirely wrong about this story, and second, you're going to lose Charley Mohr." Fuerbringer insisted that the story was just fine, and Clurman argued that the consequences were far more serious than Fuerbringer realized and that they ought to take some more time to discuss it. They agreed to have lunch. The two men deeply disliked each other, which did not bother Luce a bit ("Come on, Otto," he once said about another collision of executives, "you know I like to pit people against each other").

Clurman came from an intellectual Jewish background; his uncle was the distinguished theater critic Harold Clurman. He was brisk and intrusive; he had gone to the University of Chicago and had worked for *Commentary*. If he was not exactly an intellectual himself, he was certainly an intellectual fellow traveler; if not a liberal by the standards of *The New Republic*, he was by the standards of *Time* magazine. ("Dick really is an intellectual, isn't he?" Jim Shepley, a *Time* colleague, said of him. "He's not only Jewish, he's got ulcers.") He had first headed *Time*'s domestic bureaus, and then, when editor Emmet Hughes left the magazine, he had taken over the foreign ones as well.

Luce had called him in and said grandly, "I'm giving you the world." Clurman knew exactly what that meant. He reported, as Harry Luce wanted it, not to Otto Fuerbringer but to Harry Luce. He had, however, no control over the magazine at all; Fuerbringer's control was total. Clurman's only weapon in the struggle for power was the quality of his people; the better they were and the better their files, the more difficult it was for writers and editors in New York to ignore them.

So that day they went to lunch, Fuerbringer and Clurman and Fuerbringer's deputy, Jim Keogh. Keogh took notes at the lunch, and at one point Clurman suggested that these might be the notes for his subsequent court-martial. Clurman, who had been in Vietnam and who had met, liked, and in fact tried to hire some of the reporters there, told Fuerbringer that he was entirely wrong, that the reporters *did* see a lot of battle and, as he had himself observed, were more realistic in their appraisals than the high military. The lunch was reasonably pleasant, there were no heated words, and Clurman felt that he was making an impression. At the end of lunch, Fuerbringer said he would take another look at the story. Luce himself was away at a football game in Atlanta.

About seven o'clock that evening, Clurman saw a new version of the piece in what at *Time* was called hard copy, which is the final version. Nothing had been changed. Clurman was furious, and he went to Fuerbringer and told him again that it was a terrible story, it was wrong, there was no supporting evidence for it, it was going to cause terrible problems. He also sent out an immediate cable to Mohr saying, "Forthcoming Press section of *Time* has story which I know you'll regard, and I regard, as most seriously compromising your position," and asking to meet Mohr in Paris immediately.

He took off that night for Paris, meeting Mohr there. Mohr had not yet seen the story, but when he did, he announced that he was going to quit. Clurman told him not to, that Luce was not yet involved and therefore they didn't know how it was going to come out. It was a curious scene. They were fond of each other and they were being torn apart by the issue, and rather than getting drunk, they rode aimlessly all night through the Paris streets in a hansom cab, both of them exhausted and bitter and frustrated. Mohr said that he would stay only if there was a retraction. Clurman said he would try, but that he didn't think he could get it. Luce would be loath to do it. A retraction would mean a repudiation of Fuerbringer, and a repudiation of the managing editor, given the *Time* system, was like a repudiation of the magazine. Clurman flew back to see Luce and to tell him that Mohr was going to quit. Luce said that he did not like the story either. He called Fuerbringer in and talked to him alone for a while. Then he talked to Clurman again. Finally he said that when Kennedy was confused about Vietnam, he had dispatched McNamara for an on-site visit, and he announced he was sending Clurman on a similar mission. Fuerbringer was very unhappy with the idea. "I don't think it'll do any good," he said. "I think it's very chic," Luce answered, which made Fuerbringer think Luce was being a little mischievous.

Clurman flew that afternoon to Saigon, where he had dinner with the resident correspondents, whom he found fatalistic about the story, feeling that the problem was *Time*'s not theirs, that in the long run it would just make *Time* look silly. He dined with Henry Cabot Lodge, the new ambassador, who told him Saigon had the best resident American press corps he had ever seen and that, regrettably, its reporting was better than that of his own embassy.

Back in New York, Clurman decided that the gap between what *Time* had said about the press and what it should have said was too great, that it could not be bridged, not in the magazine as it was then edited. He determined to write not a story but a memo that he would circulate within the company. But Luce insisted on a story, and when Clurman explained the problem, he said, "Okay, we'll do a story saying we were wrong." John Koffend was also there; he was to be the typist for the meeting. Koffend sat there while Luce, Fuerbringer, and Clurman worked it out; the new story was written five times by Koffend. It was as if Clurman were the correspondent and Luce the editor. The story contained a sentence that for *Time* was absolutely extraordinary: it said that *Time* had erred in its previous evaluation. At the end of the meeting, Luce said, "Well, it's a compromise, but at least the story says that *Time* was wrong." "Yes," Clurman answered, "we've never said that before." Luce said, "Yes, I think it's a first."

Luce then asked Clurman if he was satisfied; Clurman said yes, that's about as good as we can do and now maybe we can keep Charley Mohr. At that point, Luce initialed the story. Thus it was locked up, with the approval of the editor-in-chief. After everyone had gone, Fuerbringer, who hated the story, hated the idea of saying that *Time* was wrong, who saw the story—correctly—as a repudiation of himself, decided to change it. Despite Luce's initialing, he took out the crucial sentence, the sentence admitting error, and revised the story to make it in essence concur with the earlier one. That night, when Clurman came in to check page proofs, he was flabbergasted. Whatever else Fuerbringer had been in the past, he had always been Luce's vehicle, he had never gone against Luce's orders. This was the exception. Clurman had already sent a cable to Mohr saying that the story had been rectified, that *Time* had admitted to an error; and Mohr had cabled back, saying in that case he would stay. Now it was undone. (Fuerbringer later said he had no memory of changing the second press piece. He said that he would not have changed anything that Luce approved and that the entire Charley Mohr incident had been blown up too much and his own negative role exaggerated. He also said that *Time*'s subsequent coverage of Vietnam was much fairer than critics claimed, but that liberal critics wanted *Time* to be more partisan against the war.)

On Monday morning, Clurman went in to see Luce, who was smiling and feeling very good about it, and showed him the changed story. Luce was shocked, and he began to pound the desk, shouting, "How could he do it? How could he do it?" For a brief moment, the question of whether or not he would fire his managing editor hung in the air. He called Fuerbringer in, and the two had a furious meeting. But Fuerbringer knew Luce better than the others did. He knew that Luce would not fire a managing editor, not on a question about Communism and anti-Communism. He knew he was closer to Luce's real vision than anyone else, that he was doing what Luce really wanted, even though Luce did not at first realize it. So he challenged Luce and got away with it.

Clurman told Luce that Mohr would quit, that a man had to draw the line, that to Mohr, *Time* had reneged and humiliated him again in front of his colleagues. Mohr, with his colleague Mert Perry, who was in effect also a full-time correspondent, did quit. At that point, Clurman sent a cable to all *Time* correspondents throughout the world, announcing Mohr's resignation and adding that Mohr was correct in the struggle and that the journalistic side had fought and lost. We win some and we lose some, he said. It was an open message, sent to everybody, and it enraged Fuerbringer. He immediately complained to Luce that Clurman was doing everything he could to undermine him. "I thought we all worked for the same company," he said. Luce angrily asked Clurman why he had sent the cable, and Clurman answered that the press-story incident was already a worldwide issue among journalists and there was no way in the world to keep it secret. The best thing in a bad situation was to be as honest as possible, he said.

"It certainly caused trouble with Fuerbringer," said Luce.

"Well, look at the trouble he's causing me," Clurman answered.

Luce paused and then asked, "Why does everyone tell me Fuerbringer is such a bastard?"

"I don't tell you that, but he is, of course."

"Why don't you?"

"Because I assume you're getting what you want out of him."


In April 1964, Harry Luce, of his own volition, stepped aside as editor-in-chief of Time and was replaced by Hedley Donovan, his own choice. Why Luce, who had just turned sixty-six, decided to move aside was a matter of some conjecture. It was clearly his own decision. He owned the largest block of Time Inc. stock, some 16 percent. There was no rival faction set to challenge him, though some people in the company were a bit restless with Luce's Ma-and-Pa way of doing business, his failure to understand the modern game of corporate acquisitions. Harry Luce was stronger than any figure on the business side of the organization. There was no one to oppose him. He was Time Inc. Yet the question of succession was a teasing one. How do you change power in so autocratic a company? How did you replace Harry Luce, so strong and individualistic a man? Few who knew him could imagine Luce turning over power lightly. Time Inc. without him seemed almost a contradiction in terms.

He had suffered a serious heart attack in 1958, though the news had been suppressed for fear that it would harm the Time Inc. stock. In his later years he had taken to reading the Bible with great intensity. Clearly his thoughts were more and more with the future and his own mortality. He wanted to settle the question of succession while he still had control of his faculties and could exercise as much leverage as possible on the choice of his successor.

In 1959, a year after his heart attack, he had dined with Donovan and had first broached the idea that Donovan become his successor. He did this in his own special way. He told Donovan that he intended to accept a ninth term as editor-in-chief, but that he wanted Donovan to serve as editorial director of the various publications and in a few years succeed him. He did not name a date. Donovan, the most careful and judicious of men, answered in kind. He told Luce he was flattered, but had some reservations about the choice of himself for the job. Perhaps, he said, it was a mistake to freeze the decision so soon, perhaps things might change and in the next few years some other editor might catch Luce's fancy, and he might want to change. But Luce had made up his mind; the heart attack had affected him, he was under strict medical instructions to take it somewhat easier. Besides, Donovan had a sense that more than three decades of the job had taken their toll, that Luce was feeling a little battered. At the end of the evening Luce told Donovan, "Well, it is left then that you are complimented by my suggestion and will at least think about it, and I am complimented by your suggestion that the present editor-in-chief is good at his job." Shortly afterward Donovan became editorial director of Time Inc.

Luce's top people were often in some way surrogate sons, and they tended to be tall and handsome and impressive. Certainly Hedley Donovan was of that cut. He would have made some network a wonderful anchorman. He was tall and husky and his looks were rugged without being too rough and he had a deep and commanding voice. He projected weight and presence. In style and temperament he could not have been more different from Luce. He was a careful, controlled man. He was aware of everything he did, and more, he was aware of why he did it. Nothing was left to chance; there was a reason for every decision and every decision must wait its turn, it must not be rushed. One of his sons once told an interviewer that if he misbehaved, Donovan did not shout or become angry, he simply patiently explained why the son had been *foolish* in his actions. Phil Graham, who had known him first when they were both bright young men around Washington and had carefully watched his career, once said that Hedley Donovan had never made a professional mistake; Graham did not mean this as a compliment. Luce was the founder, rough-cut and original, a man who had taken his ideas and had made them come to life; Donovan was the new man of the new more corporate generation, no rough edges, careful, thoughtful, a man looking for the *sound* and *responsible* and *fair* thing to do. He was slow and careful and honorable in his opinions. One did not sense in him a passion to inform, but rather a passion to weigh and judge. He would, thought friends, have made as good or better a judge than a newspaperman. One could readily imagine Hedley Donovan rising to the top in a company presided over by Harry Luce; one could not so readily imagine Harry Luce rising to the top in a company presided over by Hedley Donovan.

He was managing editor of *Fortune* at the time of his selection. Certainly that was an important reason for choosing him: whoever took over the company would have to have served as managing editor of one of the magazines. But *Fortune*, steady, serious, respectable, was also a somewhat sheltered place to have worked; he was protected from the intrigue and factionalism that permeated *Time*. Of the upper echelon of Time Inc. people, Donovan, if not the most talented, was the least scarred; he was the most acceptable man to the largest number of people. He was not a wildly creative or innovative man, but if he failed to project a great sense of excitement, he projected something almost as important and perhaps, at that moment in Time Inc.'s history, something even more important—trustworthiness. He was fair, serious, on occasion very pedantic, and Luce thought his by far the safest hands in which to leave the company. He was *sound*. Besides, and this was central, Luce had become in the late fifties increasingly disturbed by the complaints about *Time*. He did not agree with the complaints about *Time*'s lack of fairness, he always defended the magazine, but he was bothered by the fact that there were so many complaints, and that they often came from people whose respect he would have preferred to have. He knew that a different era was approaching, which would demand a somewhat different magazine. When in 1959 he had first broached the idea of succession to Donovan, one of the doubts Donovan had put forth, with some slight hesitation, was his own misgivings about *Time*. He was bothered by *Time*'s overt partisanship, its willingness to depart from an acceptable norm of fairness. To Donovan's surprise, when he mentioned this, Luce, if not actually agreeing with him, at least appeared sympathetic to his reservations. Clearly Luce knew this had become a serious problem for the magazine.

When Luce turned the job over to Donovan, most of the senior people wondered whether and to what degree Harry would actually move aside, succession or no. It was, after all, a somewhat unnatural act. What surprised them was the degree to which he did in fact let go. On the occasions when he was in New York, perhaps six months of the year, Luce attended the managing editors' meetings, and while he was careful to defer to Donovan, the power of his personality was still magnetic, he was forceful and driving, involuntarily domineering. But it was also clear that Luce wanted Donovan to take hold and be more aggressive. He seemed, if anything, bothered by Donovan's grayness, his lack of panache. "Can't you," he once asked a subordinate, "try to get Hedley to use the company plane more often?" Once when Luce had finished one of his prolonged, erratic, and brilliant monologues, he had turned to Donovan and said, "Okay, Hedley, now analyze that out of existence."

So now in 1964 the magazine was his. He was a man of the center, much more so than Luce, a fairer man than Luce, and a far more orthodox man than Luce. The engrossing question to those inside the company was the degree to which he would change the company and particularly *Time*, and if so, how quickly he would do it. Asia, where *Time* had traditionally encountered serious problems, seemed a likely testing ground of the new regime. At the time of the succession China in particular was still *Time*'s albatross; Asia still imprisoned the magazine. Luce knew it. Just a few years earlier, T George Harris, one of Luce's best reporters, had brought Amaury De Riencourt, the French historian and social critic, to lunch, and De Riencourt had made a brilliant case for there being two Chinas. A magazine like *Time,* he said, had to come to terms with the mainland. After the lunch, Luce said something very revealing; he took Harris aside and praised De Riencourt's performance and then added, "George, I want you to understand that there are some things that are not open to discussion as long as Chiang is alive. My father's obligation was such that I cannot do anything about that." But when Luce told Donovan that the magazine was his, he also said that if Donovan felt it was time to change and modernize the magazine's China policy, he was free to go ahead. Donovan could recognize Communist China if he wanted to.

But Donovan was a cautious man. He had taken a trip around the rim of Asia in 1965, talking with various American officials and local Asian leaders at the time and he had been impressed by their negative view of China. China and the Soviet Union were clearly regarded as hostile aggressive nations, and the war in Vietnam was the most obvious manifestation of that. Everyone told him that China had to be contained, and Donovan saw no point in rushing to recognize a nation that he and the people he respected considered an aggressor. More, he found himself committed to an American combat presence. In some way he thought we were *already* committed there. It was as if a decision already existed; we were there, we could not do less, and therefore we had to do more. Donovan had spent some time with Lyndon Johnson, and he was moved by the fact that Johnson appeared to hate this decision to go to war. He thought that Johnson probably disliked the idea of war more than any other recent President. If Donovan himself had no great enthusiasm for the job in Vietnam, he nonetheless thought it should and could be done. He was favorably impressed by the quality of American officials in Vietnam, and he believed that the lessons of World War II, of stopping an aggressor at Munich, were applicable here. The idea of helping this country to help itself, using American combat troops in the process, seemed a reasonable one and he believed that it could be accomplished within a reasonable time frame. He did not want to normalize our relations with China because he saw it as an aggressor in Vietnam. It was an important moment, for there were those who believed that had we mended our relations with China much earlier, first, Vietnam would have seemed less threatening, and second, the war would have been viewed as a manifestation of nationalism, rather than of monolithic Communism.

So Donovan cast *Time*'s policy in support of the status quo in our relations with China, and approved of the American combat commitment to Vietnam. Though in the years to come many people saw *Time*'s often harsh, jingoistic support of the war as a reflection of Fuerbringer, Donovan himself believed that the great responsibility was his. He had set the course, he believed in the war. He and Fuerbringer were very different men and there was no closeness between them, and clearly at times Donovan was bothered by the harsh and abrasive tone of *Time* in writing about the war, but nonetheless the essential decision was his. And so the stage was set for another prolonged confrontation between *Time* in New York and *Time* in Asia. *Time* knew what it wanted in Saigon, it knew what should happen. If the war had been fought along the lines it wanted, if ARVN had only been as strong, and the other side as illegitimate, as *Time*'s New York editors wanted, then its reporting would have been very accurate. Unfortunately, what took place in the field and what New York *wanted* to take place were very different. Once it had been known in New York as the Hong Kong Syndrome. Now it was the Saigon Syndrome.

When Charley Mohr quit *Time* it had been extremely damaging to the magazine, if not with its readers, then at least with other journalists. It had reactivated all the old doubts about *Time* as a magazine that simply fixed facts to suit its own preconceptions. There was also the immediate problem of choosing Mohr's successor, for almost anyone who replaced Mohr would be suspect among his peers. Anyone, perhaps, but Frank McCulloch. Before leaving for the Los Angeles *Times,* McCulloch had been one of the most respected and senior reporters at *Time*—a correspondent in Los Angeles, a bureau chief in Dallas, and then bureau chief in Los Angeles. In the fall of 1963, Clurman, at Luce's request, made him an offer to return, typically Luceian and grandiose, not just the L.A. bureau, but the L.A. bureau and *everything west of the Mississippi.* A big territory for a big man. McCulloch said yes and began preparing to take over for *Time* where Lewis and Clark had left off. But this happened to be the moment when the beheading of Charley Mohr was taking place. Clurman called again. Could McCulloch please take Hong Kong–Saigon instead? They had a terrible situation there, and it was the most important story in the world. Would he go? Of course he would, one of the reasons he had come back to *Time* was the fear that he might never report again. Besides, he was an ex-Marine who had never seen combat and he badly wanted a shot at this war. McCulloch visited Luce, who told him how important the story was, how humiliating the Mohr incident had been, and that only he could restore *Time*'s reputation. Everyone at *Time* was delighted by the return of McCulloch, with one possible exception: Otto Fuerbringer. Hearing that McCulloch was coming back, he allegedly told one friend, "What do we need with another managing editor?"

Frank McCulloch was a legend in Vietnam. It is characteristic of the war there that he was one of its best reporters and that no one outside of his profession knew his name, partly because of the anonymity of *Time* and even more because of the unwillingness of his magazine to accept his reporting. He covered Vietnam with great energy and style and courage, and he left the country a deeply disillusioned and disappointed man, dissatisfied with his magazine, dissatisfied with himself. When he first arrived in 1964 he was very typical of his generation, he was very upbeat, the Marine drill instructor as journalist. He believed in the American fighting machine and what it could do. It could *all* be done. The first team was coming and he was part of it. To a generation of Americans, Vietnam ended one kind of consciousness—confident and exuberant—and brought on another, but for McCulloch the transition, the coming to terms with a new set of premises and images, was more difficult than for most. In general, it was easier for the younger reporters, those who were post–World War II, pre–Korean War, whose sense of war was not set in the past, and who had nothing to unlearn. McCulloch was much older, a man who believed deeply in order and authority, a man who had served in the Marines Stateside during two wars, who deeply respected the military and its system, and who was probably closer to and had more genuine affection and sympathy for the upper-level American military than any other major American reporter. He was, for example, fond of Westmoreland and close to him, and he often argued with his younger, more disaffected colleague, Jim Wilde, over this friendship. Wilde disliked Westy deeply. He had once asked the American commander whether he had read any of the books in French about the Indochina War. Westmoreland had answered that he had not. Why not? Wilde had asked. "Because they lost," Westy had said, and that had ended it as far as Jim Wilde was concerned; what more could you learn or expect from a man like that? But McCulloch saw Westy differently. Part of him was drawn to these men and their bravery and their mission, it was where he wanted to be, it was his first war and he wanted to do it well and be part of it.

But part of him was simply too smart and too honest. He came to see what the generals, whom he liked and with whom he shared so much, could not see —that it could not be done, that the price was too high, beyond that which a civilized society could pay. Gradually but inevitably his vision grew darker. It put him in ever greater conflict with his magazine. His ability to see what others of his generation did not, to reach beyond his own background and traditions, made him something of a heroic figure to the younger men in the bureau, who often felt that no one listened to them. Later, a new reporter assigned to the Saigon bureau from New York was warned by colleague Jerry Schechter, "The first thing you have to understand is that those people don't work for *Time,* they work for McCulloch."

There were, Frank McCulloch later decided, several stages that most of the better American reporters in Vietnam went through. The first stage: very upbeat, Americans can save these people and they really want to be saved and will be grateful for it. Second stage (usually about three months later): we can do it but it's harder than I thought and right now it's being screwed up. Third stage (perhaps six to nine months later): you Vietnamese (always the Vietnamese, never the Americans) are really screwing it up. Fourth stage (twelve to fifteen months later): we are losing and it's much worse than I thought. Fifth stage: it isn't working at all, we shouldn't be here and we're doing more harm than good. McCulloch made his own passage through these stages, not a single straightforward passage at all, finding himself after five or six months being very dubious and then going out with a good American unit and marveling at their firepower and their excellence and coming back and believing that *yes, it could be done.* But there was an inevitability about his drift toward a more and more pessimistic view of the war. What struck him then, and even more so after he had left Vietnam, was his difficulty in trying to transmit the reality of the world he found in Saigon to the understanding of Americans, his editors, his readers, his friends. Americans did not for a moment doubt that somehow they could manage it all. After all, they were Americans.

Thus as the months passed and he felt his frustration mount in trying to explain to New York what he was witnessing, General Westmoreland and Otto Fuerbringer often seemed very similar to him, good innocent men, sure of themselves and what they were doing, unable to understand a totally different set of perceptions. At times he became very angry with Fuerbringer, but he also realized that this was too easy, that Otto was the magazine, and the magazine was Luce, and all of this was an extension of more than simply Luce, it was a reflection of something deep in the American grain that not only had produced Luce but had allowed *Time* to flower. *Time,* he thought, printed a certain kind of story each week telling of events, but in a very different and equally important way, it told a great deal about its readers and about its country.

What he was watching, and what was happening to him, he realized much later on, was a central part not just of his own education or the education of his magazine, but of the education of his country. Later he was able to see some pattern to the events, and he realized that it had begun for him with a trip by Luce to Asia in 1964. For some five weeks—or, more precisely, thirty-five lunches and thirty-five dinners—McCulloch traveled with Luce. One particular night in Saigon, McCulloch gave a dinner for him and very deliberately brought together, not the might and majesty of the American government, since most high American officials specialized in giving silly predictions for the visiting Harry Luces of the world, but rather the cream of diplomats and intelligence agents from other ranking nations, knowing that they were much tougher-minded and more independent in their judgments. There was the French chargé, the Australian military mission chief, the British MI-5, the Australian ambassador; and at one point in the evening, McCulloch had gone around the room asking each man how long he thought it would take for the Americans to win in Vietnam. He had begun with the Australian military adviser, Colonel Francis Serong, who was an expert on this kind of warfare, and Colonel Serong, rather modestly, said he hoped the Americans would not enter unless they were thinking of coming and staying forty years. *Forty years.* McCulloch went on from there, going around the table, and the answers were incredible. Twenty-five years. Thirty years. Twenty years. Forty years. But none of this made any impression on Luce at all, he simply dismissed it, it was as if he had not heard a single word, and when they were finished he simply brushed them aside and said, "It's not very hard to solve all this. All we really need is an American proconsul, just get the right man in charge here and give these people the right orders and we can solve this. We can do all this. Isn't that right?" At that point he looked at Jim Wilde. He was a Canadian, not an American, and he had covered the French war in the fifties and those memories had never left him. When Luce posed his question Wilde was absolutely startled. He had an abiding fear of company brass and he was very drunk and his hair was spilling in all directions, and suddenly he was drawing himself up and saying, his voice at once shrill and loud and angry, "No, Mister Luce, that will have no consequence whatsoever. Your American proconsul will make not the slightest difference here. Mister Luce, let me tell you something and you better remember it. This war will change when there is a South Vietnamese battalion out there with fire in their guts. Do you know what that means, Mister Luce?" Luce, suddenly very nervous from this intense assault, said no, and Wilde kept repeating, "Do you know what that means?" It was an extraordinary moment, there was such tension and passion and truth in the air, such a sudden reversal of roles, that it ended the evening.

There was one other incident on the tour that in retrospect told McCulloch about the magazine and the problems he was going to have. He and Luce were in Thailand and he had managed to have them invited for lunch at the home of an elderly Thai princess named Princess Chumbwot. She was a very gracious and sophisticated lady and she lived in an authentic Thai house and McCulloch thought it a special privilege to be able to eat with her. He also felt that an afternoon with her was a vast improvement over the endless high Thai officials who were so brilliant at playing back to American visitors what the visitors wanted to hear. That day at lunch the conversation was very pleasant and casual, and at one point McCulloch, looking for a conversational link with the princess, suggested that perhaps a partial limit inherent in journalism was that most events were a product of cause and effect whereas journalists, because of the nature of the mechanics of their trade, far too often reported only the effect and not the cause. This, he said, created a kind of imbalance. The princess seemed about to agree when suddenly Luce, quite furious, interjected himself, all missionary systems go, Presbyterian sense not dimmed by a Thai world and a Thai lunch. Worse, instead of taking his fury out on McCulloch, the rightful recipient, he went after Princess Chumbwot with a very rigid theology: man was in control of his destiny, of course he could determine events, events need not be overwhelming. "If you don't understand this," he said, looking straight at her, "you are weak and unworthy." It was an astonishing performance, Luce at his absolute worst, rude, arrogant, and insensitive, and it was an arrogance that was not even personal, it was national. There was, McCulloch thought, a sense of cultures passing each other in the air. The princess very quickly dismissed both Americans, and McCulloch was struck, on the way back to the hotel, that Luce did not realize, first, that he had been extraordinarily rude to the princess, and second, that she had dismissed him. It was, thought McCulloch, going to be harder and harder to find worthy Asians who came up to the Luce standards and terms. Some of them still existed in Vietnam—smart, brave, tough, Calvinistic—but they were almost all on the other side.

. . .

Otto Fuerbringer liked Lyndon Johnson better than he had Jack Kennedy; he had always thought Johnson slightly tougher, with a slightly harder line, and Johnson, sensing this in him, played to it just a little. Lyndon was not above playing his Johnsonian games, even on Otto. When Johnson was still Senate Majority Leader, Fuerbringer had wanted to come down and talk with him and he had told Hugh Sidey there were no problems involved, he and Johnson were old friends. So Sidey put in the request and shortly afterward he got a call from Johnson, who loved to get people's names wrong, it was a favored form of putdown, and Johnson was saying, "Now, who is this old friend I'm supposed to see? Otto Foofinger? Otto Fingerbinger?" But Johnson was moving toward a harder line on Vietnam; in late 1964, before the elections, he may have been signaling to much of the country that he was likely to be dovish on Vietnam, but in personal conversations with Otto Fuerbringer he was signaling quite the opposite. Indeed, Fuerbringer was wondering, as 1965 began, what was taking him so long. He was ready for the war, ready for victory.

In 1965 Frank McCulloch was not a dove. The terms *hawk* and *dove* did not yet exist. Hedley Donovan, meeting with him in Saigon in 1965, thought McCulloch had very complicated views on a very complicated war, but in sum he felt McCulloch essentially supported the effort. But McCulloch was already becoming frustrated. Some of his most important stories were being shot down in New York. In early January, for instance, while Johnson was still claiming he would not send in American troops, McCulloch had met with an old Marine buddy who had told him that U.S. Marines were going to land at Da Nang shortly and would quickly slip into combat roles. McCulloch had filed this, slipping the story out by mail to Clurman because there were no such things as closed cables. But the story, which was terribly important, for it showed that the United States was in fact going to war despite protestations to the contrary from the President, did not reach print. McCulloch's letter had been turned over to the Washington bureau for checking and the story, of course, had been denied. The denial cables eventually found their way back to Saigon and what stunned McCulloch was the access. The denial had not come from any lowly government figure, no lowly White House or State Department spokesman. No, this was for big stakes and the denial came from the President of the United States himself. Or, in the words of *Time*'s cables, "highest source in land." A denial by Highest Source in Land was no small denial, and so the story died, and a few months later, just as McCulloch had forecast, the Marines landed at Da Nang.

Johnson had killed the story brilliantly—he had opened the entire top echelon of the government to *Time* to stop this one story. And McCulloch realized immediately that Lyndon Johnson, with his innate political skills, had learned how to neutralize *Time*. Clearly, thought McCulloch, Fuerbringer was a hawk, but he was not a totally closed man. But if what reporters in Saigon were reporting was countermanded by Washington, and if the Washington file was inside stuff, indeed highest-level inside stuff, irresistibly presented, and *Time* had access which no one else did, then this allowed Fuerbringer to hear what he wanted to hear and not hear what he did not want. If it was a choice between four-star generals and the President of the United States on the one hand and some correspondent in Saigon on the other, whom did you believe? Highest Source in Land, of course. All newspapers were vulnerable to this, and so the reporting on Vietnam was always schizoid, with Saigon bureaus often essentially pessimistic and Washington bureaus essentially accepting the word of the government. From then on, McCulloch noticed, the same procedure was followed again and again, always at crucial junctures—Johnson giving super-access to *Time* magazine in order to kill stories he did not want in *Time*. He was always trying to minimize the size of the war while maximizing the success of what he was doing, and field reporters with their eyewitness reporting were a threat, whereas Washington reporters—trained over several generations to accept the word of high American officials at face value, to prize above all else special access—were raw meat.

Any time McCulloch had a particularly big story that went against the official line, somehow the Administration shot it down through the Washington bureau. In the fall of 1965, a time when Johnson was still trying to minimize the size of the American commitment, McCulloch found out by chance that the number of U.S. troops in Vietnam was scheduled to go up sharply. At that point there were 200,000 Americans either in the country or on their way, and Johnson was still telling the nation it was a small war. McCulloch had the best sources in Saigon—Luce's correspondents, after all, were not just correspondents, they were ambassadors from *Time*'s empire as well. *Time*'s hawkishness was a considerable asset to him in terms of access; the American military mission saw *Time* as a friendly force, and McCulloch, whose reporting they did not read but whose sympathy they perceived, as a friend. Thus he had supreme access to the military, better than that of any other reporter in Saigon; he was a friendly face among an increasingly difficult and potentially hostile press. In the fall, with rumors of an American troop increase swirling through Saigon, McCulloch had dinner with Maxwell Taylor, the outgoing American ambassador, and he found Taylor curiously ambivalent about the entire undertaking. There was no way, Taylor was saying, that if the Americans added 100,000 more men, the North Vietnamese could not match it. McCulloch quickly sensed something important, a growing tension between Westmoreland and his long-time sponsor, Max Taylor, and he decided to go by MACV and see Westy himself.

He made the appointment and he expected considerable reluctance to deal with him, a wariness that he had encountered in the past when the subject of troop buildups had come up, but this time it was very different: Westy, McCulloch came to understand later, had just been promised his troops by McNamara and he was confident and he was also very anxious to sign Washington onto the buildup, to get the deal as far out in the open as possible. He was, after all, now pledged to fight a very big war, but his country had still only pledged to fight a very small one. Westy was friendly, very friendly. After talking with McCulloch for a few minutes, he called in his chief of staff, Bill Rossen, and told him, "Tell Frank here all our plans. All about the buildup." They really want me to have the full story, don't they? thought McCulloch, trying not to salivate. They are not doing this because I am good-looking or sweet-tempered, they really want this out. Rossen proceeded to give him the story. It was, of course, classified information, and it was by all standards of judgment a leak, and it was given out by precisely those people, the military, who are most critical of leaks to a free press. But the game is there and everyone plays it. The figure that Rossen quoted to McCulloch was *a minimum of 500,000 troops*. Minimum. The balloon—that was the word Rossen used, and McCulloch long remembered it—the balloon might go up as high as 635,000. McCulloch was staggered. It was the biggest story of the war; the war was going to be very, very big, it was no longer some small hidden war of limited units and limited resources. This was going to be an enormous test of will, something the American people were completely unaware of. McCulloch filed it immediately; even as he did, Johnson became the head of the Presidential News Service. Of all the stories he did not want printed—he was still keeping the scope of the war hidden from the Congress, the press, the budget directors—this was the one. It could stimulate domestic protest and it could kill the Great Society.

When the advisory cables from Washington reached Saigon, McCulloch was furious. The Washington bureau had shot him down again. *Time* again had its story, from Highest Source in Land. Again Johnson ridiculed the idea. "Sheer insanity," he said. No one was talking about a half million men. Under the wildest circumstances, Highest Source in Land said, it might go up to 200,000. Highest Source in Land—the cables were again perhaps mischievously made available to Saigon—says that bald-headed guy in Saigon has been out in sun too long without a hat. They loved that, of course, in New York —that Lyndon Johnson knew McCulloch was bald-headed was a plus—and that he was taking time to put down their man was a plus as well. For McCulloch, it was the *Time* system at work, giving New York exactly what it wanted. So far as he was concerned, his opposite number in Washington was John Steele, the bureau chief, and it seemed to him that whenever he had a particularly important story, Steele's files canceled it out. Steele, of course, was only doing his job and his job was access, and no one in Washington had better access to the top level of the Johnson government than Steele. He was the classic journalistic insider. Only during the Kennedy administration had he been on the outside, and that was because he had refused at one point to be bullied by Bobby Kennedy; it cost him dearly for a time. But Steele's ties with Johnson were unusually strong, extending far back into Johnson's congressional days. A close relationship indeed; when Johnson was Vice-President and the New York office replaced Steele as the Johnson specialist, assigning in his place a young reporter named Loye Miller, Johnson was deeply wounded. Only Steele suited his status. Steele liked to tell of the time he was checking

out a big story on Vietnam with CIA head Richard Helms, and got a call from
Johnson right there in Helms's office telling him not to waste time with Helms,
but to come see the President himself if he wanted to be briefed.

In 1965 John Steele was very hawkish himself, very much a reflection of
his magazine's attitudes. And hawkish he remained. In 1968, when most of
*Time*'s senior people were beginning to change, Steele remained resolute.
Clurman tried to ease him up slightly in that period by getting him to go to
Saigon, but he did not go. He was a man of Washington. There he knew
everyone, there he had access. He was a man of probity; he had given his trust
and it had been badly used. He was surprised later to find that McCulloch and
many in his bureau were angry over what had happened. He had no awareness
of what the Washington bureau had done to the Saigon bureau. They had both
simply done their jobs.

McCulloch was always trying to change things. In the latter part of 1965
Otto Fuerbringer made a trip to Vietnam, and McCulloch decided to break
up the normal tour that the Pentagon laid on, smart slick briefings, two- and
three-star generals clustered around as escort officers every day. The bureau
prepared for Fuerbringer's trip and McCulloch scheduled visits that would
show Otto the size of it all and, he hoped, the complications and difficulties.
It didn't work. McCulloch quickly saw that he was not penetrating, that Otto
had already made up his mind about everything, and that everything was
wonderful. Late in the week McCulloch took Fuerbringer to Cam Ranh Bay,
where the Americans were fashioning a massive new port, their final gift, it
would turn out, to the North Vietnamese regime. McCulloch wanted Fuerbringer to see Cam Ranh because he thought it symbolized the disproportionate quality of the war. Fuerbringer's eyes swept across the awesome scene and
he turned to McCulloch and said, "I know how to end the war tomorrow,
quickly." How? asked McCulloch. "Bring five Vietcong generals here to see
this and they'll surrender." The story became legend in the bureau. The trip,
McCulloch decided, was doing more harm than good. McCulloch seemed
almost desperate after the Fuerbringer trip.

Frank McCulloch became an almost tragic figure in Vietnam. He loved
what he was doing and he felt a terrible failure in doing it. He hated what
*Time* was doing to him, yet he loved the story too much to let it go. Once he
had come home from a day in battle with Peter Arnett of the Associated Press,
and they had spent the night drinking and bitching about their respective home
offices, and when Arnett had dropped McCulloch off at the Continental,
McCulloch had looked at him and said, "What do we do for an encore?"

At one point McCulloch went home to New York for a brief break and
sat in on a weekly story conference, but that only depressed him even more.
"They don't even read our fucking suggestions," he said angrily upon his
return. He had talked at length with Otto, and Otto had been uncommonly
gracious but he had not listened. It was not that Otto thought reporters were
fools, McCulloch decided, he just felt they were not important. By early 1966,
McCulloch was becoming more and more pessimistic and angry and there was

growing anger in the bureau and a feeling both in Saigon and in certain quarters in New York that the entire bureau might yet resign en masse. McCulloch had by then been covering Vietnam, the most dangerous of America's wars for journalists, for more than two years, with a fierce disregard for his personal safety. It was as if he was always testing himself, making sure that no young reporter would take more risk than he.

In early 1966, New York made an attempt to reassign him and Wilde, which he fiercely resisted. Wilde, deeply suspicious, immediately told McCulloch that this was New York's way of trying to break up what it considered the Saigon cabal. For a time McCulloch argued with Wilde, preferring to believe the official version and telling Wilde that he had become *too* paranoiac, even by Saigon standards. Later he decided Wilde *was* right, that New York's prime interest was to break up the secessionist bureau. Soon there were other suggestions of plush jobs. Perhaps he could return to New York in a high editorial capacity? Perhaps another bureau? Then one night the members of the bureau were all sitting in the Saigon office when a Telex began clicking. A message from Clurman to McCulloch. Personal and Confidential. "Do you want the London bureau?" London! It was the symbol not just of the British empire, but of the Luce empire. The London bureau chief had a Rolls-Royce and a beautiful house and perks galore. The London correspondent lived as Luce wanted him to, as a surrogate Ambassador to the Court of St. James's. "No," typed McCulloch without hesitation, while the other members, ready to try on their bowler hats, watched mute. "Do you understand what I'm offering you?" Clurman typed. "Yes," answered McCulloch, "I'm happy here." But finally they reassigned him, first to be Washington bureau chief of *Life*, then to be the New York bureau chief for *Time*.

He did not leave Saigon a very happy man, the sense of his own failure was immense, he felt he should have communicated more of the darkness. His last letters to his wife were filled with anger and depression, he told of waiting anxiously for his replacement. "I am sick of this country, sick of it all," he wrote her. "I cannot wait for my replacement to get here." He felt he had been part of something important and that it had not worked and he had failed. Finally in the late spring of 1966 came the day that Frank McCulloch was leaving and everyone lined up to say good-bye, the Vietnamese assistants, the reporters, the drivers, everybody, and McCulloch, emotional and desperate, not knowing what to say and how to express his feelings toward these people who had meant so much to him, not wanting to be maudlin, feeling a failure, looked at them awaiting his words, and then he spotted the football they kept in the office in those years, to toss around in moments of tension and boredom. He saw David Greenway, one of his younger reporters, catch his look and nod in approval, and McCulloch picked up the football and threw it as hard as he could through the window, so carefully taped to keep grenades from being thrown in. Glass shattered in all directions. Thus he bid farewell to Saigon.

.   .   .

Not surprisingly there was no rush for the Saigon job. A number of senior *Time* correspondents were approached and they very quickly turned it down. There were varied reasons—the dislocation involved for a man with growing children, the danger—but these were not insurmountable problems for a quality reporter being offered a great story. Rather, it was the knowledge that the stain was there, everyone in the company knew it was a no-win situation. So Clurman finally turned to Simmons Fentress, a low-key, quiet, and very able Southerner who had come to *Time* from the Raleigh, North Carolina, paper. Fentress, who was covering the Justice Department, was considered a very good reporter, serious, decent, not very dramatic. After the offer was made he agonized over it for three or four weeks—he knew he was putting himself in a terrible bind and Clurman had been very blunt about the problems that existed and the lack of control over copy. Clurman could offer the job, but he could not protect the reporter who took it. Still, knowing all that, he accepted. He accepted finally because he could not say no, and he could not say no because it was the biggest story in the world. In Saigon, of course, the bureau was appalled; that anyone could replace the beloved McCulloch was unthinkable, and here was someone coming from the most detested of cities, Washington, someone who probably lunched with high officials every day and took as gospel everything they said. Long before Fentress arrived in Saigon the bureau had a nickname for him. Simple Simon, they called him.

Fentress, of course, was very much aware of the divisions within the bureau and the company, and in particular the hothouse frenzied atmosphere in Saigon, and he vowed to himself that despite all the pressures on him he would make no judgmental decisions for three months. There was an inevitability to Fentress's own passage. He found himself, despite all the fine briefings in Washington and Saigon, despite his own instinct to support the effort, steadily and quickly disillusioned. About three months into his tour he went to dinner with the men in his bureau and looked at them and said: Well, you were right. I've kept my counsel and I've looked it all over and it's the way you said it was.

By mid-1967 Fuerbringer was still a major roadblock, but now for the first time there were senior editors who were telling the reporters both in personal meetings and in private letters to make their files stronger, always stronger. Double their facts. Anticipate Otto's objections. If you get a cable from one of us with too many checkpoints, don't blow your cool, Fentress was warned by an editor, that's just our way of trying to head off Otto. Still, secret allies were not very much help. Fuerbringer was still very much in charge, and Donovan was still in favor of the war.

.   .   .

Hedley Donovan had signed on to the war in 1965. He had visited Saigon then and there had been a considerable amount of tension between him and the bureau members. At the end of the visit McCulloch had said to Donovan: We've been very rough on you and told you what we thought of the magazine and the war. What do you think about us? Donovan had answered in his very measured way that on the whole he thought the bureau had done a good job, but that if he had any additional thoughts he would write McCulloch. McCulloch thereupon took him to the airport and put him on a Thai International plane, and sure enough a few days later he received a handwritten letter from Donovan on Thai International stationery which said, "You personally should try to be less abrasive." By 1967 things were different. Hedley Donovan was very much a man of the center, and slowly, very slowly, the American political center was moving against Vietnam, not for moral reasons but for pragmatic ones. The cost of the war was simply becoming too great and the promises of victory were becoming too frail and too distant. Men like Donovan were being changed and were changing others. It was a slow, difficult, painful process, they were responsible men and patriots, and they did not lightly back away from their own, let alone America's, commitments. They, as much as Lyndon Johnson, had encouraged this course, and they, as much as he, were stuck on this tar baby. Donovan did not like excessiveness, he had not liked McCulloch's excessive combativeness, and now he was slowly becoming bothered by Fuerbringer's excessiveness on the war, by the fact that his magazine sounded more strident than it should. He was by mid-1967 responding to the doubts of his friends, people, like himself, traditionalists, conservatives, internationalists, who did not doubt America's place in the world and who did not use the word *imperialism,* but who thought there was something wrong going on out in Saigon. It was costing too much, it was out of proportion to the nation's goals, and perhaps it was not even workable.

If much of McCulloch's and Fentress's reporting had failed to get into the magazine, nonetheless Hedley Donovan was reading all the raw files very carefully, and he was reading *The New York Times,* where the reporting being published was far more pessimistic. In April 1967 he took a second trip to Vietnam. There were 500,000 Americans there and he was hearing from very reputable people that even a half million might not be enough. This trip was sobering and a bench mark. It did not turn him around on the war, he did not go from hawk to dove yet, but it jarred his confidence, it made him far more receptive to doubt and it meant that from then on Lyndon Johnson was working on a far more limited timetable with what was perhaps his most formidable ally in all of American journalism. There were small signs of change. Donovan had gone to see General Westmoreland and in the past the Saigon bureau had despaired of those high-level meetings, they had always worked against the bureau's credibility—Westy's *son et lumière* show, Westy so impressive, so handsome, with so many medals, all the charts, the brisk quick sense of Westy's intimacy. He was four-star talking to *Time*'s two- and three- and even four-star officials. They were all big men and they all understood the big things in the world. This time it didn't work; it had been a long session and when Donovan came back he was not impressed. That night he went out to dinner with the bureau. "He's not really very bright, is he?" Donovan said. "All those words and charts and there's really not that much there. . . ."

McCulloch met Donovan in Hong Kong and immediately got a feeling that his editor was different now. Listening more. Perhaps he had not changed, but he was preparing to change. At a dinner with the bureau members he did not seem so peremptory. (Yet if he was ready to change, change was still far from easy; he and *Time* magazine were very far out on a limb. Upon his return to New York, he wrote an article for *Life* that was sent to the Saigon bureau for checking. Most of the members of the bureau were appalled by the optimism of its tone.) Returning home that spring, he became increasingly aware of the corrosive effect the war was having on American domestic life. He was a man caught between what he had once been and what was still to come. That spring he gave a commencement address at NYU which on the surface seemed more hawkish than not; there was a prediction that there were surprises ahead in Vietnam and that the graduating class would like them. The usual line, gleaned, his reporters in Saigon thought, from being around too many high officials who always had the inside word and knew secrets which they could not reveal to anyone else. But there was one statement in the speech that struck some people who were astute Donovan watchers, people like Henry Anatole Grunwald, as a sign that the editor-in-chief was indeed changing; that there might be more doubts than anyone realized. It was a seemingly mild sentence. "Vietnam," he said, "will continue to be a very divisive issue until the Johnson policy has unmistakably failed or succeeded." It was, Donovan would later admit, the first visible display of his doubt. Many more would come shortly. He was now changing very quickly, and as he talked to others on the magazine he became increasingly aware of *their* growing doubts. The war had turned out to be so much bigger, slower, and more costly than he had expected. The opposition within the country distressed him, but it was a factor. Could a democracy have conscription and fight a war when so large a part of the society did not accept the war or the cause? It was no longer, he thought, a question of whether the protesters were right or not, their very existence was reality.

So it was that in the late summer of 1967 Hedley Donovan did something that was very important and dramatic at *Time* magazine. He came downstairs and for three weeks of Otto Fuerbringer's vacation he personally edited the magazine. He had intended to do this anyway; he periodically edited the various magazines and he was long overdue to edit *Time*. But the timing was extraordinary, for it coincided exactly with his change of heart on Vietnam. To the upper echelon inside *Time* there was absolutely no doubt about what he was doing, he was deliberately trying to soften the belligerence of the Fuerbringer line, to open up and ventilate the magazine. He had only done this a few times before in his tour as editor-in-chief. He seemed, the men underneath him thought, almost to welcome Saigon's doubts now. In Saigon the word was passed very quickly to the bureau, and there was a cautious kind of rejoicing, it was like the breaking of an ice jam, and for the first time Fentress and his people felt they could get some of their material in. Suddenly Saigon was pushing very hard to get in all the qualifications and doubts which had been excised for so long. The magazine, caught now between hawk and dove, between wanting to win in Vietnam and accepting reporting that proved the impossibility of winning, never turned back to its harder line. A few weeks later *Time* ran a cover photograph of the Marines at Con Thien. It showed a Marine hunkering down almost in the fetal position, and the photograph itself seemed more dramatic than any words, the exposed vulnerability of the American position.

There were those around Otto Fuerbringer who did not think he was particularly happy with the change. Fuerbringer may have been entertaining his own doubts about Vietnam (they would increase considerably in a few months, after Tet), but *Time* was still *his* magazine. Nor did he have any particular affection for Donovan. Fuerbringer was a man of *Time* and *Time* was the heart of the Time Inc. operation and Donovan was a man of *Fortune,* which was to Fuerbringer relatively small potatoes. Thus he was the real editor within the shop, the real pro. He seemed almost to condescend to Donovan. When in 1967 Fuerbringer returned to work he told close friends—as a means of putting Donovan down—that Hedley did not even know his way around the office, that the first thing he, Fuerbringer, had found on his desk when he returned was a note in Donovan's handwriting saying: "The men's room is the first door on the left."

There was one person absolutely appalled by the change in Hedley Donovan, and that was Lyndon Johnson. All during the years of escalation he had seen Donovan regularly and kept in touch with him and let him know what a vital role, *Time* magazine played, particularly given the betrayal of those people at *The New York Times* and CBS. *Time* was good, *Time* was what the country needed. *Time* was worth two divisions to him. Now, Johnson sensed that *Time* was changing. Going soft on him. Johnson became very uneasy. There were now more and more omens. A summing-up piece by McCulloch for *Life* described the United States as standing in its Vietnam agony distraught before the world. Donovan approved the piece and approved the word. *Distraught.* Not, thought McCulloch, a word that would have entered *Time* or *Life* six months earlier. Donovan and the men around him had come to the conclusion that there had to be limits, that some way had to be found to extricate the United States as mercifully as possible from Vietnam. Anything that would break the impasse. Bombing halts. Anything to set limits and to start moving away.

In early 1968 *Time* and *Life* began to call for a change in U.S. policy, a softening of U.S. objectives. Johnson was immediately alert to it, he had become suspicious of *Time* in preceding weeks, and he called Donovan to tell him that *Time* was wrong about this, that it was not the time for a bombing halt or a time to make a sign of concession, that he had tried it before, but every time he did, Ho Chi Minh socked it to him. Perhaps, he said, the best idea would be to fly Dean Rusk up tomorrow to brief the entire Time Inc. board. But Donovan had anticipated the move, he knew that Johnson would offer Rusk—McNamara would have gotten the call six months earlier, but McNamara was going soft himself—and he had already decided that he and the others had passed that particular watershed. It would be futile, he thought; the decisions at *Time* had not been easily reached, as many as twenty senior executives had participated in them, and these decisions were unalterable. It would be terribly unfair to have Rusk come up, he thought; it would embarrass everyone in New York and it would waste Rusk's time. The offer was refused, and *Time* continued to slip gradually away from official U.S. policy.

Lyndon Johnson, who was becoming increasingly encircled by domestic critics, grew very bitter at the mention of Hedley Donovan's name. He made this very painfully and bitterly clear to Donovan himself and even more so to others, citing *Time* and Donovan's switch as the worst kind of serpent's bite. Why hell, he said, he had only been trying to do out there what *Time* had wanted in the first place. Later Johnson told people that, as far as he was concerned, the turning of Donovan ranked with the turning of Walter Cronkite in costing him his war. He could not prosecute the war if people like that were going to oppose him. If he lost *Time* he was losing that much more control over the center of the country, becoming that much weaker in his ties to the feared and dreaded Eastern Establishment. He was bitter about this. "Hedley Donovan betrayed me," he told mutual friends. It was all very painful, and a few months later Otto Fuerbringer was at the White House visiting the President, and on this occasion Johnson was as courteous as ever, sensing probably that it was Donovan he had lost more than Fuerbringer, but there was a touch of sadness to the visit. "I like to see you more than I like to read you," the President said.


There were still thousands of words to come in *Time* and *Life* on the war, but there was one issue of the Luce publications that probably had more impact on antiwar feeling than any other piece of print journalism. This was the June 27, 1969, issue of *Life* magazine, and almost nothing else printed during this long war, so well and completely covered by so many journalists, brought the pain home quite so fully. Ralph Graves had just taken over as editor of *Life* three weeks earlier, and one of his closest associates on the magazine, Loudon Wainwright, had come to him with an idea. Wainwright was, like many Americans, frustrated and numbed by the war, and more, as a journalist he was disturbed by the fact that this war seemed so distant and disconnected from the rest of American life. There was a body count every week, people were clearly dying there, but it was no real way for him and most of his friends to visualize it. Indeed, even the body count seemed to reflect the dehumanization of it all, a scorecard, like some baseball statistic. So he suggested something very simple, that they run the photos of all the young men killed in a given week, all the American war dead. Nothing more. No statement, no text. Just the faces. America, meet your sons. Graves had immediately liked the idea and had taken it to Hedley Donovan, who gave it quick approval. Perhaps two years earlier an idea like this might have died, but now it was the kind of idea that once born had an irresistible force of its own. The only questions centered on how to carry it out. There had, for example, been a fierce battle up-country that week at a place called Hamburger Hill, where stupid World War II–type strategy had seen young kids ground up by ceaseless North Vietnamese fire from heavily entrenched positions. Graves and his associates decided that this was *too* dramatic, that they should go for a flat week, nothing special, no great battle, to show that there were drama and pain and death and real faces with real names in every anonymous week of this anonymous war. In the end they decided to use nothing but photos. The photos would do the talking. Even for the cover, instead of doing something dramatic, they simply blew up a passport photo of a kid. Graves mobilized the full resources of Time-Life to come up with the pictures; of the 242 young Americans killed that anonymous week, only a tiny handful of parents refused permission; a few others simply could not be located.

The effect was devastating. There was more than a little touch of class distinction to death in Vietnam—this had been a truly unfair war in which the upper class went to college and received draft deferments, and the poor and the rural and the black and the blue-collar went to Vietnam. Yet the story was so plainly done, there was the air of a high school yearbook to it; one did not know these kids, but one did—they were the kids who went to high school and who, upon graduation, went to work rather than college. Nor were these photos by Karsh of Ottawa. Their very cheapness and primitive quality added to the effect, the pride and fear and innocence in the faces, many of them being photographed in uniform, half scared and half full of bravado. It was almost unbearable. It was an issue to make men and women cry. Graves thought that only *Life* could have done it. It was, he thought, beyond the resources of a daily newspaper; television had the resources, but he thought the networks would have been afraid of an idea like this. It was considered a high-water mark of *Life*'s journalism. Some three years later when *Life* folded, Graves was bothered that in his remaining tenure as editor he had never again run anything as important or powerful as this story.

# 18/CBS

The power balance in the United States had gradually but radically changed. The President dominated all. The ability of the Congress to balance him, particularly in the area of foreign policy, had been diminished by events and by new forces, and chief among the new forces was television. It was more often than not a weapon of the executive branch, making the President even more powerful, helping him to define events on his terms, particularly when an issue was still in flux, encouraging him to extend his reach; but it could from time to time work against him as the consensus seemed to change, and twice in our era, as the President seemed to be overreaching his powers, it became a crucial element of the anti-state, of the essential opposition. The first occasion was during the Fulbright hearings on the war in 1966, the second during the Ervin hearings on Watergate.

The President could set certain things in motion but he could not, despite the vast number of public relations men on the government payroll, control events. In the sixties events suddenly moved with their own energy, for with television an event was electric and explosive. Television could reach the nation (not just the elite, but the *nation*) so much more quickly than the normal political system that events could sweep past politicians, sweep past their calculations and scenarios. Nothing could control this, not the correspondents who were covering the events, not the top-floor network executives who wanted as little confrontation with the President as possible, not the great politicians who did not wish these events to occur. The politicians had learned to manipulate, and the radicals had learned to manipulate, but there were times when events simply outstripped everyone. So it was that Lyndon Johnson at the time of Tonkin could, both by himself and with the help of men like McNamara, manipulate the media and through the various levers of power dissuade CBS from covering the more dubious side of that venture. But he could not control the events he had set loose in Vietnam and he could not control Morley Safer. Fred Friendly, who was good with tag lines and who had come up with the phrase "the electronic presidency," had another good phrase. He called Vietnam "Morley Safer's war."

Morley Safer was a very good, very professional television correspondent, a Canadian by birth, who had worked for several years for the Canadian Broadcasting Company. He was thirty-five in the summer of 1965 and he was not, by journalistic standards—it is a young man's profession—a kid. Indeed, he had covered combat and guerrilla warfare for the better part of a decade, first in the Middle East, then in Cyprus, and then again for several prolonged tours in Algeria. He was in no way naïve about the harshness and cruelty of political warfare, knowing that it was infinitely more personal and bitter than great global warfare. He had joined the London bureau in the spring of 1964, expecting to cover England and the Continent. But then Vietnam began to blow up again and CBS asked him to go to Saigon for six months; he was, after all, experienced in covering warfare, he was new at CBS (and thus more expendable), and he was single (and thus even more expendable—editors do not like the idea of bereaved widows, it plays on their consciences). It was Safer's impression that he was chosen because no one really expected the war to last long, and thus the idea of sending a young single Canadian seemed rather attractive. And probably no one else in the office was interested.

When he first arrived in Saigon what struck him most about the American military mission was its innocence. The American public information officers were so helpful, so little aware of the new forces at work and the new complexity of press relations that the war would evoke. They were graduates of previous wars in previous eras, wars of survival to be sure, and they thought the rules were the same—our side, their side. There had been, of course, a few minor confrontations; Peter Arnett and Horst Faas of AP had done a story on poison gas in the spring of 1965, and there had been a flap, and the President himself had gone on television to deny that they were using tricky gases. That had been a little unsettling, the first inkling that a broader confrontation might be building in Vietnam.

There was at that time a skilled public relations officer at the embassy named Barry Zorthian, who was generally considered the ablest press officer in the State Department and who had been sent to Saigon for that precise reason. Zorthian was exceptionally deft at being avuncular, and at mock candor, trying to make reporters feel a little guilty about what they had done —not an all-out assault upon their patriotism but a gentle exhortation to be a little better the next time; if they had covered a bad battle, perhaps they had missed the *big picture;* one isolated little battle—well, yes, granted the Vietnamese cut and ran—did not a whole war tell. Veteran correspondents noted in late 1964 and early 1965 a new dimension of candor among certain military spokesmen about the behavior and quality of the South Vietnamese troops; in the past it had been the official American line that the Vietnamese always fought well. The American propaganda machine had worked exhaustively to sell the valor of the little tigers, as they were known. Now for the first time the spokesmen were admitting that Vietnamese had fled from battle and there was a very good reason: General William Westmoreland had come to believe that the Vietnamese couldn't cut it, that Americans were going to be needed. Now, every time there was a defeat in the highlands, the mission rushed the American adviser back to Saigon to meet with reporters and tell how badly the Vietnamese had fought. It was candor of a certain kind, and soon, in July

1965, the decision was made to send American troops in large numbers.

In August 1965, Safer went up to Da Nang, the Marine staging area. He had no exact idea why he had gone there, it was just that he had not covered the Marines lately. In the trade Safer was known as having exceptional combat luck. Two kinds of luck. The luck that wherever he went he found plenty of action. And the second kind of luck, the luck to live to narrate it. He was having coffee with some young Marine officers and trying to get a feel for the area and the kind of action that was going on, and one of the officers said he had an operation going the next day and would Safer like to go along? Safer would. So the next day they went on amphibious carriers to a place called Cam Ne, which was not so much a village as a complex of villages. On the way the young lieutenant was expansive and he confided to Safer that they were going to level it, really tear it up. Safer asked why, and the lieutenant said because they had been taking a lot of fire from the goddamn village and the province chief wanted it leveled. (Years later a reporter named Richard Critchfield of the Washington *Star,* who had done a book on villages in Vietnam, told Safer that the reason Cam Ne was leveled had nothing to do with the Vietcong, but simply the province chief. This potentate was furious with the locals, who had refused to pay their taxes, and he wanted their village punished. The Americans who were to do the punishing were not aware of these facts. Vietnam was like that.) The Americans got out along a small tributary and walked toward the village in single file, everyone firing, and one thing stuck in Safer's mind, that it was all friendly fire and though there were three Marines wounded, all three, as often happened in this war, were wounded in the back by their own men. But this only added to the American anger and when they finally took the village, without any return fire, the Marines simply tore the place apart. Safer was never worried about the impact of the story he had filed; to the degree that he was worried at a professional level, it was whether the story, explosive as it was, had been too soft, and whether he should have written a harsher story, for the reality itself was uglier than he had said: the Americans were throwing in grenades and using flame throwers in holes where civilians were cowering and where they would be either burned to death or asphyxiated. At one point, Ha Thuc Can, a Vietnamese cameraman who worked for CBS and who was fluent in both French and English, as well as Vietnamese, saw a group of Americans about to fire a flame thrower down a deep hole; the voices of women and children could clearly be heard, and Can, the only really heroic figure of the day, started arguing with the Marines, screaming at them not to do that, there are Vietnamese women and children in there. He argued with the Marines for several minutes, and since he was the only one present who spoke both Vietnamese and English (Safer asked the Marine officer why he had no one in his group who could speak Vietnamese and the lieutenant said he didn't need anyone), he began to talk the people out of the hole. It took some time and some risk on his part, but he finally did it, saving perhaps a dozen lives (for which heroism Arthur Sylvester, the public relations man for the Defense Department in Washington, tried to have him fired, complaining that one of the keys to this evil story was that CBS had used a *South Vietnamese* cameraman, a sure sign of alien influence).

Safer, who had covered a good deal of fighting in his career, watched all this in shock. He was not innocent, but nonetheless this was something new to him. Part of it was the fact that it was the *Americans* who were doing it. He had become accustomed to French cruelty in Algeria, but these were Americans and, like most people, including most Americans, he thought they were different. And part of it was the senselessness of it all, for even when the French had applied torture they had usually done it with a certain precision, they knew exactly what they were trying to find out. This seemed, in addition to everything else, so haphazard and sloppy and careless, not as deliberate as the French cruelty and perhaps thus even worse. He filed his story right on the spot, a decision he later regretted, thinking that if he had had more time he might have made it better and tougher.

At CBS in New York, when Safer's report came in, there was an immediate awareness of the force and power and danger of it. Fred Friendly was called and awakened at home. At this point all they had was Safer's *radio* broadcast, which they were about to use on the "Morning News Roundup." Friendly was groggy and not entirely enthusiastic about the prospect of the story, but he asked one question: Is Morley sure of his facts? The CBS deskman at the other end of the phone answered, "Not only is he sure of his facts but he's on the Q circuit [a kind of hold line] and they've just talked to him and not only does he have it right—but wait until you see the film!" With this, Friendly immediately felt nervous and frightened, he was going to have to decide whether or not to put this film on the air and he knew the implications, the potential explosion; CBS had not assigned the story, CBS, God knows, did not want American boys to burn down Vietnamese hutches, but if the hutches had to be burned down, CBS probably would have been just as pleased if Morley Safer had missed the helicopter that would have taken him there. Who wanted anything like this to happen and who wanted it on film? Friendly's nervousness showed. He immediately called Stanton to warn him about it and then called Arthur Sylvester in the Pentagon to tell him to listen to the CBS radio station in Washington, which Sylvester did; Sylvester later denied the story and called it inaccurate.

At this point the CBS news executives decided to buy a line to Los Angeles so they could look at the film, which had to be flown in from Asia and thus reached Los Angeles first. In those days a line cost three or four thousand dollars and so they were usually reluctant to hire one, but in this case the money looked very small. So Friendly and Ernie Leiser, the executive producer, and Cronkite, sat in a small room in New York City and watched on their screen film of American Marines setting fire to Vietnamese thatched huts, Americans leveling a village. It was awesome, the full force of television, the ability to dramatize, now fastening on one incident, one day in the war, that was going to be shattering to an entire generation of Americans, perhaps to an entire country. They knew they had to go with it. It was not so much that they wanted to as that *they simply could not fail to use it.* They looked and they were shocked. But once the film arrived they were the prisoners of it. The only talk was about whether Morley had gotten the context of the story right, and so they called Safer again to be sure that they had the full reason why something as terrible as this could happen. And then they went with it. It was an eerie evening for Friendly. He stayed at his desk that night to answer the phone calls. The evening news has a kind of ripple effect because it goes out at different times to different time zones, and so each hour on the hour or the half hour a new time zone's worth of good Americans called in to scream their anger at CBS for doing something like this, portraying our boys as killers, American boys didn't do things like that. Many of the calls were obscene.

Among the obscene phone calls was one received the next day by Frank Stanton, he of the President's Advisory Commission on the USIA, an organization dedicated to selling the United States to foreign countries and promoting a benign image of Americans, and it came from his great and good friend, the President of the United States. (Stanton, asked about the call years later, said he could not remember it, but it and the reaction to it remained vivid in the memory of other CBS officials.)

"Frank," said the early-morning wake-up call, "are you trying to fuck me?"

"Who is this?" said the still sleepy Stanton.

"Frank, this is your President, and yesterday your boys shat on the American flag," Lyndon Johnson said, and then administered a tongue lashing: how could CBS employ a Communist like Safer, how could they be so unpatriotic as to put on enemy film like this? Johnson was furious, he was sure that Safer was a Communist and he sent out a search party to check his past, and the Royal Canadian Mounted Police checked out everything about Safer, including his sister, finding that he was indeed totally above suspicion and law-abiding. (Johnson was not very happy about the result and went on insisting that Safer was a Communist, and when aides said no, he was simply a Canadian, the President said, "Well, I knew he wasn't an American.") He was also, and this was more serious because it suggested some of the paranoia that was to come, absolutely convinced that Safer had bought the Marine officer, that he had bribed him to do this. "They got to one of our boys," he told his staff. He immediately called through to the Joint Chiefs to launch an investigation of the officer in charge, to make sure that he had not been bribed by a Communist reporter, that he had not taken money, and even after a serious investigation brought back the report that there was no bribing, it was just one of those things, those tricky press people had fooled a green young officer, the President of the United States believed there had been a conspiracy.

It was a shattering thing; it marked the end of an era, the end of a kind of innocence. No wonder the Vietnam War cut more sharply to the inner soul of America, to questions of morality and of American culture, than anything else in this century, no wonder it spawned an entire generation of revisionist film making and historiography (in particular on the American West and the

Indian), raising not questions of who and what the Vietnamese were, but questions of who *we* were. Just twenty years earlier, editors at *Life* had been arguing whether or not they dared to print photos of the bodies of American Marines strewn on the beaches of Tarawa. And now this. Coming right into people's homes. Some print reporters might and did write about atrocities, and there would be a mild reaction from the elite, a senator or two offended, a brief flurry of headlines, but this, this was something different, this was like a live grenade going off in millions of people's homes. Watching American boys, young and clean, *our boys*, carrying on like the other side's soldiers always did, and doing it so casually. It was the end of the myth that we were different, that we were better. In the American myth, born of a thousand Westerns, it was the cowboys who saved women and children, it was the Indians who were savages and committed terrible indecencies on the helpless; and now here was just the opposite.

Safer's film not only helped legitimize pessimistic reporting by all other television correspondents (they all resolved that if they witnessed a comparable episode they would film it), it prepared the way for a different perception of the war among Americans at large. There was simply, from that moment on, a greater receptivity to darker news about Vietnam, to accepting the fact that despite all the fine words of all the expensive public relations men the Defense Department and the President employed, and all the fine postures of high administration officials on "Meet the Press," there was something terribly wrong going on out there. Overnight one correspondent with one cameraman could become as important as ten or fifteen or twenty senators.

CBS executives, talking to Stanton in the days following the incident, knew that Stanton had it in for Safer, that he would have dearly liked to dump him. For several days they thought you could actually hear Lyndon Johnson's voice in Stanton's mouth, and then it became more subtle, it was Johnson's doubts—what do we really know about Safer, how did he get with us, what's his real background? The questions were similar to those being asked by the Defense Department (whose effort to discredit Safer failed although Arthur Sylvester, who was working as McNamara's truth squad, continued a personal vendetta against him, claiming among other things that of course Safer was biased because he had a *Vietnamese* girl friend). And there was at CBS in the next couple of weeks a constant effort to get more positive things on the air to balance the Safer report. But the Safer story stood.

Which caused terrible problems for Frank Stanton. For as the decade of the sixties developed, the conflict between Stanton's two roles—enthusiast for the News Department and denizen of the Washington corridors of power— was more and more irreconcilable. It was no longer possible both to stand up for a good public service broadcasting network and to be the closest friend of the liberal and well-intentioned President of the United States, the contradictions in American life were too great, the raw edge of power was too harsh for all that. And so the bad part was that Frank Stanton never liked Morley Safer, that his face grew cold at the mention of Safer's name, that if there had been any way of undoing what Safer had done, an honorable way of making it not happen, he would have unmade it. The good part was that Safer himself never knew this. The other news executives of CBS protected him and he went on working in Vietnam, a legendary figure among correspondents, admired as much by print journalists as by those in television.

The Fulbright hearings were a constitutional confrontation of the first order, long, long overdue. They ended more than a generation of assumed executive branch omniscience in foreign policy, and congressional acquiescence to that omniscience. They came almost a year after the combat commitment to Vietnam had begun; up until then, the national media, in particular the television networks, had belonged exclusively to the executive branch. There had not been a declaration of war, there was not a national emergency, but there was presidential action, and with presidential action, governmental consensus, and that, for the networks and much of the print press, was good enough; they had accepted, with very little questioning and debate, the President's case for military intervention in Vietnam. They—particularly the networks—had moreover not only amplified the case of the government, but silenced its most serious critics and doubters as well.

It was at about this time that the relationship between Frank Stanton and William Paley was defined once and for all. They could not have been more different in style, taste, manner, and values—Paley so hedonistic, so sensual, Stanton so tight, so cold in his taste, even in art. They were like two people locked into a terrible marriage, two people who need each other, and dislike each other, and need to dislike each other. Divorce was unthinkable, there was too much in the relationship for each of them. The tensions had grown as the calendar moved toward 1966, the year that Paley was supposed to retire and let Stanton, seven years his junior, take control of CBS. As 1966 approached, Stanton cast a longer and longer shadow. They became more irritable with one another. At one point in the mid-sixties Paley grabbed a friend: "What the hell does Frank really want?" he asked. The friend answered that Stanton wanted to be the chief executive officer of CBS, as he had been promised. "Why does he want that?" Paley complained. "Why should he want that? Look at all I've done for him! I've made him a millionaire. I've made him a big man in broadcasting—the statesman of broadcasting. Why does he want to be head of the company?"

But he did, and it had been promised. By February 1966 all the arrangements for Stanton's succession had been made. But Paley could not go through with it. The company was his, it was his life. He could not give it all up and become an old man overnight. In retrospect it seems the most predictable of Bill Paley's decisions, but Stanton was surprised and broken. It was said that the CBS publicity department had even printed up releases announcing Stanton's take-over. Stanton told close friends that he learned of Paley's turnabout only five minutes before the promotion was to have become official. By chance the events coincided with the furor over the decision not to show the Senate Foreign Relations Committee hearings and to go with "I Love Lucy" reruns. Fred Friendly, enraged over what was happening to *him,* cornered Stanton later that day and started lecturing to him about the disgrace of the great CBS News tradition. Stanton to his surprise was barely paying attention. "This is the worst day of my life," he said. Why? Friendly asked. "Because the Chairman has a resolution that somebody else will offer, asking that his term be extended. I was promised that I would run the company and now it's all gone." Later another friend asked Stanton why, rather than be treated so poorly, he didn't just quit. "Because I just bought fifty acres on the Big Sur and I'm damned if I'm going to take my stock options to pay for it," he said.

So the future of William Paley and Frank Stanton was settled for seven more years. Paley would run the company as he always had, and Stanton would do everything he could to make the company look honorable and attractive as *he* always had.

The media had played an equally important though unconscious role in making the executive branch more confident of its course in Vietnam. They gave the impression that the government was not just unified but confident of its course. Any doubt about the course ahead was not to be found within the government. Quite the reverse was true. Over fifteen years of Cold War competition with the Soviets, the American government had begun to take on some of the coloration of its adversary; in particular its preoccupation with secrecy. The rationale was that if we debated our national security openly it could only aid our adversary. So gradually, with the acquiescence of both the Congress and the press, more and more of the American processes of government began to take place in secret. Functions that had once belonged to the State Department were moved over to the CIA; key congressmen like William Fulbright, rather than playing their true constitutional roles, were often handled as friends of the White House family, they consulted and agreed, usually after the decisions were in essence already made. The real decisions were made inside the White House itself, where secrecy was far easier to control and enforce, the role of the adviser to the President on national security (Bundy, Rostow, Kissinger) gradually becoming more and more important because he, unlike the Secretary of State, was *completely* the President's man and because he never had to testify before the Congress. The kind of serious public debate that the Founding Fathers had envisioned between the presidency and the Congress over transcending issues like Vietnam did not exist, the Congress was becoming a silent partner; the only real debate was inside the executive branch itself.

So on Vietnam the media portrayed a government that was decisive and optimistic, sure of itself and of its course. In fact, the government was badly divided; at the upper levels in crucial institutions, such as the CIA, the State Department, and the United States Army, the doubters and critics might have numbered two thirds or more of the most important officials. Even men like

Bundy and McNamara and Rusk and Johnson himself were filled with doubt, the consensus in the room was a very fragile one, and different men were signing on with very different policies and scenarios in mind. But the media and particularly the networks reflected very little of the indecision, the failure to clarify what the objective really was, and the size of the interior doubt. The image that the networks projected, privy as they were to the public confidence but not the private doubts, was of a very confident government, supported by all the information given to it by experts, moving steadily ahead, having truth on its side. At the same time, the television portrait of doubters was not of serious, anguished government officials who had been passed over, or not listened to, but mostly of long-haired, angry, alienated students in the streets. It was, consciously or unconsciously, or both, legitimizing the government's case.

Thus Bill Fulbright's challenge to the President, which came a year after the United States intervened in Vietnam, was a landmark event. It was the first time in almost fifteen years of national television that the new mass media had given a national platform to a major congressional figure to challenge the centrist foreign policy of the United States.

Bill Fulbright, who had once been Lyndon Johnson's private Secretary of State and closest adviser, watching how television handled the decision to go to war and how television reflected the government position in the first year of the war, was absolutely appalled by the degree to which it had become a presidential vehicle. It was a phenomenon he had not recognized before because, he decided, it was clearly a matter of whose ox was being gored. Now for the first time it was his ox. He had dissented in the past from some of Dulles's policies, but the centrist coalition had more or less held in the fifties, and besides, Dulles had never really been a major television figure. When the new more modern media people had come in with Kennedy, he had welcomed them; Kennedy's use of television had not disturbed him, Kennedy after all was from his own party, they were friends, and by and large he approved of Kennedy's policies. So it had not bothered Fulbright when the Kennedy people had dominated the airwaves, and he had taken some mild pleasure in watching the clumsy way the Republicans had tried to strike back with the Ev and Charlie Show. But now he was watching the nation embarked on a course that frightened him. He found, first, that the policy was being systematically sold on television and second, that he himself, despite his position as head of the Senate Foreign Relations Committee, was curiously powerless to do anything about it. The President could get on the air, the Secretary of State and the Secretary of Defense could get on the air, and, what was even more galling to Fulbright, White House aides, people like McGeorge Bundy who held no real constitutional position and thus did not have to appear before his committee, could get on the air more readily than the head of the committee himself. Oh, he could get on some of the evening news shows for a minute or two on occasion, but it was nothing of substance. If he had something to say, somehow the guts of it seemed always to lie on the cutting-room floor, not out of an attempt to censor him directly but because their air time was so valuable they dared not allot more than ninety seconds to him. Against that ninety seconds was an entire flow of television coverage going the other way. All of this emphasized his own sense of loneliness (and, thought some of Fulbright's aides, his least attractive quality, his instinct in certain situations to bask in self-pity); he knew it affected how many of his otherwise sympathetic colleagues felt on an issue this sensitive. It was difficult enough to dissent on an issue that had become an issue of flag; it was even harder if a senator dissented and had less access to air time in his own state than the President did.

But at first he did not feel the need to challenge the President, or to complain to the networks. That was not his nature. It was not that he was too self-effacing, for Bill Fulbright was not really a self-effacing man. But he was not a man who sought the public spotlight. In particular he did not like television and its machinery, which he considered uniquely intrusive. (In his last Senate campaign, in 1974, when he most desperately needed exposure against the more modern Dale Bumpers, a candidate who used media expertly, he was capable of turning in rage to a CBS cameraman as he started to film Fulbright lunching with some local Arkansas officials in a small town. "Get away, get away!" he shouted. "This is private, these are my friends!" Though, of course, it was a political function.)

There were, naturally, some senators who worked the corridors of the Senate, their eyes ever poised for the sight of a few cameramen setting up their stands and lights, and who were drawn to the lights like moths to flame; but to the degree that a senator played to the media and rushed to the cameras, to the same degree he was shunned by his colleagues. Fulbright was of the old order, the Senate was a club, and he epitomized the clubman. He did not particularly like the representatives of the media, excepting of course a few titans like Lippmann, he judged them not so much for what they might do for him and for his career, as most contemporary politicians did, but rather, in an old-fashioned way, for what they represented in themselves, how learned and erudite they were. As such he almost always found them lacking. They were not quite serious, they were interested in the wrong things, they were quite capable—even the ones who wanted to help him—of exaggeration and distortion. They brutalized and trivialized serious debate. They were intruders. All of this was an irony because in the mid-sixties Fulbright became a major media figure, a role he neither sought nor cherished. After his Foreign Relations Committee hearings on Vietnam were televised, Dean Rusk, who had been something of a victim of them, was particularly angry, and had complained bitterly to Fulbright's staff that the chairman had deliberately ambushed him in a rigged circus atmosphere, and that Fulbright had promised the networks hot exciting hearings if they would come and cover them. The truth was quite different. His staff, of course, had loved the entire business of getting the cameras in but he had hated it. He did not particularly want television disturbing his hearings—television was loud and noisy and distracting and above all he hated the lights. But his hearings had been open in the past, and open was open, it meant not just print, but anyone who wanted to come, though of course he doubted whether television really wanted to come and use so much of its valuable time.

He had not really sought the confrontation with the executive branch and he had not by any means sought to be so public a figure and so forceful a dissident. It just worked out that way. He was a curiously diffident man, part aristocrat, part snob, part intellectual, part dilettante; yet there was also a part of him that was pure steel, and once he was set on something he considered to be important, he would not be pushed aside. He had his own sense of right and wrong and, moved by it, was without fear.

Lyndon Johnson, who respected no one's motivation save his own, later said with no small bitterness that Bill Fulbright had dissented on the Dominican Republic and Vietnam mostly out of jealousy, that he had always wanted to be Secretary of State himself, and that envy of Dean Rusk was behind his break on foreign policy in those years. Rarely was Johnson further from the truth: J. William Fulbright was almost unique among first-rank United States senators in that he did not try to use the Senate as a steppingstone to the presidency. The hurly-burly of fierce political infighting that went with major positions of power he found distasteful; he wanted only to be what he was. Nor could he have been anything else. Indeed, in 1960 when Lyndon Johnson was pushing him hard to be Jack Kennedy's Secretary of State, Fulbright had shrunk from it. He had turned to his closest friend in the Senate, Dick Russell, and told him to have Lyndon *cease and desist,* and as an added incentive for Russell, a Georgian, Fulbright had said that his own candidate was Russell's fellow Georgian Dean Rusk. Fulbright wanted no part of State. He knew that Kennedy intended to be his own Secretary of State and Fulbright did not want to hold an office which was largely ceremonial. "All it will be is going out to the airport to meet all those people," he told friends, "and I hate that." Besides, he saw all the people he wanted, he was *Fulbright,* a man who was special to foreigners. They beat a path to his door, not the ceremonial titled ones, who often bored him, but the intellectuals and the ones in exile, who usually were more knowledgeable and more interesting to talk to. Above all, he really loved the Senate, it was the perfect place for him. He liked to do things at his own speed in his own way and the Senate afforded him that special pleasure; it was a rare place in the modern world where a politician could, if he chose, hide and think, retreat when he wished and come forward when he wished, which was precisely what Fulbright liked to do. The gentleman as public figure. He still liked to come into his office late in the morning, meet with the minimal number of constituents, spend too much time at crucial hours working out in the Senate gym, and eventually, as his attention turned to Asia in the midsixties, spend long hours in his office reading every single book available on China and Vietnam.

For twenty years, the increasing acquiescence of the Congress to the President had been based on a number of things: the fear of a democracy's vulnerability to a totalitarian aggressor, a belief that the speed of war had outstripped a democracy's capacity to debate it, an abiding guilt about what the Senate in a previous era had done to the League of Nations, a fear of taking on the President and looking soft on Communism, and a belief that the President had genuine experts in foreign policy, that he had *all* the information. That, and a trust of the President as an extension of the nation. Above all, trust, Fulbright liked to say, the key to the relationship between the Congress and the executive branch was trust, a belief in the President's word, as indeed, in the clubbiness of the Senate, the belief in a fellow senator's word was a final act. Now he was about to challenge the word of the President, challenge the trust, and to open a major schism between the presidency and the Congress, and indeed to do it with a President of the United States who had been extremely close to him, who had in fact been his sponsor. Fulbright had come to believe that Lyndon Johnson could no longer be trusted, that by the nature of his own ferocious drive for power and the nature of the present institutional imbalance, he had exceeded the restraints and balances that were necessary in a democracy. In the beginning Fulbright's challenge was a lonely and ineffectual one; in the end it was enormously influential, he brought to it such intelligence, such reason, that he had gained the most extraordinary of powers, the power to convert. He was just a senator and he lacked the control of and access to information that the President had; similarly he lacked the President's access to the media. But he was no ordinary senator, he was the chairman of the Foreign Relations Committee, which expanded his platform considerably, and besides, he was *Fulbright,* he was special, he had the respect if not the love of colleagues in the Senate and of the Washington press corps, he was a man to be taken seriously as few senators were. He was a friend and confidant of Lippmann, which by itself was special—like the Pope, Lippmann mounted invisible battalions.

If the rising power of communications had loaded the institutional balance vastly toward the executive branch, making it far too powerful on the landscape, there were still times when circumstances could help right the balance. A good example of this was the Fulbright dissent on Vietnam; it saw the press feeding a key senator who used his position to amplify and legitimize the information and then feed it back to the press, slowly and inevitably making a case rival to that of the executive branch. But in mounting his challenge, Fulbright was opposing not just all the powerful machinery of the presidency, but all the assumptions of the last twenty years of the Cold War, which had made the President the curator of an American national interest. Much of the nation, and particularly people in the intellectual and journalistic worlds, had been to some degree touched and affected by the New Deal, and they reflected the New Deal legacy of the presidency as a center of enlightened action, and the Congress as a center of potential reaction. The Kennedy years had, if anything, heightened this, they had focused attention not just on the Kennedy family but on the presidency, they had brought style and gloss and glamour to the office, it was to be the center of the action. Talented, highly visible academics, who might never have worked for a congressman—except one with presidential ambitions—came down to work for the Kennedy White House. It helped give that office even more of an aura of intellectual and historical legitimacy and of being above politics; a generation of Washington reporters found their old professors working at the White House, dazzling them, manipulating them, and, on some occasions, lying to them.

Thus, in taking on the executive branch, Fulbright was taking on the prejudices of almost two generations of opinion makers, intellectuals who looked down on the Congress, the elite of a national press corps which preferred the excitement and action and movement of the White House, action which always translated into front-page stories or film clips which made the evening news shows, and finally newspaper editors who were also almost unconsciously contemptuous of the Congress and who were more at ease with the simplicity of presidential news. Presidential news, after all, was so much more straightforward, the Congress so much more complicated. That it was Fulbright taking on Johnson was irony enough and it made the confrontation special, for it meant that it was steeped in blood. They had been close friends, even closer allies, and each was convinced that the other had betrayed him. Johnson believed that he had made Fulbright, had given him his beloved chairmanship; Fulbright in turn believed that he had played a crucial role in the rise of Lyndon as a truly national figure, that he had been Lyndon's closest foreign-policy adviser until he had dared dissent. Both of them were right.

There was a rich contrast between the two men and the two families, the aristocratic diffidence of Fulbright, the relentless driving animal energy and sheer roughness of Johnson. But there was also a strong sense of mutual admiration. Each saw in the other the qualities that he most lacked. Fulbright cerebral, respected if not liked by his peers, the resident don of the Senate, was totally incapable of twisting an arm and pressuring a colleague to vote his way. He believed you voted as you thought. Johnson, by contrast, had none of the conceptual ability of Fulbright, he felt himself weak in foreign policy, but he could get things done, twist the arms, pressure and lean on colleagues. Fulbright's doubts about the course of American policy had been growing even before the Kennedy administration had taken office. He had been bothered by the Dulles years, by the righteous tone of the American rhetoric, the sense that we could impose our values everywhere. Perhaps, thought one of his aides, it was his southern background, the fact that he came from a defeated nation, that gave him a sense of what the rich and the powerful looked like to the less powerful.

His hopes that the Kennedy administration might be different were dampened by the Bay of Pigs. In early 1961 he had heard rumors of the impending clandestine operation, and with Pat Holt, one of his top staff people and his Latin-American expert, he had written a prophetic and forceful memo to the President arguing against it, using, among other arguments unique for that era, moral arguments, saying that the abstention from this kind of operation—a policy of force is right and that powerful and big are, of themselves, good—

is what differentiated us from the Communists. Kennedy had considered the memo carefully, and indeed Fulbright thought for a time that he had stopped the operation. Ned Kenworthy of the *Times,* who was covering the Hill at the time, heard of the memo and asked Fulbright staff man Carl Marcy for it— "Give me that memo, I know you have it"—and Marcy, almost desperate, wanting it out, had refused, saying simply he could not do it, he could not do it; Kenworthy had argued on, but to no avail, and he believed later that if he had gotten that memo he might have been able to stop the Bay of Pigs (though there was just as much chance that the *Times* would have killed his story, as it subsequently did that of his colleague Tad Szulc).

That was the first point of contact for Fulbright with the Kennedy-Johnson administration and it was disturbing. The Dulles years had been one thing, that had been Dulles and jingoistic right-wingers. Here were people he knew and vouched for following similar policies. Perhaps it was no longer just the men themselves, perhaps it was the thrust of the institutions and the society itself that was too powerful. The Bay of Pigs intensified his doubts and increased his own confidence; he was just a senator and technically he had much less information than all the great men in the executive branch, but he had been dead right and they dead wrong. Perhaps, he began to suspect, it tailored its information to its ambitions. He was becoming very suspicious of the information *and* the ambitions.

And he was becoming more and more dependent upon journalists. An axis was developing between the members of his own staff who were far more critical of the foreign-policy drift than he, and who were younger than he was, and some of the top Washington correspondents and foreign correspondents. When members of his own staff traveled, more and more their prime sources were not the people in the American Embassy but the resident foreign correspondents. In addition, he was being profoundly influenced by Walter Lippmann. Lippmann's private doubts about the course of American policy and of the men executing it were, if anything, more severe than his public columns, which were already highly critical.

Fulbright had been a dedicated Johnson supporter in 1964; Goldwater epitomized the things he hated most, a kind of American jingoism, too great a reliance on nuclear weapons and the military, military solutions to political problems. Whatever doubts he had about the growing threat of Vietnam were neutralized by his almost obsessive fear of Goldwater. He sent his entire staff down to Arkansas to work for Johnson. Johnson had sensed his vulnerability accurately and had asked him to perform one other bit of service, the shepherding of the Tonkin Gulf resolution through the Senate. Johnson had used the Goldwater argument with Fulbright, the need to protect himself from the barbarian on the right. There was a private commitment from Johnson that no ground troops would be sent to Vietnam, and so with some misgiving Fulbright undertook the assignment; it was the public act which he later most bitterly regretted. He was horrified by Tonkin, by the quick flash and possibly reckless use of American power, but he was more horrified by Goldwater, and went along. Yet he was being affected by what reporters in Vietnam were writing, by what his friend Bernard Fall was telling him, by his conversations with Lippmann. In part under Lippmann's influence, Fulbright wrote Johnson a very precise note saying that America could live with a unified Vietnam under Ho Chi Minh and that it would not affect our vital interests. Both Fulbright and his staff found it ominous that he did not receive an answer. Still, Fulbright tried to ease his staff's fears. He knew Lyndon, he said; and he knew how to deal with him. "You cannot challenge him head on, you've got to take your time and bring him along slowly. We'll educate him." So he continued to try to talk to Johnson on a subject where there was less and less listening.

Curiously enough, the split began not over Vietnam but over events in the Dominican Republic. The Dominican episode was a miniature Vietnam. In one sense the United States got lucky with its quick massive show of force, the insurgents there were not so powerful and not so deeply rooted in the society as to engage in a permanent war. In another sense the nation was unlucky; the ease with which the United States moved in and out of the Dominican Republic encouraged the President and his advisers to believe that American power would work as quickly in Vietnam. In that sense the Dominican adventure encouraged the arrogance that led to Vietnam. Fulbright had disliked the Dominican operation from the start. It was too quick and too brutal in its application of power, a symbol of Yankee imperialism to other countries, and there was no real congressional consultation. He had been very much impressed by the reporting of Tad Szulc of *The New York Times,* a reporter with uncommonly good sources in Latin America and uncommon energy and intelligence. (Lyndon Johnson had ranted and raved about Szulc during the entire Dominican affair. "That fucking Shoe-lack," he said—the name, he was well aware, was pronounced "Schultz"—"that fucking Shoe-lack. If we could just get him in jail we could liquidate the entire thing in two weeks.") Fulbright's staff people finally arranged to get from Szulc carbons of the manuscript of the book he was writing on the events, and they became the basis for committee hearings.

The hearings roused little interest in Congress; the times were not ready for dissent on presidential foreign policy. But when Thomas Mann, the Assistant Secretary of State for Latin-American Affairs and one of the architects of the intervention, came by to testify, he had sensed the reservations and he had delivered, rather grandly, the classic Cold War line: If you could just see the cables yourself, you'd know we were right. *If you could just see the cables, if you could see what we see.* It was the ultimate weapon, and nothing, nothing was more antithetical and more dangerous to the spirit of a democracy than a tiny minority—an inner club of men less mortal and more patriotic—knowing what everyone else should know, but being privileged and allowed to make secret judgments. When Mann had said that, Fulbright, prompted by his staff, had said, yes, show us the cables, and the Administration in its innocence, intoxicated by its power and its own inner lack of dissent, had turned over the cables. Pat Holt went to State and in a small room systematically checked the cable traffic, having already an alternative version of events as produced by Szulc and other reporters. To him the cables were devastating. They confirmed not the Administration's version but the Szulc history. They showed the Administration moving ahead without information, then trying to fit its information to its operations in a manner very different from what Lyndon Johnson and Dean Rusk had said.

Fulbright had pondered for a time what he was going to do with Holt's memo—his committee, after all, was divided, and it could not be a committee report—and finally he said, "The hell with it, I'll give a speech." That meant taking on the President of the United States, and it was not an act, given the nature of *this* President, to be taken lightly, nor was Fulbright the likely man to do it. But there was a part of him that was absolutely fearless. He was a politician, and a shrewd working one; he had paid a terrible price to be one; if he had accommodated on the race issue in Arkansas he had done it quite calculatedly and cold-bloodedly and for very real reasons. He was, because of that issue, a tainted man, a big man flawed.

But one did not challenge the President of the United States frivolously. It was not just a matter of comfort and safety, it was a matter of effectiveness. Fulbright's staff argued the point. Lee Williams, the senator's principal administrative assistant, knew the character of Lyndon Johnson particularly well; he could see that if Fulbright made this speech, it would be all over and he could kiss his friendship with the President, and more importantly the relationship, goodbye. His influence would be dead. *Dead.* It will not, he argued, be seen as a constitutional issue, President versus Congress, not even as an issue of policy, a debate over the limits of the American empire. Not with Lyndon B. Johnson of Johnson City, Texas. It would be seen as a betrayal of blood by blood. But it was curious, the aides thought, it seemed as though Fulbright had already decided to give the speech, and if anything, Williams's arguments probably moved him even more toward it, showing how the system was so imbalanced that to choose the constitutional path was to be injurious to his cause. *That the only way to dissent was by secret dissent.* His relationship with Johnson, he already knew, was fragile. Johnson was listening less and less to him, combat troops were already on their way to Vietnam despite the Johnsonian promises. So Fulbright simply listened and when his aide Carl Marcy made exactly the same arguments as Williams he cut him off. "Is the speech accurate?" he asked. "That's all I want to know." "Yes," said Marcy, "it's accurate, but if you give it, it's going to cause terrible political problems." Which angered Fulbright: "I don't want you to worry about my political problems, I'll worry about them. Is the speech accurate?" So Marcy agreed it was accurate. At Fulbright's request, the speech was rewritten slightly to place as much blame as possible on the President's advisers and as little on the President himself. It was simply Fulbright trying to give Johnson an out. Someone suggested he send over an advance copy of the speech to Johnson, but Fulbright rejected this. "I know him and he'll talk me out of it," he said. Instead, at the last minute, he sent over a copy with a personal covering note saying that this was in no way personal, that it was institutional and his own most serious judgment.

All of that was in vain. Johnson's reaction, as Lee Williams had predicted, was violent and final. Here he was getting ready to hunker down on Vietnam, a course he did not particularly want and was dubious about himself, and here was this breach of loyalty. He did not want advice or wisdom or lessons on constitutionality. He wanted loyalty. He immediately had friendly senators like Tom Dodd and George Smathers savage Fulbright on the Senate floor, and he set out to cut off Fulbright as completely as he could. Big things and little things. No more access. No more phone calls. No more warmth. No more Air Force One. Fulbright and a few other senators could go to a major meeting of parliamentarians in New Zealand by prop plane. Not long after the speech Johnson went into the hospital for stomach surgery, and Fulbright, who had suffered serious abdominal illness himself, sent the President a handwritten note, wishing him well, sharing his own feelings about being sick, and how to overcome it. It was an attempt to heal the wound. He received a curt answer from Jack Valenti which acknowledged that the President had received the Fulbright letter. A few weeks after that the President was returning from a foreign trip, and the Fulbright staff and Betty Fulbright pressured Fulbright to go out to Andrews Air Force Base. He did not want to go, and he argued that it would not make any difference, but they were insistent and so he went, on a miserable rainy night, and for his efforts he got not a nod, Lyndon Johnson looked right through him. So there was a breach, seemingly personal and ultimately constitutional. It was the end of trust and thus the end of an era.

A few weeks after the speech Carl Marcy went to see Dean Rusk to talk about the larger issues between the Secretary and the chairman. Marcy was disturbed by reports from very good sources in the Department that the people at State, on Johnson's request, were going to blacken Fulbright's reputation. He never got to the larger issues. He found Rusk in a rage, curt, snappish, almost unable to leave the subject of the Dominican speech, which he believed to be an assault upon both his honor and his competence (and which, in truth, it was). Marcy was stunned, he had never seen this side of the Secretary before, and Marcy quickly recognized that Rusk—like the Johnson administration— was more reasonable in public than in private. Rusk had the facts, he kept insisting, he and McNamara and the President, they had the real facts. If Fulbright had wanted any facts, why hadn't he just come to Rusk and Rusk would have given them to him. Then Fulbright would have understood. How could Fulbright take information from people like Szulc and that Pat Holt— genuine scorn there—what kind of people were these? Only we know why we sent so many troops, he said; if you wanted to know, why didn't you ask us? As for Fulbright's speech, Rusk said, he had taken the seven major points that Fulbright had made and graded them like a teacher, giving a score of one for each valid point, and the total he had come up with was one. *One.* So much for Fulbright's speech, but it was even sadder about Fulbright himself; he had known him a long time and he was fine as a college president, but he was a maverick and while the world needed mavericks, perhaps in universities, they were dangerous as chairmen of the Foreign Relations Committee. That was a serious place. Why, he added, the committee was coming apart under Fulbright, he couldn't control it any more. It made Rusk sad just to see what was happening, how chaotic the hearings were. His last appearance before the committee had been embarrassing. He did not know that his next appearance, coming up very soon, was going to be even more embarrassing.

So it was all set now for the confrontation. In Bill Fulbright's mind, Lyndon Johnson had broken a sacred promise dating back to 1964, when he had asked Fulbright to steer the Tonkin resolution through the Senate. There would be no ground troops, he had pledged to Fulbright. Fulbright, Johnson had said, should trust him. Fulbright had. A year later, without further consultation, Johnson had sent combat troops. Fulbright had raged at the White House and raged at himself, and he had apologized on the floor of the Senate to Gaylord Nelson, whose amendment prohibiting the dispatch of ground troops to Vietnam he had seen killed, the most bitter and humiliating moment of Nelson's long career. As Johnson escalated the war, Fulbright's bitterness had deepened, in part over the escalation of the war and in part over the fact that he had been an instrument of that escalation.

His sense of impotence had also increased; he could not get a purchase on policy. Johnson and his men were always outside his reach. There were no hearings on Vietnam policy, instead there were *consultations* with the Congress, where the congressmen had no other function than to listen, and these consultations were held in the White House, where the congressmen might properly be awed and intimidated. It reminded Fulbright of the divine right of kings. Except there was an additional power that the kings had never had, the use of television. The king and his princes were on television every day.

In late January 1966, Fulbright was restless, angry at the war, dissatisfied with his role, dissatisfied with his own behavior, searching for a constitutional role and a chance to ventilate the issue. The occasion he seized on was part of a hearing for a supplemental foreign aid bill. On January 28, 1966, Dean Rusk was testifying. Normally it would have been the most cut-and-dried of sessions, but Fulbright and Wayne Morse had both been growing more and more frustrated and angry, and they jumped Rusk. This was not the gentlemanly exchange between chairman and Secretary of State, between courtly Arkansan and courtly Georgian, between Rhodes Scholar and Rhodes Scholar, the exchanges that Senate buffs had become accustomed to. This was a fire fight, angry, bitter, and hostile. Fulbright lost his temper and he made no attempt to conceal it; what was on the inside came out. These were two serious, powerful men on totally different courses, and their exchange and what they represented were at the very core of a democracy, the entire atmosphere was charged and highly dramatic.

The networks, of course, had not covered it live and the network executive levels were not particularly prepared for it; their arrangements for covering public affairs did not at that moment envision a major debate between two coequal branches of the government on the most vital issue of the decade. It was the most dramatic film from the Congress in years. CBS gave it three minutes on the air, and NBC gave it five. When Fred Friendly, the president of CBS News, saw the three minutes that his network had used, he knew immediately that he had blundered and blundered big. Most of his deputies had been pushing him hard to use more film and he had resisted. After the show, when Friendly yelled at Ernie Leiser, the executive producer, asking why they had not used more, Leiser answered correctly that there had simply been too much other news. Then Friendly called Washington and talked to his bureau chief, Bill Small, who was already angry over the lack of coverage, and who complained to Friendly that the bureau had twice as much excellent film as had been used. Friendly listened and then asked if the committee would have permitted live coverage. "Certainly they would have. But you could never have gotten the air time and you know it," answered Small angrily. That was usually true, said Friendly, but maybe not true here; in any case, he would have liked to make the decision himself. He knew that as CBS had been judged in the past on how it covered great events, it was now going to be judged on how it covered Vietnam.

Six days later he got his chance. David Bell, the head of the AID program, was scheduled to testify in the same supplemental foreign aid bill hearing. Friendly decided to cover Bell's testimony live. When he called the network president's office to ask for the time, he did not realize he was beginning a confrontation of his own. He and John Reynolds, one of the network officers, talked briefly about how long they would stay live. There was some talk of thirty minutes. Thirty minutes was fine with Friendly, that should take care of all the questions and all the answers on America's involvement in the expanding war. Reynolds was pleased; this meant that it would probably interrupt only "Captain Kangaroo." There might be some complaints from mothers, Reynolds said, but there wasn't much money involved. Reynolds asked Friendly to keep it to a half hour. Fred Friendly did not realize that Bill Fulbright and Wayne Morse and Albert Gore were angry and spoiling for a fight and believed the Constitution entitled them to more than thirty minutes with the executive branch's representative, and could not care less if they exceeded the time allocated to "Captain Kangaroo." AID's Bell was a proxy for Rusk, who was himself a proxy for Johnson, and the assault upon Bell was intense; the television it produced was dramatic and absorbing. It was television doing what television was supposed to do. Gordon Manning, Friendly's chief deputy, called Friendly at home and told him to stay put, he did not want Friendly out of reach in case a decision had to be made to stay on.

A half hour passed and the hearing continued; Friendly had no intention of cutting it off, nor did he have the will; his own people were now pushing too hard. Manning had been haranguing him regularly about more live coverage, and Friendly was a prisoner of his own speeches. He believed in live television. When he had taken over the presidency of CBS News less than two years earlier, he had pledged himself to run more live television; but that had been an unfulfillable pledge, as air time became more expensive and more precious. His own news people were not just pushing him, they were baiting him, and now with the Bell hearings becoming richer and more fascinating by the minute, he did not dare tell his people to take them off the air. On and on into the morning and then the afternoon Bell's testimony went, canceling more and more expensive shows. It was no longer small money. NBC, pushed by CBS, stayed with it live too, but NBC had a weaker daytime schedule and it was losing less money. By the end of the day the cost to CBS was an estimated $175,000. (As the pressures subsequently mounted and as CBS executives began to squeeze Friendly, he often wondered, given the rocketing cost per minute in the mid-sixties, whether anyone in 1966 would have dared to cover the Army-McCarthy hearings. The cost by today's standards would be something like a half million a day, or roughly fifteen million dollars, a higher price for democracy than most network executives would be willing to pay.) By the end of Bell's day, the CBS business executives were highly displeased. So was Frank Stanton's great friend Lyndon Johnson, who announced in a sudden decision that he was flying his entire Administration to Honolulu to meet with Air Marshal Nguyen Cao Ky. It was classic presidential politics; his Administration was losing control of the media, and he wanted it back.

When Bell was finished, Friendly immediately started pressuring to cover the next witness, Lieutenant General James Gavin, a partial critic of the war. Stanton seemed opposed and distant, and only reluctantly gave his permission. This meant that the next struggle would be over George Kennan, the most reflective and cerebral man in the field of American foreign policy, the author of the containment policy, perhaps on this subject the single most important voice in the country. His testimony proved to be the most significant of the hearings. But this time Stanton was ungiving. Kennan might be the wisest voice in America, but he did not have a *title,* and it was important to have a title. Jack Schneider, on the business side, told Friendly that housewives didn't care about these hearings anyway. This time there was no give and there was no George Kennan. NBC, prodded by CBS, covered Kennan, but CBS did not. It was playing old reruns of "I Love Lucy."

At the same time, Friendly found out something else: that he had pushed and shoved and threatened resignation once too often, and his superiors were tired of him and his arguing, particularly his arguing on an issue where his case was so strong. So now, despite the promises that, as head of the News Division, he would have direct access to Paley and Stanton—which was crucial, because access to them meant access to air time—Friendly now found that there had been a bureaucratic reorganization designed to keep the News Department at a greater distance. Even as he was pleading with Stanton to cover Kennan, he discovered that he did not report to Stanton and Paley any more. There was a major new filter between him and Paley-Stanton in the person of Schneider, who ran something called the broadcast group. So Friendly had lost his access and he had lost his voice, and he was boxed in, perhaps precisely as Paley and Stanton wanted him boxed in. When in a few days he resigned, his superiors seemed not very surprised; indeed, they seemed more concerned with whether Friendly made a public issue of it than with the resignation itself. They did not want a messy resignation. Image, of course, was always crucial.

So it was that NBC carried George Kennan and CBS did not, although CBS carried General Maxwell Taylor for the Administration and Dean Rusk again; and so it was that Fred Friendly, talented, volcanic, ambitious, egocentric, but a reminder of some of the best days of CBS, left the network, wondering always whether his departure from CBS had been expedited by Lyndon Johnson through his close friend Frank Stanton. And so it was that never again were there televised hearings on the Vietnam War, though that war was to threaten the spirit and the soul of America for another nine years.

These were the first real public hearings on the Vietnam War, the hearings that should have been held two years earlier at the time of Tonkin; this was the congressional debate on essences that the nation had a right to expect. There was a certain irony to the coverage of those hearings: what legitimized them in the public mind, what forced the networks, usually so timid, to cover them, was that the witnesses were by and large Administration witnesses. The lead witness was not some antiwar critic, but Dean Rusk. Dean Rusk was the Secretary of State, and what the Secretary of State said was news. If the first witness had been James Gavin or George Kennan, there probably would have been no coverage, because it wasn't warranted. It was the first time that the Administration, however involuntarily, had allowed its major architects to go before a body of serious critics—men with titles—where the questions and doubts that the war evoked would be fully raised.

Television in the beginning had trivialized both the debate and the forces involved in Vietnam. It had confirmed the legitimacy of the President, made his case seem stronger than it was, and made the opposition appear to be outcasts, frustrated, angry, and rather beyond the pale. The Fulbright hearings gradually changed this balance. Like the Ervin hearings some seven years later, they were the beginning of a slow but massive educational process, a turning of the tide against the President's will and his awesome propaganda machinery. It was the ventilation of a serious opposition view (without it seeming to be the opposition party—most of the key members of the Fulbright committee were from the President's own party). From that time on, dissent was steadily more respectable and centrist. It was not that the opposition witnesses made such powerful cases against the war (the most formidable witness, George Kennan, was barred from CBS, and perhaps the single most important potential witness of all, General Matthew Ridgway, chose not to be a witness; he could not bring himself publicly to criticize a war he doubted while American troops were still fighting), it was the failure of the Administration under intense questioning to make a case *for* the war. It was not the opposition that won, it was the Administration that failed. This strengthened the frail heartbeat of the networks; they could always claim to the President, and quite rightly, that they had put on far more of his own witnesses than those of the opposition.

What the television cameras did to this particular war was to magnify, slowly but surely, its inconsistencies and brutalities. It was not a quick process; at the beginning, with the exception of an occasional devastating film clip, television was, in fact, very much on the team. It showed the government side far more than the antiwar side and there was often a pejorative tone to the voices of commentators in the early days of the antiwar protest, a certain distaste evinced. The major news shows accepted almost unquestioningly American goals and American statements and one did not often see I. F. Stone or Peter Arnett or Neil Sheehan as an interrogator on the Sunday newsmaker question-and-answer programs. It was, as Bill Paley had said, a consensus medium. (Even Eric Sevareid's major exclusive about Adlai Stevenson's decision to resign from his position as U.N. Ambassador under Kennedy was in *Look* magazine, not on CBS.) In the early days much of the film seemed to center on action rather than the more substantive qualities of the war, an emphasis on what the television correspondents themselves called "bloody" or "bang-bang." There was a group of younger correspondents for CBS who felt that somehow the network was always managing to sanitize the war, that there was nervousness about using some of the harsher and bloodier footage.

If it was a consensus medium, then in the early days, the consensus was for the war, although gradually that changed. For two things happened: First, the war turned out to be very difficult and victory did not come quickly, the predictions of the great men in Washington were wrong; the other side controlled the rate of the war and they could either speed up or slow down the tempo depending on their, rather than our, needs. Thus the slowness, the cumulative sense of the war went against Washington, which had hoped for and planned a quick victory. And second, the camera caught the special quality of *this* war, magnified the impropriety and brutality of it, emphasized how awesome the American firepower was and that it was being used against civilians, that you could not separate civilian from combatant. The camera also magnified the length of the war; the beginning of the combat escalation came with the bombing in February 1965, and the Tet offensive, which sealed the doom of the American mission, came three years later, and three years was, in the television age, an infinitely longer time than it used to be. The war played in American homes and it played too long. It made the American involvement there seem endless, which it was.

·  ·  ·

But in the early days of the war television was quite respectable. No one seemed to symbolize the consensus and television's acceptance of it more than Walter Cronkite. Later he changed as the nation changed, and he helped the nation to change faster. It was hard to tell who was leading whom; his own feelings on the war and his own responses a precise echo of American attitudes. In 1968 when Cronkite disassociated himself from the war, Lyndon Johnson knew it was all over, but in the early days Cronkite had accepted the government line and had in fact used his own credibility to amplify it. At his best he seemed to reflect the best of a kind of American tradition, essential good faith and trust; as a journalist he knew how hard to look and how hard not to look, and he had almost automatically given his trust to those who had titles and positions, often men he knew from World War II, men who had been his peers then and who were his peers now. He shared not just their perceptions (some but not all of them); more important, he shared their position. They were four-star, he was four-star. They had to know what they were doing because he knew what he was doing, the top of one hierarchy dealing with the top of another hierarchy. It was the great danger for the journalist as superstar superfigure; the instant access to the very top of the ladder before doing all the hard grounding out in the field, finding out the difference between theory and practice, between policy and reality, the difference between what was going on in the field and what the top brass said was going on, and *why* there was such a difference. The ordinary journalist based in Saigon had roots in the story, and would have dealt with the top of the command only after reporting from the field for several months, personal doubt and skepticism always growing. At the highest level, everyone is civilized, everyone is a good guy, everyone is aware, yes, of the problems, but these problems can be overcome. Cronkite was not the only first-rate war correspondent from War Two, as it was known, who had a bad first trip to Saigon.

He was, when he went to Saigon, what he himself termed a Kennan containment man; he did not doubt the seriousness of the corruption and the weakness of the South Vietnamese government, and he did not expect to see democracy flower, but he had been conditioned for a long time to the rhetoric of a generation, indeed he had helped push some of that rhetoric. In spite of all the dark shadows, he felt it was something we ought to do. Why bother to figure the cost, we were that rich. We might buy them some time, perhaps we could hold an umbrella long enough over the South Vietnamese so that something might grow there. A beginning. Besides, Cronkite was in essence a conventional man and this was the conventional wisdom at the time. He did not feel at ease in the early days with the people who were attacking the conventional wisdom, they were not his kind of people, and when he finally arrived in Saigon in 1965 he did not like the brashness of the younger correspondents who sat at the military briefings, tearing into the military officers.

So he gave the men who briefed him, men with several stars on their uniforms, the benefit of the doubt; he, like the rest of the country, was simply not ready to accept the idea that these same men who had fought and won the greatest war of the century did not know what they were talking about and, worse, were not to be trusted. Morley Safer, who was then the CBS bureau chief and whose perceptions were set in an entirely different era, tried to put Cronkite in touch with younger officers, men who knew the day-to-day reality of the war. It was an uphill struggle. Cronkite had done a number of CBS documentaries on airpower during the fifties and he had high-level contacts in the Air Force. The Air Force now reached out to him and showed him all its finest toys, the newest weapons; he was simply unwilling to go against the past, against all those ties and associations.

It was, thought one old friend of his watching the pressure the military put Cronkite under, as if they were using his trust and decency against him. His mistake was not so much in the way he reported as in making the trip in the first place. Some of his friends back in New York knew this and had not wanted him to go and had warned him that he would be used. But he could not resist, a war was a war, the action was the action, and he wanted to be part of it and so he went and he reported precisely as the military wanted him to; he was, in effect, on the team. But there was one thing that had bothered him. All the generals told him it was going to be a small war and a quick one, and yet they were already bulldozing Cam Ranh Bay, and it seemed to him that the huge establishment at Cam Ranh Bay was what you needed in a very big war.

He was also, whatever his sympathies on the war, the man who, as managing editor of the show, ultimately passed on the reporting of the younger, more alienated reporters from Vietnam, and while the CBS report from Saigon had its faults—the lack of time, the lack of a cumulative meaningful texture, an emphasis on bang-bang in film—it nonetheless distinguished itself by its coverage of Vietnam. To the American military it was known as the Communist Broadcasting Station. But CBS was better than the other two networks, and by journalistic consensus, the two best television reporters of the war were Safer and his younger colleague Jack Laurence. It was the CBS tradition that made the network special, the tradition that had begun with Murrow and still lived and meant that CBS attracted better people and had higher professional standards. Though the CBS correspondents themselves often rebelled at the limits of their craft, at the brevity that forced them to trivialize, at their inability to say what they really felt and to vent their own growing anger and frustration, nonetheless television subliminally caught that even when the words were edited out, and the war as broadcast on CBS gradually came to seem both endless and hopeless.

As the sum of this kind of reporting began to mount, as the dates for victory set by the architects came and went, as the war dragged on, the country began to be affected by the hopelessness of it, and so too did Walter Cronkite. Not the morality of it, war to him was war; but the disproportion of it, the fraud of it, increasing doubts about the credibility of the men running it. So he was changing and so was his audience and Walter Cronkite was always acutely aware of his audience and its moods; he was very good at leading and being led at the same time. The consensus was slipping and changing, time was beginning to work against Lyndon Johnson, as the President well knew, and he became even more sensitive to television. (In 1967 when Harry Reasoner, signing off from the CBS weekend news, happened to mention that he would not be there for the next few weeks because he was going to Saigon, he was not out of the booth before the phone rang and it was the President of the United States. Could Reasoner see him before he went overseas? So Reasoner did, receiving a marvelous Johnsonian lecture on how to cover a war, how to be a patriot, how to help his country. Was there anyone in the government Harry Reasoner wanted to see before he left? Well, said Reasoner, groping . . . McNamara, and even as McNamara's name was coming out of his mouth, Johnson was on the phone to the Secretary of Defense: Bob, was it convenient to see Harry Reasoner, which of course it was. Reasoner left for Vietnam with a profound sense that McNamara and Johnson were depressed, cornered men.)


Fulbright had held his hearings in 1966; a year later, in 1967, the war seemed hopelessly bogged down, the word *stalemate* began to appear in centrist journalistic dispatches, a Marine general held a background briefing to say the war was stalemated, the balance was changing, the enthusiasts for the war were now more and more on the defensive as 1968 opened; the President in late 1967 had felt compelled to bring both Westmoreland and Bunker home to rally support.

Thus as 1968 opened, even the President was on the defensive. Television was no longer an asset to him, he had done his television thing, and he could use McNamara and Rusk and Rostow only so many times, he could get only so much television theater out of moving the government to Manila or Hawaii or Saigon. The war had played too long, the glib predictions of White House officials had been put on once and then twice too often. Now television was about to start aiding the other side. Until January 1968, Hanoi and the Vietcong had always fought in a highly specialized way, shepherding their resources, fighting always at night and in the country because they had no airpower and little artillery or technological weaponry. Always gone before dawn. Daylight was a foe, daylight meant much heavier casualties, but daylight was required to film them. All of this meant that the enemy's sheer professionalism and toughness were rarely caught on film, and that at home in America the enemy was perceived as evasive, and perhaps not entirely serious, by the time the television camera crews arrived the Vietcong had slipped away. Indeed, network reporters even had a kind of brand name or label for that type of battle and film: "The Wily VC Got Away Again."

But the Tet offensive of 1968 changed that. For the first time the other side fought in the cities and fought in the daylight, day after day, where the American military could use the full force of their great technological might —and where American cameras could film the force and resilience and toughness of the enemy. Each day the battle went on television—showing the battlefield valor of the enemy—reduced the credibility of the Washington leadership. The first casualty of the battle was the Washington propaganda machinery. Fighting like this in the cities cost Hanoi infinitely more in human terms, but it made clear to millions of Americans the toughness and durability of the North Vietnamese. Whether Hanoi was sophisticated enough in its knowledge of American television to have scheduled the battle is debatable; no one knows (although the fact that it was perfectly timed for the upcoming presidential election is clear). What is not debatable is the effect. It changed the country, it forced the beginning of the end of the American combat participation, and it changed Walter Cronkite.

For this was crucial to the press coverage of the Tet offensive. The great impact of the offensive was not on the journalists who had covered it, reporters who had long ago become pessimistic about the eventual outcome of the war and who believed that the other side was resilient and in fact was controlling the rate of the war. Many journalists had in some form or another been reporting this or suggesting it for several months; by the middle of 1967 there were increasing numbers of stories that the war was stalemated. The real impact of the Tet offensive was on the editors and many of the readers at home, people of a different generation, of World War II, who had had great difficulty in accepting that America might be on the wrong course, that the various generals in Saigon might be wrong, that the President might be both misled and misleading. The events of that month changed the way men like Walter Cronkite and Hedley Donovan and Ben Bradlee viewed the war, and that was significant, for it meant that their powerful news institutions would no longer be so cautious in reflecting the doubt and pessimism of their reporters in Saigon.

When Tet happened Cronkite decided to go to Saigon. He was not entirely easy about making the trip and doing his own special from Vietnam because he knew that he was stepping out of his natural role, that he would be perceived differently by his viewers and that his role would never be quite the same again. He had studiously avoided revealing his real opinions and his real feelings on the evening news, and there was no doubt that this was bound to change, and that even people who agreed with him would have a new kind of suspicion about him, that Walter was somehow not quite so straight any more, that he was a different man. He was very good at anticipating the reaction. He talked it over with the various producers at CBS and Dick Salant, head of CBS News, and they decided that, whatever the misgivings, the real obligation, if you were the signature figure of a great news department, was to cover a major story at a moment when the nation was so confused and divided. So with the encouragement of Salant and others, and not without a good deal of reservation, he went again to Saigon at the time of Tet.

It was an Orwellian trip—Orwell had written of a Ministry of Truth in charge of Lying and a Ministry of Peace in charge of War—and here was Cronkite flying to Saigon, where the American military command was surrounded by defeat and calling it victory. He and Ernie Leiser, his producer, flew out together and they had trouble landing in the country. All the airports were closed. When they finally reached Saigon there was fighting going on all around them. The requisite briefing with Westmoreland was truly Orwellian, those pressed fatigues, the chromed AK-47, the eyes burning fiercely, the voice saying that little had happened, almost surprised that Walter was there, though of course it was fortunate that he was, since Tet was a very great victory. Exactly what the Americans had wanted.

Then Cronkite headed north with Leiser and Jeff Gralnick, his favorite young producer, who had just come to Saigon as a correspondent. They tried to get into the Khe Sanh base, which was undergoing very heavy fighting, but no one would write the insurance policy, it was simply too dangerous. So he went instead to Hue. Just the day before, Westy had said that the battle was over, but it was clear now that the North Vietnamese were very much around; the Marines were fighting desperately to retake the city and no great victory had been achieved. There was fighting right up and down the center of Hue, and Walter seemed slightly envious when the team got separated and the others seemed to have seen more action. The younger CBS men were impressed by the sight of Cronkite striding right into the center of the street fighting; the old war-horse, they thought, takes all the risks.

But it was a crucial moment for him because for the first time the credibility gap had surfaced in front of everyone's eyes, newcomer and all; in the past someone had to search for the difference between what Saigon said and what was happening, it was somehow subsurface, but here now was this ferocious fighting and yet in Saigon, American generals, four-star commanding generals, could sit and brief very senior American correspondents—correspondents who would go on television and speak to all the American people—and say the battle was over, when it was in fact still very much in doubt. Which meant that the generals were liars or fools, and if they lied about something like this, they might as easily lie about everything else. Cronkite was shocked not so much by the ferocity of the fighting as by the fact that the men in charge of the war were not to be trusted. Even his way of leaving Hue was symbolic: there were exceptional precautions, extra weapons aboard, and, besides the best-known commentator of the day, twelve dead GI's in body bags from a supposedly pacified city. That was how Walter Cronkite left Hue and a very great victory—with the bodies of GI's.

Cronkite and his team stopped on the way back to Saigon at Phu Bai to meet Cronkite's old friend Creighton Abrams. Abrams was then the deputy commander scheduled eventually to replace Westmoreland, and now, meeting with Cronkite, he was strikingly candid about the dimension of the catastrophe, the degree to which the command had been taken by surprise, and the psychological import of it. It was an important moment: here was the number-two man in the American command not only confirming Cronkite's own doubts and sounding like one of the much-maligned Saigon journalists, but also explaining how and why the mission had been so blind. From there Cronkite returned to Saigon to meet with his CBS colleagues.

That night with his colleagues he seemed different, moved by what he had seen, the immediacy and potency of it all, the destruction and loss and killing, and the fact that it was begetting so many lies, first by the command here in Saigon and then by the Administration in Washington. The final night he had dinner with a bunch of correspondents on the roof of the Caravelle Hotel and he kept asking, again and again: how could it have happened, how could it have happened? Peter Kalischer, the senior and most knowledgeable of the correspondents, spoke movingly: it had been happening for years, it was all lies from the start, we had been building on a false base, and we were essentially intruders in the lives of the Vietnamese.

Later Cronkite stood on the roof of the Caravelle with Jack Laurence, the youngest and perhaps the most anguished of the CBS reporters, and watched the artillery in nearby Cholon. Laurence seemed to resent the situation; he hated that breed of older correspondents who observed the war from the Caravelle roof. He and his contemporaries much preferred on their off days to sit in their rooms and get stoned on pot. He did not know if this was less moral or more moral, but it allowed him on occasion to forget the war and the bodies. Cronkite, who was trying to measure the distance of some of the artillery rounds, must have sensed this resentment, for he talked to Laurence in an extraordinary way, not so much as a senior correspondent to a very junior one, but almost father to son. He said he was grateful to Laurence and the other reporters who had risked so much (the combat losses among correspondents in Vietnam, in relation to American combat deaths, were infinitely higher than they were among correspondents in previous wars) day after day for the news show and he understood how restless and frustrated a younger man could become with the bureaucracy of journalism, and what seemed like the insensitivity of editors; he had undergone similar frustrations in World War II, the difficulty of communicating with older men thousands of miles away who were not witnessing what he was witnessing. Laurence was touched. He was left with the strong impression that Cronkite had been moved by the war and by what he had seen.

So for a man who cherished his objectivity above all, Walter Cronkite did something unique. He shed it, and became a personal journalist. He had already talked it over with his superiors in New York and they all knew the risk involved, that it was likely to be a severe blow to the reputation for impartiality that he and CBS had worked so hard to build, that it was advocacy journalism and thus a very different and dangerous role. (Later, when Nixon attacked the press, Cronkite knew that he was more vulnerable because of his Tet role, that all of the press was in bad odor, including Cronkite himself, and that Nixon had exploited this.) It was not something that he wanted to do, but something he finally felt he had to do. He broadcast a half-hour news special which he insisted on writing himself, in itself unusual. He said that the war didn't work, that a few thousand more troops would not turn it around, and that we had to start thinking of getting out. These were alien and hard words for him but he did not feel he could do otherwise. He was ready for it and the country was ready for it; he moved in part because the consensus was moving, helping to shift the grain by his very act. It was an act that made him uneasy and was in some ways sure to damage him, but he believed that it had to be done. A few weeks later a hoped-for and much-prized visa for North Vietnam finally came through. Cronkite had applied for it a whole year earlier; he had wanted badly to go and file a report from the other side of the line. But only now, after his Tet broadcast, had it come through, and Cronkite realized that it would be impossible to accept it without giving the impression that it had been issued as a reward. He believed that one act against the grain was all right, but two was too much, and he passed it on to Charles Collingwood.

Cronkite's reporting did change the balance; it was the first time in American history a war had been declared over by an anchorman. In Washington, Lyndon Johnson watched and told his press secretary, George Christian, that it was a turning point, that if he had lost Walter Cronkite he had lost Mr. Average Citizen. It solidified his decision not to run again. Though Johnson respected their power, he did not trust or like most people from television very much. He thought that they hyped their stories too much, often at his expense. Pretty boys, that's what they were, he often told his staff. Actors, wanting everyone else to be actors. In his heart he much preferred print reporters, who he thought were harder-working and smarter. But Walter Cronkite, almost alone among major television figures, held both his respect and his affection. He believed that Walter cared about the good of the country. He had liked Walter early on, and he had never thought of him as one of those Kennedy-type media people. As the war dragged on he had not liked the CBS show, the CBS reporters were the worst, but he had exempted Walter from this. In his mind Walter had tried to remain straight and tried to report the war as it was. So when Cronkite gave his post-Tet report, this affected Lyndon Johnson in two ways. First, he realized that he had lost the center, that Walter both was the center and reached the center, and thus his own consensus was in serious jeopardy. Second, because he liked and admired Cronkite so much and thought him so fair a reporter, he found himself believing that if Walter Cronkite was reporting these things, he must know something, he was not doing this just to help his own career, the way so many other reporters were. The Cronkite reporting coincided with the effort that Clark Clifford, another trusted friend, was making to convince him to pull back, so it had an added effect. Later, after Johnson had left the presidency, Cronkite, hearing of what the President had said about him, tried on several occasions to raise the subject with him, but Johnson knew the game, and began instead several long, rather incoherent tirades against the press in general and in particular the press's sinister betrayal of the national interest.

.  .  .

The last gift of CBS to Lyndon Johnson was seed money for the Lyndon
Johnson Library. It contributed this by overbidding handsomely on Johnson's
memoirs, via its subsidiary, the publishing house Holt, Rinehart & Winston.
Frank Stanton had made clear that he wanted Holt to publish the Johnson
book, and there was no doubt that Holt would win the bidding. No matter that,
given the still-strong public feelings about Vietnam and Johnson's role in it,
the memoirs were not regarded as a particularly hot literary property. Holt
went for a huge advance, more than $1.6 million, it was said. It was also said
that no other publishing house was within $700,000 of the Holt offer. Some
younger Holt editors protested that their firm would take a million-dollar bath
on the book. They were told to muzzle their opinions; the word had come from
the top.

Johnson got a million straightaway and, shrewd as ever, told some
of his rich Texas business friends that he was in a position to put up a million dollars from his own pocket for the library if they would come
through with a comparable amount. The additional money was raised very
quickly. Almost as quickly, Johnson's book was written and delivered to
Holt, which in the end laid out, as promised, $1.6 million in all. And took
a bath. The book earned back roughly $600,000. It *was* a million-dollar
bath.

Holt was chagrined, but not devastated, because the Johnson contract had
called for *two* books, and he still owed them a second volume from which they
could expect to retrieve some of their losses. But Johnson quickly put an end
to that bit of optimism. The contract, he pointed out, had called for two books
of 150,000 words each. He had delivered *300,000* words the first time and thus
had fulfilled all his obligations. If they wanted another book they would have
to advance more money. Some Holt executives were outraged; at the time of
Johnson's death there was some discussion of whether or not to sue the former
President of the United States.

# 19/ The Washington Post

Kay. She had sat in the background all those years, painfully shy, unsure of
herself, feeling very much in Phil's shadow. She felt awkward and dowdy and,
as she felt awkward and dowdy, she *was* awkward and dowdy. The Kennedy
years, which had been the most glittering period in Washington, and a wonderful time for Phil with all his connections, had been the worst time for her.
During the Eisenhower years it was permissible to be a little dowdy, dowdy
was in, but the Kennedy years were different and harder, the Kennedy stan-

dards were unrelenting. The Kennedys liked bright active men and pretty young women, and she was neither; if you were a middle-aged housewife, she thought, you simply had no role. They were invited everywhere because of Phil and the properties, but never because of her. Phil had the power and the charm, she was the appendage. She knew that at dinner parties the hosts would seat her at the worst table possible, so that she did not slow down the bright animated talk that they thrived on. When men talked to her they often asked her what Phil was up to. At a farewell party for Chip Bohlen, they were to go for a cruise on the presidential yacht, and everyone was sitting in a large circle, and the President was late and at the last minute he had arrived and taken the extra chair, which was next to Kay. She had been terrified; how, she thought, could she talk to Jack Kennedy, what would she say, and the terror had shown on her face, and she had looked across the circle and caught Phil's eye—her look at once frightened and plaintive—and he had laughed.

But it was not just Phil Graham who had over the years systematically eroded the confidence of Kay Graham, it had begun much earlier with her mother, a fierce, deeply dissatisfied woman. Physically she was formidable, intellectually she was fearsome—a tough, driving, audacious, independent woman who seemed to have sprung from a Wagnerian opera. My mother, Kay Graham later told friends, was a Viking. Agnes Meyer was a woman who seemed emotionally involved first with her father and then with her son-in-law, but not very much with her husband. She passed on to her various children a sense that somehow they were unworthy of her, or had let her down. Her marriage with Eugene Meyer had not been a calm or happy one, the sense of tension and discord was powerful. He was successful and he was solid and Agnes Ernst had needed those qualities at the time of her marriage. She had a powerful sense of herself, an enormous ego; chapter six of her memoirs was entitled "The Female Egotist Gets Married." (After she was married she once complained to Meyer that his ego was too small, that he took too little credit for what he accomplished. "That's all right," he replied, "you have enough for both of us.") She had gone to Barnard, taken a job as a reporter for the New York *Sun;* she was a romantic young woman, determined not to be a housewife but to live a full and adventurous life. When she first met Meyer in 1902 he was already thirty-two, successful and rich and accomplished.

There were disappointments almost from the start; it was a difficult marriage, short on love and warmth. Shortly after they were married, Meyer showed some of her letters to a friend. "Very intelligent, aren't they? But there is no love there," he said. He wanted children, she had no great desire to have them, and even less to mother them. Seeing her first-born daughter, Kay, she remarked that it was a "wretched little object, made even more hideous by abrasions on her poor little temple made by the forceps." She had such an unpleasant time of it during her first pregnancy that she asked her obstetrician why any woman would have a second child; and though she did have more children, they were reared primarily by nursemaids. Children were never part of the life she envisioned for herself.

So Kay Meyer never learned from her mother the things most children learn from their mothers about life. She was in her freshman year at Vassar, the possessor of two skirts and two sweaters, when one of her roommates took pity on this daughter of one of the richest men in America and told her that she needed more clothes because the ones she had were beginning to smell. She remembered waiting, as a child of ten in the huge Meyer family estate in Mount Kisco, for a friend to arrive for the weekend, and innocently asking her mother what they would do when the friend got there. Her mother flew into a rage. How dare she ask that when there were horses to ride and a swimming pool and all these wonderful things? And Kay remembers saying yes, but she did not know how to do any of those things. Even as a grown woman Katharine Meyer Graham felt very much in her mother's shadow, unsure of herself, unsure of her taste and her womanliness. Her mother encouraged her in the idea that she was no more than a housewife; once many years after Kay had married, she wandered up, a couple of children in tow, to where her mother and Phil Graham were talking about something. "Pardon us, dear," said her mother, "but we are having an intellectual discussion." Even late in her life, when she was publisher of the *Post*, Mrs. Graham still seemed to live under her mother's shadow. Kay had become a friend of I. M. Pei, the architect, whom Agnes wanted to meet. A luncheon was arranged. Pei said something very perceptive. "I didn't know that," said the Publisher of the Washington *Post*. "What's surprising about that?" asked her mother, "you've never known anything." The relationship always festered; these were stories she told on herself.

One of the abiding pains of the Meyer family was anti-Semitism. Agnes Meyer had discovered that no amount of success on her husband's part ever quite erased it. The discrimination she experienced affected her seriously and she came to hate it, and to blame her husband for it, at least in some ways; Eugene was expected to "rise above it," to be, by force of will, more accepted than it was in fact possible for him to be. The Meyer home was made to seem thoroughly Protestant. Kay Graham was sitting with some classmates at Vassar when one of them asked her what it was like being Jewish. She had no idea because no one had ever mentioned to her that she was. (In a book written about Jews in America by Steve Isaacs, then a reporter for the Washington *Post*, in language checked back with her, Mrs. Graham was described as "raised as a Christian by her German Lutheran mother, but she considers herself her father's daughter.")

When she first took over the paper after Phil's death, she was Poor Kay, someone convinced that she was the ugly duckling. No one knew her, nor did she know herself. (Perhaps a few of the older *Post* executives like Al Friendly and Russ Wiggins knew her, but they were like family, she was less shy with them, it was as if they had all grown up together.) To most people in Washington, in the last twenty years she had had no role to play and accordingly she had played none. On the day of the funeral she chose to meet with the board of directors of the paper and a few other executives. It was a very bad and

uncertain time, there were already offers coming in for the paper and rumors
that it would be sold. She asked to speak at that meeting. She began by saying
that she knew how much everyone there had been through in the last few years,
she knew the strain they had been under and the love and loyalty they had
showed, and she thanked them for holding the paper together. Then she said:
"This has been, this is, and this will continue to be a family operation. There
is another generation coming, and we intend to turn the paper over to them."
It was for the men gathered around her—and they were all men—an epiphany.
It was simple but it was impressive, and it left no doubt what the future would
be; it was also exactly what everyone wanted to hear. She meant it, and in
particular at that very moment she meant it about Donnie, her oldest son, still
in college. In those days, indeed in the first year or two after Phil's death, she
talked constantly about just holding on to the paper until Donnie got out of
school, how she wished he would hurry up and graduate from Harvard so he
could come down and take over. Then gradually she began to say it less
frequently. As Donnie grew older and more ready to assume responsibility,
there was no rush on her part to turn the paper over; when he reached the age
when Phil Graham, only a son-in-law, had received the paper from Eugene
Meyer, Donald Graham, son of the publisher, was still caught in the upper
level of the *Post* bureaucracy. Donnie, it turned out, would have to wait.


There were men everywhere. That was the first thing about the new job. She
had to deal with men who were quick and verbal and ambitious and self-
assured and who had risen through the ranks against other men who were also
smart and ambitious. These men seemed to know what they were doing at all
times and they always had the answers and they talked in a kind of insider's
shorthand. It was very easy to feel slow among them. They were not just men,
that was bad enough, but a special breed of high-powered men who were
always ahead of the game, always on the inside, always in the know. It
sometimes seemed as if they were speaking another language. They sometimes
terrified her and she felt unworthy, they knew so much more about so many
things. She confessed her terror to Walter Lippmann and he, old friend,
comfortable with his own intelligence, suggested that she read her own paper
every day and if there was a story she did not understand, she should simply
call in the reporter and ask questions and learn conversationally, at her ease
and in her office. Remove a subject from the arcane world of experts and make
it conversational. Clare Boothe Luce suggested that she be careful not to
intimidate men. "You're a woman in a world of men and you're not really
prepared. So every time men come to your office to talk, try and move away
from your desk to the sofa. Try not to be intimidating. You're going to need
all the help you can get." Still, in those early months she was unsure, she often
woke up wondering where she was and how she was ever going to do it all,
she felt she had had no training, that she had never shared in Phil's career,
they had never really talked about his world.

What surprised her the most in those early months was that people she knew and respected in the field of journalism did not think that the Washington *Post* was a particularly good newspaper. That stunned her; she had always assumed that the *Post* was a wonderful paper because Phil, after all, was wonderful and therefore any paper he published must be equally wonderful. What she was realizing now was that Phil's professional peers had liked him personally but they had made a distinction between Phil the friend and mover, whom they liked and admired, and Phil the publisher, about whom they had serious doubts because he was in fact a flawed publisher. Scotty Reston of the *Times,* whom she trusted and whom she believed to be the best newspaperman in town, told her it was a mediocre erratic paper that had no discipline, and asked her whether or not she intended to leave a better paper to her children than the one she had inherited. That disturbed her and made her think; Reston was not a man to make casual unjust criticism. Equally important, Walter Lippmann was highly critical. He thought the paper sluggish and not very adventurous. What was most disturbing about the Reston and Lippmann comments was that these men were personal friends of Russ Wiggins and Al Friendly, the men who actually ran the paper, there was no personal rancor involved. Quite the reverse in fact. But she was listening to outsiders, and her doubts about her own people were growing, particularly about Friendly. Friendly, people were telling her, was going deaf. Besides, he now took two months' vacation a year, one as his regular due and a second that had been awarded by Phil Graham for some feat of arms, and that made his control over a daily newspaper weaker. Other people, she began to notice, were coming by and in effect applying for the job. Much of the criticism seemed to center upon Friendly. Even her *Newsweek* editors in New York were subtly undermining him; they did not think the *Post* a good paper; with their New York vision, accustomed to *The New York Times,* they thought it essentially parochial.

She did not really wait very long. She spent 1964, an election year, gradually taking over, gradually gaining confidence. (Some dated her new confidence to the moment when, Democratic convention in Atlantic City finished, Lyndon Johnson had literally swept her off her feet and taken her back to the ranch, and there had not been enough time to be afraid, to feel the doubts, she had not had time to worry about whether she was ready or what she should wear. She had just gone with him, and it had proved to her that she was in fact the publisher of the Washington *Post.*) She had begun in that year to sign her name Katharine Graham instead of Mrs. Philip Graham. By the end of 1964 she was convinced that there was something wrong with the *Post,* although she was not sure what it was. It was murky over there, decisions were not sharp and creative. "You're my team," she had told Wiggins and Friendly after Phil's death. But now she had doubts. Perhaps Al was too nice. Perhaps he had been at the job too long. She was, by early 1965, beginning to think seriously of some kind of change.

And so it was that in the early spring of 1965 she called up Ben Bradlee, the Washington bureau chief for *Newsweek,* and asked him to lunch. She was very uneasy about the encounter. They were going to the F Street Club and she had never been there before and she was going to have to pay for a man's lunch and that unnerved and embarrassed her, indeed so much so that she never did it again. Besides, she did not know Bradlee very well and what she did know she did not particularly like. He was *Newsweek,* which in those days was not a very great plus, *Newsweek* in her mind being a symptom of Phil's sickness; he was more of Phil's world than hers, one of those bright dashing young men around Jack Kennedy who had ignored dowdy middle-aged ladies. In addition, he was—there was tangible proof of it—a Phil Person rather than a Kay Person; he had very clearly been on the other side during the great struggle. Phil had called Ben and said he wanted to have dinner at the Bradlee house with Robin. Bradlee said okay. Phil said that he had better check with Tony, his wife, because most Washington wives were not accepting Robin. So Bradlee checked with Tony, who said it was all right, and the four of them dined at Bradlee's house. It had not gone unnoticed. In addition, as the tensions between Kay and Phil had mounted, each had monitored the activities and loyalties of people caught in between, and Ben Bradlee, to her mind, had been one of the worst offenders. He had, she heard, been dining out around town saying that there was nothing wrong with Phil Graham that a quick divorce would not cure. (Years later she would tell people that story, pointing out that she had no cause to love Ben Bradlee. But she would quickly add, for by then he had become her editor and her friend, at least he had been aboveboard about it.) He had offended her in another way, it turned out. Bradlee had been in Europe when Phil had killed himself and he had hurried back for the funeral, but he had not come to the house after the ceremony. (He had not come because he had not been invited, and, as he told friends, where he grew up in Boston you did not go where you were not invited.) So there were two strikes against him. On the other hand, he had the reputation of being professional and good and brash, and above all, attracting very talented people to his bureau and getting a lot out of them. Everyone spoke well of the *Newsweek* Washington bureau, it was clearly an ornament to the magazine, with all the talented young men there—Ward Just, Jay Iselin, Phil Carter. She thought it was time that she saw the *Newsweek* bureau chief, particularly because she had just heard that Bradlee had for the fourth time turned down a job on the *Newsweek* escalator, allegedly because it would involve moving to New York and he was very happy where he was. What kind of a man was he, anyway, this Bradlee, a man who ignored the executive ladder and was happy where he was?

He was then forty-three years old and he was handsome and dashing in a rough, almost riverboat-gambler manner. Someone had once described him as looking like the corner bookie. Another said he had the face of an international jewel thief. But if someone were looking for a dashing, somewhat rakish journalist, then Bradlee was perfect for the part. Years later when Jason

Robards won an Oscar for playing Bradlee, it seemed to some an easier role than most outsiders suspected; Bradlee, after all, had been playing the same role with equal success for some fifteen years. Part ultimate cosmopolite, part street tough. All professions have some theater to them—academe, medicine, law, and journalism. Some professors, less brilliant than others, can dramatize their lectures better than others. Some politicians are brilliant at the theater of their profession. Jack Kennedy was wonderful at it, Scoop Jackson was dreadful; Henry Kissinger, short, pudgy, nominally unattractive, was superb at it, making himself the focal point of media coverage, until in fact he seemed more the creation of the media than of the Department of State. Scotty Reston, with his Spencer Tracy looks, his bouncy confident walk, was good at it. Dan Rather, with his cool deputy-sheriff eye, had it. And probably Ben Bradlee, more than anyone else in contemporary journalism, was good at the theater of his profession, the style, the timing, the sense of his audience, whether it was the larger audience outside or his peers inside. It was as if the camera was always on him: the hair sleeked down. The rough-handsome face. The little strut to his walk. The suits slightly out of fashion. The almost harsh voice, raspy but patrician raspy. The ability to have it both ways, to play upon a wonderful Boston upper-class background and yet disown it whenever necessary. "Humphrey Bogart in a button-down shirt," Douglass Cater of *The Reporter* said of him. He made other men want him to like them, want his approval. His intuitions about people were incredibly subtle and delicate, and he hid this well behind his rough exterior, which made the effect of his personality all the more powerful. It was not by chance that after he went to the Washington *Post* and was given an office in the new *Post* building, he demanded that the walls of his office be torn down, not just so he could see his staff, but so the staff could see him. When one of his best editors, Ben Bagdikian, was leaving the *Post* under less than happy circumstances, the two of them went to a lunch which was not particularly pleasant. Harsh words were exchanged. At the precise moment that they reentered the newsroom, with the rest of the staff watching, Bradlee reached out and put his arm around the shoulder of Bagdikian, a much-respected figure, as if in fact they were buddies and had parted buddies, and bade him farewell in such terms. *Beau geste.*

He was, to the young journalists he had assembled in the *Newsweek* bureau, a wildly romantic figure. He was a friend of the Kennedys, he had been a foreign correspondent (they would later learn that he had been a good but hardly a brilliant one), and he *looked* the way a former foreign correspondent should look, he was irreverent and audacious and frequently blasphemous. The young *Newsweek* and *Post* reporters who desperately admired him and who looked up his old clips hoping to emulate him were often a little disappointed. He had been all right, but they wanted him to be better. But he had the ability to inspire and stimulate young reporters. More, he had the ability, which was crucial for an editor or bureau chief, to make a reporter feel that if Bradlee himself were doing that particular story, he could do it easily, a piece of cake, and they *therefore should not let him down.* He projected the aura of being a great newspaperman and so they believed him and they reached a little further.

He was a great ivory hunter in a city where up to then only Scotty Reston and to a lesser degree Bob Donovan had been great talent scouts, and he was very quickly picking up some of the best young reporters around. More, he had their total loyalty. He fought with their editors in New York, they could hear him screaming at New York, and they loved that, for in the world of news magazines, New York was the enemy. He always seemed to bring excitement to stories. Ward Just, at the time a young reporter in the *Newsweek* bureau, had casually mentioned an idea about all the bright young men of the Kennedy era then in their late twenties and early thirties who really wanted to be Presidents themselves in the future. A casual mention, but Bradlee sprang alive, "Oh shit, yes! Just drop everything else, get on that! Oh, that is a wonderful goddamn idea!" Then, when Just had finished it, he had looked and said, "Just, this is a hell of a goddamn file, I'll give you that." One of his favorites, a young reporter named Phil Carter, had gone down to cover the racial trouble in Cambridge, Maryland, and he had been tired and he had filed too long and he was depressed by events and what he thought was his failure to really get hold of them. He was sitting in the wire room next to Bradlee's office when he heard That Voice on the phone to New York, and Bradlee was talking about some reporter who had done a hell of a goddamn job, that this kid was the best damn young reporter they had and it was the best goddamn file they had gotten in a long time and New York better goddamn read it and run every word without change. Slowly it dawned on Carter that Bradlee was talking about him. Just at that moment Bradlee had looked through the doorway and seen Carter and he had shouted, "Get the fuck out of here, Carter," slammed the door, and gone on with his conversation. Carter had walked back to his office in euphoria, thinking: *Bradlee loves me, Bradlee thinks I'm good.* They all loved the excitement he brought, the zest, the desire for action, the hatred of drudgery. Once when Bradlee had just gone over to the *Post* from *Newsweek,* Jay Iselin, one of his *Newsweek* stars, visited him there and watched as he took a perfectly respectable if rather dull story on the State Department and spiked it. Why? asked Iselin. "Because it's a room emptier," Bradlee said. *A room emptier!* Ben Bradlee wanted no room emptiers in his publication, he wanted neither to bore nor be bored.


Katharine Graham, feeling shy and awkward, took Ben Bradlee to lunch in order to find out what he wanted to be when he grew up. She was, of course, totally charmed by him—the intelligence, the laughter, the candid quality of his intense ambition. He did not want to go to New York, he said, because he liked Washington and he thought a Washington bureau chief ought to have some longevity, the magazine should not change its chiefs too quickly. In fact, that was exactly what he had told Phil when he had first taken over. So, she asked, is there any position in the company you might be interested in? "Well," he answered, in these exact words, for it was the way Bradlee talked and why in part he charmed her so much, "if Al Friendly's job at the *Post* ever came open, I'd give my left one for it." At the time he did not think there was any likelihood, it simply was not in the cards. Al Friendly was her best friend, they had grown up together, they played bridge every night. The last thing that Bradlee expected was that this nice pleasant woman, clearly so unsure of herself, would move against an existing editor who was virtually a member of her family. But she was already uneasy with the direction of the *Post,* and she had in some unconscious way decided to make a change, and now, talking to Bradlee, she could understand why everyone spoke so highly of him, why all the young reporters at *Newsweek* admired him. He was wonderful company, he was charming and he made her laugh. When he was around everything seemed to move faster. He was audacious and almost obscene. He reminded her very much of Phil Graham. And she was, in the same way and for the same reasons, captivated by him. Like Phil, he had the ability not just to make her laugh but to make her feel prettier and more at ease. He had, like Phil Graham, the ability to be outrageous, yet still highly respectable.

Bradlee, she thought; Bradlee at the Washington *Post.* She mentioned it to Scotty Reston, who was somewhat noncommittal and reserved (Reston, Bradlee suspected, would have preferred a more traditional editor, someone self-evidently serious, like Max Frankel of the *Times*). But she also mentioned it to Lippmann, and to her surprise Lippmann was quite positive. With that typical Bradlee hard luck that had plagued him all his life and put him five doors down the street from Jack Kennedy, it turned out that Lippmann was an old friend of the Bradlee family. Mrs. Lippmann and Bradlee's mother had gone to the Chapin School in New York City together and at one point had been co-holders of the Chapin School high-jump record. That friendship had lasted, and every year when the Lippmanns had left Washington for their summer vacation in Maine, they had made one stop, for dinner with Ben and Josephine Bradlee in Beverly, Massachusetts. (Although the young Bradlee had hated the literal way Jo Bradlee had questioned the sage—"Now Walter, tell us about this dreadful Russian situation." When she started asking questions, Ben Bradlee would leave the room.) But it was a fortunate friendship. When Bradlee had come to Washington as a journalist, Walter Lippmann had reached out to him and invited him to parties, which was a very big ticket in those days, not many young reporters were invited to the home of Walter and Helen Lippmann. It was Lippmann who had convinced Bradlee to change his early by-line at the *Post* from Ben Bradlee to Benjamin Bradlee, telling him that Ben Bradlee sounded too much like a sports by-line. Thus Walter Lippmann, who was shooting down Al Friendly, was also setting up Ben Bradlee.

The more she saw of him after the first lunch, the more she liked him. He kept pushing her for the job, in a nice way, hungry but not too hungry, and she liked that, she felt she needed to be pushed. From the moment at lunch when she had let him know it might just be in the cards for him to come to the *Post,* he had kept on it relentlessly. When are we going to do it? When am

I going over to the *Post?* There was a certain ruthlessness to him, she thought, but a civilized ruthlessness, the civilized predator, or the predatory gentleman. Everyone seemed to speak well of him. Oz Elliott spoke very highly, and Fritz Beebe, who also had a connection, liked him. She had a feeling that she needed him, that he would push her and drive her as Russ and Al would not, and she was absolutely sure she should be pushed. Because of that she could put aside her personal reservations. So it was that in June 1965 she finally decided to go ahead and bring Bradlee to the *Post.* Wiggins and Friendly were very unhappy with the idea, they sensed an immediate threat. They felt that Bradlee's style was not in keeping with their own, which was true, and they also felt that if he was coming to the *Post,* he would not be content to sit for very long on the sidelines, which was also true. They suggested that if he was coming aboard perhaps he should start as the top political reporter, it would be a good way to find out how good he really was (plenty of room for him to stumble there). Friendly in particular was in no rush; he was scheduled to become the head of the American Society of Newspaper Editors in three years, which would be the climax of a fine career, and he did not want to lose his place on the ladder. But she was impatient too, once she had decided that something was wrong, she wanted to move.

Finally she brought Bradlee in as deputy managing editor, an idea that pleased neither Wiggins nor Friendly, nor, for that matter, Bradlee. There was no fixed timetable for the succession, but in her mind Bradlee would probably take over in a few years. When she explained this to Bradlee he was very cool about it, he had no desire to become number three at the *Post* under Wiggins and then to wait for three or four years. A deputy managing editor's job is crap, he told her. She answered that perhaps she could cut the time to one or two years. "Make it a year," Bradlee said. But there was no final date set and when he went to work at the *Post* in August 1965 she believed that Bradlee would succeed Friendly in a year or two. The first thing Bradlee did was tell Friendly that he did not intend to wait three years to take over, that he would work hard and loyally for Friendly before that, but that three years was too long, one was the maximum. Don't be in such a hurry, Friendly told him, there's time for you and time for me. Neither clearly heard the other. So, with the date still unresolved, he arrived, charged with energy and ambition, staying up late every night putting out the paper. Lillian Hellman told Tony Bradlee that if Ben went to the *Post* she would lose her husband to his new job, and in a way that was true, it pulled him into a much faster orbit, here was an operation worthy of his energy. He seemed to bloom. It was as if *Newsweek* with its one deadline a week had been too slow for him. When Friendly went on his vacation to Turkey, Bradlee was clearly in charge. When both of them were in the shop there were never any fights, but the tension was enormous. It was only a matter of time.

Ben Bradlee became managing editor of the *Post* in November 1965. He had taken out Al Friendly in only three months. Anyone who in later years was surprised to find out how tough Kay Graham could be in dealing with problems need only have looked at the Bradlee ascension. She had, some two years after her husband's suicide, though still very unsure of herself and still very uncomfortable with her role, changed the top level of the *Post* management, removing the closest friend she had in the business and putting a new man in, a man who had in the previous family division seemed to be on the other side. It was her first act of independence, and she had moved very quickly and decisively once she had made up her mind.

The Washington *Post* that Ben Bradlee took over in 1965 was a good and genteel liberal newspaper. It was not as good as its reputation. It always seemed on the verge of becoming a great newspaper but it was not yet a great paper. Its editorial page was distinguished, but there was a certain softness to its reporting, as if good will and good intentions could substitute for hard work and toughness of mind. It dominated its market in advertising, and the possibility for greatness was there. "Brazil and the *Post* are alike," Bernard Nossiter, a *Post* writer, once said, "they both have a lot of potential." Part of the problem was the financial weakness of the past, which still cast a shadow, part of it was that the top people at the paper all knew each other, they were of the same generation and they liked each other and they all had the same essential attitudes. There was a certain chumminess to their decisions. There was an essential decency to the paper's political outlook: the *Post* clearly wanted the city and the nation and the world to be a better place, and it was, on occasion, prepared to use its news columns to expedite that process if the world seemed a little reluctant to turn in the right direction. It was a paper that very clearly had a moral compass and it did have conscience, much of that coming from Wiggins, a highly moral, forceful man. There was a sense in reading the *Post,* not just the editorial page but the news pages as well, of a paper that cared about right and wrong. Yet it was a very different kind of paper from the one Bradlee wanted. He prided himself that he was above ideology, above politics. He disliked what he considered the liberal do-goodism of the paper, and he constantly told his reporters and editors to take the liberal spin out of their stories. Though Wiggins, who had not even been to college, was much more the product of the meritocracy, it was Bradlee who seemed the more modern man, propelled by enormous career drive, and who produced a paper reflecting it. It was Bradlee who took over the paper at the moment when it was no longer just a family paper but was becoming part of a conglomerate, listed on the big board; when the pressure from the front office for constant increase in profit was relentless. It made the city room a more talented, driven, and cold-blooded place.

Even as the paper became Bradlee's, Wiggins's hand was still there. If he had no control over the front page, much to his consternation, he still controlled the editorial page, and in the decade ahead, the decade of Vietnam, his was to be a strong, clear voice; he was unbending in his belief in the rightness of the American cause, and he locked the paper into the war in a way which

finally embarrassed Mrs. Graham, herself a hawk for a long time. And Russ
Wiggins was a formidable hawk. He was a forceful man, James Russell Wiggins, a man of great intellectual energy and appetite, and he was not a man
to leave others uncertain about where he stood. He was intelligent and endlessly hard-working and he believed there was a moral center to politics, and
that events were all of a piece. If in the years to come some of Bradlee's critics
were bothered by what they considered the paper's flexible morality, there was
nothing flexible about Russ Wiggins's morality. He was a man of stern, almost
rigid belief in right against wrong, in good against evil. A touch of the prairie
preacher to him. Always, Wiggins told younger editors, edit with your hat on.
Which meant that you had to be willing to walk out of a job if the wrong things
were required of you. He was a man of virtue—perhaps, thought one of his
best friends, too much virtue.

He was the man who had given the *Post* its regulations prohibiting
reporters and their spouses from moonlighting and from holding any jobs that
might create a conflict of interest (even while, of course, Phil Graham was
constantly wearing two hats and wheeling and dealing all over town). He hated
disorder, hated dirty desks. He was capable of going through the city room
with a barrel and cleaning off desks. Reporters could not eat or drink coffee
at their desks in the city room. The *Post* had a rule that it did not raid its
competitors, the Washington *Star* or *The New York Times,* for talent (a rule
erected in no small part in self-defense when the paper was poorer). Bradlee
had barely been in office when he went out and raided the *Times* for David
Broder, one of the top political writers in America.

Wiggins was an old-fashioned, almost old-maidish man, a man formed by
a very different era with very different values from those that surged into
American culture in the sixties. A figure more from James Gould Cozzens than
from John Updike. It was not surprising that Thomas Jefferson was his hero,
and he was a serious Jefferson scholar. He was a self-educated man and proud
of it, a voracious reader. It was Russ Wiggins, long before it was fashionable,
who had made the *Post* drop racial designation in stories. He hated gossip in
his paper. He disliked the decay and disrepair of institutions, their inability to
perform as he thought they should. (Chief among his frustrations was the U.S.
Postal Service. Like many Americans he was disgusted by its inability to
deliver mail promptly, and went so far as to conduct a small private war
against it. From his summer house in Maine he sent a letter by post, and on
the same day dispatched another letter, to the same destination, by oxcart.
Predictably, the oxcart won, which pleased James Russell Wiggins no end.) He
did not like most of the assaults being made upon old values; the new definitions of honor and life style and patriotism. This new culture might have been
spawned by the turmoil of the sixties, but he wanted no part of it and he did
not want it in his paper.

In 1969 a young reporter for the Washington *Post* named Carl Bernstein
had noticed a new phenomenon right there in his hometown. Black radio.
There was a 50,000-watt radio station there and it was obviously the central

means of communication within the black community, since what the two white newspapers wrote in terms of black news barely touched the real feeling of the community. This in a real sense was *theirs,* and the texture was rich, and funny, and often angry, and there was a new tone to it. Watch out, honky, we're going to get you now. . . . It was also more sexually explicit than white radio or journalism, there were warnings for Big Mama to watch out, *her man was coming home.* It was, Bernstein immediately decided, an authentic voice, a genuine reflection of the community, blacks talking to blacks without white filters. So he asked to do a magazine piece for *Potomac,* the *Post*'s Sunday magazine, and since Bernstein in that period was very much into his Tom Wolfe phase, he had written a very impressionistic piece liberally sprinkled with quotes from the station and from one of its main disc jockeys. He had handed it in and his editors had liked it, it was at least *different* from what the *Post* usually ran, and it included a photo of a big black disc jockey who seemed to be sweating away while working, which was not exactly what the good white middle-class people of Washington were accustomed to seeing.

Wiggins got an early copy of the magazine a week in advance and he was absolutely appalled and enraged by it—the tone, the sexuality, the not so veiled threats to whites. He immediately investigated whether he could have the entire press run of the magazine destroyed although that turned out to be too expensive. On the Monday before publication, as Bernstein came into the office, he was grabbed by Larry Stern, one of the editors, who said, "Don't go in the office! We've got to go to lunch. Right now! Stay away from Wiggins!" So Bernstein went to lunch with Stern and Nick von Hoffman, and they briefed him on how to behave, the proper level of apology and humility, emphasizing that this was serious, jobs hung in the balance. Otherwise it was still possible that the copies of the magazine might be destroyed. So, properly briefed and properly humble, Carl Bernstein presented himself to J. Russell Wiggins. It was the first time he had ever met Wiggins and he began by saying that he gathered he had made a terrible mistake. "No, young man, it isn't your fault. It's the editors' fault. The editors should have caught this." This type of journalism, Wiggins said, was absolutely wrong. Excessive. "Language like this does not belong in a family newspaper. Why, we're giving credence to this black-power thing. That's racist. We mustn't do that. Carl, this doesn't belong in a newspaper like ours." It was, Bernstein later thought, the almost classic generational story, the sensibility was so different, there were new voices and Russ Wiggins could not listen because he could not hear. It was not a question of whether these were real voices or not, rather in some unconscious way he was deciding what people should know and hear and how wide the range of acceptable voices should be.

There was nothing small or petty about Wiggins. He was humane and essentially liberal, with a shrewd distrust of easy sentimental liberalism, and he was strong, almost rigid. If anything, one friend of his thought, he was finally, with Vietnam, made vulnerable by these strengths—his rock-hard integrity, his old-fashioned patriotism, his love of both country and President.

Like Dean Rusk, he saw China as the great threat in Asia, and the North Vietnamese as the pawns of the Chinese. When Karl Meyer, one of the younger editorial writers, upset by the growing American commitment in Vietnam and the *Post*'s support of it, tried to balance the briefings Wiggins was getting in the White House by putting him in touch with Bernard Fall, the French journalist-historian and Indochinese expert, he found that Fall's warnings met deaf ears. Wiggins did not like either Fall or his arguments. He thought him arrogant and abrasive, and wrote off his strictures as nothing but French chauvinism. The French had failed in Indochina and no Frenchman would ever admit that America could succeed where France had failed.

Vietnam was to Wiggins not a problem of colonialism versus nationalism, but part of a larger cloth; when an attack by the Vietcong took place at Pleiku in February 1965, an incident the Administration seized on to start its long-planned systematic bombing campaign, Wiggins wrote: "The violent words and violent acts of the past few days disclose with dreadful clarity that Vietnam is not an isolated battlefield but a part of a long war that the Communist world seems determined to continue until every vestige of Western power and influence has been driven from Asia." Lyndon Johnson had drawn the lines at Pleiku. So had Russ Wiggins.

Nor did he look back. In June 1965 he took a trip to the Soviet Union and did not like the cold response he received from a North Vietnamese representative there, nor the bellicosity of the Soviet officials and the Soviet press. The trip confirmed what he had already thought, that everything was connected, that we had to stand fast. The *Post* editorial page was committed, and committed with increasing belligerence, to the cause of the Administration. In this moment, in the vacuum created by Phil Graham's death and Kay Graham's still tentative assumption of control of the paper and Bradlee's embryonic attempts to take over the *news* side, Wiggins was the dominating editorial voice. He was the editor, Bradlee was the managing editor; Wiggins no longer could influence reportorial assignments, which frustrated him a good deal, particularly on Vietnam, but he could set the paper's editorial tone. His decision to cast the paper with Lyndon Johnson and the war was significant, for it meant that the most important and liberal voice in Washington fully supported this venture, thus making liberal dissent on the war, be it congressional or journalistic, that much less respectable. It gave the war—and this was of ultimate importance—a crucial liberal imprimatur, and it moved the war's critics that much further away from the center. More, because many of the nation's better newspapers, like the Milwaukee *Journal* and the St. Louis *Post-Dispatch,* took their editorial cue from the *Post* (as their managing editors weighed heavily how *The New York Times* played stories on page one each day), it helped legitimize the war in much of the interior of the country and removed a potentially powerful network of adversaries.

Johnson was aware of how powerful an ally he had gained. He and McNamara and Bundy and Rusk and later Rostow were always available to Wiggins, praising him for what he had written, filling him in on the latest top-secret information. On the phone to him all the time. This was important. As the war progressed, as predicted levels of success failed to materialize, Wiggins did not falter, nor did he have second thoughts. Meanwhile, many of Wiggins's colleagues became more dubious, and tension mounted within the editorial meetings. For the first time there was a genuine undercurrent of hostility. This was something new, a serious split between the editor and an increasingly large number of his editorial writers. By 1967 it was no longer a split but a chasm. A great deal of White House effort went into keeping Wiggins lined up. With a lesser man it might have been seen as playing on his ego, but Russ Wiggins was too fine a man for that, with him it was playing on his patriotism. One day after a reception at the White House, Johnson took Murrey Marder aside and told him that Russ and the editorial page were worth two divisions. Marder passed that on to Wiggins, who looked up, not at all displeased, thought for a second, and then asked, "Did he say *two* divisions?"


Phil Graham had been bothered by the American presence in Vietnam during his final months (he had, in fact, been so irate about it that he had, among other things, begun the conversion of his friend Emmet Hughes from hawk to dove), but his widow was different. She was new at her job, new to grave issues of foreign policy, she liked being respectable, and was very uneasy about being different from the norm. In the highest circles of Washington in 1965, those who dissented on Vietnam were different, were not quite with it, and Katharine Graham did not like being different or not with it. Her relations with Lyndon Johnson were more awkward than anything else. He was very much Phil's friend, and he had not been at ease with her, each had seemed to emphasize the other's awkwardness. She had liked the earthiness in Lyndon; once in the late fifties she had visited the ranch with Phil, and Lyndon had first decided to work on her and then decided she was a typical eastern liberal, a little too refined. "Do you know how civil rights came to Johnson City?" he had asked. "Well, there was this road gang and they had these niggers working on it, and the town bully said, 'Get those niggers out of here by sundown.' But the foreman of the gang was getting a haircut, and he was a big man, and he went down the street and he beat the hell out of the town bully. And every time he punched him he would ask, 'Can my niggers spend the night here?' What! 'Can my niggers stay?' and that's how civil rights came to Johnson City." She was at once enchanted and intimidated by him, he was very much a part of a world she feared and which Phil seemed so much at ease with. Lyndon had not gone to Phil's services, he had an absolute dread of funerals, and now he seemed awkward with her. On occasion he would tell her how much he missed Phil, how much he owed him, but there was little transfer of friendship. That bothered her, she felt she should be closer to him than she was, and for a time she wrote him a series of flattering notes about how well he was doing, how pleased she was with his choice of Hubert Humphrey at the convention. ("I thought hard about four years ago yesterday and today but I felt that unlike

Phil—*I* should not offer *you* political advice. I did want you to know how great it was, and how well done. Devotedly . . .")

But although Johnson was not at ease with her, he had other connections to her; McNamara was an old and close family friend, he dined regularly at her house, too regularly, some of her staff thought, and was a close personal adviser; years later she told friends rather innocently that she could not believe that he would lie or mislead her on questions of policy. (In fact, she told an interviewer for the Johnson Library that she became disillusioned with the war "when he got rid of McNamara in that really terrible way.") Bundy was a friend too, and the White House was not above using that connection. Of her immediate circle, Walter Lippmann was the only person who was not going along, but Walter was offset by Joe Alsop, who, in a family-tribal sense, was closer to her than Lippmann. Alsop was obsessed by the war and talked about it incessantly, though in fact he was wrong in almost everything he said or wrote. So she was at the start hawkish. Everyone said that the job had to be done and so Kay said that it had to be done. In 1965 she made a world tour with Oz Elliott that included a stop in Vietnam; the trip had begun in the White House, where Lyndon had told them what he hoped they would see. In Vietnam, to the dismay of some *Newsweek* staffers, Elliott seemed to be very sold on the war and the high-level mumbo jumbo of the generals. As Oz was sold, so was Kay. She came home and talked with members of the editorial board and some of them were dismayed by her tone. It was as if she had made a USO tour out there, it was all so wonderful.

Which meant that the only thing that might balance and potentially neutralize the editorial effect of the *Post* was the reporting from Vietnam. But here the *Post* was surprisingly weak. Vietnam had become a major issue while the *Post* was making the transition from a small staff to a major one. *The New York Times* had employed a staff reporter in Vietnam from the moment when Kennedy had escalated from 600 to 15,000 troops at the end of 1961 and it had frequently kept two reporters there. The *Post* did not send a full-time reporter until 1964. That was still the Wiggins-Friendly era and Friendly sent a young man named John Maffre, who was chosen not because he was the ablest reporter on the staff—he was in fact somewhat untested—but because he was, first, a Canadian and second, an ex-Air Force officer, as if somehow the former quality would give him added detachment and the latter would liberate him from the tension that had marked the relationship between most reporters and most government officials in Vietnam. Maffre's work did not stir the hearts of his employers and he did not stay there long, nor did he stay with the paper long after his return.

The play was to Bradlee. He was new at the paper; by the end of 1965, when Vietnam was becoming the major story in the world, he was just taking over as managing editor. Vietnam seemed very distant to him. He was not particularly interested in foreign affairs. Besides, despite his friendship with Kennedy, which was largely personal—a winner covering a winner, a Wasp patrician covering an Irish patrician—Bradlee was an almost totally apolitical person. Politics did not interest him much in the classic sense that they reflected different values and attitudes; he was interested in politics tactically, as he might be in a football game—who was ahead, who was behind, who was gaining. Politics was like sports. He prided himself on not having political attitudes and political commitments and he was deeply suspicious of those who did, which meant, in the world of journalism, younger reporters who might be too committed to causes, who might, in his phrase, try to put spin on a story. In the early days of the war he had no sympathy for the reporters in Vietnam who were challenging the official (Kennedy) version; he thought they were spinners, and he did not like the fact that a lot of their coverage was political. It was a war, you covered a war. There was more than a little traditional patriotism to him too; he greatly admired acts of courage, even as ends in themselves. Bradlee was, for all his intuitive sense of people, his extraordinary antennae, his Harvard background, a very old-fashioned journalist, like a man from another generation. He liked straight and simple stories, crime stories, stories with a measure of sex appeal to them, stories that did not necessarily have larger implications. He did not like issue stories and he was wary of the path that they took reporters on. He was to become a very successful editor at the *Post* in part because, in the words of a friend, he was a wondrously elegant man with wondrously common taste. He hated things that were dull, that slowed him down; issues, more often than not, were dull. He did not like having political opinions, he did not think it becoming to the editor of a major paper; whatever his thoughts on Vietnam, he kept them to himself. Once at a meeting of her top editors, Kay Graham went around the room asking each editor what he thought about Vietnam. When she came to Bradlee he refused to answer, and there was a quick verbal scuffle between them, she kept insisting that he give an opinion and he kept ducking, and it was briefly a tense moment. He simply would not yield.

Ben Bradlee was, in fact, irreverent in style rather than substance, in language but not in deed. He had, by the standards of his upbringing, many near-Bohemian friends—Irwin Shaw, Art Buchwald, lawyer Edward Bennett Williams—but they were very successful as well as unconventional. Like Jack Kennedy, he was one of that wonderful new breed of supremely egocentric men whose charm seems to lie in not taking themselves too seriously. Yet he was also new at the paper, he was just taking command, Vietnam was distant, Wiggins was a hawk, Kay was a hawk, most of her peers were superhawks, the town was filled with hawks, and so, to a large degree, he let Vietnam go by. He almost deliberately did not involve himself. He did not send reporters who had a sharp political cutting edge; the young Carl Bernstein, for example, asked to go as many as four times and was always turned down. In a way Bradlee was very careful whom he sent, and he stayed out of it as an issue and avoided its larger implications. He did not like the reporters who were causing the trouble out there; indeed, the very kind of reporter he would feel closest to and sponsor on Watergate, he felt very alien to on Vietnam. He did not object to employing a reporter he felt was committed to the war, but he was uneasy, as late as 1971, about sending his friend Larry Stern because he knew Stern was against the war. He did not feel the special quality of Vietnam as an issue nor did he feel any particular sympathy for those in America who were reacting to the war.

In 1965 the *Post* was thinking of hiring a talented young man named Steve Zorn, who had just graduated from Berkeley, even then an enclave of political dissent and radicalism. Steve Isaacs, then city editor, a man with a special instinct for talent, who had hired some of the best *Post* reporters of a generation (Bob Kaiser, Peter Osnos, Dick Cohen, Bernstein), was very high on Zorn. In the course of his interview Zorn mentioned that if he were drafted he would leave the United States. That did not bother Isaacs, who told Zorn it was his decision and he could do what he wanted. It never occurred to Isaacs that Bradlee would be offended, but he was, intensely so, it offended his sense of patriotism. "There's no way I'm going to hire that son of a bitch," he said, "he's not a patriot." Isaacs and Bradlee argued at length, Isaacs claiming that a reporter had as much right to a conscience as anyone else, and at the end of it, Bradlee, to his credit, went to see his boyhood friend the Reverend Paul Moore, who later became bishop of Washington, and a man profoundly affected by the war. Bradlee spent half the night talking over the problem of the draft and personal conscience with Moore. Moore was an ex-Marine, so his alien ways were more legitimate to Bradlee. The next day Bradlee told Isaacs he had changed his mind, they could hire Zorn, but there was one small hooker: Zorn first had to see Russ Wiggins. Zorn and Wiggins did not seem an ideal couple to Isaacs, who warned Zorn what was ahead. "The hell with this. I don't want to work for any goddamn paper that puts me through something like this," Zorn said, and went and took a job with the Boston *Globe,* where he did quite well before going on to take a Ph.D.


The *Post* never made a commitment to cover the war with any real intensity; as *The New York Times* was to fail on Watergate almost seven years later, in large part out of failure to commit itself, so the *Post* failed on Vietnam. By 1965, with the beginning of the American combat commitment, the *Times* had expanded to a three-man bureau. Nor was it just any three men. It was an all-star bureau of three exceptionally talented reporters, two of whom were already experienced Vietnam hands and who had a sense of the political limitations of Americans on Indochinese soil. The bureau chief was Charles Mohr, who had resigned from *Time* over its coverage of the war, intelligent, tough, a great war reporter, perhaps the closest thing now on the paper to the legendary Homer Bigart; the other two reporters were Neil Sheehan, who had in 1963, at the age of twenty-six, been the boy wonder of UPI and who had just barely missed a Pulitzer for his reporting, and who perhaps more than any other American reporter in Vietnam had a sense of what the experience of the French Indochina war had done to the present conflict; and Johnny Apple (his by-line read R. W. Apple), fresh from national politics, a talented young reporter whose star was still ascending, hustling, brash, full of himself, very quick and very energetic. It was a formidable bureau, all three men were stars and it typified what made *The New York Times* a great newspaper. From the start the *Times* had staffed Vietnam and sent its best reporters there, it had not stinted on resources and it kept men there even when the story seemed to be dying. Long after the American troops had left, and with them most American reporters, the *Times* kept a two- and three-person bureau. It had depth and it had talent and this showed in its coverage of Vietnam. It won its first Pulitzer for Vietnam in 1964, before the American combat troops arrived, and it won its last in 1976, after they had gone.

Against this, the *Post*'s coverage was for the most part very ordinary and very conventional. The one exception to it was the reporting by Ward Just, which was brilliant in its sense of mood. Just, a protégé of Bradlee, almost the first person he had brought over from *Newsweek,* was probably the most talented writer on the paper. Perhaps no reporter working for a major daily paper wrote as well from Vietnam or with as much subtlety and grace as he did. His were stories of men at war, and they were wonderful, in the best sense timeless. But Just was in no sense a political writer and this was a political war; he did not want to be another Teddy White or John Gunther, he wanted to be a novelist and in fact he became a very good one. In Vietnam he was a reporter in search of Hemingway. He was fascinated by the bravery of men at war and he took exceptional risks in combat. Bradlee loved his stories, they were part of the new *Post,* not stodgy but alive and human, they had impact, they caught people's attention. But at least in the beginning they were not about the essential issue of the war, the fact that no matter how brave the Americans were it was finally not our country, that nothing we did worked, and that the other side simply kept coming. He caught the bravery well, but not for a good while the fact that it was wasted bravery. That was the key story and for a long time the *Post* missed it.

It was only gradually that Just's stories began to have a second level of impact. Not in the first months or even the first year, but gradually. In part it was his darkening vision of the war, and the futility of it, in part it was the simple cumulative effect of the individual stories—so much heroism but no real victories. In June 1966, after a year in Vietnam, a year of almost reckless personal bravery, he was with a long-range reconnaissance patrol of the 101st Airborne near Dak Tho when it was ambushed and overrun. He was badly wounded, hit with fragments of a grenade in the back and legs. Just minimized his own wounds at the time and when the medevac chopper came in, he made sure that the enlisted men went out first, which enhanced his reputation greatly with the military. He came out of Vietnam for a few months and then when he returned his stories grew even darker, it was as if the wound had liberated him in his own mind, it was his own red badge of courage, he no longer had to feel partially guilty about being some Ivy League kid straphanging around real men who were fighting a real war.

When Just came back to Washington for his brief R & R in 1966, Bradlee was very pleasant and warm, but they did not, of course, discuss the war. That was not in the cards. They were as close as reporter and editor could be. Just was a protégé, a favorite son, and Bradlee was enormously pleased by his stories, by the fact that you could not tell what Just thought of the war from his stories. But Vietnam was still not something he thought very much about or wanted to know very much about. That Vietnam was beginning to divide and tear apart the paper, just as it was dividing and tearing apart the city and the nation, did not really affect him. Yet while the top level of the paper was committed to the war, in the working echelon there was increasing doubt, then dissatisfaction, and finally dissension. In December 1966, when Harrison Salisbury of *The New York Times* went to North Vietnam, some of the *Post*'s younger reporters were dismayed by how their own paper responded. Chalmers Roberts, the senior national security reporter and the very embodiment of an establishment reporter, wrote that Ho Chi Minh, by admitting Salisbury, was trying out a new tactic, "one as clearly conceived as the poison-tipped bamboo spikes his men emplanted underfoot for the unwary enemy. . . ."

When Just came back in 1966 after being wounded, several somewhat dovish people on the *Post* had suggested that he go by and talk with Wiggins. They thought that even if Just could not persuade him to change, which was not particularly likely, and in any case Just was certainly no dove, he might at least soften Wiggins and give him a sense of the complexity of the war. Wiggins, as it turned out, was not pleased with Just's reporting, he thought it too flashy and too little given to support of the war; in sum, too vaguely pessimistic. They did not have a successful conversation. An eavesdropper might have thought that it was Wiggins who had been out in Vietnam, and Just who had been writing from Washington. Just did not seem to be able to finish a sentence, most of the talking was done by Wiggins. If Just had his war, and it was messy and endless and probably not going very well, then Wiggins had *his* war, and it was a war he had heard about from the highest sources in the land, from the most secret of cables, and he backed it up with a thousand precedents from other wars, be it French and Indian or Boer. His was a paper war, and it was winnable. There was a long lecture from Wiggins to Just on responsibility and patriotism, admonitions against losing sight of the real issues and the big picture. It was as if they were talking about different countries and different wars. In a way Wiggins was right: if the war had been fought on paper he would have won and the war would have been won. It was not his fault that it was being fought in Indochina, among the rice paddies.

Bradlee at the time was fighting a war of his own, and Vietnam was very distant from his thoughts. For if his first major victory at the *Post* was his lightning conquest of Al Friendly, then a far greater internal struggle was now beginning to take place, the battle with the *Post*'s business side. The *Post* by 1966 had been successful for a dozen years, and yet very little of the profits had been pumped back into the paper. Phil Graham had not hesitated to pour money into *Newsweek* but he had not done so at the *Post,* and he had been sick, and during his sickness there was a vacuum, which meant that John Sweeterman, the business manager, dominated. Sweeterman was strong and able and he knew far more about the mechanical side of the paper than either Wiggins or Friendly, and also of course more about the financial side. But Bradlee represented a new era. He had come to the paper when it was extremely profitable, he believed that the key to a new, more effective *Post* was talent, and he had to be able to hire good young reporters and open new bureaus. The first thing he had told Kay Graham when she was thinking of bringing him over from *Newsweek* was that, if she was serious, she had to freeze all vacancies on the paper until he arrived. Which she did, but that was only a beginning. Bradlee had gone to his first budget meeting with Sweeterman, and Sweeterman, smart and informed, had eaten him alive and spit out the pieces. Bradlee had not done his homework, he had been talking ideas and ideals, and Sweeterman had been talking facts. Sweeterman was marvelous with figures, he could in one breath make the *Post* seem the best-run and most successful newspaper in the country, and in the next breath, without any change of voice or loss of credibility, could show how vulnerable the entire operation was, how inflation was eating the profits away.

The first time, the ball game had gone to Sweeterman, and Bradlee, with his great visions of his own new empire, of many foreign correspondents (in spite of the fact that foreign news bored him), had settled for one foreign reporter. The next year Bradlee prepared himself; he studied the finances of the paper as no editorial executive before him had ever done, he studied the mechanical side too, and he knew where the fat was; he knew what correspondents cost, and what he was entitled to. He had a further advantage in the fact that he could deal readily and easily with Kay Graham and Sweeterman could not; Sweeterman was awkward with her. Ben Bradlee made plain that he had been anointed by her, and that she had committed herself to the idea of a great national newspaper. He made sure that in the ensuing months Sweeterman heard his ideas—from Kay's mouth. That was his ace. He had charmed her at the first lunch and kept right on doing it. He allowed her to be publisher without being uncomfortable. He could tell her to go to hell in a way that absolutely delighted her. He was her editor and yet he did not seem to need her or be dependent upon her. That was a sure sign of his worthiness. More, he *was* delivering, the paper seemed alive; she had the feeling that Bradlee had opened the windows. When he put resources into the paper there seemed to be almost a direct tangible result, an almost immediate display of dramatic exciting stories. Which was not surprising, Bradlee believed above all in the star system and the best thing about the star system was the immediacy of its impact, it was high-visibility journalism, a hot reporter on a big story; this was very different from building a paper slowly, piece by piece.

In the year since he had taken over, their relationship had become stronger and stronger. That Ben Bradlee, she would say, he makes me laugh. He was particularly good with her on that score. The moment she felt fear or uncertainty in a man's attitude toward her, she lost her respect for him, as many a high executive of the Washington Post Company learned, but not Bradlee. His own personal self-image, developed long before he went to the *Post,* simply did not permit him to show fear. He could at once tease her, stay outside her reach, and never seem beholden to her. Bradlee, she told many of her friends, reminded her of Phil. By that she meant the good days. There was an unofficial luncheon club that Bradlee belonged to, Ben and Ed Williams and Art Buchwald, and they often asked her to join them and they amused her. It was a wonderful club, there was a Wasp and a Jew and a Catholic, and there was talk of making her a member, the first woman member, but each time they voted she was blackballed, and Art said he had voted for her, and Ed said he had voted for her, and Ben said he had voted for her. (When in 1978 Bradlee married Sally Quinn, his long-time lady friend, the three witnesses at the ceremony were Buchwald, Williams, and Kay Graham.) It was great fun. Scotty Reston, she said, Scotty who had been the preeminent journalist of Washington and whom she had thought of giving the paper to, Scotty isn't much fun, is he? So her relationship with Bradlee was strong and, in an increasingly corporate age in journalism, intensely personal. It was a source of special power for Bradlee: challenging him was like challenging Kay. Their relationship, close friends thought, was unconsciously almost sexual. When she was around he seemed to strut just a little bit more, his walk, already jaunty, became a little jauntier, his voice, rough and raspy, became a little rougher and a little raspier. She, the same friends thought, seemed almost schoolgirlish. No wonder Tony Bradlee did not like Kay Graham, and no wonder that Kay Graham did not like *her.* When Bradlee was trying to put together a new Style section and she was pushing him a little too hard, he had turned to her and said, "I can't edit this section unless you get your fucking finger out of my eye," and she had loved that. Ben Bradlee, it turned out, had one special skill that other talented journalists lacked: the ability to evoke from Kay Graham, a woman of both great intelligence and great personal uncertainty, most of what he wanted from her; to make her be what he wanted her to be.

John Sweeterman, being very smart, was very much aware of this. Bradlee had let Sweeterman know, in a very pleasant way, that Kay was on his side. It meant that Bradlee had a great card, a card that Sweeterman did not want Bradlee to play. He did not want a confrontation that he might lose in front of other executives; if he lost to Bradlee he might lose elsewhere. Bradlee made his demands, and outlined what they were going to accomplish for the paper, and these were big numbers, a jump in the budget of several million dollars over a very brief period. Sweeterman quickly gave in. The first time it happened the other executives sitting there had been spellbound, stunned by the change in the tide, and Harry Gladstein, the circulation manager, had scribbled a note on a piece of paper and passed it to a friend: "Score: Bradlee 100. Sweeterman 0." At the end of it, Bradlee had turned and smiled at Sweeterman and said, "A pleasure to do business with you, John." Sweeterman had been vanquished. More victories followed. It set the tone for the future; for the first time in the modern era the editorial side of the *Post* had power equal to that of the business side. It was a crucial moment. The paper was rich, it was unchallenged in its circulation area, it had a publisher and an editor committed to a new dimension of excellence which the publisher was willing to pay for. Journalism of excellence was becoming expensive, and for the first time the *Post* was willing to meet the price. Thenceforward, year after year, Bradlee dominated those meetings; it was not altogether surprising that three years after Bradlee joined the *Post* Sweeterman asked for early retirement. At the end of one annual budget meeting, Gladstein, who, like Sweeterman, was a vice-president, had turned to an editor and said, "That Bradlee. He never loses. I've never beaten him and no one else has."

Benjamin Crowninshield Bradlee, a man of great ability and talent, of extraordinary quick insights and highly tuned instincts, was accustomed to being on the winning side. He had little patience for people he did not think were smart or who could not verbalize their intelligence. He was a man lucky in his choice of profession. Academe was not for him, he lacked the patience for slow, dogged, serious work; journalism, with its adoration of the new at the expense of the old, was exactly right. That or perhaps criminal law; it was not by chance that one of his two or three closest friends was Ed Williams, the noted criminal lawyer. So journalism it was, though it was not a choice his parents had been particularly pleased with. It was not a profession for people of their kind. That was a line from the Bradlee household: *We don't see people of that kind. People like us don't go to countries like that. We don't do that sort of thing.*

He was, of course, upper-class. It was always there, even when he was pretending it wasn't, even when he was playing his street-smart role; it was there in the walk, that little strut, and in the voice. He was simply showing that he was so good he didn't need to flaunt it. After Watergate, when his very considerable success was assured, when Watergate had made him the most famous editor in the world, he talked semi-wistfully with friends of how at times he wished he had come from a Jewish ghetto, then he would be sure he had made it on his own, pure and simple (a willingness to exchange backgrounds that probably would have been snapped at by most people who had sprung from ghettos). A few years ago a researcher found out that one of the family names, Crowninshield, might originally be Kronenfeld or something similar, and he might be part Jewish. He was inordinately pleased, not unlike Lyndon Johnson, who was always trying to make his origins seem humbler than they actually were.

His father was Frederick Josiah Bradlee, known as Be, a much-admired and much-loved man, a great Harvard football player, All-American in 1914. He was very Bostonian. He felt ill at ease and uncomfortable in other cities, as if deprived of his surroundings and roots. He was not a particular success in business, but in his early years he did not need to be. He came from a reasonably wealthy family, and there was family money, though by the rules of trust funds he did not come into it until rather late in his life. He had married Josephine deGersdorff, and her people were even more high-powered than his. They were New Yorkers, which in Boston was a little suspect. Her father was the deGersdorff of one of the great New York law firms, then called Cravath, deGersdorff, Swain and Wood. Her mother was a Crowninshield, as was his maternal grandmother, so they were distant cousins, which made the respective families that much more willing to accept the match. By contrast with the deGersdorff-Crowninshield clan, Be Bradlee seemed a little conventional. Josey deGersdorff Bradlee was an ambitious driving woman, goals set, goals attained. When she had been at the Chapin School in New York she had gotten the best marks there ever. She was a woman of formidable self-discipline, ambitious for herself, ambitious for her three children. Saturday was given over to lessons so that the young Bradlees would measure up to her expectations and the expectations of the right people everywhere. French lesson at nine o'clock. Piano lesson at ten. Riding at eleven. Skating, if there was ice, at noon. Every Saturday. Ben Bradlee hated Saturdays. His memories of his mother were not especially fond; it was his father he loved, and he could recall that when Be Bradlee was quite old he had said to his son, "You know I've always loved you." "That's the one thing in my life I've always been sure of," Ben Bradlee had answered.

In 1932, Be Bradlee's brokerage job collapsed. Up until then they had been very comfortable. In those Depression years it was Josey Bradlee who carried the family; she had a rather generous allowance from her family through trust funds, about $5,000 a year, and during the bad years she gave up her singing (she loved to sing and had given recitals) and took a job at a dress shop, where she made some more money. Quietly, power in the Bradlee family passed from Be to Josey; she made the decisions, and his drinking stepped up a little. They had moved to a house in Beverly that was owned by the Lowells and was offered to them, as friends, rent-free. It was a huge sprawling place, and Be Bradlee in effect became the caretaker of the property, he chopped wood and he made and repaired furniture; there was a series of jobs provided by friends. Be Bradlee worked hard to retain his dignity in what was a difficult and painful time for him. (Ben Bradlee always hated Wall Street. It was, he felt, the place that had wounded his father. As an editor, he distrusted it and he often encouraged his reporters to break the big one there, the big scandal, there surely was a Pulitzer in it.)

The fall from financial grace did not affect the young Bradlee directly. He went off to St. Mark's, an excellent school favored by Bostonians of the better sort, where he was doing very well in all things when in 1936 a terrible epidemic of polio struck. At least thirty students caught the disease, including Bradlee. He was very sick for several months and when he recovered it was clear that he was no longer going to be a great athlete. His legs were weaker, he had lost a crucial step or two in speed (though he is still an exceptional tennis player he almost never plays; he cannot bear to play below his own expectations). Two things happened as a result of the polio. First, he was forced to read a great deal, to use up the extra time created by his illness, and second, he had to work hard to build himself up; in consequence he developed an abnormally powerful chest and shoulders, which made him seem even stronger and more powerful and which added to his *macho* look.

He went on to Harvard, as father and grandfather and great-grandfather and great-great-grandfather had before him, joining the right clubs. He was bored with Harvard as many well-bred young men are. The one interest he might have had was athletics and that, because of the polio, was out. His interests were narrow. "Before the war I didn't give a shit about anything," he once said. He was in fact on the very precipice of flunking out. But the war was coming, and he made a choice, not out of character for him; rather than flunk out he would accelerate. He took up classics, which he loved, doubled the number of classes he was taking, and graduated a year ahead of time, in 1942, going immediately into the Navy, which put him into destroyer duty in the Pacific, gave him nine battle stars, and changed him.

World War II for those upper-class young men like Bradlee who survived was at once a toughening and liberating experience. He had gotten married just as he entered the Navy, to a Saltonstall, but by the time he returned it was over. He did not want to go back and do conventional things, go to an office, make the allotted amount of money working the allotted amount of hours in the allotted office. Some friends of his were going to start a new daily newspaper in New Hampshire to challenge William Loeb's reactionary paper, and he raised some money and joined them. Almost everybody else connected with the paper was an executive and the staff turned out to be Bradlee. In particular, he became the hot exposé reporter. Bradlee found that he liked the work. He also became restless for a slightly larger pond, and got a job at eighty dollars a week on the Washington *Post*. He stayed there three years, covering police and courts, and he had loved it, but he had also felt very frustrated. The national staff was tiny, the waiting list endless. He had finally quit and gone to Paris, where a friend had promised him work as a press attaché in the embassy. His work as press attaché was not memorable except for one moment in 1953 when Cohn and Schine made their famous tour of Europe in search of left-wing books in American libraries. They wanted a press conference and so Bradlee had set up a press conference, and because feeling among Americans and journalists in Europe was far more bitter about McCarthy than in America, he had prepared a real ambush. He had called every reporter in town, particularly those that he knew hated McCarthy, and some sixty reporters of various nationalities had shown up. The very first question had been from Sy Friedin of the *Herald Tribune*. "How the hell old are you, Schine?" he had asked. The next question was from the Reuters man, and he had asked in as British a manner as he could, "Mister Cohn, are you happy in your work?" It had gone downhill from there.

Bradlee switched eventually from the embassy to *Newsweek*, from Paris to Washington, to the Kennedy connection. His first marriage broken, he fell in love with and married an absolutely beautiful young woman named Tony Pinchot. (The event occasioned a small epiphany for his brother, Fred. Before the wedding, they were dining together one night and Ben began explaining why he meant to marry Tony. "Fred," he said, "I guess I just need a pretty blonde to tell me I'm marvelous around the clock." Until then Fred had always regarded Ben as something like a Mack truck, rolling over anything in his way, always successful, admirable but not entirely lovable. Suddenly he seemed to Fred Bradlee, whose own life had been very different and a good deal more difficult, possessed by the same uncertainties as other men.) The Washington *Post* came next. And now, as never before, it was all up to him.


The first thing he did, given victory over Sweeterman and the budget bosses, was to hire an uncommonly talented staff. He was young himself and he knew where all the bright young reporters were. He had a special feeling for talent. He brought over Ward Just and Phil Carter from *Newsweek;* Stan Karnow (who had been with *Time* and *The Saturday Evening Post*), David Broder from *The New York Times.* Nick von Hoffman came from the Chicago *Daily News* to serve as the house iconoclast. Von Hoffman, impressed by the paper's huge, brightly lit, somewhat sterile city room, looked at his new office for the first time, turned to Bradlee, and asked: "Do they take American Express?" Suddenly bureaus were opened everywhere, the paper was on the move. It was a wonderful, expansive time, when everything was possible, when everyone was a star, when, if *The New York Times* was larger and bulkier and more respectable, there was a belief that the *Post* was better, livelier, more exciting. It was the successor to the *Herald Tribune,* a writer's paper. Impact, Bradlee said, he wanted everyone to have impact. That and relevance. He was, in the early days, always quoting Lippmann on the need for newspapers to be relevant (and in almost the same breath deriding foreign news). He was openly critical and almost contemptuous of the old regime, they had put out a slow and dowdy paper, and he would not be accused of that. When Bradlee had been a young reporter he had felt the *Post* paid too little attention to its young reporters. He was determined to give talent a chance.

He dominated the paper, a driving, charming, charismatic force. He seemed to want strong deputy editors under him, but in truth he was the only real editor in the paper's hierarchy. He was a man of extraordinary sensitivity and very real humanity, who seemed, in the words of one associate, to control his humanity ruthlessly, protecting himself rigorously against himself. When someone at the *Post* no longer measured up, it was not an entirely pleasant experience, it was as if Bradlee did not quite see the person any more. His style dominated the daily news conferences. He was bright and quick and verbal, wonderful with one-liners, and soon his subeditors seemed to mirror this, they knew what interested him and they became bright and quick and verbal and good with one-liners. The problem with this, of course, was that the news conference was where you should explore ideas and concepts, and should be free to stumble, and where you should not necessarily seek a laugh line. Bradlee seemed bored with that kind of talk. The meetings became a reflection of his style, everyone emulating him, everyone coming up with a tart skeptical phrase.

If Bradlee wanted to increase impact, he wanted also to reduce the "liberal" tilt in the news columns. Bradlee saw as his main opponent in this area Ben Gilbert, the old city editor. Gilbert had been the chief instrument of Phil Graham's will at the local level. He was smart, knowing, abrasive, feared by much of the staff, and by far the hardest-working news executive on the paper. He did not go to the genteel Georgetown dinner parties; his world was harder and less social. Much of the staff disliked him; his orders always seemed to be shouted, and it was office legend that he smiled at a reporter only twice, once when he hired him and once when he fired him. He was a man who had been victimized by prejudice himself, and he was passionate in his desire for racial progress. He was proud of the fact that in the late forties and early fifties, when Washington was totally segregated, the *Post,* at his and Phil Graham's direction, had worked to integrate the city, and do it with the minimum of hatred and passion. That was not the worst thing a paper could do, he thought, fight for racial justice, before it was fashionable. But if there was some sympathy for that attitude in the city room, for the belief that a newspaper needed moral coordinates, it was diminishing as the sixties moved along. There had been integration, there had been racial change, but there were now also, clearly, serious social problems arising from that change. The old attitudes, it appeared, were making the *Post* blind to resulting new racial tensions. Stories about racial riots after a football game between a black high school and a white high school for the city championship were sanitized. A story about white migration from the inner city because of problems in the school system was killed. The story had come from the city's health department and had been written by Morton Mintz, one of the most respected and most socially conscious reporters on the paper. "No goddamn clerk at the D.C. Health Department is going to set policy for the *Post,*" Gilbert said.

That was it, *policy.* An unofficial policy of encouraging good things, and discouraging bad ones. Much of it had come from Phil Graham. It was precisely what Bradlee had disliked so much about the old *Post,* and he put most of the blame for it on Gilbert. There was one memorable moment of confrontation during the 1968 riots in Washington that followed the assassination of Martin Luther King. In the middle of the riot a *Post* photographer came back with a brilliant photo showing a white clothing-store owner and two of his friends waiting inside the store, holding shotguns. The scene was framed, it seemed, by shards of glass from the window. Bradlee saw it and loved it, all the drama and tension and fear in the riot were in that photo. "Page one!" he shouted, and Gilbert, just as quickly, shouted, "No!" There was to him in that photo an inflammatory incitement to passion and anger. So they screamed at each other, and though there had been arguments before, there had never been anything as violent as this. For a moment it looked as if Bradlee might push

Gilbert's head through a pillar, it was so heated. Finally the picture ran on page one—though not quite so large as Bradlee had wanted it.

What really embittered Gilbert was the way Bradlee handled the story saying that Lyndon Johnson was going to name Walter Washington mayor of Washington. Walter Washington was black and he was Ben Gilbert's closest friend, and Gilbert used to tell people that back in the days before Washington became mayor, he used to come by Gilbert's house every night for coffee and the two of them would talk. In 1967 it was very clear that, as the city achieved a larger amount of home rule, Johnson intended to appoint Washington. Gilbert, knowing how Johnson reacted when news of appointments leaked out, wanted nothing in the paper. Joe Califano and Harry McPherson had even come to the *Post* from the White House to clear the appointment, privately and off the record, at a luncheon. Bradlee said they ought to run the story— he had assigned a reporter who got the story on her own—but Gilbert argued against it. He was furious, and afraid that his friend Washington would lose the job if the story ran. He called Califano to enlist his aid, and Califano in turn called Kay Graham to try to kill the story. If you run it, Califano said, it won't happen. But Mrs. Graham backed Bradlee; it was not, she said, the *Post*'s job to make Walter Washington mayor. The decision marked a change in attitude toward local news at the top level of the *Post*. Johnson was predictably furious, and held the appointment up for several months before finally announcing it. Eventually Gilbert left the paper, somewhat bitter at Bradlee. He had represented one era on the *Post* and there was no place for him in the new era. He sometimes complained to friends that he did not know what Bradlee really believed in or what his activism was. Perhaps, he said, the only thing he really believed in was the Washington Redskins.

Washington had turned out to be the worst possible city from which to follow the war in Vietnam, particularly for men steeped in the codes and attitudes of another generation. Russ Wiggins could only see what the most powerful people were seeing, and it blinded him. As 1966 passed and 1967 came along and domestic conflict intensified over the progress of the war and whether or not it was winnable, the *Post* editorial meetings became increasingly unhappy. There was mounting dissent from other editorial writers, and at one point it appeared that Wiggins, who had always held sway by virtue of his moral and intellectual authority as well as his position, might stand alone on this issue. For a time Alan Barth argued with Wiggins, but he made no headway, this was not the Supreme Court, they were contending on Wiggins's own ground. So Barth simply pinned up a huge photo of atrocities in Vietnam—an ARVN half-track dragging the body of a dead Vietcong. It was his form of dissent. Others followed—Selig Harrison, Harvey Siegel, Steve Rosenfeld, recently returned from Moscow. But they did not dent Wiggins; as his onetime colleagues began to desert him, Wiggins, some friends thought, became even more jingoistic. Like Lyndon Johnson, he was hunkering down.

In early 1967 Kay Graham decided to hire Phil Geyelin for the editorial page. Wiggins was to retire at the end of 1968 and Geyelin was clearly arriving as the heir apparent; there was no doubt that the choice of Geyelin marked Mrs. Graham's own disillusionment with Wiggins and in part with the war. Geyelin, who had worked for the *Wall Street Journal* Washington bureau, was one of those people everyone in journalism tried to hire. He was a Philadelphia Main Liner, very smart and very sophisticated and very subtle, and he exuded a kind of class rarely found among working reporters. *The New York Times* had tried to hire him and the Los Angeles *Times* had offered him a job writing foreign-policy articles, but he did not think he could write from that base, and there had been talk of him taking another top job there. The *Post* had tried to get him on other occasions. Geyelin, unlike most Washington journalists writing about Vietnam, had been there several times and had grave reservations about the war; he did not think it could be won, not in any manner acceptable to a democracy. He was thus quite critical of the war, but in a very genteel civilized way that did not seem offensive to people who were for the war. He had, in 1965, published a highly prophetic book about Johnson that antedated Vietnam but that warned of qualities in Johnson which might cause him trouble overseas. It was not a book that Johnson had read but he had hated it anyway, and Geyelin was, to him, an enemy. Johnson lumped Bradlee and Geyelin, who were close friends, together. He called them the Stacomb kids: that meant Georgetown smart boys, eastern Ivy League kids, Kennedy favorites. He sensed Bradlee condescended to him in private and he was right. (Bradlee referred to him as "old Clyde over there," and on occasion as "L B and J." The element of putdown was unmistakable. Johnson, for his part, had always disliked Bradlee. At one point, in 1964, when Johnson was thinking of replacing J. Edgar Hoover at the FBI, Bill Moyers had leaked the story to Bradlee. Bradlee had gone into print with it, and Johnson had immediately called a press conference, and there, before the assembled television cameras, he had announced the appointment of J. Edgar Hoover for life. When it was over Johnson had turned to Moyers and said, "Now call up your friend Ben Bradlee and tell him I said, 'Fuck you.' " For years after Bradlee was known as the man who got J. Edgar Hoover a lifetime appointment.) As Johnson had earlier regarded the arrival of Bradlee at the *Post* as a dangerous ascension, the rise of a Kennedy loyalist, he now watched the arrival of Geyelin with even greater dissatisfaction. He liked the *Post* the way it was, with Russ Wiggins in charge. And he missed Phil Graham. In 1967 he had seen Alan Barth at a ceremony where he had signed the home-rule bill and he had, much to Barth's surprise, asked him to come by and see him. Barth had once worked for a Beaumont, Texas, paper, and had known Johnson in the old New Deal days, but he was perplexed as to why a busy man like the President wanted to see him. Barth found Johnson in a very troubled and somber mood. He wanted to talk about Vietnam, how difficult it was. "If only *Phil* were still alive . . . *Phil* could deal with this." Gradually it dawned on Barth that Johnson was telling him that he was totally impaled on Vietnam, but that if Phil

Graham were alive, Phil who was the best fixer Lyndon knew, then Phil would think of something, some way out.


When Geyelin was about to go to the *Post* in 1967, Walter Lippmann took him aside. Lippmann was then at a moment of great personal disillusionment. He, almost alone on the upper level of Washington Georgetown society, had dissented and dissented hard on the war, and he had taken a full measure of abuse from the President, and a good deal of additional social unpleasantness. Washington, the city he loved, was no longer very much fun. It had turned cold and heavy. Geyelin was, however, one of his young protégés. Now Lippmann was counseling Geyelin: he should wait for the right moment, go to the mat with Wiggins, and then go to Kay. Force the issue, Lippmann had said, she's picked you, she'll have to back you up. But Geyelin was not at ease with so aggressive a strategy, it was out of character for him. So he went to the *Post* and he and Wiggins struggled with each other for almost a year. It was all very urbane. (Geyelin once told Wiggins that if Wiggins was worth two divisions, then he, Geyelin, was worth a company of Vietcong.) There were never any acrimonious exchanges: Russ Wiggins, Geyelin thought, was a fine and good and honorable man even though he disagreed almost 100 percent with Wiggins over the war.

It was very clear to Geyelin that Johnson and Rusk and Rostow were working Wiggins very hard. There were visits and phone calls and Geyelin was bothered when sometimes he would cite pessimistic information and Wiggins would counter with a more optimistic appraisal, obviously from a very high-level briefing, Johnson or Rostow, he was sure, and then Wiggins would refuse to cite his source, saying he did not feel free to do so, but clearly his source was very high. Geyelin respected Russ Wiggins immensely and did not believe, as some people in Washington did, that Wiggins had been corrupted by a fondness for power. He was too honorable for that. But Wiggins, Geyelin was sure, did have an exaggerated sense of the power and the greatness of the President, and an exaggerated belief in the commitment he owed to a President. He had trusted Presidents in the past and he saw no reason to change.

So they coexisted, despite their sharp arguments over the war. In late 1967 and early 1968 Vietnam obsessed serious Americans and obscured all other issues. Those who believed in the war thought victory just around the corner, others thought it a hopeless stalemate. The *Post* itself, with Ward Just writing his farewell piece from Saigon in almost complete contrast to the editorial optimism, seemed to have a split personality. Just's valedictory in June 1967 had said: "This war is not being won, and by any reasonable estimate, it is not going to be won in the foreseeable future. It may be unwinnable." Lyndon Johnson, who had disliked Just's reporting for a good bit more than a year, sensed he was losing control of the *Post*'s news columns, so he increased the pressure to hold the editorial page, which put more pressure on Geyelin. Sometimes it seemed as if Geyelin's strategy was two steps backward and one step forward. If Wiggins were away, the tone might be softer for a bit; if Geyelin were away, the tone might harden. At the time of the battle of Con Thien in 1967, there was a sharp debate between the two. Geyelin thought (as many high Marine officers believed privately) that it was a grotesque misuse of troops, a grinding down of Marines in static positions, but Wiggins wanted to give Westmoreland anything he wished. There developed between the two men a two-key system: Geyelin could not pass one of his editorials without Wiggins's approval, and Wiggins could not pass one without Geyelin's approval. That meant that Wiggins was still the force on the page but somewhat toned down by Geyelin. They had a very sharp argument when the North Koreans captured the American spy ship *Pueblo*. Wiggins was enraged by the act, Barbary piracy, he was ready to hurl down thunderbolts and wrote a fiery editorial to that effect, damn the torpedoes, full speed ahead. Geyelin, who was not sure that the North Koreans were entirely in the wrong, was concerned mainly about getting our men back. The two argued back and forth. Finally, Geyelin told Wiggins that Wiggins was the editor of the paper but he, Geyelin, was editor of the editorial page, and he would not send the piece to the composing room; if Wiggins wanted it printed, he would have to do it by going past Geyelin. Wiggins was quiet for a moment and then he opened his drawer and put the editorial inside, then slammed the drawer closed and locked it. He looked for a very long time at Geyelin and then said, "In six months I'll take this piece out and prove that you were wrong." Then they went back to their other work, and gradually the anger subsided, and that night Russ Wiggins drove Phil Geyelin home. Russ Wiggins did not personalize things and he was not a man for feuds. But there was no doubt that he hated what was happening.

When Tet came Wiggins was genuinely shaken by it; it had caught him by surprise as it had caught most of his prime sources by surprise. But as he was entertaining doubts, he was also constrained by one of the most potent arguments of the Administration, that any writing that reflected doubt aided and abetted the enemy. Weakened the fiber of our boys. Encouraged the dissenters, which rallied the otherwise exhausted enemy. So he stifled his doubts. But Tet had changed the balance of public opinion, and had strengthened Geyelin. Wiggins, like Lyndon Johnson, was falling more and more under siege. The end was coming for both of them; they were both, in effect, lame ducks.

On September 24, 1968, Russell Wiggins was asked by Johnson to become the United States Ambassador to the United Nations. Johnson was by then on his way out, it was little more than an honorary appointment. Some friends thought it was his way of showing contempt for the United Nations, an organization essentially hostile to his Vietnam policies. For years Russ Wiggins had set a special code of ethics for working journalists—accept no gifts, moonlight on no other job, be cleaner than Caesar's wife—and many of his friends hoped he would turn the offer down. It was clearly, in Johnson's eyes if not in Wiggins's, a payoff for Vietnam. To their dismay, Wiggins accepted the job. For some of his friends it took a career which had seemed to be special and concluded it on a sour note. He was just about the only person who did not think it was a violation of his own principles.


Vietnam brought a strange dénouement to the career of another Washington *Post* fixture. Walter Lippmann had been from the first very taken with John Kennedy. During the 1960 campaign, as Kennedy hit his stride, he became Lippmann's idea of the perfect public leader, open, modern, above all contemporary. His personal grace had touched the older man as well, and Lippmann's columns had become increasingly enthusiastic about Kennedy, this modern young man who had captured the mood and the spirit of the nation as no one since the young Franklin Roosevelt, until one day Arthur Krock, the other venerable columnist of Washington, had come out of his office, chomping on his cigar, bellowing smoke, and saying, "Well, I may be getting old and I may be getting senile, but at least I don't fall in love with young boys like Walter Lippmann." Lippmann's approval had helped Kennedy immensely with other journalists, it meant that his personal charm was backed up by a form of historical acceptance. If during Kennedy's administration Lippmann had on occasion been critical of the White House, on the whole he seemed to like the spirit of the Kennedy people, the mold of the young men around Kennedy, and he had taken the assassination very hard, there seemed an extra pain for an old man to accept the death of so young a leader. Fred Friendly, then still at CBS, had asked Lippmann to do a CBS special talking about the Kennedy years, the Lippmann television specials had been great hits (in fact, Lippmann hated the medium, and he insisted that if he did television there be no commercials, though he finally relented for Friendly's sake and allowed one). Lippmann was interested in the idea, but he decided in deference to the new President to turn it down, he felt it would seem to be casting Johnson in a shadow, and measuring him against a myth, and that seemed unfair at so delicate a juncture. He did not so much want to mourn the past as he wanted to look forward to the future.

Lippmann had great hopes for the new President. He did not entirely like him; Johnson's attempts to stroke Lippmann in the past had been unusually inept, the more personal contact there had been, the worse the impression given. But he respected Johnson and he was very much aware of the man's energy and ambition. On the whole he thought it was potentially good ambition. He told friends privately that Johnson's ascension might, because of his greater domestic political skills, be *providential* (a very Lippmannesque word), that his skills might serve the nation better than Kennedy's at that particular moment. Lippmann watched with hope and anticipation. His friends in the Administration like McGeorge Bundy kept telling him how much more restrained Johnson was than people thought. Lippmann was bothered from the start by only one issue, Vietnam, and he had started his dissent on that in the

Kennedy years. The Johnson people seemed to be deferring to him. In the early days they consulted with him and gave him many assurances that the Administration did not intend to escalate, for Johnson did not want Lippmann's enmity on a venture like that. For a time his columns praised the Administration's restraint. He felt he had received a promise. When the Administration had nevertheless escalated, Lippmann had felt betrayed. They had lied to him, he said. *Lied to him.* He was very bitter. He told friends that he had dealt with Presidents for fifty years, since Woodrow Wilson, and no one of them had ever lied to him before.

Washington became for him a hostile city. Friend had turned against friend. Lippmann, the most senior journalist of the city, was cast as the symbolic dove, the enemy of the Administration. He had loved Washington, had loved living there. Now it all turned sour. The talk at his table became hostile and harsh. People left his home in anger. Others refused to accept his invitations. All of this was entirely alien to his style, which was to dissent and criticize without personalizing an issue. He was very unhappy about it. "What this city and this country need most," he told friends, "is comity." Comity means civility and courtesy and they were words that Lippmann had lived by, but they had been swept away by the war in Vietnam. Lippmann's annual parties, great events in Washington, changed in nature and style. All the brightest and best-connected people in Washington had once trooped to them, for a Lippmann invitation was a cherished offering. But the war had changed it. Old friends refused to come. Now there were different faces at his parties, people who were there merely because they were against the war. The old friends asked among themselves: What had happened to Walter? Who *was* he seeing? Who *were* these people, certainly not his kind of people.

Lyndon Johnson took Lippmann's dissent very seriously. He was furious, Lippmann was like a burr to him. It seemed to him that people were always quoting Lippmann back to him. His aides told him to let go, to stop worrying so much about Lippmann and others like him, but he did not let go, it was unsettling for him to have someone like Lippmann criticizing his administration, particularly in foreign policy, where Lippmann traditionally had been so strong and he traditionally had been so weak. Why was Lippmann doing this to him? he complained. Why, he had let Lippmann in on the policy, had listened to him, had adopted some of his suggestions. Where was the gratitude? So gradually he cut Lippmann off. He sent out orders that Lippmann was not to be invited to ceremonial White House functions and assigned White House aides to look through every word that Lippmann had ever written in his life in search of mistakes. They had, of course, found some dillies—there were moments when no writer in America had been as wrong as Walter Lippmann. In 1967 at a state dinner honoring the President of Turkey, Johnson toasted his guest with a verbal attack on Lippmann, reading from some twenty-year-old columns on Turkey; Lippmann in turn reprinted some of the columns to show that the White House had taken them out of context. Soon Johnson was beginning all his informal meetings with a certain story about Walter Lippmann. It became, as the war dragged on, his favorite story.

The story began with Fred Friendly, who, after leaving CBS, had been teaching a course at the Columbia School of Journalism. One of his bright young students had written a script for a documentary on the peace movement. There would be, she proposed, an early cut to a bumper sticker which said, "Make Love, Not War." Friendly said that was fine as long as this was done with good taste. "The trouble with you," she told Friendly, "is that you don't know the difference between making love and getting laid." The incident quickly got around and Friendly soon began to tell it himself. It was the time of the generation gap and it seemed to Friendly the perfect generation-gap story. He told it to his friend Lippmann and Lippmann liked the story immensely. "I'm going to London next week and I'd like to tell the story there as a generation-gap story," Lippmann told Friendly. "I have only one question: What does 'getting laid' mean?"

Lyndon Johnson heard the story and embellished it. In his version Friendly went home that night and told the story to his family, including the Lippmann rejoinder. At the end in the Johnson version, Friendly's fifteen-year-old daughter, very puzzled, looked at her father and asked: *"Who is Walter Lippmann?"*

The story summed up Johnson's disdain for Lippmann. It also represented to Lippmann the growing hostility of a city which he loved and in which he had lived as a kind of prince for some thirty years. In 1967 Walter Lippmann left Washington for New York. He had no more taste for the adversarial life he was leading in Washington; it was alien to his nature. He felt he had been harried and run out of town. His friend Herblock wrote an article for the *Post* on Johnson's war against Lippmann and drew a cartoon showing Johnson hurling thunderbolts at a fleeing Lippmann. In New York he tried living in an apartment house but he hated it and he spent the remaining years of his life living in an apartment in a hotel.

Geyelin moved the Washington *Post* editorial page slowly off the Wiggins course. He had looked forward to this for a long time, but he was a careful man. Even when he dissented he did not go against the grain. When, in April 1968, Ward Just, who was by then writing editorials, very good ones in fact, published his first book on Vietnam, he used as his title a quotation from Thucydides about the futility of war: *To No End.* Geyelin suggested that he soften that just a bit and call it *To What End.* There was, after all, no need to be too hasty. Nor did he want Just to lose his reputation for objectivity. Geyelin thought you did not switch a major institution overnight, as many of his friends wanted to. Rather, he thought, you did it by degrees, the style suited a large institution better, and by doing so you were more effective, you had more chance of carrying a large number of people along with you. So, slowly, he changed the course of the paper five degrees at a time, until by the middle of 1969 the *Post* was very much against the Vietnam War. It was one of the last of the major eastern journalistic establishments to take the position. By chance—and with a certain amount of irony—the *Post*'s assumption of the role of serious critic of the war coincided with the arrival of Richard Nixon in the White House.

# 20 / Time Incorporated

In May 1968, some three months after the Tet offensive, Hedley Donovan chose Henry Anatole Grunwald to replace Otto Fuerbringer, and few in the upper echelons of *Time* doubted that Vietnam had something to do with the choice and the timing. Fuerbringer had served the rough approximation of a managing editor's tour, it was true, but he was still in his prime and normally he might have stayed in charge for a few more years. Fuerbringer's own choice was Jim Keogh, who had been his chief deputy, and who usually edited the magazine in Fuerbringer's absence. At *Time* it had always been said that Otto was Luce's Luce, and Keogh was Otto's Otto. By no means was Grunwald Fuerbringer's choice; if anything, Fuerbringer had always seemed to condescend to him just a little bit, making it clear that he did not entirely respect Grunwald's news judgment. Fuerbringer's friends thought the news of the change had taken him by surprise. The day it was announced a friend found Fuerbringer in his office. He was very subdued. "I'm leaving," he said. "Henry's going to take my job." He did not seem to want to talk about it, indeed his lack of comment seemed in some way comment enough. Clearly this was Donovan's most important move in trying to edge the magazine more toward the center. Not to remove *Time* from its essential viewpoint and from all ideology, but to tone it down slightly, to make it fairer within that viewpoint.

For Henry Grunwald was a conservative man in a far more classic sense than Fuerbringer; he was an émigré from Hitler's Austria and more than most American intellectuals he had a conservative's respect for traditional institutions and a deeply personal fear of what happens when those institutions are assaulted and weakened. He trusted order, and was wary of forces that brought too much political turbulence and disorder, no matter how just their motivating causes. At the same time he was a cosmopolite; liberal in the sense of being finely tuned to the tempo of social, intellectual, and cultural change. He was thus a man of conservative instincts but not of conservative certitudes. He was intellectually very open, and uncommonly erudite as well. If Fuerbringer had been deeply mistrustful of the New York intellectual world, then Grunwald was a man nourished by it. He was also a true child of *Time* magazine. He had gone there in 1944 at the age of twenty-two as a part-time copy boy, and he had never as an adult worked anywhere else. Older men like Max Ways and Whittaker Chambers had been startled by this man-child who already knew so much and was even hungrier to learn more. He had from the start been serious and respectable. He had risen quickly through the ranks; in 1951, when he was twenty-nine, he became the youngest senior editor in *Time*'s history. He was considered one of the quickest and most talented writers on a magazine that valued writers more than it valued reporters, and it was part of his mystique that on one memorable occasion, with deadlines pressing forward and a totally inadequate cover story in hand, the young Henry Grunwald had called in a secretary and had stood and *dictated* an absolutely flawless cover story, his voice speaking not the cadence of normal speech but the highly specialized style of a *Time* cover.

Within *Time* he was very much a man of the office. There had been one brief tour in the field, in London, but it had not been comfortable. Field reporters were by and large more boisterous and audacious. The office was his home, it had always been his home. His mind was analytical, he seemed to take subjects and strip them of passion and emotion. He was also, in contrast to Fuerbringer, very much at ease in the back of the book, and increasingly pushed cultural reporting from the back of the book to the front. He wanted, above all, ideas in the magazine, always more ideas. He once told a group of younger *Time* writers at dinner, "Writing is ideas, all good writing is ideas." The greater the intellectual range, the better the story. Words should serve ideas; words without ideas were empty. It was a comment that told a good deal about the man and a good deal about the magazine he intended to edit.

He did not have the hard-news credentials that Fuerbringer had possessed; he did not move as readily or as surely to the news beat, it was not his source of strength. A few of the old-timers, not entirely happy with Grunwald's ascension, judged him to be indecisive as managing editor, prone to ordering up two cover stories instead of one, and deciding only at the last minute which would run. That made a lot more work for everybody. They much preferred the decisiveness of Fuerbringer. Yet he brought so many other skills to his work that his rise was constant. He avoided entirely being caught up in the bogs of office politics or recruited into one or another warring clique.

By the early sixties it was clear that Grunwald was a serious contender to become the next managing editor. There was only one thing that might hold him back and that was the fact that he was Jewish. *Time*, in the past, had always been a very Protestant empire, it was a fact of life. In the late fifties the news service had been opened to Jewish reporters as it had not been a decade earlier, and by 1960 the chief, Dick Clurman, was Jewish. But whether the most important and sensitive job in the entire company would go to someone whose background was so alien was another question. It weighed heavily on Grunwald; in moments of deepest privacy, Grunwald, always so careful about revealing himself and his feelings, would talk about it with close friends. Would this hold him back? Could *Time* have a Jewish managing editor? Most people assumed that if Luce were still alive it could not happen. (Not that Luce did not like Grunwald; in fact, Luce was fascinated by him, loved the idea that Grunwald was so smart, so original, so different, and yet so familiar. But it was unlikely, colleagues believed, that Harry Luce would ever hand Henry Grunwald the keys to the printing press. Delight in his company, yes, but never make him managing editor of *Time*. Grunwald had shared these doubts about his chances, though once in 1964 Luce invited him to a private dinner and, aware of Grunwald's uneasiness, told him that he was very much in the running for the job.) This was a new era; Hedley Donovan was a different man. He was less tied to the past than Luce, they were men of different generations, and he was a man of greater fairness. And so he chose Grunwald, in full awareness of how the choice would appear.

For the failure to choose Keogh was viewed within *Time* as a partial repudiation of Fuerbringer's magazine. Keogh was a very conservative man and a man of certitudes. He had once taken a leave of absence to write a (favorable) biography of Richard Nixon, and when he left *Time* he went to work for Nixon, first as a speech writer in the Nixon White House and then to be head of the USIA. There was a going-away party for him right after Nixon's election, and the *Time* brass turned it into a rather lavish show. As is the style at functions like this, there was a lot of good-natured joking about good old Jim Keogh going to work at the good old White House, which was a terrific place, and what a good thing it was for good old Jim and good old *Time* magazine. All of this was with a pleasant, executive-style good fellowship. But then the mood was shattered by Keogh's valedictory. He had wanted to be managing editor, he said, and he accepted the decision, although he did not agree with it. Well enough, they thought. But then he took out after them, no longer a man of *Time,* now a man of Nixon: We know who you are, we know you all voted for Humphrey (which was probably not true, perhaps half of them had and half had not), we know you favored him in your news columns, and if you think you're going to get any favors from us, forget it. Just forget it. . . . For the various editors assembled there who prided themselves on how fair the magazine had been, how evenly it had reported the campaign, it was a cold, cold moment.

So *Time* magazine had a new and quite different managing editor, and it was due to change markedly as a magazine. Two developments expedited that, and Grunwald helped sponsor them both. The first was the acquisition of the Time-Life news service by the managing editor, something that Luce had always held outside Fuerbringer's grasp. The tensions between Clurman and Fuerbringer symbolized all the divisions within the magazine, but Clurman and Grunwald had been good friends and when Grunwald took over Clurman felt it no longer made any sense to keep the division separate. A year later Clurman himself left and was replaced by Murray Gart, and after some bureaucratic shuffling and despite Gart's opposition Grunwald did take over the news service; the reporters would report to Gart, who would report to him. It was a major change in the balance of the magazine. Grunwald immediately suggested that reporters in the field file for *publication*. In the past they had simply sent in raw files, sometimes brilliant and sometimes remarkably undisciplined, in which there was on occasion curiously little responsibility displayed by the reporter, since the field exercised so little control over what the magazine ran. Now that might change.

And to support this, there was to be a second step giving the field reporters a greater role in their work. In the fall of 1969, with the cooperation of both Grunwald and Gart, *Time* in New York offered reporters in the field the chance to see prepublication versions of their stories, by means of a sort of instant playback system. As the edited version went into the computer on its way to print, the same perforated tape of the story that would be used for typesetting was fed into telex machines and, at an astonishingly high speed, arrived in some foreign capital for a *Time* reporter to see. If the correspondent disagreed with the story or found a serious factual error, then there was still time to file a dissent to New York. It marked the final fusion of a once badly fragmented and faction-ridden system and overnight it changed the balance and nature of the magazine, making it infinitely more fair and, at least potentially, more accurate.

Now the reporters in the field were an extension of Grunwald. He believed that the magazine had to trust them; if it did not trust a given correspondent, then it ought to get someone better, but failing that it had to go with its own people. There was accountability for the first time—to the reporters, and through them to events. When there were conflicts between their versions and those of other sources, the *Time* reporters found to their surprise that Grunwald usually came down on their side. It was, thought many of the senior people, a step long overdue, one that was now being expedited, consciously or unconsciously, by the magazine's performance on Vietnam. As New York had not listened to its people in Saigon, it had failed to perform adequately on Vietnam; because of that it had changed, and the new process would help make possible the magazine's striking and contrasting performance on Watergate. If on Vietnam *Time*'s performance had been something of a scandal within the profession, on Watergate its journalism would be truly distinguished.

# 21 / The Los Angeles Times

The late sixties were extraordinary years for the Los Angeles *Times*, it was like a comet in constant ascent, nothing but growth, bureaus opened, reporters hired, the world conquered, old friends alienated, new friends made. The circulation had nearly doubled in the Otis Chandler years. But the tensions within the shop, the uneasy semi-truce between the eastern paper and the western paper, had never abated, the resentments were real and mutual. In the sixties all this had been held in check by a number of things: the sheer upsurge of the paper, the desire of the editors to exploit its new talent, and the fact that Nick Williams was able to handle its split-personality monster. His close personal relationship with Bob Donovan kept the Washington bureau from being too isolated. But by 1970 this was changing. Two things were happening. For the first time the impact of a major national recession was being felt. It was not that the *Times* lost money, far from it. But for the first time in the Otis Chandler regime it failed to break an existing record. In Washington and among the national reporters there was an almost immediate feeling that for the first time play on their stories was diminishing and waning, that local and regional stories were getting better play, that the national economic softness had caused the paper to pull back a little, to focus less on its national ambitions and more on its local constituency, and to play news that was of more immediate interest to local readers. There was no exact proof of this, it was almost impossible to calibrate, but there was a strong feeling among the Easterners and foreign correspondents that the California part of the paper was taking over, that it was constantly getting good play on stories that by their standards had little validity. Part of it was the way the paper was made up; there was only one place where a national or foreign story could be showcased, that was page one, but there were three places where a Los Angeles or California story could be showcased: page one, page three (which was a high-display page), and the first page of the separate Metro section. By contrast, special long takeouts by foreign or national reporters, failing page one, often fell back into what were known as the gooney-bird sections, areas deep in the paper where tiny islands of newsprint existed in a vast sea of real estate and truss ads, and where highly significant national or foreign stories might be jumped seven or eight times, demonstrating to the star reporters the paper's ambivalence toward their work. There seemed to be on the one hand a commitment to hire a quality reporter and give that reporter the time to do a major takeout, and on the other a lack of commitment in playing it, the reportage finally printed more out of obligation than out of belief. The coming of the recession seemed to show to the Easterners that they were, in effect, an adjunct, however highly visible, to this paper and that the real root was in California.

The other thing that was affecting the paper was that Nick Williams was nearing retirement and it was time to choose a successor. At one time it had seemed to most working reporters that the two likeliest successors were Jim Bellows and Ed Guthman, with Bill Thomas, the metropolitan editor, very much the outside choice. Bellows at first had seemed to outsiders at least the most natural successor, indeed it was perceived that he had been brought in by Nick Williams with that very much in mind; only a confident man like Williams would have brought in so high-powered an aide. Bellows was a man of very special editorial skills, creative, imaginative, he loved to venture into areas where journalists had never been before. He was a man of great energy, and for a major editor, little caution. His wife, Maggie, had been the society editor in Phoenix, where she had done the usual coverage of rich women going to each other's homes in furs and jewels, but her years married to Bellows and working in New York had gradually affected her and made her a far more involved woman, with a growing sense of her own professional mistreatment as a woman. The deal that had brought Bellows to Los Angeles had not been a package deal, originally there was no job for Maggie Bellows, but Nick Williams was very taken with her, and he had asked her to take over the women's page. She had, deciding that the women's pages were mired in another century. She had quickly modernized the section and there was less automatic heralding of conventional society functions. Some Los Angeles socialites complained to Buff Chandler, whose turf this had always been in the past. There were other irritants—stories on abortion, stories on what was to become the women's movement before it was really a movement—that put her ahead of where Buff thought the paper should be. Then a few incidents. Maggie Bellows getting some names wrong in a story about the music center and receiving a terrible tongue lashing administered by Buff in front of other people. In 1967, early in the Bellowses' tour in Los Angeles, Norman and Buff had co-hosted a dinner for the Nixons. White tie, tails. Indeed, the Bellows had had to go out and rent the uniform, white tie had not been de rigueur back in the old days on the *Trib* in New York. Later, after the party, Maggie had asked Jim whether in writing it up she should mention that the Chandlers were co-hosts. Bellows, thinking of eastern journalistic propriety instead of western, said no, the Chandlers would not want their names in, and he was wrong, very wrong; indeed, it was not possible, he found out, to be more wrong.

Little things like that had not helped his career, or for that matter his wife's, but he was not a particularly good careerist. He was a serious man who did not seem serious, in a world of unserious men who always seemed very serious, and by the standards of the upper echelons of the *Times,* he was quite outspoken. He once told Buff Chandler there ought to be a black and a woman on the board of the *Times.* He was affected by the Vietnam War, and the vast changes taking place in the society, and he was outspokenly liberal at the daily editorial board meetings. He was particularly bothered by the war, he did not know very much about Southeast Asia but he simply did not believe all the official reports, he sensed it was all futile, and he was very tough in editorial meetings, attacking those who spoke for the government. He knew, in the way that smart people know these things, that he was crossing an invisible line as far as the Chandler sense of propriety was concerned and yet he could not stop.

The editorial board meetings were crucial not just to the formation of the editorial policy but to the essential tone of the paper, which voices were listened to, which issues were legitimized, which editors carried how much weight. They were held every day and Otis and Nick Williams and the editorial writers and the top editors attended; Otis Chandler was generally somewhat reticent; he did not want to dominate his editors, and there was a time in the late sixties when the lines were very sharply drawn on Vietnam, and Guthman and Bellows were constantly embroiled in long arguments with Jim Bassett, the more conservative editor of the editorial page. It was as if Bassett were caught in a buzz saw, he was getting it from two forceful men: the paper's editorial policy, its support of the war, was being savaged daily by its own editors. Finally Nick Williams, who thought the arguments too long and somewhat embarrassing, took Bellows's name off the list for the editorial board meetings.

"I know what that means," Bellows said.

"It doesn't mean a damn thing," Williams said, but of course it did, it was clear confirmation that he was off the executive list. He simply was not suitable to the Chandlers, they did not take him seriously. He was not of their cloth.

Among working reporters who had little sense of the balance and whim of the Family, probably Guthman was the prime choice to succeed Williams. He was the paper's most prestigious editor, he had won the Pulitzer Prize, when *Time* or *Newsweek* needed a quote it was Guthman they called. But Guthman was never in the running. Perhaps if Robert Kennedy had not been assassinated it might have been different, perhaps he might have been managing editor. Guthman, in fact, was never on the real executive escalator; he had come along at an important moment for the *Times,* he had lent it instant prestige and credibility in certain circles, he had helped build a great staff, but his value to the Chandlers was, for a variety of reasons, declining by 1970; it would not be Guthman.

At one point, in late 1969, Otis Chandler, bothered by the lack of choice that awaited him, tried to bring Frank McCulloch back to the paper. McCulloch, having finished a very difficult and painful passage for *Time* in Saigon, was interested. He was restless with *Time,* even more restless after the death of Harry Luce, his only real protector in the *Time* hierarchy. In the fall of 1969 he was the *Life* bureau chief in Washington, unhappy there, sensing that *Life* might be terminally ill. A mutual friend told Otis Chandler that McCulloch might be available, and Chandler, who liked McCulloch very much and was reasonably at ease with him, had snapped at it, he had flown McCulloch out to Los Angeles and had offered him a national column with national syndication, he could write anything he wanted. There was an implicit suggestion that McCulloch might also move back into the *Times* executive apparatus. It was Armistice Day, 1969, and the building was almost empty, and Otis Chandler and McCulloch had shaken hands on the deal, with Chandler offering about $10,000 a year more than McCulloch was making at *Life.* Then, flying back to Washington, his mind ran through all the people who believed they might be the next editor and who might also be dealing with his copy, and who would, consciously or unconsciously, resent his coming. He remembered his struggles with the bureaucracy in the earlier period and he decided it was all too much and, not liking himself very much, he wrote a letter to Otis Chandler breaking the handshake agreement.

In 1970, with Williams's retirement approaching, Otis Chandler mentioned to Nick that Bob Donovan might be a possibility. Williams's first reaction was that he wanted to think about it. The more he thought, the more he liked the idea. Donovan did not know the interior of the paper, the working guts of it, and he did not know Los Angeles, but he had great élan and style, and he was by both instinct and training elegant and smart. Donovan, Williams thought, knew nothing of the complicated act of putting together a paper in Los Angeles. But there were a lot of good carpenters already there, and all Donovan had to do was let them do their work and give good general directions. So Williams came to accept the idea, and made the offer. It was an offer that Bob Donovan could refuse, and refuse he did at first. He had absolutely no desire to go to Los Angeles, he was totally a creature of Washington, as was his wife, Martha; they had lived there for twenty years, all their friends were there, the city was an extension of their work and their lives. In addition, he had no desire to run something. He had in truth never even run a bureau, he had always had a good number-two man who had dealt with the menial chores and liberated him for what he loved best, which was writing the big story. Of Bob Donovan it was said, with more than a grain of truth, that he could barely do his own expense accounts, much less run a big bureau. There was more money in the new job, but he did not want or need more money; he already had everything he wanted. Nick Williams, now sold on the idea, persisted; the paper needed Donovan, he could do great things for it. So reluctantly Bob Donovan accepted the offer and moved to Los Angeles to sit by Nick's side for a year on his way to becoming editor of the Los Angeles *Times*.

The Donovan appointment shook Guthman; he had, a friend thought, made the mistake of believing the rumors, and the rumors had always been better than the reality. The appointment of Donovan did not necessarily please Frank Haven either, and it pleased him even less when Donovan wanted to turn the Washington bureau over to Dave Kraslow, his number-two man. It was Kraslow who had been in constant direct conflict with Los Angeles, and Haven actively disliked him. So though Kraslow was Donovan's choice, it was not immediately accepted; Haven in a long meeting in Los Angeles argued vehemently against it. Finally Nick Williams asked Donovan if it was that important to have Kraslow, and Donovan said yes, the bureau would not stand for anyone else. If that's what you want, Williams said, that's what you get; you could not, after all, ask a man to become editor of a national paper and then turn him down on his first appointment. But it was a clear warning of how much resentment there was, how much antagonism had been built up. It was another defeat for Haven, but it came when the balance of power was about to change.

. . .

The decision to move Bob Donovan to Los Angeles seemed natural enough. He was the most prestigious reporter on the paper, and in fact the Washington bureau was not known in Washington journalistic circles as the *Los Angeles Times bureau,* it was *Bob Donovan's Los Angeles* Times *bureau.* He was a man of vision and grace and he would now, many younger California reporters were sure, bring that vision and grace to Los Angeles; they too would be touched by his magic presence. The entire paper would become what the Washington bureau had been. Nick Williams gave a series of six parties to introduce Donovan to the entire staff, and young staff members watching these two talented, urbane men dealing so easily with each other felt an excitement about the future. But prestige and power are curious things; like wine, they do not necessarily travel well. Bob Donovan had been prestigious and powerful in Washington because he had known everyone and everything and had worked for powerful outlets; in Washington he was the ultimate connected man, a deeply ambitious man without seeming ambitious, few men with as much ambition managed to be so self-effacing. That trait gave him a special style in his rough and harsh profession and added to his reputation as an important journalist in a city where journalists, even unimportant ones, are taken seriously. But who knew his name in Los Angeles? There were very powerful figures in Los Angeles but they did not need to deal with Bob Donovan; if they wanted a contact at the *Times* they need only call Otis. Who knew of all those years covering Ike and Truman, and who cared? Was self-effacement a valuable quality in a new man moving into the top job in what might be very hostile waters?

Bob Donovan was confronted by a remarkably complex city, perhaps the most complex city in America, about which he knew precious little. He headed an equally complex newspaper where much of the energy was devoted to covering things in which he was not particularly interested. He was three thousand miles from the people he knew and who knew him, and three thousand miles from the events that excited him. He was fifty-eight years old, a difficult age at which to retool himself and create new interests. He was installed in an office not in the newsroom but at the executive level, which removed him that much more from the one thing he might have been good at—newspapering.

Nor did he really know the city or the paper. Donovan at staff meetings was always telling people: "I don't know anything about that. I don't know what they're talking about." It had been charming in Washington, where, of course, he had known everything that everyone was talking about, but it was less charming here because he was telling the literal truth, he really didn't know. He said it to everyone—copy boys, colleagues. He could return from a party at Nick Williams's and tell a colleague: "I shouldn't be editor of this paper, I don't know what they're talking about." He was saying it too much and he was saying it in front of people who were quite ready and indeed eager to exploit his lack of knowledge. It was easy to make him look awkward and alien and, it turned out, there were quite a few people willing to do so. Donovan had never been interested in the interior numbers of journalism—budgets, circulation, news-to-ad ratios—and Otis cared about those numbers, he was very good at them, better in fact than anybody in journalism, it was his great strength and it had allowed him to change and modernize the paper while keeping his family happy. Nick Williams, who had seemed to working journalists a man interested only in the editorial product, was superb at the numbers, he had a total mastery of the interior of the paper and of the community it served. At the Los Angeles *Times,* mastery of the numbers was crucial to editorial freedom, and it was crucial to gaining Otis Chandler's respect. Replacing Nick Williams was going to be difficult, more difficult than anyone imagined, but for Donovan, with his lack of knowledge of both the community and the paper, it was going to be impossible. For Otis Chandler, having an editor who did not care about the figures was like having an editor who spoke another language.

There were other problems: Martha Donovan had on occasion deprecated Los Angeles, in contrast to her beloved Washington, in front of the Chandlers, and worse, had deprecated the *Times* in contrast to the Washington *Post.* That was not done, not to people who were already deeply sensitive about being Westerners. Then too Bob and Martha were seen frequently on social occasions with Norman and Buff Chandler; it was as if they were, in age and style, more at ease with the senior Chandlers than with Otis and Missy, who were some fifteen years younger than the Donovans. Perhaps it was just a natural gravitation, but it did not help. Otis had just finished a decade with one editor who was some twenty years older than he, and the image seared deep, the younger Otis being led by the older, wiser Nick Williams. It did not help that the next editor was also older. Perhaps too Donovan had not moved forward forcefully for fear of crowding Nick Williams.

So it did not work, though most of the people at the paper did not know that it did not work, including Bob Donovan, who came, in the brief time he spent in Los Angeles, to like the idea of the city and the idea of the job, and had become increasingly confident of his ability to edit the paper. He thought he was doing well. But in Otis Chandler's mind Donovan simply wasn't taking charge, he was not exhibiting what was known as leadership. Maybe he wasn't tough enough. Nick Williams had some sense of Chandler's opinion, but not much. Otis was keeping things very close to his vest and he did not talk to anyone about what was bothering him. Then one day, a very short time before Williams was to retire, Otis Chandler called his editor in and said that he did not feel comfortable with Donovan. Williams said that he was confident that Donovan could do the job, that the machinery was there and he could handle it. But Otis was insistent: that was not entirely the point, he did not feel *comfortable* with Donovan. Finally Williams said all right, but Otis had to break the news himself. Which he did, in a particularly callous way, calling Donovan in, telling him he had been right in the first place, he was a reporter not an editor, and finally asking how long it was before he retired. When Donovan answered six years, Otis said—he was never a particularly graceful man—"We'll try and carry you that long." It was a staggering insult to a man who seemed to epitomize the best of a profession, and it was the beginning of the end of Otis Chandler as the White Knight of American Journalism. About a year later, walking up Park Avenue in New York, he saw one of his ablest reporters, Don Bruckner, and asked him if people were upset about the Donovan thing. Bruckner had answered that people were *very* upset. Why? asked Otis Chandler. "Well, their attitude is, if you can do that to someone like Donovan, what about me?" answered Bruckner. "I never thought about that," said Chandler.

Donovan was shattered by the news. He called Kraslow that night and told him that it was all over, he was coming back to Washington. Bellows told him he should have quit right there on the spot, but Donovan said he could not afford to, it was too late in his career, he was not a young man, he needed the pension benefits. So he came back to the Washington bureau, working on a major history of the Truman administration, writing occasionally for the Los Angeles *Times*. He was deeply wounded; for a long time after he came back he felt publicly humiliated and did not show himself. But, as always, he was painfully honest and when a colleague suggested that Donovan had never really liked California anyway, he answered, "No, I really liked it out there very much."

So the choice for the next editor was Bill Thomas, the metropolitan editor, a man who had been the dark horse from the start. He was the acceptable choice, the best and most modern of the California group, a good editor, serious, very good on soft news, which was what the *Times* increasingly favored, acceptable to the board, acceptable to the Family. He knew the city and the greater community far better than any of the Easterners. He was very smart and very ambitious and yet he was never contentious. The new people might be a little suspicious of him, he might strike them as being a little cautious, perhaps also to eastern eyes a little parochial and lacking in vision, but they also thought him smart and professional. He was not exactly their type: he dressed differently, he was an avid golfer—which was not an eastern journalist's game, tennis was, tennis in the sixties was more a game of the meritocracy—and there was a touch of the golf course to him, and sometimes the bureau members complained that his trips to Washington seemed to center as much upon visits to the Burning Tree Country Club as to the bureau. He had none of the hard, unyielding drive of Guthman, nor the creative flair of Bellows, he was not as easy to engage in conversation as either of them, but he was sound and smart and he was not going to get anyone in a lot of trouble, people above him or people below him. If, as many people suspected, Otis Chandler consciously or unconsciously was pulling back a little for economic reasons, emphasizing local and regional coverage, then Thomas looked even better. Guthman in some way had symbolized the society's concern with its social issues and its belief that these issues were soluble, a mirror of national concern of the sixties, the journalist as activist; now, with the Vietnam War beginning to wind down, with Nixon in office, with the recession and inflation persisting, those concerns were diminishing, in terms of both the government's interest and journalistic interest. As the country's dreams contracted, under pressure of economic problems, the withdrawal affected newspapers, just as it affected the government.

The last phone call Richard Nixon had made before flying back East after his 1968 election had been to Norman Chandler, to thank him for the help over the years. There had been no call to Otis Chandler; the sins of 1962 had not yet been washed away. In 1968 Otis had been ambivalent about the endorsement, he had not by then particularly approved of the war; his wife, Missy, had pushed him hard for a long time and slowly, very slowly brought him along on that issue. He had in 1968 liked Hubert Humphrey personally, finding him good of heart and generous of spirit, and Richard Nixon was less his than his father's. But there were certain obligations that went with the paper. The orbital thrust of Republicanism was very powerful in presidential years, the Family was on guard, and so in 1968 the paper had endorsed Nixon with some reservations. Unlike his grandfather, who loved personally directing the Family's economic and political fortunes, and unlike his father, who deputized Kyle Palmer, Otis Chandler seemed almost deliberately to create a political vacuum around himself. But the responsibilities were always there and flashed publicly from time to time, as in 1970, when the *Times,* on the last day of filing for the Senate race, said editorially that George Murphy, the tap-dancing actor, was not fit to represent California in the Senate. Which was demonstrably true, but which also was, in the Family's eyes, a somewhat bold thing to say, though basically harmless. Except that reading the paper that day was Norton Simon, the brilliant eclectic businessman and Republican liberal, who was a friend of Buff and Norman and Otis, and who agreed with the editorial and thereupon put down his paper and went out and filed as a senatorial candidate in the Republican primary. He immediately went by the *Times* office to see Otis, with whom he felt very comfortable on most issues, explaining that he had just acted upon the *Times*'s editorial advice. Norton Simon pointed out that he was, like the paper, on the liberal Republican side, that he agreed with the paper on almost all issues, as Murphy did not; he was a successful businessman and hardly a radical figure, in fact he was precisely the kind of candidate the *Times* seemed to be summoning in its editorial. Therefore would the paper please support him. The very idea seemed to strike terror into Otis Chandler's heart. The reaction was almost visible. "My God, Norton, do you know how much hell I caught on that editorial?" Chandler said. "I just can't do it, I just can't support you!" There was, thought Norton Simon, a lack of conviction there, a piece missing in some way. Yet he understood that Chandler was caught among powerful forces; it was known that both Otis and Buff had preferred Pat Brown to Ronald Reagan in 1966 and yet the paper supported

Reagan, who was subsequently elected. That did not end the Reagan problem, rather it began it.

It was not just the *Times*'s reporting of the Reagan campaign, which was very tough-minded, it was Conrad, the passionate cartoonist, who seemed to have an unerring instinct for the huckster in Reagan, and with great regularity hit the raw nerve in Reagan and Reagan's influential friends. Conrad Unexpurgated. Very regularly the phone at Otis Chandler's house would ring early in the morning and it would be the Governor of the State of California calling the Publisher of the Los Angeles *Times* to complain about the latest outrage. There were so many calls that Otis Chandler finally refused to take them, at which point *Nancy* Reagan called, it was harder to turn her down, to complain regularly about what the dreaded Conrad had done to her Ron, how Conrad ruined their breakfast. Finally Otis would not take her calls either. But these calls, and many like them, were not without effect, the antagonism to Conrad was so deep and so personal because his drawings seemed so personal; in February 1967 Otis Chandler put at the top of the editorial page a small note saying that the editorials and the editorials *alone* reflected the policy of the paper. Conrad, somewhat amused, referred to it as "the Reagan Disclaimer." It was, some people thought, a small but important bench mark of retreat. It did not by any means stem the tide of protest. It was one thing to claim that only your editorials spoke for the paper, but it was hard to take that claim seriously when some equivocating editorial was matched against a Conrad cartoon, remorseless, unsparing. In September 1973 the paper made a further retreat and moved Paul Conrad from the editorial page to what is known in the profession as the op-ed page, that is, the page for *other* voices. It was another semi-disclaimer of Conrad, and he did not like it in that sense, though in a practical way he welcomed it, it made his life easier with his superiors; he could argue more readily that he did not speak for the paper, he spoke only for himself.

In the early years of Nixon's administration, Otis Chandler's relations with him were guardedly pleasant. The Los Angeles *Times* Washington reporters were very aggressive, but the paper as a whole did not seem antagonistic; it had supported Nixon in 1968, it would support him again in 1972. Haldeman was something of a thorn, there seemed to be a history of tension between him and the paper that contradicted Nixon's own personal feelings. Otis and Missy Chandler were invited with some regularity to White House dinners (Buff told friends she thought they went too often, but others thought this more a reflection of the fact that *they* were being invited instead of Norman and her). At one point the Secret Service, in order to protect Nixon, cut off surfing at Dana Point beach at the San Clemente White House, a place considered to have some of the finest surfing in the country. Other surfers had asked Chandler, a great surfer himself, to petition Nixon to open it for them. Nixon had told the publisher that this was impossible, but that *he* was welcome to surf there himself any time he wanted. Otis Chandler accepted that offer and went surfing one afternoon and he was enjoying himself when a young man swam over and began to surf too. Chandler tried to explain to the young man that he had special presidential dispensation, but just then a Coast Guard cutter moved over to pick up the kid; as the young man was being fished out of the water by the Commander-in-Chief's men, Otis Chandler heard him shout angrily, "Fuck Nixon! Fuck Nixon! And fuck you too, mister," which made him feel that perhaps special surfing rights were not really worth it and he did not surf at the President's pleasure thereafter.

Guthman had symbolized the aggressive quality of the paper in the sixties, a passion for coverage of social change, always pushing reporters to an extra dimension. He more than anyone else in the top echelon had cared about investigative reporting, about the responsibility journalism had to help protect citizens from governmental or corporate abuse. Upon the retirement of Nick Williams he became the one person Paul Conrad would go to voluntarily with the outline of a cartoon, and the only person who could talk Conrad out of a cartoon. Guthman was an unusual—and unusually important—figure on a paper like the *Times,* situated comfortably as it was in a place like Southern California, where the very climate seemed to soften the edges of daily life, where the hard edge of New York or Washington journalism often seemed out of tune with the life style, where there were beaches everywhere, where the sun always shone, and the rain and snow never fell. (The difference between the two worlds, many of the reporters thought, was symbolized by those pleasant Christmas cards from the publisher showing that handsome Chandler family, all lined up on the beach, each member with a surfboard.) That, plus the fact that Otis Chandler had deliberately styled his paper to be in large part a daily magazine, away from the breaking story. All this made the paper prone to a kind of softness, a lack of aggressiveness, a certain complacency. If some major newspapers were too keyed to what was alleged to be daily news, making themselves vulnerable to managed news and events, then the Los Angeles *Times* sometimes seemed headed toward the other extreme, almost oblivious to daily events, measuring its own pace in its own way, affected as much by the climate at hand as by the tensions in Washington, unhurried, almost leisurely. There was, and this was rare for a newspaper, almost too little pressure. The drive and the push on the *Times* came not, as on most papers, from the editors, but from the reporters; they, more than at most papers, held the initiative. The one driving relentless editor was Guthman, always pushing his reporters to make that one more phone call. In fact, there were some who thought that this counted against him within the bureaucracy, that he spent too much time on the phone talking to reporters, talking to his own sources, and too little time reading the stories as they were coming in, so that when he went into scheduling meetings he lacked the mastery of his own stories that an editor like Bill Thomas possessed.

Guthman had always been a man of rough edges, and now as the seventies arrived his edges at the paper seemed if anything a little rougher, a little more, rather than less, alien. He in turn seemed a little disappointed with the paper. He had liked Otis Chandler, but Otis somehow seemed now in this new decade more remote. There were divisions within the paper now; Guthman and Conrad were binding closer and closer together, wary to some degree of Thomas and of Tony Day, the young chief of the editorial page, whom Donovan had picked off the Philadelphia *Bulletin* and whose arrival they had at first both welcomed but with whom they had become gradually more disappointed. In the earlier period when the *Times*'s editorials had been conservative, Guthman had put the blame on Jim Bassett, now with Day as editor and the page still disappointing him, Guthman came to the reluctant conclusion that Otis Chandler had been getting exactly what he wanted all along.

# 22/ The Washington Post

The paper that Ben Bradlee was now editing was very much a reflection of Bradlee himself. It was lively and zestful, and on occasion serious. It was a wonderful showcase for talent. Haynes Johnson from the Washington *Star* with his Pulitzer Prize, Nick Kotz from the Des Moines *Register* with his, David Broder soon to win his, Dick Harwood, Ben Bagdikian, Ward Just, Phil Carter. Bradlee's All-Stars. They were the brightest journalists of a generation, and anyone who had been around Washington for any length of time knew them all, knew how good they were. As Scotty Reston had been the best ivory hunter of his generation, now Bradlee was proving to be the best of the next, creating his own journalistic galaxy. That was good for the *Post;* they brought energy and drive and style; they hit the big stories while they were big. There was danger in those tactics too, of course; some of the most important stories, like Vietnam, were at their most sensitive and most crucial when they were only tiny blips on the journalistic radar screen. Someone said that the *Post* had a style of sophisticated sensationalism, and there was more than a touch of truth to that. And that too was a reflection of Bradlee. Some people who preferred Bradlee to Wiggins and Friendly, who vastly preferred the new paper to the old and thought it a better and fairer paper, less committed in its news columns to causes, nonetheless worried about the attitudes that the newspaper reflected. Did it have a moral center? *Should* a paper have a moral center? What worried many of the reporters and some of the editors about Bradlee was that a story was an end in itself. Get the story, beat the opposition, stick it to them before they stick it to us. The story without any sense of the large context or implication. Bradlee was classically, for all his modern style, of the old Chicago school: the story was everything. It made his attitude toward journalism clean, but it disconcerted many of his colleagues—well-educated, middle-class—who thought journalism had some measure of social responsibility.

With all that talent, all those egos, Bradlee erected a system he called "creative tension." Creative tension was not arrived at by happenstance. It was very deliberate. The people who ran the *Post* were very much aware of what had occurred at the *Star,* how quickly it had fallen from its place of power, and they were determined that this would never happen at the *Post.* If there was virtually no direct economic competition on the street (there was competition with *The New York Times,* but it was psychological rather than economic), then the true competition, the determination to keep the operation honed and sharp, had to come from within. So within the *Post* staff people were deliberately played off against each other and kept on edge. It might not be the most sympathetic way to deal with talented, often sensitive people, it might not create a happy shop, but it worked. No one would get fat, no one would get sloppy. It was not by chance that Bradlee repeatedly promoted Dick Harwood to positions of executive power, for despite certain flaws in dealing with colleagues Harwood was, in Bradlee's words, great at kicking ass.

All of this made the Washington *Post,* as the sixties moved forward, a complicated paper. It was a more exciting and a fairer paper than it had been before, and it was infinitely richer and more powerful. It could on occasion be original and indeed brilliant. It was in some ways a more congenial place for a talented reporter to work than *The New York Times;* there was less bureaucracy to filter out the individualism of the reporter. But the *Post,* like its editor, lacked the attention span, the cumulative seriousness of the *Times.* It still reflected both the strengths and the limits of the city in which it was published, the company town where government and precious little else flourished. In the *Post,* Edmund Wilson's obituary was a small, bland, unreflective story on an inside page; so much for America's greatest man of letters of a generation. Assistant secretaries of state did better. That somehow told a great deal about the paper. What it lacked, Bradlee and his friend Phil Geyelin sometimes agreed, was cruising speed. *The New York Times* had cruising speed, the *Times* was not a product of one or two men's talent and brilliance, it was the sum of its many parts, often at the expense of the individual talent. The *Times* was special because of its awesome and often stifling structure, it could carry weaker reporters and raise them to the general level of the product just as frequently as it pulled more talented reporters down to that same level. The *Times* was on a plateau, a moderately high one, all by itself; the *Post* was a series of peaks and valleys.

*The New York Times.* There was, Bradlee often thought, the *Times* and then there was everyone else. Only the *Times* had the money, the resources, the prestige, the tradition to do great things, an institution that seemed the very equal of any governmental institution, a power unto itself. The *Times* was the

*Times,* and the others were simply newspapers. Only the *Times* had the money and the power and the prestige to stand up to the government, to hire the lawyers, to stand equal to the Solicitor General of the United States, to fight if necessary not just City Hall but 1600 Pennsylvania Avenue. It was money, but it was not just money, there were by the late sixties many newspapers in America more profitable than *The New York Times;* it was tradition, duty, obligation, something so ingrained in the system that the *Times* remained stronger than its weaknesses. On the *Times* strong reporters could on occasion carry weaker editors, and on other occasions, the system, the editors, could carry weaker reporters. The force of the *Times* was just too great, the commitment to a high standard of journalism too forceful for any individual to weaken it. The *Times* could even carry a weak publisher. Few at the *Times* thought that Punch Sulzberger was the ideal publisher. He had in no way been trained for the job—his older brother-in-law, Orvil Dryfoos, was supposed to be the publisher in his generation. But Dryfoos had died of a heart attack shortly after taking over, and Punch it would be, and the *Times* would remain the *Times.* There was a general feeling in the newsroom, long after Sulzberger acceded, that he was a pleasant well-meaning young man whose main preoccupation was with the business side and making money. There was also a belief that Sulzberger, an ex-Marine, did not particularly like the reporting his correspondents had done from Vietnam, nor for that matter the domestic protest that much of their reporting had in part helped inspire. Visiting the *Times* bureau in Paris in the late sixties, Sulzberger had begun a fierce tirade against peace protesters. Sydney Gruson, then the paper's foreign editor and the executive closest to Sulzberger personally, had listened for a time and had said, not in an unkind way, for people were not unkind to him, "Arthur, you're a disgrace to the paper you publish." It was the kind of story that told why the *Times* remained a special newspaper.

By the late sixties the *Post* was clearly gaining on the *Times.* It had been upgrading its staff, and gathering momentum, improving its position as an outlet for important public figures eager to debate national issues. That was a key to status: which paper would a major political figure, wanting to ventilate a crucial issue, go to? Which paper was more central in defining the national agenda? The *Post* was important in Washington, but that had a touch of parochialism to it. The joint news service with the Los Angeles *Times* had helped the *Post,* but there was still no doubt that *The New York Times* was the dominant paper. It always had been.

So it was not surprising that in the spring of 1971 the *Post* was behind the *Times* from the start on what was to become known as the Pentagon Papers. When Daniel Ellsberg decided to make the Papers (a secret bureaucratic history of the war compiled by Robert McNamara) public, he had tried elsewhere. He had tried Senator Fulbright, but Fulbright was uneasy with the role, it was out of character for him, the idea of receiving vast amounts of purloined classified documents left him cold. In *his* club you did not do that sort of thing. So the *Times* became the perfect outlet and Neil Sheehan the perfect reporter. Ellsberg had gone through a conversion of his own over the previous five years; he had begun as one of the Pentagon's bright young civilians, and he had believed in the war, and activist that he was, he did not feel that he could stay behind in Washington while great events were taking place in Vietnam. Once he was there, his own intelligence and will had taken him to every corner of the country. He had subjected Vietnam to what one colleague had called his "laser-beam intelligence," and thus from the start he had seen the difference between what Washington wanted to happen and what *was* happening. Daniel Ellsberg, in whatever incarnation and in any job, was no ordinary man, he was an obsessive man; that which he saw, others must see, that which he believed, others must believe. Thus as he became increasingly disillusioned he also became a force. No one entered an argument with him lightly or left it exactly the same. As he became dovish, he was no ordinary dove; he was extraordinarily well informed, and his dovishness was that of formidable intelligence, of a mind that never stopped. As he reached each increment of doubt, he had to push on to one further level of knowledge and insight. First, beginning in 1966 and 1967, he had to prove to himself that Vietnam did not work; by 1968 he was obsessed by the origins of the struggle, by why it had happened. For others obsessed by the same question he was a rare colleague, forceful, original, and illuminating. But whereas others might have been content with having come to the core of the rational explanation for the war (to the extent that there was a rational explanation for something so irrational) he pressed on. He was a man who saw political events in terms of moral absolutes. Now he sought moral explanations as well, and became fascinated by the question of war crimes. Had there been war crimes and who had committed them? What were the levels of guilt?

At almost the same time, Neil Sheehan, then a reporter for the *Times,* was also becoming fascinated with the issue of war crimes. Sheehan had been one of the early reporters whose pessimistic view of the war had angered American officials. He had arrived in Vietnam in 1962 for UPI at the age of twenty-five, being paid seventy-five dollars a week. He had no previous reportorial experience, but he was quick and energetic. After just missing a Pulitzer Prize in 1964, he left Vietnam, joined The New York Times, and returned in 1965 for a second tour. His reporting for the *Times* reflected his own increasingly pessimistic view, grounded as it was on his strong sense of the legacy of the past, of the French Indochina war. (In 1963, at Tan Son Nhut air base, he had coined one of the war's most prophetic lines while listening to a newly arrived American general make his airport speech about imminent victory. Sheehan had turned to a colleague and said, "Ah, look, another foolish Westerner come to lose his reputation to Ho Chi Minh.") There was in Sheehan's stories a sense of what the war was doing to the country, a sense reflected in the copy of few other reporters. Where most American reporters new to Vietnam saw the war through the prism of the Americans, he saw it through the prism of the Vietnamese. He became increasingly depressed at what the sheer might of the American commitment was doing to a place he loved, and he left for the second time in 1967, saddened over what had already happened and what he was sure was going to happen next. He was haunted by what he had seen and what he had been part of. His obsession did not necessarily please his employers, who felt that he was too close to Vietnam and that it influenced his other work, which of course it did; a generation that had covered Vietnam was never again so trusting of its government. Nonetheless, there were benefits for the *Times*. Sheehan's story, right after the Tet offensive in 1968, about the 206,000-man troop request by Westmoreland was a story of major proportions and affected the 1968 political campaign. (It had also enraged Benjamin C. Bradlee, who, the night it was published, was at a dinner of the Gridiron Club where all the power elite of Washington were gathered. Hearing of the *Times* story, Bradlee immediately began interviewing people on the scene, trying to match the story despite the Gridiron rule that no journalists can work at the dinner. "There are no journalists at a Gridiron dinner," a club executive had said to him. "Not tonight there aren't," said Bradlee, working until he and senior *Post* reporter Chal Roberts could finally put together a weak competing story.)

So Sheehan had, mostly on his own initiative, stayed on the case. In 1970 the *New York Times Book Review* editor had asked him to review a book by Mark Lane about alleged American atrocities in Vietnam. The book had not smelled right to Sheehan and, being a meticulous reporter, he had started checking Army records for units, names, officers, and had found that the officers mentioned in the book did not exist, the units were not where they were supposed to be. Sheehan had given the book a scorching review, saying that perhaps a good book on war crimes was needed, but surely this was not it. But the response to the review had fascinated him. A number of very serious people who were very concerned about American crimes in Vietnam had written him and had made a strong case that there had indeed been war crimes, and had compiled a vast bibliography. They made the bibliography available to him. Sheehan mastered it, spent months reading every book on the subject, and as a result he wrote, on March 28, 1971, a long and powerful review of thirty-three books. John Leonard, the *Book Review* editor, devoted an entire issue to this review. In the article Sheehan said that though he had not realized it at the time, he had himself witnessed war crimes in Vietnam. It was a landmark piece of commentary, and it took uncommon courage for Leonard to print the review; for a centrist institution like the *Times,* it was straying far from the accepted norm. In some ways, printing it was a more audacious act than the printing of the Pentagon Papers, which were, of course, official papers and thus buttressed by their own legitimacy. When Leonard, knowing that the Sheehan review was something special, had asked his editorial superiors to promote the piece in their house ads, they had refused. It was as if the *Times* was uneasy with what it was doing, and that reflected something of the divided personality of the paper. The *Book Review* was closer to the counterculture and more sympathetic to the protest on Vietnam than the front page of the paper, which was more traditional, more wedded to the official version.

The essay on war crimes had reached one reader in particular, Daniel Ellsberg. Sheehan had known Ellsberg in Vietnam and they had stayed in touch, part of that small underground of people who had been in Vietnam and could not let go, who sought each other out to share their particular madness. Ellsberg had hinted over the previous few months of something big that he had and might break. It was not exactly easy to tell what it was or what it was about. There were hints, subtle references. He had something he wanted out, but he still had to be wooed. Sheehan's war-crimes piece cinched it; here for Ellsberg was the right man with the right outlet. So he made his proposition. There was a vast classified secret history of the war, compiled by a staff under Robert McNamara. If he turned it over to Sheehan, would the *Times* guarantee to use it, promise not to back out under governmental pressure? It was, he said, very big stuff. Sheehan went to his superiors, principally A. M. Rosenthal, the chief news executive of the paper, who had never been considered a particular friend of the reporters in Vietnam.

Rosenthal was the son of immigrants and his feeling for American values and institutions bordered on the reverential. His own germinal reporting experience had been in Poland, where he had hated the ruling Communist Party and whence he had been expelled. There was a suspicion among the *Times* reporters in Vietnam that Rosenthal had never entirely accepted their reporting, that he was ill at ease with it and them. To him, Communism in Poland and Communism in Indochina were the same. The young *Times* reporters who had covered the social protest that the war had wrought considered Rosenthal decidedly unsympathetic to their reporting. Rosenthal had told Sheehan that he could give no guarantees on documents he had yet to see, he could not judge their newsworthiness, but that the toughness of the documents, that is, the degree to which they offended the government, would not be a problem. If, as Ellsberg seemed to promise, the documents were highly critical of American actions and revealed great discrepancies between alleged American aims and real American aims, they would be considered highly newsworthy.

It was the key decision. The moment Sheehan secured the papers, Rosenthal would set something in motion; to refuse publication would be journalistically unthinkable, a decision of even greater magnitude than the decision to publish. Nor, in the gossipy world of journalism, could it have remained a secret for very long. Rosenthal's answer satisfied Ellsberg and he passed on the mammoth study to Sheehan, who spent the next three weeks studying the documents and then briefed his top editors on their contents. It was very strong material, he said, clearly showing the government to have been highly duplicitous. Rosenthal was very supportive, despite his own view of Vietnam. (He told one colleague, "This stuff is really going to help people that I don't agree with at all, but that's that, you can't worry about it.") To his credit, he was bothered by only one thing. Were these documents, he asked repeatedly, truly authentic? Was there any chance that they were fakes, that the *Times* was in some way being set up? Sheehan, who was extremely knowledgeable about the war, was absolutely sure of their authenticity. That was enough.

A task force started working on the study in secret at the Hilton Hotel. Eventually the *Times*'s lawyer, James Goodale, was brought in; but he was brought in after the commitment to go ahead had been made to Sheehan. Goodale came from the *Times*'s old traditional law firm, and had been planted at the paper by Louis Loeb, the doyen of the firm, when it became clear that the *Times*'s business, in an increasingly litigious world, was so great that the paper needed a lawyer of its own. He enjoyed a surprisingly good reputation among working journalists at the paper. Unlike most lawyers, who in moments of crisis seek a reason not to publish, Goodale seemed to study each case as a means of finding a way *to* publish. Now, however, he was somewhat unhappy that a decision of this magnitude had been taken without consulting him first, and he wanted his colleagues at Lord, Day and Lord to see the documents. He felt this was vital to the *Times*'s interests if there were ever a court case. Sheehan and the various editors were nervous. There seemed too great a chance that word of the *Times*'s project might reach the government. But Goodale insisted that these were honorable men and would not betray the *Times.* Rosenthal, along with James Reston, who was a strong force in the decision to publish, were not all that interested in what the lawyers had to say; their position was that it was the editors' job to publish, to decide what was of news value and not to worry about the legal consequences. Later, if they had to go to jail they would go to jail. Rosenthal also thought he had the right to decide what to publish. He was wrong. In cases like this, it turned out, the *Times* was a monarchy and only Punch Sulzberger could decide.

Meanwhile the documents went to the law firm, where Louis Loeb was appalled. Loeb was then seventy-two years old, an old-fashioned man respectful of power and authority. He did not, unlike the younger men at the *Times,* make a distinction between documents that had been classified for *political* reasons, that is, to hide the government's true aims for domestic political reasons or to cover up its mistakes, and classifications for true reasons of national security, secrets which if they got out might cause a ship to be sunk, a battalion to be wiped out, a weapons system to be invalidated. His position was that to publish these documents would violate the espionage act. He said that if the government did not bring criminal action, it would bring a civil suit and it would also bring an injunction to stop the paper from publishing. The government, he predicted, would win. Most frightening of all, he said that his law firm would not defend the paper in court, because he believed what the *Times* was doing to be illegal and unpatriotic. It was harsh stuff. He had been counsel to the paper for twenty-five years, his firm had helped win the landmark First Amendment Sullivan case for the *Times.* Fortunately for the *Times,* Goodale had been studying both the papers and the law carefully, and though he was truly Loeb's man at the *Times,* he had grown beyond that, he had ambitions of his own, he was younger, and the more he read the papers, the more convinced he became that there was no violation of security in them at all. No codes were compromised, no soldier at the front made more vulnerable. These papers simply made the government look foolish and two-faced;

these were classifications not of security but of politics. Goodale told the editors he felt they could go ahead and that they could win any case that developed, because the *Times* was within its rights under the First Amendment.

For a while the argument became very heated at the *Times;* some of the business people, scared about the government's power over the paper and its television station, weighed in with Loeb. John Oakes, the editorial-page editor, who had been much tougher on the war than almost any major editor in America, came up with the compromise idea of not really using the documents, but either paraphrasing from them or quoting them very sparingly. Some people, caught between the law and their desire to print, liked the Oakes compromise. A middle position, honorable and semi-genteel. Rosenthal and Reston were appalled. The documents were of the essence. Finally, Punch Sulzberger rendered a decision; they would print as they had intended and promised, but they would only print half the length. With that, the project went ahead. The various editors were still unsure of Sulzberger. He had never inspired great confidence in the city room, journalism had always seemed to mystify him. How heavy was Punch? Would he stay the course? The editors were afraid that the government might find out, might pressure him and he might fold. The closer it got to publication day, the more nervous they became. They wanted him on vacation and indeed there was great insistence on Saturday, June 12, 1971, the day before publication, that he must go ahead with his scheduled golf game; the editors did not want him reachable.

The stories were finally ready, Rosenthal shrewdly (and much to the annoyance of some of the reporters) took out the words "top secret" from all references in the main body of type, and the *Times* published. Punch had held firm, had seemed to feel very little pressure. He was good at delegating authority. Eventually the government enjoined the *Times.* And eventually the *Times* won in court.


The publication of the Pentagon Papers by the *Times* caught the *Post* flat-footed, even though the editors there knew that the *Times* was up to something, that a team of journalists had been hidden away working on some secret project. For Bradlee it was an intensely personal thing; later he would say of those days that every word in the *Times* was printed in his blood. It was not really a matter of substance; neither he nor Rosenthal, after all, had been so fascinated by the question of how and why the United States had gone to war in Vietnam as to assign a team to find out. It was, in his eyes, that the *Times* had a big one, and he wanted to catch up. He just hated it, hated being in second place every morning, while everyone talked about the *Times.* At once he made the decision to rewrite and credit the *Times* while at the same time trying to secure a set of papers for the *Post.* Some people from the Institute for Policy Studies, a radical-left think tank in Washington, called. They had a book that was based on the Papers and they offered to let the *Post* serialize their book. But it would be their writing, their tone, their definition. Bradlee read the manuscript and was disturbed. Too much spin, he decided. So the *Post* continued to rewrite the *Times.*

But Ben Bagdikian, the national editor of the *Post,* had worked for a time at Rand, and he had known Dan Ellsberg there, and when the *Times* had printed the Papers, he was sure almost from the start that Ellsberg was the source. There were in those days about twenty or thirty people, journalists and government officials, in the Vietnam underground. Passionate, obsessed people who could not deal easily with those who had not been there and who spoke mostly to each other. Even among people like this Ellsberg was special, he was so obsessed. He seemed to suck the oxygen out of the room, nothing else mattered or existed. So when the papers appeared, Bagdikian began making telephone calls in search of Ellsberg, finally locating him, and began discussions about how the *Post* would use the material (Ellsberg was a tough negotiator, he wanted good serious play, he was not going to perform this particular act just to keep Benjamin C. Bradlee from being scooped by A. M. Rosenthal). When Bagdikian sensed that he finally had the connection, he went to Eugene Patterson, the managing editor, who was in charge since Bradlee was out of town, and asked whether the *Post* would go with the Papers if he got a set. Yes, said Patterson. But they agreed that Bagdikian ought to check with Bradlee later in the day. Bradlee told him that if he got the Papers and the *Post* did not publish them, it would have to get a new executive editor. That was the commitment.

There was no small amount of irony in the fact that it was Bagdikian who was rescuing Bradlee with what was to become, up until Watergate, the paper's foremost coup. The two men were completely different. Bagdikian was not interested in scoop but in the social implications of stories. Bradlee was only interested in issues when they were personalized and dramatized; Bagdikian was fascinated by the more subtle changes and movements, changes in a social structure that were by no means dramatic. If Bradlee liked winners, Bagdikian was fascinated by the plight of losers. There was, after the Pentagon Papers, a moment of high tension between the two of them. Bagdikian at the time was serving as the paper's ombudsman and had attended a meeting of blacks at Harvard where a black militant had charged, in the rhetoric of the moment, that it was the purpose of the media to oppress black people. Bagdikian had dissented, saying that the primary purpose of the people who controlled the media was to make money. The two men had quickly got into a shouting match and finally Bagdikian, losing his temper, had said that in a city like Washington, which was 70 percent black, there was a choice for blacks. Either they could call the publisher of the *Post* a racist and feel better, or they could boycott the paper and make their numbers count. The meeting was open and there happened to be an Associated Press reporter there, and the AP story, oversimplified as wire news stories often are, had led with the fact that a key editor of the Washington *Post* had called for a boycott of his own paper. Bradlee was furious; more than anything else, he placed a high premium on loyalty. He gave loyalty to his reporters, and in turn demanded loyalty to him, and the company, in public. When Bagdikian returned, Bradlee threw the AP story down on his desk and asked if it was true. Bagdikian had said yes, in effect it was. Bradlee said he could not believe it, could not believe that kind of disloyalty to the paper, and from one of his own lieutenants. Bagdikian had answered that he was not loyal to Bradlee, he was the ombudsman and he must not be loyal to an editor. They went on arguing, until Bagdikian said that he thought his resignation was being asked for, and Bradlee answered that it was up to Bagdikian. So Bagdikian typed up his resignation and then there was an early-morning phone call from Bradlee apologizing, saying that he still needed Bagdikian. But there was, Bagdikian felt, a division from that day on, and it did not end happily between the two of them and between Bagdikian and the *Post*.

But that was still to come. In June 1971 he was the one man who could save the *Post* on the Pentagon Papers. He went to Cambridge and brought back the Papers on June 17. That morning, even as Bagdikian was returning to Washington, the *Post* executives had met and Gerry Siegel, the in-house counsel, a man who had come from Lyndon Johnson's old senatorial office, not knowing the *Post* had a set of the Papers, had begun to talk about what the *Times* was doing. He hoped to God, Siegel said, that the *Post* would not do anything like that, so unpatriotic, such a disservice to the country. Siegel went on and on, a tirade against the *Times*. Katharine Graham, who knew the *Post* had a set of the Papers, said nothing. She simply sat and listened and her eyes were absolutely cold. By the afternoon Bagdikian had returned. With great secrecy, he raced, not to the newsroom, but to Bradlee's house. Right then it seemed as though the whole world, and in particular the government of the United States, was in hot pursuit of Dr. Daniel Ellsberg and anyone else who might have a copy of the Papers. Bradlee carefully selected the reporters he wanted to work on the project, and went up to them quietly, one by one, rather than calling them all to his office, which would tip off that something big was up. He chose them—Chal Roberts and Don Oberdorfer and Murrey Marder—for speed and for knowledge of the subject, and they all slipped out of the city room one by one and went to his house. There they looked at the Papers— some 4,000 sheets of paper, all unsorted, all shuffled cards. No order, no index. So, working against a desperate set of deadlines, they began reading and writing while the editors were meeting with corporate executives and lawyers in another room. By the time the *Post* received the Papers, the *Times* had already been enjoined by the government. There was a restraining order against printing more, and the conflict was going through an accelerated process of adjudication on its way to the Supreme Court. Which in the minds of the *Post* people placed them in a more vulnerable position than the *Times,* since when the *Times* had published originally, there had been no government injunction (in the minds of the *Times* executives, of course, *their* decision had been harder, since they were the first). Might the *Post,* by publishing now, be violating that same injunction which restrained the *Times?* Might that make its legal position even weaker than the *Times*'s?

The second problem was purely financial. The Washington Post Company had coincidentally gone public only two days before. On June 15, 1971, the *Post* stock had been listed for the first time, with 1.35 million shares of Class B common stock going on sale. Within forty-eight hours the crucial editorial meetings on the Pentagon Papers had taken place. The shadow of the stock issue hung very much over the editorial deliberations, the timing for everyone concerned could not have been worse. In addition to everything else, there was one little clause in the legal agreement for the sale of the stock that said that the sale could be canceled if a catastrophic event struck the company. Perhaps a government injunction halting distribution of the paper if it published the Pentagon Papers might be considered a catastrophic event, or an indictment for contempt, for violating a restraining order. There were several very real possibilities. It was just the type of pressure that Katharine Graham had feared in the first place when the idea of going public was broached to her.

While the reporters were working in one room of Bradlee's house, the executives, lawyers, and businessmen were meeting in another room, and it was not going well. Bradlee, sensing that it was going to be a longer day than he had imagined, moved to keep the reporters as distant from the legal struggle as possible; he did not want them distracted and depressed by the possibility that their work might go for naught. It was difficult enough trying to sort out that mass of papers and write for a deadline.

For what was going on in the main room was fast turning into a classic legal-journalistic struggle. It is an established belief of most serious working reporters that almost all conventional lawyers, men not steeped in the First Amendment, when asked for an opinion on whether or not to publish, on almost any issue, will always advise against publication, because they are sound and conservative, because they have no particular love of controversy and harsh truths, and most important of all, because if nothing is published, no one will sue. It is what might be called no-fault advice. There are exceptions to this, lawyers who believe fiercely in the First Amendment, lawyers whose own iconoclasm makes them anxious to see society's dark side in print. But the young men who were representing the *Post* in this case were not of that breed, rather they were from an entirely different tradition, and it was not their fault, it was the fault of the *Post.* Because the *Post* was tilted mostly to liberal, Democratic causes, the paper, in part to hedge its bets, had chosen Bill Rogers's law firm, a connection to the Republicans, a connection to Nixon. The *Post* had liked that, it was a good sound conservative practice. But the young lawyers from the firm of Royal, Koegel and Wells were, in the minds of the editors, creatures of Bill Rogers, sound, conservative, and cautious. And now they were in no way receptive to the idea of publication. Their former senior partner was at the right hand of Richard Nixon, and they did not like the legal, the political, or the moral course that publication implied. What became increasingly clear to the editors as time passed was that this was not going to be some light exercise in caution. The *Post*'s lawyers, Roger Clark and Tony Essaye, unlike James Goodale, seemed to be looking for reasons *not* to publish. They appeared to be very rigid. Bagdikian, moving back and forth between rooms, was appalled by how unyielding the lawyers were. They were saying that to publish now with a restraining order already pending against the *Times* was to flout the court deliberately. Besides, they added, there was no need to test the right to publish, that right was already being tested by the *Times;* all the *Post* had to do was wait for the *Times*.

That argument simply enraged Bradlee. "I want a piece of the action too," he said, arguing that what the court had done to the *Times* was all the more reason for the *Post* to publish. For him and for the other editors, the *Post* had reached a crucial moment. They had come so far toward becoming a great national newspaper, it was as if they were now poised on the brink, but if they were defeated here, defeated by their own lawyers, it would all come apart. That was uppermost in Bradlee's mind. He was on the threshold of making the *Post* big-time, the resources and muscle of a great paper were there, but the tradition and instinct were not. He desperately wanted to publish, he had made a commitment to Bagdikian that he *would* publish, and the alternative to publishing, *not* publishing, would cost him his best people. He held in his pocket the ultimate deterrent, the threat of his own resignation, but it was something he was loath to use, it would have to be the ultimate gesture. It simply put too much pressure on the publisher, it was like putting a gun to her head and it violated his own sense of loyalty.

Meanwhile, Bagdikian was being very very eloquent and forceful. If this kind of fight for a free press was somewhat new and alien to Bradlee, it was as if Bagdikian, press critic and press scholar, had been waiting all his life for it. He was telling the lawyers that other newspapers did not have to feel bound by the government's decision, that each paper had to follow its own destiny. The *Post* had some of the most serious and professional journalists in the country, they had covered this story for more than a decade, they were more than competent to judge what damaged and what did not damage national security. As for the *Times,* if the *Post* did not print now it would seem to be failing to support the *Times* and taking the government's side against it. The best way to help the *Times* was to publish the Papers, rather than to let it stand alone. Then he stopped and said, and it affected everyone in the room: "The only way to assert the right to publish is to publish." Bradlee had never admired Bagdikian more.

But the lawyers went on talking law, talking their arcane specialty. They owned the law and Bradlee did not. He was suspicious of them. He didn't believe that the case against publishing was as airtight as they made it seem, or the *Times,* after all, would not have published. He was annoyed that, rather than acting as colleagues explaining the risks, they seemed to be adversaries fighting him. He decided he needed to talk to a lawyer of his own and he quietly slipped out of the room and tried to call his friend Edward Bennett Williams.

Williams he trusted; if Williams agreed with Clark and Essaye, then that was it, the risks were too great. Williams was trying a divorce case in Chicago and, according to his office, was unreachable. Bradlee thought for a minute and called his friend Jim Hoge, the editor of the Chicago *Sun-Times,* and asked him to pass an urgent message to Williams to call Bradlee. Williams called back ten minutes later, having got the message while in a phone-equipped limousine on the way to the airport. Bradlee explained his dilemma and what the lawyers were saying and Williams laughed. "That's bullshit, Bradlee. Pure bullshit." Bradlee felt better. "Bradlee," the owner of the Washington Redskins continued, "I have never seen you so far behind so late in the game. It's 21–0 against you and there are eight minutes left in the fourth quarter." Bradlee felt even better. What about the law? "Bradlee, I've been in this city for thirty years and for thirty years I've watched responsible and respectable journalists tell the Congress and the executive branch to go fuck themselves. What's Nixon going to do? Put every major editor and publisher in jail? Let me tell you about Nixon, Bradlee. He doesn't have the balls to go after you, Bradlee. He hates you. He probably thinks about going after you more than any man who ever sat in that office. He'd love to go after you, but he doesn't have the balls." Ed Williams, Bradlee thought, was wonderful. This was precisely what Bradlee himself thought. The essence of it was not the law, it was politics. Bradlee went back into the room reassured that his position was not so lonely. He could not mention to the *Post*'s lawyers that he had consulted with another attorney, but he felt much better.

Still, it was a very tense situation. In addition to the lawyers, Fritz Beebe was there, and Beebe was the single most respected and admired figure in the entire company. It was Fritz who had held the entire organization together during the worst of Phil Graham's sickness and it was Fritz whom Kay had turned to more than to anyone else both for sustenance and for counsel on the difficult decisions in the ensuing years. Working reporters liked Beebe, they had a sense of a commitment to their profession, rare among businessmen and lawyers. He was intelligent and he was just, and he had always given reporters a sense that he genuinely admired what they did. If Beebe sided against publication, then it was serious, for at the moment Fritz Beebe, even more than Ben Bradlee, could probably carry Kay. Beebe began by saying that he did not want the decision to go public to affect the decision to publish, even though, as he said, if they were judged to be criminals it could cause the company to lose its television licenses. He meant well, but it made them all, if anything, even more conscious of the business jeopardy, more nervous about what was on the line. When Bagdikian made his statement about how to assert the right to publish, Beebe answered that that was all well and good, they were worried about the right to publish, but he was worried about the future of the newspaper. "You have your responsibilities," he said, "and I have mine, and they are very different responsibilities." The courts, he said, have found that a criminal indictment is a catastrophic act. Thus the underwriter's contract to go public could be canceled. Bradlee, watching Beebe, was intrigued. Beebe was a man he loved, Beebe came from the same firm where Bradlee's grandfather had worked, and they had always been friends and allies. But here was Beebe on the other side, though Bradlee sensed a difference between Beebe and the two younger lawyers. Beebe did not seem so rigid. It was a little as if he were arguing not so much his real view as his responsibilities.

So they continued arguing back and forth, trying to settle in one afternoon issues that the editors of the *Times* had discussed for weeks. Bradlee, Bagdikian, Geyelin on one side, the lawyers and business people on the other, everyone getting more tired, everyone looking for some means of compromise. At one point there was the beginning of a compromise idea. The *Post* would not publish that night, would hold the Papers one day, but would notify Attorney General John Mitchell that it had the Papers and intended to publish them the next day. This was never firmed up or settled on as a compromise. Like the Johnny Oakes suggestion at the *Times,* it was the product of men and women exhausted by their struggle and desperately seeking some middle ground to hold them all together. In this case it was also part of an attempt to bring Beebe over to the side of the journalists. At 7 P.M., with deadlines drawing closer and closer, the compromise was still hanging in the air when the reporters, taking a quick breather from their writing to eat some sandwiches, happened to wander into the other room and heard of the idea. Up until then they had no idea at all that the question of publication was in doubt, that their work was in jeopardy. Angered that anyone would hesitate a moment over publishing, angered even more by the timidity of the compromise, they all exploded. "That's the shittiest idea I've ever heard," Don Oberdorfer said.

Then Chal Roberts spoke. He was the top reporter on the paper, scheduled to retire in two weeks, the epitome of the establishment reporter; he was a journalistic extension of the national security complex, he judged dangers and enemies on the same scale as the people he covered, and he had almost unconsciously over a career accepted the limitations that his sources had wanted him to accept. He was the kind of reporter high officials judged to be sound. If the Pentagon Papers showed the top level of the American government to be liars, as they surely did, then they also showed reporters like Chal Roberts to have been at least partial collaborators in a shell game performed on the American people. But Roberts was now a powerful, forceful advocate of publication. The very fact that he had such seniority and that his colleagues viewed him as so traditionalist a figure gave his words an extra dimension. The compromise idea was like crawling on your belly to the government, he said. "If you don't want to risk running it, then to hell with it, don't run it," Roberts said. But if the paper did not run it, then he would move his own retirement up two weeks and he would issue a public statement disassociating himself from the decision of the paper where he had spent most of his professional life. That from Chalmers Roberts, one of the most traditional reporters on the paper. It was a warning of how the rest of the paper would react. "You're going to get a full-scale revolt from the staff," Bagdikian whispered to Bradlee.

It was not that the battle had been lost yet. Bradlee, after all, had not played his full hand. But the reporters stiffened the editors and in some way affected Beebe. It had brought home to him very dramatically the editorial consequences of failing to publish. That Chal Roberts especially felt so strongly made him less sure of his overall judgment. He knew what was wise from a business standpoint, but what was wise from a business standpoint was not necessarily what was wise from a general standpoint. Journalism was different from all other businesses, it was based on creative talent, and it was important to coddle talent, not to limit it. So, with deadlines approaching and the room still divided, they decided to call Kay Graham. She had stayed out of the decision until now, but there was no time left. If they missed the deadline and waited a day, then that in itself was a decision, because everyone in town would know they had the Papers, and had waited, and perhaps by then the government would hit them with an injunction. They reached Mrs. Graham at her house, where she was giving a large farewell party for Harry Gladstein, who was retiring as the paper's circulation manager. She had some forewarning: Gene Patterson, who was managing editor of the paper, knew what was brewing, had gone to the Gladstein party and taken Mrs. Graham aside. He had told her that she was going to have to make the ultimate decision. Patterson's warning stunned her. She had expected a minor squabble after which the Papers would be printed. It had never occurred to her that *she* might be called in to make the final decision. "I don't envy you," he had said, "you're really going to have to make the decision, and if we don't publish, then we'll be the ones pulling the rug out from under the *Times.*" "Jesus, Gene," she asked, "is it that bad? Is it really going to come to that?" "I think so," Patterson, a Southerner with a love of biblical cadence, said, "I think the immortal soul of the Washington *Post* is at stake. If we don't print it, it's really going to be terrible because the government knows we have the Papers, and we'll be used as evidence against the *Times*. They'll be the bad paper which defies the government and we'll be the good paper which believes in the government." Now the call from Bradlee's house caught her in the middle of a farewell toast. "Let me finish my toast to Harry and I'll come right over," she said. No, Beebe answered, there wasn't time for that, they were right on deadline. "You're asking me to do something over the phone that *The New York Times* took three months to do," she said. At which point Beebe quickly summarized the lawyers' position. Then he gave the editorial position. Then both Bradlee and Geyelin came on and outlined how much was at stake, how much momentum the paper had built up, how if the paper failed to publish now, all that would be lost as well as some of the best reporters on the staff. Then Mrs. Graham asked Beebe what he thought, and he said, "On balance, I think no." Hearing him, Bradlee thought *oh no*. But then he realized that it was not so much what Beebe had said as what he *hadn't* said. It was not a hard no, he did not make a passionate, intense, personal plea against publishing, he was not laying his body down on the railroad tracks. It was as if he were saying: I'm a lawyer and I can't go against what the lawyers are saying, but it's close and my instincts are divided. At which point Bradlee came back on the phone saying, "We've got to go, we've got to go." And at that moment, with Paul Ignatius, the president of the paper (and until very recently the Secretary of the Navy and a McNamara protégé; he had gotten his job at the *Post* through Bob McNamara), telling her to wait one day, shouting into one ear, and Ben Bradlee shouting into the other, Katharine Graham had to make the decision. Fritz Beebe's answer had surprised her at first, she and Fritz had always been together on everything, but then she had heard what Bradlee had also heard, that Fritz was not closing the door, Fritz was permitting her to go against him. "All right," she said, "let's go, let's publish." Hearing her say it, Beebe knew immediately that she had made the right decision.

It was, they all thought later—Bradlee and Geyelin and Mrs. Graham— the first moment of the *Post* as a big-time newspaper, a paper able to stand on its own and make its own decisions. Without it, they were sure, there never would have been Watergate. Because of the decisions that were taken that night, there were never any decisions needed on Watergate; never during Watergate did Ben Bradlee have to call Katharine Graham about whether or not they should print a particular story. If you had it, you went with it. It was the key moment for the paper, the coming of age.

In the days that followed the decision to publish, as the resistance from the government mounted and the *Post* fought its battle through the courts, Ben Bagdikian, the hero of the affair, noticed a curious phenomenon. Not only was Katharine Graham not friendly or warm toward him, but she was downright cold. There was no doubt about it, she was being very unfriendly. In meeting after meeting with the lawyers that they were both now part of, she refused to talk to him and managed not to look at him or catch his eye. On the third day they were on their way to a meeting and she turned to him and said, "Well, what kind of trouble did you get us in today?" And she said it, Bagdikian thought, in a cold, hard way. Later he mentioned it to one of his assistants, and the word got out, and a few days later when the Supreme Court had ruled for the *Times* and the *Post,* during the moment of triumph when everyone at the *Post* was a hero or heroine, Mrs. Graham came by to see Bagdikian and tell him that she had only been kidding. But it was very clear to Bagdikian that she had not been kidding. If she was making the right and courageous decisions, he thought, she was nonetheless unhappy and somewhat resentful about doing it.

Shortly afterward the Washington Post Company changed legal firms. William Rogers's firm was let go. Edward Bennett Williams's was hired.

Bagdikian had not been terribly surprised by the coolness from his publisher. It was, he thought, a part of her ambivalence, and part of the ambivalence of the paper, so close to so much power, so awed by it. Washington was built around politics, and politics was the distillation of power. Thus always the contradiction of the *Post:* covering power and yet staying apart from it. The great men of Washington, up until the Nixon administration, came regularly to Mrs. Graham's dinner parties, the best ticket in town, and as they socialized over good food and wine, the adversarial role diminished. They were close, they were friends, these were not just men of power, they were men of good will, events were seen as they wanted them seen. There was at the *Post,* as there was throughout Washington, a more than subtle reverence for power, for title, an instinct to respect it. In the Pentagon Papers struggle, the *Post* had in part risked power in its conflict with the government in order to hold power in its position within journalism. If it was not respected within journalism, then it could not be respected by exterior institutions. The balance was always delicate.

But the ambivalence was always there too. The photos on Kay Graham's walls were not of her with distinguished journalists like Walter Lippmann, but with a variety of Presidents. That was where legitimacy came from in Washington, and it was clear that the *Post* and its publisher felt most comfortable with the least amount of tension with the White House. The number-two source of power in Washington did not like the number-one source of power to be angry with it. Yet despite the *Post*'s support of even the worst of Johnson's policies, the relationship had been uneasy. The breach was there even in the good days, when he had first committed U.S. combat troops to Vietnam. It was Mrs. Graham who had tried to heal the breach and who tried to bridge it, but he was not comfortable with her, he kept her at a distance. He told his aides that she was going around telling her editors that Lyndon Johnson was trying to buy her with dinners (there had been an element of truth in that, even if she had not said it) and when she made overtures to him he answered with a very cold note. At one point she mentioned to Bobby Kennedy the cold shoulder she was receiving from Johnson, and he angrily reminded her that without Phil's intervention Lyndon Johnson would not be in the White House. Then in December 1967, as the pressure against Johnson mounted, as Gene McCarthy entered the race, Johnson fired her close friend McNamara. At that point Mrs. Graham wrote the President a letter. It was a warm, personal letter, but whether it was the kind of letter a powerful working journalist should send a powerful working politician was another matter:

> These times are so difficult that my heart bleeds for you. I think so often of the story you tell of Phil's letter to Jack Kennedy after the Bay of Pigs. Of course there's no parallel event—quite the contrary. And yet it seems that the burdens you bear, the issues you confront, the delicate line you must tread, are almost too much for one human being. The only thanks you ever seem to receive is a deafening chorus of carping criticism. Unlike Phil, I find it hard to express emotion. I can't write in the eloquent words he used. But I want you to know

I am among the many people in this country who believe in you and are behind you with trust and devotion.

This had not, of course, charmed or comforted Lyndon Johnson, besieged as he was. He regarded Russ Wiggins as a friend, but he did not trust either the paper or the magazine any more. Even in the old days his attitude toward the press had always been: "Those who aren't for me are against me"; now, under terrible pressure because of Vietnam, that was more true than ever. He did not forgive Kay Graham or her reporters, and he did not pronounce a benediction upon her until long afterward. By then he had left the presidency and had returned to the ranch, and had started going through his papers. There he had come across old memos from Phil, suggestions for what had become the Great Society, and old memories had stirred. He had thought fondly of Phil and decided to forgive the *Post*. On a trip back to Washington he sought an invitation from the *Post* and went there for lunch, staying for five remarkable hours in which he sought to prove his case, declassifying documents on Vietnam right and left. At the end he said that no matter what the *Post* had done to him on Vietnam (it had done, by and large, remarkably little against him) he forgave them all because he loved Phil so much and owed him so much. It was a great and moving performance. They gave him a standing ovation.

Lyndon Johnson was driven out of office not just by the war, though that certainly was part of it, but for a more complicated reason—a cumulative feeling among many of his fellow citizens that he had lost control of the processes and that the processes were in turn out of control. The decade of the sixties had simply seen and felt too much tension, too much raw conflict in the society, and Lyndon Johnson was at the center of it all. He seemed to have associated himself with everything, the good and the bad, the civil-rights advances and the war, the protesters and those horrified by the protests. Television had personalized the presidency, but where in the past this had aided the office, had served to bring the President closer to the people in a positive way, now as things went sour it had boomeranged. As things came apart the good citizens of America no longer blamed their congressmen, who were largely invisible, or the party leaders, who had become ciphers, they blamed the President of the United States. He was too large; he invited too much trouble.

It was ironic that it should have happened to Johnson for he was above all a politician, in the best sense. His greatest skill, and it was not to be sneered at, was the art of making 51 percent. It was an art that demanded shrewdness and talent and strength and persistence. There was simply no one better at the act of governance. There were, regrettably for him, many people far better at the act of explaining and selling governance. In this new world of television, of media politics, of young men coiffed and tailored who knew how to hide their craftiness, Lyndon Johnson's mastery counted for much less. *His* cunning somehow showed in his face. The new breed would look less like politicians, but whether they would be as good at governance as their elders was another matter.

The decision to go public in 1971, to sell Washington *Post* stock, had not been one that Katharine Graham had particularly wanted to make. To her mind the *Post* had always been a family newspaper—first her father, then her husband, now her, next her firstborn son. The paper and the family were one. From the time Donald Graham had been born, he had been regarded in that special way of publishing families, not as just a nice young man, but as the heir to the paper and the tradition. It was a very strong current within the family. During the final terrible conflict with Phil, the family lines had been strictly drawn. Agnes Meyer, who in all past disputes favored her son-in-law over her daughter, who often mused aloud about why she seemed to like her Graham grandchildren better than her Meyer children, had come down fiercely on Katharine's side, not just to help her own daughter, *but to make sure the Post stayed in the family for the next generation.*

Given that strong a tribal instinct, the idea of going public had at first seemed a threatening one to Mrs. Graham. It was like letting strangers into the house. But Fritz Beebe, as her lawyer and chief financial adviser, argued that given current inheritance laws, the only way to safeguard orderly transition to the next generation and avoid crushing inheritance taxes was to go public. Indeed, Beebe said, if they waited too long and something unexpected happened to her, it was possible that Donald Graham might lose the paper because of taxes. Besides, he said, they had a more immediate problem, the matter of cash flow. In the fifties, when the paper was poor and stock options seemed nothing more than Monopoly money, Phil Graham had been uncommonly generous with stock options to his senior people. Now these plans had matured and were being cashed in. It was said that John Sweeterman had received more than $2 million, Al Friendly more than $1 million, and Ben Gilbert, the former city editor, nearly $1 million. This money must come directly from the paper's own resources unless they could lay the bill off on new stockholders. So though she had resisted at first, Beebe and others had eventually convinced her. But she remained unhappy about it. She did not like the idea of going public and she did not like the idea of having to go before the top Wall Street people and hustle her paper. The idea of asking all those rich men for money was appalling. She feared that in some intangible way it might compromise both her and the paper. Others on the editorial staff were not entirely enthusiastic either. What Wall Street gave it also took back; if you accepted Wall Street's money, then in some way, direct or indirect, you accepted some of Wall Street's definitions on how your paper should be run. Wall Street liked companies to be run in a modern highly structured way, with a cost-accounting system built in; it did not like them to be run in random

old-fashioned paternalistic ways. But the future called: if going public was
what was demanded, then go public Katharine Graham would. "Otis," she
said somewhat plaintively to her friend Otis Chandler, whose family had
preceded her in this course, "do I really have to make my salary public?" Otis
assured her that she did.

That upset her some but not nearly as much as it upset Ben Bradlee, who
decided that he could not edit the paper if every reporter knew his salary, then
about $100,000. So he resigned from the board. (Some of his colleagues thought
his resignation a mistake since it removed from the paper's governing body the
one true spokesman for the editorial side.) But his salary remained a secret;
the salary of Oz Elliott, his friend and counterpart at *Newsweek,* was made
public and if nobody at *Newsweek* was annoyed at the news, it certainly
annoyed Benjamin Crowninshield Bradlee, since it turned out that good old
Oz of St. Mark's and Harvard was making $5,000 a year more than old Ben
of St. Mark's and Harvard. (But there is no need to feel sorry for Bradlee; a
few years later his name turned up in a list of *Post* stockholders who had 1
percent or more of the paper's stock. His own reporters did some rough
calculations and decided that his stock was worth at least $3 million. When
it was brought to his attention that this might in fact mean he was a wealthy
man, Bradlee answered: No, no, if anyone knew how far he had had to go into
debt to buy that stock, no one would think him wealthy.) He had, he explained,
been given a lot of stock options by Phil Graham as a finder's fee for the
*Newsweek* deal. In order to pick them up then he had to borrow money. Why,
half of that $3 million was borrowed, he said.

So Katharine Graham went public. In the end she did it because she felt
she had no choice. It was that or sell one of the television stations, which would
provide instant cash but would narrow the base of the company. During the
months that they prepared the stock issue Fritz Beebe, whose office was in New
York, talked frequently with the *Post*'s New York financial writer, Phil Greer,
who was unusually knowledgeable about the workings of the market. Greer
was pessimistic about the entire enterprise, and considered it a drastic mistake.
Wall Street, he believed, was a brutal partner, it was not interested in journalism or good writing, and it demanded not just profit but a relentless kind of
profit; Wall Street wanted systems, and cost accounting, and a monitoring of
expense accounts and higher productivity and lower expenditures. None of
these things had anything to do with talent or covering the news. Greer did
not believe that the *Post* could embrace Wall Street without changing. The
*Post* would inevitably become, if not far more conservative on its editorial
page, then far more conservative as an institution. When editors thought about
covering stories or opening bureaus they would think of the accountants and
the costs. What had made certain family-owned papers like *The New York
Times* and the *Post* special in the past was a certain obliviousness to materialism, the power of the editors over the accountants, a willingness to settle for
less than maximum profit. Now, however, simply being in the black would not
be enough, the margin of profit would have to be larger, 15 percent or more

a year to satisfy the stockholders. That was a powerful weapon for the *Post*'s accountants, for they could go into budget meetings and when editorial expenses were being discussed they could argue, not that the paper was losing money, but that the margin of profit was too low and that the stock might fall. The stock fall? What editor could argue back against that? Was a bureau in Johannesburg worth endangering the stock? The old paternalistic norms, some of them good and some of them bad, would be replaced by new modern computerized ones, some of them good and some of them bad, and all of them cold.

Curiously enough, the Pentagon Papers struggle seemed to have had no real effect on the *Post* stock. But the stock had not done well. It had opened at twenty-six, and then leveled out there, and then because it had not gone up, it went down. It fell, steadily. Lazard Frères had issued the stock. It was a somewhat stodgy firm and it did not know how to push this particular kind of stock. But in addition the *Post* was running into Wall Street's reservations, which were many. There had been Phil, brilliant, talented, erratic. Would you trust Phil with your own money? Then there was the fact that Kay was, well, a woman, and Wall Street, all things being equal, did not really care for corporations that were headed by women. Women were too unpredictable, not really sound. Could women make hard decisions? Then there was the fact that the *Post* was a traditionally liberal paper, and liberalism smacked of sentimentality. Were the people who ran a liberal paper as sentimental in their business dealings as they were in their editorial columns? The analysts knew the *Post*'s television stations were well run, and the television side had depth of management. But what about the paper? Sure, Bradlee was good, but what if Bradlee keeled over dead one morning? Who would replace him? The market wanted not just profitability, but a guarantee of the future, it wanted insurance on its investments, what was called depth of management. It would be good for the *Post* to buy some small papers where it could send its promising young executives—like a farm system—and then bring them back when they were ready.

So when the stock just lay there, Katharine Graham, reluctantly, unhappily, nervously, went before a major meeting of Wall Street analysts to push it. She hated public speeches anyway, they summoned all the hidden terrors in her, and this was worse. This was the alien camp, a room of men, and not the kind of men she knew in the profession, newsmen she had come to understand, but financiers, men who knew and cared above all about money and who probably disliked her paper. She was absolutely terrified that day. The words came pouring out, nonstop; the sentences ran into each other. She seemed to take not a single breath during her speech. But she was, as she usually is, enormously impressive. She had done her homework, she knew what to say. Here was a strong, impressive, attractive woman talking about maintaining a tradition and making money while doing it. She told them how much she had resisted the idea of speaking to them, how much she hated the idea of huckstering her paper and her stock. Then she spoke of the paper and its proper role in the society, and why that too would make it profitable. Phil Greer, watching, knew she had won. And sure enough, within days the stock went up three points. Katharine Graham had conquered Wall Street. And not long after that, she began to receive an endless series of requests to grace the boards of America's great corporations—because she was a woman and because, in addition, they thought she was tough. Shortly after, the *Post* bought a paper in Trenton, New Jersey, where it sent Dick Harwood, as a promising young editor, out for seasoning. It was also not very long after that that the *Post* began to get much tougher about expense accounts and about reporter productivity. Phil Greer found himself in a two-man bureau in New York where the total travel budget was ten dollars a week, barely enough for a taxi trip to Wall Street. In the old days it had been talent and style and brilliance and now it was more and more productivity. The new breed would have to be more straight-arrow than the old.

In all those years since Phil Graham's death Kay Graham had been changing. In the beginning, right after Phil's death, everyone had felt sorry for her. She had been mother and wife, and that was all. But power has magic qualities, it can bestow glamour and style on whoever has it; because people are powerful, they are treated as if they are attractive, and when they are treated as attractive, they often *become* attractive. So it was with her. Very soon she realized that she did in fact hold the power, that the others, all those men who were bright and quick and facile, were *totally dependent upon her*. That was the ultimate realization. No matter how brilliantly they wrote, how cleverly they politicked, they were dependent upon her. There were many of them, they could be replaced; there was only one of her, she could do the replacing. So too it was with the great and mighty of the government. Gradually she became more confident of her role. For the first few years after Phil's death, though she was publisher of both *Newsweek* and the Washington *Post*, she tended to make her luncheon appointments using her guest's name. Then about 1968 it began to change, she used her own name. If she went to lunch with Truman Capote, as she did regularly, now the reservation was in the name of Katharine Graham.

She held power, others coveted it. Within a few years others would describe her as the most powerful woman in America, perhaps the world. A queen and her court, McGeorge Bundy had called the world of the Washington *Post.* Mother, some of her very highest editorial executives called her, though they did not call her that to her face. At first she had frozen and turned white during her public appearances, but gradually she became good at it, cool, practiced, professional. The power was like a cosmetic, Katharine Graham became more stylish, more sure of herself, finally more imperious. It was not by accident that when Capote decided to give the ultimate party he chose her as the one to be honored; she could, after all, pull not just the literary-social world of New York, but the power world of Washington as well (she was allowed to invite five couples on her own; Capote was a tough taskmaster). She could at her best be open, intelligent, and fair-minded, and there were many who thought she might have become the best major publisher in America, far better and far more fair-minded than Phil Graham (Mad Philip, she was calling him now on occasion), who was part publisher, and part politician.

But the scars of the past were still there, she had borne a lot of burdens for too long, and the insecurity was always there, she could go from being absolutely elegant in a professional sense, to being unsure, erratic, and imperious. She was a talented and volatile boss. Those around her soon learned that she could be petty and unpleasant on unimportant things, but that the larger the issue, the greater the challenge, the better she responded, summoning what was best in the tradition of the paper and in herself. She was not particularly gracious to women who reminded her of what she had once been, nor was she gracious with the wives of her top executives. They quickly learned their place, they did not talk. Once during a tour one of them had been asking a foreign official a question when she heard Katharine's voice saying, "We'll all learn a lot more if you stop talking." As she became stronger, she also became tougher, and there were old friends who had known her since she was a girl, and who admired her for what she had done at the *Post* and *Newsweek,* who began to mind not so much the toughness as the fact that she had begun to enjoy her reputation for toughness. (She could also make fun of herself on occasion, and of the top business people, all males, who came to visit her and who during the course of the visit would by nature make a number of gestures signaling their sexual availability. She liked watching them, she told a close friend, and thinking: You'd really like to fuck a tycoon, wouldn't you?)

She became an exacting employer, and the number of high executives who joined and left her employ, hired quickly and fired quickly, was legion: four presidents or publishers of the *Post* in a very brief span, the best men available hired and then arbitrarily dismissed, careers shattered. Of the key personnel, only Bradlee remained and survived and held power. It was a symbol of Bradlee's personal power with her that when he had done the unthinkable, which was to leave his marriage and take up with Sally Quinn, a younger woman—a most touchy thing to do at the Washington Post Company, recalling too many bitter memories—she had permitted this. She had not liked it at first, but she had reconciled herself to it, and had said that if Ben needed his Sally to be a good editor, as Grant needed his liquor to be a good general, then so be it. Even though she became fonder of her power, the doubts never left her. She was easily unsettled. She did not like to feel or look awkward, to feel herself out of things. There was a notion about Kay, among some who knew her well, that the last person who talked to her often won the argument. Which made the role of Bradlee that much more important. He was the one who survived, who could always handle her and evoke the best in her. He could always charm her and make her laugh. The fact that other executives were falling by the wayside did not rattle him or make him obsequious; if anything, he seemed ever more outside her reach. She liked the fact that he went around saying that she had the guts of a cat burglar, and she liked the fact that when she was being pompous he could tell her that only the most powerful woman in the world could say something that arrogant. She also liked the fact that he delivered; when he said he was going to do something, he did. It was an interesting combination, Graham and Bradlee. She was courageous and intelligent and insecure, and it was not the least of Bradlee's skills that, in addition to running the paper, he could tune her, bringing out her better instincts and filtering out her lesser ones.

# IV

# 23/CBS

He had started his political comeback in late 1967 and he was, at the beginning, something of a joke in national politics. Reporters assigned to cover Richard Nixon did not regard it as a prime assignment. It was as if by being assigned to a loser they were in some way losers too. Their last memory of him was his 1962 valedictory, when he had promised that they would not have Nixon to kick around any more, and reporters had believed him. They were print men, and they followed politics seriously. That disastrous, embarrassing farewell scene, so unforgivable, was etched permanently in their minds. A terminal scene. Yet they were wrong, for if their minds were formed and framed by print, they now belonged to a profession defined by film. Television had changed memory, time passed more quickly, fewer impressions held. It would not do for the Democrats to rerun that 1962 film clip, it would surely backfire if they did, and so the clip could be replaced by newer, better, warmer film of him.

Nixon by 1968 was in some curious way a beneficiary of that last terrible moment; he returned to politics as both outsider and underdog and that evoked a certain reluctant undercurrent of sympathy for him, even from people who in the past had never found him a particularly sympathetic figure. For this and other reasons his early press relations during the 1968 campaign were among the best of his career. Part of it was sympathy, and part of it was the fact that of the handful of reporters covering him in the early days of the campaign, most were young, about thirty years old. They had not been even teen-agers during the worst of the McCarthy period, and they had no memory of Nixon's role in that period. They had heard from their older colleagues what an ogre he was, but he had not seemed in the early days of the campaign to be anything like that. Rather he seemed to be a painfully shy, somewhat awkward, and clumsy man trying, in spite of himself, to be a good guy. (Typically, during one of the late primaries Walter Cronkite had flown out to do a piece on Nixon. He was invited up to the candidate's hotel room, where Nixon offered him a drink while declining one himself. Then Nixon realized that refusing a drink didn't look good, it kept him from being one of the boys. "I'll tell you what," he told Cronkite, "I'll have a sherry." A sherry? *That* was hardly being one of the boys. "In fact," he said, trying to sound enthusiastic, "I'll make it a *double* sherry." Thus Nixon as one of the boys.)

In those early weeks and months, when the odds against Nixon were very long, covering him had turned out to be a surprisingly pleasant and informal assignment. Nixon was at his best. He was the ghost of politics past trying desperately to come alive again, badly in need of exposure and legitimacy. He seemed to be a minor and not particularly threatening figure on a political landscape where the central issue was the war, and in which the party of record was the Democrats, a party locked in its own fratricidal death struggles. He was accessible in those days, reasonably friendly, there was small talk between him and reporters. If he was not especially graceful at it, then at least in some way he was trying. This brief open-door policy served Nixon well. Many of the reporters wrote about a changed Nixon, a man mellowed and humanized by defeat and exile. A mellower man. A New Nixon.

Some of the absence of strain, of course, stemmed from the fact that many of the reporters did not take Nixon very seriously as a candidate. George Romney seemed the odds-on favorite, the new Wendell Willkie, attractive, handsome, a wonderful shock of hair, a proven track record in Michigan, a man of the people, a wizard with small cars, not as unacceptable to the right as Rockefeller. The nomination seemed his for the asking. But then Romney had stumbled over the English language in the primaries, and there was no one else to challenge him until Rockefeller entered far too late, and very quickly the nation's political experts and reporters looked up and realized that the nomination was going to go to Richard Nixon. As that happened, as the unlikely became increasingly likely, the Nixon press relations changed dramatically. By coincidence or not, at about the same time Bob Haldeman came aboard (some of the other Nixon people believed, in their anger, that Haldeman had waited until Nixon looked like a winner, and had *then* come aboard). It all happened very quickly. The New Nixon disappeared, the mellowness was gone. A wall went up between the candidate and the press. There was less and less access. The Nixon people became preoccupied not so much with reaching more and more people as with not making a mistake, not stumbling. (By contrast, in 1964, when things had been going well for Lyndon Johnson, he had gloried in it all, he had grabbed reporters and demanded that they be with him at all times, morning, noon, and night, in the swimming pool, in the shower, in the bathroom, until finally, desperately, they had wished for less access, not more.)

By the time of the Republican convention there was a totally sanitized, almost monastic quality to the Nixon campaign; he was the least accessible, least open, most secretive presidential candidate in years. It made fools of the reporters who had written of a New Nixon (not such big fools that they were inclined to admit it), and there was something very chilling about it and the campaign that was to follow. He was, even some who were politically sympathetic to him thought, almost anti-democratic in his aloofness. There was in him fear of and resistance to the political processes that went beyond normal cautiousness. When reporters complained, the Nixon people didn't care, they didn't need the press, they had long ago written it off. They were, by their own schedule, right on track. They had the nomination, and they had television, and that was all they needed. Now they could go over the heads of the working press. They knew they could get on the evening news shows whenever they wanted, and by and large in the way they wanted.

Television was the key. Television, Nixon was convinced, had cost him the election in 1960, and now it held the key to the current election. (One of the first things Ronald Reagan's public relations people had decided was that Nixon in 1968 would be a better candidate than Nixon in 1960 because of the advent of color television; his shadowy dark appearance was much less pronounced in color than it had been in black and white.) He was obsessed by television, and the people around him—Frank Shakespeare, who had come from CBS, Frank Treleaven, who did political spots for candidates, and Haldeman—worked out, in vague concert, a television strategy. They hoped to control the atmosphere around him, to show him when he wanted to be shown, to protect him from exposure on those bad days when he was exhausted and likely to make major faux pas (they knew that he tired easily, and that under stress he tended to come apart; they were determined above all else that this would not happen in public in 1968). Their overt campaign would be a very controlled, very limited one; the real campaign, the one which the press would never cover, would be a commercially produced one of Nixon in controlled and sanitized situations, speaking with chosen people. Paid commercials that would not look like commercials. Place, crowd, interrogators carefully selected, adjusted, and regulated. A campaign structured, in the words of its best chronicler, Joe McGinniss, as the Astrodome was built, so the wind would never blow, the rain would never fall, and the ball would never bounce the wrong way.

That the presidency was an office subject to relentless, unyielding, exhausting, and unpredictable pressure—precisely the conditions that Richard Nixon tended to fall apart under when he was tired—did not bother Nixon's men. They never doubted that they had the right man or that they were doing the right thing; they could create their own image of what he should be, and sell that. And if they could control events while he was a candidate, make the unexpected go away, then surely they could do the same for him when he was President, for then both he and they would have infinitely more power, and thus more control. They wanted to create a new Nixon, not Nixon as he was, but Nixon as he should be.

They would obliterate the past. And to do that they needed new people. They wanted no part of Ted Rogers, whom they associated with past failure, and very early on they hired Roger Ailes, a young and ambitious television producer on the Mike Douglas show, whom Nixon had taken a liking to. Nixon and Ailes had first met in 1967 when Nixon had made a brief guest appearance on the Douglas show. There had been some small talk. At one point Nixon had said that it was a shame a man had to use gimmicks like this to get elected. Ailes, twenty-eight years old at the time, brash and self-confident, told him it was not a gimmick, and that if he felt it was, he was going to lose again.

"Explain that to me, young man," said Nixon, suddenly serious.

So Ailes did. "The problem is that it's not a gimmick," he said, "it's not a toy. Flip Wilson was right. What you get is what you are. The secret is confidence in yourself." Shortly thereafter, Ailes was hired to produce Nixon's television commercials, a curious figure among the Nixon old guard and young guard, the long-haired counterculture child among the purists.

The first thing Ailes did was to go back and look at all the old Nixon footage from campaigns past. He was appalled. It was all of a kind: Nixon sitting there, speaking seriously, inevitably flanked by an American flag. The head that talked. Ailes had decided immediately that among the first things he would show the world was that Richard Nixon had arms and legs and could walk and talk informally with other human beings who were informal too. He would catch the informality of the man. This, he soon realized, was not easily done. During those years on the Douglas show, he had spent a lot of time with politicians and show-business people and he had soon realized that the best and most talented of them had a force and an energy and a presence all their own. They did not necessarily need a title or a reputation to intrigue the camera or to hold a room. Ailes had come to call that quality "control of the atmosphere," and by that he meant the capacity of a person to walk into a room and have things his or her way. Nixon, of all the prominent people he had ever dealt with, had the least control of atmosphere, the least natural chemistry. On his own, without a title, he had no physical power, he was doomed to be on the periphery of the people in any given room, someone who was almost always ignored, whose advice was never requested.

Yet in some way, Ailes assumed, it was that very quality that drove Nixon so relentlessly in a profession in which he was by nature so painfully ill at ease. His was the most public of callings and he was the most private of men, and yet, often in pain, often awkwardly, he had pursued his chosen career with a singlemindedness matched by almost no one else in politics. He above all was the long-distance runner, and surely, Ailes thought, it had to do with recognition, with the desire to be someone, the knowledge that he had once been nobody and might soon be again. But Nixon's intense desire to be President did not diminish Ailes's problem. For clearly the candidate's awkwardness and gracelessness combined with his burning ambition had already been projected into millions of American homes and had long been part of what was called his image problem. Nixon, Ailes had told Joe McGinniss in one memorable moment, was the kind of person "you put him on television, you've got a problem right away. He's a funny-looking guy. He looks like somebody hung him in a closet overnight and he jumps out in the morning with his suit all bunched up and starts running around saying, 'I want to be President.' I mean, this is how he strikes some people. That's why these shows [the controlled artificial shows the Nixon team was then putting together] are important. To make them forget all that." *To make them forget all that.*

. . .

Ailes's shows were carefully orchestrated, and they were something of a first in American politics, shows designed to erase a man's past and reinvent him. The reincarnation of Richard Nixon. They would be done in a simulated town-hall style, to give an impression of Richard Nixon among the people, although of course the people were all carefully chosen—a farmer with a clean God-fearing look, a cab driver who reflected the rough salty edges of the city's streets, a black who did not look too black and too threatening, a housewife warm and comfortable enough to sell the nation's most popular detergents as well as Richard Nixon. All carefully cast. An American chorus. They were picked for their own qualities and above all they must not seem in the least hostile to the candidate, for Richard Nixon responded very negatively to hostility, and there must be no psychiatrists on the panel, that was a No-No, for RN hated psychiatrists, he did not want anyone peering into his soul on television. So it was a selected group of friendlies, there to lob easy ones, and it was like the old town hall, but with a difference—it was completely loaded, and totally artificial, and it cost millions and millions of dollars.

They did a series of these shows, showing them around the country, buying the time to show them, which was no problem, they had plenty of money. They let in, of course, not just the panel, but a studio audience of about three hundred people, all good Republicans, and of course they kept out the working press. That was crucial, and it was a major change from the past, a symbol of the fact that television could create and project its own reality. Its strength was that it could appear open and be so closed. Frank Shakespeare, an old CBS man who deeply disliked that network's News Division, feeling as Nixon did that it was too liberal, had helped make that decision: no correspondents could come into the studio while the shows were being taped. Herb Klein, in charge of the press, argued with him, telling Shakespeare that the working reporters were already angry. But Shakespeare was adamant. They would do it their way. Klein was dismayed—he told Shakespeare it smelled like a repeat of the 1960 campaign and that this was a very dangerous thing. But the order held. Ailes agreed with Shakespeare. Television had the power. If they let reporters in, he said, they would only write how stagy it all was. Who needed that? Why, his assistant, Jack Rourke, would be inside warming up the crowd, telling them when to applaud Nixon and when and how to mob him at the end, and that would be all the print press would write about. So they decided—and it was a crucial decision, for nothing reflected the thinking of the Administration-to-be so clearly—to keep the press in an adjacent studio and let them see the monitors, that and nothing more. The print reporters grumbled, but by and large they did little, and no one really wrote about how staged the essence of the campaign was until long afterward when Joe McGinniss published *The Selling of the President*. So it was a new kind of campaign, a mostly closed one. The press would cover what the Nixon people wanted it to cover.

Much of that was Haldeman's thinking. Haldeman had his own view of the press, which was one of total distrust and dislike, and with the Democrats so badly divided he was convinced that Nixon held the whip hand and was therefore in a position to exert genuine control. He handled the technical part of the strategy. Haldeman was a media man. He considered himself an expert on television and disdained the overkill of old-style campaigns, thought them far too demanding and draining, which they were, and like many of the men around Nixon, he worried about the candidate's self-control when he was exhausted. There was always a fear among insiders that *RN would blow,* would come apart, would repeat the scene that had marked his exit from politics in 1962. Thus he must be shielded and protected for his own good. (Roger Ailes, the newcomer to the team, was appalled at how little confidence Nixon's closest aides had in their candidate; the regulars, he sensed, all seemed to feel that Nixon might collapse under any undue or unforeseen pressure. Ailes was always surprised that he had more confidence in Nixon than the loyalists did.)

Haldeman had a true right-wing hatred of the press. It was his belief that if you gave the press and particularly the networks two chances a day to cover your candidate, two opportunities to film him among the people of his land, the networks would always choose the more damaging film, the film of Nixon stumbling as he walked up to a platform, or of Nixon being booed or hassled. Or of the smaller of the two crowds. Haldeman therefore devised a campaign in which there would be only one opportunity to film Nixon each day, and that opportunity would come under the tightest possible controls, to make sure that the film was positive and exemplary, and to make sure that the networks *had* to use it, and only it. One-a-day media opportunities.

At almost the same time that Haldeman was evolving this strategy, reporters noticed that Nixon himself was becoming more skilled at handling the camera, at giving them precisely what he knew they wanted, and what he wanted, the forty-five-second segment of a speech tied to a national issue, the accusation, the promise, facing the camera and looking sincerely into it for the allotted segment. News. *Nixon Promises. Nixon Accuses.* (Indeed, he once tied a segment about atomic power into his speech, knowing that there was national news about atomic energy that day and he could easily make the news shows, and when the CBS producer on the trip, Peter Herford, missed it, not knowing the connection was there, all hell broke loose in New York—the Nixon people complained so bitterly and so quickly about the failure to use it that for a time it appeared that Herford might be pulled off the campaign.)

It was all modern and all controlled. The faster the campaign moved, the more control the Nixon people had, and the more the journalists were prisoners of the airplane, prisoners of whatever circumstances Nixon propelled them into. The faster the motion, the less time to think. Fuselage journalism, Hugh Sidey of *Time* later called it. Reporters encapsulated, never having time to smell or feel or find independent news sources, and thus dependent upon the scenario scripted for them by the Nixon staff. So it was a slightly rebellious press corps that covered Nixon in 1968, reporters knowing how he was exploiting the rules of their craft against them, making just enough news to get into the papers and on the network news shows, but running what was to them a plastic campaign.

It worked, though in the narrowest sense. He was elected, though the manner of his campaign finally backfired and his lead over Hubert Humphrey steadily diminished. Hubert Humphrey was not by any means the most attractive of candidates in 1968. He was saddled with the war, saddled with a bitterly divided party, saddled with a petulant incumbent President who was doing everything he could to make Humphrey's life miserable (such as holding back campaign funds in the Democratic Party coffers). But Humphrey was, whatever else, intensely human and he was putting on his show, flaws and warts and all, in front of the American people, and somehow they sensed that and responded. In the last few weeks of the campaign Humphrey began to close and close quickly on Nixon. In some subtle, intangible way Nixon's aloofness had become an issue, he was running as if he were already President, and that was resented. What might have been a landslide became a cliff-hanger. More, the campaign had been deeply disturbing to a large segment of Americans, who if they were not exactly neutral about Nixon were determined to give him a fresh start and who had greeted the early reports of this different and more mellow man with enthusiasm; the campaign had re-created not a new figure, but images of the old one.

For there was a price to it all, particularly with the press. At the heart of the relationship between politician and journalist is a sense of trust. The one has to trust the other, each knowing the limits and frailties of the other's profession. Politicians are allowed by reporters to dissemble within certain limits, particularly if they signal those limits; reporters, in the eyes of politicians, are permitted to analyze and criticize within certain limits. But at the heart is a common denominator: each is trying to be essentially straight and honest, trying to be fair and accountable within the codes of their very different professions. The common bond had traditionally been a mutual love of politics, a love of the game itself. But Nixon did not really love the game. Beyond that, trust had never really existed between Nixon and the press: the early Nixon had never trusted reporters, and Washington reporters who trusted most major politicians in the early fifties did not trust Richard Nixon. His radar, so finely tuned for hurt and slight, had picked up that distrust and it had intensified his own, which they, of course, had quickly picked up on *their* radar screens. In the early days of the 1968 campaign, that feedback had seemed for a brief moment to change and reporters had come to trust him, and he in turn seemed to reciprocate. But the campaign itself was a disaster. Once he no longer needed them, he put himself beyond their reach. During the campaign he was asked to come to New York to talk to the editorial board of *The New York Times*. It was the usual thing and, in the past, presidential candidates had always accepted. Nixon turned the invitation down. "Don't you understand?" Herb Klein told Harrison Salibury, "he doesn't see any point in going up there and answering a lot of questions from people who have always been against him and are still against him. He sees no future in it. He's not going to do it." A few days later a bunch of top *Times* executives had a private lunch with Klein in Washington to make sure that there was no serious breach. Klein was absolutely relaxed about it all. No problem, said Klein (who was himself to be moved out shortly after the election). Once Nixon was elected he would feel more confident. It would all change.

It did not change after he was elected. The struggle with the press had become something deep and visceral in him. Moreover, Nixon had begun to realize that there could be political gain in it. He was in the process of creating a new political constituency for himself, in part from alienated elements of the Democratic Party both in the South and in blue collar areas of the North. These people were angry and restless, showing it by their support of George Wallace. There had been too much change for them to accept, too many assaults on what they had been taught to respect and revere. Much of that change seemed to them to have been fostered by the network television shows. The Democratic convention of 1968, with the young rioters in the streets of Chicago, had been the symbol of what horrified and dismayed them. The social changes too—particularly in race relations—were difficult for them to swallow, and they resented too, the relentless reporting of the war in Vietnam. All this was easy to blame on the messenger who brought the news, the press. And if they were ready to slay the messenger, it was only good politics for Nixon to help. He sought to annex a new political constituency already angry at his oldest enemies.

The press became an irresistible target. It had always been there and beckoned to his predecessors. It had been hard for Lyndon Johnson to resist but resist he had. Even as Johnson was leaving office he had offered Spiro Agnew the new Vice-President some advice. "Young man," Johnson said, "we have in this country two big television networks, NBC and CBS. We have two news magazines, *Newsweek* and *Time.* We have two wire services, AP and UPI. We have two pollsters, Gallup and Harris. We have two big newspapers, the Washington *Post* and *The New York Times.* They're all so damned big they think they own the country. But, young man, don't get any ideas about fighting." But Nixon had no intention of resisting. By the fall of 1969, the assault on the media was a central part of Nixon's domestic political policy, and his chosen weapon was none other than Spiro Agnew. The Vice-President made the first of what was to be a series of speeches in mid-November 1969. The occasion was a meeting of the Midwest Republican Conference in Des Moines. Up to then the Vice-President had been, like so many of his predecessors, a man in search of a role. In Des Moines he found it. He complained about the media, specifically about the coverage of the President's recent speech on Vietnam (among other things he attacked ABC, the most timid of the networks on Vietnam, for its use of Averell Harriman as a guest commentator). It was the first shot in a larger assault on the media and its leading figures, and in particular upon the television networks. They were, he said, a special, arrogant, small but far too influential elite, unrepresentative, unelected, and highly paid. They all lived in the same two unrepresentative cities, Washington and New York, spoke only to each other, and constantly reinforced their own peculiar viewpoint. What was worse, he argued, the television figures did not just report, they constantly editorialized.

Though Agnew had talked on occasion before in a somewhat similar vein, there was no doubt that this was by far his harshest and most calculated attack. Besides, unlike previous Agnew attacks, this one came directly from the White House, where Pat Buchanan, one of the President's favorite speech writers, had written it. Agnew clearly was becoming, in the words of some critics, Nixon's Nixon, the hit man who would do the heavy work in the field while the White House retained deniability. The Des Moines speech, and the others to follow, were deeply disturbing to senior journalists. Though many of them accepted the truth of some of Agnew's charges, and were in fact privately bothered by some of the same failings in their profession (the sketchiness of the half-hour news show, the tendency of reporters to hang out together too much), there was nonetheless something chilling in the way that the Vice-President lashed out, a certain harshness and bellicosity. This was not just a man looking for a better or longer news show, or more public-affairs programs, this was a man looking for a fight. Beyond that, Agnew's criticism was basically partisan, a fact that became clearer in ensuing weeks as he attacked monopoly tendencies in the media, citing only liberal monopolies and never conservative ones.

Agnew's speeches were not merely words, there was an element of threat in them. Coupled with the other assaults upon the media by the Administration the effect was powerful. For Agnew's words hit a raw nerve in the society: they came in the final weeks of 1969, after a decade of jarring events. The events and the reporting of them had been particularly upsetting to the television audience, first because they seemed so much more powerful when seen in color instead of simply printed, and second because much of the audience watching the evening news show was composed of people who had never been serious newspaper readers and who were thus unprepared to deal with such charged material. The White House, delighted by the response, pressed forward. There were more Agnew speeches; clearly the network people were now on the defensive. (Walter Cronkite in 1971 would state flatly in a major speech that the Nixon-Agnew attacks were a part of a *conspiracy* to destroy the credibility of the press. Joe Wershba, an old Murrow hand, congratulated Cronkite on the speech. But *conspiracy,* Wershba said, he had a little trouble with that word. In 1973, as the details of the Nixon clandestine assault on the press began to surface, Wershba went back to Cronkite to apologize.)

The Agnew attacks were of course, excellent journalistic theater. In contrast to the increasing blandness of most American speeches, here was a high official using tough, often brutal, language. Everyone knew what he was talking about. He made good copy, he was covered live on television; after all, he was the Vice-President and the networks could put him on without an obligation to give equal time to a Democratic Vice-President. He was overwhelmed

with requests for speeches articulating long-harbored middle-American grievances against the press and those people back East. If before this he had been
something of a joke (Spiro Who?), he was now a national folk hero. He had
become precisely what he had criticized. Spiro Agnew had become a media
event.

By 1972 it appeared that the Nixon campaign against the press had been more
than partially successful; the great newspapers and broadcasting corporations
seemed on the defensive, the Administration's technical skills in using television seemed greater and greater (there were those who suspected that the
Nixon administration used bombing as a weapon in the continuation of the war
rather than ground troops because, among other things, television did not
cover bombing raids); television had turned a mild diplomatic triumph in
China into an unparalleled television spectacular—it was not just Nixon's trip
to China, it was television's trip to China, and the extent to which the networks
wanted to cover it surprised even the Administration. The presidents of the
various news divisions of the networks, men whose job it was to limit the
President's exploitation of television, scrambled to get aboard the trip, listing
themselves as sound technicians in order to get credentials. Cheerleaders and
spear carriers all. Even as tough and combative a reporter as Dan Rather was
totally defused on the China trip, there was simply no way that he could
provide serious analytical coverage. It was a classic case of journalistic overkill,
the greatest names of broadcasting following devotedly and breathlessly behind Pat Nixon on the days when the President was busy and she became a
media opportunity. It became, in the words of one top Nixon aide, the third
political convention of the year. No matter that bombs were still falling on
Vietnam, no matter that the trip was a triumph of televised picture postcards
over substance. And if it was good for the media, then it was, to paraphrase
Charley Wilson, good for the nation. No matter that it was all rigged for
television, that events were scheduled to hit prime time in America, that the
closest watch kept on the trip was not of the Chinese but of the daily playback
book of what the networks were using and saying. It was the finest political
theater, on the air hour after hour. Exotic. Different. Brilliantly cast: *Mao,
Chou En-lai, and a supporting cast of 800 million.* It was the ultimate media
trip.
    In a way the 1972 campaign was over before it started. What Democratic
candidate could run against the ticket of Nixon-Chou, or the slightly less
exotic one of Nixon-Brezhnev? But in 1972, as events proved, the Republicans
were taking no chances, there would be no Dan Rather to muck things up this
time, because they had put together their own White House television team,
which had studied the television rhythms at previous national conventions,
broken the code in effect, and written the scenario for their own convention.
They knew at which point the networks took breaks, and how long the breaks
lasted, and so if there was something they wanted to slip by, they used the

breaks as the cover for them, while the cameras were off the podium. They had the convention timed to the second, they had a list of young attractive Republican stars whom they doled out carefully to the networks throughout the festivities. It was the logical extension of the 1968 campaign. Control was at the heart of it; they would control every second of the convention, show only what they wanted, hide what they wanted. And all of it went very well, right according to script; dissent—to the degree that it existed—was properly stifled or, even better, ignored. All things done in their proper moment, balloons, scheduled to be released at 8:07 P.M., released at 8:07 P.M. Even when a reporter got hold of the entire script and published it, there was little embarrassment. So be it. Perhaps it all made for a boring convention and boring television, but there was, above all, order; that was what they wanted. Boredom was better than the chaos of their predecessors. One reason that Richard Nixon was elected in 1968 and reelected in 1972 was a sense, beyond ideological or partisan politics, that Lyndon Johnson had simply lost control of the country, there was too much disorder, and inevitably, if unconsciously, people connected that chaos to him.

So as the summer of 1972 approached, Richard Nixon seemed in a commanding position. His trip to China had overshadowed the one great issue against him, the failure to end the war in Vietnam (Nixon, Murray Kempton wrote at the time of the China trip, had an absolute genius for making peace with countries with whom we were not at war). The opposition party was tearing itself apart for precisely that reason, it was political cannibalism of the first order, the antiwar faction which had been out of power in 1968 was in command and was now savaging the other faction, angrier at its own other wing than at Nixon. The Administration's assaults upon the media seemed to have borne genuine benefits. The press, both written and electronic, seemed on the defensive, more cautious, and perhaps more than just a little frightened; the Nixon-Agnew assault on the media in his first term had been quite sharp, a major attempt to reduce the credibility of a free press, and there was reason to believe (the Watergate tapes would confirm it) that the Administration intended to be even harsher and more punitive in a second term, particularly if that term was initiated by a landslide. Those who in 1968 had hoped that election to the highest office might make Nixon mellower were wrong, he had become if anything more vengeful against those whom he considered his traditional enemies. He saw the press as committed against him, deliberately amplifying the importance of his opponents. The previous decade had been one of immense and tumultuous social change, much of it an assault on traditional American mores, and the Nixon administration deliberately sought to portray the American press as promoters of this change, fellow travelers of the counterculture. The press was in fact centrist establishment (at the publisher-owner level) and semi-liberal, semi-establishment, and quite longingly capitalistic (at the working-reporter level), and in all as much surprised by (and sometimes resentful of) the forces suddenly loosed in the country as anyone else.

The systematic attacks by Agnew and others in the Administration had been aimed at putting the press on the defensive, but the Nixon administration had also found and sliced at the soft underbelly of the networks, their affiliate stations. Herb Klein, the good guy of the Administration, gently worked the communications boondocks, using the soft-cop approach, not many headlines, but stirring up the natives against the networks, the aliens, the impudence of Dan Schorr and Dan Rather in Washington, the lack of patriotism and Americanism in the Saigon bureau. (So effectively was this done that Dick Salant, the head of CBS News, had to spend two days at one point arguing a committee of angry affiliate representatives out of a suggestion—Klein-inspired, Salant thought—that it visit the Saigon bureau on a kind of inspection tour. Not only would they go to Saigon, the affiliate owners suggested, but Salant would go with them; they would express their displeasure with the negative reporting being done and then, with Salant's assistance, they would shape up the bureau and increase the level of its Americanism. It was a delicate time for Salant. The average affiliate owner is likely to share the political attitudes of a car salesman, have little roots in journalism, little sense of the tradition of the free press. For two exhausting days Salant and his deputy, Gordon Manning, sat with the affiliate owners trying to explain the nature of journalism and why a group of owners should not visit Saigon to lecture reporters on patriotism; that it might be resented and cause angry resignations.) But there was no doubt as the Nixon administration orchestrated its assault against the network news teams that it found a receptive response among affiliate owners, most of whom were Republicans. The things that Nixon disliked, *they* disliked; they too preferred a world where if there were to be political wars, they should go largely uncovered, and if there were serious protests against the war, they too should go uncovered. They began to keep up a constant pressure on the news shows, particularly against Dan Schorr and most of all against Dan Rather.

As the tension between CBS and the Nixon administration mounted, and as the Nixon people turned the full force of their anger and hostility toward the networks, there was one official in Washington who despised what the Nixon people were doing on television but who, curiously, had no sympathy at all with CBS or Dan Rather. Charles Ferris worked in the office of the Senate Majority Leader. His specific job was to get Democrats, as members of the opposition party, on television, a job that showed him the networks at their worst, at once greedy and timid. He was disturbed by what presidential television had done to the traditional balance of power in Washington. In his opinion, the networks were in no way accountable for their power and influence: they took, but they did not necessarily give. He thought they were intimidated in part by the President, but that commercial greed was more at the heart of it. For example, when he pressured them for time to answer the President, he found them extremely generous with *radio* time and increasingly willing to give soap opera time on television, but hard and unbending about prime time in general, and totally unbending in giving prime time equivalent to that usurped by the President.

Ferris found irony in the fact that the networks were being attacked by the very people who exploited them. It was, Ferris thought, absolutely the networks' own fault and the price they paid for their arrogance and their tightness; in his opinion, they had become the victims of their own bottom-line mentality. They were so reluctant to give time to the opposition, to put on specials at night that might ventilate complicated issues and give the Congress a chance to respond to presidential television, that they had built up too much political pressure, like forcing too much gas into too small a bottle. Simply in order to save their precious air time they had inadvertently assumed the role of proxy opposition. This was not doing the real opposition very much good; nor, as the mounting resentment of the networks showed, was it doing the networks any good. The role of proxy opposition, he thought, was extremely dangerous and playing it had politicized the networks more than was healthy. It would be more natural to let political figures speak for themselves. When Ferris made this point to the networks, he was shocked by what he viewed as their arrogance; yes, they would say, his points had some merit, but few congressmen were as good—as *professional*—on television as their own people. Television reporters were professionals and were disinterested, and congressmen often digressed, went off on tangents, wasted time. Thus, their own people did it better. Which was probably true, Ferris conceded, but it was beside the point; in a democracy it was not the job of an anchorman or a White House correspondent to dissect a partisan speech of the President. There were people *elected* to do precisely that job.

But the networks did not listen to Ferris on arguments like this, as much as anything because they did not want to part with the extra time the politicians would be likely to consume. (You could always tell your White House correspondent to wrap up a presidential analysis in two minutes, but it was not the sort of thing you could demand of Hubert Humphrey.) Yet because the President got time and his opposition did not, he was encouraged to ask for more and more time, precisely because he never received any opposition. In this new electronic forum—the only one with much immediate meaning to most Americans—true political opposition as conceived of by the Founding Fathers was nonexistent.

Ferris's frustration with network practices persisted, and on one occasion, he had an opportunity to vent it. In October 1973, after Spiro Agnew resigned because of his involvement in Maryland kickbacks, the former Vice-President asked the networks for prime time to make one final statement. They granted it. Charles Ferris was absolutely appalled; here was the most precious time imaginable being given to a man who had first abused the networks, then been caught with his hand in the cookie jar, then had pledged an all-out fight to clear his name, and had finally copped a plea. *And he was getting prime time to clear his name.* Ferris, half in jest but quite bitter, picked up the phone and called his friend Bill Small, the head of the CBS bureau in Washington. He asked Small for prime time to answer Agnew. He listed a number of available Democratic senators. "Of course, Bill, we've got a problem," he said. "None of them is a convicted felon."

. . .

In the summer of 1972 the news shows were on the defensive. At CBS, after the Agnew attacks, Charles Kuralt found it easier to get broadcast time on the news show for his roving reports on America. He had been doing his charming bits of Americana, reflecting the complexity of the texture of the society, before Agnew, but now they were greeted with greater eagerness in New York, this was, after all, positive news. There was a deliberate effort to find human-interest stories—good stories, but stories that did not jar people's nerves. There was even a name for them: HI, human interest, like a slogan, get more HI; and much of the sensitivity to this came from Cronkite himself, who had very good political antennae, who traveled a great deal lecturing to various groups, and who knew that television news departments were in genuine bad odor, that Nixon had hit a very vulnerable nerve end. So there was a subtle attempt to balance criticism with, for instance, a special with Cronkite answering Agnew-like charges against television news from his hometown. What would be better than St. Joe's own Walter Cronkite responding to questions from the home-town folks; what better hometown? Just to put on some softer stories. Not to back down from important ones (or to remove Rather from the White House, which was a prime Nixon priority). But to make sure that with the hard and often abrasive news there was a certain amount of sugar-coating now. TV correspondents as good guys. Being at least a little lovable.

So in 1972 Nixon seemed to have the upper hand with most of his enemies, particularly with television journalists, who were feeling very frustrated. He had learned the disastrous lessons of 1970 when he had taken time off to campaign in behalf of Republican congressmen (not so much for them as against certain Democrats, the negative factor was always more natural to him) and he had done so with all the subtlety and grace and finesse of a man running for sheriff in Mississippi; he had appeared at that time very unpresidential, the darkness and hostility had come exploding out of him, and he had seemed unworthy of his office. So now his advisers were buttoning him up, keeping him inside the White House. McGovern, because of the Eagleton affair, had been on the defensive from the start. He had reversed the order of the usual presidential campaign, in which the issue was normally the incumbent. In this case, it was the challenger. So it was that Nixon ran, not as the Republican nominee, but in the age of television as the President. He campaigned with Chou in China and with Gromyko in the Oval Office. Having lost the 1960 election because of the debates, he wanted no part of debates with George McGovern in 1972. If in 1968 he had resisted the pressure to campaign in an uncontrolled atmosphere, now in 1972 he was even more Olympian. No one could smoke him out. Like Lyndon Johnson in 1964, he was (on the surface at least) above politics.

At one point during the 1972 campaign, Gordon Manning suggested to Walter Cronkite that Cronkite call the President to see if he could set up some

kind of exchange or interview: Cronkite Meets the President, Nixon Faces
Walter. "And," said Manning, "don't take Ziegler on the phone. Go directly
to the man." So Cronkite called the White House and twice Ziegler called
back, but Cronkite refused to take Ziegler's calls. Finally Nixon himself came
on the phone. "You know," Cronkite began, "there are all these issues and you
yourself have said that the choice has never been so clear. So I wonder if you
would come on the show so we could talk about the differences." Implicit in
this was the understanding that McGovern would get an equal shot. Nixon's
immediate reaction—and both Manning and Cronkite were impressed by how
acutely he was attuned to the media and knew how to deflect something he
did not want to do—was: "I'd love to, but what will I tell Howard Smith and
Jack Chancellor?"

Immediate. Without hesitation.

Later in the campaign, both CBS and ABC, with NBC dragging its feet,
suggested that the networks give both candidates a chance to explain their
positions on all the major issues—the economy, amnesty, the war. They could
even make the tapes themselves, and then the tapes would be run side by side.
Not exactly a debate, a little more artificial, but as close to a debate as anyone
could get. The idea was broached to Ziegler, who clearly hated it. Nixon would
have no part of it; he had nothing to gain and a considerable amount to lose,
and twelve years ago, faced with a comparable choice, he had lost a very great
deal.

# 24/ The Washington <u>Post</u>

It was, Ben Bradlee thought much later on, the supreme irony that Richard
Nixon, who hated the Washington *Post* so desperately, was responsible for the
*Post*'s greatest moment of glory and, in effect, for confirming that the *Post* was
a great newspaper. That Nixon had always hated the *Post,* there was no doubt.
The attempts on the part of the *Post*'s owners to deflect the anger had always
failed in the past—Phil Graham's brief, flawed courtship of Nixon in the fifties,
the subsequent use of Bill Rogers, allegedly the public figure most influential
with Nixon, as the *Post*'s lawyer. Those who knew Nixon thought that his
dislike of the *Post* exceeded, if that were possible, his dislike of *The New York
Times.* Art Buchwald, who had thought about it a long time, was convinced
that the source of Nixon's original anger was not the *Post*'s editorial page or
news columns, it was very simply Herblock. Buchwald was sure it was Herblock who had most deeply penetrated that fragile psyche. A news story, after
all, was something that flashed in and out of the minds of readers, it was hardly

permanent, it was easily deniable and often gone with the next day's garbage. But Herbert Block was something else, a Herblock cartoon was not deniable, it hung there in the atmosphere, a permanent vision: Nixon taking the low road, Nixon needing a shave, Nixon as a kind of political thug. Herblock had seized on all the visual vulnerabilities of Nixon, the beard, the jowls, the nose, and had, as all cartoonists do, accentuated them and somehow created a figure that exactly matched the liberals' vision of Nixon. It was as if Herblock with his pen had caught the liberal view of Nixon as no print journalist or editorial writer ever did: the fake piety, the mawkishness, the disregard of civil liberties, the ability to exploit passions while pretending that he was only trying to calm them. It stemmed from those earlier years when Nixon was the connection between the McCarthy wing and the center of the party, a role that Nixon liked to exploit and then deny, and Herblock caught it and made it permanent. If television was something new journalistically, an instrument that politicians loved because it had no memory, then Herblock was the direct opposite, his memory was enduring, the past always lived for him.

Around 1954, as Vice-President, Nixon began to complain publicly about the cartoons, and at one point he canceled his subscription to the *Post* because he did not want his daughters to see the Herblock drawings. He would, he said, take the paper at the office. A few years after that, while still Vice-President, talking with Chal Roberts of the *Post*, he went on at great length about Herblock. What a wonderful cartoonist he was. Herblock was really terrific. Would Roberts please pass on Nixon's respect to Block? He didn't take the paper at home because of the girls, but he himself really loved the cartoons. Then he spoke about the image Herblock had created. "You know," he said, "a lot of people think I'm a prick but I'm really not."

Clearly, Herblock haunted Nixon. The Herblock image was not just an idle mosquito bite of an irritation. Herblock was printed in Washington but he was syndicated throughout the country, and somehow his cartoons became part of Nixon's permanent political dossier, reflecting all the public doubts and questions about him; they stamped him and defined him as no Democratic politician could. In the fifties a lot of Americans, thinking of Richard Nixon, thought automatically of the Herblock cartoons. It would be troubling for any politician, but to a man whose psyche was so vulnerable, so totally sensitive to criticism, it was a far deeper wound. In 1960, for example, when Nixon ran against Kennedy, many Republicans were bothered by the rather genteel, somewhat namby-pamby campaign that he ran (Herblock even drew him wearing a clean-shaven Nixon mask over his real, darker face). Why don't you step up the attack? high Republicans asked him at a policy meeting. "I have to erase the Herblock image first," he answered. There it was, the permanent scar; indeed, part of the problem with the first debate with Kennedy, when his hastily produced makeup had been washed away by sweat and the bearded Nixon had been unveiled, was that it seemed to many that Kennedy was in fact debating the Herblock Nixon.

.  .  .

Thus, in addition to the tension and resentment that Nixon brought to any eastern liberal or semi-liberal publication, he brought to the *Post* a dimension of anger and hatred. It was the *Post* that sponsored Herblock; they could, in his opinion, easily stop him (as, in fact, Phil Graham *had* stopped him in the final weeks of the 1952 presidential campaign, in order to help *Ike*). Nixon could, as President, easily have charmed and handled the *Post* and the sophisticated slightly snobbish eastern Georgetown political-journalistic-intellectual world that was encamped there. If there was a liberal axis there, it was not *that* liberal, certainly never unseemly in its liberalism. It was above all pragmatic, and pragmatic in Washington meant being respectful of power. Almost any gesture from him and Georgetown would have responded. Nixon, after all, was a man of the center, a nonideological man, his politics were never the politics of the left or the right, they were the politics of self. His views on racial policy were about the same as Georgetown's, his foreign policy was not notoriously different from Georgetown's—after all, no one tap-danced his way through Georgetown so neatly as Nixon's principal foreign-policy adviser, Henry Kissinger. Georgetown, in fact, was eager to find new dimensions in him, to share his heavy burden. It had already hailed signs of a new Nixon before they were really signs.

But Nixon, for his part, was having none of it. He chose not to build bridges to Georgetown; it had not been with him before, it had always belittled him, and now that he was in power, the hell with Georgetown, let them all suffer. It had snubbed him: Georgetown's sins were not ideological, they were social. Now he would get back at them. Kissinger, by contrast, went regularly to Georgetown, it was as if he had special dispensation to go, and there was no major Katharine Graham party that he did not show up for, no matter what else was going on. He made the late show if nothing else. He played it all with suavity and skill, charming Mrs. Graham, becoming not a public figure, but a friend, a marvelous conquest, taking credit for Nixon's foreign policies when they were good ones, or when they were disastrous ones, like the invasion of Cambodia, raising an eyebrow slightly to let friends know that the fault was not his, it was that of Nixon, or Haldeman or Ehrlichman. Thus the difference in the coverage he got, tonal, but crucial. Their Haldeman. Their Ehrlichman. Our Henry. When he protested around town that he had nothing to do with the Cambodian invasion (of which he was a principal architect), they believed him. No one, after all, likes to think of a friend as a warmonger or a liar, and he had become their friend. Henry Kissinger specialized in, above all else, telling very different people what they wanted to hear, which, in the case of the Georgetown axis, was always reassuring, since it was hearing its own opinions, again and again.

Katharine Graham clearly would have liked access, would have liked normalization of relations, and she just as clearly was uneasy about the lack of it, the fact that there was no photograph of Richard Nixon in her office to

go with those of previous Presidents. These things are problematical; if Nixon
had built bridges to places like Georgetown and encouraged and even allowed
access to his White House for the upper tier of the press, perhaps there would
have been no Watergate. But if Nixon had been able to do that, he would not
have been Nixon. Enemies had always been essential to him, they fueled his
drive, he had always, in some deep psychic way, needed them, as some people
need to bite against a sore tooth. Now, now that he was President, he would
make them pay; he would not coopt them, that was too easy. Rather he would
cut them off, crush them. Friends of his and students of his career who had
hoped that his ascension to the highest office in the land would ease his
insecurities, would give him confidence and temper his anger, were bound to
be disappointed. It did not lessen his anger, he seemed if anything to demand
more vengeance than ever against his old opponents, people who had always
been against him. In 1972, right after the election, Bill Buckley dropped by the
White House and was startled by Nixon's mood. The President was deep in
a tirade: those eastern Ivy League sons of bitches, they had always been against
him, well, he would get them now, he knew who they were, he would show
them. Even a landslide had not tempered him. He was the kind of man who
remembered, not those who voted for him, but those who had voted against
him. His grievances were a source of inner strength to him. The people who
had belittled him and snubbed him made him, in some terrible dark way, more
resilient, they enabled him to stay in politics when other men might have quit.
He did not forget, and he personalized all criticism. As Jack Kennedy was at
his best with reporters from organizations, like *Time,* which were potentially
hostile, Nixon could only deal with reporters who were already for him. That
made things very difficult indeed.


For such a landmark story in American journalism, Watergate was filled with
ifs. Compared to Vietnam, which was out there, inevitable, waiting to be
covered, and which was a difficult story primarily because it was a matter of
fighting not just the government information service but a mind-set in the
nation at large, including readers and editors, Watergate was a will-o'-the-wisp
that could have evaporated completely on several occasions. In Vietnam, the
problem for reporters was not so much the compilation of an accurate picture
of events as it was an acceptance by their editors and readers of so unflattering
an account of American actions. Watergate was more evanescent. If the story
had broken on a weekday instead of on a weekend, perhaps the *Post* might have
assigned a senior political reporter from the national staff, a reporter already
preoccupied with other work, and the story might have died quickly. If the first
marriages of both Bob Woodward and Carl Bernstein had not ended, leaving
them both bachelors, they might have been pulled away by the normal obligations of home and might not have been willing to spend the endless hours that
the story required . . . If Howard Simons, the managing editor, had not in some
way been titillated by the story, and had not decided on his own to assign two

reporters full-time . . . If Woodward in the early weeks of Watergate, anxious for advancement and eager for a better story, had gotten the assignment he coveted, the District Court beat . . . If Carl Bernstein in the summer of 1972 had been a little further along in his negotiations with Jann Wenner of *Rolling Stone* to become a top national reporter . . . If, if, if.

It began as a crime story. Off the police blotter. No politics. There had been the break-in and the burglars had been clumsy and they had put the tape on the door the wrong way, and a black janitor had happened to notice it. So simple in the beginning. Five men arrested at 2:30 A.M. breaking into the Democratic national headquarters. On Saturday morning, Howard Simons got a call from Joe Califano, the *Post*'s lawyer and general counsel of the Democratic National Committee. Califano was a very ambitious, very hungry young influence broker in Washington, close to both Bradlee and Geyelin (indeed, far too close, thought some members of the staff who regarded Califano as a considerable hustler and thought that his sins in the Johnson years had come under too little scrutiny in the *Post*). Califano told Simons that there had been a break-in at the DNC headquarters, and so Simons immediately called his subordinate, Harry Rosenfeld, and told Rosenfeld, not knowing which way the story was going, that they had something special, all the ingredients were there, "Harry, I'm going to tell you a *great* story." Rosenfeld, equally titillated, called his subordinate, Barry Sussman, who was the *district* editor, and Sussman in turn called Bob Woodward at home. Woodward was young and very dogged and very hard-working. He went to the courthouse on that first Saturday, was there when the lawyers tried to shake him off, and was there when the judge asked one of the five men what he did for a living. Security consultant, the man answered. Where? the judge asked. The CIA, said the man, whose name was James McCord.

That had begun it. It was still not really political, but it was fascinating, a break-in at the Democratic headquarters featuring a CIA man and a bunch of Cubans. Like a bad thriller. When Woodward came back from the court, Howard Simons listened to his summary and then said, "That's a hell of a story." It was the weekend and Kay Graham liked her editors to stay in touch with her, so later that day Simons called her. There had been another good story that day, a car had gone through a house, and he told her she had two good ones. They put the break-in on page one that first night but they could not grasp the ramifications. None of the top editors were thinking Nixon, at least not yet. It was just a very good story, it had a beginning and it clearly ought to go somewhere. Page one was good play. Sussman wanted even bigger play; Sussman, intuitive, shrewd from the start, was the editor who first sensed and smelled the real implications of the story.

But it was a local story. In a local court. Off the police blotter. Covered by local reporters. That says something about why the *Post* did so well—it was right in its own domain. Other national news organizations had very good reporters based in Washington, but they did not cover local Washington stories, they did not even know where the courthouse was, they would not have time to cover a court hearing. The *Post* was deep in manpower, its editors were close to the implications, and it was on the story early. The editors handling the story were not preoccupied with other stories of global importance. Besides, since it started as a Washington story, every potential source who wanted to talk could, by talking to *Post* reporters, reach exactly the audience he or she wanted. That helped put the *Post* out ahead, and later, when other organizations began to pick up on it, the *Post*'s two reporters were far ahead and had locked up the best sources.

So the *Post* was in an enviable position. Now for the first time, almost twenty years after the merger and seven years after Bradlee's ascension to power, the *Post* had plenty of talented reporters; like the *Times,* it had the pick of the best and most ambitious young journalists in America. It not only had a star system at the top, it had quietly for some time been stockpiling an uncommon staff of younger reporters who were pushing hard for a coveted place on the national staff, young reporters, in fact, who would have been stars on any other newspaper in the country. The division at the *Post* between the national staff and the local staff was very sharp, the desire of most local reporters to go national almost total. National reporters covered big stories in distant places on large expense accounts. Local reporters were unknown, covered sewage meetings, and fought for their cab fares. The national staff was Bradlee's pride and joy; Howard Simons was in effect responsible for the metropolitan staff, where young men and women sat and looked enviously at the big-name reporters on the other side of the room. Simons was a former science reporter, an intelligent quiet man who distrusted the star system. He served at Bradlee's convenience; Bradlee by no means would tolerate a chief aide who might be a challenge to dethrone him. If Bradlee was a star, brilliant at the theater of journalism, Simons again was the opposite. There was nothing dramatic about his looks, he looked slightly harassed and rumpled, he was at ease being not the top figure but part of the bureaucracy. It was believed generally that part of his job was to soothe and calm the egos Bradlee had ruffled. At the *Post,* going from local staff to national, from Simons to Bradlee, was like changing papers, indeed, it was like changing worlds.

Among the young reporters on the Metro staff, Bob Woodward was regarded as a comer, and it was not surprising that Sussman had selected him to go to the courthouse the first day. He was new on the paper, he had been there less than a year, but he was already a favorite of many of the editors. He was smart and he was eager and hard-working, indeed he had on occasion complained to his superiors about the work habits of some of his young colleagues, claiming they were ripping off the paper. (Substitute for the word "colleague" the name "Bernstein.") Sussman liked Woodward immensely and they were friends from the start; he admired his eagerness, his intelligence, his obvious burning ambition and yet the control he had over his ambition. Woodward quickly had become a protégé of Sussman, which was rare. They would talk for long hours about journalism, and soon Woodward and his girl friend were invited out to Sussman's house for the weekend, where there would be dinners and touch football and putting the Sussman children to bed, all of which was unusual for a young reporter at the *Post.*

So Sussman thought Woodward would be excellent on the break-in, and when he mentioned the assignment to Rosenfeld, Rosenfeld immediately approved. It was he who had helped bring Woodward to the paper, after Woodward had harassed him persistently for a job. Woodward, Rosenfeld thought, was a very good hire, perhaps the hardest-working young reporter he had seen in ten years. Indeed, after a decade of young counterculture reporters sitting around dictating the terms under which they would consent to work, Rosenfeld, a traditionalist and a very conservative man at heart, welcomed a young man like Woodward, willing to accept any kind of story without question. He was also good, Rosenfeld thought, at poking around, and this story demanded someone to poke around. No matter where he went or what he did, he seemed to fit in and seemed to be able to get people to talk. When Rosenfeld had sent Woodward down to police headquarters, he had, unlike most journalists of his age, liked it there and made friends.

So Woodward it would be. Rosenfeld and Sussman did not agree on many things, they were very different men, Rosenfeld more emotional and more conservative, Rosenfeld a great shouter, emotions right on his sleeve as if to conceal his intelligence; Sussman quieter, more reflective, almost Talmudic. But they agreed on Woodward.

Robert Woodward of Wheaton, Illinois, came from the heartland of America and he looked like it. He seemed modest and pleasant and self-effacing and he was also, in a very pleasant and not very abrasive way, a totally compulsive person, a classic workaholic, wildly ambitious, utterly obsessed by his work and his career. He performed with great gentility, only a few rough edges showed, he did not try to steal stories from his friends and he kept his word to his sources. He simply worked harder than anyone else, accepting assignments filled with drudgery. Later, Woodward would seem by far the more normal of the Woodward-Bernstein team. The truth was that he was just as driven as Bernstein, strung just as tight, perhaps tighter. If anything, friends of both thought, Bernstein had more safety valves while Woodward kept more of his tension inside himself. "Woodward," the writer Timothy Crouse once said, "has a block of ice in his gut." Yet though Woodward did not flash his brightness around, he was very clever at guessing people's relationships, in knowing that people led private lives very different from their public ones. He was very good at sensing this and yet seeming so honorable, so decent, that people trusted him and, on very short acquaintanceship, confided their deepest secrets to him. It was a wonderful trait for a reporter to have.

His father was Al Woodward, the leading resident of Wheaton, a small conservative town about eighteen miles from Chicago, harboring a small conservative evangelical Christian college and about sixty churches, probably fifty-five of which were evangelical Protestant. (Wheaton College placed a mark on Bob Woodward at an early age: a generation of Wheaton coeds, introduced as baby-sitters into the Woodward household, made it their personal mission to save his soul. It was a pattern repeated perhaps a dozen times. "Have you taken Christ?" the baby-sitter would ask, and the eight-year-old Woodward would answer, very seriously, "Yes, I have." "Well," continued the baby-sitter, "have things changed in your life?" At eight Robert Woodward was not very good at dissembling and he would answer that they had not changed very much.) Al Woodward was the top local attorney and later the judge, the mainstay of the community, a man rooted in the area. His own father had run the local John Deere plant. He not only had all the local values, he could not easily conceive of other values. He had captained the Oberlin football team at a hundred and fifty pounds and he had gone on to law school. He seemed to embody the town's values. Upstanding. Hard-working. Restrained. Conscientious. Decent. He was puzzled by those who did not like the things he liked; if he liked broccoli he found it odd that his son did not. Things were the way they were for a good reason; he was wary of modern liberalism, years later he could still refer to that bad period on the local Wheaton paper as the time it had flirted briefly with liberalism and had supported John Kennedy. He was a reserved, controlled, strong man, much trusted and much respected. When he ran for judge he did not give speeches extolling his own virtue, rather he gave a nice little speech about the judicial system and how it worked, not a bit unaware of the value received in making so high-minded a speech. In later years his son was inclined to think that Al Woodward was very much like Gerald Ford; he reminded Bob Woodward of Ford, he looked like him, and talked like him, and they were both good guys and both of them were pillars of the community, and both knew where more bodies were buried than anyone else. Indeed, as Robert Woodward pursued Watergate, he had, in his own family, the perfect barometer of how traditional Republicans felt about Richard Nixon. For Al Woodward trusted Nixon, and did not accept what was happening. Only the publication of the White House tapes changed him.

The young Bob Woodward was the role model for others in that tight little community, but despite appearances his own boyhood was painful. The marriage of his parents was not very good and on occasion even messy, and the young Woodward was aware of the messiness. He became, some friends thought, very close with his emotions. His parents divorced when he was twelve and young Bob Woodward chose to live with his father; it was as if he was resentful of his mother for letting him down in some way. He drew constantly closer to his father, which made him unusually privy to his father's world. His father was the local lawyer and knew about the secret life of the town, and he shared much of this with his son. This was the beginning of Bob Woodward's real education. Unlike most young men who grew up thinking that life was as it was supposed to be, Bob Woodward learned that just about everyone had a secret life. When he saw people on the street he knew not just the official lives that they displayed, but their secret lives as well. In those days he was working as a janitor in his father's office at $11.75 a week and he was very good at going through his father's papers. The investigative reporter at the age of twelve.

Everyone played football at Wheaton High School, and so Bob Woodward played, though he did it badly. He was not fast and he was not particularly well coordinated, but he made the team, and spent most of the time on the bench. The coaches liked his clumsy steadfast quality: "You're not very good, but you have the right attitude, Woodward." In later years it struck him as one of the few things he had in common with Richard Nixon.

In his senior year he ran for student body president and he was considered a shoo-in; he was, after all, the best boy in town. He gave very good and serious speeches in the campaign, and he lost, which surprised him and his friends. Perhaps, he thought later, he had been too perfect, too clean, too aloof. Being the best boy at Wheaton High, he had, of course, given the graduation speech in 1961, a speech borrowed more or less from the then favored of Wheaton classics, Barry Goldwater's *Conscience of a Conservative*. He had assaulted, to the applause of many parents, the federal government for being the major predator in the lives of the average American. It seemed in keeping with being Al's boy. After all, he had scarcely ever even met a Democrat. During his senior year Nixon ran against Kennedy; he regarded Nixon as a kind of savior and John Kennedy as a curious person with a funny accent. In fact, he thought Kennedy was a *homo* (as the expression for a homosexual then was) because his voice and manner were so peculiar. The Kennedy-Nixon debates were reassuring to him because he was sure that the country would now not make the mistake of electing anybody as patently queer as Kennedy. Election night, he was cleaning his father's office and listening to the results on the radio, and when it became clear that Kennedy was going to win he could not believe it. Oh God, he thought, the country's going to be run by a *homo*. When he was a freshman at Yale (where he went on a Naval Reserve Officer's Scholarship), a young political science instructor had listened to him talk in class and had told him, in front of other students, that he was a crypto-fascist. But Yale gradually changed him. He had arrived with a narrow view of society and social responsibility and Yale had broadened his horizon. By the end of his stay there he was a crypto-liberal.

He was also considered a young Yale poet. Subsequently this struck some of his Washington *Post* friends as odd, because as a journalist he had a reputation as a clumsy writer. He was interested in fiction, took courses in creative writing, wrote one novel under the critic-professor Cleanth Brooks, and completed half of another one. The first novel was very autobiographical, about a sensitive young man with troubled roots in the Midwest, and Brooks was very encouraging. It was sent to Scribner's and there was some interest though nothing came of it. When his four years at Yale were up, paid for by the government, the bill was due. It was generally considered a good deal: the bright young men went off to eastern colleges and they got full scholarships and in the end they owed the Navy only four years. Not a bad swap. Except that Bob Woodward by chance graduated in June 1965, which was the exact moment that Lyndon Johnson was sending American combat troops into Vietnam. Suddenly the Navy not just wanted him, it needed him. Woodward in his last two years had watched what was happening in Vietnam and he did not like anything about it. He thought for a time about going to Canada, but that was not the sort of thing a Wheaton boy did. So in he went for the requisite four years (which became five years through the courtesy of Lyndon B. Johnson, who added a year on because of the war). He was twenty-two, and he had just married his high school sweetheart.

Woodward hated the Navy. He hated the boredom of it. He felt imprisoned when he was at sea, and imprisoned when he was not. Days filled with endless shifts during which nothing happened. All he could think of was getting out. He read continually, taking every correspondence course he could from the University of Wisconsin. He worked on a novel, unsuccessfully. He was, in the years 1966 and 1967, increasingly restless and alienated. In 1967, when he was stationed in Washington, he got orders to go to Vietnam as a tactical watch officer in Can Tho, the heart of the Mekong Delta. He knew about that particular duty. It meant going out in the canals of the Mekong Delta at night on Navy riverboats. The word was out about it, it was very dangerous duty. Men were getting killed doing that. He did not want to go. He was certain in his own mind, an absolute certainty, that if he went he would be killed. He did not want to die in the Mekong Delta. He began to think of how to get out. He was methodical about this, as always. He knew that he could not plead either a lack of sympathy for the war or a fear of death. He was then a lieutenant junior grade and he decided that the way to get out of the Mekong Delta was to imply that he wanted to go career Navy, because if you went career Navy you went destroyer, which was the main ticket. There were no destroyers in the Mekong Delta. So he got hold of the Pentagon phone book and he made a list of everyone who might have some control over his destiny, and he sat down and wrote them each a letter, a very sincere letter saying that he had decided to go career Navy, and that meant that he wanted to go destroyer because he wanted to get ahead. Before the board he made, as always, a very good impression, smart, attractive, good background, Yale, good fitness reports. He got the destroyer duty. He could never summon the courage to go and look up the records of the man who replaced him in Can Tho, though he thought of it often, and he was sure his replacement had been killed.

He got the destroyer duty and then Lyndon Johnson extended his tour for another year. He served his last year in the Pentagon. By then his marriage had come apart. Desperately restless, feeling that he had been cheated of five years, he was anxious to get to work, to be involved in something that mattered. Other people his age were already practicing law, doing important things. He gave up the idea of going to graduate school, it would take too long and pull him too far from the real world. He had liked the feel of the year in Washington, the sense of the rhythm of the government and the energy that the city seemed to possess, intense, serious young men and women on their way to something larger, convinced of their own worth and the worth of their vision. He thought he might try law school and he applied to Harvard Law School and was, of course, accepted, and he sent in his fifty dollars. But he was also thinking of journalism. He had met a few young journalists in Washington and their lives seemed more exciting than the law and government. The idea attracted him more and more. A few of his friends worked on local papers, and he would ask about the personalities that went with different by-lines. One day there was a protest story under the by-line of someone named Carl Bernstein. Bernstein, he asked a friend, who's he? "A very old guy," his friend answered, "been around a long time. A real old-timer." Carl Bernstein, having availed himself neither of college nor of the U.S. Navy, was a year younger than Woodward. That summer he visited friends in Cambridge, where he talked about his desire to go to work for the *Post*. "Why do you want to do that?" asked a young man named Tom Farber, who worked for an underground newspaper. "They'll never print what you write." That summer he decided against Harvard Law, and for journalism. He epitomized a new trend: journalism, for a variety of reasons, not the least of them the Vietnam War, had become an attractive profession. Journalists now did important things. They were respected, often surprisingly powerful, and well paid. In the past, mostly offbeat, somewhat funky young people had gone into journalism; now sure winners like Bob Woodward were turning down Harvard Law School to become reporters.

Filled with quiet midwestern chutzpah, Woodward had gone to the *Post* to ask for a job. He saw Harry Rosenfeld, the metropolitan editor, and Rosenfeld said it was ridiculous, his wanting a job, why, he had no experience. "This is a fast league, a big-time paper, we can't take time to teach you," Rosenfeld said. But Woodward, in that stubborn insistent manner of his, kept pushing, kept demanding a chance; it was one of his special gifts, the ability to make those who denied his requests feel that *they* were in the wrong. Finally Rosenfeld caved in. Woodward would be given a three-week tryout. During the tryout he wrote some fifteen stories, none of which was printed. "See, you're lousy," Rosenfeld said, but Rosenfeld in truth was impressed, Woodward had intelligence and true grit. With the help of the *Post* editors he got a job on the neighboring Montgomery *Sentinel.* His first story was very routine, a piece about the deadline for filing for local elections being 11 P.M., and all the other reporters in the pressroom laughed when they read Woodward's piece, which began: "At 10:53 P.M. last night . . ." There was a good joke in that, the green kid putting in the hour as if it were of any importance.

It was about the last time they laughed at Woodward. Within weeks it was clear that Woodward was very good, that he took nothing for granted, that he worked harder than anyone else, and he was soon scoring off some of the regulars on the beat, including reporters for the *Post*. If he did not know exactly what a story was, all an editor had to do was point him in the right direction and he picked up on it from there. He did not write very well, but he very quickly picked up a sense of what news was, and he could get almost anyone to talk with him. It was a wonderful combination for a reporter, the exterior so comforting, the interior so driven. Within a few weeks *Sentinel* editor Roger Farquhar was telling everyone that Woodward was going to be a great reporter. Jim Mann, one of the *Post*'s brightest young reporters, was then covering Montgomery County. He and Woodward became good friends and it was very clear that Woodward wanted to get back to the *Post*. He was constantly asking Mann questions about it. What was Bradlee like? What about Howard Simons? Rosenfeld? Sussman? Always in a pleasant nonhustling way, never saying that he wanted a job. But it was always there. After a while Mann began to sponsor Woodward. He was convinced that the *Post* needed more investigative reporters and that Woodward had a special gift for working on his own, at once dogged and subtle. At first there seemed to be some resistance to him from Rosenfeld, who wanted no part of an Ivy League kid who could not write. But Woodward kept hounding him, calling him on weekends, until finally Rosenfeld complained to his wife. "But isn't that the type of young man you always said you wanted?" his wife asked.

After a very successful year with the *Sentinel* Woodward was finally at the *Post*. He learned early how to break the code of the *Post* and get in the paper, and he did it regularly. He also told his superiors that there were some reporters there who took three days to do a story that could be done in one day. No doubt it was true, and no doubt it did not endear him to all of his contemporaries. Most young reporters there did not like the newer system at the paper. They thought it had changed markedly since Harry Rosenfeld had replaced the less structural Isaacs as city editor. He was less tolerant of staff idiosyncrasies. There was a much greater emphasis on production as an end in itself. Woodward seemed to have been produced by it. Some, like Carl Bernstein, were put off by his ambition and thought his stories a little dinky. Some felt that he was a little too reverential of the paper's power system. It was a quality that he was himself quite aware of; he could say later of Jeb Magruder, the wonderfully clean young corporate hustler of the White House, whose qualities on the surface at least seemed so familiar, "There but for the grace of God go I."

But his editors were pleased with him; he was, they hoped, the embodiment of a new kind of reporter, post-counterculture, harder-working, a winner. He got lots of stories. He impressed not just Sussman and Rosenfeld but Simons and *Bradlee* as well. Soon there was a magic day, Bradlee lunching with some of the newer reporters. Bradlee: "Which one of you is Woodward?" "I am," said the new boy. "You're all over the paper. That's good. Keep it up." Was there ever a day so sweet? He had been anointed. Soon thereafter, Bradlee came up with a story for him. Bradlee's buddy Doc Dalinsky, who ran the Georgetown pharmacy, had told him there was a big scandal in Medicaid, the selling of drugs was becoming big business. Woodward was assigned to it. "There's a Pulitzer Prize in that one, kid," said Bradlee. Did a reporter ever work harder? Woodward dressed in old clothes and pretended he had lost his Medicare credentials and tried to buy drugs, yet though he worked desperately hard he did not produce a Pulitzer Prize or, for that matter, a very good story. These things, it turns out, take time.

Woodward did not really want the Watergate story at first. There were other stories he was working on. He had been in pursuit of a local drug dealer, said to sell millions of dollars' worth of heroin in Washington, and was beginning to build up a considerable case on him. Besides, what he really wanted and was really pushing for was his buddy Jim Mann's assignment, covering the District Court beat. Mann was going on a sabbatical for a year to Italy, accompanying his wife, Caroline, an architectural student, for her year abroad (this was to hurt him badly at the *Post,* where it was considered a serious breach of *machismo,* to follow his wife to a foreign country in the midst of a great story. Rosenfeld later referred to him as "the reporter who walked away from Watergate"). Mann's beat was a prestigious assignment. Many of the best people on the paper had held it in the past, including Bradlee. Woodward had no larger vision of Watergate at first, as both Sussman and Bernstein did relatively early on. Woodward went at Watergate in the early days with a single-minded ferocity because he went at *everything* with a single-minded ferocity.

On the Sunday after the break-in, Woodward had some help from other reporters. Carl Bernstein worked on a story on James McCord, whom the Associated Press had identified as the security coordinator for the Committee for the Re-election of the President. The story was not particularly brilliant, nor did it open very much new ground. Late that night, however, the paper got its first big break. Eugene Bachinski, the *Post*'s night police reporter, who had very good police sources, discovered that the cops had found two address books on the Cubans, and in them were the name and phone number of Howard Hunt, with the notation "W. House" and "W.H." There was also an unmailed envelope containing Hunt's personal check for $6.36 made out to the Lakewood Country Club in nearby Rockville. It was the first big connection. Woodward worked on the story on Monday and near deadline time he called the White House and asked for Hunt. There was no answer at one extension. The White House operator, ever helpful, then said she would try Mr. Colson's office. The secretary in Colson's office gave him the number of a Washington public relations firm. Hunt came on the phone. Woodward, his heart beating very quickly, trying to be as calm as possible, asked him why his name and phone number were in the address book of two of the men picked up in the Watergate break-in. "Good God," Hunt said. Then he added: "In view of the fact that the matter is under adjudication, I have no comment," and slammed down the phone. That was the beginning, the first major link. The story the next day headlined: WHITE HOUSE CONSULTANT LINKED TO BUGGING SUSPECTS.

From then on Sussman gave the story special care. He was, the young reporters on the *Post* generally agreed, by far the best of the young editors at the paper. He liked softer leads and did not insist, if the substance of a good story was there, that a reporter had to fall back on the traditional and mechani-

cal "who, what, when, where." When a reporter came back to the office with
the outline of a story, Sussman was often very valuable, not only fulfilling the
editor's function but also running the assembled facts through his mind as a
reporter would, sometimes making better sense of them than the reporter was.
He was a dreamer in the best way, and when he had flashes of insight they
were seldom pedestrian. He was the first of a new generation of editors to deal
with the new generation of reporters. He could ask the larger questions.

Thus almost from the start, before anyone else at the *Post,* Sussman saw
Watergate as a larger story, saw that the individual events were part of a larger
pattern, the result of hidden decisions from somewhere in the top of government which sent smaller men to run dirty errands. He did not smell Nixon on
the very first day, but he sensed the President's role earlier than almost anyone
else, and he brought to the story a combination of suspicion and logic that
allowed him to see the whole matter in perspective sooner than anyone else.
If these events were taking place at the Washington *Post* instead of the White
House, he wondered, would Bradlee know? If there were a series of incidents
that seemed to be threatening Bradlee's future, somehow Bradlee would know,
he decided.

From the start, the *Post* was thus unusually lucky. It had the perfect
working editor at exactly the right level. Sussman was not simply encouraging,
he brainstormed the story, trying to put the pieces together, fitting them and
refitting them until finally, slowly, there was the beginning of a pattern. More,
he believed in the story, he was sure there was something there. Simons from
the start had been good because, in the best old-style newspaper sense, he had
thought that it sounded promising. Sussman, working at the foot-soldier level,
was even better; where other editors on a story so difficult might have cast
doubt upon the fragments the young reporters were bringing in, Sussman
offered only constant encouragement. Sussman always believed there was
more, and given Richard Nixon and Watergate, there always was.


Because Sussman was an original himself and did not believe in stereotypes,
he was, and this made him unusual, one of the very few editors at the Washington *Post* who thought Carl Bernstein a considerable asset. He could handle
Bernstein and evoke quality work from him. Though technically Bernstein was
supposed to be in Virginia when Watergate broke, as was his wont he had
sniffed around the story on the first day and ended up drawing a sidebar. On
the second day Sussman asked him to come in, and he ended up helping
Woodward, finally taking Woodward's version and rewriting it and improving
it. But Bernstein in the early days was not assigned to Watergate. It was still
Woodward's story. Bernstein was assigned to cover Virginia, which was perhaps going to be his last assignment. His string at the *Post* had worn very thin.
The *Post* hierarchy by then was quite resentful of Carl Bernstein and he in turn
was resentful of it, and he was looking for jobs elsewhere, perhaps at *Rolling
Stone,* where his life style would be more acceptable.

He worked for the first two or three days on Watergate and then was sent back to Virginia. But he wanted a piece of the story very badly, and he did not at the beginning respect Woodward very much, and he felt he should be on it, not Woodward. So he had written a highly original five-page memorandum which he called the "Chotiner Theory." It said in effect that there was a tradition of dirty tricks around Nixon going back to his earliest campaigns under Murray Chotiner, and that Colson was Chotiner's linear descendant. His editors were impressed by the memo and temporarily at least Bernstein was put back on the story. Almost immediately, he picked up a story about Howard Hunt, working out of the White House, investigating and haunting Teddy Kennedy. He brought the story into Bradlee's office, but Bradlee, sensitive to his own ties to the Kennedy family, was not taken by it and watered it down and put it on an inside page. Bernstein stomped out of the office muttering darkly about Bradlee and the fucking Kennedys. Two years later, when the Senate Watergate Committee came up with the same story, the *Post* played it on page one. Woodward and Bernstein reminded Bradlee that it had taken two years to get it out front.

In those early days he went around telling friends, "What's with Woodward on this? Why doesn't he get going?" The story seemed to him to be hanging there, without commitment on Woodward's part. To him, Woodward was some upper-class kid who was making it on the *Post* through social connections rather than ability. He thought Woodward was something of an ass-kisser, someone so eager that he came in on his day off; as Bernstein was not the beau ideal of a young Washington *Post* reporter, so Woodward did not fit Bernstein's conception of what a colleague should be.

By July the paper seemed to be slowing down on the story. Bradlee was on vacation. Rosenfeld was on vacation. Woodward was on the story but he was on other stories as well. Howard Simons was in charge of the paper, and he was bothered by what was *not* happening on the Watergate story. He thought it was dying and he was not sure why. There had not been many Watergate stories recently and the trail seemed to be growing cold. Woodward alone was assigned to it. But Simons did not want the story to die, something about it had fascinated him from the start. It was bizarre, so many different pieces. The Cubans. The CIA. The DNC. The White House. Who were they and what were they really looking for that night at the DNC? It was by far the best unresolved story around. He did not believe that one man, only partially committed, was enough. On July 25, Simons arrived at his office and read a story in *The New York Times* about fifteen calls being made from Bernard Barker's phone in Miami to an office at CREEP shared by Gordon Liddy and another lawyer. That was it for Simons, there *was* more to the story, although it was always coming out in dribs and drabs and each piece seemed to raise more questions than it answered.

At this point Simons made the most important decision of any editor at the Washington *Post* or, for that matter, any editor in the country during Watergate. His was, in fact, the fateful decision. He decided to create a two-man team to cover the story. To do so, he did not go to the national desk for his reporters, though this might easily have been the procedure, given the *Post*'s star system. Instead, he went to Sussman, the district editor, and he showed him the *Times* story. "Why didn't we have that?" he asked. He had deliberately gone to Sussman for a number of reasons. For one thing, Sussman was clearly fascinated by Watergate. Besides, Simons wanted hungry young reporters and he did not particularly like the *Post*'s caste system; it was unhealthy for those who were not stars and unhealthy for those who were. Good reporting, he believed, was made up more of drudgery than of glamour, and a star system did not necessarily encourage drudgery. So he told Sussman to assign two reporters full-time to it and to create in effect a full-time Watergate desk. Sussman was delighted. He too thought the story needed more manpower, and here was a superior giving him the perfect mandate—a strong commitment, enough manpower, and clear but minimal instructions.

A little while later Sussman went back to Simons's office. "I've decided to assign Woodward." Simons smiled. Sussman smiled. "And," he continued, "sit down when you hear this . . . Bernstein." Simons screamed. Just the day before, Simons had looked at Bernstein's expense account for Virginia and had been enraged. Bernstein, one of ten reporters assigned to Virginia, had used up exactly half of the entire ten-person budget for the whole year. *Half the budget.* There had been a typical Bernstein atrocity story involved: Bernstein had gone to Richmond and rented a car, used it a few times, and then left it behind in a parking garage because he preferred getting around on bicycle. He only remembered the car several months later when the Hertz people wrote him a letter saying they were delighted he liked their car so much, and did he by chance want to buy it? Simons had always rather liked Bernstein in the past, had been something of a Bernstein defender against the rising chorus of other editors, but the Virginia expense account had been too much. Enough of Bernstein. "Yes, I know," said Sussman, "but I can handle him and he's very good when he's involved." Sussman had decided on Woodward automatically, he was so hard-working, so clean, so easy to handle. But he wanted Bernstein too. If the circumstances were right, Bernstein would work as hard as Woodward. Besides, Bernstein was better with the phone than almost any other reporter on the paper, he was a magician with it. If Woodward was serious and hard-working, then Bernstein was more imaginative, more creative, and, Sussman thought, not only would they both work tremendously long hours but their styles would complement each other. "Bernstein," said Simons, "Bernstein just spent more money covering Virginia than Murrey Marder did covering the Paris peace talks. Okay, you can have Bernstein." Actually, he thought it was a rather good choice.

Sussman called Bernstein at home, where he had come in from Virginia on his day off, and told him he wanted him to follow up on the *Times* story. Bernstein exploded at Sussman over the phone, he was tired of being shuttled on and off the goddamn story, he was goddamn well tired of being a go-fer for Bob Woodward, he had damn well been in the business longer than Woodward, and he wanted to be in on the story once and for all or be out, he didn't want to be pulled in at their pleasure just because he had good phone contacts. Sussman told him not to worry, he would be in on the story, he could go down to Miami on this one. Bernstein loved out-of-town travel, it smacked of the national desk and the big-time, hotels, credit cards. So Bernstein came in. The commitment had been made, a two-man team. Two very young reporters. Woodward and Bernstein.

Sussman had wanted Bernstein partly because he was something of a throwback, an old-fashioned reporter with all kinds of old-fashioned tricks, and unlike most young reporters, he used the telephone like an old-time rewrite man. It was as if he had been born with the knack. He could call people other reporters would not think of calling, he was very clever, and his fingers were quick. Even as he was ending one call, his fingers would flick across the buttons, starting a new call. Much of that came from his training as a rewrite man on the *Star*. When other reporters failed it was Bernstein who seemed to be able to come up with the crucial unlisted phone numbers that the paper desperately needed. (That was not by chance; as a young reporter around town he had deliberately cultivated, not the top people at the White House or the State Department, but some insiders at the phone company. He had learned the advantage of this early on. It was amazing what such friends could do in moments of crisis.)

He was also considered the prize office screw-up. Nothing more, nothing less. Young reporters on the paper believed that management was keeping a list of Metro staff members who were going to be fired and at the head of the list was the name of Carl Bernstein. Certainly Bradlee had gone to Gene Patterson, the managing editor, often enough and said, "Can't we fire that goddamn kid? He's driving me crazy! Can't we do anything?" Certainly his closest friends thought he was in dire straits. Just before he went overseas for his assignment in Moscow, Bernstein's buddy Bob Kaiser had gone in to say goodbye to Bradlee, and the last thing he remembered saying was that it would be a great mistake to fire Bernstein, that he was difficult but very talented. Then another friend, Phil Carter, the *Post*'s southern reporter, had been in town and, hearing that Bernstein was in trouble again, had told Bradlee not to fire him, that he was worth all the trouble. When Bernstein had been given the Virginia assignment it was made clear that this would probably be his last chance on the paper and he had, in true Bernstein fashion, turned in some wonderfully original stories, stories of exceptional texture and flair, stories no one else would have thought of. But he had also managed to infuriate management. He had shown himself skilled at finding not only very good stories but the most expensive hotels and restaurants in the entire commonwealth. (To this day, other *Post* reporters planning vacation trips to Virginia always check with Bernstein for his remarkable knowledge of the state's finest establishments, a knowledge acquired on the company trough.)

He was legendary as the office deadbeat, legendary for borrowing money, less so for paying it back; he smoked cigarettes endlessly, rarely his own. He was the one person always available for a coffee break. He was the terror of guild meetings, swaggering around in boots and an Army fatigue jacket, shouting what he was going to do to management; Bernstein, it seemed, was a reporter perennially in search of a grievance. When the *Post* moved to its new building in 1972, much to Bradlee's fury Bernstein was soon discovered destroying the floor around his desk, dropping his cigarette butts on the floor and not even bothering to grind them out. Thus the entire area was pitted. Bradlee took this as a personal affront. It was Bernstein who would sidle up to a new reporter, find out what he or she was making, promising that he would treat this information with confidence, and if it turned out that the reporter was making more than he, blab it angrily all over the city room. Then there was Bernstein the office cutup; Bernstein watching one day as Bradlee escorted an absolutely beautiful young woman named Bernadette Carey through the city room, apparently preliminary to hiring her, Bernstein jumping on top of his desk, shouting, "Hire her! Hire her! We'll teach her to type." Bernstein once covered City Hall when there was a big demonstration going on. Steve Isaacs, the metropolitan editor, happened by and found no *Post* reporter covering the demonstration, and so he looked a little further for his man, who happened of course to be Bernstein. Isaacs finally found him lying down on a couch in the press shack, eyes closed, far from the madding crowd. To this day Isaacs insists that Bernstein was asleep and Bernstein for his part insists that he was recuperating from a terrible migraine attack. It is the stuff of Washington *Post* legend.

It was, in fact, believed that one of the reasons that Rosenfeld was brought in to replace Isaacs as metropolitan editor in 1970 was to clean up the city room and end the kind of abuse from some of the young reporters that was symbolized by Bernstein. Bernstein seemed classically of the Isaacs era, offbeat, irreverent, a lot of talent, some of which on occasion showed in the paper. Perhaps only Isaacs would have hired him. His interview with Bernstein had gone rather well; the first thing that Carl Bernstein had said to the man who was possibly going to hire him was that he wanted Isaacs's job. Isaacs liked that. It was typical of Bernstein, he may have been insecure but he was also brash and cocky; he did not believe that rules applied to him. He had talent and that was for him quite sufficient, and he had not yet bothered to discipline it. He was a person who saw himself as a victim and who therefore permitted himself to victimize others (that was one thing, friends thought, he had in common with Richard Nixon). He could be wildly insensitive to others and yet there was also an engaging sweetness to him. At the nadir he could flash a quick winsome little-boy look full of beguiling charm and he would be forgiven and allowed another chance.

He was, and this was of added value to the paper, a Washington kid. It was an irony of journalism in the nation's capital that almost none of the working reporters knew anything about the city of Washington itself, the community apart from the government. For most reporters working there,

Washington the city was simply a backdrop to the political world. They had little or no feel for the texture and the subculture of the city. Bernstein did. He had grown up there and he knew and loved the city, and he was by nature street-smart. The best stories he had done for the *Post* were about the different neighborhoods of the city, indeed Bradlee had once offered him a local column, to write what he wanted about the city. The night in April 1968 when Washington had burned in the wake of the assassination of Martin Luther King, Bernstein had gone through the burning streets with a colleague, pointed at different shattered stores, and talked about the people who had run each store. He seemed to know them all.

He was the child of left-wing parents, people of the thirties, New Dealers who had moved further left with the force of events, and who had been blacklisted during the worst of the anti-Communist hysteria. Alfred Bernstein, born in this country in 1910 into a middle-class home, had gone to Columbia and Columbia Law. He had thought for a time of staying on as a teaching fellow at Columbia, but in the mid-thirties when he had graduated from law school all the bright young men were going to Washington. He was not in those early days particularly radical, if anything he was a conventional New Dealer. He joined a major investigation of the railroads being run by Senator Burton Wheeler and worked as an investigator. He also became active in the United Public Workers' Union and that was quickly the focal point of his life. The great issues of the day for him were not the inevitable decline of capitalism, but Jim Crow and the escalating civil war in Spain, issues of conscience and passion rather than polemic and dogma. Washington was a very segregated southern city, the union was committed to ending Jim Crow long before it was fashionable, and it was representing black workers. All of this was pushing him gradually further and further to the left. During the war he went out to San Francisco, where he worked for a time for the Office of Price Administration, but even there his day was dominated by the union and he became a union organizer. He was very good at organizing, he had an easy open manner with people and they seemed to respond to him.

He had in 1939 married Sylvia Walker, originally Walkovicz. She was the daughter of tailors, people so poor that often they could barely support their family. Sylvia Walker had at first not been terribly political, the family had been too poor for that, but as a young woman she had become quite active in the local Democratic organization. Then in the late thirties Spain had become the dominant issue and this moved her and her husband further left. Fascism was on the rise in Europe, the war in Spain seemed to be the testing ground, not a political choice but, far more emotional, a moral one, this was the chance to stop fascism. Sylvia Bernstein had campaigned to get the United States to intervene and the failure had affected both of them.

By the time he entered the Army during World War II, Alfred Bernstein was spending more time on the union than on his job; when he was discharged in 1946 he went back to Washington to work for the union full-time as an organizer. The union had merged with another and it was called the United

Public Workers. It was one of the far-left CIO unions, it was—and this was considered very radical in those days—spending a lot of time organizing blacks. America's sense of social good will seemed to be shrinking under the pressure of exterior events. The Cold War was echoing ominously across the land; innocent acts of good will and good intention were no longer judged as innocent, but as part of a conspiratorial pattern. Premature anti-fascism and premature civil-rights commitments were suddenly liabilities. As the pressure mounted from the conservative right, Harry Truman moved to coopt it by instituting his own program of loyalty oaths. It was a terrible moment; overnight thousands of loyal citizens were put out of their jobs for lack of political purity, completely stranded, absolutely without means. The only group that would come to their aid at that dark moment was their union. The union's lawyer happened to be Alfred Bernstein. In the period 1946–48 he probably handled more Truman loyalty oath cases than any other lawyer; he went before countless congressional committees defending people who had been summarily fired, and he was very good at it. He won more than 90 percent of his cases. But he did not make a lot of friends in high places, and when James Eastland's Internal Security Committee began investigating Communist influence in unions, one of the first unions they went after was his, and one of the first witnesses they summoned was Alfred Bernstein. Rather than testify, he took the Fifth Amendment. At almost the same time there was a great struggle within the CIO over whether or not to expel the left-wing unions, and Bernstein's union, which had supported Henry Wallace in the 1948 campaign, was quickly drummed out.

To all intents and purposes, the union was finished and Alfred Bernstein overnight was not just unemployed, he was unemployable. He had never been particularly interested in practicing law and had never taken the bar exam, so the law was closed. He could not teach; universities were not looking for scarred left-wing professors with little teaching background. They were, in fact, looking to unload tenured professors with leftist connections. No political or social institution wanted him. So he bought a small neighborhood laundry and he became a local laundryman, 3218 Georgia Avenue, a largely black neighborhood, thirty Bendix machines, selling a little laundry soap on the side. He worked very very long hours for very little money.

He was a lawyer who could not practice law, a government official who could not work for the government, an intensely engaged man who could no longer be involved in any serious centrist way, a political man who was now politically unemployable. Carl Bernstein, even as a reporter who had broken Watergate and was a national celebrity, knew only that his parents had been very far left, and never knew whether or not they had actually been members of the Communist Party. It was a sensitive subject, not one they talked about. Carl Bernstein much admired and loved his father and thought of him, not as a man of polemics or ideology or rigid positions, but as a humanist committed at a very personal level against injustice. When his parents in the sixties and seventies talked about their politics and the politics of their families, they said they were progressives. *Progressives,* it was an odd word in the seventies, left over from another time, days of the Spanish Civil War and benefits by Paul Robeson.

Yet the Bernstein home was always a political home; even in the colder, chillier years of the fifties there was a commitment against injustice. The people who came to the Bernstein house, even in the bad days, were *involved* people, people who had been his father's clients in the loyalty oath fights or people who were allies in the struggles against segregation. That was a big cause. In the fifties Washington was still a Jim Crow town, and it was a matter of clear and simple justice. When Carl Bernstein was a little boy there were blacks constantly coming to his home; that was unusual in itself. There were, from the time he was a little boy, picket lines, usually protesting segregation in public facilities; he remembered walking on a picket line when he was six.

Eventually Alfred Bernstein became employable again, though not politically. This time it was as a fund raiser, first for the Eleanor Roosevelt Foundation for Cancer Research; eventually he became chief fund raiser for the National Conference of Christians and Jews. In 1955, much to Carl's dismay, the Bernsteins moved to the suburbs, they needed more room with two daughters as well as Carl. Could a family live in the suburbs and still be radical? Their home seemed to friends of Carl's hardly the home of political radicals, it seemed so comfortable, so middle-class. There seemed to be few tangible artifacts of the political left. The post–World War II suburbs seemed an alien place for radicalism. To live in the suburbs was to be thoroughly Americanized, happiness, after all, was guaranteed among the dishwashers and station wagons of the suburbs, they reflected the comfort and affluence of American technological and industrial victories, the fact that capitalism had not failed. But the Bernsteins were living in Silver Spring, Maryland. They did not, like many of the radicals of the sixties, identify themselves by their clothes or their hairstyles. Rather, they looked very much at home in Silver Spring. Their conversation was very nice and pleasant with a slight edge of political commitment. It was, one friend of Carl Bernstein's thought, a commitment so deep and so strong and so personal that Alfred and Sylvia Bernstein did not have to flaunt it or inflict it on people. It was there, they had lived it, it was a very real part of their lives.

How much all of that left-wing background had affected Carl Bernstein was not easy to measure. He was certainly left of center, though he was not in the classic sense a political person. His passion in his early years was far more for music than for politics. He seemed too iconoclastic, too distrusting of politics, to be a devoted radical. Sometimes his friends thought that the politics of another generation had surfaced in this new, more affluent generation in Bernstein's resistance to and distrust of the system of large companies (including the Washington *Post*) and his essential distrust of formal politics. Thus the resistance to playing the game by the *Post*'s rules. A suspicion of all things large and powerful. Sometimes, though, they thought it was as much that he was simply the slightly spoiled middle-class Jewish kid who had learned early on how to have things his way, and how to get away with the minimal amount of work, while breaking as many rules as he could and flouting authority as much as possible. Sometimes, his friends thought, it was a combination of both.

He had as a teen-ager hated Silver Spring from the start. In his own mind he was a city kid and he had loved living in a working-class neighborhood. He did not work at school, he spent as much time gambling as possible, accumulating from the time he was in junior high school a string of major gambling debts. His teachers were constantly disappointed, *Carl is very bright but he just won't apply himself.* There were bitter fights over school. His parents insisted that he had to do better, that otherwise he would not get into a good college; he in turn hated it all, the school and the lectures on studying things that seemed so meaningless. The only thing he was really interested in was the AZA, the youth organization of B'nai B'rith. For a time he was far more interested in it than in school, he became the regional president, a very important young man, a sixteen-year-old kid with a huge travel budget. There was suddenly a purpose to his life. In 1960 he wanted the AZA to become involved in the black sit-in movement taking place in the South, he worked to get his group, the Washington-Maryland-Virginia chapter, to picket in North Carolina. Jews, he felt, must lead the way in the South. Not everyone agreed; there was a cabal of middle-class parents that most definitely did not want Jews to be too associated with this civil-rights thing, to be out front on an issue of such emotion, it was not good for the Jews. At one point it appeared that he might run for international president, but when it became clear that the anti-Bernstein feeling was too strong, he pulled back.

He had not done well in high school, and he finally went to the University of Maryland, largely, in his own words, because it was the only college that would have him. At Maryland the only thing he excelled in was the accumulation of parking tickets. He had no feel for college. It did not connect with his real life. But his teachers had always told him that there was one thing he could do and do well and that was write. It was his specialty, it had bailed him out of trouble again and again on exams. So at the age of sixteen he walked into the Washington *Star* looking for a job. He got a job as a copy boy. It was as if his life began. The real world had reached him. He was very young and very green. In those days newspapers used carbon paper to produce duplicate copies. On Bernstein's first day there, dressed to the teeth, wearing his new cord suit, an assistant city editor handed him a batch of carbons and told him it was the copy boy's job to wash them. Bernstein dutifully went to the men's room and started washing the carbon paper, fouling himself and his handsome new suit. Just at that moment Newbold Noyes, the editor of the *Star,* wandered into the room and asked Bernstein what he was doing. "Washing the carbon paper," said the *Star*'s newest employee. At which point Noyes strode back into the city room and told the assembled editors, "I'm not asking the name of whoever did this but if it ever happens again, he's fired."

He loved the *Star*. It was a home and it was a connection to a larger and more real world. By the time he was nineteen he seemed to be part of the woodwork there, part of the *Star*'s establishment. Indeed, young reporters and copy boys older than Bernstein were intimidated by him; he was very tough, very aggressive, part of the city desk apparatus, connected to the big boys. He was not like a kid copy boy but rather a staffer who was on the inside, who knew all the gossip before anyone else. It seemed to some of his young peers quite scary, this tough little street kid who was a part of the desk operation and who was quite willing to throw his weight around. There was, not surprisingly, a considerable anti-Bernstein faction, those of his own age resentful of his swaggering arrogant connection to power. Bernstein did not tolerate fools lightly, but they were not all fools. He was the kind of person, one young colleague of his said, that if you were not his friend and simply judged him on his actions, you would not like him. If you were his friend and sensed some of the complexity to him and the sweetness there, it was easy to like him and look past the other qualities.

At first he had been a Dictaphone man, which was a step below a reporter; there was an unofficial rule at the *Star* that you could not be a reporter unless you had a college education. He was still in a somewhat haphazard way going to the University of Maryland, and in the summer of 1964 he was slowly growing out of his role as Dictaphone man. They needed an obit man, and so they jumped him ahead; he was even getting occasional by-lines. He wrote obits and then some split-page features and in September of that year it had been agreed that he would stay on the staff and return to college and work a four-day week whenever he didn't have classes. At the last minute, however, I. William Hill, the managing editor of the paper, said that Bernstein could not be on staff until he graduated from college. "Carl," he said, "you've really put your shoulder to the wheel and we're proud of you, but we want you to finish your education. Besides," he said, in words that Bernstein long remembered, "experience is no substitute for our training program." That meant going back from obits and occasional features to the Dictaphone.

He asked for, and got, a job on the Elizabeth, New Jersey, *Journal,* where one of the *Star*'s assistant city editors had just gone to be editor. Once there, he quickly let the other reporters know that he was better than they were, which, in most cases, was true, though perhaps it might have been better if they had found out on their own. He dropped the names of the Washington biggies he knew. They in turn had a nickname for him. The Rotten Kid. Someone who was good and knew the editor and was a bit of a show-off. He wanted to make it as a reporter that year, it was his big chance, and make it he did. The paper won two first prizes in the New Jersey Associated Press competition and both were won by the Rotten Kid. One was a lovely story he did traveling around New York City on the night of the 1965 blackout, and the other was on teen-age drinking, New Jersey kids going over to Staten Island and New York City, where they could drink at eighteen instead of twenty-one. He was, for all of that, still very undisciplined, his life was very much in disorder. He was living in Greenwich Village and he had again gotten himself very seriously in debt from gambling and from being a big spender. Household Finance knew Carl Bernstein and knew him well. When he went to Atlantic City to pick up his two awards, his father came up and with several thousand dollars they drove along the eastern seacoast paying off his debts.

He stayed at the Elizabeth *Journal* for a year and that gave him the credentials to go back to Washington. There appeared to be a job at both the *Star* and the *Post* and he chose the *Post.* Isaacs hired him, Isaacs who seemed to take pleasure in hiring the unconventional. Isaacs had called Charley Puffenberger at the *Star,* Bernstein's old editor, and Puff said, "You ought to hire that kid." Why? asked Isaacs. "Because someday he'll win a Pulitzer Prize for someone." He did not do well at the *Post.* There was never any doubt about his talent. He was absolutely convinced of his own ability; he wanted to emulate the two best nonfiction writers of the sixties, Gay Talese and Tom Wolfe, but his editors wanted more mundane treatment of more mundane subjects. He was very quickly a problem child. He did not work well except for brief flashes of talent; he was subject to migraine headaches, his debts mounted. He fell in love with a young woman reporter named Carol Honsa and married her (on the day of his wedding he turned desperately to his old friend Warren Hoge, a reporter on the *Star,* and said, in evident panic, "Hoge, get me out of here"). For a brief time his life seemed more orderly, his bills were paid, and he seemed to have more control of himself, but in a year he was slipping again, the marriage did not work, and his life started to unravel again. Most of the tension seemed to be between the *Post* and him. He would not play by their rules. The *Post* wanted him to wear his hair shorter, so he wore it longer. The *Post* wanted him to dress in a proper way, so he dressed in a fatigue jacket. The *Post* wanted him to have a proper well-ordered life, so he made it chaotic. The *Post* wanted him to abide by the subtle unwritten rules of big institutions, to hide his ambition to be on the national staff, as other promising young reporters did, so he wore it on his sleeve. The *Post* wanted him to sing the praises of covering the sewer commission, so Bernstein showed his contempt. He knew what the rules were but he refused to abide by them. He spoke badly of many of the lower-level editors, which was a cardinal sin: to get ahead you must praise all editors. He fought with them over editing and he often hung around at night to be sure that his stories came out as he wanted, that some late-night surgery was not performed upon them. That too was a sin.

Yet he was clearly very talented. He would do stories about Washington and about the neighborhoods that no one else on the paper could do. Bradlee was intrigued by him, by how street-smart and cunning he was. But Bradlee was annoyed that he was also ripping off the paper, and thus ripping off Bradlee, which bordered on another cardinal sin, disloyalty. Bradlee could never quite make up his mind whether Bernstein was a winner or a loser. A winner determined to be a loser, most probably. Whenever he was in trouble he seemed to be able to talk his way out of it, he was glib and there was a sweet inner charm which he could shyly flash and he could talk an editor into yet another chance. Years later, when Dustin Hoffman was trying to understand and master the personality of Bernstein for the movie version of *All the President's Men,* he came to Washington, studied him, and finally said, "I've got it. I understand why Carl did so well on Watergate. Carl is essentially a fuck-up and he has to fail and Nixon is a fuck-up and has to fail and so Carl could always understand Nixon."

All he really wanted was to be on the national staff. He also had tried several times to go to Vietnam, but he was not the kind of reporter Bradlee was going to send to Vietnam, not by a long shot. He *dreamed* of the national staff, and he was always busy concocting fascinating, exotic stories that would take him to distant parts of the United States, Carl Bernstein of the Washington *Post,* credit cards in hand, always first-class, always for the Washington *Post.* The *Post* instead wanted him to cover local news, to show discipline and respect. Finally his editors approved one of his trips. He had heard about the large number of deserters who had taken refuge in Canada and he wrote a memo suggesting a long piece on them. He sent in the memo and miraculously it was accepted. What he did not realize was that the moment he crossed into Canada he was in effect a foreign correspondent and he was on the staff of Harry Rosenfeld, then foreign editor. Rosenfeld, already deeply suspicious of Bernstein, was not very happy about the story under any conditions, but Bernstein made the trip and then when he came back to do the story he absolutely froze. He simply could not write. Rosenfeld kept demanding the story and Bernstein could not produce. Finally Bradlee came by and gave Bernstein an ultimatum: the story the next day or else. That night Dick Cohen and Peter Osnos, Bernstein's friends, gathered at Bernstein's house and the three of them worked on the story together. It became very clear to Cohen that Bernstein had all the parts of the story, that he had done a very good job, but was now so awed by doing a foreign-staff story that he choked. Shortly thereafter Rosenfeld became metropolitan editor and there was a feeling that Rosenfeld was keeping a ledger of Bernstein's mistakes. By the end of 1971 the paper had learned to deal with Bernstein; the way to deal with him was to sidestep him, in general not to count on him or expect anything from him, and if he did something good, count that as a bonus. The real problem between the Washington *Post* and Carl Bernstein was that at its core journalism is built upon trust, reporters have to trust editors and editors have to trust reporters, and in essence the Washington *Post* editors did not really trust Carl Bernstein. If he had left the *Post* for *Rolling Stone,* nothing would have pleased his editors more.

The first night after the break-in Carl Bernstein had dinner with Cohen and Cohen's wife, Barbara, who worked as an editor at the *Star.* They were all talking about the break-in (as young journalists in New York were not) and both Bernstein and Barbara Cohen kept saying what a great story it was. Dick

Cohen, who had already been covering the Maryland legislature and was beginning to make a considerable reputation at the *Post,* was disdainful. "It's a great story," Bernstein kept saying. Cohen did not agree. Big-time politics simply didn't operate like this. Besides, he thought, Carl always had a tendency to generalize. He liked Bernstein but he did not think of him as a political person. He was annoyed that Bernstein thought something so small was so important.

Barry Sussman was the editor who understood Bernstein best and handled him with the greatest skill. He had wanted Bernstein on the story from the beginning. When Simons had finally set up the Watergate team, one of the main reasons Sussman assigned Bernstein to it was his skill with the telephone and his contacts at the phone company. Bernstein had often been troubled by the ethics of getting confidential information from inside the Bell System. He would not have liked anyone doing anything like that to him. It was, he knew, a violation of privacy. Nonetheless, he called a source at the company and quickly confirmed that the calls reported by *The New York Times* to have been made to CREEP by one of the burglars, Bernard Barker, had in fact been made. But, his friend said, he could not give him any more information because the records had been subpoenaed by the Miami district attorney's office. You mean the FBI or the U.S. Attorney? asked Bernstein. No, said the source, it was the local district attorney. With that Bernstein grabbed a flight to Miami. After a long frustrating wait he met with Martin Dardis, one of the district attorney's assistants, and Dardis finally showed him Barker's bank statements, including the four Mexican checks and then a fifth check for $25,000 from Kenneth Dahlberg, drawn on a Boca Raton bank and deposited in Barker's account.

He was in Miami and he was alone and he did not know where the story was going, or who Kenneth Dahlberg was, but he was very good on the telephone, very good and very creative. He did not have time to get to Boca Raton and the bank was closed, but he figured the local cops would know someone who could write a check like that, the cops always knew the very rich, they often served as special security for these people's parties. So he began by calling the cops, and the cops, true to form, gave him the name of a bank officer who could be reached in an emergency. Bernstein reached the officer. He did not know Dahlberg. Finally Bernstein reached the president of the bank, James Collins. Collins knew Dahlberg, indeed Dahlberg was a director of the bank. Why, Dahlberg, Collins said casually and admiringly, had headed the Midwest campaign for Richard Nixon in 1968. Bernstein passed that information on to Woodward. Woodward called Dahlberg, who seemed stunned by the call. A few minutes later he called Woodward back to say yes, he had raised that $25,000 from campaign contributions in the Midwest for Nixon. He had turned that very large check over to either Maurice Stans or Hugh Sloan. All of a sudden it was a very big story, money raised for Richard Nixon's campaign had been deposited in the bank account of Bernard Barker, one of the five men arrested in the Watergate break-in. It connected in one swoop the Nixon campaign to the break-in. Sussman read the last piece of copy. "We've never had a story like this," he said with a touch of awe, "just never." It was the start of the momentum, the *Post* getting hotter and hotter on the story, the cover-up by the Nixon administration slowly crumbling. Events, Emerson wrote, are in the saddle and ride mankind. It was just beginning.

So it was that Woodward and Bernstein—Woodstein as they soon became known in the city room—were born. Sussman's intuition had been sound. Woodward was driven and obsessed, the young man who when he had worked for the Montgomery *Sentinel* had saved every issue of the paper just in case he might need them one day. Relentlessly he pursued every tip, whether it was from an impeccable source or an anonymous tipster. His work habits were terrifying. Even before Watergate the regular work hours of the *Post* were not enough for him, he had once come in very late at night on his own, bored with his life, and had gone out, in lieu of anything else, to interview construction workers building the new subway system in Washington, the only available interviewees at that hour. Now he would have enough work. He was a very methodical man, but bright and surprisingly supple and complex. Bernstein, who had not respected him in the past, came quickly to admire him, particularly the fact that Woodward wanted to know everything about everything, was fascinated by detail, was fascinated by how things worked. If he did not synthesize material especially well, that was not a great problem, others could help. What was attractive about him was his endless curiosity. Whereas other reporters might be touched by cynicism at the fact that some kind of political skulduggery had been taking place for years, that meant nothing to Woodward, it did not mean that it was not important, that it was not fresh, and that his readers would not want to know. That was a quality Bernstein liked about Robert Woodward, that he was not blind or bored or cynical.

Woodward was literal-minded, Bernstein was more gifted conceptually, he could think in broader sweeps, and he could put together the odds and ends of seemingly disparate bits of information and make a pattern. Better yet, he could sit there in the city room of the *Post* and put himself in the role of the people he was writing about and imagine what they were doing; it often helped a great deal in the questioning, it allowed him to ask imaginative questions that seemed lucky but were in fact not lucky at all, just imaginative and shrewd questions that anticipated what had happened. At first Woodward regarded Bernstein with some distaste. His reputation had preceded him and he seemed difficult to get along with. "He's very abrasive, isn't he?" Woodward said of him in the early weeks to mutual friends. "Very difficult to get along with." But gradually he came to respect him; Bernstein could think of calling people Woodward would never have thought of, he knew how to cast a much wider net. Besides, Woodward came to realize with some astonishment, Bernstein, despite his reputation for chaos, was on this story very meticulous, he kept very good notes and files and he was very good about recording telephone numbers for the future. Bernstein, he realized, was more careful than people thought. This did not mean that the team was without its difficulties and shouting matches, usually Woodward shouting at some lapse of Bernstein's. But it meant that their talents balanced well and they were smart enough to know it, and they pushed each other hard as young reporters will, each working harder and harder to satisfy the other.

They were wonderfully young, too young and too innocent to be impressed by Washington titles or positions. When Henry Kissinger, the cleverest manipulator of the press in Washington, tried to impose ground rules on Woodward *after* he had finished an interview, Woodward would have none of it. Others often fell for it, Kissinger was not a man they wanted to offend and he could be persuasive, alternating bullying and beseeching, threatening and whining. But Woodward and Bernstein covered the whole affair (Kissinger included) not as a political story but as a police story, indeed they never wrote of the story's political implications. In fact, just before the election when George McGovern had seized on one of their stories and exaggerated it with campaign rhetoric, Woodward, rather than being pleased as many reporters might have been, seemed appalled. He was having a drink with his friend Jim Mann and Mann was impressed, a presidential candidate picking up your stories meant you were big-time. But Woodward was angry, he did not like the use that was made of it; it's so overblown, he told Mann, the rhetoric is so exaggerated. He thought it was stupid.

They had no other obligations, no worrying about the presidential campaign or covering the Congress or the Supreme Court. They had only one assignment—Watergate. No other paper made so clear a commitment to the story so early. The *Post,* published in the city of the crime, had more manpower and more energy. But the two reporters also covered the story like old-time reporters. It was in direct contrast to most Washington reporting, clubby, part social, analytical, reporters and government officials who saw each other during the day and often dined with each other at night, so that the lines between them became increasingly blurred. It was old-fashioned police reporting. They were the ones who in the early days kept the story alive, and kept extra pressure on the prosecutors, who were, consciously or unconsciously, being intimidated by the top people in the White House, or at least allowing their witnesses to be intimidated.

What gave Woodward and Bernstein their special hold on the story was the code of CREEP. They got hold of the CREEP phone book and they checked the phones and the extensions and they put together a portrait of the structure, who worked for whom, what the interior connections were. Thus they realized from the start what few others did, that CREEP was simply the White House's way of disguising its own hand, of taking over the campaign and the financing of it without having it traceable to Nixon. CREEP was, in effect, a covert operation, a form of deniability; something made possible in an election year because of television and the rise of the presidency and because of the decline of the party system. The President no longer needed the party system, he could personalize the running of his campaign, invent his own party —CREEP—make it a separate organization, and siphon the money off to his account rather than to that of the party.

Woodward and Bernstein had gone out and started knocking on doors and from the very start they had smelled the fear of the workers at CREEP. Like most reporters, they were accustomed to people who did not want to talk to them, and in particular they were prepared for people who worked for Richard Nixon not to like them. But this was something entirely different. These people were terrified of them, afraid to be seen with them, afraid to have them come to their houses. They were getting this fear from very ordinary people, secretaries, people in the very low echelons. If the prosecutors had worked the case in the same way, Bernstein often thought, they might have smelled the fear as well, and they might have pushed harder. But the prosecutors were seeing the witnesses in a different setting, after they had been carefully prepared by their superiors, and accompanied by their attorneys from CREEP, men who were themselves deeply involved in Watergate. The witnesses were, Bernstein suspected, far more afraid of the attorneys from CREEP than they were of the prosecutors. The fear was there, naked and stark, with a smell of its own. It did not slow Woodward and Bernstein down, it made them work harder, it was in a curious way a confirmation of the accuracy of their trajectory. When someone denies something and that denial is made in cold terror, then it is no longer a denial. A lie told to a good reporter does not discourage that reporter, it simply makes him or her work harder. Fear was an even greater incentive, it made each fact loom larger, not just to them but to their editors, for they were telling their editors not just what they were getting but the atmosphere in which it was told. The two reporters were struck by the simplicity and loyalty of these people and the fact that they were absolutely terrified, scared for more than their jobs. They were, naturally, loyal to Nixon. On the occasions when they would talk, they would say that of course the President was not involved, but some of his aides were.

# 25/ The Los Angeles Times

The Watergate year was a bad year for the Los Angeles *Times* and an even worse year for Otis Chandler. Almost simultaneously with the events at Watergate, he became mired in what was known as the GeoTek scandal, and when it was over, the kindest thing that could be said of his role in it was that he had been stupid and greedy, and perhaps something of an innocent and a dupe. An old friend of his, Jack Burke, had put together during the sixties an exploratory oil-drilling company called GeoTek. Burke was someone special to Otis Chandler, one of the few people in the world who could make him relax, could make him laugh. They had been on the track team together at Stanford, they had hunted together in Mongolia, and Burke was the godfather of Chandler's firstborn daughter.

In the mid-sixties Burke told Chandler that he had this terrific deal in oil and Chandler might want to help find some wealthy investors in Los Angeles. After all, who would be better at getting a young enterprising go-getter connected in Southern California than Otis Chandler? Who bore a better name? So Otis Chandler, he of the good name, enviable reputation, and impeccable connections, between 1964 and 1968 helped Jack Burke find several million dollars' worth of investors. Eventually Otis Chandler, in addition to stock, received some $109,000 in finder's fees from Burke. Chandler later said that when he had been introducing people to Burke he had not known there would be finder's fees or gifts of stock, but that Burke had come to him later and thanked him and given him a check and said, "This is for you." In addition, Chandler had been given $373,000 worth of shares by Burke in two GeoTek offshoot companies, and he and his wife owned $278,000 worth of additional shares for a total of more than $600,000 worth. Even if Chandler did not receive them until later, GeoTek investors were unaware of the fees and the shares he was getting, and circulars for the fund did not mention his full financial interest. He may indeed, as he says, merely have been trying to help some friends, but it was nonetheless shadowy and tawdry. *The New York Times* in covering the story quoted an unnamed investor as saying that Otis Chandler as late as 1972 told him he had received no payments from Burke.

The trouble was that Burke was a crook, that the company was bust. The oil reserves, said to be worth $25 million or so, were worth at best $5 million. In September 1971 the Securities and Exchange Commission, hearing rumors of fraud, began to investigate the case. In February 1972, after the SEC had begun to move, Chandler and several others on the board threw Burke out as president and filed a civil suit against him and his family for fraud and misappropriation of funds. No story about it appeared in the Los Angeles *Times.* But the word was already getting out. In August 1972 the *Wall Street Journal* printed the first of what was to be a major series on GeoTek, noted Chandler's involvement, and said that Burke had taken some $30 million worth of investors' money. It was a humiliating moment, particularly for a man who had been the handsome young hero of American journalism, who cared so much about his image. Chandler was enraged by the *Wall Street Journal* stories, which, he felt, emphasized his own involvement in the case; he was, he believed, as much a victim of Burke as anyone else, perhaps more so, because his own reputation had been damaged. (Friends also think the *Wall Street Journal* stories may have dampened some of his enthusiasm for investigative reporting, since in effect he had been a victim of it.) It seriously affected his position in American journalism. "It's funny how much they like to throw mud at you when you've been Mr. Clean," he told one friend in some surprise.

There was some talk among senior reporters in the Los Angeles *Times* city room of asking him to resign as publisher or at least step aside temporarily; this was dropped when it was decided that anyone else the Family or the board supplied would probably be worse. His position with the Family became even more shaky. The older members, always suspicious of him, understood little of GeoTek and were shaken by the idea of scandal. He made personal visits to each older member, trying to explain that he considered himself an innocent victim of a fallen friend; he also made sure that anyone knowing of these visits did not mention them to his mother. Buff Chandler would have been shocked by his humbling himself to her enemies.

Throughout 1972 the case hovered over Otis Chandler, even as Watergate was beginning to pick up. In May 1973, with Nixon still in the White House, Chandler and eleven others were accused by the government of making false and misleading statements with respect to investments. Chandler decided to fight the charges; his legal bills eventually came to over a million dollars. He believed that he was innocent, as much wronged as anyone else, he also became convinced that there was no eagerness at the upper level of the Securities and Exchange Commission for going ahead, but that Haldeman wanted the case alive. Even though Haldeman was the grandson of one of Harry Chandler's closest friends and son of one of Norman Chandler's, Otis was sure that he had never liked him. Haldeman was always complaining to him about how *The New York Times* or the Washington *Post* had played San Clemente stories bigger than the Los Angeles *Times* did. Finally Otis had written Haldeman a letter saying that he would prefer to edit the *Times* himself, without Haldeman's help. Now, he was sure, Haldeman was enjoying both his discomfiture and the potential for leverage it gave. A member of the Watergate staff told Chandler that there were tapes on which Haldeman had talked with glee about sticking it to him, though he never heard them. In January 1975 a federal court sentenced Burke to ten to thirty months in jail; in March 1975 the charges against Otis Chandler were dropped, although civil suits for fraud were still pending.

It was a blemish of massive proportions, and it did not quickly go away. It was impossible for most of those who had liked him and looked up to him to see him in quite the same way as before. There was now always a little question about him. People who cared about him wondered how could he have done it, what was the flaw, what was the lapse? It also, in subtle ways, seemed to make the paper somewhat vulnerable during the period, which happened to coincide with Watergate. It was an odd situation; the government was pursuing him while his reporters were pursuing the government.

Nineteen seventy-two was not turning out to be a good year for Ed Guthman either. The first flag had gone up during the burglary itself in June. But then he had gone to Miami for the Republican convention. It was like no other political convention he had ever been to in his life. The totality of security procedures had first chilled and then depressed him. It was as if the Nixon people had totally isolated themselves from the traditional political processes and dug an immense moat around themselves. It was almost impossible for working reporters to cut through all the security procedures and carry out their jobs; it was harder for a reporter to interview a third-level press secretary at this convention than it was to reach a major presidential candidate at others. There was, he thought, something menacing and arrogant about the whole thing. He had pushed his reporters, who were similarly appalled, to emphasize those aspects of the convention. When he returned to Los Angeles he found that his superiors had not particularly liked the coverage; they had thought it too shrill. They had seen the convention on television, and it had not seemed so sinister. Guthman was first angered that the *Times* management sided with television, not its own reporters. Later he was willing to put the blame on himself for having failed to make the point in the coverage that there were, in fact, two different stories about Miami: the harshness of the control and the wonderful antiseptic benign spectacular that all that control had produced for millions of Americans, carefully scripted and faithfully beamed out by national television. Though Guthman put the blame on himself, he also realized that it reflected a gap between the paper's editors and the paper's reporters.

That fall, Otis Chandler had taken Guthman aside after an editorial board meeting and said, "I know you don't like this, but we're going to support Nixon." Guthman was shocked, it was in effect a denial of everything the paper had printed. There had been some strong aggressive stories on Watergate, and it was as if the paper's editors did not read the paper's reporters. Endorsing Nixon was a serious rejection of what he thought a newspaper was supposed to be, its editorial policy following the lights that were lit by its reporters. It meant that all those people at the editorial conferences pretended to listen but did not listen. He was a part of something without being a part. It was a depressing way to start every working day and he felt that his time was not well served. So he told Bill Thomas that he did not want to go to the editorial board meetings any more and in early 1973 his request was granted. It was, he knew, a bureaucratic mistake, he was isolating himself even more from the center of the paper, but he felt better about himself.


Like other papers, the Los Angeles *Times* was from the start behind on Watergate. The Washington *Post* had broken the story, and the *Times* was to spend the next two years playing catch-up. The paper in this period had both assets and liabilities, though the liabilities on this particular story outweighed the assets. The assets were first and foremost its reporters: Jack Nelson, one of the two or three best-known and most respected investigative reporters in Washington, a man of almost unique abilities, plus two additional investigative reporters who were very well thought of, Ron Ostrow and Bob Jackson. No other Washington bureau had that much talent in investigative reporting. Three men in Washington, by the standards of American newspapering, was a very large commitment. But the liabilities of the paper were even greater. The first was that its investigative reporters were well established and well connected and hard at work on other stories, which slowed their taking hold of Watergate. The second point—which was very important—was that because Woodward and Bernstein of the *Post* were less established, they could not, at that moment, be outworked; they were simply more willing to put in longer hours. The third, which was perhaps even more crucial, was the comparative weakness of the Los Angeles *Times* platform. The *Times* had become a national newspaper, but its natural base was Los Angeles, not Washington or New York, and it was always difficult for the *Times*'s reporters to tie up a source concerned about Washington impact.

Yes, there might be a joint Los Angeles *Times*–Washington *Post* news service, but on a story like this Ben Bradlee's adrenaline was running, this was war, and he was not about to give the *Times* even a tiny hold in his own domain, and thus weaken not only his own prestige but the leverage of his reporters. This was to become a point of considerable friction between the *Times* and the *Post*, with the Los Angeles people absolutely convinced that on a number of occasions their best Watergate stories were stolen by the *Post* and not properly credited.

Then too, if Watergate began as a Washington story, it meant that the *editors* of the *Post* were truly engaged in it from the start, *their* friends and peers were fascinated by the story, they pushed their reporters, made sure that the fullest possible resources were committed. By contrast, the editors of the Los Angeles *Times* were three thousand miles away, *their* friends, peers, and readers were on their way to tennis courts. The locale of the *Times* did not produce much urgency in general, nor did the general style of the paper; it was more like a magazine in tempo, events could wait, Southern California readers were in no rush.

The chief editor of the *Times*, Bill Thomas, unlike Bradlee, did not care passionately about Watergate; Guthman did, but there was no pressure from above to be more aggressive. Quite the contrary. It was not Thomas's style to push on a story like this, and Frank Haven, the managing editor, was clearly quite uneasy with Watergate. There was too much obscurity, too few certifiable facts, too few press conferences at which things were announced and confirmed. Watergate was an impossible story; when there finally was confirmation of a series of implications, it did not mean that the story was over and they could all relax and wipe the sweat off the brow, it simply meant that they were working at a higher level of authority, a higher level of implication, a more pressurized existence, the roll of the dice was for bigger stakes. So with the exception of Guthman, Los Angeles was soft on the story, the play given in the early months, even on stories where the *Times* was beating the *Post*, was somewhat weak and uncertain. And that was a little discouraging to the Washington reporters. There was also, almost from the start, what the Washington bureau defined as a California attitude about Watergate, that this was not a true national story, that the people in the country were not really that interested in it, that it was Washington navel gazing.

Guthman did not share that belief. Guthman was passionate on Watergate from the start. In later years he faulted himself for having let Jack Nelson cover the Berrigan trial through much of early 1972 and then work on a book about the trial. When Nelson was through with his Berrigan work, Guthman assigned him to Miami to scout the security setup for the Republican convention and to get to know the cops, so that if there were trouble at the convention the *Times* would be wired in. Guthman was later convinced that if Nelson had been in Washington in June, he would have been drawn to the smell of Watergate. Guthman thought Nelson was the best all-around reporter he had ever seen, that he could get *anyone* to talk. He often wondered what would have happened if Nelson had been in on the story from the beginning. He might have taken hold and *he* rather than Woodward and Bernstein would have locked up the best sources, because of the smell of it.

The smell. That was crucial. Woodward and Bernstein were new and young, and no one knew their names, they had no established sources, they had no wives or children to go home to, all they had was hunger, and they were out on the street every day visiting the homes of the people from CREEP. The Los Angeles *Times* reporters were hardly, by Washington standards, establishment reporters, they were diggers and boat rockers and outsiders, but they were not kids, they were not as young, and they were no longer police reporters, they had done *that*. They had families and they were established and they had established sources, people whom they had learned to trust over the years. So they went by instinct to their sources, many of whom were in the Justice Department or on the Hill, and they did a lot of checking by phone and dropping by at offices, and they never did what Woodward and Bernstein did, which was to knock on every door. Years later, reading their first book, *All the President's Men,* Jack Nelson felt somewhat sick, he knew immediately what had happened and why he had been beaten on the story, why the two younger reporters had been better. They had picked up the fear, he had not. In Los Angeles, Guthman, impressed from the start by the reporting of Woodward and Bernstein, had sensed the difference and understood that the other paper had its reporters closer to the pulse of the story. He somehow realized that his own people were doing it by more traditional means, and he knew that this story was too explosive for phone work, that it had to be done by foot. No one he knew passed such confidential and delicate information over the phone, not in contemporary Washington. If he had confidential sensitive information to give out, Guthman thought, would he do it over the phone? Did anyone in America consider the phone a confidential instrument any more?

So he began to push Dennis Britton, the bureau manager, to get the reporters out of the office, telling Britton again and again that it could not be done on the phone. Every day he would call Britton and tell him to get them off the phones. "They've got to get off their asses and knock on doors. Dennis, get them outside," he said. Finally Britton had a small sign made up saying GOYA/KOD: Get Off Your Ass and Knock On Doors. Britton kept putting it on the desk of his three investigative reporters, GOYA/KOD, but there was an age difference, it was hard for journalists in their forties, men who had reached some status in life, to knock on doors, knocking on doors was something you did before you came to Washington. It was for the three *Times* reporters very frustrating, particularly for Jack Nelson, who had never been behind on a story before. No matter how hard they worked, Woodward and Bernstein always seemed to be just one step ahead. *Woodward and Bernstein!* Who the hell were Woodward and Bernstein? Bernstein, it was said through the journalistic grapevine, was some flaky semi-hippie who had been hanging around the *Star* and the *Post* forever, usually screwing up, and Woodward was some fresh-faced kid just out of the Navy. Yet there were Woodward and Bernstein, always ahead, locking up the best sources, and their stories—and this some-times made Nelson and Ostrow and Jackson especially envious—always got good play, which surely led to other stories. So the Los Angeles *Times* people kept driving and pushing, and occasionally they would be slightly ahead on a story, and hearing that the kids were moving on it too, they would move a little faster, but they were usually in second place at best, there was no doubt about it.

Guthman was right. One of the *Times*'s first big stories, one of the most important in the entire episode, came precisely because Nelson was out in the field, knocking on doors, in effect camping out. The story broke in early October 1972, at a time when the Los Angeles *Times* was distinguishing itself, not by brilliant Watergate stories, but by being one of the very few papers in America doing any Watergate stories at all. In late September, Jack Nelson had been down in Miami tracking the Cuban end of the story, talking with Henry Rothblatt, the lawyer for the Cubans. While he was there, Ostrow, Nelson's colleague in Washington, picked up a rumor that there might be an eyewitness to the bugging and break-in and so he doggedly began to call sources on Capitol Hill, picking up a few bits of information, and then someone mentioned the name *Baldwin* to him, *Alfred Baldwin.* Baldwin was in fact an ex-FBI agent who sat in for McCord monitoring the wiretaps the night of the bugging and who had, from the Howard Johnson motel across the street, watched the police capture his colleagues. So Ostrow quickly got on the phone to Nelson in Miami and said, "Try out the name Baldwin on your man Rothblatt." Nelson did, catching Rothblatt by surprise. "How did you know about him?" Rothblatt said, startled, and Nelson knew he was on to something very good. They had the story and they played it well. There was an eyewitness to events: he had been monitoring the raw stuff the Plumbers were tapping and he had seen the events. This was a very big story, and Nelson sensed there was more to come, this might tie the break-in even closer to the White House or the Attorney General's office. Besides, for the first time the *Times* was ahead of the *Post* and Nelson did not want to lose the advantage.

So he began camping out in Connecticut, where Baldwin lived and where his lawyers, Bob Mirto and Jack Cassidento, both lived. At first it was very low-key, just getting to know the lawyers, trying to separate himself from the rest of the pack of reporters, sensing finally that they wanted to talk, that Baldwin was unhappy over what he had been part of, feeling that he had been used by what he had thought was the government and now was doubtful that the government would protect him against the government. The reaction of Mirto and Cassidento was, Nelson thought, somewhat encouraging. Nelson suggested that in this case, since the normal protective agency, the Justice Department, was under control of some of the men who had operated the Watergate break-in, perhaps Baldwin's greatest protection in the long run was to get his story out. Otherwise he might end up a fall guy. A first-person story that would get his side out, and why not in the Los Angeles *Times?* If it was a first-person story, Nelson said, Baldwin would have some measure of control, it would be his story, and it was the only way he could get to see a story before it was published.

Mirto and Cassidento were interested and Nelson went back to Washington, only to reappear a few days later. By then the two lawyers were talking about selling Baldwin's story, perhaps to the *Times* or *The New York Times* or the *Post,* or some magazine. Nelson argued vehemently against it; it was not the money, he insisted, but the idea; if the Los Angeles *Times* paid for the story it would cast an immediate cloud over Baldwin's motives and credibility. The White House, which had powerful information instruments at hand, would find it easy to discredit him. He was very insistent. At about the same time, Bob Woodward called Cassidento trying for the same story. "Ugly fuckers, you reporters," Cassidento said. But Nelson was pleased by the fact that they were talking about money; it was an encouraging sign, it meant that they wanted the story out. Victory number one, he thought.

He went back to Washington. He called a few days later and Mirto said that nothing had changed, there was no need to come back up, but Nelson insisted, he wanted to come up anyway, you never can tell, besides, he told Mirto, he and Cassidento had promised Nelson a look at the famous Baldwin. "Hell, I've been up there all those times and I've never even met him." He thought they were ready to talk, but there was one problem, Baldwin was under subpoena from the Patman committee in the House and that prevented him from talking with the press, otherwise he might be in contempt of Congress. So Nelson spent the afternoon with Cassidento and Mirto, being a good old boy, explaining the danger of being locked in to the feds, sure somehow that Baldwin was in the same building, wanting to get a look at his man. Then in the late afternoon the phone rang. Cassidento talked to someone for a few minutes and when he was finished he turned to Nelson. "Hey, you still got your tape recorder with you?" he said. Nelson asked why. "Because the Patman committee just called and said it wasn't going to subpoena Baldwin." Did Jack Nelson have a tape recorder? It was in the car, he had in fact checked the batteries earlier, and Nelson walked very slowly and deliberately out of the office, so as not to tip off his eagerness. Then, outside the building, he ran like hell for his car before they could change their minds.

It was about 5 P.M. when he returned. The lawyers said it was a little late, why didn't they start in the morning, but Nelson did not want to wait, he was nervous about their changing their minds or about the prosecutors moving in and stopping him. With the Patman subpoena lifted, Baldwin was like a minnow among sharks, and Nelson wanted to move, and move quickly. So they went out to Mirto's house and worked for five hours that night, sending out for sandwiches, and Baldwin was wonderful. The ideal source, he had total recall, he was enjoying it, there was almost, in fact, a danger that he was embellishing it and Nelson had to slow him down on a few occasions. Baldwin insisted that John Mitchell knew about the break-in, and Nelson demanded proof, and Baldwin just insisted he *knew*, but there was no proof, and so Nelson made him drop the reference. It was a fascinating story of how Baldwin had been recruited by McCord and taken through CREEP, of taking logs from the bugging to the Nixon reelection headquarters, of dealing with Hunt and Liddy, of sitting across from the Watergate the night of the break-in, and of seeing Hunt casually slip away from the Watergate as the police closed in.

It was powerful stuff. It brought Watergate right to the heart of the Nixon reelection campaign, in a more dramatic way than any other story so far. Near the end of it Baldwin made one request of Nelson. What was it? the reporter asked. Well, said Baldwin, he had this girl friend out in Wisconsin, and perhaps Nelson could refer to him in his story as a husky ex-Marine. Nelson looked at Baldwin, who struck him as being somewhat pudgy and overweight, and thought, well, every story has its price, and so it was that Al Baldwin was described in the Los Angeles *Times* as a husky ex-Marine. They almost finished the first night and then they went back the next morning for a few hours. Then Nelson called Guthman and said that he had the story; Guthman sent Ron Ostrow up to help Nelson by writing the regular news story that would accompany the first-person story, and to get a copy of the tapes. That night, with the story done, Nelson went over it line by line with Baldwin and Cassidento, getting their approval; Mirto was to read it the next morning. But Nelson had their approval and so, because he was afraid of the prosecutors, he stayed up until 3 A.M. dictating the story to Los Angeles. When it was done he was relieved; it was now the property of the home office.

The next morning, sure enough, there was a call from Cassidento at 7 A.M. telling Nelson he could not run the story. Why not? Nelson asked. "Because we've just gotten a call from Earl Silbert and Silbert knows about the *Times* story and he says if you run it he'll revoke Baldwin's immunity." Nelson, very noncommittal, said he would talk to his editors. A few minutes later there was another phone call from Cassidento, and this time he said, "Now I *know* you can't run it!" Why not? asked Nelson again. "Because Judge Sirica has just issued a gag order," Cassidento said. Nelson again said he would talk with his editors and immediately called both Guthman and Thomas, and with Ostrow helping him, argued ferociously that the story must run, that the *Times* already had it, that they had lived up to their part of the bargain—they had the story as Baldwin had dictated it, with his approval and with his lawyer's approval. It was not Baldwin who had changed his mind, it was the *government* that did not want the story out. In this case, Nelson argued, Baldwin really wanted the story out, there was no doubt in his mind on that score; clearly Baldwin thought he was better protected that way. The only obligation in a case like this, Nelson argued, was to the source, and in this case they had honored the source's request. In fact, said Nelson, despite what Cassidento was saying on the phone, which was what as a lawyer he *had* to be on the record as saying, both Cassidento and Baldwin wanted it out. They did not trust the government, there was no reason to, no one was sure what role the prosecutors were playing; were they trying to get information in order to suppress it or were they trying to build a real case?

In Los Angeles, Bill Thomas had to make this decision himself. Otis Chandler was away at the time and was unreachable. Guthman wanted to go ahead with it, and Thomas knew it was a very important story. The *Times*'s lawyers read it and they were very nervous; their judgment was that if the *Times* printed the story it was running an enormous risk, not just to the paper but to the corporation as well. The lawyers pointed out that if Baldwin were penalized in any way because the story ran, he stood a very good chance of collecting from the paper, and collecting big. Thomas, who was normally a very cautious man, thought about it, and he thought that the story had been obtained honorably and fairly, and he said go with it. It was a very tough call. Sirica was furious, there was an immediate legal hassle and at one point Sirica ordered John Lawrence, the Los Angeles *Times* Washington bureau chief, to jail. It also looked for a moment as if Nelson and Otis Chandler might also have to go to jail. Nelson, coming out of the Washington courtroom, was interviewed by a radio reporter, and said rather casually that he was ready to go to jail and he was sure that Otis Chandler would be proud to go to jail on a case like this too. The Washington *Post* picked up Nelson's quote and made a parenthetical insert to it: "In Los Angeles, Otis Chandler had no comment." The next day Nelson's phone rang and it was Ed Guthman saying, "Goddamn! What have you said about Otis?" This much amused most of Nelson's colleagues, his volunteering his boss for prison, but a year later his friends Chuck and Camille Morgan were with the Chandlers in Los Angeles and Mrs. Morgan told Otis that even though she had never met him before, she had always liked him, ever since she had heard her friend Jack Nelson say that he would be glad to go to prison. "I would have been proud to have gone," Otis Chandler said. Meanwhile the government's case against the *Times* came apart quickly. The *Times*'s lawyers were well prepared, it was a quick (and costly) legal battle, five days, all the way to the Supreme Court, and the *Times* won.

The story ran on October 5, 1972, perhaps the most important Watergate story so far, because it was so tangible, it had an eyewitness, and it brought Watergate to the very door of the White House. It ran in most papers that carried the Times-Post news service. But it did not run in one paper, and that was the Washington *Post*. There had been a tendency not to use the Los Angeles *Times*'s stories or, on occasion, to rewrite them without giving credit.

Ben Bradlee was not the most generous of souls. But this was really too much, a story of this magnitude could not be lightly rewritten; you could not rewrite an eyewitness story. So the *Post* did nothing with it. The next day the managing editor of the Washington *Star* called the Los Angeles *Times* and asked to use the Baldwin story. Bill Thomas said that was fine but the *Star* had to clear it with the *Post* because the *Post* had jurisdiction over syndication within the area. A few minutes later Bradlee called Thomas and said, "Hey, old buddy, you can't give that one away. We're going to use it tomorrow." Which they did, almost reluctantly.

It was a great victory for the Los Angeles *Times,* and the Washington bureau was particularly proud. It was a strong bureau and there was a feeling in it that, journalist for journalist, they were now the best bureau in Washington. Privately many of the members thought the *New York Times* bureau was vastly overrated, that it had slipped and its members too often simply reflected the official government viewpoint. The Washington *Post,* they thought, was good but erratic, it had some excellent people, but it seemed undisciplined. If anything, the fact that the Los Angeles *Times* reporters did not get good play on their stories in Washington made them more closely knit and tougher-minded. With several hundred papers subscribing to the news service, it was now a real force in American journalism. More than a decade had passed since Bob Donovan had come over from the *Trib,* and if in some way he had failed in Los Angeles, he had nonetheless succeeded to an uncommon degree in his first intention, which was to bring New York standards to West Coast journalism. The Washington bureau of the *Times* was genuinely distinguished, the rest of the paper was getting better and better. In the early days of Watergate the one paper dogging the Washington *Post* was the Los Angeles *Times.* And this was important; it made the story that much more national, and it meant that Richard Nixon could not say that he was being pursued only by eastern outlets or liberal outlets. He was being pursued, if that was the word, by the very people who had helped to invent him.

# 26/ The Washington Post

Time was on the side of Woodward and Bernstein. A story like Vietnam or Watergate has a balance of forces of its own. At first the charges are deniable, the existing structure holds, powerful men with powerful positions can keep their troops in line. All the weight is on one side, and reporters like Woodward and Bernstein are a tiny minority, seeming puny by comparison. But there is the momentum. The denials slowly weaken, events undermine the denials so that there have to be more denials, and each denial is a little weaker than the previous one. The structure turns out not to be so awesome, it flakes away a little, and each chip makes the next chip easier. Slowly the people who are issuing the denials lose credibility, and the reporters begin to gain in credibility. At first they had been scorned by officialdom and their peers, but they turn out to have been right. They begin to gain reputations, they gain confidence in themselves. They become legitimized, precisely as the once awesome structure is losing its legitimacy. More people are emboldened to talk to them; they seem by then to have a copyright on the story. The balance has shifted, the established order becomes constantly less respectable and more endangered, encouraging once true loyalists to betray it. Outsiders—like Woodward and Bernstein—replace it, becoming more respectable, more honored. So it was with Watergate.

In the beginning they were very much alone, although well protected within the paper. Sussman was very good with them, sheltering and shrewd, pushing them for more, brainstorming with them, suggesting ideas, sorting out facts. He was keeping them moving, yet helping them avoid mistakes; he was imaginative and he was careful. He was almost like a third member of the team. Then Harry Rosenfeld would come into the act. Rosenfeld was tough, old-fashioned, certainly less trusting of Bernstein than Sussman was (he told Woodward to watch out for Bernstein, not to let him generalize), but Sussman could sell him a story. At that point it became a Metro story, it was on Rosenfeld's home ground, and he fought for it fiercely. Rosenfeld felt that no one at the *Post* took him seriously unless he shouted, and so he would go roaring into the news conferences. If at the news conference he did not get page one, then he had a great fallback position, the Metro front, the first page of the second section. If Bradlee and Simons were not going to use the story on page one, Rosenfeld would keep it for his own section and give it very good display; the flexibility was another advantage the *Post* had over other papers.

So the machinery of the *Post* was working properly, from bottom to top. There was also, in those crucial months, Howard Simons. He was shepherding the story through. He had made the original commitment to Sussman and so the story was in a way his property too, and he was protective of it. Bradlee had not yet come in on the story. In the early period, when the lifeline of the story was so delicate, when it all could so easily collapse, Simons was very good, very sensitive and supportive. When the two reporters were disappointed in the play, if the day's piece for some reason was going inside the paper, he was very reassuring. Don't worry, he would tell them, people will see it. He was very good at calming the two of them. Once in August when things were very tense, he looked out his window and remarked that it was snowing. Woodward of course nodded that yes, it was snowing, and Bernstein predictably began to argue. "Carl," Woodward said, "if Howard says it's snowing out, then it's snowing out. You and I can argue about it later between us."

It was, particularly in the early months, a voyage into the darkness. There was a considerable amount of uneasiness about what the two reporters were doing. Some of the national reporters did not trust the story or the reporters, particularly Bernstein. Some of the sniping both in news conferences and around town came from Dick Harwood, the national editor. Harwood was one of Bradlee's first hires, an unusually talented and aggressive reporter, and he had become in the early seventies the paper's interior house critic, its ombudsman. In the view of many of the reporters, he seemed to be delivering on the inside a somewhat toned-down version of what Agnew was saying on the outside: that reporters on the *Post* and other leading papers had a liberal, eastern elitist view of the society, that there were too many stories in the paper automatically favorable to Ralph Nader or grape pickers or women who wanted abortion. Harwood was brash and abrasive, he was an ex-Marine and he made those around him very much aware of that fact. If Harwood's attitude had not exactly endeared him to working reporters at the *Post,* Bradlee liked him. Moreover, Harwood was a convenient instrument for Bradlee. His flame burned brightly with what he was interested in and what he knew, he could pursue a story that he understood with great energy and excellence, and he could also handle other reporters' copy with skill. But some of his colleagues thought there was also something limiting in his vision, anything that was new or that he did not understand he distrusted by instinct, and he would, almost as a reflex, fight. Some *Post* reporters had the impression that he automatically put down stories belonging to others, either on the *Post* or on other papers. Watergate was not a story that he was easy with. He was worried that it was taking the paper into an unwanted, unwinnable confrontation with an already hostile government at a delicate moment. He thought a great deal was being risked on it.

He began sniping at the story in news conferences. Who are their sources? Can we really count on them? Do they really have these sources? I hear differently. There was no doubt also that he was talking outside the shop in much the same manner, which bothered some of the other editors. Much of it was aimed at Bernstein, but some of it at Woodward as well, and some of it at Sussman, who on occasion had made what seemed like a raid into Harwood's territory. Later, in October, as the story began to grow, he moved to take the story away from Metro and give it to his own national staff, where all the big hitters were. Bradlee, whose essential instinct was that big stories deserved big reporters, was quite tempted to go with him. In the movie of *All the President's Men,* it is Simons who goes to Bradlee and asks to give the story to the national reporters, and it is Bradlee who holds the fort and says: We'll stay with the kids. This was obviously done for dramatic reasons, to build up an already strong character role for Jason Robards, Jr. In fact, it was Bradlee who, on more than one occasion, went to Simons and said it was probably time to give it to national and Simons who said no, the story should stay with the kids, they are doing well.

Fortunately, Bradlee was learning to trust Carl Bernstein. It was not easy, it was on-the-job training. Woodward he liked, Woodward was a winner, clear and simple. Bernstein was more difficult, Bernstein was somehow outside his reach. Bernstein was sly, that was the word. He could be a winner but there was a part of him that wanted to piss it away and be a loser. But Bradlee liked the way Bernstein was stalking this story. Besides, Bradlee thought, the White House denials were curious. They were odd, incomplete, just a little tricky. They denied things that had not been written and failed to deny things that *had* been written. It was as if they were written for people who had never read the *Post*'s stories.

So slowly the stories built. Not one great story that said it all. Just small pieces, one after another. Another chink and a little closer to the truth. The *Post* as a major institution found itself involved in a total confrontation with the White House in a gradual way. Each story led to another, always connecting Watergate to a higher level. The secret-fund story. The involvement of lesser White House and Justice figures like Magruder, LaRue, and Mardian, overseeing the destruction of CREEP records and telling CREEP employees what not to talk about. Sloan gradually becoming a source. Woodward, straight and decent and ambitious, going out to Sloan's house one day and talking to Sloan, straight and decent and ambitious; Woodward volunteering to do housework. Woodward seeing Sloan in obvious anguish and consoling him, saying that perhaps one day Sloan would become President, half, in the tradition of great reporters, meaning it, and half using it. Sloan had tightened the noose just a little, and his information, coupled with what they were getting elsewhere, had led gradually to John Mitchell. Mitchell as Attorney General had personally controlled the secret fund to gather information. Mitchell was one of five who could control the secret fund, and Woodward and Bernstein had explained that to their editors, that they were going to be able to get the names of the other four. Even as they were explaining, Bradlee was preoccupied, doodling on a piece of paper (were they boring him with the news that the Attorney General of the United States had helped control a secret fund?). Bradlee interrupted his doodling to ask if they were sure about Mitchell. They said they were. "Absolutely certain?" the editor asked. They nodded. "Can you write it today?" he asked. Bradlee did not want to wait for the other four names, they too would be stories. Bernstein called Mitchell in New York and Mitchell had screamed over the phone, *Jeeesus,* a primal scream, Bernstein thought. Katie Graham (it was typical of the Nixon people, they did not get the names right, it was Kay, or to truly close associates, Katharine, never Katie) would really get her tit caught in the wringer if the *Post* printed that. "Do you have any more messages for me?" Mrs. Graham later asked Bernstein.

So on September 29, they ran the Mitchell story and the window opened a little wider. A few days later Woodward got a call from the desk telling him that the Los Angeles *Times* had beaten him to the Al Baldwin story. Woodward had wanted it badly, and when the story had gone to the Los Angeles *Times* because of Jack Nelson's doggedness and energy, it had hurt Woodward, but it had also strengthened his credibility and Bernstein's, the story was so strong and so tangible, it had real people with real names, not just saying things but reenacting the drama of Watergate.

In October, Bernstein, responding to an anonymous tip, began the work that led the paper to Donald Segretti and the secret campaign of dirty tricks, spying, and sabotage against the Democrats. Bradlee monitored that story very carefully. The two reporters had originally thought there was enough material for three stories but Bradlee had thought no, it was only one, and he sat down and typed out the lead himself. It was a very big story and *The New York Times* quickly confirmed it by talking to various lawyers who had been approached by Segretti to take part in his game.

The day that story was published Bradlee walked over to Woodward's desk and told him he wanted to have lunch with the two reporters. Bernstein was out of town. Then just the two of us, Bradlee said. They went across the street and Bradlee said that it was time to get serious, he wanted a fill-in on where the story was and where it was going. He had heard secondhand from Simons and the other editors, but now he needed to know firsthand. Everything. He wanted to know who their sources were, or at least what their titles were, and he wanted to be sure that these were not people grinding their axes on the pages of the *Post*. Woodward was not entirely comfortable. Telling editors the names of sources could be a tricky thing, an editor might tell another editor, and it might get around town. An editor knowing the name of a source might have the leverage to replace the two of them with more senior reporters. Woodward told Bradlee as much as he could without giving names. At the end of the lunch Bradlee was satisfied. "Now what have you got for tomorrow?" It was an important moment: it meant that Bradlee was in on the story. Not that he had any real choice, events had come to him as much as he had come to them. But it meant that his own drive was now harnessed to the story. It would be Bradlee pushing the two young reporters, not just his deputies, and that energized the reporters more and it energized the paper too.

Now all the wheels were in motion. The stakes, Bradlee knew, were large and becoming larger by the day. The denunciations of the *Post* by the Nixon administration, carefully orchestrated, were harsher and harsher. They were often highly personal, directed at both Bradlee and Kay Graham. Other newspapers which covered Watergate were exempted, but the *Post* was singled out. After the Segretti story there had been a barrage of attacks. Ehrlichman. Ziegler. Robert Dole. Clark MacGregor. The theme was the same, the *Post* was a vehicle for McGovern. Bradlee was intrigued by the MacGregor attack; they had been friends in the past and their children had played together, and yet MacGregor had savaged the paper. But Bradlee had noticed something very interesting about the MacGregor attack. He had refused to answer questions. He had come to his press conference, read a statement for the benefit of the many cameras there assembled, and then departed. The denials did not really hold water. (A few years later Bradlee asked MacGregor why he had attacked a newspaper and its credibility without having checked out any of the stories or put any effort into it himself, and MacGregor simply said that the White House had asked him to read the statement and so he had done it; he saw nothing wrong with that.)

But Bradlee was worried. Suddenly it was not just a good story or a good running story that was causing heat, but a story on which the entire paper might be riding. They really, he often thought, could lose the whole damn paper. He was hearing from people around town that the Nixon people were planning to be particularly vindictive toward the *Post* if and when Nixon was reelected, and reelection appeared increasingly certain. The word was that they would go all out after the *Post*'s television stations. (The word was right, they did go after the stations, and interrogation of Chuck Colson by the Special Prosecutor's office later showed a direct connection from the White House through Colson to the challenges to the licensing of the stations, the defense of which cost the Washington Post Company millions of dollars. The tapes, and the interviews with Colson, were never made public because the prosecutors talked to Colson with the provision that the information would not be used unless it was part of a prosecution, which Jaworski finally decided against.)

So the Nixon people looked like electoral winners and for that matter very angry electoral winners. Colson was going around town boasting of what was going to happen to the *Post* in the second term. Henry Kissinger, whose ability to have it both ways in so divided a city was probably his most conspicuous diplomatic triumph, was warning Kay Graham in quite chilling terms about the course her paper was on. "Don't you believe we are going to be reelected?" he asked her. What made it particularly difficult for Bradlee was the amount of freedom he was receiving from his publisher. It was not the guidelines and the strictures that she imposed that were so difficult, it was the very absence of them. What was troubling was the degree to which she trusted him and was entrusting her entire newspaper and in effect her company to him. It was as if, having passed the moment of truth on the Pentagon Papers, she now totally accepted his judgment. The degree of faith was a burden in itself. Of course he and the other editors had the advantage of living in the same city as his two reporters and seeing them every day, and he knew not just each story but the context of each story; not just what they were printing, but also, and this was important, what they were *not* printing, what they had but could not quite use, which was often even more potent. The secret knowledge—the knowledge that the sources were often very serious, very legitimate high-ranking Republicans —strengthened Bradlee's position.

He was reassured by his friend Ed Williams. "Ben," Williams had said repeatedly, "the kids have got to be right because otherwise why are the Nixon people lying so goddamn much? If they're clean why don't they show it? Why are there so many lies? I'll tell you why. Because you've got them." That made him feel better momentarily, he always trusted Williams's cunning and shrewdness. But still, all in all, it was based on trust, there were so few moments when things were tangible, the sourcing was always so delicate. It was putting more on trust than he had ever done before, perhaps more than any editor on so big a newspaper had ever done before. Sometimes during the long months of 1972 and into early 1973 he would simply close the door to his office and sit with Howard Simons and they would think what for editors was truly the unthinkable. They knew the stories were based on facts. On solid information. They really had the sources. But what if, *what if* it was all part of an elaborate setup designed to get the *Post* way out on a limb and then saw it off? What if it were all some black trick or elaborately baited trap? Suppose these sources of Woodward and Bernstein's who were giving out information so reluctantly were in fact loyal Nixon people systematically setting up the *Post,* leaking stories, creating an atmosphere of conspiracy. Could the Nixon people be that devious? They had displayed, after all, a clear pattern of dirty tricks and covert operations in the past and during the campaign. Was a newspaper any more immune than a presidential candidate? If that were the case, then perhaps Bradlee really would lose his paper, the *Post* would be finished and so would their careers. He and Simons never discussed this with Woodward or Bernstein, they did not want to pass on any unnecessary paranoia.

Bradlee, of course, was cool throughout all those months. Above all, he would never show fear or doubt. In that sense he was the perfect editor for this story. Courage, more than anything else, he understood and valued, and this was a story which demanded that. He judged other men on their physical courage (the only time he had ever expressed personal admiration for his distinguished colleague Ben Bagdikian was when Bagdikian had voluntarily entered prison for a series of articles. "I got to hand it to you, buddy," he had said, "you've really got big ones"); when the *Pueblo* was captured there had been a part of Bradlee, old Navy man, that had wanted to take the ship and make a run for it, North Koreans or no. Courage for him was of the essence, far more important than ideology. If in this story he was editor of a newspaper struggling with vengeful powerful forces, then so be it, there was a part of him that gloried in it. His very presence, his sense of confidence in the reporters, increased their confidence in themselves; if Bradlee believed in them, then things were all right; Bradlee was without fear, without tension. Inside, of course, he was constantly on edge. None of this was being done without a price. In the summer of 1973 Bradlee developed what appeared to be a very serious illness. One of his eyelids began to droop. At first it did not bother him, but finally, as much because it was unattractive as anything else, he went to see a doctor. His own doctor was on vacation but his partner was there and the doctor examined Bradlee very carefully and told him, "I'm afraid you've got Horner's syndrome." That was not particularly pleasant news, it meant a brain tumor. "Or," the doctor continued, "perhaps an aneurysm." It was terrifying. Bradlee was at the peak of his career, he had always thought himself in wonderful shape, and now he seemed on the verge of death. For ten days he shuttled back and forth between Washington specialists who were trying to determine whether or not he had a brain tumor. In the end it turned out to be nothing but nerves. He was simply bearing too much tension over too long a period.

It was right before the election that they made their first major mistake on a story. Worse, it was on a very big story, connecting Bob Haldeman to the secret fund. The Haldeman story had been building for several weeks; each previous story had always somehow pointed the way to a higher level, and most certainly to Haldeman. First they had named Mitchell. Then they had run the Segretti stories and that had been tied in directly to Dwight Chapin. And Chapin was Haldeman's man. Chapin's arms and legs were wired to Haldeman's brain. Chapin did nothing that Haldeman did not want or approve of. Woodward and Bernstein were moving toward naming Haldeman but they were moving very slowly. Haldeman was very big game indeed, the tough guy at the White House. Sources who talked relatively easily about other men, even Mitchell, became frozen at the very mention of Haldeman's name. He was clearly a man who generated fear. A formidable and vindictive enemy, with total access to Nixon. Their sources had seemed to indicate that they were right about Haldeman. Hugh Sloan had already told them that a high White House official was involved. The man they called Deep Throat, Woodward's most sensitive source, equivocated about Haldeman, but he refused to deny that Haldeman was involved. Woodward had ended his conversation with Deep Throat by saying that failure by Throat to warn Woodward off a bad story would damage their friendship. Throat had not warned Woodward off Haldeman.

It was always that way, skating on such thin ice. The failure to deny was a confirmation. They would talk their story through with a source, and if the source failed to deny and did not tell them not to run it, then it was all right to go ahead. It was dicey stuff, but they were playing in a tense and scary atmosphere. This always allowed their sources to tell their own superiors that they were not in fact the sources of the reporters' stories. Bernstein had been uneasy with Woodward's confirmation and they had gone to see Sloan, who had already talked with the grand jury. Sloan was very careful with them. He specifically denied that the keeper of the fund was Ehrlichman, and he specifically denied that it was Colson, and he specifically denied that it was Nixon. If that was so, said Woodward, it had to be Haldeman. "Let me put it this way," Sloan said, "I have no problem if you write a story like that."

But they were still wary and they continued to talk with other sources, somehow picking up the fact that the grand jury had the same information that they had. It was logical, if Sloan had talked to the grand jury and Sloan were in effect confirming Haldeman for them, then Sloan had told the grand jury about Haldeman. So they had Haldeman. They went through a long and searching session with Bradlee and the other editors, with Bradlee serving as the prosecutor, trying to tear the story apart. Bradlee by then was convinced that Haldeman was behind the whole thing, but he was wary of going too soon, of being premature on a story so important. At the end they decided to go.

Only Simons had doubts, he seemed to want another source, so Bernstein had gone to a phone and called a lawyer in the Justice Department. But the lawyer had not been particularly helpful. Bernstein had devised a test; he would count to ten, and if the story was wrong, if there was anything wrong, the lawyer would hang up before he reached ten. Reading tea leaves, it was. Bernstein counted to ten and the lawyer did not hang up. Thus they had their confirmation.

Unfortunately the lawyer had misunderstood the test. The story ran on October 25. The next day the two reporters heard from their colleagues that Sloan's attorney was denying the story, saying that Sloan had not named Haldeman at all. They were stunned, they had no idea what had gone wrong. Later they would come to realize that they had only assumed that what Sloan told them he had also told to the grand jury; it was a sign that they were for a moment ahead of the prosecutors. If they had simply gone with the Haldeman story and left out the part about the grand jury, they would have been all right. But they did not know that at the time; at the moment the denial seemed so total. What could they do, tell James Stoner, Sloan's lawyer, that his client was their source? Bradlee was sick. It was for him the lowest moment in Watergate. He saw it all on television. Dan Schorr, he thought, big tough Dan Schorr, who had been a friend for twenty-five years, laying it not to Richard Nixon or Bob Haldeman but to Ben Bradlee. Kay Graham had called earlier and she had asked, "Oh Jesus, Ben, what went wrong?" and he had answered that he did not know, he hadn't talked to the boys yet.

The boys were shattered. This was their biggest story and they had blown it. They had no idea what had gone wrong and they began to retrace their steps. They had been so sure they had it right. Already the denials from the White House had a new tone, they were angrier. Really virulent. The White House was on the offensive. The two of them started checking back on their sources (stopping to have a prearranged lunch with Dick Snyder, their New York publisher; which enraged Rosenfeld, who thought they should be out working exclusively for him while the paper was in the balance). They were exhausted and they were frightened. Woodward kept thinking, if only he could set the clock back one day. Why did we write that story? he kept thinking. Why did we write it? Somewhere, he was sure, was a small stupid mistake and it was going to bring both of them down; he was sure that both of their careers were finished. He and Bernstein talked of resigning from the paper. They were certain they had permanently damaged the paper's credibility. There were, he and Bernstein noticed, small smiles on the faces of other reporters in the city room. But Bradlee in those hours was at his best. Let's find out what happened, he said, and so they set to work. At one point as the day progressed Woodward became so frustrated that he wanted to blow the name of a source at the FBI, but Bernstein hesitated, and Dick Harwood had argued vehemently against it.

In the early afternoon Woodward called Stoner. Stoner told him the story was wrong. "Wrong on the grand jury" were his words. Their conversation was oblique. What about the main theme of the story, that Haldeman had control of the fund? Woodward asked. "No comment," Stoner said. But wasn't that important? Woodward continued. They talked some more, Woodward groping for ways of confirming, of piercing Stoner's lawyerese answers. Did the *Post* owe Sloan an apology? asked Woodward. No, said Stoner. Woodward thought about his next question, whether the *Post* owed Haldeman an apology. It was a tricky question, because Stoner might say yes and then Woodward might be cornered into having the *Post* apologize to Haldeman. He thought for a moment, and decided things were so desperate that there was little to lose. So he asked it. "No comment," said Stoner. No comment, Woodward thought. For the first time since he had heard the denials, Woodward began to breathe a little easier. Emboldened, he pushed forward: it was very important for a newspaper to be accurate, if there had been a wrong, it was important to right it. Finally Stoner said he would not recommend apologizing to Haldeman. For the first time Woodward relaxed. He and Bernstein filled Bradlee in.

Bradlee had been receiving calls all afternoon from other news organizations demanding a response to the White House and the Stoner denials. Now he was convinced that the essence of the story had been essentially right and that the mistake was a minor one, an assumption about the grand jury. All afternoon he had been typing various answers for the other news organizations and then tearing them up. Finally he sat down and typed: "We stand by our story." It was vintage Bradlee. The captain before the mast in the stormiest of seas, never daunted. He felt relieved. So did Woodward and Bernstein. They had not been wrong on substance, but they had made one small mistake. Later Bernstein reached Sloan and Sloan said that Haldeman's name had never been given to the grand jury because he had never been asked about it.


But the trail had gone cold. They had written about Haldeman, they had made an error, they had been put on the defensive. The incident seemed to strengthen the White House and add to the legend that Haldeman was invincible. Deep Throat was furious with Woodward and lectured him about his mistake: you have to build slowly on something like this and as you get nearer the top you have to be very careful, not to shoot and miss. "You put the investigation back months," Deep Throat told him. "It puts everyone on the defensive—editors, FBI agents, everyone has to get in a crouch after this." He was right. Woodward and Bernstein felt embarrassed after the Haldeman story. They did not want to go to the White House for briefings; for the first time on the story they felt young and foolish. A few days later Nixon was reelected by a huge majority, and that temporarily made the trail even colder. Watergate, it seemed, had not become an issue, it had not reached most Americans yet.

# 27 /CBS

It was a bottled-up story, covert instead of overt, often intangible, usually invisible. It was a very easy story not to see and not to cover and not to film. During the campaign, when Woodward and Bernstein were writing some of their most important stories (and the period when the Nixon administration least wanted Watergate covered), from the middle of September to election day, NBC devoted a total of only 41 minutes and 21 seconds to covering Watergate. ABC gave it 42 minutes and 26 seconds. Even that coverage was more often than not perfunctory; the Democrats and Larry O'Brien Charged, the Republicans Answered. The networks were in no rush to get out ahead on this story. Yes, the Washington *Post* was legitimizing the story every day, but in the headquarters of television executives and television news executives the *Post* was hardly the index of the day's events that *The New York Times* was. The *Times* was doing poorly on Watergate, and Jack Gould, its famed television critic, was becoming convinced that the *Times*'s failure was playing a role in the networks' lethargic attitude. He was outraged by the degree to which his own paper was letting the networks off the hook.

NBC, which like CBS had a fine deep news staff, was always a little ambivalent about Watergate, always unsure of how hard to ride it, and wary that it might blow up in everyone's face. This was true not just during the campaign but right up until the time when McCord broke the story open and it all came apart. The NBC reporters in Washington were constantly complaining to colleagues about troubles they were having with New York and its lack of enthusiasm for Watergate stories, and nothing illustrated this, and the timidity of the network, better than an incident involving Carl Stern of NBC in the spring of 1973. Stern was both a lawyer and an able reporter. In early 1973 he had very good sources on Watergate, including a young White House aide, then largely unknown, named John Dean. Stern was reasonably frustrated in those days about failing to get his stories on the air, but one day he learned that E. Howard Hunt, one of the Watergate plotters, was blackmailing the White House and threatening to tell all. It was a powerful, important, and entirely correct story; his source, he knew, had a very good record for accuracy. So he immediately went on the radio with it—radio, being far less powerful, is virtually unedited, a reporter calls the radio desk, tells what he has, and asks for a certain amount of time. None of the corporate filters that reach into television hang over radio. The story quickly went out over NBC radio—it was, in fact, broadcast with an NBC imprimatur and was the most important news of the day. Stern thereupon called the television news desk and explained what he had for the "Nightly News" broadcast and said that he had already used it on radio. But the executives of the "Nightly News" wanted no part of Hunt's blackmail and they told Carl Stern that it was no story. NBC television was afraid to broadcast what NBC radio had already broadcast. So much for NBC during Watergate.

Of the three networks, only one covered Watergate with any sense of real obligation, and this was CBS. What happened there—the slowness in covering it, the amount of energy required to do two major Watergate pieces, the difficulty in getting them on the air, and the intensity of the pressure they created—reflected the weakness of the networks, even the best network with the best people in charge of its news department, and demonstrated how difficult it was to go against the grain.

The decision to do two major Watergate pieces in the fall of 1972 began with a decision to do a long segment on the wheat deal. From the start the Soviet wheat deal had offended Walter Cronkite, with his old-fashioned values. He told his closest associates in the late summer that there was something terribly wrong with the wheat deal, that it smelled wrong, very wrong, and that this, not Watergate, was going to be the Teapot Dome of the Nixon adminstration. The great strength of Cronkite on the "Evening News" is that he wears two hats, he is both the anchorman and the managing editor, and he can, within the limits and as long as he doesn't push too hard too often, get what he wants on the show. His successors in future years almost surely will not wear two hats and will not have this kind of power. But in 1972, on those occasions when he willed it, Walter Cronkite had a special power and in this case he wanted the wheat deal.

It was not a story that television could easily dramatize; it was subtle and complicated, almost too intricate for print, there were few opportunities for film, and CBS, like the other networks, lacked the facilities, resources, manpower, and, above all, the inclination to do serious investigative reporting. Television did those stories best that told themselves, or appeared to tell themselves; television liked what was on the surface and was made uneasy by what was beneath the surface. Yet on CBS the wheat story was a striking success. Cronkite assigned Stanhope Gould, considered by most CBS people to be the most talented young producer there, and his graphics and his illustration of the story were simply brilliant. Gould was aided by a young assistant named Linda Aminoff, who was particularly skillful at breaking down the scandal into comprehensible parts. The great strength of the piece was that it broke out of the language of networkese, that short, hard, semi–wire-service exposition, trying to do something very complicated in twenty seconds by nuance and implication. The wheat deal was difficult for economists, let alone ordinary citizens, to understand, and so CBS explained it by repetition. Normally television would have covered it with lots of film of wheat fields, with the wind rippling through, that and a few bland paragraphs of narration. Not this time. This time they concentrated on reporting about exports and commodities, and conflict of interest, going back again and again to Cronkite, explaining once and then twice and then three times, always with that repetition, and repetition was something television hated, repetition wasted time. At one point Walter Cronkite came out of his chair to do some graphics, and the audience immediately knew it was important, *Walter would not have come out of his chair for just anything,* and yes, there he was showing his legs, which of itself was unique, Walter did not show his legs lightly. Proof that it was not your average story.

It was a considerable triumph for CBS News, it had scooped much of the print press, editors at the *Times* and other major newspapers called CBS News to express admiration, a reversal of the normal pecking order—print leads, television follows—and the CBS executives and Cronkite were encouraged to try some Watergate specials. Again the problems for television were immense: it was a complicated story without proof and without film. Earlier that summer the word to members of the Washington bureau who had wanted to go all out on Watergate was that no, it was not a television story, it would have to wait on events. It was Cronkite's decision that changed it, his imprimatur that made the difference. But Watergate posed even more problems than the wheat deal; it was not only complex, it was almost totally subsurface, it demanded great and careful cultivation of sources, enormous patience on the part of reporters and editors, and staff—something CBS, infinitely richer than the newspapers, lacked. The top dozen CBS reporters were excellent, but the staff was spread thin after that, there were no bodies to be spared for investigative reporting. Now, suddenly, with the election approaching, CBS, wanting to bring extra density to its Watergate coverage, found itself dependent on the Washington *Post.* Gordon Manning of CBS had worked with Ben Bradlee at *Newsweek,* and Manning (as Spiro Agnew might have suspected) had called Bradlee to ask for the *Post*'s help on the story, to turn over sources or, even better, its documents (CBS had heard that the *Post* had great numbers of FBI and Justice Department documents and the idea of the camera moving across those documents—good film—appealed to them as the security blanket they would provide in case of lawsuits). But Bradlee had answered (in a way that would have surprised Agnew)—Manning could fuck off, there would be no help, there would be no documents, indeed there *were* no documents—and when Stan Gould of CBS had gone to see Bradlee (another Manning brainstorm, Gould had gone to Harvard, Bradlee had gone to Harvard, thus they would get on well; they had, it turned out, gone to very different Harvards), Stan Gould came away with the very strong impression that Ben Bradlee, very much like Ted Agnew, did not like network newsmen, and even more, that Bradlee, who knew that he and his two boy wonders were skating on very thin ice, was supersensitive to the charge of collusion and conspiracy.

So the CBS team had come down from New York, and though men like Schorr and Rather were very helpful, it was nonetheless a very derivative story, putting together what had been in the *Post,* crediting mostly the *Post*'s sources. It was all there and yet nothing was there; what Stan Gould was telling his

superiors was that here was an important story, although they did not have
the sources of their own to confirm it; that it was strong stuff; that the
Washington *Post* and the Los Angeles *Times* were clearly on to something and
that the White House denials were very odd, very carefully phrased. Partial
denials, in fact. But if they went with it, like it or not, he emphasized, they
were going to be in bed with the *Post* (which is not unusual, it is accepted
journalistic practice for the networks to run stories that have appeared only
in the *Times* or some other paper, giving the proper credit). In effect, the
choice was to do the Washington *Post* story or do nothing.

They decided to go. Part one was the espionage itself, the break-in plus
Segretti and the spy campaign. It ran slightly more than fourteen minutes.
Fourteen minutes was the real breakthrough, more even than the content. The
entire news show is twenty-two minutes, which means that all news items are
equal and equality is enforced by brevity. Everything is two minutes. Three
minutes for the apocalypse. Four minutes if it's an American apocalypse. And
now here was fourteen of twenty-two precious minutes going to Watergate; it
was like the *Times* playing only one story on two thirds of its front page. It
was very strong reporting.

The triumph was totally Stanhope Gould's. He was the in-house iconoclast, a genius at and true child of television, who raged at what the News
Division had done to it. A man of undisputed talent and originality, he considered it a cowardly medium, and he frequently wondered if he had wasted his
life by choosing a career in which there were so many restrictions and limitations. He had despised the network's coverage of the Vietnam War, he was
convinced that his superiors had sanitized footage from the field, and that they
had never really used the camera as they might have, to close in on the gore.
In particular he hated, more than any television critic could have hated it, the
formula of network news reporting, the two-minute reports, so often empty
and superficial, so often determined by the government's news managers.

In the two Watergate pieces Gould deliberately set out to get beyond the
self-imposed limitations of formula. When the first was screened in New York
(the second segment was only a tattered rough draft), Cronkite was immediately enthusiastic. Not everyone else was so pleased. Sandy Socolow, the
producer of the show, was furious. First because of the length. Gould had
pulled off a kind of subversive assault against the New York producer system
—he had usurped virtually the entire news show (Socolow, his victim, realized
this immediately). And, second, he was so late. The show came in on Friday,
ten days before the election. It was much too long and there was almost no
time to rework it. Gould, Socolow knew, had presented him with a *fait accompli.* There was a part of him that believed, probably accurately, that lateness
was tied to the length, that Stanhope Gould, who hated the limits of the news
show, had deliberately waited until the last minute so that his superiors would
have no real chance to cut back on the length of the piece. So Socolow was
at once impressed and unhappy with it.

When it was screened there was one other unhappy witness and that was

Dick Salant, the president of CBS, a man who had attained his job not because he was a creative, original newsman, filled with the ideas and excitement of news, but because he was a lawyer, and a corporate figure, and a man expert in the *implications* of news, what it might mean legally and politically; a man who was caught between the forces coming down from the executive levels of Black Rock—the CBS headquarters—and the forces pushing up from the newsroom. Salant during the Johnson and Nixon years had stood as a figure of very considerable integrity, he had grasped what was important about CBS News and he had shepherded it through an increasingly difficult time; he loved the news business, for which he was not trained, and despised the law, for which he was, and as he had gotten closer and closer to retirement he had seemed to those around him an increasingly liberated man.

But now, sitting in the screening room, Salant was clearly upset: "Isn't this a little old? . . . Do we really have to go with this? . . . Isn't this quite long? . . ." He could sense the problems ahead, and that they would not be pleasant ones. But Gordon Manning was very enthusiastic about the piece, he had become the executive force behind it, and Socolow, still privately irritated with Gould, was backing his man now (it was now News Division against the corporation), and besides, they had the most important of all CBS forces going for them, the backing of Walter Cronkite. Fourteen minutes it was, and fourteen minutes it would be. There would be a Part Two scheduled.

> CRONKITE: At first it was called the Watergate caper—five men apparently caught in the act of burglarizing and bugging Democratic headquarters in Washington. But the episode grew steadily more sinister—no longer a caper, but the Watergate affair escalating finally into charges of a high-level campaign of political sabotage and espionage apparently unparalleled in American history. Most of what is known of the Watergate affair has emerged in puzzling bits and pieces, through digging by the nation's press and television newsmen. Some of the material made public so far is factual, without dispute—those men caught in the act at the Watergate, for instance. Some is still allegation, uncovered by the press but as yet legally unsubstantiated. We shall label our sources carefully as we go along. But with the facts and the allegations we shall try tonight to pull together the threads of this amazing story, quite unlike any in our modern American history. . . .

So it began. The show aired on Friday night, October 27, 1972, and it had a power and authority special for television. Though CBS was extremely careful to name the Washington *Post* sources and equally careful to carry the White House denials, there was no doubt about the force of the report, this much time on a national news show, Walter Cronkite's stamp of approval on it—if that's what Walter said, then that's the way it was. For the first time Watergate became a real national story; and there was demonstrated by the length of the report a rare willingness of television to accept the implications of news.

Among those who watched the show that Friday night was Charles Colson. Colson was the chief monitor in the White House and he was regarded by colleagues there as being the cobra of the operation. He was deputized by Nixon to deal with the networks, the bad cop to Herb Klein's good cop. Colson was a man in his forties before he found Jesus, full of swagger and a touch of the bully; he played heavily on his background as an ex-Marine, and he was frequently described in newspaper columns as being tough and hard-nosed. He had been quoted as saying that he had a grandmother whose body he did not disdain to walk over on behalf of his Chief of Staff. Just as the confidence and swagger of John Mitchell impressed Richard Nixon, he of so little physical confidence and such terrible shyness, so did the confidence and swagger of Colson impress him. All of Colson's reports back to the White House starred, of course, Chuck Colson; Colson telling off people, network executives cringing as Colson laid down the law. Nixon delighted in all this. It was an enviable job, not just because Nixon was obsessed by what the networks were doing, but even better because there was no way Colson could lose. The relationship to the truth in the playing back of his daring deeds was questioned by some of his associates, but that never mattered.

Chuck Colson watched CBS that Friday night and he was furious; it was, so far as he was concerned, a violation of journalistic ethics. He was quick to the phone; the Nixon White House was not going to stand for reporting like this. Frank Stanton, who liked to deal with the big boys himself, had encouraged calls from Colson; if there was something wrong with CBS News, just call your friendly Dr. Stanton and they would talk. Stanton's position, oft expressed to the newsroom, was that he was simply protecting its interest, taking the flak, but there were those in CBS News who believed that it was Stanton trying again to have it both ways. Stanton's way of handling things meant that the News Department never knew what the White House was saying and doing and whether in fact the CBS corporate structure was bending and trading them off.

Frank Stanton was regarded in the last years of his tenure at CBS as being more and more the inheritor of the Murrow mantle, and some of the CBS News people thought of him as being very good, very intelligent, very protective, and very devious, and they were very uneasy about the duality of his role. (For example, Colson later accused Stanton of bartering the CBS White House coverage—perhaps softer reporting—for White House help in lobbying in the congressional fight over the anti–military-establishment program "The Selling of the Pentagon." There are people at CBS who like and admire Stanton, and do not like and do not admire Colson, who think Colson may be telling at least a partial truth here.)

So Colson, having watched the long segment on Watergate, on Saturday made his first call to Stanton, who was, not by chance, away from home. At the moment Colson called, Mrs. Stanton happened to be on the phone long-distance with a friend; the White House operator brusquely cut in to announce that the White House was calling and that Mrs. Stanton should get off the phone. She did, thinking that there were some very crude people in power these days. She tried to reach her husband, missed him a couple of times, and by the time she got him, it was too late, Colson had already gone to Bill Paley, who had *also* encouraged White House calls. (Later, after Watergate, Paley told a few close friends almost lightly —nothing really serious there—that he had made a slight mistake with the Nixon people, taken a few phone calls that he shouldn't have.) When Stanton realized that Colson had already gone to Paley, he became a little nervous, he could guess what was in store and he had a sense that Paley was not ready for it. He, Stanton, had shielded Paley too long, Paley might be particularly vulnerable. The timing of all this is extremely important: it was immediately before the election, Nixon seemed a sure winner and a landslide winner to boot. Charles Colson found in William S. Paley a very willing listener, and shortly thereafter William S. Paley summoned Richard S. Salant. It was the classic moment, the corporation coming down on the newsroom under great pressure from the White House.

Colson, filled with the arrogance of the White House at that moment, had told Paley that this was the most irresponsible journalism he had ever seen, that it was pure McGovern work, journalists pretending to be journalists but working for McGovern, that it was much too long, that it was too close to the election, that it was all old stuff, and old stuff that had been lies to start with, and that it was just CBS using the Washington *Post* stuff, and CBS would live to regret it. On Monday, Paley had made these exact same charges to Salant, with one exception: he did not say where they came from, and he did not mention the White House or Colson (although Salant suspected that Colson was the real source; unlike Johnson, Nixon never liked to make his calls himself, and Johnson calls were more volcanic, the Nixon ones more calculated, and more deniable, if someone heard about them). Paley and Salant went back and forth on the subject of the show's legitimacy and fairness; they had had sessions like that before, but never so continuously, and for so long, and so intense. Each one's position had a certain fragility; Paley liked to have things both ways with the News Department. He wanted to keep it reasonably contained and to minimize its obstreperousness. (A good deal of brilliant corporate planning had gone into setting the limits while at the same time keeping it from looking as if there were any; significantly, at the time of Watergate there was no Ed Murrow figure who spoke for the network and had the access to time and who could put together and explain what all these complicated bits and pieces really meant. The audience, almost deliberately, had been left on its own to grope.) Yet at the same time he liked to be able to say to outsiders that he never told the News Department what to do. Salant was not Paley's man; Salant had come first from the law firm that handled the CBS account. Stanton had found him there when Salant was a young lawyer working on the color-television case, and Stanton had immediately liked him and sensed that his interest went far beyond the law. He had pulled Salant into the News Division, making him in the process his protégé.

Salant from the start had been Stanton's man. He admired and esteemed Stanton and his vision of broadcasting. This meant that his feelings for Paley were necessarily mixed, since he had picked up some of Stanton's prejudices and attitudes and Stanton could barely control his hatred of Paley any more. Yet if Salant was not entirely admiring of Paley, if he was bothered that the Chairman's value system seemed so different from his own, he nonetheless had a grudging respect for the man. He was proud of CBS News, it was the best, and much of the credit for that had to go, like it or not, to Paley. Salant had served one earlier term as the head of news, had been tumbled by a combination of pressures, including a more or less orchestrated campaign against him by Friendly, who wanted the job himself. When Friendly had left in 1966, there was a desperate need for a replacement, and a sense that Paley did not particularly want Salant again but had accepted him because of the belief that in the turmoil caused by Friendly's resignation, it would be reassuring to have someone in charge coming from within the shop. And Salant had, in the pressurized years since 1966, years of endless assault upon the News Department, shown to correspondents that if he was a less creative and exciting figure than Friendly, he was somehow steadier and firmer; he had won in those years the very considerable respect of working reporters, and there were few who mourned for the days of Friendly. He was nonetheless Stanton's protégé, not Paley's, and thus it was not surprising that at this meeting both Paley and Stanton were there.

Stanton quietly sat by while the Chairman repeatedly invoked his name and associated it with his own views. What Bill Paley was saying again and again was that this had been bad journalism, and that it was unworthy of CBS's traditions. More, Paley said, this was not just his view, *it was that of Dr. Stanton.* Salant looked at Stanton. Stanton said nothing. But the tactic affected Salant and made him take the accusation more seriously. It would not have surprised him at all to learn that Bill Paley could be reached and bent by the White House in a situation like this. But Frank Stanton, that was another matter; Stanton was a man who had virtually written the book on broadcasting fairness. Curiously, during all of this meeting, it was only Paley who spoke. Stanton remained absolutely silent as his name was invoked. He did not disagree and he did not correct Paley. He knew that Paley was in fact giving an order to Salant to kill Part Two. Stanton was then less than a year away from retirement. Later, much, much later, after he had left the company, he told Salant that he had not agreed with Paley. Those at CBS who knew both Stanton and Salant well later realized that something fascinating had happened in that meeting, that the protégé had passed the professor, that Salant, the more liberated man, the man who was not afraid of losing his job, had in some way absorbed Stanton's lessons and done more, had been willing to act upon them. He had outgrown the man he revered, and would in the future revere him just a little less.

Salant had never seen Paley like this before. The session seemed to go on and on. Salant, good lawyer that he was, had immediately sent out for a list of the *other* long news segments they had done on the show, to prove that this was not unique, and he was buttressed there, on what was the single most important point of the show, the sheer length of it. Salant was in a reasonably strong position. No one had expected him to last that long in a job known increasingly for brevity of tenure, but he had been there six years and the constant very public pressures against CBS News over the years had also strengthened him; to let him go now was to give in to the Nixon-Agnew barbarians at the gate. He was not that far from retirement, was independently wealthy, and simply didn't need the job that much. He also knew that he had an additional protection. For whatever fire CBS was taking at the moment from the White House might be nothing in the long run to the barrage loosed if Salant resigned in protest over CBS's buckling to the White House. If Salant quit over this issue, it might absolutely tear the News Division apart, and it might end right then that special tradition that still lived on from the days of Murrow. That in itself was a pretty good card.

During this long session Salant was at first puzzled by Paley's insistence and firmness. It was unlike the Chairman. But gradually as Paley began to ask more and more about the second segment, Salant guessed what had happened. Paley had almost certainly made a promise to Colson that there would be no Part Two and was trying in as polite a way as he could to order the News Department not to run it. That was what all this bullying and repetition was about, Paley was letting Salant know how important it all was and how much was at stake. No one ever ordered anyone to kill a story at CBS, but it was absolutely clear to Dick Salant during all this byplay that William S. Paley was in a pleasant, subliminal way, telling him to kill the second part, and it was equally clear in what Salant was saying that Paley would have to fire him first.

Those who were working with Salant at the time thought that he had left Paley's office on Monday morning visibly shaken, that it had been a brutal morning for him. Immediately word got around in the gossipy world of television news that the White House had intervened, that Salant had been ripped apart and that Part Two was in jeopardy. That made the screening of Part Two a uniquely tense occasion. It was one of those moments when everyone in the room was aware that he was no longer simply a journalist, that outside considerations were playing a role, and that the corporate side was coming down. The decisions were no longer entirely theirs. The second piece was scheduled for approximately the same length as the first one, about fourteen minutes. It was also very strong, and again its strength was the essential violation of networkese, its brevity, its speed, its unwillingness to uncomplicate the complicated. This one had a segment on laundering money in Mexico, something that was extremely difficult to explain in print, let alone on television, but Gould had come up with vivid graphics, plus segments with Dan Rather explaining the importance of Haldeman and Chapin and Mitchell and somehow bringing everything very close to Richard Nixon. And finally a very strong closing by Cronkite saying that all this was very important and that the White House denials were not very convincing.

The meeting on the second segment included Salant, Socolow, Manning, Paul Greenberg, Cronkite's executive producer, and Gould, who had produced the two segments. Cronkite did not attend, because the smell of trouble was in the air, and Gordon Manning had decided at least temporarily to hold Cronkite out of battle, like a reserve battalion. Gould, seeing that Cronkite was not attending, knew that things were going badly, that the news side was on the defensive. He knew that Cronkite was a weather vane. The Manning view was that Walter was a precious commodity, you could only use him and his special resource so often and then it was expended, and so you did not erode him in battles like this if at all possible. Perhaps if it became a question of no second segment at all, you brought him in, otherwise you tried to save him for another day; it was really like an old-time rifleman conserving his powder, and in a way it illustrated the dilemma of network news: the pressures against doing anything controversial are so great, and so exhausting, that you must be very careful not to undertake battle too often, or on anything but the most favorable grounds. The forces against you do not ration their energy.

So Cronkite was not there. Salant was, and he was very strong for cutting back. It was too long, they simply could not run anything this long on the "Evening News," it was not what the "Evening News" was all about. Besides, he argued, a great deal of it was very repetitious. But that was *precisely* what Stan Gould wanted, he felt the repetition was the essence of the piece. Then Salant said a very odd thing: "I hope I feel this way because I'm a fair and honest newsman." It was an oblique remark, admitting that he did not even understand his own feelings, that there was now so much pressure on him that he hoped the reasons he was stating were his own, not Paley's, and not, dear God, those of Richard Nixon or Chuck Colson. Then he cited an old piece that Dan Schorr had done on a Labor Day weekend special; the Schorr segment had been on laundering money and Salant wanted to know how this new section was different from the old Schorr one. (One great difference was that a piece on a weekend special, particularly a Labor Day weekend special, when no one is presumed to be watching the news, is different from the Cronkite news. A weekend special is hit or miss and the audience accepts it or rejects it, but the "Evening News" is CBS, it has the authority of Walter Cronkite, it means that these things are true and real and guaranteed and one must take them seriously.) He had the text of the old Schorr piece and they began to compare them. The other executives in the room, all of whom had forgotten about the Schorr piece or, like most CBS listeners, had never heard it, shook their heads, thinking that Salant is one smart lawyer son of a bitch, how did he ever remember that one, what a great argument to take to the News Department.

Gould argued strenuously on behalf of the second segment, pleading that it not be cut, that it was new, that Watergate needed above all to be summed up, not nickel-dimed, that above all the time and the repetition were crucial. Everyone at CBS, Gould argued, was hearing the same thing from Middle America, that Watergate was too complicated to understand. This was a journalistic failure, he said, and in particular it was a failure of network news departments, who were charged with reaching the great mass audience and making it understand these things. Manning and Socolow also argued for the piece; Manning was very strong and he said that it would ruin morale in the newsroom if it were dropped or severely cut, particularly since they had already announced on the air that the second piece was coming up, they had committed themselves.

But there was also a sense in the room that the curtain was coming down. Socolow was charged with taking the old Schorr script and trying to remove overlap and repetition, and then cutting the second segment down to size. He was to make it shorter and make it as different from Labor Day as possible. There was a sense that the cold breath of Black Rock was upon them. Socolow had a feeling that they all might be out of jobs the next day and he told his wife as much that night. Finally he managed to cut the segment from fourteen minutes to eight minutes; he showed it to Cronkite, who bought it. Gould was furious. As far as he was concerned, the script had been raped, they had cut the guts out, and even if the segments were similar in words, they were vastly different in graphics and thus in impact. He believed they had backed down to pressure and ripped up a good show, and he could be heard telling friends that the first thing they must remember about television was that it was a timid medium. A timid goddamn medium. Cronkite took the script to Salant, who approved it: Well, let's go, but this may be it. Paley was absolutely furious when it was broadcast, and he and Salant went around one more time. He told Salant in a very pleasant and gracious way that CBS News must never do something like this again. Never. But it was done. Or almost done.

A few days after the election, when the Nixon administration was riding at its highest, when the President was talking to his aides about how they were really going to get their enemies this time, Chuck Colson called Frank Stanton on another matter, and this time he bullied and threatened Stanton at great length. This administration was not going to play gentle games any more. No more Mister Nice Guy. The Nixon administration knew who its friends were and who its enemies were and it was going to bring CBS to its knees on Madison Avenue and Wall Street. The CBS stock was going to collapse. When Richard Nixon got through with CBS there was going to be damn well nothing left. They were going to take away the five owned and operated stations (the real source of CBS's wealth). "We'll break your network," Stanton heard him say. On he went with a litany of things the Administration was going to do to CBS, including throwing its support behind pay television. Stanton was not surprised, but he was upset, there was a dimension of fury to it, a kind of arrogance that even for this administration was chilling. He was appalled but he said nothing at the time. If a CBS reporter had found a comparable Nixon official making similar threats to the head of U.S. Steel or General Motors it would have been the lead story, but Frank Stanton, who loved the News Department but also loved to lobby, said nothing. He was not about to challenge this administration, though later, long, long after the Nixon administration was on the defensive and coming apart, he put all this in an affidavit. In the spring of 1973, when Frank Stanton had retired from CBS, there was a small party given for him, and it was by chance the same day that all the Nixon people fell out of the tree. Mitchell, Haldeman, Ehrlichman, Dean. And Stanton, usually so mild-mannered and correct and proper and reserved, had turned to a friend and said, with truly shocking ferocity, "I hope they get that little son of a bitch Colson too."

Soon after the two CBS segments ran, Katharine Graham of the Washington *Post* happened to see Bill Paley at a party. Until then she had felt herself very much alone on Watergate, but now CBS was with the *Post*. CBS had enlarged the story, made it national. So she ran over to Paley and kissed him. "You saved us," she said. He seemed to freeze just a little bit, it was precisely what he did not want to hear.

The people who had put together the two segments were very pleased with what they had achieved. Stan Gould complained about the cutting of the second segment, but on the whole he and the others felt that they had done something important that went beyond the regular television news routine. Repeatedly in the months to come, as Watergate continued to fill the news budgets, they suggested doing further long special segments for the "Evening News." With a variety of excuses, they were always turned down.

In June 1973, without any real consultation with his News Department, Bill Paley suddenly issued an order ending Instant Analysis, the innocuous form of criticism network reporters and commentators were accustomed to indulge in following the broadcast of a presidential speech. (It was often little more than a review of the speech with practically no editorial comment.) It had long been a sore point with the Nixon White House; Haldeman felt that the reporters were in effect piggybacking on the President's audience. When Paley announced his decision, most of his Washington reporters were outraged. They did not doubt that he was bowing to pressure from Nixon and Haldeman, and he was doing so at a moment when it was sure to be taken as a victory by the White House over CBS. It was regarded by CBS bureau members as the concession of an old and scared man, and there was great resentment over the fact that they had not been consulted. Roger Mudd went so far as to do a piece protesting the order, which was never broadcast. The top reporters—Mudd, Schorr, Marvin Kalb, and Rather—drafted a letter to corporate management, Mudd doing most of the work on it, stiffening the language of it several times. Finally Rather balked at signing it—it was *too* strong—and said he would write his own letter, which infuriated the others. The situation was hardly eased when a day or two later CBS News president Dick Salant said he approved of the joint letter being sent and Rather, seeing the ground a little more clearly now, volunteered to come in again, an act which notably infuriated Mudd, his potential rival as Cronkite's successor. (Five months later, in an equally perfunctory manner, Paley restored Instant Analysis; with the White House so weakened by Watergate by then, no one regarded the move as particularly heroic.)

At the time Watergate broke open Gordon Manning and Bill Paley were in China, out of touch with the incredible events of those days. When they finally got back to Hong Kong there was a whole stack of *The New York Times* waiting for them, and on the long flight back to the U.S. Paley read them, one after another, saying very little, just the sound of a man sucking in his breath, a light gasp or two. After several hours he turned to Manning and asked how it could have happened, these were all educated men, they had all been to law school.

Manning said it was simple.

"Why?" asked Paley.

"Because they lacked character," said Manning.

There was a long pause. "I guess you're right," Paley said.

# 28/ Time Incorporated

The relationship between *Time* and Richard Nixon had always been odd. It should have been a happy one, each side getting exactly what it wanted. Certainly *Time,* during the crucial early years of Nixon's career, took pains to portray him as the bright young fellow on the rise, filled with all the best of American virtues. "Fighting Quaker," *Time* typically titled one early cover story. That one, which ran in August 1952, called him "a good-looking, dark-haired young man with a manner both aggressive and modest, and a personality to delight any political barker. He seemed to have everything—a fine TV manner, an attractive family, a good war record, deep sincerity and religious faith, a Horatio Alger–like career." Other cover stories found him brisk, efficient, filled with principle, respected by colleagues, trusted by Ike: "When the press of other business calls Ike away in mid-meeting, Ike turns to Nixon and says, 'Dick, you take over.' " The darker side of Nixon's nature, which worried his political peers, many of the reporters who covered him, and in fact Luce himself, never reached print.

*Time* was very Republican in those days, it was very anti-Communist, and it was getting from Richard Nixon exactly what it wanted. In truth, many of the *Time* senior people had serious doubts, not about the politics of the man but about his character, the anger, the quick flashes of hostility, and finally the stilted quality of the man. He had once come to a meeting of the Time-Life editors, and he had looked across the room and seen Jack Jessup, the man who wrote most of the *Life* editorials, and he had asked, "Jack, how's that house of yours that burned down?" Jessup had been startled and he had finally managed an answer, "Mister Vice-President, that was six years ago." Nixon had jarred not just Jessup but everyone in the room. It was always like that, he had no capacity for small talk, and as he could not put himself at ease he could not put others at ease. He had no ability, as most skilled politicians do, to meet journalists and editors halfway, to sense what they want and what they do not want. He could not do this, he feared so much what they wanted, each encounter—given the fragility of his makeup—bordered on a trespass. Unlike other politicians, he could not separate those reporters worthy of trust from those who were not, and deal accordingly. He could give trust to almost no one; the fact told more about him than it did about the press corps.

That was particularly puzzling for the people at *Time:* here was a young man upon whom they had showered their most favorable notices and yet they could never really understand him, or reach him. Even Luce found Nixon a puzzling figure: he was internationalist, he was smart, he was ambitious, he was tough on both Communists and Democrats, he had, thus, all the proper virtues. Good Calvinist that he was, Luce was sure the fault was *his,* that if Nixon were as fine a specimen as *Time* regularly proclaimed, he should be likable as well. But it was not easy, he found, to force himself to like someone.

Certainly *Time* wrote gently of Nixon in his first presidential run in 1960, but it wrote fairly of Kennedy that year as well; *Life* had come out editorially for Nixon but it was a somewhat cautious endorsement. Later, after Kennedy's victory, Luce was bothered by his own role, perhaps he had let the good side down, perhaps he should have been more partisan. But it was never easy, *Time* would make a bid for access, for friendship, and somehow the response was always chilly. On the eve of Nixon's trip to the Soviet Union in 1959, the Vice-President had called in the two reporters from the two leading Republican outlets who were going to make the trip with him, Charley Mohr of *Time* and Don Irwin of the *Herald Tribune.* "You're different from the other reporters," he had begun, "I can trust you. So I'm going to give you a special briefing." Though they did not particularly like the implication that they were truer to the Republican cause than the others, both Mohr and Irwin leaned forward, quite willing to pick up a few extra points against their opposition. But then Nixon went into the standard Cold War, Communism-against-the-Free-World briefing that he gave to every farmer and businessman from out of town.

Even Jim Shepley, who had been *Time* magazine's connection to the Republican center-right in the fifties, had been disillusioned by Nixon. Shepley had been the *Time* Washington bureau chief in the late fifties, and he had gotten quite close to Nixon. He had taken a leave of absence from *Time* in order to work for Nixon during the 1960 campaign. For a very brief time, when Shepley first came aboard, he had been the golden boy with special access and the candidate seemed to solicit his opinion on almost everything. The Nixon old-timers smiled at each other and wondered how long it would be before Shepley was treated like everyone else, that is, badly. It was about a month. Shepley, who was in charge of issue research, became very discouraged. He had worked doggedly to prepare the research for Nixon's first debate with Kennedy and he was no more able than anyone else to reach the candidate. It was all a waste and in years to come his association with Richard Nixon was not one he liked to reminisce about.

In 1968 the magazine had been very fair and generally kind; at the end of the campaign, though he did not consider it an easy decision, Hedley Donovan had decided to endorse Nixon in a *Life* editorial. Donovan had thought about this a long time in his own judicious way. He was certainly not a Nixon hater, but he found Nixon a puzzling figure, at once able and awkward and graceless, terribly self-defeating in personal relationships. He was an odd package, Donovan thought, but he was by no means below the permissible level. Not very likable though. Humphrey was clearly more likable. Hearing that *Life* had decided to endorse him, Nixon telephoned Donovan to thank him. Donovan was not sure whether Nixon had actually seen the editorial or whether he had only heard of the decision. So he took pains to point out that it was a somewhat measured endorsement.

Perhaps, Donovan thought, Nixon might, like many of his predecessors, grow in office, there might be a new dimension of magnanimity. But Donovan, like others, was wrong in this. Nixon did not forgive. Among others he did not forgive was *Time* magazine. If many of its readers had been convinced that it had in the past been uncommonly pro-Republican and pro-Nixon, one person who did not share that opinion was Richard Nixon. On the eve of his 1968 campaign he could tell aides that there was no way in the world he could get a sympathetic cover story out of *Time*. It was too eastern, too liberal. Its people were always against him. Take Sidey. Nixon did not like Hugh Sidey, the *Time* bureau chief in Washington and the White House correspondent. Though Sidey was immensely likable and truly a man of two institutions— *Time* and the presidency, hired by one, wooed by the other—Nixon could not accept Sidey, could not open the door, though Sidey was predisposed to like *any* President and offered the President a marvelous opportunity to have his voice heard once a week in a very influential national magazine. But that was not good enough for Nixon. To him Sidey was a Kennedy pal, a Johnson pal. He must first pay for his past and renounce his earlier sins. The Nixon people took pains to cut Sidey off, to keep him as far away as possible. Haldeman worked long hours to keep Sidey off Air Force One and to cut off his sources.

All of this was astonishing to Sidey, who worked for what had long been an essentially Republican magazine and who had covered two previous Presidents, both of them Democrats; he had, after all, dealt with Lyndon Johnson at his most irascible and had never been cut off like this. *Time* magazine was ready and willing and anxious to be a forum for Richard Nixon, but instead the President simply pulled his own circle tighter around him; all others were alien and not to be trusted. Whereas Jack Kennedy had usually seen Sidey every two or three weeks, Hugh Sidey saw Richard Nixon only twice in six years. One was a straight trade-off. *Time* was thinking of doing a Nixon cover, and Nixon, about to leave for a European tour, badly wanted to be on the cover here and in the international edition. He would see Sidey if the cover was guaranteed, not just the American edition but the international edition as well. The bargain was struck.

Sidey accepted his own lack of access but he felt the magazine should have some connection at the top. He thought that perhaps Donovan might be able to establish more rapport. Donovan after all was more senior and as Luce had seen Presidents on a regular basis, perhaps Donovan could now see Nixon on a regular basis. But little came of it. It was not the kind of contact that Nixon sought. A meeting was scheduled and the Nixon office said that it looked very good, and so at Sidey's suggestion Donovan flew down to Washington. He waited with Sidey at the Washington bureau, two blocks from the White House. Time passed. First a half hour, then an hour, then two hours, then more. Still the White House kept saying that it still looked good. Finally they called to cancel. They were very sorry. It was very clear that Hedley Donovan had been stood up. Sidey was appalled but Donovan took it very well. Well, he said, that's Nixon.

"A news magazine with an exclusive story is like a whore with a baby." Roy Alexander, the former managing editor of *Time,* had said it, and there were tales (by no means mythical) of *Time* correspondents with exclusives having to give their stories to their colleagues from *The New York Times* so that they could be legitimized in the *Times* and thus seem newsworthy in the minds of their editors. But journalism had changed and so had *Time;* the Washington bureau of *Time* was filled with talented journalists who could work for any paper in the country and the magazine was now competitive not just with *Newsweek* (which had itself steadily improved the quality of its reportage) but with *The New York Times* and the Washington *Post* and the Los Angeles *Times.* The magazine that Henry Grunwald edited was very different from that of his predecessor, it relied much more on its reporters in the field, and it liked nothing better than an occasional exclusive of its own, sending out press releases on Sunday night so there would be stories (duly credited) in the daily papers on Monday morning.

Thus the magazine was readier for Watergate than it might have been ten years earlier. It was much more a reporter's magazine, and Vietnam had profoundly affected the editors in New York. One question was whether it had the manpower to handle so specialized a story. Most national bureaus in Washington had talented reporters, but precious few of them, and most of them were already overcommitted on their essential beats. But *Time* had Sandy Smith. He was the most unlikely of *Time* reporters. If in the fifties and sixties there was a *Time* magazine stereotype, it was a man who was Ivy League–educated, eastern if not in origin at least in manner, tweedy of dress, filled with a certain amount of social grace, good at lunching (which was a particular news magazine skill, for Luce's people were not just journalists but instant ambassadors of the empire, and it was important for his ambassadors to lunch well, and there was a breed of *Time* magazine foreign correspondent, charming and graceful at social discourse, who spoke not a word of the indigenous language, but lunched brilliantly). It was their job to know the right people, to be liked by the right people, so that when some member of the top brass arrived in their distant outpost there was no one of consequence who could not be produced for lunch.

Sandy Smith was different. He knew no one famous. He never bothered with lunching. He avoided the New York brass like the plague. He was, thought one colleague in the Washington bureau, the only reporter in Washington and New York who actually craved anonymity. He was a big rough-hewn man of fifty-three years who was as different from the *Time* or any other journalistic mold as it was possible to be. He was, thought his former bureau chief Frank McCulloch, probably the single best investigative reporter in the country. He was smart and tough and relentless and totally apolitical. No reporter in America had sources in the FBI and the Justice Department like Sandy Smith's. Whereas most *Time* reporters loved being in the weekly publisher's letter, Smith repeatedly turned down mention. He did not attend bureau meetings. He did not list his home phone on the office bulletin board. He did not see fellow reporters from *Time* or other publications either for lunch or for dinner. He was the absolute lone wolf in his work. He thought the cult of journalists as stars and public figures demeaning. Given the ego drive of most reporters, this alone made him unique. His life was his work and his family, and his work was his sources, and his sources were people vulnerable in their work, vulnerable to publicity. It was the most sensitive kind of relationship that a reporter could have and it required absolute discretion on his part. There was nothing he could learn by being around other reporters; if he was going to hang around, he would hang around with people who might have some information.

Smith was the odd man out in the *Time* system; most of the *Time* field reporters were connected, but connected at the top. He was connected everywhere else. *Time* had very few reporters who had real sources, people hidden away in the heart of the government at the middle and lower levels; rather, *Time* operated off the big story on major events and that required connection to the top people. Like most reporting of its kind, that meant it reflected the essential governmental positions. To Smith high-level sources reflected *policy,* not reality. If you wanted real information you had to have good sources not just at the bottom but secreted away in the upper echelons as well, high enough to know what was going on but not so high that they were voices of policy. By 1970 his sources were remarkable; he had never violated his word to any of them. He had spent years as an investigative reporter in the highly competitive world of Chicago journalism. There he had covered the mob and he had developed uncommonly good sources in the FBI and the Justice Department. By the time he went to work for *Time* in the late sixties (after working for a period on *Life* magazine's investigative unit) many of his sources had moved from Chicago to Washington where they held increasingly influential positions in the government.

Time magazine had never known exactly how to use Smith, and he was on occasion quite restless there. He and McCulloch talked often about the difficulties of developing truly original stories for *Time*. The magazine was getting better than it had been, but it was still uneasy about being first and being alone on a story. "They don't like being on the point," McCulloch liked to say, using a phrase from Vietnam. In the spring of 1972 Smith had spent much of his time working on the Clifford Irving case, a story that caused no end of embarrassment to the executives of Time Inc., since *Life* had bought the rights to the bogus book. On June 15, 1972, Clifford Irving had pleaded guilty in a New York court and Sandy Smith had turned to Frank McCulloch and asked, "Now what the hell do we do?" Within forty-eight hours he read the first story of Watergate.


Because his superiors did not entirely understand him or know what to do with him, Sandy Smith could assign himself to any story that he wanted. The moment he read of the break-in he assigned himself to Watergate. He had that instantaneous suspicion, the old familiar feeling about a big story in the air. He knew nothing of the White House, nothing of Nixon beyond what everyone knew, but he smelled it and he knew that things like this did not happen by themselves. Unlike most reporters reading the stories about clumsy burglars, Sandy Smith thought not of the men who had been caught but of the men who had given them orders. He was absolutely sure that, in some way or another, it went much, much higher in the White House, probably to Nixon himself. After he read the story he immediately flew to Washington and talked to his old friends, and found that the head of the FBI, Patrick Gray, and top officials of the CIA were trying to derail the investigation. That confirmed, as he had suspected, that the impulse for the break-in had come not from the bottom but from the top. Nor was it just medium-level White House people. Only the very top White House people would be able to go to the FBI or the CIA and rein in an investigation. As far as Smith was concerned, the flag was up and the White House was the likely sponsor.

He became, second only to Woodward and Bernstein, the top digging reporter on Watergate, particularly in the early stages. The *Post* men had better sources at the White House, but he had better sources at the FBI and at Justice. They had a daily outlet, he had a weekly outlet. In the past, to a degree that was unusual for the magazine on risky stories, his superiors had shown confidence in him. Now the only question was, would they have the nerve to listen to him and publish him on so uniquely sensitive a story as this? He had a reputation for uncommon accuracy, a reputation that grew as Watergate developed and story after story panned out. Still it was very tricky. One factor working against him was that *The New York Times* was not doing well on the story. The Washington *Post* was pushing the story very hard, but the *Post,* for the editors of *Time* in pre-Watergate days, was not as legitimate an index of the day's news as the *Times.* Consciously and unconsciously his editors took their cues from the *Times.* Still, he had several things going for him.

One was Hugh Sidey. Sidey was absolutely appalled by the break-in. Over the years he wrote a column that was institutionally committed to the presidency, but he was nonetheless a knowing and reasonably detached observer of the men who held the office. More, he was one of the most influential members of the Washington press corps, not just for what he wrote but in the way he was listened to by his colleagues. He was low-key and smart and never precipitous, there was little ideological about him, and his influence had been amplified by the fact that for many years he had worked in tandem with Peter Lisagor of the Chicago *Daily News.* Not very much of what Lisagor wrote was read in Washington either by his colleagues or by public officials, but his personal authority was so immense, he was so smart, funny, and tough of mind, so unconnable, that he was taken very seriously by his peers. It was Lisagor, smart, quick, verbal, who always seemed to be able to define an event in a few words. Other reporters were always quoting Lisagor. Despite working for a dying newspaper he had ultimate peer power. Sidey's influence in Washington was that much greater for his teamwork with Lisagor. Lyndon Johnson had been acutely aware of that, he had called Sidey and Lisagor the stud ducks of the press corps, and he had seen them far more often and far longer than the rest, trying not just to influence *Time* and the Chicago *Daily News* but through them to influence the entire press corps. Johnson would forgive Sidey transgressions in print for which he would not so readily forgive other reporters. Thus Sidey was an important man. He had great influence with his peers in Washington and that influence was reflected in New York; his New York editors knew he was taken seriously by his peers and consequently they took him a little more seriously.

In June 1972 Hugh Sidey decided immediately that Richard Nixon was behind the break-in. He did this not out of ideology but out of an intimate knowledge of how the Nixon White House worked and the way Nixon had handled sensitive political issues in the past. To him Richard Nixon was the ultimate paranoid in American politics, a man who trusted no one and delegated almost nothing of a sensitive nature; Nixon had always tried to control every detail of his own political operations, he was both candidate and campaign manager. Sidey had watched Haldeman and Ehrlichman with dismay

for several years, and if he did not write harshly of them, he nonetheless
considered them frightened and insecure men; to him they were very simply
yes men, there to carry out Richard Nixon's orders, to question nothing and
to report back to Nixon what others were doing. There was nothing about the
Nixon White House that the President himself was not aware of and was not
responsible for, in Sidey's opinion. His friend Lisagor agreed even more
strongly and the two of them talked about it regularly. Very soon after the
break-in the two of them had had lunch with Larry O'Brien, who had his own
sources in Justice and the FBI, and O'Brien's sources had told him that this
ran very deep, and that it would be almost impossible for Richard Nixon to
turn off the processes beginning to work against him. Strengthened by Lisagor,
Sidey became very early on a formidable advocate within the *Time* system for
the argument that Watergate was a serious issue, that Nixon was in some way
or another implicated, that it would not go away, and that *Time*'s proper role
was to cover it.

Sidey's warnings, coupled with the hard facts that Smith was digging up,
had a powerful effect on what the reporters in the field called the Zeppelin
Pilots, the top editorial people who ran the New York office, the Zeppelin
Factory (would they fly or would they not fly?). (At *Newsweek* it was much
the same, the executives there were known as the Flying Wallendas.) The head
Zeppelin Pilot, of course, was Donovan. He steered a steady course and flew
if at all possible, it was said, above storms; Grunwald was said to fly in the
more exotic European style, though it was also said that Grunwald did not
particularly like to take the airship out in turbulent weather. Still, as Watergate
moved along in the early fall, there was a general feeling among the reporters
that the Zeppelin Pilots were behaving better than expected on this story,
although there was still a lot of indecision in New York. Sandy Smith was
doubly careful, when he came up with his exclusives, to make sure that the
New York editors understood them, and he would often call and patiently
explain a story personally. On occasion there would be a quick flash of Smith's
anger when New York seemed cold to a particular story ("Yeah, that story
is filled with lies and distortions, but all the others I filed and they printed were
accurate"). But in general New York was listening more than the field men
might have expected.

Grunwald was second only to Donovan as the most important Zeppelin
Pilot. (In 1978 he would in fact be appointed to succeed Donovan as editor-
in-chief of Time Inc.) *Time* was his magazine. He had to make the crucial
decisions, not just whether he should print Watergate stories but the degree
to which he should open up the magazine for them, thus legitimizing them.
Grunwald, his associates thought, was from the beginning somewhat ambivalent about Watergate; it was not so much that he doubted the accuracy of
the stories, or the White House's culpability, as that he was very much the
European skeptic and he was thus in his political outlook a good deal more
cynical than the normal American innocent. He found it very hard to believe
that Watergate as a process would go as far as it did, and that the Nixon

administration would prove to be as stupid as it finally did. He was in some ways a little wary of moving the magazine too far out ahead on the story; it seemed to him probable that Nixon would at some point quickly settle the matter. If that happened he did not want *Time* magazine to look foolish. Grunwald tended to see the White House as being more in control of events than in fact it was. The shabbiness and clumsiness of the burglary he could believe, the compounding of that stupidity week after week was harder for him to deal with. On July 24, 1974, when the Supreme Court had ruled on the White House tapes, Grunwald sat with Jason McManus, head of the Nation section, as they waited for the White House's response. Hours passed and still the Administration remained silent. Grunwald kept asking McManus, "What are they doing? What are they doing?" McManus answered that the White House was in total disarray, that the Nixon people had no control of events, that they had had no idea the Court would rule against them. Thus they had no contingency plan. "No," said Grunwald, "they've got to have it worked out, they've got to have their answers. They've had plenty of time to get a sense of this." "No," said McManus, "you don't understand, they really are that desperate. They thought it would never come this far, and when it comes this far, they just aren't ready." Grunwald shook his head, it was all very hard for him to believe. Not so much the arrogance of it all as the stupidity. He did not really believe, for example, that Nixon would be so stupid as to tape himself and then turn over the tapes; he assumed that if the tapes had been turned over they constituted in some form or another an ambush for his critics. The press would be out on a limb and Nixon might saw it off. Watergate was terribly alien to his experience; some of his colleagues thought he was more puzzled than offended by it. But he was open. Very early in the story Sandy Smith began to file what were exclusive stories based on his sources at Justice. They were always met by White House denial. In the beginning New York seemed uneasy; but now Smith was able to plead his case to Grunwald and Grunwald thought about it and then went ahead. It was an important bridgehead. It was a new departure for *Time* magazine.

But Grunwald was only a part of the decision making at the top. The other part was Hedley Donovan. On a story of this magnitude, reaching as it did to the center of *Time*'s existence, for *Time* had always loved the presidency and here was a genuine Republican President under attack, it was a corporate decision as well. Here Donovan was crucial. He was not a man of driving relentless curiosity and great creative impulse, but he was a man of overwhelming rectitude. Those who knew both Grunwald and Donovan well thought they brought very different attitudes to Watergate: Grunwald looked at it through a somewhat jaded eye which assumed a certain level of evil and corruption; Donovan, much more the American innocent, looked at government in terms of honor and moral tone and acceptable patterns of behavior. He had been troubled by the entire Nixon presidency.

Like most establishment figures, he had given Nixon reasonably high marks in foreign policy and had been reassured by the presence of Henry Kissinger. But he had been constantly bothered by what he felt were Nixon's defects of character, the isolation he had brought to the office, the instinct to lash out and personalize criticism. In particular he had been bothered by Agnew. Donovan knew that in politics the selection of a Vice-President was based on a number of things, but he felt nonetheless that Agnew was a deeply unworthy man, unfit to succeed the President if that were necessary. Why would a President choose a man like Agnew? Donovan had watched Agnew carefully and had found the Vice-President a narrow and dangerous man with a genuine capacity for bigotry. He did not consider Spiro Agnew as Vice-President an extension of politics as usual. Earlier in 1972 *Life* had run an article calling upon Nixon to choose a different Vice-President for the good of the country. Agnew, a proud and very sensitive man, had been deeply offended by the editorial and had immediately asked to meet with the editors of *Life.* What followed was an extremely unpleasant lunch. Donovan and the others had expected some mild measure of civility so that they could talk and answer questions and the *Life* people would get some additional measure of the man. But they had seriously misjudged Agnew, he had a skin as thin as Nixon's and they had wounded him. He had raged at them from the beginning of the lunch, lecturing them, telling them how improperly they had behaved. Donovan listened and at the end he had said that he was sorry that Agnew felt as strongly as he did, that there was nothing to be ashamed of, *Life* had not said that he was a bad human being, just that he should not be President. That wasn't so bad, why, there were a lot of people in the United States who were perfectly pleasant who should not be President. Hedley Donovan was surprised that Spiro Agnew had taken it so personally.

Thus Donovan was the type of man most distressed by Watergate. He had not paid a great deal of attention in the first two or three months of reporting, but gradually he became more and more involved. Those who knew him and knew the world he moved in, among the top businessmen in America, thought he was affected not just by the bureau's coverage and what he was reading elsewhere, but also by what he was hearing from his friends in the business world about the kind of pressures that Maurice Stans and Herbert Kalmbach had applied during the successful fund raising for CREEP. Little of that had surfaced in the public prints, but in the world of top businessmen there was a back-channel knowledge that it was smutty and dirty and that the smell was very foul.

So, regretting that Nixon had not grown in the presidency, Hedley Donovan gradually became a Watergate fan. By September he was hooked. He brought it up regularly at his weekly managing editors' meeting, and that was an important sign, it showed that he cared and it put everyone else there on alert that they had better care too. He was very deliberate and very cautious.

He did not accept the Nixon story, but he also did not want the magazine to go too far, he wanted to weigh the evidence very carefully. He was not afraid of where the evidence was taking them and, this was crucial, did not think the events out of character for the Nixon administration. Thus he was not persuaded by the denials. In mid-October, for example, *Time* ran an unusually tough and very intelligent essay saying that Watergate simply would not go away and that the Nixon denials simply did not stand up. It was signed by Lance Morrow, a senior New York writer, and by Hugh Sidey, and it was one of the toughest editorial pieces to that date on Watergate.

This was not to say that *Time* totally committed itself. It was always uneasy. It moved forward and backward on the story. The target, after all, was the President of the United States and it was totally out of character for *Time* to go after the President. There were times when the editors seemed to go a little colder, when they thought perhaps Nixon might beat it after all, and thus the magazine might look a little foolish, and they pulled back a bit. Then there would be some new evidence and they would become tougher again. Some of the *Time* reporters were dismayed when in January 1973 the magazine named Nixon and Kissinger as Men of the Year. Not everyone on the magazine was entirely happy, but there it was, the China trip, the Moscow trip, by *Time*'s standards it could be no one else. The writing of the piece seemed to dismiss Watergate or at least minimize it. But then a few weeks later the reporting began to come in very strong and the magazine opened up for it. What was happening was that *Time* magazine, so essential to the political center in America and particularly to the Republican center, was coming down hard on Watergate, giving the story increasing legitimacy and systematically cutting the center away from Nixon.

# 29 / The Washington <u>Post</u>

Bradlee had not taken the CBS team very seriously and he had not been particularly cooperative, but as soon as the two Watergate pieces were aired he realized he had been wrong. CBS had not broken any new ground, but it had changed the public setting of the story. The *Post* was no longer alone, CBS had made the story national. Cronkite, Bradlee thought, half admiringly, half skeptically, the Great White Father, had given his blessing to the Watergate stories and if Walter had given his blessing that made a great deal of difference to all those editors out in the interior of the country, they all felt safer with Walter aboard. Up until then Bradlee had felt that he was very much alone and so was his paper. It was a classic example of how television had the power to amplify print; it was not a television story, for the reporters for the CBS stories were not the CBS staffers, but Carl Bernstein and Bob Woodward. CBS had put the essence of the *Post* stories on the air and given it the power and the force of its twenty-million audience. What surprised Bradlee was the effect that the CBS stories had on regional editors; usually print led the way and television followed, but in this case it was almost the reverse. So many of the editors out there were, for social and cultural reasons, not at ease with the world as described by the Washington *Post* and *The New York Times.* But they were at ease with Walter. Not that Ben Bradlee liked most of those editors anyway, or cared what they thought, he did not really respect them or their papers or the way they went about their business. He considered them second-raters and cowards. He had once walked into a meeting of the American Society of Newspaper Editors with his sidekick Gene Patterson, looking around and feeling very much the outsider, and had said to Patterson, "There aren't but two or three people in this whole goddamn place that I'd hire." Patterson had laughed and told him, "Don't worry, Bradlee, there aren't but two or three who would hire you either."


Katharine Graham was subject to serious attacks of insomnia and Watergate had not made her life easier. It was now almost ten years since she had been thrust into taking charge of the paper, and she had grown steadily in ability. She had become very good at the representational part of it, making speeches, holding lunches. (She had once invited Billy Graham the evangelist to lunch and he had talked about his revivals, and she had asked him, "What is your retention rate?" What? he had answered. "Well, in the magazine business when we try for new subscribers we talk about a retention rate, and I just wondered what yours was," she said.) The men who worked for her were impressed by her, by her intelligence and decency of judgment, but they were also made uneasy by her, she could on occasion be imperious, demanding, and insecure. Some staff members were bothered by the degree to which she could become socially close to powerful figures like McNamara and Henry Kissinger and the degree to which they played her. (One top *Post* editor had once told her that Kissinger was a congenital liar and could not be believed on any subject. "Do you think so?" she asked. "I don't believe that at all. I just can't imagine Henry lying.")

To many of her top people, she could be difficult and uncertain, but she never showed a closed mind. The best thing about Katharine Graham, they thought, besides her intelligence, was her sense of duty and tradition. The paper in the best sense was *of* her, and *of* her family; in moments of crisis, she would envision both its past and its future. She could be petty and almost snobbish, and the most dangerous situation was when she was made to feel clumsy or awkward or alien. Above all, she did not like to be surprised. That was part of the great skill of Bradlee. On very rare occasions he forgot, and then very quickly it could get ugly. Once in 1971, when the *Post* was barred from access to a prison, Bradlee without checking had filed an access lawsuit, and the next day Kay had stormed into his office and screamed at him, "Goddamnit, Ben, I told you no more lawsuits without my permission. No more goddamn lawsuits! You had no business bringing this suit," she shouted. Those in the room—Bradlee, Simons, Bagdikian—had never seen her like that. Which meant that Ben Bradlee worked very hard to keep her informed and never to surprise her, and she in turn granted him not only total trust but more, she felt at ease with him and his instincts; if Bradlee was on a given course, then it was less alien.

She still felt awkward at times in her roles. She knew she was a good publisher, and she knew in a way that she was a better publisher than Phil, certainly enough people had told her that. But it was so much a world of men, and they always seemed so bright. Once at a meeting of the Allied Chemical board, her father's old company, an executive had been showing slides of hundreds of women in a huge factory working at sewing machines. He called them "girls." "Oh, God," she thought, "I'll let it go by." Then he did it again. "These girls are . . ." he said. "Women," she heard her voice say. He did not hear her. "These girls are . . ." he resumed. "If you call them girls, then call the other people boys," she said. Then she went home and collapsed. She had felt some of that indifference at *Newsweek,* not so much with Oz Elliott as with some of the other editors, who condescended to her and who barely tolerated her questions, and tended to make her feel particularly clumsy, listening to her as one might listen half patiently to some intrusive mother-in-law. Once there had been an opening at *Newsweek* for a culture editor and she had cautiously suggested Aline Saarinen, the very talented widow of the great architect. Others explained why Mrs. Saarinen would not do, she could not work the long hours. She had accepted it at the time but it had bothered her, and there would be more turnovers of top personnel at *Newsweek* than at the *Post.* That was what was so good about Bradlee. He treated her not so much as a boss, but more as an equal.

Nonetheless, Watergate was scary. Her decisions might cost her family the paper. There had been so many threats, some spoken, some unspoken. Kissinger had tried to warn her off the story several times. In the world of very powerful people in which she felt at ease, there were very few who believed that the paper was on the right course. Too many people she knew thought that even if the boys were right it was not worth the struggle, it was risking too much for too little. Colson was going around town talking about their national advertisers, about what the Administration would do to her, about hurting her on the big board. A close friend, Andre Meyer, a Wall Street financier with very good sources, told her she was being bugged and being followed and that she should not go anywhere alone. That was not the most reassuring call, and there were other warnings like it. She would often wake in the early hours of the morning in cold terror and wonder what was going to happen. Would there ever be any resolution to this, or would it simply drag on forever? All of this was taking place before Alex Butterfield had let the world know that the words and deeds of Richard Nixon were on tape, recorded by Richard Nixon himself, and so there was very little sense of clarity and certainty about the eventual outcome.

Bradlee, she thought, was very good. As the story mounted he was being very careful, and he was assuring her that the boys were being very careful, and she took some solace in the fact that apparently a lot of their sources were Republicans and high ones at that. Bradlee reassured her that one of the advantages of being so lonely on the story was that the boys were under less competitive pressure than usual and thus had more time to check their sources. But it seemed so endless. Would they really have to face four full years of this kind of struggle, could they survive it? She decided that somehow they could. She had no illusion about how little support the *Post* had among other newspapers; since Watergate began she had been isolated and snubbed by most of her erstwhile colleagues, treated at various professional meetings like a pariah. It was clear that most of them did not like papers like the *Post* and *The New York Times,* and it was also clear that they approved far more of Richard Nixon. But she also knew that there was somehow a certain point beyond which it would be difficult for Nixon to go in punishing the *Post* without antagonizing his own friends in print and broadcasting. If a Nixon administration could so easily punish a liberal newspaper, then the corollary was there, and not too subtle: a liberal administration might in due time punish conservative editors and conservative broadcasters. So she would get finally that kind of peer protection, the protection of self-interest. But it was cold and chilly, and it was going to be messy.

She trusted her reporters and most of all she trusted Bradlee. Still, it was a long dark journey. On occasion she communicated her uneasiness. In early January 1973, just as the trial of the Watergate Seven (the five men arrested at the Watergate, plus Liddy and Hunt) was starting, she asked to meet with Woodward and Bernstein and go over the stories. They lunched and it was reasonably pleasant. Nothing much was happening at the trial, there was a sense that the Nixon cover-up might succeed at this level, and at least in this round. That was hardly comforting news, but expectable. Mrs. Graham asked, almost plaintively, "Is it all going to come out? I mean, are we ever going to know about all of this?" Woodward thought it was a very nice way of asking: what have you boys done to my newspaper? He said that he and Bernstein were not sure that it would ever come out. "Never?" she asked, and she seemed momentarily depressed. "Don't tell me never," she said. During the lunch she passed on bits of information about Kissinger's attempt to protect Haldeman, that Henry—he was, after all, Henry to her—was very upset and thought that the *Post* had been very unfair to Haldeman. Woodward told her that if there was anyone who had not been wronged, it was Haldeman. "Oh," she said, "I'm glad to hear you say that, because I was worried."

So the story went on, with a drive and a momentum of its own, accompanied by a good deal of uneasiness. It was as if the Watergate coverage was separated from the rest of the paper, and the rest of the paper—except for the editorial page, which with Roger Wilkins was very strong—adopted an attitude of nonrecognition toward it. The national staff did not write of the implications of Watergate or the liabilities it brought on. In January 1973, on the occasion of Nixon's second inaugural, the *Post* published a multipage special section on Nixon. It never mentioned Watergate. Woodward, Bernstein, and Sussman were not pleased; Sussman in particular felt that the national staff was looking the other way. In February 1973, when Nixon lost a crucial struggle with the Congress over additional aid to Vietnam, Sussman was convinced that part of the reason was that Nixon was by then a wounded President, and he was angry that the *Post*'s coverage made no mention of it.

Deep Throat had warned that things would be much harder if they took a shot at Haldeman and were seen as having missed, and he was right. Sources were more frightened and editors were more cautious, and the reporters were less sure of themselves, more defensive. After the election and after the Haldeman story, Woodward and Bernstein seemed slower. They were tired, some friends thought they were a little discouraged by the size of the Nixon win, as if in some way it was a repudiation of their stories. December was a slow month and as January 1973 came along the *Post* seemed sluggish. There were no new sure leads. Some people at the *Post* who were involved in the story thought that in this period the paper was being very cautious and feeling the pressure, that it was in no rush to be out alone and push too hard after Nixon. The White House was at its peak of strength, Nixon had just been reelected, his retention of power had cooled off sources and allowed his lieutenants to hold their subordinates in line. They were all working hard to keep the lid on, and for a moment it appeared that they might be able to do it.

In January, as the trial of the Watergate Seven was about to start, Woodward and Bernstein wanted badly to cover it. They asked for the assignment, expecting to get it, and were turned down by Rosenfeld. They were furious. Woodward argued that only the two of them understood the nuances of the case. To turn them down would be a denial by their own paper of their credibility on this story. Rosenfeld, quite correctly, said that on a story like this the paper had to be objective and that if the two of them covered it, no matter how fairly they reported, it would look to outsiders as if they were trying to justify their own coverage. Their reporting, no matter how fair, would be suspect. Woodward argued strenuously that they had earned the right to cover it. A few days later Rosenfeld announced that Larry Meyer, the regular court reporter, would cover it, but that one of them would attend each day with Meyer, looking for Watergate leads in the testimony. They were both angry. They thought it might be a reflection on them and a sign that the *Post* was pulling back from the story. They did some additional legwork and became convinced that the trial was going to be a sham, that the essential White House strategy would be to let the Seven take the rap and that probably there was some quid pro quo in the deal. None of the larger questions would be asked. But it would be made to appear that all the questions *had* been asked and all the answers given. Woodward and Bernstein wrote a story saying as much. Rosenfeld rejected it. We'll see what happens and then report on it, he said. He was wary of having the *Post* anticipate the judicial system. The reporters repeatedly pushed for the story about the unasked questions of Watergate during the trial, and the story was always held up. When it finally ran, it was an important one. For the trial truly was a sham, such a sham that it infuriated the judge, but all the story's verbs were in the past tense. It was not a story about which questions *weren't* being asked, but a story about which questions *hadn't* been asked.

Thus in the early days of the trial Woodward and Bernstein were discouraged. Sussman was probably more optimistic at this point; he had always suspected that a cover-up could not work, that there were too many people involved, that the loyalties were too fragile, that whereas some people with a great deal at stake would be totally loyal, others were only partially involved and partially loyal. Thus inevitably the cover-up would unravel all by itself. There would be too many people going in too many different directions for it to hold together. For the moment it appeared he was wrong. But during the days immediately preceding the trial Bernstein had picked up rumors that Hunt was pressuring the four Cubans to keep quiet, to use the same defense he did. There was a rumor that he had said there would be something in it for them if they did. On the Friday of the last week of the trial, a group of reporters were clustered outside the courthouse when Bernstein saw Henry Rothblatt, the lawyer for the Cubans, standing on a corner trying to hail a taxi. Bernstein turned to Woodward and said that they would lose Rothblatt unless one of them went, and Woodward agreed, and with that Bernstein, with the audacity of the young, rushed toward Rothblatt and the Cubans and, as they were getting in their car, he, quite uninvited, joined them and rode with them to the airport and from there, since they were going to Miami, to Miami as well. He helped one of the Cubans carry luggage onto the plane and it was all very friendly and in the course of it he learned how Hunt had recently visited the four men in Miami and spent a week urging them to change their pleas from not guilty to guilty and promising them that their families would be cared for, and that they could count on executive clemency in a few months if they went to jail. Rothblatt had been furious when he heard of Hunt's attempt at friendly persuasion. Rothblatt had told them to stay away from that son of a bitch Hunt. But it had been too late.

It was a very important story and it had special implications, it meant that the government, which had broken the law in the past, was still breaking the law, and was still trying to keep the lid on. Woodward and Bernstein took the story to Howard Simons. The editors were uneasy about running it. Judge John Sirica, who had already hauled the reporters into court for trespassing on what he considered his domain, might do it again in an attempt to find their source. That might mean that one of them would have to go to jail for obstruction of justice. Simons asked the *Post*'s lawyers for their opinion and got a divided answer. The deadline for that edition of the paper was drawing near. Finally Simons shrewdly decided to run the story with only one of their by-lines, so that if that one went to jail, the other could still operate. Nonetheless, they decided to hold the story for one day, for a little more checking; the shadow of the Haldeman incident was still there. After all, the Watergate story was not really competitive and they still had plenty of time, or so they thought.

They did not. Seymour Hersh of *The New York Times* beat them on the story, that very night. Except that his version was better. Hersh had found out that the Cubans were *still* being paid. That was electrifying, one of the biggest stories of the entire Watergate history. It meant not only that the main story of Watergate was very much alive again but that a secondary and perhaps even more important story, that of cover-up or obstruction of justice, had begun. It also meant that for the first time *The New York Times* was in for keeps, that it was committed. For Hersh was the *Times*'s most distinguished and most ferociously competitive investigative reporter, and he had with this story done something that he had resisted for five or six months. He had signed on to Watergate. And this meant that the pressure against the Administration was much greater, at precisely the moment when the capacity of the White House to prop up its case was becoming weaker. Whatever regrets Woodward and Bernstein had about being scooped were overshadowed by their pleasure in having Hersh and the *Times* aboard.

Hersh made his paper big-time overnight on Watergate. He would never entirely catch up with Woodward and Bernstein, for they were too far out in front, they had locked up some remarkable sources and their work habits were relentless and there were two of them and only one of him, but to the degree that one reporter could push them, Seymour Hersh did. The *Times* had never been particularly strong on investigative reporting in the past, it was in effect part of the snobbery of the paper, as if it fancied itself above the fray, distant from events. Its reporters were not supposed to scurry around in dark alleys looking for corruption and injustice, they were supposed to take it in stride as the gentlemen or gentlewomen they were. The *Times* was Olympian; it represented the final memo on the history of a given day, and the paper preferred not to prod history very much, that was not its role. In the late fifties and sixties the *Times* hired many of the best young reporters in America, serious, intelligent, well educated, but very few of them, whatever their private doubts, openly challenged official versions, and very few of them tried to knock down walls, or work the darker side of the tracks of investigative journalism (investigative journalism meant inevitably that reporters dealt with unsavory characters; only the unsavory, after all, were intimate with and expert on their unsavory fellows). In the fifties and indeed even during most of the sixties the idea of someone like Hersh working for *The New York Times* and doing his type of investigative reporting would have been inconceivable. If he had been hired at all, which was unlikely, he might have been assigned to cover the daily briefing at the State Department and at best he might have lasted a few weeks.

But journalism had changed in the sixties as the society had changed;

some talented reporters, restless with the narrow confines of daily journalism, had left the *Times* at relatively early ages. The *Times* had slowly adapted, the limits of what was respectable and acceptable had widened considerably, the strictness of the past at the *Times,* when a reporter could not leave the city room at night until an editor had formally said good night, and the reporter in turn had said good night, had been discarded. In self-defense, in keeping with a more volatile and iconoclastic era, the paper had begun to hire people whom it would never have hired in another day, including Seymour M. Hersh, who had broken the story of the My Lai massacre, and, lacking any outlet except a fragile radical connection called Dispatch News Service, had tried to sell the story to the *Times.* For that act he had been called, by one highly respectable *Times* editor, a peddler. He was clearly very good but was he respectable? Was he a *Times* type? But in 1972, with some misgivings and with warnings from some former *Times* colleagues that it would never work out, he had joined the *Times* and had been given exceptional freedom, doing a sustained amount of remarkable reporting. He was driven, brilliant to a degree that was almost terrifying, bullying and knowing. Starting with My Lai he was responsible for a series of formidable stories with national implications. He was an illustration of the degree to which the paper was changing, but even so he was a world unto himself; few other reporters would have been given the freedom to write what he wrote or to comport themselves the way he did. He got away with it because he was *sui generis,* there was no one else like him there, and because he always delivered. Still, his work was like a paper within a paper, as if at another time, thirty years earlier, the *Times* had printed on occasion, with great flourish, alongside its regular reporting, I. F. Stone's newsletter.

Hersh had not gotten into Watergate in the beginning because he had been working on a series of stories about General John Lavelle, who had been bombing North Vietnam in November 1971 and March 1972 without any apparent authorization. That was no small story, it was important in itself, a general seemingly disobeying orders, and Hersh suspected from the first that it might lead even higher and that it might, pleasure of pleasures, keeping his fingers crossed, lead to Henry Kissinger. He was very suspicious of Kissinger. Hersh thought he was the prime liar of Washington and the prime manipulator of his colleagues, and nothing would have pleased him more than taking the Lavelle stories right to Kissinger's door. He had suspected for a long time, with a great deal of proof, that Kissinger was very skilled at talking one way at Washington journalistic dinner parties after dark, and acting another way in the high councils of government the next day when the Nixon team was measuring *machismo.* He liked the Lavelle story for a number of reasons: for one thing it was very much his own, a Sy Hersh special, and for another thing he believed that it would lead to a conclusion. In contrast, and this was very important for an investigative reporter wondering whether or not to commit six or seven or eight months to a story, he did not think that Watergate would really come to an end, he thought it would fizzle off in some indeterminate, unsatisfactory way. On one or two occasions his bureau chief, Max Frankel, had suggested that he go on Watergate, but he had no great respect for Frankel, whom he considered the embodiment of the Washington establishment reporter and a prime journalistic friend of Kissinger (Frankel seemed to Hersh always to be telling him to check his stories with Kissinger, which did not, to Hersh, seem the ideal manner of confirmation).

But Frankel did not push Hersh very hard, and Hersh had a feeling that Frankel only called him when Woodward and Bernstein, or "the boys," as he referred to them, broke off a big one and New York told Washington to clean up, they never made a real commitment to the story, never created a desk or made it a priority. He felt no real pressure from either *Times* managing editor Abe Rosenthal or Frankel to get on Watergate, no sense that they wanted to redirect the paper's true energy, which, when committed, was awesome, to get Watergate. It was, Hersh thought, as if the *Post* was so far ahead on the story and the *Times* was being beaten so badly that the *Times* in some unconscious way did not really *want* the story to be true, not because of bias, but because of pride. If it *was* all true, it was not only going to make Richard Nixon look very evil, it was going to make *The New York Times* look very foolish. What was it Bradlee had said in the middle of the crisis, when Woodward and Bernstein had come up with a big one? "Eat your heart out, Abe." He was talking to his real adversary, not the White House, but the managing editor of the *Times.*

Until Hersh came in the *Times* did not do well. It simply did not seem to know how to go about it. Very early, for example, right after the break-in, the *Times* had wanted to get someone into the Howard Johnson motel across the street from the Watergate, the headquarters from which part of the unit had watched the burglary. But the motel was made off limits for reporters by the authorities, and no one in the bureau knew how to get inside. By chance Bill Kovach of the Boston bureau of the *Times* was in town that day and Kovach, who had been a considerable investigative reporter for the Nashville *Tennessean,* went over, registering as an out-of-town salesman, requesting a room high up for medical reasons, then went back to the bureau and gave his colleagues his motel key.

Hersh came into the story in November 1972. He had learned from Bob Loomis, his editor at Random House, that there was a book going around town in which Frank Sturgis, one of the Cubans, told all, in conjunction with a free-lancer with strong Cuban connections named Andrew St. George. Loomis had seen the outline and it sounded like strong stuff, as if the Cubans were ready to tell their side of the story. St. George, who had once been with Castro in the hills, and who had worked for both *Life* and *Look,* had fallen on thinner days as a journalist, and Hersh made a connection with him. Later St. George felt badly used by Hersh, but meanwhile he cooperated, and made a fatal mistake for any reporter: he allowed Hersh to meet Sturgis, his prime source. Sturgis was on the make, St. George was a connection for him, but Hersh with the might and majesty of the *Times* was clearly a better one. Traditionally, reporters do not let their superiors or any of their colleagues meet their best sources for precisely this reason, a source may decide to trade up. Sturgis, having met Hersh, bypassed St. George. Sturgis told Hersh how the funds from the White House had continued after the burglary, and how Hunt had lobbied for the Cubans to perjure themselves.

It was powerful stuff, and Hersh wrote a five-part series based on it. But the *Times* sat on the series, seemed immobilized by it. Where was confirmation? There was no confirmation. But Hersh knew, absolutely *knew,* that Sturgis was telling the essential truth and that he could go on it. It was something a reporter has to know. He was irate over his superiors' indecision: flying back to Washington one day he told a colleague, "If I had to meet the *Times*'s standards I could never have written My Lai. I believed that kid at My Lai and I know these guys are telling me the truth. There's just no formula for sources." The *Times* sat on the story for a few weeks; finally it was scheduled to start on January 7, but St. George, hearing of what was happening, feeling he had been had by Hersh, called Rosenthal and claimed that perhaps his sources weren't reliable and delayed the story another week, when it finally ran on January 14, 1973.

It was a terribly important story. It marked the beginning of the unraveling of the White House defense. It appeared while the case of the Watergate Seven was being tried in Judge Sirica's court and it infuriated Sirica, convincing him even more that he was being confronted by a fraud and made a patsy. It committed the *Times* to the Watergate story as it had not been committed in the past, which meant that the two most powerful papers in the country were now pursuing the story with equal intensity. If Woodward and Bernstein had been on a downer since the election, the entrance of Hersh to the lists was a spur and incentive, the story was hot again. A few weeks later Hersh developed a story based largely on grand jury material and was told by his superiors that the *Times* did not publish that kind of thing. When the *Post* printed essentially the same story the next day, that policy went out the window. The *Times* did not want to be number two any more. The restraints of both papers were being pulled aside; either you trusted your reporters or you were out of the game. The competition was mounting.

It was for Hersh an exhilarating time. It was not really his story, it belonged to the boys, but it seemed to be getting bigger and bigger and there was a sense now that there *might* be a conclusion. Woodward and Bernstein were always ahead; he was amazed at how good they were and how hard they worked, he who had always outworked everyone else, he was in awe of their energy and drive. His recurrent nightmare was of arriving at some lawyer's office and seeing Woodward leaving it. Often that nightmare turned out to be true. Once he was interviewing a lawyer and he asked if Woodward had been there that day and the lawyer assured him that Woodward had not, though of course he was coming by in an hour. So Hersh left a note for Woodward saying *Kilroy was here.* A small victory. There were not many of them. Even when he beat them, he usually found out that they had the story but were not quite ready to break it yet. It was an unusual feeling for Seymour Hersh, the feeling that someone was always just a little ahead of him.

# 30/ The Los Angeles Times

If the Baldwin story had been a victory for the Los Angeles *Times,* it was a short-lived one; 1973 was, despite occasional victories, a frustrating year. Exactly like Sy Hersh of *The New York Times,* Jack Nelson and Ron Ostrow and Bob Jackson had always to face the fact that Woodward and Bernstein were just a little ahead of them. The Los Angeles *Times* reporters would work on a story, and just when they were about to wrap it up, there it would be in the *Post,* with a by-line for the two kids. The *Times* platform was simply weaker than the *Post*'s or *The New York Times*'s or, as the story developed, the news magazines. Nor was Los Angeles at ease with the story. In the Washington bureau there was a sense of constant nervousness and uncertainty about the home office, a sense that Los Angeles was not pushing. This was heightened in late September 1972 when the Washington bureau picked up word of the Segretti campaign sabotage against the Democrats and wanted confirmation of it. They had the story but they could not run it until someone talked to Segretti. Territorial imperative, very important on newspapers, required that Segretti, who lived in Los Angeles, be approached by a Metro reporter. A reporter was assigned, but nothing seemed to happen, there was no push from the Metro desk. Days passed. To Washington it was a big story, Nelson knew that Bob Woodward was on it, which meant that the clock was ticking and ticking fast, and he kept pushing Guthman, but Guthman assured him that he had a good relationship with Mark Murphy, the Metro editor (which was wrong, he had no relationship at all, Murphy spoke of him privately with barely concealed contempt; Murphy had the power, *the juice,* he called it now, not Guthman). Washington thought of sneaking its own reporter into California, anything to get the story. Finally, after about a week, Murphy assigned Ken Reich, a top political writer who was a former national reporter, and Reich camped out by Segretti's door. He finally got him, though by then it was too late, the *Post* already had the story. It was a bitter experience. To the Los Angeles *Times* men in Washington it showed that the paper did not really care much about their very big story.

. . .

There were other good stories, but even the good stories had a price. In March 1973 the Los Angeles *Times* broke a very big story, a story that all the other papers envied, but the price was, in journalistic terms, exorbitant, for it cost the paper John Dean as a source. From the beginning of Watergate, by a fluke of Washington social connections, the *Times* had an odd and unusual link to one of the Watergate criminals. Jim McCord, the ex-CIA man who had been picked up the night of the break-in, had a mentally handicapped daughter, and Bob Jackson, one of the three investigative reporters in the *Times*'s Washington bureau, had a daughter who was deaf. Both the McCords and the Jacksons had been extremely active in a Washington group of parents who lobbied for better educational facilities for exceptional children. McCord had been president of the group, and Mrs. Jackson vice-president. Bob Jackson had liked big Jim McCord, thought him a good man, obviously very religious, a family man, an exceptional listener at these meetings, which were often highly charged and emotional, quite good at hearing everyone out (later, knowing McCord's real profession, Jackson thought him very well equipped to be an eavesdropper) and then summing up in a fair and equitable way, so that everyone went away satisfied and encouraged. The moral, law-abiding, concerned citizen, the very pillar of the community, Jackson had thought. On the first Sunday of Watergate, when Powell Moore, an assistant press officer for CREEP, reached Jackson at the *Times* bureau and read a statement for John Mitchell that mentioned among others the name of security officer James McCord, Jackson did not quite believe it. *Jim McCord, it can't be.*

But it was the same Jim McCord, and it was a connection, and he worked it hard, keeping in touch with McCord, trying to open him up and get information out of him. It was an exceedingly difficult task; McCord was by nature and even more by training an extremely taciturn man. He did not like going public and speaking to reporters, going in effect against the government to people he had always considered the enemies of the government, people who pried. It was deeply alien to him and he felt a powerful conflict of loyalties and instincts. Nevertheless, the pressure to justify his acts, particularly to his children, who were appalled that their law-abiding father was perceived as a criminal, had a powerful effect. It was terribly difficult, even as he edged closer and closer to going public, even with a reporter that he genuinely trusted like Jackson; long hours would be spent in which Jackson would learn nothing, at the end of which McCord would say how lucky he was to have a friend like Jackson whom he could really trust. McCord had been of some help to the Los Angeles *Times* right after the break-in, but the pressures on him from the government not to talk were considerable, and Jackson quickly found himself with an enormously trusting but largely silent source. Nonetheless, he kept in touch with McCord and his family during that period, visiting when he could and when McCord was not in prison. (He was in prison for most of the early period and Jackson did not visit him because that would have cost McCord a family visit.) But Jackson knew that on some level McCord wanted to talk, that he wanted to clear himself, and in January 1973 Jackson received a couple of anonymous notes, clearly from McCord, one saying that Magruder was going to perjure himself, which he did, and another saying that Magruder knew of the Watergate planning but would deny it. Jackson in turn sent back an anonymous note saying that this was too thin, that he could not get into print on the basis of something like this, he needed details. McCord sent back another anonymous note saying he could not give details at that moment.

Then in March 1973 McCord came out of jail, and he began to be, at least for McCord, more and more open. Jackson was using the Jack Nelson approach, simply camping on the doorstep, being there as often as possible and in as friendly a manner as possible. He was pushing hard for a first-person story from McCord like the one Nelson got from Baldwin; he knew that McCord had liked the Baldwin story. Yet getting information out of McCord was like mining gold from a very shallow vein. McCord was the wiretapper who saw wiretaps everywhere and was suspicious of everyone and everything. He trusted no phone; so far as Jim McCord was concerned, they were all bugged. He spoke in the most cautious governmentese. Jackson would ask a question and the answer would come back as if from a government memo. What happened then? Jackson might ask. "The appropriate individual responded," McCord would say. In what way? Jackson would ask. "The appropriate way," McCord would answer. Who? Jackson would ask. "An individual at the White House." Who? "I don't think I can tell you that." He was, Jackson knew, always giving just a little and always holding back a good deal more, as if to protect himself, as if giving all his information out at once was to give out all his chips, to leave him nothing to negotiate with. "Have you told the Watergate committee about it?" "I don't think I can tell you that." Then, on the day of the sentencing, McCord gave his wife a letter with instructions to give it to Jackson if he was hustled off to prison. This was the famous McCord letter of March 25, 1973. Sirica read the letter aloud in court and Jackson lost a precious exclusive.

But they got it back a few days later. Jackson went out to McCord's house again and they spent the afternoon talking about the first-person story, but it was very, very difficult. McCord was trying to help him, there was clearly something on his mind—almost, Jackson thought, on his tongue—but he was very tight and very nervous. Jackson kept saying that McCord could now talk, but McCord was saying that there was still the grand jury to deal with and he still couldn't talk. Jackson spent three quite fruitless hours with McCord and at about five-thirty, feeling very discouraged and frustrated, he got ready to go home, sure that there would be no first-person story. He was putting on his coat and was going out the door when the phone rang. McCord picked it up and Jackson heard his voice say, "Oh . . . is that right? . . . No, I can't comment on that. . . ." Then he hung up. "That was Bob Woodward," he told Jackson. That damned Woodward, Jackson thought, he really is good, isn't he, and Jackson was impressed, for in those days McCord kept changing his phone number every two or three days and there was Woodward on the phone. That alone was impressive.

"Woodward says that Sam Dash just had a press conference and that I furnished two key names," McCord told Jackson.

"Jim, did you?" asked Jackson, feeling suddenly very tense. It was important, he remembered, to ask McCord one question at a time. Small bites.

"Yes."

"Jim, what did you tell him?"

"I told him that Magruder and Dean had knowledge of the pre-Watergate planning and were involved in it." Jackson took off his overcoat.

"In what way, Jim?"

"I didn't tell Dash what way."

"Did he ask?"

"Yes."

"Why not?"

"I wasn't prepared to tell him yet."

"Was there any documentation?"

"Yes."

"An affidavit?"

"Yes."

"Jim," said Jackson, "that's sensational. I wish I had more details."

"I can't tell you any more."

But that of itself was enough. It tied Watergate that much closer to the White House, McCord naming both Magruder and Dean, Nixon's own lawyer. It connected Watergate that much closer to the President himself, it made the Nixon attempt to clean it up that much more of a sham. It was a very damaging story and the White House saw it as such. That night Nixon was in Key Biscayne, and Jackson and Ostrow told their White House man, Bob Toth, to go to Ziegler for the obligatory denial. "We've denied this before and we deny it again," Ziegler said. Later that night Jackson got a strange call from Toth. "Listen, I don't know what all this means and I'm just passing it along for what it's worth. I'm calling you from a restaurant and Ziegler just came up to my table, which means he had to work very hard to find me because I didn't tell anybody where I was going. I mean, he put in a lot of work to find me. And he said, 'We've known each other a long time and been friends a long time, right, Bob?' And I said right. 'And I've always been very straight with you, right?' Right, Ron. 'Okay, I'm being very straight with you now, your boys are doing that story tomorrow about Dean and Magruder, and you have our denial. But I'm saying this now to you as a friend, because we've always been friends, if you print that story, you're flat-ass wrong and we're going to tear your ass apart, we'll leave nothing behind. I'm passing this along as a friend and because I respect you and I don't have to tell you this.' " So Toth, somewhat bewildered, passed along Ziegler's guidance and told them they'd better double-check their sources. And Jackson and Ostrow knew two things: they knew that their source was absolutely sure and straight, Jim McCord himself—it couldn't be better, he wasn't some clerk in a small room passing on something he thought he'd heard, he was an eyewitness, a mover in the game, and so you could put your money on the story; and they knew that the fact that the White House had used Ziegler to call in his connections in so unusual a manner with so personal a denial meant that the White House was scared, very scared.

But the story cost the Los Angeles *Times* John Dean as a future source. Dean was a crucial figure, he, more than anyone else below the rank of Haldeman and Mitchell, knew the interior of the White House and sensed midway through that he was being fitted for a noose by his superiors, they had selected him to be the one to hang in the wind. This was not a role he relished, and so in March and April, after McCord's letter blew it apart, Dean began to switch sides, and he did this with great shrewdness, using the press as his main vehicle, becoming a prime source for both investigators and journalists, drawing the noose closer around the White House and at the same time trying to negotiate the best possible deal for himself and to place himself in the most attractive light possible. John Dean had, among other qualities such as driving ambition and the ability to read the desires of his superiors, total recall, and he now proved to be as clever in understanding the uses of the media as he had been in dealing with superiors in the Nixon administration. He understood immediately which papers had the most leverage and which magazines might portray him in the most favorable light and how best to dole out his information. He was furious with the Los Angeles *Times,* he thought the *Times* had libeled him and made it look as if he were a partner to the planning, and he held this against the *Times,* though had the circumstances been different, had the *Times* been a platform he wanted, he would surely have made his peace.

# 31 / Time Incorporated

The day after the McCord letter Carl Bernstein went on his rounds, checking Watergate leads. Part of his tour that day took him through the courthouse. Everywhere he went there were packs of reporters waiting and television crews staked out. It was a surprise; up to that point he and Woodward had worked Watergate more alone than not, far from the journalistic pack. Whatever competition there was, was quiet. He had rarely seen other reporters. Now they were everywhere. Everyone wanted a slice of the story. Bernstein suddenly felt very good. The crowd of other newspapermen were watching him, watching what he was doing, surreptitiously trying to figure out who he was seeing. That was a confirmation itself of what he and Woodward had been doing all along.

Woodward too felt the change in the attitude of his colleagues. Clearly the McCord letter had vindicated them. There was no doubt that his and Bernstein's stories had played a key role in Judge John Sirica's attitude. They were so much different from what he was getting from the Nixon people. Sirica was sure that he was being mocked and toyed with. So he kept reading and kept following the case. He never said anything to the two reporters at the time. But long after Watergate was over, John Sirica called Bob Woodward into his chambers and introduced him to his daughter. Woodward was touched; Sirica showed unusual kindness and warmth in his gesture. It was almost as if, Woodward felt, Sirica was saying that we were in this together, we were all part of something that worked.


After the McCord letter it all began to break and break quickly at *Time*. The White House front was coming apart and the magazine seemed wide open. Cover story followed cover story as Watergate became increasingly readable and, to the surprise of *Time*'s editors, salable. Suddenly all the big editors were hungering for more Watergate, encouraged as they were by hungry readers. Watergate by May 1973 had become the great national detective thriller. Ben Bradlee in Washington was perhaps the first to recognize it. His close friends would start calling him in the early evening trying to find out what story he had for the next day. It was like a stimulant to them, Bradlee thought, they were calling in for their Watergate fix. In New York the editors of *Time* were also among the first to realize how important Watergate was becoming, how deep into the veins of the society it had reached, for the editors of *Time*, unlike the editors of local newspapers, have a ready national index, the newsstand sale of a given issue. Nixon covers had never, to the regret of the editors, sold very well. Now, for the first time, Richard Nixon was becoming a salable commodity. Just a few months earlier, when he had been named with Kissinger as Man of the Year, the sales were very disappointing. The average *Time* cover in 1972 sold about 245,000 copies on the newsstand and the Man-of-the-Year covers traditionally sold a good many more than that. Richard Nixon, in that moment of triumph, sold 214,000. A few months later, as Watergate hung heavily over him and *Time* produced an endless series of Watergate covers, the issues sold remarkably well, 280,000, then 290,000, then 300,000. Only in his disgrace was Richard Nixon a hot commodity; only in his decline did readers want to know more about him.

The whole magazine seemed to pull together. The Washington bureau spoke well of the New York writers, who were careful and courteous and deferential with the raw files. The New York editors were proud of Washington. When a Sandy Smith file was about to come in there was a genuine excitement in the New York office. Smith liked to file as close to deadline as possible, largely, it was said, to avoid nit-picking and lawyers. New York admired Smith, he was so smart, so low-key, so unflappable, and there was so much laughter as he explained a file to the doubters. A Sandy Smith file had few anecdotes and very little color. It was much shorter than the files of almost everyone else. All he had was facts, usually facts that no one else had.

There was a dynamic to it. Once McCord began to talk, the White House defense began to crumble. It was like a ship on which the rivets of loyalty were more fragile than they seemed and now as the ship began to sink everyone was running for the lifeboats, stopping only long enough to betray his best friends. At the center of it was John Dean, and John Dean was about to become a press industry. He had been right at the center of the cover-up, and if he did not know the details of the original break-in he was a certifiable authority on how the White House had tried to cover it up ever since. He was smart and cold and very much on the make. Different White Houses had been filled in recent years with the John Deans of the world, selected because they were so hungry, would work such hard hours, and had no real value system or constituencies of their own; instead of values they had what were more useful to superiors —burning ambitions and flexible ethics. Dean was one of the brightest of the young men around Nixon; he even reminded some old-timers there of a young Richard Nixon; he was so eager, so clearly determined to get ahead. The big men of the White House, Haldeman and Ehrlichman, had drafted him to do the dirty work on Watergate and involuntarily he had become privy to the seamy side of the White House. He was so low in rank and the President was so awesomely powerful—a god to pawns like Dean—that it never occurred to them that Dean would not take the fall for Nixon. That had not occurred to Dean either, particularly in the good days, but they had not reckoned with two remarkable qualities that were to surface in him—a highly refined sense of exactly how to survive and a remarkable memory.

Dean quickly became aware that he was being fitted to take the fall, and that helped him see things more clearly than before. And among the things he now managed to see was that the President, because of Watergate, was no longer an all-powerful figure; instead, he was an erratic and clumsy man whose power was diminishing daily before Dean's eyes. The more Richard Nixon spent his time reminiscing about what was clearly the high point of his career, the Hiss case, the more terrified Dean became. To Nixon, the Hiss case was a triumph of the lonely congressman-prosecutor against all odds, including the President of the United States; to Dean, Watergate could become an ironic repeat of the Hiss case, the triumph of lowly government agencies against the President of the United States. He was surprised that Nixon failed to see any irony in it. And he found himself less and less anxious to take the fall for the White House and for this strange, awkward, distant man. There were simply too many good things that John Dean wanted to do; even as Watergate had begun he had been taking Berlitz lessons in hopes of becoming ambassador to some small French-speaking nation. John Dean wanted to be an ambassador, not a felon.

So it was that in early 1973 he began cooperating with the prosecutors and, because he and his lawyers did not trust the prosecutors, with the press as well. One of his lawyers, Bob McCandless, was quite sophisticated about the nature of the Washington press corps and Dean quickly learned from him. McCandless and Dean did not at that moment entirely trust the prosecutors, and they saw in the press a means of keeping the processes open and moving. They dealt with the press with speed and skill, doling out a little bit of information here and a little there, never giving too much, because if Dean gave too much, a paper or a magazine might not need him any more and they then might become tougher in what they said about him; he had learned that as the papers and magazines needed him, they became friendlier. He was clearly using the press corps in his struggle for immunity. Everyone wanted a slice of John Dean and there were turning out to be quite a few slices indeed and he was rationing himself with great skill. He was very good with the Washington *Post.* He cut out *The New York Times* for quite a while because the *Times* seemed to him to be reflecting the Chuck Colson anti-Dean line. Finally there was a breakfast between Scotty Reston and Bob McCandless. Reston wanted to know how the *Times* could get back in on the John Dean industry and it was decided that if the *Times* did not actually call for immunity for Dean, it would nonetheless say that people should start listening to him. Shortly after that, Seymour Hersh was assigned Dean by the *Times,* and soon after that, the *Times*'s coverage was right up there with that of the *Post.*

Time magazine had more difficulty at first. In the beginning, right after the McCord letter, it simply could not reach John Dean. That was puzzling, and the people in New York could not understand it. *Newsweek* had made an early Dean connection and *Newsweek* had beaten *Time* badly on some Dean-related stories. Advised by McCandless, Dean learned early on that news magazines were very good outlets for him, they had the space, and the form required a narrative story, and because they did not appear daily, they needed the little human touches the daily papers had no time for. The news magazines humanized and dramatized stories. What was it Ben Bradlee, then at *Newsweek,* had once said of his friendship with Jack Kennedy? That it was great access because it gave the personal touch that his magazine liked, the fact that the candidate had chalked his fingernails to make them stand out better.

The early *Newsweek* connection had been a problem for *Time,* and there had been a major *Newsweek* story based on material from Dean that was different from other stories. It not only recounted what Dean knew, but said that Dean would accuse the President of being a part of the cover-up. That was a very big story. Woodward and Bernstein had a strong Dean connection; McCandless had gone quickly with the *Post,* and Bernstein had been trying to get the story, the Dean-will-accuse story, in for some two weeks and it had been taken out by his editors, who were feeling both confident and cautious. The story was coming their way and they saw no need to rush it. Bernstein was irritated by those decisions. Then, while he was out in Omaha speaking at a convention of journalists, he picked up *Newsweek* and saw the story there and he cursed angrily and bitterly. His anger was nothing to that of Henry Grunwald in New York. "I don't want to have to quote *Newsweek* on this," he kept telling the *Time* bureau.

Hays Gorey had been covering that part of Watergate for *Time* and he was assigned to make the Dean connection. Gorey was a very sound and personable man, one of whose great strengths was his ability to convey to sources that he was as much interested in their welfare as he was in his story. The only conduit to Dean in those days was McCandless. McCandless had read *Time* and *Life* as a boy in Oklahoma, where memories of the Depression were very strong, and he had powerful memories of Harry Luce's magazines, with Tom Dewey always on the cover telling him and his folks what was good for the country. He had grown up a working Democratic lawyer and he believed that *Time* magazine was a key part of the Republican political machinery. So when a Mr. Gorey of *Time* magazine, along with hundreds of other reporters, kept calling him, McCandless did not return the calls. Finally, unable to reach McCandless any other way, Gorey went out to McCandless's apartment house. There he tipped the doorman to make it seem he was delivering a package. Presumably McCandless would come down to pick up the package and Gorey would intercept him. Instead, Mrs. McCandless descended.

Eventually he succeeded in tying down McCandless for lunch. "Why are you killing us?" Gorey asked. "Because you're so Republican you'll murder us on this story," McCandless answered. "Things have changed," Gorey said. The two made their peace and, true to Gorey's good fortune, *Newsweek* had blown a Dean story that week; New York had exaggerated it over Washington's objections. So McCandless decided to give Gorey a chance, based on Gorey's pledge that he would guarantee control in New York over anything he wrote, a pledge he could not have uttered five years earlier. McCandless sent Gorey to see John and Maureen Dean, suggesting that he bring Mo flowers and John wine, and armed with these trinkets and the power of the Time-Life empire, he soon found himself very tight with John Dean, so tight that not only did *Time* start beating *Newsweek* (which was now being punished for its sins) but he eventually ended up ghost-writing Maureen Dean's book. Such is charm.

But if Gorey was very good with Dean, then Dean in turn was very good with Gorey. He doled out his material very carefully, never giving too much, for he did not want them to tire of him, he wanted them to stay hooked. More, he did it at two levels: material they could use in the magazine, and material even more titillating, wonderful tidbits of things to come that they could know of and talk about among themselves but not use. Dean had tried to bargain for immunity with Gorey, and Gorey had immediately arranged a lunch with Grunwald. There Dean made his pitch, and there was no doubt that *Time* would be the beneficiary of excellent stories if it played the game. Grunwald, to his credit, said that *Time* could not do that, they could not swap their pages for a recommendation of immunity, but that *Time* would treat Dean fairly and honestly and with courtesy. Grunwald made a good impression on McCandless, not just directly with Dean, but in a more subtle way; for Grunwald had clearly paid attention to Gorey at the lunch and made clear that he would honor Gorey's relationships. That helped Gorey immensely in McCandless's eyes.

It came faster and faster. In New York, Hedley Donovan was fascinated. He and Grunwald were early convinced of one crucial fact: the need for Nixon to go. In the fall of 1973 the Agnew scandal broke and Agnew subsequently resigned. Shortly after that, *Time* called for Nixon's resignation. That was very much Donovan's hand. He did not feel that he could call for Nixon's resignation as long as Agnew might become President. From time to time Donovan met with the members of the Washington bureau and he kept congratulating them on their files. It was clear that he himself was reading raw files, not waiting to see what appeared in the magazine.


In December 1973 the top executives of *Time* flew down to Washington for an exploratory dinner with Judge Sirica. The reason, as they had earlier explained to the judge, was that they were thinking of making him Man of the Year. Hays Gorey, who had covered Sirica for the magazine, had warned his superiors that Sirica on occasion sounded like a bit of a hack, until you realized that he really believed the platitudinous things he was saying; that he was a very sincere man and a tough one as well, very much the immigrant's son who took his role seriously and simply could not be pushed around. Gorey's warning was effective. The world of John Sirica was light-years away from the world of most of the top editors of *Time,* but as the evening wore on it became quite pleasant and warm and the editors grew increasingly impressed with Sirica. To them, Sirica, with his very lack of grace, was proof not just of the judicial system working, but of America working. They warned him that Man of the Year was a chancy thing, but at the end of the evening he turned to them and said that he didn't want to presume, but did they think it was all right if he told his wife he was being considered for that honor? With that comment he won their hearts. A month later he became Man of the Year. Whereas Richard Nixon the year before had sold 214,000 newsstand copies, Judge John Sirica sold 291,000.


Then in February 1974 it began to slow down. The information in 1973 had moved faster than the processes, the information flow had been so immense that the expectancy it created for immediate action was tremendous. Now the legal and political processes were working, but they were working more slowly, in older rhythms, and there was in the world of the media a sense of disappointment. Nixon seemed to be holding together while the case was in the hands of the Special Prosecutor. Perhaps, some of the top editors thought, Nixon might make it, and if he did it was going to be embarrassing to most of journalism's major figures. Like it or not, they were not just covering him now, the very nature of the story had made them adversarial. No matter what the validity of the stories they had run, no matter how damaging the evidence, if Richard Nixon was able to remain in office they might in some court of public opinion be judged wrong and he judged innocent, however guilty he might really be.

It was at this point, in late February 1974, a time of some uncertainty, that *Time*'s top editors and writers from New York had a quiet dinner in Washington with Leon Jaworski. The bureau liked arranging such gatherings because they kept New York both informed and involved. Hays Gorey had set it up. It came at a crucial time for the Special Prosecutor's office. The staff there had just received the tapes and was bitterly divided over whether to indict Nixon or simply to name him as an unindicted co-conspirator. Jaworski had thought a lot about the *Time* meeting; it was clearly very important to him. He was a bantam rooster of a man, a second-generation American, both vain and clever. He liked being with important people. When he first came to Washington, Meg Greenfield and Phil Geyelin, the two editorial-page editors of the *Post*, had written kindly about him and helped ease the general suspicion against him. Then Tony Lewis of *The New York Times* had proved helpful. Now he wanted a comparable connection with *Time*. He wanted the sympathy and the guidance of the top people there, for he was about to walk a very tight rope indeed.

Jaworski had usually been careful and restrained with the press, but that night, needing help and needing allies, he deliberately decided to stretch his discretion to its absolute limits. The dinner seemed to be progressing pleasantly enough when Jaworski turned and asked the editors a question. "Let's suppose, hypothetically, just hypothetically," he said, "that we have come across evidence that the President of the United States had committed an impeachable offense. What do you think the President will do?" Someone asked what an impeachable offense was, but Jaworski neatly sidestepped the question and simply posed his own question again, "What would the President do?" Implicit in his question was that there were facts to show Nixon had indeed committed such an offense. Ed Magnuson, the chief *Time* writer, who was writing all the *Time* cover stories and had in fact established a modern record for *Time* cover stories (on his fiftieth one they had given him the cover painting for his office; it was, of course, a Watergate cover of Richard Nixon, "The Push to Impeach"), had answered, "He will resign." A couple of people started laughing. Jaworski stopped them. "Well, let's not laugh at that, let's just think about that for a moment." Then he placed himself in Nixon's position: what was the easiest, most honorable, and least humiliating thing to do if there was hard evidence of crimes in the hands of the prosecutor? (Later the *Time* editors realized that Jaworski was referring to the June 21 tape, the bribery tape.) "Suppose," Jaworski continued, "the President knows we have this tape which is so damaging, knows we have this information. Wouldn't he think this is a good time to get out and give a self-sacrificing speech and say he was doing it as a magnanimous gesture?" It was clear that Jaworski was trying to decide what to do himself; he clearly did not want to name the President of the United States as a conspirator. No one in the room was laughing any more. Jason McManus, who was editing the Nation section, took out a pencil and scribbled a note and passed it to Magnuson. "We've got him," the note said. Jim Doyle, who was Jaworski's press secretary, was amazed by his own man's indiscretion. Even as he was marveling at Jaworski's performance and dreading the consequences, David Beckwith, a young *Time* reporter sitting next to him, leaned over and said enthusiastically, "This is the best dinner we've ever had!" I believe that, Doyle thought, I believe that.

It was Jaworski trying to keep *Time* informed, trying to get their sense of what he should do, and of course trying to get on the cover of *Time,* which meant a great deal to him. (He did, some two weeks later, a cherished moment, a cover that sold 325,000 copies on the newsstand.) He did it very deliberately. He was trying to keep potential allies lined up, he did not want them falling away. Later, after the meeting, Magnuson wrote Jaworski a letter asking why he had been so outspoken and Jaworski answered that he believed in being candid; that unless they knew which way the process was going, they could easily be misled. The effect of this on the Zeppelin Pilots in New York was electrifying. They were more excited now than their reporters, and more confident; it was as if the tension and uncertainty that had hung over New York for the last few weeks had broken. They knew now that it was only a matter of time.

# 32/CBS

The reporters covering the President had been frustrated in 1972 by his unwillingness to come out and campaign, and by his expert ability to use them, to make them part of the campaign, be it in China or the Soviet Union, but rarely on the hustings. (At one point Rather signed off a commentary as "Dan Rather with the Nixon campaign at the White House.") But by late 1973 the situation was reversed. Watergate was in the public domain and it would not go away.

Sam Ervin of North Carolina, a curiously old-fashioned man who was also something of a country slicker, had not particularly wanted to head the Senate Select Committee. His time in the Senate was getting short, he did not intend to stand for reelection, and he had several other issues that he wanted to pursue with his subcommittees in the limited time in Washington left to him. But Mike Mansfield, a mild-mannered man, had been deeply bothered by what he had been reading on Watergate, and in the fall of 1972 when he had been campaigning he had promised, almost casually, that he intended to look into Watergate when he returned to Washington. Normally the task might have gone to Jim Eastland of Mississippi, the head of the Judiciary Committee, but Mansfield and Eastland both knew that Eastland was, for a variety of political reasons, too close to the White House and any investigation of his would seem a farce. Ervin, by contrast, was ideal for the job, he was the Senate's leading constitutional expert, unlike some of the young bloods in the Senate he was not a man running for the presidency, he was a very conservative man, his essential political constituency was not unlike that of Richard Nixon, and he was allied with the President on any number of issues, be it race or Vietnam. (As his fame increased during Watergate, civil-liberties groups came to admire him and seek him out as a speaker. He would then mention Vietnam in his speech: "I'm a howk," he would say, and the chill in the room was immediate.) He was the man Mansfield wanted. A subcommittee headed by Ted Kennedy had turned up some serious allegations on Watergate in 1972 but Mansfield thought the entire subject so grave that it must not be a partisan show, there must be no Kennedy on it. Indeed, as he put together the Democratic side of the committee he took care to add none of the Senate's rising young media stars. If there were rising young stars on the committee, they would be the young Republicans, Howard Baker and Lowell Weicker. Mike Mansfield intended to be scrupulous about this proceeding. If there was nothing there, that was one thing, but if it was, as he suspected, and almost feared, a serious matter, then the Democratic side of the committee must be above reproach.

The Senate Select Committee came into being on February 7, 1973, by a 77–0 vote of the Senate. At the time Watergate was not yet a story that the networks had picked up on. Ervin was still dubious about the whole thing. In early February he talked informally with Bob Woodward of the *Post*, and Woodward had found him very pessimistic about the forthcoming proceedings. The White House wall was still made of stone, there had been no real crack in it, and Ervin saw little real hope of penetrating the cover-up. Ervin told Woodward he thought they would be lucky if in getting people to talk they reached as high as Jeb Magruder. One of the first questions he had to confront was that of television. Sam Ervin did not particularly like television, and he was not, by normal standards, a media figure; no advertising company in North Carolina had ever made very much money doing fancy televised clips for an Ervin reelection campaign. His press secretary's main job seemed not so much to get him on television shows as to keep him *off* them. He did not like the entrance of television into politics, he considered it an intrusion, all those lights, all that equipment. But he and Mansfield had talked about television from the start and they had agreed that since Ervin was investigating a cover-up the hearings must by demand be as open as possible. That meant television, if television was willing to come. At his early meetings with his committee Sam Ervin had raised that point, and there had been unanimous agreement that they must be open. But, everyone agreed, they must not become a circus. No one was sure how much of the proceedings the networks would really want to cover, whether they would go live, whether they would only come for the big stars. No one had any idea of how important the hearings were to become. Most committee members thought it was going to be rather limited in scope.

The networks, in the preliminary talks, were very interested. Not just polite, but very interested. They seemed ready to cover the hearings, but their representatives kept saying cautiously that there was no guarantee on how long they would go with these things. That was always in higher hands. In early March, as the Select Committee was still preparing its case, trying to put together its own procedures, studying witnesses, a lawyer named Bernard Fensterwald came by to see the committee with his client, James McCord. There was some talk that McCord had a very strong letter with him and that there would be important developments. Fensterwald said he had a copy of the letter, which he had given to Rufus Edmiston, Ervin's top assistant. Edmiston could not find it. Suddenly everyone in the room was stripping off jackets and searching pockets, looking for the letter. It was found in Fensterwald's jacket. Ervin read it aloud. He looked at Edmiston and they realized that it was all going to come apart. The effect upon the Select Committee was electric. Suddenly, overnight, there were journalists everywhere, and the demand for seats at the proceedings was unparalleled in Senate hearings. Watergate in the days following the McCord letter became an awesome story; the White House was beginning to collapse, the stone wall had been breached. By the time the hearings began on May 17, it was the biggest story in the country; there was no way the networks could do anything but cover it live, gavel to gavel. Those regular watchers of soap operas who had at first complained because their favorite programs were being crowded off soon became hooked. The ratings were very good.


Friends had told Sam Ervin that television seemed to magnify his warts, that it made him look heavier and made his eyebrows look too large. He feared that some people watching him made fun of his accent and manner. He often grumbled about television lighting. As the hearings approached, someone who knew a lot about television told him to wear a light suit because it was cooler in the heat of the lights. Someone else who knew a lot about television told him to wear a dark suit because it set him off against the background and made him look better.

At first he was awkward and stilted. He received thousands of letters from viewers telling him to leave his eyebrows alone and to stop blinking his eyes. Others, hundreds of others, wrote to ask why his hands were so gnarled. His staff answered that he had arthritis. Slowly, gradually, Ervin became comfortable. He began to realize from the mail that he was reaching not merely the cameramen or the television reporters, whom he had long distrusted, but the very people he had always talked to. Soon he was enjoying it, quoting the Bible, quoting Shakespeare.

Ervin became the perfect counterpart to the Nixon White House. He was so artfully unartful, so clearly a man from an era now past, that he gained an extra legitimacy. He was not sleek and pretty. He was what he was, that which he had always been. Television was incidental. Television had found him, he had not found television. The contrast between him and the Nixon White House was striking, these men who knew all the tricks and scheduling techniques of television and lived by it. They had always been skilled at showing television what they wanted it to see—skilled speeches, or two-minute segments of film, or carefully orchestrated visits to foreign countries. Now for the first time people were seeing the other side of the modern imperial presidency, the arrogance of power that had become a part of it, the lack of accountability. Haldeman and Ehrlichman had been good at directing the television eye where they wanted it to go, they themselves had never deigned to go before it and answer questions. Now they had to go before the camera and it was a terrible mismatch, Ervin so human and skilled in the art of persuasion, Haldeman and Ehrlichman so hard and evasive. When it was all over, the balance had changed, Watergate was national, the White House in the truest sense had lost control and lost the center.

The polls reflected it very accurately. Right before the Ervin committee hearings 69 percent of the American people approved of Nixon's presidency; by July that figure was down to 40 percent. A Harris poll in May had shown the country against Nixon's resignation by a margin of 77 to 13; by mid-June 67 percent of the American people thought Nixon was involved in Watergate. Haldeman and Nixon had always seen television as a PR tool and were confident because they controlled it. They knew, as Ehrlichman put it, what played in Peoria. Now the hearings were over, and Sam Ervin had played better in Peoria than Bob Haldeman and John Ehrlichman.


By October of 1973 the net was closing all too tight, and Richard Nixon did what no other citizen under the shadow of a crime in this country could do, he fired the Special Prosecutor pursuing him, and thereby guaranteed the resignation of an Attorney General. If it cost him credibility with millions of people, it bought him time, and time was becoming more important than credibility. But even then Watergate did not go away. He had underestimated how deeply it had penetrated into the political bloodstream. What Nixon was saying could now be checked against a vast and growing public record, by an increasingly knowledgeable and aware public. Truth was not as it had been for five years, merely anything that the President said; truth was instead a record, an accounting. Firing a Special Prosecutor would not make Watergate go away, public pressure now demanded that a new Special Prosecutor be hired.

But the President was still different; other men seriously involved in criminal charges could not fire their prosecutor, or deal privately with the Justice Department; and no other citizen closely linked to a crime could get very much of his side of things into a newspaper, let alone usurp prime television. The President could. And so now, backed into a corner, his popularity dwindling, time and time again Richard Nixon took prime television time, not in the national interest, not to clarify public policy, but to defend himself by implying that he was still popular. To go on as he wanted: rarely in press conferences, where the number of crucial unanswered questions was growing, but more often in special presidential appearances, with Brezhnev in California, in the Middle East with assorted leaders. The role of Dan Rather and other White House correspondents thus became more and more important; they were the link between the growing number of questions posed by Watergate and the one man who might answer them but who did not have to go before the Ervin committee, Richard Nixon. For though Nixon could get television time whenever he wanted it, none of his political opponents could, and this left Rather in an extraordinary position. In America's new world of televised politics, he was the proxy opposition.

So if Watergate would not go away, neither would Dan Rather. In the spring of 1974, as Richard Nixon was trying to save himself from drowning, the need for a way of fending off Watergate, for the right forum where he could be unveiled as safely as possible, where he could seem to be popular and yet be under minimum pressure, was ever more desperate. The White House was in straits: the evidence against it was mounting, the number of ways of relaxing the pressure was diminishing. Nixon could fire a Cox but he could not fire a Jaworski after a Cox. By April it was clearly no longer a judicial matter, it was a political matter, impeachment proceedings were looming larger, and the President needed to hold the conservative wing of the Congress against impeachment. Consequently, he badly needed to hold as much of public opinion as he could, particularly in the South. So each appearance became more and more important—the right place, the right setting, the right audience. Earlier in the year Nixon had stumbled onto a suitable formula when he went before a meeting of the Associated Press Managing Editors Association in Florida. It had been reasonably successful political theater, that is, the impression of a press conference without the full reality of it; the managing editors were by and large older, more respectful of authority, and less precisely informed than their reporters, and the appearance had been judged by the White House as something of a success, exhibiting the kind of mock candor that was so vital to the President's case.

Now the White House came up with another theater for Nixon, the meeting of the National Association of Broadcasters in Houston, in March 1974. It had all the necessary ingredients. It was in the South, perfect for their purposes since the South was the citadel of conservatism and it would be easier to get enthusiastic crowd response there than elsewhere, a chance to get scenes of the President being cheered for the evening news shows. The setting was even better because in the public's mind "broadcasters" were authentic Nixon antagonists, were men like Cronkite or Rather or Schorr or Carl Stern or Fred Graham, enemies of Richard Nixon, men who had covered all of Watergate and caused all these problems. In truth, however, this convention was far from being a lion's den for Richard Nixon. These were different broadcasters, pussycats, affiliate owners, ill informed; more often than not anti-press, wedded to profit, possessing a chamber of commerce mentality, and likely to be extremely reverential to the President. Perfectly designed to play the game the President expected of them.

Rather and his superior, Bill Small, the head of the CBS Washington bureau, were wary of the Houston meeting from the start. They saw it immediately as a potential ambush for them. It was, in Rather's opinion, a brilliantly conceived setup for using reporters as Nixon wanted them used, and Rather did not want to be a bit player for Haldeman and Nixon. So he decided not to ask a question this time. His doubts were reinforced when he arrived at the auditorium and found that the Nixon people had rigged the crowd even more carefully than usual—they were, after all, fighting for their lives—and the rigging was worthy of Mayor Daley; they had given press credentials to young Republicans and conservatives from the University of Houston. So Rather found it easy to stick to his decision not to ask a question—until midway through the evening he heard Richard Nixon, the thirty-seventh President of the United States, say that he had fully cooperated with the Special Prosecutor, Leon Jaworski.

It was a direct contradiction of the record, what used to be called in a simpler age a bald-faced lie, and it was at the heart of the struggle then going on between the White House and the forces now massing against it, the constant delaying actions (trying to tire the country and thus make it turn away from Watergate), the refusal to turn over tapes, the making of promises by Nixon, the subsequent hedging on them. And here was the President of the United States deviating, so to speak, from the truth, with no Special Prosecutor to call him on it, no Senate leader to come on and clear the record, the President going completely unchallenged into perhaps 60 million homes. Rather waited a few minutes, hoping that someone else would ask Nixon about this very basic contradiction, but no one did, the affiliate owners either did not know the record or, if they did, preferred not to embarrass the President. Asking a question implying that the President of the United States was a liar was sure to be embarrassing, if not to the President then at least to the questioner, and they did not want to return to the country-club bars in their hometowns to be looked upon as men who had been uppity with the President. So, reluctantly, Rather rose, and as he did, and as he tried to identify himself, he seemed to hear an enormous amount of booing (a subsequent examination of the tape reveals that there might have been cheering as well). Booing or cheering, or perhaps the noise of rising crowd expectation, the arrival of the moment of truth, here was the confrontation that everyone wanted, the last inning of a close baseball game, the last two minutes of a football game, the ultimate confrontation between bull and bullfighter. What everyone had come to see and hear. To Rather, however, it was the sound of boos and he tried three times to pierce it: "Mister President . . . Mister President . . . Mister President . . ." In New York, watching the press conference, Dick Salant, the head of CBS News, became apprehensive; it was all getting out of hand and he was worried about Rather, he knew that his correspondent had been under a special kind of pressure for a long time. In Houston, Richard Nixon, hearing the noise, warmed to it—"Are you running for something?" he asked. And Rather made, in his prolonged confrontation with the President, his first major tactical mistake. He had decided long ago not to take anything from Nixon or any member of the White House staff, he believed they were all bullies, that they always wanted to break your stride, to throw you off and put you on the defensive. The moment it happened, the moment they pressured him, he decided, he had to stand his ground.

And so he answered the President—"No, sir, Mister President, are you?" It was a mistake, and he knew it almost as soon as the words were out of his mouth, he had finally walked into the ambush they had set. The question he had asked was soon forgotten, the fact that it was a response to a clear presidential lie; it was the act of confrontation that people remembered, that he had left his proper role and had, so it seemed to many people, abused the President, been flip and rude. In New York, Salant felt slightly sick. The President had provoked him and he had gone for it. A serious mistake, Rather had with great discipline resisted provocations like this in the past, but this time he had been trapped into becoming part of the story. Rather sensed it himself. The next day he saw Pat Buchanan, the President's conservative speech writer, and Buchanan was grinning, delighted; Rather hadn't seen many White House smiles lately, and he knew that he had gone too far this time, that they had him now, and that they had drawn a little of his blood. He also knew that for several years the White House had been encouraging the affiliate stations to bring pressure on the network aimed at taming the Washington coverage and that the main targets of the pressure were Rather and Schorr; now they would have more ammunition against him. Later that next day Salant called and Rather knew he was very upset, though he said nothing critical. "Well, we may get a lot of heat on this," Salant said, "but I want you to know that you were the White House correspondent yesterday and you're the White House correspondent today and you'll be the White House correspondent tomorrow." Rather was touched by the gesture. He knew that a different boss might not have done it.

But the Houston meeting was followed in only a few weeks by the meeting of the CBS affiliates, and the pressure was clearly mounting against Rather, and potentially against Salant. The intelligence network indicated that a formal move might be made against Rather, based on the Houston incident. Salant asked Rather to go to the meeting, not to speak, or to apologize, but just to show himself, to be available to be a good guy. Rather wanted no part of it; the whole thing, as far as he was concerned, was humiliating, it was beneath a working journalist to politic among affiliate owners; but he went to the meeting anyway. He was aware that CBS was genuinely worried about the pressure, that there was a feeling that there might be a vote of the affiliate stations against him (while the affiliate stations cannot directly determine the policy and personnel of CBS News, they can express their sentiment). The tactics of the CBS News people were multilateral. First, to try to prevent any kind of formal vote—even if the vote finally turned out to be pro-Rather, the very fact that it had been taken was a judgmental act, a bad precedent for working journalists. A second tactic was the decision by Salant himself to meet the pressures against Rather head-on in a speech, and to defend CBS's overall coverage of Watergate.

On the Sunday night before the meeting there was an attempt to gain votes for some sort of censure against Rather. Some lobbying in the hotel corridors. CBS News, an elite organization, might now have a mass base and mass political consequence, but the system had a built-in counterbalance in the uneasiness of the affiliates with journalistic elitism. But where a year or two earlier, at the height of the Agnew assault, there might have been strong support for a censuring of Rather, in the last two years things had changed and few affiliate executives, despite their innate conservatism, were anxious to stake themselves on a man like Richard Nixon, who was becoming less and less believable. They displayed little enthusiasm for a movement against Rather, and a distinct wish to avoid any vote on the question even if, as seemed to be the case, the essential mood of the affiliates was supportive. A news story saying that 15 or 20 percent of his own stations lacked confidence in a working newspaperman would set a dangerous precedent. Those opposed to Rather had a hearing, but there was no vote; the move against him was vitiated from the start.

It was further weakened later that day by Salant's speech; Salant said that he regretted the Houston incident and he suspected that Rather regretted it too. "And by the word 'it' I mean to include the applause that punctuated a serious and otherwise excellent presidential press conference; the applause and boos that greeted Dan Rather when he stood to ask a question; the President's question to Dan; and Dan's reply to the President. The last would never have happened if the first hadn't happened. And I'm sure that Dan, the next morning, could—like you and me—have thought of better things to say, or not to say. And I'm also sure that all of us, including Dan, wished he'd said those better things—or not said them." Nor would he transfer or reassign Rather, Salant said. With that he defended the entire CBS coverage of Watergate. It was a speech that went over well. Besides, time was on his side.

Systematically now, events were moving against Nixon, and thus against his defenders. But for Rather the affiliates' meeting had been a disturbing event, the pressures were getting too close and too direct, and it was disquieting. He had a sense of his growing vulnerability. He was also aware, as a colleague pointed out, that one of the things that had protected him was not so much the love of the affiliate owners for a free press and the First Amendment as the fact that CBS entered the meeting far ahead in the ratings, with eighteen of the top twenty shows in the country, and the affiliate owners, in a time of national recession, were all making more money than ever before. Such things soothed anger. Moreover, there was less and less pressure on the networks now. The impeachment proceedings themselves were about to begin, it would no longer be the President against the media, now it would be the President against the traditional processes. The Ervin committee hearings had played their role, largely educational, and now the House Judiciary Committee was to sit in judgment on the President's guilt—*in televised sessions.* It was a remarkable departure; in the past the only time members of the House had been seen on television in their own chambers was during the annual visit of the President when he came to deliver his State of the Union message, and used congressmen as warm-bodied props. There was irony in the fact that this very medium that did so much to shift the balance of power away from Congress and to the presidency would now cover the beginning of the President's humiliation.

Not everyone in the media or in the House felt that the televised hearings were a good idea. They might become a zoo, a circus. But the worriers were wrong. The hearings became instead the kind of rare, deeply democratic function the Founding Fathers had in mind. The House members were a cross section of America; knowledge that the whole country was watching them evoked the best in them; and as they performed so well the nation in turn came to understand, more clearly than ever before, the true scale and nature of the issues involved. It was an uncommon instance of democratic process ventilating a society in the best way. Watching the proceedings an observer could sense why there was so much frustration in the country on so many other issues; so seldom were they discussed in this way, informing and involving the people. The proceedings spelled the end for Nixon. The only question was the time and manner of his going. On August 9, 1974, Richard Nixon resigned.

It was not Dan Rather's finest hour, nor the finest hour for CBS News. All of Rather's doubts and vulnerabilities showed that night. He had clearly been under too much tension for too long. Events had finally caught up with Nixon, all the delaying tactics were exhausted, the tapes proved him a liar (his lawyer, James St. Clair, had finally bothered to check out the evidence that had been more or less available to him for months, and the evidence proved that Nixon had lied to his lawyer as he had lied to the country; though apparently to St. Clair the former sin was the greater), and now at the urging of St. Clair and the President's Chief of Staff, Alexander Haig, Nixon had to admit that he had deliberately lied; his support completely crumbled in the House Judiciary Committee, even among his die-hard supporters (most of whom, nonetheless, were rewarded for their misguided loyalty to Nixon by defeat in the upcoming elections). Nixon had to resign, the alternative was certain impeachment with only a tiny handful of Deep South senators and congressmen supporting him.

His statement of resignation was, true to his career, ungenerous and ungracious. Perhaps by Nixonian standards of behavior it might have been worse, there was less snarling in it than in his previous farewell to politics in 1962, but it nonetheless accepted no real blame for the crimes of Watergate, nor, and this was worse, for keeping the country ensnarled in the nightmare of Watergate when he and he alone knew best that he was guilty of involvement in the cover-up; he was resigning, it seemed, because he had inexplicably lost support in the Congress. If there was any blame to be laid for his leaving office, it seemed it was to be placed on Congress.

It was not an attractive performance, nor did it come to terms in any way with the issues raised by Watergate. But that night the commentary on CBS was a disaster. It was Cronkite at his worst, Sevareid at his worst, and Rather at his worst; only Roger Mudd, the major CBS correspondent who had been least involved in the Watergate coverage, had any real insight into what Nixon was doing or spoke with any candor. The people at the top in CBS had been nervous all day and some of that had trickled down—there was a belief that Nixon might go out with a blast at the press and perhaps at CBS, and so the word had been passed down to some correspondents not to seem vindictive, not to seem to gloat. And indeed CBS was part of the story and part of the struggle; that night an extremely high percentage of real Watergate buffs were watching CBS because it was CBS, more than the other networks, that had been in confrontation with the President and thus it was going to be more interesting to watch how CBS handled the dénouement.

How they handled it was badly. The bone-deep political instincts of the network news shows rarely showed through more clearly: the desire not to offend, to be good winners. The desire for centrist respectability. It was like interviewing the victorious presidential candidate after a close defeat of the opposing candidate, nothing but magnanimous statements about how worthy the other fellow was, and in this case a desire to tidy up CBS's own constituency, to show that they were all good fellows after all, not anti-Nixon, that they knew presidential graciousness when they saw it, and perhaps even when they didn't. To Cronkite, the Nixon speech was conciliatory. To Sevareid, it was as effective and magnanimous a speech as Nixon had ever made—"Few things in his presidency became him as much as his manner of leaving the presidency." To Rather, it was one of Richard Nixon's finest hours—"if not his finest hour. . . . He did give—and I would agree with, Walter, what you said—he gave to this moment a touch of class—more than that—a touch of majesty—touching that nerve in most people that says to their brain: Revere the presidency and respect the President; the Republic and the country comes first . . ." They were playing their part in the politics of the country, trying to ease the transition of power, trying to tidy their own slates and reduce antagonism against them, more interested in protecting their own political base as a mass instrument than in doing their assigned jobs.

Rather himself was later aware that he had blown it, that he had simply gotten it wrong, and there was a certain edge of bitterness in the fact that his rival for Cronkite's job, Mudd, who had really covered Watergate very little, had come out so well when he, Rather, had borne the main part of the burden for so long. It was Mudd alone who caught the pettiness in Nixon's speech, his unwillingness to accept responsibility. Rather's own explanation for the weakness of his commentary was that he had not had time to think about it, that he had been running all day long, reporting on events live as they were breaking, that he had not had time to think, that ten minutes before Nixon went on the air he had been at the White House and his superiors told him to get back to the CBS studio, some fifteen blocks away, and that he had double-timed back, gotten in breathless, and had had no time to think in his own mind of what he wanted to say for Nixon's epitaph (which was, finally, who cared about Richard Nixon?—now was the time to get on with running the country and to put the past away). But friends of his thought his dilemma was different, that he had been so closely associated with the confrontation, that he had been in the pit so much, and that he was acutely aware that night of everyone looking at him as if somehow his fingers were on the gun—what will Dan Rather be like, will he be gloating?—and he had very simply bent over backward, Dan Rather was a good citizen, what was past was past. He was, thought his friends, showing the results of the pressure of the job; it was the first time they felt that his instincts were not true and that he had allowed his role in the story to affect his coverage of the story seriously. Much more so than the incident at Houston. If television gave the press a new power base, then it never showed so clearly as that night in Washington, when Rather, Cronkite, and Sevareid were not so much like reporters covering a story as politicians wanting to get 51 percent of the vote.

A month later all that sensitivity, all that touchiness and distrust, came to a head. Rather had always been aware of the pressure against him from the affiliates, from the government, and the fact that the corporation itself was not easy with his role, that Salant might well be a very lonely embattled figure within CBS, that many people in high places in CBS wished that he had never left Texas. And so it was that when his superiors offered him a better job, Dan Rather, so sensitive to the pressure against him and so nervous about the company's backing, at first resisted it. Salant, whom he had always trusted, offered him a job as the anchorman of "CBS Reports," one of the prize plums within the company, and Rather thought they were trying to dump him. It had all gotten that bad. The idea went back several months to the time when the CBS documentary people had met with Bill Small (then being groomed as Salant's successor) and had expressed their desire for a single anchorman for their documentaries, reminiscent of what Murrow had been at the crest of his power. They were aware that the "CBS Reports" were not as strong as they had been and were not making a strong impression on the public, and they thought that the addition of a highly visible figure might give the programs greater strength and greater public identity. The figure they asked for was Dan Rather.

It was still the height of the Watergate confrontation, and as far as Small was concerned, the idea of switching Rather was inconceivable, it would be misinterpreted and would look as though CBS was bowing to pressure. He rejected the idea flatly, never even mentioning it to Rather. By August 1974, however, Nixon was out of the White House. Rather had, in effect, been vindicated and there was the problem of what to do with him. He was controversial, but more than that he was a superstar, and there were precious few positions on the air for a superstar. At which point Small remembered "CBS Reports" and mentioned it to Salant; it seemed like the perfect answer to their dilemma. It was a position for a star, it would give Rather—who had been too long at the White House, a very confining assignment—a chance to grow, and it seemed likely to strengthen "CBS Reports." Rather was a strong figure, he did have weight and authority. They were offering Rather what Hughes Rudd called the best job in the company. As far as they were concerned, the essential battle with the Nixon White House was over, Rather had been vindicated, CBS had clearly weathered the pressure. Besides, there was the sneaking fear that Rather, as forceful as he was, as perfect as his style was for the Nixon years, was the wrong man for the Ford White House. He might simply be too strong, and that would in the end work against him.

So he was invited to lunch in New York. It was casual and Rather thought it was just going to be an easy lunch with Small, who was one of his closest friends in the organization. Just before they left for the restaurant Small mentioned that they were having company, and Salant and Bill Leonard showed up. There had been no previous mention of any reassignment, or any job change. But Rather could see that this was not just another lunch. Salant made the offer of the new job; so far as he and Small were concerned, he was making it clear that Rather could either stay at the White House or take the "CBS Reports" job. If he took the "CBS Reports" job he would also get another anchor shift on the weekend news, which would give him additional exposure. Either way there would be a 50 percent pay raise; Salant did not want Rather to think he was making a crucial job decision based on money. But if that was what Salant thought he was saying, Rather thought he heard something very different. He was not at all convinced, as the lunch progressed, that he was being given any choice. He kept bringing the subject up because it was, after all, his career and his life they were talking about. It seemed to him that Salant and Small wanted him to take the other job (and wanted him out of the White House), that this was their preference, and he got the strong impression that he had little choice. He kept asking whether he had a choice in the matter and he did not hear them say yes.

He left depressed and getting more depressed by the minute. He was shocked by what had happened, it was apparent to him that CBS *was* bowing to pressure, that it wanted to get him out of the White House as soon as it could do so without loss of face. He went back to Washington and stayed up all night talking about the lunch; the more he talked, the more he became depressed, and the more convinced he was that CBS was backing down. The next day he could not bring himself to go to work; CBS owed him a good deal of time, and so he called in and said he was taking some time off, and decided to go fishing with his son in Virginia where he would be unreachable. Off he went. Two days later the story leaked out of Chicago that CBS was trying to move Rather out of the White House; Rather insists he did not leak it, though he says if leaking it had occurred to him, he would have. The reverse pressure on CBS was now enormous; print reporters are—with good reason—extremely suspicious of the networks and a number of them concluded that what they had long expected to happen was now happening. Rather was out of touch, but Salant and Small started calling his house—they needed another meeting, all hell was breaking loose. They set up a second meeting in Washington and they went through it all again. Rather asked Salant bluntly whether there was any pressure that they were responding to. Salant said no. Pressure from the affiliates? No. From others within the corporation? No. Was this from anyone above? No. Salant pledged that they were not buckling to pressure. This time Salant made it very clear that Rather had a choice, and this time Rather accepted the job. And so a month after Richard Nixon left the White House, so did Dan Rather.

# Epilogues

# 33 / The Washington Post

The Pulitzer Prize jury had already submitted their decisions in March of 1973 when the Watergate story was suddenly validated by the news of the McCord letter. Watergate had not been a particularly popular story with the regional editors who made up the jury. The *Post* stories had been entered in the Public Service category and had come in fourth. *Fourth.* At that point the *Post* was apparently in line to receive three Pulitzers—one to David Broder as columnist, one to Dan Morgan and Bob Kaiser for distinguished reporting from Eastern Europe, and one to William Claiborne on conditions in local jails. Three was a lot and there was some question about whether they could all be awarded to one paper. Then, between the time the judges submitted their decisions and the announcement of the prizes, the McCord letter became public.

At that point the senior editors who serve on the advisory board, a sort of Pulitzer governing board, realized that the whole thing was about to blow up in their faces, that the biggest story of the year was about to be ignored, and that the scandal might diminish the value of the Pulitzer Prize itself. A few top officials, men like Newbold Noyes and Scotty Reston, went to Ben Bradlee, told him they were going to do something about it, and asked him which category he would like the Watergate Pulitzer to be awarded in. Public Service, he said, which meant that the prize would go to the paper instead of to Woodward and Bernstein. (If the category had been Investigative Journalism, the prize would have gone to the two reporters.) A little while later the executives came back to Bradlee and told him that the *Post* would be getting two Pulitzers, one for Public Service on Watergate, and one for Broder. Just for a moment, Bradlee's face fell. "What's the matter, Ben?" Noyes asked. "You want four?" Bradlee looked at him coldly. "Yes," he said.

Woodward and Bernstein were very upset when they heard that Bradlee had taken the Pulitzer for the paper (and in effect for himself), instead of deeding it over to them; after all, if they won, the paper won as well. They were both furious and after fuming for a time, they went to see Harry Rosenfeld, who had of course known what was coming and knew why Bradlee had done what he did. It was a loyalty decision, loyalty to the paper first and foremost. Rosenfeld was very good with them. He warned Bradlee, and later that day

Bradlee received the two of them. The two reporters had prepared themselves very properly, they knew what they were going to say, and they walked in on Bradlee dressed in their best suits. He was very cool, wearing a black turtleneck sweater and looking, Woodward thought, a lot like Kirk Douglas playing a U-boat commander. Woodward began, saying that he felt it should have gone the other way, that if the paper had put them up, then they would have won it and the paper would have won it too. The paper owed them that much. You get so few chances at it, he said. Then Bradlee took over. "Listen," he said, "this paper had its cock on the chopping block." He talked about the economic pressures on the paper, and the threats against Mrs. Graham. They did not, he said, have a sense of what the stakes were, they had been deliberately insulated from that, but it had been very tense for a long time. It was a matter of loyalty. The paper had been loyal to them and supportive of them and it was the paper that they owed so much to; no other paper, he said, would have done it. It was, Woodward thought, Bradlee at his most seductive, attractive, and charming, and soon Woodward felt a little guilty. How could he and Bernstein have been so crass and greedy as to have wanted the prize for themselves?

Bradlee, his colleagues thought, lost concentration and passion in the months after Watergate. It was as if after scaling the highest mountain, the challenges remaining were not great enough. He was a man by nature geared for big events, not little ones, and the biggest event of all had already come his way. On occasion a particular story—the scandal of Congressman Wayne Hays, Bob Woodward's story on the CIA's connection to King Hussein—moved and energized him, but he seemed different, less driven. Sometimes when the *Post* went into head-to-head competition with *The New York Times,* he came alive; then it was all very personal, not just the *Post* on a good story, not just the *Post* against the *Times,* but Bradlee against Abe Rosenthal. The competition between the two papers did not bring out the best in either: good stories were often underplayed (if the other had gotten there first) and weak stories (the choosing of a new president of Yale, for example) seriously overplayed. That did not bother Mrs. Graham as much as her fear that the tempo of the *Post* might be changing. There was some kind of post-Watergate letdown taking place in Bradlee, she told close friends, and it bothered her for a time. She told friends that at times she pictured Jim Bellows of the *Star* walking around in his city room, his sleeves rolled up, right on top of the action. Bradlee no longer seemed like that to her. She hoped it was only a temporary phase. It worried her.

It was not certain at all who would succeed him as editor. None of his deputies was considered a likely replacement. The *Post* had a history of bringing in attractive deputies for Bradlee, and Bradlee had a history of at once wanting them and at the same time, because he did everything so personally, making life intolerable for them. David Laventhol had appeared briefly as an assistant managing editor, and he ended up editing *Newsday;* Gene Patterson had had a distinguished career at the Atlanta *Constitution,* and served for a time as managing editor of the *Post* before escaping to edit the St. Petersburg *Times;* and Dick Wald had come in as assistant managing editor before very quickly going to NBC, where he became head of NBC News.

Kay Graham wondered about succession, partly because Wall Street wondered about succession, and she mentioned it to Bradlee from time to time. Bradlee said he was aware of the problem. In the fall of 1978 he was fifty-seven; his health was good, and the question of succession did not bother him as much as it did Wall Street or Mrs. Graham. He had never liked Wall Street anyway.

The Washington *Post* had been a somewhat funky disorganized place, and in the fifties and early sixties many of the best people had gone to it, not because of its size or richness, but because it was different and idiosyncratic; if it was flawed, it was also humane, and for all its flaws it seemed to stand for something. It was not an airless place.

By the mid-seventies many of Phil Graham's dreams had been realized. The *Post* was a world-famous newspaper. If it was not as complete and final an index of what had happened in the world each day as *The New York Times,* it was nonetheless formidable, dominating the nation's capital and for the first time being taken seriously in the executive reaches of New York. No serious government official dared not read it. It now could rival the *Times* as an outlet for a politician wanting to leak an important story. Ben Bradlee, because of Watergate and the film that portrayed him in a flattering role, had become, if not the most prominent editor in the world, certainly the most celebrated. After Jimmy and Rosalynn Carter, he and his friend (later wife) Sally Quinn, a reporter on the *Post,* were the most sought-after couple in Washington, and when at the screening of a new movie the two of them arrived, *Ben and Sally,* the two of them immensely glamorous, there was a craning of necks equal to that at the arrival of superstars at a Hollywood screening.

Yet all its new fame and riches had not necessarily made the *Post* a happier place. There was considerable institutional pride in the Watergate triumphs, but all of that had also increased the pressures and the tensions in an already stress-laden, egocentric institution. The intensity of ambition within the paper was greater than ever. Normal, non-Watergate stories now somehow seemed smaller. Because the *Post* was so famous, the people who came to work for it were supercharged themselves, all bearing the best of college degrees and the fiercest of ambitions. Yet there were only so many good stories, so many choice assignments. Ironically, the more highly talented people the paper hired, the greater the level of dissatisfaction on the staff. Life at the *Post* was beginning to resemble life at *The New York Times,* where the system, not the individual, prevailed. A reporter could appear to be a star at one moment, reporting a big story in an exotic foreign capital, then a month later be only one of a hundred reporters covering the city side. That was happening now at the *Post.*

Perhaps Watergate had brought the paper too much glamour, too much success. Reporters and editors were at their best when motivated by instincts of social conscience, and belief in justice. But those very instincts, given the curious value system in America, often made them stars. It was heady stuff, this new touch of the bitch goddess. Barry Sussman, who had once befriended the young Woodward and Bernstein, felt betrayed by his two former protégés, left out of their book. He no longer talked to either of them. Bernstein felt himself harassed by Simons, his former defender, and left the paper. Simons was said to be less than happy with his portrait in Alan Pakula's movie about the *Post* and Watergate. Woodward remained at the paper, though he worked primarily on books. He married for a second time, but his work habits remained, as before, obsessive, and the marriage did not last.

Looking back, perhaps the happiest period at the paper had been that explosive time when Bradlee first took over and began hiring. In those days there were room and stories for everyone, an entire new world to conquer. Many of the reporters who had shared in that time—Karnow, Bagdikian, Kotz—had already left, and not all of them spoke well of Bradlee and the *Post.* One of the ablest of them, Nick Kotz, had, on the occasion of his departure in June 1973, left a note on the bulletin board that some thought uncommonly troubling. A very talented reporter who had won a Pulitzer Prize in Des Moines for exposing malpractice in the meat-packing industry, Kotz at the *Post* had specialized in writing about social issues, welfare problems, and race relations. The drift of the paper in the early seventies was, as in the nation itself, away from concern about these areas. Kotz's note read: "I think that the dedication, the skills, and the commitment exhibited by the newspaper in the Watergate story can launch a new era in which the *Post* seeks to become an even better newspaper. I hope that the commitment and sense of responsibility that has characterized the Watergate coverage can and will be extended to the *Post*'s coverage of other issues, including the social issues that now divide the country. Best wishes and friendship to all of you." A tough note to read for those left behind.


Watergate, like Vietnam, had obscured one of the central new facts about the role of national journalism in America, a fact that helped explain the not entirely latent discontent at places like the *Post* and CBS and *The New York Times,* rich and powerful and successful as they were. Only very rich, very powerful corporate institutions like these had the impact, the reach, and above all the resources to challenge the President of the United States. Yet the price of that external influence was high to those institutions in an internal sense. The bigger and richer and more powerful the journalistic institution, the more bureaucratic its way of dealing with its own best people, the more distant and aloof its management. The *Post* was now part of a big rich corporation, 452nd in the *Fortune* list. Its standards and goals now resembled, not the standards and goals of small old-fashioned newspapers, but those of the other giant corporations on that list. For a highly individualistic profession like journalism there was an inherent contradiction in this. Even those *Post* reporters who were not entirely enamored of Bradlee, who thought his attention span too short, who objected to the fact that he sometimes preferred sexy stories to what they considered more serious ones, and who thought him too star-oriented, nonetheless welcomed his presence, highly personalized as it was, as a defense against the corporation. They believed that he was buying the newsroom time, that his connection to Mrs. Graham was so close that he could secure freedom of a sort that his successor could not.

Yet the corporation was being felt in the newsroom as it had not been felt before. Not necessarily directly; no one ever told a *Post* reporter to tailor a story to an advertiser's wish, and Bradlee was wonderful in telling a group of Washington retailers, come to protest against a series of stories on housing practices, to go to hell (even though he had not read the yet-to-be-published stories). But reporters were aware that in recent years Kay Graham had committed herself more and more to profit, to winning Wall Street's approval. In late 1975 she had gone before a meeting of securities analysts in New York and she had told them she would like to win a Pulitzer Prize for management. She knew she was not a good manager. On the business side, top executives came and went, their tours becoming, it seemed, ever briefer. When in November 1972 John Prescott came from Detroit to run the business side of the paper, most people in the profession were pleased and thought Mrs. Graham had finally hired the perfect man. But three years later Prescott was unceremoniously let go, and it was said that Mrs. Graham did not think Prescott was tough enough. She seemed to relish the notion of being tough herself. She liked the idea of bridging two worlds, that of the nation's top corporate executives, who welcomed the toughness of her words, her talk about bringing 15 percent profit to the newspaper, and who were made uneasy by what they considered the liberal eccentricities of the *Post*'s editorial pages; and the world of the newsroom, where 15 percent sounded like an ominous figure indeed (although, as she pointed out, much smaller a figure than the 20 or 25 percent some of the big chains were now demanding). The paper, after all, had been very profitable in the late sixties. But then in the seventies there had been a recession, followed by inflation. Costs were up, and profits, sizable as they might be, were down. The margin of profit had dropped to 8 and 9 percent of revenue. Wall Street did not like margins like that, or the kind of management that accepted them; it sounded as though the people who wrote the editorials were also running the paper.

Indeed, the reporters for the *Post* found themselves caught in a more and more ambivalent position. They worked for what had traditionally been a liberal institution, an institution that regularly dictated the humane, honorable solution to the conflicts of other institutions, but was now a liberal institution that followed the norms of Wall Street, and Wall Street was not necessarily committed to humane, honorable solutions. What brought home the schizophrenic nature of their position was the pressmen's strike of 1975–76. It was a terribly bitter experience for everyone involved. Mrs. Graham—who had undergone great personal tragedy during her husband's illness, and who had been under great stress during Watergate—called the strike the worst thing she had ever been through in her life. It divided the paper, labor from management, reporters from labor, reporter from reporter; finally, it seemed to cut the paper off from part of its past.

The story is immensely complicated; these are merely the essential facts. There is no doubt that the *Post* through the years had lost control over the small factory where the paper was actually put together and printed, its printshop and pressroom. Yet, like many other newspapers, the *Post* needed desperately to move gradually into more modern, relatively labor-free technology, which in the past the unions had successfully fought. Within the profession the *Post* was regarded as having unusually high production costs, and it was competing for advertising dollars with television stations that were hampered by few labor restrictions and had the most modern technology available. In the past the *Post* executives had been somewhat intimidated by the unions and unwilling to risk a strike. Not only had the paper's profits been considerable, but the instinct and desire to *publish,* not to be censored by anyone, be it government or labor union, was so intense that the company had made concessions that some of its executives later regretted.

But by the mid-seventies the atmosphere of accommodation had changed. Profits were no longer just a private matter within the family, they were of concern to Wall Street and public investors. The new management people who represented the *Post* with labor had brought with them reputations for being much tougher. The company had signed an agreement with a firm in Oklahoma that to all intents and purposes specialized in helping newspapers to break strikes. Management could send its own top personnel there for lessons in the intricate mechanical work required to issue a basic newspaper. *Post* people trained in Oklahoma set up their own school in suburban Virginia for the training of even more personnel. The unions called it, very simply, a scab school. It was the company's way of letting the unions know that it intended to enter negotiations in an entirely new frame of mind. It was in a position to put out a paper, using photo typesetting, without the help of any of the traditional craft workers.

Slowly the *Post* changed the labor balance. In late 1974 it signed a contract with the printers' union that allowed the company to begin introducing cold-type technology. With their own agreement, printers were being phased out now in return for sizable cash bonuses. As they left they were replaced by machines. The remaining pressmen were more militant. On October 1, 1975, negotiations failed and the pressmen went on strike. Before they began the strike, however, some of them went on a rampage inside the printshop, beating the night foreman, sabotaging all nine of the presses, destroying the fire extinguishers and starting a fire on one of the presses.

That single act obscured everything else that happened; because of it, the strike was over before it began. The pressmen had handed Mrs. Graham and management a total public relations victory. The management might have learned how to use the new cold-type machines and how to run the presses, but there was one element missing that would have made it impossible to put out the *Post* during a strike: the reporters. And to the reporters the assault upon the *Post*'s presses had been an act of sacrilege. Above all, the right to publish was sacred, and the reporters saw, in the pressmen's vandalism, a hint of something sinister, something from Nazi Germany. The Newspaper Guild, the reporters' relatively weak union, voted to stand by the company and not to observe the strike. Twice more the Guild voted on the strike, and twice more it voted to continue working, though by narrower margins each time. Those decisions were crucial; they allowed the *Post* to keep good faith with its most devoted readers, those who took the liberalism of its editorial page seriously. After the vote Mrs. Graham came down to meet with the reporters and to tell them how brave they were, and how grateful she was. It was very moving: they felt as one with her as they had during Watergate. The paper missed publishing only one day. Slowly, steadily, it regained its full size as the top executives handled the most menial of pressroom chores. Within six weeks it was publishing a fifty-six-page paper. By December it was advertising for nonunion help. Seven hundred applicants appeared the first day. Washington, unlike New York, is not a strong union town. It is a black city and no member of the pressmen's union had been black. In mid-February the mailers voted to come back to work. The printers then followed. The strike was over. Mark Meagher, the general manager, boasted that the strike had left one union dead on the battlefield and others severely chastened.

Yet the strike had badly divided the city room, and seriously weakened the Guild. Some old members had honored the picket lines and were bitter against the reporters who had crossed. There were charges of elitism—many of the paper's best and most celebrated reporters had ignored the lines. At first, after the strike was over, the Guild was a weak, almost despised union. But gradually many of the best reporters on the paper began to have second thoughts about the strike. More than two years later, management had failed to reach a new contract with the Guild. There had been two raises, and the pay at the *Post* was very good, but these raises had come at the whim of management, not as the result of union negotiation. Many of the more senior reporters decided to come back to the Guild, knowing that their very act of joining, however belated, was a signal to management. There was among many of them a feeling of being used, and worse, a feeling that their loyalties had been exploited. The one violent act of the pressmen, they now felt, had obscured a much more significant fact: that management had been utterly prepared to bust a union.

With the union beaten, with the way open to modernize its technology, profits at the *Post* began to soar. Where before the strike the net income had averaged about $13 million a year, even though the strike had extended into part of 1976, the figure for that year was almost double the average: *$24.5* *million.* In 1977 it was $35.5 million, an increase of 45 percent, and the figures for 1978 looked even better, a further increase of about 25 percent. Predictably, the *Post* was suddenly a hot stock, worth more than three times what it had been before the strike. Wall Street approved. There was nothing soft or sentimental about the Washington Post Company now.

Her staff was left with very mixed feelings about Katharine Graham. They liked the fact that the bigger the journalistic issue, the better she performed. But many were also dismayed to recognize that there was a part of her that was imperious, cold, and hard, and that she now seemed to want to impress Wall Street more than working journalists. The magic figure of 15 percent was in the air. Everything had to measure up. If the *Post* was interested in acquisitions, it was because Wall Street liked acquisitions. A certain kind of acquisition. Unfortunately it often turned out that the more profitable the acquisition, the more second-rate the property: some newspaper with a monopoly on its town, or a third-ranked television station in some small city. When a colleague rather casually mentioned that Kay might think of acquiring one of America's distinguished monthly magazines, worthy but hardly prosperous entities which often lost money, Mrs. Graham had no interest at all. But it could be, said the colleague, a complement to the *Post*'s and *Newsweek*'s existing journalism—the Washington Post Company could absorb the losses—and it might even be a place to transfer senior reporters who had become restless with daily reporting. But she had no interest. The company, she insisted, could only buy properties that made a *profit,* every property had to justify itself. It was an interesting attitude for a company already making so handsome a profit. It meant that a dinky television station that showed nothing but reruns was more valuable than a distinguished magazine that ventured into the world of ideas and opinions. Indeed, it was an attitude which, if held by Eugene Meyer, would have prevented his buying and subsidizing the Washington Post Company.

Much of the toughness of her position, close friends thought, was her desire to keep the *Post* a family paper and a family company and to pass it on to her son, Donald. When the company acquired the *Times-Herald* in 1954, Eugene Meyer had said that the importance of this is that it means the paper is safe for Donnie. That was her next ambition, to turn the paper over to him. But not immediately, there was no rush. Wall Street had a lever on her now, although all the voting stock remained in family hands. Wall Street could, in its own way, vote no confidence, and people would lay off the stock and its value would go down until finally outside management would take over. These things happen. So it was in part her desire to keep the paper in the family that dictated her tough-minded policy, that and the fact that she also liked being known as someone who could make it in the big corporate world.

In 1976, at the age of thirty-one, Donald Graham was named general manager of the Washington *Post*. In the next-to-last step in a thoroughly and carefully prepared career. At the time he was already past the age Phil Graham had been when he was made publisher. (The announcement of Donald Graham's appointment noted that he was the grandson of Eugene Meyer and the son of Katharine Graham. There was no mention of Philip Graham.) Donnie Graham was a serious, modest young man with none of his father's flair; indeed he seemed determined to live his life in a manner that contrasted as much as possible with his father's style and, among other things, he never took a drink. Since, from the time he was born, he had been the publisher apparent, it was not surprising that he was filled with a sense of obligation and self-imposed restraints and control. Right out of college, he had gone to Vietnam because he thought that it was his duty, and when he returned he had worked for a time as a cop in Washington. Then he undertook a job program not unlike that followed by Otis Chandler some three thousand miles to the west, starting at the bottom and moving through virtually every employment level in different departments of the *Post*. Groomed and ready he would be. He seemed to know the name of everyone on the paper, he was intelligent and pleasant. But no one was prepared to say what the intelligence meant, what Donnie Graham really *felt*. He appeared to be wound terribly tight, to be conscious of what was demanded of him, and indeed he seemed to excel at everything he touched. He had been a fine student at Harvard, president of the *Crimson* and a gifted athlete. (The summer he returned from the Army he turned up at the *Post* staff picnic and in the last inning of the softball game hit the longest ball anyone had seen that summer. "They teach you that at prep school," remarked Carl Bernstein, then a young reporter, to a friend.) If none of his peers knew exactly what was inside him, they nevertheless liked his commitment to the paper and his respect for quality.

He had been clearly ready to graduate from his apprenticeship long before his mother gave a sign that she was ready to turn over the paper. She was obviously possessed by a fear that if she did step aside, her telephone might not ring any more, that she might lose her power in the city. But she had another fear: that she might be stifling her son. She often talked about the succession with close friends, and they could see that she hesitated, worried over it; Donald Graham for his part was a good soldier and never complained. In January of 1979 the business section of the *Post* interviewed him about his work as general manager, and he spoke enthusiastically about how much he liked it and how he intended to stay there for a long time. His mother heard of the story and killed it before it could run. She had decided that the time had come.

Less than a week later, Kay Graham announced that she was stepping aside as publisher of the *Post*, while retaining the position of chief executive officer, and that Donald Graham would become publisher. It was plain that she did not want to relinquish any real power, but she did want less day-to-day responsibility and more personal freedom. There were those who thought she chose to make the transition while Ben Bradlee was still in his prime so that there would be a certain generational overlap. Thus, at thirty-three, Donald Graham became publisher of the *Post*; at the same time Otis Chandler was grooming his son Norman Chandler to take over the Los Angeles *Times*, and at *The New York Times* there was a new by-line in the Washington bureau, that of young Arthur Ochs Sulzberger, Jr.

# 34/ The Los Angeles Times

In 1973 Norman Chandler was dying of cancer. He had cancer of the mouth. It was very painful and he bore it well, a proud man as ever; those who were his friends and saw him during this time were impressed with the dignity of this fine and handsome man, still elegant, in terrible pain, trying to pay no attention to his own anguish, trying to put others at ease, still interested in what was going on. In the last couple of months of his life, it was decided by someone, perhaps Rose Mary Woods, that it would be a very nice touch if Richard Nixon dropped by to see his old friend Norman Chandler. Norman was staying at his country place at Dana Point, about fifteen minutes from the Western White House at San Clemente. Early in the spring of 1973, with Watergate still going on, Richard Nixon arranged to drop by. A quick visit. Just for old times' sake. Norman Chandler was delighted. Watergate was a very distant thing to him, he knew he was dying and he was appreciative of this gesture. A President was a President. He got ready for the visit with the aid of Buff, which was not easy, as he was already quite weak, and it took a great deal of his dwindling energy. When he was ready he waited and he waited, while Buff talked about the difficulty of being President, long schedules, unforeseen appointments, Presidents were always late. In the end Nixon did not come, nor did he call and cancel. Norman Chandler hid his disappointment. A little later there were, through Rose Woods, some muffled apologies, a hint (because Rose Woods was always very discreet, one did not get to be a Los Angeles *Times* Woman of the Year without discretion) that it had been Haldeman who blocked the trip because of the *Times*'s coverage of Watergate. But it could be rescheduled for a few months later, Rose said, and it was. Nixon would drop by briefly. And this time, at even greater effort, for Norman Chandler was even weaker, he was readied and he was pleased, he was an old-fashioned man and a President was coming by to see him. Again the minutes passed and then the hours and Richard Nixon did not show, nor did he call. This time there was no doubting Norman's disappointment.

On October 20, 1973, a Saturday, Norman Chandler died at the age of seventy-four, and the next day's *Times* gave considerable prominence to the obituary, though the story did not lead the paper; the lead story was by Ron Ostrow and ran under the headline: NIXON FIRES COX, ABOLISHES HIS OFFICE; RICHARDSON QUITS.

Buff Chandler was furious with the Nixon snubs, but she did not do anything at first. Instead she waited and fumed, and finally she wrote Richard Nixon a blistering letter that said that he was a dreadful man, which was proved by the fact that he would stand up Norman Chandler—who had been his friend and who had done so much for him—when he was terminally ill. Nixon had failed even to visit Norman Chandler, yet had given a medal to Sam Goldwyn, who, she wrote, was senile anyway, had never done anything for anybody. That just proved to her that Nixon could be a friend to no man. *A friend to no man.* She wrote the letter by hand and had it hand-delivered so that there would never be any question of whether or not it got through. She did not hear from Richard Nixon.


That the *Times* did as well as it did in covering Watergate did not help national editor Ed Guthman with his colleagues at the paper. It did not increase his power or leverage. Rather, if anything, the entire episode had underscored again the fact that Guthman was too passionate, too committed. He was not a very good bureaucrat and he was slow to realize that his power was shrinking. He took his superiors' assurances that he was doing well at face value. Then in 1976 there was a critical slip in the gradual decline of Ed Guthman. The political coverage of the presidential race was taken away from him. It was nothing personal, they said, simply better for the paper. But it represented, within the bureaucracy of a newspaper, a considerable loss of power and influence. At the heart of a national editor's power is control over the political coverage and the ability to reward the top reporters with what are considered plum assignments. If an editor cannot determine assignments like that, then a reporter no longer pays any attention; in a presidential year top political reporters leave great newspapers over such issues. It was a clear slap at Guthman, though presented as just another routine step in the modernizing of the structure of the paper. Shortly after the campaign, talk arose of appointing a permanent political editor, an even more final incursion into Guthman's territory. It was clear that he was in real jeopardy. He was fifty-seven years old, he liked living in California, he had just bought a new house, and there are not a lot of slots for fifty-seven-year-old editors. "You must get a lot of offers," one of his national reporters said to him. "No," he replied, very much aboveboard, "I don't get any offers at all." But in February he did get lucky. The Philadelphia *Inquirer,* run by a very able editor named Gene Roberts, was looking for an editorial-page editor, and Guthman, somewhat resentful over what was happening to him and the way it had been done, and not anxious to stay around for eight powerless years of shuffling papers, quit and went to Philadelphia.

It caused a good deal of uneasiness among the paper's better reporters. Most of them saw Guthman not only as the ablest and most aggressive editor on the staff but as a kind of conscience as well. On his last day there Guthman went by to say goodbye to Otis Chandler, but it was a very formal, very stiff meeting, and the thing that bothered Guthman in retrospect was that Otis

Chandler never asked him any questions, and he had a feeling that some fire, some taste for publishing and being in the pit, had gone out in the publisher, whom he had always liked and respected. It was as if, despite the thirteen years together, they had nothing in common after all.

Though some of the national reporters were apprehensive about what Guthman's departure meant, Dennis Britton, who was considered a Guthman protégé, was named to replace him. That reassured many of the reporters. It did not help the mood of Paul Conrad, who had lost his closest friend on the paper, and who took all of this as a sign that things would be less adventurous than in the past.

The paper continued to grow richer and richer. Early in 1978 Otis Chandler surprised almost everyone by deciding to make a major move into the San Diego area, opening a twenty-six-person editorial bureau there and printing an additional seventy thousand copies of the *Times* with a large special San Diego section. The reasons for the move were many: the San Diego papers had always been weak and vulnerable, the San Diego area was now growing faster than Los Angeles, the *Times* was so incredibly rich that it could easily afford the move. Finally, and perhaps most important, the demographics of Los Angeles were changing. There was an out-migration of middle-class whites to suburban Orange County and even farther south toward San Diego. Those shifts in population were reflected in the *Times*'s own circulation: in 1977 it dropped below a million for the first time in several years. The Chandlers were not the kind of people to wait until things got serious.

Otis Chandler remained perhaps the most successful publisher in America among those who sought some measure of editorial excellence. His company in 1977 was big and becoming bigger, 232nd on the *Fortune* 500. To the journalists he employed he remained an aloof, distant, enigmatic figure. His passions seemed so vastly different from theirs. Reporters liked to tell the story, which they insisted was not apocryphal, of a late-morning editorial meeting at the *Times* when someone walked in to hand Otis a note. The publisher read it, crumpled it up, and quickly ended the meeting. Later a new editorial writer picked up the piece of paper. It had said: "The surf is up at 12:30."

Most of the top reporters felt they got a better sense of who Otis was and what he wanted from his wife, Missy, than from the publisher himself. Yet they considered him a good and serious man and they liked his taste for quality in top-level people. He had acquired the Dallas *Times Herald* and he had quickly improved it, both editorially and financially; if *Newsday* on Long Island had been a successful paper before Chandler acquired it, it had remained as good as ever after the acquisition. In a single generation the Los Angeles *Times,* one of the worst newspapers in the country, had become one of the very best. It had an exceptionally able staff, and its flaws seemed if anything to reflect the community itself; they both sprawled and each, to a degree, lacked definition and sharp edges.

The financial success of the *Times* in its own area was staggering. It had, thanks to General Otis and Harry Chandler, remained a nonunion shop in a profession otherwise bedeviled by union contracts that had slowed down the arrival of new technology. This had made the *Times* infinitely more flexible and successful. It served an unusually prosperous region, it was a morning newspaper in a place where no afternoon paper would have a chance, given the geography. (The *Times* had 93 percent of the advertising in its territory.) It ran more classified ads than any other paper in the country, and there was nothing sweeter for a newspaper publisher than classifieds, automatic money coming in with no editorial expense. All of this meant that there was virtually no bit of commerce in the greater Los Angeles area, be it large or small, that the *Times* did not take a slice of. All that advertising required that the *Times* print countless pages. The sheer amount of editorial space the ads made available, some professional observers thought, was not entirely healthy. Filling gave a quality of softness to the paper, a sense that the need to fill space, rather than editorial imperative, dictated much of the paper's content. Some stories were endlessly long, jumping from page to page to page, until finally they simply ran out, exhausted. It was as if Southern California's growth demanded that the stories be that long.

Otis Chandler and Bill Thomas rankled over the failure to get adequate national recognition for the *Times*. The paper, they thought, was the victim of a kind of eastern snobbery. The population might have shifted westward, but news still moved from east to west and the nation's taste making was still done in the East. They believed that since the paper was not often seen in New York and Washington, for most Easterners it did not exist, and probably could not, on the principle that a serious newspaper of any excellence simply could not be published on the West Coast by Westerners. When Tom Griffith wrote an essay in *Time* magazine about the nation's top newspapers, he placed *The New York Times* and the Washington *Post* on a plateau above all others. This infuriated Thomas. He wrote Griffith a letter of two words: "Parochial bullshit."


Not surprisingly, the figures for the Times Mirror Company were always very good. Some chains, like Gannett and Newhouse, made higher levels of profit, but among newspaper groups where quality was of the essence, no one ran an operation like Otis Chandler. He produced editorial quality *and* continued business success. His profit margin was consistently satisfactory, always, it seemed, 15 percent, 16 percent. In 1977 the Times Mirror newspapers brought in $510 million in revenue and $81 million in pretax profit; those figures in 1978 were expected to be $600 million in revenue and about $100 million in pretax profit, of which roughly two thirds came from the *Times* alone. The Times Mirror Company was now generating more money than it knew what to do with.

The company had been one of the early leaders in the game of acquisition. Now it found that the competition was becoming tougher and tougher. Given America's current tax laws, all kinds of newspapers that had once been considered very small and of no particular value (especially to those poor souls who had to read them) were suddenly hot properties. These were often small-town nonunion monopoly situations as well as big-city morning newspapers in certain prosperous cities. They were now viewed, with some accuracy, as companies with a license to print money. Suddenly the competition between the various chains—Newhouse, Knight-Ridder, Gannett (which by 1977 had more than seventy papers in it)—seemed touched by madness. The Times Mirror had made a serious pass at the Kansas City *Star* in 1977 but another chain, Capital Cities Communication, snagged it, for a staggering $125 million. Then the Chandlers attempted to buy the Booth newspapers, a string of small papers in Michigan plus *Parade* magazine. The Times Mirror entered the bidding actively and three of the Booth directors had pledged their stock to Otis at $40 a share. That meant an offer of roughly $250 million for the operation. Then Newhouse entered the bidding. S. I. Newhouse seemed to collect papers the way other men collected postage stamps, and was known as a man who gave little thought to the editorial product. As a result, it was said, his papers returned profits just short of 30 percent on the revenue. Newhouse already owned 25 percent of the Booth papers; now he offered $47 a share for the remaining interest. It meant a sale of $300 million, *three times* the book value of the property. It was accepted. All of this left Otis Chandler momentarily discouraged. The competition, he thought, was getting out of hand.

But his disappointment did not last very long. Very soon he and the men around him realized that the prime lesson of the Booth venture was not the rate at which the price escalated, but the willingness of the banks to underwrite so expensive a take-over. Two hundred and fifty million dollars was a staggering amount to a firm like the Times Mirror Company, yet the banks had very readily come along. The experience taught Chandler how much muscle he really had, how respected his company was not just by banks but by sizable companies that he might want to buy. The assault upon Booth had brought his firm publicity and recognition of a kind not normally accorded a West Coast outfit, and Times Mirror was now being accepted as big time. Almost immediately, he began a dazzling series of purchases as part of a $500 million program of expansion and acquisition: *Sporting News,* a statistic-laden bible of sports journalism, located in St. Louis, for $18 million; two Connecticut papers, the Greenwich *Times* and the Stamford *Advocate,* for about $20 million (a purchase made especially attractive by the fact that both were located in Fairfield County, a center for corporate headquarters); M. Grumbacher, a leading art supply company, for $15 million; Graphic Controls, a Buffalo company that produces paper used in scientific calibrations, for $47 million; a new cable television company, Communications Property Inc., for $85 million, making the Times Mirror the sixth largest cable company in America; and, for $82 million, five Newhouse television stations, in St. Louis,

Syracuse, Birmingham, Harrisburg, and Elmira, let go because Newhouse was forced to sell stations in cities where he also owned newspapers. It was all done in less than two years, and it stunned and surprised the Times Mirror executives themselves to find that they could expand so quickly, that other companies would so readily welcome their arrival. Nor would it stop there; the new properties were all so lucrative that there were certain to be more and more profits and, inevitably, more and more acquisitions.

# 35 / Time Incorporated

It was 1966, in the last year of his life. Harry Luce was tired then, but he still loved being a part of his magazines, editing them, arguing with writers, editors, copy boys if there was no one else around. *Life* magazine that year happened to be doing a special three-part series on the history of modern China, from the Opium War through the Communist take-over in 1949. It was a subject that was not just close to Luce's heart, it was in fact his very soul, and the two *Life* editors in charge, John Thorne and Chuck Elliott, had found him fascinated with the layouts for the forthcoming story. Luce was particularly interested in the second installment, which dealt with China in the twentieth century before the Japanese invasion. In his opinion it seriously understated what a positive moment the 1930's had been for both China and Chiang. In that period everything had looked so bright, he claimed. Chiang had been unchallenged, the economy was on the upswing, the nation seemed secure, proving what it could do under a sound government. Elliott, who had worked for *Life* in Hong Kong and was something of a China scholar, dissented. He and Luce argued back and forth for several minutes. Finally Luce walked to his desk, sat down, swiveled his chair so that he did not face Elliott and Thorne, but instead looked out over the Hudson, and perhaps back all the way to his childhood. "All right," he said, "go ahead. You'll do it the way you want to anyway."

He was right, now they would do it the way they wanted to. In a year he was dead, and the company was changing, and changing rapidly. It had once been a highly personal company, his own creation, where his own presence was uniquely palpable, his touch on everything total, intense, and personal. It was a company whose business was printed words and pictures. A decade after his death Henry Luce would not recognize his own company. Part of the transformation had occurred during his lifetime, and very little of it had brought him any pleasure. In 1964, right after the company went on the big board, Luce had been at a Republican convention and the Time stock had gone up several points that day. One of the business people had whispered this to Dick Clurman, who was sitting next to Luce, suggesting that he pass on the information. Surely it would gladden Luce's heart. Clurman did just that, and Luce, rather than being pleased, was outraged by the interruption. "Why would I want to know that now? Why are you telling me that?"

Though in fact under other circumstances Luce had a very healthy interest in the value of his company's stock (he after all owned a great deal of it), he had little tolerance for the corporate idea, the world of acquisitions and different units, companies brought together only by a desire for profit. When he had been in communications he had not even liked the idea of broadcasting, he wanted words on paper, not words in the air. At a very early date he had turned down a chance to take over what was to become the ABC network, for precious little money, and he had seemed over the years somewhat offended by the profits made by Time Inc.'s five television stations. His idea of the company was old-fashioned, it was a business of words and every word was, in a real sense, his own. If he published a magazine, it was because he willed that magazine to exist, and not merely for profit. Very late in his career the Time Inc. business people decided to buy a textbook company. They had checked it out very carefully, it was a good buy. It was all but approved, when, at the last moment, Luce balked. "I don't want to do it," he announced at the final meeting. Patiently, as if talking to an elderly retired parent, Luce's modern young corporate executives explained what a good acquisition this was, that it was a sure thing, a guaranteed profit center. "No, no, that's not it," Luce said, "I can barely read all the words we print now, and I know I can't read all these textbooks. I don't want them going out with my name on them if I haven't read them."

But cooler heads prevailed, the textbook company was purchased (although there was some shaking of heads over poor Harry, who did not quite understand). In his last months, his friends thought, Luce, who always appreciated profit, began to understand the need to change the company and to diversify. Certainly it came quickly after his death. In any case, Time Inc., unlike most communications companies, was never a family business, Luce had never believed in nepotism, his real family had been the company, and it was not surprising that he intended to leave the running of his company to the men he had worked with all those years. The family stock went into a foundation. His son Hank worked in the company but Luce's real heirs were Hedley Donovan on the editorial side and Andrew Heiskell and Jim Shepley on the business side.


Even while he was alive the magazine world was drifting rapidly into crisis. *Life,* which had publicized Luce's idea of the American Century, was to close down, overtaken by the very technology that the Century symbolized. *Life* had been the perfect vehicle for mass national advertising, but that ended with the coming of television. The issues of the early fifties had been thick and rich. By the mid-sixties they were painfully thin. Instead of trying to adapt to television, making the magazine smaller but more sophisticated, informing their readers about what they had just seen on their tubes (Ralph Graves, the last editor of the weekly *Life*, felt in retrospect that the furious bidding between *Life* and *Look* for the rights to William Manchester's *Death of a President* had been so intense mainly because readers had seen all of these events on their screens and thus were involved), the executives of Time Inc. decided to make a frontal riposte and escalate its circulation. *Life* was thus caught in an immense dilemma, risking its true constituency of *readers* in competition with television and its *watchers*. It was to be a hopeless numbers game. Television had audiences of 15 and 20 million for some programs, and so *Life* was being pushed by mail-order hucksters to people who did not particularly want it, at a price per copy far below the cost of production, just for the sake of showing advertisers that the magazine medium was competitive. The last promotion for *Life* offered 78 copies for $11.95 or roughly fifteen cents a copy for a magazine that was costing at least twice that to produce. That meant that every time *Life* bought another chunk of circulation—six million, eight million—the magazine was in truth not gaining, but losing, subsidizing that many more households. And there was a Catch 22 built in. Because the losses per copy were so great, *someone* had to pay for part of the cost, and that turned out to be the advertisers. The rates thus became so high that the game was lost at the outset—it was an attractive outlet for advertisers that most advertisers couldn't afford. All the big national magazines were caught in the same dilemma, and one by one they perished, *Collier's, The Saturday Evening Post, Look*, and finally *Life*. When *Collier's* died, its circulation list was for sale and the *Life* people, chary of the pitfalls, refused to bid. But *Look* bought the circulation, making *Look* bigger than *Life*, and when *The Saturday Evening Post* folded, *Life* decided it had to react in order to be number one again. The *Post* list took *Life* from 7 million to 8.5 million. It was like buying cancer.

By then some of the *Life* people were arguing for the idea of making the magazine smaller, with a readership that actually wanted the magazine, priced honestly on the newsstand. In the final three years of *Life*'s existence, Garry Valk, the last publisher, cut its list twice, first from 8 to 7 million, then to 5.5. Valk's dream was to cut it to 3 million, which he thought was the true readership. He thought he had a chance at that figure. But in the last five or six years of *Life*'s existence it had lost some $30 million. In 1972 a smart advertising man named Bob Liddell of Compton Advertising met with a group of merchandisers from Procter and Gamble to discuss how they should spend their advertising dollars in the years ahead. Among other things, Liddell told them not to advertise in *Life*. It was, he predicted, going out of business very soon. Time Inc., he said, was in the process of selling its five television stations to McGraw-Hill and when they were sold the profits would be enormous. At that point, he was sure, the company would fold *Life* and write the loss off against the television profits. It was a chilling prediction and it hurt *Life* around town. Soon the television stations were sold, and soon *Life* was closed down, not, thought some of its employees, with a whimper, but for a tax deduction.

The death of *Life* left the company much weaker in terms of influence. But at a time when other companies seemed to be expanding their communications properties, the once mighty Luce publications seemed to be sidling away from them. A few years after the death of *Life, Time* entered the marketplace with a new magazine, *People*. It could be regarded as either a much lighter version of *Life* or an expansion of the People section of *Time*. *People* was finely tuned to the new volatility of celebrityhood in America, quick entrance, often quicker departure; it was pleasant, lightly gossipy, it largely accepted people and their reputations as they wished to be accepted. It told neither too much nor too little about the celebrities it discussed, and its editors seemed to know their audience very well. Most of the old *Life* people looked down on it. But it bore several advantages over *Life*. First, it was sold mostly at supermarkets and newsstands, so it could avoid the vagaries and expense of the U.S. Postal Service. Second, its price was realistic, it covered the cost of producing the magazine, no one was trying to push cut rates in order to increase circulation. Third, it complemented television rather than competing with it. It covered exactly the right people, and they were with uncommon frequency the people that readers had just seen on a television screen. It was a very big moneymaker for the company, and its very success increased stirrings to bring out a new, statelier monthly version of *Life* that would be free, among other things, of its old circulation lists.

But the magazines, successful or no, were nonetheless becoming a smaller part of the company every year. Slowly but surely the giant communications empire that Harry Luce had spawned was turning into a forest-products giant.

The first step had come in 1952 with the acquisition of Eastex—East Texas Pulp and Paper company—a large pulp company with 585,000 acres in Texas. The original reason for the purchase seems almost trivial now; it was to be a hedge against the day when magazine paper might become exorbitantly expensive. *Time* would have its own source. Besides, it had been a good buy. Then, in 1973, *Time* entered into a dramatic merger with Temple Industries, a huge timber company in East Texas headed by Arthur Temple. Temple was in communications too, in a somewhat more modest way. He was the owner of the *Angelina Free Press* (circulation 4,200) of Diboll, Texas. On the day the merger was completed, the Time shareholders met at Rockefeller Center in Manhattan while the shareholders of Temple Industries met at the Pine Acres Community Center in Diboll, whose population is 3,558. Temple Industries was an immensely profitable lumber company with more than 400,000 acres of pine trees in East Texas.

The merger made Time Inc. overnight the largest landholder in Texas, bigger than the King Ranch. Temple, a roughhewn man given to wearing his hat in the office and coming to work in overalls, automatically became an immense force within Time Inc. He and his colleagues found themselves the possessors of very sizable blocks of Time stock. His eighty-four-year-old aunt became the largest individual stockholder in Time with 4.2 percent of the stock. All told, the Temple people owned about 15 percent of the Time stock, roughly the same as the Luce family, the Time board members, and the company executives all put together. Temple went immediately on the board and was soon a vice-chairman; people talked of the future, when he might become chairman of the board. Bill Broyles of the *Texas Monthly* noted as early as 1973 that Temple Industries would boost Time's pretax revenues from forest products to 42 percent of the company's revenues.

The whole arrangement was troubling to many Time traditionalists. It gave people who were unknown, people who had no background in national journalism, people who were *Texans* (and Texas was not considered a center of enlightened journalism), an immense lever on the company. Would Time lose control of its own house? Would voices from the corporate room, voices that wanted to hear only what was good about America, now dominate the professional journalists within the company? Would the board impose upon the journalists too brutal a form of budgeting? (Some Time people felt that the 1976 strike at Time was in fact, among other things, a result of harsher budgeting procedures.) The coming of the Texans was bothersome: journalists by nature have been trained to listen to the voices of dissent and discontent and they feared that these were people who by nature preferred the voices of success and assent.

But the people who had put the deal together held the day easily. If you wanted to sustain editorial excellence in difficult economic times, they argued, then you had to diversify, and this was ideal for the company. Look at how profitable it all was. Look at how the stock was going up. Publishing, after all, was subject to many kinds of variables, technology was working against print, the history of *Life* proved that, and magazines had to be balanced with other, more stable properties. What could be more stable than pine trees? So the companies merged and in the early years the Texans showed great respect for the journalists. They did not move in editorially. It turned out that they had other interests.

Arthur Temple very quickly began to exert influence within Time Inc., but not in the way that working journalists had feared. To him the world of magazines was alien and small. He was a lumberman, he did not particularly want to be a big man in Washington and New York media circles, he wanted to be dominant in the world of paper and pines and building. He intended to expand Time Inc., but in a way familiar to him, along a road he knew and knew well. For he had all those thousands and thousands of acres of trees, trees growing every minute, and Time Inc. could not make use of them. If trees growing did not necessarily make him a profit, trees being cut and sold did, and he needed outlets for them. Temple was a very good and old friend of Henry Goodrich, the head of Inland Container Company, a company which made cardboard containers and which needed, more than anything else, a lot of trees to make its containers. Thus it was no surprise to those who knew Temple, though perhaps a considerable surprise to others in the company, when in 1978 Time Inc. acquired Inland Container for about $280 million.

Time Inc. was changing significantly and quickly. Yes, it had added cable-television companies and bought the Book-of-the-Month Club, and yes, it was making some tentative moves into television, but it was not the same company. The dog had become the tail and the tail had become the dog. It was no longer a communications business with a resource ancillary, it was more and more a forest-products company or a resource company that also had some magazines. It was, with the acquisition of Inland, a $2 billion company, roughly the 150th-largest company in the country. Time executives estimated that with Inland the traditional Time Inc. editorial core operations—magazines and books—would now account for only about 45 percent of revenue, with the same amount or more coming from forest products. Some Wall Street analysts believed that the magazines alone accounted for no more than 25 percent. There would surely be more acquisitions. Those who knew Arthur Temple well suspected that he would move quickly to expand the Texas-Inland axis, he would acquire, they thought, some lumber-mill capacity to cut his trees, and what was called in the trade a liner-board mill, which turned out the cardboard that went into containers. That would complete a fully integrated paper company.

Arthur Temple and Jim Shepley and Andrew Heiskell got on very well, it was said, and Temple was described by those who knew him as a man who respected the prerogatives of journalists. Yet clearly the role of the magazines within the company was diminishing, and their voice within the company was becoming less important. Time Inc. was still a company that produced magazines, but it did so, so to speak, with its left hand, while thinking about other, possibly more serious things. There may have been some awareness of this in Time's higher echelons when in 1978 Time surprised everyone by announcing that it was buying the Washington *Star*. The *Star*, a perennially floundering newspaper, did not appear to be a particularly good buy. It was an afternoon newspaper in a city whose core population was neither rich nor white. But it cost only $20 million, and tiny papers in tiny towns sold for more than that. It had lost money regularly in recent years and it would almost surely continue to lose money. Its very life, until Time moved in, seemed to hang in the balance. What Time was buying was a voice in the nation's capital, and a chance to bring the Washington *Post* some daily competition. It was also a connection to the past.

# 36/CBS

Bill Paley did not like the people who were always accusing his network of timidity. Now, in his final years, when he spoke to reporters he made clear his belief that he had not been given enough credit for the Murrow show on McCarthy. He particularly disliked the insinuation that it had ended badly between Murrow and him professionally. Why, if anything he had tried to get Ed to cut back on his work schedule because he was ill and needed rest. When versions less sympathetic to his side of the story began appearing in print, Paley decided to act. CBS commissioned a young documentary film maker in Hollywood named Alan Landsburg to produce an original film on Murrow and McCarthy and Murrow's last days. About twenty-five thousand dollars in seed money, a handsome sum, was put up. Landsburg was promised complete artistic freedom. No one would try to censor him, he was free to find out the facts, judge them, and write his script accordingly. Landsburg proceeded to interview everyone connected with the story, some of whom, like Fred Friendly, warned him that his work would never see the light of day. His final version of the script reflected the view that Murrow and Friendly had enjoyed less than enthusiastic support from the company during the period of the McCarthy show, and that Murrow's final days were not particularly happy ones. Landsburg eventually handed in the script. No one from CBS ever commented on it or argued with him about it. But a few months later he was notified that the script did not meet CBS's present needs. Bill Paley had not ceased to wrestle with history. He was at about this time becoming expansive about the company's role in Watergate. Why, he told a young interviewer, he was very proud of the way CBS had stood almost alone, had taken the Washington *Post*'s story and made it national. When the reporter mentioned the struggles between Salant and Paley over doing the Watergate shows at all, he had no memory of them.

The years after Watergate were troubled ones for Paley. As he came closer to retirement he became more and more concerned with his public image, how he wanted his stewardship at CBS to be remembered, the Paley he wanted to be. But coincidentally he was for the first time in his career coming under much closer scrutiny from print journalists, a scrutiny produced by a growing public awareness of the power and influence of network television. Accustomed to fending off doubters by the invocation of the names of Murrow, Stanton, and others, Paley took the newer, tougher criticism personally and reacted badly to it. When a reporter for *The New York Times* named Robert Metz wrote a book about CBS, Paley's publicity people sent all reviewers a "fact sheet" filled with what they claimed were inaccuracies in the book. The controversy this inspired helped sell that book. When *The Atlantic Monthly* printed two sections from the present book, Paley became very upset and for a time there was serious discussion at the upper levels of CBS about buying the magazine so that nothing like that could ever happen again. Angered by books that he thought unflattering, he hired a professional writer named Martin Mayer at a very high price to prepare a house-produced narrative of the company. Mayer's report was to be a narrative history of CBS News, roughly twenty thousand words long, and Mayer believed that he was writing it for eventual distribution to all stockholders. Mayer, who regarded CBS News as a worthy institution, agreed to do the work with one proviso: that no one could edit any part of it without his permission. He worked very hard on the piece, which finally ran to forty thousand words and failed to receive the Chairman's approval. It was plain that Mayer's principal fault had been in not assigning enough credit to Paley for the early victories of CBS News, and in mentioning Paley's nervousness over the phone call from Colson at the time of the CBS Watergate programs. CBS would not, thank you very much, care to print the Mayer narrative. Thus frustrated, Paley was also working on his own memoirs, but he was having trouble. Writers appeared, worked on them, and disappeared.

By the time Frank Stanton, the self-proclaimed statesman of broadcasting, left CBS in 1973, the feeling between the two men had turned very bitter. Stanton had hoped to run the company, had lost his chance at that, and then had hoped to stay on past retirement age. But when he had reached sixty-five in 1973 he had been cast aside, used goods, nothing more. After Stanton's retirement there had been arguments over the size of Stanton's office (located, at Paley's insistence, outside the CBS building) and the amount of secretarial help. The dispute had become angry. For a time it seemed that it might even go to court. That was an intriguing idea, the man most responsible in recent years for the creation of the CBS image suing the very network he had helped create. At the last minute cooler counsel prevailed and Stanton did not sue. But the bitterness remained. Stanton felt totally cut off from the company, which was precisely what Paley intended. When Stanton talked with old friends he could no longer control his anger about the Chairman. He felt used, badly used. It was beyond him to say a kind word about Paley. While he was still at CBS he had been bombarded with offers from almost every corporation, foundation, and university in the country, but when he reached retirement at sixty-five there were suddenly fewer offers than he might have expected. He was sixty-five and his price had automatically gone down. He took a job as head of the American Red Cross, which was at least partly ceremonial. Old friends found him restless, frustrated, and underemployed, obsessed by CBS and Paley. He knew that his successor, Arthur Taylor, was trying to "de-Stantonize" the company and wipe out his memory.

He had a consultancy without consultation. He and his wife, Ruth, had never had children. He was restless at the Red Cross. It was far from the action that he was accustomed to. There was some talk about a position with the Carnegie Endowment. The job needed the approval of Bill Paley, and Paley shot it down. Then in the winter of 1977 there was to be an opening for the chairmanship of the Public Broadcasting System. Stanton heard of the job and began to hint of his interest in it. The people at PBS were themselves immediately intrigued; Frank Stanton was the perfect man for the job, he knew broadcasting and, whatever his flaws, he was a man of taste. He knew the value system in which broadcasting had to operate, and there could be, above all, no better fund raiser for the poverty-stricken public network. His friends were pleased with the idea, it would be the ideal job for him. Indeed, some of them thought it was probably the place where he always should have been. The offer was made. Stanton was delighted and very interested. But he told the people from PBS that they would have to check with a CBS lawyer named Lloyd Cutler before he could take the job. After all, he was on the CBS board and he had that CBS consultancy. The PBS people were a little surprised, either you wanted a job or you did not. Besides, they had heard reports that he was about to be dumped from the board. The call was made to Cutler; he said CBS would get back to Stanton. CBS did get back to Stanton. It was not Bill Paley, with whom Stanton had worked intimately for thirty years, who called, but Cutler again. The word was clear enough. Bill Paley did not want Frank Stanton to take the PBS job. He was sick of Stanton taking the credit for the public-spirited decisions that *he,* Bill Paley, was making. Stanton at PBS, being even purer, would be too much. Of course, Stanton could go to PBS. But he would have to give up the position on the CBS board and the consultancy. Stanton was perhaps as upset by the fact that Paley had used Cutler and had not called him directly as he was by the answer.

Though it was a job that Stanton desperately wanted and though he was terribly restless with the American Red Cross, and though his personal net worth was estimated at $30 million dollars and though he was said to be the second-largest stockholder at CBS, Frank Stanton did not give up the consultancy with the office and the secretary and the car, or his position on the board. Bill Paley had been right about him: Paley had decided Stanton was weak, and weak he had been.

Stanton did not stay very long on the CBS board. In 1978, Daniel Schorr, irate at his former employers, published a book in which he quoted Stanton as saying that in 1964 he had told Paley not to come to the Republican convention because every time he did, Paley, in Stanton's words, was guilty of "really screwing up the works." Before the book was published, Stanton got wind of the quote and called Schorr from London, claiming that he had said no such thing. Schorr got out his tapes. Yes, Stanton had indeed said it. Stanton suggested that Schorr take out the reference anyway. Schorr said that he could not, that the book was already in galleys and that if he took it out everyone would know and it would prove far more embarrassing. So it remained in and Frank Stanton believed that it was the reason that shortly afterward he was removed from the board of CBS.

The short happy life of Arthur Taylor as Frank Stanton's successor, and as Paley's heir, lasted from 1973 to 1976. Taylor had come highly recommended and touted from International Paper, and he was said to be the best of the new generation of corporate managers. He had a Ph.D., he had once taught at Brown, and he was very bright and very ambitious. He knew nothing of broadcasting, either the programming side or the public-service side. He did, however, want to be a statesman, just as Stanton had been. There were those who thought that he also intended to be not just President of CBS but President of the United States. He did not make an entirely favorable impression upon people in the News Department, many of whom thought him a vain and bumptious man. He once told Morley Safer, the CBS correspondent, that when he grew up he wanted to be a CBS foreign correspondent, and Safer sensed subtle condescension in the joke. Taylor told news executives at one point that he would be willing to go ahead with a controversial piece of film if they would assure him that it would not cost the company $50 million worth of business. The executives explained that one of the problems with the news business is that there are no such guarantees. It would be a much easier business if there were. Gradually, however, some of the news people came to like him, most noticeably Dick Salant, who thought that Taylor's immense ambition and desire for recognition made him a potential corporate ally. Taylor, Salant decided, might help Salant get what he wanted most, and what the network for reasons of greed was unwilling to give him, the one-hour news show.

Taylor seemed to be doing very well on the corporate side. He was much better at corporate management and above all at acquisitions than Stanton, and it was said that he rather quickly brought more organization to the corporate side of the company. Bill Paley in the early days of their association spoke well of Arthur Taylor. He was coming along well, learning fast. Mike Dann, listening to Paley praise Taylor, heard a certain unconscious reserve in the Chairman's voice and knew that the jury, composed of twelve Bill Paleys, good and true, was still out on Arthur Taylor. Those close to Arthur Taylor thought he was doing well and was very happy in his work; those who were close to Bill Paley or who had known him in years past did not envy Arthur Taylor, they thought he was caught in a hopeless dilemma. If he did poorly at CBS, he would anger Paley, for that would hurt the company and the company must be protected. If, however, he did very well, that would not necessarily help him, because it would be the most feared thing of all for the Chairman, a sign of Paley's own mortality. The better he did, the closer the image of mortality would hover, an indication that Paley would someday have to let go of the company. Bill Paley's friends began to notice that Paley became increasingly reluctant to praise Arthur Taylor. Perhaps the success he brought the company was too great. In October 1976, much to Arthur Taylor's surprise, he was fired. He was given a one-million-dollar settlement. He did not understand what had happened to him. He had made the company very rich, he had become rich himself, but he had scared an old man.

He was replaced by John Backe, who had come from the CBS book division, who had no background in broadcasting, and who was viewed not as a man of books but as a man of systems. Backe seemed to think, one associate believed, that the *system* was the answer to everything. He had no particular link to the News Department and when he became President of CBS he made no attempt to get to know people there. He seemed, colleagues thought, to share the general corporate belief that CBS News was trouble and the less seen of it, the better. He met Dick Salant at the regular monthly meetings of the presidents of the different sections and that was enough for him. He did not bestir himself to see Salant more. Salant felt more cut off from Black Rock than ever, his oxygen line ever frailer. A bright new young CBS executive named Peter Derow, who knew both Backe and Salant, managed to bring them together, but there was an element of mild humiliation in even this for Salant, who had to go through a much younger and less senior person to have any genuine access to his boss. That did not bode well. It was a sign that the News Division mattered less and less in the scheme of things, and that the new people like Backe—unlike Paley and Stanton—had no feeling for that special tradition in which the News Division was measured, not by its financial contribution, but by its social and moral importance. It was being judged more and more by corporate standards, by how much money it could make (or lose). Thus it had no real weight in the new scheme of things.

Nothing showed that more than the brief career of Bill Moyers at CBS. Moyers was one of the most talented and attractive young men of his generation in the area of public affairs, and after he had left the White House he had become editor of *Newsday,* where he had done very well until Harry Guggenheim decided he was a bit too liberal. From *Newsday* Moyers had gone to the Public Broadcasting System, where he had instantly displayed an uncommon talent for television reporting. He seemed at once intelligent, incisive, and humane. PBS gave Moyers, its main star, easy access to air time, a good deal of freedom, and, by the standards of the networks, very small budgets. CBS, coveting what it did not allow itself, hired him away in 1976. Moyers had been uneasy about making the switch to so large a network, but he was seduced not just by the money but by the chance to address so large an audience from so powerful a platform. He soon found that he was given the platform on very rare occasions indeed, usually when most of the audience was supposed to have gone to bed. He found himself working with highly professional people who were also very clearly the stepchildren of the corporation. That which they did they did very well, but it was also clear that no one very high up cared much about what they did. Moyers found himself far more frustrated at CBS than he had been at PBS: there the frustrations were those of too little money, and faulty equipment, not a feeling of irrelevancy. At CBS the equipment was wonderful, the money was wonderful, and the people who ran the network did not really care.

Yet the network did care about Moyers. He was a star. He was what network television executives dream about, someone so smart, so intuitive, and yet so subtle that he could deal with the most explosive of subjects in a strong and intelligent way without tearing the house apart. Bill Moyers had always, first with Lyndon Johnson, then with Harry Guggenheim, shown an ability to charm older men and, true to form, Bill Paley became very enamored of him. Paley admired his work, and decided that Moyers was the CBS type because he was classy. Besides, Paley was absolutely charmed by him personally. But none of this kept Bill Moyers from being very unhappy at CBS and he soon began to think of returning to the smaller audiences and faultier equipment and greater access to air time of PBS. The executives of CBS, including William S. Paley, were appalled. No one that CBS *wanted* ever left for PBS; if people had left in the past, it was because the network no longer needed them. The word went out to hold Moyers at all costs. They promised him everything they could think of. Sevareid's job (Eric was soon to retire), Salant's job when Salant retired in 1979. There was a mention of money, lots of it. There was even talk of Cronkite's job, though there was no guarantee of it.

But Moyers did not bend. He liked the people at CBS but he did not like the system, a system in which many good intentions were always being expressed about what the network intended to do, in spite of which the network went on very much as before. Bill Paley, hearing that Moyers was becoming restless, met with him to find out what would make him happy.

"A regular prime-time show," said Moyers, who had learned very fast. "Much like Murrow had. On a regular schedule and a set hour."

The man who answered was the real Bill Paley, a man shorn of his speeches and his public relations division. "I'm sorry, Bill," the Chairman said. "I can't do it any more. The minute is worth too much now." So Moyers left. It briefly shocked Bill Paley. It was strange to offer so much to so fine a young man and be turned down.


It was a curious thing. Bill Paley had invented the system, but now the system was in the process of swallowing him up. It was his company but now it was no longer his company, the system was too powerful for him, the index on Wall Street too important. There had been a time when he had truly controlled it and he had put on what he wanted when he wanted, and it had been his decision to go for constantly greater profit. Now in his final years it was beyond him. Even if he had wanted to return to a more pluralistic schedule it was too much. The company was too big, Wall Street watched too closely. It was his company but it was no longer his company. He had ridden on the tiger and now he might just as well be inside. Nothing seemed to go well for him, he was getting older, seventy-four in 1975, and he was losing touch. In that year he lost his best programmer to a rival network without even knowing he was losing him. He was soon to start losing in the ratings too.

He lost Freddie Silverman to ABC. No one had paid much attention at the time because Freddie Silverman, though a very talented commercial programmer, did not cut a wide swath in New York media circles and because, in addition, no one took ABC seriously. It was the perennial third network, last in everything but sports. Everyone laughed at it and there were endless ABC jokes: about how they should take the Vietnam War and play it as a sit-com on ABC and it would all be over in a few weeks; about the Arab oil millionaire who came to America with his son and they stayed at the Plaza Hotel and the son liked it, so the Arab bought it for him, and they flew to Los Angeles by American Airlines and the son liked the trip, so the Arab bought American Airlines for him, and they went to Disneyland and the son liked *that,* so the Arab bought Disneyland for him, and finally, the trip an almost complete success, the father asked if there was anything else the son wanted, and the son said yes, he wanted a Mickey Mouse outfit. So the father bought ABC.

Freddie Silverman was a very good commercial programmer. He was a link to the great days when CBS dominated the two other networks year after year in commercial programming and always got first look at all the new hot series. Like most people in his chosen profession, he was not particularly concerned with the social obligation or the moral consequences of what he did. His life was the Nielsen ratings, he knew what worked and what did not, and he had a good sense of the limits of the public taste and what was the right moment to try new areas. He was intense, totally driven by his work. He knew how to rig a schedule to protect a new show in the lee of a stronger show. He had a very good instinct for mass taste and he was an ultimate professional in a profession built on rendering unto Mammon what is Mammon's. He was the classic workaholic and it was said of him that if he were visiting China he would make sure that the previous day's Nielsens would be delivered to him by bicycle rider. At CBS he had done very well, but mastery of the ratings had been taken for granted there. Fred Silverman felt frustrated and neglected. He had little genuine access to Bill Paley. The company was too big, the structure was too heavy, and there were too many people between him and the Chairman, men like Jack Schneider and Bob Wood. It was hard to believe, but Paley was also starting to show his age, although, of course, he did not *think* he was showing his age, and he simply wasn't paying attention any more. Silverman, a volatile man, was reaching a boiling point over his lack of access to Paley, his salary (only about $140,000 when people who were taking credit for his work had senior vice-presidencies and perhaps $500,000), the fact that he had no company car or private dining room. Yet Bill Paley did not seem to know that his key man was feeling desperately unappreciated. When Silverman quit, Bill Paley had not even known that he was angry. Silverman was not even given a goodbye party, although *everyone* at CBS got a goodbye party. He was replaced as head of programming by someone who had been in sales. That broke a sacrosanct rule at CBS, that programming belonged to no one but programming people. It was a sign, some old-timers thought, of a growing arrogance at the top. People within the profession saw the manner of Silverman's departure as a sign that Bill Paley was out of touch. Now, with Silverman using all the tricks and techniques that he had learned at Bill Paley's hand, ABC moved up faster than anyone had expected. (One of his early successes at ABC was a truly terrible show called "Charlie's Angels." It featured equal parts of mindless scripts and female flesh. When Bill Paley first saw it, he reportedly asked, "Where are *our* beautiful girls?") In a stunningly short time ABC was number one.

Time seemed to pass for everyone else, but not necessarily for William S. Paley. But his later years were not necessarily happy ones. Babe Paley had died a lingering death in 1978, and it had shaken him. Even those men and women who did not like him, who thought him cold and tough, were touched by the degree of his sensitivity during her illness. It was a Bill Paley they had never seen before. Meanwhile, he endured. He was still the Chairman, he had out-lived everybody from the old days, friends, aides, critics. They were all gone, some dead, some retired. Potential successors had foolishly checked his age in *Who's Who* and settled in, expecting to replace him. They had waited, and their time had never come, and they had left, some bitter, all disappointed. It was still his company. Many friends thought he had stayed on too long. More than fifty years after he had come to CBS, Bill Paley was seated at a dinner party next to Mike Dann, who had been one of his bright young men in programming, and who was not so young any more. Paley turned and said, almost wistfully, "Where are the young Mike Danns today?" Dann answered, "They're all around you," but even as he said it he realized that Paley was no longer in touch. But for all that it was still his company, he was still the invincible man. He had survived, the others had left.

Nor was William Paley in any rush to change things. In 1973, near the end of Watergate, he had taken a trip to Europe and done something that he had not done in years. He met with his foreign correspondents. They were concerned about the future, concerned that various kinds of interference, political and otherwise, were in store for CBS. Nixon was to them but a symptom of what was to come. Winston Burdett, one of the last correspondents from the Murrow days still working in Europe, had asked Paley about it. "You've been good to us," he said, "but the pressures against the News Division are terrible. What's going to happen after you've gone?" William S. Paley smiled and replied, "I suggest you find a way for me to stick around for another twenty-five years." Not everyone who knew Bill Paley thought he was kidding.

# Acknowledgments,
# Bibliography,
# and Index

# Acknowledgments

This book is the product of five years of work. It began as a small idea in 1973 and it grew, constantly changing incarnations. At first it was going to be merely a book on a television network and the presidency; gradually it evolved into a book on the rise of modern media and their effect on the way we perceive events. In selecting the four institutions that have the major role in this book, I tried to give as fair a cross section of the national press as I could. I chose CBS because it has traditionally represented the best in broadcast journalism; *Time* because among national magazines it reflects something special in the American character; the Washington *Post* because it has become a serious national newspaper and because this is in part a book about the road to Watergate; and the Los Angeles *Times* for those reasons and also because it played so large a part in the career of Richard Nixon. I did not write as fully about *The New York Times* as about the other two papers because it has been written about so much in the past, most notably by my friend and colleague Gay Talese, and because I did not want to write at length about an institution where I worked and about which my own feelings were so personal and ambivalent.

Although hundreds of people were interviewed for the book, I would like to cite in particular two whose help was special: the first is my friend Fred Dutton, who, perhaps because his roots are in California politics, started talking to me about the changing role of the media and politics long before anyone else, and who was extremely helpful in the embryonic stages when I needed help the most; the other is the late Jim Bassett of the Los Angeles *Times,* a man of great personal kindness, who, although he was doing an authorized (and thus potentially competitive) book on the Los Angeles *Times,* was uncommonly generous in helping me with the history of the *Times* in general, and especially with the early relationship between Richard Nixon and the *Times.*

I would like also to acknowledge the help of these editors: first Jim Silberman, formerly of Random House, my editor for eight years and the original editor of this book, who lost it only because he switched to Simon & Schuster and I was legally unable to follow him; and Charles Elliott of Knopf, diligent, steadfast, intelligent, who in a brief time took an immense and complicated manuscript and helped fuse it together. What a worthy man he is. In addition, Robert Kotlowitz, my editor at *Harper's* some twelve years ago, and in all these years a colleague who has offered me a rare combination of friendship and professional sustenance. I would like also to thank Roberta Pryor, my agent, and Alan Schwartz, my lawyer; Lesley Krauss, production editor at Knopf, for her assiduous and painstaking work; the wondrous Irene Smirnoff, who transcribed most of the interview notes and typed the manuscript, more as friend and enthusiast than as employee; Carol Clurman, now of the Nashville *Tennessean,* who worked as a researcher and checker for me for some eight months near the end. (I had advertised at the Fletcher School for an assistant and she responded to the ad; I pointed out that I knew her father, Richard Clurman, formerly of Time Inc., and was indeed writing about him; she said she should not be penalized for that. We settled by my hiring her with the agreement that she would do no work on the Time section.)

Most of the material upon which the book is based comes from my interviews. A large number of people were extremely generous in seeing me, sharing memories and ideas. Only a tiny handful of people refused to see me (including Richard Nixon—when I called, his office said that he was working on his own book). Very very few of the interviews were conducted on the telephone. By and large I do not like using the phone for magazine and book reporting; it is depersonalizing and there is too little sense of the other person. The average interview lasted between ninety minutes and two hours. Some people saw me five and six and seven times. The interviews are a curious thing: they are at once the most exhausting part of this kind of journalism but, in the end, the best part of it, the most valuable, not just in a narrow professional sense of getting information, but in a larger human sense.

What follows is a list of the people I interviewed. It includes about 95 percent of them; the rest, for personal or professional reasons, felt too vulnerable to be listed. The list is broken down into five major categories: those interviewed about each of the four major media covered in the book, and a miscellaneous group.

# CBS

David Adams, Martin Agronsky, Roger Ailes, Michael Arlen, Aaron Asher, Russell Baker, Homer Bigart, Ed Bliss, Joel Blocker, Carter Burden, Frank Bourgholtzer, Mike Burke, Truman Capote, Ann Chambers, John Chancellor, Dwight Chapin, George Christian, Blair Clark, Ralph Colin, Charles Collingwood, Goeff Cowan, Louis Cowan, Ken Cox, Walter Cronkite, Charles Crutchfield, John Culver, Charlotte Curtis, John Charles Daly, Michael Dann, Johanna Davis, Peter Davis, Peter Derow, Dick Dorso, Bill Downs, Paul Duke, Fred Dutton, Douglas Edwards, John Henry Faulk, Charles Ferris, Fred Friendly, Ed Fuohy, David Garth, Manny Gerard, Peter Goldmark, Jack Gould, Stanhope Gould, Fred Graham, Jeff Gralnick, Jap Gude, Pamela Colin Harlech, John Hart, E. William Henry, Peter Herford, George Herman, Don Hewitt, John Hightower, Gladwin Hill, Dorothy Paley Hirschon, Richard Hottelet, Nicholas Johnson, Tom Johnson, Alex Kendrick, Robert Kintner, Robert Landry, Jack Laurence, Ernie Leiser, Bill Leonard, Ike Levy, Blaine Littell, Gordon Manning, Robert McCormick, Aileen Mehle, Sig Mickelson, Les Midgely, Newton Minow, Herbert Mitgang, Edward P. Morgan, Bill Moyers, Roger Mudd, Janet Murrow, Carroll Newton, Shad Northshield, Kenneth O'Donnell, Margaret Osmer, William S. Paley, Tom Pettit, Robert Pierpoint, Harry Rasky, Dan Rather, Victor Ratner, Harry Reasoner, George Reedy, Rosser Reeves, Hubbell Robinson, Ted Rogers, Hughes Rudd, Morley Safer, Richard Salant, Pierre Salinger, Harrison Salisbury, John Scali, Franklin Schaffner, David Schoenbrun, Daniel Schorr, Herbert Segal, Tom Seigenthaler, Irene Selznick, Eric Sevareid, Jim Seward, Frank Seyferts, William L. Shirer, Hugh Sidey, Bill Small, Carleton Smith, Howard K. Smith, Sandy Socolow, Ben Sonnenberg, Frank Stanton, Carl Stern, Tom Stix, Bill Stout, Jack Valenti, Richard Valeriani, Sander Vanocur, Sylvester (Pat) Weaver, Doris Klauber Wechsler, Sylvia Westerman, Wallace Westfeldt, Joseph Wershba, Theodore White, Bill Wilson, Perry Wolff, Robert Wussler.

# Los Angeles Times

Rudy Abramson, Jay Allen, Seth Baker, James Bassett, Herb Baus, Leone Baxter, Muriel Beadle, Olive Behrendt, Earl (Squire) Behrens, Jim Bellows, Dick Bergholz, Martin Bernheimer, Harry Bernstein, Gene Blake, Dennis Britton, Pat Brown, Don Bruckner, Ron Buttons, Asa Call, Will Campbell, Ed Carter, Al Casey, Dorothy Buffum Chandler, Otis Chandler, Nancy Chotiner, Paul Conrad, Tony Day, Ken Dean, Digby Diehl, Bob Donovan, Dick Dorso, Dick Dougherty, Helen Gahagan Douglas, Fred Dutton, Robert Erburu, Robert Finch, Harold Fleming, Donald Frost, Carl Greenberg, Ed Guthman, Joyce Haber, Ken Hahn, Robert Hartman, Coleman Harwell, Gladwin Hill, Chet Holifield, Don Irwin, Bob Jackson, Tom Johnson, Phil Kerby, Herb Klein, Virginia Knight, Sid Kossen, David Kraslow, Tom Kuchel, Jack Langguth, Art Larow, Harry Lerner, Stuart Loory, Frank Mankiewicz, Richard Matheson, Frank McCulloch, Helene Melzer, Freddie Miller, Chuck Morgan, Franklin Murphy, Mark Murphy, J. Edward Murray, Bryce Nelson, Jack Nelson, Ronald Ostrow, Bill Price, Ken Reich, Vern Scoggins, Donald Shannon, David Shaw, Norton Simon, Merrill Small, Bill Stout, Bill Thomas, Tex Thornton, Jack Tobin, Jim Toland, Robert Towne, Dick Tuck, Jerry Voorhis, John Weaver, Paul Weeks, Ted Weisman, Art White, Nick Williams, Nick Williams, Jr., Jules Witcover, Mickey Ziffren, Paul Ziffren.

# Time Incorporated

John Anderson, Robert Sam Anson, Peter Arnett, Edward Atorino, Louis Banks, Felix Belair, Jesse Birnbaum, Richard Burgheim, Richard Clurman, Shirley Clurman, J. L. Dabbert, Ken Danforth, Ralph Davidson, Michael Demarest, Joan Didion, Gaylord Donnelley, Hedley Donovan, Martha Duffy, John Gregory Dunne, Charles Elliott, Osborn Elliott, John Fairbank, Barry Farrell, Clay Felker, Simmons Fentress, Otto Friedrich, Otto Fuerbringer, John Kenneth Galbraith, Murray Gart, Burt Glinn, Hays Gorey, Ralph Graves, Tom Griffith, Allen Grover, Henry Grunwald, T George Harris, John Hersey, Nancy White Hilles, Emmet John Hughes, Annalee Jacoby, Jack Jessup, Stanley Karnow, James Keogh, Andrew Kopkind, Ronald Kriss, Jon Larsen, Roy Larsen, Marshall Loeb, Christopher Luce, Ed Magnuson, Robert Manning, Dwight Martin, Frank McCulloch, Jason McManus, John Milliken, Charles Mohr, Norma Mohr, Beth Luce Moore, Lance Morrow, Carl Mydans, Shelley Mydans, Don Neff, Curt Pendergast, Karsten Prager, Jon Randal, Jerry Schechter, Israel Shenker, James Shepley, Hugh Sidey, Sandy Smith, John Steele, Ed Thompson, James C. Thompson, Calvin Trillin, Friedel Ungeheuer, Gary Valk, Max Ways, Don Weaden, Frank White, Theodore White, Jim Wilde, James Wright, Barry Zorthian.

# The Washington Post

Deirdre Elliott Adler, John Anderson, Scott Armstrong, Harry Ashmore, Ben Bagdikian, Bobby Baker, Alan Barth, Carl Bernstein, Lester Bernstein, Herbert Block, Ben Bradlee, Fred Bradlee, Art Buchwald, Bob Campbell, James Cannon, Truman Capote, Philip Carter, Marquis Childs, Blair Clark, Richard Clurman, Barbara Stubbs Cohen, Richard Cohen, James Daly, Peter Derow, Dorothy de Santillana, Len Downie, Jim Doyle, Fred Dutton, Willard Edwards, Osborn Elliott, Francis FitzGerald, Anne Taylor Fleming, Karl Fleming, Eddie Folliard, Otto Friedrich, Al Friendly, Katharine Graham, William Graham, Philip Geyelin, Ben Gilbert, Meg Greenfield, Phil Greer, Bill Greider, Edwin Gritz, Louis Harris, Richard Harwood, Brooks Hays, Coit Henley, Seymour Hersh, Warren Hoge, Richard Holbrooke, Emmet John Hughes, Steve Isaacs, John Jay Iselin, Leon Jaworski, Haynes Johnson, Ward Just, Robert Kaiser, Stanley Karnow, Nick Kotz, Ferdinand Kuhn, Joe Laitin, Kermit Lansner, Jim Mann, Gordon Manning, Murrey Marder, Myra McPherson, Betty Medsger, Karl Meyer, Morton Mintz, Paul Moore, Martin F. Nolan, John Oakes, Don Oberdorfer, Eugene Patterson, Phil Potter, Shirley Povich, Ed Prichard, Sally Quinn, Maxwell Rabb, Joe Rauh, James Reston, Harry Rosenfeld, Steve Rosenfeld, Richard Salant, Arthur Schlesinger, Jr., Neil Sheehan, Susan Sheehan, Gerald Siegal, Howard Simons, George Smathers, Larry Stern, Barry Sussman, John Sweeterman, Sander Vanocur, Frank Waldrop, Lally Graham Weymouth, Roger Wilkins, Edward Bennett Williams, Thomas Winship, Geoffrey Wolff, Robert Woodward, James Wooten, Steven Zorn.

# Miscellaneous

Les Aspin, Dick Aurelio, Bill Bader, Wes Barthelmess, Andrew Biemiller, Homer Bigart, Dick Bolling, John Brademas, Jack Brooks, Horace Busby, Joe Califano, Liz Carpenter, Turner Catledge, Robert Chartrand, Frank Church, Clark Clifford, Tony Coelho, Jeff Cohelan, David Cohen, Richard Conlan, John Culver, William Darden, Robert Eckhardt, Rufus Edmiston, Frank Eleazar, David Fine, John Finney, Don Fraser, Alton Frye, Eugene Fubini, J. William Fulbright, Leslie Gelb, K. Dun Gifford, Charles Goodell, Albert Gore, Len Hall, D. B. Hardeman, Bryce Harlow, Michael Harrington, Joseph C. Harsch, Russell Hemenway, Pat Holt, Tom Hughes, Gary Hymel, Frank Ikard, Walter Jenkins, Doris Kearns, Tom Keenan, Edward Kennedy, E. W. Kenworthy, Larry L. King, Robert Kotlowitz, Bill Lawrence, Ted Lewis, Henry Cabot Lodge, Winston Lord, James Lowenstein, Anthony Lukas, George Mahon, Carl Marcy, Charles Mathias, Earl Mazo, Robert McCormick, Rick Merrill, Lee Metcalf, William Lee Miller, Joseph Mohbat, William Moorhead, Margaret Moose, Richard Moose, Michael Moriarty, Wayne Morse, Bill Moyers, Gaylord Nelson, John Newhouse, Martin Nolan, Anthony Oettinger, William Phillips, Walter Pincus, Richard Pollak, John Pomfret, Sam Popkin, Dan Rapoport, David Riesman, Tom Ross, Frank Ryan, Alan Schwartz, Robert Semple, John Siegenthaler, Hall Smith, John Chabot Smith, John Stewart, Stuart Symington, Tad Szulc, Don Tacheron, Frank Thompson, Seth Tillman, Bascom Timmons, Morris Udall, Stewart Udall, Ivan Veit, Tom Wicker, Francis Wilcox, Lee Williams, Richard Wilson, Sid Yates.

To all of them I give thanks for time spent, and information given.

# Bibliography

Certain books were particularly valuable for this work. The Robert Elson two-volume authorized history of Time Inc., *The Intimate History of a Publishing Enterprise,* is uncommonly fair and open (published by Atheneum, the first volume, covering the years from 1923–41 appeared in 1968, the second volume, from 1941–60 was published in 1973); Chalmers Roberts's history of the Washington *Post,* again an authorized work (*The Washington Post: The First 100 Years* [Boston: Houghton Mifflin, 1977]) is intelligent, judicious, and quite tough minded. *Thinking Big: The Story of the Los Angeles Times, Its Publishers and Their Influence on Southern California* (Robert Gottlieb and Irene Wolt [New York: G. P. Putnam's Sons, 1977]) is by no means authorized and it is exceptionally valuable in its treatment of the Chandler economic empire and its influence. For anyone writing about broadcasting, one source above all else is valuable and that is Erik Barnouw's three-volume history of American broadcasting. These books represent a remarkable achievement. They are literate and intelligent and intensely human; anyone traveling through this largely uncharted region owes an immense debt to Mr. Barnouw (*A History of Broadcasting in the United States* [New York: Oxford University Press, 1966, 1968, 1970]). The first volume, *A Tower in Babel,* covers broadcasting up until 1933; the second volume, *The Golden Web,* goes from 1933 to 1953; the third volume, *The Image Empire,* runs from 1950 to the present.

Meyer Berger's book on the history of *The New York Times* (*The Story of the New York Times: The First One Hundred Years* [New York: Simon & Schuster, 1951]) is helpful, but being a house history, carefully sanitized; Gay Talese's book (*The Kingdom and the Power* [New York: World, 1969]), by comparison, is quite the reverse. Not only is it an exceptional document on the *Times* itself, but it is a pioneer attempt to see journalists and editors beyond their own mythology.

I have also read for this book virtually all the books on the Eisenhower, Kennedy, Johnson, and Nixon administrations, as well as all the Watergate memoirs, and virtually the entire shelf of Vietnam books as well.

Allen, Frederick L. *Only Yesterday: An Informal History of the Nineteen Twenties.* New York: Harper & Row, 1957.

Arlen, Michael J. *The Living Room War.* New York: The Viking Press, 1969.

Aronson, James. *Press and the Cold War.* Indianapolis: Bobbs-Merrill, 1970.

Bagdikian, Ben. *Information Machines: Their Impact on Men and the Media.* New York: Harper & Row, 1971.

Barth, Alan. *The Loyalty of Free Men.* New York: The Viking Press, 1951.

Bernays, Edward L. *Biography of an Idea.* New York: Simon & Schuster, 1965.

Block, Herbert. *Herblock's State of the Union.* New York: Simon & Schuster, 1972.

Boorstin, Daniel J. *Image: A Guide to Pseudo-Events in America.* New York: Harper & Row, 1961.

Bradlee, Benjamin. *Conversations with Kennedy.* New York: W. W. Norton, 1957.

Braestrup, Peter. *Big Story.* New York: Doubleday Anchor, 1978.

Brown, Les. *Television: The Business Behind the Box.* New York: Harcourt Brace Jovanovich, 1974.

Burlingame, Roger. *Don't Let Them Scare You.* New York: J. B. Lippincott, 1961.

Burns, Joan S. *The Awkward Embrace: The Creative Artist and the Institution in America.* New York: Alfred A. Knopf, 1975.

Childs, Marquis, and Reston, James, eds. *Walter Lippmann and His Times.* New York: Harcourt Brace Jovanovich, 1959.

Cogley, John. Fund for the Republic. *Report on Blacklisting.* New York: Meridian Books, 1956.

Cohen, Richard M. and Witcover, Jules. *A Heartbeat Away.* New York: The Viking Press, 1974

Crouse, Timothy. *The Boys on the Bus.* New York: Random House, 1973.

Darrow, Clarence. *The Story of My Life.* New York: Charles Scribner's Sons, 1932.

Diamond, Edwin. *The Tin Kazoo: Television, Politics, and the News.* Boston: MIT Press, 1975.

Downie, Leonard, Jr. *The New Muckrakers.* Washington, D.C.: New Republic Books, 1976.

Epstein, Edward Jay. *News from Nowhere: Television and the News.* New York: Random House, 1973.

Faulk, John Henry. *Fear on Trial.* New York: Simon & Schuster, 1964.

Fielding, Raymond. *The March of Time.* New York: Oxford University Press, 1978.

Friendly, Fred W. *Due to Circumstances Beyond Our Control. . . .* New York: Random House, 1967.

Fulbright, J. William. *The Arrogance of Power.* New York: Random House, 1966.

Goldmark, Peter. *Maverick Inventor.* New York: Saturday Review Press, 1973.

Hamblin, Dora J. *That Was the Life.* New York: W. W. Norton, 1977.

Harris, Louis. *The Anguish of Change.* New York: W. W. Norton, 1973.

Hoge, Alice A. *Cissy Patterson.* New York: Random House, 1966.

Kendrick, Alexander. *Prime Time: The Life of Edward R. Murrow.* Boston: Little, Brown, 1969.

Keogh, James. *President Nixon and the Press.* New York: Funk & Wagnalls, 1972.

Kobler, John. *Luce, His Time, Life and Fortune.* New York: Doubleday, 1968.

Lukas, J. Anthony. *Nightmare: The Underside of the Nixon Years.* New York: The Viking Press, 1976.

MacNeil, Robert. *The People Machine.* New York: Harper & Row, 1968.

Mayo, Morrow. *Los Angeles.* New York: Alfred A. Knopf, 1933.

Mazo, Earl. *Richard Nixon.* New York: Harper & Row, 1959.

McGinniss, Joe. *The Selling of the President.* New York: Trident, 1969.

McLuhan, Marshall. *Understanding Media: The Extension of Man.* New York: McGraw-Hill, 1965.

McWilliams, Carey. *California: The Great Exception.* New York: A. A. Wyn, 1949.

————. *Southern California: Island on the Land.* Layton, Utah: Peregrine Smith, 1946.

Meyer, Agnes. *Out of These Roots.* Boston: Little, Brown, 1953.

Mickelson, Sig. *Electronic Mirror: Politics in an Age of TV.* New York: Dodd, Mead, 1972.

Miller, Merle. *Only You, Dick Daring!* New York: William Sloane, 1964.

Minow, Newton, et al. *Presidential Television: A 20th Century Fund Report.* New York: Basic Books, 1973.

Mowry, George. *California Progressives.* New York: Quadrangle/The New York Times Book Co., 1963.

Murrow, Edward R. *In Search of Light: The Broadcasts of Edward R. Murrow (1938–61).* Edited by Ed Bliss. New York: Alfred A. Knopf, 1967.

Nadeau, Remi A. *The Water Seekers.* New York: Doubleday, 1950.

Nixon, Richard M. *Six Crises.* New York: Doubleday, 1962.

Nizer, Louis. *Jury Returns.* New York: Doubleday, 1960.

Oberdorfer, Don. *Tet.* New York: Doubleday, 1971.

Olin, Spencer C., Jr. *California's Prodigal Sons: Hiram Johnson and the Progressives.* Los Angeles: University of California Press, 1968.

Pollard, James. *The Presidents and the Press.* New York: Macmillan, 1947.

Powers, Ron. *The Newscasters: The News Business as Show Business.* New York: St. Martin's Press, 1977.

Pusey, Merlo J. *Eugene Meyer.* New York: Alfred A. Knopf, 1974.

Rather, Dan, and Herkowitz, Mickey. *The Camera Never Blinks.* New York: William Morrow, 1977.

Roberts, Chalmers. *First Rough Draft.* New York: Praeger, 1973.

Rosten, Leo C. *The Washington Correspondents.* New York: Harcourt Brace Jovanovich, 1937.

Rowse, Arthur. *Slanted News: A Case Study of the Nixon and Stevenson Fund Stories.* Boston: Beacon Press, 1957.

Schorr, Daniel. *Clearing the Air.* Boston: Houghton Mifflin, 1977.

Seldes, George. *Lords of the Press.* New York: Julian Messner, 1938.

Sevareid, Eric. *Not So Wild a Dream.* New York: Alfred A. Knopf, 1946.

Shirer, William L. *Berlin Diary.* New York: Alfred A. Knopf, 1941.

Steffens, Lincoln. *Autobiography of Lincoln Steffens.* New York: Harcourt Brace Jovanovich, 1958.

Steinberg, Alfred. *Sam Rayburn.* New York: Hawthorn Books, 1975.

Stone, Irving. *Clarence Darrow for the Defense.* New York: Bantam Books, 1958.

Swanberg, W. A. *Citizen Hearst.* New York: Charles Scribner's Sons, 1961.

Swanberg, W. A. *Luce and His Empire: A Biography.* New York: Charles Scribner's Sons, 1972.

Szulc, Tad. *Dominican Diary.* New York: Delacorte Press, 1965.

Unger, Sanford. *The Papers and the Papers.* New York: E. P. Dutton, 1972.

White, Theodore H., and Jacoby, Annalee. *Thunder Out of China.* New York: William Sloane, 1946.

White, Theodore H. *The Making of the President 1960.* New York: Atheneum, 1961.

———. *The Making of the President 1964.* New York: Atheneum, 1965.

———. *The Making of the President 1968.* New York: Atheneum, 1969.

———. *Breach of Faith.* New York: Atheneum, 1975.

———. *In Search of History: A Personal Expedition.* New York: Harper & Row, 1978.

Wiggins, J. Russell. *Freedom or Secrecy.* New York: Oxford University Press, 1964.

Wills, Garry. *Nixon Agonistes.* Boston: Houghton Mifflin, 1970.

Woodward, Bob, and Bernstein, Carl. *All the President's Men.* New York: Simon & Schuster, 1974.

# Index

# A NOTE ABOUT THE AUTHOR

David Halberstam's unsurpassed personal knowledge of the media goes back to the mid-fifties. He went from Harvard to work as a reporter on the smallest daily paper in Mississippi, then spent four years on the Nashville *Tennessean,* and for six years served as a foreign correspondent for *The New York Times* in the Congo, Vietnam, and Poland. His remarkable reporting from Saigon in 1962 and 1963 earned him a Pulitzer Prize and estabilshed him as one of the country's most admired and respected journalists. His books include *The Making of a Quagmire* (1965), *The Unfinished Odyssey of Robert Kennedy* (1969), and an extended essay on North Vietnamese leader Ho Chi Minh, published in 1971. In 1972 came *The Best and the Brightest,* his masterly study of the era that began with the hope and promise of Kennedy's inauguration and ended in the disorder and public anger of the late sixties.

After leaving *The New York Times* in 1967, Halberstam was for four years a contributing editor of *Harper's.* Since 1972 he has devoted all his working time to this book.

# A NOTE ON THE TYPE

The text of this book was set via computer driven cathode ray tube in a face called Times Roman, designed by Stanley Morison for *The Times* (London), and first introduced by that newspaper in 1932.

Among typographers and designers of the twentieth century, Stanley Morison has been a strong forming influence, as typographical adviser to the English Monotype Corporation, as a director of two distinguished English publishing houses, and as a writer of sensibility, erudition, and keen practical sense.

Composed, printed and bound by The Haddon Craftsmen, Inc., Scranton, Pennsylvania.

Typography and binding design by Virginia Tan.